Racial and Ethnic Diversity in Higher Education

Third Edition

ASHE Reader Series

Edited by
Shaun R. Harper and Sylvia Hurtado

Series Editor
Jerlando F. L. Jackson, University of Wisconsin

Learning Solutions

New York   Boston   San Francisco
London   Toronto   Sydney   Tokyo   Singapore   Madrid
Mexico City   Munich   Paris   Cape Town   Hong Kong   Montreal

Pearson Learning Solutions, 501 Boylston Street, Suite 900, Boston, MA 02116
A Pearson Education Company
www.pearsoned.com

Printed in the United States of America

1 2 3 4 5 6 7 8 9 10 V0CR 15 14 13 12 11 10

000200010270575077

SB/CB

ISBN 10: 0-558-84857-5
ISBN 13: 978-0-558-84857-6

TABLE OF CONTENTS

ACKNOWLEDGMENTS REPORT   viii

PREFACE | SHAUN R. HARPER AND SYLVIA HURTADO   xi

ABOUT THE EDITORS AND ASSOCIATE EDITORS   xv

ADVISORY GROUP MEMBERS   xvii

PART I   HISTORY   1
MARYBETH GASMAN AND CHRISTOPHER TUDICO, ASSOCIATE EDITORS

CHAPTER 1
THE CHOCTAW NATION: CHANGING THE APPEARANCE OF AMERICAN   5
HIGHER EDUCATION, 1830–1907 | STEVEN CRUM

CHAPTER 2
THE AFRICAN AMERICAN FEMALE ELITE: THE EARLY HISTORY OF AFRICAN   18
AMERICAN WOMEN IN THE SEVEN SISTER COLLEGES, 1880–1960 | LINDA M. PERKINS

CHAPTER 3
WHAT'S IN A NAME? A HISTORICAL LOOK AT NATIVE AMERICAN-RELATED   45
NICKNAMES AND SYMBOLS AT THREE U.S. UNIVERSITIES | MARK R. CONNOLLY

CHAPTER 4
"LIFE BEGINS WITH FREEDOM": THE COLLEGE NISEI, 1942–1945 | THOMAS JAMES   65

CHAPTER 5
RACE, MERITOCRACY, AND THE AMERICAN ACADEMY DURING THE IMMEDIATE   79
POST–WORLD WAR II ERA | JAMES D. ANDERSON

CHAPTER 6
SCYLLA AND CHARYBDIS: NAVIGATING THE WATERS OF ACADEMIC FREEDOM   94
AT FISK UNIVERSITY DURING CHARLES S. JOHNSON'S ADMINISTRATION
1946–1956 | MARYBETH GASMAN

CHAPTER 7
"THIS HAS BEEN QUITE A YEAR FOR HEADS FALLING": INSTITUTIONAL AUTONOMY   109
IN THE CIVIL RIGHTS ERA | JOY ANN WILLIAMSON

CHAPTER 8
FROM VISIBILITY TO AUTONOMY: LATINOS AND HIGHER EDUCATION IN THE U.S.,   124
1965–2005 | VICTORIA-MARÍA MACDONALD, JOHN M. BOTTI, AND LISA HOFFMAN CLARK

PART II   STUDENTS   147
KIMBERLY A. GRIFFIN AND WALTER R. ALLEN, ASSOCIATE EDITORS

CHAPTER 9
MINORITY-STATUS STRESSES AND THE COLLEGE ADJUSTMENT OF ETHNIC MINORITY   151
FRESHMEN | BRIAN D. SMEDLEY, HECTOR F. MYERS, AND SHELLY P. HARRELL

CHAPTER 10
THE BLACK BOX: HOW HIGH-ACHIEVING BLACKS RESIST STEREOTYPES ABOUT   164
BLACK AMERICANS | SHARON FRIES-BRITT AND KIMBERLY A. GRIFFIN

CHAPTER 11
"I AM NOT A RACIST BUT . . . ": MAPPING WHITE COLLEGE STUDENTS' RACIAL   178
IDEOLOGY IN THE USA | EDUARDO BONILLA-SILVA AND TYRONE A. FORMAN

CHAPTER 12
NINE THEMES IN CAMPUS RACIAL CLIMATES AND IMPLICATIONS FOR INSTITUTIONAL   204
TRANSFORMATION | SHAUN R. HARPER AND SYLVIA HURTADO

CHAPTER 13
DECONSTRUCTING WHITENESS AS PART OF A MULTICULTURAL EDUCATIONAL   217
FRAMEWORK: FROM THEORY TO PRACTICE | ANNA M. ORTIZ AND ROBERT A. RHOADS

CHAPTER 14
RACIAL DIVERSITY MATTERS: THE IMPACT OF DIVERSITY-RELATED STUDENT   230
ENGAGEMENT AND INSTITUTIONAL CONTEXT | NIDA DENSON AND
MITCHELL J. CHANG

CHAPTER 15
ENHANCING CAMPUS CLIMATES FOR RACIAL/ETHNIC DIVERSITY: EDUCATIONAL   254
POLICY AND PRACTICE | SYLVIA HURTADO, JEFFREY F. MILEM, ALMA R. CLAYTON-
PEDERSEN, AND WALTER R. ALLEN

PART III   FACULTY   269
JENNY J. LEE, ASSOCIATE EDITOR

CHAPTER 16
FACULTY OF COLOR IN ACADEME: WHAT 20 YEARS OF LITERATURE TELLS US | 273
CAROLINE SOTELLO VIERNES TURNER, JUAN CARLOS GONZÁLEZ, AND J. LUKE WOOD

CHAPTER 17
COLORING THE ACADEMIC LANDSCAPE: FACULTY OF COLOR BREAKING THE SILENCE   305
IN PREDOMINANTLY WHITE COLLEGES AND UNIVERSITIES | CHRISTINE A. STANLEY

CHAPTER 18
'TEACHING WHILE BLACK': NARRATIVES OF AFRICAN AMERICAN STUDENT AFFAIRS   330
FACULTY | LORI D. PATTON AND CHRISTOPHER CATCHING

CHAPTER 19
RACE-RELATED SERVICE AND FACULTY OF COLOR: CONCEPTUALIZING CRITICAL   343
AGENCY IN ACADEME | BENJAMIN BAEZ

CHAPTER 20
INTERRUPTING THE USUAL: SUCCESSFUL STRATEGIES FOR HIRING DIVERSE FACULTY | 361
DARYL G. SMITH, CAROLINE S. TURNER, NANA OSEI-KOFI, AND SANDRA RICHARDS

CHAPTER 21
WOMEN OF COLOR IN ACADEME: LIVING WITH MULTIPLE MARGINALITY | 380
CAROLINE SOTELLO VIERNES TURNER

CHAPTER 22
THE CONTRIBUTION OF FACULTY OF COLOR TO UNDERGRADUATE EDUCATION | 394
PAUL D. UMBACH

PART IV   CURRICULUM, TEACHING, AND LEARNING   415
CAROLINE SOTELLO VIERNES TURNER AND STEPHEN JOHN QUAYE, ASSOCIATE EDITORS

CHAPTER 23
HIDING IN THE IVY: AMERICAN INDIAN STUDENTS AND VISIBILITY IN ELITE   419
EDUCATIONAL SETTINGS | BRYAN MCKINLEY JONES BRAYBOY

CHAPTER 24
TALKING ABOUT RACE, LEARNING ABOUT RACISM: THE APPLICATION OF RACIAL   438
IDENTITY DEVELOPMENT THEORY IN THE CLASSROOM | BEVERLY DANIEL TATUM

CHAPTER 25
TRANSFORMANDO FRONTERAS: CHICANA FEMINIST TRANSFORMATIVE PEDAGOGIES | 457
C. ALEJANDRA ELENES

CHAPTER 26
RACIAL AND ETHNIC DIVERSITY IN THE CLASSROOM: DOES IT PROMOTE STUDENT   469
LEARNING? | PATRICK T. TERENZINI, ALBERTO F. CABRERA, CAROL L. COLBECK,
STEFANI A. BJORKLUND, AND JOHN M. PARENTE

CHAPTER 27
MINORITY STUDENTS IN SCIENCE AND MATH: WHAT UNIVERSITIES STILL DO NOT   484
UNDERSTAND ABOUT RACE IN AMERICA | RICHARD TAPIA AND CYNTHIA JOHNSON

CHAPTER 28
CLASS, RACE AND GENDER AND THE CONSTRUCTION OF POST-SECONDARY CURRICULA   492
IN THE UNITED STATES: SOCIAL MOVEMENT, PROFESSIONALIZATION AND POLITICAL
ECONOMIC THEORIES OF CURRICULAR CHANGE | SHEILA SLAUGHTER

CHAPTER 29
CURRICULUM MATTERS: CREATING A POSITIVE CLIMATE FOR DIVERSITY FROM THE   515
STUDENT PERSPECTIVE | MATTHEW J. MAYHEW, HEIDI E. GRUNWALD, AND ERIC L. DEY

CHAPTER 30
BRINGING HOME DIVERSITY: A SERVICE-LEARNING APPROACH TO TEACHING RACE   530
AND ETHNIC RELATIONS | SAM MARULLO

PART V   ORGANIZATIONS, LEADERSHIP, AND GOVERNANCE   545
JAMES T. MINOR AND ALMA R. CLAYTON-PEDERSEN, ASSOCIATE EDITORS

CHAPTER 31
CLOSING THE ACHIEVEMENT GAP IN HIGHER EDUCATION: AN ORGANIZATIONAL   549
LEARNING PERSPECTIVE | ESTELA MARA BENSIMON

CHAPTER 32
CAMOUFLAGING POWER AND PRIVILEGE: A CRITICAL RACE ANALYSIS OF UNIVERSITY   557
DIVERSITY POLICIES | SUSAN VANDEVENTER IVERSON

CHAPTER 33
UNDERSTANDING LEADERSHIP STRATEGIES FOR ADDRESSING THE POLITICS OF   574
DIVERSITY | ADRIANNA KEZAR

CHAPTER 34
DEVELOPING LEADERS OF COLOR IN HIGHER EDUCATION: CAN CONTEMPORARY   597
PROGRAMS ADDRESS HISTORICAL EMPLOYMENT TRENDS? | BRIDGET R. MCCURTIS,
JERLANDO F. L. JACKSON, AND ELIZABETH M. O'CALLAGHAN

CHAPTER 35
HISPANIC PRESIDENTS AND CHANCELLORS OF INSTITUTIONS OF HIGHER EDUCATION   614
IN THE UNITED STATES IN 2001 AND 2006 | ALFREDO G. DE LOS SANTOS JR. AND
IRENE I. VEGA

CHAPTER 36
DECISION MAKING IN HISTORICALLY BLACK COLLEGES AND UNIVERSITIES: DEFINING   635
THE GOVERNANCE CONTEXT | JAMES T. MINOR

CHAPTER 37
BAKKE AND STATE POLICY: EXERCISING INSTITUTIONAL AUTONOMY TO MAINTAIN   647
A DIVERSE STUDENT BODY | PATRICIA MARIN AND STELLA M. FLORES

PART VI   POLICY, FINANCE, AND ECONOMICS   659
BRIDGET TERRY LONG AND STELLA M. FLORES, ASSOCIATE EDITORS

CHAPTER 38
THE EFFECTS OF AMERICA'S THREE AFFIRMATIVE ACTION PROGRAMS ON ACADEMIC   663
PERFORMANCE | DOUGLAS S. MASSEY AND MARGARITA MOONEY

CHAPTER 39
WAS JUSTICE O'CONNOR RIGHT? RACE AND HIGHLY SELECTIVE COLLEGE ADMISSIONS   680
IN 25 YEARS | ALAN B. KRUEGER, JESSE ROTHSTEIN, AND SARAH TURNER

CHAPTER 40
WINNERS AND LOSERS: CHANGES IN TEXAS UNIVERSITY ADMISSIONS POST-*HOPWOOD* | 689
MARK C. LONG AND MARTA TIENDA

CHAPTER 41
STATE DREAM ACTS: THE EFFECT OF IN-STATE RESIDENT TUITION POLICIES AND   714
UNDOCUMENTED LATINO STUDENTS | STELLA M. FLORES

CHAPTER 42
THE NEW MERIT AID | SUSAN DYNARSKI   739

CHAPTER 43
RACE-CONSCIOUS STUDENT FINANCIAL AID: CONSTRUCTING AN AGENDA FOR   764
RESEARCH, LITIGATION, AND POLICY DEVELOPMENT | EDWARD P. ST. JOHN,
BRITANY AFFOLTER-CAINE, AND ANNA S. CHUNG

CHAPTER 44
DO COMMUNITY COLLEGES PROVIDE A VIABLE PATHWAY TO A BACCALAUREATE   787
DEGREE? | BRIDGET TERRY LONG AND MICHAL KURLAENDER

PART VII   CRITICAL PERSPECTIVES ON RACE AND RACISM   811
IN HIGHER EDUCATION
LORI D. PATTON AND ROBERT T. TERANISHI, ASSOCIATE EDITORS

CHAPTER 45
HIDING THE POLITICALLY OBVIOUS: A CRITICAL RACE THEORY PREVIEW OF DIVERSITY   815
AS RACIAL NEUTRALITY IN HIGHER EDUCATION | OTONIEL JIMENEZ MORFIN,
VICTOR H. PEREZ, LAURENCE PARKER, MARVIN LYNN, AND JOHN ARRONA

CHAPTER 46
ACCESS AND EQUITY FOR AFRICAN AMERICAN STUDENTS IN HIGHER EDUCATION: 829
A CRITICAL RACE HISTORICAL ANALYSIS OF POLICY EFFORTS | SHAUN R. HARPER,
LORI D. PATTON, AND ONTARIO S. WOODEN

CHAPTER 47
CHALLENGING RACIAL BATTLE FATIGUE ON HISTORICALLY WHITE CAMPUSES: 845
A CRITICAL RACE EXAMINATION OF RACE-RELATED STRESS | WILLIAM A. SMITH,
TARA J. YOSSO, AND DANIEL G. SOLÓRZANO

CHAPTER 48
CRITICAL RACE THEORY, RACIAL MICROAGGRESSIONS, AND CAMPUS RACIAL   861
CLIMATE: THE EXPERIENCES OF AFRICAN AMERICAN COLLEGE STUDENTS |
DANIEL SOLÓRZANO, MIGUEL CEJA, AND TARA YOSSO

CHAPTER 49
NIGGERS NO MORE: A CRITICAL RACE COUNTERNARRATIVE ON BLACK MALE   875
STUDENT ACHIEVEMENT AT PREDOMINANTLY WHITE COLLEGES AND
UNIVERSITIES | SHAUN R. HARPER

CHAPTER 50
CRITICAL RACE THEORY AND RESEARCH ON ASIAN AMERICANS AND PACIFIC   888
ISLANDERS IN HIGHER EDUCATION | ROBERT T. TERANISHI, LAURIE B. BEHRINGER,
EMILY A. GREY, AND TARA L. PARKER

CHAPTER 51
TOWARD A TRIBAL CRITICAL RACE THEORY IN EDUCATION | BRYAN MCKINLEY   896
JONES BRAYBOY

CHAPTER 52
CRITICAL RACE THEORY, LATINO CRITICAL THEORY, AND CRITICAL RACED-   911
GENDERED EPISTEMOLOGIES: RECOGNIZING STUDENTS OF COLOR AS HOLDERS
AND CREATORS OF KNOWLEDGE | DOLORES DELGADO BERNAL

CHAPTER 53
GETTING BEYOND THE 'SYMPTOM,' ACKNOWLEDGING THE 'DISEASE': THEORIZING   925
RACIST NATIVISM | LINDSAY PEREZ HUBER, CORINA BENAVIDES LOPEZ,
MARIA C. MALAGON, VERONICA VELEZ, AND DANIEL G. SOLÓRZANO

CHAPTER 54
TOWARDS A CRITICAL THEORY OF WHITENESS | DAVID S. OWEN   937

ACKNOWLEDGMENTS REPORT

Grateful acknowledgment is made to the following sources for permission to reprint material copyrighted or controlled by them:

Copyright Acknowledgments

"The Choctaw Nation: Changing the Appearance of American Higher Education, 1830–1907," by Steven Crum, reprinted from *History of Education Quarterly* 47, no. 1 (February 2007), by permission of John Wiley & Sons, Inc.

"The African American Female Elite: The Early History of African American Women in the Seven Sister Colleges, 1880–1960," by Linda M. Perkins, reprinted from *Harvard Educational Review* 67, no. 4 (winter 1997).

"What's in a Name? A Historical Look at Native American-related Nicknames and Symbols at Three U.S. Universities," by Mark R. Connolly, reprinted by permission from *The Journal of Higher Education* 71, no. 5 (September/October 2000).

"Life Begins with Freedom: The College Nisei, 1942–1945," by Thomas James, reprinted from *History of Education Quarterly* 25, no. ½ (spring/summer 1985), by permission of John Wiley & Sons, Inc.

"Race, Meritocracy, and the American Academy during the Immediate Post-World War II Era," by James D. Anderson, reprinted from *History of Education Quarterly* 33, no. 2 (summer 1993), by permission of John Wiley & Sons, Inc.

"Scylla and Charybdis: Navigating the Waters of Academic Freedom at Fisk University During Charles S. Johnson's Administration (1946–1956)," by Marybeth Gasman, reprinted from *American Educational Research Journal* 36, no. 4 (1999), by permission of the American Educational Research Association.

"'This Has Been Quite a Year for Heads Falling': Institutional Autonomy in the Civil Rights Era," by Joy Ann Williamson, reprinted from *History of Education Quarterly* 44, no. 4 (winter 2004), by permission of John Wiley & Sons, Inc.

"From Visibility to Autonomy: Latinos and Higher Education in the U.S., 1965–2005," by Victoria-María Macdonald, John M. Botti, and Lisa Hoffman Clark, reprinted from *Harvard Educational Review* 77, no. 4 (winter 2007).

"Minority-Status Stresses and the College Adjustment of Ethnic Minority Freshmen," by Brian D. Smedley, Hector F. Myers, and Shelly P. Harrell, reprinted from *Journal of Higher Education* 64, no. 4 (July/August 1993), by permission of The Ohio State University.

"The Black Box: How High-Achieving Blacks Resist Stereotypes about Black Americans," by Sharon Fries-Britt and Kimberly A. Griffin, reprinted by permission from *Journal of College Student Development* 48, no. 5 (September/October 2007).

"'I am not a racist but . . .': Mapping White College Students' Racial Ideology in the USA," by Eduardo Bonilla-Silva and Tyrone A. Forman, reprinted from *Discourse & Society* 11, no. 1 (2000), by permission of Sage Publications.

"Deconstructing Whiteness as Part of a Multicultural Educational Framework: From Theory to Practice," by Anna M. Ortiz and Robert A. Rhoads, reprinted by permission from *Journal of College Student Development* 41, no. 1 (January/February 2000).

"Racial Diversity Matters: The Impact of Diversity-Related Student Engagement and Institutional Context," by Nina Denson and Mitchell J. Chang, reprinted from *American Educational Research Journal* 46, no. 2 (June 2009), by permission of American Educational Research Association.

"Enhancing Campus Climates for Racial/Ethnic Diversity: Educational Policy and Practice," by Sylvia Hurtado et al., reprinted from *The Review of Higher Education* 21, no. 3 (1998), Association for the Study of Higher Education.

"Faculty of Color in Academe: What 20 Years of Literature Tells Us," by Caroline Sotello, et al., reprinted from *Journal of Diversity in Higher Education* 1, no. 3 (2008), American Psychological Association.

"Coloring the Academic Landscape: Faculty of Color Breaking the Silence in Predominately White Colleges and Universities," by Christine A. Stanley, reprinted from *American Educational Research Journal* 43, no. 4 (winter 2006), by permission of American Educational Research Association.

"Women of Color in Academe: Living with Multiple Marginality," by Caroline Sotello Viernes Turner, reprinted by permission from *Journal of Higher Education* 73, no. 1 (January/February 2002).

"Teaching While Black: Narratives of African-American Student Affairs Faculty," by Christopher Catching and Lori D. Patton, reprinted from *International Journal of Qualitative Studies in Education* 22, no. 6 (November/ December 2009), Taylor & Francis Group.

"Race-related Service and Faculty of Color: Conceptualizing Critical Agency in Academe," by Benjamin Baez, reprinted from *Higher Education* 39, no. 3 (2000), by permission of Kluwer Academic Publishers, a division of Springer Science and Business Media.

"Interrupting the Usual: Successful Strategies for Hiring Diverse Faculty," by Daryl G. Smith et al., reprinted by permission from *Journal of Higher Education* 75, no. 2 (March/April 2004).

"The Contribution of Faculty of Color to Undergraduate Education," by Paul D. Umbach, reprinted from *Research in Higher Education* 47, no. 3 (May 2006), by permission of Springer Science and Business Media.

"Hiding in the Ivy: American Indian Students and Visibility in Elite Educational Settings," by Bryan McKinley and Jones Brayboy, reprinted from *Harvard Educational Review* 74, no. 2 (summer 2004).

"Talking about Race, Learning about Racism: The Application of Racial Identity Development Theory in the Classroom," by Beverly Daniel Tatum, reprinted from *Harvard Educational Review* 62, no. 1 (1992).

"Transformando Fronteras: Chicana Feminist Transformative Pedagogies," by C. Alejandra Elenes, reprinted from *Qualitative Studies in Education* 14, no. 1 (2001), Taylor & Francis Group.

"Racial and Ethnic Diversity in the Classroom," by Patrick T. Terenzini et al., reprinted by permission from *Journal of Higher Education* 72, no. 5 (September/October 2001).

"Minority Students in Science and Math," by Richard Tapia and Cynthia Johnson, reprinted from *Doctoral Education and the Faculty of the Future,* edited by Ronald G. Ehrenberg and Charlotte V. Kuh (2009), Cornell University Press.

"Class, race and gender and the construction of post-secondary curricula in the United States: Social movement, professionalization and political economic theories of curricular change," by Sheila Slaughter, reprinted from *Journal of Curriculum Studies* 29, no. 1 (1997), by permission of Routledge, a division of Taylor & Francis Group.

"Curriculum Matters: Creating a Positive Climate for Diversity from the Student Perspective," by Matthew J. Mayhew, Heidi E. Grunwald and Eric L. Dey, reprinted by permission from *Research in Higher Education* 46, no. 4 (2005).

"Bringing Home Diversity: A Service-Learning Approach to Teaching Race and Ethnic Relations," by Sam Marullo, reprinted from *Teaching Sociology* 26 (October 1998).

"Closing the Achievement Gap in Higher Education: An Organizational Learning Perspective," by Estela Mara Bensimon, reprinted from *New Directions for Higher Education* 131 (fall 2005), by permission of John Wiley & Sons, Inc.

"Camouflaging Power and Privilege: A Critical Race Analysis of University Diversity Policies," by Susan VanDeventer Iverson, reprinted from *Educational Administration Quarterly* 43, no. 5 (December 2007), by permission of Sage Publications, Inc.

"Understanding Leadership Strategies for Addressing the Politics of Diversity," by Adrianna Kezar, reprinted by permission from *Journal of Higher Education* 79, no. 4 (July/August 2008).

"Developing Leaders of Color in Higher Education," by Bridget R. McCurtis, Jerlando F. L. Jackson, and Elizabeth M. O'Callaghan, reprinted from *Rethinking Leadership in a Complex, Multicultural, and Global Environment,* edited by A. J. Kezar (2009), by permission of Stylus Publishing.

"Hispanic Presidents and Chancellors of Institutions of Higher Education in the United States in 2001 and 2006," by Alfredo G. de Los Santos, Jr. and Irene I. Vega, reprinted from *Journal of Hispanic Higher Education* 7, no. 2 (April 2008), by permission of Sage Publications, Inc.

"Decision Making in Historically Black Colleges and Universities: Defining the Governance Context," by James T. Minor, reprinted from *The Journal of Negro Education* 73, no. 1 (winter 2004).

"Bakke and State Policy: Exercising Institutional Autonomy to Maintain a Diverse Student Body," by Patricia Marin and Stella M. Flores, reprinted from *Realizing Bakke's Legacy: Affirmative Action, Equal Opportunity and Access to Higher Education,* edited by Patricia Marin and C. L. Horn (2008), by permission of Stylus Publishing.

"The Effects of America's Three Affirmative Action Programs on Academic Performance," by Douglas S. Massey and Margarita Mooney, reprinted from *Social Problems* 54, no. 1 (2007), by permission of the University of California Press.

"Was Justice O'Connor Right? Race and Highly Selective College Admissions in 25 Years," by Alan B. Kreuger, Jesse Rothstein, and Sarah Turner, reprinted from *College Access: Opportunity or Privilege?,* edited by Michael McPherson and Morton Schapiro (2008), College Board.

"Winners and Losers: Changes in Texas University Admissions Post-Hopwood," by Mark C. Long and Marta Tienda, reprinted from *Educational Evaluation and Policy Analysis* 30, no. 3 (September 2008), by permission of American Educational Research Association.

"State Dream Acts: The Effect of in-State Resident Tuition Policies and Undocumented Latino Students," by Stella M. Flores, reprinted from *The Review of Higher Education* 33, no. 2 (winter 2010), Johns Hopkins University Press.

"The New Merit Aid," by Susan Dynarski, reprinted from *College Choices: The Economics of Which College, When College, and How to Pay For It,* edited by C. M. Hoxby (2004), by permission of the University of Chicago Press.

"Race-Conscious Student Financial Aid: Constructing an Agenda for Research, Litigation, and Policy Development," by Edward P. St. John, Britany Affolter-Caine, and Anna S. Chung, reprinted from *Charting the Future of College Affirmative Action,* edited by G. Orfield and P. Marin (2007), Civil Rights Project at UCLA School of Education.

"Do Community Colleges Provide a Viable Pathway to a Baccalaureate Degree?" by Bridget Terry Long and Michal Kurlaender, reprinted from *Educational Evaluation and Policy Analysis* 31, no. 1 (March 2009), by permission of American Educational Research Association.

"Hiding the Politically Obvious," by Otoniel Jimenez Morfin, Victor H. Perez, and Laurence Parker, reprinted from *Educational Policy* 20, no. 1 (January/March 2006), by permission of Corwin Press.

"Access and Equity for African American Students in Higher Education: A Critical Race Historical Analysis of Policy Efforts," by Shaun R. Harper, Lori D. Patton, and Ontario S. Wooden, reprinted by permission from *Journal of Higher Education* 80, no. 4 (July/August 2009).

"Challenging Racial Battle Fatigue on Historically White Campuses," by William A. Smith, Tara J. Yosso, and Daniel G. Solórzano, reprinted from *Faculty of Color: Teaching in Predominantly White Colleges and Universities,* edited by C.A. Stanley (2006), by permission of John Wiley & Sons, Inc.

"Critical Race Theory, Racial Microaggressions, and Campus Racial Climate," by Daniel Solórzano, Miguel Ceja, and Tara Yosso, reprinted from *Journal of Negro Education* 60, no. ½ (winter/spring 2000).

"Niggers No More: A Critical Race Counter Narrative on Black Male Student Achievement at Predominantly White Colleges and Universities," by Shaun R. Harper, reprinted from *International Journal of Qualitative Studies in Education* 22, no. 6 (November/December 2009), Taylor & Francis Group.

"Critical Race Theory and Research on Asian Americans and Pacific Islanders in Higher Education," by Robert T. Teranishi and Laurie B. Behringer, reprinted from *Conducting Research on Asian-Americans in Higher Education—Special Issue of New Directions for Institutional Research* (2009), by permission of John Wiley & Sons, Inc.

"Toward a Tribal Critical Race Theory in Education," by Jones Brayboy, reprinted from *The Urban Review* 37, no. 5 (December 2005), Springer Science and Business Media.

"Critical Race Theory, Latino Critical Theory, and Critical Raced-Gendered Epistemologies," by Dolores Delgado Bernal, reprinted from *Qualitative Inquiry* 8, no. 1 (February 2002), by permission of Sage Publications.

"Getting Beyond the Symptom, Acknowledging the Disease: Theorizing Racist Nativism," by Lindsay Perez Huber and Corina Benavides Lopez, reprinted from *Contemporary Justice Review* 11, no. 1 (March 2008), by permission of Taylor & Francis Group.

"Towards a Critical Theory of Whiteness," by David S. Owen, reprinted from *Philosophy & Social Criticism* 33, no. 2 (2007), by permission of Sage Publications.

PREFACE

The election of a person of color to the presidency of the United States supposedly signified an instantaneous shift to a post-racial America. Thus, some may understandably question the necessity of a third edition of the ASHE Reader on Racial and Ethnic Diversity. If racism ended in November 2008, then why publish a new volume that engages many of the same old topics pertaining to people of color and their problems in the postsecondary educational context? Continually focusing on racism only sustains it, right? Wrong. It would have been miraculous if barriers to college access and completion for students of color instantly vanished when Barack Obama was elected our nation's 44th president. But unfortunately, they remain and are often accompanied by racial toxins that make navigating certain institutional environments particularly tough for student populations that have long been underrepresented and underserved. We wish the appointment of Ruth Simmons to the presidency of Brown University suddenly stimulated an increase in senior-level administrators of color at predominantly white institutions. A decade later, representation rates are still dismal. And during the 18 months that Elsa Murano served as the first Hispanic president in the 132-year history of Texas A&M University, tenure and promotion rates for faculty of color rapidly increased, yes? No.

Considerable progress can occur under the leadership of a dynamic leader, but on their own, presidential appointments and the promotion of an occasional person of color are weak signals of racial progress. Stronger indicators include, but are not limited to, fewer reports of marginality and differential treatment among racial/ethnic minority students, faculty, and staff; narrower gaps between students of color and their White peers on a range of achievement indicators; more full professors and senior administrators of color; and a willingness among postsecondary professionals to talk openly and honestly about racism and how it undermines espoused institutional values concerning diversity. In the absence of these and a host of other meaningful signifiers, we are reluctant to pronounce the long-awaited demise of racism. As indicated across the 54 chapters that follow, much about this enterprise called higher education is inequitable and race still matters.

This book is organized around six focal areas of study in the field of higher education: (1) History; (2) Students; (3) Faculty; (4) Curriculum, Teaching and Learning; (5) Organizations, Leadership and Governance; and (6) Policy, Finance and Economics. The Association for the Study of Higher Education (ASHE), the premier professional organization for those who conduct research pertaining to colleges and universities, uses these topic areas to organize sessions for its annual meeting. Higher education scholars have grown accustomed to situating important problems in one or more of these domains—we see racism as a historical and contemporary problem that spans all six. Hence, we deliberately framed the ASHE Reader in this way to show how race, racism, and racial injustice are persistently reinscribed into every aspect of American higher education—from access and admissions to students' sense of belonging, faculty hiring and promotions, racial underrepresentation among chief administrators and institutional decision-makers, culturally unresponsive curricula and pedagogy, etc.

Taking Account of Race: Toward Personal Responsibility and Institutional Transformation

"In order to get beyond racism, we must first take account of race. There is no other way." These words from Supreme Court Justice Harry Blackmun in a landmark affirmative action case ring as true today in higher education as they did more than 30 years ago. For example, a rope fashioned into a noose recently hung in the library at the University of California, San Diego (UCSD), an incident that routinely occurs at several institutions across the country. Just two weeks prior, a predominantly white UCSD fraternity hosted the "Compton Cookout," a racist theme party that reinforced numerous offensive stereotypes about African Americans. These and other race-related problems serve as vivid reminders of our need to continually educate college students and higher education professionals about the history and continuing legacy of racism. Ignorance is not an excuse for racist behaviors or the cyclical perpetuation of racial/ethnic power differentials in institutional norms. As educators and administrators, it rests on our shoulders to increase our individual and collective awareness about the importance of race and explain how it frames experiences, perspectives, outcomes, and positionality on college and university campuses. We are also charged with improving the success of racial and ethnic minority persons who pay intercultural costs as they advance in higher education—from college entry to the tenured ranks of academia.

It is essential to acknowledge that we are educated and socialized within distinct racial contexts that can be culturally enriching or psychologically debilitating if framed by inequality and differential privilege across racial/ethnic groups. If racism still exists in society, then no campus environment is immune to it. Even the most diverse institutions operate within a larger social context plagued with longstanding inequities and racial disparities. Educators, researchers, and administrators remain in the unique position to affirm the value of diversity and actively disrupt existing institutional norms and social structures that perpetuate inequality based on race, ethnicity, and national origin. Responsibility for this must be both individual and collective. It may be difficult to accept for those who do not see race or racism as significant and permanent, but it is nonetheless important for us to educate ourselves and others while working individually and collectively to transform colleges and universities into institutions that responsibly enact espoused values concerning diversity, inclusive excellence, and social advancement.

Scholarship on race, ethnicity, national origin, and the continuing legacy of racial oppression in the U.S. helps us to "first take account of race"—to become cognizant and comprehend how American higher education has yet to fulfill its promise of equal opportunity. For example, some campuses focused on achieving diversity goals under "race neutral" policy constraints, that cannot take race into account, are now required to finally acknowledge how current practices and policies are not race neutral in their effects. These campuses must remain accountable to increasingly diverse populations and rely on those who can help identify institutional actions that sustain racial inequity. Furthermore, those campuses that have achieved some level of diverse racial/ethnic representation at different levels of the institution are now required to learn how to become a functioning multicultural learning environment. The benefits of such environments are now evident for learning and innovation, as research in this volume documents; we now need to learn how to optimize the conditions to achieve these benefits. In short, improving racial/ethnic diversity in higher education and desired outcomes for society requires not only more sophisticated research and practices, but also critical self-examinations and new mindsets. In many cases, incremental change in institutions no longer suffices—institutional transformation is required.

The 54 readings in this book can help identify problems and solutions, shape classroom and broader campus discussions, and facilitate processes leading to institutional transformation. The 3rd edition of this particular ASHE Reader acknowledges the dedication of several researchers who have had the courage and expertise to identify and name the issues, develop a language that enables us to discuss race and racism, and illuminate the remarkable experiences of American Indians, African Americans, Asian Americans, and Latina/os that signal resilience despite institutional barriers to equity and opportunity. Many scholars whose work is included in this volume have pushed the boundaries of existing knowledge, theory, and research methods to raise consciousness concerning the permanence and prevalence of racism. Moreover, their work challenges educators and institutions to act responsibly when taking account of race.

Why So Critical?

As previously noted, this ASHE Reader is mostly organized around the major areas of study in the field. However, we have also included a seventh section devoted entirely to critical perspectives on race and racism in higher education. Consistent with the ASHE Institutes on Equity and Critical Policy Analysis, we believe it is important to infuse critical perspectives and use critical race methodologies in the study of higher education policy and practice. Institutional change for equity is unlikely to ensue unless researchers and administrators are constructively critical of structures, people, and practices that contribute to the cyclical reproduction of racism and racial disparities. The section includes 10 chapters written by scholars within and beyond the borders of our field. Using Critical Race Theory and perspectives from Critical Whiteness Studies, the authors reveal much about the permanence and pervasiveness of racism in U.S. higher education. They also use these frameworks to show how policies sustain inequities, how especially debilitating racist campus environments are for faculty and students of color, how campus leaders often act in their own self-interests concerning racial matters, and how critical race epistemologies can be used to disrupt unidimensional understandings of particular populations (e.g., Asian Americans and Black men). Readers may notice that these chapters are more focused on *racism* than are several others in the volume. Producing this comprehensive resource on race without including critical readings on racism would have been shortsighted and disrespectful to our brilliantly courageous colleagues who are publishing important critical race work. In our view, more studies such as these are needed to counterbalance traditional research methods employed to study race in higher education.

Race All by Itself: A Limitation

One fundamental shortcoming of this volume is the absence of more scholarship that considers the intersection of race with other social identities that are typically oppressed in hegemonic postsecondary education systems. Caroline Sotello Viernes Turner (in Chapter 21) and Shaun R. Harper (in Chapter 49) both consider the intersection of race and gender for women and men of color, respectively. Otherwise, little else is included here that captures the multiple dimensions of identity that sometimes lead to experiential differences, navigational challenges, onlyness (i.e., being the only out lesbian faculty person of color at the institution), and discrimination on college and university campuses. In large part, our omission is reflective of the research that presently exists in the field. Indeed, more scholarship is needed on the intersection of race with sexual orientation, (dis)ability and health status, gender, class, age, size and body type, religion, and linguistic difference. Much remains to be published on the collision of racism with other –isms in higher education.

Cross-Generational Pairings

With the exception of the section on faculty, all others include a pair of Associate Editors who are differently situated in their careers—one is more senior than the other. The pairings include a doctoral student with a tenured faculty member, an endowed chair with a third-year assistant professor, a vice president of a national association with a newly-tenured associate professor, and so on. Despite their generational differences, we recognized that each partner in the collaborative parings possesses tremendous expertise on racial and ethnic diversity. We predicted the early career partner would learn much from her or his more senior collaborator, and vice versa. Furthermore, we thought the volume would be strengthened by having two scholars who have studied (and experienced) race for varying lengths of time work together on a section that is relevant to their research. Such substantive engagement across age, rank, and position has resulted in what we believe to be an outstanding contribution to the field, one of which all who participated in producing are proud. Also noteworthy is that we and 12 of the 13 Associate Editors are scholars of color.

Acknowledgments

We extend our appreciation to colleagues and students at Penn and UCLA with whom we learn, critically analyze, and collaboratively research important problems related to race, equity, and American higher education. We are also indebted to Ryan J. Davis for his assistance in the early phases of this project. A portion of any praise we receive for the 3rd edition of this ASHE Reader rightfully belongs to our pioneering predecessors who edited the first and second editions: Caroline Sotello Viernes Turner, Mildred García, Amaury Nora, Laura I. Rendón, anthony lising antonio, Berta Vigil Laden, and Cheryl L. Presley. Additionally, we salute a handful of eminent scholars, past and present, whose writings on race, racism, and racial justice continue to inform our own in extraordinarily powerful ways. Among them are W. E. B. Du Bois, Derrick Bell, Walter R. Allen, Kimberlé Williams Crenshaw, Patricia Gándara, Michael A. Olivas, John B. Williams, Estela Mara Bensimon, and Daniel G. Solórzano. Last, but certainly not least, our sincerest gratitude belongs to the 13 Associate Editors and the 32 colleagues who participated in advisory groups for this project. Praiseworthy is their generosity, expertise on race and racism, and personal commitments to racial justice.

Dedication

This volume was proposed and accepted for publication under the leadership of Dr. Lenoar Foster, former Editor-in-Chief of the ASHE Reader Series. We dedicate this third edition of the ASHE Reader on Racial and Ethnic Diversity to him. Indeed, Len's untimely and unexpected death continues to bring great sadness to us and other colleagues in the ASHE community who benefited from his goodness. While doing our work for this Reader, Dr. Foster remained on our minds for at least three reasons. First, he was so deeply committed to racial justice and the broadening of opportunity for persons of color in American higher education. Many of the ideals conveyed in this book were reflected in Len's scholarly and service work. Second, several colleagues whose research was selected for inclusion in this Reader had meaningful relationships with Len. We have found it impossible to bring together this extraordinarily rich collection of works without thinking about the man who generously encouraged, supported, and applauded generations of minority scholars and diversity researchers. And third, it unfortunately remains the case that Dr. Foster was among the first and very few Black full professors in our field. While we are continually disappointed by the underrepresentation of professors of color, we remain inspired by Professor Foster's ascension to the highest academic rank at his former institution, Washington State University.

We also dedicate this volume to Eric L. Dey, a beloved member of the ASHE community who was personally and professionally dedicated to equity and diversity. He worked actively with many campuses to assess and improve their climates for diverse populations of students, faculty, and staff. Dr. Dey's work was central to the University of Michigan's evidentiary case regarding affirmative action in higher education, which influenced the 2003 U.S. Supreme Court decisions. He was a brilliant member of the research team that linked cross-racial interactions to learning outcomes for all students, thus highlighting the educational benefits of diversity. Eric's unassuming and jovial manner will be missed by those who knew him and encountered his good work, particularly his former graduate students and colleagues in higher education communities of research and practice.

Shaun R. Harper, University of Pennsylvania
Sylvia Hurtado, UCLA

ABOUT THE EDITORS AND ASSOCIATE EDITORS

Shaun R. Harper is on the faculty in the Graduate School of Education, Africana Studies, and Gender Studies at the University of Pennsylvania. His research focuses on racism and gender inequities in U.S. higher education, Black male college access and achievement, the effects of college environments on student behaviors and outcomes, and gains associated with educationally purposeful student engagement. He has published nine books and more than 60 peer-reviewed journal articles, book chapters, and other academic publications. His books include *Student Engagement in Higher Education: Theoretical Perspectives and Practical Approaches for Diverse Populations* (Routledge, 2009); *College Men and Masculinities* (Jossey-Bass, 2010); and the fifth edition of *Student Services: A Handbook for the Profession* (Jossey-Bass, 2011). *The Journal of Higher Education, Journal of College Student Development, Teachers College Record, American Behavioral Scientist,* and several other well-regarded journals have published his research. Additionally, Harper has delivered over 40 keynote addresses and presented more than 125 research papers, workshops, and symposia at national education conferences. His professional honors include the 2010 Outstanding Contribution to Research Award from the National Association of Student Personnel Administrators, the 2010 Early Career Award from the American Educational Research Association (Division G: Social Context of Education), and the 2008 Early Career Award from the Association for the Study of Higher Education. His Ph.D. in Higher Education is from Indiana University.

Sylvia Hurtado is Professor and Director of the Higher Education Research Institute at the University of California, Los Angeles. She has written over 100 publications that focus on student development in college, sociology of education, and diversity in higher education. Hurtado is best known for her research on campus climate as it affects different racial/ethnic groups. Her books include *Intergroup Dialogue: Deliberative Democracy in School, College, Community, and Workplace* (University of Michigan Press, 2001); *Enacting Diverse Learning Environments: Improving the Climate for Racial/Ethnic Diversity in Higher Education* (Jossey-Bass, 1999); and *Defending Diversity: Affirmative Action at the University of Michigan* (University of Michigan Press, 2004). She is a past president of the Association for the Study of Higher Education. *Black Issues in Higher Education* (now *Diverse Issues in Higher Education*) named Hurtado among the Top 15 Influential Faculty who personify scholarship, service, and integrity and whose work has had substantial impact on the academy. She has conducted several national studies on diverse learning environments and retention, diversification of the scientific workforce, preparing students for a diverse democracy, and innovation in undergraduate education. Hurtado received her A.B. degree in sociology from Princeton University, master's degree in education from Harvard University, and Ph.D. in education from UCLA.

Marybeth Gasman is Associate Professor of Higher Education at the University of Pennsylvania, Graduate School of Education. She is also Vice President of the American Educational Research Association (Division F: History and Historiography). Her Ph.D. in Higher Education is from Indiana University.

Christopher Tudico is a researcher and archivist at The Josiah Macy, Jr. Foundation. His Ph.D. in Higher Education is from the University of Pennsylvania.

Kimberly A. Griffin is Assistant Professor and Research Associate in the Center for the Study of Higher Education at The Pennsylvania State University. Her Ph.D. in Higher Education and Organizational Change is from UCLA.

Walter R. Allen is the Allan Murray Cartter Professor of Higher Education and Distinguished Professor of Sociology at UCLA. His Ph.D. in Sociology is from the University of Chicago.

Jenny J. Lee is Associate Professor and Director of the Center for the Study of Higher Education at the University of Arizona. Her Ph.D. in Higher Education and Organizational Change is from UCLA.

Caroline Sotello Viernes Turner is a Professor in the Educational Leadership and Policy Studies doctoral program at California State University, Sacramento. She is also Professor Emerita and founding director of the doctoral program in Higher and Postsecondary Education at Arizona State University. Her Ph.D. in Administration and Policy Analysis is from Stanford University.

Stephen John Quaye is Assistant Professor of Education at the University of Maryland, College Park. His Ph.D. in Higher Education is from The Pennsylvania State University.

James T. Minor is a Senior Program Officer and Director of Higher Education Programs at the Southern Education Foundation. Formerly, he was a tenured Associate Professor in the Higher, Adult and Lifelong Education program at Michigan State University. His Ph.D. in Higher Education is from the University of Wisconsin–Madison.

Alma R. Clayton-Pedersen is Vice President for Education and Institutional Renewal at the Association of American Colleges and Universities. Her Ph.D. in Higher Education is from the Vanderbilt University Peabody College of Education and Human Development.

Bridget Terry Long is Professor of Higher Education at the Harvard Graduate School of Education. Her Ph.D. in Economics is from Harvard University.

Stella M. Flores is on the faculty in Higher Education, Public Policy, and Sociology at Vanderbilt University. Her Ed.D. in Higher Education is from the Harvard Graduate School of Education.

Lori D. Patton is Associate Professor of Higher Education at the University of Denver. Her Ph.D. in Higher Education is from Indiana University.

Robert T. Teranishi is Associate Professor of Higher Education at New York University. His Ph.D. in Higher Education and Organizational Change is from UCLA.

ADVISORY GROUP MEMBERS

The 13 Associate Editors consulted 32 experts in their respective content areas for advice and recommendations on the publications that were ultimately selected for inclusion in this Reader. Listed below are colleagues who generously contributed to the seven advisory groups.

Michael N. Bastedo, University of Michigan
Estela Mara Bensimon, University of Southern California
Bryan McKinley Jones Brayboy, Arizona State University
Alberto Cabrera, University of Maryland
Mitchell J. Chang, UCLA
Frances Contreras, University of Washington
Gertrude Fraser, University of Virginia
Kassie Freeman, Southern University System
Sharon L. Fries-Britt, University of Maryland
Juan Carlos González, California State University–Fresno
Evelyn Hu-DeHart, Brown University
Jerlando F. L. Jackson, University of Wisconsin–Madison
Victoria-Maria MacDonald, University of Maryland
Michele S. Moses, University of Colorado at Boulder
Michael A. Olivas, University of Houston
Gary Orfield, UCLA
Nana Osei-Kofi, Iowa State University
Linda M. Perkins, Claremont Graduate University
Laura W. Perna, University of Pennsylvania
Robert D. Reason, The Pennsylvania State University
Riyad A. Shahjahan, Miami University
Daryl G. Smith, Claremont Graduate University
Daniel G. Solórzano, UCLA
Edward P. St. John, University of Michigan
Christine A. Stanley, Texas A&M University
Terrell L. Strayhorn, The Ohio State University
John R. Thelin, University of Kentucky
Marta Tienda, Princeton University
Frank Tuitt, University of Denver
Joy A. Williamson, University of Washington
Tara J. Yosso, University of California, Santa Barbara
Ximena Zúñiga, University of Massachusetts, Amherst

PART I

HISTORY

MARYBETH GASMAN AND CHRISTOPHER TUDICO, ASSOCIATE EDITORS

Historians of higher education have often focused on elite and traditional institutions, as well as the upper and middle class students who have attended them. For instance, in 1965, when Laurence Veysey published his highly influential *The Emergence of the American University*, the bulk of the volume was littered with names of institutions such as Harvard, Columbia, Johns Hopkins, Stanford, Chicago, Michigan, and the University of California at Berkeley. Veysey's fascination with the history of elite universities, like other historians of higher education after him, obscures the stories of countless educational institutions in the United States—the grand majority of which are neither universities nor elite. Similarly, Frederick Rudolph's *The American College and University: A History*, written in 1962, devoted most of its attention to "established" colleges and universities. The collective result of this phenomenon was a very narrow portrait of the history of higher education, one that too often omitted the stories of Blacks, Latinos, Asian Americans, American Indians as well as lower-income students. Even John Thelin, who has arguably written the most comprehensive and inclusive history of American higher education, spent only a few pages discussing historically Black colleges and universities. Moreover, although Thelin alluded to the influence that Latino college students would have on the future, there was barely a mention of them in his expansive volume.

More recently, scholars have broadened their research agendas to include the histories of a wide range of institutions and peoples—from academic freedom and McCarthyism at historically Black colleges and universities to the experiences of the Choctaw Indians in higher education, and from the development of Hispanic-Serving Institutions (HSIs) to the enrollment of Japanese Americans in college during World War II. Each of these topics, as well as others, is featured in this section on the history of racial and ethnic diversity in higher education.

The section begins with Steven Crum's illuminating chapter, which chronicles one Indian nation's participation in higher education for nearly three-quarters of a century. Crum recounts how education became a primary goal of the Choctaw after the nation was forced to move from their ancestral homeland in Mississippi to Oklahoma in the early 1830s. He contends that Choctaw elders viewed college as a "survival tactic" and a means to educate future generations, who would, in turn, lead and serve the nation. As a result, the Choctaw sent students east, to Delaware College and Union College (among others), to earn an education. Crum concludes, over time, that the Choctaw gradually came to view formalized European-American education as one of the best ways to interact with the larger White majority. However, this Indian nation also simultaneously maintained its own history and culture.

In Chapter 2, Linda M. Perkins recounts the often painful experiences of young Black women who attended elite women's colleges of the Northeast. These young women persevered despite being ostracized and marginalized by their White classmates. According to Perkins, the Seven Sister colleges replicated American society, and in effect, racism and prejudice followed the women to campus. Ironically, even though White women faced discrimination and sexism themselves, they neither felt a kinship with the Black women nor saw them as equals. Perkins's research also reveals that Black women who attended the Seven Sister colleges were highly successful upon graduation, despite the challenges they faced.

Mark R. Connolly examines in Chapter 3 an entirely different aspect of race and ethnicity in American higher education. He uses case studies of Miami University, Eastern Michigan University, and the University of Illinois to examine the role of American Indian names and symbols attached to each institution. These manifestations typically appear in the form of sports teams' names and mascots. Connolly includes a brief history of the Indian names each institution became affiliated with, the universities themselves, and the nicknames that became synonymous with the schools. Throughout the course of the 1920s and 1930s, the names of the Redskins, Huron, and Fighting Illini were attached to Miami, Eastern Michigan, and Illinois, respectively. Connolly's study highlights the complex relationship between the objectification of American Indians (in the form of nicknames and symbols), the growth of intercollegiate athletics, the perspectives of alumni and donor, and regional pride.

Thomas James details in Chapter 4 the bittersweet story of the 4,000 Nisei (2nd generation Japanese Americans) who left interment camps to attend college. The reflections of the Nisei lay the foundation for James's narrative, one that uncovers the hope and trepidation of the students who left their families behind to enroll in colleges and universities. James's study of the experience of the Nisei college students offers valuable insight into the sudden concentration and dispersal of Japanese Americans during wartime. Moreover, the reflections of the students illuminate the many challenges and complexities faced by a group of people attempting to gain acceptance into a society where citizenship and social status were racially predetermined.

In Chapter 5, James D. Anderson examines the pervasive institutional racism that stood in the way of Blacks joining the faculty at White colleges and universities following World War II. Anderson highlights the seemingly hypocritical nature of the leaders of these institutions: college presidents vigorously promoted the idea of meritocracy, yet prevented highly qualified Blacks from becoming professors. According to Anderson, there were virtually no exceptions to this pattern of discrimination. At roughly the same time that White college presidents restricted access to their faculty ranks, the specter of McCarthyism swept across America and college and university campuses, including those of Black colleges. Marybeth Gasman examines in Chapter 6 the unenviable task that faced the president of one Black college: whether or not to fire a productive faculty member rumored to be associated with the Communist Party. Gasman argues that in a politically charged setting, Charles S. Johnson chose to let a faculty member from Fisk go in order to protect the Black college from demise. She predicts that the institution's White donors would have pulled their financial support had the president not fired the faculty member. Gasman's study of Fisk complicates the issues of academic freedom, civil rights, and the sometimes precarious position of Black colleges in the age of McCarthyism.

Similarly, Joy Ann Williamson explores in Chapter 7 how Tougaloo College's support of the Civil Rights Movement affected the historically Black college. She notes that private Black colleges faced threats to their institutional autonomy that their larger public counterparts were spared. Being indebted to philanthropists and having a smaller enrollment placed undue reliance on outside benefactors of the school. While supporting the Civil Rights Movement coincided with the fabric of Tougaloo's mission, the college's liberal leanings and support of racial equality marked the institution as radical within the social order of the South. Consequently, it became a prime target of racists. Ultimately, Williamson contends that Tougaloo's role in the Civil Rights Movement became a liability in lean economic times. In contrast to Fisk University's president, Charles S. Johnson, Tougaloo's president, Adam Beittel, was White. Juxtaposed, these two historical case studies provide a complex look into race relations in the South at the nation's Black colleges.

Victoria-Maria MacDonald, John M. Botti, and Lisa Hoffman Clark chronicle the Latino experience in American higher education in Chapter 8. Their analysis begins with the Higher Education Act of 1965 to the designation of Title V in the Act's 1998 reauthorization. The authors note that along this pathway the Latino experience in higher education evolved from establishing visibility and legitimacy to self-determination, self-scrutiny, emulation, and finally, autonomy. MacDonald, Botti, and Clark compare and contrast the story of Latinos in higher education with that of African Americans, and conclude their chapter by looking at the role of Hispanic-Serving Institutions in American higher education.

Conclusion

Whether the history of individual peoples such as the Choctaw or Nisei, or that of specific colleges like Fisk or Tougaloo, each chapter in this section contributes much to the historical study of race in American higher education. Together, these histories represent an expansion in the range of institutions and populations studied by scholars. And yet, the historians who authored the chapters only scratch the surface of the history of racial and ethnic diversity in higher education. There are countless other stories that have not yet been written. Exploring and documenting these accounts is crucial to illuminating the voice of people of color in the history of higher education. With this enlightenment, students of color will see themselves reflected in the history of our nation's colleges and universities. Moreover, White students will have greater access to historical narratives pertaining to populations and institutions that they are unlikely to encounter in popular higher education history books.

References

Rudolph, F. (1962). *The American college and university: A history*. New York: Alfred A. Knopf.

Thelin, J. R. (2004). *A history of American higher education*. Baltimore: Johns Hopkins University Press.

Veysey, L. (1965). *The emergence of the American university*. Chicago: University of Chicago Press.

CHAPTER 1
THE CHOCTAW NATION: CHANGING THE APPEARANCE OF AMERICAN HIGHER EDUCATION, 1830–1907

STEVEN CRUM

In September 1830 the U.S. government negotiated the Treaty of Dancing Rabbit Creek with some leaders of the Choctaw Nation. The treaty reinforced the congressional Indian Removal Act of 1830, which paved the way for the large-scale physical removal of tens of thousands of tribal people of the southeast, including many of the Choctaw. It provided for the "removal" of the Choctaw from their traditional homeland in Mississippi to Indian Territory. Over a two-year period, from 1831 to 1833, roughly thirteen thousand to fifteen thousand Choctaw, or about half of the tribe, moved to the region we now call southeastern Oklahoma.[1]

The Treaty of Dancing Rabbit Creek proved to be a mixed blessing. If it paved the way for tribal removal, which the Choctaw viewed as something negative, it also had other provisions, which benefited them. One was a higher education provision. Article Twenty directed the President of the United States to provide for the education of "forty Choctaw youths for twenty years."[2] Although the treaty did not specify a collegiate education, both the treaty negotiators and the tribal leaders understood that advanced education was an ultimate goal of the Choctaw Nation. After all, the Choctaw people, as noted in the treaty, were "in a state of rapid advancement in education" and wanted a delegate sitting in the U.S. House of Representatives.[3] Political representation thus became part of the treaty negotiations as the Choctaw wanted some amount of future political power.

There was more than one reason why some Choctaw leaders favored higher education for their tribal membership. One was the need for highly educated leaders who would lead the Choctaw Nation into the future. Moreover, by the second quarter of the nineteenth century, the Choctaw people came to view formalized Euroamerican education as a way to interact effectively with the white Americans.[4] To use the words of Choctaw historian Clara Sue Kidwell, "Choctaw leaders, both full bloods and mixed bloods, wanted education that would allow their children to deal with the white men on their own terms."[5] Lastly, the Choctaw viewed education as a "survival" tactic in an ever-changing world. According to Choctaw educator Grayson Noley, the Choctaw "accepted change as inevitable," and formalized schooling in the early nineteenth century was a manifestation of surviving in a shifting world, which included complex interactions with white America.[6]

Even before the signing of the 1830 treaty, a certain percentage of the Choctaw had accepted American-styled education. Several students had attended the missionary-run Choctaw Academy established in Kentucky in 1825. Although possessing the Choctaw tribal name, this school was actually run by the Baptist denomination. The school officials firmly believed that Native Americans needed to become "civilized" as the dominant society viewed native cultures as savage like. The teachers offered the tribal students basic American subject matter, including English reading and writing, and math. The highest numbers of students were Choctaw, and their education was paid for by funds coming from a Choctaw treaty negotiated the same year the school came into existence.[7] Besides the Choctaw Academy, a few Choctaw had briefly attended some colleges in the 1820s before the 1830 treaty.[8]

It appeared that a large number of Choctaw had firmly accepted the white man's so-called "civilization" by favoring formalized Euroamerican schooling. Hence, the general public labeled the Choctaw tribe as one of the "Five Civilized Tribes."[9] Yet the Choctaw remained different from the larger dominant society because of their distinct tribal culture and political identity.[10] They viewed themselves as a nation within a nation. For several decades up to the dissolution of Indian Territory in 1907, they gave a new appearance to their higher education experience. Owing to their cultural and political distinctiveness, they took some American practices and reshaped them. The first way was by carrying out groupness behavior; the second was by returning to their native homeland; and the third was by carrying out equal gender representation, especially in the last two decades of the nineteenth century.

The first way the Choctaw Nation gave a new appearance to higher education was by sending students in groups to particular mainstream colleges. This stood in contrast to white American municipal governments, state governments, and the federal government, which played no role in determining where college students pursued their higher education. Instead, individual families and the students themselves made this decision. The end result was that Euroamerican students attended hundreds of colleges and universities of their choice across the nation.

The Choctaw, as an Indian nation, applied a tribal or group behavioral pattern to a new situation; in this case, earmarking specific postsecondary institutions. This groupness orientation—"Itapela Hosh Nana Yakomichi," or "Doing things as a Group"—became evident in 1842 when the Choctaw national council, in accordance with the 1830 treaty, decided to send four groups of students to the following colleges: ten to Jefferson College in Pennsylvania; ten to Indiana Asbury University (today's Purdue); ten to Ohio University; and ten to an unspecified college, later determined to be Lafayette College in Pennsylvania.[11]

But if the Choctaw leadership had intentions of sending four groups of students to the named colleges, it soon after backed away from this effort for several reasons. First, Choctaw students attending the missionary-run Choctaw Academy were not ready for a collegiate education at this time. Second, the Choctaw leadership wanted to build its own tribally run high school and send the graduates to college at a later date. That school became a reality in 1844 when the Nation created Spencer Academy.[12] Third, by the early 1840s, most of the treaty money earmarked for "forty youth" had been largely spent sending more advanced students to the Choctaw Academy in Kentucky. The council thus resolved that a new fund needed to be created from the remaining treaty money, and once the interest had accumulated, the fund would be used for college-bound Spencer graduates. According to one commentator, the council's position stood as follows: "The Choctaws have also set apart a fund for the collegiate education of which they propose, after it shall have accumulated for a few years more, to apply annually to this purpose. The young men are expected to pursue their preparatory studies at their own schools, for which provisions are made, and to be subsequently sent to colleges in the United States."[13] Thus, the "Forty Youth Fund" officially came into existence in the early 1840s.

Finally, in 1848, the Choctaw leaders decided to send some of the Spencer graduates to college. As there was no postsecondary institution in Indian Territory, they chose to take the students to an unspecified eastern college. Tribal leader Peter Pitchlynn accompanied five young Choctaw men (Leonidas Garland, Joseph Hall, William Howell, Lycurgus Pitchlynn, and Allen Wright) and two Chickasaw (Holmes Colbert and Frederic McCarley) to Washington, DC. The delegation visited William Medill, commissioner of the Office of Indian Affairs (today's Bureau of Indian Affairs, BIA), who quickly realized that the Choctaw had not selected a college. He therefore recommended nearby Delaware College (today's University of Delaware) in Newark, Delaware. Some eighteen years after the signing of the Dancing Rabbit Creek Treaty, the first Choctaw students thus entered college. But instead of forty, there were only seven Spencer-educated students, primarily because a larger number of Choctaw students were not academically prepared for a higher education. Nevertheless, the Nation finally carried out the educational provision of the treaty.[14] Of equal significance was the fact that the Choctaw Nation had sent a group of students to a single college. As already noted, this action was due to the Choctaw thinking in terms of groupness, a native practice which predated the white Americans.

Life did not go well for some of the seven Indian students at Delaware College. William Howell died in early 1849. There were conflicting accounts about his death. One college official stated that he died of tuberculosis. Another account states that someone pushed him down a stairway. College officials regarded Lycurgus Pitchlynn and Leonidas Garland as troublemakers. Pitchlynn eventually withdrew and returned to Indian Territory where his undesirable behavior continued. Garland remained but he complained frequently about the weather, the size of the college, and the students' housing and money problems. Some of his complaints were legitimate, especially about money and housing problems, which were universal for students in general.[15]

On a more positive note, most of the Indian students joined ranks with the larger student population both socially and academically. Four became members of the campus-based Athenaean Literary Society, and two belonged to the Delta Phi Fraternity. Even though some of the students needed preparatory work, they quickly became full-fledged collegians. After one year of attendance, the Choctaw were sophomores and the Chickasaw freshmen.[16]

However, Indian attendance at Delaware College did not last long. In early 1850, college president James Wilson declared that the college would no longer offer collegiate work, and rumors surfaced that the college would close. The students pursuing a liberal education were required to leave and attend another college. Wilson saw to it that the Indians, along with a larger number of whites, transferred to Union College in Schenectady, New York. In April of that year, the three remaining Choctaws—Garland, Hall, and Wright—and the two Chickasaws moved to upper New York to adjust to a new environment all over again.[17]

As had been the case at Delaware College, some Indian students had problems at Union. Officials described Leonidas Garland as "gloomy" and depressed. He left college, returned briefly, but left a second time permanently and returned to Indian Territory. James Hall and Holmes Colbert showed signs of homesickness by late 1850. Eventually, by 1852, all the Indian students, except for Allen Wright, had withdrawn from Union and returned to the Choctaw Nation. As is already apparent, their reasons for leaving were multiple. They had been sent half way across the continent and were bound to become lonely, isolated, and homesick for their families and tribal kinfolk. Money was also a problem. Because of the great distance from home, they were unable to secure funds immediately from their families or from the Choctaw Nation.[18]

The one big success story, however, was Allen Wright, who earned his bachelor's degree from Union College in 1852. He then pursued graduate study at the Union Theological Seminary in New York City and earned a master's degree in 1855, thereby becoming the first tribal individual from Indian Territory to finish graduate school. Wright, of course, received financial support under the Forty Youth Fund while pursuing his higher education. He went on to do great things. The Choctaw Nation elected him as Principal Chief in 1866. He has been credited for popularizing the name "Oklahoma" ("Red People" in the Choctaw language) which became the name of what was left of Indian Territory in 1907. In short, Allen Wright had traveled a long path. He was born in Mississippi in 1826, was part of the Choctaw removal to Indian Territory in 1832, entered Spencer Academy in 1844, and ended up earning two college degrees a decade later.[19]

Upon finishing his higher education in 1855, Allen Wright chose not to remain back east or to live out his life in the larger dominant society. Instead, he chose to return home to the Choctaw Nation. He stated his position in a letter to Indian Bureau commissioner G.W. Manypenny in May 1855: "I am through . . . then I must think about making preparation to return to the Choctaw Nation whence I have been so long absent."[20]

There were several reasons why Wright returned home. One reason was that, like other Choctaw, he was not a citizen of the United States. Rather he was a member of the Choctaw Nation, which had subsidized his higher education. Thus he felt an obligation to return home and serve his nation. Another reason is that the Choctaw people had a strong traditional kinship system that had existed for generations before Euroamerican contact. Concerning the importance of kinship, Choctaw historian Donna Akers writes: "The most basic type of relationship was that of kinship.

Kinship provided identity to the individual, the family, the clan, and the village. It defined all Choctaw people and, therefore, all people who were not Choctaw. Kinship dictated behavior and ordered the way each human related to all others."[21] Like other Choctaw, Wright was an individual who belonged to a kinship network, and returning home allowed him to rejoin his kinship. Owing to the above reasons, most or perhaps all Choctaw college students also returned to the Choctaw Nation from the 1840s forward. Returning home became the second way of giving a new appearance to their higher education experience.

One might argue that perhaps the Choctaw returned home because of racial and job discrimination. Certainly, discrimination applied to African-American teachers of the nineteenth century, for only 8.3 percent secured jobs outside the southern states by 1890.[22] However, there is little if any evidence that college-educated Choctaw sought jobs back east. Instead, like Allen Wright, they chose to return home either before or at the time of college graduation.

In marked contrast to the Choctaw, a significant number of Euroamerican students in the mid-nineteenth century did not return home on a permanent basis after leaving or finishing college. Instead, they viewed higher education as a way to move out and up, not to return to the communities of their origins. In his examination of the graduates of South Carolina College between the years 1830 and 1860, historian Michael Sugrue asserts that "almost half of the alumni left the state [South Carolina], and nearly all went to the lower South."[23] This example was fairly typical of white college graduates of the nineteenth century. Historian Burton Bledstein concludes that the "Mid-Victorians," or the rising Euroamerican middle class of the nineteenth century, had "cultivated a new vision, a vertical vision that compelled persons to look upward." In doing so, they "rejected horizontal social unity."[24] In short, white American students came to view higher education as the appropriate path to upward social and economic mobility. They looked at the world vertically whereas the Choctaw viewed it horizontally, and the Choctaw vision led Choctaw students to return home. By returning home to the Choctaw Nation, the Choctaw college student had gone "Full Circle" (from home to college, then back home), to use a phrase made popular by twentieth century Iroquois educator Ron LaFrance.[25]

As for the four Choctaws and two Chickasaws who did not graduate from Union College, the larger dominant society would have labeled them as failures or college dropouts. But perhaps there is another way of looking at their experience. Instead of viewing them as dropouts, perhaps we can view them as drop-ins; that is, dropping back into tribal society where some of them became prominent individuals. For example, Holmes Colbert became a politician and delegate for the Chickasaw Nation by the 1860s.[26]

Despite the fact that only one Choctaw had graduated from Union College, the Choctaw Nation did not become discouraged in its effort to send students to college. Yet, at the same time, some leaders implied that they made a mistake by sending five young men roughly a thousand miles away from home. The Choctaw national council therefore initiated some changes. In 1850, it sent four students (Thomas Jefferson Bond, David Folsom, L.D. James, and George W. Harkins) to Centre College in Danville, Kentucky. Not only was this college closer to Indian Territory, but Kentucky was familiar territory as many Choctaw students had lived in the region earlier while attending the former Choctaw Academy before the early 1840s.[27]

In contrast to the first group of students, most of the second group graduated from college. Thomas Jefferson Bond earned his bachelor's degree in 1854, pursued a medical education at Pennsylvania Medical College in Philadelphia, returned to Indian Territory in 1858, and ended up being a prominent Choctaw leader until his death in 1879. He served as superintendent of Choctaw national education, as Choctaw national treasurer twice, and was elected as a senator from the Atoka district on the Choctaw national council. David Folsom also earned his bachelor's degree in 1854, returned home and became a successful businessman. Although George Harkins did not graduate from Centre, he transferred to Cumberland University in Lebanon, Tennessee where he earned a law degree. He too returned to Indian Territory and later became superintendent of the nearby Chickasaw national board of education. Little if any information exists about L.D. James, except for his student status at Centre College in 1853.[28]

Although the Choctaw Nation sent a group of students to a particular college, it did not always follow this practice. In the 1850s alone, a few tribal members attended other colleges, not as part of a group, but singly. Hiram Pitchlynn first attended DePauw University in the late 1840s and later transferred to the Jefferson Medical College in Philadelphia. Kenan Pitchlynn briefly attended the Indiana Central Medical College in the early 1850s. Mary Pitchlynn briefly attended the Southern Masonic Female College and then the Virginia Female Institute in the mid-1850s. All were related to a major leader of the Choctaw at that time, Peter Pitchlynn. Joseph Folsom entered Dartmouth College in 1850 and graduated four years later. Like other college-educated Choctaw, Folsom also returned home. As a tribal leader, he later compiled Choctaw laws published in 1869 under the title of Constitution and Laws of the Choctaw Nation and Treaties of 1855, 1856, and 1866. He participated in the Okmulgee Council of 1870, which sought to create a unified inter-tribal government in Indian Territory, consisting of the Choctaw and other tribes.[29] Here again are examples of returning home.

However, sending an individual student to a college, independent of a group, was the exception rather than the rule. In 1857 alone, the Choctaw Nation sent three students—Claudius Kincaid, Edwin McKinney, and James Riley—to Wesleyan University (today's University of North Alabama) in Florence, Alabama. Little is known about two of these students, largely because the oldest historical records of the university no longer exist. What is known is that James Riley probably graduated, as he was identified as a senior in 1860. Upon finishing his schooling, he too returned home, immediately became Choctaw National Secretary, and then was elected to the Choctaw National Council in 1861. In 1858, the Nation sent two women to the Eldgeworth Seminary in Pittsburgh, Pennsylvania. Little if anything is known about one of them. The other, Jane McCurtain, graduated in 1861, returned home, and later married a prominent Choctaw politician.[30]

Choctaw Nation higher education came to an abrupt halt when the Choctaws became engrossed in Civil War politics and war. Because of the Nation's proximity to the South, and because some of its leaders owned Black slaves, the Choctaw government made a treaty with the Confederate government in 1861 to support the Confederacy against the Union. No Choctaw students experienced higher education from 1861 to 1865. Nor would the tribal students pursue a higher education in the immediate years after the end of the war, while the Choctaw went through a period of financial and economic recovery. Like the other tribal governments of the Five Tribes of eastern Indian Territory, the United States government punished the Choctaw for having sided with the Confederacy. In April 1866, the Choctaw and nearby Chickasaw jointly signed a Reconstruction treaty that compelled them to free their slaves and to cede part of their tribal domain.[31]

Not until 1868 did the Choctaw Nation start to once again consider advanced education for its students. But the Nation had serious problems with limited financial resources. Very little was left of the Forty Youth Fund to subsidize students. Limited resources prompted Thomas Jefferson Bond, earlier graduate of Centre College and superintendent of Choctaw education, to make the following comment to the federal Indian Office in Washington, DC in March 1868: "I would respectfully request that such sum of money known as the 'Forty Youth Fund' that may be due up to this time, be paid once to me for the use and benefit of the Choctaw youths who are now in the states at school."[32] By 1869, whatever was left in the fund disappeared as the Choctaw Nation made the decision to use it to pay postwar debts that stemmed from a legal matter.[33] The fund thus became a victim of postwar hard times.

In an effort to secure funds for college students, the Choctaw leaders turned to the Indian Bureau in the late 1860s and early 1870s. Peter Pitchlynn asked the Bureau to provide funds for his son Thomas who was attending Pennsylvania College. Apparently, the Bureau had promised $300 in 1869, but that money had not been forthcoming by 1870. Soon after, Pitchlynn asked the Bureau to provide funds for Choctaw student Thomas Howell, who was attending Kings College in Tennessee and who wanted to pursue a medical education at the University of Maryland. Pitchlynn asked for funds from the Bureau's "civilization fund," used to pay the education of Indian students in mainstream schools. But the Bureau refused to provide funds, arguing that Howell was too advanced in his education.[34] There was perhaps another reason why the Bureau did not issue support under its civilization fund. It used this congressional source, in existence since 1819, to support private and missionary schools who were in the business of "civilizing" Native Americans with the basics of education.

Limited funding had become such a serious issue that the Choctaw national council passed a law in November 1871 to provide one thousand dollars to bring home the few Choctaw college students who were still away attending school. But the Choctaw treasury had no funds for this purpose.[35] At least one Choctaw student, G.W. Folsom, asked the Indian Bureau if it could provide emergency funding so that he could return home to the Choctaw Nation. In February 1872, while finishing his medical education at St. Louis University, Folsom wrote to the Bureau: "I have just finished my course in Medicine, and am anxious to *return home* [emphasis mine] to the Nation and finding myself much reduced of means."[36] The Bureau however provided no travel money.

The postwar Choctaw financial crisis most likely prevented some Choctaw students from earning college degrees. Oliver Jones attended Howard University in Washington, DC, for three years, from 1869 to 1872, took two years of college preparatory work, but withdrew after his freshman year in college.[37] A. Frank Ross attended Baylor College in Waco, Texas, but also did not graduate. Jacob B. Jackson, who also did not graduate, presents one of the more interesting cases of financial need. He attended Roanoke College in Virginia from 1872 to 1874. While in college, tribal leader and college graduate Allen Wright appealed on his behalf. Wright wrote to the Bureau and emphasized that Choctaw college students in the early 1870s had been "sent home on account of the want of funds to defray their expenses at schools." He went on to note that the "Choctaw Nation" was "no longer able to support" Jackson. Wright thus asked the Bureau for $270.00 from the "civilization fund" to pay Jackson's college expenses.[38] In the end, the Bureau agreed to provide support, but bureaucratic slowness and foot-dragging forced Jackson to remind the Bureau repeatedly of the needed money.[39] In the end, another Choctaw leader, Peter Pitchlynn, appealed on Jackson's behalf. In April 1874, Pitchlynn wrote the following to the Bureau: "we respectfully request that the sum of $200 be advanced to Jacob B. Jackson a Choctaw to pay expenses incurred by him while a student at Salem Virginia and to enable him to *return home* [emphasis mine] . . . He has finished his course and wants to go back to his people."[40] After the Bureau turned down the request, Jackson returned home in the spring of 1874 without a college degree and without federal support.

One development became obvious in the late 1860s and early 1870s in the period of instability and financial need. The Choctaw Nation did not send a group of students to a particular college. Rather, the few who pursued a collegiate education went to particular colleges singly.

By the mid-1870s, the Choctaw Nation had recovered from the postwar crisis and developed a stable economy. One major source of income came from the selling of natural resources, including coal, rock, and timber. With a markedly improved financial state, the Choctaw national council appropriated $4,534.00 in 1875 for the postsecondary education of Choctaw students. This new fund no longer had the old name of the Forty Youth Fund. Rather it was called "Choctaw Students in the States" (outside of Indian Territory) or the "Royalty Scholars" program, named after the royalties coming from natural resource income.[41] College-educated Choctaw leaders were largely responsible for making sure the Nation provided sufficient funds for students. Thomas Jefferson Bond, superintendent of Choctaw education, stressed the "great importance or necessity of pushing forward the cause of education . . . it is for the Choctaw people, through their National council, to act in the matter of increasing the amount of the [higher education] school fund."[42]

Having recovered economically, the Choctaw Nation once again carried its practice of sending a group of students to a particular college. In the fall of 1876, Edmund McCurtain, the new superintendent of Choctaw education, escorted eight Choctaw students to Roanoke College in Virginia. Without doubt, the reason why the Nation chose Roanoke was owing to the influence of Jacob B. Jackson. By this time, Jackson was one of twelve elected senators sitting on the Choctaw national council.[43] Although he himself did not have a college degree, Jackson looked upon his college experience as a positive force, and he held a high opinion of his alma mater. In the second half of the 1870s and into the following decade, a substantial number of Choctaws attended Roanoke.

Like the earlier group sent to Delaware College and later Union College in the late 1840s and early 1850s, only one Choctaw from the 1876 group earned a degree from Roanoke. N.B. Ainsworth earned an AB degree in 1881. Like the earlier groups of Choctaw students, Ainsworth and the rest of the Roanoke group also returned to the Choctaw Nation. Ainsworth later became the official auditor of the Nation.[44]

Following the 1876 group, the Nation sent other groups to Roanoke. Of the latter groups, four more earned degrees: William Harrison McKinley, AB degree in 1883; James Bower, AB in 1890; Solomon James Homer, AB in 1893; and James Alfred Dukes, AB in 1896. These tribal members also returned home. McKinley pursued graduate school at the Yale Divinity School and returned home to become an evangelist. Homer pursued a legal education at Harvard and the University of Kansas, then returned home and became National Secretary and also superintendent of Armstrong Academy, a lower-level Choctaw school. Dukes became the Speaker of the House of the Nation in 1899.[45]

As in previous periods, not all Choctaw ended up as part of a group in the 1870s and 1880s. A few went singly. Allen Wright's sons chose to attend the alma mater of their father. Eliphalet N. Wright, who graduated from Spencer Academy in 1878, attended Union College from 1878 to 1882. Upon earning his bachelor's degree, he pursued a medical education and earned an MD degree in 1884 from the Albany Medical College. He returned to the Choctaw Nation and became a physician. In 1895, the Choctaw populace elected him to the national council. His brother Frank also graduated from Union, pursued religious training at the Union Theological Seminary, and returned to the Nation to become a Christian missionary.[46] William A. Durant graduated from Arkansas College in 1886. Likewise, William F. Semple graduated from Washington and Lee University in Lexington, Virginia, in 1907.[47] Both Durant and Semple returned home and became Choctaw politicians.

Regardless of a few Choctaw students going to particular colleges on an individual basis, the Choctaw Nation adhered to its practice of sending groups to certain colleges up to the end of the nineteenth century. In the 1880s and 1890s, besides Roanoke, the Nation sent sizable groups to Baird College in nearby Missouri; Drury College, also in Missouri; and Henry Kendall College, a Presbyterian-run college established in Muskogee, Indian Territory in 1894. Although most did not graduate, they all returned home. Some graduates and nongraduates became noted figures in Choctaw history. Peter J. Hudson, after earning his AB degree from Drury in 1887, returned home to become a national interpreter owing to his native language fluency. Victor Locke, Jr., who attended Drury in 1895–96, became a noted tribal politician after the turn of the century. Gabe Parker graduated from Henry Kendall in 1899, taught at Spencer Academy briefly and then became principal of Armstrong Academy from 1900 to 1904.[48]

The third way the Choctaw Nation gave a new appearance to their higher education experience was by sending equal numbers of tribal men and women to college, especially in the last two decades of the nineteenth century. The Choctaw people, according to linguist Jacob Bohanon, had a phrase for this arrangement: "Nakni micha ohoyo etilawit holisso apisa ashachi tok" (men and women were equally placed in school).[49] The Choctaw gender balance stood in marked contrast to the larger dominant society in which college-going was largely a male enterprise in the second half of the nineteenth century. Noted educational historian Lawrence Cremin asserts that American higher education at the turn of the century was "overwhelmingly" male.[50] In 1873 less than 15 percent of the postsecondary education population in the U.S. was women. By 1889, it stood at around 20 percent, or slightly higher, depending on whom we read.[51] If the Choctaws had a 50/50 ratio, the white Americans had an 80/20 (or 64/36 on the high end) ratio around 1890.

For the Choctaw decision to pursue gender representation in higher education, there were perhaps two possible influences. One was the earlier precontact Choctaw matrilineal tradition in which a person's identity was based on the mother's side of the family. In this earlier indigenous world, women played an important role in the home education of children as well as other aspects of life.[52] Even after contact, both men and women recognized the influence of women. Two Choctaw male leaders, Allen Wright and J.B. Turnbull, made the statement that "it is more important to educate girls than boys, because mothers have the larger influence in training and educating children."[53] The second was the acculturation process of the nineteenth century. Like the other Five Tribes of Indian Territory, the Choctaw had also been affected by Euroamerican missionaries both before and after removal. In the first half of the century, the Congregationalists under the American Board of Commissioners for Foreign Missions (ABCFM) made a visible inroad into the Choctaw world. After ABCFM withdrew in 1859, the Presbyterians became the most visible entity.[54] A missionary legacy was to view formalized education as a way to "uplift" the people and to serve as a "civilizing" agent. In this process, native women also came to be viewed as uplifting educational agents who could serve their children, husbands, and of course the larger tribal population.[55]

After some Choctaw accepted formalized American education in the early nineteenth century, there was a tendency to follow the Euroamerican model. In the initial stages of the Choctaw pursuit of American-styled higher education, only a few women attended. We have only the names of Mary Pitchlynn and Jane McCurtain for the pre–Civil War period. As the years went by, however, the Choctaw male leadership realized that women too needed higher education. Because most of the pre–1870 educational records of the Choctaw Nation no longer exist, we have only isolated Choctaw statements of both men and women receiving equal treatment in the early years of the Forty Youth Fund. Allen Wright stated in 1873 that the "Choctaw Nation usually sends and maintains about twenty youths of both sexes equal in numbers in the states to be educated out of the fund known as 'Forty youths fund'."[56]

In the last quarter of the nineteenth century, however, the Nation made certain that the men and women who received higher education support were equally represented. The national council asserted in 1890 that the students "shall be selected from the various districts . . . and the number of each sex shall be kept equal."[57] By 1899, the Nation provided twelve thousand dollars to send forty Choctaw students to college, twenty men and twenty women. Many of the women ended up at Drury and Baird, such as Anna Dwight, Junia Folsom, Mary LeFlore, Lorinda Maytubby, and Florence Turnbull. A few of them graduated, including Lutie May Walcott, who earned her bachelor's degree from Baird in 1892.[58]

College-educated Choctaw women, in stark contrast to the men, were less visible in the nineteenth century. This development was due to more than one factor. One was that men continued to serve as the public political leaders as had been practiced in traditional times. Males naturally received more attention, especially after the American government and its Indian Bureau dealt with Indian male leaders, but not women. On the other hand, Choctaw women remained influential advisors and indirect politicians, even though they were not elected to political positions.[59] Additionally, women took the last names of their husbands, thus making it difficult to trace their postcollege lives. The end result is that, compared to men, we know much less about the highly educated Choctaw women.

Some women, however, became highly prominent individuals. In 1894, the Choctaw government selected Jane McCurtain as superintendent of the tribally run Jones Academy, an all-male school. As a school administrator, wife, and mother, she encouraged her two daughters, Ida and Lucinda, to pursue a higher education in the 1890s.[60] Perhaps the most eminent college-educated Choctaw woman was Czarina Colbert Conlan, who attended Mary Baldwin College in Virginia for two years, in 1889 and 1890, but did not graduate. Upon returning to Indian Territory, she helped found more than one Indian women's organization. Conlan became the first President of the Indian Territory federation of women. After the turn of the century, she became supervisor of the Oklahoma State Historical Society Museum for some twenty years.[61]

In the end, Choctaw Nation support for higher education came to an end at the turn of the twentieth century. The end was due to the federal government choosing to dissolve the Indian governments as well as Indian Territory itself, paving the way for the creation of Oklahoma. Congress passed the Curtis Act in 1898 to dissolve the Indian national governments in Indian Territory by March 1906. One scholar, Sanda Faiman-Silva, appropriately called this act "tribal termination."[62] The Choctaws saw the handwriting on the wall. In 1900, when Spencer Academy burnt down, the Nation made no effort to rebuild it.[63] As noted in this chapter, Spencer was the big feeder school for those who pursued a postsecondary education. In 1903, the Nation dissolved the position of superintendent of public instruction, a position held by various college-educated Choctaw leaders in earlier years.[64] Choctaws could no longer elect their leaders, and beginning in 1910, the President of the United States appointed the principal chiefs. With the end of Indian Territory, and the establishment of Oklahoma in 1907, the federal Indian Office took over many of the earlier functions of the Choctaw Nation.[65] Choctaws no longer had a distinct tribally based higher education program, nor would the tribe re-create one until the last quarter of the twentieth century.

However, it did not matter that the "Students in the States" or "Royalty" scholars program had ended at the beginning of the new century. On their own, individual Choctaw parents, especially those who had earlier experienced higher education, encouraged and supported their children and grandchildren to pursue a higher education. Vivia Locke, the daughter of Victor Locke, earned a bachelor's degree in English from the University of Oklahoma in 1939. After earning a master's degree, she went on to become a Professor of Theater at Oklahoma State University from 1950 to 1981. Muriel Wright, the granddaughter of Allen Wright and daughter of Eliphalet Wright, temporarily attended Wheaton College in Massachusetts and then earned a bachelor's degree from East Central State College in Ada, Oklahoma, in 1912. She went on to become a recognized person within the Oklahoma Historical Society. Irene Hudson Heard, the daughter of Peter Hudson, attended both Drury College and Southeastern State University in Durant, Oklahoma, in the early twentieth century.[66] In short, what the Choctaw people of the nineteenth century had done was to create a higher education legacy that has extended up to the present time.

Of equal significance, several of the pre-1907 college-educated Choctaws became recognizable Choctaw leaders and administrators in the early twentieth century. Victor Locke Jr., served as Principal Chief from 1911 to 1917, William F. Semple as chief from 1918 to 1922, and William Durant as chief from 1937 to 1948. Gabe Parker served as Indian office superintendent of the Five Civilized Tribes agency of eastern Oklahoma from 1915 to 1922.[67]

Before concluding this essay, a word needs to be said about the elitist appearance of Choctaw Nation education. Some scholars maintain that Choctaw education of the nineteenth century was elitist; that is, the tribal students who attended preremoval missionary schools and postremoval tribal schools, including Spencer, were primarily mixed-blood students who came from wealthy Indian families.[68] In examining Choctaw higher education from 1830 to 1907, there appears to be truth in such a claim. For example, of the five Choctaw students who attended Delaware College in 1848, four were mixed-bloods, and only one was a full-blood. Most came from prominent Choctaw families. Two of them, Leonidas Garland and William Howell, were the nephews of Choctaw leader Peter Pitchlynn. Of the dozens of women who attended college in the 1880s and 1890s, many came from leading families: four had the last name Folsom, one LeFlore, two McCurtains, and two Pitchlynns. Many, both men and women, had a small degree of Choctaw blood, including the following: Victor Locke Jr. (1/4), Czarina Hebert (1/16), Goldie Lowery (1/8), and Lula Parshall (1/8).[69]

By contrast, not all Choctaw college students fit the wealthy, mixed-blood profile. Two of the well-known graduates, Allen Wright and Peter J. Hudson, were full-bloods. Several of the women of the 1880s and 1890s were near full-bloods, including Susie Conser (3/4). Moreover, the national council believed in geographic representation and made certain that the students, both men and women, regardless of blood quantum and socioeconomic background, were selected equally from the four districts that had Choctaw names: Apukshennubbee, Hotubbee, Mushulatubbee, and Pushmataha.[70] Thus, an unspecified percentage of students did not fall into the elitist profile.

A second point that needs to be made is that many college-educated Choctaw, even though they maintained various aspects of their indigenous culture, had become more acculturated. They did so by having accepted visible mainstream white American practices after having returned to Indian Territory. In 1884, one group of Choctaw, including father and son Allen and Eliphalet Wright, created a business company called the Choctaw Oil and Refinery Company to process and sell oil to potential buyers.[71] By doing so, they had accepted American-styled capitalism of the late nineteenth century.

College-educated Choctaws also helped to create American-styled political parties in the closing years of the nineteenth century. In the 1890s, various leaders established the National Party and the Progressive Party. The former opposed the recently created federal Dawes Commission whereas the latter reluctantly favored it. The Commission was another federal initiative to dissolve the land base of the "Five Civilized Tribes" and issue individual land allotments to tribal members. The commission eventually developed census or tribal rolls so that listed tribal members could eventually receive allotments.[72]

As for some of the college-educated Choctaw leaders, Jacob Jackson and Victor Locke joined the National Party whereas Solomon Homer and Eliphalet Wright supported the Progressive Party.

Although Wright initially favored allotment and even cooperated with the Dawes Commission, he ended up opposing land allotment after realizing that the overall intent was to dissolve communal and tribal domains, and thus ending Indian Territory itself.[73]

In conclusion, the Choctaw Nation appeared to have become visibly Americanized in the years after Indian removal. This was a major reason why the larger society labeled them as one of the "Five Civilized Tribes" of eastern Indian Territory. Although the Choctaws did accept many aspects of the white American way-of-life, including American-styled higher education, at the same time, they maintained their own cultural and political identity. Owing to their distinctiveness, they reshaped some white American practices. In short, they gave a new appearance to their own American higher education experience.

Notes

1. Donna L. Akers, "Removing the Heart of the Choctaw People: Indian Removal from a Native Perspective," *American Indian Culture and Research Journal* 23 (1999): 63–76; Ronald N. Satz, *American Indian Policy in the Jacksonian Era* (Lincoln: University of Nebraska Press, 1975), 82–83. For an excellent bibliography on Choctaw history, see Clara Sue Kidwell and Charles Roberts, *The Choctaws: A Critical Bibliography* (Bloomington: Indiana University Press, 1980). The author thanks Dr. Jane Haladay at the University of California, Davis for reviewing this manuscript. I also give thanks to Choctaw historians Dr. Charles Roberts at California State University, Sacramento, and Dr. Donna Akers at the University of Nebraska-Lincoln for also reviewing this article. I assume responsibility for any errors within this work.

2. "A Treaty of Perpetual Friendship, Cession and Limits," *Treaties between the United States and the Indian Tribes: The Public Statutes at Large of the U.S. of America* 7 (Boston: Charles C. Little and James Brown, 1848), 333–341.

3. Ibid.

4. Grayson B. Noley, "The History of Education in the Choctaw Nation from Precolonial Times to 1830," PhD diss., Pennsylvania State University, 1979, 172.

5. Clara Sue Kidwell, "Choctaws and Missionaries in Mississippi before 1830," *American Indian Culture and Research Journal* 11, (1987): 69.

6. Noley, "The History of Education in the Choctaw Nation," 170. For general sources on the history of Native American education, see the following: David Wallace Adams, *Education for Extinction: American Indians and the Boarding School Experience, 1875–1928* (Lawrence: University Press of Kansas, 1995); Jon Reyhner and Jeanne Eder, *American Indian Education: A History* (Norman: University of Oklahoma, 2004); Margaret Connell Szasz, *Education and the American Indian: The Road to Self-Determination since 1928* (Albuquerque: University of New Mexico Press, 1977); and Amy C. Schutt, "'What will become of our young people?' Goals for Indian Children in Moravian Missions," *History of Education Quarterly* 38, (Fall 1998): 268–286.

7. Francis Paul Prucha, *The Great Father: The United States Government and the American Indians*, Abridged (Lincoln: University of Nebraska Press, 1984), 56; Clara Sue Kidwell, *Choctaw and Missionaries in Mississippi, 1818–1918* (Norman: University of Oklahoma Press, 1995), 101.

8. Jesse O. McKee and Jon A. Schlenker, *The Choctaws: Cultural Evolution of a Native American Tribe* (Jackson: University Press of Mississippi, 1980), 71; Peter Pitchlynn letter, 5 October 1826, Letters Received (LR), Microfilm (M) 234, Roll 773, Frame (F) 409, Record Group (RG) 75, National Archives (NA); W. David Baird, *Peter Pitchlynn: Chief of the Choctaws* (Norman: University of Oklahoma Press, 1972), 30; Thomas McKenny to David Folsom, 20 October 1829, Letters Sent (LS), (M 21,R 6, F 64), RG 75; Carolyn Thomas Foreman, "The Choctaw Academy," *The Chronicles of Oklahoma* 9 (1931): 382–411.

9. Grant Foreman, *The Five Civilized Tribes* (Norman: University of Oklahoma Press, 1934).

10. Noley, "The History of Education in the Choctaw Nation," 172.

11. "About Some of Our First Schools in Choctaw Nation," *The Chronicles of Oklahoma* 6, (1928): 386, 392. I thank Choctaw tribal language teacher Richard Adams for providing the quote concerning group behavior.

12. "About some of our first schools," 386, 392; W. David Baird, *The Choctaw People* (Phoenix: Published by the Indian Tribal Service, 1973), 44; Baird, "Spencer Academy: The Choctaw 'Harvard,' 1842–1900" (MA Thesis, University of Oklahoma, 1965), 1; Choctaw Leaders to Samuel Rutherford, 14 January 1848, LR (M 234, R 171, F 616–17), RG 75, NA.

13. American Board of Commissioner for Foreign Missions, *Annual Report of the American Board of Commissioners for Foreign Missions, 1846* (Boston, The Board, 1847), 200.

14. Pitchlynn to William Medill, 29 March 1848 (M 234, R 171, F 581–84), RG 75; Pitchlynn to Thompson, 13 December 1848, Jay L. Hargett Collection, Gilcreast Institute, Tulsa, Oklahoma; Medill to Delaware College President, 17 April 1848, LS (M 21, R 40, F 220), RG 75, NA; Report of the Commissioner of Indian Affairs (CIA), 30 November 1848, 407, in *The New American State Papers, Indian Affairs* 2 (Wilmington, DE: Scholarly Resources Inc., 1972), 231.

15. James Wilson to William Medill, 19 March 1849, LR (M 234, R 784, F 1407); John A. Munroe, *The University of Delaware: A History* (Newark: University of Delaware Press, 1986), 92; William Graham to Orlando Brown, 20 July 1849, LR (M 234, R 784, F 939), RG 75, NA; James Wilson to Orlando Brown, 15 March 1850, LR (M 234, R 784, F 939), RG 75, NA; Baird, Peter Pitchlynn, 87; Leonidas Garland letter, 30 January 1850, LR (M 234, R 785, F 168–171), RG 75, NA.

16. Munroe, *The University of Delaware*, 92; Report of the Five Choctaw Youth and Two Chickasaw at Delaware College, 1849, LR (M 234, R 784, F 1454). RG 75, NA.

17. James Wilson to Orlando Brown, 21 February 1850, LR (M 234, R 785, F 701–4), RG 75, NA; Munroe, The University of Delaware, 93; Alex Holland to Orlando Brown, 27 April 1850, LR (M 234, R 785, F 205), RG 75, NA.

18. Holland to Brown, 16 July 1850, LR (M 234, R 785, F 216), RG 75, NA; L.H. Willard to A.L. Longberg, 26 October 1850, LR (M 234, R 785, F 753), RG 75, NA; North to Luke Lea, 31 December 1850, LR (M 234, R 785, F 1302–8), RG 75, NA; L.H. Willard to Lea, 16 October 1852, LR (M 234, R 785, F 503), RG 75, NA; Holmes Colbert Letter, 8 January 1851, LR (M 234, R 785, F 850–852), RG 75, NA.

19. Biographical information about Allen Wright, Union Theological Archives, New York; John Bartlett Meserve, "Chief Allen Wright," *The Chronicles of Oklahoma* 19, (December 1941): 314–321; Allen Wright, Principal Chief of the Choctaw Nation, 1866–1870, Muriel H. Wright Collection, Box 4, Oklahoma Historical Society (OHS).

20. Allen Wright to G.W. Manypenny, 19 May 1855, LR (M 234, R 788, F 647–48), RG 75, NA.

21. *Akers, Living in the Land of Death: The Choctaw Nation, 1830–1860* (East Lansing: Michigan State University Press, 2004), 43.

22. Michael Fultz, "African-American Teachers in the South, 1890–1940: Growth, Feminization, and Salary Discrimination," *Teachers College Record* 96, (1995): 552.

23. Michael Sugrue, "'We desired our future rulers to be educated men': South Carolina College, the Defense of Slavery, and the Development of Secessionist Politics," in *The American College in the Nineteenth Century* ed. Roger Geiger (Nashville: Vanderbilt University Press, 2000), 114.

24. Burton J. Bledstein, *The Culture of Professionalism: The Middle Class and the Development of Higher Education in America* (New York: W.W. Norton & Company Inc., 1976), 105.

25. "Going Home, Improving Communities," *Indian Country Today*, 12 December 2001, A4.

26. Annie Heloise Abel, *The American Indian and the End of the Confederacy, 1863–1866* (Lincoln: University of Nebraska Press, 1993), 303.

27. General Catalogue of Centre College of Kentucky, 1890 (Danville: The Kentucky Advocate Printing Company, 1890), 174–75; Choctaw leaders to Orlando Brown, 29 January 1850, LR (M234, R 785, F 267–69), RG 75, NA; William Wilson to Luke Lea, 10 September 1850, LR (M234, R 785, F 124–25), RG 75, NA.

28. General Catalogue of the Centre College, 1890, 174–75; John C. Young to Sir, 9 April 1885, LR (M 234, R 788, F 697–99), RG 75, NA; Daniel F. Littlefield, Jr., and James W. Parins, *A Bibliography of Native American Writers, 1772–1924: A Supplement* (Metuchen, New Jersey: The Scarecrow Press, 1985), 224.

29. James D. Morrison, Schools for the Choctaws (Durant, Oklahoma: Choctaw Bilingual Education Program, 1978), 244, 277; George B. Manhart, DePauw through the Years 1 (Greencastle: DePauw University Press, 1962), 150; Kenan Pitchlynn to CIA, 15 December 1851, LR (M 234, R 785, F 614), RG 75, NA; Kathleen Garrett, "Dartmouth Alumni in the Indian Territory," *The Chronicles of Oklahoma* 32, (Summer 1954): 130, 137.

30. R.H. Rivers to CIA, 23 July 1858, LR (M 234, R 791, F 432), RG 75, NA; Anna Lewis, "Jane McCurtain," *The Chronicles of Oklahoma* 11, (1933): 1026–1031.

31. LeRoy H. Fischer, *The Civil War Era in Indian Territory* (Los Angeles: Lorrin L. Morrison, 1975), 58, 137.

32. T.J. Bond to N.G. Taylor, 7 March 1868, LR (M 234, R 796, F 553), RG 75, NA.

33. Allen Wright to Acting CIA, 22 February 1873, LR (M 234, R 466, F 878), RG 75, NA.

34. P.P. Pitchlynn to E.S. Parker, 2 February 1870, LR (M 234, R 797, F 1200), RG 75, NA; Pitchlynn to Parker, 9 August 1870, LR (M 234, R 797, F 1241), RG 75, NA; Acting CIA to Pitchlynn, 29 August 1870, LS (M 21, R 98, F 17), RG 75, NA.

35. Forbis LeFlore to Senate and House of Representatives, 13 March 1872, CTN 87–1, OHS.

36. G.W. Folsom to Parker, 24 February 1872, LR (M 234, R 799, F 128), RG 75, NA.

37. Khalil Mahmud (librarian) to author, 16 October 1991, Letter in possession of author.

38. Allen Wright to Acting CIA, 22 February 1873, LR (M 234, R 466, F 878– 880), RG 75, NA.

39. H.L. Clum to Wright, 25 February 1873, LS (M 21, R 109, pp. 362–363); H.L. Clum to J.B. Jackson, 23 April 1873, LS (M 21, R 111, p. 32), RG 75, NA; E.P. Smith to W.B. Yonce, 6 September 1873, LS (M 21, R 113, p. 214), RG 75, NA.

40. P.P. Pitchlynn to E.P. Smith, 21 April 1874, LR (M 234, R 181, F 480–481), RG 75, NA.

41. To the Honorable Senate and House, 9 October 1877, Box IX, F 1, Choctaw Nation Papers (CNP), Western History Collections (WHC), University of Oklahoma (OU); J.B. Jackson to General Council, 11 November 1881, CNP, Box XIII, F 40, WHC, OU.

42. "Let us Progress," *Vinita Vindicator*, March 27, 1875, 2.

43. "Our Indian Students," Roanoke Collegian, December 1876, 29.

44. William Edward Eisenberg, *The First Hundred Years, Roanoke College, 1842–1942* (Salem, Virginia: Trustees of Roanoke College, 1942), 206.

45. Eisenberg, *The First Hundred Years*, 207.

46. "Dr. E.N. Wright to Olney announces for Congress," *The Coalgate Courier*, 29 May 1924, 1; "Organ honors memory of Indian Evangelist," *The Daily Oklahoman*, 1 May 1927.

47. Choctaw Nation List of Chiefs, Revised, 26 June 1998, Choctaw Nation, Durant, OK.

48. "Peter James Hudson," *The Chronicles of Oklahoma* 18 (1939): 4; "Gabe E. Parker, Father and Son Funerals Pend," *Daily Oklahoman*, 10 May 1953, 16A.

49. Telephone conversation with Jacob Bohanon, 24 February 2003, regarding translated phrases in the Choctaw language.

50. Lawrence A. Cremin, *American Education: The Metropolitan Experience, 1876–1980* (New York: Harper & Row, Publishers, 1988), 592.

51. Ellen Goodman. "College-Educated Women Beware!." *San Diego Union Tribune* 3 (September 2002): B6. For sources that highlight the male/female rations in higher education in the late nineteenth century, see Roger Geiger, "The Era of Multipurpose Colleges in American Higher Education, 1850 to 1890," *History of Higher Education Annual* 15, (1995): 67, 77; Nancy Woloch, *Women and the American Experience* (New York: Alfred A. Knopf, 1984), 543.

52. Sandra Faiman-Silva, *Choctaws at the Crossroads: The Political Economy of Class and Culture in the Oklahoma Timber Region* (Lincoln: University of Nebraska Press, 1997), 8–10, 12.

53. Twenty-Third Annual Report of the Board of Indian Commissioners, 1891, 109.

54. Akers, *Living in the Land of Death*, 139.

55. For an excellent study on Cherokee women viewed as agents of uplift in the nineteenth century, see Devon A. Mihesuah, *Cultivating the Rosebuds: The Education of Women at the Cherokee Female Seminary, 1851–1909* (Urbana: University of Illinois Press, 1993), 3, 21, 39.

56. Allen Wright to Acting CIA, 22 February 1873, LR (M 234, R 466, F 878–880), RG 75, NA.

57. "The cause of Higher Education among the Choctaws," William Stigler Papers, Box 8, Folder 47, Carl Albert Center, OU.

58. "An Act making appropriations for Students in the States," 15 April 1899, Foreman Transcripts, Supt for FCT, Vol. 2, 184, OHS; "Students from Indian Territory, 1873–1907," Special Collections, Drury College, Springfield, Missouri; Peter J. Hudson, "Choctaw Nation-Schools, Students in the States," Indian Archives, OHS; *Indian Pioneer History*, Vol. 68, 439, OHS.

59. Faiman-Silva, *Choctaws at the Crossroads*, 8, 10.

60. Dr. Anna Lewis, "Jane McCurtain," 1026, 1031.

61. "Necrology," *The Chronicles of Oklahoma* 8, 3 (September 1930): 242; Muriel H. Wright, "Contributions of the Indian People to Oklahoma," *The Chronicles of Oklahoma* 14, 2 (June 1936): 160; Czarina C. Conlan to Society of University Indians of America, 20 August 1935, Arthur C. Parker Papers, University of Rochester Archives.

62. Faiman-Silva, *Choctaws at the Crossroads*, 4.

63. W. David Baird, "Spencer Academy, Choctaw Nation, 1842–1900," *The Chronicles of Oklahoma* 45, (Spring 1967): 38.

64. "Abolishing the Office of Superintendent of the Schools and Repealing the Law in Relation thereto," Choctaw Nation Papers, Box 39, Folder 32, WHC, OU.

65. C.J. Rhoads to Joshua Anderson, 23 January 1933, Central Classified Files, 25472–28-Five Tribes-803, Pt. 1, RG 75, NA.

66. "Vivia Locke," Oklahoma State University Outreach 52:5 (July 1981); "Professor is named 'Indian of Year'," Oklahoma State Alumnus 12, no. 9 (December 1971): 22; "Muriel Wright," Bishinik, August 1992, 10; "Irene Hudson Heard," Bishinik, August 1998, 12.

67. Choctaw Nation List of Chiefs, Revised, 26 June 1998, Choctaw Nation, Durant, OK.

68. Kidwell, Choctaw and Missionaries in Mississippi, 1818–1918, 102; Joel Spring, *The Cultural Transformation of a Native American Family and Its Tribe, 1763–1995: A Basket of Apples* (Mahwah, NJ: Lawrence Erlbaum Associates, 1996), 3, 56; Morrison, Schools for the Choctaws, 286.

69. Final Rolls of Citizens and Freedman of the Five Civilized Tribes in Indian Territory, T 529, R 1, RG 75, NA.

70. Final Rolls; Fischer, *The Civil War Era in Indian Territory*, 69.

71. Angie Debo, *The Rise and Fall of the Choctaw Republic* (Norman: University of Oklahoma Press, 1934), 130–131.

72. Debo, *The Rise and Fall*, 162–174; Prucha, The Great Father, 258–59.

73. Debo, *The Rise and Fall*, 162–174, 250–259.

CHAPTER 2
THE AFRICAN AMERICAN FEMALE ELITE: THE EARLY HISTORY OF AFRICAN AMERICAN WOMEN IN THE SEVEN SISTER COLLEGES, 1880–1960

LINDA M. PERKINS

The Seven Sister colleges are well known for producing some of the nation's most successful women. At the turn of the century, they were recognized as the leading institutions for elite White women. In this chapter, Linda Perkins outlines the historical experiences of African American women attending the Seven Sister colleges from the institutions' founding to the civil rights era of the 1960s, a period during which approximately five hundred Black women graduated from these institutions. Through an exploration of university archives, alumni bulletins, and oral interviews with alumnae, Perkins shows that the Seven Sister colleges were not a monolithic entity: some admitted African American women as far back as the turn of the century, while others grudgingly, and only under great pressure, admitted them decades later. Perkins illustrates how the Seven Sister colleges mirrored the views of the larger society concerning race, and how issues of discrimination in admissions, housing, and financial aid in these institutions were influenced by, and had an influence on, the overall African American struggle for full participatory citizenship.

The seven private, elite northeastern women's colleges—Mount Holyoke, Vassar, Wellesley, Smith, Radcliffe, Bryn Mawr, and Barnard—commonly known as the Seven Sister colleges, are recognized for their academic excellence and distinguished alumnae. Founded in the nineteenth century in response to the leading private, elite male institutions' refusal to admit women, the Seven Sisters offered curricula of equal quality to these male institutions. Only Mount Holyoke was founded originally for the middle classes. By the turn of the century, Mount Holyoke and the other Seven Sisters became identified with the daughters of the White Anglo-Saxon Protestant of the middle and upper classes. The era of their founding was also one of much skepticism and hostility towards the higher learning of White women and of African American men and women, as both groups were believed to be intellectually inferior to White males. This chapter focuses on the history of African American women attending the Seven Sister colleges from the institutions' founding to the civil rights era of the 1960s, a period during which approximately five hundred Black[1] women graduated from these prestigious institutions. This exploration is important because these institutions are well known for producing some of the nation's professionally most successful women. The presence of African American women and their academic success in these institutions refuted the notion of Blacks' intellectual inferiority. Further, while these institutions did not explicitly prepare women for the world of work, the majority of the African American women who matriculated at the Seven Sisters did work, contributing their talents to both the Black community and the larger society.

By the 1890s, the Seven Sister colleges had evolved into institutions of academic excellence and were educating the daughters of the most wealthy and socially prominent citizens of the nation.[2]

Although many histories and studies have been done on the Seven Sister colleges, none focuses on the presence (or absence) of African American women attending them.[3] This focus is nonetheless important, because the growth of these institutions paralleled the African American struggle to obtain full citizenship, as well as educational and economic rights. Exploring the experiences of African American women in these colleges will provide insight into the extent to which these institutions mirrored the views of the larger society concerning racial issues. As many White women sought parity in education and other aspects of American life, they in turn often denied the same to African American women. Black women found themselves unwanted and frequently barred from most White women's organizations and activities.[4] In a 1900 study conducted by African American scholar W.E.B. DuBois on Black college students, he noted that it was easier for a Black male to gain entrance into a White men's college than for a Black woman to enter a White women's college. DuBois noted that the White women's colleges were "unyielding" in their opposition to admitting African American women:[5]

> Negroes have graduated from northern institutions. In most of the larger universities they are welcome and have on the whole made good records. In nearly all the western colleges they are admitted freely and have done well in some cases, and poorly in others. In one of two larger institutions, and in many of the large women's colleges [referring to the Seven Sisters], Negroes while not exactly refused admissions are strongly advised not to apply.[6]

Yet, a small number of African American women did begin to attend the Seven Sister colleges in the late nineteenth century. As will be discussed, when photographs were not required with a college application and/or the applicant was light-skinned enough to be mistaken for a White person, these institutions sometimes unknowingly admitted African Americans; in other instances, they were admitted in token numbers. When DuBois became editor of *Crisis* magazine in 1910 (the publication of the National Association for the Advancement of Colored People [NAACP]), he tracked assiduously the status and treatment of Black students in U.S. higher education. Each year, DuBois contacted the presidents of all the nation's major White colleges and universities for an update on the status of African Americans in their institutions. In 1913, *Crisis* began publishing an annual issue on Blacks and higher education. By the 1920s, members of the NAACP began speaking on White college campuses to engender support for racial integration and equality from the students. As a result of these activities, along with the NAACP's continued legal efforts to integrate public education during the 1940s and 1950s and the heightened civil rights activities of the 1960s, the Seven Sister colleges began actively recruiting Black women by the 1960s.

This chapter outlines the historical experiences of African American women attending the Seven Sister colleges. First, I provide a general discussion of the historical context of African American women attending these colleges in the late nineteenth and early twentieth centuries. I address how these women differed from their African American counterparts at other types of institutions, as well as from their White classmates on their respective campuses. Second, I discuss how each of the Seven Sisters responded to the presence of African American women on their respective campuses and provide a look at the campus life of these students. I also explore why some institutions opened their doors to African American women while others kept theirs firmly closed.

The discussion of race and the presence of African Americans in these institutions becomes murky at times. Many of the African American women who attended the Seven Sisters were physically indistinguishable from White women, thus it is reasonable to assume that they passed as Whites and their actual race was not recorded or known. For example, Vassar, one of the last of the Seven Sisters to officially admit African American women, had a Black woman graduate in the class of 1897. However, the student appeared to be White, and Vassar discovered only shortly before commencement that she was, in fact, partially African American—or in their eyes, Black. This discussion centers around those African American women who self-identified as such and around the Seven Sister colleges' knowingly admitting them.

The number of African American women attending all the Seven Sisters combined was rarely more than one or two per class until the 1950s, and the information available on these women is uneven. The archives of the institutions that admitted African American women in more than token numbers—Smith, Radcliffe, Wellesley, and Mount Holyoke—are rich with biographical data, enrollment information, oral histories, and lists of these students. Barnard, Vassar, and Bryn Mawr, the last of the Seven Sisters to admit Black women, did not maintain such records and have less information on these students. When appropriate, oral interviews with some of these Black women supplement the written record.

The Black Elite[7]

Studies of Black communities in the nineteenth and early twentieth centuries acknowledge the existence of class differences. In his 1899 study, *The Philadelphia Negro*, DuBois noted the presence of what he defined as a small upper class of Blacks, which included caterers, government clerks, teachers, professionals, and small merchants. DuBois noted that many of these individuals had significant wealth, elite education, political influence, and connections.[8] Another study on the Black upper class at the turn of the century noted that this group was usually college educated, attended Episcopal or Presbyterian churches, and included community leaders. This group's wealth was not as great as its White counterpart's, and status stemmed primarily from occupation, education, and family background. The Black upper class included women who attended the Seven Sister colleges, and who came primarily from families in which both parents had a formal higher education.[9] This is not an insignificant fact, for as historian James Anderson found, until the mid-1930s, "almost all of the southern rural communities with significantly large Afro-American populations and more than half of the major southern cities failed to provide any public high schools for Black youth."[10]

By the late 1890s, the majority of African Americans resided in the South, where they suffered the economic, educational, legal, and social barriers of segregation. The *Plessy v. Ferguson* Supreme Court decision of 1896 established the "separate but equal" doctrine, which furthered legal restrictions on Blacks in the South, commonly known as "Jim Crow" laws. These laws suppressed any meaningful progress for African Americans in the South; even the Black middle class was subject to the same restrictions (e.g., segregated schools, public accommodations, etc.) as poorer African Americans. However, a different situation existed for those African Americans living in the North, at least those with money. DuBois observed that two classes existed among northern African Americans—"the descendants of the northern free Negroes and the free immigrants from the South."[11]

This group of elite northern African Americans lived in a self-contained, exclusive world of restrictive clubs, with memberships based on complexion, education, and wealth. Adelaide Cromwell Hill observed in her study of upper-class Boston Blacks that this group often preferred White tutors and servants because they believed "more gentility and culture would come from exposure to Whites." She noted further that this group gave "lavish and always tasteful entertainments, including catered dinners of many courses, dances with well-known orchestras, debutante balls, select musicales and literary gatherings. They were most often Episcopal and shunned denominations associated with emotionalism or lower-class African Americans." Their daughters were often well traveled and tended to spend their summers in such spots as Martha's Vineyard, Saratoga Springs, and Newport, Rhode Island.[12]

Willard B. Gatewood writes of these upper-class African Americans in *Aristocrats of Color: The Black Elite 1880–1920*. He notes the central role of higher education within the African American elite, stating, "No matter how significant family background, complexion and church affiliation might be as stratifiers, they were singly and collectively less important than the disciplined, cultivated mind produced by higher education."[13]

Higher education opportunities for African American women in the nineteenth century included a growing number of Black colleges in the South, which were mostly still of high school grade.[14] Even though they were called "colleges," in reality they were actually more like high schools. Outside of the South, African American women were admitted to some state universities, a few private White women's institutions, and teacher-training schools. Public sentiment during this period was often against educating African Americans of either gender on an equal basis with Whites. Thus, few White colleges admitted qualified African American women, and those institutions that did enroll them encountered hostile reactions. For example, when Prudence Crandall, a

Quaker, attempted to enroll twenty-one Black girls at her Canterbury, Connecticut, Female Boarding School in 1833, local opposition to the notion that African American women should be educated similarly to White women was so great that Crandall's house was burned down, her well was poisoned, and she was ultimately driven out of town.

A 1979 study of the education of African Americans in New York State noted that, of the more than 150 academies and seminaries that existed in that state between 1840 and 1860, no more than eight admitted African Americans.[15] Throughout the northern and New England states, few White institutions during the antebellum period would admit Blacks; one exception was Oberlin College in Ohio. Oberlin, an institution founded by abolitionists, began admitting African Americans and women in 1833. Many African American families relocated to Oberlin so that their children could have an opportunity to obtain a higher education. From 1833 until 1910, more than four hundred African American women attended Oberlin College.[16] In sharp contrast, during the period addressed by this chapter—the 1890s through the 1960s—the Seven Sister colleges combined graduated approximately five hundred African American women.

By the turn of the century, the Seven Sisters were recognized as the leading institutions for elite White women. These institutions offered African American women from prominent families not only intellectual growth and stimulation, but also entrance into a world of White power and privilege. Most of the Black women who attended the Seven Sisters between the 1890s and 1960s were from these educated, solidly upper- and middle-class families. Education was expected to endow them with the refinement and culture essential for entry into the highest stratum of African American society.

Early History of Black Women in the Seven Sister Colleges

The early women's colleges were significant because they offered women a higher education degree equivalent to that of the leading men's colleges. Wellesley College in Wellesley, Massachusetts, and Smith College in Northampton, Massachusetts, were both founded in 1875. Radcliffe College (formerly known as the Harvard Annex) was founded in 1879. Although these three institutions are not the oldest of the Seven Sisters, they have the longest and most continuous history of Black women students and graduates. African American women began attending Wellesley, Radcliffe, and Smith in the mid-1880s in token, yet steady, numbers. Both Mount Holyoke, founded in 1837, and Vassar, founded in 1865, also had Black women students in the late nineteenth century; however, as will be discussed later in this chapter, these students were not known to be African Americans until after they arrived. Neither Barnard, founded in 1889, nor Bryn Mawr, founded in 1884, admitted African Americans until well into the twentieth century. Although the number of Black women who attended these institutions prior to 1960 was small (around five hundred), their influence within the African American community was significant. They went on to serve on faculties of African American high schools and colleges, and became prominent lawyers, physicians, and scientists.

Wellesley College

Wellesley College was founded in 1875 in Wellesley, Massachusetts, by Henry Durant, a Harvard graduate and successful lawyer. Durant, a trustee of Mount Holyoke Seminar and a devout Christian, sought to model Wellesley after the religious Mount Holyoke. Religion permeated the Wellesley campus with chapels, Bible classes, and questions to students concerning their religious condition. The college statute read, "The college was founded for the glory of God and the service of the Lord Jesus Christ, in and by the education and culture of women. . . . It is required that every Trustee, Teacher, and Officer, shall be a member of an Evangelical Church." According to Horowitz, Durant enforced these statutes literally.[17]

The first African American to graduate from Wellesley College was Harriett Alleyne Rice of Newport, Rhode Island. Rice, the daughter of a steward on the steamship "The Pilgrim," lived on campus in a single room, according to the campus directory.[18] After graduating in 1887, Rice earned a medical degree in 1893 from the Women's Medical School of the New York Infirmary. From all indications, Rice's experience at Wellesley was positive. She kept in touch with the college and returned there in 1920 to lecture on her experiences as a medical assistant in France during the First World War. Rice's services had been refused by the American Red Cross because of her race, and she worked instead for the French government.[19] In response to a 1937 alumnae questionnaire that asked, "Have you any handicap, physical or other, which has been a determining factor in your [professional] activity?" Rice replied, "Yes! I am colored which is worse than any crime in this God *blessed Christian* country! My country (100%) tis of *thee!*"[20]

While it appears that the African American women who attended Wellesley in the first two decades of the twentieth century did not articulate publicly any instances of discrimination at the institution, Jane Bolin, class of 1928, did. Bolin was from New York City and the daughter of a prominent lawyer who had attended Williams College, an elite men's college in western Massachusetts. She recalled that she and Ruth Brown, the only other Black woman admitted as a first-year student in 1924, were assigned to the same room in an apartment in which they were the only college students. Bolin notes a number of incidents that revolved around her race. For example, although African American women were allowed to eat in the dining hall, Southern students refused to sit with them; Bolin's roommate was asked to play the role of Aunt Jemima in a skit (including wearing a bandanna); and, although Bolin was an honors student, she was rejected from one of the sororities that claimed to be concerned with social problems. Her rejection letter was an unsigned note left under her door.

Bolin's "sharpest and ugliest" memory of Wellesley occurred during a mandatory conference with a guidance counselor in her senior year. Bolin wrote that the counselor was in shock when she heard that Bolin wanted to be an attorney. Bolin recalled, "She threw up her hands in disbelief and told me there was little opportunity in law for a woman and absolutely none for a 'colored' one. Surely I should consider teaching."[21] Despite this discouragement, Bolin had a distinguished career in law: after Wellesley she attended Yale Law School, earned an LL.B. in 1931, and in 1939, at the age of 31, was appointed the first Black woman judge in the United States by New York City Mayor Fiorello LaGuardia. Bolin recalled bitterly that, although her historic appointment was widely publicized and she received letters and telegrams from all over the world, "not a single note from teacher, president, dean, house mother" or anyone in an official capacity at Wellesley during her four years there acknowledged her achievement.[22]

However, from the perspective of a White southerner in the 1920s, Wellesley was extremely accommodating to African Americans. Virginia Foster Durr, Wellesley class of 1925, grew up in a prominent Birmingham, Alabama, family. A quintessential southern belle, Foster said that her family wanted her to be well married and that Wellesley was an investment in achieving that goal. After arriving at Wellesley in 1921, Foster met a southern woman in Cambridge whose Southern Club sponsored parties and dances for southerners. As a freshman she lived off campus in Wellesley village, as was customary; after her first year, she was able to live on campus. Of her first night in the dormitory, she wrote:

> I went to the dining room and a Negro girl was sitting at my table. My God, I nearly fell over dead. I couldn't believe it. I just absolutely couldn't believe it. She wasn't very black, sort of pale, but she was sitting there eating at the table with me in college. I promptly got up, marched out of the room, went upstairs, and waited for the head of the house to come. She was a tall, thin, New England spinster. She wore glasses on her nose and she would cast her head down and look over them at us. I told her that I couldn't possibly eat at the table with a Negro girl. I was from Alabama and my father would have a fit. He came from Union Springs, Bullock County, and the idea of my eating with a Negro girl—well, he would die. I couldn't do it. She would have to move me immediately.[23]

According to Foster, the house mother informed her that Wellesley had rules, and that students had to eat at the table to which they had been assigned for a month, after which Foster could move. If she did not want to comply, she was told, she could withdraw from the college without penalty on her academic record. Foster said that when she presented her dilemma to her southern girlfriend, her friend convinced her of what was at stake. Foster was enjoying her college years: "I was having the time of my life at Wellesley. I was in love with a Harvard law student, the first captain of VMI, and life was just a bed of roses. But I had been taught that if I ate at the table of a Negro girl I would be committing a terrible sin against society."[24] Ultimately, Foster decided to stay and simply not mention to her father that she had to eat at the same table with a Black woman:

> So I didn't tell Daddy and I stayed. But that was the first time I became aware that my attitude was considered foolish by some people and that Wellesley College wasn't going to stand for it. That experience had a tremendous effect on me. . . . There were other Southern girls at Wellesley. We were all a little ashamed of breaking the Southern taboos, and yet we didn't want to leave. I didn't know whether I had acted rightly or wrongly, whether I should have stood by Southern tradition and gone home or not. I only knew I had stayed because I didn't want to miss the good times I was having.[25]

Segregated housing remained an issue at Wellesley into the 1930s. The faculty in the Department of Biblical History addressed the problem in a letter to President Ellen F. Pendleton, protesting the college's policy of housing discrimination:

> We wish cordially to express our recognition of the courtesy and kindness which the college administration has always shown to underprivileged groups at Wellesley, and our realization of the expenditure of time and effort in their behalf; but we feel that we must state our deep regret that the administration has felt it necessary to adopt a new policy—the definite ruling that students of different race [sic] may not room together.

> Such a regulation made by the dominant group must inevitably be interpreted as an endorsement of race prejudice. Such an endorsement seems to us inconsistent with Wellesley's heritage, and with the teaching of Jesus as that teaching has been interpreted at Wellesley.

> We therefore sincerely hope that the college will find it possible to modify its recent formulation of policy.[26]

There is no other correspondence concerning either the letter or the policy. College records make no further mention of segregated housing until 1948, when Dean of Residence Ruth H. Lindsay telegrammed a southern woman named Mary Chase to inform her: "It would be entirely contrary to the policy of the College to assign a white freshman and a negro freshman to [the] same room. Any rumor of such assignment is without slightest foundation."[27]

Three Black women attended Wellesley in the last two decades of the nineteenth century. Two of them earned baccalaureate degrees, one in 1887 and the other in 1888.[28] Only one other Black woman earned a degree from the school over the next twenty-five years. Portia Washington, daughter of prominent educator Booker T. Washington, attended for only one year. By 1960, seventy-five Black women had attended Wellesley; forty-five earned baccalaureate degrees, others were in graduate programs, and some attended without earning a degree.

Wellesley's first two Black alumnae were happy with their college experience. As noted above, Harriet Rice, Wellesley's first Black graduate, kept in touch with her alma mater. Ella Elbert Smith, who earned her degree in 1888, when asked in an alumni questionnaire about the weaknesses and strengths of Wellesley, wrote, "I think that one of Wellesley's finest characteristics now and from the beginning is that it makes no distinction as to race, color or creed."[29] When asked in 1952 to reflect on the most important aspect of her college experience, Smith noted, "personal contact and often fine and lasting friendships with members of the faculty. These were possible and priceless in the Wellesley of my day."[30] Upon Smith's death in 1955, her family requested that donations in her memory be sent to Wellesley College. In addition, Smith donated more than 1,300 books, pamphlets, and rare manuscripts related to slavery and the Civil War to Wellesley College.[31] As will be discussed later, most African Americans considered Wellesley, along with Smith College, to be the most welcoming of the Seven Sister colleges. The administration stood behind them when issues of racism arose, as was evidenced by Virginia Foster Durr's recollection. Although its housing was segregated in 1913, Wellesley was the only Seven Sister college that allowed Blacks to live on campus.

Radcliffe College

Originally known as the Harvard Annex, Radcliffe College was founded in 1879 in Cambridge, Massachusetts, by the Society for the Collegiate Instruction of Women. Women had to meet the same admission requirements as for Harvard. Radcliffe students were taught by Harvard faculty, and were awarded degrees and honors according to the same standards as Harvard.[32]

Radcliffe enrolled African American women continuously from the 1890s. Though barred from campus housing, they participated in all other aspects of campus life and extracurricular activities. The first Black Radcliffe graduate was Alberta Scott of Cambridge. Scott graduated from Cambridge Latin High School and entered Radcliffe in 1894. There, Scott was active in the Idler, a dramatics club, and in the German Club. She was also involved in music. After graduating in 1898, Scott went to Tuskegee Institute at the invitation of Booker T. Washington. She taught there until she became ill and had to return to Cambridge in 1900. She died in 1903 at the age of twenty-seven.[33]

Most of Radcliffe's earliest Black students were from Cambridge and the greater Boston area. Because African Americans could not live on campus, students from farther away had to find accommodations with members of Cambridge's Black community. As I describe later, the issue of discrimination in campus housing was revisited over and over by African American students, as well as by the NAACP. In 1913, Mary Gibson became the first African American from outside the Cambridge/Boston area to enroll in Radcliffe and was also the first student from a Black high school, Dunbar High School in Washington, DC. Her enrollment presented the first major racial problem for Radcliffe officials. Although Gibson was a brilliant student and had outstanding credentials, she needed financial aid. Her parents were both college educated. Her father had been a lawyer and her mother had taught at Tuskegee Institute, but her father's recent death had left them without financial resources.[34] Gibson's mother was eager for her daughter to receive a first-rate education, and they moved to Cambridge together to set up an apartment for Mary. Gibson had a recommendation from Roscoe Bruce, a prominent African American Harvard graduate. Bruce was assistant superintendent of the Washington, DC, Public Schools and a friend of Radcliffe President Lebarron Russell Briggs. Apparently the Gibsons felt confident that their connections through Bruce would give Mary an excellent chance for a scholarship, but this was not the case. Briggs told them that very few scholarships were awarded to first-year students.[35] Instead, Radcliffe Dean Bertha Boody found Mary a job doing domestic work. Her mother was outraged. She refused to allow her daughter to accept the position, saying the job offer was racist and insisting that Radcliffe could find scholarship monies or a job more suitable and less demeaning, such as working in the library.

President Briggs frantically attempted to raise money for Mary from outside supporters of Radcliffe. In the meantime, Mrs. Gibson refused to allow Mary to work and her tuition was not paid. The college hurriedly obtained a loan for Gibson. While Briggs worked intensely on Mary's behalf, Mary and her mother believed that her biggest obstacle at Radcliffe was Dean Boody. They believed Boody, a southerner, was racially prejudiced and under no circumstances wanted Gibson to be awarded a Radcliffe scholarship. Boody's influence was considerable, and she convinced Briggs that the Gibsons were ingrates and basically uppity Negroes.[36]

The Gibsons were from Washington, DC, where many prominent Black families had children attending Seven Sister and Ivy League colleges. Briggs was concerned about their interpretation of this problem, especially since Radcliffe had always been perceived as a liberal, welcoming institution to African American women. Mary Church Terrell was a prominent African American clubwoman, civil rights leader, and former educator (she had taught at Dunbar High School). In a letter to Terrell, who had spoken at Radcliffe in 1912 on "The Progress of the Colored Women," Briggs apologetically explained the situation from his perspective:

> If you don't mind my saying so, there is, I suspect, a little difficulty in regards to Miss Gibson, a difficulty which probably comes from the fact that her mother has been a teacher and feels, naturally enough, a certain superiority in herself and in her daughter which makes her shrink from letting her daughter do certain kinds of honorable service. We have girls who have been with us a year or two, whom everyone respects who go as mothers' helpers or serve in any capacity whereby they may honorably help themselves along. . . . I suppose the fact that her daughter is a colored girl makes her the more cautious, so that she is unwilling that her daughter should do many things which the most earnest of our white girls do not hesitate for a moment to do and which everybody respects a self-respecting girl for doing.[37]

Mrs. Gibson secured employment in Boston and Mary found a part-time job selling magazine subscriptions, so they were able to support themselves during Mary's first year at Radcliffe. When

Mary was refused a scholarship the second year, Mrs. Gibson went to prominent clergy in the Cambridge and Boston White communities to garner their support. Briggs admitted in a letter to one of the clergymen, the Reverend Dr. van Allen, that Radcliffe had not awarded Gibson a scholarship her second year because they did not want her to return to Radcliffe. However, he said that the question of the moment was "whether she will be saved by being forced out or by being kept here with uninterrupted college education, after which she can take care of herself and her mother too." Briggs ended his letter saying that Mary was an excellent student.[38]

Briggs always appeared torn about Radcliffe's treatment of Gibson, and his conscience ultimately haunted him. Within a month of his letter to van Allen, Briggs wrote in a confidential letter that he believed Radcliffe had been unjust in not awarding Mary a scholarship. He said that in spite of her financial difficulties and in the face of starvation and destitution, Mary had remained an outstanding student. He wrote: "The persistency with which she has done good work—even, as I have learned, at a time when she had insufficient food, is a mark of something which I believe should be encouraged."[39] He said that every visible avenue of help to Mary had been deliberately stopped. But, he now agreed, given Mary's academic record, it was reasonable for her to expect a scholarship. In fact, the person with whom she had tied for a scholarship in her second year came from a home of comfortable financial circumstances. With a change of heart and reason, Briggs said that he believed that Radcliffe's actions toward Mary were "harsh and unnatural," considering that the girl had no home or resources.[40] Dean Boody vehemently disagreed and said she would be "ashamed" if Radcliffe awarded anything to Gibson.[41] Boody's decision prevailed, but Briggs was able to secure a personal, interest-free loan from an anonymous donor for the remainder of Mary's stay at Radcliffe. After she graduated in 1918, she repaid the loan in full.[42]

Despite Mary's financial woes, she led an active, full life at Radcliffe. She was a member of the student government, the Science Club, and the Cosmopolitan Club; she was also class accompanist and wrote the Class Song for 1918. After graduating, she returned to Washington, DC, and taught at her alma mater, Dunbar High School, and sent many of her students to Radcliffe during the course of her years there. At her fiftieth Radcliffe reunion in 1968, Mary recalled with pleasure her years at Radcliffe, but stated, "the fly in the ointment was the dean from Baltimore, who demanded that I work as a domestic if I ever hoped to get her recommendation for a scholarship. In spite of her persistent persecution, I found consolation in the president, an ideal Yankee whom I adored."[43] Mary Gibson remained a loyal and devoted Radcliffe alumna throughout her life.

Black students had varying opinions about the discrimination they experienced. Margaret Perea McCane, who graduated from Radcliffe in 1927, recalled years later that

> it was fortunate that all of us lived at home, because in those days Black students could not live in the dormitories at Harvard or Radcliffe. It wasn't until my junior year in college that a Black girl was admitted to the dormitory at Radcliffe and it was a few years later that black boys at Harvard could live at college. But, McCane rationalized, those were some of the things that one took in one's stride then. I do not say that it was fair and that we should have been able to accept it. It was a situation [in] which one dealt with the problems that one had, with the handicaps that one met, and one did not let those things stand in the way of one's getting an education, a good education for that was why you were there. And you recognized the fact that your contacts and what you did and the record you made were going to influence other young black people who followed you. I think that always stood as a goal before all of us.[44]

Radcliffe's African American graduates contributed greatly to the education of their race at both historically Black colleges and Black public high schools. Beginning with the first, Alberta Scott, who taught at Tuskegee Institute in Alabama, all but one of Radcliffe's Black graduates during the first decades of the twentieth century taught at some point at Black education institutions.

By the second decade of the twentieth century, Radcliffe graduated more than one Black woman each year. By 1920, four Black women graduated in the same class. This was unheard of at the other Seven Sister colleges, where such numbers would not be achieved until the 1940s and 1950s. By 1950, Radcliffe had graduated fifty-six African American undergraduates and thirty-seven African American graduate students. It was by far the leader in the number of Black women graduates among the Seven Sister colleges.

Smith College

Smith College in Northampton, Massachusetts, was endowed by a wealthy single woman, Sophia Smith, in 1868. A devoutly religious woman, Smith sought to establish a college at which women could have an education equal to that offered by the leading men's colleges, but also wanted the college to be "pervaded by the spirit of evangelical Christian religion."[45] Thus, like its sister institutions of Mount Holyoke and Wellesley, religion was central to the life of Smith College.

The first African American woman to graduate from Smith was Otelia Cromwell of Washington, DC, who graduated in 1900. Her father, John Wesley Cromwell, was a prominent educator and, after earning a law degree, a chief examiner in the U.S. Post Office. Otelia Cromwell was a product of the segregated schools of Washington. She transferred to Smith College in 1898 from the all-Black Miner's Teachers College. As was the case at most White institutions, Cromwell was not allowed to live on campus and was housed in the home of a Smith College professor. Despite this, she apparently enjoyed her education; in a letter to her father in 1899, Cromwell expressed her happiness with Smith and her pleasure with classes and professors. She wrote, "I am having a very happy time of it this year." After graduating from Smith, Cromwell studied in Germany, earned a masters degree from Columbia University in 1910, and a Ph.D. in English from Yale University in 1926. She spent her life as an educator of Black youth in Washington, DC.

In 1913, Smith faced a situation that forced it to reconsider its discriminatory housing policy. The situation came to a head when Carrie Lee, the daughter of a letter carrier from New Bedford, Massachusetts, was admitted to Smith. Because photographs were not required for admission at the time, and because Lee was from a predominantly White high school, Smith officials were unaware of her race until she arrived on campus. Her race became an immediate problem because she had been assigned a room with a White student from Tennessee. When the White roommate protested, Smith told Lee to find accommodation within the approved housing of the Northampton community. The only approved housing available to Lee required that she be a servant and not use the main entrance of the house.

Insulted and outraged, Lee's parents contacted the NAACP. Minutes from an NAACP board meeting note that Dr. Joel. E. Spingarn, one of the organization's founders who served as chairman, treasurer, and president, met with Smith's president to discuss the matter. He told the school's dean that he would "unloose the dogs of war at Smith" if the situation was not resolved favorably.[46] In the face of such negative publicity, the college found housing for Lee in the home of a Smith professor, Julia Caverno, who had housed other African Americans. Although *Crisis* magazine did not name Smith College as the culprit, W.E.B. DuBois did cover the story. He reported that a "refined young girl of cultured parents who had won a scholarship in one of the large colleges" had been denied housing. He wrote that after the White student from Nashville complained,

> the colored girl was asked to leave and was unable to secure a room on the campus or anywhere in the college town. One of the teachers, a staunch friend, took her in but was unable to solve more than the room problem. Then began the wary search for board which was finally only secured on condition that the young lady would act as waitress. Though she had never done work of this kind she pluckily determined to stay on the ground and fight out her battle. Meantime, the Association was working hard to reach the proper authorities. Fortunately, a friend of the colored people on the board of trustees of the college became interested and succeeded in getting the girl on the campus in a delightful room where she is entitled to all the privileges of the college, including, of course, the dining room. Best of all, she is becoming popular with her classmates and through her charming personality is winning friends for her race.[47]

Members of the NAACP board played a prominent role in changing Smith's housing policy. Moorfield Storey, a successful Boston lawyer and chairman of the NAACP board of trustees, wrote Smith's president, the Reverend Marion Burton, that if the story about Lee's housing dilemma was true, "I think it is the very greatest discredit to Smith College." Storey continued:

> For a Massachusetts College to so far forget the principles which have made Massachusetts what it is, and to weakly abandon the rights of colored people in order to conciliate Southern prejudice is to the

last degree weak and discreditable. I sincerely hope that this statement I have received is not true, or that if it is true the policy will be abandoned. Otherwise I hope the facts will be published throughout the breadth and length of this state in order that the citizens of Massachusetts may understand how little regard the trustees of Smith College have for the principles of justice.[48]

Ruth Baldwin, an NAACP board member, Smith alumna, and the first woman to serve as a regular member on the Smith board of trustees, used her influence to have Smith's housing policy changed.[49] Baldwin discovered that Smith had no official policy about Blacks living on campus, but that this discriminatory practice was based on the individual decisions of college officials. Baldwin felt that the fact that Wellesley College allowed African American women to live on campus would influence Smith trustees who were sympathetic to the issue. The matter was resolved in October 1913, when the trustees affirmed the rights of African American women to live in Smith housing.[50]

The NAACP's influence at Smith widened with the appointment of William Allan Neilson as the college's third president in 1917. Neilson was a member of the national board of the NAACP. Walter White, a general secretary of the NAACP, recalled that Neilson "devoted a great portion of his extracurricular activity to service as a member of the board of directors of the NAACP."[51] White wrote:

> Thanks to Dr. Neilson and others on the Smith faculty, the college maintained leadership among American educational institutions in ignoring artificial lines of demarcation based on race, social position, wealth, or place of birth. Few colleges I have known have been more free from cant and hypocrisy or more ready to examine new ideas than Smith.[52]

He stated it was because of Neilson's and Smith's leadership that he and his wife decided to have their daughter Jane educated there.

The Lee incident led Smith officials to inquire about housing policies at the other Seven Sisters. Wellesley was the only institution that claimed not to discriminate in admissions or housing against African Americans. Mount Holyoke, which had graduated two African Americans in the late nineteenth century, did not admit Black women in 1913, nor did Barnard, Bryn Mawr, and Vassar admit African Americans that year.

After Otelia Cromwell, Smith consistently admitted African American women, usually one per year. It was not until 1925 that two Black women graduated in the same class. This was repeated in 1926, and then not again until 1934.[53] By 1964, sixty-nine Black women (including African women) had attended and/or graduated from Smith.

Mount Holyoke College

Mount Holyoke College in South Hadley, Massachusetts, is the oldest of the Seven Sisters. It was founded as a women's seminary in 1837 by Mary Lyon. Its mission was to train teachers, missionaries, and wives of missionaries, and did not achieve collegiate status until the 1890s.

In 1845, the Mount Holyoke trustees voted not to admit Black women. After the vote, Mary Lyon received a long letter from a White male resident of nearby Springfield. He protested the college's policy, which he believed was hypocritical, considering the Christian principles espoused by the school. He wrote that public sentiment was undergoing a rapid change, and that the events that occurred at Prudence Crandall's Canterbury Female Boarding School would not be repeated. He noted that Dartmouth College had recently decided to admit colored students, and concluded by stating, "I hope that the religious influence that goes out of the Mount Holyoke Seminary will no longer be contaminated with this hatred or that it will not *deliberately* decide to reject colored applicants."[54] Another letter to Lyon, from a former student, urged her to take a stand on the question of slavery, pointing out that while Mount Holyoke expressed interest in foreign missions, Black slaves in this country were ignored.[55] Lyon, who died in 1849, never took a public stand on slavery.

Mount Holyoke's earliest known African American graduate during its seminary years was Hortense Parker of Ripley, Ohio, in the class of 1883. The first Black to obtain a collegiate degree from Mount Holyoke was Martha Ralston of Worcester, Massachusetts, in the class of 1898. According to a letter from the dean of Mount Holyoke in 1913 to Ada Comstock, dean of Smith College, the race of both Ralston and Parker was a surprise to the officials of the college when they first arrived.[56] All students were required to live on campus at Mount Holyoke, and though records are missing for the years of Parker's matriculation, subsequent records indicate that African American students who were enrolled in the early years lived in single rooms in the Seminary Building.

Alumnae records state that Ralston's father was an Englishman and that her home "is located in one of the wealthiest sections of Worcester."[57] A musician whose education was financed by a patron, Ralston had planned to study in Europe, but the death of her patron in her senior year prevented her from being able to go abroad.[58] Ralston apparently made friends at Mount Holyoke. One of her White classmates wrote to her mother upon Ralston's arrival in 1894, "There is a colored girl here in the freshman class. She comes from Worcester, Mass. and the other girls who come from that place like her very much and say that she is of a very good family."[59]

Mount Holyoke's first African American graduate of the twentieth century was Francis Williams of St. Louis, Missouri. Until her death in 1992, Williams was the school's oldest living Black alumna. Like Otelia Cromwell, the first Black graduate of Smith College, Williams was a product of a Black segregated high school in the South. Her parents were college graduates, as were her three siblings. Her father was principal of the well-known Charles Sumner High School, a Black public school in St. Louis. After graduating as valedictorian from Sumner, Williams attended the University of Cincinnati for one year. She found the campus too large and impersonal, and decided to transfer. Her mother sent Williams's transcript to Mount Holyoke in 1916, and only after she had been accepted did her mother inform the college that Williams was African American. She received a letter from the college stating that they did not believe her daughter would be happy at Mount Holyoke, to which she responded that she wasn't sending her daughter to be happy, but to receive an education. Williams, who had a light complexion, recalled that many of her fellow students would not sit with her at meals, although some were not concerned about her race. Williams held a double major in chemistry and economics, and graduated Phi Beta Kappa in 1919. Her parents paid for her education at Mount Holyoke, but she received a fellowship from the college after graduation to attend the New York School of Social Work. After earning a certificate there, she earned a masters in political science from the University of Chicago. Williams spent her professional career working in the area of race relations for the National Young Women's Christian Association (YWCA) and various other civil rights organizations.[60]

More than the other Seven Sister colleges, Mount Holyoke attracted African American women from Black high schools and the South, including several from Atlanta, Georgia. There was one Black graduate in the Mount Holyoke class of 1926 from Wilmington, Delaware; the next five Black students at the school were from Atlanta and Washington, DC. Of this group, two were graduates of the prestigious all-Black Dunbar High School in Washington, which had a long history of sending its graduates to elite New England colleges. The other three were transfer students, two from Spelman College in Atlanta, and one from Atlanta University (an affiliate of Spelman).[61] The Atlanta connection was due to a prominent White alumna of the class of 1909, Florence Read. In 1927 Read was appointed president of the all-Black Spelman College, a women's college founded in 1881 and modeled in part after Mount Holyoke.[62]

Few African American women graduated from Mount Holyoke prior to the mid-1960s; by 1964, only thirty-nine had graduated since Hortense Parker in 1883. One African American graduated from Mount Holyoke during the twenties, six in the thirties, twelve during the forties (due to increased pressure from religious and civil rights groups), twelve during the fifties, and five from 1960 to 1964.[63]

Despite their small numbers, the African American women at Mount Holyoke participated fully in campus organizations and events. The institution and its environment nurtured the women intellectually and spiritually. The Black women who attended Mount Holyoke before the 1960s all said that they would attend the institution again.

Bryn Mawr College

Bryn Mawr College in Bryn Mawr, Pennsylvania, was founded in 1885 by Orthodox Quakers "for the advanced education and care of young women, or girls of the higher classes of society."[64] Bryn Mawr's mission, as interpreted by the institution's president, the formidable M. Carey Thomas, who reigned from 1893 to 1922, excluded Black women. Although Thomas explained the absence of Black students as being due to the "difficulty of the admissions examination and the fact that we do not admit on certificate of high school graduation," in reality it was her deeply held belief in the inferiority of African Americans that kept them out. Her bigotry, according to Thomas's biographer Helen Horowitz, was rooted in her Baltimore upbringing in which her only interactions with Blacks were with servants.[65]

In 1903, Jessie Fauset, an African American from Philadelphia, graduated at the top of her class at the city's Girls' High. It was customary that the school's top student would enter Bryn Mawr on scholarship, but when it was discovered that Fauset was Black, President Thomas raised money for Fauset to attend Cornell (Thomas's alma mater) rather than have a Black woman attend Bryn Mawr. In 1906, Thomas received an inquiry from M Street High School in Washington, DC, an important source of talented African American students to elite private colleges in the North, concerning the suitability of Bryn Mawr for its students. Thomas responded that their students should seek admissions to other New England colleges rather than Bryn Mawr, due to the large number of students those schools admitted from the middle and southern states. She reasoned:

> As I believe that a great part of the benefit of a college education is derived from intimate association with other students of the same age interested in the same intellectual pursuits, I should be inclined to advise such a student to seek admission to a college situated in one of the New England states where she would not be so apt to be deprived of this intellectual companionship because of the different composition of the student body.[66]

While Thomas implied that Bryn Mawr students would not feel comfortable with African American classmates, these sentiments actually reflected Thomas's own inhibitions.

In her opening address of the 1916 school year to the Bryn Mawr student body, Thomas expressed her belief in the intellectual superiority of the Anglo-Saxon race:

> If the present intellectual supremacy of the White races is maintained, as I hope that it will be for centuries to come, I believe it will be because they are the only races that have seriously begun to educate their women. . . . One thing we know beyond doubt and that is that certain races have never yet in the history of the world manifested any continuous mental activity nor any continuous power of government. Such are the pure negroes of Africa, the Indians, the Esquimaux, the South Sea Islanders, the Turks, etc. . . . These facts must be faced by a country like the United States which is fast becoming, if it has not already become, the melting pot of nations into which are cast at the rate of a million a year the backward people of Europe like the Czechs, the Slavs, and the south Italians. If the laws of heredity mean anything whatsoever, we are jeopardizing the intellectual heritage of the American people by this headlong intermixture of races. . . . If we tarnish our inheritance of racial power at the source, our nation will never again be the same. . . . Our early American stock is still very influential but this cannot continue indefinitely. For example, each year I ask each freshman class to tell me what countries their parents originally came from and for how many generations back their families have been on American soil. It is clear to me that almost all of our student body are early time Americans, that their ancestors have been here for generations, and that they are overwhelmingly English, Scotch, Irish, Welsh, and that of other admixtures, French, German, Dutch largely predominate. All other strains are negligible. Our Bryn Mawr college students therefore as a whole seem to belong by heredity to the dominant races. You, then, students of Bryn Mawr, have the best intellectual inheritance the world affords.[67]

Not surprisingly, given Thomas's views, no African American women attended Bryn Mawr while she was president, regardless of their qualifications.

Although Thomas retired as president of Bryn Mawr in 1922, she remained a director and member of the board of trustees for life. Thomas's successor was Marion Edwards Park, a former dean of

Radcliffe College. Soon after Thomas's retirement, an African American student from New England enrolled at Bryn Mawr, but she left after one week. Her identity and circumstances, even the year she came, remain a mystery. College records indicate that this woman requested that her name never appear on any list concerning Bryn Mawr.[68]

In 1927, the Bryn Mawr board of directors voted to authorize President Park to reply to inquiries regarding the admission of African American women, but with the proviso that she make it clear that such students would be admitted "only as non-residential students." Board member Thomas's opposition to the admission of Black students was steadfast, but the college nevertheless moved forward in this regard.

Enid Cook entered Bryn Mawr in 1927. She majored in chemistry and biology, and in 1931 became the first African American woman to graduate from the college. Cook lived in the home of a Bryn Mawr professor her freshman year, and then with a Black family in the town during her remaining years. She earned a Ph.D. in bacteriology from the University of Chicago in 1937. The second Black woman to graduate from Bryn Mawr was Lillian Russell, in 1934. Russell, who was from Boston, was discouraged from attending Bryn Mawr by the Boston alumnae chapter. They did not believe it was a good place for a "coloured girl" and they felt she would not be happy. But Russell insisted that she wanted to attend, and was awarded the New England Regional scholarship. The Boston alumnae chapter was unable to have the housing restriction waived; thus Russell lived her first few weeks at the college with President Park, and subsequently with Black families in the area. She majored in chemistry and philosophy and was active in extracurricular activities. After graduating from Bryn Mawr, Russell did graduate study in physical chemistry at the Massachusetts Institute of Technology.

As mentioned earlier, M. Carey Thomas, while no longer president of Bryn Mawr after 1922, remained a trustee. Her biographer Helen Horowitz noted that after 1922, Thomas "kept her hand in Bryn Mawr," even to the point of interference.[69] In 1930, in the midst of Bryn Mawr's discussion of housing restrictions, Thomas wrote to Virginia Gildersleeves, dean of Barnard College, asking what Barnard's policy was on this matter.[70] Thomas confided to Gildersleeves her concern that, since Philadelphia had become a center for African Americans, she anticipated continued inquiries concerning admissions and housing from that community. Thomas expressed her concern about the presence of African American men if African American women were allowed to live on campus. She said that when four Black women were allowed to live on Bryn Mawr's campus during summer school, "whenever entertainments are given by the summer school a solid block of negro men from the neighborhood of Bryn Mawr appears in the audience, last summer I am told from twenty-five to thirty."[71] Gildersleeves responded that no African American woman had ever lived on campus at Barnard, but that they were allowed to live in graduate housing at Columbia.[72]

The debate on the admission of African American women and their right to be housed on campus clearly revealed that President Park, former dean at Radcliffe, was quite different from M. Carey Thomas. When a Bryn Mawr alumna wrote to the school's Alumnae Bulletin voicing her opposition to African American women living on campus, President Park responded:

> I agree with all the premises of your letter and arrive at the opposite conclusion as to Bryn Mawr's responsibility, but officially I shall not bring up the matter of the residence of negro students this year. There is much difference of opinion, I think, in all groups connected with the college . . . but I shall be unwilling to propose that a negro student should come into residence while there is strong undergraduate feeling against it, even although the feeling, as I believe it is, is actually on the part of a minority.[73]

Although a couple of Black women graduate students lived in the residence halls in the 1930s and early 1940s, the housing issue was not resolved until 1942, when the executive committee of the board of directors ended the restriction that Blacks could not live on campus. The board voted that "hereafter all students be admitted [and housed] according to the rules and regulations in force as adopted by the Faculty from time to time."[74] The first Black woman moved into unrestricted campus housing in 1946.

Even after African Americans were allowed to attend Bryn Mawr, beginning in 1927, few did. Considering the school's long history of discriminatory practices and attitudes towards African Americans, it took a courageous Black woman to seek admission to Bryn Mawr. By 1960, only nine

African American women had graduated from the institution: two in the 1930s, one in 1948, one in each of the years from 1954 to 1960, except for 1956.

In a 1979 oral history, Evelyn Jones Rich, the African American graduate of the class of 1954, said that she felt she was graded harshly at Bryn Mawr and the marks she received did not fairly represent her work.[75] Rich, who later earned a Ph.D. from Columbia, believed that unjust grades prevented her from graduating cum laude. However, she also recalled that in her senior year, when she and a Black male friend were refused service at a restaurant in the town of Bryn Mawr, the Undergraduate Association, other students, and the college president pressured the restaurant to change its discriminatory policy. When the college lawyer found that the policy violated a Pennsylvania law, the restaurant owner stopped barring African Americans from eating at a booth.[76]

The 1958 Black Bryn Mawr graduate, Camilla Jones Tatem, became a doctor, but said she felt this was in spite of, and not because of, Bryn Mawr. She said she never felt a part of the biology department where she majored, and that the department members discouraged her academic pursuits.[77] In contrast, Christine Philpot Clark, a Black graduate of the class of 1960 who later earned a law degree at Yale, recalled that she liked Bryn Mawr and "even loved particular faculty." She said her Bryn Mawr years coincided with the Little Rock, Arkansas, push to integrate its Central High School, and that this created enormous guilt feelings in some of her White classmates.[78] She noted that two of the four Black women attending Bryn Mawr at that time (one per class) were elected class presidents. "I was approached by some classmates trying to enlist me to be the third," she recalled, "but I knew then the distorted motivations behind it all. I remember, too, the hate letters the two black presidents were receiving."[79]

Clearly, by the 1950s, when a few African American women began to attend Bryn Mawr, the other Seven Sister colleges offered more favorable options. Bryn Mawr and Vassar were the last of the Seven Sisters to admit African American women. For those few African American women who were the early graduates of these institutions, their greatest reward was the power of the degree to advance their career objectives and to demonstrate to the world their ability to compete with the majority members of society.

Vassar College

Vassar College was founded in Poughkeepsie, New York, in 1865, with the endowment of a wealthy brewer, Matthew Vassar. This was a significant event for women's higher education, as Vassar was established as a full-fledged liberal arts college from its inception. Vassar's academic reputation and its affluent alumnae probably account for its being the most resistant to the admission of African American students.[80] It was the last of the Seven Sister colleges to knowingly admit African American students.

The first known Black student at Vassar was Anita Florence Hemmings, from Boston. She enrolled in 1893 and graduated in 1897. A scandal erupted throughout New England when it was discovered that Hemmings, who was light-skinned and passed for White, was actually African American. The event drew significant press coverage. One headline read: "Negro Girl at Vassar: the handsomest girl there. Yale and Harvard Men among those who sought favor with the 'brunette beauty'"[81] Another article reported that "Vassar girls are agitated over the report that one of the students in the senior class of '97 is of Negro parentage. She did not disclose the fact until just before graduation when statements made to Hemmings' roommate led to an investigation."[82] The article said that Hemmings had been noticed as being very bright as a young child, and that her early education was financed by a wealthy White woman. Hemmings studied hard, passed the required examination, and entered Vassar. The article noted that "Vassar is noted for its exclusiveness, and every official of the college refuses to say aught regarding this girl graduate."[83] Another source reported that the faculty was debating whether Hemmings should be denied her diploma. "Never had a colored girl been a student at aristocratic Vassar, and professors were at a loss to foresee the effect upon the future if this one were allowed to be graduated."[84] In the end the faculty did consent to her graduation, reasoning that she was but a few days from commencement and, after this event, the girl would be gone and forgotten.

While at Vassar, Hemmings was active in the Debate Society, College Glee Club, and the Contemporary Club Literary Organization. After graduating she worked at the Boston Public Library in the foreign cataloguing division. She married a physician, and her daughter, Ellen Parker Love, graduated from Vassar in the class of 1927.[85] Presumably Love passed for White as well, since her application stated that she was English and French. Hemmings's husband's race was unknown.[86]

Vassar officials clearly felt that the presence of African American women, even those with a slight tinge of Black blood, would detract from the image it sought to project as an institution for the aristocratic and genteel woman. Historian Lynn Gordon points out that during this period, students from Vassar came almost exclusively from upper-middle-class families. By 1905, attendance at Vassar had become a tradition in many families and a Granddaughters Club was started for students whose mothers and aunts had attended the school.[87]

Continuing his pressure on White institutions, W.E.B. DuBois wrote Henry MacCracken, president of Vassar in 1930, to inquire into Vassar's policy on admitting African Americans. The letter read, "For many years the *Crisis* magazine has secured annually information concerning colored students in northern institutions. The answer from Vassar has always been that you have no colored students. I write to ask you if there has been any change in this rule recently. Are there any colored students in Vassar College today? If a properly equipped colored woman should apply, would you admit her?"[88] MacCracken returned a curt, two-sentence reply, saying that DuBois should read the statement in the Vassar catalogue that read, "No rules other than those there stated govern the admission of students."[89] Despite this response, the reality was that African Americans were neither admitted nor welcome at Vassar. In a 1932 issue of the *Crisis*, DuBois noted that "Vassar is the only first grade women's college in the North which still refuses to admit Negroes. Bryn Mawr and Mount Holyoke held out long but finally surrendered, although Bryn Mawr still keeps its dormitories lily White."[90]

A prominent African American minister from Harlem, the Reverend James Robinson, gave a lecture at Vassar in the late 1930s at a conference cosponsored by the college and the YWCA. In his lecture, Robinson challenged the White women students to improve race relations by getting Vassar to open its doors to Black women. When the students responded that they did not know any Blacks, Robinson offered to find a Black student for the college.[91]

Robinson's congregation included an outstanding student, Beatrix McCleary, the daughter of a physician and an extremely light-skinned Black woman who could have passed for White. "Beatty," as she was known, entered Vassar in the fall of 1940. McCleary excelled in her studies and was elected to Phi Beta Kappa. She was also the first Black to be a member of the Daisy Chain.[92] McCleary obtained the highest rank in zoology while at Vassar, and was awarded four Vassar College fellowships. McCleary went on to become the first African American woman graduate of the Yale University School of Medicine and went into the field of psychiatry.[93]

During the six years after McCleary's entrance into Vassar, six additional African American women were admitted. Separate dormitory rooms for the Black women were still required during this period. June Jackson, from Cambridge, Massachusetts, arrived at Vassar in 1941, the year after McCleary. Jackson had been an active member of the NAACP Youth Council in Cambridge, and had been accepted and awarded scholarships to both Vassar and Radcliffe. Her aunt, Geneva Jackson, had graduated cum laude from Radcliffe in 1919. Her aunt's accomplishments were a great source of pride in their family, and Jackson said she knew she would have to compete with her aunt's record. She said her parents were concerned about reports of snobbishness at Vassar, but after speaking with McCleary, whose views of Vassar were positive, Jackson decided to attend. Jackson noted in her housing request that she would like a roommate, but the president of the Boston Vassar Club told her, in a "genteel but firm manner," that Jackson would be happier if she had a single room. The woman said further that the college had been courageous enough to increase the student body of African Americans by admitting Jackson and another Black woman that year, but that the school was not ready to integrate the dormitories.[94]

Jackson's recollections of Vassar differ from McCleary's, who wrote two years after her graduation that she felt she had been treated fairly at Vassar. Jackson, who was much darker than McCleary in complexion and appeared to have a more heightened consciousness about racial issues, said she was denied entrance into a Poughkeepsie skating rink where she had gone with a group of students because she was Black. She recalled that she could not find a room to rent for her freshman prom date, who was also visibly African American; in her sophomore year, a White roommate rented a room for her. Jackson said that a professor expressed surprise about a well-written paper she submitted, stating that "it didn't sound like a Negro's writing." Most of the White students' only previous interaction with African American women had been with their maids, and they repeatedly asked Jackson simplistic questions about race and told her she didn't talk like an African American. Their surprise at meeting an articulate, intelligent Black woman was symptomatic of the prevailing view of most Whites toward African Americans. As Jackson recalled, "Sometimes my personal pain at racist incidents was so deep that I could not share it with my new-found White friends until a greater sense of trust had developed." During Jackson's last years at Vassar, she lived in a cooperative house on campus where twenty women lived, studied, cooked, ate, and socialized together. Jackson was the only African American housemate, but she recalled that another woman of color lived in the house.[95]

Several other African American women were admitted to Vassar during World War II. These included Marie Lawrence, a day student from an old and prominent Poughkeepsie family who graduated in 1945 and later earned a masters degree in social work from Smith College; her sister, Stadella Lawrence, who graduated in 1947; and Olive Thurman, the daughter of renowned theologian Howard Thurman, then dean of the chapel at Howard University, who graduated in 1948. W.E.B. DuBois spoke at Vassar in 1942 and challenged the college of twelve hundred students to admit one hundred African American women, stating that the token number of African American women was ridiculously small, given the size of the student body. He pointed out that the acute racial problem in the United States caused most Blacks to be excluded from the best education, the best jobs, the best living accommodations, and everything that would allow them the opportunity to display their ability. DuBois noted that the cultural patterns of the United States, which continually upheld White superiority, must give way to the democratic ideals that were "preached much but practiced so little."[96]

But neither Vassar nor the United States was ready for true integration or the practice of democratic ideals. In the 1940s, only seven Black women graduated from Vassar. For nearly twenty-five years after McCleary was admitted in 1940, Vassar admitted no more than three African Americans in any given year. In some years, none were admitted.

Like its sister institution Bryn Mawr, Vassar had a long history of excluding African American women. Through the protests of people like the Reverend James Robinson and the work of the NAACP and other organizations, the doors of Vassar slowly opened to African American women. June Jackson writes that World War II and the heightened expectations of African Americans had created an activist spirit among Black women students in the 1940s. By the fifties, however, most Vassar students had become more apathetic about issues of race and social justice, and Black women students received a different message:

> Even though they were few in number, they were now expected to be there. It could be said that Vassar did admit Negroes. The implicit message was one that fostered assimilation and denial of differences, as expressed by "We don't see color," or "I never think of you as Black." This imposes a different burden, that of denying a part of your identity even though consciously acknowledging your race.[97]

By 1960 only twenty-three African American women had graduated from Vassar. These women were solidly middle to upper middle class, the daughters of professionals. They were the products of integrated high schools of New York and New England, and the renowned Dunbar High School of Washington, DC. These women excelled at Vassar, and most continued their education in graduate and professional schools. But, as June Jackson noted, despite their accomplishments, the early Black students at Vassar paid a huge personal cost:

> For the Black woman who entered Vassar during these early years, the lone Black student entered to live the demanding life of being the "one and only," a life many remember as lonely in an atmosphere which was unaccepting and, at times, hostile. Administrators and faculty who might have provided support and guidance or served as role models were lacking. For most of those early students, the college community did not provide a sense of being valued or belonging.[98]

Barnard College

Barnard College was founded in 1889 as the "sister" institution to the all-male Columbia. Given its New York City setting, Barnard should have provided a convenient location for college-bound African American women; however, this was not the case. Members of the Black community believed that Barnard discouraged applications from African American women and placed quotas on their numbers when it finally began to admit them.

Famed Harlem Renaissance writer Zora Neale Hurston enrolled at Barnard College as a transfer student in 1925. Hurston, who was the personal secretary of writer Fanny Hurst, had received a scholarship to Barnard after impressing one of its founders, Annie Nathan Meyer. Hurston was a day student and commuted from Harlem to the campus. Hurston was apparently the first African American woman to attend Barnard and was the only Black student during her three semesters there. A witty and eccentric personality, Hurston stated that she encountered no prejudice at Barnard. In fact, Hurston felt it gave White students status to say they had lunched with her. In her autobiography, *Dust Tracks on a Road: An Autobiography*, Hurston wrote:

> I have no lurid tales to tell of race discrimination at Barnard. I made few friends in the first few days. The Social Register crowd at Barnard soon took me up, and I soon became Barnard's sacred black cow.[99]

Hurston recognized the opportunity attending Barnard afforded her:

> I felt that I was highly privileged and determined to make the most of it. I did not resolve to be a grind, however, to show White folks that I had brains. I took it for granted that they knew that. Else, why was I at Barnard? . . . So, I set out to maintain a good average, take part in whatever went on, and just be a part of the college like everybody else. I graduated with a B record, and I am entirely satisfied.[100]

Hurston also expressed her indebtedness to Annie Nathan Meyer: "Mrs. Meyer, who was the moving spirit in founding the college and who is still a trustee, did nobly by me in getting me in. No matter what I might do for her, I would still be in her debt."[101]

Belle Tobias and Vera Joseph enrolled after Hurston's graduation in 1928. Tobias, a botany major, and Joseph, a chemistry major, had both attended New York City public schools. Tobias was the daughter of prominent civil rights and religious leader Channing Tobias, who was secretary of the Colored Department of the National Council of the Young Men's Christian Association, the first African American to serve as director of the Phelps-Stokes Fund, and a member of the board of the national NAACP. Belle Tobias graduated Phi Beta Kappa in the Barnard class of 1931, and went on to earn a masters degree from Wellesley College in 1932.[102]

Vera Joseph was an immigrant from Jamaica who had graduated from George Washington High School in Harlem. She had taken the commercial rather than the college preparatory curriculum in high school to prepare herself for the world of work, since her family had no financial resources for her education beyond high school. However, one of her teachers, Irene F. Gottesman, recognized Joseph's academic talents and insisted that she go to college. As a result, Joseph stayed an additional semester in high school to take the college preparatory courses that qualified her for admission to college. Joseph recalled that she had envisioned herself on a residential campus, but Barnard was the only college that her teachers suggested she consider. She enrolled in 1928 and graduated in 1932. Her first year at Barnard was financed by a scholarship from a group of African American businessmen and educators from Harlem, and by a Barnard scholarship; her subsequent years were financed through scholarships and jobs.[103] Joseph also graduated Phi Beta Kappa, entered Columbia Medical School in 1932, and later became a physician. Joseph, by now Dr. Peterson, said that she and Belle Tobias became good friends and recalled few slights or acts of discrimination at Barnard. As she recalled:

> I never looked for evidence of racial slights or discrimination, so if they occurred I may not have been aware of it. I was making great discoveries in my books and classes and was quite happy with my life at Barnard. It was not until my senior year when I discovered I was not being invited to join the Barnard Club in New York City after graduation that I recognized that I was being discriminated against, and resented it. But more important things than admission to a social club were happening in my life; I was going to medical school.[104]

Jeanne Blackwell transferred to Barnard in 1934 after spending three years at the University of Michigan. Blackwell had graduated in 1931 as valedictorian of her class from the segregated Douglass High School in Baltimore. She had wanted to attend a Seven Sister college, but her family could not afford the tuition. Thus, she enrolled in the University of Michigan, a public institution with an outstanding academic reputation. Blackwell's dream was to become a physician and she was a pre-med student at Michigan, where she also struggled for three years for the right to live on campus. Her mother became concerned about the amount of effort Blackwell was spending on the housing battle and felt she should transfer to another institution. Thus Blackwell transferred to Barnard, mistakenly believing the situation there would be better.

Barnard officials, unaware of Blackwell's race before she arrived, refused to allow her to live on campus. She instead lived in the nearby International House, which was integrated. Despite being refused permission to live on campus, Blackwell recalled her year at Barnard as positive. She recalled that one of her professors was quite embarrassed that Blackwell was refused dormitory housing and expressed her regret to her. Blackwell graduated in 1935, earned a B.S. from the Columbia School of Library Science the following year, and went on to become a prominent authority on Black literary and scholarly collections. In 1955 Blackwell was appointed curator of the renowned repository of African American collections, the Schomburg Center for Research in Black Culture of the New York Public Library.[105]

Throughout the 1930s and 1940s, the NAACP waged legal battles against discrimination against Blacks in higher education. With Black soldiers fighting and losing their lives in World War II, protests mounted against the discrimination and exclusion of African Americans in all aspects of U.S. life. When the Reverend James Robinson addressed an interfaith conference on the campus of Teachers College in February 1943, he spoke out again on the discrimination that talented African American women experienced in applying to certain Seven Sister colleges. Robinson said that it was well known that Barnard and Vassar had quotas for Black women, admitting no more than four every two years. Virginia Gildersleeves, dean of Barnard, issued a written response in the pages of the *Barnard Bulletin* vehemently denying Robinson's accusation:

Dear Mr. Robinson:

It has been reported to me that you stated in an address at the Teachers College Chapel yesterday that Barnard discriminated against Negro students and had a Negro quota which permitted the admission of four students every two years. This is quite untrue. We have no Negro quota. We never receive many applications for admission from Negroes. If we are going to have a quota, we certainly would not have such a foolish one as that reported in the strange rumor which seems to have reached you.

We always have some Negro students in Barnard. This year our most valuable graduate fellowship is held by a Negro, and one of our most distinguished alumnae is a Negro, of whom we are very proud.

I am anxious to do anything I can to further the solution of this serious race problem, and I shall be glad to discuss it with you, if you would like to call and see me. I regret you have such a bad opinion of us.[106]

An editorial in the same issue of the *Barnard Bulletin* commented that while the school might not have quotas for African American women, the issue of race should not die there, and that much should be done. While there were Black colleges for African Americans, the editorial continued, "there are, however, Negro students who are willing to sacrifice personal happiness in return for the opportunity of 'proving themselves' in the North." The editorial suggested that a certain number of scholarships should be earmarked for African American women students at Barnard.[107]

As a result of the editorial, a group of politically active White students established a Committee on the Investigation of Educational Opportunities for the Negro at Barnard. The committee concluded that two factors contributed to the dearth of Black women at Barnard. The first was financial, since most Black candidates could not afford to attend. Second, those who could afford to attend Barnard preferred to attend either a Black college in the South, or Radcliffe or Smith, which admitted more Blacks. The committee concluded that it should inform local high school counselors that Barnard did welcome African Americans and that no racial quotas existed.[108] However, since most of the Black students in the Seven Sister colleges paid their own tuition and many won scholarships after arriving on these campuses, this first explanation does not accurately reflect the reality of the situation. Barnard's location in New York, a city with a large Black population, made it accessible to a large pool of Black women who could have commuted to the campus. It appears that the primary reason Barnard had so few Black students was that Black women believed the school did not welcome them.

Charlotte Hanley was the immediate beneficiary of the effort to increase African American enrollment at Barnard. Hanley graduated from Yonkers High School in 1942 and planned to enroll in New York University, but she could not afford to attend. She moved to New York City to live with her maternal grandmother in hopes of attending the tuition-free Hunter College, which both her grandmother and aunt had attended. However, shortly after Robinson's lecture and the subsequent reaction, a social worker friend of Hanley's family informed them that Barnard was prepared to offer a full tuition scholarship to a deserving Black student. Hanley and her mother met with Reverend Robinson, after which she initiated the application process to Barnard, which she had always thought to be an expensive school available only to the daughters of the affluent. Barnard accepted Hanley and provided her with a full tuition scholarship (except for $50) to cover the entire period of her studies. She lived in Harlem with her godparents and worked in the community center of Reverend Robinson's church, to earn money for books and living expenses.[109]

Hanley entered Barnard as a mathematics major but changed to economics, which she felt would make her more employable. Hanley recalled her years at Barnard as being very enjoyable, and said that her degree meant a great deal in terms of social contacts and employment opportunities. She said that her professional success was due to a Barnard economics professor who offered her a job working as a researcher in the Department of Financial Research for the National Bureau of Economic Research. Several years later she became the first African American hired at the Federal Reserve Bank of Chicago as an economist, where in time she was appointed assistant vice president.[110]

Barnard did not maintain student rosters by race, and thus an exact count of African American women at the college prior to 1960 is not available. However, it is believed that Zora Neale Hurston was the first known African American graduate, and that she was followed by Black women graduates in the classes of 1931, 1932, and 1935. Both Hurston and Blackwell, who graduated in 1928 and 1935, respectively, said that there were no other African American women on campus while they were students. The publicity surrounding Reverend Robinson's challenge to Barnard increased the college's awareness and efforts to attract more African American women in the years after World War II. Charlotte Hanley pointed out that Barnard recruited Black women from New York City public schools who were not as socially or economically advantaged as many of the Black women at the other Seven Sister colleges.[111] The small number of African American women who attended Barnard in the middle of the century remember the classes and faculty fondly. Though Black students were barred from living on campus, the only other remembered racial slight was Vera Joseph's recollection stating that she was not invited to become a member of the Barnard Club of New York after graduation.[112] While all of the Black alumnae who commented on their Barnard years said they had made many friendships across racial lines, their primary concern at Barnard had been the value the degree gave them in their careers and professional growth.

Conclusion

In terms of policies related to race, the Seven Sister colleges are not a monolithic entity. Some admitted African American women as far back as the turn of the twentieth century, while others grudgingly, and only under great pressure, admitted them decades later. Discrimination in housing, however, was a constant problem for African American students at every Seven Sister institution. Even when they were finally allowed to live on campuses, they remained segregated within the dormitories. In 1927, Smith College's President Neilson informed a parent that "legally the College had no right to exclude colored girls . . . but we take care that a colored girl and a White girl never have to share the same room, and we advise colored girls for their own comfort to room outside the college."[113] Frances Monroe King, a Black Mount Holyoke graduate in 1942, recalled that "we did have a dean of residence who did not permit interracial rooming. I had a single room all four years, not always by choice."[114] In fact, White students' views on this issue often differed from the administration. King said that when a White and an African American student from the class of 1943 requested a room together, the college's rejection of their request caused an "outrage" on campus among students.[115]

Many White students joined the struggle for racial equality on the Seven Sister campuses. Interracial and Christian student groups, for example, were very active. June Jackson recalled that the early leaders of the Interracial Group at Vassar, many of whom were Jewish, were criticized for being "too interested in Negroes"—a charge tinged with anti-Semitism.[116] In 1937, the Student Christian Movement sent a letter to Radcliffe President Ada L. Comstock inquiring about the situation of "Negro" students: they asked how many had ever been admitted, whether quotas existed, what the school's housing policy was, and to what extent Blacks were allowed to participate in campus life.[117] Charlotte Hanley, a 1947 Barnard graduate, acknowledged that the efforts of certain White classmates made her scholarship possible:

> I celebrate Shirley Sexauer Harrison, Miriam Gore Ruff [member of the Committee on the Investigation of Educational Opportunities for the Negro at Barnard], the editors of the *Barnard Bulletin* for the editorial of March 4, 1943, and all the other Barnard women, who, along with Jim Robinson, caused Dean Gildersleeves to reflect on Barnard's student recruitment policies. Their strong commitment to the importance of having more Negro students at Barnard had lasting effects. Guidance counselors at high schools in Harlem and elsewhere thereafter were invited to locate promising candidates for admission. By the time of Dean Gildersleeves' retirement in 1947, the number of Negro students attending Barnard, as I recall, had risen to eight—the largest number in its history—an improvement, but still a small fraction of the 1,400 strong student body.[118]

Despite the resistance they faced, the small number of African American women who attended and graduated from the Seven Sister colleges overwhelmingly asserted that they would attend the same institution again. Many of their daughters and granddaughters have since attended these same institutions. Most of these women minimized any discrimination they experienced on these campuses, saying the pursuit of the degree was their primary goal. While they experienced discrimination, primarily in housing, these limitations did not paralyze them. Most were outstanding students, active in campus activities, and many formed lifelong friendships across racial lines during their years at the Seven Sisters.

Despite these positive feelings, however, not all Black alumnae from that era share the sentiments. For example, when some of Radcliffe's earliest Black graduates were asked to comment on their experience, one woman vehemently refused. The interviewer observed, "[Although] she had an interesting career . . . she is very, very bitter about Radcliffe because of her experience there. And she deeply resents Radcliffe's failure to recognize its early Black graduates and their accomplishments."[119]

The early Black graduates of the Seven Sister colleges were a privileged group, and they were aware of it. Their African American sisters in the South who attended Black colleges were often channeled into teacher-training, vocational, and home economics programs. While African American women who attended White coeducational institutions found themselves barred from many "male disciplines," the Seven Sister graduates were among the earliest Black women scientists, lawyers, and doctors: Harriet Rice, Wellesley's first Black graduate in 1887, became a physician; Jane Bolin, a 1928 graduate of Wellesley, became the first African American woman judge in the country; Eunice Hunter Carter, from Smith's class of 1921, became the first African American woman district attorney in the state of New York, whose work in the 1930s resulted in the biggest prosecution of organized crime in the nation; Evelyn Boyd, a 1945 Smith graduate, became one of the first Black women to earn a Ph.D. in mathematics (Yale, 1950). A 1988 study found that, of the twenty-eight living Black alumnae of Mount Holyoke, fourteen became prominent physicians and research scientists.[120]

Shirlee Taylor Haizlip, a 1959 graduate of Wellesley, noted that there were only two other Black women in her class and eight on the campus in total, but to her their small numbers did not matter. She said her closest friends were White, and that there was no consciousness concerning Blackness among the African American women at Wellesley, that they wanted to be viewed just like any other students. Haizlip explained that the thinking of the period was that "to be overly friendly with others of color would . . . set them too much apart," thus Black students deliberately avoided one another.[121] June Jackson recalled that in the 1940s at Vassar, African American women were expected to be assimilationist and integrationist, the unquestioned goals of most middle-class African Americans prior to the 1960s. She was told by college officials and faculty to think of herself as an American and not a Negro American.[122] Barbara P. Wright, Mount Holyoke class of 1943, also remembered that "there were few Black students [at Mount Holyoke], and although we were friends, we all went about our business."[123]

African American women appear to have preferred Wellesley and Smith, which were perceived as the most welcoming to Blacks of the Seven Sisters. In a letter to the dean of Radcliffe College in 1946, Mary Gibson Huntley, a 1918 graduate of Radcliffe, said that Smith and Wellesley were the fairest towards African American women in terms of scholarship awards and housing policy. She added that the alumnae clubs of these two institutions were more accepting of Black women.[124]

Early African American graduates of the Seven Sisters were frequently loyal alumnae. They attended reunions, were active in alumnae clubs, gave money to their alma maters, and served as trustees. Having earned degrees from these institutions gave these Black women unprecedented access to people of power and privilege. Fifty years after graduating from Radcliffe, Mary Gibson Huntley wrote: "The prestige of my degree brought contacts in emergency, when professional or racial problems arose."[125] Charlotte Leverett Smith Brown, a 1920 graduate of Radcliffe and the first Black woman at Radcliffe to graduate with a degree in science (chemistry), concurred with Huntley's assessment. Writing at age sixty-nine, Brown stated, "I always have been and always will be proud that I am a Radcliffe graduate, and find that when questioned the mention of Radcliffe seems to settle all arguments and discussions."[126] Frances M. King, Mount Holyoke class of 1942, agrees, "I continue to be grateful for having had the opportunity for a Mount Holyoke education. It stacks up well in the world and makes me proud to be an alumna."[127] Evelyn Rich, Bryn Mawr class of 1954, who did not enjoy her college experience and felt that she was given grades she didn't deserve, nevertheless stated in an interview, "I'm very supportive of the college now. . . . I give them money, and more importantly I give them time and my commitment because I feel . . . that the life I live now is largely a result of my Bryn Mawr experience."[128] In recent discussions, early Black Barnard College graduates shared the perspective that a degree from such a distinguished institution opened doors and provided invaluable contacts.[129]

While not every Black Seven Sister student was affluent—many worked to earn money while in college—the socioeconomic status and life experiences of most of them were far removed from those of the average African American. Wellesley graduate Shirley Taylor Haizlip, class of 1959, reflected on her fellow Black Seven Sisters:

> The hue of their skin barely distinguished them from other students. Like other young women in the Sister Colleges and men in the Ivy League schools, the Negroes generally came from life styles similar to that of the majority of the student body. More often than not, their parents were professionals, conservative in their politics, and moderate in their racial practices. . . . The Northern Negro student's identification with the economically and socially less fortunate of his brothers was tenuous at best. Although in each successful black family there were always some close familiar links with the poverty and the peculiar degradation of being black, strong attempts were made to ignore or avoid any contamination by association. These, and I, too, were blacks of a different color.[130]

The roster of Black Seven Sister graduates from the mid-1960s reads like a "who's who" of elite Black America. The daughters of doctors, religious and civil rights leaders, educators, and other professionals dominated. Jane White and Gladys White, the daughter and niece of NAACP President Walter White, graduated from Smith in 1944 and 1942, respectively. Channing Tobias's daughter Belle graduated from Barnard in 1931; Black Nobel laureate Ralph Bunche's daughter Joan was a member of the Vassar class of 1953; Olive Thurman, the daughter of prominent Black theologian and dean of Howard University Divinity School Howard Thurman, was in the Vassar class of 1948; and Gail Lumet Buckley, daughter of actress Lena Horne, graduated from Radcliffe in 1959.

Many of these women were so light complected that they were easily mistaken as White. June Jackson commented that her classmate at Vassar, Beatrix McCleary, "was so light in complexion, and the student body so unused to the varied shades of Afro-Americans, that she was generally mistaken for any ethnic background other than Black."[131] Nevertheless, these women's high achievements often didn't change Whites' attitudes towards them, as they were viewed as atypical Blacks. For example, in 1914, when Radcliffe President Lebarron Russell Briggs attempted to help Mary Gibson get financial aid, he repeatedly mentioned to donors that Gibson did not look African American. In one letter, he wrote, "this girl is almost White," and assured them that Gibson was extremely bright, and, although colored, that "she is a colored girl who would easily be taken for a Spanish girl."[132] However, these women's light skin did not prevent their schools from keeping them in segregated housing.

In many ways these African American women's Seven Sisters' education set them apart from most women of their race. It gave them the freedom, exposure, and opportunity to prove themselves intellectually on the same basis as Whites, and opened to them opportunities for a wider range of careers, including medicine, science, and law. In fact, Wellesley College alumnae records reported in 1964 that the number of African American alumnae who had earned graduate and professional degrees was "especially striking" and far exceeded that of the college population as a whole.[133] In contrast to many of their White classmates, who often married and stopped working outside the home, the early Seven Sisters' Black graduates overwhelmingly both married *and* maintained careers. These women knew that they were expected by other Blacks to be "a credit to the race," and that their success or failure had an impact not only on them as individuals, but on the African American race as a whole. They were race representatives regardless of how unrepresentative they were in other respects (e.g., social and familial backgrounds).

Mount Holyoke, Wellesley, and Smith, which were founded in part on Christian beliefs, were challenged when their policies and practices conflicted with these beliefs. At Smith, the strong influence of the NAACP made the school popular among African American women. Radcliffe was a favorite among African American women for both undergraduate and graduate study. Radcliffe President Lebarron Russell Briggs was close friends with NAACP board members, and was considered a fair and liberal man by African American students. Vassar, Barnard, and Bryn Mawr were the most resistant to admitting African American women. As noted above, throughout the presidency of M. Carey Thomas, no African American woman attended Bryn Mawr. Her negative and stereotypical views of African Americans are a matter of record. Key personnel at the Seven Sisters made the difference in the treatment of African Americans and their ability to matriculate in these institutions. Historian Rosalind Rosenberg noted that Virginia Gildersleeves, dean of Barnard from 1911–1946, "welcomed Jewish students and faculty only so long as they were thoroughly assimilated, and she included African Americans only so long as they were well spoken and did not ask to live in the dormitories."[134]

In written and oral histories, early African American students at the Seven Sister colleges stated that these institutions had a quota of no more than two Blacks per class. Though there was in fact no written policy limiting the number of African American students at these colleges, there was an unwritten policy, like the one contested at Smith in 1913. Francis Monroe King, Mount Holyoke College class of 1942, recalled:

> When I was a freshman, the only other Negro was a senior. By my sophomore year there were two in the freshman class, thus shattering a long-standing unwritten quota among the Seven Sister colleges of "only two at a time on campus." When I was a senior, two more Negroes were freshmen, bringing our total to five![135]

Charlotte Hanley Scott, Barnard class of 1947, recalled that there were usually two women a year during her tenure. By the 1950s, more Blacks were being admitted. An article on Black students at Barnard noted that in the 1950s, when as many as three African Americans were admitted per class, Black women at the school referred to themselves as "The Holy Twelve" because there were never more than twelve Black women on campus in any given year.[136]

As noted above, the increased presence of African American women on the campuses of the Seven Sister colleges during the twentieth century was influenced greatly by the people in the leadership of those institutions and the protest efforts of the NAACP. Public condemnation and negative press also forced this issue to a head. Even with the most liberal of the Seven Sister colleges, the issue of social equality remained. The refusal to assign African American women rooms with

Whites, regardless of their background or hue, clearly communicated to the Black community that in many ways these campuses reflected society's attitude towards them. In addition, the women were often viewed in racial terms. Letters of references from professors often noted that they were the brightest "colored or Negro" student. College student affairs records with comments like "well bred, deeply thoughtful, possible future leader of her race" reflected the bias and expectations that were envisioned for many of the Black women students.

It was sometimes believed by the administrators of these institutions that most of the African American women graduates would be employed in a Black setting. Mary Gibson recalled that Black women college graduates routinely faced discrimination in hiring and had little choice but to go South to teach in segregated high schools. She noted that a few also taught in New England schools and in New York City. While at Radcliffe, she relates,

> in June, 1917, a rare opportunity made me the first colored bank clerk in Boston, where I worked two summers for the Tremont Trust Company on State Street. President Briggs had advised me to go back home and give my training to my people. That was the ideal of service for many decades. It was the hope of my widowed mother, a former Washington teacher. It had been the dream of my father, a Baltimore lawyer.[137]

Thus, despite the "rare opportunity," duty and service to her race prevailed. Gibson spent forty-five years teaching in public schools. She stated that this position brought "problems and sacrifices as well as many rewarding experiences."[138] Many graduates did break through racial barriers and had stellar careers outside of the African American community. However, some often reported limitations in their careers because of their race. Most of the women reported some active involvement with civil rights, community organizations, and interracial groups throughout their lives. As mentioned earlier, the expectation of the African American community was that those who had achieved academic and professional success would return and assist the community.

The Seven Sister colleges were certainly not utopias, but to many of the African American women who attended these institutions prior to the 1960s, it was an experience they valued enough to encourage the following generations of Black women to continue in their footsteps.

Notes

1. The terms "African American" and "Black" will be used interchangeably in this chapter.
2. Helen Lefkowitz Horowitz, *Alma Mater: Design and Experience in the Women's Colleges from Their Nineteenth-Century Beginnings to the 1930s* (Amherst: University of Massachusetts Press, 1993), p. 147.
3. See Arthur C. Cole, *A Hundred Years of Mount Holyoke College: The Evolution of an Educational Ideal* (New Haven, CT: Yale University Press, 1940); Cornelia Meigs, *What Makes a College? A History of Bryn Mawr* (New York: MacMillan, 1956); L. Clark Seelye, *The Early History of Smith College, 1871–1910* (Boston: Houghton, Mifflin, 1923); Florence Converse, *Wellesley College, a Chronicle of the Years, 1875–1938* (Wellesley, MA: Hathaway House Bookshop, 1939); Marian Churchill White, *A History of Barnard College* (New York: Columbia University Press, 1954); Horowitz, *Alma Mater*; Patricia Ann Palmieri, *In Adamless Eden: The Community of Women Faculty at Wellesley* (New Haven, CT: Yale University Press, 1995).
4. For a discussion of this, see Rosalyn Terborg-Penn's "Discrimination against Afro-American Women in the Women's Movement, 1830 to 1920," in *The Afro-American Woman: Struggles and Images*, ed. Sharon Harley and Rosalyn Terborg-Penn (New York: Kennikat, 1978); Linda M. Perkins, "The Impact of the 'Cult of True Womanhood' on the Education of Black Women," *Journal of Social Issues*, 39, No. 3 (1983), 17–28.
5. W.E.B. DuBois, "The College Bred Negro," in *Proceedings of the Fifth Conferences for the Study of the Negro Problems* (Atlanta, GA: Atlanta University Press, 1900).
6. W.E.B. DuBois, "The College Bred Negro," p. 30.
7. W.E.B. DuBois held a lifelong interest in the "talented tenth" of the race, those individuals who were formally educated. Beginning in the late nineteenth century, he surveyed and kept data on the progress of African Americans in higher education. In his 1900 study, "The College Bred Negro," he summed up the progress of Blacks in gaining admission to White institutions.
8. W.E.B. DuBois, *The Philadelphia Negro: A Social Study* (New York: Schocken Books, 1970), p. 7.
9. See Adelaide M. Cromwell, *The Other Brahmins: Boston's Black Upper Class, 1750–1950* (Fayetteville: University of Arkansas Press, 1994), p. 10, and Willard Gatewood, *Aristocrats of Color: The Black Elite, 1880–1920*. (Fayetteville: University of Arkansas Press, 1990), pp. 247–271.

10. James D. Anderson, *The Education of Blacks in the South* (Chapel Hill: University of North Carolina Press, 1988), p. 186.
11. DuBois, *The Philadelphia Negro.*
12. Cromwell, *The Other Brahmins*, p. 139; Gatewood, *Aristocrats of Color*, p. 114.
13. Gatewood, *Aristocrats of Color*, p. 247.
14. For more on this topic see Anderson, *The Education of Blacks in the South.*
15. Carlton Mabee, *Black Education in New York State: From Colonial to Modern Times* (Syracuse, NY: Syracuse University Press, 1979), p. 104.
16. Roster of African American Women Students at Oberlin College, compiled in 1984 by Michon Boston, in History of Black Women at Oberlin Project. In possession of the author.
17. Quoted in Horowitz, *Alma Mater*, p. 54.
18. Wellesley College Directory of Students, Wellesley College Archives, Wellesley, MA, 1887–1888.
19. Harriett A. Rice, "On the Mountain Top," *Wellesley Magazine,* June 1943, p. 298.
20. Biographical records of Harriet A. Rice in Harriet A. Rice folder of Wellesley College Alumnae Association Records, Wellesley College Archives, Wellesley, MA.
21. Jane Bolin Offset, "Wellesley in My Life," in *Wellesley After-Images: Reflection on Their College Years by Forty-Five Alumnae,* ed. Wellesley College Club of Los Angeles (Los Angeles: Wellesley College Club of Los Angeles, 1974), p. 92.
22. Offset, "Wellesley in My Life," pp. 91–92.
23. Virginia Foster Durr, *Outside the Magic Circle: The Autobiography of Virginia Foster Durr,* ed. Hollander F. Barnard (University: University of Alabama Press, 1985), p. 56.
24. Durr, *Outside the Magic Circle*, p. 58.
25. Durr, *Outside the Magic Circle*, p. 58. In 1926, Virginia Foster married Clifford Durr. Durr was a former Rhodes scholar and prominent lawyer in Birmingham, Alabama. Despite Foster Durr's attitudes towards race while at Wellesley, by the 1950s she and her husband were living in Montgomery, Alabama, and had become active civil rights advocates. Her husband Clifford accompanied African American attorney E. D. Nixon when he bailed Rosa Parks out of jail after she was arrested for refusing to give up her bus seat to a White rider in 1955.
26. Letter from the Department of Biblical History to President Ellen Pendleton, Wellesley College, May 6, 1932, President's Office Papers, Residence Halls (1918–1967), Wellesley College Archives, Wellesley, MA.
27. Ruth H. Lindsay, Dean of Residence. Wellesley College, to Mary Chase, Charlotte, North Carolina, May 9, 1949, President's Office Papers, Residence Halls (1918–1967), Wellesley College Archives, Wellesley, MA.
28. As mentioned earlier, Mount Holyoke graduated a Black woman from its seminary in 1883.
29. Ella Elbert Smith, class of 1888, Alumnae Questionnaire of 1951, Wellesley Alumnae Records, Wellesley College Archives, Wellesley, MA.
30. Smith, Alumnae Questionnaire of 1951.
31. Ella Elbert Smith, class of 1888, biographical folder, Wellesley College Alumnae Records, Wellesley College Archives, Wellesley, MA.
32. Henry Parsons Dowse, *Radcliffe College* (Boston: H. B. Humphrey, 1913), n.p.
33. Alberta Scott biographical data sheet, Radcliffe College Collection of Biographical Data on African American Students, p. 1, Schlesinger Library, Radcliffe College, Cambridge, MA.
34. Mary Gibson Huntley, "Radcliffe in My Life," May 1968, Mary Gibson Huntley Papers, Box 10, folder 4, Schlesinger Library, Radcliffe College, Cambridge, MA.
35. Lebarron Russell Briggs to Mary Church Terrell, October 16, 1914, Briggs Papers, Box 7, folder 53, Schlesinger Library, Radcliffe College, Cambridge, MA.
36. See various correspondence on this issue in the Mary Gibson Huntley Papers, Schlesinger Library, Radcliffe College, Cambridge, MA.
37. Lebarron Russell Briggs to Mary Church Terrell, October 16, 1914, Briggs Papers, Box 7, folder 53, Schlesinger Library, Radcliffe College, Cambridge, MA.
38. Lebarron Russell Briggs to Rev. W. H. van Allen, October 21, 1916, Briggs Papers, Box 2, p. 677, Schlesinger Library, Radcliffe College, Cambridge, MA.
39. Lebarron Russell Briggs to Mrs. S. Burt Wolbach, November 7, 1916, Briggs Papers, Box 2, p. 713, Schlesinger Library, Radcliffe College, Cambridge, MA.
40. Lebarron Russell Briggs to Mrs. S. Burt Wolbach, November 7, 1916, Briggs Papers, Box 2, p. 714, Schlesinger Library, Radcliffe College, Cambridge, MA.
41. Lebarron Russell Briggs to Miss Elizabeth Hoar Storer, February 28, 1917, in Briggs Papers, Box 2, vol. 3, p. 829, Schlesinger Library, Radcliffe College, Cambridge, MA.

42. Lebarron Russell Briggs to Mary Gibson, March 5, 1920, Briggs Papers, Box 2, vol. 4, p. 573, Schlesinger Library, Radcliffe College, Cambridge, MA.

43. Gibson, "Radcliffe in My Life," p. 1.

44. Interview of Margaret McCane by her daughter Charlotte McCane on January 1, 1981, The Margaret McCane Papers, Box 1, folder 4, Schlesinger Library, Radcliffe College, Cambridge, MA.

45. Quoted in Horowitz, *Alma Mater,* p. 70.

46. Partial transcript of NAACP meeting [n.d.], "Discussion in re Carrie Lee," in Office of the President Files, Smith College Archives, Northampton, MA.

47. W.E.B. DuBois, "A College Girl," in *Crisis,* 8 (1913), 293.

48. Moorfield Storey, Boston, Massachusetts, to Reverend Marion Lercy Burton, Smith College, October 14, 1913, in Carrie Lee folder, Individuals 1917, Box 1789, Smith College Archives, Northampton, MA.

49. Biographical Sheet, Faculty Records Bo-Br, Box 42, in Ruth Bowles folder, Smith College Archives, Northampton, MA.

50. Mary White Ovington, Brooklyn, New York, to Joel Spingarn, October 23, 1913, in Individuals 1917, Box 1789, Carrie Lee folder, Smith College Archives, Northampton, MA.

51. Walter White, *A Man Called White: The Autobiography of Walter White* (Bloomington: Indiana University Press, 1948), p. 336.

52. White, *A Man Called White,* p. 337.

53. Roster of Black Undergraduates Who Attended Smith College, 1900–1974, Admissions Office Records, Black students folder, Smith College Archives, Northampton, MA.

54. Jefferson Church, Springfield, Massachusetts, to Mary Lyon, November 17, 1845, Mary Lyon Collection, Series A, sub-series 2, Mount Holyoke College Archives, South Hadley, MA.

55. Francis Gillette, Bloomfield, Connecticut, to Mary Lyon, May 29, 1846, Mary Lyon Collection, Series A, sub-series 2, Archives and Special Collections, Mount Holyoke College, South Hadley, MA.

56. Florence Paringtow, Dean of Mount Holyoke College, South Hadley, MA, October 11, 1913, to Dean Ada Comstock, Smith College, Northampton, MA, in Individuals 1917, Box 1789, Carrie Lee folder, Smith College Archives, Northampton, MA.

57. History Department, Course Records for History 265, paper by Martha Ralston Perkins, Archives and Special Collection, Mount Holyoke College, South Hadley, MA.

58. Alumnae Biographical file for Hortense Parker, Class of 1883, Archives and Special Collections, Mount Holyoke College, South Hadley, MA.

59. Helen B. Calder Papers, Calder to "dear mamma," November 14, 1894, Archives and Special Collections, Mount Holyoke College, South Hadley, MA.

60. Interview with Frances H. Williams, October 31–November 1, 1977, Black Women Oral History Project, Schlesinger Library, Radcliffe College, Cambridge, MA; Interview with Frances William, October 9, 1991, Frances Williams, Class of 1919 Alumnae file, Archives and Special Collections, Mount Holyoke College, South Hadley, MA; (Massachusetts) *Transcript-Telegram,* February 2, 26, 1983.

61. Alumnae files of Alice Stubbs, 1926; Miriam Cunningham, 1932; Ida Miller, 1933; Laura Lee, 1936; Mabel Murphy, 1937; and Ruth Smith, 1937, Archives and Special Collections, Mount Holyoke College, South Hadley, MA; (Massachusetts) *Transcript-Telegram,* February 2, 26, 1983.

62. Beverly Guy-Sheftall and Jo Moore Stewart, eds., *Spelman: A Centennial Celebration, 1881–1981* (Charlotte, NC: Delmar, 1981), p. 47.

63. History Department, Course Records for History 265, "Black and White Americans," Fall 1973, folder 1: Background Material, Archives and Special Collections, Mount Holyoke College, South Hadley, MA.

64. Quoted in Dean Karen Tidmarsh, Bryn Mawr College, "History of the Status of Minority Groups in the Bryn Mawr Student Body," p. 1, Collection 9JG, Bryn Mawr College Archives, Bryn Mawr, PA.

65. Helen Lefkowitz Horowitz, *The Power and Passion of M. Carey Thomas* (New York: Knopf, 1994).

66. M. Carey Thomas, Bryn Mawr College, to Georgiana R. Simpson, Washington, DC, May 2, 1906, M. Carey Thomas Papers, letter book 34, p. 320, Bryn Mawr College Archives, Bryn Mawr, PA.

67. M. Carey Thomas address to 1916 College Opening, reprinted in *The College News,* Bryn Mawr, October 11, 1916, p. 1.

68. Quoted in Dean Karen Tidmarsh, Bryn Mawr College, "History of the Status of Minority Groups in the Bryn Mawr Student Body," p. 3, Collection 9JG, Bryn Mawr College Archives, Bryn Mawr, PA.

69. Horowitz, *The Power and Passions of M. Carey Thomas,* p. 444.

70. M. Carey Thomas, Bryn Mawr, to Virginia Gildersleeves, Barnard College, New York City, December 12, 1930, Gildersleeves Papers, Barnard College Archives, New York, NY.

71. M. Carey Thomas, Bryn Mawr, to Virginia Gildersleeves, Barnard College, New York City, December 12, 1930, Gildersleeves Papers, Barnard College Archives, New York, New York.

72. Virginia Gildersleeves, Barnard College, to M. Carey Thomas, December 15, 1930, Gildersleeves Papers, Barnard College Archives, New York, NY.

73. Prue Smith Rockwell, Paris, France, February 7, 1931, to Marion Edwards Park, Bryn Mawr College, in *Bryn Mawr Alumnae Bulletin,* April 1931, p. 11; Marion Edwards Park to Prue Smith Rockwell, February 24, 1931, *Bryn Mawr Alumnae Bulletin,* April 1931, p. 11.

74. Karen Tidmarsh, "History of the Status of Minority Groups in the Bryn Mawr Student Body," 1988, Dean of the Faculty Papers, Bryn Mawr College Archives, Bryn Mawr, PA.

75. Evelyn Jones Rich, "Reflections on the Bryn Mawr Experience," July 24, 1979, audiotape, "Oral History Collection," Bryn Mawr College Archives, Bryn Mawr, PA.

76. Jones, "Reflections."

77. "Rediscovering Bryn Mawr—Past and Present, from a Black Perspective," conference held February 7 and 8, 1975, Summary 9, Bryn Mawr College Archives, Bryn Mawr, PA.

78. Christine Philpot Clark, "As It Was and As It Is," in *Bryn Mawr Alumnae Bulletin,* Spring 1969, p. 5.

79. Clark, "As It Was and As It Is," p. 5.

80. Based on statements made by June Jackson Christmas's recollection of Vassar and its reputation in the eyes of African Americans. See June Jackson Christmas's "A Historical Overview: The Black Experience at Vassar," in *Vassar Quarterly,* Spring 1988, p. 5.

81. Newspaper clipping, 1897, in Anita Florence Hemmings folder, Vassar College Archives, Poughkeepsie, NY.

82. Quoted in 1897 newspaper clipping, "Negress at Vassar," in Anita Florence Hemmings folder, Vassar College Archives, Poughkeepsie, NY.

83. Quoted in 1897 newspaper clipping, "Negress at Vassar," in Anita Florence Hemmings folder, Vassar College Archives, Poughkeepsie, NY.

84. Various newspaper clippings of the Hemmings affair, in Anita Florence Hemmings folder, Vassar College Archives, Poughkeepsie, NY.

85. Various newspaper clippings of the Hemmings affair, in Anita Florence Hemmings folder, Vassar College Archives, Poughkeepsie, NY.

86. Christmas, "A Historical Overview," p. 4.

87. Lynn D. Gordon, *Gender and Higher Education in the Progressive Era* (New Haven, CT: Yale University Press, 1990), p. 140. The club included students whose grandmothers, mothers, or aunts were alumnae.

88. W.E.B. DuBois to Dr. Henry MacCracken, May 15, 1930, in Presidential Papers, May 1930, Vassar College Archives, Poughkeepsie, NY.

89. Dr. Henry MacCracken to W.E.B. DuBois, May 17, 1930, in Presidential Papers, May 1930, Vassar College Archives, Poughkeepsie, NY.

90. W.E.B. DuBois. "Postcript," *Crisis,* August 1932, p. 266.

91. Christmas, "A Historical Overview," pp. 4–5.

92. The Daisy Chain was a prestigious Vassar commencement activity dating back to 1884. Vassar students were selected in their sophomore year based on leadership and willingness to assist seniors with commencement activities. Those chosen carried chains made of daisies.

93. Christmas, "A Historical Overview," pp. 4–5.

94. Christmas, "A Historical Overview," pp. 4–5.

95. Christmas, "A Historical Overview," pp. 4–5.

96. Quoted in article, "DuBois Suggests That Vassar Have 100 Negro Students," in *Vassar Miscellany News.* April 4, 1942, p. 1.

97. Christmas, "A Historical Overview," p. 8.

98. Christmas, "A Historical Overview," p. 3.

99. Zora Neale Hurston, *Dust Tracks on a Road: An Autobiography* (Urbana: University of Illinois Press, 1984), p. 169.

100. Hurston, *Dust Tracks on a Road,* p. 171

101. Hurston, *Dust Tracks on a Road,* p. 171.

102. Biographical entry on Channing Tobias in Rayford W. Logan and Michael R. Winston, eds., *Dictionary of American Negro Biography* (New York: W. W. Norton, 1982), pp. 593–595; Roster of Black Students, Publicity Office Files, Wellesley College Archives, Wellesley, MA.

103. Telephone interview with Vera Joseph Peterson, MD, and Linda M. Perkins, June 12, 1997, and comments in *Different Voices: The Experiences of Women of Color at Barnard* (New York: HEOP Office of Barnard College, 1996), pp. 11–12.

104. Vera Joseph Peterson, *Different Voices,* p. 12.

105. Interview with Jean Blackwell Hutson by Linda M. Perkins, New York, June 5, 1997.

106. Virginia Gildersleeves, Barnard College, to the Reverend James H. Robinson, n.d., reprinted in the *Barnard Bulletin,* March 1, 1943, p. 1.

107. Editorial, "Where Do We Go from Here?" in *Barnard Bulletin,* March 1, 1943, p. 2.

108. "Report on Educational Opportunities for Negroes," *Barnard Bulletin,* June 4, 1943, p. 1.

109. Statement written by Charlotte Hanley Scott to Caroline Niemczyk in Barnard College Archives, African American Student folder, New York, NY.

110. Telephone interview with Charlotte Hanley Scott by Linda M. Perkins, June 9, 1997.

111. Telephone interview with Charlotte Hanley Scott by Linda M. Perkins, June 9, 1997.

112. Vera Joseph Peterson, in *Different Voices,* p. 12.

113. Memo to file, President's Office, quoting President Neilson to parent, February 2, 1927, Black Students, 1929–1945, Neilson Papers, Smith College Archives, Southhampton, MA.

114. History Department, Course Records for History 265, Frances M. King Drue, Cleveland, Ohio, to Regina Elston, South Hadley, MA, November 26, 1973, in Regina Elston's student paper, folder 1, Archives and Special Collections, Mount Holyoke College, South Hadley, MA.

115. History Department, Course Records for History 265, Frances M. King Drue, Cleveland, Ohio, to Regina Elston, South Hadley, MA, November 26, 1973, in Regina Elston's student paper, folder 1, Archives and Special Collections, Mount Holyoke College, South Hadley, MA.

116. Christmas, "A Historical Overview," pp. 4–5, 7.

117. David Klugh, Chair, Interrace Group, to President Ada L. Comstock, January 8, 1937, Ada L. Comstock Papers, folder 217, Schlesinger Library, Radcliffe College, Cambridge, MA.

118. Charlotte Hanley Scott, class of 1947, letter to the editor of *Barnard Alumnae Magazine,* Winter 1996, p. 3.

119. Margaret P. McCane to Ellen Henle, January 9, 1982, in Margaret P. McCane Papers, folder 5, Schlesinger Library, Radcliffe College, Cambridge, MA.

120. Janet Novas, "Black Women in Science from Mount Holyoke: A Biographical Sketch of Two Mount Holyoke Alumnae," in History Department records, Series D, Course Records, Papers for History 381, Spring 1988, Archives and Special Collections, Mount Holyoke College, South Hadley, MA.

121. Shirlee Taylor Haizlip, "Only the Robes Were Black," *Wellesley Alumnae Magazine,* Fall 1985, pp. 10–11.

122. Christmas, "A Historical Overview," p. 8.

123. Quoted in Midge Nealon's history paper, "Barbara Penn Wright, class of 1943," in History Department, Course Records for History 265, "Black and White American," Fall 1973, folder 4, Archives and Special Collections, Mount Holyoke College, South Hadley, MA.

124. Mary G. Huntley to Dean Mildred P. Sherman, Radcliffe College, Cambridge, Massachusetts, April 8, 1946, in the Mary Huntley Papers, Box 4, folder 45. Schlesinger Library, Radcliffe College, Cambridge, MA.

125. Mary Gibson Huntley, "Radcliffe in My Life," Huntley Papers, Schlesinger Library, Radcliffe College, Cambridge, MA.

126. Charlotte Leverett Smith Brown biographical data in Radcliffe College of Biographical Data on African-American Students, p. 29, Schlesinger Library, Radcliffe College Archives, Cambridge, MA.

127. Frances L. Monroe King, History Department, Records Series D, Course Records, Papers for History 265, Fall 1973, Archives and Special Collections, Mount Holyoke College, South Hadley, MA.

128. Evelyn Jones Rich, "Reflections on the Bryn Mawr Experience," July 24, 1979, audiotape, "Oral History Collection," Bryn Mawr College Archives, Bryn Mawr, PA.

129. Interviews with Jean Blackwell Hutson and Charlotte Hanley Scott by Linda M. Perkins, June 5 and June 9, 1997 respectively.

130. Shirlee Taylor Haizlip, "Reflections," *Wellesley Alumnae Magazine,* Winter 1969, p. 45.

131. Christmas, "A Historical Overview," p. 5.

132. President Lebarron Russell Briggs, Radcliffe College, to Miss Harriet D. Buckingham, Bournedale, Massachusetts, August 4, 1914 in President Briggs Papers, Box 2, vol. 3, p. 91, Schlesinger Library, Radcliffe College, Cambridge, MA; President Lebarron Russell Briggs to Mrs. Storey, Bournedale, Massachusetts, August 4, 1915, Briggs Papers, Box 2, vol. 3, p. 93, Schlesinger Library, Radcliffe College, Cambridge, MA.

133. Negro Alumnae and Present Negro Students at Wellesley College list, June 1, 1964, Publicity Office, Black Students File, Wellesley College Archives, Wellesley, MA.

134. Rosalind Rosenberg, "The Legacy of Dean Gildersleeves," *Barnard Alumnae Bulletin,* Summer 1996, p. 21.

135. Francis L. Monroe King to Regina Elston, November 26, 1973, in History Department Senior Papers, Francis L. King Paper, Archives and Special Collections, Mount Holyoke College, South Hadley, MA.

136. Andree L. Abecassis, "Black at Barnard: A Survey of Policy and Events," *Barnard Alumnae Journal,* Spring 1969, p. 4.

137. Huntley, "Radcliffe in My Life," p. 2.

138. Huntley, "Radcliffe in My Life," p. 2.

CHAPTER 3

WHAT'S IN A NAME?

A HISTORICAL LOOK AT NATIVE AMERICAN-RELATED NICKNAMES AND SYMBOLS AT THREE U.S. UNIVERSITIES

MARK R. CONNOLLY

"Hoyas" . . . "Leathernecks" . . . "Dons" . . . "Hoosiers"—the colorful and sometimes peculiar nicknames of college athletic teams have long been a source of identity and affection for students, staff, faculty, and alumni. Such nicknames are frequently accompanied by equally compelling logos, such as the University of Notre Dame's scrappy leprechaun, the unmistakable Michigan "M," and the silhouette of the Texas Longhorn (Franks, 1982; Lessiter, 1989; Sloan & Watts, 1993). Athletic nicknames and logos are powerful cultural symbols because they not only evoke allegiance to an institution's athletic teams but also may be instrumental in shaping the image of the entire college or university (Gilbert, 1998; Slowikowski, 1993).

However, some nicknames are not so uniformly appreciated. At most recent count, more than 60 colleges and universities currently use nicknames—such as "Indians," "Braves," "Chiefs," "Tribe," and "Savages"—that are deeply disliked because they either refer to Native Americans or are associated with institutional symbols (e.g., logos or mascots) that depict Native Americans in denigrating ways (Rodriguez, 1998).[1] The use of such nicknames and symbols, say their critics, demeans Native Americans by reducing them to caricatures and stereotypes. Yet, to alumni, students, and other faithful supporters of these institutions and their athletic teams, the nicknames and logos represent long-standing traditions. And they agree that rather than denigrating Native Americans, such nicknames serve to honor tribes that might otherwise be forgotten.

As a result of such passionate and contentious opinions about Native American-related nicknames for collegiate athletic teams, many colleges and universities find themselves responding to critics of these symbols as well as to boosters who dearly embrace them (Monaghan, 1992; Shea, 1993). For these institutions, what was originally chosen as a clever nickname for a college sports team often prompts rancorous debate and pitched battles that reach even beyond the campus to involve state and federal policymakers. How can a nickname or image that once seemed innocuous and played a key part in fostering institutional affiliation become so divisive? To understand the importance of these nicknames to an institution and its stakeholders, more must be learned about the history of these nicknames—namely, how they were chosen and how they evolved to occupy a place in the institution's culture. Such analysis might provide useful insights into not only what social attitudes may have influenced the selection but also to what extent attitudes toward the use of Native American-related nicknames have changed.

In this chapter I examine the origins of three postsecondary institutions' Native American-related nicknames and symbols, trace their evolution, and discuss the controversies that have surrounded them during the past three decades. These three particular U.S. universities were selected for study because the particulars of each case promised to be illuminating (Stake, 1995).

The University of Illinois at Urbana–Champaign (UIUC) is the largest university in the nation with a Native American-related nickname, the "Fighting Illini." The U of I, which enjoys national prestige for both its academic and athletic endeavors, has been steadfast in its refusal to change its nickname or discontinue the performances of its well-known mascot, "Chief Illiniwek," at athletic events. The second institution, Miami University in Ohio, is distinctive in that, up until recently, the nickname "Redskins" was formally sanctioned by the Miami Tribe of Oklahoma. The university deflected criticism of its use of the nickname and related images by pointing to its unique relationship with the Miami Tribe, which in 1972 issued a statement formally proclaiming its support for the "Redskins" nickname. However, in 1996 the leadership of the Miami Tribe voted unanimously to withdraw its endorsement of the nickname, leading the university to change its nickname to "Red-Hawks." Eastern Michigan University in Ypsilanti was selected as the third case because it changed its nickname from "Hurons" to "Eagles" in 1991. EMU's decision to drop entirely its use of the "Hurons" nickname and associated symbols was met with vociferous and persistent opposition, providing a glimpse of the resistance and consequences that may accompany institutional efforts to abandon Native American-related nicknames.

The following questions were used to focus the cases:

- When and how were these nicknames chosen, and to what extent did their selection reflect social attitudes of the age?

- How were logos and other symbols (e.g., an Indian head) developed and used over time to reinforce the identity suggested by the nickname?

- How have institutions responded to concerns of Native Americans and others who claim that such names and symbols are racist and can no longer be considered appropriate or honorable?

Historical data were gathered using archival documents located at UIUC, MU, and EMU that included yearbooks, newspaper articles, memoranda, and sports information publications. This information was supplemented by drawing upon sources of historical information about Native American tribes as well as current and historical information about the three institutions.

Because most people know so little about contemporary Native Americans and their history, some background information about the Native American tribe associated with the nickname introduces each case. Then, after a brief description of the institution, the selection of the nickname or mascot is examined. A summary of the controversy over ending the use of the nickname concludes each case. Following the review of the three cases is a discussion of the two social attitudes that likely influenced the selection and promotion of the institutions' nickname and symbols and how these attitudes still shape the justifications for keeping them. Finally, implications for institutional policy are discussed.

The University of Illinois at Urbana–Champaign

The Illinois Tribes

Prior to the late 18th century, the mid-Mississippi River valley was dominated by the Illinois, or Illini,[2] a confederation of Algonquin-speaking tribes that included the Cahokia, Kaskaskia, Michigamea, Peoria, and Tamaroa. As a result of intertribal conflicts spurred by European encroachment, the Illini were nearly eradicated by 1769, and their lands were claimed first by other tribes and then by White settlers moving westward. After ceding their remaining land to the U.S. government in 1803, remaining members of two Illini tribes, the Peoria and the Kaskaskia, were relocated first to Kansas, then to Oklahoma. Although the Peoria's status as a federally recognized tribe was terminated by the federal government in 1950, it was eventually restored in 1978. Today, the Peoria Tribe of Oklahoma owns 39 acres in northeastern Oklahoma and has a tribal enrollment of nearly 2000, 400 of whom live in the trust area. The Peoria maintain what little of Illini culture remains, presenting traditional songs and dances of Illini people at tribal ceremonials (Davis, M. B., 1994; Grant, 1994; Sultzman, 1997b).

The University

The University of Illinois, the state's land-grant institution, was founded in 1867 as Illinois Industrial University in a field halfway between the Urbana courthouse and the Illinois Central train station in Champaign (Ebert, 1967; Rudolph, 1965/1990). It adopted its current name in 1885, and in 1895 the U of I was one of seven founding institutions of the Intercollegiate Conference of Faculty Representatives, an organization now known as the Big Ten Athletic Conference (Eubanks, 1976; Hyman & White, 1977). Today, the U of I in Urbana-Champaign is the state's flagship campus and among the nation's largest universities. It enrolls almost 28,000 undergraduates and 9,000 graduate and professional students (UIUC Office of Public Affairs, 1998), and its alumni association has more than 122,000 members (J. Rank, personal communication, December 16, 1999).

"Chief Illiniwek"

The adoption of the nickname "Illini" by the University of Illinois has an uncertain origin. It first appeared on the campus in 1874 when the student newspaper changed its name from the *Student* to the *Illini*. When this name was first used by the university's athletic teams is not clear, according to the University Archives (R. Chapel, personal communication, April 6, 1996).[3] However, although Native American activists and supporters have been critical of the nickname "Fighting Illini," they have tended to focus more of their effort on ending the appearances of "Chief Illiniwek," the university "symbol." Its history at the institution is more certain and its symbolic significance under greater debate.

Although published accounts describing the first appearance of "The Chief" disagree on minor details, they all claim that Chief Illiniwek first appeared on October 30, 1926, during half-time of a football game between Illinois and the University of Pennsylvania (Borchers, 1959; Pearson, M., 1995).[4] As part of a stunt, an Illinois student, Lester Leutwiler, appeared in a homemade Indian costume and met at mid-field another Illinois student dressed in a Quaker outfit as Pennsylvania's founder, William Penn. After the two shook hands, Leutwiler became the first to perform what would become an Illinois tradition: the dance of Chief Illiniwek.[5] The stunt was so well received that Leutwiler was asked to perform the half-time dance at subsequent football matches, which he did through the 1927 season, when Illinois claimed its fourth national football championship in 13 years, and until his graduation in 1929 (Eubanks, 1976).

The second Chief Illiniwek, Webber Borchers, was the first to appear in a costume made by Native Americans. After hitchhiking to the Pine Ridge reservation in South Dakota in the summer of 1930, Borchers was put in contact with "an old Indian woman" who agreed to oversee the making of an "authentic" costume. When the University of Illinois' football team traveled to New York City to play Army in Yankee Stadium in November 1930, Borchers appeared in the new costume as the Chief, leading the Illinois band down Fifth Avenue prior to the game and performing a dance at half-time (Borchers, 1959). Since then, students playing Chief Illiniwek have worn five different outfits made by Native Americans, the most recent of which was presented to the university in 1983 by Chief Frank Fools Crow of the Oglala-Lakota Sioux (Official Fighting Illini Sports Website, 1998).

Beginning in the late 1960s, increased Indian activism forced the United States to acknowledge the many concerns of Native Americans, and among them was the use of Native American-related nicknames and logos by both professional and collegiate sports teams. Institutions of higher education such as Stanford University and Dartmouth College, whose teams were called the "Indians," and the University of Massachusetts, whose teams were named the "Redmen," discontinued the use of their Native American-related nicknames during this era (Monaghan, 1992). The University of Illinois, too, was forced to confront this issue. Concern over the use of the Chief was first documented in 1975. Bonnie Fultz, an executive board member of Citizens for the American Indian Movement (AIM), was quoted in the *Illio*, the university's yearbook: "Chief Illiniwek is a mockery not only of Indian customs but also of white people's culture" ("A challenge to the Chief," 1975, p. 154). AIM member and U of I professor of anthropology Norma Linton added that Chief Illiniwek was an inaccurate composite: "The idea of symbols from several different tribes mashed together angers Indians" ("A challenge to the Chief," 1975, p. 154). Efforts to bring an end to Chief Illiniwek during this time had little support. The University's only response to AIM's demands was to remove the symbol of Chief Illiniwek from all official stationery ("A challenge to the Chief," 1975).

However, this concession became moot just a few years later when the university adopted a new official logo—a depiction of a male Native American head with a feather head dress and chest plate—that was used not only by athletic teams but also throughout the university (McGovern, 1995).

The controversy aroused in the 1970s eventually subsided, and public antipathy toward Chief Illiniwek and the "Fighting Illini" nickname remained muted until the late 1980s, when the movement to force the university to discontinue the use of the Chief again gained momentum. In 1989 a student-led group fought to raise the issue with the university's administration (Chang, 1989). Charlene Teters, an UIUC student and Spokane Indian who performed traditional dances, explained in a public debate that the Chief Illiniwek dance was not an authentic Indian dance but "a gymnastics routine" (Anderson, 1989, p. 1). Although UIUC Chancellor Morton Weir decided to allow the Chief to remain, he did stipulate that "inappropriate derivatives" of the Indian symbol, such as war paint on the faces of cheerleaders and a painted Roman letter "I" on the Chief's face would no longer be allowed (Davis, R., 1989; Monaghan, 1992). Weir also asked Illini fans to stop wearing costumes and war paint.

Because the UIUC chancellor's decision did not quell the controversy, the university's Board of Trustees agreed to address the issue and set university policy regarding the use of the Chief. After hearing testimony in October 1990 from two Native American groups that objected to the use of Chief Illiniwek, the United Indian Nation of Oklahoma and the Indian Treaty Rights Committee of Chicago, the board voted 7–1 to keep the Chief (Griffin, 1990; Jouzaitis, 1990; Lederman, 1990). In an effort to articulate its own stance in the campus debate, the UIUC Student Government Association voted 34–2 in March 1991 to approve a resolution stating that the university should cease using the Chief as its symbol (Sherman, 1991).

By this time, the controversy over Chief Illiniwek reached beyond the UIUC campus. Fellow Big Ten institutions Minnesota and Wisconsin enacted policies in 1993, stating that their football teams would no longer play teams outside the conference that had Native American nicknames, such as the Florida State Seminoles. Although the policies did not apply to these institutions' contests with conference rival Illinois, they nevertheless sent a message about the propriety of such types of team nicknames and symbols ("U. of Wisconsin," 1993). In the same year, the University of Iowa forbade images of Native Americans—including Chief Illiniwek—on its campus during its homecoming football game with Illinois because American Indians were offended during a homecoming event two years earlier when students drew pictures of Indians being stabbed ("Two Campuses Debate," 1993).

In 1994 a group of Native Americans affiliated with the university filed a discrimination complaint with the U.S. Department of Education's Office of Civil Rights (OCR), claiming that the use of the Chief contributed to a racially hostile environment for them (Pearson, R., 1992). In December 1995 the Office of Civil Rights concluded a 20-month investigation and ruled that the use of offensive symbols by universities did not by itself constitute illegal discrimination against Native Americans by the University of Illinois (McGovern, 1995). Although the OCR acknowledged the "perceived offensiveness" of the Chief Illiniwek symbol, the OCR said this was irrelevant to the legal issues in the case, which rested upon finding sufficient evidence that Native Americans were subjected to a racially hostile environment at the Urbana-Champaign campus. Because this case was the first the OCR had considered regarding a college or university mascot, it was viewed as a test of how the Education Department would balance free-speech rights against the complaints of minority students. University officials, in praising the decision, acknowledged that "some are offended" by the use of the Chief and added that the university would make every effort to continue the tradition "in a respectful manner" (Jaschik, 1995, p. A29).

Debate over the continued presence of the Chief has persisted in various forms. A documentary titled *In Whose Honor?*, produced and directed by an Illinois alumnus who favored the elimination of Native American-related nicknames and mascots, introduced the university's controversy to a national audience (Rosenstein, 1997). In March 1998 the Urbana-Champaign Faculty-Student Senate voted 97–29 to pass a non-binding resolution to retire the Chief (Olson, 1998). In spite of this and numerous other efforts by students and faculty to demonstrate growing support for dropping the Chief (Farnell, 1998; Gunderson, 1998), the UIUC trustees have remained resolute, indicating they will not consider any further action on the matter of Chief Illiniwek until "substantive, important, and new information" is brought before them (Hendricks, 1998, p. 1).

Miami University of Ohio

The Miami Tribes

The Miami Indians, like the Illini, once were an Algonquin-speaking association of tribes who lived around the Great Lakes, primarily in Ohio, Indiana, and Illinois.[6] The Miami first made contact with Europeans in 1668; later, they provided the scouts who guided Father Jacques Marquette and Louis Joliet to the Mississippi River in 1673. Like other tribes, the Miami were pushed from their homelands as White settlers moved westward. The Miami lost most of their homeland in Ohio (11.8 million acres) with the signing of the Treaty of Greenville in 1795, and in 1809 (the year Miami University was founded) they ceded another 3 million acres in southern Indiana and Illinois to the United States government. By 1840 the Miami had lost nearly all of their remaining land in Indiana. In 1846 the U.S. government forcefully divided the Miami into two groups. One group of more than 600 Miami were relocated to Kansas territory in 1846 and then moved again to Oklahoma in 1867. The second group of between 500 and 1,500 Miami remained in Indiana, where they gradually lost their land to land speculators and tax sales by 1900. Although both the Miami Tribe of Oklahoma and the Miami Tribe of Indiana were initially accorded federal recognition, an administrative order by the assistant U.S. attorney general terminated the federal recognition of the Indiana Miami in 1897, claiming that the Miami who had been relocated to Oklahoma were the "official" Miami nation. The Oklahoma Miami, with a tribal roll of more than 1,600, currently have 160 acres held in trust near Miami, Oklahoma, where the tribe maintains its tribal headquarters. However, the Indiana Miami, concentrated principally in Allen, Huntington, and Miami counties and numbering more than 6,000 members, have been denied recognition by the U.S. government as recently as 1992 and consequently do not share the education, health care, and legal rights given their Oklahoma kin (Davis, M. B., 1994; Grant, 1994; Sultzman, 1998).

The University

Chartered by the Ohio General Assembly in 1809 and established in the town of Oxford, Miami University enjoys the distinction of being the second oldest state-assisted institution of higher learning west of the Allegheny Mountains and the seventh oldest in the nation. Known as "Miami University" from the time of its inception, the institution was named in honor of the Miami Tribe, who had occupied southwestern Ohio prior to 1795 and were yet living in what would later become the state of Indiana. The Miami were closely associated with the area where the campus was established; to construct one of the university's first halls in 1812, Miami burial mounds had to be leveled (Havighurst, 1969; Rudolph, 1990).

Today, MU enrolls more than 20,000 students, including 16,000 at its Oxford campus and more than 2,000 at each of its Hamilton and Middletown campuses. Considered a "public ivy," MU has been earned national recognition for its outstanding undergraduate instruction (Miami University, 1998).

The "Redskins" Nickname

Intercollegiate athletics started at MU in 1888. Through the first twenty years of organized competition, MU teams had no nicknames, although they adopted their team colors of red and white during this time. For the next two decades, sports teams at MU were known by a variety of nicknames— "the Miami Boys," "the Big Reds," "the Reds," and "the Red and Whites" ("A Chronology," 1993; Miami University Office of the President, 1996). In 1928, forty years after MU athletics were first organized, publicity director R. J. McGinnis began calling the MU teams "Redskins." An alumni newsletter offered this explanation for the choice:

Since the state is overrun with Bearcats, Wildcats, Bobcats, Musketeers, and other such-like small deer, members of the Athletic Department went into a huddle not long ago and decided that Miami teams ought to have a moniker and a symbol. As the very name of Miami is taken from an Indian tribe and the term "Big Reds" smacks of Redskins and the warpath, an Indian brave in warlock and feathers was thought to be a suitable insignia. This will be found displayed at appropriate places and on appropriate occasions. It is hoped that with the injection of the Big Reds into the Buckeye forests some of the wildcats, bearcats, and other cats will be exterminated or at least tamed. (" 'Big Reds'," 1930, p. 22)

During the 1950s the use of Indian caricatures at athletic events became more prominent. Students dressed as Indians appeared as part of the marching band, and the band's bass drum featured a cartoonish depiction of an Indian. In the 1960s, the band's Indian mascot was replaced with "Hiawabop," a student dressed as a Plains Indian in a war bonnet and painted face who wielded a tomahawk and helped lead cheers ("A Chronology," 1993).

Spurred in part by the increase in Indian activism during the late 1960s, the university established a formal relationship with the Miami Tribe of Oklahoma. In 1972, when other institutions including Stanford and Dartmouth were eliminating their Native American-related nicknames, MU president Phillip Shriver appointed a task force to examine the ways in which the university was using Indian symbols and consider whether the "Redskins" nickname should be abandoned. Although the review committee voted 5–2 to retain the "Redskins" nickname, it acknowledged the importance of eliminating derogatory caricatures of American Indians. In its report dated August 1972, the committee's recommendations included eliminating all derogatory caricatures of Indians (including Hiawabop), using only authentic Indian symbols and artifacts, changing the name of a campus dining hall to something other than "The Redskin Reservation," and creating scholarships for qualified applicants from the Miami tribe ("Report of Ad Hoc," 1972; "A Chronology," 1993).

To show its support of the university and its decision to retain the "Redskins" nickname, the Miami tribe passed a resolution in September 1972 affirming the emerging relationship between it and the university. The resolution stated, in part, the following:

Whereas, it is our counsel that the name Redskins is a revered and honored name in the eyes and hearts of the people of Miami University, and that it signifies to them as to us the qualities of courage, self-discipline, respect, kindness, honesty, and love exemplified by generations of young athletes, therefore, know all peoples that we of Miami blood are proud to have the name Miami Redskins carried with honor by the athletic representation of Miami University on the playing fields of Mid America and in the arena of the world in international Olympic competition. (Miami Tribe of Oklahoma, 1972, n. p.)

Throughout the 1970s the university implemented many of the recommendations made by the task force, such as the establishment of full scholarships for qualified members of the Miami Tribe of Oklahoma and the creation of a formal liaison between MU and the tribe ("Effort To Dignify," 1972). Hiawabop's replacement, "Chief Miami," made his debut in 1977 at a basketball game between MU and the Eastern Michigan "Hurons" ("Chief Miami To Make," 1977). The MU student who first played the Chief had prepared for his performance by visiting the Miami tribe in Oklahoma and appeared during the MU-EMU game wearing a red-and-white costume created with the assistance of the head of protocol and dance instruction for the Miami Tribe. Like Chief Illiniwek, Chief Miami was considered a dignified representative of an American Indian tribe who performed a ceremonial (and purportedly authentic) dance during athletic competitions.

The Miami Tribe's 1972 endorsement appeared to allay some concerns over the University's use of the "Redskins" nickname. However, the issue reemerged on campus in the early 1990s, when the appearance of both the Cleveland Indians and the Atlanta Braves in the 1993 World Series brought national attention to the issue of using Native American-related nicknames. MU President Paul G. Risser, perhaps influenced by a bill introduced in the Ohio legislature seeking to force teams such as MU's and the Cleveland Indians to drop their American Indian nicknames, promised to address the university's use of the nickname ("Ohio Hopes," 1993). In 1993 the MU campus community discussed whether to replace the "Redskins" nickname, and a university task force was convened to examine the issue. The compromise that President Risser subsequently suggested to the university's Board of Trustees reflected the difficulty of crafting a solution that would please all concerned groups. Emphasizing the importance of each individual's personal choice to use a term that may or may not be considered disrespectful, Risser asked that

> (a) Only those University athletic organizations and athletic publications currently using the nickname "Redskin" may continue to use the nickname. . . . The use of the nickname "Redskin" shall not be expanded beyond representations where it currently appears. . . . [and] (b) All other organizations sponsored by the University and official publications of the University not covered above will use the term 'Miami Tribe' as the nickname of the athletic teams. . . . The University's linkage with a proud Native American people, even in the very name of the institution, can be preserved with dignity indefinitely through the use of the words "Miami Tribe." (Risser, 1993)

Rather than mandating that the "Redskins" nickname no longer be used, which ran the risk of angering MU alumni and possibly the Miami Tribe, Risser's plan sought to offer a different yet related nickname as an attractive alternative and then encourage individuals to adopt it (Risser, 1996). In time, the president hoped, a collective choice of "Tribe" would lead to the eventual disintegration of "Redskins." In December 1993 the Board of Trustees approved President Risser's plan in a vote of 4–3 ("Board Votes to Accept," 1993; Wolff, 1993). The Miami Tribe, which had been consulted during the decision-making process, had agreed in advance to support the university's decision regardless of the outcome (Leonard, 1993). With the trustees' approval of the president's plan, official campus debate was closed.

However, Risser's attempt to craft a "win-win" solution satisfied few in the campus community. The director of the Miami Valley Council for Native Americans called the trustees' decision "a cop-out" (Wolff, 1993, p. 1), and an MU professor said "Risser left everyone despairing at the sheer wishy-washyness of his non-resolution" (Lesniewski, 1996). The time and energy expended by the campus community to resolve this issue seemed to have borne little meaningful change.

In July 1996 the long-standing foundation beneath the university's justification for keeping the "Redskins" nickname—the explicit endorsement of the nickname by the Miami tribal leadership—was suddenly withdrawn. In a formal resolution that rescinded its earlier statements of support, the leadership of the Miami Tribe unanimously declared:

> Whereas: We realize that society changes, and that what was intended to be a tribute to both Miami University and to the Miami Tribe of Oklahoma, is no longer perceived as positive by some members of the Miami Tribe of Oklahoma, Miami University, and society at large;

> Therefore, be it resolved that the Miami Tribe of Oklahoma can no longer support the use of the nickname Redskins and [we] suggest that the Board of Trustees of Miami University discontinue the use of Redskins and other Indian related nicknames, in connection with its athletic teams, effective with the end of the 1996–97 academic school year. ("Miami Tribe No Longer," 1996; "Miami U. Abandons," 1996)

In order to comply with the Miami Tribe's wishes and maintain what the university had long described as its deeply respectful relationship with the Tribe, the MU Board of Trustees voted 7–1 in September 1996 to discard the "Redskins" nickname, following the Tribe's July proclamation by less than two months. However, in keeping with a particular request of the Miami Tribe, the university acknowledged it planned to keep its Indian-head logo, such as that appearing on its football stadium (Lesniewski, 1996). Newly appointed president James Garland was charged by the trustees with overseeing the selection of a new nickname. In April 1997 the MU trustees voted unanimously to accept "Red-Hawks" as the new nickname for its athletic teams ("Miami U. To Shed," 1997). Although the university began using the new nickname in Fall 1997, a lawsuit was filed in county court seeking to block the nickname change on the grounds that the MU trustees violated Ohio's sunshine law by secretly discussing the nickname change ("Miami U. To Shed," 1997).

Eastern Michigan University

The Huron Tribes

The Huron/Wyandot nation once was a powerful federation of four Iroquois tribes that occupied a small portion of the northern banks of the Saint Lawrence River in central Ontario.[7] However, their numbers began to drop precipitously following European contact as a result of epidemics of hitherto unknown diseases and a series of trade-related conflicts with other tribes. After being nearly wiped out in 1647 in a fierce Iroquois attack, the remaining Wyandot spent the next 50 years wandering as refugees through Wisconsin, Minnesota, and upper Michigan. By 1701 the few Hurons who had not been either captured by Iroquois tribes or given refuge by other tribes had settled in the Ohio Valley between what are now the cities of Detroit and Cleveland; there they were known as the Wyandot. In March 1842 the Wyandot were forced to cede their lands in Michigan and Ohio to the U.S. government and were relocated to Kansas in 1845 and later to Oklahoma in 1857. Today, there are two tribes, Oklahoma Wyandot and Kansas Wyandot; only the Oklahoma Tribe has federal recognition, having regained it in 1978 after it was terminated in 1956. The Oklahoma Wyandot have a tribal enrollment of nearly 4,000 and collectively own 192 acres (Davis, M. B., 1994; Grant, 1994; Hinsdale, 1930; Sultzman, 1997a).

The University

Michigan State Normal School was founded in 1849 in the town of Ypsilanti, a site on the Huron River where Wyandot burial grounds were located until about 1851, when White residents disinterred "relics" such as skeletons, weapons, and jewelry (Colburn, 1923). Chartered as a teachers college, the institution underwent subsequent name changes in 1899 (Michigan State Normal College), 1956 (Eastern Michigan College), and 1959 (Eastern Michigan University). As Michigan's fifth-largest state-assisted institution, EMU currently offers more than 200 undergraduate and graduate programs to an enrollment of more than 23,000 students. Ninety percent of their students are Michigan residents, and roughly 1,500 are graduate students. The alumni association claims more than 110,000 known members. EMU's athletic teams compete at the NCAA Division I-A level (Eastern Michigan University, 1998a; Eastern Michigan University, 1998b).

The "Hurons" Nickname

Like those of Miami University, EMU's athletics teams were first known by a number of unofficial nicknames such as "Men from Ypsi" and "Normalites." In 1929 the Men's Union of the Michigan State Normal College, in cooperation with the Women's League, initiated a contest to choose an official nickname for the college's sports teams. The nickname "Hurons" was selected from student suggestions by a committee of three faculty members; the second-choice nickname was the "Pioneers" ("Nickname Contest," 1929; "Hurons Is Chosen," 1929; Lessiter, 1989).

The "Hurons" nickname remained in use by athletic teams at the Ypsilanti campus despite two subsequent changes of the institution's name. Eventually, a logo depicting an Indian was created and used as a graphic identity for both the athletic teams and the institution. How EMU responded to complaints about its "Hurons" nickname during the early 1970s is unclear, but like Illinois and Miami, EMU opted to keep its nickname (Franks, 1982).

In 1988 the Michigan Civil Rights Commission recommended that all state educational institutions, including four colleges and universities, discontinue their use of Indian names and logos, which they said were "stereotypic, racist, and discriminatory" ("EMU Drops Nickname," 1991; McLean, 1991). At the request of EMU President William Shelton in February 1989, a campus committee surveyed students, staff, faculty, and alumni and organized debates and discussions regarding a change in the use of the nickname and logo. After nearly a year, the committee voted 8–6 to keep both the "Hurons" nickname and Indian-head logo. At a September 1990 meeting, the EMU Board of Regents received the committee's recommendation and asked President Shelton to provide them with a final decision on the matter (McLean, 1991).

In January 1991 Shelton subsequently asked the regents to approve the discontinuation of the "Hurons" nickname and authorize the adoption of a new identity. As Shelton explained in a statement to the regents, "There was really only one dominant issue which steadfastly drew my attention: What is the responsibility of an institution of higher learning? Is there a higher obligation entrusted to the academic community in a democratic society?" His answer: "As an educational institution, I do not believe that we can justify the continued use of symbols which we now know offend and denigrate, however unintentionally, members of our community" ("Use of the Huron," 1991). On January 30, 1991, the regents voted unanimously to drop the nickname and the logo ("EMU Drops," 1991; "EMU To Change," 1991).

At their May meeting, the regents selected "Eagles" as the university's new nickname, and in August 1991, they approved a design for a new athletic logo that was created by several EMU students ("EMU Committee Selects," 1991; "EMU Logo Unveiled," 1991).

The decision to replace both the "Hurons" nickname and the Indian-head logo was met with vociferous and persistent opposition. Among those protesting their elimination were two representatives of the Huron-Wyandot tribe, Grand Chief Max Gros-Louis and Chief Leaford Bearskin. Gros-Louis said in a letter to President Shelton, "I can assure you the Huron logo of EMU is viewed by our nation as a symbol of honor and integrity." Stating his case more strongly, Bearskin said, "The action taken to discontinue the Huron logo was much more degrading to the culture of my people than leaving it alone and viewing it as a symbol of honor and integrity" ("Once A Huron," n. d.). Following the decision in May to adopt the "Eagles" nickname, a group known as EMU Huron Restoration, Inc. mounted a campaign to restore the tribe's name and even attempted to secure a legal injunction to prohibit the university from using the "Eagles" nickname and logo ("Huron Fans Consider," 1991; Eshenroder, 1991). Within several months of the decision, more than 75 alumni canceled their memberships in the EMU alumni association, and several alumni angrily removed EMU from their will. According to records obtained by Huron Restoration, EMU's total donations dropped from $2.3 million in fiscal 1990 to $1.9 million in fiscal 1991. As one graduate said, "No Hurons, no money" ("Hurons Become Eagles" 1991; "Eastern Michigan U. Alumni" 1991). In early 1995, more than three and a half years after the trustees' decision, the university administration warned the Huron Restoration Alumni Chapter to stop using the "Hurons" nickname and logo, saying its continued use amounted to copyright infringement ("Cheer Eagle, Not Indian," 1995). As late as 1996, heated letters about the nickname issue continued to appear in the student newspaper at least weekly. Although the controversy diminished in magnitude, many angry alumni and students continue to promise that "Huron restoration is not a matter of if, but when."

What's in a (Nick)Name?

These three institutions share noteworthy similarities. All three are Midwestern, state-assisted institutions that currently provide a large number of degree programs to enrollments of at least 20,000 students. At all three universities, their nicknames and symbols sparked bitter and persistent debate between campus stakeholders, leaving the president and institution's governing board with the impossible task of making a decision that would satisfy them all. Finally, and perhaps most telling, all three institutions chose and popularized their nicknames (in the case of MU and EMU) or mascot (in the case of UIUC) about the same time, the late 1920s and the early 1930s. What was it during this era that permitted, if not encouraged, the adoption of this type of nickname?

Two social trends likely contributed to the selection and development of these institutions' nicknames and symbols. The first was the objectification of Native Americans as "good Indians," and the second was the rise of the collegiate "booster culture." Although both social phenomena existed at a national level of consciousness, the latter trend affected postsecondary institutions in particular.

Objectification of Native Americans

Since the arrival of Columbus, Euro-Americans have consistently portrayed Native Americans stereotypically (Berkhofer, 1978; Mihesuah, 1996). Whites' misrepresentations of Native Americans were often dualistic, portraying them either as bloodthirsty, "uncivilized" savages or as friendly, subservient "noble" innocents. How Native Americans were represented depended largely on the hegemonic objectives of Whites. When Euro-Americans sought to dominate the North American continent, their portrayal of Native Americans as being aggressive, wild, godless, and duplicitous justified Euro-American efforts (usually aggressive and duplicitous themselves) to "civilize" the native inhabitants. However, around the turn of the 20th century, when the national project to remove Indians was largely completed, Whites grew nostalgic for this "vanished race." Consequently, sympathetic (yet nevertheless stereotypical) representations of Native Americans became more common in popular entertainment, beginning with Wild West shows and continuing in movies and other popular media that featured "sidekick" characters such as the Lone Ranger's, Tonto, who epitomized White notions of Indian trustworthiness, stoicism, stamina, natural athleticism, and dignity in bearing (Berkhofer, 1978; Davis, L. R., 1993). These romanticized representations were in turn exploited by commercial businesses to sell products such as Red Cloud chewing tobacco, Indian motorcycles, and Kickapoo Indian medicinal salve (Green, 1979).

It was during an era when popularizing and merchandising the "good" Indian had become commonplace that the nicknames of Miami and Eastern Michigan and the Illinois mascot were chosen. In fact, many college sports teams that have adopted Native American nicknames did so during the 1920s (Davis, L. R., 1993; Franks, 1982). Whether consciously or unconsciously, choosing these nicknames capitalized on the objectification of the Native Americans and the admiration for the idealized traits associated with Indian stereotypes, such as "endurance, rhythm, time, coordination, sense perception, an uncanny ability to get over any sort of terrain at night, and . . . an enthusiasm for fighting" (Ickes, as cited in Takaki, 1993, p. 389). As the explanation given for Miami's adopting the "Redskins" nickname suggests, these institutions wanted names and symbols that reflected desirable characteristics associated with "good" Indians: natural athleticism, stamina, stoicism, modesty, bravery, and just enough aggression and ferocity to satisfy the competitive nature of athletics (" 'Big Reds'," 1930, p. 22).

What this practice meant, however, is that the only Native Americans most Whites ever "knew" were stereotypes appearing in movies, dime novels, and on commercial products. Instead of seeing *Native Americans* as fellow human beings who were struggling to resist marginalization, mainstream America saw only *Indians*, frozen in time, a face on an Indian head nickel. Rather than dealing with the painful reality of Native Americans' marginalization, Whites preferred to cling to "the White man's Indian"—sentimentalized stereotypes and caricatures of their own construction. Indian-related symbols—including product names, nicknames and symbols—did not represent Native Americans; rather, they were souvenirs of White cultural domination.

Regional Pride and Booster Culture

The second significant social trend that likely influenced the selection and legitimization of the three institutions' nicknames and symbols was the rise of collegiate athletics and its role in fostering regional pride. The decades of the 1920s and 1930s were a propitious time for U.S. higher education. Not only did student enrollments swell by nearly five times between 1917 and 1937, but America also fell in love with college life and especially collegiate athletics (Michener, 1976; Thelin, 1994). Successful football programs brought national recognition to otherwise undistinguished institutions (e.g., the University of Notre Dame, Centre College in Kentucky), and at public universities and colleges, winning football teams also fostered regional pride. According to one historian of higher education, "The state university came increasingly to be seen by ambitious governors, state legislators, and mayors as a conscious instrument of aspiration. And intercollegiate athletics joined agricultural extension services as a means by which the state university could extend real and symbolic affiliation to all citizens of the state or region" (Thelin, 1994).

As a result of the growing popularity of intercollegiate athletics—first football and later basketball—citizens who had never attended the state university were cheering for its sports teams and claiming them as their own. Over time there emerged a group of people who not only shared an outward and enacted affection for their region's university sports teams but also often felt an implicit pride in the region itself. Membership in this group of enthusiastic athletic boosters had no admission requirements other than to belong to or affiliate with the region or state, believe in and perpetuate the team's saga or myths, and participate in the group's various rituals, be they attending the team's games, wearing or displaying emblems of support, or simply talking positively and passionately with others about the team's fortunes. Because groups of boosters shared values, assumptions, practices, and beliefs, they constructed and participated in what might be called *booster culture*.[8]

Although university alumni, often known for their enduring affection and zeal for an institution's athletic teams, were perhaps the most obvious and largest segment of booster culture, others who may have adhered to the culture's tenets and participated in its activities included high-level administrators, undergraduate students, community members, politicians, influential business officers, members of the news media, university staff, and faculty. Frequently, those most invested in the booster culture were White upper- and middle-class men. Because of significant overlap among their members, booster culture typically shared many values and assumptions, such as prejudices and stereotypes about persons of color, with dominant social groups or cultures (namely, Whites, males, upper-SES, Christians, and heterosexuals). And, booster culture, like dominant social cultures, acted in ways that ensured its survival, although often in unacknowledged or unseen ways. When plans to discontinue Native American-related nicknames or symbols became evident, it was those who adhered to booster culture who rose to defend what were to them beloved traditions, in the process making explicit their culture's fundamental values and tacit assumptions.

During the 1920s and 1930s, politicians and college administrators both capitalized on the fervor of their region's or state's variation of booster culture. Politicians hoping to gain political advantage from being associated with a "winner" regularly directed the attention of their constituency to the successes of their regional teams, and universities benefitted from increased national prestige and regional affiliation in the form of increased financial assistance from state government and other financial supporters. Because the valuable resources gained from enthusiastic supporters could be used to build up an institution and enhance its prestige, universities encouraged booster culture, sometimes by picking a nickname such as "Buckeyes," "Sooners," or "Hoosiers" that would appeal to and ostensibly represent the citizens of the entire state.

Based on the historical evidence, booster culture appeared to have affected the adoption of the three institutions' nicknames and symbols to different degrees. At Michigan State Normal College (i.e., Eastern Michigan), where the nickname was selected in a week's time by a faculty committee and did not include input from administrators, alumni, or athletics staff, the process for selecting the school's nickname did not necessarily suggest the direct involvement of "members" of the booster culture. Yet, choosing a regionally distinctive nickname like "Hurons" did provide the residents of Ypsilanti and Eastern Michigan with the sort of symbol that could establish and reinforce a region's booster culture. At Miami University, the "Redskins" nickname was simply coined by the university's publicity director, and considering the university took its name from the Miami tribe, the nickname then seemed a sensible way to emphasize a distinctive characteristic of the university as well as acknowledge the history of the region and the institution.

However, it is at the U of I—which clearly had the most established "big-time" athletics program of the three institutions—where the influence of the booster culture is most evident. A founding member of the Big Ten athletic conference, the University of Illinois was regularly playing other well-established football teams such as Chicago, Michigan, Notre Dame, and Penn during the 1920s. Illinois attracted a national audience during this era, largely as a result of the remarkable athletic accomplishments of its star football running back Harold "Red" Grange and winning its third and fourth national football championships in 1923 and 1927.

It was thus significant to the history of Chief Illiniwek and his role in fostering Illinois booster culture that he debuted before a standing-room-only crowd in a large Eastern city while playing the University of Pennsylvania, a well-respected and formidable opponent that also had a sizable national following. The stunt of having "Chief Illiniwek" greet "William Penn" was more than half-time entertainment; it was "East meets Midwest." Making his first appearance during a decade that represented a critical time in the history of both the institution and its athletic programs, "Chief Illiniwek" was given special symbolic significance by the booster culture, for the Chief represented not only the institution, but—like William Penn—he also represented the state that took his name. Consequently, the Chief became a booster icon—a cultural symbol ardently embraced by the U of I boosters that represented the pride they felt for the Illinois athletic teams (and, indirectly, the state and the institution).

These two social trends of the 1920s—romanticized depictions of Native Americans and the emergence of regional boosterism—not only provide a context for better interpreting the institutions' decisions to adopt Native American-related nicknames and symbols during that era, but they also appear to explain why these institutions defended their nicknames and symbols for so long. The reasons used by supporters of the Native American nicknames and symbols at all three institutions were consistently similar and can be distilled into three themes.

Claims of respect and cultural sustenance. Unlike many institutions that used Native American-related nicknames and symbols, each of the three institutions profiled in this case study associated its nickname and symbols with a particular Native American tribe that formerly lived in the geographical region where the institution is located.[9] However, historical records suggest that, other than in name, these universities made no effort to portray the tribes realistically or authentically; rather, these institution's symbols were nothing more than virtually interchangeable amalgams of headdresses, war paint, fringed buckskin suits, and red-skinned faces. Because all Native Americans were obscured by these stereotypes, Whites considered any differences between tribes to be insignificant. Such an example is found in Chief Illiniwek's "authentic" costume, made by Lakota-Sioux, a Great Plains tribe, to wear by someone who is supposedly a chief of an Illini tribe, which belonged to a different culture area (Woodlands) and language family (Algonquin)(Farnell, 1998; Gone, 1995).

When such inaccuracies were exposed, boosters responded by *authenticizing* the symbols, or imbuing them with a false, manufactured authenticity. For example, when Chief Hiawabop was exposed as a degrading representation of the Miami tribe, the university responded by making its new mascot, Chief Miami, supposedly more "authentic" with a more realistic costume. Likewise, the University of Illinois responded to complaints that the Chief was nothing more than an institutional invention by authenticizing Chief Illiniwek (i.e., removing the Chief's inappropriate face paint and giving him a more "realistic" dance). The process of authenticization also included making the spurious distinction between authenticized symbols and traditional team mascots and equating public exhibitions of human mascots with cultural performances, not cheerleading. Boosters attached only the noblest intentions to authenticized symbols, saying in effect, "See how respectful and proud we are of Native Americans that we would make such efforts to portray the tribe more realistically." Oftentimes, boosters not only claimed that Native American cultures were being remembered and sustained with authenticized symbols, but they also suggested that doing away with these symbols would encourage forgetting Native Americans' history as well as overlooking their current political interests (Gone, 1995).

However, authenticizing symbols proved not to be a reliable defense for boosters. In many cases, protesters asserted that making a mascot or logo less cartoonish and more realistic only emphasized how humiliating and oppressive using a Native American image as a sports logo or halftime cheerleader feels to living Native Americans. When defending human mascots, such as Chief Illiniwek, boosters sometimes attempted to dodge this charge by claiming the mascot, although authenticized, was nevertheless fictitious and should not be interpreted as the misrepresentation of an actual human being (Fontenot, 1997). An Illinois state representative and UIUC alumnus implied why an invented mascot was nevertheless important to keep:

> I realize that there was probably no such person as Chief Illiniwek, and to some extent, it's mythological, I suppose. It's an attempt, I think, by people in Illinois to try to remember a vanished tribe, the Illini tribe, that was apparently annihilated by an opposing Native American tribe in the 1760s—to try to remember their heritage, to do it in a way that's respectful. (Rosenstein, 1997)

Defending Native American-related nicknames and images as being respectful of Native Americans was a tactic used most often by boosters holding positions accountable to public constituencies (e.g., trustees, legislators, administrators) who wanted to appear sensitive and inclusive while at the same time seeking to retain symbols that objectified Native Americans.

Comparing Native Americans with other groups. One of the most frequent responses given to Native Americans' complaints about being used as nicknames and mascots is that U.S. ethnic groups did not protest being represented by nicknames such as "Fighting Irish" or "Quakers" or "Britons."

> Should ranchers get upset about the Dallas Cowboys? . . . Scandinavians about the Minnesota Vikings? Greeks about the [Michigan State] Spartans? Should people of Irish Catholic descent get upset over the silly fighting leprechaun of Notre Dame? Should the Audubon Society fight over names like the Lions, Tigers, Cardinals, and Orioles? (Begnoche, 1991)

Because Native Americans appeared to be the only group protesting, their concerns were consequently portrayed as being nothing more than cases of "political correctness" and over-sensitivity. Thus, it was suggested, particularly in the popular press, that acknowledging the legitimacy of complaints about Native American nicknames would unleash a flood of similar objections from other over-sensitive groups. In an effort to trivialize the complaints of Native Americans, critics of political correctness made their cases with extreme arguments, as illustrated by one college president's response to nickname controversies:

> Our struggle with the PC Police must surely be nearing its zenith. How else can we justify a serious debate about the political correctness of sports mascots. . . . Let's settle this once and for all. I suggest that all college football teams adopt the names of flowers so that we will not offend anyone, anything, or any political movement, correct or otherwise. How about the Florida State Forget-Me-Nots? Who could be offended by the Illinois Fighting Chrysanthemums? Or the UABegonias? The Ole Miss Marigolds would be far less offensive, as would the UMass Hollyhocks. Let's try the Arkansas State Statice! (Jones, 1993)

To Whites, such arguments, while patently absurd, seemed justifiable, because Whites often did not recognize or acknowledge the uniquely oppressive conditions for Native Americans in the United States. As opponents of Native American-related nicknames were fond to point out, the objectification of other ethnic or religious groups as sport nicknames and mascots (e.g., the Detroit Junglebunnies, the Phoenix Wetbacks, the Boston Popes, the New York Shylocks) would seem unimaginable, especially in light of the efforts people of color had made to eliminate other harmful stereotypes (e.g., "Little Black Sambo"). Yet, the Washington Redskins, Kansas City Chiefs, and Cleveland Indians were considered defensible and "harmless" nicknames. The difference with Native Americans, it appeared, is that they were, as Ward Churchill (1993) writes, "(falsely) perceived as being too few, and therefore too weak, to defend themselves effectively against racist and otherwise offensive behavior" (p. 45). The seeming invisibility of Native Americans was perpetuated by popular media that usually represented historical or contemporary Native Americans as "vanished" mythic figures. In spite of their continued efforts to dispel invidious stereotypes held by the dominant White culture, contemporary Native Americans were nevertheless overlooked in favor of manufactured misrepresentations of them—replicas with no original—that White Americans used to satisfy their nostalgia for a past that never occurred (Davis, L. R., 1993). Speaking to the importance of giving White Americans authentic—not authenticized—representations, one Native American explained:

> It will only be when American people realize that Indians are living, twentieth century, honest-to-goodness human beings that our lives, hopes, ideas, and lands will be respected and appreciated. As long as we are stereotyped and abstracted into college and product names, cowboy movie backgrounds, advertising gimmicks and tourist attractions, we will continue to be unreal shadows on the American scene. Even if our request to abandon the use of our names for college teams is irrational and emotional, we ask that it be honored for one reason that should be sufficient if it is really true that you give us respect: We, the people you call Indians, ask that you not use our name that way. That should be reason enough. (Akwesane Notes, as cited in "Report of Ad Hoc," 1972)

Divided opinions among Native Americans. Not *all* Native Americans agreed that the institutions' nicknames and symbols were inappropriate. In the cases involving both Miami University and Eastern Michigan University, leaders of federally recognized tribes endorsed the use of nicknames and symbols that national organizations such as the American Indian Movement and National Congress of American Indians called offensive and racist. Because the University of Illinois claimed that the Illini were extinct (and also would not acknowledge the Peoria Tribe of Oklahoma as the Illini's cultural heirs), the university could not consult with the tribe it was purportedly representing. Although both national and local Native American advocacy groups pressed the U of I to drop the Chief, the university ignored their protests and instead featured the opinions of a few Native Americans not affiliated with the institution who were willing to state publicly they found nothing offensive about the Chief.

When a particular tribe authorized the continued use of a nickname, or when a Native American individual said publicly that nothing was wrong with such nicknames, boosters would smugly claim, "If even the Indians themselves are for this, then who can be against us?" The fact that not all Native Americans held identical opinions on the matter of nicknames and symbols was routinely exploited by boosters, who said that the symbols need not be discontinued as long as some Native Americans agreed they were not objectionable. Implicit in this argument seemed to be the assumption that only when *all* Native Americans were in agreement would the institution have to acknowledge the legitimacy of their complaint; thus, the institution need not act until Native Americans resolved the matter for themselves first. Yet, as EMU's Shelton demonstrated, institutional leaders did not need to be immobilized by different opinions among Native Americans; like Shelton, they could comply with the wishes of national representative organizations and take the risk of ignoring or defying other Native Americans who may be more immediately involved in the controversy (Shelton, 1991). However, to disregard Native American opinions in order to make a decision that was supposedly "for their own good" appeared patronizing and further reinforced the power disparity between the predominantly White institution and the Native Americans. Thus, while it was essential to include Native American voices when addressing these controversies, it was a mistake for institutional leaders to rely on getting "the" Native American perspective. And, although numerous organizations and tribes that represented Native Americans nationally said unequivocally that Indian nickname and symbols must be eliminated, boosters continued to focus selectively on dissident voices.

The reasons the three institutions used to justify keeping their Native American-related nicknames and symbols were sorted into three general themes that might be summarized as thus: (1) using such nicknames and symbols is a way of respecting and remembering Native Americans; (2) Native Americans are no different from other groups used for nicknames and symbols; and (3) only a militant minority of Native Americans has a problem; the rest of them do not take offense. These themes revealed that the same social attitudes that shaped the selection and popularization of these nicknames and symbols at the three institutions still lay beneath the arguments used to defend them. That is, booster culture, by arguing that Native American-related nicknames did no harm, continued to objectify Native Americans, trivialize their complaints, and ignore their efforts to be recognized and respected. At the heart of the boosters' defense of objectionable nicknames and symbols was a pervasive belief that Native Americans should be invented and not heard.

Moreover, the powerful positive feelings—e.g., pride, affection, nostalgia—that boosters associated with such misconstructed Native American *symbols* as Chief Illiniwek and the Miami Indianhead logo were clearly not felt about Native American *people*, as boosters often claimed. What these symbols actually represented—and what boosters defended so vehemently—was the strong sense of pride and affiliation boosters felt toward the traditions and values of their *own* culture—of boosterism. Thus, to threaten these dearly loved symbols was to threaten how boosters constructed their own cultural identity.

Why Native American-related Nicknames and Symbols Persist

Over the past decade, numerous institutions—including Miami University and Eastern Michigan University—have replaced Native American-related nicknames and symbols over the objections of their boosters. Although there was some variation, the processes by which institutions arrived at a decision to drop the nickname or symbol followed a consistent pattern: the administration acknowledged the problem, gathered history and input on the issue from an array of campus stakeholders, reviewed the evidence, and following what was often represented as dispassionate and logical deliberation, the administration announced that as an institution of higher learning it must disassociate itself from what was now seen as offensive. However, if discarding a racist nickname was only a matter of implementing this ostensibly linear, rational process, then what explains the continued resistance at nearly sixty institutions?

To understand why some institutions feel justified in their continued use of Native American-related nicknames, important clues can be found in looking at how booster culture strives to preserve itself. To every institution's booster culture, athletic nicknames, colors, and mascots are important cultural symbols that represent shared values and assumptions (e.g., belief in the goodness of the team and university) and foster group affiliation (e.g., fans wear clothing with team colors to indicate team loyalty). Although nicknames and mascots are intended for use by athletic teams, at institutions composed of increasingly heterogeneous groups and perspectives they may be one of the few things that constitute a common institutional identity. In some cases, distinguishing for which group the symbols are meaningful or symbolic is difficult, as when an institution adopts a logo that is used outside of athletic contexts (e.g., on official stationery and publications), paints campus structures with "school colors," or uses a nickname to refer to members of the campus community who are not student athletes. Thus, to the booster culture and perhaps to the entire institution, nicknames, mascots, logos, and other symbols play a fundamental role in constructing a common culture.

However, to Native Americans, Native American-related nicknames and other images also have highly symbolic meanings that are largely offensive and demeaning; same symbol, very different interpretations. The often emotional conflict over Native American-related nicknames and symbols, then, is like a "custody battle," a cultural struggle over who is rightfully entitled to control these nicknames and symbols. On one hand, the movement to eliminate Native American-related nicknames and symbols is an effort to end the use of racist stereotypes and return control to Native Americans over a cultural element crucial to their survival: authentic images and representations of themselves in U.S. society. On the other hand, these same symbols have become embedded within the culture of the boosters, who (1) do not consciously associate the nickname or symbol with modern-day Native Americans, and (2) embrace the nickname or symbol for their own group. Thus, it seems inconceivable to boosters that they must sacrifice a central part of their cultural identity and "return" those symbols and images to a group that they hardly recognize. As long as boosters of Native American-related nicknames and symbols are unable to "see" Native Americans as they truly are—and not as the stereotypes that are incessantly promoted—then they see little reason to make such a significant cultural sacrifice.

Furthermore, although many boosters may hold positions of formal authority at the institutions (e.g., campus administrators, trustees, athletics personnel), alumni are boosters who often wield tremendous yet unacknowledged influence in forming institutional policy. For, not only do alumni threaten to end their generous contributions when campus leaders begin discussing dropping a controversial nickname, but state-assisted institutions may face the additional pressure of public policymakers (many of whom are true-blue alums) who seek to resist institutional changes, either through force of law or with threats of decreased state allocations. Even at institutions (such as UIUC) where faculty and student governance bodies have formally supported efforts to retire its nickname or mascot, the power exercised by booster culture may be nearly impossible to overcome. Indeed, in spite of what might cautiously be called a trend among numerous institutions to drop or change Native American-related nicknames or symbols, there is no compelling evidence that this study's lone holdout—UIUC—will join their ranks anytime soon, in spite of continued opposition by numerous students, faculty, staff, and even alumni.[10] Because of the tremendous influence booster culture holds at large, state-assisted (in some cases, flagship) institutions as well as in the regions they serve, it is quite likely that large public universities with Native American-related nicknames and symbols (e.g., UIUC, Florida State University, the University of Utah) will face the most stubborn and widespread resistance, leaving them among the last to change—if ever.

Implications

Native American-related nicknames will continue to be a contentious issue not only for the sixty or so institutions still using them but also for institutions that have recently changed them, such as Miami and Eastern Michigan, where members of the booster culture still feel angry, betrayed, and resentful toward the institution. Although each of these institutions may seek to meet the same short-term goal of replacing their nickname or mascot, the larger project of facilitating meaningful changes in campus cultures occurs in different ways at differing rates, particularly when such changes include the redistribution of institutional power and influence. It would be overpromising, therefore, to suggest any single recipe for change would work equally well amid the unpredictable and unique factors of each particular institutional context. Rather, it would be more helpful to offer campus leaders useful insights gleaned from the particulars of the cases covered in this study.

First, the case studies suggest that perhaps the most contentious method for addressing a controversial nickname or symbol is for an administration or governing board to uproot the nickname and symbols all at once, as Eastern Michigan did. This is not to say this sort of "shock therapy" might not be effective, but from a cultural perspective, this approach strips an important and influential campus constituency of a part of its identity, which, if taken, they will fight to retain. In contrast, a negotiated approach, characterized by some sense of give-and-take, may help the booster culture surrender shared symbols while giving them time to adapt to changes.

For example, changing the Miami University nickname while keeping the Indian-head logo indicated the institution's willingness to change an offensive practice but also ameliorated boosters' concerns about losing their cultural symbols. Bradley University kept its nickname "Braves" but discontinued using Native American-related symbols, a strategy other institutions have taken ("Bradley To Keep," 1993). Perhaps one of the most creative solutions was crafted by the University of Tennessee at Chattanooga, which had used an Indian logo with the nickname "Moccasins." In 1996, UTC changed its nickname to that of the state bird, "Mockingbirds," which not only provided a new nickname that could enhance regional affiliation but also allowed their sports teams to still be referred to as the "Mocs" ("Changes In Mascots," 1997). Of course, the saying that compromise makes a good umbrella but a poor roof applies here as well. Aiming for a "win-win" situation may eventually leave all concerned parties deeply dissatisfied and unwilling to cooperate. How much change to impose depends on the institutional context.

Second, gathering and disseminating historical information—about both the symbols and the Native Americans associated with them—is crucial to sustaining a change process. Boosters often cleave to inaccurate assumptions about the origin and longevity of their institution's nicknames and symbols. However, such misconceptions can be revised with historically sound data, perhaps demonstrating to boosters that nicknames and especially graphic identities (i.e., logos and mascots) are not as deeply rooted in the institution or as authentic as they might believe.

Likewise, getting boosters to understand how their symbols are stereotypical and racist depends on helping them gain more accurate information about Native Americans as both historical and contemporary peoples. As Stage and Manning (1992) explain in their cultural brokering approach to fostering multicultural environments, moving an institution from a predominantly monocultural perspective to one more multicultural depends on creating opportunities for persons to learn to think more contextually and span cultural boundaries. To truly respect Native American cultures and experiences, boosters must be encouraged when possible to "walk a mile in another's moccasins," which, however unpleasant, should include learning more about the injustices Whites have perpetrated against Native Americans.

Third, once institutional leaders concede that the institution's nickname and symbols are indeed offensive and racist, they often believe (mistakenly) that eliminating the offending nickname will resolve the problem and end the conflict. However, to Native Americans, these nicknames and symbols are not causes of prejudice and stereotyping but instead they are reflections of a greater social disorder. Consequently, when administrators and trustees see the nickname as the only problem, they are treating only symptoms and not the oppressive attitudes and practices they reflect. Because the controversy surrounding a Native American-related nickname can easily become a statewide spectacle, it is not surprising that institutional leaders wish to focus primarily on bringing the controversy to closure. However, as an institution of higher education, the college or university should use the controversy as an opportunity to teach its staff, students and faculty how to identify and expose other emblems of discrimination and prejudice.

Conclusion

So, what *is* in a name? As far as Native American-related nicknames and associated symbols go, not enough to be concerned about, it seems. When ticking off the most urgent social concerns on U.S.

college campuses—the erosion of affirmative action, an increasing incidence of incivility, violence, and hate speech—offensive nicknames appear much less compelling. Presenting this issue to most people outside of higher education, even to well-meaning Whites, often elicits responses ranging from outrage to eye rolling. Within the academy, PC-fatigued faculty and students muster only polite indifference, and many persons otherwise sensitive to the problems of institutional racism may not think twice about sitting down to enjoy the sixth game of the World Series between the Braves and the Indians.

These responses reveal how difficult it can be even to direct attention to this issue, let alone reevaluate its priority on the issues "list." However, one need only ask a president, alumni director, trustee, coach, or protester from an institution embroiled in conflict over a Native American-related nickname what it has meant to them and the institution for the importance of the issue to become more evident, on as well as off the campus. The strong feelings that surface in the midst of these controversies—Native Americans' anger and embarrassment, boosters' deep affection for their teams and disaffection for "troublemaking" activists, indifference toward Native American history—otherwise remain unacknowledged elsewhere in U.S. society. Thus, Native American-related nicknames and symbols are a challenge for all of higher education—not just because the nicknames themselves are offensive to Native Americans and their allies, but because the controversies surrounding them expose the lack of will that characterizes the ways in which numerous colleges and universities respond to complaints of institutional racism. In spite of the temptation for many campus leaders to give thanks that Native Americans mascots and nicknames are a problem only at *other* institutions, the persistence of institutionalized "isms" across higher education shows that the bell tolls also for them.

Notes

1. Although Rodriguez (1998) attempts to document which two- and four-year institutions use Native American-related nicknames, his list is a bit out of date. A more comprehensive and accurate list of college and university nicknames can be found at the web site <*http://www.afn.org/~recycler/sports.html*>.
2. "Illinois" is the French variation of "Illiniwek" (pronounced ill-EYE-neh-wek), their name for themselves, which meant simply "men" or "people." The tribes are sometimes referred to by a shortened form, "Illini."
3. Robert Chapel, UIUC University Archives technical assistant, confirmed that the origin of the athletic use of the nickname "Illini" is poorly documented. This claim also appeared in Lessiter (1989).
4. The discrepancies between the accounts are generally minor. According to a letter written by the person who was the second "Chief Illiniwek," the game was played in Pittsburgh, not Philadelphia (Borchers, 1959). Pearson, M. (1995) says the game was played not in Pennsylvania but in Illinois at the U of I's brand-new Memorial Stadium.
5. The mascot's name, "Chief Illiniwek," was supposedly suggested by legendary Illinois football coach Robert Zuppke (Lessiter, 1989).
6. The Miami called themselves "Twightwee," their name for the cry of the crane and the symbol of the Atchakangouen (the Miami proper tribe). "Miami" is a French and English variation of their Ojibwe name, "Oumami," which means "people of the peninsula."
7. The Huron called themselves "Wyandot" or "Wendat," an Iriquoisan word meaning "island people" or "dwellers on a peninsula." They were called "Hurons" by French explorers, a pejorative name derived from the French word *hure*—meaning "wild boar"—which alluded to the Wyandots' bristly hair. Today, members of this tribe living in Quebec still refer to themselves as "Hurons."
8. Although culture is a concept with multifarious definitions, Kuh and Whitt (1988) provide a definition applicable to higher education organizations and settings that appears to justify applying the term "culture" to the shared practices and meanings of regional athletic boosters.
9. This connection between an institution's Native American-related nickname and a particular tribe is not always the case. Most institutions using these kinds of nicknames are more generic (e.g., the Marquette Warriors, the Bradley Braves, the Arkansas State University Indians).
10. Other institutions that have recently dropped their nicknames or symbols include Bradley University (IL), Knox College (IL), Marquette University (WI), Ripon College (WI), Saint John's College (NY), and the University of Tennessee-Chattanooga.

References

Anderson, H. (1989, October 19). Ire raised during talk about Chief. *Daily Illini*, p. 1.

Begnoche, S. (1991, Fall). Viewpoints. *Eastern Today, 8*, 3.

Berkhofer, R. F. (1978). *The white man's Indian: Images of the American Indian from Columbus to the present*. New York: Knopf.

"Big Reds" is short for "Tribe Miami." (1930, May). *Miami Alumni Newsletter*, p. 22.

Board votes to accept decision on "Redskins." (1993, December 16). *Miami Report*, p. 1.

Borchers, W. (1959). *Personal letter in possession of University of Illinois Archives*.

Bradley to keep nickname "Braves." (1993, May 2). *The New York Times*, p. 28.

A challenge to the Chief. (1975). *The Illio* (pp. 154–155). Urbana, IL: University of Illinois.

Chang, I. (1989, October 16). U. of I. urged to scrap Indian mascot. *Chicago Tribune* [News Section], p. 3.

Changes in mascots and logos lead to trouble on two campuses. (1997, February 28). *Chronicle of Higher Education*, p. A10.

Cheer Eagle, not Indian, university tells alumni. (1995, January 20). *Chronicle of Higher Education*, p. A37.

Chief Miami to make debut at EM game. (1977, January 26). *Hamilton and Fairfield Journal-News*, p. 13.

A chronology. (1993, December 16). *Miami Report*, p. 2.

Churchill, W. (1993, March). Crimes against humanity. *Z Magazine*, 43–47.

Colburn, H. C. (1923). *The story of Ypsilanti*. Ypsilanti, MI [no publisher information].

Davis, L. R. (1993). Protest against the use of Native American mascots: A challenge to traditional American identity. *Journal of Sport and Social Issues, 17*, 9–22.

Davis, M. B. (1994). *Native America in the twentieth century: An encyclopedia*. New York: Garland.

Davis, R. (1989, November 15). U. of I. won't send Chief Illiniwek to sideline. *Chicago Tribune* [News Section], p. 1.

Eastern Michigan U. alumni angry over nickname change from Hurons to Eagles. (1991, September 18). *Chronicle of Higher Education*, p. A37.

Eastern Michigan University. (1998a). *About Eastern Michigan University*. Retrieved September 29, 1998 from the World Wide Web: http://www.emich.edu/emu/aboutemu.html.

Eastern Michigan University. (1998b). *University Profile*. Retrieved September 29, 1998 from the World Wide Web: www.emich.edu/public/gradcatalog/generalinfo/profile.html.

Ebert, R. (1967). *An Illini century: One hundred years of campus life*. Urbana, IL: University of Illinois Press.

Effort to dignify nickname. (1972, September 14). *The Miamian*, p. 2.

EMU committee selects three nicknames for athletic teams. (1991, May 1)[Eastern Michigan University press release]. Ypsilanti, MI: Eastern Michigan University, Public Information Office.

EMU drops nickname "Hurons." (1991, January 31). *Grand Rapids Press*, n. p.

EMU logo unveiled amid protests. (1991, August 10). *Ypsilanti Press*, p. 2A.

EMU to change Huron name and logo. (1991, February). *EMU Alumni Action News*, p. 1.

Eshenroder, O. (1991, November 22). State urged to void EMU vote on logo. *Ann Arbor News*, p. A1.

Eubanks, L. (1976). *The fighting Illini: A story of Illinois football*. Huntsville, AL: Strode.

Farnell, B. (1998, April). Retire the Chief. *Anthropology Newsletter, 39*, 4.

Fontenot, C. J. (1997, September 15). Stereotypes, traditions, fantasy, outrage, and the Chief. *Urbana–Champaign News-Gazette*, pp. B-1, B-5.

Franks, R. (1982). *What's in a nickname? Exploring the jungle of college athletic mascots*. Amarillo, TX: Ray Franks Publishing Ranch.

Gilbert, B. (1998). Rah, rah, ruffians! *Smithsonian, 29*, 74–81.

Gone, J. (1995). *Chief Illiniwek: Dignified or damaging?* Retrieved September 29, 1998 from the World Wide Web: http://fantasia.ncsa.uiuc.edu/~jayr/gone.html.

Grant, B. (1994). *Concise encyclopedia of the American Indian*. (Rev. ed.). New York: Wings.

Green, R. (1979). American Indian stereotypes. In *Festival of American folklife program book* [program](pp. 18–21). Washington, DC: U.S. Government Printing Office.

Griffin, J. L. (1990, September 14). Illiniwek protests to be heard. *Chicago Tribune* [Chicagoland Section], p. 9.

Gunderson, M. (1998, September 28). Protests at game meet controversy, students react with mixed feelings. *Daily Illini Online*. Retrieved September 29, 1998 from World Wide Web: http://www.illinimedia.com/di/sept_98/sept28/news/news01.html.

Havighurst, W. (1969). *The Miami years, 1809–1969*. (Rev. ed.). New York: Putnam.

Hendricks, D. (1998, April 14). BOT finished with Chief issue, board refuses to hear more arguments without new anti-Chief information. *Daily Illini*, p. 1.

Hinsdale, W. B. (1930). *The first people of Michigan*. Ann Arbor, MI: G. Wahr.

Huron fans consider lawsuit. (1991, September 4). *Eastern Echo*, p. 7.

Hurons become Eagles; lose money. (1991, July 3). *Chronicle of Higher Education*, p. A37.

Hurons is chosen as Ypsi nickname. (1929, October 31). *Normal College News*, p. 1.

Hyman, M. D., & White, G. S. (1977). *Big Ten football, its life and times, great coaches, players, and games*. New York: Macmillan.

Jaschik, S. (1995, December 15). U.S. upholds use of Chief Illiniwek, U. of Illinois mascot. *Chronicle of Higher Education*, p. A29.

Jones, S. W. (1993, December 8). Ditch team names in favor of mascots. *Chronicle of Higher Education*, p. B5.

Jouzaitis, C. (1990, October 12). U. of I. board votes to keep Chief Illiniwek. *Chicago Tribune* [Chicagoland Section], p. 6.

Kuh, G. D., & Whitt, E. J. (1988). *The invisible tapestry: Culture in American colleges and universities* (ASHE-ERIC Higher Education Report No. 1). Washington, DC: Association for the Study of Higher Education.

Lederman, D. (1990, June 2). Illinois trustees vote to keep Indian mascot. *Chronicle of Higher Education*, p. A27.

Leonard, F. E. (1993). Statement of the Miami Tribe of Oklahoma, copy in possession of Miami University Archives.

Lesniewski, B. (1996, July 18). Secret visit to Miami Tribe may have spurred secret Redskin resolution. *High Street Journal* [Oxford, OH], pp. 1, 3.

Lessiter, M. (1989). *The college names of the games*. Chicago: Contemporary Books.

McGovern, L. A. (1995, November 30). *Letter from Department of Education's Office of Civil Rights to UIUC Chancellor Michael Aiken*. Retrieved September 29, 1998 from the World Wide Web: http://chronicle.com/che-data/focus.dir/data.dir/1204.95/aiken.htm.

McLean, D. (1991). *EMU President Shelton recommends that university drop Indian name and logo* [press release of EMU Public Information Office], p. 1.

Miami Tribe no longer supports use of term "Redskins" for athletic teams. (1996, July 18). *Miami Report*, p. 1.

Miami Tribe of Oklahoma. (1972). *Formal resolution*, copy in possession of Miami University Archives.

Miami U. abandons "Redskins" name at tribe's request. (1996, October 4). *Chronicle of Higher Education*, p. A8.

Miami U. of Ohio to shed "Redskins" nickname for "RedHawks." (1997, May 2). *Chronicle of Higher Education*, p. A9.

Miami University Office of the President. (1996). *Message to Miamians* [mass mailing]. Oxford, OH: Author.

Miami University. (1998). *Miami at a glance*. Retrieved September 29, 1998 from the World Wide Web: http://www.muohio.edu/aboutmiami/ataglance.html.

Michener, J. A. (1976). *Sports in America*. Greenwich, CT: Fawcett.

Mihesuah, D. A. (1996). *American Indians: Stereotypes & realities*. Atlanta, GA: Clarity.

Monaghan, P. (1992, January 8). New debates rage over American Indian symbols. *Chronicle of Higher Education*, p. A39.

Nickname contest started by union. (1929, October 24). *Normal College News*, p. 1.

Official Fighting Illini Sports Website. (1998). *Traditions: Chief Illiniwek*. Retrieved September 29, 1998 from the World Wide Web: http://www.fightingillini.com/htm/main2/traditions/traditions_par ent.html.

Ohio hopes to force teams to drop Indian nicknames. (1993, September 1). *Chronicle of Higher Education*, p. A47.

Olson, E. (1998, March 10). Vote opposes Chief, U-C senate votes 97–29 in favor of retiring mascot. *Daily Illini*, p. 1.

Once a Huron, Always a Huron. (n. d.). Brochure published by EMU Huron Restoration, Inc.; photocopy in possession of Eastern Michigan University Archives.

Pearson, M. (1995). *Illini legends, lists, and lore: 100 years of Big Ten heritage*. Champaign, IL: Sagamore.

Pearson, R. (1992, December 19). State urged to force U. of I. to get rid of Chief Illiniwek. *Chicago Tribune* [News Section], p. 5.

Report of ad hoc committee to investigate the university's identification with the Miami Indians and with the use of the term "Redskins." (1972). Oxford, OH: Miami University.

Risser, P. G. (1993). *Regarding the use of the term "Redskin" as a nickname for the university's athletic teams.* Oxford, OH: Miami University Office of the President.

Risser, P. G. (1996). Confronting value conflicts. In J. B. McLaughlin (Ed.), *Leadership transitions: The new college president* (New Directions for Higher Education No. 93, pp. 33–40). San Francisco: Jossey-Bass.

Rodriguez, R. (1998, June 11). The assassination of Little Red Sambo. *Black Issues in Higher Education, 15,* 20–24.

Rosenstein, J. (Producer & Director). (1997, July 15). In whose honor? In L. Heller (Executive Producer), *P.O.V.* New York: Public Broadcasting Service.

Rudolph, F. (1990). *The American college and university: A history.* Athens: University of Georgia Press. (Original work published 1965.)

Shea, C. (1993, November 10). Mascots under fire. *Chronicle of Higher Education,* p. A33.

Shelton, W. E. (1991, Summer). Higher education, higher values: The anatomy of a logo decision. *Educational Record, 72,* 36–38.

Sherman, E. (1991, March 16). Student government vote puts heat on Illini's chief. *Chicago Tribune* [Sports Section], p. 1.

Sloan, J., & Watts, C. (1993). *College nicknames and other interesting sports traditions.* Northport, AL: Vision.

Slowikowski, S. S. (1993). Cultural performance and sport mascots. *Journal of Sport and Social Issues, 17,* 23–33.

Stage, F. K., & Manning, K. (1992). *Enhancing the multicultural campus environment: A cultural brokering approach* (New Directions for Student Services No. 60). San Francisco: Jossey-Bass.

Stake, R. E. (1995). *The art of case study research.* Thousand Oaks, CA: Sage.

Sultzman, L. (1997a). *Huron history.* Retrieved September 29, 1998 from the World Wide Web: http://www.dickshovel.com/hur.html.

Sultzman, L. (1997b). *Illinois history.* Retrieved September 29, 1998 from the World Wide Web: http://www.dickshovel.com/ill.html.

Sultzman, L. (1998). *Miami history.* Retrieved September 29, 1998 from the World Wide Web: http://www.dickshovel.com/mia.html.

Takaki, R. T. (1993). *A different mirror: A history of multicultural America.* Boston: Little Brown & Co.

Thelin, J. R. (1994). *Games colleges play: Scandal and reform in intercollegiate athletics.* Baltimore, MD: The Johns Hopkins University Press.

Two campuses debate the futures of their mascots. (1993, October 27). *Chronicle of Higher Education,* p. A4.

U. of Wisconsin at Madison considers athletic boycott. (1993, June 2). *Chronicle of Higher Education,* p. A27.

UIUC Office of Public Affairs. (1998). *University of Illinois at Urbana–Champaign: Facts 1998.* Retrieved September 29, 1998 from the World Wide Web: http://www.oc.uiuc.edu/pubaff/facts96.html.

Use of the Huron logo and name. (1991, February 19). *Focus EMU,* p. 3.

Wolff, C. (1993, December 12). Miami Tribe or Miami Redskins? *Cincinnati Enquirer,* p. 1.

CHAPTER 4
"LIFE BEGINS WITH FREEDOM": THE COLLEGE NISEI, 1942–1945

THOMAS JAMES

EDUCATION, wrote Margaret Mead in 1943, creates a "drama of discontinuity" between parents and children in modern life. By encouraging children to be different from their parents, education holds forth the possibility, unknown to traditional societies, of introducing new values, even bringing new worlds into being. The dark side of this possibility is that education can degenerate into "techniques of power," teaching through indoctrination and locking the future into coercive relations of superiority and inferiority while conditions of life change in other respects. To avoid such a prospect, she argued, education should be placed at the service of learning instead of manipulation, spontaneity instead of control. A proper use of the discontinuity between parent and child would be to "devise and practice a system of education which sets the future free."[1]

During the year before Mead published these views, the United States government evacuated more than 110,000 Japanese Americans from their homes in western states, placed them in temporary "assembly centers" under the control of the U.S. Army, then moved them inland to ten "relocation centers" in wilderness and barren lands, guarded by military police and administered by a civilian agency of the government. The reflections of an anthropologist may seem ethereal when compared to the reality of fenced enclosures with rows of barracks inside and guard towers at intervals around the perimeter. Nevertheless, her perspective illuminates the dilemma of the camps in relation to democratic traditions of education in the twentieth century. Mead located the menace of totalitarianism as a potential within her own society, where a "spurious sense of superiority" had corrupted education. What was true for education in general was even more real and present for Japanese Americans during the war. For them, the value of education depended, in part, on deciding whether freedom might possibly exist in the future, even when their current investment in learning was being made under circumstances of manifest oppression. This decision about the future, unlike the order to build the camps or the administrative policies that ensued, had to be made by the Japanese Americans themselves, and it could be no more than a guess, whether informed by hopeful conviction or bitter disillusionment. Educators, social scientists, and camp administrators, no matter how gracious their motives, could not promise that the future would be free.[2]

The wartime evacuation came at a crucial juncture in the experience of Japanese Americans. Indeed, the camps heightened the drama of discontinuity between the Issei and Nisei, the first and second generations. Nisei outnumbered Issei by 79,642 to 47,305 in 1940. By 1942 the median age of the Nisei was 17, almost time for college and work. Although some had been born as early as 1910 and others were still being born in the 1940s, a great many Nisei entered the camps during the throes of their transition from youth to adult life. The discontinuity would have been dramatic even if there had been no evacuation in 1942. Born in the United States, the Nisei were citizens by birth; born in Japan, the Issei were permanent aliens by law. By the time the war began, the dominant language of the Nisei was English; the first language of their Issei parents was Japanese. Both generations had developed their own distinctive organizations and styles of leadership; the Issei had emphasized cultural preservation, community solidarity, and ethnic enterprise, while the Nisei were more attuned to political participation as citizens and assimilation into the dominant culture of the United States. Both generations left remarkable records of adjustment to social and economic conditions, both suffered from racial discrimination, but by the early 1940s the Nisei had participated more widely in the world outside of ethnic enclaves, especially in public schools.[3]

Surrounded by techniques of power in the camps, not only those of barbed wire and military police but the more subtle instruments of a benevolently coercive administration intent on making the best of its planned communities, the Nisei had to decide whether accommodation would make them patriots or quislings, whether the future would make their people Americans or "another Indian problem." Without knowledge of where their actions would lead them, who could say what ends might materialize to justify the different means available for coping with incarceration? Which agenda was most plausible, and to what extent would present beliefs influence future success?[4]

Out of the evacuated population several groups came forward with strategies for action. This essay explores the history of one of those groups, the college Nisei. These were more than 4,000 students who were allowed to leave the camps to study in institutions of higher education outside of the restricted zone of the Western Defense Command. The purpose of this inquiry is not to gloss over the importance of other sources of leadership among Japanese Americans. Rather, it is to understand the experience of a group that served as a living argument about future society for the entire racial minority. The argument suggested a transition from camp to college, from oppression to opportunity even in the darkest of times. For many students it was a journey across space, time, culture, and class position. If their experiences were unusual when compared to life in the ten wartime camps, this made it all the more central to the dilemma created by evacuation from their pre-war homes. In many respects, theirs was the vision of the future—and theirs the new problems and predicaments—that came about for many more Japanese Americans in the post-war world.

Fortunately, there is an ample record with which to interpret the experience of the college Nisei. The files of the National Japanese American Student Relocation Council, including hundreds of letters written by the Nisei students, have been preserved at the Hoover Institution, Stanford University. The organizational history of the student relocation has been well told by Robert O'Brien in his pioneering study, *The College Nisei,* first published in 1949. A tremendous wealth of documentary evidence on the history of the camps has been amassed at Bancroft Library in Berkeley and the National Archives in Washington, D.C., among other places. It is time now to reappraise the experience of these young people and to delve more deeply into their consciousness and initiative as related to the discontinuity created by the camps. The experience of the college Nisei offers valuable insight into the sudden concentration and dispersal of Japanese Americans during the war. Their reflections also throw light upon the complexities faced by any group of people trying to achieve acceptance in a society where the terms of citizenship, social status, and economic well-being are often racially determined.[5]

Of the approximately 25,000 Nisei attending college in western states at the beginning of World War II, only about two hundred were reported to have transferred to other schools in the Midwest and East before being evacuated. If the rest were excluded from higher education, what was to become of them, and what hope was there for the many other Nisei students graduating from high school each year? In 1942 more than 28 percent of the evacuated population was 15–24 years old, compared to slightly more than 17 percent of youth in the same group for the entire U.S. population. From the rising generation of Nisei almost four thousand boys and girls had attended twelfth grade in the 1941–42 school year before being evacuated. Within the camps there were few opportunities beyond high school, and nothing approaching a genuine college education. For most of the evacuees in 1942 the best alternative was work, which in the camps was regulated by the government so that no "colonist," as the Japanese Americans were often called by administrators, could receive more than $19 per month regardless of skills or productivity.[6]

As students inside the camps realized that "all we held dear to us could be swept away," outside it dawned on a few liberals, educators, and religious groups that concentrating citizens and their immigrant parents behind barbed wire was inimical to democratic ideals. *The Christian Century* featured an editorial in the summer of 1942 asserting that there was a "strategic necessity" for immediate action to protect "a whole generation of young Americans in one of our minority groups." The editorial spoke to the conscience of the white majority in American society: "To validate our many declarations of purpose and goal in this world struggle, all the rest of us must extend to them every chance for fuller assimilation into our national life." During the evacuation in 1942, a small coalition formed to help the dislocated Japanese Americans, giving special attention to helping the college-educated elite, partly because of their importance as a vanguard that was seen to be leading the group into the mainstream of American life, but also because other strategies of assistance seemed impossible in the face of the anti-Japanese hysteria and the so-called "military necessity" in western states.[7]

Educators and concerned citizens working to help the Nisei from outside the camps were also protecting the norms of open competition and individual freedom that gave higher education its legitimacy as a democratic institution in American society. The list of advocates included nationally known educational leaders like Robert Gordon Sproul of the University of California and Ray Lyman Wilbur of Stanford University. Besides advocating the interests of the Nisei, educators were defending their own position in the moral order of U.S. society as keepers of enduring values, sorters of intellect, managers of assimilation. In support of the student relocation from camp to college, educators argued that it was essential to avoid the waste of human resources brought about by the evacuation. The Nisei were citizens who would play a role in American society after the war, and sending them to college would cost no more than maintaining them as wards of the government in the camps. Those who went to college, the argument continued, would symbolize to their families and friends in the camps that education was still the best route to a successful future. Finally, the process of assimilation would be enhanced among young Americans in midwestern and eastern communities, where the relocated students would be received more generously than on the west coast.[8]

For many Nisei students there was little doubt that that the brighter prospects were *outside*. This word acquired new meanings for those who had been forced to live inside the camps. As one student wrote from Amache, the camp in Colorado, while awaiting leave clearance so that he could go to college, "this is taking on more and more of a concentration camp atmosphere. Spotlights will start glaring soon . . . a fence is being built . . . closer and closer the net winds. And we sit speechless . . . either in astonishment or from lack of interest, or from lack of any direction to the voices raised here and there." Some people complained that the family unit was breaking down, leaving children without ~~~~ded to prepare them responsibly for the future. Those within the camps, deprived ~~ re whether their former communities on the west coast would remain forever out ~~ were now in danger of losing their capacity to imagine where they might go and ~~ to rebuild their lives after such a calamity.[9]

~ of special channels for student relocation proceeded quickly as soon as the gov-~ving Japanese Americans from their home communities to temporary assembly ~ onfusion and uncertainty of the mass evacuation, it helped considerably that the ~nt of the Nisei found a sympathetic audience in the nation's capital. On May 21, ~ the Assistant Secretary of War, wrote to Clarence E. Pickett of the American ~nittee: "Anything that can legitimately be done to compensate loyal citizens of ~ the dislocation to which they have been subjected, has our full approval." Suc-~ucators and concerned groups in the spring of 1942 led to the formation of the ~erican Student Relocation Council, with offices first in several cities, then cen-~ during 1943. The council, a voluntary agency operating on private funds out-~, became a strong advocate for the interests of Nisei students eligible to go to ~ gressive role in persuading institutions of higher education to participate. It ~ocedures for college application, then screened candidates and coordinated ~ d funds to help the Nisei pay for college, since the government would pro-~~~~ ~~pport. The council also pressured federal authorities for expanded educational rights for the Nisei, and it tried in several ways to boost the sagging morale of young people in the camps.[10]

Some colleges right away refused to participate. One would not even issue transcripts of former students of Japanese descent, arguing that they should all be treated as prisoners of war, whether citizens or not. Despite such occurences, the response from colleges was favorable enough overall that hundreds of students were able to relocate in the year following evacuation. By the fall of 1942 the council had administered and collected from the camps more than 2,000 questionnaires filled out by Nisei interested in attending college. Japanese Americans matched their energy with their own as they raised funds—more than $3,000, no mean sum in those days, from the camp at Topaz alone—to give scholarships to Nisei students leaving the camps for college. The effort to get students out of the camps became known as an "Underground Railroad" among those who kept it going during the early months of the war. The metaphor suggested a transit not merely from camp to college, but from slavery to freedom.[11]

For students, thanks to the council and the willingness of the government to cooperate, there was a way out of the camps, though only for a few during the first year of incarceration. For a time early in the war, the journey for a select few from camp to college was one of the only available niches in the world of normal communities beyond the fence. The journey was a quest for educational opportunity and for a brighter future, but it was also a choice offered on terms set by those who directed higher education, terms that were at the same time checked and controlled at every step by the government. Social advancement was to be had through sponsorship by designated officials who selected students according to criteria based on cultural traits as well as cognitive aptitude. A committee of deans, registrars and personnel administrators evaluated the Nisei applicants, reviewing scholastic performance, character, professional ambitions, contacts with Caucasians, and special interests or unusual talents. This sponsorship by a philanthropic organization working to create opportunities for a disadvantaged group—an arrangement new to the Nisei and, in fact, to most minority groups—operated within the constraints of government policy and the receptivity of communities and local institutions. To obtain leave from the government to attend college, the Nisei aspirants needed proof that they had been accepted at an institution outside of the Western Defense Command. The government required evidence in advance of adequate financial resources, testimony from a public official that the student would be acceptable to the local community, proof that the institution had been cleared by the U.S. Department of War, and certification that the Federal Bureau of Investigation had completed a security check and granted the student a clearance. At first, Nisei students were not allowed to attend most major universities because of defense-related research and production on campus or in the cities where these institutions were located. When the restriction was lifted in 1944, Nisei students applying to such universities were subjected to an additional "personal security" questionnaire.[12]

Beyond these general policies controlling the selection of Nisei to leave the camps in pursuit of higher education, notes taken by the field staff of the student relocation council reveal that government officials took an interest in regulating the process. Camp authorities often required advance appointments for interviews. Outside educators and staff of the council found their movements constrained and monitored when they tried to gain access to evacuated students. Within the camps the government allowed only sole-purpose interviews, focusing on the college admission procedure, not on family or community life. The presence of a member of the internal security staff of the administration was mandatory in meetings between students and field staff of the council, and all communication had to be conducted in English. Perhaps most importantly, those given indefinite leave to go to college found it difficult to go back to the camps, except for one small group of college Nisei who returned under the auspices of the student relocation council to recruit other students for college.[13]

In summary, three features stand out from the early history of student relocation. First, educators and humanitarian groups organized a system for selecting and sponsoring individual Nisei to leave the camps to attend institutions of higher education. Second, the system of sponsorship functioned within narrow constraints set by governmental authority and local willingness to receive Nisei students into the community. Third, the conditions placed upon the admissions process and upon college attended impeded communication about the family and community of Nisei students, and for the most part prevented those who attended college from returning to the camps for the duration of the war.

The people on the outside who helped Nisei students in the camps were nourishing the hope that persisted among Japanese Americans, hope that educational opportunity was still alive, that equal citizenship and social mobility were still plausible images of the future. In working to keep alive such hopes, educators and other Caucasian allies created a system of sponsorship that, by design, dispersed individual aspirants away from the concentrated community and impeded their return. Exactly when the median age of the second generation was on the threshold of the college years, individual students faced a choice between rapid dispersal, high achievement and isolation away from their racial group, or the slow, dispiriting but nonetheless still recognizably communal life of being concentrated in segregated camps as wards of the government. This was the design of educational opportunity that surrounded and helped to shape the relationship between the college Nisei and the incarcerated population in the camps.

One student, writing from Smith College, said she knew what it was to fly from a cage. She soon found that this was also to fly into a chasm between two worlds. Many Nisei students recognized the contradictions of their flight to freedom and acknowledged their ambivalence as they tried to untangle opportunity from oppression. They wrote hundreds of letters to the few Caucasians they felt were genuinely working to help them. These letters piled up at the offices of the American Friends Service Committee, for the Quakers had reacted to the evacuation in 1942 by extending what they called a "spiritual handshake" to the victims, helping in various ways to soften the impact of anti-Japanese hysteria during the nation's mobilization for war. At the invitation of the federal government, the Quakers had played a central role in setting up the National Japanese American Student Relocation Council. Perhaps because these pacifists had offered unequivocal support to Japanese Americans at a time when even most liberals were rationalizing the oppression as a regrettable consequence of military necessity, they were privileged to hear voices among the Nisei that others could not hear. The evidence offers glimpses of self-awareness during an extreme crisis for Japanese Americans. Such evidence could be seen as limited, to some extent, by the fact that the Nisei students were writing to enlist the sympathies of Caucasians who had power to help them, but the range of written reflections in the letters suggests that a deeper and more authentic communication was taking place. To go back and read these letters is to realize that later explanations often leave out the role played by the Nisei as subjects of their own experience, not merely the objects of history. The college Nisei, vanguard of a minority group that excels in higher education, helped to construct their place in American society in part by how they chose to understand what was happening to them.[14]

Even good fortune spawned bizarre predicaments for those who went from camp to college. Riding trains eastward across the country, the Nisei students traveled with servicemen returning from such places as Pearl Harbor and Guadalcanal. They arrived to college towns where no Japanese American had ever set foot before. These young people immediately confronted their own insecurities, the fear of having the wrong face and being in the wrong place. Venturing forth as a tiny elite, the Nisei students saw themselves as "ambassadors of good will" whose charge was to open the way for racial tolerance. In the words of a play staged at Amache, they were "eastward pioneers," their frontier good relations with the white majority. "Living in the same dorms as others and studying together," wrote three Nisei students from a college in Missouri, "we are testing a type of relation that we were never able to experience on the Pacific coast." Writing from Wellesley College, a student told her friends in camp that "those who have probably never seen a Nisei before will get their impression of the Nisei as a whole from the relocated students." The ones who went first were clearing a path for others to follow.[15]

Education presented the college Nisei with opportunity, but it also impelled the select few into a diaspora. Before the war most of the college group would have been concentrated in a half dozen universities on the west coast. A relocated Nisei student wrote from Ohio that "seeing America, the larger America, for the first time . . . we are creeping out of a shell that we have unconsciously been in." Once on the outside, the college Nisei confronted a stark dichotomy between past and present, children and parents, school and home. Quite often they found themselves to be the only Japanese Americans in an entire college town of Caucasians. For most of them the separation from what they had known before was total, since they could go back neither to the camps nor to their pre-war homes during the war.[16]

Techniques of power intruded upon their good fortune wherever they went. The sole means of escape for the college Nisei was exceptionally high levels of performance and verifiably conventional behavior on terms set by their Caucasian sponsors in the new world they were entering. Having been instilled with a strong commitment to education by their immigrant parents—who, as

Charles Wollenberg has observed, "may well have been the best-educated immigrant group ever to come to America"—the Nisei now found it necessary to prove themselves worthy of equal treatment or else fall back into the enclosures where their race had been concentrated. In this way, the cultural affinity of the minority group for educational achievement was channeled by racial oppression and liberal sponsorship, first into a pattern of dispersal away from parents and the concentrated community, then into an obligatory challenge of maintaining high levels of performance and conformity to defend the second generation's status as citizens in American society.[17]

This predicament added a frightening dimension to the usual concerns of students about success and failure. A quest for confirmation replaced the self-evident truths of citizenship, and for the time being the alternative to assimilation was not the familiar ambience of an ethnic neighborhood and family businesses, but existence as wards of the government in a controlled, completely segregated environment. The Nisei were fully aware of this predicament: "the long stay in the camp has etched in my mind the value of freedom," wrote one of them from Salt Lake City. "So I say again," she continued, "Life begins with freedom." But freedom was no longer an inalienable right since the shock of evacuation. It depended on successfully managing the perceptions of others, persuading them that one deserved to be free. One had to gain recognition and the approval of whites to be selected and sponsored to leave the camps. Once free to go to the place approved by the government, one still had secured only the right to begin convincing others that freedom was appropriate, not yet the secure enjoyment of that status. While one Nisei journeyed to the Statue of Liberty and marvelled that "she still carries a torch for me," another remarked that "the fellows out here treat me very well so I haven't got a kick coming anywhere."[18]

In spite of the risks and disenchantments, higher education was a channel to the free world, the world outside the camps. Education brought the Nisei into contact with people whose alliances could help them to turn around public acceptance of the intolerance and political opportunism that had swept Japanese Americans out of their homes at the beginning of the war. While a history of both accommodation and resistance developed inside the camps, the college Nisei fought for connections with the outside world, a mixed world of oppressors and friends and mostly indifferent people. Even when they met with hostility, the college Nisei were in a position to learn more about the circumstances that were causing their oppression.

"As we face the future," wrote a Nisei woman in an education magazine, "our horizon is darkened by the possible threats of movements taking place to exclude all the Japanese from the United States after the war and to deprive us second and third generation American citizens of our citizenship." A coalition of southern and western congressmen was pushing to keep all Japanese Americans, including the college Nisei, inside the camps. Bills were proposed to deprive the Nisei of their citizenship. Government officials had even discussed the possibility of using evacuees as a "reprisal reserve" to insure the survival of American prisoners of war in Japan. The fortunes of Japanese Americans were fragile material amid the violent movements of public opinion and the machinations of special interest groups. Total war was just then coming of age—the terror bombing of civilian populations was one example. It was not clear how the worldwide obliteration of moral scruples about the limits of warfare would affect the status of Japanese Americans. Among the groups that mobilized to oppose their interests were the American Legion, the House Special Committee on Un-American Activities, and the congressional delegation from California. In an editorial in its *National Legionnaire*, the American Legion found it

> hard to understand why, at this time, men whom the Government does not see fit to trust with rifles are permitted to pursue uninterruptedly their college and professional courses. . . . There is a rankling hurt in the bosom of good, honest, patriotic, loyal, and devoted Americans when they see their sons come to the crossroads—their sons take the road that leads to war and the battlefield. The Japanese boy takes the road that leads to college and, to use a trite phrase worn rather thin and threadbare, the abundant life.[19]

Many traces of this resentment remained among local agitators and officials even after the Nisei were allowed to serve in the U.S. Army after the second year of the war.

Colleges wishing to accept the Nisei students were sometimes confronted with a fusillade of local protest. When politicians and pressure groups agitated against the presence of Japanese Americans on campus, they were guided by reasoning that pronounced guilt by racial association with the enemy. In some places, trustees feared sabotage or fifth column activities, and enterprising administrators wanted military personnel on campus to boost war-depleted enrollments. The presence of the military in programs designed to further war aims would mean that no Nisei could be admitted to the institution. Among educators, though, many instances of resistance to the relocation of Nisei students probably stemmed less from prejudice than from timidity, a fear of undermining the prestige of their institution among conventionally minded citizens who, unnerved by the war emergency, had little patience with the nuances of educational opportunity in a democratic society. It is remarkable in retrospect that a majority of college officials welcomed the Nisei and defended their rights even when highly vocal segments of the surrounding community disapproved.

Recognizing that the challenge was, above all, one of persuasion and public relations, many college Nisei spoke far and wide to community groups while they were going to school. A star pupil who became class president in his college and served on the executive committee of the local YMCA spoke nine times a month to different groups around the state where he lived. Another was elected student body president at a college in Kansas, but decided, without prompting from college officials or fellow students, to step down when local pols downtown staged a fiery meeting to denounce his election and decry such subversive activity on the campus. It was a delicate process for the Nisei students, balancing self-determination and accommodation under these circumstances. "Understanding will have to come through seeing, feeling, experiencing—and then believing," reflected one of them. "I know we Japanese Americans will first have to develop a philosophy of understanding others and their reactions in order to *be* understood and to comprehend in a small way our own problems in relation to others." In spite of the realities of total warfare and some instances of public resistance to their presence in college, it was still possible for this group of young people to believe that "our acceptance in the American community must germinate from us, from our activities." They realized that they were struggling not only against external oppression but against self-imposed limits, their assumptions about what was possible.[20]

Some of their deliberations touched upon the appropriate response to injustice—and to success when it came. The college group was well aware of the conflict among Japanese Americans in the camps over whether it was possible to hope for anything but discrimination and exclusion in a racist society. One young Nisei wrote that he preferred to be treated badly because "the race situation is what it is and there isn't anything we can do about it. I expect prejudice." Another asked her peers rhetorically, "What can you and I expect in a country where they tolerate slums like those of Chicago, or the Okies in California, or the poor whites in the South and the lynching of Negroes?" Many others among the college Nisei felt that the only answer was total assimilation and one-hundred percent Americanism. For some, though, this doctrine raised the specter of Nisei racism as the college-going elite adopted the racial attitudes of the dominant white majority. One student warned that "our hope is to gain equality with the Caucasians, and the Negro is forgotten in the rush. . . . We've got to combat this racial feeling. . . any group in trouble finds it so much easier to shove the blame onto some other minority group, and we are as guilty as any other racial stock." There were also signs of solidarity between the races. Those who went east, where there was less stigma attached to being Asian than in the west, found friends in various stages of nascent critical consciousness about the democratic promise of the United States. One Nisei student reflected on the patterns of prejudice standing in the way of other minority elites attending college: "There were several Jewish boys who tell me that they cannot enter medical school; the Catholic boys here have similar problems to tell, the Negro chap can talk endlessly of the south, the fellows of Italian descent speak of the disparagement they often receive, and on it goes." In Chicago a Nisei woman attending college lived in a cooperative house that was battling its landlord to keep a black student member on the premises. The example was one among many of how the college Nisei were learning to recognize the contradictory position of education—and educated elites—in a society that continued to be sharply divided along lines of race and class. It was a poignant reminder of the burden of race in America when blacks offered expressions of sympathy as government propaganda attacked Japanese racial characteristics.[21]

The racial stigma would not wash away easily. Many Nisei students wrote of the need to avoid forming cliques when several Japanese Americans attended the same school. But this strategy was not enough. The quest for social acceptance was not to be consummated merely through rapid dispersal of the race. One problem was sheer indifference, the tendency of the majority to lump minorities into a single insignificance as far as the dominant culture was concerned. One student complained that a teacher "actually asked me whether the rest of the Niseis spoke English, and another *history* teacher asked me why the Isseis were not citizens." These more subtle forms of prejudice were cause enough for desperation at times: "I feel like tossing my books into the fire and taking the first train to Topaz," the camp in Utah. This melancholy correspondent confided that he had begun to discover "something unreal" about his experience at college, a "slow, subtle change . . . it seems harder to make Caucasian friends . . . I can't help feeling that I am putting a wall deliberately between myself and others."[22]

Such feelings of powerlessness no doubt recurred as the dispersed elite graduated from college, moving on to job discrimination, dual wage scales for white males versus minorities and women, and further exclusionary policies set in their path, education and the good will of some Caucasians notwithstanding. Even so, the college Nisei also felt empowered as they advanced. Accepting an unfair challenge and proving themselves, through education, to be fully part of the nation at war with the nation of their grandparents, many of them gained an appreciation of the larger arena of contending forces that made the United States so paradoxical in its freedoms and tyrannies. The letters they wrote suggest another gain as well. Inasmuch as the college Nisei were leaders who saw themselves as clearing a path for others to follow, they recognized that part of their task was to create a shared understanding beyond themselves, a way of symbolizing to others the social faith that would turn tragic events into a future reconciliation. As one of them reflected in a long letter:

> When misfortune falls we tend to wallow in it, and completely ignore the forces working to counteract this situation; we concentrate on those who brought about the misfortune and forget those who under severe handicaps are fighting to ease and correct the misfortune; one suddenly realizes the gross injustice one has done to those who have kept faith and courage in the ideal he himself has given up for lost and useless. The ideal becomes more beautiful and real than ever because it is now devoid of its superficial members and we see it in its purer working forms. It becomes clearer than ever before and finally we grasp the inner meaning of such terms as "faith," "courage," and "democracy." The course of the past two years had been thus with me.[23]

It would be beautiful indeed if this were the whole story. But whatever hopes or fears the college Nisei might have had, were they not still the chosen few? By what means did their leadership come to be known in the camps? How did it fit into the drama of discontinuity there? Who responded to their ideals from within the dislocated community?

Life in the camps, it must be remembered, had a history of its own, marked by such high points as riots, work programs, strikes, shootings, loyalty tests, segregation of supposed "disloyals," the drafting of young men into the army, draft resistance, and a family resettlement program that met with resistance from Japanese Americans because they were wary of what might happen to them in the outside world. While some of the college Nisei wrote ecstatically about barbecues and pillow fights with their Caucasian peers, young Nisei in the camps were losing heart. By late 1943 the field director of the student relocation council was appalled by the contagion of "lose-fight" he encountered. Most disturbingly, the percentage of graduating high school seniors who were applying for leave clearance to attend college was declining as the war progressed. A Nisei poet in the camps found shadows gathering inside while others on the outside professed hope and promise:

> Oh—
> Is it only a vanished mirage
> That I though the land of the future—
> Hope, success, happiness, fulfillment of humanity?
>
> In the falling dusk—
> I hear discouraged, disillusioned voices—
> "Why is it wrong to be colored?"
> "We have served, and want to serve! Are we given no place in this land?"[24]

The educators and government administrators involved in student relocation had thought of ending the council in 1943, since by then it seemed to many that the path to college had been cleared. Obviously, a new problem had arisen, intensifying the need for active sponsorship of students, and thus, as it turned out, extending the life of the council for another three years. Now that the energies of the council were not needed so much for persuading colleges, communities, and all levels of government to make way for the Nisei students, the focus turned inward, into the camps, where it appeared to those on the outside that the younger generation was "thinking up reasons for staying put," perhaps even losing its will to live in the United States. Even worse, it was becoming evident to some advocates of Nisei educational interests that the schools inside the camps were contributing to the problem.[25]

Touring all ten camps in the summer of 1943, staff of the student relocation council learned that many Caucasian teachers were, despite the progressive rhetoric of their profession, advising Nisei students not to go to college. "Some of this hostility," observed the field director, "is born of race prejudice, particularly among the teachers who are attracted to the projects by the relatively high salaries paid by the Federal Government." But, he added, the lack of support for Nisei educational aspirations also arose from

> an attitude which the teachers describe to you as realism. They will tell you that it is a mistake for a Japanese American to think in terms of a college education since he is destined to be only a manual laborer anyway. They point out that if he goes to college and gets "high falutin" ideas about what he can do in life, it will only lead to unhappiness and disillusionment when he finds that the fields for which he trained are not open to him.

Such attitudes became an even more serious factor in 1944 when the college placement function of the student relocation council was absorbed by the counseling staff in the camp schools. This policy change meant that the council would henceforth engage only in supportive activities such as raising funds and coordinating communications. In that year the field director of the council discovered that students at Topaz were not able to take more than four academic subjects in school. By design, then, they were not being prepared adequately for college. One of the thirteen college Nisei who returned to the camps under the auspices of the council in the summer of 1944 said that the evacuated students "sensed a diabolical plot which had as its end the un-education of the Nisei, in the hope of having our mental processes compete with the Digger Indians of yore in excavating for a living."[26]

There were other reasons as well for the drop in college applications. Many students in the camps who could have gone to college refused to do so. If they were the oldest children in their families, they often felt a responsibility to care for the young and for their aged parents. An illness in the family was enough to keep many students in the camps, since the parents often depended on their children to communicate with authorities in the English language. Many boys preferred to wait and show their loyalty with derring-do instead of sitting in college classes. "Maybe after the war when Freedom comes, I might again ask you for advice," wrote one lad to the student relocation council as he enlisted in the army. More than 16,000 Nisei from the mainland United States served in the armed forces during World War II. Some Nisei males, however, refused both college and military service. From Heart Mountain, the camp in Wyoming where the draft sparked bitter and organized resistance, one student who spoke up probably reflected the attitude of others who remained silent:

> It is true that I applied for student relocation . . . but I did so under the influence of another man, and I was not sufficiently independent in my thinking. I had left college toward the end of my sophomore year because of a distaste for the methods and philosophical bases evident in the educational system in practice—and also because of a basic readjustment of my views wherein lay true service in life and wherein lay right and wrong.

Though girls were often preferred by colleges (they aroused less suspicion), many were discouraged by their parents from leaving camp for fear of what might happen to them in distant places. Other young people stayed in camp to help their families eventually resettle in outside communities instead of using scarce family resources for their own education. A smaller number merely awaited the end of the war and expatriation.[27]

The college Nisei who returned to camp ran into a wall of questions about the future, social life on the outside, reasons for the council's altruism, and a sense of foreboding that one interviewer summarized as follows: "I wonder if there's any use going to college in these kind of circumstances. Broken down: How will they treat you? Eats on the train? Call you a Jap? Stare at you: Cost a lot?"

Encountering resistance, one of the college-educated elite complained of students in the camps that "they do not see the whole problem of democracy, and therefore, cannot argue constructively, and when pressed, fall back onto the constitutionality of the evacuation as a basis for disbelief in America." There was also the issue of guilt for the college Nisei. To witness the lethargy of the "colonists" while they, the racial pioneers and ambassadors of good will, advanced to new occupations and a more normal life on the outside, was deeply disturbing, for it was "heartrending to think of the 100,000 others who should have the same opportunities I have, but who are instead being subjected to that environment of mass internment." One returning Nisei admitted that "defeatists in the Center have expressed their disapproval of my beliefs and I can feel the effect of their words digging into me."[28]

Hoping to expand family resettlement by creating a positive impression of the outside world, the camp administrators allowed the "returnees," as the college Nisei visiting the camps under official auspices were known, to circulate freely in the barracks and speak with parents as well as children. The reason for this belated liberality is to be found in the predicament of the government after it had built segregated camps for a racial minority. Once people have been excluded, dispossessed, concentrated together against their will, it is no easy task to disperse them with a second act of coercion. From the perspective of the government in 1944 and 1945, not enough evacuees were leaving the camps to resettle in American communities. The total population of all ten camps in January of each year went from 110,240 in 1943 to 96,576 in 1944 to 80,878 in 1945, even though there were few obstacles to obtaining leave clearance in the last two years of the war. The remaining population within the camps showed a higher and higher proportion of young and old people, as the most employable and educable left for opportunities outside. Thus, the complement to elite sponsorship for the few—the shadow of opportunity and dispersal—was an even greater concentration of those members of the evacuated population who, having lost the security of their pre-war ethnic communities, did not have the resources, the attitudes considered appropriate, or the will to master the channels of sponsorship that were available for reincorporating themselves into the world outside on favorable terms. Those of the college elite who returned to the camps, sponsored by the same Caucasians who had helped them to get out, now faced the concentrated community and tried to persuade its younger members that they should disperse themselves widely, as the vanguard had done, into niches that awaited them in places they had never seen. The records of the student relocation council suggest that the returning college Nisei were successful in making known their views and reaching many ambivalent high school students in the camps, but that they also encountered varieties of resistance that were deeply rooted in the crisis of the generations and not likely to be resolved through individual opportunities for exit and dispersal.[29]

Among school-aged Nisei who remained in the camps, one of the chief obstacles to higher education was parental objections. Knowing how much the parents supported the education of their children under normal conditions, the college Nisei who returned saw right away that this was a more complex problem than it had appeared from the outside. A torturous communication was taking place between the remaining Issei and Nisei in the camps. After experiencing the imposed authority and opportunity that had divided the generations in so many ways, those who still inhabited the camps by 1944 were, paradoxically, moved to consider what they had in common. Mirroring the drama of discontinuity, which was carrying the young from the inside to the outside world, was its exact complement, a drama of continuity, as the generations lived at close quarters in a coercive setting, drawing the attention of dispersing individuals back to their concentrated point of origin as a racial group. The demand of many Issei for family solidarity, even when they believed strongly in the value of education, became a way of negotiating the future on their own terms. The reports of the few college students who returned to the camps suggest that the Issei were demanding an awareness of collective needs as the college-bound Nisei pursued individual opportunities.

The students who returned came to see, therefore, that their role was not merely to persuade fellow Nisei to enter the channels of outside sponsorship so that they could leave the camps and attend college. Their role was also to serve as examples to the Issei, showing them that a settled life in America was again possible through the education of their children, that families would surely benefit from new opportunities in the post-war world. Returning students found that the prospect was not an outlandish one to the Issei if it was presented in the right way. "Parents will listen," concluded one who returned, "to children who show determination and initiative in their thoughts about education. It is the Niseis who waver like a pendulum or toss like corks in a sea who succumb to the objections of their parents." The educated Nisei, returning to the camps as children of character and accomplishment, exemplified the plausibility of the future to the older generation. They gave Japanese Americans who were inside the camps an occasion to speak directly with those who had ventured forth into the outside world and showed that it could be done.[30]

Certain subtleties in this message made the returnees convincing to many high school students and their parents in a way that educators, administrators, and social scientists in the camps could never be, no matter how altruistic their intentions. The written reflections of the college Nisei indicate that both assimilation and resistance were at play for those who sought higher education through the sponsorship of the student relocation council. The college Nisei had demonstrated through great effort that future success was not ruled out by present suffering in the camps. But they had also encountered shadows—isolation, fear of rejection, marginal status—that crisscrossed their social mobility. They were forced to acknowledge these shadows, even as they achieved greater acceptance than in the past. Theirs was, they believed, a path that many others would follow in the post-war world. And so it was, beginning with another important leadership group, Japanese American soldiers returning to the generous educational benefits of the G.I. Bill.

Watching the new generation on the rise, the Issei had mixed feelings about the opportunities of their children, a spectrum of emotions ranging from disgust to adulation. The legal isolation of the elders remained unchanged, reaching back to the permanent denial of citizenship or any right of naturalization that had conditioned their lives in the United States from the beginning. There is no shortage of evidence to reveal the tensions between old and young over the cultural consequences of assimilation. "I find myself stumbling over words," said one Nisei son, "as I make vain attempts to talk to my father. I don't understand him; he doesn't understand me. It is a strange feeling to have such a barrier between my father and myself." Yet, it also appears from the letters of the college Nisei that many Issei did enter into an unstated pact of reconciliation with their children, or at least one of tragic acceptance.

> My father is old, 78 years old, and he knew I would miss him greatly and that he may never be able to see me again. But as I left, he strengthened me with these words. "I am old, someday you will hear that I am dying, perhaps while you are still in school. Forget about me. Make my dying days happy in the knowledge that you are studying and preparing yourself for service. My life is in the past, yours is in the future."

Fathers who lived long enough to leave the camps at the end of the war often found that the niches their children attained in school and jobs became the new home of the family.[31]

One student, mindful that her family had come to the camp with little more than a suitcase each, having lost their home, their land, and most of their possessions, wrote that "the only place in the world for us is America." A momentous communication occurred among Japanese Americans during World War II. It was a threshing time of symbols for the future. The drama of discontinuity was magnified by official policies that concentrated and dispersed the group, and it was played out amidst the passing of cultural authority and community leadership from one generation to the next. Inasmuch as the college Nisei were a vanguard, a leadership group, they carried within them and transmitted to others a sense that this journey they were making outward from the concentrated community was the journey of their people. It was, as we have seen, a paradoxical vision, isolating those who believed in it and dispersing them, while those who were in doubt, who were not able to gain the sponsorship of Caucasians, or were frightened by what they saw, remained inside for a longer time. Meanwhile, both inside and outside the camps, young and old alike wanted more than anything to be home. This was the ground of human dignity that joined the experience of people who otherwise disagreed. But their home of the future was a pioneering venture, not a foregone conclusion. The college elite had realized that they must learn to speak to the majority to preserve the rights of the minority group. Many of their letters reflect a conviction that Japanese Americans must work in combination with others to construct a future society in which the security of their race would be guaranteed. A Nisei student wrote to one of his sponsors from Chicago, where he was studying: "If no one speaks, no one will ever know what an experience America passed through in using expediency instead of justice, and falling prey to fear instead of rising to understand. God grant that it never happens again, to any minority in this country!"[32]

Notes

1. Margaret Mead, "Our Educational Emphases in Primitive Perspective," *American Journal of Sociology* 48 (1943):633–39.

2. War Relocation Authority, *The Evacuated People: A Quantitative Description*, U.S. Department of the Interior, 1946, p. 4. Mead, "Our Educational Emphases," p. 638.

3. For the 1940 figures, see U.S. Bureau of the Census, *Historical Statistics of the United States*, Part I (Washington, D.C., 1975), p. 14. These figures are for the continental United States and do not include Hawaii. For a comparison with previous decades, see Roger Daniels, *Concentration Camps USA: Japanese Americans and World War II* (New York, 1972), p. 21. The figure for median age was computed by the Evacuation and Resettlement Study at the University of California; see Dorothy Swaine Thomas, *The Salvage* (Berkeley, 1952), p. 19.

4. The phrase "another Indian problem" appears in the weekly reports and field notes of the National Japanese American Student Relocation Council (NJASRC), Hoover Institution Archives, Stanford University.

5. Robert W. O'Brien, *The College Nisei* (Palo Alto, 1949). The organizational files of the NJASRC at Hoover were augmented in 1982–83 with files of John W. Nason, an NJASRC official and president of Swarthmore College, and the papers of Thomas Bodine, a Quaker who served as field director of the council. The Bodine papers include transcripts of hundreds of letters sent by Nisei students to NJASRC staff. A comparison between a sample of these transcripts and originals in the NJASRC organizational files, which are also at Hoover, shows the transcripts to be accurate, including grammatical errors. Since only a small percentage of the individual student files of NJASRC were saved in the Hoover collection of the organizational files, the Bodine papers are an invaluable source of Nisei views during the relocation from camp to college. The Bodine papers will be referred to as Bodine-Hoover in subsequent notes; the NJASRC organizational files will be referred to as NJASRC-Hoover Archives; and other NJASRC materials at Hoover but not in the archives will be known as Hoover Library. Archival restrictions do not allow use of individual names for the letters written by students, so the letters are identified by their dates for the Bodine-Hoover papers and by student identification number for NJASRC-Hoover Archives.

6. Margaret Cosgrave, "Relocation of Japanese American Students," *American Association of Collegiate Registrars Journal* 18 (1943):221–26; John H. Provinse, "Relocation of Japanese-American College Students." *Higher Education* 1 (16 April 1945):1–4; O'Brien, *College Nisei*, p. 34; War Relocation Authority (WRA). *Evacuated People*, pp. 95, 100, 81. For an overview of the work program and compensation, originally published by WRA, see Edward H. Spicer et al., *Impounded People: Japanese Americans in the Relocation Centers* (Tucson, Arizona, 1969), pp. 88–96.

7. George Sakata, University of Toledo, as quoted in "Nisei Students Speak for Themselves," *Junior College Journal* 14 (1943–44):246. Robbins Barstow, "Help for 'Nisei' Students," *Christian Century* 59 (1942):836.

8. "Bulletin No. 2. Student Relocation Committee, May 16, 1942," quoting a written statement by Monroe E. Deutsch, vice president and provost, University of California, Berkeley; in President's File, Bancroft Library, CU5 Box 588. University of California, Berkeley. Also relevant is the testimony provided by Deutsch and other university officials and faculty for the Tolan Committee, *Hearings*, Select Committee Investigating National Defense Migration. 77th Congress, 2nd Session (Washington, D.C., 1942).

9. Student letter, January 29, 1942. Bodine-Hoover.

10. Letter from John J. McCloy to Clarence E. Pickett, May 21, 1942. John W. Nason Collection, Box 1, Hoover Archives. Executive Committee Minutes and Staff Reports, NJASRC-Hoover Archives. For a description of meetings, organizations, and people involved in the formation of the NJASRC, see O'Brien, *College Nisei*, pp. 60–73.

11. Cosgrave. "Relocation of Japanese American Students." *Education for Victory* 1 (15 September 1942):2, 24. On funds raised for scholarships at Topaz, see *Newsletter* 6 (5 August 1943):2, in NJASRC-Hoover Archives. The newsletter was prepared by NJASRC staff for student counselors in the camps. Letter from Thomas Bodine to Joseph S. Daltry, May 24, 1942, Bodine-Hoover.

12. Student application forms, staff reports and memoranda, NJASRC-Hoover Archives and Bodine-Hoover. Cosgrave, "Relocation of Japanese American Students," *Education for Victory*, p. 2. Provinse, "Relocation," pp. 3–4. Also see official list of conditions for leave clearance in letter from John J. McCloy,

Assistant Secretary of War, to Dillon S. Myer, Director, War Relocation Authority, August 5, 1942, Japanese Evacuation and Resettlement Records, Bancroft Library 67/14 C1.08, University of California, Berkeley.

13. Notes and correspondence of the field director of NJASRC. Bodine-Hoover. Restrictions on movement and communication of NJASRC field staff were gradually relaxed later in the war at most of the camps.

14. Student letter from Smith College, 1942 (undated), Bodine-Hoover. "Japanese Evacuation Report #5," March 10, 1942. Bodine-Hoover.

15. The notion that Nisei leaders were cultural ambassadors bridging the gap between East and West had a history going back more than two decades before World War II. For a discussion of this background and the alternate visions of Nisei leadership before the war, see Jere Takahashi, "Japanese American Responses to Race Relations: The Formation of Nisei Perspectives," *Amerasia* 9 (Spring/Summer 1982):31–32 and *passim*. "New Pioneers for America," a play presented at commencement services, Amache High School, May 19, 1944, p. 18, Bodine-Hoover. Student letter, January 3, 1943, Bodine-Hoover. *Trek* 1 (February 1943):34, where the final quote appeared in an article from a student at Wellesley College, was a literary magazine produced by evacuees at Topaz, Utah. The word Nisei was not capitalized in the article.

16. Student letter, June 22, 1943, Bodine-Hoover. According to Section 60.4.21.A–C of the WRA Administrative Handbook, return to the camps by those who had been granted indefinite leave was allowed only with the permission of the authorities. Evacuees were encouraged not to return, but could reapply for residence if they could persuade a Relocation Officer that they could not keep outside employment. Visitors to the camps were required to give up their indefinite leave permits in order to enter. Although the permits were returned to them upon leaving, the procedure seemed unpleasantly akin to giving the authorities the power once again to determine conditions of exit.

17. Charles Wollenberg, *All Deliberate Speed: Segregation and Exclusion in California Schools, 1855–1975* (Berkeley, 1976), p. 51. On the affinity of Japanese Americans for education, see William Caudill and George DeVos, "Achievement, Culture and Personality: The Case of the Japanese Americans," *American Anthropologist* 58 (1956) 1102–26; Isao Horinouchi, *Educational Values and Preadaptation in the Acculturation of Japanese Americans*, Sacramento Anthropological Society, Paper No. 7, 1967; Audrey J. Schwartz. "The Culturally Advantaged: A Study of Japanese-American Pupils," *Sociology and Social Research* 55 (1971):341–353; Darrel Montero and Ronald Tsukashima, "Assimilation and Educational Achievement: The Case of the Second Generation Japanese American," *Sociological Quarterly* 18 (1977):490–503; Bob H. Suzuki, "Education and the Socialization of Asian Americans: A Revisionist Analysis of the 'Model Minority' Thesis," *Amerasia* 4 (Fall 1977):23–51; Ki-Taek Chun, "The Myth of Asian American Success and Its Educational Ramifications," *IRCD Bulletin* 15 (Winter/Spring 1980):1–11, published by the Institute for Urban and Minority Education, Teachers College, Columbia University.

18. Student letters, April 16, February 9, and January 21, 1943, Bodine-Hoover.

19. Gloria Kambara, "Nisei Students Speak for Themselves," *Junior College Journal* 14 (1943–44):251. On the idea of a "reprisal reserve" and the correspondence in which the phrase appeared, see Michi Weglyn, *Years of Infamy* (New York, 1976), pp. 54–56. *National Legionnaire* editorial quoted in its entirety by Rep. Paul W. Shafer of Michigan in the *Congressional Record*, 78th Congress, 1st Session, Vol. 89, Part 9, Appendix, p. A358.

20. Student quoted in *Newsletter* 6 (24 September 1943), Bodine-Hoover. Student letters, May 25 and 29, 1944, Bodine-Hoover.

21. Student quoted in letter to NJASRC, December 22, 1943, from psychologist working for American Friends Service Committee, Bodine-Hoover. Rhetorical question from letter of Nisei girl quoted in Otis D. Richardson. "Nisei Evacuees—Their Challenge to Education," *Junior College Journal* 13 (1942–43):10. Student letters, November 28, 1942, March 17, 1943, and March 31, 1943, Bodine-Hoover. For an example of black opinion toward the situation of Japanese Americans, see Harry Paxton Howard, "Americans in Concentration Camps," *Crisis* 49 (1942):283–84, 302. For additional perspectives on the attitudes of blacks toward racist propaganda during World War II see Delbert C. Miller, "Effect of the War Declaration on the National Morale of American College Students," *American Sociological Review* 7 (1942):631–44; Wallace Lee, "Should Negroes Discriminate Against Japanese?" *Negro Digest* 2 (September 1944):66, wherein a national poll of blacks found them strongly opposed to the discrimination taking place against Japanese Americans because "discrimination against the Japanese is based on color, much the same as prejudice against Negroes"; Gunnar Myrdal, *An American Dilemma* (New York, 1944), pp. 814–15; and Richard Polenberg, *One Nation Divisible: Class, Race, and Ethnicity in the United States Since 1938* (New York, 1980), pp. 72, 78–85.

22. Student letters, April 11–14 and March 12, 1943, Bodine-Hoover.
23. Student letter, October 24, 1943, Bodine-Hoover.
24. "Report of the Field Director, September 29, 1943," NJASRC-Hoover Library. Memorandum from Thomas Bodine to John W. Nason, November 7, 1943, Bodine-Hoover. Poem entitled "From the Dusk," two of twenty-three stanzas, student letter circa July 1942, Bodine-Hoover.
25. "Report of the Field Director, September 29, 1943."
26. Ibid. It should be noted that there were some teachers who strongly encouraged the educational aspirations of Japanese Americans. There were also some teachers and many assistants who were themselves Japanese Americans, but because they were working at a maximum of $19 per month alongside Caucasian teachers who were making many times as much, their lower status tended to confirm the view that opportunities were limited by race even as they worked hard to encourage Nisei students to seek advancement through education. Notes of NJASRC field director, 1944, Bodine-Hoover. Student letter. January 1, 1943, Bodine-Hoover.
27. Student letter, April 19, 1943, Bodine-Hoover. On the induction of Nisei into the armed forces during World War II, see *Special Groups,* Special Monograph No. 10, Vol. 1, Selective Service System (Washington, D.C., 1953), pp. 113–142; induction figures on pp. 141–42. Student letter, March 14, 1943, Bodine-Hoover.
28. Notes of NJASRC field director, 1944, Bodine-Hoover. Student letters, June 19, 1944, and October 6, 1942, "Final Composite Report of the Returnee College Leaders, Summer of 1944," NJASRC-Hoover Library.
29. WRA, *The Evacuated People,* p. 18; these figures include camp residents who were on short-term or seasonal leave (such as agricultural laborers) but who were still under the control of the War Relocation Authority. "Final Composite Report," NJASRC-Hoover Library. Returnee reports, Bodine-Hoover.
30. "Final Composite Report," NJASRC-Hoover Library. Also see Box 28, "Student Returnee Project" file, NJASRC-Hoover Archives.
31. The quote from the Nisei son is in a file on "Education—Commencement Addresses and Reports by Students," Poston Project Reports, Headquarters Files, Box 18, Record Group 210, National Archives, Washington, D.C. Student letter, May 19, 1944, Box 36, File 676, NJASRC-Hoover Archives.
32. Student letters, July 2, 1943 and January 19, 1944, Bodine-Hoover.

CHAPTER 5
RACE, MERITOCRACY, AND THE AMERICAN ACADEMY DURING THE IMMEDIATE POST–WORLD WAR II ERA

JAMES D. ANDERSON

This address concerns the initial integration of African American scholars into the American academy. It traces an interesting and unusual national campaign that first opened the doors of northern white universities to African American scholars. The primary focus is on what this campaign reveals about the interrelationship of race and meritocracy in mainstream American higher education during the immediate post–World War II period. It is also a story about a select pool of highly qualified African American scholars and their opportunities for employment at northern white universities. Finally, this is also a history of a particular process of institutional racism. One underlying purpose is to explore the usefulness of the social science concept of institutional racism for framing and explaining the formation and development of specific types of racial exclusion or discrimination in educational systems that operate with explicitly race-neutral or "color-blind" laws, procedures, and policies.

This is perhaps the most appropriate point at which to define institutional racism and note the controversy that has surrounded the concept since its invention in 1965. Institutional racism is a form of ethnic discrimination and exclusion through routine organizational policies and procedures that do not use ethnicity or color as the rationale for discrimination, but instead rely on nonracist rationales to effectively exclude members of ethnic minority groups. Some scholars have argued that the concept is of little value to social scientists and other scholars. Nathan Glazer, for example, contends that "institutional racism" is "obviously something devised in the absence of clear evidence of discrimination and prejudice." He views the emergence of the term as evidence "that racism pure and simple is less often found or expressed." The concept "institutional racism," however, was constructed to apprehend a process in which forms of overt discrimination against ethnic minorities are displaced from the level of race, color, or religion, to the level of merit, privilege, class, or other principles that appear to be above the bigotry of commonly practiced racism and ethnic prejudice. When such a process develops, one should not expect to discover racism pure and simple. One is more likely to find traditional patterns of discrimination couched in politely phrased objections. Such objections justify the exclusion of ethnic groups on such grounds as merit, the mission of the institution, professional standards, or convenience, but without the implication that exclusion carries any prejudiced or racially discriminatory intent.[1]

The historical questions involved in a study of institutional racism are similar in some respects to the legal questions. The question of discriminatory "effects" versus "intent" has dominated civil rights debates for several years. Lawyers for minority groups and women generally prefer to use a test of discrimination based on the effects of institutional and legislative behavior, rather than the intent of a particular individual or practice. Whereas one can offer substantial evidence to demonstrate the effects of ethnic or gender discrimination in areas as diverse as housing, employment, voting, and education, a discriminatory purpose is far more difficult to prove. Further, the emphasis on proving intent increases the burden of proof for those who charge discrimination. The standard of intent is a tremendously difficult, if not impossible, burden for individual litigants to meet in most cases. The United States Supreme Court itself has recognized the difficulty of trying to identify the intent of a body such as a university, school board, or legislature. Hence, the Court tends to operate with two standards. In school desegregation cases from the South, for example, the Court has focused on the effects, not the intent, of school board actions, holding that local authorities have a duty to dismantle dual school systems that resulted from legally mandated segregation as of 1954 (*Brown v. Board of Education*). In northern cases, where it is presumed that local governing bodies started with a clean slate as of 1954, the Court tends to hold that there is no violation of the Constitution without proof of discriminatory intent. Nevertheless, the discriminatory effects of school segregation exist independently of whether a superintendent or school board intended them. The challenge for historians is to demonstrate the effects of institutionalized discrimination and yet focus on the behavior of individuals within institutions in order to grasp how beliefs about race and ethnicity, coupled with other beliefs, influence the execution of standard policies and routine organizational behavior.

In 1940, for example, neither southern nor northern white universities had any African American scholars on regular academic appointments. There was no mystery as to why southern white universities had none. Racial discrimination in the South was overt, manifested in frequently hostile interactions between whites and blacks, and generally prescribed by law. Southern white universities proclaimed the virtues of white supremacy and acknowledged that African Americans were excluded by law and custom on the basis of "race." In northern white universities racial discrimination was customary, but it was not prescribed by law, and at least by World War II meritocratic principles specifically rejected race and ethnicity as criteria for determining the qualifications of scholars for faculty appointments. Nonetheless, in 1940, northern white universities were just as effective as southern white universities in excluding African American scholars from regular faculty appointments.

Whereas virtually all scholars would attribute the exclusion of African Americans from the faculties of southern white universities to racial segregation, many focus on nonracist causes to explain the absence of African Americans from northern white institutions. Some scholars allege that publishing requirements, as those established by Harvard University in the 1930s, operated effectively to restrict the appointment of African American scholars to northern white universities. They maintain that most African American scholars carried heavy teaching loads in historically black colleges which limited their time to write and thus left them poorly qualified for positions in northern white universities. Other scholars presume that "career characteristics" (i.e., the absence of Ph.D.s and research publications) and "choice" (i.e., the desire to teach in black colleges) account for the virtual exclusion of African American scholars from northern academia. The "separate and unequal" explanatory framework that accounts for many developments in southern education is not so easily applied to the northern context. Capturing the form and meaning of racial discrimination in northern white universities requires different conceptual frameworks. The concept of institutional racism modified for purposes of historical investigation may offer a different and useful angle of vision for understanding developments in northern higher education.[2]

Until 1941 no African American scholar, no matter how qualified, how many degrees he or she had earned, or how many excellent articles and books he or she had published, was hired in a permanent faculty position at any predominantly white university in America. The absence of African Americans from these positions reflected at least one form of racial discrimination that was common to both the North and South. A few African American scholars were hired to fill part-time positions, others to fill visiting faculty posts, and still others to hold nominal professorships. Yet none was hired in a regular faculty position. In 1941, Dr. Allison Davis, distinguished anthropologist, author, and lecturer, was hired as professor of education at the University of Chicago, becoming the first African American scholar of record to serve with full status in a predominantly white university in America. Some students of American higher education regard Julian H. Lewis, a research scientist who held a Ph.D. in pathology from the University of Chicago and an M.D. degree from Rush Medical College, as the first African American scholar to attain a "regular" academic appointment at a northern white university. Lewis received an appointment as "Associate Member" of medical research in the University of Chicago's Sprague Memorial Institute in 1915. He rose to instructor in 1917, assistant professor in

1922, and associate professor in 1931. Lewis, a pathologist at Provident Hospital in Chicago, was retained by the Sprague Memorial Institute to investigate pathology among black people in all countries. He acquired only a nominal appointment in the University of Chicago's Department of Pathology. All evidence points to Allison Davis's appointment in 1941 as the starting date for the employment of African American scholars in regular faculty positions at northern white universities.[3]

This study of the initial integration of African American scholars into northern white universities and what that process reveals about the interrelationship of race, meritocracy, and institutionalized discrimination is possible because of a unique campaign conducted by agents of the Julius Rosenwald Fund on the eve of World War II. In 1945, Fred G. Wale, the Fund's director of education, spearheaded a nationwide campaign to introduce a select group of distinguished African American scholars to the faculties of northern white universities. One of the many ironies of this campaign is that Wale was prompted to conduct it because of a request he received from the president of Black Mountain College, an all-white institution in North Carolina. The president of Black Mountain College requested names of African American scholars who might be interested in faculty positions at his institution. Beginning in the summer of 1945, Black Mountain College hired four African Americans as visiting faculty members. Percy Hayes Baker in biology and Carol Brice, Mark Fax, and Roland Hayes, all in music, taught at Black Mountain College between the spring of 1945 and the second semester of the 1945–46 academic year.[4]

"Some of us wondered," Wale later wrote, "why if a bi-racial faculty could be contemplated there, it could not be considered by every institution above the Mason-Dixon line." During the summer of 1945, he answered his own question by sending out a letter to "about six hundred college and university presidents," asking them if they would hire qualified applicants who happened to be African American. Wale drew up a list of approximately 150 African American scholars with outstanding qualifications and mailed it to the same presidents. He also included a list of African American scholars who, since January 1945, had received temporary or permanent appointments to northern white faculties where formerly no African American had been hired. The first replies to his inquiry came within two days, and over the next month responses were received from approximately one-third of the original list of 600 college and university presidents. About 400 of the original 600 never responded, and in Wale's view, their silence spoke for them. Approximately 200 presidents answered the second correspondence. Until 1947, when the organized campaign ended, extensive correspondence developed between Wale and the presidents over the question of why African American scholars were or were not considered for faculty positions at northern white universities. Meanwhile, Wale followed up his correspondence with a few personal contacts, and over the course of the two-year campaign, he wrote to, and received letters from, other university and college administrators and faculty. The record of this campaign—the correspondence between Wale and college administrators and faculty from Maine to Oregon—affords rare insights into the role of "race" in the American academy during the immediate post–World War II period.[5]

It seems clear that Wale's campaign to desegregate northern white faculties was motivated by his convictions that African American scholars were unfairly barred from employment because of race, that predominantly white institutions were depriving themselves and their students of a particular pool of well-educated personnel, and that faculty in general should be selected on the basis of intellectual merit. He also believed that meritocratic principles and procedures affirmed democratic values and eliminated traditionally racist and therefore antidemocratic values. As Wale put it: "Negroes have been denied admission to college faculties for about the same reason that many Jewish scholars have been, or that Japanese and Chinese Americans and occasionally Catholics have been. Too often, the college administrator, like many restaurant keepers, real-estate agents, and hospital trustees, has accepted the unchallenged way of our past. Consciously or unconsciously, he has never seriously considered a Negro as eligible for a faculty. If perchance he had, previous to 1940, he would have put the idea behind him as too controversial." Although he recognized that discrimination adversely affected many groups, Wale decided to conduct his campaign on behalf of African American scholars because, in his words, "Negroes more than any other people bear the brunt of discrimination." With such convictions in mind he proceeded to attack discrimination against

African American scholars, believing that his efforts would open the doors of academe to all qualified scholars irrespective of race, color, religion, and national origins.[6]

In Wale's view, there was no better time for his campaign than the eve of World War II. "With the Negro Marine, officer and private, fighting side by side with his white brother, with Navy ships manned by mixed crews, with Americans of all creeds standing side by side at the factory bench, it was no longer a daring thing . . . for a college to add a Negro to its staff," he contended. Further, the war had been fought against fascism in the name of democracy which made all forms of American racism and discrimination seem even more inhumane and irresponsible, and also hypocritical. The United States could no longer maintain a pervasive system of discrimination at home while playing the leader of democracy and the "free world" abroad. "American higher education will have to answer to the charge of a deliberate policy of door-slamming in the face of the qualified Negro," wrote Wale to President Ralph Cooper Hutchison of Washington and Jefferson College. "This charge can be for us as serious as some of those we bring against the enemies of democracy," he concluded. Moreover, Americans could not tolerate racial discrimination, said Wale, "lest in winning the war abroad, we lose in some measure the benefits of peace here at home." It would be wrong, Wale's letters generally concluded, "to appoint an unworthy person just because he was a Negro, but it would be equally wrong to turn down a worthy candidate because he was a Negro."[7]

There were other forces that made the post–World War II era an opportune time to press for the elimination of the color bar in academe. The short- and long-term enrollment trends indicated clearly the need for many new faculty members. From 1900 to 1940 American higher education enrollments increased 529 percent. During the same period the nation's total population increased only 73 percent, and the population of individuals aged 18 to 21 increased 63 percent. The G.I. Bill was largely responsible for another sharp increase in enrollment during the post–World War II era. In 1945, the total college enrollment was 1,676,851, among whom 88,000 of the 927,662 males were veterans. By 1946, the total college enrollment had jumped to 2,078,095, and of the 1,417,595 males, 1,013,000 were veterans. The nation's college enrollment increased sharply again in 1947. Then there were 2,338,226 college students; 1,659,249 were male, and 1,150,000 were veterans. Although the percentage of veterans in the total college enrollment began to decline after 1948, the total college enrollment itself continued to increase until 1950. The growth in college enrollments, created in part by the influx of veterans, significantly augmented the need for new faculty personnel. America, it seemed, needed all qualified scholars to staff its colleges and universities. A 1946 study of the demand for college professors found that 142,982 new faculty members were required to provide instruction for the minimum projected enrollment of 1,630,000 students. It seemed ideal, therefore, to launch the campaign to integrate African American scholars into northern white universities at a moment when there was a serious shortage of teaching personnel. Aside from other favorable circumstances, there was no reason to fear that white scholars, highly qualified or minimally qualified, would go jobless because colleges and universities hired African American scholars.[8]

Finally, there was yet another important reason that 1945 was a good year for Wale to initiate his campaign. For the first time in American history there was an emerging pool of African Americans with advanced degrees. In the six years preceding World War II, 30,000 African Americans were graduated from college and professional schools, as many as in the entire previous period of American history. By the mid-1940s there were approximately 3,000 African Americans holding master's degrees and more than 550 with Ph.D.s. One might expect virtually all of these Ph.D.s to seek academic posts in the historically black colleges, and undoubtedly most of them were needed in those institutions. However, traditional patterns of southern race relations and a renewed postwar campaign by African Americans for first-class citizenship combined to make working and living in the South increasingly unattractive. Nearly all African Americans with advanced degrees had attained them in either northern white universities or European universities. They had become accustomed to living in societies more open and democratic than southern society. Many African American scholars simply preferred to live and work in the North, while others, preferring to live in the South, refused to do so because of the repressive conditions of Jim Crow society.[9]

The manner in which Wale conducted his campaign had much to do with the kind and quality of responses generated over the course of two years. The first letter simply asked college and university presidents if they were willing to employ qualified African American scholars, and thus invited the presidents to state their principles regarding the question of employing African American scholars. When responding to this letter, the presidents and other college administrators were quick to affirm the merit system. "We have no negroes on the Bryn Mawr faculty at present," wrote President Katherine McBride, "but we should be glad to consider candidates on the same terms as any others." R. D. Hetzel of The Pennsylvania State University concurred: "In appointing members of the faculty we shall continue to try to select the best person irrespective of color, race, or religion."[10]

Virtually none of the respondents viewed the complete absence of African American scholars from their staffs as even suggestive of racially discriminatory hiring practices. "I assure you that the university has steadily sought to choose its faculty, and its students as well, solely on the basis of their qualifications and without regard to race, ancestry, religion, or color," wrote Monroe E. Deutsch, the acting president of the University of California at Berkeley. "It is true that we have no Negro on our faculty," Deutsch continued, "but I believe in all sincerity that there has been no prejudice against Negroes." Similarly, Alvin C. Eurich, president of Stanford University, said: "For each position we fill at Stanford we are concerned with the matter of appointing the most competent person we can find; we have placed no restrictions on race, creed, or color." Few presidents were more emphatic about the absence of race prejudice or affirmed the merit system more than Edward J. Scanlon of the Massachusetts State Teachers College at Westfield. "There is not now and never has been any discrimination against the employment of Negroes in any of our state teachers colleges, and should an opportunity arise they should be given the same consideration as any other candidate, the most qualified person being selected for the position," wrote Scanlon to Wale on 27 September 1945.[11]

Scanlon saw no contradiction between the fact that the state teachers colleges had never employed African American scholars and his claim that there never had been any discrimination against their being employed in faculty posts. President L. M. Gould of Carleton College in Northfield, Minnesota, held the same view: "One of the most cherished traditions of Carleton College is its genuine racial and religious tolerance," he wrote to Wale in December 1946. "We have no quotas here either among the students or the faculty. Protestants, Catholics, Jews, and Gentiles are part of both student and faculty groups." However, Gould continued, "It happens that we do not have any colored students at the moment, but this is merely a coincidence." Carleton also had no African American faculty members, and Gould made no effort to account for that condition, except to assure Wale that it was certainly not due to racial discrimination. Dean A. Chesley York of Calvin Coolidge College in Boston reported: "I do not at the present time, have any Negroes on our faculty [the incorrect inference being that he had employed some in the past], but this is not because of any design." Similarly, at the University of Rochester, according to President Alan Valentine, "Questions of race, color and other factors are largely irrelevant." President George D. Stoddard of the University of Illinois at Urbana, during a time when African American students were not permitted to live in the university's residence halls, assured Wale that "the appointment of competent Negro staff members would be considered without prejudice." Whether it was a small religious college in Iowa, a major state university in Pennsylvania, or a prestigious private university in California, throughout the northern states the presidents of colleges and universities maintained strongly that qualified scholars were not excluded because of race, color, religion, or national origins.[12]

Undoubtedly, there were many presidents who were unaware of the qualifications, availability, and aspirations of African American scholars. Since the door to northern white colleges and universities had always been closed to African American professors, they did not as a matter of course apply for positions in those institutions. Other presidents were probably aware of the acute shortage of Ph.D.s in the historically black colleges and might have assumed that African American scholars would naturally take positions in those institutions. However, Wale's follow-up correspondence clarified all such concerns and misperceptions. He included a long list of qualified African American scholars who had indicated a willingness to consider faculty positions in northern white universities. This second correspondence challenged the presidents' commitment to meritocratic principles in a much more direct manner. Prior to being presented with a list of qualified African American scholars, they could easily approach the question on an abstract level. Having received a list of highly qualified African American scholars, they were forced to make a more realistic appraisal of the relationship between race and merit in the academy. This appraisal began a long process of correspondence between Wale and various college and university presidents regarding the roles of race and merit in the hiring of faculty. Their responses reveal the peculiar manner in which practices of racial exclusion and meritocratic principles were merged to build a bridge across the contradictory creeds of equality and ethnic discrimination.

The Rosenwald Fund's list of African American scholars who were qualified for faculty posts at northern white colleges and universities was certainly impressive. Indeed, not one president questioned the qualifications of the black scholars on the Rosenwald list. The list included African American scholars in anthropology, art, biology, creative writing, drama, economics, education, history, home economics, language and literature, law, library science, mathematics, mechanical engineering, medicine, music, philosophy, photography, physics and chemistry, political science, psychology, religion, social service, sociology, and zoology. The main list was frequently supplemented by smaller lists in particular subject fields as the Fund discovered more and more African American scholars with each passing month. The scholars as a class were highly qualified to hold faculty posts in any American college or university. More than one-third of the African American scholars on Wale's list had received their Ph.D.s from the University of Chicago (20), Harvard University (15), Columbia University (10), the University of Michigan (6), or the University of Pennsylvania (5). Other institutions that had more than two Ph.D.s on the list were Yale University, Cornell University, the Massachusetts Institute of Technology, Radcliffe College, Brown University, Western Reserve University, and the University of Wisconsin. Wale had taken care to stock his list with African American Ph.D.s from the nation's most distinguished graduate schools. He understood that his mission required a list of applicants whose credentials could not be questioned.[13]

In physics, chemistry, and biology the list included Birtill A. Lloyd, James Raymond Lawson, James E. LuValle, Percy L. Julian, Thomas H. Bembry, Henry Aaron Hill, Kimuel Alonzo Huggins, Nathaniel Oglesby Calloway, Edward M. Chandler, Samuel Milton Nabrit, Percy Baker, Fred W. Alsup, and W. Montague Cobb. Lloyd, then employed at Picatinney Arsenal in Dover, New Jersey, received his Ph.D. in physical chemistry from the University of Illinois. Before moving north, he had taught physics and chemistry at Kentucky State College, a historically black college in Frankfurt, Kentucky. Lawson was head of the Department of Physics at Fisk University in Nashville, Tennessee. He received his Ph.D. in physics from the University of Michigan in 1939. By 1945 he had published several articles in the *Journal of Chemical Physics*. LuValle received his Ph.D. in physical chemistry from the California Institute of Technology in 1940. In 1945, he was a research chemist for Eastman Kodak Company in Rochester, New York. He had also taught at Fisk University in Nashville. Percy L. Julian was chief chemist in the Soya products division at Glidden Company in Chicago, Illinois. Having received his Ph.D. in organic chemistry from the University of Vienna in 1931, Julian had taught at Fisk University, West Virginia State College, and Howard University before taking his position with the Glidden Company. Thomas H. Bembry, a visiting instructor of chemistry at the College of the City of New York, had been head of the Department of Chemistry at Livingstone College, a black college in Salisbury, North Carolina. He received his Ph.D. in chemistry from Columbia University in 1942 and by 1945 had published several articles in the *Journal of the American Chemical Society*. Henry Aaron Hill had been employed for several years as a research chemist at Atlantic Research Associates in Newtonville, Massachusetts. He earned his Ph.D. in organic chemistry from the Massachusetts Institute of Technology in 1942. Kimuel Alonzo Huggins, a professor at Morehouse College in Atlanta, Georgia, received his Ph.D. in chemistry from the University of Chicago.

Nathaniel Oglesby Calloway's education was obtained at Iowa State College where he earned his bachelor's degree in science and his Ph.D. in chemistry. He had taught at Tuskegee Institute and Fisk University. He then completed training for an M.D. at the University of Chicago and the University of Illinois in Chicago. In March 1946, the Chicago *Defender* reported that "Dr. Calloway completed his medical training at the University of Illinois after he was forced to withdraw from the University of Chicago Medical School because he was a Negro." His internship and residency requirements were completed at the University of Illinois. Calloway reported in 1946 that he had published "approximately seventeen papers" and "four more are now in process." His research was in the fields of chemistry, pharmacology, and internal medicine. Another important chemist was Edward M. Chandler, who received his Ph.D. from the University of Illinois in 1917, becoming the second African American to earn a doctorate in chemistry. In 1945, Chandler was an assistant professor of chemistry at Roosevelt College in Chicago. Much of his research on triphenylmethane dyes, synthetic drugs, and pelleting characteristics of explosive powders was held confidential by industrial organizations and never published.

The biologists included Samuel Milton Nabrit, a Ph.D. from Brown University. In 1945, he was a professor of biology at Morehouse College. Percy Baker, an associate professor of biology at Virginia State College, earned his Ph.D. in biology from the University of Michigan. Fred W. Alsup was an instructor of zoology at Howard University in 1945. At that time he was studying medicine under the Army Specialized Training Program. Alsup studied at the Marine Biological Laboratory at Woods Hole, Massachusetts, before earning his Ph.D. from the University of Pennsylvania in 1941. W. Montague Cobb was one of the most accomplished African American biologists. A professor of anatomy in Howard University's School of Medicine, Cobb received his M.D. from Howard University and his Ph.D. in biology from Western Reserve University. Cobb was associate editor of the *American Journal of Physical Anthropology* and associate editor of the *Journal of the National Medical Association,* the official journal of the African American medical professional society.

David Blackwell headed the list of African American mathematicians. A Ph.D. from the University of Illinois at Urbana, Blackwell had studied at the Institute for Advanced Study at Princeton University. In 1945, he was professor of mathematics and physics at Southern University in Baton Rouge, Louisiana. He later became a member of the National Academy of Science. William W. Schieffelin Claytor, also a professor of mathematics at Southern University, received his Ph.D. from the University of Pennsylvania. Wade Ellis was a "special instructor" in mathematics at the University of Michigan where he received his Ph.D. in mathematics. He had taught at Fort Valley State College in Fort Valley, Georgia, and at Fisk University. J. Ernest Wilkins, an associate physicist in the Metallurgical Laboratory at the University of Chicago, earned his Ph.D. in mathematics from the University of Chicago. He had taught mathematics at Tuskegee Institute and published various papers in the *Duke Mathematical Journal, Annals of Mathematics, Bulletin of the American Mathematical Society, Annals of Mathematical Statistics,* and the *American Journal of Mathematics.*

By the 1940s there were scores of African American social scientists and historians who were eminently qualified to serve on the most distinguished faculties in northern colleges and universities. Moreover, it was not the case, as is sometimes argued, that African American social scientists and historians were not employed in northern white colleges and universities because of a shortage of such scholars, or because they were needed so greatly by black colleges. In 1947, three of the outstanding African American economists were employed by the United Nations Organization, the National Housing Authority, and the American Council on Race Relations. William H. Dean, a Ph.D. from Harvard in 1938, had graduated summa cum laude from Bowdoin College in 1930. While at Bowdoin, he also earned membership in the Phi Beta Kappa Society. Selections from his doctoral dissertation, "The Theory of the Geographical Location of Economic Activities," became assigned class reading at Harvard and Yale. The dissertation was published by Edward Brothers of Ann Arbor, Michigan, for the Harvard University Press in 1938. Dean taught at Atlanta University from 1942 to 1946 before becoming head of the Africa Area Unit in the Division of Economic Stability and Development of the United Nations in October 1946. Booker T. McGraw received his Ph.D. in economics from Harvard University in 1939. The title of his doctoral dissertation was "French Monetary Policy, 1927–1938." In 1947, McGraw, formerly a professor of economics at Lincoln University in Jefferson City, Missouri, was employed by the National Housing Authority as principal housing analyst. Robert C. Weaver, another Ph.D. from Harvard University, was executive director of the Chicago Mayor's Committee on Race Relations. Weaver completed his doctoral dissertation in 1934 on "The Wage Theory of Prosperity." He was employed by the American Council on Race Relations. Some other outstanding economists were Abram L. Harris, Brailsford R. Brazeal, and William J. Trent, Jr. Harris was widely known for his books *The Negro Capitalist* and the *Black Worker.* He received his Ph.D. in economics from Columbia University in 1931 and, in 1946, was professor and head of the Department of Economics at Howard University. Brazeal, chairman of the Department of Economics at Morehouse College, received his Ph.D. in economics from Columbia University in 1942. His dissertation, "The Origin and Development of the Brotherhood of Sleeping Car Porters," was later published as a book.[14]

There were a number of excellent African American sociologists in the country, among whom the best known were William Edward Burghardt DuBois, Allison Davis, Charles Spurgeon Johnson, E. Franklin Frazier, Ira De A. Reid, and Horace Roscoe Cayton. DuBois, at age seventy-six, was already past the normal retirement age, but was still very active as director of Special Research for the National Association for the Advancement of Colored People. By 1946, he had published more than ten books and hundreds of articles, editorials, reviews, and addresses in a variety of national journals, magazines, and newspapers. Having written a seminal study in sociology, *The Philadelphia Negro,* and in history, *Black Reconstruction,* DuBois continued to be one of America's most distinguished scholars. He might have served well as professor emeritus for any university.

Davis, Johnson, Frazier, and Cayton all studied sociology at the University of Chicago. In 1946, Johnson was president of Fisk University. He had published more than ten books, including *Shadow of the Plantation, Growing Up in the Black Belt,* and *Economic Status of the Negro.* Although Johnson did not have a doctoral degree, he was a member of the editorial board of the *American Sociological Review.* Horace Cayton was another sociologist who did graduate study at the University of Chicago but stopped short of writing his doctoral dissertation. However, Cayton co-authored the classic two-volume study, *Black Metropolis,* with St. Clair Drake, and thereby established himself as a very capable sociologist. In 1946, he was director of the Parkway Community House in Chicago.

E. Franklin Frazier was head of the Department of Sociology at Howard University. He received his Ph.D. in sociology from the University of Chicago in 1931. By 1946, he had published three books and numerous articles in sociology, education, and psychology journals. His research and writing on the history and sociology of the African American family were probably the best of his era. He later became president of the American Sociological Association. Reid, a professor of sociology at Atlanta University, earned his Ph.D. from Columbia University in 1939 and did one year of postdoctoral study at the London School of Economics. By 1945, he had published four books, several monographs, and many articles in social science journals. Allison Davis, assistant professor of education at the University of Chicago, received his Ph.D. in anthropology from that institution in 1942. His books, *Children of Bondage,* co-authored with John Dollard, and *The Deep South,* were excellent studies, as were his many other scholarly contributions in education and sociology journals. Other highly qualified anthropologists were Mark Hana Watkins (Ph.D. from Northwestern in 1945), and Lawrence Foster (Ph.D. from the University of Pennsylvania in 1931).

Ralph J. Bunche headed the list of African American political scientists. Bunche was employed by the State Department as an area specialist in the Office of Special Political Affairs. He received his Ph.D. in political science from Harvard University in 1934. The title of his doctoral dissertation was "French Administration in Togoland and Dahomeys." Bunche later won the Nobel Peace Prize for his diplomatic efforts in the Middle East. John A. Davis, Allison's brother, was also among the political scientists on Wale's list. He was just completing his doctoral dissertation in political science at Columbia University in 1946. Davis, then assistant professor of political science at Lincoln University in Pennsylvania, had been director of the Fair Employment Practice Committee's Division of Review and Analysis. He had written articles for several social science journals and was writing the last two chapters of his dissertation, "The Regional Organization of the Social Security Administration." Other excellent social scientists were sociologists Edward Nelson Palmer (Ph.D. from Michigan), Harry W. Roberts (Ph.D. from Yale), and Preston Valien (Ph.D. from the University of Wisconsin), and psychologist Kenneth Bancroft Clark, who received his Ph.D. from Columbia University.

Wale's list also contained an impressive selection of African American women social scientists. It included Merze Tate, Adelaide Cromwell Hill, Mamie Phipps Clark, Bonita H. Valien, Estella H. Scott, and Mabel Murphy Smythe. Merze Tate, an associate professor of political science at Howard University, completed her doctoral work at Radcliffe College in 1941. Her major field was international relations. She wrote her thesis on "The Movement for a Limitation of Armaments to 1907." Her books, *The Disarmament Illusion* and *American Disarmament Policies,* were significant contributions to the study of international relations. Adelaide Hill received her A.B. from Smith College,

A.M. from the University of Pennsylvania, and Ph.D. in sociology from Radcliffe College. Mamie Clark received her Ph.D. in psychology from Columbia University. Both Estella Scott and Bonita Valien earned their doctorates in sociology, Scott from the University of Pennsylvania and Valien from the University of Wisconsin. Mabel Smythe completed her doctorate in economics at the University of Wisconsin in 1942. She wrote her doctoral dissertation on "Tipping Occupations as a Problem in the Administration of Protective Labor Legislation."

The historians comprised a group of sterling quality. They included Rayford W. Logan, A. A. Taylor, Charles H. Wesley, and John Hope Franklin, all Harvard Ph.D.s who then held positions at Howard University, Fisk University, Wilberforce University, and North Carolina College for Negroes, respectively. The list of historians also included Lorenzo Johnston Greene (Ph.D. from Columbia University), Luther Porter Jackson (Ph.D. from the University of Chicago), Eric Williams (Ph.D. from Oxford University), and Benjamin A. Quarles (Ph.D. from the University of Wisconsin). This was a group of unusually talented and well-published historians. Many of their scholarly works became standard-bearers in American history.

In the fields of creative writing, philosophy, literature, and religion there were such eminent scholars as Sterling A. Brown, Shirley Graham (DuBois), Langston Hughes, Lawrence D. Reddick, J. Saunders Redding, Margaret A. Walker, Richard Wright, Alain L. Locke, Lorenzo D. Turner, Benjamin E. Mays, Harry V. Richardson, and Leon Edward Wright.

All of the scholars on Wale's list were highly qualified to hold faculty posts in the most outstanding American colleges and universities. As a class they were well published even by today's standards and were far ahead of the standards of their own time. Although Harvard University in the 1930s set up a variety of publishing and research criteria for tenure, such requirements did not really take hold in many American colleges and universities until some years later. In many major universities faculty were still being tenured through the early 1960s primarily on the strength of their teaching record. Research and publishing requirements, however, would have worked in favor of the African American scholars on Wale's list, for virtually all of them had excellent records of research and publication.

In the face of this talented pool of African American scholars, the presidents affirmed their belief in meritocratic principles and hiring procedures, and then searched for reasons unrelated to race to account for the long-standing exclusion of such outstanding African American scholars from their colleges and universities. The door had never been closed to black scholars, asserted Robert G. Sproul, president of the multi-campus University of California. He offered proof as to the absence of "group" prejudice on the Berkeley campus. "To the best of my knowledge there is no group prejudice against Negroes on the staff at this University. We have employed a Negro for a part-time coaching position with the football team for many years," wrote Sproul to Wale. Sproul meant to imply that any university that would integrate its football staff, even with a part-time coach, would not tolerate racial bias in selecting its faculty. After some encouragement by Wale, officials at Berkeley decided to experiment with the appointment of an African American lecturer. Provost C. A. Dykstra, while ignoring the scholars on Wale's list, informed Wale that "We might get for a try-out one of our own graduates who is now with the Department of State." On 24 August 1946, the *Los Angeles Times* reported that "one of the few Negroes holding a master's degree in engineering, Joseph T. Geir, of East Oakland, was last week named to the faculty of the University of California at Berkeley as a lecturer in electrical engineering." Geir, who received his master's degree at Berkeley, was employed by the testing bureau of California's Automobile Association and had just formed an electrical engineering company with two of his fellow alumni. Fred G. Wale, having read the *Times* article, wrote to Sproul for information about Geir's background. Sproul maintained his posture of color-blindness. "I was not personally aware of the fact that Mr. Geir is of Negro blood."[15]

Throughout the North the presidents of colleges and universities maintained strongly that in selecting faculty there was no discrimination on the basis of race, color, religion, or national origins. There were virtually no exceptions to this pattern of self-denial, and even the complete absence of African American scholars from their faculties did little to shake their faith in the mythical color-blind meritocracy. They could always point to what they believed to be nonracist rationales for the exclusion of African American scholars.[16]

Some presidents reported that they had considered the exclusion of African American scholars from northern colleges and universities a matter of grave importance for many years, but as yet had taken no positive action. President Clair S. Wrightman of the State Teachers College at Paterson, New Jersey, said to Wale: "For ten years I have been hopeful that a Negro with outstanding ability would apply to me for a position, but we have not had one application from a Negro in the ten years that I have served as president." "I have wavered much about the desirability of recommending a Negro for an instructorship at our college," he wrote to Wale in June 1945. Ultimately, he decided against recommending an African American for an instructorship at his college. During one year, however, Wrightman "considered the desirability of offering a clerical position to a Negro." He felt relieved of acting when "the Negro clergyman in town had no one available for us." Moreover, "my Negro friends" have "cautioned me to go slowly about the matter." Hence, Wrightman could see himself as not violating the meritocratic principles in which he believed so dearly; he was merely following the advice of his "Negro friends," and, in his view, no one could fault him for that.[17]

Sometimes personal interviews revealed the fundamental conflict between meritocratic beliefs and racial attitudes. In June 1945, Virginia E. Gildersleeve, dean of Barnard College, wrote to Wale virtually boasting of her commitment to a racially neutral hiring policy: "We have at this institution no rule or policy preventing us from engaging a Negro to teach, and we should be happy to consider suitable candidates in connection with any vacancy." Wale was so encouraged by the response that he went to Barnard College for a conference with Dean Gildersleeve. He soon realized that she, too, was, wittingly or unwittingly, engaged in meritocratic rhetoric which camouflaged traditional institutionalized practices of racial discrimination and exclusion. As Wale recorded, "to put it mildly, I was quite disappointed in the outcome." Wale had learned to expect some resistance to hiring African American scholars, but not as much as he encountered with Gildersleeve. During the interview, Dean Gildersleeve said that she was very much interested in the attitude of people who occasionally came to her and asked, "How many Negro students do you have at Barnard?" To such a question she always replied, "Frankly, I do not know, and frankly, what is a Negro?" Later in the interview Wale asked her how many "Negro" students were enrolled at Barnard, "and without smiling, she said, 'eight or nine.' " Dean Gildersleeve, as so many of her colleagues across America, was strongly committed to meritocratic principles and, as her colleagues, held this commitment with a religiosity that was disconnected from practice. Indeed, this commitment constructed a defense against the practice of equality of opportunity. When Wale discussed the idea of Barnard hiring African American scholars, he found "a defensive, rather than a sympathetic, national and international figure."[18]

Several presidents reconciled the practice of racial exclusion with their beliefs in meritocracy by attributing the reality of ethnic exclusion to factors they perceived as unrelated to ethnicity, such as geography and population. President John C. West of the University of North Dakota replied: "The University of North Dakota is so far North, being the most northern university in the United States I think, that we have no colored students neither do we have colored members of the faculty. This is due to geographical location rather than to any prejudice one way or the other." President A. L. Strand of Oregon State College in Corvallis, Oregon, could easily agree that Wale's list of African American academicians was one of "outstanding artists and scholars." Still, in Strand's view, they were inappropriate for his university. "It seems to me," he wrote, "that it would be less difficult to gain acceptance for Negroes on the staff in states where Negroes comprised a higher percentage of the population than has been the case in Oregon." President William A. Shimer of Marietta College in Ohio argued that although he did not discriminate against people because of their race, he was convinced that African American scholars "would be happier in certain other institutions where they would have Negro companions." Toward that end, it was for their own happiness that Shimer kept them out of Marietta. Instead of facing squarely the ugly reality of racial discrimination, Shimer found a way to avoid that confrontation by focusing on the positive belief that he was actually helping African American scholars by not bringing them into a racially isolated environment. Benjamin E. Schwartz, chancellor of Nebraska Wesleyan University in Lincoln, Nebraska, informed

Wale that at various times his institution had as many as five Negro students enrolled. "However, we have not as yet had any Negroes on the college faculty. I doubt whether this would be advisable under present conditions," Schwartz concluded. He did not explain what those "conditions" were.[19]

Some responses foreshadowed contemporary arguments against affirmative action. President Herbert G. Espy of the State Teachers College at Geneseo, New York, replied: "I do not know whether they [department heads] will feel that the educational needs of our students now warrant our making any special effort to employ Negro teachers or to discriminate against white applicants." Wale was surprised at Espy's suggestion that his requests for presidents to consider African American scholars for faculty posts constituted discrimination against white scholars. "I had not felt before," responded Wale to Espy, "that the consideration of a Negro applicant was to discriminate against a fellow white applicant." Espy remained convinced, however, that it was "some degree of discrimination against white applicants if I made in behalf of colored applicants certain special efforts not made in behalf of white applicants." Instead of responding to Wale's call for northern white colleges to broaden their faculty memberships to include African Americans, Espy evaded the issue by arguing that such considerations amounted to reverse discrimination against white scholars. This particular response to demands by African American scholars for equality of opportunity in higher education would find its greatest use during the early 1970s and beyond. Yet, like so many other dimensions of the meritocratic defense of racial discrimination, it too was honed during the post–World War II era.[20]

There were, of course, many ways to evade the question of considering African American scholars for faculty posts in northern white institutions. About a third of the replies were bare acknowledgements. Presidents wrote to Wale thanking him for the lists of African American scholars and promising that they would give the matter due consideration, as one president stated, "should the problem ever arise." Such was the response of Thomas S. Gates, chairman of the University of Pennsylvania: "I will be glad to keep in mind the file of information you have on American Negro scholarship and to call upon you if any need to explore it should arise." Some presidents gave more detailed reasons for not having African American faculty. Occasionally one or two were quite straightforward. President Clarence E. Josephson of Heidelberg College in Tiffin, Ohio, said, "Our college is not ready for it quite yet." However, the most dismal aspect of the whole campaign was that 400 presidents failed to reply to Wale's letter. This fact, together with the overall thrust of the respondents' answers, added up to one unmistakable total: there was virtually no opportunity for highly qualified African American scholars in northern white colleges and universities at midcentury.[21]

The evidence proves conclusively that the respondents held two basic and contradictory positions. The presidents in general simply did not want to appoint African American scholars to their faculties, even at a time when there was a great shortage of qualified scholars. Yet, they were strongly committed in principle to the idea that the best scholar should get the faculty post without regard to race, religion, color, or national origins. Wale's campaign forced the presidents to grapple with the fundamental contradiction between their philosophy of meritocracy and their practice of ethnic discrimination. None of them chose to sidestep the issue by arguing that the African American scholars on Wale's list were unqualified to hold regular faculty posts in their universities and colleges. Wale had selected a list of scholars with virtually impeccable credentials, all of them being trained at America's most outstanding universities. There was simply no way that college and university presidents could challenge the academic qualifications of these scholars. This is probably why 400 presidents chose the easy way out by refusing to reply. The respondents were forced to rely on the most specious arguments.

One approach to reconcile meritocratic principles with traditional patterns of racial discrimination was threefold: first, affirm one's commitment to a color-blind hiring policy; second, ignore the request to hire African American scholars; and third, focus on what was being done for African Americans in nonacademic areas. A. D. Henderson of Antioch College in Yellow Springs, Ohio, informed Wale that his college had no policy or practice against hiring African American scholars. "We, too, believe that no candidate should be turned down because he is a Negro, and we are anxious to bring about natural inter-racial situations wherever possible. President Henderson then proceeded to enlighten Wale about the college's track record in hiring African American staff in other areas:

> The man who trains many of our students at the Antioch College Dining Hall is a Negro, and he has been given the equivalent status of instructor by our Administrative Council because of his counseling work. The secretary to our librarian is a Negro. We have other Negro members on our office staff. . . . We have Negro students and are continually looking for outstanding young Negroes who would be interested in our program of education. We have brought in a number of Negro lecturers to the college on our assembly program.

Since Wale was compiling a list of all African American scholars employed in northern white colleges and universities, he wrote to Henderson requesting the official title of the person who had been accorded the status of instructor. Henderson replied with the following description: "The Negro person who is on our faculty in full-time employment is Mr. Kenneth Hamilton, whose title is listed in our Catalogue as *Service Manager, Tea Room*." "In this Capacity," Henderson continued, "Mr. Hamilton trains and supervises our students who work in the tea room as waiters, waitresses, kitchen workers and so on." To President Henderson, these developments were solid evidence that Antioch operated a colorblind hiring policy. Likewise, President James P. Baxter of Williams College informed Wale: "There are no colored men teaching at Williams College, but we have just engaged William Morgan, a colored veteran who will graduate tomorrow, as an assistant in the college library." Apparently, the geographical, population, and other circumstances that allegedly worked against hiring African Americans as professors did not preclude their employment as library assistants and service managers in tea rooms.[22]

Many college and university presidents were quick to point to the uniqueness of their institutions as legitimate reason for having no African American faculty members. The Very Reverend Msgr. Carl J. Ryan of The Teachers College Athenaeum of Ohio, a Catholic college in Cincinnati, pointed out that his school was run primarily for the education of Sisters for Catholic parochial schools. Although the school had enrolled African American students "at various times," Ryan was convinced that "the time is somewhat distant when we shall have either Negro priests or Sisters qualified for a position on the faculty." John C. Baker, president of Ohio University in Athens, Ohio, argued that his institution's commitment to take back many faculty members, then on leave with the military, precluded the employment of any new scholars.[23]

President Russell D. Cole of Cornell College in Mount Vernon, Iowa, thought that the size of his college accounted for the fact that he had no African American scholars and for the reason that he should make no attempt to appoint any. Said Cole to Wale: "Your suggestion as to Negro faculty members comes as a new idea, for I had not thought of such men on a small college faculty." Wale responded with a cryptic observation. "I do not believe size is necessarily a factor, willingness and readiness are greater determinants." He also informed Cole that Olivet College in Michigan and William Penn College in Oskaloosa, Iowa, had recently appointed African Americans to full-time permanent faculty positions. Cole, however, was not persuaded to follow the examples of Olivet and William Penn colleges. Harvey L. Turner, president of Hillsdale College in Hillsdale, Michigan, was very favorably impressed with the qualifications of Wale's list of African American scholars. "I must admit," he conceded, "that the list that you have submitted indicates candidates with excellent qualifications." Nonetheless, Turner argued that the size of his institution precluded hiring African American scholars and thus, from his vantage point, he had legitimate reasons not to hire anyone from Wale's list. As he put it:

> I appreciate the fact that you are promoting a worthy cause, but I must confess that it would seem to me eminently unwise for a college as small as Hillsdale, located in a community of our type, to consider at this time the employment of a negro staff member. This is not because we differentiate against the negro race as such but because our student body consists almost entirely of white students. In fact, we had only one negro student enrolled during the past year. Our community likewise has a population of only 7,500, and there is only one negro family in the community. Therefore, it would seem to me unreasonable to expect Hillsdale College to employ a negro staff member at this time.[24]

President W. C. Giersbach of Pacific University in Forrest Grove, Oregon, also assured Wale that his school "had no written or unwritten rules concerning the employment of colored folk." In Giersbach's words, "our usual question leads to the matter of whether or not they are well trained, whether they can teach and whether they are in sympathy with the thinking and acting of a liberal Christian institution." However, according to Giersbach, there was a problem. "The problem is one of community reaction to the employment of people who are Chinese, Japanese, Jewish or Negro," he explained to Wale. Such rationales shifted the burden of racial and ethnic exclusion or discrimination from the university to the community. Such rationales enabled college and university presidents to convince themselves, and attempt to convince others, of their firm commitment to fair and equitable principles while continuing to close the academic door to scholars from particular ethnic groups.[25]

A small number of college presidents were encouraged by Wale's campaign, and they took affirmative steps to pursue the scholars on his lists. Dean Arthur J. Mekeel of William Penn College informed Wale that he was searching diligently for a professor in the fields of biology and chemistry. By September 1945, William Penn College hired Madeline Clarke Foreman as a professor of biology; she was one of the scholars from Wale's list. In October 1945, President Cecil E. Henshaw reported: "Mrs Foreman is working out very well at the college and there seems to be universal appreciation of her among the students and faculty." However, he added, "A few local people are disturbed by the action which we have taken and it has cost us some in students and local financial support." Mearl P. Culver of Southwestern College in Winfield, Kansas, gave the following response: "The purpose of this letter is to advise that I am interested in the possibility of placing a negro on the faculty of Southwestern College, or at least investigating the possibility of the same." Likewise, Arthur W. Calhoun, dean of the faculty at Sterling College in Sterling, Kansas, said: "You may put me on the list of those interested in placing Negro teachers in college positions." Between the summer of 1945 and the beginning of the 1946–47 academic year, twenty-three African American scholars from Wale's list received permanent faculty positions in northern white universities, and another twenty-seven earned temporary appointments. Roosevelt College in Chicago set the pace by appointing four African American scholars to permanent positions. Edward Chandler (chemistry), St. Clair Drake (sociology), Alyce Graham (psychometry), and Lorenzo Turner (English) were all teaching at Roosevelt by the fall term of 1946. The actions of the presidents at these institutions contrasted sharply with those who defended the status quo. Their behavior demonstrates that not all college leaders synthesized racial discrimination with meritocracy. Nonetheless, they formed a distinct minority and, despite their efforts, could not change the prevailing ethic that merged ethnic discrimination and meritocracy into a single objective.[26]

Usually meritocracy is viewed as the antithesis of racism, ethnic and religious prejudice, and related forms of exclusion and discrimination. The beliefs and behavior of the overwhelming majority of northern white college and university presidents, however, tell a radically different story about the relationship between race and meritocracy as it evolved in the American academy during the post–World War II era. The practice of proclaiming one's devotion to meritocratic principles, while actually perpetuating traditional patterns of ethnic discrimination and exclusion, transformed theoretical enemies (i.e., racism vs. meritocracy) into pragmatic friends. Meritocracy became the fragile bridge across the intolerable contradictions between equality and racism. Indeed, the presidents of northern white universities resorted to meritocratic principles as their most ardent defense of traditional racial and ethnic discrimination. In this marriage between racism and meritocracy, nonracist rationales meant not only a defense of the traditional exclusion of African American scholars from northern white universities, they defined that tradition of exclusion as the consequence of fair and equitable principles and procedures. Over time there developed in the American academy an ethic which held that African American scholars were justifiably excluded from faculty positions because somehow there was always a mismatch between their circumstances and the particular needs of the white-dominated academy. Instead of viewing racial and ethnic exclusion as the antithesis of merit, the presidents found a way out of this uncomfortable confrontation by constructing a set of rationales that effectively defined African American scholars as the antithesis of merit. To be sure, their definitions of merit extended beyond strict academic achievement. They included "institutional needs," "geography," "population," and "local community attitudes," and other criteria that were used to justify the exclusion of African American scholars on "merit" grounds. Thus, they could hold on to their faith in meritocracy while excluding African American scholars from faculty positions in their institutions.

This peculiar marriage between race and meritocracy in the academy has survived through stormy times and remains a problem in our contemporary institutions of higher education. The post–World War II rationales that justified the exclusion of African American scholars from the academy and thereby defined them as the antithesis of merit, placed on African American scholars a badge of inferiority that continues into our own present. Even in today's environment, the question of hiring African American scholars at traditionally white universities is invariably followed by the question of "qualification" or "merit." African American scholars are often suspicious of the process in which their quest for integration is surrounded by an exacerbated debate of meritocratic principles and a strong emphasis on hiring only "qualified blacks." One cannot help but be reminded of the post–World War II era when the presidents of white colleges and universities employed meritocratic principles to shield the widespread and deep-seated resistance to the presence of African American scholars in the academy.

Notes

1. Joe R. Feagin and Clairece Booher Feagin, *Discrimination American Style: Institutional Racism and Sexism* (Malabar, Fla., 1978); Nathan Glazer, *Affirmative Discrimination: Ethnic Inequality and Public Policy* (New York, 1975), 69.

2. Glazer, *Affirmative Discrimination,* 69.

3. Jessie P. Guzman, "Persons Appointed to Positions in White Institutions of Higher Learning," *Negro Year Book,* ed. Guzman (Tuskegee, Ala., 1947), 16–18; University of Chicago, *Annual Register: 1917* (Chicago, 1917), 59; NAACP, "Negro Higher Education in 1921–22," *Crisis* 24 (June 1922): 108.

4. Fred G. Wale to Leon W. Scott, 14 Feb. 1946, and Wale to James H. M. Henderson, 24 Jan. 1946, folder 2, box 308, Julius Rosenwald Fund Papers, Special Collections, Fisk University Archives, Nashville, Tenn. (hereafter cited as JRF Papers).

5. Wale to Josephine Glasgow, 21 Nov. 1945, folder 2, box 308, JRF Papers; Fred G. Wale, "Chosen for Ability," *Atlantic Monthly* 180 (July 1947): 81–84.

6. Wale, "Chosen for Ability," 81–84.

7. Ibid., 83; Wale to Ralph Cooper Hutchison, 17 Sep. 1945, and Wale to Nicholas Murray Butler, 11 June 1945, folder 2, box 309, JRF Papers.

8. Keith W. Olson, *The G.I. Bill, the Veterans, and the Colleges* (Lexington, Ky., 1974), 44; John Dale Russell, ed., *Problems of Faculty Personnel,* in *Proceedings of the Institute for Administrative Officers of Higher Institutions* (Chicago, 1946), 18: 6.

9. Harry Washington Greene, *Holders of Doctorates among American Negroes: An Educational and Social Study of Negroes Who Have Earned Doctoral Degrees in Course, 1876–1943* (Boston, 1946).

10. Wale, "Chosen for Ability," 82; Wale to Butler, 11 June 1945, Wale to Hutchison, 17 Sep. 1945, Katherine McBride to Wale, 2 Jan. 1947, and R. D. Hetzel to Wale, 3 July 1945, folders 2, 4, boxes 308, 309, JRF Papers.

11. Monroe E. Deutsch to Wale, 19 June 1945, and Edward J. Scanlon to Wale, 27 Sep. 1945, folders 2, 4, box 308, JRF Papers.

12. Scanlon to Wale, 27 Sep. 1945, L. M. Gould to Wale, 25 Dec. 1946, A. Chesley York to Wale, 20 June 1945, Hetzel to Wale, 3 July 1945, Alan Valentine to Wale, 21 June 1945, and George D. Stoddard to Wale, 20 Jan. 1947, folders 2, 8, 13, 15, 20, boxes 308, 309, JRF Papers.

13. For the selected list of African American scholars, see list in box 308 or 309, JRF Papers.

14. Thomas Sowell contends that historically most black academics preferred to remain in black colleges because of choice and because their career characteristics did not match the research publication requirements of major research universities. These factors, however valid, would not account for the African American scholars on Wale's list. Thomas Sowell, *Education: Assumptions versus History* (Stanford, Calif., 1986), 77–78.

15. Alvin C. Eurich to Wale, 19 June 1945, Deutsch to Wale, 19 June 1945, Robert G. Sproul to Wale, 20 June 1945, and C. A. Dykstra to Wale, 20 June 1945, folder 4, box 308, JRF Papers; *Los Angeles Times,* 24 Aug. 1946.

16. Scanlon to Wale, 27 Sep. 1945, Gould to Wale, 25 Dec. 1946, York to Wale, 20 June 1945, Hetzel to Wale, 3 July 1945, and Valentine to Wale, 21 June 1945, folders 2, 13, 15, 20, boxes 308, 309, JRF Papers.

17. Clair S. Wrightman to Wale, 24 Dec. 1946, and Wrightman to Wale, 21 June 1945, folder 19, box 308, JRF Papers.

18. Virginia E. Gildersleeve to Wale, 28 June 1945, "Negroes on Northern College Faculties," 16 Oct. 1946, record of interviews with President Horvde of the New School for Social Research, Professor Counts of Teachers College, and Dean Gildersleeve, folders 2, 20, box 308, JRF Papers.

19. John C. West to Wale, 28 June 1945, A. L. Strand to Wale, 25 June 1945, Harvey L. Turner to Wale, 23 June 1945, Turner to Wale, 18 Sep. 1945, Turner to Wale, 28 Dec. 1946, Russell D. Cole to Wale, 14 June 1945, William A. Shimer to Wale, 5 Oct. 1945, and Benjamin F. Schwartz to Wale, 16 June 1946, folders 1, 10, 14, 17, 22, 23, boxes 308, 309, JRF Papers.

20. Herbert G. Espy to Wale, 31 Dec. 1946, Wale to Espy, 17 Jan. 1947, and Espy to Wale, 24 Jan. 1947, folder 20, box 308, JRF Papers.

21. Thomas S. Gates to Wale, 21 June 1945, and Clarence E. Josephson to Wale, 23 June 1945, folders 2, 23, boxes 308, 309, JRF Papers.

22. A. D. Henderson to Wale, 25 June 1945, Henderson to Wale, 10 Dec. 1945, and James P. Baxter to Wale, 6 Feb. 1947, folders 13, 23, box 308, JRF Papers.

23. Very Rev. Msgr. Carl J. Ryan to Wale, 21 June 1945, and John C. Baker to Wale, 9 July 1945, folders 9, 23, boxes 294, 308, JRF Papers.

24. Russell D. Cole to Wale, 14 June 1945, Wale to Cole, 17 Sep. 1945, Wale to Cole, 20 Sep. 1945, Turner to Wale, 23 June 1945, Turner to Wale, 18 Sep. 1945, and Turner to Wale, 28 Dec. 1946, folders 23, 14, boxes 294, 308, JRF Papers.

25. W. C. Giersbach to Wale, 5 July 1945, folder 1, box 308, JRF Papers.

26. Arthur J. Mekeel to Wale, 14 June 1945, Cecil E. Henshaw to Wale, 4 Oct. 1945, Mearl P. Culver to Wale, 20 Dec. 1946, and Arthur W. Calhoun to Wale, 11 July 1947, folders 10, 11, box 308, JRF Papers.

CHAPTER 6

SCYLLA AND CHARYBDIS: NAVIGATING THE WATERS OF ACADEMIC FREEDOM AT FISK UNIVERSITY DURING CHARLES S. JOHNSON'S ADMINISTRATION 1946–1956

MARYBETH GASMAN

A prominent sociologist and race relations activist, Charles S. Johnson dedicated his life to the advancement of Blacks. His presidency at Fisk University, a historically Black college, was the culmination of his career. During the latter part of his administration, he faced a dilemma involving an outspoken professor named Lee Lorch, who, in 1954, was accused of being a communist. Johnson and the Board of Trustees dismissed Lorch because he refused to answer a congressional committee's questions about his previous political affiliations. In 1959, the American Association of University Professors found the late President Johnson guilty of violating the principles of academic freedom. This chapter explores the ways in which academic freedom, civil liberties, and civil rights clashed in the Lee Lorch case. Furthermore, it examines the ways in which the setting of a historically Black college alters traditional assumptions about the application of these principles.

In a decision overturning an Oklahoma law requiring instructors to swear that they were not members of a subversive or communist organization, Justice Felix Frankfurter wrote:

> [Instructors] . . . must be exemplars of open-mindedness and free inquiry. They cannot carry out their noble task if the conditions for the practice of a responsible and critical mind [are] denied to them. They must have the freedom of responsible inquiry . . . into the meaning of social and economic ideas, into the checkered history of social and economic dogma.[1]

In Frankfurter's mind, "open-mindedness and free inquiry" included the right to free association. This decision in *Wieman v. Updegraff* was one of many in which the courts upheld the rights of academic freedom both inside and out of the classroom.

During the McCarthy era, there were many instances in which academic freedom, particularly the extent of faculty members' rights to express themselves outside of the classroom, was challenged. Charles S. Johnson's presidency at Fisk University, and more specifically a controversy involving Professor Lee Lorch, provides an example of the collision of academic freedom with civil rights and the cause of Black higher education. Not unlike most college and university presidents, Johnson had many difficult decisions to make during his tenure at Fisk University. He was forced to balance the opinions of his constituents (i.e., faculty, staff, trustees, donors, alumni, students, and local Nashville citizens) with his own convictions and agenda. Like his counterparts at predominantly White institutions, Johnson faced the pressure of meeting donor expectations that accompanied monetary contributions.

However, in addition to these pressures, Johnson was confronting issues that weighed heavily on the shoulders of historically Black college and university (HBCU) presidents. Johnson had to contend with the race-laden political agendas of donors and southern Whites who feared that the equal education of Blacks would lead to demands for equality in other areas. Above all, Johnson's presidency took place at what may have been the most important turning point in the history of Black civil rights during the 20th century: the *Brown v. Board of Education* decision.[2] The uncertainty surrounding this decision created a need for Johnson to weigh his actions carefully in terms of their effects on the future of race relations in the South. It was in this context that Johnson was handed the dilemma of dismissing one of his faculty members, Lee Lorch, or putting the future of Fisk in jeopardy. In making a decision, Johnson stayed close to his overall pragmatic philosophy, which he best expressed in a 1942 interview with the *Chicago Defender*:

> The difference between random behavior and a program is largely that of the ends in view. The thing that gives meaning to any single act is the larger context in which it is set. No strategy is sound that does not envisage the total picture in such a way that a person can be helped in deciding, in smaller individual cases, what is soundest and most important to stress and what, on the whole, is of minor consequences.[3]

Charles S. Johnson's interaction with Lee Lorch pitted this pragmatic philosophy against that of an outspoken activist. This chapter explores the ways in which academic freedom, civil liberties, and civil rights clashed in the Lorch case. Furthermore, it examines the ways in which the setting of a historically Black college alters traditional assumptions about the application of these principles.

Academic Freedom at Fisk: A Checkered Past

Questions of academic freedom at Fisk are not unique to Charles S. Johnson's presidency. Throughout the university's history, Fisk presidents battled with these issues. Established in 1866 through a joint effort by the government's Freedmen's Bureau and the American Missionary Association, Fisk University gave educational opportunity to the former slaves. Under its first president, Erastus Milo Cravath, Fisk received the majority of its funding from local and national grassroots missionary organizations. Because of this support, the institution was able to develop a rigorous liberal-arts-based curriculum while maintaining independence from the local southern White political structure.

As operating costs increased and missionary funds dried up, later Fisk presidents had to look for alternative funding sources. It was at this point that several White northern industrialists, who had previously supported only primary and secondary education for Blacks, began to support Black colleges. The motivation behind the shift in interest was most likely a desire by the industrial philanthropists to control all forms of Black education. In contrast to a liberal arts curriculum that encouraged political and social advancement, the philanthropists advocated industrial education that provided Blacks with skills appropriate for menial positions only. Rather than learning about literature, philosophy, and science, Blacks were trained in household duties, planting, field work, personal hygiene, and horse shoeing.[4]

During the same time period, the General Education Board (GEB) was established by John D. Rockefeller. The board was a conglomeration of major industrial philanthropists and some lesser known but influential individuals. Because of the tremendous financial backing and the influence of its members, the GEB gained a virtual monopoly on education and philanthropy for southern Blacks. The GEB was primarily concerned with the prosperity of the South's agricultural economy and the role of Blacks in this prosperity. It wanted to provide Blacks with skills, morals, and enough education to keep them in the South as the laboring class.[5]

The motives of the GEB and other industrial philanthropists have been characterized by some historians as benevolent and by others as self-serving and reactionary. Christopher Jencks and David Reisman, as well as Merle Curti and Roderick Nash, depict the northern philanthropists as pragmatic contributors who supported Black education for genuinely philanthropic reasons. These historians generally accepted the northern industrialists' own explanation for their support of industrial education: that support of anything more forward would have "incurred White supremacist vengeance." Raymond Fosdick, a member of the GEB, offered this type of apology in 1962 when he wrote:

The Board was aware from the start of the dangers inherent in a Northern institution working in the highly charged emotional atmosphere of a biracial South. . . . A single misstep could be disastrous . . . consequently its role was marked with caution and modesty. . . . That the philosophy of [Wallace] Buttrick [former head of the General Education Board] and his contemporaries was based on the idea of gradualism cannot be denied. But his was the thinking of the time. . . . Their strategy was strongly pragmatic. To raise the level of education in the South . . . it was necessary to work through the race in power. Sixty years ago there was no alternative to this approach; there was no public opinion to support any other cause.[6]

In contrast, Edward Berman and several other historians note that the industrialists wanted to focus their resources on a small group of "safe" southern Blacks in order to perpetuate an educational structure that repressed the social and economic advancement of all but a selected few. The GEB's use of its financial resources to gain power over institutions parallels Rockefeller's monopolistic business strategies in his other enterprises.[7]

The first of the Fisk presidents to accept contributions from industrial philanthropists was James Merrill. The GEB contributed to the establishment of an applied sciences program at Fisk. Upon receiving the financial support, President Merrill said:

It must not be understood in the least that I decry industrial training; on the other hand, as a source of mental development it is of great value to the college student, and I hope the day is not far away when, for this reason if for no other, Fisk can have a well-equipped industrial department. The two types of education [liberal arts and industrial] are not antagonistic and can be made so only as those who are at the head of the different schools lack breadth of view.[8]

Under President Merrill's leadership, Fisk University's curriculum continued to shift toward industrial education. In addition to his cooperation with the GEB, Merrill asked Booker T. Washington, the chief Black promoter of industrial education, for his support in raising funds for Fisk. A product of the Hampton Institute, Washington advocated educating students to meet the present-day conditions in the South. He stressed the dignity and beauty of labor to students: "to send every graduate out feeling and knowing that labor is dignified and beautiful—to make each one love labor instead of trying to escape it." This shift and the narrowing of academic freedom that accompanied it caught the attention of Fisk's most prominent alumnus and staunch advocate of liberal arts, W. E. B. Du Bois. He thought that only liberal arts education would provide Blacks with the resources to obtain intellectual, social, and political equality. When asked to deliver the Fisk graduation address in 1908, Du Bois took the opportunity to rebuke the university's administration:

And so today this venerable institution stands before its problem of future development, with the bribe of Public Opinion and Private Wealth dangling before us, if we will either deny that our object is the highest and broadest training of black Men, or if we will consent to call Higher Education that which you know and I know is not Higher Education. And I say we in this case advisedly; for my brothers and sisters, if this happens: if the ideal is lowered or the lie told, the responsibility rests on us.

According to Du Bois, it was this speech that led to President Merrill's resignation and the demise of the Department of Applied Sciences. In his own explanation, Merrill essentially acknowledged the issues that Du Bois had raised, although he did not admit that it was Du Bois in particular who caused him to resign. Upon his departure, he told the Board of Trustees, "The only real difficulty is the money side and this difficulty is so great that I have come to the conclusion that I have no longer a right to continue in my present position."[9]

Perhaps the most serious attempt to alter the curriculum at Fisk was during Fayette McKenzie's reign. In his inaugural address in 1915, he assured the White southerners and northern philanthropists that Fisk would aid in restoring the South to economic prosperity and increase the wealth of the nation—precisely the goals of these groups. Satisfied with McKenzie's leadership, the GEB agreed, in 1920, to support a campaign to raise a $1 million endowment for Fisk. With such large sums of money pledged to Fisk, the philanthropists were easily able to take control of its board of trustees from the former alliance of Black educators and White missionaries.[10]

In 1923, a General Education Board memorandum called for the collection of more financial support for Fisk and emphasized the urgent need to train "the right type of colored leaders"—leaders who would assist the Negro in becoming a capable worker and a respectable citizen. Following up on this memo, McKenzie curtailed the liberal arts curriculum, suspended the student newspaper, and refused to allow a campus charter of the National Association for the Advancement of Colored People (NAACP). Furthermore, he arranged special Jim Crow entertainment for the White benefactors of the university. Clearly, the "right type of colored leader" was one who would acquiesce in the segregationist social order in the South. As a result of his suppression of student initiative and narrowing of the curriculum, McKenzie was able to gain not only the support of the industrial philanthropists but the praise of the local southern White population. In what was perhaps the first instance of a southern city supporting Black higher education, the White citizens organized a campaign to raise $50,000 for the university.[11]

McKenzie's high-handed tactics were a clear violation of the accepted principles of academic freedom. While the definition of academic freedom was and continues to be fluid, it had, in McKenzie's time, come to focus on two German concepts: *Lehrfreiheit* and *Lernfreiheit*. Roughly, *Lehrfreiheit* was the professor's right to research and teach what he or she pleased; *Lernfreiheit* was the student's right to study what he or she pleased. Of the two concepts, *Lehrfreiheit* was adopted wholeheartedly by the American academic community. For example, the 1915 American Association of University Professors (AAUP) statement on academic freedom set forth guidelines to ensure that the college professor would have both freedom within the classroom and freedom to research and publish on the subjects of his or her choice—roughly the same as the German concept of *Lehrfreiheit*. By curtailing the curriculum, McKenzie clearly violated the AAUP's interpretation of the German concepts.[12]

McKenzie's repression of students and pandering to the southern Whites caused unrest and alienation among many of the Fisk alumni and students. Alumni contributions were at an all-time low during McKenzie's presidency. The feelings of disgruntled alumni and students spread rapidly across the country and eventually caught the attention of W. E. B. Du Bois. When invited to give the commencement address at Fisk in 1924, Du Bois openly criticized the Fisk administration:

> I have come to address you and, I say frankly, I have come to criticize. . . . I come to defend two theses, and the first is this: Of all the essentials that make an institution of learning, money is the least. The second is this: The alumni of Fisk University are and of right ought to be, the ultimate source of authority in the policy and government of this institution. . . . Fisk University is not taking an honest position with regard to the Southern situation. It has deliberately embraced a propaganda which discredits all of the hard work which the forward looking fighters for Negro freedom have been doing. . . . It continually teaches its students and constituency that this liberal white South is in the ascendancy and that it is ruling; and that the only thing required of the black man is acquiescence and submission.[13]

During the months following Du Bois's speech, alumni and student anger escalated against the university's policies and conduct. In January of 1925, alumni groups from all over the United States met in New York City for the sole purpose of agitating for McKenzie's resignation. On February 4, 1925, the Fisk students revolted. In a protest the day after the student revolt, more than 2,500 Black Nashville citizens called for McKenzie's ouster. Several historians believe this was a major factor in McKenzie's resignation 3 months later. After the revolt, Fisk encountered much difficulty in securing funds. Philanthropists were reluctant to give money to an unstable university, and the White citizens of Nashville withdrew their support. In contrast, Hampton University, which maintained its industrial curriculum, was able to amass an $8.5 million endowment during this period. The conflict during McKenzie's presidency left a permanent mark on the history of Fisk.[14]

The Rise of Black Leadership at Fisk

In 1946, Charles S. Johnson was selected as Fisk's sixth president and its first Black president. With years of research and teaching experience as well as excellent connections with philanthropic organizations, Johnson came well prepared. He was born into a religious, middle-class family in Bristol, Virginia. Heavily influenced by his father, an educated Baptist minister, Johnson had aspirations of attending college at a young age. He graduated with an AB from Virginia Union College in 1916. With Chicago sociologist Robert E. Park as his mentor, Johnson earned a PhB from the University of

Chicago in 1917. During World War I, Johnson interrupted his studies at the University of Chicago to enlist in the military. Upon returning to Chicago in 1919, he found himself in the midst of a city torn by race rioting. The stoning of Eugene Williams—a young Black man who accidentally swam into the "White side" of a Chicago beach—spurred one of the country's worst race riots. This incident sparked Johnson's involvement with the Chicago Race Relations Commission as associate executive secretary. In 1922, Johnson and the Chicago commission published *The Negro in Chicago: A Study of Race Relations and a Race Riot.* He received national acclaim for his involvement with the study and the commission.[15]

In 1921, he moved to New York to work as the director of the department of research and investigations at the National Urban League. In addition, Johnson edited *Opportunity: A Journal of Negro Life* during his 7-year stay in New York. Many credit this publication with the spawning of the Harlem Renaissance.[16]

Near the close of the Harlem Renaissance in 1928, Charles Johnson returned to the South to establish a nationally known department of social science and an internationally known race relations institute at Fisk University. In addition to his work on race relations within the academic setting, Johnson served as a trustee for the Julius Rosenwald Fund from 1934 to 1948, working specifically as the co-director of the race relations program. From 1944 to 1950, he served as the director of the race relations division of the American Missionary Association. During his career, Johnson also conducted research for the government and worked as a cultural ambassador under Presidents Hoover, Roosevelt, Truman, and Eisenhower.

Despite his strong interest in race relations, Charles Johnson was not an activist in the tradition of W. E. B. Du Bois, Martin Luther King, Jr., Marcus Garvy, or Paul Robeson. A self-proclaimed "sidelines activist," Johnson advocated a well-thought-out, research-based approach to advancing the rights of Blacks. Methodical research, in his opinion, was "a necessary prelude to liberal reform and change in public policy." As evidenced by the many books and articles he published—notably *Into the Mainstream: A Survey of Best Practices in Race Relations in the South, Shadow of the Plantation,* and *Race Relations: Adjustment of Whites and Negroes in the United States*—Johnson had very specific ideas about race relations. He thought that "social science could be joined to advocacy—in various degrees of militancy—in the sense that a solid foundation of research would serve the advocates [he among them] in demonstrating the depth and scope of racial inequality preventing millions of African Americans from achieving 'full American citizenship.' "[17]

Charles Johnson spent a lifetime working toward Black equality, with his most valuable contribution being his creation of venues for dialogue, self-expression, and change. Whether he was publishing artistic works in *Opportunity,* helping an emerging scholar obtain a Rosenwald Fellowship, or giving a very young Martin Luther King, Jr., an opportunity to speak at the renowned Fisk race relations institutes, Johnson made significant contributions to the advancement of Blacks in the United States.

While Johnson admitted to being a "sidelines activist," he fought on many occasions for the exchange of diverse ideas and freedom within the academy. For example, during the summer of 1944, when Johnson began holding the race relations institutes, he received extensive criticism from the local press. Fisk was chastised for its mixed-race conference sleeping facilities, interracial dancing and dining, and, in particular, the discussion of "radical" ideas. The White citizens of Nashville threatened to censor the institute, and then-President Thomas Elsa Jones intended to accede to their wishes. In response, Johnson threatened to leave Fisk and invited his colleagues in the social science department to go with him. Eventually, Jones conceded to Johnson and left the race relations institute intact. Johnson's insistence on open discussion at the race relations institute clearly falls within *Lehrfreiheit*—the right of the professor to teach. The radical ideas discussed (integration, voting rights, and socioeconomic advancement for Blacks) were part of Johnson's research, and surely he had a right to teach them.[18]

While *Lehrfreiheit* was generally accepted as a core principle of academic freedom, there was much controversy over whether it should apply outside of the classroom and outside of the professor's discipline. Should a professor's controversial statements and affiliations with so-called radical groups be protected under academic freedom, even if they put the institution in jeopardy? Should a professor be free to make pronouncements on topics beyond the scope of his or her expertise? In its 1940 statement of principles, the AAUP clearly favored an expansion of academic freedom to include broad-based civil liberties as well as the right of the professor to research and lecture freely within his or her field: "When he [i.e., the college or university teacher] speaks or writes as a citizen he should be free from institutional censorship or discipline." The AAUP's statement implies that professors merit the same freedoms within the institution as do citizens of the United States under the Constitution.[19]

Although his involvement in the race relations institutes showed Johnson to be a staunch defender of civil rights, his advocacy of civil liberties is a more complex issue. In some instances, he clearly defended the right to free speech and association. In 1948, for example, he was called before the Tenney Committee (Joint Fact-Finding Committee on Un-American Activities, State Senate of California) as a result of his affiliation with the National Sharecroppers Fund. In a strong defense of civil liberties, Johnson denounced the committee's inquiries as "witch-hunts" and stated that they were "much more un-American than the un-American activities being pursued." In 1949, when called to testify on the alleged communist infiltration of HBCUs, Johnson assured the House Un-American Activities Committee (HUAC) that there was no evidence to substantiate this claim.[20]

However, in other cases, particularly those dealing with internal university affairs, Johnson's defense of civil liberties was less clear. In 1949, Fisk physics professor Giovanni "Ross" Lomanitz took the Fifth Amendment when called to testify about his alleged communist affiliation. Lomanitz was cited for contempt of Congress. Shortly afterward, President Johnson informed Lomanitz, who was untenured, that his contempt charges made it impossible for Fisk to offer him another year of work under contract. Although offered the opportunity to work without a contract, Lomanitz refused and left Fisk. Johnson had been "officially" in the Fisk presidency only 2 years when the Lomanitz controversy came across his desk. Coupled with the pressure of being the first Black president of Fisk, his newness in the role may have had an impact on his decision. The Lomanitz situation was not the kind of publicity that Johnson wanted as he was attempting to build the university's endowment, attract top-rate scholars, and move Fisk into the mainstream of American higher education.[21]

Again in 1951, Johnson was faced with a question of defending civil liberties or remaining silent when W. E. B. Du Bois was indicted on the flimsy charge of failing to register as an agent of a foreign power. Although offering support to Du Bois may have seemed logical on the part of HBCU presidents, only Charles Johnson spoke out on his behalf. According to Du Bois, "Of the 50 presidents of Negro colleges, every one of which I had known and visited—of these only one, Charles Johnson of Fisk University, publicly professed belief in my integrity before the trial; and only one congratulated me after the acquittal." Perhaps because Du Bois was strongly connected to Fisk alumni, Johnson thought it important to support him. Regardless of his reasoning, Johnson's support is evidence of his unconditional respect for Du Bois—the same man who fought rather vehemently against Johnson's selection as president and labeled him "reactionary."[22]

The Case of Lee Lorch

Perhaps the most complex incident in Johnson's record regarding civil liberties and academic freedom is the case of Lee Lorch. This incident pitted Johnson's philosophy of gaining equality for Blacks against his belief in academic freedom. A math professor and PhD from the University of Cincinnati, Lee Lorch came to Fisk in September 1950 with excellent credentials but also as a controversial civil rights activist. When Charles Johnson appointed Lorch for an initial 3 years, he was well aware of Lorch's activism. Lorch had been denied reappointments at both the City College of New York and Pennsylvania State College because of his political activities on behalf of Blacks. Despite Lorch's reputation, Johnson gave him an opportunity when other institutions did not. According to Ellen Schrecker, "To get such a job, a full-time, tenure-track position in an American college, a black-listed professor would have to go to the South to the small, poor, denominational Negro colleges that were so desperate for qualified faculty members that they would hire anybody with a Ph.D., including teachers other educational institutions dared not touch."[23]

Although Schrecker's description of private HBCUs during the 1950s is representative of many of these colleges, Fisk University was a special case. While speaking of the majority of HBCUs in the most scathing terms—as "academic disaster areas"—Christopher Jencks and David Riesman, writing in 1968, placed Fisk among an elite group of Black colleges. Although meager relative to that of predominantly White institutions, Fisk had a sizable endowment of just over $4 million and no operating deficit. Furthermore, the Fisk University that had accepted Lee Lorch on its faculty was the same institution that attracted Sterling A. Brown, Horace Mann Bond, E. Franklin Frazier, James Weldon Johnson, Robert E. Park, Arna Bontemps, John Hope Franklin, Robert Hayden, and Aaron Douglas. Johnson was instrumental in persuading the majority of these scholars to come to Fisk and saw the hiring of the academically well-respected Lorch as yet another step toward moving Fisk into the mainstream of American higher education. Johnson may have had a chance to hire someone less controversial than Lorch, but perhaps he believed that Lorch would adapt his methods to the specific situation of the South and that the two of them could work together. Other activists for Black equality would be less direct in their approach when working in the South than in the North. Johnson may have expected Lorch to do the same.[24]

Lorch proved to be a model faculty member in terms of his teaching, research, and involvement with students. Upon accepting the appointment at Fisk, Lorch was made the acting chair of the mathematics department; after a year, he officially became chair of the department. Following his initial 3-year contract, he was reappointed for another 2-year period, although the question of his tenure was deferred until 1955. Lorch easily moved from associate to full professor, and, according to his colleagues, he was a respected member of the Fisk community. In fact, the Fisk math department reached its highest level of excellence as a result of the work of Lorch and Drs. Robert and Gertrude Rempfer. During Lorch's stay at Fisk, five of his students went on to get PhDs in math or math education—"a very high percentage in a school whose total enrollment was about 400." Lorch's students were among the first from Fisk's math department to pursue a PhD.[25]

At Fisk, Lorch continued his efforts on behalf of civil rights for African Americans. Along with three other faculty members, Lorch made a concerted effort to end discrimination within the American Mathematical Society and the Mathematical Association of America. In a 1951 *Science* article, Lorch stated, "It is our view that the scientific societies, with their talk of the international character of science, must recognize its interracial character and put an end to discriminatory practices at meetings, etc." Lorch also became active within the NAACP, serving as state vice president and a member of the Nashville chapter.[26]

Although White, Lee Lorch lived near Fisk, "in the heart of the Black community." Following the Supreme Court's 1954 decision that declared segregation in public education unconstitutional, Lorch and Robert and Gertrude Rempfer petitioned the Nashville school board to admit their daughters to Pearl Elementary School, an all-Black school near the Fisk campus.[27] According to Lorch, he and the Rempfers felt compelled to establish "an atmosphere of peaceful compliance with this decision [the *Brown* decision] and to show there was white support in the South for it." Their requests "were denied pending a final implementation decree by the United States Supreme Court." Upon hearing the school board's decision, Z. Alexander Looby, a Black city councilman and attorney for the NAACP, announced that legal action would be taken against the school board. On September 7, 1954, Lorch was subpoenaed by HUAC and was required to testify in Dayton, Ohio, on September 15 of that year.[28]

According to Lorch, the *Nashville Tennessean* knew about the subpoena before it was served and informed President Johnson immediately. He thinks that it is likely that the *Tennessean* provoked the subpoena:

> At that time the *Nashville Tennessean* was a very prominent newspaper, and it was busy backing Gordon Browning for governor. Browning was running on a platform of preservation of segregation. He said that one hundred percent of the whites and ninety-nine percent of the blacks wanted things to stay as they were. He would see that they did. This was his program. And of course our action showed that the one hundred percent wasn't quite one hundred percent. The *Nashville Tennessean* then began to make inquiries about me, and I was immediately subpoenaed by the House Un-American Activities Committee.[29]

In response to HUAC's questioning, Lee Lorch testified that he was not a member of the Communist party during his appointments at Fisk. In the opinion of both Warren Taylor and Frank Fetter of the AAUP, Lorch offered this testimony "contrary to his conscience, in order to safeguard his institution against unfavorable publicity." Lorch believed that "one of the purposes of this shotgun expedition was to smear Fisk University and to procure unfavorable publicity for it." An "unfriendly witness" (his words), he refused to answer questions regarding his past membership in the Communist party in 1941 during his graduate study at the University of Cincinnati, noting that political affiliations and activities were personal and guarded by the First Amendment. Although reported by one researcher as having invoked the Fifth Amendment so as to not incriminate himself, Lorch did not. As a result of his lack of cooperation with the HUAC, Lorch was cited for contempt of Congress.[30]

The next day, both the *Nashville Tennessean* and the *Nashville Banner* gave substantial coverage to the hearing and published a statement, released in advance, by Charles S. Johnson. Johnson stated, "Fisk's position regarding communism, in the present state of the nation and world, is forthright and unequivocal. We do not knowingly, employ or retain faculty members who hold this allegiance." Furthermore, Johnson declared that, "in these times, invoking the Fifth Amendment [sic] when there is a clear opportunity to affirm or deny is for all practical purposes tantamount to admission of membership. Under any such circumstances Fisk University would have to take prompt steps to release the person from its faculty."[31]

In preparing the advance press release, Charles Johnson most likely alluded to the wrong amendment. According to the AAUP, Johnson, who issued the statement without formal consultation with the Board of Trustees, probably drew no distinction between the First and Fifth Amendments—invoking either brought about the possibility of negative publicity. In making this statement, Johnson clearly placed avoiding the backlash from the local White community in front of defending the civil liberties of his faculty member.[32]

Over the next few weeks, Johnson let the Nashville papers know that the Board of Trustees would be reviewing Lorch's case and considering his dismissal from Fisk. On October 28, 1954, Lee Lorch appeared before the Fisk Board of Trustees at the request of President Johnson, who told him to "hold himself in readiness to answer questions." Ironically, charges were never brought against Lorch by the university, nor did he receive any official statement from President Johnson. In fact, Lorch's main source of information on his status within the university was the local press. During his appearance before the Fisk Board of Trustees, Lorch gave a prepared statement that was 13 single-spaced pages in length. The majority of the statement criticized the HUAC and its procedures. However, Lorch also made it clear that he believed this incident was a retaliation by Nashville segregationists, who disagreed with his activism on behalf of Black civil rights.[33]

The decision to dismiss Lorch did not come quickly. On November 19, 1954, with one member dissenting, the Fisk Board of Trustees voted not to renew Lee Lorch's appointment at the university. According to Lorch, the Fisk board initially voted 17 to 2 in favor of retaining him, but "then one of the white members of the board, a local manufacturer, got up and . . . said that if . . . [the] decision stands, he . . . [would] resign from the board and spread his resignation in the press, and that the other dissenting member would do the same." Although Lorch attributes a great amount of power to this local manufacturer (Dan May), according to John Hope Franklin, who was present at the board meeting, "Dan May didn't have great influence and usually didn't understand the issues being discussed."

Several months later, at the next quarterly board meeting, a board-appointed executive committee voted 10 to 1 not to renew Lorch's contract. Although Lorch continued to petition the Fisk board, the executive committee's decision was approved on April 29, 1955, by the full board, with all White members present voting for Lorch's dismissal and most Black trustees voting to retain him. However, a few Black trustees, including John Hope Franklin, supported Johnson and felt that Lorch was given due process. It is clear that Johnson was as responsible for the move to dismiss Lorch as the White trustees.[34]

Prior to and after Lorch's "official" dismissal, many Fisk faculty, staff, alumni, and students pledged their support for him. Along with several other faculty members, Professor Nelson Fuson of the physics department offered to take a cut in pay to make up a salary for Lee Lorch. Furthermore, the local chapter of the AAUP came to Lorch's defense. Faculty and students circulated petitions, wrote letters, held meetings, and spoke to the administration on Lorch's behalf. A later AAUP investigation noted that "twenty-two student leaders, 150 alumni, 157 citizens, . . . [and] forty-seven of seventy eligible faculty members, . . . made representation to President Johnson and the Board in behalf of the retention of Professor Lorch." Although this investigation reprimanded Johnson for a violation of academic freedom, the authors do not give a detailed definition of academic freedom; they merely refer to Lorch's constitutional rights as a citizen. As Ellen Schrecker points out in her 1986 publication *No Ivory Tower*, as late as 1953 there was not a single agreed-upon definition of academic freedom.[35]

On the subject of the campus-wide uproar that arose over the Lorch controversy, Patrick Gilpin states, "Lorch did nothing to discourage this support and apparently was a participant, if not an organizer." Although he may have assisted in the organization of activities, it is apparent that Lorch's friends were profoundly loyal and defended his integrity and rights. They admired his steadfast fight for civil rights, respected his professional competency, or valued his personal right of association and his academic right to freedom. However, it was precisely these activities on his behalf that the board cited as a reason for Lorch's dismissal: "There has been continual agitation of the question on the campus to the detriment of the pursuit of teaching and studying . . . stimulated by some person or persons who had little or no regard for the adverse effect that it might have on the healthy pursuit of learning."[36]

In Johnson's mind, the greatest good for Fisk was to disassociate the university from Lorch. Perhaps this is the reason why he returned Lorch's National Science Foundation (NSF) award. According to Lorch, "Shortly after my appearance before HUAC, the National Science Foundation approved my application for a research grant [the first such for Fisk]. Without consulting me, Dr. Johnson returned the check to NSF."

A Decision to Secure Fisk's Future

Why would Charles Johnson, an ardent advocate of civil rights, not have fought to retain a man whose views on Black advancement were similar to his own? On the surface, the decision not to renew Lorch's contract seems merely an example of the denial of academic freedom and the reasonable safeguards of academic due process. However, to reach this conclusion ignores the important issues of Johnson's leadership style, the history of Fisk, and the context of the South in the 1950s.[37]

Charles Johnson's dismissal of Lorch had little to do with the difference between invoking the First or Fifth Amendment or Lorch's right to do so under the concept of academic freedom. Instead, the dismissal was most likely based on a difference in the type of civil rights activism practiced by Johnson and Lorch. Charles Johnson knew the South. Johnson doubted the effectiveness of large-scale protest events because he thought that, under southern conditions, they might lead to violence and be more detrimental than helpful. Instead of promoting acts of civil disobedience, Johnson took a pragmatic approach and tried to find allies within the White power structure. He used research to convince these allies, such as Edwin Embree, Will Alexander, and John Hay Whitney, to change the direction of Black higher education from industrial to liberal in the early 1930s and to assist young Black scholars in their quest for educational funding. Whereas other race relations leaders, including Du Bois, tended to fight racism primarily in the Northeast, Johnson chose to stay in the South.[38]

In contrast to Johnson, Lorch was from the Northeast and was much more idealistic and confrontational in his approach. In one instance, Lorch sublet his Stuyvesant Town apartment to a Black family in open defiance of that New York housing project's policy of excluding Blacks. In the words of Nelson Fuson, Lorch's colleague, "Lorch was an activist for integration. Many people were afraid that they, or the breadwinners of their family, would risk being fired if they publicly supported an unpopular cause like desegregation even if it was the correct cause. But Lorch was not one of these!"[39]

As a college president, Johnson wanted to make sure that his style prevailed. In the past, Johnson had sometimes been possessive of his creations. For example, Johnson was criticized by several other Black sociologists—W. E. B. Du Bois, E. Franklin Frazier—for hoarding research resources for Fisk and acting as the gatekeeper of Black sociological research. According to Butler Jones, as head of the Fisk race relations institute, Johnson had exercised control over the field of Black sociology and race relations research. However, Jones also notes that Johnson was praised by many Black sociologists. They "freely admitted [their] indebtedness to him for his work in maintaining at Fisk a center for the education and training of blacks in the intricacies of sociological research." Johnson continued this diligent yet controlling style of management as president of Fisk. He was known among the faculty as a demanding leader. Certainly, this style of leadership would have come into conflict with Lorch's forward actions.[40]

Although his decision to dismiss Lorch was not honorable, in making it, Johnson was being true to his own agenda of securing Fisk's future. Johnson knew well the potential backlash Fisk might receive from a decision to retain Lorch. Even Lee Lorch acknowledged that Johnson was under a great amount of pressure:

> It must be understood what a black institution is. It's not an institution controlled by African-Americans; it's one attended by them. The control still rests in the hands of those who control the rest of society. With some of the historically black institutions of the South, in those days, every single member of the board was white. . . . The then president of Fisk was the first nonwhite president in its history.[41]

As under the presidency of McKenzie, when Nashville Whites criticized Fisk for being too "radical," northern philanthropists became nervous about supporting the institution. Although his defense of Du Bois and the subject matter at the race relations institutes showed that he would not cave in to outside pressure under every circumstance, Johnson understood that Fisk's survival depended on at least a few allies within the White community. In the Lorch incident, it was apparent that those few allies had retreated. Although not merely a puppet of philanthropists, as McKenzie had been, Johnson had to be particular about the battles he fought. He made his decisions with the best interest of Fisk in mind.

Just as Johnson was detailed, almost meticulous, about the research and activities of the Fisk race relations institutes, he had his own vision of how Fisk would react to the *Brown* decision. After *Brown,* the atmosphere in the local community was tense, and Johnson chose to put the survival of Fisk before the testing of *Brown.* That he made this decision was no accident when we consider his philosophy on integration. Although he supported *Brown* by contributing research toward Kenneth Clark's studies and making affirmative public statements after the decision, Johnson clearly believed that integration alone would not bring about Black equality. When asked in 1942 whether Blacks should insist upon integration, he replied, "No, because integration is not something that can be commanded or conferred. They should insist upon equality of status in their own right as Negroes and without social and economic penalties for their physical differences." Contrary to those who thought that the legal end to segregation made HBCUs unnecessary, Johnson saw a continuing need for these institutions. At the 1956 United Negro College Fund campaign meeting, Johnson said with conviction:

> The time is now to strengthen these colleges; to give their virtues greater power in this crisis. These institutions are not beggars; nor are they or should they ever become the pathological and apologetic symbols of the intellectual products of their nurturing. The time is now to help them set the example for the nation, of a democratic and dynamic education, that can save the nation itself for its greater destiny in the world.

Although the vehemence of Johnson's statement could be attributed to the "rhetoric of fund raising," Johnson "rarely practiced the art of hyperbole" during his career. It is likely that Johnson, a lifelong champion of Black colleges, was expressing a deeply felt conviction.[42]

For Charles Johnson, dismissing Lee Lorch was not an easy decision. In fact, he told Nelson Fuson in confidence that Lorch was wronged but that he had to do it for the institution. Perhaps this is why, in writing to the president of Philander Smith College regarding Lorch's future employment, he gave a shining recommendation of Lorch and went to great lengths to avoid mentioning the controversy: "I shall only say that Dr. Lorch is a very competent mathematician. Our decision not to renew his contract was not on the basis of his mathematical ability or his racial attitudes."

From the perspective of the post–civil rights era, it is difficult to understand why Johnson might have dismissed such a strong supporter of Black equality. Was he forced to make this decision?

Although Johnson was under a great amount of pressure from southern Whites, his history of independent decision making proves him to be more than just their pawn. Johnson most likely viewed Lorch's dismissal as a necessary sacrifice for the long-term benefit of Black higher education, specifically at Fisk. In certain instances, values collide in ways that make it impossible to take the "right" course of action from all viewpoints. Such was the case in Johnson's decision to dismiss Lee Lorch. Johnson saw Fisk as an institution that would meet the needs of Blacks in a transitional era—an era free of legal segregation but without a guarantee of full integration. Johnson understood that to secure Fisk's future existence and prosperity he needed, at various times, cooperation both from southern Whites and from the Fisk community. Given the current backlash against affirmative action, it is apparent that this transitional era is not yet over. Colleges such as Fisk still have a role to play in guaranteeing equal education to Blacks and providing diverse cultural centers.[43]

The questions of academic freedom raised by the Lee Lorch case are unresolved to this day. Although the American academy adopted the German concept of academic freedom, the extent of this professorial right has always been unclear. Because of the pragmatic nature of American higher education, with its increasing attention to social, political, and applied sciences, American professors were more likely to operate within the public sphere than their German counterparts. Unlike the Germans, the Americans were operating under a constitutional guarantee of free speech, one that was afforded to all American citizens. These factors led them to demand greater freedom in public utterances outside of their discipline. When the AAUP first created the guidelines for academic freedom, there was an effort to expand the German concept to include free speech and even political activism outside of the classroom. This effort provoked a backlash by some who thought that this kind of freedom shielded professors from any responsibility for their actions—including actions that were detrimental to their own institutions. Unlike other public figures, who were given free speech but were expected to bear the consequences of unpopular opinions, professors were asking for a broad mandate to express their opinions on all subjects without negative career consequences.

The final statement of the AAUP regarding "extramural utterances" was ambivalent. On the one hand, it noted that professors should not be prohibited from "expression to their judgments upon controversial questions, or that their freedom of speech outside the university should be limited to questions falling within their own specialties. . . . [Furthermore, they should not be denied the right to] support . . . organized movements which they believe to be in the public interest." On the other hand, it was quick to point out the need for professors to avoid making "hasty or unverified or exaggerated statements, and to refrain from intemperate or sensational modes of expression." As stated in 1955 by Richard Hofstadter and Walter Metzger, the extent of academic freedom continues to be a "vexing question."

The Lorch incident provides a good example of how this debate over the extent of academic freedom plays out in a politically charged setting. No one challenged Lee Lorch's competence as a researcher and teacher; instead, the decision to dismiss Lorch concerned his right to participate in a form of political activism that could have harmed the university. Similar incidents continue to occur today. In a recent interview, historian Ellen Schrecker stated:

> Professors may be losing their ability and willingness to speak out on issues outside the classroom. Because of the job crunch, junior faculty are so insecure that they cannot now openly take political positions as they did in the 1960s. Junior faculty—and this, of course, would apply to adjuncts as well—are deprived of the opportunity to act in their capacity as citizens.

Today, universities are increasingly adopting a corporate model—downsizing, outsourcing, and replacing tenured faculty positions with adjuncts. These practices put pressure on faculty members to curtail political involvement that might bring negative publicity to their institutions. Just as the fear of negative public opinion in a racially hostile, segregated South was the impetus for dismissing Lorch, today's universities are being pressured to adopt a narrow view of academic freedom that prohibits professors from advocating on behalf of unpopular causes. The context of a Black college shows the impact of economic pressure on the academic setting. When an institution is constantly under pressure to garner funds from remotely connected sources, there is a strong tendency to follow the status quo. The lack of financial resources of many alumni and parents of Black colleges means that these institutions must rely more heavily on foundation support.[44] This helps us to understand the actions of Charles S. Johnson at Fisk but also underscores the need for clarification of how far the concept of academic freedom should reach.[45]

Notes

This work was generously funded by both the Indiana University Center on Philanthropy and the Rockefeller Foundation. I wish to thank the staffs at the Fisk University Special Collections, the Rockefeller Archive Center, and the Indiana University library for their assistance with this project. Furthermore, I am grateful to the following individuals who took the time to review this chapter prior to its publication: Andrea Walton, B. Edward McClellan, Michael Parsons, Jonathan Zimmerman, Ellen Schrecker, Patrick Gilpin, Anthony E. Hargrove, Robert S. Evans, and Edward Epstein. Their critical review is appreciated. An earlier version of this manuscript was presented at the Organization of American Historians annual meeting in Indianapolis, Indiana, 1998.

1. Jack Dvorak and Jon Dilts, "Academic Freedom vs. Administrative Authority," *Journalism Educator* 47 (Fall 1992): 3–12; *Wieman v. Updegraft,* 344 U.S. 183 (1952).

2. *Brown v. Board of Education of Topeka,* 347 U.S. 483 (1954).

3. Charles S. Johnson, "Famous Sociologist Asks, Answers Some Key Questions for Negroes," *The Chicago Defender,* 26 September 1942, 32–33.

4. Joe Richardson, *A History of Fisk University, 1865–1946* (Tuscaloosa: University of Alabama, 1980); James A. Anderson, *The Education of Blacks in the South, 1860–1935* (Chapel Hill: University of North Carolina Press, 1988).

5. James D. Anderson, "Philanthropic Control Over Private Black Higher Education," in *Philanthropy and Cultural Imperialism: The Foundations at Home and Abroad,* ed. Robert Arnove (Boston: G. K. Hall & Co., 1980).

6. Christopher Jencks and David Riesman, *The Academic Revolution* (Chicago: University of Chicago Press, 1968); Merle Curti and Roderick Nash, *Philanthropy in the Shaping of American Higher Education* (New Brunswick, N.J.: Rutgers University Press, 1965); Stephen Peeps, "Northern Philanthropy and the Emergence of Black Higher Education—Do-Gooders, Compromisers, or Co-Conspirators," *Journal of Negro Education* 50 (Summer 1981): 265; Raymond Fosdick, *Adventure in Giving: The Story of the General Education Board* (New York: Harper & Row, 1962), 323.

7. Edward Berman, *The Influence of the Carnegie, Ford, and Rockefeller Foundations on American Foreign Policy: The Ideology of Philanthropy* (New York: State University of New York Press, 1983). The reference to several others includes Anderson, "Philanthropic Control"; Anderson, *The Education of Blacks in the South;* Ronald Butchart, *Northern Schools, Southern Blacks, and Reconstruction: Freedmen's Education, 1862–1875* (Westport, Conn.: Greenwood Press, 1980); Butchart, "Outthinking and Outflanking the Owners of the World: A Historiography of the African American Struggle for Education," *History of Education Quarterly* 28 (1988): 333–366; Vincent P. Franklin and James A. Anderson, eds., *New Perspectives on Black Educational History* (Boston: G. K. Hall & Co., 1978); Manning Marable, "Booker T. Washington and the Political Economy of Black Education in the United States, 1880–1915," *Teaching Education* 3, no. 1 (1990); Peeps, "Northern Philanthropy"; Robert Stuckert, "The Negro College—A Pawn of White Domination," *The Wisconsin Sociologist* (January 1964); William Watkins, "Teaching and Learning in the Black Colleges: A 130-Year Retrospective," *Teaching Education* 3, no. 1 (1990).

8. James Merrill, quoted in American Unitarian Association, *From Servitude to Service* (Boston: American Unitarian Association, 1905), 211–212.

9. Charles Willie and Ronald Edmonds, *Black Colleges in America: Challenge, Development, Survival* (New York: Teachers College Press, 1978), 76; W. E. B. Du Bois, *The Education of Black People: Ten Critiques, 1906–1960,* ed. H. Aptheker (New York: Monthly Review Press, 1973); Minutes of the Board of Trustees of Fisk University, 25 June 1908, Fisk University Archives, Nashville, Tennessee.

10. Anderson, *The Education of Blacks in the South.*

11. Fisk Endowment Campaign, Memorandum, 25 May 1923, Box 23, General Education Board Papers (Rockefeller Archive Center, Tarrytown, New York); Minutes of the Board of Trustees of Fisk University, 9 November 1915 (Fisk University Archives, Nashville, Tennessee); Minutes of the Board of Trustees of Fisk University, 2 May 1921 (Fisk University Archives, Nashville, Tennessee).

12. Richard Hofstadter and Walter P. Metzger, *The Development of Academic Freedom in the United States* (New York: Columbia University, 1955).

13. Richardson, *A History of Fisk University;* W. E. B. Du Bois, "Diuturni Silenti," in *The Education of Black People,* 41; Anderson, *The Education of Blacks in the South.*

14. Both Richardson, *A History of Fisk University,* and Anderson, *The Education of Blacks in the South,* claim that the student revolt was a major factor in Fayette McKenzie's resignation. For more information on student revolts on Black college campuses during the 1920s, see Raymond Wolters, *The New Negro on Campus: Black College Rebellions of the 1920s* (Princeton, N.J.: Princeton University Press, 1975). For information on the disparaging difference between the Fisk and Hampton endowments, see Peeps, "Northern Philanthropy," 251–269.

15. Although commonly referred to as Dr. Johnson, he did not have a PhD. His graduate work at the University of Chicago was cut short, and he received a PhB (bachelor of philosophy).

16. Those who credit *Opportunity* with the spawning of the Harlem Renaissance include Mary Schmidt Campbell et al., *Harlem Renaissance: Art of Black America* (Harlem, N.Y.: Abradale Press, Harry N. Abrams, Inc., 1982); Patrick Gilpin, "Charles S. Johnson: Entrepreneur of the Harlem Renaissance," in *The Harlem Renaissance Remembered,* ed. A. Bontemps (New York: Dodd, Mead & Co., 1972); Gilpin, "Charles S. Johnson: An Intellectual Biography" (PhD dissertation, Vanderbilt University, 1973); Blyden Jackson, "A Postlude to a Renaissance," *Southern Review* 25 (1990): 746–765; David Levering Lewis, *When Harlem Was in Vogue* (New York: Oxford University Press, 1981); Guichard Parris and Lester Brooks, *Blacks in the City: A History of the National Urban League* (Toronto: Little, Brown & Co., 1971); Ralph Pearson, "Charles S. Johnson: The Urban League Years" (PhD dissertation, Johns Hopkins University, 1971); Ralph Pearson, "Combating Racism With Art: Charles S. Johnson and the Harlem Renaissance," *American Studies* 18 (1977): 123–134; J. Vincent, "Philadelphia's Afro-American Literary Circle and the Harlem Renaissance" (PhD dissertation, University of Pennsylvania, 1980).

17. Robert King, *Civil Rights and the Idea of Freedom* (New York: Oxford University Press, 1992); John Kirby, *Black Americans in the Roosevelt Era: Liberalism and Race* (Knoxville: University of Tennessee Press, 1980); Charles S. Johnson, *Into the Mainstream: A Survey of Best Practices in Race Relations in the South* (Chapel Hill: University of North Carolina, 1947); Charles S. Johnson, *Shadow of the Plantation* (Chicago: University of Chicago Press, 1934); Willis Weatherford and Charles S. Johnson, *Race Relations: Adjustment of Whites and Negroes in the United States* (Boston: D. C. Heath, 1934); Richard Robbins, *Sidelines Activist: Charles S. Johnson and the Struggle for Civil Rights* (University, Miss.: University of Mississippi Press, 1996).

18. Gilpin, "Charles S. Johnson: An Intellectual Biography"; Gilpin, "Charles S. Johnson: Entrepreneur of the Harlem Renaissance."

19. Warren Taylor and Frank Fetter, "Academic Freedom and Tenure: Fisk University," *American Association of University Professors Bulletin* 45 (March 1959): 33.

20. The National Sharecroppers Fund was labeled a communist front by HUAC. Charles S. Johnson, quoted in Robbins, *Sidelines Activist,* 149.

21. Ellen Schrecker, *No Ivory Tower: McCarthyism and the Universities* (New York: Oxford University Press, 1986).

22. *A Soliloquy on Viewing My Life From the Last Decade of Its First Century: The Autobiography of W. E. B. Du Bois,* ed. H. Aptheker (New York: International Publishers, 1968), 391; Herbert Aptheker, ed., *The Correspondence of W. E. B. Du Bois* (Amherst: University of Massachusetts Press, 1978), 306–307.

23. Lee Lorch was recommended to the university by Judge Hubert T. Delany, who was one of the first African American judges in New York City and a close friend of Charles Johnson. For more information on Lee Lorch's political activities prior to his position at Fisk, see Cedric Belfrage, *The American Inquisition, 1945–1960* (Indianapolis: Bobbs-Merrill, 1973); David Caute, *The Great Fear: The Anti-Communist Purge Under Truman and Eisenhower* (New York: Simon & Schuster, 1978); Griffen Fariello, *Red Scare: Memories of the American Inquisition. An Oral History* (New York: W. W. Norton & Co., 1995); Gilpin, "Charles S. Johnson: An Intellectual Biography"; Patrick Gilpin, "Charles S. Johnson and the Second Red Scare: An Episode," *Tennessee Historical Quarterly* 37 (1978): 76–88; Robbins, *Sidelines Activist;* and Schrecker, *No Ivory Tower,* 289.

24. Jencks and Riesman, *The Academic Revolution,* 433. For evidence of Johnson's instrumental role in bringing prominent scholars to Fisk, see Folder 14, Box 41, Charles S. Johnson Papers (Fisk University Archives, Nashville, Tennessee). For information on Johnson's goal of moving Fisk into the mainstream, see Gilpin, "Charles S. Johnson: An Intellectual Biography," and Gilpin, "Charles S. Johnson and the Second Red Scare." Robbins, *Sidelines Activist,* discusses Black activists who were less confrontational in their approach when in the South.

25. Several of Lorch's former colleagues have commented on his stature on the Fisk campus: Nelson Fuson to author, 20 February 1998; Marian Fuson to author, 24 February 1998; Gladys Forde, interviewed by author via telephone, 27 March 1998. For additional information on the views of Lorch's colleagues at Fisk, see Gilpin, "Charles S. Johnson: An Intellectual Biography," and Gilpin, "Charles S. Johnson and the Second Red Scare." In a letter to the author dated 15 February 1998, Lee Lorch noted the high percentage of PhDs. For more information on the Fisk math department under Lorch's direction, see Vivienne Mayes, *American Mathematical Monthly* (November 1976).

26. Lee Lorch, "Discriminatory Practices," *Science* 114 (1951): 161; Fariello, *Red Scare*.

27. Lorch initially asked the principal of Pearl Elementary whether his daughter could enroll. The principal, who had known Lorch's daughter for years, said that he would welcome her.

28. Lee Lorch, interview by author, 15 February 1998; Lee Lorch, quoted in Fariello, *Red Scare*, 493; "Fisk May Ask Lorch to Resign: Professor Dodges Queries on Links With Communism," *Nashville Tennessean*, 16 September 1954.

29. Lee Lorch, interview by author, 15 February 1998; Lee Lorch, quoted in Fariello, *Red Scare*, 493.

30. Taylor and Fetter, "Academic Freedom and Tenure," 44; "Lorch Says Committee Broke Rules Calling Him," *Nashville Banner*, 16 September 1954. Fariello, *Red Scare*, 493; Robbins, *Sidelines Activist*.

31. "Lorch Says Committee Broke Rules Calling Him," *Nashville Banner*, 16 September 1954; "Fisk May Ask Lorch to Resign: Professor Dodges Queries on Links With Communism," *Nashville Tennessean*, 16 September 1954.

32. Taylor and Fetter, "Academic Freedom and Tenure."

33. Gilpin, "Charles S. Johnson and the Second Red Scare," 82; Gilpin, "Charles S. Johnson: An Intellectual Biography." The hearing was held to investigate communist infiltration in Dayton, Ohio. Lorch, who had only resided in Cincinnati, was not told this until he arrived before the committee (Fariello, *Red Scare*); Taylor and Fetter, "Academic Freedom and Tenure."

34. Lee Lorch, quoted in Fariello, *Red Scare*, 493. The other dissenting member of the board was Wendall Phillips, the vice president of a major Nashville bank at the time. The one Black trustee was L. Howard Bennett, who went on to become assistant secretary of defense for the United States government and chair of the Fisk Board of Trustees. According to John Hope Franklin, "Charles Johnson assumed that Howard Bennett was his friend and would support him—when it came to Lee Lorch he did not" (John Hope Franklin, interview by author, 5 June 1998). Detailed information regarding the April 1955 board meeting is located in the Fisk Board of Trustee Minutes and Charles S. Johnson Papers (Fisk University Archives, Nashville, Tennessee). For more information on the specific voting patterns, see Fariello, *Red Scare*, and Taylor and Fetter, "Academic Freedom and Tenure."

35. Taylor and Fetter, "Academic Freedom and Tenure," 35; Schrecker, *No Ivory Tower*.

36. Supporters included Dr. William J. Zeigler, a Fisk alumnus and Chicago dentist; Dr. Percy L. Julian, the second Black ever elected to the National Academy of Sciences and a leading figure in organic chemistry; Reverend Henry Allen Boyd, president of the Citizens Savings Bank; and W. E. B. Du Bois. Although August Meier states, in *A White Scholar and the Black Community, 1945–1965* (Amherst: University of Massachusetts Press, 1992), that W. E. B. Du Bois was not willing to oppose Lorch's dismissal, this assertion is inaccurate. See Du Bois's collected works, published by the University of Massachusetts (1973–1978), for his unambiguous opposition to Lorch's dismissal (Lee Lorch, interview with author, 26 February 1998). Robbins, *Sidelines Activist*; Warren and Fetter, "Academic Freedom and Tenure," 41; Gilpin, "Charles S. Johnson and the Second Red Scare," 83, 85; Gilpin, "Charles S. Johnson: An Intellectual Biography."

37. Gilpin, "Charles S. Johnson and the Second Red Scare," 82; Gilpin, "Charles S. Johnson: An Intellectual Biography"; Taylor and Fetter, "Academic Freedom and Tenure." Lorch reapplied from his next post at Philander Smith College in Little Rock even before his trial on charges of contempt of Congress. To its credit, NSF again awarded Lorch a grant. According to Lorch. "The president of PSC happily activated it" (Lee Lorch, interview by author, 15 February 1998).

38. Taylor and Fetter, "Academic Freedom and Tenure"; Robbins, *Sidelines Activist*. Edwin Embree was the president of the Julius Rosenwald Fund until its closure in 1948. Will Alexander was the head of the American Missionary Association. John Hay Whitney was the founder and chair of the Whitney Foundation. Anderson, *The Education of Blacks in the South*; Jane Belke, "To Render Better Service: The Role of the Julius Rosenwald Fund Fellowship Program in Graduate and Professional Degrees of African Americans" (PhD dissertation, Indiana University, 1994); Kirby, *Black Americans in the Roosevelt Era*. Du Bois did spend time at Atlanta University in Atlanta, Georgia (as an instructor [1897–1910] and department chair [1934–1944]).

39. Nelson Fuson to author, 20 February 1998.

40. Gilpin, "Charles S. Johnson and the Second Red Scare"; Gilpin, "Charles S. Johnson: An Intellectual Biography"; Anthony Platt, *E. Franklin Frazier Reconsidered* (New Brunswick, N.J.: Rutgers University Press, 1991); Robbins, *Sidelines Activist*; John Stanfield, *Philanthropy and Jim Crow in American Social Science* (Westport, Conn.: Greenwood Press, 1985); Butler Jones, quoted in John Bracey, August Meier, and Elliott Rudwick, *The Black Sociologists: The First Half Century* (Belmont, Calif.: Wadsworth Publishing Company, 1971), 136.

41. Robbins, *Sidelines Activist*; Gilpin, "Charles S. Johnson and the Second Red Scare"; Lee Lorch, quoted in Fariello, *Red Scare*, 494.

42. Charles S. Johnson, Statement on Supreme Court Decision, 17 May 1954, Folder 34, Box 174, Charles S. Johnson Papers (Fisk University Archives, Nashville, Tennessee). The Southern Educational Reporting Service was organized in 1954 in Nashville as a race relations information dissemination center to assist peaceful transitions in the midst of the *Brown* decision and afterward. Kenneth B. Clark, *Prejudice and Your Child* (Boston: Beacon Press, 1955); Charles S. Johnson, "Famous Sociologist Asks, Answers Some Key Questions for Negroes," *The Chicago Defender*, 26 September 1942. Charles S. Johnson, "The Time Is Now," Remarks at the United Negro College Fund campaign meeting, Detroit, Michigan, 18 July 1956, Charles S. Johnson Papers (Fisk University Archives, Nashville, Tennessee); Ralph Pearson, "Reflections on Black Colleges: The Historical Perspective of Charles S. Johnson," *History of Education Quarterly* 23 (1983): 55–68.

43. Nelson Fuson, interviewed by Richard Robbins, Nashville, Tennessee, 12 June 1975; M. LaFayette Harris to Charles S. Johnson, 8 July 1955, Charles S. Johnson to M. LaFayette Harris, 13 July 1955, Folder 6, Box 29, Charles S. Johnson Papers (Fisk University Special Collections, Nashville, Tennessee). *American Association of University Professors Bulletin*, No. 1 (December 1915): 35–37. Hofstadter and Metzger, *The Development of Academic Freedom*, 411.

44. According to the *Journal of Blacks in Higher Education* (Winter 1998/1999, no. 22) and the U.S. Census Bureau, the most striking evidence of racial inequality in the United States is that the median net worth per Black family is $4,418, as compared with the median net worth of a White family, which is $45,740.

45. Stanley Katz, "A Conversation With Academe's Ellen Schrecker," *Organization of American Historians Newsletter* 27 (February 1999): 1, 4.

CHAPTER 7

"THIS HAS BEEN QUITE A YEAR FOR HEADS FALLING": INSTITUTIONAL AUTONOMY IN THE CIVIL RIGHTS ERA

JOY ANN WILLIAMSON

Historically Black Colleges and Universities (HBCUs) and their students played a pivotal part in the Civil Rights Movement of the 1950s and early 1960s. Private HBCUs, in particular, provided foot soldiers, intellectual leadership, and safe places to meet and plan civil disobedience. Their economic and political autonomy from the state enabled the institutions and their students to participate in activism without the constant fear of legislative retribution. Their private status did not shield them completely from the state's wrath, however, particularly when college aims collided with state interests. Some constituents argued that HBCUs should agitate for constitutionally protected freedoms; others maintained that HBCUs should shun politics and focus on purely educational concerns. Debates over the role of HBCUs raged on and off campuses. Those with the greatest degree of commitment to the movement faced severe penalties.

Events at Tougaloo College dramatized the consequences of HBCU participation in the Civil Rights Movement. Located outside of Jackson, Mississippi, Tougaloo is a private liberal arts institution committed to African-American equality. Civil rights activists considered its white president, Reverend Dr. Adam D. Beittel, a friend of the cause. Beittel resigned in September 1964. Observers alternately accused the Board of Trustees, Brown University, the Ford Foundation, and the Mississippi Sovereignty Commission of conspiring against Beittel and precipitating his departure. One side of the story was that of a financially strapped institution seeking to reinvent itself through a partnership with Brown University funded by the Ford Foundation. The other involved the Sovereignty Commission and that agency's admonition to keep politics out of education and education out of politics. Tougaloo's role in the Civil Rights Movement triggered the debate and placed it in a precarious position. Its liberal leanings and dedication to the principles of racial equality served as a beacon for civil rights activists and a target for segregationists. Accelerating civil rights activity severely worsened the already uneasy relationship between Tougaloo and the state. The College's financial status left it in dire need of economic assistance and at the mercy of philanthropic agencies with little interest in questions of institutional integrity. These external and internal pressures collided and destabilized the institution in 1964.

Beittel's resignation offers a portal for an investigation of the delicate balance of finances and state pressure at a private HBCU during the Civil Rights Era and the costs HBCUs paid in institutional autonomy. Tougaloo's quandary is an example of what HBCUs across the South debated: could it afford to be involved in the Civil Rights Movement? Could it financially afford to spend multiple hours and resources defending itself and its constituents in lean economic times? Could it politically afford to be committed to African-American equality in the face of constant state pressure? Under different circumstances Tougaloo may not have entertained such questions. In 1964, its place in the movement and financial reality forced the institution to examine its mission.

Tougaloo in the Heart of Dixie

The end of the Civil War forced the nation, and the South in particular, to grapple with integrating freedmen and freedwomen into the social order. Formal schooling became an important part of that process, and African Americans sought education at all levels. Individual southern states and industrial philanthropists created institutions that educated African Americans to occupy a lowly position in the southern racial caste system. The school curriculum taught the dignity of manual labor, respect for the racial order, and the proper limits of African-American aspirations. Students rarely participated in academic pursuits. These reformers never intended to create academic institutions and only grudgingly admitted that African Americans deserved a college education. They invested in higher education not for African-American uplift but to insure social stability, to create a separate African-American professional class, and to keep African Americans from attending historically white institutions.

Other organizations, usually missionary associations, created institutions that defied the racial caste system and educated African Americans for full equality.[1] The American Missionary Association (AMA) pioneered the creation of these types of colleges for African Americans. AMA-supported institutions followed a classical curriculum, employed both African-American and white faculty, appointed African-American and white members to the Board of Trustees, and created a climate that supported African-American participation in civic and political life. Their ideas on African-American equality and racially mixed campuses marked them as radicals.[2] In 1869, the AMA, in cooperation with the Freedmen's Bureau, purchased a 500-acre plantation seven miles north of Jackson, Mississippi, to build a school for African Americans.

In 1871 the State of Mississippi granted Tougaloo University its charter and incorporated its Board of Trustees with the understanding that the property, both real and personal, be limited "to the amount of five hundred thousand dollars."[3] The AMA moved quickly to craft it into an institution imbued with a liberal and egalitarian spirit. The new university, a generous description since it included only a primary, secondary, and normal school, was "accessible to all, irrespective of their religious tenets, and conducted on the most liberal principles for the benefit of our citizens in general." A combination of tuition, AMA contributions, individual church donations, and philanthropic foundation funds supported the new institution. The school day mixed academics and vocational training, but liberal arts dominated the curriculum.

In the early 1930s the institution, now called Tougaloo College, became a four-year accredited liberal arts college—the only African-American college of the sort in the entire state.[4] Its prestige grew throughout the first half of the twentieth century as Tougaloo received the honor of being the only African-American college to gain an "A" rating from the Southern Association of Colleges and Secondary Schools in 1948. By the early 1950s, none of the faculty held less than a master's degree. The institution also focused on the college curriculum and phased out the primary and secondary school. Tougaloo's reputation brought students from Louisiana, Arkansas, Texas, Tennessee, Alabama, Michigan, and Illinois though most students came from Mississippi. The student body remained exclusively African American despite Tougaloo's open attendance policy.[5] The faculty, administrative staff, and Board of Trustees were racially mixed.

Tougaloo's curricular focus, national reputation, freedom from state control, and race-liberal attitudes rankled white Mississippians. Its mere existence contradicted the educational reality of most African Americans in the state. In 1950, 70 percent of African Americans over twenty-five years of age had less than a seventh-grade education; only 2.3 percent finished high school.[6] Wary of the approaching decision in the *Brown v. Board of Education* case, the state, which spent $122.93 per white child and $32.55 per African-American child, hurriedly attempted to equalize funding.[7] Its attempts were lackluster at best.

Segregationists reorganized after the Supreme Court's *Brown* decision. The Mississippi White Citizens' Council, founded less than six months after the decision and headquartered in Jackson, declared itself "dedicated to the maintenance of peace, good order and domestic tranquility in our Community and in our State and to the preservation of our States' Rights."[8] The Sovereignty Commission grew out of the same antidesegregation spirit, and the two groups worked in tandem to defeat desegregation efforts in general and school desegregation in particular. Created by the Mississippi legislature on 29 March 1956, that commission sought to "do and perform any and all acts and things deemed necessary and proper to protect the sovereignty of the state of Mississippi, and her sister states, from encroachment thereon by the Federal Government or any branch, department, or agency thereof."[9] The commission conducted investigations, participated in the national campaign to thwart passage of the 1964 Civil Rights Act, created a Speakers Bureau to present Mississippi's case to the nation, and donated money to groups and individuals (including African Americans) who favored segregation.[10] With the assistance of the Citizens' Councils and the Sovereignty Commission, Mississippi successfully stalled student desegregation in every primary, secondary, or collegiate school into the 1970s—except Tougaloo.

Tougaloo, like other HBCUs, maintained an uneasy agreement with the surrounding white community: Tougaloo constituents did not aggressively agitate against the racial status quo in exchange for being left alone by hostile whites. Individuals at Tougaloo, however, were not completely complacent. Activism grew in the mid-twentieth century and exacerbated Tougaloo's tense relationship to the state. In 1946, Reverend William Albert Bender, Tougaloo's sixty-year-old African-American chaplain, attempted to vote in the Democratic primary but was denied. He later filed a complaint with the state attorney general. Hostile whites burned a cross on the Tougaloo campus in retaliation.[11] In the early 1950s, Ernst Borinski, a German Jew who was Head of the Department of Sociology and Chairman of the Division of Social Science, sponsored a Social Science Forum in which he invited speakers to discuss politics, race, popular culture, and government. That Forum drew an interracial audience since students and faculty from Millsaps College, a private white institution in Jackson, often patronized the series.[12] At the same time, Reverend John Mangram, an African American and the new Chaplain, participated in one of the most hated civil rights organizations: the National Association for the Advancement of Colored People (NAACP). Bringing further unwanted attention to Tougaloo, Mangram helped organize the Fourth Annual Southeast Regional NAACP Conference in 1956 and the Tougaloo youth branch of the NAACP in 1960.[13] These individual acts of resistance primed Tougaloo for the role it assumed in the burgeoning Civil Rights Movement.

Students at HBCUs across the South entered the Civil Rights Movement and inaugurated a period of sustained mass activism in 1960. Their brand of activism broke with the past and shifted civil rights agitation from the courts to the streets. Four students from North Carolina Agriculture and Technical College, a public HBCU, staged a sit-in at the local Woolworth store to protest segregation and discrimination in eating establishments on 1 February. Other HBCU students in North Carolina followed their example, and soon HBCU students in other states conducted their own sit-ins. Shaw University, a private HBCU in North Carolina, hosted a conference to organize the sit-in movement in April. The Student Nonviolent Coordinating Committee (SNCC) grew out of that conference and enabled a coordinated attack on segregation by HBCU students across the South. SNCC turned its attention to voter registration as proprietors desegregated their facilities. HBCU students and interested others fanned out across the South to encourage African Americans to register and vote in elections. They traveled to the deep South and provided voter education classes, transportation to registration and voting locations, and psychological sustenance to disenfranchised African Americans.[14] Activists used local churches, homes, and HBCU campuses like Tougaloo to organize their attack on racial domination.

Not all HBCUs proved hospitable to such aims. The institution's relationship to the state often determined its role in the movement.[15] Southern legislatures closely controlled public institutions. States invested in racial hierarchy refused to support black public schools heavily involved in the destruction of the southern social order. Mississippi's Board of Trustees of Institutions of Higher Learning carefully selected amenable presidents to head the state's three public HBCUs. The Board bullied those college presidents, worked with the Sovereignty Commission, and overtly threatened to curtail funds if presidents did not maintain the Board's vision of a proper Mississippi. Public HBCUs did not want to alienate the Board. At Jackson State College, only six miles from Tougaloo, the president supplied the Sovereignty Commission with the names and home addresses of activist students, refused to allow students to form an NAACP chapter, and dissolved the Student Government Association after it spearheaded a demonstration on campus in 1961. Any violation of campus policies resulted in suspension or expulsion, a power the president used more than once. He similarly ruled the faculty, all of whom were African American as segregation laws required. Tenure did not exist, and the president fired members of the faculty without due process. Those who criticized the Mississippi way of life or the campus incurred the wrath of the president and the Board of Trustees.[16] Campus constituents were interested in racial equality, but they treaded softly.

Private institutions like Tougaloo enjoyed autonomy absent at public institutions.[17] HBCUs founded by missionary philanthropists had long histories of dedication to racial uplift in civic and political life, and their ideas on African-American equality made them an anomaly in the South.[18] Unlike public HBCUs, they solicited money primarily from northern interests not southern interests or state governments, they maintained headquarters outside the South, and their Boards of Trustees included both southern and northern members. Institutional autonomy forced southern interests to find creative ways to harass the private colleges in Mississippi and elsewhere. Students at neither public nor private campuses overwhelmingly participated in direct-action, but those at private institutions like Tougaloo did so with a degree of freedom not shared by students at public HBCUs.

Conditions in Mississippi stalled full-blown direct action in the state. When NAACP Youth Council members solicited advice on conducting a sit-in shortly after events in North Carolina, conservative Mississippi NAACP leadership dissuaded them from participating in such protests and suggested they refocus their energies.[19] White political and economic terror reigned in the state, and conservative leaders feared that direct action would only led to violent retaliation. Militant NAACP members ignored the advice. Medgar Evers, Jackson resident and Mississippi Field Secretary for the NAACP since 1954, organized an Easter boycott of downtown Jackson stores to protest poor treatment and discrimination in 1960. Local college students, including several from Tougaloo, publicized that boycott, but it lasted only a short while and met with limited success. The same April, NAACP members on the Gulf Coast organized a wade-in in Biloxi to protest regulations that prevented African Americans from patronizing beaches along the Gulf of Mexico. A white mob chased and assaulted the swimmers as police watched.[20] Intense racist scrutiny and reprisals forced Mississippi activists to regroup. Almost an entire year passed before African-American Mississippians initiated another direct-action attack on Mississippi's racial hierarchy.

Nine Tougaloo students inaugurated the rebirth of direct action in Mississippi with a sit-in at the Jackson Municipal Library in March 1961. That sit-in, arrests, and media coverage reinvigorated African-American Mississippians, particularly those in Jackson. The North Jackson NAACP Youth Council, West Jackson NAACP Youth Council, Tougaloo NAACP youth branch, and other interested individuals planned and executed a variety of assaults on segregation and discrimination in the city in the next few years. Between 1961 and 1964, activists in Jackson launched another longer lasting and more effective boycott of white stores, conducted sit-ins, pickets, mass marches, and letter-writing campaigns, and initiated a school desegregation suit. Police arrested over 600 people between 1961 and 1962 alone.[21] The assault on Jackson, the urban center and capital of the state, infuriated white Mississippians. Citizens' Councils, local police, and state agencies bloodied, jailed, and killed activists to stem the tide of protest.

Tougaloo provided a refuge to plan many of these direct-action attacks. The institution itself welcomed Freedom Riders, hosted civil rights conferences and planning sessions, and sponsored a work-study program through which SNCC workers earned college credit. Tougaloo students worked with national organizations like the NAACP and SNCC but also created their own organizations to attack racial domination. One such organization was the Student Nonviolent Group. In fall 1963, that organization's Cultural and Artistic Committee focused on discrimination in live entertainment and initiated a massive letter writing campaign to dissuade entertainers from performing in front of segregated audiences in Mississippi. The Committee contacted artists, agents, and management to support their cause, "The issue is no longer one of merely appearing before a segregated audience. To appear is to endorse and condone segregation in toto."[22] Another wing of the group targeted segregated churches, some of which Tougaloo professors attended. Together white Tougaloo professors, black and white students, and other activists carefully planned visits to certain prominent Jackson churches.[23] Students took full advantage of the liberal campus climate and directly confronted Mississippi's racial caste system.

By 1964, Mississippi's dismal record on civil rights and opposition to African-American political participation made it unique, even when compared to other southern states. The state's rabid resistance earned it international attention; it also brought increased activism. In the spring, local Mississippi activists created the Mississippi Freedom Democratic Party, an alternative to the state's Democratic Party that barred African-American participation. They lobbied unsuccessfully to unseat the Mississippi Democrats at the Democratic National Convention in August, but their appearance at the convention drew a national audience. Meanwhile, SNCC spearheaded preparations for the Mississippi Summer Project, which brought hundreds of mostly white volunteers to Mississippi to teach in Freedom Schools and work in voter registration. Mississippi segregationists braced for the "outside agitators" and harassed locals working in concert with activists. Tougaloo became a favored target.[24]

Reverend Dr. Adam D. Beittel stepped into this context. Born of Quaker roots, he nurtured his liberal philosophies at progressive institutions like Oberlin and the University of Chicago where he received a master's and doctoral degree, respectively. Beittel then worked in a variety of religious colleges including one exclusively white Quaker institution, Guilford College, in North Carolina, and one exclusively African-American AMA institution, Talladega College, in Alabama. His educational credentials, religious dedication, and administrative experience made Beittel attractive to the Tougaloo Board of Trustees who lured him away from his position as Dean of Chapel and Professor of Religion at Beloit College. His decision was difficult because of his age (sixty-one) and the thought of leaving a comfortable job in Wisconsin for the hostile environment of Jackson, Mississippi. According to Beittel, the Board convinced him: "[B]ecause I had spent many years in the South and had a good deal of experience on college campuses in the South, I could be very useful to Tougaloo College at a time which seemed to them to be a somewhat critical one."[25] The Board of Trustees also assured him job security until age seventy, provided he remained healthy, with the option to continue on a yearly basis after age sixty-five.[26] He agreed to the conditions and became Tougaloo's eighth president effective 1 September 1960.

Beittel brought with him an aggressive liberalism. His opinion on racial equality contributed to his 1952 dismissal as president of Talladega College, a private HBCU in Alabama, and a sister institution to Tougaloo under the AMA. In 1948, three years after he assumed the presidency, Beittel closed the primary and secondary school on Talladega's campus. The secondary school was the only institution in the entire county in which African-American students received high school diplomas. A source of pride and example of interracial cooperation, the closing of the desegregated schools infuriated faculty and staff (particularly the African-American faculty and staff) with children enrolled. Beittel believed their presence absolved the city of Talladega from providing a high school education for African-American youth. Off campus, Beittel's vocal desegregationist sentiments angered local whites. He openly condemned racial discrimination in education, recreation, and health care and even wrote the governor to express his opinion. He also tried to attract white students to Talladega; his own son received a degree from the College in 1950. With internal and external opposition to Beittel, the trustees dismissed him along with other key administrators.[27] Eight years later Beittel became the president of Tougaloo.

Beittel's dismissal from Talladega did not dissuade the Tougaloo Board of Trustees. The Talladega Board of Trustees only fired him because of pressure from the faculty, pressure the Board believed was unfounded but led to such internal strife as to "make it impossible for him to carry on as president of the college."[28] Beittel also proved his loyalty during the crisis over the primary and secondary schools. A majority of the Board supported closing the schools despite faculty attitudes to the contrary. Beittel, not the Board, suffered the consequences. The AMA's paternalistic attitude toward its colleges made the appointment of a white president at Tougaloo highly likely, and Beittel's familiarity with AMA schools and his qualifications made him competitive for the position. His experience with southern attitudes and sensibilities solidified the Tougaloo Board's decision. These same trustees requested Beittel's resignation four years later.[29]

Overt activism at Tougaloo accelerated in the early 1960s and coincided with Beittel's arrival. During his tenure, individual acts of civil disobedience transformed into organized direct action as Tougaloo constituents helped initiate the Jackson phase of the civil rights struggle. Beittel's presence did not precipitate campus activism, but his liberal ideals meant participation in civil rights protest went unpunished. Between 1961 and 1964, Tougaloo students, faculty, and staff participated in a variety of public attacks on segregation in Jackson: sit-ins at the Jackson Municipal Library and the local Woolworth's, kneel-ins at Jackson churches, pray-ins on federal property to protest police brutality, pickets at the segregated county fair, and boycotts of Jackson stores. The new chaplain and first white man to hold the post, Reverend Ed King, participated in some of the direct-action initiatives and even ran as the Mississippi Freedom Democratic Party's Vice Presidential candidate. John Salter, a white professor of sociology, became the North Jackson NAACP Youth Council's adult advisor and spearheaded the planning for several acts of civil disobedience. Beittel never punished campus constituents for their activism though the state pursued criminal prosecutions. Beittel further angered the white Jackson community by voicing his own race-liberal and desegregationist sentiments on a local television show, participating in a sit-in, and allowing civil rights organizations to host meetings on campus. Adding insult to injury, Tougaloo now enrolled four white students, some of whom participated in the direct-action campaign. It seemed, at least to the State of Mississippi, that the entire campus was involved in the Civil Rights Movement by 1964.

Tougaloo attendance remained small in the middle 1960s, approximately 500, an even smaller number of which participated in direct-action. Many campus constituents admonished activists to focus on academics and graduation rather than civil rights. Regardless, the state took steps to quell the activism centered at what the local press called Cancer College. In June 1963, President Beittel, Chaplain King, Professor Salter, and Tougaloo student Bette Anne Poole (an African American) were named along with other individuals, the NAACP, the Congress of Racial Equality, Tougaloo Trustees, and "their agents, members, employees, attorneys, successors, and all other persons in active concert with them" in a writ of temporary injunction preventing them from demonstrating in any way, shape, or form.[30] The state even attempted to disestablish the institution in 1964. On 17 February, Lieutenant Governor Carroll Gartin called for further investigation of the college's role in demonstrations and civil rights activities. Gartin reportedly told a local civic club that Tougaloo provided a haven for "quacks, quirks, political agitators and possibly some communists."[31] Other state leaders joined his cause, and three days later three state senators introduced a bill to revoke Tougaloo's ninety-four-year-old charter in the name of "public interest."[32] They maintained a twofold argument: First, Tougaloo's original charter restricted the campus to $500,000 worth of assets, a figure Tougaloo passed years earlier without repercussions. Second, and more to the heart of the matter, Gartin and others accused the College of completely neglecting its charter: "The big question to be decided is whether the school has substituted civil disobedience instruction for the curriculum it was authorized to have under its charter."[33]

At the same time, the Mississippi legislature contemplated Senate Bill 1794, which allowed discretionary powers to the Commission on College Accreditation.[34] That bill attacked Tougaloo without mentioning it by name. Passage of the bill revoked reciprocal accreditation from the Southern Association of Colleges and Schools and the state, and the loss of state accreditation prevented education students from receiving state teacher's licenses. The state hoped the loss of accreditation would tarnish Tougaloo's reputation, limit attendance, and force those teachers who received their degrees from Cancer College to leave the state to teach their integrationist propaganda elsewhere.

The legislature introduced both bills to punish Tougaloo for its support of civil rights activism, and the legislature never pretended otherwise. Such drastic and public measures brought the state unwanted scrutiny, particularly since Tougaloo mounted an aggressive publicity campaign to call attention to the situation and embarrass Governor Paul Johnson into either vetoing or limiting the influence of each bill. President Beittel enlisted the assistance of the American Association of University Professors, the United Church of Christ, Tougaloo's sister institutions, the Southern Association of Colleges and Schools, and other institutions and organizations with a vested interest in protecting higher educational autonomy.[35] Tougaloo's efforts proved successful. The bill to revoke Tougaloo's charter died in the Judiciary Committee, and though passed, the act separating accreditation held no teeth. The entire episode demonstrated the level of hostility toward Tougaloo and its importance to the Civil Rights Movement.

A financial crisis in 1964 also plagued Tougaloo. As a private institution, Tougaloo relied on various sources of religious and foundation philanthropy. By the 1960s, the College struggled to meet its financial goals and trustees worried about the status of the institution. Their experience with the Southern Association of Colleges and Secondary Schools fed their fears. In 1951, that Association planned to revoke Tougaloo's accreditation based on the college's financial situation. To be accredited, an institution needed a certain amount in its operating budget, a reputable library with a number of holdings, an adequate physical plant, faculty with advanced degrees, and a salary minimum for faculty members.[36] Tougaloo, with philanthropic support, succeeded in maintaining its accreditation and meeting the financial requirements but remained scarred by the experience. The campus's physical plant needs and rising student enrollment exacerbated the funding demands.[37]

Despite their best efforts Tougaloo Trustees found themselves with an operational deficit of $34,982.67 in 1961.[38] The trustees broadened sources of income both to erase the deficit and to improve the physical and academic quality of the campus. Beittel worked hard to solicit funds from individual donors and philanthropic agencies and was in large part successful. Certain financial sources, however, turned away from Tougaloo. For instance, the Mississippi branch of the Christian Churches (Disciples of Christ) withdrew its financial support after Tougaloo activists targeted their segregated churches for pray-ins in 1963.[39] Trustees identified the Ford Foundation's Fund for the Advancement of Education as one possible funding source. That fund supported partnerships between HBCUs and predominantly white northern colleges. Tougaloo and Brown University already maintained a friendly relationship: they sponsored a student and faculty exchange program, and two of Tougaloo's trustees were connected to Brown University.[40] Tougaloo and Brown contemplated expanding their relationship and pursuing Ford funding. Tougaloo trustees considered the partnership a viable source of income and an opportunity to receive assistance in improving the quality of the academic program. Brown considered the partnership an opportunity to assist a struggling college in the spirit of institutional cooperation. In fall 1963, Tougaloo and Brown began the application process for Ford funds.

Enter Brown University and the Ford Foundation: The Role of Finances

Tougaloo Trustees Wesley Hotchkiss, Emory Ross, and Board Chairman Robert Wilder, all of whom were white, broached the subject of Beittel's retirement at special meeting in New York in January 1964.[41] The three-man committee reported that Tougaloo's financial situation demanded quick action. Tougaloo's trustees hoped that other philanthropic agencies would follow the Ford Foundation's example and donate funds for the college. Trustees envisioned it as an exciting new period in Tougaloo's existence and the beginning of substantial campus growth. Such a venture necessitated consistent leadership over a period of at least ten years. According to the trustees, Beittel did not share the Board's enthusiasm, and his age, sixty-five years by this time, prevented him from providing the institution with the type of permanence necessary to translate into practice the new vision for Tougaloo. The committee confronted Beittel with the decision and indicated they were "pleased with the reasonable response of the president to the suggestion."[42] Trustees decided to announce the decision at the official spring meeting in April rather than issue an immediate press release.

The relationship between Beittel and the trustees dissolved soon after the January meeting. Beittel refused to accept the Board's decision and began a semi-public campaign to halt his forced resignation. Trustees accused Beittel of changing his mind and attempting to use public opinion to maintain the presidency. Beittel accused the trustees of acting in bad faith, questioned if a quorum existed at the January meeting, and invoked his contract that gave him the discretion to continue as president until his seventieth birthday—five years away.[43] Beittel fired off a set of letters asking for further clarification, and his supporters wrote their own letters of inquiry. He concluded that Brown University managed to influence the Board's decision and worried about the implications for institutional autonomy.

The relationship between Beittel and the trustees had become openly hostile by April 1964. Beittel, unswayed by the Board's explanation of his forced retirement, wrote to Brown University President Barnaby Keeney. In his letter, Beittel referred to a 1 April meeting between himself and Trustee

Chairman Robert Wilder in which Beittel gathered that Brown University played a role in the Board's decision. Beittel repeated what he gleaned from the conversation, "It was indicated that Brown University would not continue our promising cooperative relationship unless I am replaced, and that without Brown University the Ford Foundation will provide no support, and without Ford support other Foundations will not respond, and without foundation support the future of Tougaloo College is very uncertain."[44] Keeney assured Beittel that he played absolutely no part in the trustees' decision to seek Beittel's retirement in January and emphatically denied that Brown attempted to interfere with the internal affairs of Tougaloo.[45]

Both President Keeney and the Ford Foundation did play an important role in Beittel's removal from office, however. Keeney himself substantiated Beittel's accusations in a letter to a Tougaloo Trustee in which he requested the trustees assure the Ford Foundation that Tougaloo would appoint a new president in 1964. According to Keeney, Ford "will not do much, if anything, until they have this assurance."[46] Beittel's civil rights stance and Tougaloo's role in the Civil Rights Movement became stumbling blocks, and Ford money became conditional. To mask his own role in the negotiations, Keeney counseled the trustees: "This must be handled very carefully because it would be disastrous if the word got around that Brown was interfering in the internal affairs of Tougaloo."[47]

The accusation that Brown University attempted to interfere in Tougaloo business angered the trustees.[48] The trustees considered the Brown-Tougaloo partnership pivotal to the future of the college, but only insofar as the relationship improved the quality of education at Tougaloo and increased the amount of monies filtering into the college. Beittel's lack of interest in the partnership (an inaccurate description of Beittel's attitude according to Beittel) demonstrated he was not acting in Tougaloo's best interest. By April, Trustee Wesley Hotchkiss lamented: "It has become apparent that Dr. Beittel simply cannot become the leader of the kind of development program necessary to keep Tougaloo afloat."[49] Beittel could save Tougaloo's reputation only if he stepped down gracefully.

Beittel failed to retain the presidency. The Board of Trustees held their annual spring meeting 24 and 25 April at which they announced Beittel's retirement effective 1 September.[50] Three weeks after the meeting, President Beittel and President Keeney announced in a joint statement that the two institutions "entered into a wide-ranging agreement under which Brown has pledged its educational and administrative resources to an intensive academic development program at Tougaloo."[51] The Ford Foundation, through its Fund for the Advancement of Education, donated $245,000, while other foundations and an individual donor contributed another $118,000. The press release announced that Brown chose Tougaloo because of its liberal arts focus, integrated faculty and student body, and "its commitment to the highest ideals of academic freedom."[52]

Beittel backed away from his initial accusation that Brown University officials requested his resignation but remained firm in his conviction that the Board forced his retirement under dubious circumstances. He challenged the Board's portrayal of Tougaloo's financial status by providing evidence that the campus emerged out of debt and reached a surplus during his tenure.[53] Beittel pressed the trustees regarding their decision even after the announcement of his retirement. If asked about the situation, "Should I tell them the unvarnished truth that in spite of an agreement with the Board for a longer term of service, I am being sacrificed with the hope that this will result in larger financial gifts to the College? Shall I say that while Brown University has not demanded a change of administration at Tougaloo, a change of administration is being made with the thought that it will be pleasing to Brown University and perhaps to the Ford Foundation?"[54] Rather than entertain Beittel's argument, the trustees thanked Beittel for his service to Tougaloo and refused to reconsider their decision.

Enter the Sovereignty Commission: The Role of Civil Rights Activism and the State

The Sovereignty Commission entered the picture in April 1964 with its own agenda. Harassing Tougaloo became a top priority for Director Erle Johnston, Jr., who believed that curtailing activism at Tougaloo could be a vehicle for his own career advancement.[55] The Commission sought assistance in their objective and did not wait long. On 2 April, an unnamed source reported that Dr. John Held, a white male and Chairman of Tougaloo's Department of Philosophy and Religion, agreed to be an informant.[56] Held accused Beittel and others of hijacking education for civil right aims and transforming Tougaloo into a center for political activity. He also had designs on the presidency. At Johnston's invitation, Held visited the Sovereignty Commission office 13 April and informed the Commission about "the dissension among faculty and students" regarding the policies of President Beittel and Chaplain King, threatened to resign if Beittel was not removed, and offered to identify documents linking Beittel to a communist organization. The Commission thanked him and requested a list of students and faculty opposed to and in support of Beittel and King as well as the names of trustees who might be open to Commission concerns. Held and Johnston "worked out a code system for communication and relaying information which would not involve Dr. Held with those at Tougaloo who would be opposed to his contact with the Sovereignty Commission."[57] Days later, "Mr. Zero" submitted a list of trustees considered "most vital and influential" (all of whom were white) and those "probably more easily influenced by pressure" (all of whom were African American). The communication also included a list of notable students and a Tougaloo College catalog in which Mr. Zero categorized the faculty.[58]

On 17 April, Johnston contacted Wesley Hotchkiss (one of the trustees Mr. Zero identified as most vital and influential) and asked to meet with the trustees to discuss materials gathered by the Commission and to offer a trade: the resignation of President Beittel and Chaplain King for institutional safety. In his letter to Hotchkiss, Johnston accused Beittel and King of tarnishing Tougaloo's good name by inciting activism. "The people of Mississippi, both white and colored, would like to see Tougaloo College restored to its former reputation as a qualified, accredited private school for education only." The Mississippi legislature and the Mississippi Accrediting Commission promised punitive action against the school if the trustees refused to act and Tougaloo maintained its present course. Johnston suggested replacing Beittel and King with "dedicated persons interested only in the education of students."[59] Hotchkiss arranged a meeting on 21 April in New York, a date that coincided with the annual Board of Trustees meeting.

Johnston and attorney Shelby Rogers flew to New York and met with Trustees Robert Wilder (Chairman), Wesley Hotchkiss, and Lawrence Durgin, all of them considered most vital and influential by Mr. Zero. L. William Nelson, a white man and Chairman of the Buildings and Grounds Committee for Tougaloo, also attended. Johnston and Rogers presented themselves as individuals, "not as representatives of any governmental group" though they clearly acted in the state's interest and with the consent of the governor, if not the legislature.[60] Johnston outlined their agenda in his report,

> At the meeting it was our purpose to show that the image of Tougaloo as represented by the President, Dr. A. D. Beittel and [Reverend Ed King], had inspired such resentment on the part of state officials and legislators that a showdown clash appeared imminent. We suggested that if Tougaloo had a good man as president and a good man as [chaplain], the institution could be restored to its former status as a respected private college. We also suggested that if such a move could be made by the trustees, the college would have ample time to prove good faith and a change of attitude and possibly avoid punitive action from the Legislature.[61]

Johnston then showed the trustees copies of the two bills introduced into the legislature that attacked Tougaloo and assured the trustees that "we would do all in our power" to halt such punitive measures if the trustees followed the Commission's advice. "The state gives wide latitude on policy to private schools," attorney Rogers explained, but "we prefer peace and respect instead of agitation and demonstration."[62]

Johnston and Rogers employed a different tactic after realizing the trustees were not as easy to convince as they hoped. They accused Tougaloo of harboring communists. Johnston and Rogers linked Tougaloo to a communist conspiracy by associating Beittel with John Salter, a former member of the faculty who then worked with the Southern Conference Educational Fund (SCEF).[63] Chaplain King's association with the Council of Federated Organizations (COFO) and the work-study arrangement between SNCC and Tougaloo also demonstrated Tougaloo's complicity with communist sentiment.[64] Such charges proved to be a common ploy to discredit the Civil Rights

Movement and organizations that supported racial integration. The Sovereignty Commission's accusations against SCEF, COFO, and SNCC were not grounded in fact, nor were the trustees convinced that communists had infiltrated the African-American freedom movement. Sovereignty Commission officials, however, cared less about proving their accusations than they did about poisoning public sentiment toward Tougaloo.

The trustees dismissed the Commission's claim of dissension and dissatisfaction with Beittel as "normal complaints on any college campus and normal diversity of thought" rather than adopting the Commission's interpretation of Tougaloo student and faculty activism as a direct threat to the state. The trustees further rejected the Commission's interpretation by stating that students "had a right to be interested in the rights of human kind" and that the off-campus actions of Tougaloo students and faculty were not under the board's purview. Clearly annoyed with this interpretation, Johnston and Rogers "wondered out loud" if Tougaloo fulfilled its charter's duties and accreditation requirements. The trustees bristled at the threat, and according to Rogers, became very nervous and concerned.[65]

L. William Nelson asked what "sort of deal" the Commission wanted in order to keep Tougaloo's charter and accreditation. Although Rogers and Johnston clearly identified such a deal as part of their agenda, they begged off and "promptly told them that we had no deal and no authority to make any commitment on behalf of any official body." Rather, they suggested the removal of Beittel and King to improve the general climate and image of Tougaloo, which, in turn, would open the lines of communication between Tougaloo, legislators, and other governmental bodies. Rogers was not confident that the state could close Tougaloo, but he left the meeting pleased since it sufficiently scared the trustees to act, caused further division between the trustees, the president, and the students, provided fodder for finding "actual technical reasons" for revoking the charter, and helped the Commission identify trustees they could trust.[66]

Trustees announced Beittel's retirement four days after that meeting. The news thrilled Erle Johnston who believed the Sovereignty Commission had successfully intimidated the Board into action. The Board's explanation for the resignation lifted his spirits further: "Our pipeline of information from Tougaloo says the trustees gave as their reason for dismissal of Dr. Beittel that he was 'inefficient.' This will certainly work to our advantage. Had Dr. Beittel been asked to resign because of racial agitation or collaboration with communist front organizations, he could have made a martyr out of himself. As it is, he can say nothing because the trustees would naturally answer any statement he made by stating he was discharged for inefficiency."[67] The Commission hoped Beittel's departure would negatively influence civil rights participation and limit Tougaloo's role in the Civil Rights Movement. Satisfied with their results, Johnston and the Sovereignty Commission set their sites on one of Mississippi's other private HBCUs, Rust College, in the hopes of achieving the same success.[68]

The implication that the Sovereignty Commission played a role in Beittel's firing rocked the campus. Students, faculty, and staff rallied to Beittel's side. A poem written by Elizabeth Sewell, a white faculty member, represented one wing of campus sentiment. She placed Beittel among martyrs in the civil rights struggle:

This has been quite a year for heads falling.
Not a thing one is accustomed to
In the ordinary everyday life we all suppose
Is ours.
That small-girl head, torn from its body, was the first
At Birmingham . . .
After there was that other, the strong virile head,
Sun-tanned and ruddy
With two smashing bullets in it
At Dallas . . .
Promises devalued as if they were only dollars,
Current coin worthless now if not
For ever.

For which reason a poet goes back
To old words
And I think of two for you,
Integrity and valor,
Because they came to me when I first met you
That hot September
Half a year, or a lifetime, ago,
And nothing since to make me change my mind.[69]

Not all Tougaloo constituents mourned Beittel's dismissal. John Held, the Sovereignty Commission informant, applauded the Board's decision and hoped his retirement would end Tougaloo's active role in the Civil Rights Movement. He worried, however, about Beittel's handling of the situation and accused him of using any speaking engagement as a platform to discuss his dismissal. "I do not mind a little boasting and tears," Held said, "but this sort of thing can alienate the Negro public from the new president and his administration." The problem of Chaplain King remained. Held fumed at King's continued involvement in COFO and the student body's use of direct-action tactics to desegregate Jackson facilities. "Now, I am in favor of the Negro having every right that he can obtain—but I do not believe it to be the purpose of Tougaloo College to sponsor agitation." Held suggested it was time to clean house, sever Tougaloo's ties with activist organizations, and dismiss both Beittel and King. Generously, he offered his services: "If I were made president of this college, I believe I could make the college respectable and acceptable in the eyes of the power structure of the state—at the same time, preserving its place in the Negro structure. I seem to have the confidence and respect of the State and of the Negro community."[70]

Off-campus agencies wrote the trustees to express their dismay over Beittel's firing and to inquire about the rumors of Sovereignty Commission involvement. Paul Anthony, Director of Field Activities for the Southern Regional Council, refused to argue with the Board's decision, not because he felt they were right, but because: "My affection for Dr. and Mrs. Beittel is so great that I am relieved that they will be leaving Mississippi. That society is a hell in which the best of men of the strongest conscience should not be asked to endure."[71] Three Mississippi religious leaders reminded the trustees that "a change in the Presidency at this juncture will so complicate current critical issues about Tougaloo and race relations that the advances of the past few years will be seriously endangered. The reaction of the enemies of Tougaloo has already been made obvious in the press: Dr. Beittel's leaving is a victory for them and the first step in the control which must be exercised by the racists of Mississippi on the campus. Tougaloo is finally surrendering to intimidation."[72] Off-campus activists understood Tougaloo's place in the Civil Rights Movement and lamented the fact that its role might be sacrificed.

The trustees then initiated a campaign to squash rumors that they fired Beittel and denied that his involvement in and support of the Civil Rights Movement hastened the Board's decision. The Board explained that Beittel had reached retirement age, Tougaloo needed at least ten years of presidential continuity in this new era (impossible for Beittel since he was sixty-five), and Beittel's lack of interest in, and commitment to, the Brown-Tougaloo partnership necessitated new leadership.[73] A friend and colleague of the trustees alluded to the fact that Beittel's civil rights activities influenced their decision: "One of the behavior patterns of some civil rights enthusiasts which I find myself resenting is their easy assumption that every institution and every available person can justifiably be used as a tool in the service of this cause."[74] In the communications with their critics and friends, however, trustees resented such an implication.

Wesley Hotchkiss addressed the delicate situation triggered by the Sovereignty Commission's visit. He explained that a few Board members met with Commission representatives in April but that the Board requested Beittel's resignation months prior to the meeting. The Commission's threats were of little consequence though their visit put the trustees in an embarrassing position: Beittel's retirement was not public knowledge, and the timing of the Commission's visit could be construed to make the trustees appear complicit with Commission aims. The Board, according to Hotchkiss, refused to be swayed from its course despite anticipated rumors. They proceeded to request Beittel's retirement and bristled at the suggestion that an outside agency had the power to select someone for the presidency. Hotchkiss regretted that such rumors spread across the nation but affirmed that reasons other than Beittel's civil rights stance precipitated his retirement.[75]

Conclusion and Implications

Private HBCUs in the civil rights era faced threats to their institutional autonomy that other institutions never had to contemplate. They remained indebted to philanthropic interests in ways different than other institutions, had fewer wealthy alumni, admitted more students unable to pay tuition, and enrolled a smaller number of students on which to rely for financial contributions.[76] Chronic underfunding forced them to consider broader financial opportunities that left them vulnerable to philanthropic impulses. Moreover, their liberal leanings and support of racial equality marked them as radical within the southern social order and as prime targets for southern racists. These pressures were not new to private HBCUs. What made the 1960s different was the Civil Rights Movement. The state easily dealt with individual campus constituents who confronted the southern system. Quelling group dissent proved another matter. Their private status forced legislators and segregationists to invent creative solutions to curtail activism, but the institutions were far from invulnerable. Similarly, private status shielded HBCUs from state financial sanctions, but the institutions remained susceptible to philanthropic agencies with a clear agenda for higher education—an agenda that did not include institutional involvement in a social movement. At Tougaloo, these pressures collided and forced President Beittel's resignation.

Tougaloo's situation demonstrates both the vulnerability and worth of HBCUs, particularly during the civil rights era. Such colleges played a unique role in the preservation of egalitarian aims in an enormously hostile environment. In the early 1960s when southern state interests collided with constitutionally protected freedoms, HBCUs like Tougaloo provided a forum for dissent. Still, their financial reality and liberal ideas on racial equality left them in jeopardy. The legislative bills punishing Tougaloo illustrated the enmity with which the state held the institution. Neither bill produced the anticipated result, so a state agency, the Sovereignty Commission, tried another route: President Beittel's termination. Halting all civil rights activity at Tougaloo by revoking its charter or accreditation seemed out of reach. The next best course of action was to cut off the proverbial head to kill the body. The Sovereignty Commission's self-congratulation regarding Beittel's resignation was misplaced, but the state did play an active and important role. Each time the state attacked Tougaloo, the trustees and their financial supporters diverted personnel and funds to defend the institution. Tougaloo's role in the Civil Rights Movement became a liability in lean economic times. Together, internal and external pressures left their mark and impacted institutional autonomy.

Notes

1. Negro philanthropy also supported institutions that defied the racial caste system. James D. Anderson discusses Negro philanthropy, missionary philanthropy, and other forms of HBCU financial support in *The Education of Blacks in the South, 1860–1935* (Chapel Hill: University of North Carolina Press, 1988), chapter 7.
2. The AMA and other missionary philanthropists hired integrated faculties, but paternalistic attitudes precluded them from hiring African-American presidents. See Anderson, *Education of Blacks in the South*, 244.
3. "An Act to Incorporate the Trustees of Tougaloo University," May 1871, folder 11, box 112, American Missionary Association Archives [hereafter AMAA], Addendum (1869–1991, n.d.), Series A, Subseries Tougaloo Correspondence, Amistad Research Center [hereafter ARC]., Tulane University, New Orleans, Louisiana.
4. Mississippi had two other private four-year HBCUs, neither of which shared Tougaloo's level of prestige.
5. Tougaloo had one white student prior to the 1960s. In 1879, the first normal school graduating class included Luella Miner, daughter of Tougaloo's Treasurer. Clarice Campbell and Oscar Allan Rogers, Jr., *Mississippi: The View from Tougaloo* (Jackson: University Press of Mississippi, 1979), 14.
6. *Census of the Population: 1950, Volume II, Part 24, Mississippi* (Washington, D.C.: Government Printing Office, 1952), 148.

7. *United States Census, Volume II,* 28–29, cited in John Dittmer, *Local People: The Struggle for Civil Rights in Mississippi* (Urbana: University of Illinois Press, 1994), 34.

8. *The Citizens' Council* 2, no. 2 (November 1956), 1, Citizens' Council Newspapers, 1955–1957, Accession Number 90.25, Tougaloo College Archives [hereafter TCA], Tougaloo, Mississippi.

9. *General Laws of the State of Mississippi,* 1956, Chapter 365, Section 5, 521.

10. Erle Johnston to Federation of Constitutional Government, 4 May 1964, Erle Johnson, "Canton Lions Club Speech," 13 May 1964, Erle Johnson to Herman Glazier, 16 March 1965, and Erle Johnston to Paul Johnson, 29 March 1965, cited in "Sovereignty Commission Agency History," 3, summary report included in Sovereignty Commission Files, Mississippi Department of Archives and History [hereafter cited MDAH], Jackson, Mississippi.

11. United States Senate, 79th Congress, 2d Session, *Hearings Before the Special Committee to Investigate Senatorial Campaign Expenditures, 1946* (Washington: Government Printing Office, 1947), 19, 88–90, cited in Dittmer, *Local People,* 3.

12. Invited speakers included Ralph Bunche, James Baldwin, Otto Nathan, David Riesman, Pete Seeger, and Joan Baez. See Gabrielle Simon Edgecomb, "Ernst Borinski: Positive Marginality: 'I Decided to Engage in Stigma Management,' " in *From Swastika to Jim Crow: Refugee Scholars at Black Colleges* (Malabar, FL.: Krieger Publishing, 1993), 117–128. Borinski further angered segregationists by inviting Tougaloo students to join his German and Russian classes at Millsaps College. See folder Biography, box 1, Ernst Borinski Papers, TCA.

13. Ruby Hurley to John Mangrum, 28 March 1956, and John Mangram to Ruby Hurley, 25 January 1960, no folder, box John D. Mangram, TCA.

14. Clayborne Carson, *In Struggle: SNCC and the Black Awakening of the 1960s* (Cambridge: Harvard University Press, 1981).

15. The difference in rate of participation between public and private college students is discussed in Elton Harrison, "Student Unrest on the Black College Campus," *Journal of Negro Education* 41 (Spring 1972): 113–120; John Orbell, "Protest Participation Among Southern Negro College Students," *American Political Science Review* 61 (June 1967): 446–456; and Joel Rosenthal, "Southern Black Student Activism: Assimilation vs. Nationalism," *Journal of Negro Education* 44 (Spring 1975): 113–129.

16. Jacob Reddix to Albert Jones, 1 April 1961, Sovereignty Commission Files 10-105-0-2-1-1-1, MDAH (all Sovereignty Commission Files are from the MDAH); John A. Peoples, Jr., *To Survive and Thrive: The Quest for a True University* (Jackson: Town Square Books, 1995), 58; and "Report Classes Boycotted at Jackson State," *Jackson Daily News,* 7 October 1961, Sovereignty Commission Files 10-105-0-4-1-1-1.

17. Private institutions remained autonomous from the state, but missionary associations kept close tabs on their institutions. The AMA headquarters forced presidents to request permission on everything from curriculum to repairs. According to Joe Richardson, *Christian Reconstruction: The American Missionary Association and Southern Blacks, 1861–1890* (Athens: University of Georgia Press, 1986), 136: "seldom did the AMA delegate authority to its administrators commensurate with their responsibilities."

18. Some institutions founded by Negro philanthropy were even more radical within the Southern order since they hired African American presidents to head the institutions. Missionary philanthropists refused to appoint African American presidents until the middle twentieth century.

19. Dittmer, *Local People,* 85–86.

20. J. Michael Butler, "The Mississippi Sovereignty Commission and Beach Integration, 1959–1963: A Cotton-Patch Gestapo?" *Journal of Southern History* 68:1 (February, 2002): 107–148.

21. Charles Payne, *I've Got the Light of Freedom: The Organizing Tradition and the Mississippi Freedom Struggle* (Berkeley: University of California Press, 1995), 286.

22. Austin Moore to Gary Graffman, 2 February 1964, folder 450, box 9, Ed King Collection, TCA.

23. "Negro Girls Turned Away from Church," *Clarion-Ledger,* 14 October 1963, and "12 Arrested at Churches here Sunday," *Clarion-Ledger,* 21 October 1963, Sovereignty Commission Files 3-74-1-31-1-1-1.

24. Students and staff, including the president, traveled to the Democratic National Convention as Mississippi Freedom Democratic Party delegates. Len Holt, *The Summer That Didn't End: The Story of the Mississippi Civil Rights Project of 1964* (New York: Da Capo Press, 1965), 339–340. The campus also hosted SNCC volunteers, and a few Tougaloo students themselves participated in the Summer Project.

25. Adam D. Beittel, interview with George Henderson, 2 June 1965, Jackson, Mississippi, 1–2, folder A.D. Biettel, box 6, John Quincy Adams Manuscript Papers, Oral History Project, Millsaps College Archives, Jackson, Mississippi.

26. Robert O. Wilder to A. D. Beittel, April 20, 1960, folder 17, box 110, AMAA, Addendum (1869–1991, n.d.), Series A, Subseries Touglaoo Correspondence, ARC.

27. Beittel's experience at Talladega is taken from Henry N. Drewry and Humphrey Doermann, *Stand and Prosper: Private Black Colleges and Their Students* (Princeton: Princeton University Press, 2001), 148–152.

28. Ibid., 150, citing [no title], *New York Times,* 9 June 1952, 18.

29. The Tougaloo Board of Trustees included a racially diverse group from the North and South. African American members included Earl B. Dickerson (Chicago, IL), Blair Hunt (Memphis, TN), A. H. McCoy (Jackson, MS), B. G. Olive, Jr., (Memphis, TN), and Nelson Willis (Baldwin, MI). White members included Kenneth Brown (Clayton, MO), Hodding Carter (Greenville, MS), Lawrence Durgin (Providence, RI), Irving Fain (Providence, RI), A. Dale Fiers (Indianapolis, IN), Mary Dale Fiers (Indianapolis, IN), Wesley Hotchkiss (New York, NY), Mrs. Richard Renner (Cleveland Heights, OH), Emory Ross (New York, NY), A. C. Stone (Cincinnati, OH), Howard Spragg (New York, NY), Mrs. [Mossie] Wyker (Berea, KY), and the Chairman, Robert Wilder (Warren, PA).

30. Writ of Temporary Injunction, Chancery Court of the First Judicial District of Hinds County, Mississippi, 6 June 1963, folder 374, box 8, Ed King Papers, TCA. The state of Mississippi understood Salter to be a white male, but Salter identified himself as a Wabanaki (Abenaki) Indian. John R. Salter, Jr., *Jackson, Mississippi: An American Chronicle of Struggle and Schism* (Malabar, FL: Robert E. Krieger Publishing, 1979), 5.

31. "Tougaloo Bill Appears Dead," *Clarion-Ledger,* 14 April 1964, Subject Files Tougaloo College, 1960–1969, MDAH.

32. Senate Bill No. 1672 of the Mississippi Legislature, Regular Session 1964, folder Accreditation Revocation (state), box Tougaloo College History, TCA.

33. "Action on Tougaloo is Due for Delay," *Clarion-Ledger,* 6 March 1964, folder Accreditation Revocation (state), box Tougaloo College History, TCA.

34. Senate Bill No. 1794 of the Mississippi Legislature, Regular Session 1964, folder Accreditation Revocation (state), box Tougaloo College History, TCA.

35. A. D. Beittel to William Fidler [AAUP], 6 June 1964, A. D. Beittel to Hollis Price [President, LeMoyne College], 27 May 1964, and A. D. Beittel to Gordon Sweet [Southern Association of Colleges and Schools], 6 June 1964, folder Accreditation Revocation [state], box Tougaloo College History, TCA).

36. Campbell and Rogers discuss the attempted revocation of Tougaloo's accreditation in *Mississippi: The View from Tougaloo,* chapter 18.

37. In 1954, Tougaloo merged with Southern Christian Institute which increased foundational support but also enrollment and campus costs.

38. A. D. Beittel to Members of the Board of Trustees of Tougaloo College, 1 September 1964, folder 94.01 Beittel retirement, box A. D. Beittel Unprocessed; and Campbell and Rogers, *Mississippi: The View from Tougaloo,* 196.

39. [no author], "Church Group Cancels Support of Tougaloo," *Jackson Daily News,* 20 September 1963, folder Board of Trustees Fall 1963, box A. D. Beittel Unprocessed, TCA. The Disciples of Christ financially supported Southern Christian Institute prior to its merger with Tougaloo College in 1954. Their funding continued after the merger, but the Mississippi branch ended its giving program in 1963.

40. Irving Fain was a Providence businessman, and Lawrence Durgin was pastor of the Congregational Church in Providence.

41. Board of Trustees Minutes report their action as unanimous and with Board consent. It is unclear if any Trustees, whether African American or white, dissented. Ed King, in his interview with the author, mentioned that some of the Trustees were unaware of this special meeting and may have disagreed with the position taken (Ed King, interview with author, 28 August 2003, Jackson, Mississippi).

42. Wesley Hotchkiss to Robert Wilder, 10 April 1964, folder Tougaloo College, 1964–65, box Miscellaneous Correspondence, Barnaby Keeney Office File Register, Brown University Archives [hereafter BUA], Providence, Rhode Island.

43. Beittel mentioned these factors in his letter of resignation, Beittel to Members of the Board of Trustees of Tougaloo College, 1 September 1964.

44. A. D. Beittel to Barnaby Keeney, 5 April 1964, folder 18, box 110, AMAA, Addendum (1869–1991, n.d.), Series A, Subseries Touglaoo Correspondence, ARC.

45. Barnaby Keeney to A. D. Beittel, 9 April 1964, no folder, box 1, Brown-Tougaloo Collection, TCA.

46. Barnaby Keeney to Lawrence Durgin, 9 March 1964, folder Tougaloo College, 1964–65, box Miscellaneous Correspondence, Barnaby Keeney Office File Register, BUA.

47. Barnaby Keeney to Robert Wilder, 10 April 1964, folder Tougaloo College, 1964–65, box Miscellaneous Correspondence, Barnaby Keeney Office File Register, BUA.

48. Several letters expressed anger at the implication that Brown attempted to interfere in Tougaloo business. See Keeney to Wilder, 10 April 1964, Hotchkiss to Wilder, 10 April 1964; Merle Miller to Wesley

Hotchkiss, 13 April 1964, and Wesley Hotchkiss to A. D. Beittel, 15 April 1964, no folder, box 1, Brown-Tougaloo Collection, TCA.

49. Wesley Hotchkiss to Mr. and Mrs. George Owens, 20 April 1964, folder 18, box 110, AMAA, Addendum (1869–1991, n.d.), Series A, Subseries Tougaloo Correspondence, ARC.

50. Beittel remained in Jackson after his retirement and became Director of the Mississippi Program of the American Friends Service Committee. Reverend Ed King resigned in 1967, and joined the staff of Delta Ministry, an arm of the National Council of Churches.

51. Press Release, 18 May 1964, folder Beittel-Brown Connection, box A. D. Beittel Unprocessed, TCA.

52. Ibid.

53. In his letter of resignation, Beittel stated that the College's assets grew from $1,648,423.35 in 1960, to $2,730,421.03 in 1964. Likewise, he reported a deficit of $34,982.67 in 1961, and a surplus of $15,486.41 in 1964 (Beittel to Members of the Board of Trustees of Tougaloo College, 1 September 1964, 2, TCA).

54. A. D. Beittel to Board of Trustees, 29 May 1964, 2, folder Board of Trustees, box A. D. Beittel, TCA.

55. Erle Johnston to John Salter, 17 August 1981, folder Brown University-Tougaloo College Cooperative Program, box Brown files on Tougaloo, Tougaloo Office File Register, BUA.

56. [no first name] Hopkins to Erle [Johnson], 2 April 1964, Sovereignty Commission Files 3-74-2-18-1-1-1.

57. Erle Johnston to File, 13 April 1964,1, 2, Sovereignty Commission Files 3-74-2-17-1-1-1.

58. Mr. Zero to Sovereignty Commission, 5 May 1964, Sovereignty Commission Files 3-74-2-19-1-1-1 through 2-1-1.

59. Erle Johnston to Wesley Hotchkiss, 17 April 1964, 1, 2, folder 18, box 110, AMAA, Addendum (1869–1991, n.d.), Series A, Subseries Tougaloo Correspondence, ARC.

60. Shelby Rogers to Earle [sic] Johnston, [May 1964], 1, Sovereignty Commission Files 3-74-2-13-1-1-1.

61. Johnston to File, 24 April 1964, 1, Sovereignty Commission Files 3-74-2-16-1-1-1. Ed King's name and title were blacked out in the record, but it is certain that he is the individual to whom the report refers.

62. Johnston to File, 24 April 1964, 1 (both quotes).

63. Salter left Tougaloo in 1963.

64. For a discussion of Tougaloo's relationship with SCEF, see Johnston to Hotchkiss, 17 April 1964 and Jeff Woods, *Black Struggle, Red Scare: Segregation and Anti-Communism in the South, 1948–1968* (Baton Rouge: Louisiana State University Press, 2004), 201–204. For a discussion of COFO, see Erle Johnston, "Report on Mississippi State Sovereignty Commission, 1964–1967," 6, folder 388, box 8, Ed King Papers, TCA. For a discussion of SNCC, see Johnston, to File, 24 April 1964. SCEF, COFO, and SNCC were interracial organizations dedicated to the end of racial segregation and the fulfillment of equal rights for all American citizens.

65. Ibid., 3, 5, 6.

66. Ibid., 6, 6, 8.

67. Erle Johnston to (Governor) Paul Johnson and (Lieutenant Governor) Carroll Gartin, 5 May 1964, Sovereignty Commission Files 3-74-2-23-1-1-1.

68. Erle Johnston to Herman Glazier, 9 June 1964, folder Tougaloo College, 1964–65, box Miscellaneous Correspondence, Barnaby Keeney Office File Register, BUA.

69. Elizabeth Sewell, "For A. D. Beittel," 20 May 1964, folder 19, box 110, AMAA, Addendum (1869–1991, n.d.), Series A, Subseries Tougaloo Correspondence, ARC.

70. John Held to [Wesley] Hotchkiss, 2 June 1964, folder 19, box 110, AMAA, Addendum (1869–1991, n.d.), Series A, Subseries Tougaloo Correspondence, ARC.

71. Paul Anthony to Robert Wilder, 2 May 1964, folder 18, box 110, AMAA, Addendum (1869–1991, n.d.), Series A, Subseries Tougaloo Correspondence, ARC.

72. Reverend Bernard Law, Reverend Duncan M. Gray,Jr., and Rabbi Perry E. Nussbaum to Board of Trustees, 4 May 1964, folder 18, box 110, American Missionary Association Archives, Addendum (1869–1991, n.d.), Series A, Subseries Tougaloo Correspondence, ARC.

73. See Wesley Hotchkiss to Reverend James Lightborne, Jr., 10 June 1964, no folder, box 1, Brown-Tougaloo Collection, TCA.

74. Truman Douglass to Ray Gibbons (Council for Christian Social Action), 5 June 1964, 2, no folder, box 1, Brown-Tougaloo Collection, TCA. Truman Douglass was the Executive Vice President of the United Church Board for Homeland Ministries and a friend of Trustee Wesley Hotchkiss.

75. Wesley Hotchkiss to Robert Spike, 24 June 1964, no folder, box 1, Brown-Tougaloo Collection, TCA.

76. Daniel Thompson, *Private Black Colleges at the Crossroads* (Westport, CT.: Greenwood Press, 1973), 245–254.

CHAPTER 8

FROM VISIBILITY TO AUTONOMY: LATINOS AND HIGHER EDUCATION IN THE U.S., 1965–2005

VICTORIA-MARÍA MACDONALD
JOHN M. BOTTI

LISA HOFFMAN CLARK

In this chapter, Victoria-María MacDonald, John M. Botti, and Lisa Hoffman Clark trace the evolution of higher educational opportunities for Latinos in the United States from the Higher Education Act of 1965 to the designation of Title V in the Act's 1998 reauthorization. The authors argue that this evolution moved through stages, including establishing visibility and legitimacy, self-determination, self-scrutiny, emulation, and, finally, autonomy. The journey toward improving higher educational opportunities for Latinos is juxtaposed with the journey experienced by African Americans in the United States. Because of the enormous historical, social, and political differences between the two groups, the models utilized by and for Blacks were viewed as inadequate for serving Latino needs in higher education. However, the model established by Historically Black Colleges and Universities inspired Latino educators to found Hispanic-Serving Institutions (HSIs). The authors conclude their chapter by discussing contemporary issues surrounding HSIs and looking toward the future of Latino higher education.

More than forty years after the Higher Education Act of 1965 was passed, the Latino relationship to higher education remains a complicated one.[1] Never a simple story of progress, the Latino narrative has been marked by a dialectic of educational access and societal constraint, of opportunity achieved and expectations tempered. This hard journey is rooted in the 1960s, when the civil rights movement encouraged Hispanic Americans, particularly Mexican Americans, to seek both recognition and attention from politicians and policymakers. Indeed, before significant inroads could be made into opening their access to higher education, Hispanics had to gain national visibility as a group whose needs and voices had historically been neglected.

In contrast, the rights of African Americans had first been formally recognized by government during Reconstruction (1865–1877). Through the passage of the Thirteenth, Fourteenth, and Fifteenth Amendments, newly freed slaves were recognized as citizens and Black men were granted the right to vote. African Americans exercised the franchise, founded and attended Black colleges, and held high political positions ranging from the superintendent of education in Florida to representatives in Congress (Foner, 1988). After 1877, typically viewed as the end of Reconstruction, African Americans found their constitutional rights rolled back, as the U.S. Supreme Court ruled in 1883 that the Civil Rights Act of 1875 was unconstitutional. Furthermore, the Supreme Court's 1896 ruling in *Plessy v. Ferguson* affirming the constitutionality of separate but equal railroad cars for Blacks and Whites led to entrenched racial segregation throughout all institutions of Southern society (Litwack, 1998). It took the civil rights movement, which started in the 1950s, to prompt the federal government to again address the promise of civil rights that began during Reconstruction. In an effort to dislodge the practice of segregation, federal rulings, laws, and agencies worked to open doors to higher educational institutions that at the time were closed to Blacks.

Inspired by the success of the civil rights movement, which centered largely on the rights of African Americans, Latinos sought similar rights and opportunities in the Great Society of the Johnson era. However, they first needed public visibility and legitimacy within the national discourse. Such inroads were made slowly, beginning during the John F. Kennedy administration. Kennedy's political strategists had attempted to tap the Hispanic electoral vote through the "Viva Kennedy" gatherings, and the arrival of refugees from the Cuban revolution brought further national attention to a small but vocal Hispanic group (García, 2000). Beginning during Lyndon B. Johnson's administration and continuing into the Nixon administration, Mexican Americans and, by extension, other Latinos were increasingly defined as a minority group that merited special attention under the umbrella of the Great Society (Kaplowitz, 2003). These governmental efforts were often prompted by grassroots Latino activists who challenged both a status quo that limited their visibility and a reform agenda whose federal appointees, commissions, hearings, and press statements focused primarily on Blacks (Pycior, 1997).

Not content to accept the glacial pace of reform efforts in Washington, Latino activists pushed elected leaders and appointees within the Johnson and Nixon administrations for a national agenda focused on a variety of political, economic, and social issues, including higher education. Latinos were dissatisfied in general with the incongruity between rhetorical promises and political inaction, particularly from Lyndon B. Johnson, whom they believed would be sympathetic to their needs, particularly because of his historical relationships with Mexican American politicians and the political capital he garnered from Mexican American votes in Texas and the Southwest (Kaplowitz, 2003; Pycior, 1997).

One example of Latino activism was the Chicano and Puerto Rican youth movements of the 1960s and 1970s, which demanded meaningful access to higher education. These movements also called for curricula that reflected the changing composition of student populations, faculty members who could serve as role models for aspiring scholars, Hispanic cultural and research centers, and the financial means to realize these goals. The activities of youth movements enhanced the visibility of Hispanic concerns in higher education, which in turn stimulated actions on an institutional level, including open admission policies, a more responsive curriculum, and the creation of research centers such as the Centro de Estudios Puertorriqueños at Hunter College in New York City (García, 1989; MacDonald & García, 2003). In short, a community barely on the radar of politicians, policymakers, the media, and educators in 1965 demanded and received the type of political legitimacy that would secure the support of federal and state governments, civil rights organizations, private philanthropies, and colleges and universities to address the blatant inequities facing Latinos seeking higher education. By the 1980s, optimism reigned within Latino circles as college attendance rates soared and high school dropout rates decreased (Baker & Velez, 1996; Olivas, 1986). A generation of first-time college and graduate school attendees began to establish themselves as academics, while Latinos entered the fields of social work, law, and other professions in unprecedented numbers (Cuádraz, 1999). This Latino presence in the halls of academe helped foster permanent changes in the curricula, demographic makeup, and faculty at U.S. institutions of higher education.

By 2000, however, the sanguinity of past decades had subsided. Latinos endured a series of backlashes during the 1990s on several fronts, including education. This backlash was intensified by the results of the 2000 Census, which revealed soaring immigration rates among Latinos. By the turn of the century, Latinos had been labeled as the country's greatest demographic, economic, social, and political "challenge" (Huntington, 2004; Santa Ana, 2002). This "challenge" often expressed itself in contradictory terms: Latinos were alternatively derided as illegal aliens who siphoned off the nation's resources, while at the same time they earned praise for possessing a strong work ethic and contributing to a robust economy. Such ambiguity also characterized the Latino presence in higher education, which found itself bound up in debates over identity construction, curriculum content, financial support, generational progress, and retention rates.

This paper has at least two goals. First, as questions about Latino higher education enrollment, transfer, retention, and graduation rates persist in educational policy talk, the need to situate this discourse in a historical context stands as a primary imperative. This is not a comprehensive historical work; rather, its intention is to provide a broad overview of the complex interactions between Latinos, government institutions, private foundations, and educational policymakers over the past forty years. Building on a preliminary historical essay (MacDonald & García, 2003) in which the dearth of historical inquiry into Latino higher education was emphasized and a potential outline of periodization for such inquiry was created, this chapter examines the arenas available for future and more in-depth archival retrieval and analysis. The writing of history is a political act (Novick, 1988; Zinn, 2005), and this piece is guided by a belief that the narrative of Latino history has been neglec-ted as part of the U.S. historical imagination. Despite forty years of research and writing on Latinos (Ruiz, 2006), this historical account is again being constrained and marginalized by a dominant discourse that derides the presence of so-called "aliens" and their participation in the U.S. social, economic, or political community (Huntington, 2004). For example, the dehistoricization of Latinos appears in the stalled passage of the Development, Relief, and Education for Alien Minors Act (DREAM), legislation that would permit states to establish their own residency rules for charging in-state tuition to undocumented students.

Sadly, the public's collective memory does not include the long history of immigration legislation in the United States undergirding the origins of the DREAM Act and the humane solution it offers to children caught between U.S. immigration policies, wars, and disasters (The "Dream Act" and "The American Dream Act" Fact Sheet, 2007). From the federal government's extension of civil rights efforts under the aegis of omnibus bills such as the Elementary Secondary Education Act and the Higher Education Act of 1965, to the creation of Hispanic-Serving Institutions (HSIs) in 1992, the Latino journey to higher educational equity and access has been largely omitted from the historical record. Michael Olivas's 1982 article, "Indian, Chicano, and Puerto Rican Colleges," has been reprinted for over twenty years in higher education readers as the sole history on institutions serving Latino students (Olivas, 1982, 1997; Turner, antonio, García, Laden, Nora, & Presley, 2002). Few scholars, except the late Berta Vigil Laden, explored the modern development of HSIs (Laden, 2001, 2002). Historians of education have called for more scholars to examine the history of higher education of people of color, with only a trickle of results (Donato & Lazerson, 2000). Based largely (but not solely) on the published records of foundations, congressional hearings, and legislation, this narrative represents a initial effort at making the historical record more robust and inclusive. Alternative viewpoints and more definitive conclusions may be drawn from further exploration of primary materials, and it is the authors' hope that this research will initiate more nuanced investigations of the evolution of HSIs.

A second rationale for this essay involves illuminating the convergence and divergence of the Latino and African American historical experience in higher education. In particular, our understanding of post-1965 minority participation in higher education, including desegregation, is largely and legitimately informed by an in-depth examination of the Black experience (Drewry & Doermann, 2001; Glasker, 2002; Rojas, 2007; Rooks, 2006; Samuels, 2004; Yamane, 2002). As a consequence, current policy prescriptions in higher education rarely take into account the often divergent historical and cultural experiences of Latinos. For instance, the Hispanic civil rights strategy focused on the K–12 sector rather than pursuing equity in higher education. During the 1930s and 1940s, then, while the National Association for the Advancement of Colored People (NAACP) assailed the racial caste system of public higher education and professional schools, the chief desegregation cases concerning Mexican American children were at the elementary school level. These actions received legal and financial support from the League of United Latin American Citizens (LULAC), a civil rights advocacy organization created in 1929 by Mexican Americans (Márquez, 1993; San Miguel, 1987). Testimony from civil rights hearings, court depositions, and first-person interviews in the decades after World War II reveal that it was an unofficial practice to bar Latinos from attending high school prior to the 1950s; this custom became systemic in the 1960s, channeling Latino students into vocational/technical programs that lacked college-preparation courses (Pycior, 1997; U.S. Commission on Civil Rights, 1967, 1968; Weinberg, 1977). Until at least 1960, the highest level of education for the majority of Latinos in the Southwest was thus the eighth grade (Donato, 1997; Grebler, Moore, & Guzman, 1970).

At a time when African Americans were making inroads in higher education and consolidating the influence of Historically Black Colleges and Universities (HBCUs), Latinos lacked analogous colleges and universities and, importantly, a network of graduates from institutions of higher education; this reality was both a consequence of and a further impetus for the push for educational access centered on lower levels of schooling. In our analysis of the documents, we argue that the struggle for Latino higher education has proceeded through five stages: visibility and legitimacy in the early to late 1960s; self-determination in the early 1970s; seeking resources beyond the rhetoric in the early 1980s; emulation in the late 1980s and early 1990s; and, finally, autonomy in the late 1990s. These stages describe a narrative not marked by steady progress, but by ebbs and flows created by shifts in political power, social mores, and demographics. Furthermore, we demonstrate the tendency throughout these stages of the federal government, philanthropists, and other members of the chiefly White power structure to envision the future of Latino higher education in terms of models previously utilized for Blacks. Because of the enormous historical, social, and political differences between the two groups, however, models utilized by and for Blacks have often been incongruent with Latino needs in higher education. The one-size-fits-all approach that was applied to Latinos failed to take into account the very different paths each population group has taken to access higher education. Ultimately, Latinos needed to create their own networks and lobbies, a path that was not established until very recently, during the final stage. The prospects for Latino higher education in the twenty-first century thus continue to reflect its complex forty-year heritage, which has shaped and will continue to shape the relationship of Latinos to U.S. higher education.

Visibility and Legitimacy of the Early to Late 1960s: Putting Hispanics on the Federal Radar

By the middle of the twentieth century, African Americans had established access to a network of public undergraduate and graduate institutions that, while segregated and underresourced, demonstrated the potential value the larger society and the Black community placed on higher education. Black colleges were established before the Civil War in the North, such as Wilber-force in Ohio (by Black Methodists) and Lincoln University in Pennsylvania (by White Presbyterians). Access expanded during Reconstruction with the federal government's creation of Howard University in 1867, the founding of numerous missionary-based and independent Black colleges, and the Morrill Land Grant Act of 1890, which provided funds primarily to southern states to either create or supplement state-funded colleges for Blacks (Roebuck & Murty, 1993). Graduates of these programs formed the vanguard of an educational civil rights movement that would push for desegregation and the expansion of higher educational opportunity, particularly among state-supported institutions. Indeed, the HBCUs became, according to Brown and Davis (2001), the "purveyors" of social capital, a social capital that graduates could apply to change the political, economic, and ethical realities in which they lived (Drewry & Doermann, 2001).

Latinos were not altogether absent from higher education at mid-century; indeed, many Hispanics who had served in World War II used the GI Bill to attend college (Rivas-Rodriguez, Torres, Dipiero-D'sa, & Fitzpatrick, 2006). Because of discriminatory practices against Mexican American veterans, however, Latinos created the American GI Forum (AGIF) in the 1940s to help veterans fully access their GI benefits, including burial rights, housing, and education subsidies (Allsup, 1982; Ramos, 1998). Despite such efforts, the Latino presence in higher education at mid-century remained decidedly limited. In 1958, for example, Latinos comprised fewer than 6 percent of first-year college students in the Southwest (Carter, 1970).

The framing ideals of Lyndon B. Johnson's Great Society programs, coupled with the energies of the civil rights movement, attempted to redress historical inequities and systemic discrimination within American society. Through numerous legislative acts, including the 1964 Civil Rights Act, the 1965 Voting Rights Act, the 1965 Elementary and Secondary Education Act, and the 1965

Higher Education Act, Johnson hoped to provide a mechanism that would expand and protect the political and social/economic opportunities of the traditionally dispossessed. Although the wording of these acts did not specify a particular minority group, political and media rhetoric surrounding the legislation initially tended to prioritize the concerns of African Americans (Davies, 2002; Woods, 2006). Similarly, during the conception stage of the Higher Education Act's Title III, Congresswoman Edith Green, chairwoman of the Special Subcommittee on Higher Education, explained that it was targeted to southern Black higher education institutions. She noted that "this particular title was written in my office last year and was a separate piece of legislation. . . . *We conceived it primarily to strengthen the Negro colleges in the South* [italics added]" (Hearings on the Higher Education Act of 1965, p. 845). As it appeared in statute, Title III, "Strengthening Developing Institutions," did not specify institutions belonging to any particular ethnic or racial group. A developing institution was one that "for financial or other reasons [was] struggling for survival [and] isolated from the main currents of academic life," a definition that hinted that these were historically marginalized institutions but could have included rural Appalachian schools as well (Higher Education Act of 1965, p. 1229). Roebuck and Murty (1993) assert that Title III was in fact "interpreted as a direct intercession favoring black colleges and universities" (p. 39). This benefit accorded to racially segregated and historically underfunded schools speaks to strong and admirable African American leadership in the civil rights movement in both individual and collective action, the existence of a strong Black middle class, and the backing of established interracial national organizations such as the NAACP, the United Negro College Fund, and the Urban League (Gasman, 2007). As David Karen (1991) has argued, groups such as African Americans and women who had politically mobilized and had "official social categories" in the 1960s achieved greater access to higher education (p. 223). The specific nomenclature of HBCUs within Title III was not realized until reauthorization of the Higher Education Act in 1986 (Roebuck & Murty, 1993); nonetheless, as federal reports indicated, the lion's share of funds from Title III went to HBCUs (Brown, Rosen, Hill, & Olivas, 1980).

Though it would be years before the federal government explicitly extended these protections and provisions to Latinos and their institutions, the federal identification of specific needs for Blacks opened a gateway to higher education through which, ultimately, large numbers of Latinos would pass. As John Hope Franklin (1981) expressed so well, "the examples of their [Black's] civil rights organizations, their activities in the field of litigation, and their political influence are a source of envy as well as admiration, but what is more important and to the point is that they have provided inspiration for others" (p. 10). Nevertheless, in the 1960s Latino reformers increasingly began to express frustration that needs specific to their community were not visibly addressed (Kaplowitz, 2003; Pycior, 1997; Woolley & Peters, 1965).[2]

The expansion of Great Society programs and legislation to include Latinos specifically began as a result of three factors. First, President Johnson (1967) acknowledged the premature exclusion of Mexican Americans from the civil rights conversation, stating, "The time has come to focus our efforts more intensely on the Mexican Americans of our nation" (para. 3). Johnson also supported his rhetoric with a degree of political action. For instance, he created a Task Force on Problems of Spanish Surname Americans and helped Latinos fund organizations such as the United Migrant Opportunity Services through the Economic Opportunity Act of 1964 and its newly created Office of Economic Opportunity (Pycior, 1997; Rodriguez, 2003). Johnson's attention to Latino issues was perhaps the product of a childhood and early adulthood spent in Texas, which provided personal familiarity with the Mexican American experience. A year as a schoolteacher in a segregated "Mexican School" revealed to Johnson how poverty and discrimination could block opportunities for Mexican Americans. Also, his lifelong friendship with the son of one of his father's ranch hands contributed to an abiding sympathy for this group (Woods, 2006). The degree to which such sympathy catalyzed Johnson's contempt for social injustice is unclear; what is apparent is that he was not above using such personal experience, no matter how genuinely felt, as the currency of political opportunism. For example, while signing the Higher Education Act in 1965 at Southwest Texas State College, Johnson (1965) invoked this sentiment:

I shall never forget the faces of the boys and the girls in that little Welhausen Mexican School, and I remember even yet the pain of realizing and knowing then that college was closed to practically every one of those children because they were too poor. (para. 45)

Johnson thus translated individual biography and presidential rhetoric into the seeds of federal action. Although these steps provided a symbolic departure from policy that had almost completely neglected Latinos, the Latino community remained dissatisfied with the Johnson administration's inattention and their relative invisibility in his administration.

Self-Determination in the Early 1970s

Latinos led the second major effort to promote the expansion of higher education opportunity. Aided and inspired by the African American civil rights movement, Latino self-agency proved a significant element in cultivating access to colleges and universities, as youth efforts throughout the 1960s helped illuminate the specific concerns of the Hispanic minority. Many of the student sit-ins, protests, and walkouts were conducted in the shadow of the Los Angeles Watts riots in 1965 and amid widespread civil unrest during 1967 and 1968. These actions alarmed citizens and civic leaders throughout the country, particularly in urban areas, and virtually demanded the administration's response (Steigerwald, 1995). The government's response included Johnson's creation of the well-known National Advisory Commission on Civil Disorders in 1967, which produced the seminal Kerner Report. Garnering less attention yet of considerable import were the Office of Civil Rights (OCR) hearings on the Mexican American condition, which were held in San Francisco and Oakland in 1967 and in San Antonio in 1968. Through voluminous reports—each numbered over one thousand pages—and the efforts of the OCR, educational injustices against Mexican Americans were finally being documented and brought to the attention of federal legislators, the media, and policymakers (U.S. Commission on Civil Rights, 1967, 1968).

Latinos had learned from the African American civil rights movement that active protest—including sit-ins and boycotts, militant organizations (such as the Black Panthers, who trained the Brown Berets), walkouts, and other highly vocal and visible activity—was particularly useful in securing goals relating to higher educational access. Sometimes in tandem with Black students and sometimes alone, Latino youth worked to expand such access through a variety of grassroots efforts (MacDonald & Garcia, 2003; Muñoz, 1989; Rodriguez, 2003). Well-detailed in numerous studies, the Chicano student movement represented a more militant strategy than previous efforts among the two best known pre–civil rights era advocacy organizations, LULAC and AGIF (Allsup, 1982; Gómez-Quiñones, 1978; Márquez, 1993; Muñoz, 1989; Navarro, 1995; Ramos, 1998). This shift also mirrored increased militancy among the African American community, as activists embraced the Black Power movement led by leaders such as Malcolm X. *El Plan de Santa Barbara* (1969), often called the Magna Carta of the Chicano youth movement, articulated numerous demands for higher education institutions to ensure equitable access and opportunity. The Chicano Coordinating Council on Higher Education—a coalition of students, faculty, and staff from California institutions of higher education—called for the numerous student groups that had cropped up around the Southwest to unite in the *Movimiento Estudiantil Chicano de Aztlan* (MEChA) (MacDonald & García, 2003).

Student calls for reform were not limited to the Southwest. Through a 1969 strike and campus shutdown, Latino (mostly Puerto Rican) and Black students at the City University of New York (CUNY) worked together to promote an open admissions policy at the school (Lavin & Hyllegard, 1996). Similar joint "Black and Brown" efforts were made at Brooklyn College, as the Black League of Afro-American Collegians and Puerto Rican Alliance united to occupy the president's office and issue a series of demands. Puerto Rican students at Yale University organized themselves into the *Boricuas Unidos* to push for increased Latino enrollment (MacDonald, 2004; Traub, 1994). In addition, the creation of several grassroots Latino-centered colleges and research centers reflected Latino's deepseated desire to create and take ownership of postsecondary institutions that would put their admissions, curriculum, language, and other needs front and center (MacDonald, 2004;

Olivas, 1997). Here, too, the example of the African American experience was influential. In our analysis, Latinos viewed the network of HBCUs as models for institutions that graduated a "talented tenth" of the African American community and provided role models among its faculty and staff.[3] Seeing the utility of such schools in forwarding a civil rights agenda, Latinos moved to create parallel responsive institutions. For example, B. Roberto Cruz, founding president of the National Hispanic University, declared that the inspiration for his school came from the "success rate and high quality of education provided by Historically Black Colleges and Universities" (*History of the University and Higher Education*, 2007, para. 2).

In the late 1960s and early 1970s, at least eight grassroots experimental Chicano and Puerto Rican colleges were founded, most of whose histories remain unwritten. Notable Mexican American schools included Colegio César Chavez in Mt. Angel, Oregon (1973), and Juárez-Lincoln University in Austin, Texas (1971). Hostos Community College was created as part of the CUNY system in the Bronx (1969), and Boricua College in Brooklyn, New York (1973), represented the Puerto Rican students' demands for a bicultural and bilingual learning environment (*Handbook of Texas Online*, 2007; Maldonado, 2000; Meyer, 2003; Olivas, 1997). Practical realities ultimately limited these schools' ability to function as Latino analogs to the HBCUs because financial struggles and accreditation problems hampered the fledgling institutions. For example, Chicano colleges could not secure federal financial aid for students through Title III without at least accreditation candidacy (Maldonado, 2000; Olivas, 1997). The financial exigencies that included low faculty salaries combined with small enrollments led to their eventual demise. At Colegio César Chavez, for example, enrollment peaked in 1974–1975 at almost 140 students, before beginning a serious decline to less than a dozen at the time of closure in 1983 (Maldonado, 2000).

By 1983, among the eight Chicano colleges formed in the 1960s and 1970s, only Deganawidah-Quetzalcoatl (D-Q), which had been subsumed into the Tribal College System, remained (Olivas, 1997). The Puerto Rican schools fared a little better; both Hostos Community College and Boricua College remain in operation today and serve a large numbers of minorities, particularly Puerto Ricans, in New York City. The National Hispanic University was created in 1981 in San José, California, and is still in operation today. Although the practical failure of most of these institutions slowed the energy of the Chicano and Puerto Rican movements, their creation and existence, no matter how brief, speak to the strong sense of the emerging Latino identity in the late 1960s and early 1970s.

Private foundations interested in advancing the Mexican American and Puerto Rican civil rights agenda and educational opportunities represent another factor driving Latinos into national visibility. Throughout the history of American higher education, philanthropy has had the potential to wield transformative power on both individual institutions and across postsecondary education as a whole. Philanthropic power has sometimes sought change at specific schools, such as consolidating weaker programs and colleges or permitting experimentation with new programs. In other cases, philanthropy has leveraged its financial power to implement systemic change, such as expanding access to higher education for women or advancing a particular postsecondary curricular agenda (Anderson, 1988; Curti & Nast, 1965; Walton, 2005). Certain philanthropic foundations, taking a more global view of their responsibility, often saw higher education as a principal symbol of advancement and, by the 1960s and 1970s, were eager to include Latinos in this discourse of progress. The Ford, Carnegie, and Rockefeller foundations were notable in this regard, and subsequently expanded their traditional assistance to Black colleges to include Hispanics and other minority groups. As with the federal government, attention to the needs of Blacks had understandably absorbed the interests of numerous private philanthropies for several decades. In its 1969 Annual Report, the Ford Foundation acknowledged that in the past, "most of the grants dealt with the problems of Black Americans . . . and some new steps were taken to support special programs for Mexican American, Puerto Rican, and American Indian students" (p. 9). The expansion of foundation largesse to include Native Americans and Hispanic Americans did not come at the expense of diminished attention and resources for African Americans; rather, it represented the foundations' new awareness of formerly less-visible minority groups who had thrust themselves into the spotlight during the civil rights era. Funding for Black Studies, for example, although begun during the height of the Black Power movement, continues to the present (Rojas, 2007; Rooks, 2006). In addition, when the Ford Foundation pledged $100 million for six years to enhance minority opportunities, half of the amount was dedicated to institutional support for Black colleges and half for minority graduate fellowships (Magat, 1979). Accordingly, the foundation reported in 1970 that after having "assisted the development of Afro-American studies as a field of scholarly inquiry," it would now extend that support to other ethnic minorities, including "Spanish-speaking Americans" (Ford Foundation, 1970, p. 41). The Ford Foundation's move into the Latino arena mirrored its previous efforts within Black higher education.

Ford was particularly instrumental in creating the Mexican American Legal Defense Education Fund (MALDEF), which has litigated for Latino educational opportunities since its inception in 1968 and assisted in the creation of the Puerto Rican Legal Defense and Education Fund (PRLDEF) in 1972 (Magat, 1979). Although historical accounts of the founding of MALDEF are not unanimous in their praise of this endeavor, the Ford Foundation's grant of $2.2 million dollars to create a Latino organization modeled on the NAACP's Legal Defense Fund is not disputed (Davies, 2002; San Miguel, 1987). Furthermore, since 1967, the Ford Foundation has given millions of dollars to advance the research of and extend support to students and faculty of color in higher education. Ford's philanthropy, which particularly benefited Latinos during the tumultuous 1960s and 1970s student protest era, included grants to CUNY for the planning of what would eventually become Hostos Community College in 1969; donations to establish *El Centro Para Estudios Puertorriqueños* (Center for Puerto Rican Studies) at CUNY; training grants to schools of education to increase the number of Mexican American teachers in the Southwest; and the 1973 creation of the *Chicano Chronicle,* a newspaper to re-create Mexican American history for college and high school courses through the Claremont University Center. These contributions represent a small fraction of the benefits extended via the Ford Foundation, most of which have not received sufficient scholarly treatment and analysis.

Like the Ford Foundation, the Rockefeller Foundation has historically occupied an important role in the world of academic philanthropy. Rockefeller's foundation assistance to Latino higher education did not begin until the 1960s (Groutt & Hill, 2001). While the Ford Foundation's largest grants, which created MALDEF and PRLDEF, enabled Latinos to sue school districts or governmental agencies in court for their educational rights, Rockefeller programs benefiting Latinos in the 1960s and 1970s focused on gaining access to higher education (Groutt, 2002). Beginning in the mid-1960s, Rockefeller supported Latino efforts at numerous institutions, including Arizona State University, the Claremont Colleges cluster, California State College, Los Angeles, and Yale, to create an unbroken educational pipeline. In 1968, for example, the foundation granted $650,000 to the Claremont Colleges to create a "Program of Special Directed Studies for Mexican American and other economically and socially disadvantaged students" (Rockefeller Foundation, 1968). Through such programs, high school students were channeled into urban colleges and universities; attended summer semesters at Yale to prepare them for the rigors of Ivy League admission; and were able to utilize on-campus minority centers created and funded by the Rockefeller Foundation (Rockefeller Foundation, 1967–1978). What gave these programs particular significance was their ecumenical nature. Many social programs in the Great Society era tended to focus resources on ameliorating the historic and systemic oppression of African Americans. The Rockefeller grants, conversely, were neither earmarked for nor rhetorically extended to a particular racial or ethnic community; they were most often designed to benefit African Americans, Latinos, Native Americans, and others who had been denied their share of the nation's educational resources through racial and economic discrimination.

The foundation also backed initiatives for higher education sponsored by the federal government's War on Poverty. Chief among these governmental efforts were the so-called TRIO programs, three measures intended to equalize educational opportunity for those with low socioeconomic status. Although the first of these programs, Upward Bound (founded in 1964), was issued under the aegis of the Office of Economic Opportunity, the Rockefeller Foundation played a critical role in the design and experimental phase of the project as early as 1963 (Groutt, 2002). The foundation provided financial support and enhanced the visibility of Upward Bound and the other TRIO programs, including Talent Search and Special Services for Disadvantaged Students (Groutt, 2002). The Rockefeller Foundation was thus an important partner of the federal government in the effort to prepare underachieving students from low-income backgrounds for college. For Latinos, such efforts were vital in maintaining their nascent educational pipeline into the nation's college and university system.

During the 1960s and early 1970s, Hispanic Americans pushed themselves onto the national civil rights agenda through their participation in the Chicano student movement, the farmworker movement led by César Chavez, and other grassroots activities. These social movements led to bureaucratic responses from the federal government. Institutional structures were further consolidated and solidified during the Nixon administration, as Latino-related Great Society programs such as bilingual education continued and were even expanded. As Gareth Davies (2002) has noted, the pragmatic Nixon saw Latinos as lacking a traditional party affiliation, and thus believed that continuing social programs could help forge a Republican alliance with Hispanic Americans, an alliance that would deliver needed votes from a burgeoning population. The U.S. Supreme Court's decision in *Lau v. Nichols* (1974), which affirmed the right of children whose first language was not English to receive special services in the public schools (MacDonald, 2004), was a pressing issue during the 1970s for Latino elementary and secondary education and also essential in securing a pipeline to postsecondary schooling. An even more direct impact on Latinos and higher education would eventually result from Hispanics being added to the U.S. Census beginning in 1970 and President Nixon's O.M.B. Statistical Directive 15 of 1973, which acknowledged Hispanics as a separate federally identified group. Previously dehistoricized, Latinos' inclusion in the census and federal government agencies as an official category meant that accountability for higher education enrollment, retention, and degree attainment could finally be formally documented.

In fewer than twenty years, Hispanic Americans had emerged as a vital, viable constituency in our national political, social, and educational debates. A combination of forces had contributed to this dramatic shift in Latino visibility and influence. In the first stage, Lyndon B. Johnson's personal and political interest in Mexican Americans merged with his leadership in the War on Poverty to promote the needs of a long-neglected community. In the second stage, Latino self-determination—especially among Puerto Ricans and Mexican Americans—had exercised considerable agency on the grassroots level, both in bringing a long trajectory of systematic discrimination to national attention and in calling for educational resources to address these problems. Finally, private philanthropic foundations played a seminal role in this shift. Public attention from these entities helped legitimize Latinos in the national discourse as worthy and necessary candidates for higher education. Philanthropic organizations also helped Latino students in their effort to find and define a role in often unfamiliar academic milieu by subsidizing programs that eased financial burdens and ameliorated the students' experience of cultural dislocation. Thus, for example, as Puerto Rican students in New York City demanded that CUNY create more responsive curricula and new admission criteria, the Ford Foundation responded with a five-hundred thousand dollar grant (Ford Foundation, 1969).

Seeking Resources beyond the Rhetoric: The Early 1980s

> We are not only a "Nation at Risk," we are a nation which has already gambled away and failed to provide equal opportunity in higher education for its Hispanic Americans.
>
> Antonia Hernandez, Counsel, Mexican American
> Legal Defense and Education Fund, Washington, D.C.
> (*Hearings on Higher Education Civil Rights Enforcement*, 1983, p. 421)

The 1980s was a decade of paradox and contradiction for Latino higher education, as the promise of the 1960s and 1970s encountered a climate increasingly inimical to its progressive tendencies. The closing of several Chicano-centered colleges during the late 1970s and early 1980s epitomized the decade's uneven progression. On the one hand, retrenchment from the militant facets of the Chicano and Puerto Rican movements signaled, in part, the assimilation of Latino demands on higher education (Chicano student centers, Puerto Rican Study majors, hiring of Latino faculty, etc.) into mainstream institutions. On the other hand, this reduction in grassroots pressure also heralded a shift in popular discourse. In the post-Vietnam era, the rallying and unifying energy of the civil rights and student protests movement were slowly but inexorably abridged. Increasingly, its place in the national mindset was appropriated by an ideology of limited government and a rhetorical backlash against minority-specific programs such as affirmative action and bilingual education (Chapa, 2002; MacDonald, 2004; Rubio, 2001). It was in this context that Latinos began to question whether federal resources were being applied toward the demands made in the 1970s. Latinos were also asking for the higher education desegregation model to expand beyond a Black-White binary.

During the more conservative 1980s, Latino progress in higher education reached a plateau. The programs launched in the 1960s and 1970s, which had brought Latinos into colleges and universities in unprecedented numbers, began to stall by 1980. In 1975, the percentage of Latino high school graduates attending college was 35.4 percent. This figure declined to 30 percent in 1980, and then to 27 percent in 1985, before finally rising again in the early 1990s (National Center for Education Statistics, 2003; Olivas, 1986). This decline in minority higher education enrollment has been attributed to crucial changes in federal financial aid policies, which came during a period of escalating collegiate costs (Baker & Velez, 1996; Orfield, 1992). Traditionally, Latinos have been reticent to take out loans as a means of subsidizing education; as a result, the Reagan era shift in aid allocation—one that favored loans instead of grants—disproportionately affected lower income Latino students. This flagging momentum in collegiate access among all minority groups—not just Latinos—was confirmed by sobering findings in the U.S. government's first major report on Latinos and schooling, *The Condition of Education for Hispanic Americans* (Brown et al., 1980). Eventually, this gloomy circumstance drew the attention of activist groups and the more liberal sectors of the federal legislature. Concerned that the Decade of the Hispanic (as various media labeled the 1980s) was not translating into concrete gains in higher education (or other key economic and social indicators), these activists and lawmakers sought to recapture the hope and energy of the previous decade (Miranda & Quiroz, 1990; Valencia, 2002).

The first concrete effort on the federal level to focus resources specifically on Latino higher education was undertaken by Senator Paul Simon, chairman of the Subcommittee on Postsecondary Education. Sparked by the 1980 report "Condition of Education," Simon attempted to explore more thoroughly the degree to which the Higher Education Act's compensatory programs served the increasingly large and visible Hispanic population (*Staff Report on Hispanic Access to Higher Education*, 1985). For example, the report showed that under Title III, which allocated monies for "Strengthening Developing Institutions," mainland U.S. colleges with 20 percent or more Hispanic enrollment received only 6.4 percent of the allocated funds (Brown et al., 1980). Also, Latino participation in the TRIO programs remained at under 20 percent. Finally, Latinos earned fewer than one-fifth of Graduate and Professional Opportunities Program (GPOP) fellowships, while Black students claimed more than one-half of these awards (Brown et al., 1980). Prompted by these findings, a series of hearings was held on several campuses during 1982 and 1983. Simon subsequently introduced H.R. 5240 to the Higher Education Act Amendments of 1984, which recommended several reforms to aid Hispanic access and retention. These measures included the modification of Title III to provide direct aid to institutions with high concentrations of Hispanic students; specific monies for Hispanic students in the TRIO Programs and GPOP; and a special emphasis on teacher-preparation (Title V) programs to train teachers for Hispanic populations (*Staff Report on Hispanic Access to Higher Education*, 1985). Although H.R. 5240 was not approved, subsequent legislation as part of the 1992 Higher Education Act Reauthorization incorporated many of the bill's key points. Furthermore, Simon's data-gathering efforts provided documentation to support future reforms. A final congressional bill introduced in the 1980s to support Hispanic higher education was Albert Bustamante's Hispanic-Serving Institutions of Higher Education Act of 1989, which was designed to target funds for schools serving large numbers of Latino students. This bill also failed in Congress but opened the way for successful bills in the 1990s (Santiago, 2006).

Similarly alarmed over the slowing rate of Latino enrollment in higher education, MALDEF attempted to ensure that compliance with mandates from the Office of Civil Rights for the desegregation of higher education included Latinos, and moved away from Texas's historically narrow (and inaccurate) demographic construction of only Blacks and Whites (Foley, 1997). MALDEF's primary role since 1968 had been to use the legal system and courts to advance educational equity for Latinos. Although many of its efforts focused on K–12 lawsuits, MALDEF also hoped to protect the Latino educational pipeline to colleges and universities. In 1983, MALDEF counsel Antonia Hernandez testified to Congress that the departments of Justice and Education had failed to protect Hispanics under Title VI of the 1964 Civil Rights Act, which specified that federal funds be withheld from institutions that discriminated "on the ground of race, color, *or national origin*" (Civil Rights Act of 1964, Title VI, SEC. 601). "MALDEF is aware and sensitive to the fact," Hernandez noted, "that the national origin suspect class has been overlooked in desegregation plans and compliance patterns by the violating state, the Department of Education and the Department of Justice" (*Hearings on Higher Education Civil Rights Enforcement*, 1983, p. 411). She specifically criticized the U.S. Department of Education's review of Texas's attempts to comply with Title VI. Observing that Texas had only examined segregation of Black and White colleges, Hernandez asserted that the review "focused on Black concerns without any consideration of violations against Hispanics and national origin groups" (p. 401).

Texas, like the other nine southern states found in noncompliance with higher education desegregation regulations, had been ordered by the Office of Civil Rights to comply with the "Ingredients of Acceptable Plans to Desegregate State Systems of Higher Education" issued on February 15, 1978. MALDEF and Hernandez objected to Texas's May 1983 plan of remedy on the grounds that it (1) failed to provide for a mechanism to upgrade institutions where large concentrations of Hispanic students were enrolled, and (2) did not provide goals and timetables for Mexican American students that would remedy existing violations by 1990 (*Hearings on Higher Education Civil Rights Enforcement*, 1983, p. 410). Echoing the concern of activists during the Johnson administration, Hernandez pointed out that the term "minority" continued to be defined as "Black," and that Latinos remained the losers in this dichotomous equation. Hernandez closed her statements with a forceful condemnation of the Reagan administration's retreat from enforcement of the civil rights mandate:

> Since this administration took office, the situation has become worse. Efforts to enforce our Civil Rights laws have ceased and both the Department of Education and the Department of Justice have adopted policies which seek to limit and eliminate all preventive efforts to curtail discrimination. (*Hearings on Higher Education Civil Rights Enforcement*, 1983, p. 418)

MALDEF finally argued in the Texas State Supreme Court case *LULAC, et al. v. Ann Richards, Governor of Texas, et al.* (1987) that the method used to fund and approve public higher education planning in Texas discriminated against Latinos who were enrolled largely in the institutions along the Texas and Mexico border. The case was lost, but jurors agreed that the state had failed to create "first-class" colleges and universities on the border (Santiago, 2006). On the legal front, then, MALDEF, along with the National Council of La Raza, ASPIRA,[4] Puerto Rican Legal Defense and Education Fund (PRLDEF), and LULAC, spent much of the 1980s fighting to maintain the gains of the 1960s and 1970s.

Philanthropic organizations such as the Ford Foundation also recognized that the 1980s were tenuous times for Hispanic higher education, as the policy backsliding of the decade was exacerbated by exponential growth in the Hispanic population. Progressive philanthropists were concerned with both the impact of financial retrenchment in social welfare programs and a popular climate increasingly hostile to large government initiatives. Accordingly, private foundations stepped into this financial breach by offering critical assistance to minority higher education projects. In 1984, the Ford Foundation astutely observed that "the conservative national mood is contributing to the drying up of the public support that in the past helped to make racial progress possible" (Walker, 1984, p. 48). In response, Ford reaffirmed its commitment to support social-justice programs, particularly at the community action level and in the realm of higher education. Recognizing its autonomy from prevailing political trends that threatened the gains of the civil rights movement, the foundation sought to reclaim and even intensify momentum for a progressive agenda that would serve the needs of Blacks, Hispanics, Native Americans, and women (Walker, 1984).

As part of this endeavor, the Ford Foundation acknowledged that within compensatory measures and policies, structures of opportunity had long been geared toward Blacks. As Michael Olivas (1997) observed, a partial explanation for this imbalance lay in the "memory of slavery and its present-day legacy," which had historically driven social policies and contributed to the public perception of minority issues "as synonymous with black civil rights" (p. 678). Brown and Davis (2001) further argued that government and societal support of HBCUs in the postbellum era represented a social contract, an implicit agreement acknowledging that these institutions were a vehicle through which the nation could repair its relationship with African Americans. By the 1980s, the Ford Foundation saw the virtue in also extending this contract to Hispanics. The foundation more fully articulated this theme by comparing the Latino situation to the Black condition a generation earlier. In the past, the foundation noted, Hispanics had been viewed

> as one group among many in need. . . . Examination of the Hispanic condition, however, suggests that this approach is no longer sufficient. What Hispanics have need of today is what blacks needed twenty-five years ago: greater knowledge and understanding of their economic, social, and political situation and of the roots of their disadvantage, and the development of an infrastructure that will increase their participation in the mainstream of society. (Ford Foundation, 1984, p. 63)

Continuing its revaluation, the foundation noted that "in the sixties, the Ford Foundation and other private philanthropies launched a series of major individual and joint efforts to help this nation's black population" (p. 51). In Ford's view, Hispanics were experiencing difficulties similar to those of African Americans two decades earlier while at the same confronting the demographic challenges of a rapidly growing population. As a consequence, the foundation recommended that "in the eighties, similar major efforts be undertaken on [Latinos'] behalf as well" (p. 51). It is important to note that these Hispanic initiatives did not represent a retreat from Black programs and funding; in fact, the foundation pointedly asserted that programs for Native Americans, Blacks, and other disadvantaged groups would maintain or even increase their level of support. Ford's support of social-justice efforts remained in place in the 1980s; what was new was its acknowledgement of the special circumstances confronting Latinos (Walker, 1984). The results of the foundation's task force on education (one of five task forces created to identify critical research needs among Hispanics) were varied and far reaching. They included funding the Inter-University Program in Chicano and Puerto Rican Research (IUP) to generate comparative research on the heterogeneous Hispanic population; creating and sustaining a Border Junior College Consortium to support the students and faculty of the seven community colleges along the U.S.-Mexico border; establishing support programs to improve the transfer experience between community college "feeder" schools to four-year "receiver" schools and interrupt the high rate of attrition; continuing funding to ASPIRA's programs assisting urban high school students with college applications; and, lastly, creating a minority postdoctoral fellowship in 1985, which included Latinos, Native Americans, and Blacks, to increase the number of minority faculty in academe (Ford Foundation, 1980, 1981, 1988).

Emulation Era of the Late 1980s and Early 1990s

> We at HACU believe that the Higher Education Act, through its various titles, is well positioned to meet some of the unique needs of Hispanic students and institutions. Radical changes to current legislation would not be required to achieve progress among those population groups that are in greatest need of improving academic achievement. . . . To enable the Hispanic-serving institutions to meet this challenge, HACU recommends that an HSI initiative within the current Title III program be enacted with a concomitant authorization and appropriation commitment that would result in minimum funding for the HSI initiative of $30,000,000.
>
> Testimony of Cesar Mario Trimble, vice president, HACU
> (*Hearings on the Reauthorization of the Higher Education Act of 1965,*
> 1991, pp. 166–167)

During the 1970s, many Latino organizations worked to effect change from an outsider perspective through demonstrations, picketing, and marches (Gómez-Quiñones, 1990). Unwilling to leave the future direction of Latino higher education solely in the hands of the federal government or philanthropists, a prominent group of Latino leaders in education and business adopted a new strategy: unite the de facto Hispanic colleges and universities into one organization to garner political mobilization and direct strategic initiatives at a national level for Hispanic higher education. The Hispanic Association of Colleges and Universities (HACU) was thus created in 1986. As illustrated in Rojas's (2007) model of how social movements change bureaucracies, during the late 1980s and early 1990s Latinos were establishing their own organizations, accommodating to traditional power structures, and finding ways of bringing in additional support in terms of funding or power to their organizations. By the 1980s, a critical mass of professional, financially secure, and politically savvy Latinos were in place to enable Hispanics to utilize traditional forms of political pressure such as lobbying and leverage from the Hispanic Congressional Caucus to move higher education reform agendas forward.

HACU's initial group was composed of eighteen two- and four-year institutions, both public and private; it quickly rose to 112 institutions by 1991, and in 2003 numbered 236. Echoing the goals of organizations such as the National Association for Equal Opportunity in Higher Education (NAFEO), which had historically raised money for Black colleges and universities, HACU sought to increase Latino access to higher education and raise the quality of those institutions serving Hispanic students. It is HACU's continuing mission to promote the development of member institutions; to improve the access and quality of postsecondary opportunities for Latino students; and to meet the needs of business, industry, and government through sharing resources, research, and expertise (Laden, 2002). Through the successful acquisition of resources from private foundations, Fortune 500 firms, and the federal government, HACU created a powerful lobbying organization with offices in San Antonio, Texas, and Washington, D.C. The group also provided scholarships and internships to Latino students, and the term "Hispanic-Serving Institution," which was subsequently adopted as a federal designation, originated at the first HACU conference in 1986 (Santiago, 2006). HACU's powerful networks set the stage for its important role in reshaping Titles III and V under the 1992 and 1998 reauthorizations of the 1965 Higher Education Act (Laden, 2002). The creation of HACU not only raised the visibility of Latino higher education but also, in contrast to the civil rights era approach, created an organization both able and eager to work within established systems of power. This "insider" approach, which had worked remarkably well for the HBCU lobby, enabled HACU to have a united voice in tapping business and government networks and policymakers.

The 1980s stagnation in Latinos' progress in higher education was also countered by proactive stances from a bevy of supporters; organizations such as MALDEF, the Ford Foundation, and ASPIRA provided essential legal, financial, and academic resources. In addition, key individual efforts from academics such as Michael Olivas—both in his work with LULAC and NCES and through his academic monograph, *Latino College Students* (1986)—provided intellectual weight to the push for equal access and opportunity for Hispanics in American colleges and universities. When we consider that as recently as two decades earlier, Hispanic students in higher education had neither a network of institutions specifically designed to meet their needs nor the alumni of those institutions to provide contacts and what Vincent P. Franklin has termed "Black cultural capital," the 1980s stand as a turning point in Latino higher education (Franklin & Savage, 2004; Olivas, 1997). Faced with the potential loss of ground won during the vital decades of the 1960s and 1970s, both individual and group actors such as HACU (with the support of private philanthropy and certain segments of the federal government) fought to protect the gains Latinos had made in higher education. Together, these activists succeeded in salvaging a progressive agenda and opened up the possibility of further growth in the next decade.

Since the 1960s, the Latino community has attempted to identify and address, through special dispensations and financial support, inequities facing Hispanics seeking access to higher education. During the 1990s, the federal legislature began to address these demands more comprehensively than ever before through its 1992 and 1998 reauthorizations of the 1965 Higher Education Act. In the 1992 reauthorization, the inclusion of HSIs in Title III, the Developing Institutions Program of HEA, was a coup engineered by the relatively new HACU lobby (Laden, 2001). Through the testimonies of several key leaders in the organization and member institutions, HACU emphasized several selling points for the federal recognition and creation of HSIs. These included the national contribution that an educated Latino community would make to U.S. productivity; the consequences of not educating a relatively young and often poorly schooled immigrant population; and the systemic failure of U.S.

public high schools, which displayed increasingly troubling dropout and low college graduation rates (*Access to College and Program Simplification, 1991, Hearings on the Reauthorization of the Higher Education Act of 1965*). Furthermore, HACU tried to offset concerns that aid given to HBCUs or Tribal Colleges and Universities would be reduced due to increased attention to Latino concerns. For example, José Ramon Gonzalez, president of the Inter-American University of Puerto Rico, testified that HSI programs "would not threaten the HBCU set-aside" (*Access to College and Program Simplification, 1991, p. 724, Hearings on the Reauthorization of the Higher Education Act of 1965*). Although HACU members were careful to assuage fears of the HBCU lobby, they also recommended measures to safeguard Latino interests. Rafael Magallan, executive director of HACU, wanted to ensure that shared programs would result in "HACU-member/Hispanic-Serving Institutions [being] *fairly represented* among the grant recipients" (*Hearings before the Committee on Labor and Human Resources*, 1991, p. 64). Senator Claiborne Pell, a longtime friend of higher education, finally introduced the bill creating HSIs in 1992.

The federal definition of "Hispanic-Serving Institution" under the new legislation was stringent. Public Law 102-325 placed HSIs under Title III, Part A, Section 316 of the HEA, and they were defined as having (1) an enrollment of at least 25 percent full-time equivalent Hispanic students; (2) not less than 50 percent of its Latino students low-income and first-generation college students; and (3) an additional 25 percent of its Hispanic students *either* low-income or first-generation college students. These cumbersome requirements made it difficult for HSIs to identify qualified students. In addition, although HACU was satisfied that HSIs had finally received federal identification, designated funding amounts were not realized. Initial funding of $45 million for fiscal year 1993 was not dispersed until 1995; even then, only $12 million became available. By 1997, the appropriation to HSIs had dropped to $10.8 million. Furthermore, only thirty-seven of the ninety-two applications for funding under Title III were granted, which prompted concern and resentment that the more generously funded HBCUs were favored in the allocation process (*Hearings of the Committee on Labor and Human Resources*, 1997, pp. 14–16; Hispanic Association of Colleges and Universities, 1997, pp. 58, 71). Eventually it fell to the 1998 HEA reauthorization to address these limitations in the federal government's first broad funding program for Latinos in higher education.

The disappointments of the 1992 reauthorization were exacerbated by a social climate in the early 1990s that was increasingly conservative and anti-immigrant, particularly against Latinos. The passage of measures such as Propositions 209 (1996) and 227 (1998) in California limiting bilingual education and affirmative action, and the Fifth Circuit Court of Appeals's negative ruling on affirmative action in *Hopwood v. Texas* (1996) signaled potential backsliding for Latino higher education.

However, national leadership helped counter these setbacks. President Bill Clinton, through Executive Order 12900 in 1994, created the President's Advisory Commission on Educational Excellence for Hispanic Americans, resulting in the influential policymaking publication, *Our Nation on the Fault-Line: Hispanic American Education* (1996). Furthermore, Secretary of Education Richard Riley contributed his leadership to the White House Initiative for Educational Excellence for Hispanic Americans (1996).

Autonomy of the Late 1990s: Latino Higher Education and the Federal Government in the Twenty-First Century

In all titles where "other minority-serving institutions" are mentioned, Hispanic-serving institutions should be recognized explicitly. To best accomplish this we urge that there be a new section created under Title III strengthening institutions for HSIs, comparable to Part B for Historically Black Colleges and Universities. We recognize and respect our historical differences, but can build an equally compelling argument for equity.

Testimony of Thomas Martinez, representative of the
Hispanic Association of Colleges and Universities, Washington, D.C.,
(*Hearings on HR 6—The Higher Education Amendments of 1998*, p. 61).

As the 1998 reauthorization of the Higher Education Act approached, Latino advocates maneuvered to have HSIs placed in a separate title, which would focus more clearly on their specific interests.

The Hispanic lobby worked to quell fears among HBCUs that such a shift would result in reduced funding to their institutions. For instance, Norman Maldonado, president of the University of Puerto Rico and an HACU member, testified, "It is not our goal today to pit one favorite child against the other. We recognize that a rising tide lifts all boats" (*Hearings on the Reauthorization of the Higher Education Act,* 1997, para. 29). Both rumor and media outlets had heightened suspicion that a trade-off was coming. Many held that the reauthorization would decrease HBCU funding in order to meet the needs of the ever-growing numbers of federally designated HSIs and the Latino students at these colleges and universities. This long-simmering competition between Brown and Black in higher education, which emerged sporadically during the civil rights era, had decreased during the 1970s and 1980s but reemerged in both popular print media and scholarly journals by the early 1990s (Anderson, 1992; Martinez, 1993; Piatt, 1997; Ramirez, 1995; Rodriguez, 1994; Vaca, 2004; West, de Alva, & Shorris, 1996).

At the time of the post–civil rights reemergence, the social and political context had changed significantly. By the early 1990s, Hispanics had made considerable political headway nationally and utilized lobbies such as the Hispanic Educational Coalition to the U.S. Hispanic Congressional Caucus (*Hearings on the Reauthorization of the Higher Education Act of 1965,* 1997). Moreover, the sheer number of Latinos in the U.S. had risen dramatically (76%) between the 1980 and the 1990 Census, and demographers proclaimed that Hispanics would soon surpass African Americans as the largest U.S. census-identified minority group in the United States, a status the Black community had held since the Revolutionary War (U.S. Census Bureau, 2002). Thus, despite the reaffirmation in *United States v. Fordice* (1992, pp. 727–732) that a "sound educational justification" existed for supporting HBCUs in the social contract that Blacks and the White majority had crafted after the Civil War, the arrival of a new group that might alter that contract had not been considered (Brown & Davis, 2001; Samuels, 2004). It is entirely reasonable, then, that the Black higher education lobby reacted with concern to the increasing presence of Latinos in this realm. Historically Black Colleges and Universities are defined in Part B of Title III as institutions created *prior* to 1964; as a result, their institutional numbers are fixed. In contrast, although HSIs lacked the social capital and deep historical roots of HBCUs, their numbers continued to grow as Latino college enrollment in both two-and four-year colleges increased (Fry, 2003).

HACU's strategy to emulate HBCU strategies and models for HSIs was initially effective in getting their foot in the door. However, it became clear by the late 1990s that HSIs were culturally, historically, politically, and socially too distinct to remain in the same federal category as HBCUs; the HSIs had their own unique needs. Hearings for the 1998 reauthorization reflected these distinctions. By 1997, the federal government recognized almost two hundred members representing two- and four-year institutions whose enrollments were more than one-quarter Latino. HSIs were less than 3 percent of all higher education institutions in the United States, but they enrolled over 60 percent of all Latinos in higher education (U.S. Department of Education, 2002). Paralleling a situation that had emerged in the HBCU network, which enrolled fewer than one in five African American students in higher education but graduated over one-half, HSIs began to show similar positive trends, not only in enrollment but also in completion rates, long a matter of concern. The National Center for Education Statistics's first report on HSIs found that by 1999, these institutions conferred over one-third (37%) of all bachelor's degrees to Hispanics (U.S. Department of Education, 2002). Increases in both enrollment trends and graduation rates between 1990 and the end of the decade signaled the critical role HSIs would play in the realm of Hispanic higher education nationwide.

Supporters of HSIs in the 1998 reauthorization emphasized three principal areas of reform. First, supporters identified that the qualifying requirements for HSIs were unnecessarily restrictive and diminished the number of potential institutions able to achieve HSI status. Thus, the first recommendation was to strike the full-time equivalent requirement for identifying the number of Hispanic students. President R. Vic Morgan of Sul Ross State University argued that this restriction did "not reflect the reality of Hispanic college enrollment," as most Latino students could only afford to enroll part-time (*Hearings of the Committee on Labor and Human Resources,* 1997, p. 16). Further, HACU recommended that Congress eliminate the requirement that 50 percent of Hispanic students at HSIs not only be low-income individuals but also first generation college students. In doing so, reformers argued, Congress would permit more institutions to qualify for HSI status (Hispanic Association of Colleges and Universities, 1997). In addition to easing these eligibility measures, HACU argued for HSIs placement in their own section of HEA (titled "Part C") under Title III, instead of its current generic placement under Title A, "Strengthening Institutions." HACU offered a dual rationale for this redefinition. First, it employed a numerical angle by noting that "this redesignation is more than cosmetic. HSIs are unique because they enroll more than half of all Hispanics." Second, HACU offered a moral argument. It was time, claimed the reformers, that the needs of Latino schools were "accorded a similar degree of recognition presently reserved only for HBCUs" (Hispanic Association of Colleges and Universities, 1997, pp. 74–75). The third and final major change recommended in the 1998 reauthorization was an overall increase in funding, especially as the initial round of funding from 1992 had been inadequate and was only disbursed after 1995.

The Higher Education Act of 1965 was amended in 1998 with all three of these recommendations in place. This legislative triumph was further enhanced by the surprising placement of HSIs into its own title—Title V—which had previously concerned teacher training. Through the separate designation of Title V, the Latino community had finally established a distinct identity within federal discussion of higher education. No longer was the Latino experience simply blended with the unique narratives of African Americans or Native Americans in the unwieldy categorization of Title III; rather, Hispanics had at last been granted their own space to confront the particular challenges that faced them in higher education.

Numerous monographs have examined contemporary Latino student experiences in colleges and universities and compared their relative achievement and success in higher education with that of Whites, Asian Americans, and African Americans (Cabrera & LaNasa, 2001; Perna, 2000; Swail, Cabrera, & Lee, 2004; Terenzini, Bernal, & Cabrera, 2001). This paper, on the other hand, has attempted to discover the institutional and governmental structures and policies that affected Latino access to these very colleges and universities; it has also detailed the efforts made by Latinos themselves to cultivate meaningful access to higher education within such structural boundaries. Still, having achieved autonomy through the 1998 reauthorization of the HEA, the ultimate utility of HSIs still remains to be seen. The policy organization Excelencia in Education has begun analyses of student attainment and achievement at HSIs, but the comparative newness of these schools does not allow us to assess their efficacy in the same way that has been possible with HBCUs (Santiago, Andrade, & Brown, 2004). Furthermore, as this paper has made clear, HSIs were created after the fact, rarely originating as grassroots institutions designed solely for Latinos.[5] A small but growing number of scholars are asking for more transparency in the mission statements of universities designated as HSIs, as well as more accountability regarding graduation and community college transfer rates (Contreras, Malcom, & Bensimon, in press).

As part of this growing understanding that qualification as an HSI does not ensure academic success, four important trends in Latino higher education bear monitoring during the next decade. First, while HSIs have done an admirable job of attracting and serving Latino students, the degree to which they have done so may discourage Latinos from attempting to access the cultural capital attendant in the nation's historically prestigious and exclusive institutions, and this irony demands attention; plainly put, how do Latinos balance the need to legitimate HSIs with the necessity of attending elite schools, whose privileged station allows more immediate access to transformative power? Second, can Latinos create, as have graduates of elite women's colleges and HBCUs, their own "talented tenth" through HSIs? Third, issues of gender disparity within the Latino educational community have burgeoned. Parallel to experiences within the African American community, Latino girls and women have succeeded in the realm of higher education at considerably higher levels than their brothers (Harris, 2005). As schools already attuned to issues germane to Latino culture, perhaps HSIs have an opportunity to address this gender imbalance more thoroughly than more traditional colleges and universities. Lastly, more than half of the HSIs receiving federal funds are two-year colleges (Santiago, 2006). Community colleges certainly serve an important societal good by broadening access to postsecondary education for those who, for various social and economic reasons, cannot or do not choose to enroll in four-year colleges.

Another point to consider is that community colleges are congruent with Latino cultural mores, which place a premium on children—particularly young women—remaining at home or nearby while pursuing a college education (Ginorio & Huston, 2001). However, as Brint and Karabel first pointed out in their 1989 classic, *The Diverted Dream*, and Brint (2003) subsequently reaffirmed, community colleges pose a challenge to baccalaureate completion for all attendees, but specifically for minorities. For example, among undergraduates who begin college with the aim of completing a baccalaureate degree, only 26 percent who begin at community colleges achieve that objective within six years, compared to a completion rate of 62 percent for students beginning at a four-year institution (Fry, 2003). While HSIs enrolled 52 percent of all Latino undergraduates in 2003, the imperative not only to enroll but to graduate and to successfully transfer Latino students to a four-year degree program is one that HSIs must address as they begin and continue their journey to serve Latinos in the United States.

Notes

1. Ethnic nomenclature inevitably carries with it connotations born of social, political, and historical constructions; as a consequence, any effort to affix a label to large groups risks perpetuating stereotypes and alienating contemporary readers. That said, the authors have elected to use the terms "Latino" and "Hispanic" interchangeably. When the term "Chicano" is used, it refers to activist Mexican Americans. While Hispanic was a term created by the federal government and thus may be seen as imperious, it is included here for reasons of historical authenticity; until recently, those who saw themselves as Latino used the term Hispanic in acts of self-identification.

2. For example, at the president's news conference of March 31, 1966, a reporter asked, "Mr. President, have you heard anything to the effect that Mexican Americans feel they should have more attention?" The president responded:

   Yes, I have heard that all my life. And I agree with them. I think they should have more attention. I am going to give them all the attention I can. I haven't given them enough. I want to give them more. I think that they are entitled to more consideration in Government employment than they have received. I think they have been discriminated against in housing, in education, in jobs. I don't think we can be very proud of our record in that field. (Wooley & Peters, 1965)

3. The term "talented tenth" is utilized here as conceived by W. E. B. DuBois in his 1903 classic, *The Souls of Black Folks;* that is, an educated elite within the African American community that could provide leadership.

4. The ASPIRA Association, Inc., is the only national nonprofit organization devoted solely to the education and leadership development of Puerto Rican and other Latino youth. ASPIRA takes its name from the Spanish verb *aspirar,* "aspire."

5. One exception is The National Hispanic University, created in California in 1981.

References

Allsup, C. (1982). *The American G.I. Forum: Origins and evolution.* Austin: University of Texas, Center for Mexican American Studies.

Anderson, J. (1988). *The education of Blacks in the South, 1860–1935.* Chapel Hill: University of North Carolina Press.

Anderson, T. (1992). Comparative experience factors among Black, Asian, and Hispanic Americans: Coalitions or conflicts? *Journal of Black Studies, 23,* 27–38.

Baker, T. L., & Velez, W. (1996). Access to and opportunity in postsecondary education in the United States: A review. *Sociology of Education, 699,* 82–101.

Brint, S. (2003). Few remaining dreams: Community colleges since 1985. *Annals of the American Academy of Political and Social Science, 586,* 16–37.

Brint, S., & Karabel, J. (1989) *The diverted dream: Community colleges and educational opportunity in America, 1900–1985.* New York: Oxford University Press.

Brown, G., Rosen, N. L., Hill, S. T., & Olivas, M. A. (1980). *The condition of education for Hispanic Americans.* Washington, DC: U.S. Government Printing Office.

Brown, M. C., II, & Davis, J. E. (2001). The historically Black college as social contract, social capital, and social equalizer. *Peabody Journal of Education, 76*, 40–42.

Cabrera, A. F., & LaNasa, S. M. (Eds.). (2001). On the path to college: Three critical tasks facing America's disadvantaged. *Research in Higher Education, 42*, 119–149.

Carter, T. P. (1970). *Mexican Americans in school: A history of educational neglect.* New York: College Entrance Examination Board.

Chapa, J. (2002). Affirmative action, x percent plans, and Latino access to higher education in the twenty-first century. In M. Suárez-Orozco & M. Páez (Eds.) *Latinos remaking America* (pp. 375–388). Berkeley: University of California Press.

Civil Rights Act, 88 U.S.C. § 601 (1964).

Contreras, F. E., Malcom, L. E., & Bensimon, E. M. (in press). Hispanic-serving institutions: Closeted identity and the production of equitable outcomes for Latino/a students. In M. Gasman, B. Baez, & C. Turner (Eds.), *Interdisciplinary approaches to understanding minority serving institutions.* Albany: State University of New York Press.

Cuádraz, G. H. (1999). Stories of access and "luck": Chicana/os, higher education, and the politics of incorporation. *Latino Studies Journal, 10*, 100–123.

Curti, M., & Nast, R. (1965). *Philanthropy in the shaping of American higher education.* New Brunswick, NJ: Rutgers University Press.

Davies, G. (2002). The Great Society after Johnson: The case of bilingual education. *Journal of American History, 88*, 1405–1429.

Donato, R. (1997). *The other struggle for equal schools: Mexican Americans during the civil rights era.* Albany: State University of New York Press.

Donato, R., & Lazerson, M. (2000). New directions in American Educational history: Problems and prospects. *Educational Researcher, 29*, 4–15.

The "Dream Act" and "The American Dream Act" fact sheet. Retrieved October 15, 2007, from http://www.nclr.org/content/publications/download/43340

Drewry, H. N., & Doermann, H. (2001). *Stand and prosper: Private Black colleges and their students.* Princeton, NJ: Princeton University Press.

Foley, N. (1997). *The White scourge: Mexicans, Blacks, and poor Whites in Texas cotton culture.* Berkeley: University of California Press.

Foner, E. (1988). *Reconstruction, America's unfinished revolution, 1863–1877.* New York: Harper Books.

Ford Foundation. (1969). *Annual report for the year 1969.* Retrieved August 26, 2006, from http://www.fordfound.org/elibrary/documents/1969/029.cfm

Ford Foundation. (1970). *Annual report for the year 1970.* Retrieved August 26, 2006, from http://www.fordfound.org/elibrary/documents/1970/045.cfm

Ford Foundation. (1980). *Annual report for the year 1980.* Retrieved August 26, 2006, from http://www.fordfound.org/elibrary/documents/1980/toc.cfm

Ford Foundation. (1981). *Annual report for the year 1981.* Retrieved August 26, 2006, from http://www.fordfound.org/elibrary/documents/1981/toc.cfm

Ford Foundation. (1984). *Hispanics: Challenges and opportunities* (Ford Foundation Working Paper). Retrieved August 26, 2006, from http://www.fordfound.org/elibrary/image.cfm?img=001&xml_id=0147&pn_physical=001

Ford Foundation. (1988). *Annual report for the year 1988.* Retrieved August 26, 2006, from http://www.fordfound.org/elibrary/documents/1988/toc.cfm

Franklin, J. H. (1981). The land of room enough. *Daedalus: Journal of the American Academy of Arts and Sciences, 110*, 1–12.

Franklin, V. P., & Savage, C. J. (Eds.). (2004). *Cultural capital and Black education: African American communities and the funding of Black schooling, 1865 to the present.* Greenwich, CT: Information Age.

Fry, R. (2003). *Hispanics in college: Participation and degree attainment.* New York: ERIC Clearinghouse on Urban Education. (ERIC Document Reproduction Service No. ED480917)

García, I. (2000). *Mexican Americans in search of Camelot.* College Station: Texas A & M University Press.

García, I. M. (1989). *United we win: The rise and fall of the Raza Unia party.* Tucson: University of Arizona, Mexican American Studies and Research Center.

Gasman, M. (2007). *Envisioning Black colleges: A history of the United Negro College Fund.* Baltimore: Johns Hopkins University Press.

Ginorio, A., & Huston, M. (2001). *¡Sí se puede! Yes, we can!: Latinas in school.* Washington, DC: American Association of University Women.

Glasker, W. (2002). *Black students in the ivory tower: African American student activism at the University of Pennsylvania, 1967–1990.* Amherst: University of Massachusetts Press.

Gómez-Quiñones, J. (1978). *Mexican students por La Raza: The Chicano student movement in Southern California, 1967–1977.* Santa Barbara, CA: La Raza.

Gómez-Quiñones, J. (1990). *Chicano politics: Reality and promise, 1940–1990.* Albuquerque: University of New Mexico Press.

Grebler, L., Moore, J. W., & Guzman, R. C. (1970). *The Mexican American people: The nation's second largest minority.* New York: Free Press.

Groutt, J. (2002). *The Rockefeller programs for the disadvantaged and federal educational programs.* Tarrytown, NY: Rockefeller Archive Center.

Groutt, J., & Hill, C. (2001). Upward bound: In the beginning. *Opportunity Outlook: Journal of the Council for Opportunity in Education,* 26–33.

Handbook of Texas Online. (2007). Juárez-Lincoln University. Retrieved October 16, 2007, from http://www.tsha.utexas.edu/handbook/online/articles/JJ/kcj3.html

Harris, P. (2005, November 17). A quiet crisis: Conference highlights higher education disparities between Latino men and women [Electronic version]. *Diverse Issues in Higher Education.* Retrieved February 16, 2007, from http://findarticles.com/p/articles/mi_m0WMX/is_20_22/ai_n15950924

Hearings on higher education civil rights enforcement: Joint hearings before the Subcommittee *on Postsecondary Education of the Committee on Education and Labor and the Subcommittee on Civil and Constitutional Rights of the House Committee on the Judiciary,* 98th Cong., 1 (1983) (testimony of Antonia Hernandez).

Hearings on HR 6—The Higher Education Amendments of 1998: Hearing before the Subcommittee on Postsecondary Education, Training and Life-Long Learning of the House Committee on Education and the Workforce, 105th Cong., 6 (1998) (testimony of Thomas Martinez).

Hearings on the Higher Education Act of 1965: Hearings before the Special Subcommittee on Education of the House Committee on Education and Labor. 89th Cong., 1 (1965) (statement of Edith Green). *Access to college and program simplification: Hearings on the reauthorization of the Higher Education Act of 1965 before the Subcommittee on Postsecondary Education of the House Committee on Education and Labor.* 102nd Cong., 1 (1991) (testimony of Cesar Ramon Trimble).

Hearings on the Reauthorization of the Higher Education Act of 1965: Hearings before the *Subcommittee on Postsecondary education, training, and lifelong learning, of the House Committee on Education and the Workforce,* 105th Cong., 6 (1997) (testimony of Dr. Norman I. Maldonado). LexisNexis Congressional. Federal Document Clearing House (FDCHeMedia, Inc.) Capitol Hill Hearing Testimony. Load-date: June 27, 1997.

Higher Education Act of 1965, Pub. L. No.89–329, 79 Stat.1219 (1965).

Higher Education Act of 1965: Hearings before the Special Subcommittee on Education of the House Committee on Education and Labor. 89th Congress.1 (1965).

Hispanic Association of Colleges and Universities. (1997). *A perspective on the reauthorization of the Higher Education Act.* San Antonio, TX: Author.

History of the university and higher education.(n.d.). Retrieved August 7, 2007, from http:// www.nhu.edu/about_nhu/history.htm

Hopwood v. Texas, 78 F.3d 932 (5th Cir. 1996).

Huntington. S. (2004, March/April). The Hispanic challenge. *Foreign Policy,* 30–45. Ingredients of Acceptable Plans to Desegregate State Systems of Higher Education, 43 Fed. Reg. 6658 (Feb. 15, 1978).

Johnson, L. (1967). Memorandum establishing the inter-agency commission on Mexican American affairs. In J. Woolley & G. Peters, (Eds.) *Public papers of the presidents of the United States: Lyndon B. Johnson, book II* (American Presidency Project). Santa Barbara: University of California. Retrieved August 27, 2006, from http://www.presidency.ucsb.edu/ws/?pid=28293

Johnson, L. B. (1965). Remarks at Southwest Texas State College upon signing the Higher Education Act of 1965. In J. Woolley & G. Peters, (Eds.) *Public papers of the presidents of the United States: Lyndon B. Johnson, book II* (American Presidency Project). Santa Barbara: University of California. Retrieved August 27, 2006, from http://www.presidency.ucsb.edu/ws/index.php?pid=27356&t=&st1=

Kaplowitz, C. A. (2003). A distinct minority: LULAC, Mexican American identity, and presidential policymaking, 1965–1972. *The Journal of Policy History, 15*, 192–222.

Karen, D. (1991). Politics of class, race, and gender: Access to higher education in the United States, 1960–1986. *American Journal of Education, 99*, 208–37.

Laden, B. V. (2001). Hispanic-serving institutions: Myths and realities. *Peabody Journal of Education, 76*, 73–91.

Laden, B. V. (2002). Two-year Hispanic-serving colleges. In C. S. Turner & a. l. antonio et al. (Eds.). *Racial and ethnic diversity in higher education* (2nd ed., pp. 42–72). Boston: Pearson Custom.

Lavin, D. E., & Hyllegard, D. (1996). *Changing the odds: Open admissions and the life chances of the disadvantaged.* New Haven, CT: Yale University Press.

Litwack, L. (1998). *Trouble in mind: Black southerners in the age of Jim Crow.* New York: Alfred A. Knopf.

MacDonald, V. M. (Ed.). (2004). *Latino education in the U.S.: A narrated history, 1513–2000.* New York: Palgrave/Macmillan.

MacDonald, V. M., & García, T. (2003). Latino higher Education: Historical pathways to access. In L. Jones & J. Castellanos (Eds.), *The majority in the minority: Retaining Latina/o faculty, administrators, and students in the 21st century* (pp. 15–43). Sterling, VA: Stylus Press.

Magat, R. (1979). *The Ford Foundation at work: Philanthropic choices, methods, and styles.* New York: Plenum Press.

Maldonado, C. S. (2000). *Colegio Cesar Chavez, 1973–1983: A Chicano struggle for self-determination.* New York: Garland.

Márquez, B. (1993). *LULAC: The evolution of a Mexican American political organization.* Austin: University of Texas Press.

Martinez, E. (1993). Beyond Black/White: The racisms of our time. *Social Justice, 20*, 22–34.

Meyer, G. (2003). Save Hostos: Politics and community mobilization to save a college in the Bronx, 1973–1978. *El Centro Journal, 15*, 73–97.

Miranda, L., & Quiroz, J. T. (1990). *The decade of the Hispanic: An economic retrospective.* Washington, DC: National Council of La Raza, Washington, DC Office of Research Advocacy and Legislation. (ERIC Clearinghouse on Education, ED320972)

Muñoz, C., Jr. (1989). *Youth, identity, power: The Chicano movement.* London: Verso Books.

National Center for Education Statistics. (2003). *Enrollment rates of 18- to 24-year-olds in colleges and universities: Selected years 1980 to 2000. Status and Trends in the Education of Hispanics.* Washington, DC: Author.

Navarro, A. (1995). *Mexican American youth organization: Avant-garde of the Chicano movement in Texas.* Austin: University of Texas Press.

Novick, P. (1988). *That noble dream: The "objectivity question" and the American historical profession.* Cambridge, England: Cambridge University Press.

Olivas, M. A. (1982). Indian, Chicano, and Puerto Rican colleges: Status and issues. *Bilingual Review, 9*, 36–58.

Olivas, M. A. (1986). Research on Latino college students: A theoretical framework and inquiry. In M. A. Olivas (Ed.), *Latino college students* (pp. 1–25). New York: Teachers College Press.

Olivas, M. A. (1997). Indian, Chicano, and Puerto Rican colleges: Status and issues. In L. F. Goodchild & H. S. Wechsler (Eds.), *The history of higher education* (2nd ed., pp. 677–698). Needham Heights, MA: Simon & Schuster Custom.

Opportunity Programs: Opening the doors to higher education: Hearings of the Committee on Labor and Human Resources. United States Senate, 105th Cong., 1 (1997) (testimony of Dr. R. Vic Morgan).

Orfield, G. (1992). Money, equity, and college access. *Harvard Educational Review, 62*, 337–372.

Perna, L. W. (2000). Differences in the decision to attend college among African Americans, Hispanics, and Whites. *The Journal of Higher Education, 71*, 117–141.

Piatt, B. (1997). *Black and Brown in America: The case for cooperation.* New York: New York University Press.

Pycior, J. L. (1997). *LBJ & Mexican Americans: The paradox of power.* Austin: University of Texas Press.

Ramirez, D. A. (1995). Multicultural empowerment: It's not just Black and White anymore. *Stanford Law Review, 47*, 957–992.

Ramos, H. (1998). *The American GI Forum: In pursuit of the dream, 1948–1983.* Houston: Arte Publico Press.

Rivas-Rodriguez, M., Torres, J., Dipiero-D'sa, M., & Fitzpatrick, L. (Eds.). (2006). *A legacy greater than words: Stories of U.S. Latinos & Latinas of the World War II generation.* Austin: University of Texas Press.

Rockefeller Foundation. (1967–1978). Information on these programs in Record Group 1.2 Series 200: Box 9, folders 71–72, "Arizona State University—Minority Education, 1969–1972"; Box 17, folders 139–142,

"California State College, Los Angeles—Community Relations, 1968–1971"; Box 17, folders 143–144, "California State College, Los Angeles–Urban Education, 1968–1970"; Box 19, folders 158–163 (supplemental material in folder 164), "Claremont Colleges—Mexican American Students, 1967– 1974, 1978." Sleepy Hollow, NY: Rockefeller Archives Center.

Rockefeller Foundation. (1968, June). *Resolution to grant funds to Claremont College* (Record Group 1.2, Series 200, Box 19, Folder 158). Sleepy Hollow, NY: Rockefeller Archives Center.

Rodriguez, M. S. (2003). A movement made of "Young Mexican Americans seeking change": Critical citizenship, migration, and the Chicano movement in Texas and Wisconsin, 1960–1975. *Western Historical Quarterly, 34,* 275–299.

Rodriguez, R. (1994). Black/Latino relations: An unnecessary conflict. *Black Issues in Higher Education, 40–42.*

Roebuck, J. B., & Murty, K. S. (1993). *Historically Black colleges and universities: Their place in American higher education.* Westport, CT: Praeger.

Rojas, F. (2007). *From Black power to Black studies: How a radical social movement became an academic discipline.* Baltimore: Johns Hopkins University Press.

Rooks, N. M. (2006). *White money /Black power: The surprising history of African American studies and the crisis of race in higher education.* Boston: Beacon Press.

Rubio, P. F. (2001). *A history of affirmative action, 1619–2000.* Jackson: University Press of Mississippi.

Ruiz, V. L. (2006). Nuestra América: Latino history as United Status history. *Journal of American History, 93,* 655–672.

Samuels, A. L. (2004). *Is separate unequal? Black colleges and the challenge to desegregation.* Lawrence: University of Kansas Press.

San Miguel, G., Jr. (1987). *"Let all of them take heed": Mexican Americans and the campaign for educational equality in Texas, 1910–1981.* Austin: University of Texas Press.

Santa Ana, O. (2002). *Brown tide rising: Metaphors of Latinos in contemporary American public discourse.* Austin: University of Texas Press.

Santiago, D. A. (2006). *Inventing Hispanic-serving institutions (HSIs): The basics.* Washington, DC: Excelencia in Education.

Santiago, D. A., Andrade, S. J., & Brown, S. E. (2004). *Latino student success at Hispanic-serving institutions: Findings from a demonstration project.* Washington, DC: Excelencia in Education [Electronic Source]. Retrieved July 29, 2007, from http://www.edex-celencia.org/pdf/web-LSSatHSIs.pdf

Staff Report on Hispanic Access to Higher Education. Committee on Education and Labor. 99th Cong., 1st Sess. (1985).

Steigerwald, D. (1995). *The sixties and the end of Modern America.* New York: St. Martins Press.

Swail, W. S., Cabrera, A. F., Lee, C. (2004). *Latino youth and the pathway to college.* Washington, DC: Educational Policy Institute.

Terenzini, P. T., Bernal, E. M., Cabrera, A. F. (2001). *Swimming against the tide: The poor in American higher education.* New York, College Entrance Examination Board.

Traub, J. (1994). *City on a hill: Testing the American dream at City College.* New York: Addison-Wesley.

Turner, C.S., antonio, a.l., García, M., Laden, B.V., Nora, A. & Presley, C.L. (Eds). (2002). *Racial and ethnic diversity in higher education* (2nd ed.). Boston: Pearson Custom.

U.S. Census Bureau. (2002). *Table 1. United States—Race and Hispanic origin: 1790 to 1990.* Washington, DC: Author. Retrieved November 28, 2007 from http://www.census.gov/population/documentation/twps0056/tab01.pdf

U.S. Commission on Civil Rights. (1967). *Hearing held in San Francisco, California, May 1–3, 1967, and Oakland, California, May 4–6, 1967.* Washington, DC: U.S. Government Printing Office.

U.S. Commission on Civil Rights. (1968). *Hearing held in San Antonio, Texas, December 9–14, 1968.* Washington, DC: U.S. Government Printing Office.

U.S. Department of Education, National Center for Education Statistics. (2002). *Hispanic Serving Institutions: Statistical Trends from 1990–1999* (NCES 2002-051)

United States v. Fordice, 112 S. Ct. 2727, 120 L. Ed. 2d 575 (1992).

Vaca, N. C. (2004). *The presumed alliance: The unspoken conflict between Latinos and Blacks and what it means for America.* New York: HarperCollins.

Valencia, R. (2002). The explosive growth of the Chicano/Latino population: Educational implications. In R. Valencia (Ed.), *Chicano school failure and success: Past, present, and future* (2nd ed., pp. 52–69). London: RoutledgeFalmer.

Walker, L. (1984). *Civil rights, social justice, and Black America: A working paper from the Ford Foundation.* New York: Ford Foundation.

Walton, A. (Ed.). (2005). *Women and philanthropy in education.* Bloomington: Indiana University Press.

Weinberg, M. (1977). *A chance to learn: A history of race and education in the United States.* Cambridge, England: Cambridge University Press.

West, C., de Alva, J. K., & Shorris, E. (1996, April). Our next race question: The uneasiness between Blacks and Latinos. *Harper's*, pp. 55–63.

Williamson, J. A. (2003) *Black power on campus: The University of Illinois, 1965–1975.* Urbana: University of Illinois Press.

Woods, R. B. (2006). *LBJ: Architect of American ambition.* New York: Free Press.

Wooley, J., & Peters, G. (1965). Public papers of the presidents of the United States: Lyndon Johnson (Vol. 1). *The American Presidency Project.* Santa Barbara: University of California. Retrieved August 27, 2006, from http://www.presidency.ucsb.edu/index.php

Yamane, D. (2002). *Student movements for multiculturalism: Challenging the curricular color line in higher education.* Baltimore: Johns Hopkins University Press.

Zinn, H. (2005). *People's history of the United States, 1492 to present.* New York: Harper Collins.

PART II

STUDENTS

KIMBERLY A. GRIFFIN AND WALTER R. ALLEN, ASSOCIATE EDITORS

It is hard to ignore how college and universities have changed over the past few decades. Campuses in the U.S. have become increasingly diverse, with students from traditionally underrepresented groups becoming more represented in college classrooms that were once exclusively White. According to a recent report from the American Council on Education (Ryu, 2008), the growth in Asian American, Latino/a, African American, and Native American student populations has outpaced increases amongst White students for many years. Specifically, White student enrollments have shrunk from 70% to 61% of all undergraduates enrolled in college over the last decade. Carnevale and Fry (2000) anticipate these trends will continue and minority student enrollments will multiply at an accelerated pace, projecting that by 2015 minorities will represent almost 40% of all students on college and university campuses.

Most education scholars generally regard this trend as good. Increased diversity in the student body seemingly signifies that students from a variety of backgrounds are gaining access to college and attaining their educational goals at higher rates. These demographic shifts also hold the promise of enabling educators to create optimal learning environments. At their best, racially and ethnically heterogeneous campuses offer unique opportunities for students to engage across difference. But unfortunately, these diverse learning environments neither create nor sustain themselves—they require consciousness and deliberate action from faculty, staff, and administrators. In addition to highlighting the benefits of a diverse campus, scholars whose work is included in this section make clear how negligence in fostering productive cross-racial engagement leads to hostile battlegrounds where students of color feel marginalized, White students feel either reluctant or resentful, and most avoid engaging beyond the borders of their own racial and ethnic groups.

Ultimately, as the demographics of higher education continue to shift, scholars, policymakers, and institutional leaders must consider the following questions: will colleges and universities that have traditionally served White populations have the knowledge and infrastructure necessary to construct inclusive environments conducive to the success of students from *all* racial and ethnic backgrounds? And how can policymakers, institutional leaders, faculty, and student affairs professionals create contexts in which *all* students learn, develop, and accrue equitable educational outcomes? The seven chapters in this section engage our thinking around these issues, highlighting the significance of race and ethnicity in shaping the context of college campuses. While we may often think of an educational environment as being composed of lifeless objects like classrooms, buildings, tables, and chairs, it is also about people and relationships. Who students live, play, and learn with has great potential to influence how they experience their campuses, perform in classrooms, and develop as thinkers and citizens. These chapters afford a glimpse into how experiences with racism, diversity, and cross-racial engagement can influence learning, personal development, and other educational outcomes.

Some chapters in this section illuminate minority students' encounters with racism and racial stereotypes. In Chapter 9, Brian D. Smedley, Hector F. Myers, and Shelly P. Harrell provide a typology for understanding the experiences of minority students on predominantly White campuses, which they call "minority-status stresses." The authors acknowledge there are certain stresses that all students experience as they transition to and attempt to achieve success in college. However, there are particular stressors that racial/ethnic minority students must endure that White students do not. Similarly, in Chapter 10, Sharon L. Fries-Britt and Kimberly A. Griffin write about a group of high-achieving Black undergraduate students who faced challenges with which most academically talented students struggle. However, there were additional barriers they encountered and were required to overcome because of their race.

In both studies, it appears that others' beliefs, assumptions, and stereotypes about minority students and their academic abilities were most challenging and debilitating. Minority students reported feelings of stress around their academic abilities, preparation, or how they were being judged in comparison to their White peers. Consequently, participants in Smedley, Myers, and Harrell's study reported experiencing more psychological distress and earning lower grade point averages. Students in the Fries-Britt and Griffin study described having doubts about their academic abilities and worth, despite their membership in the campus honors program. While some found motivation amid their doubts, it is important to understand the lengths to which these students went to prove their academic worth and debunk the myths of minority underachievement.

Some might suggest these stresses are self-imposed or that students are imagining others' doubts about their academic worth. However, Eduardo Bonilla-Silva and Tyrone A. Forman's research on White students and racial ideology offers confirmatory evidence that the concerns articulated by minority students are not imagined. In Chapter 11, they present a study in which White undergraduates were sometimes challenged to articulate, but other times clearly communicated, their perspectives, values, and beliefs about individuals from racial and ethnic backgrounds that differed from their own. Many expressed colorblind ideologies; they purported not seeing race and believed little to no racism existed in contemporary American society. White participants in Shaun R. Harper and Sylvia Hurtado's study (Chapter 12) also had significant misperceptions of the experiences, engagement, and satisfaction of students of color on their same campuses—they perceived them to be much happier than was actually the case. Together, Chapters 11 and 12 reveal that White students largely interact with peers like themselves. It was rare for these students to report relationships with students who were not White; they admittedly lived segregated lives where their racial views often went unchallenged. Harper and Hurtado also highlight the tendency for White students to perceive minority student programs and organizations as the source of this segregation, taking little ownership for their own lack of engagement with individuals from different racial or ethnic backgrounds.

How can institutions encourage White students to learn in ways that challenge these perspectives? How can they improve learning environments and encourage students to interact with each other and reap the benefits of living in a diverse community? Anna M. Ortiz and Robert A. Rhoads offer some answers in Chapter 13. They highlight the lack of attention devoted to the racialized experiences of White students on most college campuses, and offer guidance on how to help White students develop positive racial identities. At a local level, Ortiz and Rhoads recommend working with White students through a multi-stage process to facilitate movement out of a colorblind ideology and into a more multicultural worldview. They note, however, that the development of a multicultural worldview requires substantive interaction with individuals from different racial and ethnic backgrounds. This is consistent with learning theories that suggest development takes place when individuals are pushed to engage ideas and perspectives that are unfamiliar and often contrary to their prior racial socialization. These experiences create disequilibrium, which spurs growth as students strive to process and incorporate new perspectives into their existing belief systems.

In addition to enhancing individual identity development, diversity researchers suggest the disequilibrium that occurs when students live and learn with peers from different racial and ethnic backgrounds also improves learning. Educators must consider strategic ways to facilitate opportunities for students to engage with each other in semi-structured settings beyond the classroom. In Chapter 14, Nida Denson and Mitchell J. Chang suggest that individual levels of interaction with diverse peers are linked to student development, particularly in terms of feeling a sense of efficacy relating to others from different backgrounds. Especially noteworthy is that students enrolled at institutions where their classmates were interacting with diverse peers learned more, regardless of their own behaviors.

Again, the findings of this research speak directly to institutional agency in creating the most optimal environments for learning. While making efforts to promote micro-level change in an individual student's attitudes and behaviors is certainly important, institutional change is also necessary. Harper and Hurtado remind us that while many educators and administrators say they are devoted to fostering an inclusive campus climate for all students, there is often insufficient institutional action and evidence to confirm such commitment. Perhaps these institutions would benefit from reading Sylvia Hurtado, Jeffrey F. Milem, Alma R. Clayton-Pedersen, and Walter R. Allen's work (in Chapter 15), which provides a framework designed to facilitate change. The framework identifies four core constructs institutions must attend to as they aim to improve campus racial climates and better address issues pertaining to race. In addition to increasing the representation of all racial and ethnic groups on campus, institutions must acknowledge and address their historical legacies of exclusion, students' variable perceptions of and experiences with the climate, and the nature and quality of interactions across difference.

Conclusion

It is important to acknowledge the changing face of U.S. higher education. In aggregate terms, the country's postsecondary institutions now enroll more women and students of color. However, it is important to acknowledge, progress aside, the considerable distance yet left to travel in terms of fundamental institutional change. As noted in the previous section of this ASHE Reader, shifts in the racial and ethnic composition of colleges and universities have required struggle and been met with resistance. By their very nature, institutions of higher education are slow moving, if not inherently resistant to change. At the same time, U.S. attitudes toward race, ethnicity, subordination, and power have also been particularly resistant to change. Our nation was founded as the world's only racial democracy, and the U.S. Constitution embraced the Enlightenment ideals of personal freedom and self-determination, yet legalizing Black slavery. Profound contradictions were also evident in gender, racial/ethnic, and social class historical patterns of subordination and exercise of power, such that women were treated as second class citizens, poor whites were denied voting rights, the land of Native Americans was stolen, and the labor of Latinos and Asians was expropriated. Over time, the very DNA of American culture and society came to assume White (and male) supremacy and privilege as natural and expected. This is the context within which we must locate and understand efforts to achieve change in core American institutions like colleges and universities.

It has been said the past is not past, but instead is very much present. This is a powerful reminder, as the task of remaking American higher education moves forward. Society, core institutions, and individuals all reflect a milieu that would deny racial, ethnic, gender, and socioeconomic oppression, both historically and contemporarily. It is the responsibility and challenge of higher education to lead the way in changing worldviews, attitudes, and practices that perpetuate exclusion, disempowerment, and denigration based on skin color, sex, language, sexual orientations, and socioeconomic status—otherwise known as "difference." This change must begin with the preparation of students who will depart colleges and universities to enter a diverse democracy. In many respects, the demographic change we noted above is superficial—enrollments of students of color continue to increase, but the structures, curricula, and culture of most institutions remain largely (and in some instances, exclusively) White. Colleges and universities must be intentionally re-designed so that students' worldviews, learning, behaviors, and outcomes are reflective of the racial and ethnic diversity they will encounter in post-college settings.

References

Carnevale, A. P., & Fry, R. A. (2000). *Crossing the great divide: Can we achieve equity when generation Y goes to college?* Princeton, NJ: Educational Testing Service.

Ryu, M. (2008). *Minorities in higher education, 2008: Twenty-third status report.* Washington, DC: American Council on Education.

CHAPTER 9
MINORITY-STATUS STRESSES AND THE COLLEGE ADJUSTMENT OF ETHNIC MINORITY FRESHMEN

BRIAN D. SMEDLEY, HECTOR F. MYERS, AND SHELLY P. HARRELL

In the ten-year period between 1969 and 1979, minority students enrolled in predominantly White colleges in increasing numbers, due in part to the greater access afforded by affirmative action programs [14]. Since the early 1980s, however, there has been a disturbing regressive trend in the enrollment, academic performance, and retention of these students. For example, African-American and other non-Asian minority students attending predominantly White colleges are less likely to graduate within five years, have lower grade point averages, experience higher attrition rates, and matriculate into graduate programs at lower rates than White students and their counterparts at predominantly Black or minority institutions [3, 6].*

Efforts to account for these regressive trends suggest that intellective and academic background factors (that is, aptitude test scores, high-school preparation, and so on) and non-cognitive, contextual, and socio-cultural factors may be differentially associated with the college adjustment and performance of minority and non-minority students [6, 23, 26, 29, 35, 36]. For example, African-American students are more likely than Whites to view predominantly White campuses as hostile, alienating, and socially isolating [1, 2, 4, 10, 16, 28, 30, 34, 35, 36], and as less responsive to their needs and interests [4]. African-American students have also been found to experience greater estrangement from the campus community [16, 34] and heightened discomfort in interactions with faculty and peers [20, 30]. In addition, Tracey and Sedlacek [35] and Nettles, Theony, and Gosman [27] have found that the academic adjustment and achievement of African-American and other minority students are influenced by different sociocultural and contextual factors (for example, student satisfaction with college, peer group relations) than those that have an impact on White students.

In order to define conceptually how these factors might contribute to minority student college adjustment, we have proposed a multidimensional stress-coping model [33] which identifies three sets of factors as important in minority college student adjustment and achievement: (1) individual attributes that enhance or moderate students' vulnerability to academic failure (for example, academic preparation, intelligence, self-confidence, social maturity); (2) the psychological and sociocultural stresses students face during their academic careers (for example, stresses that are experienced on campus, in the community, and so on); and (3) the strategies students use to cope with these stresses (for example, individual and group appraisals of stresses and the strategies used to cope with them). Consistent with a transactional model of stress and coping [22], we view the types of stresses experienced, the coping styles used, and the outcomes obtained as mutually interacting. Consequently, the pattern of relationships among these variables is likely to vary as a function of individual, group, and college campus characteristics.

---

*For purposes of simplicity, the term "Black" will be used interchangeably with "African-American" to refer to U.S. born students of African descent.

We also note that many of the experiences reported by minority students at predominantly White colleges are experienced by and affect all college students and are integral to the role of college student (for example, academic demands, relationship problems, financial worries, and so on). These student role strains constitute a generic pathway of influences and contribute to college maladjustment for all students. However, these generic role strains should be distinguished from the more unique stresses experienced by minority students that heighten feelings of not belonging and interfere with minority students' effective integration into the university community (for example, experiences with racism, questions about their right to be on campus). These experiences are conceptualized as *minority status stresses* and constitute a separate and additional pathway of risk for maladjustment (that is, an additional stress load).

These status stresses are believed to exert their pathogenic effects in at least two ways. First, they can exert a direct, independent effect, as in the case of those stressful experiences that are attributable to minority group membership (for example, experiences of overt racial prejudice or discrimination) [12, 24, 25]. Because these experiences are due to the specific physical or cultural attributes that define membership in an ethnic minority group, such experiences have limited direct relevance to White students, and affect them only indirectly (for example, being treated with suspicion and mistrust by minority students). Second, minority status stresses can exert an indirect effect by compounding the episodic and chronic stresses faced by all students, due to the marginal social, political, and economic status of many minority students [3, 21]. Such stressors as financial problems, pressures at home, conflicts with faculty and peers, and academic weaknesses may all be experienced as more stressful and may have more negative consequences for the minority student [1, 8].

The purpose of this study, therefore, was to ascertain whether the hypothesized minority status stresses confer an additional risk for poor college adjustment for minority students beyond that attributable to the chronic student role strains and episodic life event stresses experienced by these students.

Method

Sample

The data reported here were obtained in a larger doctoral dissertation study [32] that examined the role of stress and coping on the adjustment of freshmen students to college. The study was conducted in a large university whose student body was predominantly White (56 percent), and included 17.5 percent Asians, 11.8 percent Hispanics, 7.1 percent African-American, 4.1 percent Pilipinos, 0.7 percent American Indians, and 2.3 percent Others. Of the minority students, a large percentage (58 percent) were women. All 1,096 minority freshmen (African-American, Chicano, Latino, American Indian, and Pilipino students) and a random sample of 300 White freshmen entering the university in 1986 were recruited to participate. A questionnaire measuring a variety of academic, psychosocial and background variables was mailed to these students at three times during the freshman year (the summer prior to starting classes [t_1], in mid Fall quarter [t_2], and in late spring [t_3]). Potential respondents could participate at any data collection point, even if they had not returned questionnaires at t_1 or t_2.

Relevant variables for this study were measured at the last assessment point. Therefore, only data collected from the 161 minority students who responded at t_3 are reported here. These include data from 45 African-American, 54 Chicano, 25 Latino, and 37 Pilipino students. Of this sample, 91 students returned questionnaires at the two previous data collection points. Attrition analyses revealed that students who responded at all three data collection points had significantly higher high-school grade-point averages and Scholastic Aptitude Test scores than students who responded to questionnaires at t_1 or t_2 only. In addition, over 70 percent of the participants at t_3 were women (47 males and 114 females). Despite the relatively poor representation of minority group males, the sample reflects the larger proportion of women (58:42) in the population of minority freshmen attending the university.

As seen in tables 1a and 1b, the ethnic groups differed significantly on socioeconomic (SES) status, especially in terms of parental education and maternal occupation, as well as on level of educational preparation. Newman-Keuls post-hoc tests of SES, as defined by Hollingshead's (1974) criteria, indicated that Pilipinos came from higher SES backgrounds ($p < 0.05$), and had higher average high-school GPAs ($p < 0.05$) and SAT scores ($p < 0.05$) than African-Americans and Chicanos. Chicanos also had higher high-school GPAs than African-Americans ($p < 0.05$). Overall, SAT scores of the four ethnic groups are considerably higher than the national average, reflecting the academic selectivity of the university and the relatively strong academic preparation of the students in this sample.

Measures

Sources of stress. Separate scales were used to measure the two "generic" stresses and the minority status stresses which are conceptualized as important predictors of minority college student adjustment. Episodic Life Events Stresses (LES) were measured with the Life Events Survey for College

TABLE 1A

Demographic Background Variables by Ethnic Group

	Black (n = 45)	Chicano (n = 54)	Latino (n = 25)	Pilipino (n = 37)	X^2 (df)
Gender					
Male	15	15	7	10	
Female	30	39	18	27	0.53 (3)
SES					
Low	24	34	11	12	
High	21	20	14	25	8.75* (3)
Maternal Education					
Partial HS	3	20	3	3	
HS diploma	8	9	6	4	
Partial college or BA	29	19	12	23	
Prof. or grad. degree	4	5	4	7	24.98** (9)
Paternal Education					
Partial HS	8	18	1	3	
HS diploma	8	9	5	0	
Partial college or BA	24	18	13	22	
Prof. or grad. degree	4	6	6	10	27.94*** (9)
Maternal Occupation					
Unemployed	13	20	12	2	
Unskilled	4	6	0	3	
Semiskilled	6	3	1	2	
Skilled	11	13	6	11	
Sales, technical, professional	11	12	6	19	24.83* (12)
Paternal Occupation					
Unemployed	12	7	4	4	
Unskilled	3	10	2	4	
Semiskilled	3	8	3	3	
Skilled	14	12	8	10	
Sales, technical, professional	13	17	8	16	11.49 (12)
Ethnic Composition of Neighborhood of Origin					
Same race	15	15	12	12	
Predominantly White	14	26	8	16	
Integrated	16	13	5	9	6.36 (6)

*$p < 0.05$ **$p < 0.01$ ***$p < 0.001$

Students, which is a modified version of the 120-item Life Events Survey [19]. The LES includes items from several life-event lists and omits items that might be confounded with depressive symptomatology. Students were asked to circle events experienced during the past year and then to indicate whether the event occurred before coming to college in the fall, since they came to college, or during both times. Event impact ratings were made on a 7-point scale ranging from extremely negative impact (-3) to extremely positive impact ($+3$), and an overall life change stress score was obtained by computing a weighted algebraic sum. The LES has been shown to be a very reliable and valid measure of episodic life stresses among college student samples [19].

TABLE 1B

Academic Background Variables by Ethnic Group

	Black (n = 45)	Chicano (n = 54)	Latino (n = 25)	Pilipino (n = 37)	F (df)
HS GPA	3.363 (0.33)	3.598 (0.33)	3.477 (0.34)	3.802 (0.42)	10.78** (3,153)
SAT Total	941.1 (140.0)	968.2 (149.3)	997.6 (167.1)	1047.6 (160.4)	3.40* (3,153)

Note: Newman-Keuls post-hoc tests ($p < 0.05$) revealed that Pilipinos had significantly higher high-school grades and SAT scores than Black and Chicano students, and that Chicanos obtained significantly higher high-school grades than Blacks.

*$p < 0.05$ **$p < 0.01$

Chronic Student Role Strain (CRS) was measured with the Current Concerns Scale [32]. CRS reflects the ongoing stressors that are part of a student's role (for example, academic demands) and the normal life demands of late adolescence/early adulthood (for example, romance, family, friendships, financial problems, illness). The Current Concerns Scale was developed specifically for this study, and measures role strains in seven functional domains: school-academics, romance, family, adjusting to college, neighborhood/living situation, extracurricular activities, and personal life. Students rated each domain on a 4-point scale from (1) not at all, to (4) very much, to reflect the importance and the degree to which they had had problems in each domain during the past three months. They also identified the most problematic domain, described the specific problem experienced, and assigned a stressfulness rating on a 5-point scale from (1) not at all stressful to (5) extremely stressful. A chronic role strain score was calculated as the weighted sum of ratings (that is, sum of stress ratings multiplied by their importance rating), and was found to be moderately reliable (alpha = 0.61).

Minority Status Stresses (MSS) were measured with the 37-item Minority Student Stress Scale, which was developed for this project. Items for the MSS scale were obtained from student stress scales [13, 38] and from issues and experiences suggested by a pilot sample of 100 minority students who participated in a university summer school program. The MSS items reflect both unique, minority-specific stressors (for example, "Too many people of my race are employed in low-status jobs at the university"), as well as "generic" student role stresses that are compounded by a student's racial/ethnic or social class background (for example, "being the first from my family to attend college"). Students were asked to rate each item on a six-point scale, from (0) does not apply, to (5) extremely stressful.

A principal components analysis with varimax rotation identified five stable and reliable factors (Chronbach's alpha values ranged from 0.76 to 0.93) that accounted for 58 percent of the common variance. Only items with factor loadings above 0.30 were retained. The factor solution, which is presented in table 2, included: an 11-item first factor that assessed Social Climate Stresses, a 7-item second factor that tapped Interracial Stresses, a 5-item third factor that reflected students' concerns about actual or perceived experiences with Racism and Discrimination, a 4-item fourth factor that tapped students' concerns about Within-group Stresses, and a fifth factor, termed Achievement Stresses, that reflected student's concerns about their academic preparation and ability and high family expectations for their success. The items on each factor were summed to generate five minority status stress scores.

TABLE 2

Minority Status Stress Scales and Items (Factor solution accounts for 53 percent of the variance)

Scales and Items	Factor Loading
Factor 1: Social Climate Stresses (33% of variance; alpha = 0.93)	
The university does not have enough professors of my race	0.76
Few students of my race are in my classes	0.75
Racist policies and practices of the university	0.74
The university lacks concern and support for the needs of students of my race	0.66
Seeing members of my race doing low status jobs and Whites in high status jobs on campus	0.65
Few courses involve issues relevant to my ethnic group	0.61
Negative attitudes/treatment of students of my race by faculty	0.52
White students and faculty expect poor academic performance from students of my race	0.49
Pressure that what "I" do is representative of my ethnic group's abilities, behavior, and so on.	0.49
Tense relationships between Whites and minorities at the university	0.47
The university is an unfriendly place	0.37
Factor 2: Interracial Stresses (6% of variance; alpha = 0.85)	
Difficulties with having White friends	0.70
Negative relationships between different ethnic groups at the university	0.69
The White-oriented campus culture of the university	0.64
Having to live around mostly White people	0.52
The lack of unity/supportiveness among members of my race at the university	0.51
Trying to maintain my ethnic identity while attending the university	0.44
Having to always be aware of what White people might do	0.44
Factor 3: Racism and Discrimination Stresses (5% of variance; alpha = 0.87)	
Being treated rudely or unfairly because of my race	0.91
Being discriminated against	0.74
White people expecting me to be a certain way because of my race (i.e., stereotyping)	0.60
Others lacking respect for people of my race	0.48
Having to "prove" my abilities to others (i.e., work twice as hard)	0.41
Factor 4: Within-Group Stresses (4% of variance; alpha = 0.78)	
People close to me thinking I'm acting "White"	0.68
Pressures to show loyalty to my race (e.g., giving back to my ethnic group community)	0.58
Pressures from people of my same race (e.g., how to act, what to believe)	0.58
Relationships between males and females of my race (e.g., lack of available dating partners)	0.52
Factor 5: Achievement Stresses (3% of variance; alpha = 0.76)	
Doubts about my ability to succeed in college	0.74
Feeling less intelligent or less capable than others	0.72
My family has very high expectations for my college success	0.62
My academic background for college being inadequate	0.55
My family does not understand the pressures of college (e.g., amount of time or quiet needed to study)	0.41
Being the first in my family to attend a major university	0.32

Outcome measures. Three indicators of college adjustment were measured which reflect both personal/social adjustment and academic achievement: level of psychological distress, feelings of well-being, and academic achievement.

Psychological Distress (PD) was measured with the Hopkins Symptom Checklist (HSCL-58). The HSCL is a 58-item self-report measure that asks respondents to rate on a 4-point scale from (1) = not at all to (4) = very often the frequency with which a list of physical and psychological symptoms are experienced [11]. The scale yields five reliable and valid symptom clusters: anxiety, somatization, interpersonal sensitivity, obsessive-compulsiveness, and depression [11]. For purposes of the present study, only the sum HSCL score was used as a global measure of psychological distress.

Feelings of Well-Being were measured with eight items from the General Well-Being Questionnaire (GWB) [37] that measure positive adjustment [5, 9]. The GWB provides a reliable self-report of perceived psychological well-being and distress and includes items that measure health, worry/concern, energy level, mood, emotional stability, control, tension/nervousness, and positive expressions of well-being. The first six items measure the intensity or relative frequency of positive feelings and perceptions, and the last two items measure the degree of relaxation and energy felt for the past three months. Items are scored such that high scores indicate positive well-being. These two subscales of well-being have been used with multi-ethnic samples and have been found to be inversely related to stress and depression [5], and to be enhanced by the availability of social supports [5, 9].

Finally, Academic Achievement was measured using the students' official cumulative grade point average (GPA) at the end of the freshman year.

Results

Between-Group Differences

Because of the small sample size, the four SES groups were first reduced to two by combining Hollingshead levels I, II, and III into a low SES group, and levels IV and V into a high SES group. A series of two-way race X SES analyses of variance (ANOVAs) were then conducted on each of the independent and dependent variables. As shown in table 3, the four ethnic groups differed significantly on overall minority status stresses ($p < 0.001$), and specifically on social climate stresses ($p < 0.001$), within-group stresses ($p < 0.001$), interracial stresses ($p < 0.001$), and on racism and discrimination stresses ($p < 0.001$). Post-hoc Neuman-Keuls tests revealed that African-Americans reported significantly higher mean stress levels ($p < 0.05$) than the other ethnic groups on each of these sources of stress.

Significant SES differences on social climate stresses ($p < 0.001$) and on chronic student role strains ($p < 0.01$) were also obtained. In both cases, lower SES students reported higher mean stress levels. No significant race X SES interactions were obtained.

Finally, a series of two-way race X gender ANOVAs were conducted on each of the independent and dependent variables. These analyses, not shown here, revealed no significant race X gender interactions, and only one significant gender difference among the variables. Females reported significantly higher levels of achievement stresses (M = 2.41) than males (M = 1.80), F (1, 113) = 11.53, $p < 0.01$.

Relative Contribution of Minority Status Stresses

A series of setwise, hierarchal regression analyses were conducted to test whether minority status stresses would contribute to the explanation of variance for each of the three indexes of college adjustment, after accounting for the effects of race, gender, SES, prior levels of academic preparation, and "generic" student stresses. In each case, gender and SES were entered first as a set, followed by race. Dummy coding (that is, 1, 0) was used to generate three separate dummy variables for the racial groups, and gender was coded as 0 = male and 1 = female. High-school grade-point average and total Scholastic Aptitude Test (SAT) scores were then entered as a set, followed by chronic student role strain (CRS) and life event stress (LES), in separate steps. Finally, the set of five minority

TABLE 3

Race by SES Differences on Academic Background, Life Stresses, and Academic Achievement (N = 161)

SES	Black low 28	Black high 17	Chicano low 36	Chicano high 18	Latino low 13	Latino high 12	Pilipino low 12	Pilipino high 25	FRace	FSES	FR x SES
Academic Background											
High-school GPA	3.37 (0.35)	3.36 (0.32)	3.57 (0.32)	3.64 (0.35)	3.49 (0.37)	3.46 (0.32)	3.70 (0.27)	3.85 (0.47)	10.17**	0.61	0.75
SAT total score	913.5 (130.5)	971.4 (146.8)	944.4 (136.2)	1008.8 (165.0)	1002.7 (123.7)	993.6 (199.4)	956.4 (168.4)	1091.3 (139.8)	2.53	6.93**	1.06
Chronic role strain	83.3 (21.4)	68.1 (21.8)	71.8 (15.7)	63.6 (17.0)	77.4 (16.7)	73.6 (23.8)	75.2 (17.2)	72.6 (17.4)	1.99	7.45**	0.86
Life change stress	18.9 (13.3)	20.4 (9.1)	23.2 (12.7)	21.3 (10.9)	27.4 (13.1)	26.6 (12.5)	28.6 (15.7)	21.5 (12.5)	2.14	0.85	0.76
Minority-Status Stresses											
Social climate stresses	2.47 (1.03)	1.76 (1.14)	1.57 (1.10)	1.04 (0.67)	0.87 (0.24)	1.22 (0.83)	1.36 (0.66)	1.05 (0.51)	9.52**	6.12*	0.17
Interracial stresses	1.51 (0.58)	1.55 (1.06)	1.20 (0.80)	0.83 (0.35)	0.71 (0.36)	0.99 (0.43)	1.12 (0.23)	1.11 (0.31)	6.20*	0.31	1.36
Racism	2.24 (1.05)	2.19 (1.39)	1.54 (1.15)	0.92 (0.64)	1.02 (1.06)	1.23 (0.59)	0.90 (0.90)	1.40 (1.13)	8.30*	0.12	1.73
Within-group stresses	2.17 (1.09)	2.10 (1.31)	1.12 (0.84)	0.91 (0.67)	0.89 (0.60)	1.02 (0.68)	0.98 (0.69)	1.09 (0.62)	15.33*	0.09	0.28
Achievement stresses	2.33 (1.04)	1.78 (1.11)	2.42 (1.01)	1.99 (0.91)	1.91 (0.78)	2.47 (1.10)	2.29 (0.91)	2.40 (0.95)	0.63	1.33	1.83
General well-being	31.8 (8.5)	32.1 (10.0)	33.2 (7.2)	37.3 (8.5)	34.1 (8.2)	32.3 (8.9)	33.2 (6.6)	35.0 (8.7)	1.13	1.33	0.80
Psychological distress	130.5 (33.8)	124.3 (25.9)	120.7 (24.8)	109.6 (26.5)	125.7 (31.3)	117.7 (18.0)	123.7 (13.8)	125.2 (24.3)	1.99	2.37	0.40
Freshman year grade-point average	2.41 (0.60)	2.50 (0.61)	2.50 (0.52)	2.61 (0.58)	2.65 (0.42)	2.50 (0.69)	2.52 (0.55)	2.77 (0.47)	0.96	0.92	0.60

$p < 0.05$ ** $p < 0.001$

TABLE 4

Hierarchical Regression Analysis of General Well-Being from Student Background Variables, Chronic Role Strain, Life Events, and Minority Status Stresses ($N = 161$)

Step	Variable(s)	R^2 Change	F Change	Beta
1.	Gender	0.00	0.37	−0.03
	Socioeconomic status			−0.05
2.	Race	0.02	1.16	
	African-American			−0.13
	Chicano			0.00
	Latino			−0.06
3.	SAT total score	0.01	0.72	−0.04
	High-school GPA			0.03
4.	Chronic role strain	0.14	26.43***	−0.31***
5.	Life events	0.00	0.95	−0.04
6.	Minority status stresses	0.05	2.07	
	Interracial stresses			0.06
	Racism stresses			−0.18
	Achievement stresses			−0.06
	Within-group stresses			0.19
	Social climate stresses			−0.18

R^2 equation = 0.22, (adjusted R^2 = 0.16), F (equation) = 3.25, $p < 0.001$
*$p < 0.05$
**$p < 0.01$
***$p < 0.001$

status stress (MSS) scores were entered into the equation. In each equation missing data were replaced by the overall mean for each variable. To reduce capitalization on chance variation in the data, adjusted R^2 values are reported for each equation.

General well-being. A significant setwise regression equation on well-being was obtained which accounted for 16 percent of the variance in the dependent variable ($F = 3.25$, $p < 0.001$). As shown in table 4, after the effects of gender and SES (0.0 percent of variance), race (2.0 percent of variance) and high-school grades and SAT scores (1.0 percent of variance) were accounted for, chronic role strain was the only variable significantly associated with well-being. Chronic role strain accounted for an additional 14 percent of the variance and was inversely related to well-being scores (beta = −0.31, F change = 27.35, $p < 0.001$). Neither life event stress nor minority status stresses were significantly associated with well-being, although minority status stress did account for an additional 5 percent of the variance.

Psychological distress. Results of the setwise regression indicated that all three sources of stress were significantly associated with symptoms of psychological distress, and all independent variables accounted for 28 percent of the cumulative variance in symptoms ($F = 5.43$, $p < 0.001$). As shown in table 5, after the effects of gender, SES, race, high-school GPA, and SAT scores were accounted for (5 percent), chronic role strain accounted for an additional 14 percent of the variance in distress (beta = 0.21, F change = 26.28, $p < 0.001$), while life event stress accounted for an additional 3 percent of the variance (beta = 0.13, F change = 5.89, $p < 0.05$). Consistent with the stress-load hypothesis, minority status stresses accounted for a significant additional 12 percent of the variance in psychological distress (F change = 5.43, $p < 0.001$), with achievement stresses (beta = 0.32, $p < 0.001$) emerging as the most important source of status-related stress.

Academic achievement. Results of the setwise regression on student grade-point average indicated that none of the "generic" sources of stress were significant correlates of GPA. However, minority status stress accounted for an additional and significant 9 percent of the variance in cumulative grades (F change = 4.49, $p < 0.01$), after controlling for demographic attributes, prior academic preparation,

TABLE 5

Hierarchical Regression Analysis of Psychological Distress from Student Background Variables, Chronic Role Strain, Life Events, and Minority Status Stresses (N = 161)

Step	Variable(s)	R^2 Change	F Change	Beta
1.	Gender	0.01	0.92	0.01
	Socioeconomic status			0.05
2.	Race	0.03	1.56	
	African-American			0.09
	Chicano			−0.10
	Latino			−0.04
3.	SAT total score	0.01	0.72	0.04
	High-school GPA			0.01
4.	Chronic role strain	0.14	26.28***	0.21**
5.	Life events	0.03	5.89*	0.13
6.	Minority status stresses	0.12	5.43***	
	Interracial stresses			−0.12
	Racism stresses			0.04
	Achievement stresses			0.32***
	Within-group stresses			−0.01
	Social climate stresses			0.19

R^2 equation = 0.34, (adjusted R^2 = 0.28), F (equation) = 5.42, $p < 0.001$
*$p < 0.05$
**$p < 0.01$
***$p < 0.001$

and "generic" stress. Again, this finding is consistent with the stress load hypothesis. As shown in table 6, gender, SES, and race differences were found to account for a non-significant 6 percent of the variance in grades. As expected, high-school GPA and SAT scores accounted for the greatest amount of variance in college grades (23 percent of variance, F change = 24.69, $p < 0.001$), and were positively related to GPA. Status-related achievement stresses were the only minority status stressor that was significantly and inversely associated with academic achievement (beta = −0.31, $p < 0.001$).

Discussion

This study investigated the relationship of student role strains, life events stresses, and minority status stresses with the psychological and academic adjustment of minority freshmen at a major university. Specifically, we hypothesized that minority status stresses would confer an additional burden of stress and would be associated with an increased risk for negative outcomes beyond that which is attributable to the stresses of being a student at a highly competitive academic institution. Our results generally confirm this hypothesis. They indicate that chronic student role strains and life events stresses are important correlates of psychological distress in minority freshmen, and that minority status stresses make a substantial additional contribution to this correlation. Our findings also confirm previous evidence that psychological stresses, regardless of their source, are not as important as academic aptitude (that is, prior academic preparation and performance) in accounting for current academic performance. However, the significant association of minority status-related achievement stresses with lower GPA suggests that conflicts between academic expectations and questions about readiness to compete academically are an important additional source of academic vulnerability for these students. Finally, only chronic student role strain was an important and negative correlate of feelings of psychological well-being.

These results provide additional empirical support for the hypothesis that sociocultural and contextual stresses play a significant role in the adaptation of minority freshmen to a predominantly

TABLE 6

Hierarchical Regression Analysis of Grade-Point Average from Student Background Variables, Chronic Role Stresses, Life Events, and Minority Status Stresses ($N = 161$)

Step	Variable(s)	R^2 Change	F Change	Beta
1.	Gender	0.04	3.48*	0.03
	Socioeconomic status			0.12
2.	Race	0.02	1.13	
	African-American			−0.10
	Chicano			0.05
	Latino			0.09
3.	SAT total score	0.23	24.69***	0.30***
	High-school GPA			0.34***
4.	Chronic role strain	0.00	0.00	0.00
5.	Life events	0.00	0.02	−0.02
6.	Minority status stresses	0.09	4.49**	
	Interracial stresses			0.06
	Racism stresses			0.13
	Achievement stresses			−0.31***
	Within-group stresses			0.06
	Social climate stresses			0.15

R^2 equation = 0.38, (adjusted R^2 = 0.33), F (equation) = 6.55, $p < 0.001$
*$p < 0.05$
**$p < 0.01$
***$p < 0.001$

White college. Status-related pressures are associated with increased feelings of distress and pose additional demands on students' coping resources. These stresses emerge from various sources, including contact and conflict from within and between racial and ethnic groups. As described in previous studies, the minority freshmen studied here evidenced considerable psychological sensitivity and vulnerability to the campus social climate; to interpersonal tensions between themselves and White students and faculty; and to experiences of actual or perceived racism, racist attitudes and expectations, and discrimination. Such external pressures are often compounded by pressures for loyalty and solidarity from within the respective ethnic groups, which become more salient as campus race relations are experienced to be more conflictual [2, 13, 17, 35].

Our results also indicate, however, that minority students' status-related pressures are also experienced as heightened concerns over their academic preparedness, questions about their legitimacy as students at the university, perceptions of negative expectations from White peers and from the faculty, and concerns over parental/family expectations and lack of understanding of the peculiar demands of attending a highly competitive university. These more personal sources of stress may be due in part to minority students' status as entering freshmen, but also reflect a sensitivity to their stigmatized "special status" as beneficiaries of affirmative action decisions, despite their individual accomplishments. The latter is especially significant, given that the students sampled here are a very select group of minority students whose academic credentials (that is, combined SAT scores of 950–1050) are above the national average for such students.

These results are not surprising and underscore the complexity of the problem of minority student adjustment to White college campuses. The highly competitive atmosphere of the university in which this study was conducted and the consequent pressures on students for academic achievement is a normal role-related source of stress for all students. However, for some minority students this source of college student stress may be compounded by actual or perceived weaknesses in academic preparation due to limited educational opportunities relative to their White peers, doubts about their abilities, or concerns that faculty and peers may question their legitimacy as college students. All of these factors threaten the effective early adjustment to college of minority freshmen students.

Contrary to the hypothesis, minority status stresses were not significantly associated with feelings of well-being. Chronic role strain, however, was associated with lower feelings of well-being. It is possible that minority status stresses have a domain-specific effect on functioning (that is, they exert a more powerful influence on negative than positive outcomes). Alternatively, the effects of minority status stresses on well-being may be mediated by factors that help to maintain minority students' self-esteem and sense of positive health. For example, minority students' social, political, and/or cultural orientations (for example, sense of ethnic identity and collective consciousness) may serve to buffer the effects of status-related pressures on well-being [17, 18].

It is not surprising that academic performance during the freshman year was most strongly associated with prior academic preparation and achievement. Negative life events and chronic role strain were not correlated with poor academic outcomes. Minority status stresses, however, were inversely associated with academic achievement. It is important to recognize that minority status-related sources of stress may also be operative in the educational system and have an impact on student adjustment long before college. Minority students from elementary through high school may experience similar disincentives, including teacher and peer expectations for their failure, intergroup conflicts, racist policies and practices of school districts, and culturally insensitive curricula. If this is the case, then academic performance may be affected by these minority status stresses very early in a student's schooling. Therefore, what we may be observing in high-school grades and SAT scores is the cumulative impact of these status stresses over time. Our understanding of this problem would be enhanced by future studies that investigate this cumulative status-related effect on the academic achievement of minority students longitudinally from grade school through college.

Our results also indicate, somewhat surprisingly, that the more visible and attention-grabbing stresses (for example, interracial conflicts and experiences of overt racism and discrimination) were less important correlates of distress. This should not be interpreted as suggesting that such experiences have limited impact or are of relatively less concern for these students. Rather, these results may reflect the relatively low frequency of occurrence of those overt conflicts and experiences in comparison to more covert and subtle pressures. We would expect that when overt conflicts and expressions of racism occur, they magnify the effects of the more subtle but chronic minority status stresses (for example, feelings of alienation from the university).

In summary, it appears that the more debilitating minority status stressors were those that undermined students' academic confidence and ability to bond to the university. These stresses come from both internal sources as well as from the demographic composition and social climate of the campus. Initial group differences suggest that these minority status stresses may be greater for African-American freshmen than for other minority freshmen. Due to the small number of subjects sampled from each racial group, however, it is difficult to determine whether African-Americans are at greater risk for the pathogenic effects of status-related stresses than other minority students. Future studies should investigate conditional effects of minority status stresses (that is, race-by-stress interactions) to determine if these stresses tend to exert their effects differentially by racial group membership.

These findings suggest that intervention programs designed to improve minority student retention are likely to be more effective if they focus attention on helping minority freshmen to understand the interplay of the additional social and academic stresses they will face from their peers and from faculty in addition to providing academic support services. Such interventions should emphasize enhancing the effectiveness of the students' efforts to cope with these status-related demands and should target those students who are finding it particularly difficult to handle both generic student role strains and minority status stresses.

The present research also suggests, however, that it is equally important to intervene at the level of the university environment. Many of the items that minority students identified as stressful point to failures of the university structure to meet the needs of minority students. This requires that such campuses be made less alien and more culturally and emotionally accessible to a diverse student population [4, 10, 16]. Effective and culturally sensitive interventions should be developed that target not only the individual student, but also the policies, atmosphere, demographics, and structure of the university.

Finally, although the results obtained confirm our hypotheses, the relatively small sample, the overrepresentation of women, the focus on freshmen, and the single university setting require replication with other larger and more representative samples and more diverse academic settings. It would be useful to begin identifying those contextual variables that promote positive outcomes among minority students as a step toward creating university-centered solutions to the problem of minority student retention. In addition, future research is needed to identify those coping resources and styles that moderate the negative effects of the minority status stress load in order to insure more positive psychological, social, and academic outcomes in minority students who attend predominantly White colleges and universities.

References

1. Allen, W. R. "Correlates of Black Student Adjustment, Achievement, and Aspirations at a Predominantly White Southern University." In *Black Students in Higher Education,* edited by G. E. Thomas. Westport, Conn.: Greenwood Press, 1981.

2. ———. "Black Student, White Campus: Structural, Interpersonal, and Psychological Correlates of Success." *Journal of Negro Education,* 54 (1985), 137–47.

3. ———. "The Education of Black Students on White College Campuses: What Quality the Experience?" In *Toward Black Undergraduate Student Equality in American Higher Education,* edited by M. T. Nettles, pp. 57–86. Westport, Conn.: Greenwood Press, 1988.

4. ———. "Improving Black Student Access and Achievement in Higher Education." *Review of Higher Education,* 11 (1988), 403–16.

5. Aneshensel, C. S., and R. R. Frerichs. "Stress, Social Support and Depression: A Longitudinal Causal Model." *Journal of Community Psychology,* 10 (1982), 363–76.

6. Astin, A. W. *Minorities in Higher Education: Recent Trends, Current Prospects, and Recommendations.* San Francisco: Josey-Bass, 1982.

7. Burbach, H. J., and M. A. Thompson. "Alienation among College Freshmen: A Comparison of Puerto Rican, Black, and White Students." *Journal of College Student Personnel,* 12 (1971), 248–52.

8. Burrell, L. F., and T. B. Trombley. "Academic Advising with Minority Students on Predominantly White Campuses. *Journal of College Student Personnel,* 24 (1983), 121–26.

9. Cohen, P., et al. "Community Stressors, Mediating Conditions and Well-Being in Urban Neighborhoods." *Journal of Community Psychology,* 10 (1982), 377–91.

10. Crossen, P. H. "Four-Year College and University Environments for Minority Degree Achievement." *Review of Higher Education,* 11 (1988), 365–82.

11. Derogatis, L. R., et al. "The Hopkins Symptom Checklist (HSCL): A Self-Report Symptom Inventory." *Behavioral Science,* 19 (1974), 1–15.

12. Dohrenwend, B. S., and B. P. Dohrenwend. "Class and Race as Status-Related Sources of Stress." In *Social Stress,* edited by S. Levine and N. A. Scotch. Chicago: Aldine Press, 1970.

13. Edmunds, G. J. "Needs Assessment Strategy for Black Students: An Examination of Stressors and Program Implications." *Journal of Non-White Concerns in Personnel and Guidance,* 12 (1984), 48–56.

14. Evans, G. "Black Students Who Attend White Colleges Face Contradictions in Their Campus Life." *Chronicle of Higher Education* (30 April 1986), 29–30.

15. Fleming, J. "Blacks in Higher Education to 1954: A Historical Overview. In *Black Students in Higher Education,* edited by G. E. Thomas. Westport, Conn.: Greenwood Press, 1981.

16. ———. *Blacks in College: A Comparative Study of Student's Successes in Black and White Institutions.* San Francisco: Jossey-Bass, 1984.

17. Gibbs, J. L. "Patterns of Adaptation among Black Students at a Predominantly White University: Selected Case Studies." *American Journal of Orthopsychiatry,* 44 (1974), 729–40.

18. Gurin, P., and S. Epps. *Black Consciousness: Identity and Achievement.* New York: Wiley and Sons, 1975.

19. Hammen, C., T. Marks, A. Mayol, and R. deMayo. "Depressive Self-Schemas, Life Stress, and Vulnerability to Depression." *Journal of Abnormal Psychology,* 94 (1985), 308–19.

20. Keller, J., C. Piotrowski, and D. Sherry. "Perceptions of the College Environment and Campus Life: The Black Experience." *Journal of Non-White Concerns in Personnel and Guidance,* 10 (1982), 126–32.

21. Kessler, R. C. "Stress, Social Status, and Psychological Distress." *Journal of Health and Social Behavior,* 20 (1979), 259–72.
22. Lazarus, R. S., and S. Folkman. *Stress, Appraisal and Coping.* New York: Springer Press, 1984.
23. Lunneborg, C. E., and P. W. Lunneborg. "Beyond Prediction: The Challenge of Minority Achievement in Higher Education." *Journal of Multicultural Counseling and Development,* 14 (1986), 77–84.
24. Moritsugu, J., and S. Sue. "Minority Status as a Stressor." In *Preventive Psychology: Theory, Research, and Practice,* edited by R. D. Felner, L. A. Jason, J. Moritsugu, and S. S. Farber. New York: Praeger Press, 1983.
25. Myers, H. F. "Stress, Ethnicity, and Social Class: A Model for Research with Black Populations." In *Minority Mental Health,* edited by E. Jones and S. Korchin. New York: Holt, Rinehart and Winston, 1982.
26. Nelson, R. B., T. B. Scott, and W. A. Bryan. "Precollege Characteristics and Early College Experiences as Predictors of Freshman Year Persistence." *Journal of College Student Personnel,* 25 (1984), 50–54.
27. Nettles, M. T., A. R. Theony, and E. J. Gosman. "Comparative and Predictive Analyses of Black and White Students' College Achievement and Experiences." *Journal of Higher Education,* 57 (May/June 1986), 289–318.
28. Oliver, M. L., C. J. Rodriguez, and R. A. Mickelson. "Brown and Black in White: The Social Adjustment and Academic Performance of Chicano and Black Students in a Predominantly White University." *The Urban Review,* 17 (1985), 3–24.
29. Pascarella, E. T. "Racial Differences in Factors Associated with Bachelor's Degree Completion: A Nine-Year Follow-up." *Research In Higher Education,* 24 (1986), 351–73.
30. Patterson, A. M., W. E. Sedlacek, and F. W. Perry. "Perceptions of Blacks and Hispanics of Two Campus Environments." *Journal of College Student Personnel,* 25 (1984), 513–18.
31. Pierce, C. M. "Psychiatric Problems of the Black Minority." In *American Handbook of Psychiatry,* edited by S. Arieti and G. Caplan. Vol 2, 2nd ed. Basic Books, 1974, 512–23.
32. Prillerman, S. L. *Coping with a Stressful Transition: A Prospective Study of Black Student Adjustment to a Predominantly White University.* Ph.D. dissertation, University of California at Los Angeles, 1988.
33. Prillerman, S. L., H. F. Myers, and B. D. Smedley. "Stress, Well-Being, and Academic Achievement in College." In *Black Students: Psychosocial Issues and Academic Achievement,* edited by G. L. Berry and J. K. Asamen. Newbury Park, Calif.: Sage, 1989.
34. Sedlacek, W. E. "Black Students on White Campuses: 20 Years of Research." *Journal of College Student Personnel,* 28 (1987), 484–95.
35. Tracey, T. J. and W. E. Sedlacek. "The Relationship of Noncognitive Variables to Academic Success: A Longitudinal Comparison by Race." *Journal of College Student Personnel,* 26 (1985), 405–10.
36. ———. "Prediction of College Graduation Using Noncognitive Variables by Race." *Measurement and Evaluation in Counseling and Development,* 19 (1987), 177–184.
37. U.S. National Center for Health Statistics. "Plan and Operation of the Health and Nutrition Examination, United States, 1971–1973." (Vital and Health Statistics Series 1, No. 10b, DHEW Publication No. HSM 73–1310). Rockville, Md.: National Center for Health Statistics, 1973.
38. Zitzow, D. "The College Adjustment Rating Scale." *Journal of College Student Personnel,* 25 (1984), 160–64.

CHAPTER 10

THE BLACK BOX: HOW HIGH-ACHIEVING BLACKS RESIST STEREOTYPES ABOUT BLACK AMERICANS

SHARON FRIES-BRITT
KIMBERLY A. GRIFFIN

This qualitative study explores the academic and social experiences of nine Black high achievers attending a large public university. Findings indicate that despite their participation in the honors program and high degree of academic ability, Black high achievers felt that they were judged based on prevalent social stereotypes regarding the academic abilities of Black students. These external perceptions pushed students to engage in various behaviors and actively resist stereotypes with their behaviors both in and outside of classroom.

High-achieving Blacks have been described as "the best and the brightest" and are predicted to achieve the highest levels of academic and professional success (Solano, 1987). Indeed, many of these students go on to enroll at and graduate from some of the most prestigious institutions in the country (Bowen & Bok, 1998). Because they are labeled as high-achievers, university staff may assume that academically talented Blacks do not need special support services or that they experience the same issues as academically talented White students (Ford & Harris, 1995; Freeman, 1999; Fries-Britt, 1997). In reality, academically talented Blacks often need and report the desire for services that reflect their specific experiences (Fries-Britt, 1997; Person & Christensen, 1996). In addition to the normal difficulties of college life faced by all students, minority students endure strains that can interfere with their adjustment to college, integration into the campus community, and development of feelings of belonging (Smedley, Myers, & Harrell, 1993). Despite their increased academic capability, high-achievers continue to be vulnerable to these stresses and may encounter stereotypes about their racial group affiliation and their academic ability (Fries-Britt & Turner, 2001; Smedley et al.; Strommer, 1995).

The purpose of this study was to examine the collegiate experiences of a select group of high-achieving Black students. [In this chapter the terms high achiever, gifted, and academically talented are used interchangeably and are defined as having superior intelligence that is measurable by IQ and other quantitative tests (Fries-Britt, 1997) and/or exceptional academic performance (Freeman, 1999).] Black high achievers remain an understudied segment of the student population; consequently we know far less about their academic, social, and psychological needs and experiences. Understanding more about the within-group differences in communities of color is important as institutions endeavor to successfully retain and serve a diverse and complex student body. Two broad questions guided this study: (a) how do high-achieving Black students view their academic performance and academic struggles? and (b) What coping mechanisms, strategies, and support structures do high-achieving Black students utilize to relieve the stresses associated with their academic performance?

Based on the findings of this study, we argue that despite their participation in their campus's honors program, Black high-achievers are still judged based on prevalent social stereotypes regarding the academic abilities of Blacks. This pushes them to actively resist these stereotypes with their behaviors both in and outside of the classroom. Although this study confirms much of what we already know about Black high achievers, it reveals a great deal about and adds to our understanding of how Black high achievers process their experiences. Importantly, it also offers vivid examples of how these students resist the ways in which Black students are put in a stereotypical "box." In this manuscript we identify it as a Black box to capture the confinement expressed in their stories and because the box is often a racial box in which their racial/ethnic background limits how their peers and faculty perceive and interact with them. They describe how some peers and faculty see their Blackness and begin to attribute negative characteristics based on assumptions and stereotypes about the Black community. These are the experiences that create the Black box that these high-achieving students consistently resist.

Background

Freeman (1999) emphasized that for many academically successful Blacks, dropping out of college is not related to their ability to do college work or their GPA. Rather, highly talented Blacks withdraw from college often because they feel a lack of support and connection to their institution. Person-environment relationships are more closely related to persistence rates for academically talented Black students than actual ability (Ford & Harris, 1995), and dissatisfaction with one's social life can have a negative impact on grades and other student outcomes (Allen, 1988, 1992; Mow & Nettles, 1990; Person & Christensen, 1996).

Unfortunately, it appears that many high-achieving Blacks do not have the opportunity to make social connections with others like themselves. Person and Christensen (1996) found the high-achieving Blacks in their study to be more satisfied with their academic experiences in college than social ones, and 90% of the sample expressed a need for an identifiable Black community. In Fries-Britt's (1998) study of Black students in a high profile honors program, respondents expressed feeling shunned by both Black and White students at their university: White students doubted Black students' abilities and claimed that they received opportunities only because they were Black, and Black students believed the Black high achievers thought that they were better than everyone else.

Facing a hostile campus racial climate can also adversely impact the achievement, integration, and retention of high-achieving Blacks. Although all students experience certain life stresses, academically talented Blacks face racism and hostility at predominantly White institutions (PWIs) that White students do not (Fries-Britt, 1997, 2000; Noldon & Sedlacek, 1996; Person & Christensen, 1996; Smedley et al., 1993). Smedley et al. reported that minority students are subject to unique "minority status stressors," which include being the target of racist acts, having the legitimacy of one's presence on campus questioned, and feeling pressured to prove one's cultural identity to same-race peers. These stressors are debilitating to students because they undermine their confidence, heighten their concerns over their academic preparedness for college, and limit their ability to bond to the university. Consistent with this framework, another study found that 53% of sampled Black students at a highly selective institution reported having experienced discrimination and described being followed in bookstores, asked to explain the Black experience, or expected to portray certain stereotypes (Person & Christensen). These experiences may be particularly difficult for academically talented Black students due to their tendency to be perfectionists and believe in moral order (Lindstrom & Van Sant, 1986).

The racist actions academically talented Blacks are subjected to may be very blatant; however, it appears that there are many instances when the discrimination they face is more subtle. Rather than encountering blatantly racist acts, Black students may find themselves facing subtler judgments and expectations by students, faculty, and staff according to broad social stereotypes. According to cognitive and social psychologists, stereotyping is a natural function that humans employ to categorize individuals into groups that are believed to embody certain characteristics, allowing us to make sense of our environments without consuming more time in gathering information (Fiske, 1989; Stephan & Rosenfield, 1982). Stereotypes, which are often based on interactions with family, friends, and the media, allow individuals to quickly guide their interactions with others by both creating expectancies for a group member's behavior and giving them a basis for their interactions (Fiske, 1993; Neuberg, 1989; Stephan & Rosenfield). When a specific trait is associated with a group, the members of that group are believed to be homogenous and, therefore, different from other groups based on this trait (Stephan & Rosenfield).

In the larger social milieu, Blacks are often portrayed and stereotyped as criminals, gang members, athletes, and entertainers, but rarely as academics. To some "gifted Black" is an oxymoron; high levels of academic talent are associated primarily with Asian and White students, whereas expectations for the academic abilities of Black students are low (Fries-Britt, 1997, 1998; Steele, 1997). Therefore, although Black students are highly rewarded for their achievements in athletics, many Black students may fear that their academic achievements will be met with doubt, hostility, alienation, or resentment (Harvey, 1986). Overcoming these stereotypical perceptions can add additional burdens to Black high-achievers who are struggling to define their identities, and doubts of the academic abilities and talents of Black students have been found to be particularly damaging to their achievement and self-esteem (Smedley et al., 1993; Solorzano, Allen, & Carroll, 2002; Solarzano, Ceja, & Yosso, 2000; Steele, 1997).

The research literature documents many instances of academically talented Blacks being questioned about their intelligence, and some academically talented Blacks have reported feeling like they are always being watched and judged by both peers and faculty (Ford, Baytops, & Harmon, 1997; Fries-Britt, 1998; Fries-Britt & Turner, 2002). Black participants in an honors program described having their academic capabilities doubted and being accused of unfairly gaining access to the benefits and recognition associated with the program by their White peers (Fries-Britt, 1998). Black students attending predominantly White research institutions also reported enduring a less overt form of racism referred to as "microaggressions"; subtle and often unconscious racist acts that cumulatively add stress to the experience of people of color. Blacks reported many instances of peers and professors questioning their academic abilities both in and outside of the classroom and reported sensing that they were seen as being less intelligent students that could not have been admitted to college without affirmative action (Solorzano et al., 2000, 2002).

Students subjected to these stereotypes often attempt to resist and disprove negative assumptions about their intelligence. Solorzano et al. (2002) found that one response of students who had their abilities doubted was to work doubly hard and show their peers and professors that they belonged. Successful Black students interviewed by Fries-Britt and Turner (2002) shared that they often encountered students who made comments based on stereotypical images of Blacks, and that they felt that they repeatedly engaged in a "proving process" to establish themselves as worthy and academically able both in and outside of the classroom. A high-achieving Black male attending a PWI who was interviewed by Bonner (2001) also reported feeling pressure to be "ten times as smart as everyone else" (p. 11), and that he constantly had to prove himself and his capabilities. High-achieving Black males participating Shaun Harper's national study also noted that their academic achievement and engagement in campus activities and highly visible leadership positions enabled them to challenge and disprove pervasive stereotypes about Black men held by faculty and staff (Harper, 2005; Harper & Quaye, 2007). Even though there's some limited understanding of this process of resistance that Black students engage in, especially within the classroom, there's little understanding of acts of resistance students may engage in outside of the classroom and when interacting with their peers. Further, it is important to give voice to these students as they engage in the process of resistance, creating a richer understanding of these students' experiences.

Methods

This study is best described as a sociological multi-case study, which directed the researchers to give attention to the society people live in, social problems, roles individuals play in society, and different classes that individuals fall into relative to their educational experiences (Merriam, 1998). This study was designed to be interpretive—an effort to understand what Black honors students experience in college in relation to research on Black students and their experiences with subtle and overt racism and why they respond in the ways that they do. A sub-sample of the Black students enrolled in the Honors Program at State University served as the respondents in this study. We employed purposive methods (Bogdan & Biklen, 1998) to solicit the sample for this study; students were selected based on their race and engagement in the Honors Program at State University to create a sample that would provide the most insight into this study's research questions.

Institutional Data

The site for this study was "State University" (pseudonym), a large, extensive research university that serves as the flagship of its state's public university system. Census data indicates that in 2000, there were over 5 million residents in the state in which the university is located, and the state's racial/ethnic composition was 64% White, 28% Black, 4% Latino, 4% Asian, and .3% Native American (U.S. Census Bureau, 2000). State University enrolls approximately 35,000 students (25,000 are undergraduates), and just over 75% of undergraduates are in-state residents. Although not completely proportional, the undergraduate enrollment of State University somewhat mirrors the wider state population: 68.0% of undergraduates are White and 32.0% are minorities. Specifically, 12.0% of undergraduate students are Black, 14.0% are Asian American, 6.0% are Latino/Hispanic, and 0.3% are Native American.

Enrollment in State University's Honors Program was used as the characteristic that defined students as "high-achievers," largely due to the rigorous academic standards required to gain admission to this university-wide program. All State University applicants, regardless of race, ethnicity, or gender, were considered on an individual basis for acceptance into the Honors Program if they met the requirements of a 3.0 GPA and 1200 on the SAT. The students who were admitted to the Honors Program for the Fall 2000 semester had, on average, a 4.1 GPA on a four-point scale (students are able to achieve GPAs above a 4.0 by enrolling and achieving As in advanced placement [AP] courses). Further, 50% of students admitted to the Honors Program had SAT scores between 1360 and 1470. In comparison, the average high school GPA of the incoming class at State University in 2000 was 3.72 overall, and 50% of the students had SAT scores between 1170 and 1330.

Student Sample

The sample size was intentionally small because we were interested in interviewing students who were more engaged on campus and in the honors program. We wanted to have an opportunity to interview students who would have a wide range of experiences both in and outside of the classroom. Based on the input of the staff, we identified a total of 9 Black high achievers (6 females and 3 males) who participated in the study. The participants' average age was 19.6, ranging from 18 to 23. Four participants were sophomores, making them the most represented class in this study. The sample also included 2 freshmen, 1 junior, and 2 seniors. All participants were full-time students, though 7 worked part time during the academic year. Six of the students had attended public high schools before attending State University, 2 had gone to private schools, and 1 had attended both public and private high schools. Seven of the students reported having taken AP courses in high school and 4 had participated in SAT preparation courses.

There was significant diversity in respondents' family backgrounds. The reported family incomes of participants ranged from $10,000 to over $150,000. Parents' educational level also varied. Three participants reported that their mothers had obtained high school diplomas, one mother had completed some college, two mothers had bachelor's degrees, and three mothers had master's degrees. Fathers' educational levels were also mixed, with two fathers having completed some high school, two having graduated from high school, one father having completed some college, two with bachelor's degrees, one with a master's degree, and one with a professional degree.

Data Collection

Student participants in this study were recruited from the Honors Program at State University in the spring of 2001. One of the researchers met with a key administrator in the Honors Program to obtain permission to both focus the study on students in the program and obtain an initial list of potential participants who were engaged in the program and might be willing to participate. Identified students were contacted via e-mail and invited to participate in the study. We attended three meetings of the Black Honors Caucus to observe the students' interactions and to understand the concerns that students had about their campus experiences. We also recruited a member of the Honors Caucus to inform students about the project and enlist additional potential respondents.

All students who agreed to participate met individually with one of the researchers. Each participant first completed a short demographic questionnaire and then participated in a semistructured interview. Semi-structured interviews offer researchers the opportunity to respond to new ideas or emerging worldviews presented by their respondents during the course of the interview (Merriam, 1998). Consequently, many of the core questions were complemented by a series of probing questions that added depth and detail to subjects' responses and allowed exploration of issues not covered by questions in the protocol. Interviews were 60-75 minutes in length, audio taped, and later transcribed for analysis. In order to ensure their anonymity, all study participants were assigned and referred to by pseudonyms.

Analyses and Instruments

Both qualitative and demographic data were collected from participants. A 5-minute demographic survey about their background and family characteristics was administered before every interview. The primary source of data, however, came from the interview transcripts. The interview protocol was formulated based on a review of the literature on the challenges and experiences of academically talented Black students. Interview questions were composed to assess subjects' perceptions of their sources of motivation, feelings about their academic transition, views on the prevalence of stereotyping, and opinions about what factors served as barriers to their academic achievement. This protocol was tested in a pilot interview with a Black female student prior to its use in this study.

After all participants were interviewed and their narratives were transcribed, data were manually coded. The research literature on stereotyping and the experiences of academically talented Black students was reviewed to identify recurring themes, from which a coding scheme was developed. We also read through participants' narratives, adding themes that appeared in these interviews to the coding scheme, and then revisited interview transcripts, applying the codes to organize the data. Once the data were organized, the student narratives were analyzed by utilizing the "pattern matching" technique (Yin, 1994). In this process, data are compared to existing theories and research. Thus, categorized sections of narratives were compared to the findings of studies on student achievement and research on the experience of high achievers.

Findings and Discussion

The students in this study expressed a high degree of self-confidence, and they displayed humility when discussing their academic abilities. Although they were proud of their intellectual achievements, they did not feel that they had more talent than their Black peers who were not enrolled in the honors program. A female student expressed this sentiment when she described her academic ability as representing one type of accomplishment but acknowledged that other students excelled in other ways that were equally important. The majority of the students indicated that they did not reveal to others that they were in the honors program; however, if the honors program came up in conversation and someone learned that they were enrolled in the program, they did not try to hide their involvement.

As the students described their encounters on campus with peers and faculty and their experiences as high achievers, several interrelated themes emerged. First, many of the students talked about the fact that they were still the only Black person in a classroom, and they noticed the low numbers of minority professors they encountered on the campus. It also became evident that these students encountered stereotypes about Blacks both in and outside the classroom. Students felt they had to dispel stereotypes and myths about Blacks from peers and faculty and described feeling pressure to behave in ways that are considered "non-Black," involve themselves in events so that they could serve as a positive example of Blacks, and prove that they were smart so that people would not think they were accepted into the honors program because of affirmative action. Their experiences and insights illustrated the tensions that often exist for high-achieving Blacks who attend traditionally White institutions and they offered insight into the ways that high achievers cope and deal with the stresses in the environment, especially underrepresentation and stereotypes.

Challenging Stereotypes and Myths About Blacks

All participants talked about the stereotypes about Blacks they encountered on a regular basis. Although a few students expressed significant concerns about how their own behaviors may confirm stereotypes, the majority of the students expressed minimal concern about their own individual behaviors confirming stereotypes. On occasion, some students did say that they felt pressure to be aware of their actions and not to exhibit stereotypical behaviors. Usually this pressure surfaced when they were being identified as an honors student in a public forum and/or if they were asked to participate in an event on behalf of the university.

Julian described this well, explaining that he felt pressure to carry himself in a certain way, especially when he was introduced as an honors student. Anna also reported a sense of fear that she might confirm wider societal stereotypes with her behavior. She shared that she would switch the way she communicated based on who was around. Many students who have bicultural abilities and who understand the rules of communication and interaction in multiple communities will switch communication patterns and styles to apply rules and ways of communicating that are accepted in each context. Anna felt that it was important to let people know that Blacks had a range of speaking ability and could use different communication patterns.

Thompson and Fretz (1991) identified these bicultural patterns as coping mechanisms reflective of a student's ability to manage the demands of a predominately White campus. They suggested that there are a number of adaptive strategies that Black students can employ to be successful in a dominant cultural context. Two are particularly relevant to this study. First, Black students with high levels of communalism tend to be more resourceful and direct in coping in White environments. Hence it is important for Black students to connect with other Black peers to provide them with the support they need to deal with the dominant context. Another coping strategy for Black students is to simultaneously value learning about Anglo-centric stimuli and Afro-centric stimuli. Investment in learning from both of these perspectives allows Black students to relate to the dominant context while protecting their own psychological development and learning about ideas and information germane to the Black culture. Clearly Black students who attend PWIs will continue to be challenged with Anglo-centric stimuli in the social and academic milieu of the campus. However, what may be essential to their success are the opportunities they have to connect to Afro-centric stimuli. These interactions are more likely to happen if there are greater numbers of diverse students and faculty and if the experiences of White students and professors reflect an appreciation and knowledge of both Anglo- and Afro-centric perspectives.

Many students at PWIs will find themselves in a position of being the only or "token" Black student. These situations require them to develop coping skills that allow them to feel comfortable and whole. Nathan shared that sometimes he felt like a "token" when he was asked to serve on various university committees. For the most part he did not mind being involved because he felt that it was important for him to be at the table expressing his ideas and learning from the opinions of others. It was clear that Nathan struggled with his involvement and why he was being invited to participate. He shared that

> I feel like the only reason they want me to be a part of it is because I'm a Black guy and I'm a nice guy. And just because I'm a Black, nice guy doesn't mean I want to be a part of everything.

Embedded in Nathan's comment is the pressure he feels to represent a segment of the Black male population that is "nice," a tame Black man, one that the majority culture can relate to and tolerate. The stereotypes of Black males as hostile, angry, and violent may add to the pressure that Nathan felt to be involved just to demonstrate that there are nice Black males. Not far below the surface however was Nathan's anger that he may be invited because he is a nice Black guy. Although on one hand he accepted this characterization that he is a nice Black male, he was not willing to be in many respects the token Black male as a part of "everything" on campus. It was more than being a token Black male—Nathan felt particular pressure because he had been identified as a "nice Black male," as if this characteristic is unusual for Black males. If this was Nathan's identity, his particularity in the majority community, what options did he have to express his anger or disapproval on these campus committees when issues surfaced that offended him or with which he did not agree? Did he risk losing his role if he ever exhibited other types of emotions than those for which he was rewarded?

Many of the students commented that they liked to disrupt people's stereotypes by behaving in ways that are considered incongruent with being Black, and they enjoyed seeing the surprise on their peers' faces when they defied their perceptions. Janice offered the most compelling example of this, saying that she often sang Mozart in Latin while she was taking a shower in the residence hall community bathroom. She knew that as she was singing the song it would attract attention, and she commented that she enjoyed seeing the shock on people's faces when they learned that it was a Black woman singing Mozart in Latin. She was very aware that she did not fit their image or stereotype of who would be singing Mozart in the shower. Janice was very intentional about trying to be incongruent with stereotypes about Blacks, and her strategy demonstrates the level of effort that some students put into dispelling stereotypes about Blacks and into proving that Blacks have behaviors and abilities that are "normative" and like everyone else (Whites).

To be incongruent with stereotypes about Blacks means that, at some level, these students give up part of what it means to be Black. Stereotypes are in many ways over-exaggerated truths. The problem is the degree to which society over-attributes these truths to a group. Blacks tend to be assigned negative stereotypes associated with the larger Black community, both at the individual and group levels. If individuals felt like they were truly judged based on their own individual actions and not the stereotypes of the group, there might be less of a desire to be incongruent with stereotypes about Blacks. Singing Mozart in Latin was a form of coping for Janice—a way of establishing her own identity and boundaries around what it means to be Black and/or White.

Ashley's way of dispelling myths and stereotypes about Blacks was by confronting issues in the classroom that seemed to leave out the Black perspective. Whenever she found herself in a classroom where there was a lot of discussion and where different perspectives were shared, Ashley felt like it was important to explain how she felt the subject matter impacted the Black community. She commented,

> I feel like there's a whole other side of it [the topic being discussed] when it's Black, regardless of what the topic is . . . especially talking about history and things like that. You have to feel that you straightened this out. So you always have to kind of explain yourself.

Ashley was comfortable and familiar with discussing her perspective on Black issues. She felt that it was important to be

> able to talk to them [Whites] maybe in a way they will understand it, or explain it to them in a way they understand it so that they understand where I am coming from or where the majority of Black people are coming from.

Ashley's commitment to helping White students understand more about the Black experience was influenced by her early experiences with a White roommate who had little exposure to Blacks prior to college.

> [My roommate] never went to a school with a Black person before. . . . She always had so many stereotypes . . . she definitely thought that Black people did tend to do worse on the SATs just because they were dumber. . . . So we used to talk all the time about all the different types of stuff, about whether it would be, like our economic statuses, our families, our schools, and where we came from. . . . I think that she learned more from me than she could have learned from any course on[sic] the university. And she did, she did say she had learned a lot.

Ashley's attempts to educate her White roommate may be viewed as desirable by some of her White peers. In fact, interactions across race and culture have been supported by the literature as instrumental in the academic and social development of students (Hurtado, 2001; Hurtado, Milem, Clayton-Pedersen, & Allen, 1999). Although benefits are likely to accrue for Ashley and her roommate, it is important to assess the degree to which Ashley's energy was devoted to educating her roommate, peers, and faculty, thus diverting her focus away from her academics. These repeated conversations may produce different outcomes for Black and White students over time. In a study examining the experiences of Black students who attended a PWI versus a historically Black college or university (HBCU), Fries-Britt and Turner (2002) found that students at the HBCU tended to describe interactions that cultivated their energy, whereas Black students at the PWI had their energy diverted from academics. A Black male student described how the HBCU helped develop confidence and gave him the "adrenaline" to accomplish his goals. The Black students attending the PWI gave examples of having to explain to and educate their White peers.

To the extent that Black students have a primary role in explaining cultural differences and serving as cultural informants on college campuses, they are likely to encounter negative attitudes that can foster conditions that impede their academic progress. Over time, they may be typecast as hostile for always raising "racial issues," labeled as intellectually narrow-minded because they continue to place race on the agenda, and more likely to become socially isolated as their peers perceive interactions with them as confrontational.

Proving Academic Worth and Ability

As the students discussed their experiences, it became evident that, in addition to feeling that they needed to disprove negative stereotypes, they encountered pressure to prove their academic ability to White peers and, to a lesser extent, demonstrate their racial affiliation to Black peers. First, they felt like they had to prove to their White peers that they were admitted into the Honors Program because they were smart and not just because they were Black. Some students commented that this constant proving process added a layer of doubt to their sense of worthiness. Black students on White campuses have their academic competency questioned in part because of the commonly held misperception that affirmative action policies and efforts to diversify college campuses have eroded quality and excellence. Thus, it is assumed that Black students continue to be admitted to college because of policy initiatives like affirmative action and diversity and not because they are actually qualified scholars (Chang, 2001; Milem, 2001).

Several students shared accounts of how people assumed they had not earned their place in the Honors Program. Ashley noted that she had people questioning her or making statements about her admission into the program. She reflected that people made comments to her like, "'Oh, you're going to get in there because you're Black' . . . or thinking that everything that I was getting was because I was Black—that was the only reason." Similarly Nathan, who was in his senior year, had a student say to him that he had received a scholarship and was accepted to a prestigious Ivy League institution only because he was Black.

Ashley explained that, in some cases, there was a degree of competition between her and her White peers because they would ask about her scores on exams. In cases where the White students' scores were higher they would inform her and then ask her "how come they didn't get into the program," as if scores were the only criterion for selection. This question is precisely the type of question and interaction that Steele (1992; Steele & Aronson, 1995) described as inducing stress and anxiety. Steele (1997) submitted that threat of stereotype "is in the air" once students begin to talk about scores on exams and admission into the program, particularly within the context of the Honors Program. Most students are aware that Blacks tend to perform lower on standardized exams. Consequently, the assumption is that the Blacks in the Honors Program are likely to have lower scores than White students, yet they were admitted into the program. The truth is that in some cases Black students' scores were higher than their White peers in the Honors Program and in other cases lower. These types of interactions and discussion about scores divert Blacks students' energy away from academics, and they send a message to Black students that they are not perceived as capable.

The students in this study were confident that they were as prepared as other students in the Honors Program. However, the questions they encountered from White peers over time tended to chip away at their self-confidence causing them to internalize feelings of self-doubt. These findings are consistent with findings of other studies (Fries-Britt & Turner, 2002; Smedley et al., 1993), which demonstrated that Black students feel that their academic ability is constantly questioned. Perhaps the most compelling example of stereotype threat came from Janice, who felt like she encountered resentment from her White peers because she was in the Honors Program. Her perception was that individuals who were closed-minded believed she was in the Honors Program only to fill a quota. Her response to this was, "I know I'm not a quota filler . . . I don't believe that I am. . . . I don't think that [quotas] exist, you know."

A closer examination of Janice's comment reveals the damage of the stereotypes that she faced. Her observations reflect just how the threat of a stereotype can be internalized even if she does not intend to let the stereotype affect her. Janice boldly stated that she was not "a quota filler." With this assertion she was confronting the stereotype that Black students are assumed to be quota fillers. Being a Black student meant that at some level the stereotype could apply to her, even though she knew it was not true in her case. Her own truth suggested that she was not a quota filler and that her admission into the Honors Program was based on her ability. Or was it? The next part of her statement demonstrates the doubt that quickly emerged as she commented, "I don't believe that I am." In a matter of seconds, Janice moved from a bold assertion that she is not a quota filler to questioning if it could be true. If she were a quota filler, what would that mean? Would that mean that she did not belong in the Honors Program and that she was less capable than her peers? Even more important, would she ever know?

Finally, in the last part of her statement, she was able to reconcile this issue as she questioned the existence of quotas. She stated, "I don't think that [quotas] exist." If quotas do not exist, then she could not be a quota filler. In fact, quotas are illegal; however, the pervasive myths about affirmative action continue to distort images of policies and programs designed to level the playing field. The internal dialogue that Janice had with herself is an example of how energy got diverted from academics and went into affirming her right to be in the program and to reassuring herself that she was worthy. It is an example of what Steele and Aronson (1995) referred to as a race-primed condition in which the threat of being a quota is likely to create conditions that induce stress and anxiety.

Julian described the degree of pressure that he felt in the classroom to prove his ability. For Julian it was the broader stereotype that Blacks are less intelligent that made him want to perform better in the classroom.

> They still think that, you know, we are a subdivision of human folks and we are lower than they are. So it's important for me to prove that, you know, I can do everything that you [Whites] can do . . . there is no difference between you and I except our skin color."

Anna also gave a vivid description of how the proving process manifested for her:

> Well, when I find that I'm the only Black person in a class, I feel that I have to prove myself just as intelligent, just as smart, just as worthy, you know, of the same grade as somebody else who's not my race. I am not extremely competitive, but I feel competitive in that instance where I have to prove myself to be as strong student, you know, to compete with those in my classroom. It's been that way since high school because I was going up against mostly Asians and Whites . . . so I've always felt that I had to prove myself when I've always been the one Black person in the class.

In both Julian's and Anna's cases it may seem that the pressure to prove their academic ability was a self-imposed pressure and unrelated to anything in the classroom. Julian described it best when he said that the larger stereotypes about Blacks in society made him feel like he had to prove his intellectual ability in the classroom. In both examples the students felt the threat of the stereotype about Blacks as less intelligent because they were dealing with perceptions in the domain of the college classroom, which represents precisely where these abilities are evaluated. The stereotypes that are held about Blacks as a referent group in the larger society are precisely the ones that get carried over into the environment of the campus.

The challenges faced by Blacks by no means suggest that White students enter the classroom devoid of pressure or free of stereotypes. In fact, it is characteristic of most high achievers to feel a degree of pressure about their academic ability. In another study we compared the experiences of high-achieving Whites and Blacks who were participants in an honors program. These data are still being analyzed, however preliminary findings suggest that both groups experienced a degree of alienation from peers because of their interest in academics. The difference in Black and White students' experiences was the intensity and nature of the alienation. A key difference for White students is that they perceived that assessments made about their academic ability were aimed at them individually and were not applied to the larger community of Whites. Put differently, White students were less likely to perceive that others stereotype them as less intelligent because they are members of the White community. Black students described something different altogether. They perceived that individual Blacks are assumed less intelligent precisely because they are members of the Black community, a community that historically has been perceived as less intelligent.

Proving academic ability was by far the greatest test faced by these students. However, to a lesser extent, these students felt pressure to prove their Blackness, as evidenced by their choice in extracurricular activities and cultural preferences. When the students did not fit the stereotyped images that their White peers had about Blacks they were not sure how to respond to them. Janice observed, "The population feels that there is a certain way to act Black, a certain way to act White." Katrina shared that she had been referred to as "not Black" by her White friends; because she did not fit many of the societal stereotypes that people had of Blacks, her Black friends saw her as being less Black because of the way she expressed herself and because she was less fond of rap and hip-hop music, which are associated largely with the Black community. Teddi's comments capture this dilemma well:

> [J]ust because I'm Black doesn't mean I like Puffy Combs [popular hip-hop artist], you know. Just because I'm Black doesn't mean I cannot drink alcohol . . . smoke weed. I never drank any alcohol, never had any drugs; I have never carried a Glock [gun]. I have never, you know, had a boom box on my shoulder walking down the street bopping.

Implications

The findings of this study bring attention to the ways in which Black high achievers have been "boxed in" based on stereotypes about their race, assumptions about their abilities, and thoughts about their social activities and behaviors. The students in this study talked about the ways in which they felt pressure to prove that they are academically capable and to dispel myths and stereotypes about the Black community. In our work, we have found that the resistance process that Black students undertake, and the time they spend dispelling myths and stereotypes about the Black community, have the potential to divert energy away from studying. As we bring our work to a close we would like to offer several observations about the importance and impact of this work as it relates to the students ability to cope with stereotypes.

The degree to which students were able to effectively cope varied. Janice chose to sing "Mozart in Latin" as a way of dealing with the threat of a stereotype. In her own words she described this behavior as being incongruent with images of how Black students behave. In the short run this strategy may have worked for Janice, but what is the impact over time for Janice and other students who feel that it is necessary to be incongruent with images of Blacks in order to be successful? What is the emotional price that students pay as they find themselves increasingly isolated from their cultural community in order to fit into the dominant culture? Nathan, who was often referred to as a "White boy," admitted that his involvement on campus was primarily with Whites and that he did not feel as connected to the Black community.

A number of the observations offered by the students in this study occurred in the classroom with peers and faculty who either questioned their academic capability and/or made comments during class discussions that demonstrated that they held a number of stereotypes about Blacks. These interactions resulted in the participants spending significant time "teaching" others. The time that students spend "teaching" about the Black experience can be both beneficial and detrimental depending on the sustained nature of the conversations. The extent to which Black students manage conversations about race in the classroom can also be costly. Even though they do not mind talking to White peers, and in some cases faculty, about the complex factors that shape their experience, each conversation adds to the level of scrutiny they encounter about their ability to be successful at a PWI. They become more vulnerable to the judgments and views of others as they freely share their own experiences. Black students frequently reveal their feelings and experiences without the benefit of knowing what others feel and think.

Although the resistance that the high-achieving students in this study exhibited did not derail their academic success, there were emotional costs and stresses associated with the process. Solorzano et al. (2002) reminded us that, in an effort to resist stereotypes about minority students, students of color often "push themselves to exhaustion and still are not able to reap the fair rewards for their work" (p. 67). Research on stereotype threat also confirmed that high-achieving minority students are often highly aware of the stigma associated with their racial groups and that students of color are often distracted from academic tasks by their attempts to disprove social stereotypes about members of their race (Steele, 1997; Steele & Aronson, 1995). In most cases, stereotype threat does not cause high-achieving Blacks to completely give up on academic tasks. Rather, stereotype threat serves as a distraction; it diminishes students' efficiency and causes them to spend more time re-reading texts and re-thinking questions (Steele & Aronson, 1998), all of which can impact overall performance. In the most extreme cases, Black students who experience chronic stereotype threat may dis-identify with academic achievement by switching to less rigorous courses or majors, or at the extreme, dropping out of college, to escape the pressure and anxiety related to potentially fulfilling a negative stereotype (Steele & Aronson, 1998). Thus, there is a tenuous balance between resistance as motivation and resistance that is detrimental to students' academic and psychological well being. Students need support as they encounter these experiences, and it is important to create opportunities for Black high achievers to come together to provide each other with encouragement and understanding.

Black faculty can also offer an important form of support as they face these experiences. During his interview, Nathan offered a clear example of how Black professors can support their students as they struggle with their efforts to resist. He commented that "the teachers that I've had, like, real conversations with . . . that stand out to me have been Black, both men and women." The "realness" in the conversation that Nathan observed is likely to have occurred because Black faculty are in a better position to understand the spoken and unspoken experiences encountered by Black students. Black faculty are likely to have a connection because they are able to use their own experiences as additional insight to go below the surface of the conversation and to engage students on substantive issues that impact their lives on and off campus.

Many Black professors were former high-achieving college students who attended both Black and White campuses. In order to be successful in their own academic careers, they too have encountered many challenges to their academic sense of self. Hence, they are more likely to understand the challenges that Black students often face at PWIs and can instinctively know how to support Black students. Not only have Black faculty traveled similar academic paths as many Black students, they may also be encountering racial experiences on the campus that challenge their sense of self as a professor (Allen, Epps, Guillory, Suh, & Bonous-Hammarth, 2000; Banks, 1984; Johnsrud & Sadao, 1998). Consequently they are likely to have an innate understanding of the subtle cues that Black students send about their academic and social condition on campus and their overall level of satisfaction. This intuition is likely to be enhanced because they may share similar cultural understanding and knowledge of informal and formal rules of interaction and communication. These shared experiences create a connection between Black faculty and Black students that can be fundamentally unique and critical to the survival and satisfaction of both groups on the campus.

It is important to note that we do not recommend that Black students resist sharing their experiences in the classroom. What is important is that Black students feel a sense of control over what they wish to share rather than feeling like there is pressure for them to take on the role of "educating" White America. Thompson and Fretz (1991) found that Black students used a number of adaptive strategies on White campuses:

> In the classroom, Black students who have positive attitudes toward working with (cooperating) rather than against (competing) or away from their peer group may desire the opportunity for others to learn about them as individuals. These students may be of the mindset that in order to overcome racism, members of a community must be willing to break down barriers to communication by sharing thoughts and ideas rather than perpetuating stereotypes beliefs though minimal contact. (p. 440)

Although this strategy is useful for some Black students, for too long minority students have been viewed as sources of expertise on issues of race and ethnicity in the classroom. Non-minority peers and faculty have relied on the willingness of Black students to share their experiences in ways that enhance discussions on race and racial relations in the classroom.

Even though the contributions of students can be significant, faculty members must understand the important role that they have in guiding and constructing conversations about race. Faculty must understand that they too have been shaped by race in ways that are likely to influence their perceptions of students and the teaching process. In *Teaching to Transgress*, bell hooks (1994) submits that:

> despite the contemporary focus on multiculturalism in our society, particularly in education, there is not nearly enough practical discussion of ways classroom settings can be transformed so that the learning experience is inclusive. If the effort to respect and honor the social reality and experiences of groups in this society who are non White is to be reflected in a pedagogical process, then as teachers—on all levels, from elementary to university settings—we must acknowledge that our styles of teaching may need to change. (p. 35)

Encouraging discussions that include complex topics like race in the classroom can present a number of challenges. First, there are a number of curriculum changes that need to take place. To the extent possible, faculty should incorporate readings and assignments that educate from a diverse perspective. In cases where faculty may not have had opportunities or resources to enhance their teaching materials, presumably they should acknowledge that the issues being discussed are likely to have different implications for other racial/ethnic groups. It is also important to establish a climate in the classroom that invites students with differences of opinion and diverse perspectives to participate. These can be important teaching tools that help to inform the debate and enhance the exchange of ideas. Finally, on a practical level, it is important to allow time in class to process discussions that involve race. Not only do students need time to process their own thoughts and feelings, they also need time to understand the perspective held by others that may differ from their own.

Like students, faculty must also feel comfortable talking about race in the classroom. To do so, faculty must be comfortable with a degree of vulnerability and openness in the classroom as they share some of their own experiences and observations about race. For some faculty this will be a significant challenge to their teaching style; discussions of race can require more risk taking, which can enhance or impede discussions and interactions in the classroom. For some students, talking about race is likely to engage them more in the class, whereas others may feel silenced. Finding teaching techniques that are effective across groups is important. Using only one pedagogical style is not enough to respond to the needs of a multicultural classroom. In incorporating these new pedagogical techniques, faculty must take risks that are not unlike those taken by Black students everyday on college campuses.

References

Allen, W. (1988). The education of Black students on White college campuses: What quality the experience? In M. T. Nettles (Ed.), *Toward Black undergraduate student equality in American higher education* (pp. 57–85). New York: Greenwood Press.

Allen, W. (1992). The color of success: African-American college student outcomes at predominantly White and historically Black public colleges and universities. *Harvard Educational Review, 62*(1), 26–44.

Allen, W. R., Epps, E. G., Guillory, E. A., Suh, S. A., & Bonous-Hammarth, M. (2000). The Black academic: Faculty status among African Americans in U.S. higher education. *Journal of Negro Education, 69*(1/2), 112–127.

Banks, W. M. (1984). Afro-American scholars in the university. *American Behavioral Scientist, 27*(3), 325–338.

Bogdan, R. C., & Biklen, S. K. (1998). *Qualitative research in education: An introduction to theory and methods* (3rd ed.). Boston: Allyn and Bacon.

Bonner, F. A., II. (2001). Gifted African American male college students: A phenomenological study. Storrs, CT: National Research Center on the Gifted and Talented.

Bowen W. G., & Bok D. (1998). *The shape of the river: Long-term consequences of considering race in college and university admissions.* Princeton, NJ: Princeton University Press.

Chang, M. J. (2001). The positive educational effects of racial diversity on campus. In G. Orfield & M. Kurlaender (Eds.), *Diversity challenged: Evidence on the Impact of Affirmative Action* (pp. 175–186). Cambridge, MA: Harvard Education Publishing Group.

Fiske, S. T. (1989). Examining the role of intent: Toward understanding its role in stereotyping and prejudice. In J. S. Uleman & J. A. Bargh (Eds.), *Unintended thought: The limits of awareness, intention, and control* (pp. 253–283). New York: Guilford Press.

Fiske, S. T. (1993). Controlling other people: The impact of power on stereotyping. *American Psychology, 48*(6), 621–628.

Ford, D. Y., Baytops, J. L., & Harmon, D. A. (1997). Helping gifted minority students reach their potential: Recommendations for change. *Peabody Journal of Education, 72*(3–4), 201–216.

Ford, D. Y., & Harris, J. J. (1995). Exploring university counselors' perceptions of distinctions between gifted Black and gifted White students. *Journal of Counseling and Development, 73*, 443–450.

Freeman, K. (1999). No services needed? The case for mentoring high-achieving African American students. *Peabody Journal of Education, 74*(2), 15–26.

Fries-Britt, S. (1997). Identifying and supporting gifted African American men. *New Directions for Student Services, 80*, 65–78.

Fries-Britt, S. (1998). Moving beyond Black achiever isolation: Experiences of gifted Black collegians. *Journal of Higher Education, 69*(5), 556–576.

Fries-Britt, S. (2000). Identity development of high-ability Black collegians. In M. D. Svinicki, R. E. Rice (Series Eds.) & M. Baxter Magolda (Vol. Ed). *Teaching to promote intellectual and personal maturity (New Directions for Teaching and Learning*, No. 82, pp. 55–65). San Francisco: Jossey-Bass.

Fries-Britt, S., & Turner, B. (2001). Facing stereotypes: A case study of Black students on a White campus. *Journal of College Student Development, 42*(5), 420–429.

Fries-Britt, S., & Turner, B. (2002). Uneven stories: Successful Black collegians at a Black and a White campus. *The Review of Higher Education, 25*(3), 315–330.

Harper, S. R. (2005). Leading the way: High-achieving African American male students. *About Campus, 10*(1), 8–15.

Harper, S. R., & Quaye, S. J. (2007). Student organizations as venues for Black identity expression and development among African American male student leaders. *Journal of College Student Development, 48*(2), 127–144.

Harvey, M. L. A. (1986). Minorities and women and honors education. *Fostering academic excellence through honors programs (New Directions for Teaching and Learning* No. 25, pp. 41–51). San Francisco: Jossey-Bass

hooks, b. (1994). *Teaching to transgress: Education as the practice of freedom.* New York: Routledge.

Hurtado, S. (2001). Linking diversity and educational purpose: How diversity affects the classroom environment and student development. In G. Orfield & M. Kurlaender (Eds.), *Diversity challenged: Evidence on the impact of affirmative action* (pp. 187–203). Cambridge, MA: Harvard Education Publishing Group.

Hurtado, S., Milem, J., Clayton-Pedersen, A., & Allen, W. (1999). Enacting diverse learning environments: Improving the climate for racial/ethnic diversity in higher education. (*ASHEERIC Higher Education Report* Volume 26, No. 8). Washington, DC: The George Washington University, Graduate School of Education and Human Development.

Johnsrud, L. K., & Sadao, K. C. (1998). The common experience of "otherness": Ethnic and racial minority faculty. *The Review of Higher Education, 21*(4), 315–342.

Lindstrom, R. R., & Van Sant, S. (1986). Special issues in working with gifted minority adolescents. *Journal of Counseling and Development, 64*, 583–586.

Merriam, S. B. (1998). *Qualitative research and case study applications in education.* San Francisco: Jossey-Bass.

Milem, J. F. (2001). Increasing diversity benefits: How campus climate and teaching methods affect student outcomes. In G. Orfield & M. Kurlaender (Eds.), *Diversity challenged: Evidence on the impact of affirmative action* (pp. 233–246). Cambridge, MA: Harvard Education Publishing Group.

Mow, S. L., & Nettles, M. T. (1990). Minority student access and persistence and performance in college: A review of trends and research literature. In J. C. Smart (Ed.), *Higher education: Handbook of theory and research* (Volume 4, pp. 35–105). New York: Agathon Press.

Neuberg, S. L. (1989). The goal forming accurate impressions during social interactions: Attenuating the impact of negative expectancies. *Journal of Personality and Social Psychology, 56*(3), 374–386.

Noldon, D. F., & Sedlacek, W. E. (1996). Race differences in attitudes, skills, and behaviors among academically talented students. *Journal of the Freshman Year Experience, 8*(2), 43–56.

Person, D. R., & Christensen, M. (1996). Understanding Black student culture and Black student retention. *NASPA Journal, 34*(1), 47–56.

Smedley, B. D., Myers, H. F., & Harrell, S. P. (1993). Minority-status stresses and the college adjustment of ethnic minority freshman. *Journal of Higher Education, 64*(4), 434–452.

Solano, C. H. (1987). Stereotypes of social isolation and early burnout in the gifted: Do they exist? *Journal of Youth and Adolescence, 16*(6), 527–539.

Solorzano, D. G., Allen, W. R., & Carroll, G. (2002). Keeping race in place: Racial microaggressions and campus racial climate at the University of California Berkeley. *Chicano Latino Law Review, 23*(Spring), 15–112.

Solorzano, D. G., Ceja, M., & Yosso, T. J. (2000). Critical race theory, racial microaggressions, and campus racial climate: The experiences of African American college students. *Journal of Negro Education, 69*(1/2), 60–73.

Steele, C. M. (1992). Race and the schooling of Black Americans. *Atlantic Monthly,* (April), 68–78.

Steele, C. M. (1997). A threat in the air: How stereotypes shape intellectual identity and performance. *American Psychologist, 52*(6), 613–629.

Steele, C. M., & Aronson, J. (1995). Stereotype threat and the intellectual test performance of African Americans. *Journal of Personality and Social Psychology, 69*(5), 797–811.

Steele, C. M., & Aronson, J. (1998). Stereotype threat and the test performance of academically successful African Americans. In C. Jenks & M. Phillips (Eds.), *The Black-White test score gap* (pp. 401–427). Washington, DC: Brookings Institution Press.

Stephan, W. G., & Rosenfield, D. (1982). Racial and ethnic stereotypes. In A. G. Miller (Ed.), *In the eye of the beholder: Contemporary issues in stereotyping* (pp. 92–136). New York: Praeger.

Strommer, D. (1995). Advising special populations of students. *New Directions for Teaching and Learning, 62,* 25–34.

Thompson, C. E., & Fretz, B. R., (1991). Predicting the adjustment of Black students at predominately White institutions. *Journal of Higher Education, 62*(4), 437–450.

U.S Census Bureau: American FactFinder. (2000). Retrieved June 25, 2007, from http://factfinder.census.gov

Yin, R. K. (1994). Case study research design and methods. *Applied social research methods series,* (5). Sage Publications.

Chapter 11
"I am not a racist but . . .": Mapping White College Students' Racial Ideology in the USA

Eduardo Bonilla-Silva

Tyrone A. Forman

Introduction

Since the civil rights period it has become common for Whites to use phrases such as "I am not a racist, but . . ." as shields to avoid being labeled as "racist" when expressing racial ideas (Van Dijk, 1984:120). These discursive maneuvers or *semantic moves* are usually followed by negative statements on the general character of minorities (e.g. "they are lazy", "they have too many babies") or on government-sponsored policies and programs that promote racial equality (e.g. "affirmative action is reverse discrimination", "no-one should be forced to integrate").[1] Qualitative work has captured these discursive maneuvers on issues as diverse as crime, welfare, affirmative action, government intervention, neighborhood and school integration (Blauner, 1989; Feagin and Sikes, 1994; Feagin and Vera, 1995; MacLeod, 1995; Rieder, 1985; Rubin, 1994; Terkel, 1993; Weis and Fine, 1996; Wellman, 1977). For example, Margaret Welch, angry about not getting a scholarship in college, told Studs Terkel: "I've never been prejudiced, but why the hell are you doing this to me?" (Terkel, 1993: 70). Doug Craigen, a 32-year-old White truck driver, declared to Lillian Rubin: "I am not a racist, but sometimes they [Asians] give me the creeps" (Rubin, 1994: 188). Finally, Lawrence Adams, a supervisor interviewed by Bob Blauner, stated his views on affirmative action as follows:

> Now don't get me wrong. There are people . . . who are very capable and who are going to progress up the line. The fact that they would be able to progress faster than I would because of affirmative action is not the part that bothers me. The part that bothers me, I can name you as many of them who are an incompetent bunch of bastards who have no right being there, but are only there because their last name is Hispanic or Black or they are females—*and that's wrong*. (Blauner, 1989: 256)

These prejudiced expressions clash with research that suggests that racial attitudes have improved dramatically in the USA. Beginning with Hyman and Sheatsley's widely cited paper in *Scientific American (1964)*, survey research has documented substantial change in Whites' racial views (e.g. Firebaugh and Davis, 1988; Lipset, 1996; Niemi, Mueller and Smith, 1989; Smith and Sheatsley, 1984; Schuman et al., 1988; Sniderman and Piazza, 1993). Sheatsley (1966), for instance, proclaimed that:

> The mass of White Americans have shown in many ways that they will not follow a racist government and that they will not follow racist leaders. It will not be easy for most, but one cannot at this late date doubt their basic commitment. In their hearts they know that the American Negro is right. (p. 323)

The conflicting findings regarding the character of Whites' racial views based on interviews and surveys as well as the differing interpretations of survey-based attitudinal research (see Bobo and Hutchings, 1996; Hochschild, 1995; Kinder and Sanders, 1996; Lipset, 1996; Schuman et al., 1988, 1997; Sniderman and Carmines, 1997; Sniderman and Piazza, 1993) have produced a new puzzle: *What is the meaning of contemporary Whites' racial views?* How can *Whites* claim to believe in racial equality and yet oppose programs to reduce racial inequality? Why is it that a large proportion of *Whites*, who claim in surveys that they agree with the principle of integration, do not mind their kids mixing with non-Whites, have no objection to interracial marriages, and do not mind people of color moving into their neighborhoods continue to live in all-White neighborhoods and send their kids to mostly White schools? Finally, why is it that interview-based research consistently reports higher levels of prejudice among Whites?

To explore the meaning of contemporary Whites' views, this chapter examines White racial attitudes from both a different conceptual perspective and with a different methodology. Conceptually, we situate the racial attitudes of Whites as part of a larger racial ideology that functions to preserve the contemporary racial order.[2] Here we build on the work of others who have argued that the complexity of contemporary White racial attitudes reflects changes occurring in the USA since the late 1940s (Bonilla-Silva and Lewis, 1999; Brooks, 1990; Smith, 1995). Specifically, they claim that the dramatic social, political, economic and demographic changes in the USA since the 1940s combined with the political mobilization of various minority groups in the 1950s and 1960s, forced a change in the US racial structure—the network of social, political, and economic racial relations that produces and reproduces racial positions. In general terms, White privilege since the 1960s is maintained in a new fashion, in covert, institutional, and apparently nonracial ways (Bobo et al., 1997; Bonilla-Silva and Lewis, 1999; Jackman, 1994, 1996; Kovel, 1984; Smith, 1995; Wellman, 1977).

In consonance with this new structure, various analysts have pointed out that a new racial ideology has emerged that, in contrast to the Jim Crow racism or the ideology of the color line (Johnson, 1943, 1946; Myrdal, 1944), avoids direct racial discourse but effectively safeguards racial privilege (Bobo et al., 1997; Bonilla-Silva and Lewis, 1999; Essed, 1996; Jackman, 1994; Kovel, 1984). That ideology also shapes the very nature and style of contemporary racial discussions. In fact, in the post civil rights era, overt discussions of racial issues have become so taboo that it has become extremely difficult to assess racial attitudes and behavior using conventional research strategies (Myers, 1993; Van Dijk, 1984, 1987, 1997). Although we agree with those who suggest that there has been a normative change in terms of what is appropriate racial discourse and even racial etiquette (Schuman et al., 1988), we disagree with their interpretation of its meaning. Whereas they suggest that there is a 'mixture of progress and resistance, certainty and ambivalence, striking movement and mere surface change' (p. 212), we believe (1) that there has been a rearticulation of the dominant racial themes (less *overt* expression of racial resentment about issues anchored in the Jim Crow era such as strict racial segregation in schools, neighborhoods, and social life in general, and more resentment on new issues such as affirmative action, government intervention, and welfare) and (2) that a new way of talking about racial issues in public venues—a new *racetalk*—has emerged. Nonetheless, the new racial ideology continues to help in the reproduction of White supremacy.

Notwithstanding that the study of ideology is related to the examination of Whites' attitudes, it is not the same. Uncovering ideology involves finding common *interpretive repertoires*[3] (Potter and Wetherell, 1987; Wetherell and Potter, 1992), story lines or argumentation schemata (Van Dijk, 1984, 1987), thematics, and construction of the self. Consequently, although we highlight variance among our respondents—specific ways in which respondents mobilized arguments—we focus more intensely on tracking their *global* ideological views. Although we recognize that individual modalities in people's accounts matter (Billig et al., 1988; Potter and Wetherell, 1987), our conceptual premise is group-rather than individual-centered. Thus our main concern in this chapter is tracking White college students' interpretive repertoires on racial matters as expressed during in-depth interviews and comparing them to their views as expressed in responses to survey items. We do this in order to demonstrate that the survey research paradox of contemporary White views on race is not a paradox after all.

Research Design

The 1997 Social Attitudes of College Students Survey was a sample of undergraduate students at four universities. One school was located in the south, another in the midwest, and two were located in the west. Data collection occurred during the spring of 1997. All students surveyed were enrolled in social science courses. The questionnaire was administered during a class period. Students were informed that participation in the study was voluntary. Fewer than 10 percent declined to participate and a total of 732 students completed the survey. There were no significant differences on demographic characteristics between students who chose to participate and those that did not. All of the analyses reported in this chapter use only White respondents ($N = 541$). The sample sizes of other racial groups are too small for reliable statistical comparison. The remaining 191 respondents were self-identified as Asian ($N = 73$), Black ($N = 61$), Latino ($N = 34$), Native American ($N = 6$), other ($N = 14$), and no racial self-identification ($N = 3$). The questionnaire included both traditional and contemporary questions on racial attitudes that were previously used in national surveys (e.g. General Social Survey, National Election Study, and Gallup). It also included several questions on affirmative action, housing integration, and other race-related policy questions in which respondents were asked to choose an answer from a close-ended question and provide a brief explanation of their answer. Although the survey instrument was somewhat long (20 pages), the completion rate was 90 percent.

We conducted in-depth interviews with a random sample of the White college students that had completed the survey because prior research has found differences in Whites' racial attitudes depending on mode of data collection (Dovidio and Gaertner, 1986; Dovidio et al., 1989; Groves, Fultz et al., 1992; Krysan, 1998; Sigall and Page, 1971). We were able to interview students at only three of the four universities, which reduced the White student sample size to 451. However, we were able to maintain the regional diversity of the larger survey study because the university that we were unable to conduct in-depth interviews was one of two located in the west. In order to facilitate our selection of respondents for the in-depth interviews, we asked each respondent surveyed to provide on the first page of the survey their name, telephone, and e-mail address. After the students were chosen the page was discarded. Over 80 percent of the 451 White college students who completed the survey at the three universities provided contact information. There were no significant differences between students that provided contact information and the 20 percent who did not on either several racial attitude items or demographic characteristics. We randomly selected 41 White college students (approximately 10%) who had completed the survey and provided contact information. Interviews were conducted during the spring of 1997. In order to minimize race of interviewer effects (see Anderson et al., 1988a, 1988b), the interviews were conducted by three White graduate students and two White advanced undergraduate students. Whenever possible, we also matched respondents by gender (Kane and Macaulay, 1993). The interviews were conducted using an interview guide that addressed several issues explored in the survey instrument. The time of interviews ranged from 1 to 2.5 hours. The present study draws more extensively on the in-depth interview data, addressing White college students' general and specific racial attitudes, social distance preferences, and reported interactions with racial minorities.

Although this study is a convenience sample of undergraduate students and we are well aware of its limitations, we think it provides an important opportunity to examine a paradox in contemporary racial attitudes. That is, why Whites seem more tolerant in survey research than they do in interviews. Furthermore, whereas most studies that have used in-depth interviews to examine White racial attitudes have relied on lower social class White adults, we examine higher social class young adults. Given the importance of young adults in the changing racial attitude landscape it seems important to focus on them. Second, it is important to find out whether or not the racialist views of Whites expressed in interviews are an artifact of the method or because the focus has been on interviewing lower SES Whites. Here we attempt to fill a void by focusing on the young and generally higher SES Whites since these undergraduate students are probably more liberal than the total White adult population on issues related to race. Yet, there are two reasons to be less concerned about the type of sample that we have. First, since the sample is of college students taking social science courses, the expectation, based on previous work, is that they should exhibit less racist views than other segments of the population (Adorno et al., 1950; Allport, 1954; Bobo and Licari, 1989; Jackman, 1978). For example, if the students—educated and mostly middle-class—seem prejudiced, then our results are most likely underestimates of the true nature of the racial views of the entire white population. Furthermore, if the survey and interview results differ significantly, then our data cast a reasonable doubt on the almost exclusive reliance on surveys as the instruments for examining people's racial views. Thus, although we cannot make any strong generalizations on the White population based on this sample, this research design allows us to make (1) a preliminary comment about the nature of contemporary White college students' racial attitudes and (2) a reasonable assessment of the interview method as a way of obtaining more valid data on Whites' racial attitudes.

Toward an Analysis of Contemporary White Ideology

White College Students' Views: Survey Results

Table 1 shows the responses of White students to questions on affirmative action. The table provides results on the total sample (the three universities) as well as on the 41 students selected for the interviews. A number of things are clear from these data. First, the interview sample mirrors the total sample, something that holds for all the tables.[4] If anything, the interview respondents are slightly more likely to support affirmative action measures. Second, Whites seem to openly oppose or have serious reservations about these programs, regardless of how the question is worded. These findings are quite consistent with previous research on Whites' attitudes toward affirmative action (Kluegel, 1990; Kluegel and Smith, 1986; Lipset, 1996; Schuman and Steeh, 1996; Steeh and Krysan, 1996). For example, 65 percent of White respondents disagree with occasionally providing special consideration to Black job seekers, 51 percent are against and 36 percent are 'not sure' about reserving openings for Black students in colleges and universities, and 36 percent indicate that they would support a proposal to eliminate affirmative action in their locality. Third, most of the respondents fear the effects of affirmative action programs on their life chances. This fear is evident in the large proportion of respondents (70% or higher) who believe that it is "somewhat likely" or "very likely" that they will lose out on a job, promotion, or admission to a college due to affirmative action (see questions G1, G2, and G3). This finding is interesting because it goes against other research on affirmative action that shows that these programs have had little impact on Whites (Badgtee and Hartmann, 1995; Glass Ceiling Commission, 1995; Edley, 1996; Herring and Collins, 1995; Hochschild, 1995; Wicker, 1996). More significantly, the results are intriguing because these college students are from mostly middle-class backgrounds and are not in a vulnerable social position.

In Table 2 we show the results on social distance items. Our results in Table 2 are consistent with those of previous research. A very high proportion of Whites claim to approve of interracial marriage, friendship with Blacks, and with people of color moving into predominantly White neighborhoods (Firebaugh and Davis, 1988; Niemi et al., 1989; Schuman et al., 1988; Sniderman and Piazza, 1993). However, results based on two non-traditional measures of social distance from Blacks indicate something different. A majority of Whites (68%) state that they do not interact with any Black person on a daily basis and that they have not recently invited a Black person for lunch or dinner. Although suggestive, this finding is somewhat inconclusive since it is possible that Whites have changed their attitudes on social distance but do not have the opportunity to interact meaningfully with Blacks because of residential and school segregation (Massey and Denton, 1993; Orfield and Eaton, 1996; Wilson, 1987).

Finally, in Table 3 we display our results on Whites' beliefs about the significance of discrimination for Blacks' life chances. Interestingly, most Whites (87%) believe that discrimination affects the life chances of Blacks and approximately a third (30%) agree with the statement that "Blacks are in the position that they are because of contemporary discrimination" (for similar findings, see Lipset and Schneider, 1978). In contrast, a slight majority of White college students believe that preferences

TABLE 1

White Students' Views on Affirmative Action Items

Affirmative Action Questions	Survey sample (%) (N = 410)	Interview sample (%) (N = 41)
B21. An anti-affirmative action proposition passed by a substantial margin in California in 1996. If a similar proposition was put on the ballot in your locality, would you support it, oppose it, or would you neither oppose nor support it?		
1. Support	25.8	37.5
2. Neither Support Nor Oppose	38.3	25.0
3. Oppose	35.9	37.5
X^2		n.s.
C18. Sometimes Black job seekers should be given special consideration in hiring.		
1. Agree	13.3	17.9
2. Neither Agree Nor Disagree	21.6	17.9
3. Disagree	65.2	64.1
X^2		n.s.
G1. Affirmative Action programs for Blacks have reduced Whites' chances for jobs, promotions, and admissions to schools and training programs.		
1. Agree	50.8	36.6
2. Neither Agree Nor Disagree	26.2	17.1
3. Disagree	23.0	46.3
X^2		**
G2. What do you think are the chances these days that a White person won't get a job or a promotion while an equally or less qualified Black person gets one instead?		
1. Very Likely	11.1	17.9
2. Somewhat Likely	60.3	46.2
3. Not Very Likely	28.7	35.9
X^2		n.s.
G3. What do you think are the chances these days that a White person won't get admitted to a school while an equally or less qualified Black gets admitted instead?		
1. Very Likely	26.3	15.0
2. Somewhat Likely	52.9	60.0
3. Not Very Likely	20.8	25.0
X^2		n.s.
G4. Some people say that because of past discrimination it is sometimes necessary for colleges and universities to reserve openings for Black students. Others oppose quotas because they say quotas discriminate against Whites. What about your opinion—are you for or against quotas to admit Black students?		
1. For	12.4	22.5
2. Not Sure	36.7	27.5
3. Against	50.9	50.0
X^2		n.s.

Source: Social Attitudes of College Students Survey, 1997.
* p < .05, ** p < .01, n.s. = not significant.

TABLE 2

White Students' Views on Social Distance Items

Social Distance Questions	Survey sample (%) ($N = 410$)	Interview sample (%) ($N = 41$)
Traditional Items		
B2. If a Black family with about the same income and education as you moved next door, would you mind it a lot, a little, or not at all?		
1. Not at all	92.1	95.1
X^2		n.s.
B12. Do you approve or disapprove of marriage between Whites and Blacks?		
1. Approve	79.4	90.2
2. Not Sure	13.7	4.9
3. Disapprove	6.9	4.9
X^2		n.s.
B7. How strongly would you object if a member of your family had a friendship with a Black person?		
1. No objection	91.9	95.1
X^2		n.s.
Nontraditional Items		
A13. Think of the five people with whom you interact the most on an almost daily basis. Of these five, how many of them are Black?		
1. None	67.7	68.3
2. One	19.6	24.4
3. Two or more	12.7	7.3
X^2		n.s.
A15. Have you invited a Black person for lunch or dinner recently?		
1. No	67.8	75.0
2. Yes	32.2	25.0
X^2		n.s.

Source: Social Attitudes of College Students Survey, 1997.
* $p < .05$, ** $p < .01$, n.s. = not significant.

should not be used as a criterion for hiring (53.4% were "against") and 83 per cent of the White respondents also believe that Whites either want to give Blacks a "better break" or at least "don't care one way or the other". Again, these results are somewhat contradictory (Schuman et al., 1988). Although most White college students believe that Blacks experience discrimination and that this explains in part their contemporary status; at the same time, they believe that most Whites want to give Blacks a "better break" or "don't care one way or another" and that preferences should not play any part in hiring and promotion decisions.

Accordingly, based on these survey results, we could construct a variety of interpretations of White college students' racial attitudes. If we based our analysis on the respondents' answers to traditional questions, we would conclude, as most social scientists do, that Whites are racially tolerant. If we use all of our survey findings, we could conclude, as Schuman and his colleagues do (1988), that Whites have contradictory racial views. Finally, if we give more credence to our respondents' answers to the modern racism questions (B17, C18, E6, G1, G2, G3, and G4) and some of the new questions (A13, A15, B21) than to their answers to traditional items, we could conclude that Whites are significantly more racially prejudiced in their views than previous research has concluded. In the next section we use the 41 in-depth interviews with White students to make sense of our conflicting survey findings.

TABLE 3

White Students' Views on the Significance of Discrimination on Blacks' Life Chances

Significance of Discrimination Questions	Survey sample (%) ($N = 410$)	Interview sample (%) ($N = 41$)
B13. Do you agree or disagree with the following statement? Discrimination against Blacks is no longer a problem in the United States		
1. Agree	8.1	7.3
2. Neither Agree nor Disagree	4.9	4.9
3. Disagree	87.0	87.8
X^2		n.s.
B17. On the whole, do you think that most Whites in the USA want to see Blacks get a better break, do they want to keep Blacks down, or don't care one way or the other?		
1. Better Break	20.1	17.5
2. Don't Care One Way or the Other	62.9	65.0
3. Keep Blacks Down	17.0	17.5
X^2		n.s.
E6. Some people say that because of past discrimination against Blacks, preference in hiring and promotion should be given to Blacks. Others say preferential hiring and promotion of Blacks is wrong because it gives Blacks advantages that they haven't earned. Are you for or against preferences in hiring and promotion to Blacks?		
1. Against	54.1	47.5
2. Not Sure	38.6	47.5
3. For	7.1	5.0
X^2		n.s.
F5. Blacks are in the position that they are as a group because of contemporary discrimination.		
1. Agree	30.6	48.7
2. Neither Agree Nor Disagree	39.3	20.5
3. Disagree	30.1	30.8
X^2		*

Source: Social Attitudes of College Students Survey, 1997.
* $p < .05$, ** $p < .01$, n.s. = not significant.

White College Students' Views—In-Depth Interviews

"If Two People Love Each Other . . .": Whites' Views on Interracial Marriages

Our strategy for interpreting our interview data on intermarriage was as follows. First, we read carefully the respondents' answers to a specific question about whether or not they approved of interracial marriages. Then we examined their romantic history and what kind of friends they had throughout their lives. In some cases, we examined their views on other matters because they contained information relevant to interracial marriage. Based on the composite picture of the respondents that we obtained using this strategy, we classified them into six categories (see Table 4).

Five of the respondents (category 1) had lifestyles consistent with their views on intermarriages, 28 had reservations that ranged from serious to outright opposition (categories 3–6), and 7 claimed to approve of intermarriage but had lifestyles inconsistent with the interracial perspective that they presumably endorsed (category 2). For presentation purposes, we will provide one

TABLE 4

Views on Interracial Marriage (Total sample, $N = 40$)[1]

	Respondents % (N)
Support Interracial Marriage/Integrated Life	12.5 (5)
Support Interracial Marriage/Segregated Life	17.5 (7)
Reservations toward Interracial Marriage/Integrated Life	10.0 (4)
Reservations toward Interracial Marriage/Segregated Life	52.5 (21)
Oppose Interracial Marriage/Integrated Life	0 (0)
Oppose Interracial Marriage/Segregated Life	7.5 (3)

[1] The question was not asked of one of the students in the sample.

example of respondents in category 2 (since this was the hardest group to make sense of) and one of respondents in categories 4 (the modal category) and 6.

The first case is Ray, a student at a large midwestern university, an example of students in category 2. Ray answered the question about interracial marriage by stating that:

> I think that there's . . . *I think that interracial marriage is totally legitimate. I think if two people love each other* and *they* want to spend the rest of their lives together, I think *they* should definitely get married. And race should in no way be an inhibitive factor . . . (Interview # 150: 13)

Although Ray supports interracial marriages (despite using some *indirectness*), his life prior to college and during college was racially segregated. He grew up in a large city in the midwest, in an upper middle-class neighborhood that he characterized as "all *White*" (Interview # 150: 2) and described his friends as "what the average suburban kid is like nowadays" (Interview # 150: 3). More significantly, Ray, who was extremely articulate in the interview, stuttered remarkably in the question (asked *before* the one on intermarriage) dealing with whether or not he had ever been attracted to Blacks. His response was as follows:

> . . . Um, so, to answer that question, no. Um, but I would not . . . I mean, *I would not . . . I mean, I would not ever preclude, uh, a Black woman from being my girlfriend on the basis that she was Black.* Ya know, I mean . . . ya know what I mean? If you're looking from the standpoint of attraction, I mean, I think that, ya know . . . I think, ya know, I think, ya know, I think, ya know, all women are, I mean, all women have a sort of different type of beauty if you will. And I think that for Black women it's somewhat different than *White* women. Um, but I don't think it's, ya know, I mean, it's, it's . . . it's nothing that would ever stop me from like, uh . . . I mean, I don't know, I mean, I don't [know] if that's . . . I mean, that's just sort of been my impression. I mean, it's not like I would ever say, "no, I'll never have a Black girlfriend", *but it just seems to me like I'm not as attracted to Black women as I am to White women for whatever reason. It's not about prejudice, it's just sort of like, ya know, whatever. Just sort of the way . . . way . . . like, I see White women as compared to Black women, ya know?* (Interview # 150: 12)

As is evident from Ray's statement, he is not attracted to Black women, something that clashes with his self-proclaimed color-blind approach to love and his support for interracial marriages. More significantly, he seemed aware of how problematic that sounded and used all sorts of rhetorical strategies to save face.

The next case is an example of students who had reservations about interracial marriages who lived a primarily segregated life (category 4), the modal group in our sample. We found regularities (Brown and Yule, 1983) in the structure of their answers similar to the ones we found among those who responded "yes and no" to the affirmative action question. Their answers usually included the rhetorical moves of *apparent agreement* and *apparent admission*—a formal statement of support for interracial marriages followed or preceded by statements qualifying the support in terms of what might happen to the kids, how the relationship might affect the families, or references to how their parents would never approve of such relationships.

The next example is Sally, a student at a large midwestern university. She replied to the interracial marriage question as follows:

> *I certainly don't oppose the marriage,* not at all. Um . . . *depending on where I am, if I had to have a concern, yes, it would be for the children* . . . Ya know, it can be nasty and then other kids wouldn't even notice. I think . . . *I could care less what anyone else does with their lives, as long as they are really happy.* And if the parents can set a really strong foundation at home, it can be conquered, *but I'm sure, in some places, it could cause a problem.* (Interview # 221: 5)

Sally's answer included displacement (concerns for the children and the certainty that interracial marriages would be problematic in some places) and indirectness ("I could care less what *anyone else* does . . . as long as *they* are really happy") alongside her initial apparent admission semantic move ("I certainly don't oppose the marriage"). Sally's apprehension on this subject matched the nature of her life and her specific views on Blacks. Sally's life was, in terms of interactions, relationships, and residence, almost entirely racially segregated. When questioned about her romantic life, Sally said that she had never dated a person of color and recognized that "I've never been attracted to a Black person" and that "I never look at what they look like . . . it just hasn't occurred in my life" (Interview # 221: 5).

The final case is Eric, a student at a large midwestern university, an example of the students who openly expressed serious reservations about interracial marriages (category 6). It is significant to point out that even the three students who stated that they would not enter into these relationships, claimed that there was nothing wrong with interracial relationships per se. Below is the exchange between Eric and our interviewer on this matter.

> *Eric:*   Uh . . . (sighs) I would say that I agree with that, I guess. I mean . . . *I would say that I really don't have much of a problem with it but when you, ya know, If I were to ask if I had a daughter or something like that, or even one of my sisters, um . . . were to going to get married to a minority or a Black, I . . . I would probably . . . it would probably bother me a little bit* just because of what you said . . . Like the children and how it would . . . might do to our family as it is. Um . . . so I mean, just being honest, I guess that's the way I feel about that.
>
> *Int.:*   What would, specifically, if you can, is it . . . would it be the children? And, if it's the children, what would be the problem with, um . . . uh . . . adjustment, or
>
> *Eric:*   For the children, yeah, I think it would just be . . . I guess, through my experience when I was younger and growing up and just . . . ya know, those kids were different. Ya know, they were, as a kid, I guess you don't think much about why kids are different or anything, you just kind of see that they are different and treat them differently. Ya know, because you're not smart enough to think about it, I guess. And the, the other thing is . . . *I don't know how it might cause problems within our family if it happened within our family, ya know, just . . . from people's different opinions on something like that. I just don't think it would be a healthy thing for my family. I really can't talk about other people.*
>
> *Int.:*   But would you feel comfortable with it pretty much?
>
> *Eric:*   Yeah. Yeah, that's the way I think, especially, um . . . ya know, *grandparents of things like that. Um, right or wrong, I think that's what would happen.* (Interview # 248: 10)

Eric used the *apparent admission* semantic move ("I would say that I agree with that") in his reply but could not camouflage very well his true feelings ("If I were to ask if I had a daughter or something like that, or even one of my sisters, um . . . were [sic] to going to get married to a minority or a Black, I . . . I would probably . . . it would probably bother me a little bit"). Interestingly, Eric claimed in the interview that he had been romantically interested in an Asian-Indian woman his first year in college. However, that interest "never turned out to be a real big [deal]" (Interview # 248: 9). Despite Eric's fleeting attraction to a person of color, his life was racially segregated: no minority friends and no meaningful interaction with any Black person.

The results in this section clash with our survey results. Whereas in the survey the students seemed to favor interracial contacts of all kinds with Blacks, the interview data suggest otherwise. Whites' serious reservations if not opposition to interracial marriages are expressed as "concerns" for the welfare of the offspring of those relationships, upsetting the family, or the reaction of the larger community to the marriage. All these statements—a number of the respondents themselves classified these arguments as excuses—seem to be rationalizations to *discursively* avoid stating opposition to interracial marriages. This is quite significant since they could easily *state* that they have no problems with intermarriage. The fact that very few do so in an unequivocal manner, gives credence to the argument that Whites' racial aversion for Blacks is deeply ingrained into their unconscious (Fanon, 1967; Hernton, 1988; Jordan, 1977; Kovel, 1984). Finally, the respondents' comments about their romantic lives and friendships clearly indicate that rather than being color-blind, they are very color conscious.

"I Kind of Support and Oppose . . .": Whites' Views on Affirmative Action

Intentionally, we did not define affirmative action in our interview protocol. We were particularly interested in how the respondents themselves defined the various programs that have emerged since the 1970s to enhance the chances of minorities getting jobs, promotions, access to institutions of higher learning, etc.[5] Although some of the students hesitated and asked for a definition of the program, to which our interviewers replied "what do you think it is?", most answered based on what they thought affirmative action meant.

Content analysis of the responses of the 41 students interviewed shows that most (85%) oppose affirmative action. This degree of opposition was somewhat higher than the results obtained in the survey. However, unlike in the survey, only a quarter (10 out of 41) came out and opposed affirmative action in a straightforward manner. In part, this may be the result of a general belief that if they express their views too openly on affirmative action, diversity, or any other race-related issue, they are going to be labeled as "racist".[6] Although we were able to detect some of this reticence through discursive analysis, many respondents expressed their concern explicitly. For instance, Bob, a student at a large southern university and who openly opposed affirmative action, said, "I oppose them [affirmative action programs], mainly because, *I am not a racist but* because I think you should have the best person for the job" (Interview # 6: 13). Mark, a student, at a large midwestern university, who said that he couldn't give a "definite answer" on affirmative action, later mentioned that companies need to diversify because "we need diversity, and if you don't have diversity, *then people call you a racist and you have to deal with all of those accusations*" (Interview # 6: 24).

Since respondents were very sensitive to not appearing "racist", most (26 out of 41) expressed their opposition to affirmative action indirectly. Brian, a student at a large southern university, responded to the affirmative action questions by saying: "Man . . . that's another one where [laughs] . . . *I kind of support and oppose it*" (Interview # 10: 8). If we had based our analysis only on the students' responses to this one question, we would have had to conclude that most Whites are truly torn apart about affirmative action, that they have "non attitudes" (see Converse, 1964, 1970, 1974), or are "ambivalent" (Katz et al., 1986). However, we included several questions in the interview schedule that dealt either directly or indirectly with affirmative action. Therefore we were able to make sense of respondents' vacillations concerning affirmative action.

In many cases, a thorough reading of the complete response to the primary affirmative action question helped us to understand that the "yes and no" responses really meant "no". For example, Brian, the student cited earlier who was seemingly ambivalent about affirmative action, went on to say, "Pretty much the same thing I said before . . . I don't know, *if I come,* I don't know, *somebody under-qualified shouldn't get chosen,* you know?" (Interview # 6: 8). After being probed about whether he thought that what he had just described was an example of reverse discrimination, Brian replied, "Um, pretty much, I mean, yeah".

Furthermore, Brian's response to a specific question asking if he supported a program to give minorities unique opportunities in education suggests that his hesitations and his *topic avoidance by claiming ignorance* and *ambivalence* ("I don't know" and "I am not sure") in the earlier quote were just semantic moves that allowed him to voice safely his opposition to affirmative action ("somebody under-qualified shouldn't get chosen") (see Van Dijk, 1984: 109, 131–2). Brian's response to a question about providing unique educational opportunities to minorities was the following:

> *Brian:* Um . . . mmm, that's a tough one. *I don't, you mean, unique opportunities, as far as, just because you are, they are that race, like quotas type of thing or . . .*
>
> *Int.:* Well, why don't you stipulate the kind of program that you would support and where your limits might be for that.
>
> *Brian:* All right . . . Um . . . mmm, let's see, uh . . . I, I don't know (laughs), *I am not sure about like, the problem is like, I don't know, like, 'cause I don't think race should come into like the picture at all, like I don't think they should be given unique opportunities . . .* (Interview # 10: 8)

In Brian's case as well as in many of the other cases where students apparently wavered on affirmative action, we looked at their responses to questions dealing with job-related cases at the fictitious ABZ company.[7] Brian's answers to these questions clearly indicate that he believes that programs that give *any* additional opportunities to minorities to compensate for past and present discrimination amount to reverse discrimination. For instance, Brian's response to the first scenario included the displacement semantic move, "It seems like *the White guy* might be a little upset", although at the end of his statement he resorted to apparent admission by saying, "I guess I don't have a problem with it". Moments later, when probed about how he would respond to someone who characterized the company's decision as reverse racism, Brian said that "I would say, *yeah, it is*" (Interview # 6: 9).

Mark, the student cited earlier, stated his position on affirmative action as follows:

> *Yes and no.* This is probably the toughest thing I have deciding. I really . . . cuz I've thought about this a lot, but I can make a pro-con list and I still wouldn't like . . . I've heard most of the issues on this subject, and *I honestly couldn't give a definite answer.* (Interview # 6: 21)

Mark's response is illustrative of the classic apparent ambivalence of our respondents on this issue. However, later on, after recognizing that minorities do not have similar opportunities because they start "from so much lower" and even suggesting that they "should be granted some additional opportunities", Mark complained, using the displacement semantic, move that "most people [who] disagree with affirmative action think that the programs raise them to a higher level than they deserve to be at" (Interview # 6: 22). What he said immediately after reveals that Mark is actually against affirmative action.

> . . . *I don't know what I think about this.* I mean, yeah, I think affirmative action programs are . . . needed. But . . . I don't know. Because, I mean, *I'm gonna be going out for a job next year, and I'll be honest, I'd be upset if I'm just as qualified as someone else. And individually, I'd be upset if a company takes, you know, like an African American over me just because he is an African American.* I think that would—ya know? I wouldn't. (Interview # 6: 22)

Mark also did not support providing unique educational opportunities for minorities. When asked about whether he would support hiring an equally qualified (equal results in a test) Black candidate over a White at the ABZ company, he said: "If I'm that person, I'm not gonna support it. If I'm the majority getting rejected just because I'm a different race" (Interview # 6: 24).

The final case is Rachel, a student at a large midwestern university, who used the *topic avoidance by claiming ambivalence* move in her response to the direct affirmative action question.

> Um . . . affirmative action programs? Um . . . like I was saying, *I think . . . uh . . . I don't know if I do because . . . I don't I mean, I think they established it was just to make up for the 200 and some years of slavery. And . . . umm . . . it's just trying to, like, for us, just trying to make up for the past.* And, uh . . . on the Blacks', on that end, I feel that they are kind of . . . I would feel . . . bad, ya know because, oh, I . . . *I am getting in because the color of my skin, not because of my merits. And I'd feel kind of inferior, ya know, like, I'd feel that the whole affirmative action system would inferiorize (sic) me.* Just because . . . maybe I'll get a better placement in a school just because . . . the color of my skin. *I don't know.* (Interview # 276: 16)

Rachel mentioned in her response to a question on affirmative action in college admissions that people who are in colleges (Whites) "have *worked hard* to get where they are" and added:

> . . . I think . . . *the people who are in . . .* the opportunities have *worked hard* to get where they are. And they haven't just *slacked off* or anything. And they would be sad to see if somebody who's worked *really hard* to be where they are today and . . . ya know . . . just because *they, these people* are . . . ya know, not necessarily privileged, um . . . ya know, *get in ahead of you,* and maybe have done *half as much of what you have done in your lifetime.* I don't know. (Interview # 276: 15)

Rachel also did not support any of the affirmative action hiring decisions of the hypothetical ABZ company.

The student's comments on affirmative action in interviews suggest that there is even more opposition to affirmative action than our survey results indicate. Also, the opposition to affirmative action of our respondents seems to be related to racial prejudice. However, we recognize that many survey analysts doubt this interpretation and suggest that Whites' opposition to these programs is 'political', 'ideological', or that it expresses 'value duality' (Katz et al., 1986; Kluegel and Smith, 1986; Lipset, 1996; Sniderman and Piazza, 1993) Thus, to strengthen our case, we add another piece of information. In the elaboration of their arguments against affirmative action, 27 of the 41 respondents used spontaneously one of two story-lines or argumentation schemata (Van Dijk, 1984, 1987). The fact that so many of the respondents used the same 'stories' underscores the fact that Whites seem to have a shared cognition and that these stories have become part of the ideological racial repertoire about how the world is and ought to be. The two stories were "The past is the past" and "Present generations cannot be blamed for the mistakes of past generations" and were mobilized as justification for not doing anything about the effects of past and contemporary discrimination.

We present one example to illustrate how these stories were mobilized. The example is Sally, a student at a large midwestern university, who answered the question about whether or not Blacks should be compensated for the history of oppression that they have endured by saying:

> Absolutely no. How long are you gonna rely on it? I had nothing to do with it . . . I think it's turning into a crutch that they're getting to fall back on their histories . . . I just think that every individual should do it for themselves and achieve for themselves. (Interview # 221: 10)

Sally's angry tone in this answer saturated all her responses to the affirmative action questions. For instance, she stated in her response to another question that minorities feel like 'supervictims' and asked rhetorically, inspired by the arguments from Shelby Steele that she learned in her sociology course, "For how long are you gonna be able to rely on an oppressed history of your ancestors?" (Interview # 221: 11–12).

"I Believe That They Believe . . .": White Beliefs about Contemporary Discrimination against Blacks

We asked the subjects to define racism for us and then followed up with five related questions.[8] The students that we interviewed defined racism as "prejudice based on race", "a feeling of racial superiority", "very stupid . . . lots of ignorance", "psychological war", "hating people because of their skin color", and "the belief that one race is superior to the other". Only five of the subjects mentioned or implied that racism was societal, institutional, or structural, and of these only two truly believed that racism is part and parcel of American society. More importantly, very few of the subjects described this country as "racist" or suggested that minorities face systemic disadvantages, in this or in any other part of the interviews. Thus, Whites primarily think that racism is a belief that a few individuals hold and which might lead them to discriminate against some people.

Notwithstanding these findings, it is important to explore Whites' beliefs about the prevalence of discrimination against minorities and about how much it affects the life chances of minorities in the USA. Our analysis revealed that most of the subjects (35 out of 41) expressed serious doubts about whether discrimination affects minorities in a significant way. As in the cases of their responses to the affirmation action and intermarriage questions, very few respondents (14%) who expressed doubts about the significance of discrimination did so consistently in all the questions.

In the following, we provide an example of respondents who hesitated in a serious manner and another who denied explicitly and without discursive reservations that discrimination affects significantly the life chances of minorities. In general, the first group of respondents used *expressives* (Taylor and Cameron, 1987)—utterances where the speaker makes known her or his attitudes to the hearer. The students provided several examples, suggesting that minorities use racism as an excuse, that discrimination works against Whites nowadays, that discrimination is not such an important factor in the USA, and that other factors such as motivation, values, or credentials may account for Blacks' lack of mobility.

The first case is Emily, a student at a large midwestern university, and one of the 30 students who hesitated in expressing her doubts about the significance of discrimination for Blacks' life chances. She used the 'topic avoidance by claiming ignorance' semantic move to state her views.

> *I personally don't see that much racism happening, but I am White,* so maybe I don't see it that much because I never experience it myself. And there could be, *but as far as I know, I don't understand that there is really . . . There is some, but not as much as there used to be in the past.* (Interview # 339: 14)

Sixteen of the respondents used this move in answering the discrimination questions. Specifically, the respondents claimed that they could not answer because they were not Black. Although this seems like a legitimate answer, since the respondents are not Black and do not associate with Blacks often, the fact that they still answered the question and provided racially charged answers suggests that their statements were in fact semantic moves. Obviously, Emily does not believe that discrimination is an important factor affecting minorities' life chances ("there is some but not as much . . .") but, by adding the qualifying statement that because she is White she may not "see [discrimination] that much because I never experience it myself", the racial character of her doubts is concealed. Emily used the same strategy of adding some qualification in her responses to the other questions on discrimination. Accordingly, when explaining her view on the claim that some minorities have about the significance of discrimination in jobs and promotions, Emily replied, "I think *maybe some companies might do that.* But I think, generally, that they have equal opportunities in jobs, I think". In her response to the question about whether discrimination was the reason for the overall status of Blacks in this country, Emily said "I don't really think it's due to discrimination" but added that:

> I think that maybe that in the past that they were treated badly, and it is . . . I don't know. Like that they're, I don't know, maybe that their families have, like for a long time been poor, and they really don't like, see how they could get out of it. Like they don't really know about, like, opportunities they might have to better themselves. I mean, they just, they maybe, I don't know, just try to go day by day, and maybe they don't realize that they could be doing better things for themselves. . . . *But I don't really think that's because . . . I mean, maybe it was racism in the past that kinda kept it the way it is, but maybe . . . I think it seems to be getting better now.* (Interview # 339: 14)

Finally, when asked why she thought so few minorities are at the top of the occupational structure, Emily stated indecisively:

> I think it's because they don't have enough money for that. Maybe, I don't know. Just that *those jobs were for White people,* I think. And that they . . . most of the people that are in those jobs are White, and *they don't know, feel that they can really,* I don't know . . . I really, don't know what to say. (Interview # 339: 15)

Immediately after this answer the interviewer probed Emily since, despite her qualifications, she seemed to be saying that the best jobs in the economy are reserved for rich *White* people. However, in the follow-up questions, Emily restated that the best jobs go to people that "have more money" and that White employers "may be *sometimes* discriminatory, but I don't think it happens on a very large scale" (Interview # 339: 15).

If Whites such as Emily do not understand or appreciate how race matters for minorities in the USA and yet hear them complaining about discrimination, then the obvious next step is to regard minorities' complaints as whining, excuses, or untrue (Hochschild, 1995). This specific charge was made directly by 14 of the respondents. For example, Kara, a student at a large midwestern university, denied explicitly and without discursive reservations that discrimination affects significantly the life chances of minorities, in her answer to the first question on discrimination:

> *Int.:* Some Black people claim that they face a great deal of racism in their daily lives, and a lot of other people claim that that's not the case. What do you think?
>
> *Kara:* I would think, presently speaking, like people in my generation, I don't think it's . . . as much that there is racism that, *but Black people almost go into their experiences feeling like they should be discriminated against and I think that makes them hypersensitive.* (Interview. # 251: 13)

Kara went on to say that she believes that Blacks receive preferential treatment in admissions or, in her words "being Black, if you just look at applying to graduate schools or things, that's a big part". To the question of why she thinks Blacks have worse jobs, income, and housing than Whites she replied:

> . . . part of me wants to say like work ethic, but I don't know if that is being fair . . . I just don't know, I think that if you look at the inner city, you can definitely see they're just stuck, like those people cannot really get out . . . like in the suburbs . . . I don't know why that would be. I mean, I am sure they are discriminated against but . . . (Interview # 251: 13)

Immediately after, Kara answered the question about whether or not Blacks are lazy by saying that:

> *I think, to some extent, that's true.* Just from like looking at the Black people that I've met in my classes and the few I knew before college that . . . not like they're—*I don't want to say waiting for a handout, but [to] some extent, that's kind of what I am hinting at.* Like almost like they feel like they were discriminated against hundreds of years ago, now what are you gonna give me? Ya know, or maybe even it's just their background, that they've never, like maybe they're first generation to be in college so they feel like, just that is enough for them. (Interview # 251: 14)

Although some Whites acknowledge that minorities experience discrimination or racism, they still complain about reverse racism, affirmative action, and a number of other racially perceived policies. This occurs in part because in their view, racism is a phenomenon that affects few minorities or affects them in minor ways, and thus has little impact on the life chances of minorities, in particular, and American society more generally. For many Whites, racism is a matter of a few rotten apples such as David Duke, Mark Fuhrman, and the policemen who beat Rodney King rather than a 'system of social relations in which Whites typically have more access to the means of power, wealth, and esteem than Blacks [and other minorities]' (Hartman and Husband, 1974: 48). Furthermore, Whites either do not understand or do not believe the new institutional, subtle, and apparently non-racial character of the American racial structure (Bonilla-Silva and Lewis, 1999; Carmichael and Hamilton, 1967; Hochschild, 1995; Jackman, 1994; Smith, 1995). These two factors combined may explain why Whites regard the complaints of minorities about discrimination as exaggerations or excuses. If Whites 'don't see' discrimination and do not understand the systemic racial character of our society (Kluegel and Smith, 1982, 1986), then they must interpret minorities' claims of discrimination as false (Essed, 1996) and blame minorities for their lower socioeconomic status (Kluegel, 1990).

Color-Blind Racism: Toward an Analysis of White College Students' Collective Representations in the USA

In the previous sections we demonstrated that White students use a number of rhetorical strategies that allow them to safely voice racial views that might be otherwise interpreted as racist. In this section, we examine whether or not what students were saying through the rhetorical maze of "I don't know", "I am not sure", and "I am not a racist, but" fits the themes of color blind racism, the dominant racial ideology in the post-civil rights era (Bonilla-Silva, 1998). In our analysis we assume, as discourse analysts do, that people use language (talk) to construct *versions* of the social world (Wetherell and Potter, 1987). However, unlike conversational analysts (Psathas, 1995), we strive to unravel the ideological stance of interlocutors, that is, to see where people *fit* in the larger racial ideological battlefield of a social formation (Van Dijk, 1998; for a full elaboration of the notion of racial ideology, see Bonilla-Silva, 1998). As Billig (1991) has argued, opinion expressing is argumentative and thus persuasive; actors 'take sides' in social controversies and use arguments to make their opinions believable and reasonable.

The Central Themes of Color-Blind Racism

In recent work, Bobo and his coauthors (Bobo and Kluegel, 1997, Bobo et al., 1997) have labeled post civil rights racial ideology as 'laissez faire racism'. Laissez faire racism, unlike Jim Crow

TABLE 5

Central Elements of Dominant and Alternative Contemporary Racial Interpretive Repertoires in the USA

Dominant Framework (Color-Blind Ideology)	Alternative Frameworks (Cultural Pluralism, Nationalism, & Others)
1. *Abstract* and *decontextualized* notions of liberalism (e.g. "Race should not be a factor when judging people")	*Concrete and contextualized* notions of liberalism or more radical egalitarian theories for distributing social goods
2. *Cultural* rationale for explaining the status of racial subjects in society (e.g. "Blacks are *lazy*" or "Blacks lack the proper *work ethic*")	*Political* rationale for explaining the status of racial subjects in society (e.g. "Blacks have been left behind by the system")
3. Avoidance of racist language and direct racial references in explaining racially based or racially perceived issues such as affirmative action, school busing, or interracial dating. (Note: Color-blinders utilize indirect subtle and racially coded words to talk about racial matters)	
4. *Naturalization* of matters that reflect the effects arguments (e.g. explaining segregation or limited interracial marriage as a natural outcome)	Explanation of race-related issues with race-related of White supremacy (e.g. segregation as the product of the racialized actions of the state, realtors, and individual Whites)
5. Denial of *structural* character of 'racism' and discrimination viewed as limited, sporadic, and declining in significance	Understanding racism as 'societal' and recognition of new forms of discrimination
6. Invoke the *free-market* or *laissez faire* ideology thus to justify contemporary racial inequality (e.g. "Kids should be exposed to all kinds of cultures but it cannot be imposed on them through busing")	Recognition that 'market' outcomes have a racial bent and support of special programs to ameliorate racial inequities

racism, is 'an ideology that blames Blacks themselves for their poorer relative economic standing, seeing it as a function of perceived cultural inferiority' (Bobo and Kluegel, 1997: 95). Other social analysts have pointed out that post civil rights racial hostility is 'muted' (Jackman, 1994) or is expressed as 'resentment' (Kinder and Sanders, 1996). We argue that post civil rights racial ideology should be called *color-blind racism* since the notion of color blindness is the global justification Whites use to defend the racial status quo. Table 5 presents the central elements of color-blind racism and of alternative racial ideologies (Bonilla-Silva, 1998; Crenshaw, 1996; Essed, 1996; Jackman, 1994; Kovel, 1984).

Since a detailed discourse analysis of the 41 interviews is beyond the scope of this paper, we analyze two cases in each section below (one typical student and one dissenter per section for a total of four cases). Although there are many possible discourse categories for dissecting texts (see Van Dijk, 1998), we chose to emphasize two central matters. First, we examined whether or not the White respondents created a *discourse of difference* about racial minorities (Wodak, 1996). This discourse of difference as Wodak suggests (1996, 1997), is articulated by Whites by presenting the 'other' (in the USA, racial minorities) as different, deviant, or as a threat. We also examined the strategies of group definition and construction (we-they) used by the students as central to the construction of 'other' and 'same'. Second, following Billig and his co-authors (1988), Van Dijk (1997), and Potter and Wetherell (1987), we examined whether racial inequality was rationalized in a 'pragmatic' way when the ideology of liberalism did not fit some specific situations. Specifically, we checked for argumentative strategies of *Apparent Sympathy, Justification: The Force of Facts, Reversal* (blaming the victim), and *Fairness.*[9]

"They Are" and "We Are": Otherizing Talk among Students

If the USA had truly achieved the color blind dream of Martin Luther King, Whites would not see Blackness as otherness, as difference that entails inferiority. However, in interview after interview, White students constructed a 'we-they' dichotomy of Blacks and Whites.

For instance, Bob, a student at a southern university from a working-class background, argued that Blacks have a different culture than Whites. He states:

> I think it's true. Um, I think that Blacks have a lot stronger sense of family. Well at least from my own um I always hear about my friends going to family picnics and going to the park and stuff and church, um. My parents, um, I know I have over thirty cousins, and I know like three of them. So I, I think, I think it has to do with family values. (Interview # 6: 8)

Although Bob seems to have positive valuation of Blacks' culture, his next comment suggests otherwise. Bob's answer to the question, "Do you think the origins of these differences, are they natural, cultural, environmental?" was the following:

> I think it's cultural, they way they were raised, the way their parents were raised. My parents worked, my grandparents worked, so they didn't have a lot of strong family outings and gatherings, like Easter, stuff like that, that's about it, um . . . that's what I think. (Interview # 6: 8)

As evident from this statement, Bob's apparently positive evaluation of the family life of Blacks is tied to his belief that Blacks do not work. Hence, he believes that, unlike Whites, Blacks have time to concentrate on family matters. This interpretation of Bob's views was confirmed by Bob himself later on in the interview in his response to a question dealing with why Blacks have worse jobs, income, and housing than Whites. After pointing out that discrimination "may play a factor", Bob added that there were other factors. We cite him at length because his answer clearly illustrates his negative views on Blacks' culture.

> Like . . . motivation, uh, family values . . . Here I, I know I argued a minute ago that they have stronger family values but I know a lot of my [minority] friends didn't have fathers, and they don't have . . . Their mothers were gone all the time, so they'd stay out and play all day. If they wanted something, they'd go out and steal it. Um, they don't have the money to have a lawn mower, so they can't mow yards like I did. And granted, I didn't even have to do that. I mean, my parents wouldn't give me things I asked, but if I really needed something, I'd get it. Um, if I, they'd let me work it off but these kids, they couldn't do that, so they'd get stuck in a rut, they'd start making minimum wage, they get a girlfriend, get her pregnant and they get stuck stuck in a big ongoing cycle, a big circle, and their kids, and their kids, like that. Um whereas like immigrants, like say . . . Jewish people, came over this country and had, you know, they, it was like in their heads that they were going to do better. And that's why I think nowadays they own a lot of things. People who were persecuted against in other countries come here and do *real* well, but if you're here all along, well, for a long time, you get used to how you are . . . (Interview # 6: 9)

Here Bob clearly states his belief that Blacks' family values are *inferior* to those of Whites. Black families are described as pathological, Black children as out of control, and Blacks in general as lacking the work ethic. In contrast, Bob views Whites as people who are entrepreneurial (mow yards even though they don't really need that extra money), can control their impulses (Blacks get their girlfriends "pregnant" and "get stuck in a rut"), and fight against all odds to overcome life's obstacles (White immigrants struggled but were able to overcome).

Although based on our analysis of the students' responses to the interview questions on affirmative action, interracial marriage, and the significance of discrimination for Blacks' life chances, most students were not racially tolerant (36 out of 41), we classified five of them as racial progressives. These racial progressives did not subscribe to the 'we-they' dichotomy, were more likely to find problems with the way in which Whites see Blacks, and were more understanding of the significance of discrimination in society. These students formulated their positions from alternative racial ideological frameworks (see Table 5). For instance, Lynn, a student at a large midwestern university from a lower middle-class background who grew up in a small town, began her interview by acknowledging that her community was very racist. She said that her village was a "hick town" and that "there was a lot of stereotypes" (Interview # 196: 1). Whereas most White students felt quite comfortable with their segregated neighborhoods and did not even realize that they were segregated, racial progressives such as Lynn disliked the lack of diversity in their communities. In Lynn's words:

> Um, I actually disliked it a lot because there was a lot of, . . . um a lot of racist people and it was nothing for my friends to make very racist remarks . . . especially because they didn't know anybody of any other race, so it didn't bother them. And they were feeding off the stereotypes . . . that were really negative. (Interview # 196: 2)

Lynn also recognized that discrimination is central in explaining Blacks' status in the USA. For example, Lynn's response to a question on why there are so few minorities at the top of the occupational structure was the following:

> Uh, discrimination. Um . . . just cuz they've had to come back from slavery and everything, and . . . they're not fully integrated into . . . ya know . . . they just still aren't accepted. A lot of the old views are there. (Interview # 196: 10)

More significantly, although most Whites recognized that there are "racists out there", racial progressives such as Lynn were more likely to acknowledge that they themselves had problems. Lynn's response to a question on dealing with Blacks' claim that they face a great deal of racism in their daily lives elicited the following response:

> I would say . . . I'd say yeah, they do, probably. Um . . . just, um, like I know . . . I do this, I've been trained to do this. Like, when I walk down the street at night . . . by myself, and I meet a White guy on the street, I'm not as scared as if I meet a Black guy on the street. I keep telling myself that's stupid, but . . . that's how I've been trained. I mean just little things like that. I mean, I don't think they're like discriminating, I guess, on a large scale every single day, but . . . yeah, in little ways like that. (Interview # 196: 9)

Although we believe that White progressives *tended* to formulate their views from an alternative racial ideology, they were not totally free from the influence of the dominant racial ideology. For instance, Lynn, who had agreed with the decision of a hypothetical ABZ company to hire an equally qualified Black applicant over a White to increase diversity "because obviously if they're 97 percent White . . . they've probably been discriminating in the past" (Interview # 196: 12), opposed hiring the Black candidate when the justification was that the ABZ company had discriminated in the past. Using a variety of semantic moves to shield her from being perceived as prejudiced, she stated:

> I think I'd disagree because, I mean, even though it's kinda what affirmative action . . . well, it's not really, because . . . um . . . I don't think like . . . my generation should have to . . . I mean, in a way, we should, but we shouldn't be . . . punished really harshly for the things that our ancestors did, on the one hand. But on the other hand, I think that . . . how we should try and change the way we do things. So we aren't doing the same things that our ancestors did. (Interview # 196: 14)

Furthermore, although Lynn had stated that she supported affirmative action because "the White male is pretty instilled . . . very much still represses . . . um, people and other minorities" (Interview # 196: 12), she vented anger toward the program and even said that if she was involved in an affirmative action type of situation, "it would anger me . . . I mean, because, ya know, *I* as an individual got . . . ya know, ripped off and, ya know, getting a job . . . even though, even if I thought I was more qualified" (Interview # 196: 14–15). Finally, although she expressed concern about the lack of diversity in the village where she grew up, had taken classes with racial minorities while at university, and had even reported having had Black acquaintances in her first year in college, all her primary associations at the time of the interview were with Whites.

The Reasonable Racist: Liberal and Pragmatic Justifications for the Racial Status Quo

In the postmodern world not even members of the KKK want to be called racist (Berbrier, 1998). Yet, most Whites support equal opportunity, but are against affirmative action. They believe in residential and school integration, but oppose government intervention to guarantee it. They approve of interracial marriage, but qualify their support. These dilemmas (Billig, 1988) become mute as Whites find justifications to exhibit prejudicial views or support positions that maintain White privilege. Whites talk as 'reasonable racists' (Billig et al., 1988) or 'reasonable negrophobes' (Armour, 1997) and argue, using elements of liberal humanism combined with the pragmatism of free market ideologues, that little can be done to change the racial status quo.

One set of questions that elicited a lot of 'reasonable racism' concerned the hypothetical ABZ company. For instance, Sue, a student at a large southern university self-described as middle class, expressed her support toward affirmative action—albeit in a very hesitant way—in the direct question on the issue as follows:

> Um . . . affirmative action programs are programs that help the minorities? I guess I support them . . . because I think they're necessary. (Interview # 1: 9)

However, in her response to the practical questions on affirmative action (the ABZ company), she strongly disagreed with the program using *reversal* and *fairness*.

> Um, I think A, that I mean, they are being biased with like who they're gonna, who they're gonna hire just because of their race or whatever. But they do have, I mean, they do both have the same score, so I mean, I think that that would be OK to hire the Black person or whatever. But for B, I think that that would be reverse discrimination or whatever. They should not hire the person just because of their race or whatever because the White person has scored higher on that entrance thing or whatever, entrance test. [And what about case C . . . what if now they are doing it because they've discriminated in the past?] Um . . . I still think that, you know, for both of those that it still applies because you shouldn't hire someone because of their race, and that would still be reverse discrimination. (Interview # 1: 10)

Sue's opposition to the ABZ company's hiring decisions in cases B and C—again, a company that we described as 97 percent White—were framed as a matter of *fairness*. When she was pushed by our interviewer to explain the lack of diversity in the company, Sue replied:

> Um . . . I don't really . . . I mean, if they have . . . I don't see it as, yeah, sure, they might not be diverse because of the different races they have or whatever but I mean, if they're fair in who they hire and whatever, and they're giving equal opportunity to people to apply then I don't see problem. (Interview # 1: 10)

Sue, as most White students, had a *formal* and *abstract* view on fairness and equality which allowed her to defend all sorts of *substantively* unfair and unequal situations such as a company being 97 percent White. A more telling case was her view on school integration. Sue, who had attended an 'integrated' school (she acknowledged that because of tracking she basically had a White experience in her school) and claimed that integration was a good thing, opposed busing to achieve school integration. In her words:

> Um, like I said, I don't think that you should, you know, I don't think that it may be necessary to bus them miles and miles and miles away and so they have a two hour bus ride every day just to go to school. I mean, they should be provided with an equal education in the areas around them. (Interview # 1: 9)

Sue's argument here, framed as *apparent sympathy* and *force of facts* (they live far from us so busing makes no sense), amounts to a modern version of the 'separate but equal' argument.

> If they're as qualified as everybody else. If they're . . . if their credentials are lower and they're only letting him in because of his race . . . no. Because they could have taken the opportunity when they were in school to do better, and they didn't choose to take the opportunity. (Interview # 7: 8)

In contrast to the arguments used by the reasonable racists to justify the racial status quo, the racial progressives argued that discrimination was widespread, contextualized their answers, and, generally speaking, were sympathetic to state intervention to remedy the effects of past and contemporary discrimination. For example, Mandy, a student at a large western university from a working-class background, recognized the "we-they" discursive strategy of Whites. In her response to the question on whether there are fundamental differences between the races, she said that there are cultural differences "but those differences aren't negative . . . differences doesn't mean that there's anything wrong" (Interview # 504: 8). However, she recognized later on in the interview that her peers in high school believed that Blacks were inferior compared to Whites: "If they thought about Black people, they'd say 'All gangs. Nothing's [good]'. They are all gang members there and all the women are teenage mothers on welfare . . ." (Interview # 504: 9).

Mandy's description of her high school peers' views on Blacks matches what most White students in our sample said about Blacks.

Mandy, unlike most White students, believed that discrimination is a central reason why Blacks are worse off than Whites in the USA today. She even narrated a case of racial discrimination that she witnessed. Mandy said that while she was shopping in a store, the clerk totally ignored her as soon as a Black man entered the store and pointed out that she "could've stuck anything in my backpack if I wanted to" (Interview # 504: 10). Mandy narrated what happened after as follows:

> [The clerk] went over to the guns, picking out a gun, and I am standing there with money in my hand, and this guy goes "Can I help you?" to the guy. He says, "Do you need something, sir? Is there anything you need?" and just keep looking at him. And so I said, you know, "Here's my money (laughs) if you want to take it." And he's all "Sorry" and he is taking my money, but he's still keeping an eye on this guy, and I looked at the guy, and he had this look on his face that just broke my heart because you could tell . . . that he has to deal with this, and I had never had to deal with that. (Interview # 504: 10)

Whereas the typical White student interpreted Blacks' status as Blacks' own fault, Mandy acknowledged the role of discrimination and even understood the significance of White privilege. She states:

> Oh, definitely [the overall inferior status of Blacks is] due to discrimination. It's not a coincidence . . . that a large population in this country lives in substandard housing, and, and, substandard jobs and schools . . . but I went to middle school in a richer neighborhood because my mom lied about where we lived, but I think that if you were Black in the community and tried to go over to a White school that was more wealthy . . . you wouldn't be able to do that because people would know exactly where you came from . . . and I just think that there is something at work keeping people in their spot. (Interview # 504: 11)

Finally, Mandy's answers concerning the ABZ company hiring practices, exemplifies how racial progressives framed racially perceived issues differently than reasonable racists. For example, Mandy supported the company's decision in the second case (White applicant scored 85 and Black applicant 80) and pointed out that "I thought that five percentage points wasn't enough of a difference in terms of a score" (Interview # 504: 18). When she was probed about whether these decisions could be construed as reverse racism, she said that "if the country [has] a history of hiring White people over Black people, then it's about damn time they hired a Black person, and if it's discriminatory toward the White person, too bad. They need a little dose of what it feels like" (Interview # 504: 17).

Discussion

Four points emerged from our examination of White college students' views on fundamental racial issues—affirmative action, interracial marriage, and the significance of discrimination. *First,* White students exhibited more prejudiced views in the interview than in their survey responses. This cannot be attributed to 'selection bias' since the survey answers of the 41 respondents selected for interview mirrored the results of the total sample and, in some cases, appeared to have a slightly more 'racially progressive' outlook than the entire sample (see Tables 1 to 3). For example, on intermarriage the differences were quite large. The 80 to 90 percent who approved of it in the survey (see Table 2) dropped to 30 percent (12 out of 40) in the interviews, and more than half of the 30 percent approved of it without having an interracial lifestyle themselves. Although we interpret the various discursive maneuvers of the remaining 70 percent as semantic strategies to avoid voicing personal reservations toward interracial marriages, the fact remains that many of them exhibited serious 'concerns' about these unions. Therefore, Whites' support for interracial marriages as reported in our survey (80 to 90% of Whites approve of interracial marriages) may be much less in reality. We found similar patterns in their responses to the affirmative action and the significance of discrimination questions.

Second, although, based on the interview data, the respondents were more prejudiced than in the survey, they used a variety of semantic moves to save face. Interview respondents consistently used phrases such as "I don't know", "I am not sure", "I am not prejudiced", or "I agree and disagree", rather than explicitly expressing their racial views. In addition, they often incorporated discursive elements into their answers that expressed social distance (indirectness) or projection (displacement), usually followed by statements that betrayed these hesitations. Teun van Dijk explains why Whites resort to strategic talk as follows:

> Given the strict social norms against ethnic prejudice, discrimination, and racism, who wants to be considered a racist? People have, or try to maintain, a positive self-image of tolerant, understanding, cooperative citizens, on the one hand, and of kind persons, on the other. (1984: 46)

The large degree to which respondents used semantic moves was astounding. Our respondents used these moves from 68 percent of the time on the affirmative action question to 85 percent on the direct intermarriage and significance of discrimination questions. This amounts to a new *racetalk*. Unlike during the Jim Crow period, when Whites openly expressed their racial views (Dollard, 1938; Johnson, 1943, 1946; Myrdal, 1944), today Whites express their racial views in a sanitized way. (For a similar finding in South Africa, see Schutte, 1985.) Although our sample does not allow us to make generalizations to the entire White population, our results are quite consistent with the semantic moves that appear in the racetalk of White workers (Blauner, 1989; Rubin, 1994; Terkel, 1993; Weis and Fine, 1996). Although previous research has documented stylistical differences in racial talk about minorities between middle- and working-class Whites (Van Dijk, 1984), future research should examine whether or not class background affects the degree to which semantic moves are used.

Third, we showed how useful a discursive approach is for deciphering the meaning of Whites' racial views. For instance, based on our analysis, it is obvious that liberal ideology is neither racist nor progressive (Sniderman and Carmines, 1997; Hochschild, 1995; Myrdal, 1944). A total of 5 of the 41 respondents (our racial progressives) used the ideas of liberal ideology to support interracial marriage, affirmative action, and to state their beliefs about the continuing significance of discrimination as a central factor shaping the life chances of racial minorities. However, unlike most White respondents, the racial progressives used the ideas of liberal ideology *in context*, that is, they defended affirmative action or busing by recognizing the effects of past and contemporary discrimination and were concerned with *substantive* rather than *abstract* equality and fairness. In addition, the argument that Whites experience 'ambivalence' or a 'dilemma' between their commitment to equality of opportunity and their treatment of Blacks and other minorities seems to be more of an interpretive artifact rather than a reality (Hochschild, 1995; Myrdal, 1944; Schuman et al., 1988; 1997). As we showed, our respondents were not truly ambivalent about crucial racial issues. Their hesitations were part of a strategic talk to avoid appearing racist. Our respondents did not seem to experience cognitive dissonance (Festinger, 1957) because their opposition to affirmative action and other racially coded programs was couched *within* the discourse of liberalism. Thus, the apparent discursive contradictions and hesitations ("Yes and no" or "I am not sure about that one") were *resolved* by turning liberalism into an *abstract* matter. This strategy allowed them to feel that it is the government and Blacks who are being unfair. Moreover, the students' strong principled position collapsed when issues of past discrimination were raised. That is, students moved from the philosophical principles of liberalism into practical rationality (Billig et al., 1988; Wetherell and Potter, 1992). Virtually no policy alternatives were envisioned as feasible for addressing the profound inequality existing between Blacks and Whites. This casts serious doubt on arguments that suggest that class-based or color-blind policies can unite Whites and racial minorities (Sniderman and Carmines, 1997; Wilson, 1987). Finally, 27 of the respondents used either "The past is the past" or "Present generations cannot be blamed for the mistakes of past generations" anti-egalitarian story lines in their responses to the question, "Do you believe that the history of oppression endured by minorities merits the intervention of the government on their behalf?". Similar story lines have emerged in Western racialized societies such as South Africa, New Zealand, and the Netherlands (Essed, 1996; Schutte, 1996; Wetherell and Potter, 1992). This discursive flexibility in moving from strict liberalism to practical matters is central to racial ideology. In order to work, all ideologies must allow some 'room' to handle contradictions, exceptions, and change. Rather than being eternally fixed, ideologies should be conceived as processes or as ideological practices (Jackman, 1994; Wetherell and Potter, 1992).

Fourth, based on the analysis of our data, we found that the students' defense of White supremacy is no longer based on the parameters of Jim Crow racism but is instead based on a new racial ideology. As many analysts have pointed out (Bobo et al., 1997; Bonilla-Silva and Lewis, 1999; Essed, 1996; Prager, 1982), the crux of the post civil rights racial ideology is twofold. First, Whites resolutely deny that racial inequality is structural and, second, they explain it as the result of Blacks' "cultural deficiency" (e.g. they are lazy, their families are in shambles, their communities are bursting with crime). On the first issue, we showed that although the White students believe that Blacks experience discrimination, they also believe that it is due to a small number of prejudiced White individuals. They also added that Blacks use discrimination as an excuse and that they need to work harder and complain less if they want to succeed. On the matter of Black culture, as we showed in the last section of this chapter, most White students, despite their 'color blind dreams', still conceive Blacks as the 'other'. (For a similar finding, see Lewis et al., 1998.) Specifically, they construe Blacks as culturally inferior; as living in a tangle of pathology. Thus, not surprisingly, most of our White respondents blamed Blacks themselves for their lower status. At best, the students felt pity for Blacks, at worst many openly expressed contempt and hostility toward Blacks.

Thirty-six of our respondents mobilized arguments of liberal ideology such as 'fairness' and 'equal opportunity'—with little regard for the glaring group consequences of historical and contemporary racial discrimination—combined with a pragmatic stance to make their arguments. We highlighted how students used the argumentative strategies of *Apparent Sympathy, Fairness, Reversal, Justification: Force of Facts,* to justify the racial status quo. By invoking *abstract* elements of liberalism, making pragmatic claims (e.g. these are the facts), and transforming the notion of equality into 'meritocracy', our respondents could display moral fervor and indignation toward "undeserving minorities" who "take their jobs" and their "places in colleges" (for similar arguments on the role of liberal ideology, see Gans, 1973; Ryan, 1981).

We want to conclude this chapter with a comment on the politics of color-blind racism. The interview data reveal that the liberal, free market, and pragmatic rhetoric of color-blind racism allows Whites to defend White supremacy in an apparently nonracial manner (Bobo and Hutchings, 1996; Bobo and Smith, 1994; Carmines and Merriman, 1993; Kluegel and Bobo, 1993; Jackman, 1994). Color-blind racism allows Whites to appear 'not racist ("I believe in equality"), preserve their privileged status ("Discrimination ended in the sixties!"), blame Blacks for their lower status ("If you guys just work hard!"), and criticize any institutional approach—such as affirmative action—that attempts to ameliorate racial inequality ("Reverse discrimination!"). Hence, the task of progressive social analysts is to blow the whistle on color-blind racism. We must unmask color-blind racists by showing how their views, arguments, and lifestyles are (White) color-coded. We must also show how their color-blind rationales defend systemic White privilege. Analytically this implies developing new questions for our surveys and using new strategies for the analysis of contemporary racial attitudes. Politically it implies that we must concentrate our efforts in fighting the new racists, all the nice Whites who tell us "I am not a racist but . . ."

Notes

1. Semantic moves are 'strategically managed relations between propositions' (Van Dijk, 1987: 86). They are called *semantic* because the strategic function of a proposition is determined by the 'content of speech act sequences', that is, by the link between a proposition and a preceding or subsequent proposition. The overall goal of these moves, the *semantic strategy*, is to save face, that is, to avoid appearing 'racist'.
2. By racial ideology we mean the *changing* dogma that provides 'the rationalizations for social, political, and economic interactions between the races' (Bonilla-Silva, 1997: 474). The central function of racial ideology is explaining and, ultimately, justifying racial inequality (Prager, 1982). Unlike the notion of attitudes, which is bounded by methodological individualism, the notion of racial ideology regards the beliefs of actors as fundamentally shaped by their group interests. Whereas attitudes ultimately represent degrees of affect toward non-Whites, racial ideology signifies the collective views and interests of Whites. Thus it is possible for Whites to have non-prejudiced attitudes and still subscribe to the central themes of the dominant racial ideology (Hartman and Husband, 1974: 54–5; Pettigrew, 1985).

3. Wetherell and Potter (1992) define interpretive repertoires as:

> broadly discernible clusters of terms, descriptions and figures of speech often assembled around metaphors or vivid images. In more structuralist language we can talk of these things as systems of signification and as the building blocks used for manufacturing versions of actions, self and social structures in talk. They are some of the resources for making evaluations, constructing factual versions and performing particular actions. (p. 90)

4. Chi-square tests confirm that the interview sample is comparable to the larger sample for all items except two.

5. This approach is congruent with the symbolic interaction tradition in sociology. As symbolic interactionists, we believe that 'the meanings that things have for human beings are central in their own right', that those meanings 'are socially produced through interaction with one's fellows, and that in the process of interaction, the meanings of things are interpreted and reinterpreted' (Blumer, 1969: 2–5). However, unlike many followers of this tradition, we pay attention to how the larger social system produces the themes and boundaries of the meanings produced through interaction.

6. Although we recognize that all people engage in what social psychologists label as *self-presentation*, it is clear that our subjects primarily resorted to *ideal* and *tactical* rather than *authentic* self-presentation (Baumeister, 1982; Swann, 1987).

7. The specific wording of the three questions was the following:
   (a) Suppose that two candidates apply for a job at the ABZ company, a company that has a workforce that is 97 percent White. They take an examination and both applicants score 80 (70 was the minimum score required to pass the test). The company decides to hire the Black applicant over the White applicant because the company is concerned with the lack of diversity of its workforce. Under these conditions, do you agree or disagree with the decision of the ABZ company?
   (b) Suppose that the Black applicant in the above case scored 80 on the exam and the White candidate scored 85 (70 was the minimum score required to pass the test). The company, despite the fact that the White applicant did slightly better than the Black applicant, decided to hire the Black applicant because of its concern with the lack of diversity of its workforce. Under these conditions, do you agree with the decision of the ABZ company?
   (c) Suppose that the decision of hiring the Black applicant over the White applicant in the previous two cases was justified by the ABZ company not in terms of the need to diversify its workforce but because the company had discriminated in the past against Blacks in terms of hiring. Under these conditions, would you agree or disagree with the decision of the ABZ company?

8. The specific wording of the questions was:
   (1) Some Blacks claim that they face a great deal of racism in their daily lives. Many people claim that this is not the case. What do you think?
   (2) Many Blacks and other minorities claim that they do not get access to good jobs because of discrimination and that, when they get the jobs, they are not promoted at the same speed and to the same jobs as their White peers. What do you think?
   (3) On average, Blacks have worse jobs, income, and housing than Whites. Do you think that this is due to discrimination or something else?
   (4) Many Whites explain the status of Blacks in this country today as a result of Blacks lacking motivation, not having the proper work ethic, or being lazy. What do you think?
   (5) How do you explain the fact that very few minorities are at the top of the occupational structure in this country?

9. Van Dijk (1997) defines these strategies as follows:
   Apparent Sympathy = When arguments or positions that place minorities at a disadvantage are constructed as being 'for their own good'.
   Fairness = When arguments that affect the welfare of racial minorities are presented as embedded in the tradition of liberal humanism but with a concern for practical matters. In the European context, they are exemplified by the expression of being 'firm but fair'.
   Justification: The Force of Facts = Negative positions toward the 'other' are justified in terms of 'facts'.
   Reversal = This is the classic 'blaming the victim' move.

Acknowledgements

This study was supported in part by a research grant from the American Sociological Association/National Science Foundation Fund for the Advancement of the Discipline. The authors thank Jessie Daniels, Joe

Feagin, James Kluegel, Amanda Lewis, Pat Preston and Bruce Williams for comments on an earlier version of this paper. The authors also acknowledge the assistance of Aaron Ahlstrom, Colin Beckles, Joe Feagin, Thomas Guglielmo, Amanda Lewis, Janet Maki, Eileen O'Brien, and Jose Padin in the collection of the survey and interview data.

References

Adorno, Theodore, Frenkel-Brunswik, Else, Levinson, Daniel J. and Sandford, R.N. (1950) *The Authoritarian Personality*. New York: Harper & Row.

Allport, Gordon W. (1954) *The Nature of Prejudice*. New York: Addison-Wesley.

Anderson, Barbara, Silver, Brian and Abramson, Paul (1988a) 'The Effects of Race of the Interviewer on Measures of Electoral Participation by Blacks in SRC National Election Studies', *Public Opinion Quarterly* 52(1): 53–83.

Anderson, Barbara, Silver, Brian and Abramson, Paul (1988b) 'The Effects of the Race of Interviewer on Race-Related Attitudes of Black Respondents in SCR/CPS National Election Studies', *Public Opinion Quarterly* 52(3): 289–324.

Armour, Jody David (1997) *Negrophobia and Reasonable Racism*. New York: New York University Press.

Baumeister, R.F (1982) 'A Self-Presentational View of Social Phenomena', *Psychological Bulletin* 91(1): 3–26.

Berbrier, Mitch (1998) ' "Half the Battle": Cultural Resonance, Framing Processes, and Ethnic Affectations in Contemporary White Separatist Rhetoric', *Social Problems* 45(4): 431–50.

Billig, Michael (1991) *Ideology and Opinions: Studies in Rhetorical Psychology*. London: Sage.

Billig, Michael, Condor, Susan, Edwards, Derek, Gane, Mike, Middleton, David and Radley, Alan (1988) *Ideological Dilemmas: A Social Psychology of Everyday Thinking*. London: Sage.

Blauner, Bob (1989) *Black Lives, White Lives: Three Decades of Race Relations in America*. Berkeley and Los Angeles: University of California Press.

Blumer, Herbert (1967) *Symbolic Interactionism: Perspective and Method*. Englewood Cliffs, NJ: Prentice Hall.

Bobo, Lawrence, and Hutchings, Vincent (1996) 'Perceptions of Racial Competition in a Multiracial Setting', *American Sociological Review* 61(6), December: 951–72.

Bobo, Lawrence and Kluegel, James R. (1993) 'Opposition to Race-Targeting: Self-Interest, Stratification Ideology, or Racial Attitudes?', *American Sociological Review* 58: 443–64.

Bobo, Lawrence and Kluegel, James R. (1997) 'Status, Ideology, and Dimensions of Whites' Racial Beliefs and Attitudes; Progress and Stagnation', in Steven A. Tuch and Jack Martin (eds) *Racial Attitudes in the 1990s: Continuity and Change,* pp. 93–120. Westport, CT: Praeger.

Bobo, Lawrence, Kluegel, James and Smith, Ryan (1997) 'Laissez faire Racism: The Crystallization of a Kinder, Gentler, Antiblack Ideology', in Steven A. Tuch and Jack Martin (eds) *Racial Attitudes in the 1990s: Continuity and Change,* pp. 15–42. Westport, CT: Praeger.

Bobo, Lawrence and Licari, Frank (1989) 'Education and Political Tolerance: Testing the Effects of Cognitive Sophistication and Target Group Affect', *Public Opinion Quarterly* 53, Fall: 285–308.

Bonilla-Silva, Eduardo (1997) 'Rethinking Racism: Toward a Structural Interpretation', *American Sociological Review,* Vol. 62(3), June: 465–80.

Bonilla-Silva, Eduardo (1998) 'Racial Attitudes or Racial Ideology: Toward a New Paradigm for Examining Whites' Racial Views', unpublished manuscript, Texas A&M University.

Bonilla-Silva, Eduardo and Lewis, Amanda E. (1999) 'The New Racism: Racial Structure in the United States, 1960s–1990s', in Paul Wong (ed.) *Race, Ethnicity, and Nationality in the United States: Toward the Twenty-First Century,* pp. 55–101. Boulder, CO: Westview Press.

Brooks, Roy L. (1990) *Rethinking the American Race Problem*. Berkeley: University of California Press.

Brown, Gillian, and Yule, George (1983) *Discourse Analysis*. Cambridge: Cambridge University Press.

Campbell, Angus (1971) *White Attitudes Toward Black People*. Ann Arbor, MI: Institute for Social Research.

Carmichael, Stokely and Hamilton, Charles V. (1967) *Black Power: The Politics of Liberation in America*. New York: Vintage Books.

Carmines, Edward G. and Merriman, W. Richard, Jr (1993) 'The Changing American Dilemma: Liberal Values and Racial Polices', in Paul M. Sniderman, Philip E. Tetlock and Edward G. Carmines (eds) *Prejudice, Politics, and the American Dilemma,* pp. 237–55. Stanford, CA: Stanford University Press.

Converse, Phillip E. (1964) 'The Nature of Belief Systems in Mass Publics', in David E. Apter (ed.) *Ideology and Discontent,* pp. 206–61. London: Free Press of Glencoe.

Converse, Phillip E. (1970) 'Attitudes and Non-attitudes: Continuation of a Dialogue', in E.R. Tufte (ed.) *The Quantitative Analysis of Social Problems*, pp. 168–89. Reading, MA: Addison-Wesley.

Converse, Phillip E. (1997) 'Comment: The Status of Nonattitudes', *American Political Science Review* 68: 650–66.

Crenshaw, Kimberlé Williams (1997) 'Color-blind Dreams and Racial Nightmares: Reconfiguring Racism in the Post-Civil Rights Era', in Toni Morrison and Claudia Brodsky Lacour (eds) *Birth of a Nation'hood*, pp. 97–168. New York: Pantheon.

Dollard, John (1937) *Caste and Class in a Southern Town*. London: Yale University Press.

Dovidio, John F. and Gaertner, Samuel L. (1986) 'How Do Attitudes Guide Behavior?', in R.M. Sorrentino and E.T. Higgins (eds) *The Handbook of Motivation and Cognition: Foundations of Social Behavior*, pp. 204–43. New York: Guilford Press.

Dovidio, John F. and Gaertner, Samuel L. (1991) 'Changes in the Expression and Assessment of Racial Prejudice', in Harry J. Knopke et al. (eds) *Opening Doors: Perspectives on Race Relations in Contemporary America*, pp. 119–50. Tuscaloosa: University of Alabama Press.

Dovidio, John F., Mann, J.F. and Gaertner, Samuel L. (1989) 'Resistance to Affirmative Action: The Implications of Aversive Racism', in F. Blanchard and F. Crosby (eds) *Affirmative Action in Perspective*, pp. 81–102. New York: Springer-Verlag.

Edley, Christopher Jr (1996) *Not All Black and White: Affirmative Action and American Values*. New York: Hill and Wang.

Essed, Philomena (1996) *Diversity: Gender, Color, and Culture*. Amherst, MA: University of Massachusetts Press.

Fanon, Frantz (1967) *Black Skins, White Masks*. New York: Grove Press.

Feagin, Joe and Sikes, Melvin (1994) *Living With Racism: The Black Middle Class Experience*. Boston, MA: Beacon Press.

Feagin, Joe and Vera, Hernan (1995) *White Racism: The Basics*. New York: Routledge.

Festinger, Leon (1957) *A Theory of Cognitive Dissonance*. Evanston, IL: Row, Peterson, and Company.

Firebaugh, Glen and Davis, Kenneth E. (1988) 'Trends in Anti-Black Prejudice, 1972–1984: Region and Cohort Effects', *American Journal of Sociology* 94: 251–72.

Gans, Herbert J. (1973) *More Equality*. New York: Pantheon Books.

Glass Ceiling Commission (1995) *Good for Business: Making Full Use of the Nation's Human Capital*. Washington, DC: Government Printing Office.

Groves, Robert, Fultz, Nancy H. and Martin, Elizabeth (1992) 'Direct Questioning About Comprehension in a Survey Setting', in Judith M. Tanur (ed.) *Questions About Questions: Inquiries Into the 4 Cognitive Bases of Surveys*, pp. 49–61. New York: Russell Sage Foundation.

Hartman, Paul and Husband, Charles (1974) *Racism and the Mass Media: A Study of the Role of the Mass Media in the Formation of White Beliefs and Attitudes in Britain*. London: David Porter.

Herring, Cedric, and Collins, Sharon (1995) 'Retreat from Equal Opportunity? The Case of Affirmative Action', in Michael Peter Smith and Joe Feagin (eds) *The Bubbling Cauldron*, pp. 163–81. Minneapolis: University of Minnesota Press.

Hernton, Calvin C. (1988) *Sex and Racism in America*. New York: Anchor Books/Doubleday.

Hochschild, Jennifer (1995) *Facing Up to the American Dream: Race, Class, and the Soul of the Nation*. Princeton, NJ: Princeton University Press.

Hyman, Herbert H. and Sheatsley, Paul B. (1964) 'Attitudes Toward Desegregation', *Scientific American* 195 (Dec): 35–9.

Jackman, Mary R. (1978) 'General and Applied Tolerance: Does Education Increase Commitment to Racial Integration?', *American Journal of Political Science* 22(2) May: 302–32.

Jackman, Mary R. (1994) *Velvet Glove: Paternalism and Conflict in Gender, Class, and Race Relations*. Berkeley: University of California Press.

Jackman, Mary R. (1996) 'Individualism, Self-Interest, and White Racism', *Social Science Quarterly* 77(4): 760–7.

Johnson, Charles S. (1943) *Patterns of Negro Segregation*. New York: Harper and Brothers.

Johnson, Charles S. (1946) *Racial Attitudes: Interviews Revealing Attitudes of Northern and Southern White Persons of a Wide Range of Occupational and Educational Levels, Toward Negroes*. Nashville, TN: Social Science Institute, Fisk University.

Jordan, Withrop D. (1977) *White Over Black: American Attitudes Toward the Negro, 1550–1812*. New York: W.W. Norton.

Kane, Emily and Macaulay, Laura (1993) 'Interviewer Gender and Gender Attitudes', *Public Opinion Quarterly* 57(1): 1–28.

Katz, Irwin, Wackenhut, Joyce and Hass, R. Glen (1986) 'Racial Ambivalence, Value Duality, and Behavior', in John Dovidio and Samuel L. Gaertner (eds) *Prejudice, Discrimination, and Racism*, pp. 35–60. Orlando, FL: Academic Press.

Kinder, Donald and Sanders, Lynn M. (1996) *Divided by Color: Racial Politics and Democratic Ideals.* Chicago and London: University of Chicago Press.

Kluegel, James R. (1990). 'Trends in Whites' Explanations of the Gap Black–White Socioeconomic Status, 1977–1989', *American Sociological Review* 55(4), August: 512–25.

Kluegel, James R. and Smith, Eliot R. (1982) 'Whites' Beliefs about Blacks' Opportunity', *American Sociological Review* 47: 518–32.

Kluegel, James R. and Smith, Eliot R. (1986) *Beliefs About Inequality: Americans' Views of What Is and What Ought to Be.* New York: Aldine de Gruyter.

Kovel, Joel (1984) *White Racism: A Psychohistory.* New York: Columbia University Press.

Krysan, Maria (1998) 'Privacy and the Expression of White Racial Attitudes', *Public Opinion Quarterly* 62(4): 506–44.

Lewis, Amanda, Chesler, Mark, and Forman, Tyrone (1998) ' "I'm not Going to Think of You as Black, I'll Just Think of You as my Friend": Color-blind Ideologies and Exclusionary Race Relations on a Predominantly White College Campus', unpublished manuscript, University of Michigan.

Lipset, Seymour M. (1996) *American Exceptionalism: A Double-Edged Sword.* New York and London: W.W. Norton.

Lipset, Seymour and Schneider, William (1978) 'The Bakke Case: How Would It Be Decided at the Bar of Public Opinion', *Public Opinion* 1(1): 38–44.

MacLeod, Jay (1995) *Ain't No Makin' It: Aspirations and Attainment in a Low-Income Neighborhood.* Boulder, CO: Westview Press.

McConahay, J.B. and Hough, J.C. (1976) 'Symbolic Racism', *Journal of Social Issues* 32(1): 23–45.

Massey, Douglas S. and Denton, Nancy A. (1993) *Segregation and the Making of the Underclass.* Cambridge, MA: Harvard University Press.

Meertens, Roel W. and Pettigrew, Thomas F. (1997) 'Is Subtle Prejudice Really Prejudice?', *Public Opinion Quarterly* 61: 54–71.

Myers, Samuel L. (1993) 'Measuring and Detecting Discrimination in the Post-Civil Rights Era', in John H. Stanfield II and Rutledge M. Dennis (eds) *Race and Ethnicity in Research*, pp. 172–97. Newbury Park, CA: Sage.

Myrdal, Gunnar (1944) *An American Dilemma: The Negro Problem and Modern Democracy I.* New York and London: Harper and Brothers Publishers.

Niemi, Richard G, Mueller, John and Smith, Tom W. (1989) *Trends in Public Opinion: A Compendium of Survey Data.* New York: Greenwood Press.

Orfield, Gary and Eaton, Susan, E. (1996) *Dismantling Desegregation: The Quiet Reversal of Brown v. Board of Education.* New York: New York Press.

Pettigrew, Thomas F. (1985) 'New Black–White Patterns: How Best to Conceptualize Them?', *Annual Review of Sociology* 11: 329–46.

Potter, Jonathan and Wetherell, Margaret (1987) *Discourse and Social Psychology: Beyond Attitudes and Behavior.* London: Sage.

Prager, Jeffrey (1982) 'American Racial Ideology as Collective Representation', *Ethnic and Racial Studies* 5(1), January: 99–119.

Psathas, George (1995) *Conversation Analysis: The Study of Talk-in-Interaction.* Thousand Oaks, CA: Sage.

Rieder, Jonathan (1985) *Carnasarie: The Jews and Italians of Brooklyn against Liberalism.* Cambridge, MA: Harvard University Press.

Rubin, Lillian (1994) *Families on the Fault Line: America's Working Class Speaks about the Family, the Economy, Race, and Ethnicity.* New York: HarperCollins.

Ryan, William (1981) *Equality.* New York: Pantheon Books.

Schuman, Howard and Steeh, Charlotte (1996) 'The Complexity of Racial Attitudes in America', in Silvia Pedraza and Ruben Rumbaut (eds) *Origins and Destinies*, pp. 455–69. Belmont, MA: Wadsworth.

Schuman, Howard, Steeh, Charlotte and Bobo, Lawrence (1988) *Racial Attitudes in America: Trends and Interpretations.* Boston, MA: Harvard University Press.

Schuman, Howard, Steeh, Charlotte, Bobo, Lawrence and Krysan, Maria (1997) *Racial Attitudes in America: Trends and Interpretations*, rev edn, Boston, MA: Harvard University Press.

Schutte, Gerhard (1995) *What Racists Believe: Race Relations in South Africa and the United States*. London: Sage.

Sheatsley, Paul (1966) 'White Attitudes Toward the Negro', in Talcott Parsons (ed.) *The Negro American*, pp. 303–24. Boston, MA: Houghton Mifflin.

Sigall, Harold and Page, Richard (1971) 'Current Stereotypes: A Little Fading, A Little Faking', *Journal of Personality and Social Psychology* 18(2), January: 247–55.

Smith, Robert C. (1995) *Racism in the Post Civil Rights Period: Now You See It, Now You Don't*. Albany: State University of New York Press.

Smith, Tom W. and Sheatsley, Paul B. (1984) 'American Attitudes toward Race Relations', *Public Opinion* 7(5): 14–15, 50–3.

Spiegelman, Art (1997) 'Getting in Touch with my Inner Racist', *Mother Jones*. September–October: 51–2.

Sniderman, Paul M. and Piazza, Thomas (1993) *The Scare of Race*. Boston, MA: Harvard University Press.

Sniderman, Paul M. and Carmines, Edward G. (1997) *Reaching Beyond Race*. Cambridge, MA: Harvard University Press.

Steeh, Charlotte and Krysan, Maria (1996) 'Affirmative Action and the Public, 1970–1995', *Public Opinion Quarterly* 60: 128–58.

Swann, W.B., Jr (1987) 'Identity Negotiation: Where Two Roads Meet', *Journal of Personality and Social Psychology* 53(6): 1038–51.

Taylor, Talbot A. and Cameron, Deborah (1987) *Analysing Conversation: Rules and Units in the Structure of Talk*. Oxford: Pergamon Press.

Terkel, Studs (1993) *Race: How Black and Whites Think and Feel About The American Obsession*. New York: Doubleday.

Van Dijk, Teun A. (1977) *Text and Context Explorations in the Semantics and Pragmatics of Discourse*. London and New York: Longman.

Van Dijk, Teun A. (1984) *Prejudice in Discourse: An Analysis of Ethnic Prejudice in Cognition and Conversation*. Amsterdam and Philadelphia, PA: John Benjamins Publishing Co.

Van Dijk, Teun A. (1987) *Communicating Racism: Ethnic Prejudice in Thought and Talk*. Beverly Hills, CA: Sage.

Van Dijk, Teun A. (1997) 'Political Discourse and Racism: Describing Others in Western Parliaments','' in Stephen Harold Riggins (ed.) *The Language and Politics of Exclusion: Others in Discourse*, pp. 31–64. Thousands Oaks, CA: Sage.

Van Dijk, Teun A. (1998) *Ideology: A Multidisciplinary Approach*. London: Sage.

Weis, Lois, and Fine, Michelle (1996) 'Narrating the 1980s and 1990s: Voices of Poor and Working-Class White and African American Men', *Anthropology and Education Quarterly* 27(4): 493–516.

Wellman, David (1977) *Portraits of White Racism*. Berkeley, CA: University of California Press.

Wetherell, Margaret and Jonathan Potter (1992) *Mapping the Language of Racism: Discourse and the Legitimation of Exploitation*. New York: Columbia University Press.

Wicker, Tom (1996) *Tragic Failure: Racial Integration in America*. New York: William Morrow and Company.

Wilson, William Julius (1987) *The Truly Disadvantaged*. Chicago, IL: University of Chicago Press.

Wodak, Ruth (1996) 'The Genesis of Racist Discourse in Austria Since 1989', in Carmen Rosa Caldas-Coulthard (ed.) *Texts and Practices: Readings in Critical Discourse Analysis*, pp. 107–28. London: Routledge.

Wodak, Ruth (1997) '*Daus Ausland* and Anti-Semitic Discourse: The Discursive Construction of the Other', in Stephen Harold Riggins (ed.) *The Language and Politics of Exclusion: Others in Discourse*, pp. 65–87. Thousands Oaks, CA: Sage.

CHAPTER 12
NINE THEMES IN CAMPUS RACIAL CLIMATES AND IMPLICATIONS FOR INSTITUTIONAL TRANSFORMATION

SHAUN R. HARPER AND SYLVIA HURTADO

Administrators at two universities were probably less than excited about the news coverage their campuses received on April 27, 2006. Although they were located in different regions of the country, various indicators of racism and racial/ethnic minority student discontent were apparent at both institutions. On one campus in the Northeast, four alarming headlines and race-related stories were printed on the front page of the student newspaper. An incident in which a campus police officer made racist remarks to three African American female students was juxtaposed with the story of a philosophy professor suing the university for demoting him from department chair because he reported to the dean of his college that students had been racially harassed and discriminated against by his faculty colleagues. The third front-page article described a letter sent to the administration by Hillel, the Jewish student organization, demanding an apology and other concessions for the unfair cancellation of a student art exhibit on campus. Among their requests, Hillel student board members asked the university to conduct "an investigation into the discrimination, racism, and intimidation" one of their members experienced in his interactions with the art gallery director.

A protest at the Office of the President organized by Black Caucus and the LGBT (lesbian, gay, bisexual, and transgender) student organization the day before was described in the final story. Protestors said they were insulted that staff members locked the office door and the president walked by refusing to address their concerns. Therefore, they slid a letter under the door, chanted outside on megaphones, and subsequently posted a video of the entire protest on YouTube.com. The protest was in response to what students perceived to be insufficient punishment against the women's head basketball coach, a White woman, who allegedly interrogated a Black female player about her sexual orientation, repeatedly threatened to dismiss the student from the team if it was discovered that she was in fact a lesbian, and eventually demanded that the player leave the team. While this story appears to be more about sexual orientation than race, Black Caucus members were especially disturbed that this happened to an African American woman who was probably not the first or only player the coach suspected was gay. Perhaps institutional leaders believed these were isolated incidents that coincidentally occurred around the same time, hence there being no formal assessment of the campus racial climate following this day of problematic news coverage.

With support from the president and provost, the second university commissioned an audit of its campus racial climate. The day after a public presentation of preliminary findings from the audit, a reporter from the city newspaper wrote an article with a bold headline indicating the institution had received "a poor racial report card." The story included a summary of the auditor's findings and this quote from an African American male sophomore: "It is not a sensitive community for Black students. If I stay, the only reason will be to help effect change." The article was also retrieved by the Associated Press and reprinted in newspapers across the nation. Unlike at the first university, administrators on this campus felt public pressure to respond to the problems that had been exposed and were expected to use findings from the racial climate audit to guide institutional change. Within one year, the midwestern school hired a chief diversity officer, crafted a memorandum of understanding with the local chapter of the National Association for the Advancement of Colored People to improve the campus racial climate, organized a conference to examine the status of racial/ethnic minority male students, and pursued more purposefully the recruitment of a diverse faculty, among other efforts. The audit clearly raised institutional consciousness about the realities of race on campus and revealed racial toxins that had long existed but remained unaddressed.

These two predominantly White institutions (PWIs) had similar responses to racial issues on campus. Although the second university was forced to change after having been embarrassed in the local and national press, it is highly unlikely that the audit was the first indicator of racial turbulence on campus. Instead, there had been signals such as those at the first institution that had been disregarded, either intentionally or inadvertently. Unfortunately, such incidents and subsequent responses are not atypical.

In this chapter, we synthesize fifteen years of research about campus racial climates and present nine themes that emerged from a multi-institutional qualitative study we conducted. The primary goal here is to illuminate trends that persist on many college and university campuses, especially those that are predominantly White. At the end of the chapter, we use perspectives on transparency and organizational change to frame our implications for institutional transformation.

Post–1992 Research on Campus Racial Climates

"The Campus Racial Climate: Contexts of Conflict" (Hurtado, 1992) is the most widely cited study on this topic. Results were derived from the Cooperative Institutional Research Program (CIRP) fourth-year follow-up survey, a nationally representative longitudinal study of college students in the late 1980s. Among the most salient findings was that approximately one in four survey respondents perceived considerable racial conflict on their campuses; this proportion was even higher at four-year institutions that were large, public, or selective. When racial conflict was present on campus, few students were convinced that fostering racially diverse learning environments was a high institutional priority. Racial/ethnic minority students were more likely to believe espoused institutional commitments to multiculturalism when racial tension was low. Hurtado also found that White students were less likely than Blacks and Latinos to perceive racial tension on their campuses, as most believed racism was no longer problematic in society. Furthermore, she concluded that racial tension is probable in environments where there is little concern for individual students, which is symptomatic of many large PWIs that enroll several thousand undergraduates.

The Hurtado study has been reprinted in books and frequently cited by scholars who have written about racial realities on college campuses over the past fifteen years. Given the problematic nature of the results presented in this landmark study, we retrieved and analyzed empirical research studies that have since been published in education and social sciences journals to determine how campus racial climates have evolved since 1992. Although considerable effort has been devoted to studying various topics concerning racial/ethnic minority undergraduates at PWIs, we reviewed only journal articles that focused on the racialized experiences of college students and campus racial climates. Also excluded are climate studies regarding racial/ethnic minority faculty and other underrepresented populations (such as LGBT and low-income students), conceptual pieces, literature reviews, unpublished conference papers, dissertations and theses, legal proceedings, reports, and books (with one exception: Feagin, Vera, and Imani, 1996).

Findings from studies that have been published since 1992 can be divided into three categories: (1) differential perceptions of campus climate by race, (2) racial/ethnic minority student reports of prejudicial treatment and racist campus environments, and (3) benefits associated with campus climates that facilitate cross-racial engagement. Studies in which these findings have emerged as well as the methods and samples on which they are based are presented in Table 1. Seventy-one percent of the articles we reviewed are based on quantitative methods, and only one qualitative study (Solórzano, Ceja, and Yosso, 2000) was conducted at multiple institutions. Also apparent is that too

TABLE 1

Clusters of Post-1992 Research Studies on Student Experiences with Race and Campus Racial Climates

Authors	Research Design	Sites	Sample (N)	Respondents/Participants
Differential perceptions of campus climate by race				
Ancis, Sedlacek, and Mohr (2000)	Quantitative	Single	578	Asian American, Black, Latino, and White students
Cabrera and Nora (1994)	Quantitative	Single	879	Asian American, Black, Latino, and White students
Cabrera and others (1999)	Quantitative	Multiple	1,454	Black and White students
D'Augelli and Hershberger (1993)	Quantitative	Single	146	Black and White students
Eimers and Pike (1997)	Quantitative	Single	799	Asian American, Black, Latino, Native American, and White students
Helm, Sedlacek, and Prieto (1998)	Quantitative	Single	566	Asian American, Black, Latino, and White students
Johnson-Durgans (1994)	Quantitative	Single	2,957	Black and White students
Nora and Cabrera (1996)	Quantitative	Single	831	Asian American, Black, Latino, Native American, and White students
Radloff and Evans (2003)	Qualitative	Single	27	Black and White students
Rankin and Reason (2005)	Quantitative	Multiple	7,347	Asian American, Black, Latino, Native American, and White students
Suarez-Balcazar and others (2003)	Quantitative	Single	322	Asian American, Black, Latino, and White students
Racial/ethnic minority student reports of prejudicial treatment and racist campus environments				
Davis and others (2004)	Qualitative	Single	11	Black students
Diver-Stamnes and LoMascolo (2001)	Qualitative	Single	153	Asian American, Black, Latino, Native American, and White students
Feagin, Vera, and Imani (1996)	Qualitative	Single	77	Black students and Parents
Fries-Britt and Turner (2001)	Qualitative	Single	15	Black students

Study	Method	Sample	N	Population
Hurtado (1994a)	Quantitative	Multiple	510	Black and Latino students
Hurtado (1994b)	Quantitative	Multiple	859	Latino students
Hurtado and Carter (1997)	Quantitative	Multiple	272	Latino students
Hurtado, Carter, and Spuler (1996)	Quantitative	Multiple	203	Latino students
Lewis, Chesler, and Forman (2000)	Qualitative	Single	75	Asian American, Black, Latino, and Native American students
Smedley, Myers, and Harrell (1993)	Quantitative	Single	161	Asian American, Black, and Latino students
Solórzano, Ceja, and Yosso (2000)	Qualitative	Multiple	34	Black students
Swim and others (2003)	Mixed	Single	51	Black students
Turner (1994)	Qualitative	Single	32	Asian American, Black, Latino, and Native American students and faculty

Benefits associated with campus climates that facilitate cross-racial engagement

Study	Method	Sample	N	Population
antonio (2004)	Qualitative	Single	18	Asian American, Black, Latino, and White students
antonio and others (2004)	Mixed	Multiple	357	White students
Chang (1999)	Quantitative	Multiple	11,680	Asian American, Black, Latino, and White students
Chang (2001)	Quantitative	Single	167	Asian American, Black, Latino, and White students
Chang, Astin, and Kim (2004)	Quantitative	Multiple	9,703	Asian American, Black, Latino, and White students
Chang, Denson, Sáenz, and Misa (2006)	Quantitative	Multiple	19,667	Asian American, Black, Latino, Native American, and White students
Gurin, Dey, Hurtado, and Gurin (2002)	Quantitative	Multiple	12,965	Asian American, Black, Latino, and White students
Levin, van Laar, and Sidanius (2003)	Quantitative	Single	1,215	Asian American, Black, Latino, and White students
Milem, Umbach, and Liang (2004)	Quantitative	Single	536	White students
Pike and Kuh (2006)	Quantitative	Multiple	42,588	Asian American, Black, Latino, and White students
Sáenz, Ngai, and Hurtado (2007)	Quantitative	Multiple	4,380	Asian American, Black, Latino, and White students

few researchers have explored how Asian American and Native American students experience campus racial climates. What follows is a brief synopsis of recurring findings within each thematic cluster of studies.

Differential Perceptions of Campus Climate by Race

Researchers have consistently found that racial/ethnic minority students and their White peers who attend the same institution often view the campus racial climate in different ways. For example, racial/ethnic minorities in Rankin and Reason's study (2005) perceived campus climates as more racist and less accepting than did White survey respondents. Similarly, D'Augelli and Hershberger (1993) noted, "Almost all of the sampled African American students reported having borne the brunt of racist remarks and most assumed that African Americans would be mistreated on campus" (p. 77). White students in their study did not report similar experiences and expectations. Nora and Cabrera (1996) found that Whites and racial/ethnic minorities alike perceived the campus climate negatively, reported discrimination from faculty, and recognized insensitivity in the classroom. However, White students' perceptions were weaker on all three measures and not necessarily attributable to race. While both White and Black participants in Cabrera and Nora's study (1994) felt alienated in various ways on campus, racial prejudice and discrimination was the predominant source of such feelings among the latter group.

Radloff and Evans (2003) linked perceptual differences to their participants' home communities. That is, the White students they interviewed grew up in predominantly White neighborhoods and thus had limited firsthand exposure to racism prior to college. Cabrera and others (1999) found that perceptions of racial prejudice had greater effects on Black students' levels of institutional commitment in comparison to their White counterparts who had also experienced various forms of discrimination. Multiple studies have shown that Black students report lower levels of satisfaction with racial climates and perceive differential treatment on the basis of race more frequently than do their Asian American, Latino, Native American, and White peers (Ancis, Sedlacek, and Mohr, 2000; Cabrera and Nora, 1994; Hurtado, 1992; Suarez-Balcazar and others, 2003). These differences are not just in perceptions but also in the way racial/ethnic minority students experience PWIs.

Minority Student Reports of Prejudicial Treatment and Racist Campus Environments

The second cluster of studies, half of them qualitative, offer insights into how racial/ethnic minority students experience race and racism on predominantly White campuses. Consistent with the pre-1992 literature (Allen, 1988; Fleming, 1984; Loo and Rolison, 1986; Nettles, Thoeny, and Gosman, 1986), the research reviewed here consistently calls attention to the isolation, alienation, and stereotyping with which these students are often forced to contend on campuses where they are not the majority. Perhaps the title of Caroline Sotello Viernes Turner's article, "Guests in Someone Else's House: Students of Color" (1994), best characterizes a feeling that is shared among many at most PWIs. In their study of racial/ethnic minority first-year students, Smedley, Myers, and Harrell (1993) discovered that racial conflict and race-laden accusations of intellectual inferiority from White peers and faculty engendered stresses beyond those generally associated with attending a highly selective university; they also found these stresses were most pronounced among Black students. While similar research has focused mostly on undergraduates, Hurtado (1994a) confirmed that Black and Latino graduate students are not immune to the deleterious effects of campus racial climates.

In their study of Latino student transition to college, Hurtado, Carter, and Spuler (1996) suggested, "Even the most talented Latinos are likely to have difficulty adjusting if they perceive a climate where majority students think all minorities are special admits [and] Hispanics feel like they do not 'fit in.' . . . Students may internalize these climate observations, presumably because these are more difficult to identify or sanction than overt forms of discrimination" (p. 152). Reportedly, experiences with racial discrimination and perceptions of racial/ethnic tension complicated the participants' first- and second-year transitions. Beyond the first year, Hurtado and Carter (1997) found that perceptions of racial hostility had negative effects on Latino students' sense of belonging in the junior year of college. In another study (Hurtado, 1994b), 68 percent of the high-achieving Latino students surveyed felt their peers knew very little about Hispanic culture, which significantly increased the participants' feelings of racial/ethnic tension and reports of discriminatory experiences on campus.

Feagin, Vera, and Imani's study (1996) appears to be the first to involve both Black students and parents in an examination of the campus racial climate. Situated at a public university in the Southeast, the participants were well aware of the institution's racist history and the reputation it had garnered for being racially toxic. And the students described the confrontations they had with White peers and faculty, the absence of cultural space they could call their own, barriers to successfully navigating the institution, and the constant burden of disproving racist stereotypes regarding their academic abilities. Fries-Britt and Turner (2001) described how Black students' confidence in their academic abilities is often eroded by stereotypes regarding their intellectual inferiority and presumed entry to universities because of affirmative action.

Black undergraduates participating in a research study by Swim and others (2003) wrote in diaries each time (if at all) they experienced racism or perceived something on their campuses to be racist over a two-week period. Thirty-six percent documented unfriendly looks and skeptical stares from White students and faculty, 24 percent chronicled derogatory and stereotypical verbal remarks directed toward them, 18 percent kept a log of bad service received in the dining hall and other facilities on campus, and 15 percent noted other assorted incidents. The students attributed all of this negative treatment to racism. Solórzano, Ceja, and Yosso (2000) found that when Black students experience racial micro-aggressions (subtle verbal, nonverbal, or visual insults), they begin to feel academically and socially alienated in spaces where such oppression occurs, and as a defense mechanism they create their own academic and social counterspaces (ethnic enclaves that offer shelter from the psychoemotional harms of racial microaggressions). While the worth of ethnic culture centers, minority student organizations, and other counterspaces has been empirically proven in recent studies (Guiffrida, 2003; Harper and Quaye, 2007; Patton, 2006; Solórzano and Villalpando, 1998), a reality is that they often limit interactions between White students and racial/ethnic minorities.

Benefits Associated with Campus Climates That Facilitate Cross-Racial Engagement

Findings from studies in the third cluster are relatively consistent. Researchers have recently furnished a large body of empirical evidence to confirm the educational merit of deliberately creating racially diverse college campuses. Much of this evidence was used in support of testimony for the University of Michigan affirmative action cases (*Gratz* v. *Bollinger* and *Grutter* v. *Bollinger*). These studies verify that students who attend racially diverse institutions and are engaged in educationally purposeful activities that involve interactions with peers from different racial/ethnic backgrounds come to enjoy cognitive, psychosocial, and interpersonal gains that are useful during and after college (antonio and others, 2004; Chang, 1999, 2001; Chang, Astin, and Kim, 2004; Chang, Denson, Sáenz, and Misa, 2006; Gurin, Dey, Hurtado, and Gurin, 2002; Pike and Kuh, 2006).

Exposure to diverse perspectives during college could interrupt long-standing segregation trends in society. Students (especially Whites) who engage meaningfully with peers from different backgrounds and diverse perspectives both inside and outside college classrooms are unlikely to remain isolated within their own racial/ethnic communities (Sáenz, Nagi, and Hurtado, 2007), which is believed to be sustainable in environments (such as residential neighborhoods) after college (Milem, Umbach, and Liang, 2004). In contrast to those who maintained racially homogeneous friendships, undergraduates (especially first-year students) with friends outside their race held fewer biases about and expressed less anxiety toward racially different others at the end of college (Levin, van Laar, and Sidanius, 2003). Participants in antonio's study on friendship grouping (2004) agreed their campus was racially segregated and could describe the range of racially homogeneous groups that existed. Despite this, many selected best friends based on those with whom they interacted most in the first year of college, not on the basis of race. These findings illustrate the importance of institutional intent in creating spaces and opportunities for meaningful cross-racial engagement, especially for students who are newcomers to an institution.

A Multicampus Qualitative Study of Racial Climates

Solórzano, Ceja, and Yosso's article (2000) appears to be the only published qualitative study of racial climates based on data collected from more than one institution. It should be noted that their sample was composed exclusively of Black students. To explore the realities of race more deeply, we used qualitative research methods at five PWIs located in three different geographical regions of the country; two campuses were in rural towns and the others in urban areas. In light of Hurtado's finding (1992) that institutional size affects perceptions of the campus racial climate, only large institutions were included in this study. On average, White students composed 73 percent of the undergraduate populations on these campuses. The primary goals were to pursue a deeper understanding of how contemporary cohorts of students experience campus racial climates in the three areas consistently noted in the literature, while searching for additional themes that have not been captured as fully in previous research.

Focus groups were facilitated with 278 Asian American, Black, Latino, Native American, and White students across the five campuses. The composition of each focus group was racially homogeneous (for example, only Native Americans in one and Latinos exclusively in another). Administrators in academic affairs, student affairs, and multicultural affairs assisted in participant recruitment by sending mass e-mail invitations to all undergraduates from each of the racial/ethnic minority populations on the campus; each White participant led a major campus organization such as student government. In addition to interviews with students, one additional focus group was facilitated with staff persons (mostly entry- and midlevel professionals) from academic affairs, student affairs, and multicultural affairs at each institution. Interestingly, only five of the forty-one staff participants were White, even though we never specified a preference for racial/ethnic minorities who worked at the institutions.

Each focus group session was audiorecorded and later transcribed. The interview transcripts were analyzed using the NVivo Qualitative Data Analysis Software Program. Several techniques prescribed by Miles and Huberman (1994) and Moustakas (1994) were systematically employed to analyze the data collected in this study. The analyses led to the identification of nine recurring themes, which are presented in the next section. To ensure the trustworthiness of the data, we shared our findings in public forums on each campus where participants were invited to deny or confirm our syntheses of what they reported in focus groups about the racial climate, a technique referred to as "member checks" (Lincoln and Guba, 1986). Patton (2002) noted that participants with seemingly unpopular or minority points of view might not feel empowered to offer divergent perspectives in focus groups and subsequently may decide against reporting something different or controversial, a trend better known as "focus group effect." This certainly could have been the case in this study and is therefore acknowledged as a limitation. Using a different sampling and participant recruitment technique for White students, while justified below, is another noteworthy shortcoming.

Each of the five campuses in this study had its own context-specific challenges with race and racism, which are not discussed here to keep the institutions' identities anonymous. Instead, we present and summarize nine common racial realities across the institutions.

Cross-Race Consensus Regarding Institutional Negligence

Racial/ethnic minorities and White students alike expressed frustration with the incongruence of espoused and enacted institutional values concerning diversity. "The university has diversity plastered everywhere, but I have yet to see any real evidence of it," one focus group participant commented. Many were also disappointed with the lofty expectation that they would magically interact across racial difference on their own. A White student told of growing up on a ranch in Texas where he had not interacted with anyone outside his race prior to enrolling at the university. Regarding the initiation of conversations with racial/ethnic minorities on the campus, he asked: "Why should I be expected to know how to do this on my own? And the university expects us to talk about something as sensitive as racism without helping us. This is unrealistic and actually unfair." Other students wanted and needed assistance, structure, and venues in which to meaningfully engage with racially different peers, but they found little guidance from educators and administrators. Consequently, almost all of the students interviewed deemed their institutions negligent in the educational processes leading to racial understanding, both inside and outside the classroom.

Race as a Four-Letter Word and an Avoidable Topic

Participants, including the staff persons interviewed, spoke of the infrequency with which race-related conversations occurred on their campuses. Put simply, race remained an unpopular topic and was generally considered taboo in most spaces, including classes other than ethnic studies. At one institution, a midlevel staff member shared: "We don't talk about race on this campus because this state has long struggled with racial issues that trace back to slavery. So the political climate is such that the university would get into trouble with the state legislators if we talked too much about race." Students also referenced city and state political norms in their comments about the silencing of topics related to racism and racial injustice. "This campus is a microcosm of [this town] when it comes to running away from anything that even smells like race. It is just something we never talk about here, and most people are okay with that." Many participants recognized the contradiction inherent in expecting students to interact across racial lines on campuses where race is deliberately unacknowledged in classrooms and other structured venues.

Self-Reports of Racial Segregation

Like the students in antonio's study (2004), participants here were well aware of the segregation on their campuses. Few encountered difficulty naming spaces where evidence of racial segregation could be found. Chief among them was fraternity row. In fact, one Black student referred to this segregated space as "Jim Crow Row," as he reflected on fraternity parties and other events to which he had been denied access, perceivably due to his race. At the conclusion of a focus group at another institution, the participants led a guided tour through various "ethnic neighborhoods" (as they called them) in the campus dining hall, where racial segregation was visibly apparent. Beyond observable segregation trends on the campuses, most students we interviewed personally confessed to having few (if any) friends from different racial/ethnic backgrounds. Several White participants expressed an interest in building friendships with others but said they did not know how. By her own admission, a White female student leader was embarrassed that she had not even noticed until the focus group discussion that all of her close friends were White. In some instances, White students attributed their lack of engagement with racial/ethnic minority peers to the existence of minority student organizations. "If we did not have the Black frats, our chapters would have more diverse members," an Interfraternity Council president claimed. Worth acknowledging here is that only twenty-nine students held membership in the four Black fraternities on this particular campus.

Gaps in Social Satisfaction by Race

White and Asian American students often expressed feelings of social satisfaction at the five institutions and found it difficult to identify aspects of the campus environment they would change. Because all the White participants were student leaders, the universality of this finding should be interpreted with caution. While not as satisfied as the White and Asian American students, Latinos and Native Americans mostly expressed gratitude for having been afforded the opportunity to matriculate at the various campuses. Their expectations for the provision of stronger social support appeared to be modest in comparison to those of their Black peers. It should be noted that Native American undergraduates were less than half of 1 percent of the undergraduate student populations on four of the campuses we studied. In one focus group, a Latina first-year student began with an enthusiastic description of the benefits associated with attending such a prestigious university, but hearing stories from others ignited consciousness of just how little social support she had been afforded at the institution. At every university, Black students expressed the highest degrees of dissatisfaction with the social environment.

Reputational Legacies for Racism

One logical explanation for Black student displeasure was the bad reputations that preceded the universities they attended. Some entered their institutions expecting to experience racism. "My parents, sister, aunt, and just about every African American in my home town couldn't understand why I came here. They told me to go to [a black college] because this place is so racist," one woman shared. In each focus group, other Black students told similar stories of how they had been warned about the racist environments they would encounter. "Kanye West said George W. Bush does not care about Black people. Well, it is obvious [this institution] does not care about Black people, and we have known this for a few generations now." Like the students and parents in Feagin, Vera, and Imani's study (1996), Black undergraduates interviewed for this study described how negatively their institutions were viewed within Black communities across the state because of historical exclusionary admissions practices. Many Black students withdrew prematurely in the past, and those who managed to persist through degree attainment often returned to their home communities with stories of the racism they had endured. Although this was found only among Black students in the study, its salience and consistency across the five campuses makes it noteworthy.

White Student Overestimation of Minority Student Satisfaction

White student leaders were selected because they were thought to be most likely to have interacted with racial/ethnic minority peers in the student organizations they led. Moreover, we suspected they were positioned to offer more meaningful appraisals of the campus racial climates because of their levels of political leadership on the campuses. Focus groups with these participants were always conducted after those with racial/ethnic minority students. The White students were most satisfied with the social environments, and they erroneously assumed their Black, Latino, and Native American peers experienced the institutions this same way. They reported that racial/ethnic minority student engagement in mainstream campus organizations was low, but for some reason those students were thought to be equally satisfied with their college experiences. When asked about the basis of their assumptions, the White participants often responded with, "I don't know . . . I just figured everyone loves it here." Because there was so little structured and meaningful interaction across races, student leaders who were presumed to have understood the general pulse of the campus were generally unaware of the disparate affective dispositions their racial/ethnic minority peers held toward the institutions.

The Pervasiveness of Whiteness in Space, Curricula, and Activities

Beyond ethnic and multicultural centers on the five campuses, Asian American, Black, Latino, and Native American students found it difficult to identify other spaces on campus in which they felt shared cultural ownership. White interests were thought to be privileged over others, which many racial/ethnic minorities viewed as inconsistent with institutional claims of inclusiveness. These perceptions are perhaps best illustrated in this quote from a sophomore student: "Everything is so White. The concerts: White musicians. The activities: catered to White culture. The football games: a ton of drunk White folks. All the books we read in class: White authors and viewpoints. Students on my left, right, in front and in back of me in my classes: White, White, White, White. I feel like there is nothing for us here besides the [cultural] center, but yet [this university] claims to be so big on diversity. That is the biggest white lie I have ever heard." Other participants also critiqued the isolation of ethnic culture to a single center, office, or academic major. Although Asian American students generally appeared to be as satisfied as their White peers, even they expressed a desire for greater cultural representation.

The Consciousness-Powerlessness Paradox among Racial/Ethnic Minority Staff

Nearly 88 percent of the staff persons we interviewed were racial/ethnic minorities. Interestingly, they were fully aware of the degree to which minority students were disadvantaged and dissatisfied on the five campuses. They also knew about the extent to which racial segregation existed. Much of what the students shared in focus groups was confirmed (mostly without prompting) in interviews with the staff. One of the five White staff participants asserted, "Everyone around this table knows how segregated students are, but we never talk about it. It is the sort of thing that will piss the upper administration off and make them leery of you for raising the issue." Despite their consciousness of the realities of race, most indicated a reluctance to publicly call attention to these trends for fear of losing their jobs or political backlash. "I feel bad for what the young brothers and sisters go through here, but there is only so much I can do since I have only been here two years," a Latino academic advisor explained. Staff persons would complain to each other and privately strategize with students but felt powerless in voicing observations to senior administrators and White colleagues. Fear of being seen as troublemakers who were always calling attention to racism compelled many to remain silent.

Unexplored Qualitative Realities of Race in Institutional Assessment

In every focus group on each of the five campuses, student participants (Whites and racial/ethnic minorities alike) indicated that it was the first time any institutional effort was made to inquire about the qualitative realities of their racialized experiences. "You're the first person to ask us these kinds of questions" was a common remark. Furthermore, the White student leaders said no one, including their student organization advisors, had ever asked them questions about minority student engagement and satisfaction or the frequency with which they interacted with peers who were racially different. Reportedly, the institutional research offices had not conducted any formal climate assessments. Likewise, informal queries from faculty and administrators were also uncommon. "If they truly cared, they would have asked us about these things before now," a Native American male senior believed.

Implications for Institutional Transformation

The 2006 report of the commission appointed by U.S. Department of Education Secretary Margaret Spellings to explore needed areas of improvement in higher education called for more transparency regarding student learning outcomes on college and university campuses. Merely reporting outcomes, however, keeps the source of racial inequities undisclosed and does not result in better, more inclusive climates for learning. The consistency of results from fifteen years of empirical research, along with the nine themes that emerged in our study, make clear the need for greater transparency regarding racial realities in learning environments at PWIs. Even when cues are readily available (for example, a newspaper with four front-page articles related to racial injustice), the realities of race are typically made transparent only when there is a highly publicized, racially motivated incident or when embarrassing findings from an external auditor are made public.

Consistent with Kezar and Eckel's recommendation (2002a), we suggest that administrators, faculty, and institutional researchers proactively audit their campus climates and cultures to determine the need for change. As indicated in many of the nine themes, racial realities remained undisclosed and unaddressed in systematic ways on college campuses. As long as administrators espouse commitments to diversity and multiculturalism without engaging in examinations of campus climates, racial/ethnic minorities will continue to feel dissatisfied, all students will remain deprived of the full range of educational benefits accrued through cross-racial engagement, and certain institutions will sustain longstanding reputations for being racially toxic environments.

Eckel and Kezar (2003) defined *transformation* as the type of change that affects the institutional culture, is deep and pervasive, is intentional, and occurs over time. Accordingly, deep change reflects a shift in values (for example, from espoused to enacted) and assumptions that underlie daily operations (for example, the flawed expectation that cross-racial interactions will magically occur on their own). Pervasiveness indicates that change is felt across the institution in the assumptions and daily work of faculty, staff, and administrators. For example, the Black culture center on a campus cannot improve an institution's external reputation if professors routinely perpetuate racist stereotypes in classrooms. Also, racial/ethnic minority students will continue to feel like "guests in someone else's house" if student activities offices fail to sponsor programs that reflect the diverse cultures represented on a campus. Intentionality in constructing culturally affirming environments and experiences that facilitate the cultivation of racially diverse friendship groups must substitute passivity and negligence. As previous research has established, these racial climate issues have consequences for student outcomes (Hurtado, Milem, Clayton-Pedersen, and Allen, 1998). For example, attention to diversity in the curriculum and cocurriculum, particularly in the first two years of college, results in student development along many dimensions of complex thinking and social cognitive growth (Hurtado, 2005).

Eckel and Kezar (2003) also distinguished transformation from other types of change, including adjustments that continually happen in academia that are neither pervasive nor deep, such as showing a one-hour video on respecting diversity at new student orientation; isolated change that may be deep but limited to one unit or program area, as when an ethnic studies department offers a cluster of elective courses on race; or far-reaching change that affects many across the institution but lacks depth, as with a policy regarding the symbolic inclusion of an equal opportunity statement on letterhead and all hiring materials. Moreover, Kezar and Eckel (2002b) found that senior administrative support, collaboration, and visible action are among the core elements requisite for transformational change in higher education. While administrative leadership on its own is insufficient, our findings make clear that entry- and midlevel professionals, especially racial/ethnic minorities, often feel silenced and powerless to transform campus racial climates.

In their 2005 study, Kezar and Eckel interviewed thirty college presidents who had been engaged in organizational change with a significant emphasis on the success of racial/ethnic minority students. The presidents used a strategy of dialogue and discussion in the appraisal of their own and their institutions' commitments to diversity, while holding various stakeholders accountable for aligning efforts with stated institutional values and priorities. If this is to occur on other campuses, race cannot remain an avoidable topic. For instance, if accountability for student learning is a high priority, dialogue and strategic efforts must be directed toward addressing undercurrents of racial segregation that inhibit the rich learning that occurs in cross-racial engagement. Likewise, faculty and staff in academic affairs, student affairs, multicultural affairs, and other units on campus should be challenged to consider their roles as accomplices in the cyclical reproduction of racism and institutional negligence.

Despite fifteen years of racial climate research on multiple campuses, the themes of exclusion, institutional rhetoric rather than action, and marginality continue to emerge from student voices. Conducting a climate study can be symbolic of institutional action, only to be filed away on a shelf. We advocate that data gathered through the ongoing assessment of campus racial climates guide conversations and reflective examinations to overcome discomfort with race, plan for deep levels of institutional transformation, and achieve excellence in fostering racially inclusive learning environments.

References

Allen, W. R. "Black Students in U.S. Higher Education: Toward Improved Access, Adjustment, and Achievement." *Urban Review,* 1988, *20*(3), 165–188.

Ancis, J. R., Sedlacek, W. E., and Mohr, J. J. "Student Perceptions of Campus Cultural Climate by Race." *Journal of Counseling and Counseling Development,* 2000, *78,* 180–185.

antonio, a l. "When Does Race Matter in College Friendships? Exploring Men's Diverse and Homogeneous Friendship Groups." *Review of Higher Education,* 2004, *27*(4), 553–575.

antonio, a. l., and others. "Effects of Racial Diversity on Complex Thinking in College Students." *Psychological Science,* 2004, *15*(8), 507–510.

Cabrera, A. F., and Nora, A. "College Students' Perceptions of Prejudice and Discrimination and Their Feelings of Alienation: A Construct Validation Approach." *Review of Education/Pedagogy/Cultural Studies,* 1994, *16*(3), 387–409.

Cabrera, A. F., and others. "Campus Racial Climate and the Adjustment of Students to College: A Comparison Between White Students and African American Students." *Journal of Higher Education,* 1999, *70*(2), 134–160.

Chang, M. J. "Does Racial Diversity Matter? The Educational Impact of a Racially Diverse Undergraduate Population." *Journal of College Student Development,* 1999, *40*(4), 377–395.

Chang, M. J. "Is It More Than About Getting Along? The Broader Educational Relevance of Reducing Students' Racial Biases." *Journal of College Student Development,* 2001, *42*(2), 93–105.

Chang, M. J., Astin, A. W., and Kim, D. "Cross-Racial Interaction Among Undergraduates: Some Consequences, Causes and Patterns." *Research in Higher Education,* 2004, *45*(5), 529–553.

Chang, M. J., Denson, N., Sáenz, V., and Misa, K. "The Educational Benefits of Sustaining Cross-Racial Interaction Among Undergraduates." *Journal of Higher Education,* 2006, *77*(3), 430–455.

D'Augelli, A. R., and Hershberger, S. L. "African American Undergraduates on a Predominantly White Campus: Academic Factors, Social Networks, and Campus Climate." *Journal of Negro Education,* 1993, *62*(1), 67–81.

Davis, M., and others. "'A Fly in the Buttermilk': Descriptions of University Life by Successful Black Undergraduate Students at a Predominately White Southeastern University." *Journal of Higher Education,* 2004, *75*(4), 420–445.

Diver-Stamnes, A. C., and LoMascolo, A. F. "The Marginalization of Ethnic Minority Students: A Case Study of a Rural University." *Equity and Excellence in Education,* 2001, *34*(1), 50–58.

Eckel, P. D., and Kezar, A. J. *Taking the Reins: Institutional Transformation in Higher Education.* Westport, Conn.: Praeger, 2003.

Eimers, M. T., and Pike, G. R. "Minority and Nonminority Adjustment to College: Differences or Similarities?" *Research in Higher Education,* 1997, *38*(1), 77–97.

Feagin, J. R., Vera, H., and Imani, N. *The Agony of Education: Black Students at White Colleges and Universities.* New York: Routledge, 1996.

Fleming, J. *Blacks in College: A Comparative Study of Students' Success in Black and White Institutions.* San Francisco: Jossey-Bass, 1984.

Fries-Britt, S. L., and Turner, B. "Facing Stereotypes: A Case Study of Black Students on a White Campus." *Journal of College Student Development,* 2001, *42*(5), 420–429.

Gratz v. *Bollinger,* 123 2411 (S. Ct. 2003).

Grutter v. *Bollinger,* 124 35 (S. Ct. 2003).

Guiffrida, D. A. "African American Student Organizations as Agents of Social Integration." *Journal of College Student Development,* 2003, *44*(3), 304–319.

Gurin, P., Dey, E. L., Hurtado, S., and Gurin, G. "Diversity and Higher Education: Theory and Impact on Educational Outcomes." *Harvard Educational Review,* 2002, *72*(3), 330–366.

Harper, S. R., and Quaye, S. J. "Student Organizations as Venues for Black Identity Expression and Development Among African American Male Student Leaders." *Journal of College Student Development,* 2007, *48*(2), 127–144.

Helm, E. G., Sedlacek, W. E., and Prieto, D. O. "The Relationship Between Attitudes Toward Diversity and Overall Satisfaction of University Students by Race." *Journal of College Counseling,* 1998, *1,* 111–120.

Hurtado, S. "The Campus Racial Climate: Contexts of Conflict." *Journal of Higher Education,* 1992, *63*(5), 539–569.

Hurtado, S. "Graduate School Racial Climates and Academic Self-Concept Among Minority Graduate Students in the 1970s." *American Journal of Education,* 1994a, *102*(3), 330–351.

Hurtado, S. "The Institutional Climate for Talented Latino Students." *Research in Higher Education,* 1994b, *35*(1), 21–41.

Hurtado, S. "The Next Generation of Diversity and Intergroup Relations Research." *Journal of Social Issues,* 2005, *61*(3), 595–610.

Hurtado, S., and Carter, D. F. "Effects of College Transition and Perceptions of the Campus Racial Climate on Latino College Students' Sense of Belonging." *Sociology of Education,* 1997, *70*(4), 324–345.

Hurtado, S., Carter, D. F., and Spuler, A. "Latino Student Transition to College: Assessing Difficulties and Factors in Successful College Adjustment." *Research in Higher Education,* 1996, *37*(2), 135–157.

Hurtado, S., Milem, J. F., Clayton-Pedersen, A., and Allen, W. R. "Enhancing Campus Climates for Racial/Ethnic Diversity: Educational Policy and Practice." *Review of Higher Education,* 1998, *21*(3), 279–302.

Johnson-Durgans, V. D. "Perceptions of Racial Climates in Residence Halls Between African American and Euroamerican College Students." *Journal of College Student Development,* 1994, *35*(4), 267–274.

Kezar, A. J., and Eckel, P. D. "The Effect of Institutional Culture on Change Strategies in Higher Education: Universal Principles or Culturally Responsive Concepts?" *Journal of Higher Education,* 2002a, *73*(4), 435–460.

Kezar, A. J., and Eckel, P. D. "Examining the Institutional Transformation Process: The Importance of Sensemaking, Interrelated Strategies, and Balance." *Research in Higher Education,* 2002b, *43*(3), 295–328.

Kezar, A. J., and Eckel, P. D. *Leadership Strategies for Advancing Campus Diversity: Advice from Experienced Presidents.* Washington, D.C.: American Council on Education, 2005.

Levin, S., van Larr, C., and Sidanius, J. "The Effects of Ingroup and Outgroup Friendships on Ethnic Attitudes in College: A Longitudinal Study." *Group Processes and Intergroup Relations,* 2003, *6*(1), 76–92.

Lewis, A. E., Chesler, M., and Forman, T. A. "The Impact of 'Colorblind' Ideologies on Students of Color: Intergroup Relations at a Predominantly White University." *Journal of Negro Education,* 2000, *69*(1), 74–91.

Lincoln, Y., and Guba, E. G. "But Is It Rigorous? Trustworthiness and Authenticity in Naturalistic Evaluation." In D. William (ed.), *Naturalistic Evaluation.* New Directions for Program Evaluation, no. 30. San Francisco: Jossey-Bass, 1986.

Loo, C. M., and Rolison, G. "Alienation of Ethnic Minority Students at a Predominantly White University." *Journal of Higher Education,* 1986, *57*(1), 58–77.

Milem, J. F., Umbach, P. D., and Liang, C. T. H. "Exploring the Perpetuation Hypothesis: The Role of Colleges and Universities in Desegregating Society." *Journal of College Student Development,* 2004, *45*(6), 688–700.

Miles, M. B., and Huberman, A. M. *Qualitative Data Analysis: An Expanded Sourcebook.* (2nd ed.) Thousand Oaks, Calif.: Sage, 1994.

Moustakas, C. *Phenomenological Research Methods.* Thousand Oaks, Calif.: Sage, 1994.

Nettles, M. T., Thoeny, A. R., and Gosman, E. J. "Comparative and Predictive Analyses of Black and White Students' Achievement and Experiences." *Journal of Higher Education,* 1986, *57*(3), 289–318.

Nora, A., and Cabrera, A. F. "The Role of Perceptions of Prejudice and Discrimination on the Adjustment of Minority Students to College." *Journal of Higher Education,* 1996, *67*(2), 119–148.

Patton, L. D. "The Voice of Reason: A Qualitative Examination of Black Student Perceptions of Black Culture Centers." *Journal of College Student Development,* 2006, *47*(6), 628–644.

Patton, M. Q. *Qualitative Research and Evaluation Methods.* (3rd ed.) Thousand Oaks, Calif.: Sage, 2002.

Pike, G. R., and Kuh, G. D. "Relationships Among Structural Diversity, Informal Peer Interactions, and Perceptions of the Campus Environment." *Review of Higher Education,* 2006, *29*(4), 425–450.

Radloff, T. D., and Evans, N. J. "The Social Construction of Prejudice Among Black and White College Students." *NASPA Journal,* 2003, *40*(2), 1–16.

Rankin, S. R., and Reason, R. D. "Differing Perceptions: How Students of Color and White Students Perceive Campus Climate for Underrepresented Groups." *Journal of College Student Development,* 2005, *46*(1), 43–61.

Sáenz, V. B., Nagi, H. N., and Hurtado, S. "Factors Influencing Positive Interactions Across Race for African American, Asian American, Latino, and White College Students." *Research in Higher Education,* 2007, *48*(1), 1–38.

Smedley, B. D., Myers, H. F., and Harrell, S. P. "Minority-Status Stresses and the College Adjustment of Ethnic Minority Freshmen." *Journal of Higher Education,* 1993, *64*(4), 434–452.

Solórzano, D., Ceja, M., and Yosso, T. J. "Critical Race Theory, Racial Microaggressions, and Campus Racial Climate: The Experiences of African American College Students." *Journal of Negro Education,* 2000, *69*(1), 60–73.

Solórzano, D., and Villalpando, O. "Critical Race Theory: Marginality and the Experience of Students of Color in Higher Education." In C. A. Torres and T. R. Mitchell (eds.), *Sociology of Education: Emerging Perspectives.* Albany: State University of New York Press, 1998.

Suarez-Balcazar, Y., and others. "Experiences of Differential Treatment Among College Students of Color." *Journal of Higher Education,* 2003, *74*(4), 428–444.

Swim, J. K., and others. "African American College Students' Experiences with Everyday Racism: Characteristics of and Responses to These Incidents." *Journal of Black Psychology,* 2003, *29*(1), 38–67.

Turner, C. S. V. "Guests in Someone Else's House: Students of Color." *Review of Higher Education,* 1994, *17*(4), 355–370.

U.S. Department of Education. *A Test of Leadership, Charting the Future of U.S. Higher Education: A Report of the Commission Appointed by Secretary of Education Margaret Spellings.* Washington, D.C.: U.S. Department of Education, 2006.

CHAPTER 13

DECONSTRUCTING WHITENESS AS PART OF A MULTICULTURAL EDUCATIONAL FRAMEWORK: FROM THEORY TO PRACTICE

ANNA M. ORTIZ
ROBERT A. RHOADS

Based on emerging theoretical work on White racial identity, the authors argue that a central problem of multicultural education involves challenging the universalization of Whiteness. The authors propose a theoretical framework to advance a multicultural perspective in which the exploration and deconstruction of Whiteness is key.

Over the past 20 years a host of educational researchers have explored the intersections of race and schooling as part of the larger project to achieve racial equality in the United States. Such efforts have focused both on K through 12 settings as well as postsecondary educational contexts (Altbach & Lomotey, 1991; Apple, 1982; Kozol, 1991; McCarthy & Crichlow, 1993; Ogbu, 1978). More recently, and most pertinent to this chapter, theory and practice has focused on multicultural education and the goal of building culturally inclusive schools, colleges, and universities (Astin, 1993a; Banks, 1988; Delpit, 1995; Giroux, 1992; hooks, 1994; Rhoads & Valadez, 1996; Sleeter & Grant, 1994; Tierney, 1993). This movement is also evident in the field of student affairs where a variety of researchers have explored multiculturalism in relation to out-of-class learning as well as the preparation of student affairs practitioners (Manning & Coleman-Boatwright, 1991; McEwen & Roper, 1994; Pope, 1993; Rhoads & Black, 1995; Strange & Alston, 1998). The vast majority of multicultural research and theorizing has focused on the problems and complexities faced by students of color as members of diverse minority cultures in the United States. Although many of these findings are helpful in advancing multiculturalism, a major gap exists in this body of literature.

The gap in higher education's knowledge base relates to the limited exploration of White racial identity, or what may be termed "Whiteness." By ignoring the cultural complexities associated with White racial identity, practitioners and scholars may unwittingly contribute to the universalization of Whiteness, and consequently, the marginalization of non-White racial identities. Fusco (1988) addresses this very issue: "Racial identities are not only black, Latino, Asian, native American, and so on; they are also White. To ignore White ethnicity is to redouble its hegemony by naturalizing it. Without specifically addressing White ethnicity, there can be no critical evaluation of the construction of the other" (p. 9). And Roediger explained,

> When residents of the US talk about race, they too often talk only about African Americans, Native Americans, Hispanic Americans, and Asian Americans. If whites come into the discussion, it is only because they have "attitudes" towards nonwhites. Whites are assumed not to "have race," though they might be racists. Many of the most critical advances of recent scholarship on the social construction of race have come precisely because writers have challenged the assumption that we only need to explain why people come to be considered Black, Asian, Native American or Hispanic and not attend to . . . the "invention of the white race." (1994, p. 12)

We, along with others, concur with Roediger in seeing race largely as a social construction— meaning that little biological basis exists for grouping people by racial categories (Frankenberg, 1993, 1994, 1997; Giroux, 1997; hooks, 1992). However, we do not deny that as a social construction race has significant effects in terms of defining privilege and nonprivilege. As Roediger paradoxically notes, "Race is thus both unreal and a seeming reality" (1994, p. 6). For some, race is a very harsh reality, and this, ideologically and pragmatically, is what multiculturalism seeks to address.

Our goal in this chapter is to review recent scholarship on White racial identity and to suggest a theoretical framework for advancing multiculturalism in which the exploration and deconstruction of Whiteness is pivotal. Our fundamental assumption is this: If educators want to advance students' understanding of White privilege, and relatedly, racial inequality, they need to help students explore and deconstruct White racial identity, both among Whites and non-Whites. This is a pivotal step in promoting a multicultural perspective. However, placing Whiteness under the microscope is problematic; for example, significant resistance derives from the lack of consciousness among Whites about their own racial identity, and consequently, resentment is often directed at other racial groups who connect with their cultural heritage. Ultimately, our goal is to displace White racial identity as the universal norm by challenging ourselves and our students to name it. When students begin to see Whiteness as a visible aspect of society and culture, they are then in a better position to raise questions about its inequitable universalization.

Research on White Racial Identity

Research on White racial identity tends to be rooted in one of three general areas of inquiry: psychological, cultural, and educational. Psychological research on White identity development primarily revolves around Helms' work (1984, 1990). By focusing on the racial attitudes of Whites toward self and others, Helms identified six stages that Whites may pass through on the way to a more complex and integrated view of race. More recently, Helms and Piper (1994) have suggested that the stages may be best understood as statuses that do not necessarily follow a linear trajectory. The six statuses are: contact, disintegration, reintegration, pseudo-independent, immersion/emersion, autonomy. Movement between these statuses generally flows from "a superficial and inconsistent awareness of being White" (Helms, 1990, p. 55) to high levels of consciousness characterized by a realization of White privilege and a commitment to pursuing social change.

Rowe, Bennett, and Atkinson (1994) developed a similar conception of White racial consciousness and suggested seven types reflective of one's attitudes toward racial identity; avoidant, dissonant, dependent, dominative, conflictive, reactive, and integrative. As with later explanations of the Helms model, the White racial consciousness model is not to be treated as a linear stage theory. Also, like the Helms model, the White racial consciousness model suggests that attitudinal differences among Whites range from a lack of "consideration of one's own White identity" (p. 136) to those reflecting a "pragmatic view of ethnic/minority issues" (p. 141). Block and Carter (1996) criticized the final location in the White racial consciousness model because it implies, in their words, "that an individual characterized by a healthy White identity could be seen as being passive and free of guilt with regard to racial/ethnic issues and simply be content with the status quo in this country, suggesting that he or she would be a supporter of a racist society" (p. 329). We also assert that any developmental model of Whiteness must include a commitment to social action as a central facet of a vital identity.

A serious problem with the preceding psychological theories is that they only address a portion of what it means to be White: a sole focus on racial attitudes toward oneself and others does not constitute a holistic view of White identity. This, as Roediger (1994) has pointed out, is problematic given the fact that one's sense of White racial identity involves much more than simply how one views Whites and non-Whites. Just as ethnic identity for culturally different people includes aspects of culture (language, customs, religion, food), identifying elements of White culture is necessary for a wholistic view. For example, specific aspects of U.S. culture predominantly reflect the White experience; the racial segregation of sports and genres of music offer some examples. Equally assured is the fact that if particular aspects of culture are part of the White experience, then they also contribute to White identity. After all, as Hall (1990) has pointed out, "Cultural identities are the points of identification . . . which are made within the discourses of history and culture" (p. 226). Similarly, Rhoads (1997) has argued, "Identities are constituted within the parameters of culture" (p. 95). The classic statement from Geertz (1973) alludes to the power of culture in shaping identity as well: "Man is an animal suspended in webs of significance he himself has spun" (p. 5). Let us turn then to cultural analyses of the construction of White racial identity.

In cultural studies, incorporating mostly feminist, historical, anthropological, and sociological frameworks, researchers also have uncovered understandings linked to the construction of White racial identity which more directly illustrate the connection between White racial identity and the supremacy of Whiteness in U.S. society. For example, Winant (1997) has argued that White identity has been reinterpreted and rearticulated "in a dualistic fashion: on the one hand egalitarian, on the other privileged; on the one hand individualistic and 'color blind,' on the other hand 'normalized' and White" (p. 42). Nowhere is this dualistic framework more evident than in the 1990s debate about affirmative action. Whereas one group of Whites has supported affirmative action as part of an egalitarian measure, the other, as Winant argued, has situated Whiteness as disadvantage. Despite the lack of empirical support for claims of reverse discrimination, a deeply resistant form of White identity emerged after the dramatic social and cultural upheaval of the 1960s, and, as Winant has maintained, "Provides the cultural and political 'glue' that holds together a wide variety of reactionary racial politics" (p. 42). Particular constructions of Whiteness, for Winant, have tended to fall into one of five categories ranging from a belief in the biological superiority of Whites (the far right racial project) to a belief in the need to abolish Whiteness altogether (the new abolitionist racial project).

The abolitionist project is most notable in the work of Roediger (1991, 1994), who has argued that "the idea of race is given meaning through the agency of human beings in concrete historical and social contexts, and is not a biological or natural category" (1994, p. 2). This supports our contention that race is largely socially constructed; and because race is a social construction it offers the possibility of being deconstructed and reconstructed. Intellectual efforts aimed at making Whiteness visible is for Roediger part of the political and cultural project of abolishing Whiteness altogether (something that remains largely invisible and often is deeply entrenched within the subconscious realm is hard to critique). And, of course, because Whiteness is the universal standard by which diverse others are measured, and, in turn, delimited and devalued, its abolition has the potential to be emancipatory for non-Whites.

Intellectually and pragmatically, we have concerns about the goal of abolishing Whiteness as a cultural construction and source of identity, as well as the logical conclusion of ultimately eliminating the entire category of race. The presumption underlying such a strategy suggests to us that equality cannot be achieved without complete elimination of racial identity differences and the related identity politics. We believe an alternative vision does in fact exist and is rooted in the ideals of multiculturalism and the valuing of difference. Briefly, multiculturalism advances the ideal of communities of difference in which concerns for dialogue and learning about one another's lives becomes a source of community building (Burbules & Rice, 1990; Rhoads, 1997; Rhoads & Valadez, 1996; Tierney, 1993). Hence, in terms of Whiteness, its elimination is not the only solution: Displacing Whiteness as the universal standard by which all other races are gauged is also a step toward racial and cultural equity. Frankenberg (1997) has spoken to this position when she argued for the need to "resituate Whiteness from its unspoken (perhaps unspeakable?) status; to displace and then reemplace it" (p. 3). Realistically, any movement toward denormalizing Whiteness is a positive step to be taken.

From the intellectual advances associated with the recent exploration of White racial identity have come educational research and theory aimed at exposing the underlying influences of Whiteness in teaching and learning contexts. Maher and Tetreault (1997), for example, sought to reexamine their study of college classrooms conducted from a feminist perspective. "We considered ourselves feminist researchers sharing a common perspective with the women of color that we studied," they explained, only later to discover that "as White researchers, we did not fully interrogate our social position of privilege, which made us vis à vis our subjects, oppressors as well as feminist allies" (p. 322). In the reexamination of the data that previously had formed the basis for

The Feminist Classroom (1994), Maher and Tetreault sought to unearth racial privilege through the "excavation of Whiteness in its many dimensions and complexities" (p. 322). A key strategy they have recommended is the use of literature aimed in part at unearthing the effects of the cultural networks related to Whiteness. Examples of the literature they have recommended include Morrison's *The Bluest Eye* (1970) and *Playing in the Dark* (1993), McIntosh's (1992) work on White and male privilege, Ellsworth's (1997) pedagogical exploration of the effects of Whiteness, and Hacker's (1995) analysis of Black and White racial divisions and related discrimination.

Giroux (1997) also explored the educational implications of Whiteness and suggested that educators need to create learning opportunities that enable students to connect White ideology and identity with progressive social reform. "Central to such a task is the political and pedagogical challenge of refashioning an anti-racist politics that informs a broader, radical, democratic project" (1997, p. 315). The deconstruction of Whiteness, especially its advantages and privileges, helps students to discover the direct impact of living in a society where being White is favored in the distribution of social capital and opportunity. Concerned with advancing anti-racist politics, Fine (1997) offered insight into the potential of examining institutionalized discrimination in schools (e.g., tracking) "that renders Whiteness meritocratic and other colors deficient" (p. 64). Instead of focusing on students who continue to endure discrimination, Fine has suggested that institutional analyses may be better suited for exposing the ways that Whiteness is situated as advantage. Also concerned with unearthing advantage, Rosenberg (1997) found student autobiographies to be helpful tools in promoting understandings of privilege among White college students.

The preceding works reflect a belief in the political and cultural potential of educational interventions. In this regard, we agree with King and Shuford (1996), who have argued that a multicultural perspective actually depicts a cognitively more advanced view about cultural diversity. Ultimately, educational theory and practice concerned with unearthing Whiteness and advancing a more democratic, multicultural society needs to explore specific pedagogical strategies.

A Theoretical Framework

Theoretical and empirical evidence supports the development of educational strategies that challenge students to give serious consideration to the construction of Whiteness. Educational strategies that assist students in exploring White racial identity are likely to promote higher levels of White racial consciousness and at the same time offer the potential to deepen student understanding of culture and privilege. The problem, as most college and university educators are well aware, is that students, especially White students, tend to shut down when issues of race and privilege are introduced to classroom and cocurricular contexts. Students often fear that they may unintentionally make ignorant or racist statements, or that they may indeed expose prejudice and stereotypes they have. Therefore, multicultural education theories and strategies are needed for addressing this problem.

The following four assumptions undergird our theoretical approach:

1. Culture is a misunderstood construct, but one that is key for helping students understand diversity and confront their own racism.
2. Students in general and White students in particular have a difficult time identifying their own cultural connections.
3. Cultural diversity is a fact of life and efforts to build a common culture inevitably privilege the dominant culture.
4. Multiculturalism is a valued and desired view for students to develop.

Our framework follows five steps which are informed by the assumptions listed above: (a) understanding culture, (b) learning about other cultures, (c) recognizing and deconstructing White culture, (d) recognizing the legitimacy of other cultures, and (e) developing a multicultural outlook (see Figure 1). Our thinking reflects not only the work on Whiteness and White privilege by Roediger (1991, 1994), Frankenberg (1994, 1997), McIntosh (1992) and others, but

	Step 1: Understanding Culture	Step 2: Learning About Other Cultures	Step 3: Recognizing and Deconstructing White Culture	Step 4: Recognizing the Legitimacy of Other Cultures	Step 5: Developing a Multicultural Outlook
Cognitive Goal	To develop a complex understanding of culture (culture shapes people's lives and people shape culture).	To develop a more advanced understanding of diverse cultures.	To develop an understanding of how White culture has been universalized as the norm and to begin to question its privileged position.	To recognize that culture other than one's own is just as valued to another individual.	To recognize that all cultures within a given society shape each other and that the inclusion of all cultures requires the reconstruction of U.S. society.
Beginning Problem Statement	I see culture as something a society creates.	I know that differences between cultural groups exist, but the differences are only superficial.	I see culture as something that some have, but others do not.	I understand that there are many cultures, but we should agree on a common culture.	I value living in a society that is multicultural.
Ending Problem Statement	Culture is something I create, but that also creates me.	I understand that many cultural groups exist within the U.S. and each reflects deeply held norms, values, beliefs, and traditions.	I see culture as something that all people have.	I see that many diverse cultures can coexist including my own and that this is a good thing.	I can work to make society an equitable place for people of all cultural backgrounds because our vitality is intricately tied to one another's.
Activity	Understanding Culture— Observing and critically analyzing everyday events.	Exploring Cultures— Attending cultural events and reflecting on their meaning as well as dialoguing with culturally diverse others.	Analyzing White Culture— Learning to recognize White culture and to begin to challenge its normalization.	The Impact of Culture— Students identifying aspects of own cultures that play important roles in their lives and sharing these with other students.	Multiculturalism leads to Action— Discovering how institutions shape the ways in which culture is expressed.

Figure 1   Framework of Multicultural Education (Ortiz & Rhoads)

also the work of Sleeter and Grant (1994) on multicultural educational strategies and Garcia's (1995) work on culture as a key construct in multicultural training. The framework is not meant to be considered as an invariant linear model, but one in which each of the five steps contributes to an overall educational goal of enhancing multicultural education. Elements of each step may be incorporated in one educational intervention, used separately in individually designed educational programs, or the framework as a whole may be used to guide the development of curricula addressing multicultural issues.

Following the discussion of each step in the framework, we briefly discuss educational strategies that we have used to meet the cognitive goal of the step. We wish we could include student outcomes research verifying the effectiveness of the framework and thus demonstrating that we have helped students to progress toward multicultural understanding, but this is not the case, nor is such data likely to become available anytime soon. The fact is that altering attitudes involves much more than simply exposing students to alternative forms of thought through a 1- or 2-hour exercise. The pedagogical strategies suggested should be viewed as part of a long-term process through which increased exposure to alternative ways of viewing race, culture, and identity eventually challenge students to rethink their own views. As student outcomes research has clearly shown, oftentimes the effects of college are long term (Astin, 1993b; Pascarella & Terenzini, 1991). In the end then, the development of meaningful pedagogical strategies must rest a great deal on the logical extensions drawn from sound theories.

Step 1: Understanding Culture

In Step 1, the overarching cognitive goal is for students to fully understand how culture shapes their lives and how they shape culture through their interactions. This is the more complex notion of culture, in which culture is much more than simply the artifacts that a society creates. Geertz's (1973) dynamic notion of culture as "webs of significance" that are in part created through human interaction and at the same time guide human interaction is the depth of understanding sought here. The beginning problem statement reads: "I see culture as something a society creates." However, the ending problem statement reads: "Culture is something I create, but that also creates me." An activity designed to promote a more advanced understanding of culture involves some type of exercise that gets at how culture shapes the human condition, but at the same time highlights the ability people have to alter culture. An advanced understanding of culture also should incorporate knowledge about how culture shapes one's worldview and hence, how one perceives others and their cultures.

For Step 1 a myriad of activities can be used to achieve the cognitive goal. Many of these come from the work of intercultural communication practitioners and scholars who train students and business personnel to sojourn abroad (Bennett, 1986; Gudyknust & Kim, 1984; Hess, 1997; Paige, 1993; Sorti, 1990; Stewart & Bennett, 1991). In Step 1 the bulk of learning comes from critical reflection and analysis of everyday events. From this examination comes the realization that culture indeed affects individuals and that individuals through social interaction also affect culture.

Because of the cognitive complexity of this stage we recommend two activities that have been particularly effective in helping students to understand culture as a dynamic and dialectical phenomenon. In the first activity, students observe a setting on campus where their attention is focused on one particular behavior or attribute. For example, a student may choose to study how students greet each other on the central quad area of campus. Before the observation, students, guided by the facilitator, generate a list of questions about the behavior and setting they are about to observe. Sample questions might be: Were the greetings loud and boisterous or more subdued? Did students use physical contact in some way? Were students walking alone or in groups? Did they stay or move on? What were the students wearing? Once the observations are complete, students are given quiet time to write down their reflections and discoveries from the exercise (this could be done as a homework assignment as well). The group then comes together and compares notes. Attention must be paid to the many "teachable moments" as students are often drawn to different attributes in the setting and will have divergent interpretations of the same setting. At this point students begin to see how culture shapes human behavior and perception. Facilitators can encourage this process by asking questions such as: What norms did you observe and did anyone violate those norms? From where do such norms come? These questions should help students to see how social lives are indeed shaped by culture, but also they come to understand how people shape cultural norms.

A more advanced activity for Step 1 is to conduct an analysis of a "critical incident." Kappler (1998) used the following critical incident in her study of intercultural perspective-taking among U.S. students:

> Mariko is a student from Japan. Although when she first arrived she was a little uneasy, she is now used to the different routines and lifestyle and is doing quite well in school and is fluent in English. She has become good friends with one of her classmates, Linda. One afternoon, their professor asked for two volunteers to come in early the next class to help with a special project. Linda raised her hand and volunteered herself and suggested Mariko might also be willing. Mariko replied hesitantly that she did not think she could do it and that it would be better to ask someone else. Linda said that Mariko would be quite good and told the professor they would do it. The next day, Mariko did not turn up and Linda did all the work herself. The next time Linda saw Mariko she asked her rather coldly what had happened to her. Mariko apologized and said that she had to study for an exam that day and she didn't really feel capable of doing the work. Linda was frustrated and asked her why she had not said so clearly in the class at the time. Mariko looked down and said nothing.

Analysis of this critical incident challenges students to develop an explanation of what happened from Linda's point of view, from Mariko's point of view, and from the students' own points of view. The comparative analysis of the differing points of view helps to demonstrate how culture shapes our behavior and our perspectives. Additionally, the facilitator also needs to raise questions about how cultural norms might be altered by various actors in a critical incident. Of course, facilitators should be encouraged to write critical incidents that are highly relevant to the specific contexts of the students with whom they are working.

Step 2: Learning about Other Cultures

Step 2 provides the laboratory for Step 1. Much of the multicultural education that took place on college campuses in the 1980s focused on "cultural awareness." Programs and events were designed to expose students to the traditions, food, and music of distinct cultural groups. Although such programs are important in helping students experience aspects of diverse cultures, we contend that without serious reflection about culture as a construct, the potential for a deeper understanding of cultural diversity is likely to be lost. With the orientation to understanding culture that is offered in Step 1, the cultural exploration of others' lives becomes grounded in a theoretical understanding of culture. We have found through our own pedagogical efforts that students develop an enthusiasm for cultural exploration when it is enhanced by theoretical insights about culture. They begin to make connections between cultural artifacts such as food, clothing, and music, and the complex norms, values, and beliefs associated with various cultural groups. Hence, the beginning problem statement in Step 2 reads: "I know that differences between cultural groups exist, but the differences are only superficial." The ending problem statement is: "I understand that many cultural groups exist within the US and each reflects deeply held norms, values, beliefs, and traditions."

Step 2 activities should be designed to build energy and enthusiasm for learning about other cultures. Activities like this are probably a staple of multicultural education at most colleges and universities. The educational activity for this step involves motivating students to attend cultural events and programs already planned by groups on campus. Of course, an easy way to help students take the risk to attend such events is to go as a group. Although we tend to think that attending cultural events is a low-risk way to educate oneself, "I don't have anyone to go with" is a common refrain we hear from our students (and sometimes ourselves). Such outings should be accompanied by a reflection component as this will help to facilitate a more meaningful learning experience much in the way reflection adds to the community service experience.

In groups where participation is ongoing (i.e., an orientation course or student staff training), we also recommend an activity in which students engage in an ongoing dialogue with a culturally different person. We have used this strategy in courses by asking students to meet with their dialogue partner at least once a week for about 6 weeks. We do not encourage students to enter each encounter with a set of interview questions; rather, our preference is the student or facilitator determine a general topic for each meeting. We also stress that the dialogues are meant to be an exchange and not a one-way conversation in which the primary contributor is the cultural other. We have found that students learn a great deal about another culture and person through this exercise, and that their confidence level in having significant interactions with diverse others increases. The extent of this process can be quite basic or rather extensive, as in the "voice project" described by Strange and Alston (1998).

Step 3: Recognizing and Deconstructing White Culture

In Step 3, the overarching cognitive goal is helping students to see that Whites have culture, and that White culture has become in many ways the unchallenged, universal basis for racial identity. Experience tells us that in the preceding step students primarily will focus on aspects of culture typically derived from non-Whites (both White and non-White students when asked to explore a culture different from their own will rarely select White cultural groups). Because of a general lack of recognition of White culture, students are ill-equipped for deconstructing Whiteness. Recognizing and deconstructing Whiteness is particularly challenging to White students, because of White culture being so universalized. When White students begin to recognize that they in fact are culturally positioned, they are more likely to understand that others have culture too. Thus, White students begin to see the essence of racial differences. The beginning problem statement for Step 3 is: "I see culture as something that some have, but others do not." The ending problem statement reads: "I see culture as something that all people have." We call the pedagogical exercise for Step 3, "Analyzing White Culture," and we focus on getting students to reflect on aspects of White culture as a source of identity.

Step 3 is the key contribution we offer to a comprehensive multicultural educational intervention. We need to be clear here. We are not saying that White culture is in any way more significant or of greater value than any of the many other cultural identities. However, a lack of understanding of Whiteness is a major barrier to achieving a multicultural society. Therefore, we contend that the deconstruction of Whiteness must be central to educational interventions designed to challenge White privilege and advance a multicultural perspective.

The exercise we have used for Step 3 is called Analyzing White Culture and is quite simple to implement. However, although the exercise may be simple, the complications and discomforts associated with students' explorations of race need to be thought about in advance. Because the discussion has the potential to be animated and conflictual, the facilitator should establish some communicative guidelines before beginning the activity. Guidelines might include the following: only one person speaks at a time, no heckling, participants must agree to keep an open mind, and participants must agree to stay through the debriefing phase of the program. Analyzing White Culture involves asking students to list on a sheet of paper the 10 most significant characteristics, adjectives, or statements that come to mind when asked to describe White racial identity or White culture. We use the terms "White racial identity" and "White culture" interchangeably in this exercise because some students find it easier to describe one and not the other, and both capture various characteristics associated with the diversity of White experience in the U.S.

We use two basic permutations of this exercise. One strategy is to collect the lists and then pass them back to students randomly so that each student gets someone else's. Of course, to ensure anonymity, the same kind of paper should be used by all students and they should not write their names on the paper. Another option, but one that only should be used with a diverse group of students, is to ask the students to indicate whether they are White or a person of color (specific racial or ethnic categories may compromise student anonymity, depending of course on the size and diversity of the group). This adds another dimension to the discussion in that theoretically one might expect to see some differences in the lists depending on the status of the student as White or as a person of color. For example, White students often ask, "What do you mean by White culture? There isn't one." Meanwhile, students of color may already be on item five or six. This is to be expected given the fact that the universalization of Whiteness is experienced most pointedly by people of color, while its normative status may be taken for granted by Whites. The fact that students of color may have an easier time completing their lists is an important outcome of the exercise and should be a key concern in the subsequent discussion. Again, attempting this exercise without adequate representation of both students of color and White students is not advisable because a degree of discomfort related to racial exploration is a likely result and small numbers of students from one group should not be forced to confront such psychological and emotionally challenging activities.

Once the responses have been collected and then randomly distributed, the facilitator will ask for volunteers to read their lists (and to identify the race of the person who completed the list, but only if the group is diverse!). Once several lists have been read the facilitator should solicit reactions from students. Debriefing involves the facilitator reconnecting the purpose of the Exploring White Culture exercise with the larger goal of advancing racial and multicultural understanding.

Step 4: Recognizing the Legitimacy of Other Cultures

The cognitive goal of Step 4 is recognizing that culture other than one's own is just as valuable and meaningful to another individual. This involves getting students to see that many cultures exist at the same time and that such multiplicity is not a bad thing. The beginning problem statement reads: "I understand that there are many cultures, but we should agree on a common culture." The ending problem statement is: "I see that many diverse cultures can co-exist including my own and that this is a good thing."

In Step 4 students move from general and specific understandings of culture and cultures to the realization that multiple cultures have a legitimate place in U.S. society. The activity recommended for this step helps students to recognize the impact of culture on individuals by identifying which aspects of their individual cultures play important roles in their lives. The worksheet for this exercise has three columns. In the first column (titled Cultural Attribute) students list important aspects of their culture. In the second column (titled Contribution to Sense of Self) students explain what each attribute contributes to their identity, how they feel about and perceive themselves in reference to others. Finally, in the last column (titled Affects How I See the World by . . .) students record the ways in which each attribute might shape their perceptions of themselves, other individuals, cultures, and societies.

After students have completed the grid they should be placed in small groups that are as diverse as possible (up to four). They are instructed to notice what attributes they have in common and those that are different. Those with common attributes are likely to have different responses for the last two columns. Students need to pay close attention to these as they are the prime examples of the ways in which culture affects individuals.

Step 5: Developing a Multicultural Outlook

The cognitive goal for Step 5 is helping students to recognize that all cultures within a given society shape each other and that the inclusion of all cultures requires the reconstruction of U.S. society. The previous steps help students to learn more about other cultures and begin to incorporate multicultural perspectives into their own identities. Step 5 offers the potential to motivate students to take action to assist creating multicultural society. The beginning problem statement reads: "I value living in a society that is multicultural." The ending problem statement reveals a more complex understanding of the interface between culture, society, and its members: "I can work to make society an equitable place for people of all cultural backgrounds because our vitality is intricately tied to one another's." Students need to focus on embracing multiculturalism and discover how societal institutions embrace or deny cultural difference and how the status of one's culture in a society affects individuals. Educational strategies used in this step help students move away from xenophobia and toward celebrating difference in such a way that they see taking social action toward the inclusion of diverse cultural perspectives as the logical next step in their own education and liberation. In this regard, we agree with Sleeter and Grant's (1994) view: The most valuable form of multicultural education is both multicultural and social reconstructionist.

In Step 5 students are encouraged to integrate a multicultural perspective that helps them to become critical consumers of culture. At this point students should be able to recognize that their culture changes over time (and their "selves" change as well) as they and their society embrace diverse cultural perspectives. In their quest to learn about other cultures, they may find that they incorporate aspects of other cultures into their own behavior and cognitive structures. They also begin to see societal consequences for the continuing marginality of diverse cultures in the U.S. Their multicultural outlook calls for them to take action on both internal and external levels.

The activity that helps students become more multiculturally oriented is an institutional analysis of how their colleges or universities support or do not support the expression of diverse cultures. This activity may be implemented two different ways. With an ongoing group such as a staff or a class, small groups of three students are given a unit or activity at the particular institution to analyze. They visit the space or context, speak with staff and students, examine the publications related to the unit or activity, and explore the connections the particular unit or activity has with other areas of campus life. Their charge is to unearth the ways in which diverse cultural expressions are present or absent from the particular environment and what might be done to enhance cultural inclusiveness.

With a group that meets only one time (i.e., a training session or one-shot educational program), the facilitator uses the same small group method, but instead of extended study of a particular unit or activity, the facilitator collects artifacts from various units or activities around campus. The artifacts may include publications, job descriptions, applications, photos, or newspaper clippings. Small groups then have the same charge as the more permanent groups: to unearth ways in which diverse cultural expressions are present or absent from the particular environment and what might be done to enhance cultural inclusiveness.

Conclusion

We believe that this framework helps to increase the multicultural understanding of all students, but especially White students. We see multicultural understanding as a developmental journey where a multicultural outlook is created by guiding students through a process where they are confronted with more difficult challenges as they accomplish those which are less challenging. This framework also promotes attitudes that encourage cultural learning and intercultural competence as Hess (1997) outlined. These attitudes include: a high regard for culture, an eagerness to learn, a desire to make connections, and a readiness to give as well as receive.

One of the major limitations of this framework and of other frameworks or models of multicultural education or prejudice reduction is the paucity of research and evaluative findings. Although some specific interventions have been tested in small studies (Greenman & Kimmel, 1995; Suarez-Balcazar, Drulak, & Smith, 1995), we did not find widespread research on the effects of multicultural education and prejudice reduction models. We have begun to collect data for the activity described in Step 3 (Analyzing White Culture), and we will seek to examine the effectiveness of the framework and its activities in the future. We encourage other researchers and educators to collect evaluative data and share such findings through publication and conference presentations. Evaluative data need not be limited to the study of outcomes, but may also include qualitative explorations of the dynamics of facilitating such activities and reports of student reactions to them. Obviously, all theoretical frameworks should be continually refined, and we expect no less for the framework proposed here. We also encourage educators to experiment with the kinds of activities suggested for each of the theoretical steps of our framework. We have described some that have worked for us, but at the same time improvements can be made here as well. The usefulness and success of some of the activities we list will vary depending on the contexts and the students involved.

We in no way expect that this framework completes a student's multicultural journey. We see students moving from this framework to others that focus on prejudice reduction (Helms's White Racial Identity Model), ally development (Washington & Evans, 1991), and more social-action-oriented goals (Sleeter & Grant, 1994).

One lesson that we have learned in the course of our work with students in multicultural education is that if more resistant White students are to be affected by multicultural education, the intervention and facilitators must be willing to meet the students at their respective level of development. For most college-aged White students, beginning the dialogue with discussions of

White privilege or White racism provide too great a challenge. We assert that our framework of multicultural understanding begins at a less threatening point (but no less important) that teaches students basics about the importance of culture. As with other forms of learning, the goal of the educator is to foster students' enthusiasm for learning in a way that motivates them to take on greater challenges. Indeed, enthusiasm for cultural learning is at the heart of building a multicultural society and is key to the success of the framework we have proposed in this chapter.

References

Altbach, P. G., & Lomotey, K. (Eds.). (1991). *The racial crisis in American higher education*. Albany: State University of New York Press.

Apple, M. W. (1982). *Education and power*. Boston: Routledge and Kegan Paul.

Astin, A. W. (1993a). Diversity and multiculturalism on the campus: How are students affected? *Change, 25*(1), 44–49.

Astin, A. W. (1993b). *What matters in college: Four critical years revisited*. San Francisco: Jossey-Bass.

Banks, J. (1988). *Multicultural education: Theory and practice*. Boston: Allyn and Bacon.

Bennett, M. J. (1986). A developmental approach to training for intercultural sensitivity. *International Journal of Intercultural Relations, 2*, 179–96.

Block, C. J., & Carter, R. T. (1996). White racial identity attitude theories: A rose by any other name is still a rose. *The Counseling Psychologist, 24*(2), 326–334.

Burbules, N., & Rice, S. (1991). Dialogue across differences: Continuing the conversation. *Harvard Educational Review, 61*(4), 393–416.

Delpit, L. (1995). *Other people's children: Cultural conflict in the classroom*. New York: New Press.

Ellsworth, E. (1997). Double binds of Whiteness. In M. Fine, L. Weis, L. C. Powell, & L. M. Won (Eds.), *Off-White: Readings on society, race, and culture* (pp. 259–269). New York: Routledge.

Fine, M. (1997). Witnessing Whiteness. In M. Fine, L. Weis, L. C. Powell, & L. M. Won (Eds.), *Off-White: Readings on society, race, and culture* (pp. 57–65). New York: Routledge.

Frankenberg, R. (1993). *White women, race matters: The social construction of Whiteness*. Minneapolis: University of Minnesota Press.

Frankenberg, R. (1994). Whiteness and Americanness: Examining constructions of race, culture and nation in White women's life narratives. In S. Gregory & R. Sanjek (Eds.), *Race* (pp. 62–77). New Brunswick, NJ: Rutgers University Press.

Frankenberg, R. (1997). Introduction: Local Whitenesses, localizing Whiteness. In R. Frankenberg (Ed.), *Displacing Whiteness: Essays in social and cultural criticism* (pp. 1–33). Durham, NC: Duke University Press.

Fusco, C. (1988). Fantasies of oppositionality. *Afterimage, 16* (December), 6–9.

Garcia, M. H. (1995). An anthropological approach to multicultural diversity training. *Journal of Applied Behavioral Science, 31*(4), 490–504.

Geertz, C. (1973). *The interpretation of cultures*. New York: Basic Books.

Giroux, H. A. (1992). *Border crossings: Cultural workers and the politics of education*. New York: Routledge.

Giroux, H. A. (1997). Rewriting the discourse of racial identity: Towards a pedagogy and politics of Whiteness. *Harvard Educational Review, 67*(2), 285–320.

Greenman, N. P., & Kimmel, E. B. (1995). The road to multicultural education: Potholes to resistance. *Journal of Teacher Education, 46*, 360–368.

Gudyknust, W. B., & Kim, Y. Y. (1984). *Communicating with strangers: An approach to intercultural communication*. Reading, MA: Addison-Wesley.

Hacker, A. (1995). *Two nations: Black and White, separate, hostile, unequal*. New York: Ballantine Books.

Hall, S. (1990). Cultural identity and diaspora. In J. Rutherford (Ed.), *Identity: Community, culture, difference* (pp. 222–237). London: Lawrence & Wishart.

Helms, J. E. (1984). Toward a theoretical explanation of the effects of race on counseling: A Black and White model. *The Counseling Psychologist, 12*(4), 153–165.

Helms, J. E. (1990). *Black and White racial identity attitudes: Theory, research, and practice*. Westport, CT: Greenwood.

Helms, J. E., & Piper, R. E. (1994). Implications of racial identity theory for vocational psychology. *Journal of Vocational Behavior, 44*, 124–138.

Hess, J. D. (1997). *Studying abroad/learning abroad: An abridged edition of the whole world guide to culture learning.* Yarmouth, ME: Intercultural Press.

hooks, b. (1992). *Black looks: Race and representation.* Boston: South End Press.

hooks, b. (1994). *Teaching to transgress: Education as the practice of freedom.* New York: Routledge.

Kappler, B. J. (1998). *Refining intercultural perspective-taking.* Unpublished doctoral dissertation, University of Minnesota, Minneapolis.

King, P. M., & Shuford, B. C. (1996). A multicultural view is a more cognitively complex view: Cognitive development and multicultural education. *American Behavioral Scientist, 40*(2), 153–164.

Kozol, J. (1991). *Savage inequalities: Children in America's schools.* New York: Harper Perennial.

Maher, F. A., & Tetreault, M. K. T. (1994). *The feminist classroom: An inside look at how professors and students are transforming higher education for a diverse society.* New York: Basic Books.

Maher, F. A., & Tetreault, M. K. T. (1997). Learning in the dark: How assumptions of Whiteness shape classroom knowledge. *Harvard Educational Review, 67*(2), 321–349.

Manning, K., & Coleman-Boatwright, P. (1991). Student affairs initiatives toward a multicultural university. *Journal of College Student Development, 32*, 367–374.

McCarthy, C., & Crichlow, W. (Eds.). (1993). *Race, identity, and representation in education.* New York: Routledge.

McEwen, M. K., & Roper, L. D. (1994). Incorporating multiculturalism into student affairs preparation programs: Suggestions from the literature. *Journal of College Student Development, 35*, 46–53.

McIntosh, P. (1992). White privilege and male privilege: A personal account of coming to see correspondence through work in women's studies. In M. L. Anderson & P. Hill Collins (Eds.), *Race, class, and gender: An anthology* (pp. 70–81). Belmont, CA: Wadsworth.

Morrison, T. (1970). *The bluest eye.* New York: Holt, Rinehart & Winston.

Morrison, T. (1993). *Playing in the dark: Whiteness and the literary imagination.* New York: Vintage.

Ogbu, J. U. (1978). *Minority education and caste: The American system in cross cultural-perspective.* New York: Academic.

Paige, R. M. (Ed.) (1993). *Education for the intercultural experience.* Yarmouth, ME: Intercultural Press.

Pascarella, E. T., & Terenzini, P. T. (1991). *How college affects students.* San Francisco: Jossey-Bass.

Pope, R. L. (1993). Multicultural-organization development in student affairs: An introduction. *Journal of College Student Development, 34*, 201–205.

Rhoads, R. A. (1997). *Community service and higher learning: Explorations of the caring self.* Albany: State University of New York.

Rhoads, R. A., & Black, M. A. (1995). Student affairs practitioners as transformative educators: Advancing a critical cultural perspective. *Journal of College Student Development, 36*, 413–421.

Rhoads, R. A., & Valadez, J. R. (1996). *Democracy, multiculturalism, and the community college: A critical perspective.* New York: Garland.

Roediger, D. (1991). *The wages of Whiteness: Race and the making of the American working class.* New York: Verso.

Roediger, D. (1994). *Towards the abolition of Whiteness: Essays of race, politics, and working class history.* New York: Verso.

Rosenberg, P. M. (1997). Underground discourses: Exploring Whiteness in teacher education. In M. Fine, L. Weis, L. C. Powell, & L. M. Won (Eds.), *Off-White: Readings on society, race, and culture* (pp. 79–89). New York: Routledge.

Rowe, W., Bennett, S. K., & Atkinson, D. R. (1994). White racial identity models: A critique and alternative proposal. *The Counseling Psychologist, 22*, 129–146.

Saurez-Balcazar, J., Drulack, J. A., & Smith, C. (1995). Multicultural training practices in community psychology programs. *American Journal of Community Psychology, 22*, 785–798.

Sleeter, C. E., & Grant, C. A. (1994). *Making choices for multicultural education: Five approaches to race, class and gender* (2nd edition). New York: Macmillan.

Sorti, C. (1990). *The art of crossing cultures.* Yarmouth, ME: Intercultural Press.

Stewart, E. C., & Bennett, M. J. (1991) (2nd ed.). *American cultural patterns: A cross-cultural perspective.* Yarmouth, ME: Intercultural Press.

Strange, C., & Alston, L. (1998). Voicing differences: Encouraging multicultural learning. *Journal of College Student Development, 39,* 87–99.

Tierney, W. G. (1993). *Building communities of difference: Higher education in the 21st century.* Westport, CT: Bergin & Garvey.

Washington, J., & Evans, N. J. (1991). Becoming an ally. In N. J. Evans & V. A. Wall (Eds.), *Beyond tolerance: Gays, lesbians, and bisexuals on campus.* Alexandria, VA: American Association of Counseling and Development.

Winant, H. (1997). Behind blue eyes: Whiteness and contemporary U.S. racial politics. In M. Fine, L. Weis, L. C. Powell, & L. M. Wong (Eds.), *Off-White: Readings on race, power, and society* (pp. 40–53). New York: Routledge.

Chapter 14

Racial Diversity Matters: The Impact of Diversity-Related Student Engagement and Institutional Context

Nida Denson

Mitchell J. Chang

This study addressed two questions: (a) Do different forms of campus racial diversity contribute uniquely to students' learning and educational experiences when they are simultaneously tested utilizing multilevel modeling? (b) Does a campus where students take greater advantage of those diversity opportunities have independent positive effects on students' learning? Consideration of racial diversity extended beyond student composition and included social and curricular engagement. Results suggest that benefits associated with diversity may be more far-reaching than previously documented. Not only do students benefit from engaging with racial diversity through related knowledge acquisition or cross-racial interaction but also from being enrolled on a campus where other students are more engaged with those forms of diversity, irrespective of their own level of engagement.

When the U.S. Supreme Court ruled in favor of the University of Michigan in the 2003 Grutter v. Bollinger decision, contributors to campus diversity efforts viewed this as an affirmation of their ongoing work. Justice O'Connor, who wrote the majority opinion for that case, stated that "numerous studies show that student body diversity promotes learning outcomes, and better prepares students for an increasingly diverse workforce and society, and better prepares them as professionals" (Grutter, et al. v. Bollinger, et al., 2003, p. 18). Indeed, the research supporting the educational benefits associated with having a more racially diverse student body was relatively unchallenged in the courts, but those who contributed to that body of research call for sustained attention (e.g., Chang, 2005; Hurtado, 2005).

Although the evidence supporting the benefits of being educated among a more racially diverse undergraduate student body is mounting, it is a relatively new area of educational research and, subsequently, can still be strengthened in a number of ways. With this in mind, this study addresses two basic questions. First, do different forms or expressions of campus racial diversity contribute uniquely to students' learning and educational experiences when they are simultaneously tested? The purpose here is to test previous findings using hierarchical linear modeling (HLM), which better addresses the hierarchical or nested structure of large national data sets.

The added strength of HLM is that it provides a better estimate of aggregated student data, which also make it possible to test the second question of interest. That is, does a campus where students take greater advantage of key racial diversity opportunities have independent positive effects on students' learning and educational experiences? Because of statistical limitations, many previous studies examining the benefits of diversity have focused on the student as the main unit of analysis, and thus, little can be confidently said about the higher-level institution or environment effects on students. It may be the case, for example, that even those students who report being disengaged from or hostile to diversity opportunities may still be positively affected simply by being in an environment where a larger proportion of other students are engaged in such opportunities. Given this possibility, we examined whether the effects of racial diversity might be even more far-reaching than previously documented by testing a few key institution-level variables based on aggregated student responses.

Research Background

Alongside the legal controversy regarding race-conscious admissions practices, a fairly recent body of research has emerged that has contributed to understanding the potential educational benefits of racial-ethnic diversity in 4-year colleges and universities. Most of this empirical work has focused on three distinct forms of racial diversity: structural diversity (student body racial composition), curricular/co-curricular diversity (programmatic efforts that expose students to content about race/ethnicity), and interaction diversity (informal student-student cross-racial contact). We briefly review below the key research along these three forms of diversity.

Perhaps of greatest interest to the University of Michigan affirmative action cases was the research concerning the effects of enrolling a more racially diverse group of students, or structural diversity. Ironically, of the three forms of diversity, structural diversity has received the least empirical attention. One of the most well-known studies is Bowen and Bok's (1998) *The Shape of the River*. While the main findings focus on African Americans and their postcollege achievements, they found that both White and African American alumni report having benefited from structural diversity. In particular, they felt that diversity had helped them get along better with members of other races and held more positive attitudes toward affirmative action programs. Another study (Wells, Duran, & White, in press), while it focused on the effects of high school, also demonstrated long-term benefits of attending racially diverse schools. For example, graduates of racially mixed schools reported being more accepting of and comfortable with people of different racial-ethnic backgrounds, which in turn better prepared them for a global economy and society. Those graduates reported that this preparation was the most important outcome of their experiences of attending racially diverse schools.

Another (antonio et al., 2004) that used a randomized assignment design tested psychological explanations of the impact of diversity by manipulating the race of a confederate participant (Black, White) in an all-White undergraduate discussion group. Drawing upon theories of minority influence, the researchers tested the hypothesis that when minority opinions and individuals are present in homogeneous groups, cognitive complexity is stimulated among majority members. The findings of the experiment show that the presence of a Black student in an otherwise all-White discussion group enhances complex thinking, particularly when group discussions involve an issue that is racially charged. The authors concluded that racial and ethnic compositional diversity can create richer and more complex social and learning environments than racially homogeneous ones, which subsequently can serve as an educational tool to promote all students' learning and development.

Not all studies examining structural diversity, however, report positive findings. For example, Rothman, Lipset, and Nevitte (2002) conclude that diversity had few positive and even many negative effects on attitudinal and educational outcomes. They found that the proportion of African Americans in the student body does nothing to improve student perceptions of campus life and in some cases affects them adversely. Specifically, they found that when structural diversity increased, student satisfaction and perceived quality of education decreased. Additionally, the higher the structural diversity, the more likely the students were to report having experienced discrimination themselves.

Other empirical studies that have examined structural diversity suggest that the student body composition is an insufficient condition in and of itself for maximizing educational benefits, but rather, its value appears to depend on whether or not it leads to greater levels of engagement in diversity-related activities, such as curricular diversity and cross-racial interaction. Indeed, several studies have specifically examined this relationship and demonstrated that the structural diversity of an institution does indeed shape curricular diversity and/or opportunities to interact with diverse peers (Chang, 2001; Chang, Astin, & Kim, 2004; Gurin, 1999; Pike & Kuh, 2006). Given the above relationships, some researchers have argued that when there is a diverse student body, the environment enhances the chances that students will become more involved in diversity-related activities and socialize more often across racial groups; in turn, having these types of involvement and interaction can have a positive impact on students' development (Chang, 2001; Gurin, 1999).

Another form of diversity, curricular/co-curricular diversity, refers to institutionally structured and purposeful programmatic efforts to help students engage in diversity with respect to both ideas and people (Terenzini, Cabrera, Colbeck, Bjorklund, & Parente, 2001). Students encounter this form of diversity through course work and curriculum or through participation in activities such as racial-cultural awareness workshops and student organizations. Curricular/co-curricular diversity has been shown to be positively associated with outcomes such as intergroup attitudes (Lopez, 2004); racial prejudice and intergroup understanding (Chang, 2002); attitudes toward campus diversity (Springer, Palmer, Terenzini, Pascarella, & Nora, 1996); critical thinking skills (Nelson Laird, 2005; Pascarella, Palmer, Moye, & Pierson, 2001); cognitive and affective development (Astin, 1993a); learning and "democracy" outcomes (Gurin, Dey, Hurtado, & Gurin, 2002); civic, job-related, and learning outcomes (Hurtado, 2001); academic self-confidence and social agency (Nelson Laird, 2005); social action engagement outcomes (Nelson Laird, Engberg, & Hurtado, 2005); and action-oriented democratic outcomes (Zúñiga, Williams, & Berger, 2005).

Lastly, there is also strong evidence that interaction diversity, or the frequency of cross-racial interaction that occurs during the normal course of undergraduate life, contributes to students' learning and educational experiences. Interaction diversity has been shown to be positively associated with outcomes such as intergroup attitudes (Lopez, 2004); cultural knowledge and understanding and leadership skills (antonio, 2001); cognitive and affective development (Astin, 1993a); student learning and personal development (Hu & Kuh, 2003); learning and democracy outcomes (Gurin et al., 2002); civic, job-related, and learning outcomes (Hurtado, 2001); critical thinking skills (Nelson Laird, 2005; Pascarella et al., 2001); academic self-confidence and social agency (Nelson Laird, 2005); action-oriented democratic outcomes (Chang et al., 2004; Zúñiga et al., 2005); intellectual and social self-confidence and student retention (Chang, 2001; Chang et al., 2004); and student satisfaction with their overall college experience (Chang, 2001).

The recent growth in empirical knowledge concerning the educational benefits of diversity can be largely attributed to pressing debates framed by earlier U.S. Supreme Court decisions, which have constrained the defense of race-conscious admissions practices (Chang, 2005). Even though the Court supported the constitutionality of such practices in 2003, more research is still needed to understand better the scope and depth of those related educational benefits. To improve understanding, this study addresses two limitations with the existing body of knowledge.

Limitations in Analytic Approach

Although a variety of methodological approaches have been applied to examine the educational benefits of diversity in higher education, many of those that analyzed large national data sets (e.g., Astin, 1993a, 1993b; Gurin et al., 2002; Hurtado, 2001) have employed single-level linear modeling. Those approaches, however, do not accurately model the hierarchical nature of most national data sets. Whereas HLM is commonly applied in other areas of education research (e.g., K–12 literature), it is not as widely utilized in higher education research. To address this common methodological shortcoming among previous studies, we applied HLM (Raudenbush & Bryk, 1986, 2002) to more accurately model the structure of a multilevel longitudinal data set. In short, through this approach, we are able to more accurately assess the impact of the different forms of diversity at both the student and institution levels.

Limitations of Theoretical Framework

Another limitation with the existing body of knowledge is related to current explanations about how students might theoretically benefit from diversity. Since the vast majority of research has focused mainly on students as the unit of analysis, much progress has been made in explaining student-level effects by drawing from psychological theories. For example, Gurin et al. (2002) argue that at a campus with a more diverse student body, a student has a better chance of coming across opinions and situations different from her or his home environment. When they engage in this difference, according to Gurin et al. (2002), it can lead to a mental process of "accommodating" and "assimilating" new information or what psychologist Piaget (1975/1985) called "cognitive disequilibrium." This processing of new information or experience affects students' learning and cognitive growth. Thus, when there are more opportunities to engage in difference, there is greater potential for learning (Gurin et al., 2002).

Moreover, Gurin et al. (2002) draw from other established psychological concepts, such as Erikson's (1946, 1956) notion of "psychosocial moratorium," to make the case that diversity is even more educationally appropriate for undergraduate students. According to this notion, undergraduates are typically at a developmental stage where they are freer to explore new ideas, social roles, and relationships. Combining this developmental moment with a racially diverse environment that exposes students to surroundings that are dissimilar or incongruent with their home environments raises the potential for deeper and more critical thinking. Drawing from established psychological theories, Gurin et al. (2002) have provided a better understanding about how students benefit educationally from being a member of a racially diverse student body.

One limitation, however, with explaining the benefits in only psychological terms that tend to focus mostly on student-level effects is that the educational benefits of diversity may extend beyond psychological explanations. The environmental effects on students are well documented in higher education research (e.g., Astin, 1993b; Pascarella & Terenzini, 1991, 2005), suggesting that the context in which learning takes place can have a measurable impact on students, independent of a student's own behaviors and experiences. With respect to diversity, two recent studies that employed HLM have tested diversity-related environmental effects on undergraduate students.

Chang, Denson, Sáenz, and Misa (2006) tested both student-and institution-level effects associated with cross-racial interaction. They found that even though a student's own level of cross-racial interaction is a more direct and powerful way to realize developmental gains associated with openness to diversity, cognitive development, and self-confidence, students also benefit uniquely from being enrolled in an institution that sustains positive race relations. They used HLM to examine an identical set of variables reported at both the student and institution levels. This allowed them to better differentiate between the effects of a student's own behavior and the effects of the broader context associated with that behavior.

Another recent study also demonstrated benefits for four institutional measures of diversity. Although their study primarily focused on students attending liberal arts colleges, Umbach and Kuh (2006) found numerous positive benefits of (a) the "diversity density index" (the probability that a student will interact with a student from another race), (b) institutional "climate for diversity" (students' perceptions of the emphasis their institution places on encouraging contact among students from different backgrounds), (c) "diversity in coursework" (the extent to which students reported their classes included readings or discussions related to diversity), and (d) "diversity press" (a scale made up of the three other diversity measures: structural diversity, the extent to which students perceive that diversity is valued and important, and curricular diversity) on a variety of outcomes that included measures of student engagement, perceptions of a supportive campus environment, gains in learning and intellectual development, and gains in social awareness. While all four institutional measures of diversity were positively associated with many of the outcomes, the strongest positive effects were seen for engagement in diversity-related activities and gains in understanding of people from other backgrounds and cultures. Umbach and Kuh also used HLM, which allowed them to more accurately assess the effects of these institution-level diversity "contexts." While their study did not differentiate between the effects of a student's own behavior and the effects of the broader context associated with that behavior, they did simultaneously test the three forms of institutional diversity contexts against each other, which demonstrated unique effects (although to varying degrees) of each.

If similar contextual or normative effects associated with the various forms of diversity can be replicated, it would suggest that the effects of diversity are even more far-reaching. That is, having a larger percentage of students who participate in diversity opportunities may contribute uniquely to learning that extends beyond psychological explanations and may perhaps require organizational or sociological lenses to explain. With respect to organizational impact, for example, Berger (2000) found that different patterns of organizational behavior do indeed affect outcomes in various ways for different students. He claims that although there are many viable theories to explain how organizations affect students in higher education, one important effect he found in his study was that high levels of an organizational behavior create intense organizational environments that exert stronger uniform effects on student outcomes. He regards this finding as support of Clark, Heist, McConnell, Trow, and Yonge's (1972) assertion that "campuses exert a more powerful impact on student outcomes when those colleges have clear visions that are articulated through congruent and consistent sets of policies, procedures, traditions, and espousal of values in everyday campus life" (p. 191). From a sociological perspective, antonio and Muñiz (2007) refer to this effect as the "transformative potential" of higher education. In their review of the "sociology of diversity," they also conclude that impact or transformation is dynamic, so while colleges can exert an impact on students, students can also change institutions, for example, by intensifying the obligation to offer more and better diversity-related courses and/or activities.

The cursory discussion above suggests that organizational or sociological lenses can be useful in explaining the contextual effects associated with diversity. It appears that shifts in student populations or needs can have a transformative effect on a college's vision and organizational behavior. If that vision includes diversity and is articulated in a cohesive and consistent way, then higher levels of organizational behavior as measured by a student body's engagement with diversity, for example, can create more intense environments that exert stronger uniform effects on all students' capacity to engage in diversity. So, if institutional-level effects can be further documented in this study, it would add to how diversity is considered both practically and theoretically.

The purpose of this study is to examine further and in greater depth the benefits of campus racial diversity by addressing the two limitations noted above. To do this, we consider two primary research questions: (a) Do different forms or expressions of campus racial diversity contribute uniquely to students' learning and educational experiences when they are simultaneously tested? (b) Does a campus where students take greater advantage of those racial diversity-related opportunities have independent positive effects on students' learning and educational experiences?

Method

Data Source

The data for this study were drawn from the Cooperative Institutional Research Program (CIRP) at the University of California, Los Angeles (UCLA), Higher Education Research Institute (HERI). This study utilized two student surveys that were collected at two different time points. The Student Information Form was administered to full-time 1st-year entering students and was intended to gather background information prior to their having any substantial experience with college. The students were subsequently administered the College Student Survey (CSS) at the end of their 4th year, which queried students about many of the same topics on the Freshman Survey but also asked them about various college experiences that they may have had over the past 4 years.

The initial sample consisted of 21,651 students nested within 272 institutions. From this sample, we created a subset sample that excluded 2-year colleges and universities, historically Black colleges and universities, and students and institutions with preestablished thresholds of missing cases or items.[1]

This yielded a final total sample of 20,178 students nested within 236 institutions. Depending on the outcome, the final sample of students ranged from 19,794 to 19,978 students due to pairwise deletion.

Dependent Variables

To examine the relationship between diversity and student development, we focused on three outcomes similar to those used in the Gurin et al. (2002) study. We assessed the personal (self-efficacy and general academic skills) and social (racial-cultural engagement) domains. Our social outcome—racial-cultural engagement—is identical to the one used by Gurin et al. However, the two personal outcomes—self-efficacy and general academic skills—were not identical to those constructed by Gurin et al. because the items that they used to construct their measures failed to achieve strong reliability when using our more current data set. So, we constructed comparable personal outcomes that we termed self-efficacy and general academic skills. Factor analysis with maximum likelihood (ML) estimation of the 11 individual items (with promax rotation) produced three factors, confirming the three outcomes (Table 1).

Primary Independent Variables of Interest

The principal independent variables of interest were those that represent the three targeted forms of racial diversity (at both the student and institution level): curricular diversity, cross-racial interaction (or CRI), and structural diversity. At the student level (Level 1), items for the curricular diversity and CRI measures were drawn from the CSS. Curricular diversity was a composite of three items on the survey that asked the students if they participated in the following activities (0 = no; 1 = yes): taken an ethnic studies course, attended a racial-cultural awareness workshop, or participated in an ethnic-racial student organization since entering college. The CRI measure was a composite of student responses on five items from the CSS that tap into a student's level of engagement in the following activities with someone from a different racial-ethnic group at the college: studied, dined, dated, interacted, and socialized ($\alpha = .79$).

At the institution level (Level 2), we examined diversity with respect to an institution's percentage of underrepresented minority (URM) students (i.e., the combined proportional representation of African Americans, Latinos/Latinas, and American Indians), average level of curricular diversity, and average level of CRI. The percentages of students from the URM groups within institutions were obtained from the National Center for Education Statistics (NCES) Integrated Postsecondary Education Data System (IPEDS) enrollment figures. The institutional peer levels of curricular diversity and institutional peer levels of CRI were the average curricular diversity and average CRI scores of all respondents for that institution, respectively.

Control Variables

Key control variables identified by previous studies were included in the analyses (see Appendixes A and B). In addition to the pretest measures listed in Table 1, we included student background characteristics (e.g., gender, race) and also controlled for college experiences (e.g., living and working arrangements). Additionally, enrollment size, level of selectivity, control (public-private), and the aggregate measures of all the student-level control variables were included in the models so that the student- and institution-level effects can be properly differentiated. While the control variables are not of primary substantive interest, they were included in the analyses because they represent characteristics, predispositions, and college experiences of students that, unless taken into account, could lead to a miscalculation of the effects of diversity, as implied by the literature reviewed earlier.

Analytic Approach

The HLM approach and statistical software used for this study are thoroughly explained in Raudenbush and Bryk (2002). We computed three separate sets of HLM analyses, one for each outcome variable. Within each set, we developed seven models, but due to space limitations, we can present only the first and final HLM models to describe our analyses.

TABLE 1

Factor Loadings and Reliabilities for Outcome Variables and Their Pretests

Factor and Survey Items	Factor Loading	Internal Consistency (Alpha)
Dependent variables		
Self-efficacy		.703
Self-ratings of drive to achieve[a]	.565	
Self-ratings of intellectual self-confidence[a]	.707	
Self-ratings of competitiveness[a]	.466	
Self-ratings of academic ability[a]	.655	
Self-ratings of writing ability[a]	.499	
General academic skills		.736
Self-change assessments in general knowledge[b]	.599	
Self-change assessments in analytical/problem-solving skills[b]	.741	
Self-change assessments in ability to think critically[b]	.794	
Self-change assessments in writing skills[b]	.476	
Racial-cultural engagement		.722
Self-change in knowledge of people from different races/cultures[b]	.603	
Self-change in ability to get along with people of different races/cultures[b]	.941	
Pretests of the dependent variables		
Self-efficacy		.686
Self-ratings of drive to achieve[a]	.566	
Self-ratings of intellectual self-confidence[a]	.715	
Self-ratings of competitiveness[a]	.432	
Self-ratings of academic ability[a]	.660	
Self-ratings of writing ability[a]	.447	
General academic skills		.510
Self-ratings of academic ability[a]	.821	
Self-ratings of writing ability[a]	.821	
Racial-cultural engagement		.528
Importance of promoting racial understanding[c]	.824	
Importance of helping others who are in difficulty[c]	.824	

[a]Five-point scale from 1 = lowest 10% to 5 = highest 10%; items have corresponding pretests.
[b]Five-point scale from 1 = much weaker to 5 = much stronger.
[c]Four-point scale from 1 = not important to 4 = essential.

The first model. The first model was a fully unconditional model because no predictors were specified at either the student level (Level 1) or institution level (Level 2). This model, represented by Equations 1 and 2 below, provides useful preliminary information about how much variation in each of the outcome lies within and between institutions and also about the reliability of each institution's sample mean as an estimate of its true population mean.

$$\text{Level 1: } Y_{ij} = \beta_{0j} + r_{ij} \quad r_{ij} \sim N(0, \sigma^2), \tag{1}$$

where $i = 1, 2, \ldots, n_j$ students in institution j, and $j = 1, 2, \ldots, j$ institutions. In Equation 1, each student's score on the outcome measure, Y_{ij}, is characterized as a function of his or her institutional average on the outcome measure, β_{0j}, and a random effect, r_{ij}, which is unique to each individual. The r_{ij} represents random error, which is typically assumed to be normally distributed with a mean of zero and variance σ^2. The variance of the random effects (σ^2) represents the within-institution variance.

$$\text{Level 2: } \beta_{0j} = \gamma_{00} + u_{0j} \quad u_{0j} \sim N(0, \tau_{00}). \tag{2}$$

In Equation 2, the institutional average on the outcome measure, β_{0j}, is characterized as a function of the mean on the outcome measure for all institutions, γ_{00}, and a random effect, u_{0j}, which is unique to each institution. The random effect u_{0j} is also typically assumed to be normally distributed with a mean of zero and variance τ_{00}. The variance of the random effects (τ_{00}) represents the between-institution variance.

The final model. The final model was a conditional model because it contained both student-level (Level 1) and institution-level (Level 2) predictors. Before arriving at the final model, we developed intermediary conditional models (Models 2 through 6) whereby predictors were specified at Level 1 and/or Level 2 in an incremental fashion. By modeling these intermediary models, we were able to determine the incremental variance explained by each of the variables of interest (e.g., curricular diversity, CRI, structural diversity) once controlling for other student and institutional characteristics. The following equations (Equations 3 and 4) describe the model estimated in the final stage of the analyses (Model 7). All Level 1 predictors have been group-mean centered, and all Level 2 predictors have been grand-mean centered so that the intercept term (β_{0j}) represents the institutional average on the outcome measure (unadjusted mean) for institution j.

$$\begin{aligned}
\text{Level 1: } Y_{ij} = {} & \beta_{0j} + \beta_{1j}(\text{curricular diversity}) + \beta_{2j}(\text{CRI}) + \beta_{3j}(\text{part-time job on campus}) + \\
& \beta_{4j}(\text{Pretest of outcome}) + \beta_{5j}(\text{HS GPA}) + \beta_{6j}(\text{SES}) + \beta_{7j}(\text{live on campus}) + \\
& \beta_{8j}(\text{Native American}) + \beta_{9j}(\text{Asian}) + \beta_{10j}(\text{African American}) + \beta_{11j}(\text{Latino}) + \\
& \beta_{12j}(\text{Female}) + \beta_{13j}(\text{level of involvement}) + r_{ij} \\
& r_{ij} \sim N(0, \sigma^2)
\end{aligned} \tag{3}$$

In the Level 2 model, the intercept (β_{0j}) was specified as random, while all other coefficients were specified as fixed. The coefficients β_{1j} and β_{2j} represent the institutional averages of the curricular diversity and CRI slopes, respectively, for institution j. Since the student-level effects of curricular diversity and CRI were not assumed to be constant across institutions, the variances of these coefficient were calculated, separating parameter variance from error variance, and were tested to determine whether these effects varied across institutions. Based on the results of chi-square tests, the β_{1j} and β_{2j} coefficients were then respectively specified as either fixed or random in the final Level 2 model (Equation 4).[2]

$$\begin{aligned}
\text{Level 2: } \beta_{0j} = {} & \gamma_{00} + \gamma_{01}(\%\text{ URM students}) + \gamma_{02}(\text{ln Size}) + \gamma_{03}(\text{Selectivity}) + \gamma_{04} \\
& (\text{Control: Private}) + \gamma_{05}(\text{AVG: curricular diversity}) + \gamma_{06}(\text{AVG: CRI}) + \\
& \gamma_{07}(\text{AVG: part-time job on campus}) + \gamma_{08}(\text{Pretest of outcome}) + \gamma_{09} \\
& (\text{AVG: HS GPA}) + \gamma_{010}(\text{AVG: SES}) + \gamma_{011}(\text{AVG: live on campus}) + \gamma_{012} \\
& (\text{AVG: female}) + \gamma_{013}(\text{AVG: level of involvement}) + u_{0j} \\
& u_{0j} \sim N(0, \tau_{00}) \\
\beta_{1j} = {} & \gamma_{10} + \gamma_{11}(\%\text{ URM students}) + \gamma_{12}(\text{AVG: curricular diversity}) \\
& + \gamma_{13}(\text{AVG: CRI}) \, [+ \, \gamma_{14}(\text{AVG: part-time job on campus})] \, (+ \, u_{1j}) \\
& u_{1j} \sim N(0, \tau_{11}) \\
\beta_{2j} = {} & \gamma_{20} + \gamma_{21}(\%\text{ URM students}) + \gamma_{22}(\text{AVG: curricular diversity}) \\
& + \gamma_{23}(\text{AVG: CRI}) \, [+ \, \gamma_{24}(\text{AVG: HS GPA})] \, (+ \, u_{2j}) \\
& u_{2j} \sim N(0, \tau_{22}) \\
\beta_{3j} = {} & \gamma_{30} \\
& \vdots \\
& \vdots \\
\beta_{13j} = {} & \gamma_{130}
\end{aligned} \tag{4}$$

Limitations

As with most studies, this one is not free of limitations. First, as mentioned previously, the data for this study came from UCLA's HERI. Although they seek to survey the full population of 4-year institutions and students, not all institutions participate or administer the surveys as prescribed. Thus, the study's sample is limited in that the data are from only those institutions that participated between 1994 and 1998, and differences in survey administration may affect the results. To address this problem, we controlled for a range of both institution-and student-level characteristics that may bias the sample. Second, our study incorporated a longitudinal design, which offers numerous advantages in determining causality. However, even with our longitudinal study design, the data remain correlational (i.e., nonexperimental) in nature. Despite our periodical use of the term effect, as with any correlational data, cause-and-effect relationships should be interpreted cautiously. Third, all of the data collected from students are based on self-reports. Although this is a widely used and generally valid approach for obtaining student information (Pike, 1995), students may be using differing baselines when they are asked to report their own growth during college (Pascarella, 2001). The large sample size in the current study helps to offset threats to validity inherent in self-report measures by capturing a more accurate overall population average rather than relying on a few individual students' own point of reference.

Lastly, selection bias is always a major concern for any study that does not utilize random assignment. In other words, can we be confident that the effects we observe are attributable to the institutions themselves? Or do certain types of students go to certain types of institutions? Our analyses rely on nonexperimental statistical techniques to either examine or reduce the likelihood that any given association is due to self-selection (Schneider, Carnoy, Kilpatrick, Schmidt, & Shavelson, 2007). To examine the threat of self-selection bias, we created a diversity pretest that was measured at the point of college entry.[3] We then correlated the student-level score on this pretest with the institutional-level pretest score (the average entering score of the respondents' peer group or institutional average). The relatively weak correlation ($r = .26$) between the student-and institutional-level scores on this pretest suggests that students choose their institutions on the basis of a variety of other factors, and not only on the basis of their diversity inclination alone.

Additionally, our statistical modeling also reduces the possibility that our observed effects were due to selection bias. Specifically, in testing the effects of our diversity-related variables, we included a number of other key variables in the HLM analyses to minimize self-selection bias and to control for the effect of critical institutional characteristics (see Appendix A). We selected these variables based on their noted importance in previous studies cited earlier, and we used them to rule out alternative explanations for findings. Most importantly, in all three outcomes, we included a pretest for the dependent measure as a control variable in our analyses. Thus with respect to each pretest measure, any significant relationship that may exist between a diversity variable of interest and the outcome can be interpreted as a unique effect above and beyond that of the pretest. Other limitations with this study are discussed with reference to the findings.

Results

The First Model

Table 2 presents results from the first models. The table shows the ML point estimate for the grand mean and the estimated values of the within-institution variance (σ^2) and between-institution variance (τ_{00}) for all three outcomes. The ML point estimates for the grand means are 19.34 for self-efficacy, 17.16 for general academic skills, and 7.63 for racial-cultural engagement. Overall, the students in our sample tended to rate themselves on the higher end of the continuum on the self-efficacy (ranging from 5 to 25), general academic skills (ranging from 4 to 20), and racial-cultural engagement (ranging from 2 to 10) measures.

Table 2 also reports the within-institution and between-institution variances, but these numbers alone do not provide a good sense of the proportion of total variance that is due either to individual differences or to institutional differences. So, as recommended by Raudenbush and Bryk (2002), we

TABLE 2

Estimation of One-Way Random-Effects ANOVA Base Models

Fixed Effects	Coefficient	SE	t Ratio	Reliability
Factor 1: Self-Efficacy				
Intercept (γ_{00})	19.34	.05	412.99***	.74
Factor 2: General Academic Skills				
Intercept (γ_{00})	17.16	.03	620.64***	.68
Factor 3: Racial/Cultural Engagement				
Intercept (γ_{00})	7.63	.02	380.52***	.68

Random Effects	Variance Component	df	Chi-Square
Factor 1: Self-Efficacy			
Between institution (τ_{00}) (variance of intercepts)	0.38	235	1146.73***
Within institution (σ^2)	7.30		
Factor 2: General Academic Skills			
Between institution (τ_{00}) (variance of intercepts)	0.12	235	931.29***
Within institution (σ^2)	3.23		
Factor 3: Racial-Cultural Engagement			
Between institution (τ_{00}) (variance of intercepts)	0.06	235	1164.78***
Within institution (σ^2)	1.77		

***$p < .001$.

computed the intraclass correlation (ICC) to assess the proportion of variance in each outcome that is due to between-institution differences.[4] The presence of a significant ICC indicates the need for HLM. For our set of outcomes, we found that only 4.9% of the variance in self-efficacy, 3.6% of the variance in general academic skills, and 3.3% of the variance in racial-cultural engagement was due to between-institution differences. These ICC findings suggest that the majority of the variance in each of the three outcomes is due mostly to within-institution differences. At the same time, however, differences between institutions still accounted for a statistically significant ($p < .001$) portion of the variance, indicating a need for utilizing multilevel modeling.

The Final Model

Table 3 reports the results of the final HLM model for each of the three outcome measures. Given space constraints, we will focus our discussion mainly on the key independent variables of interest with respect to each outcome.

Self-efficacy. As shown in the first two columns of numbers in Table 3, the coefficients for the curricular diversity slope base ($\gamma_{10} = .08$, $t = 4.01$) and CRI slope base ($\gamma_{20} = .14$, $t = 7.39$) are statistically significant, suggesting that these two student-level characteristics have a significant positive effect on this self-efficacy measure. In other words, students who were more involved in workshops or classes that incorporated issues concerning diversity, or who interacted more with others of another race, tended to also report higher levels of self-efficacy. By contrast, none of the institutional measures of diversity had any statistically significant effect.

General academic skills. The second set of results in Table 3 shows the findings for the general academic skills measure. Again, focusing on the key variables of interest, the student-level characteristics of curricular diversity ($\gamma_{10} = .17$, $t = 10.40$) and CRI ($\gamma_{20} = .16$, $t = 9.74$) exerted significant positive effects on the general academic skills measure. That is, students who participated in more workshops or diversity-related classes or who interacted more often with students of another race tended to also report higher levels of general academic skills. Additionally, the student body's average level of curricular diversity engagement ($\gamma_{05} = .31$, t = 3.84) also had a significant positive effect on this measure. So students who attended institutions where more students participated in workshops or classes that considered diversity issues tended to also report higher levels of general academic skills, regardless of their own personal involvement.

Lastly, the random effects results for this measure reported at the bottom of Table 3 shows that the CRI slope varies across institutions for this measure ($\tau_{22} = .01$, $\chi^2 = 274.27$, p < .05). This means that some institutions have steeper CRI–general academic skills slopes, whereas other institutions have flatter CRI–general academic skills slopes, suggesting differential effects across institutions. In other words, CRI at some institutions has a greater positive effect on students' general academic skills than at other institutions.

Racial-cultural engagement. The last set of results reported in the two columns of numbers on the far right in Table 3 shows that both curricular diversity ($\gamma_{10} = .22$, t = 18.57) and CRI ($\gamma_{20} = .35$, t = 32.28) had significant positive effects on the racial-cultural engagement measure. In addition, both average level of institutional curricular diversity ($\gamma_{05} = .24$, t = 4.09) and average level of institutional CRI ($\gamma_{06} = .32$, t = 5.47) had significant positive effects on students' racial-cultural engagement, even after controlling for a student's own level of participation in those diversity-related activities. These institution-level findings suggest that students who attended institutions where students as a whole were more engaged with diversity tended to also report higher levels of self-change in knowledge of and ability to get along with people of different races or cultures, independent of their own personal involvements and interactions.

Another interesting finding concerns the influence of institutional-level CRI on the relationship between individual CRI and racial-cultural engagement. Whereas there is a strong positive association between individual engagement with CRI and knowledge of and ability to get along with people of different races or cultures, the institutional-level CRI appears to have an attenuating effect on the same outcome. That is, the positive association between individual CRI and racial-cultural engagement tends to be weaker at those institutions where the broader student body is interacting more frequently across racial lines. Put in another way, the effect of a student's own level of cross-racial interaction on this outcome is stronger at an institution with lower average levels of CRI among students than at one with higher levels. So with respect to achieving racial-cultural engagement, students' own level of cross-racial interaction is even more significant when there is a general absence of such interaction among the larger student body.

Practical Significance

To assess the practical significance of the statistically significant findings above, we followed Raudenbush and Bryk's (2002) suggestion and compared the variance estimates within institutions (σ^2) and between institutions (τ_{00}) for each type of significant engagement, then calculated the proportion of variance explained at Level 1 and also the proportion of variance explained at Level 2 in the final model.[5] These proportion-of-variance-explained indices provide another way of gauging the results. That is, variables that are stronger predictors tend to also account for a greater amount of variance in the outcome and are considered to have greater practical significance.

As shown in Tables 4 and 5, the practical significance of diversity measures varied by outcome. For the self-efficacy measure, the diversity variables accounted for only a small percentage of the total variance explained, suggesting that they have weak practical significance on this measure. By comparison, the diversity variables contributed to a larger proportion of the overall variance explained for the general academic skills outcome. At the student level, curricular diversity explained 0.8% and CRI explained 0.5% of the within-institution variability, whereas all other student-level variables explained 3.2% of the within-institution variance. At the institution level, the student body average level of curricular diversity engagement accounted for 4.7% of the total institution-level variance in general academic skills, compared to 41.8% of the between-institution

TABLE 3

Estimation of the Final Hierarchical Linear Modeling Model

Fixed Effects	Self-Efficacy		General Academic Skills		Racial/Cultural Engagement	
	Coefficient (SE)	t Ratio	Coefficient (SE)	t Ratio	Coefficient (SE)	t Ratio
Institutional mean						
Base (γ_{00})	19.31 (0.03)	712.00***	17.15 (0.02)	736.10***	7.64 (0.02)	466.65***
Control: Private (γ_{01})	0.07 (0.10)	0.66	0.20 (0.09)	2.37*	−0.02 (0.06)	−0.32
Natural log of size (γ_{02})	−0.05 (0.04)	−1.19	−0.07 (0.04)	−2.05*	0.01 (0.03)	0.22
Selectivity (γ_{03})	0.00 (0.00)	1.79	−0.00 (0.00)	−0.26	−0.00 (0.00)	−2.14*
% URM students (γ_{04})	−0.00 (0.01)	−0.28	0.00 (0.00)	0.10	0.00 (0.00)	0.12
AVG: Curricular diversity (γ_{05})	0.05 (0.09)	0.53	0.31 (0.08)	3.84***	0.24 (0.06)	4.09***
AVG: CRI (γ_{06})	0.15 (0.10)	1.44	−0.09 (0.09)	−0.97	0.32 (0.06)	5.47***
AG: Gender: Female (γ_{07})	−0.03 (0.21)	−0.16	−0.21 (0.17)	−1.25	−0.04 (0.12)	−0.31
AVG: High school GPA (γ_{08})	−0.47 (0.26)	−1.80	−0.08 (0.21)	−0.39	−0.12 (0.12)	−1.04
AVG: Lived on campus (γ_{09})	0.05 (0.25)	0.19	−0.04 (0.21)	−0.17	0.06 (0.15)	0.42
AVG: Had part-time job on campus (γ_{010})	−0.77 (0.23)	−3.34**	−0.03 (0.20)	−0.13	0.13 (0.14)	0.96
AVG: Parental education (γ_{011})	−0.07 (0.07)	−0.94	0.15 (0.06)	2.36*	−0.13 (0.04)	−3.01**
AVG: Campus involvement (γ_{012})	0.26 (0.08)	3.12**	0.01 (0.07)	0.20	0.01 (0.05)	0.13
AVG: Pretest (γ_{013})	1.71 (0.17)	10.15***	0.29 (0.14)	2.10*	0.19 (0.10)	1.98*

(continued)

241

TABLE 3 (cont.)

Estimation of the Final Hierarchical Linear Modeling Model

Fixed Effects	Self-Efficacy		General Academic Skills		Racial/Cultural Engagement	
	Coefficient (SE)	t Ratio	Coefficient (SE)	t Ratio	Coefficient (SE)	t Ratio
Curricular diversity slope						
Base (γ_{10})	0.08	4.01***	0.17	10.40***	0.22	18.57***
	(0.02)		(0.02)		(0.01)	
% URM students (γ_{11})	−0.00	−0.33	0.00	0.14	0.00	1.72
	(0.00)		(0.00)		(0.00)	
AVG: Curricular diversity (γ_{12})	0.00	0.07	0.05	0.91	0.01	0.39
	(0.06)		(0.05)		(0.04)	
AVG: CRI (γ_{13})	−0.03	−0.48	0.06	1.18	−0.03	−0.79
	(0.06)		(0.05)		(0.03)	
AVG: High school GPA (γ_{14})			−0.17	−2.02*		
			(0.08)			
CRI slope						
Base (γ_{20})	0.14	7.39***	0.16	9.74***	0.35	32.28***
	(0.02)		(0.02)		(0.01)	
% URM students (γ_{21})	0.00	1.11	0.00	0.68	−0.00	−1.18
	(0.00)		(0.00)		(0.00)	
AVG: Curricular diversity (γ_{22})	−0.07	−1.07	−0.05	−0.93	−0.01	−0.17
	(0.06)		(0.05)		(0.04)	
AVG: CRI (γ_{23})	0.09	1.33	0.02	0.42	−0.07	−2.09*
	(0.06)		(0.05)		(0.04)	
AVG: Had part-time job on campus (γ_{24})	0.32	2.60**				
	(0.12)					
Gender: Female (γ_{30})	−0.56	−15.96***	−0.04	−1.45	−0.08	−4.24***
	(0.03)		(0.03)		(0.02)	
Had a part-time job on campus (γ_{40})	−0.01	−0.16	0.08	2.68**	0.04	1.83
	(0.03)		(0.03)		(0.02)	
Level of campus involvement (γ_{50})	0.06	3.21**	0.03	2.31*	0.02	1.93
	(0.02)		(0.02)		(0.01)	

TABLE 3 (cont.)

Estimation of the Final Hierarchical Linear Modeling Model

Fixed Effects	Self-Efficacy		General Academic Skills		Racial/Cultural Engagement	
	Coefficient (SE)	t Ratio	Coefficient (SE)	t Ratio	Coefficient (SE)	t Ratio
African American (γ_{60})	−0.32 (0.11)	−2.85**	−0.10 (0.09)	−1.10	−0.21 (0.06)	−3.25**
American Indian (γ_{70})	−0.07 (0.15)	−0.46	−0.31 (0.12)	−2.58*	−0.34 (0.08)	−4.03***
Asian (γ_{80})	−0.47 (0.08)	−5.64***	−0.36 (0.07)	−5.22***	−0.28 (0.05)	−5.74***
Latino (γ_{90})	−0.30 (0.10)	−3.12**	−0.01 (0.08)	−0.08	−0.24 (0.05)	−4.28***
High school GPA (γ_{100})	0.55 (0.04)	13.47***	0.00 (0.03)	0.09	0.02 (0.02)	1.02
Parental education (γ_{110})	0.08 (0.01)	7.74***	−0.00 (0.01)	−0.46	−0.04 (0.01)	−5.99***
Lived on campus in fall 1994 (γ_{120})	−0.27 (0.07)	−4.03***	−0.14 (0.05)	−2.60**	0.13 (0.04)	3.33**
Pretest (γ_{130})	1.46 (0.02)	81.57***	0.20 (0.01)	14.18***	0.05 (0.01)	6.03***

Random Effects	Var (df)	Chi-Square	Var (df)	Chi-Square	Var (df)	Chi-Square
Between institution (τ_{00}) (variance of intercepts)	0.09 (222)	555.95***	0.07 (222)	628.28***	0.03 (222)	696.63***
CRI slope (τ_{22})			0.01 (222)	274.27*		
Within institution (σ^2)	4.77		3.12		1.57	

Note. URM = underrepresented minority; AVG = average; CRI = cross-racial interaction; GPA = grade point average; Var = variance.
*$p < .05$. **$p < .01$. ***$p < .001$.

TABLE 4

Percentage of Variance Explained at Level 1

Within Institutions (σ^2)	Curricular Diversity	Cross-Racial Interaction	All Student-Level Variables
Self-efficacy	0.1	0.2	34.2
General academic skills	0.8	0.5	3.2
Racial-cultural engagement	2.9	5.2	12.6

TABLE 5

Percentage of Variance Explained at Level 2

Between Institutions (τ_{00})	% URM Students	Peer Average Level of Curricular Diversity	Peer Average Level of CRI	All Institutions Level Variable
Self-efficacy	3.0	0.0	0.0	76.9
General academic skills	0.0	4.7	0.0	41.8
Racial-cultural engagement	0.0	14.7	14.1	30.8

Note. URM = underrepresented minority; CRI = cross-racial interaction.

variance by all of the other institution-level variables. These percentages-of-variance-explained indices for the diversity variables (at both levels) suggest modest practical significance.

The diversity variables yielded the most impressive practical significance on the racial-cultural engagement measure. Here, curricular diversity alone accounted for 2.9% of the total student-level variance, while CRI accounted for 5.2% of the variance. Comparatively, the student-level diversity-related activities account for a total of 8.1% of the variance explained whereas the student-level variables taken together explained 12.6% of the within-institution variance for racial-cultural engagement. When the institution-level variables were added in the model, the aggregate measure of curricular diversity accounted for 14.7%, and the aggregate measure of CRI accounted for 14.1%, of the total institution-level variance in racial-cultural engagement. Those two variables taken together explain 28.8% of the total between-institution variance, compared to 30.8% by all other institution-level variables. From these findings, it can be said that both student-and institution-level diversity engagement have practical significance for promoting students' self-change in their knowledge of and ability to get along with people from different races and culture.

Student Body Racial Composition

As shown above, there are positive benefits students accrue by just being in an environment where other students have higher levels of engagement with racial diversity, either through curricular activities or cross-racial interaction. Curiously, the percentage of URMs in the student body did not have a statistically significant effect on any of the outcomes tested. It is, however, premature to suggest that the racial composition of the student body does not matter. Intuitively, it would seem that having larger proportions of underrepresented students in the student body would increase diversity-related engagement among students. Indeed, institutions with larger proportions of underrepresented students tend to also have a student body that has higher average levels of both cross-racial

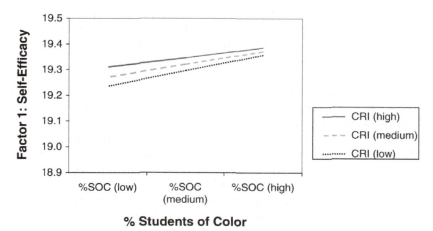

Figure 1   Interaction plot of structural diversity by average levels of cross-racial interaction (CRI) for self-efficacy.
Note. SOC = students of color.

interaction and participation in diversity-related courses and/or activities. The relationship between the proportion of underrepresented students and student body level of cross-racial interaction is particularly strong ($r = .46, p < .001$).

Given the interrelated nature of these three variables, our study does not test the possibility that student body racial composition might moderate the positive effects associated with both student body cross-racial interaction and student body participation in diversity-related courses and/or activities. We found some evidence of moderating potential when we plotted the percentage of underrepresented students by student body cross-racial interaction on self-efficacy.[6] Figure 1 suggests that the effect of the institution-level cross-racial interaction on self-efficacy tends to be stronger on campuses that have larger proportions of underrepresented students. We recommend conducting multilevel structural equation modeling (SEM) to test how racial composition might moderate the effects of student body cross-racial interaction on students' development, which is beyond the scope of this study.

Discussion

This study examines issues critical to ongoing debates concerning race-conscious admissions practices in higher education. Even though the U.S. Supreme Court ruled in its 2003 decision to allow colleges and universities to consider race in making admissions decisions, the ruling has not yet fully settled this controversy. This study builds on a growing body of research related to those debates by examining two key research questions.

First, we asked, "Do different forms or expressions of campus racial diversity contribute uniquely to students' learning and educational experiences when they are simultaneously tested, while accounting for the nested structure of multilevel data?" The findings of our study overcome some important limitations of previous research yet still confirm previous findings based on single-level statistical approaches. Using multilevel modeling, we confirmed the positive educational benefits associated with involvement in workshops or classes geared toward diversity and interaction with others of another racial-ethnic group. Specifically, the findings from our study demonstrate that a student's own frequency of engagement in diversity through curricular activities or CRI is associated with positive ratings of his or her own self-efficacy, academic skills, and self-change in his or her capacity to engage with racial-cultural differences.

Our student-level findings are particularly impressive because the effects of curricular diversity and CRI were consistently and significantly positive across all three outcomes, even after controlling for a range of relevant student and institutional characteristics, including pretests of the outcome measures. These results suggest that when students interact more frequently across race or engage with diversity by taking ethnic studies courses, participating in racial-cultural awareness workshops, or joining ethnic-racial student organizations, they also tend to report higher levels of self-efficacy and self-change concerning general academic skills and racial-cultural engagement. Both curricular diversity and CRI explained a significant proportion of the differences within institutions for all these outcomes. The positive educational benefits of curricular diversity and CRI are most remarkable for improving students' capacity to engage in racial-cultural difference, as those two activities explained most of the within-institution differences.

For our second research question, we asked, "Does a campus where students take greater advantage of those racial diversity–related opportunities have independent positive effects on students' learning and educational experiences?" By using HLM, we were able to assess the contextual effects of both curricular diversity and CRI, which previous studies have not adequately undertaken. We found that being in an environment where students are more engaged with diversity had significant positive educational effects. Specifically, the peer group average measure of curricular diversity had a significant positive effect on a student's general academic skills and racial-cultural engagement. Additionally, the peer group average measure of CRI had a significant positive effect on racial-cultural engagement. Interestingly, the peer group average measure of CRI also attenuated the relationship between individual CRI and racial-cultural engagement. The positive association between individual engagement with CRI and improving one's knowledge of and ability to get along with people of different races or cultures gets stronger as an institution's average level of CRI drops. In other words, the benefits of interacting with others of another race or ethnicity on racial-cultural engagement seem to be even more significant for students when their campus peers are interacting less frequently.

Although our measure of student body racial composition did not yield statistically significant effects on any of the outcomes, we suspect that having greater racial diversity in the student body may moderate in positive ways the benefits associated with diversity engagement, particularly, CRI. In any case, our findings do not support claims (Rothman et al., 2002) that greater racial diversity in the student body harms students' educational experiences and learning.

Similar to the student-level findings, the institution-level findings concerning students' capacity to engage with diversity are educationally meaningful. The positive educational benefits of the peer group average measures of curricular diversity and CRI explained most of the relative between-institution differences for the racial-cultural engagement outcome. It seems when it comes to practical significance, the effect of being an undergraduate on a campus where the student body is more actively engaged with diversity is most robust for cultivating students' knowledge of and ability to get along with peoples of different races or cultures.

Implications and Conclusions

This study confirms previous findings but also suggests that the benefits associated with racial diversity may be even more far-reaching than previously documented. There are appreciable educational benefits associated with racial diversity, which are independent of a student's own level of engagement and point to normative effects. Campuses where students are more engaged with racial diversity through related knowledge acquisition or cross-racial interaction have measurable positive effects on all students irrespective of a student's own frequency of engagement with diversity. Although our institutional measures do not enable us to point to exactly what institutions are doing to facilitate greater racial diversity-related engagement among their student body, achieving higher levels of student body engagement does not occur by accident but requires intentional effort.

While all institutions should theoretically have the potential of exposing students to diversity throughout their college careers (Alger, 1997), we found in the case of our academic skills outcome that the positive effects of cross-racial interaction varies by institution. Other studies have also found variations related to diversity across institutions. Hu and Kuh (2003) found that students attending large doctoral-extensive universities and liberal arts colleges had more experiences with diversity than students at other institutional types. The first finding was not unexpected, given that larger universities tend to be more racially diverse. The second finding regarding liberal arts colleges, on the other hand, was somewhat surprising, given that they tend to be located in less racially diverse and more rural locations.

In a more recent study, Umbach and Kuh (2006) found that students attending liberal arts colleges were more likely to engage in diversity-related activities and to report higher gains in understanding people from diverse backgrounds than their peers at other types of colleges and universities. The authors suggest that while liberal arts colleges tend to be structurally less diverse themselves, "it appears that a distinctive dimension of contemporary liberal arts colleges is their ability to expose students to diversity in educationally purposeful ways" (p. 172). Thus, it appears that there is a contextual effect that is unique to liberal arts colleges, which may be associated with their stronger liberal arts orientation and tradition.

Umbach and Kuh's (2006) findings suggest that certain types of institutions have a stronger capacity to realize the added educational benefits associated with diversity. In all likelihood, this capacity is not exclusive to just liberal arts colleges but can be intentionally developed. Richardson and Skinner (1990), for example, concluded in their study of nine 4-year institutions that the coordination of a wide variety of strategies is more critical than the implementation of a particular program or policy for determining the success of how institutions adapt successfully to diversity. According to Chang (2002), campus diversity efforts should move beyond striving toward superficial changes and seek to transform the normative context by addressing deeply held institutional values and practices. Campuses where students are offered more diversity-related opportunities and are encouraged to take advantage of them are also those that are likely to possess a unique normative context that embraces diversity and are serious about eradicating racism. From a practical standpoint, our findings suggest that students benefit from being educated in such a context.

Such findings also have theoretical implications. Although psychological theories advance understanding of how students benefit from diversity, they do not fully capture the broader normative benefits accrued by students. Those benefits can be explained by organizational and sociological frameworks that were discussed earlier (antonio & Muñiz, 2007; Berger, 2000). If higher levels of student body engagement with diversity signal more cohesive and consistent positive organizational behavior toward diversity, then the positive effects of greater student body engagement can be interpreted as a result of a more intense environment shaped by institutional practices and shifting student needs, which enhances the benefits of diversity. If so, then our institution-level findings appear to support Clark et al.'s (1972) assertion that campuses will have a more powerful impact on students when those colleges have clear interests, in this case, with diversity, which are articulated through congruent and consistent sets of policies, practices, ideals, and communication of values in everyday campus life.

Hurtado, Milem, Clayton-Pederson, and Allen (1998) have specifically discussed the importance of similar institutional qualities in maximizing the educational benefits associated with diversity. Their conceptual framework, however, focuses on how those institutional qualities shape students' capacity to engage successfully with diversity, which in turn leads to educational benefits. The findings from this study extend that thinking by suggesting that the context that facilitates engagement can itself directly advance benefits for students, which are independent of a student's own frequency of engagement. Thus, as explained by certain organizational behavior and sociological frameworks, even students with low personal levels of involvement and CRI also benefit from being educated in a context that facilitates higher average levels of involvement and CRI among all students.

One issue with contextual effects identified through HLM, however, is that they are open to widely varying interpretations (Raudenbush & Bryk, 2002). On the one hand, such contextual effects may occur because of the normative effects associated with an organization as described above. On the other hand, the contextual effect may instead be a proxy for other important institutional characteristics that were omitted from the statistical model (e.g., racial climate, resource allocation). Thus, even though this study demonstrates possible normative effects of curricular diversity and CRI, it is unclear as to what exactly is the source of these effects. Future research should attempt to examine more closely the actual causes (or sources) of these contextual effects. Additionally, future studies should also examine if and how involvement and interaction in diversity-related activities, as well as their contextual effects, exert long-lasting benefits for students even after they leave college. Although this study was able to assess the positive effects associated with different types of diversity-related activities near the end of a student's undergraduate studies, this line of inquiry would also benefit from longitudinal research that follows up on students in the years after graduation.

It would also be beneficial to explore the role of diverse administrators, staff, or educators in higher education as a related line of inquiry into contextual effects. There has been research that suggests that faculty of color are vital to American higher education for a number of reasons, such as providing students with diverse role models, providing support and mentoring to minority students, and being supportive of and engaging in nontraditional scholarship areas (antonio, 2002; Brown, 2000). Future research should explore how faculty of color may contribute to the contextual effect of an institution.

It should also be noted that in a narrow consideration of the broader educational benefits associated with diversity, as is the case here, it is easy to lose sight of how different groups of students are differentially affected by various diversity-related efforts on campus. When it comes to implementing or dismantling institutional policies, practices, and programming, the stakes can be quite different depending on a group's vantage point. For example, Espenshade and Chung (2005) found that eliminating race as a factor for making admissions decisions could lead to a significant drop in admission offers for African American and Latino applicants yet no significant gains for White applicants. Although we consider diversity in terms of its added benefits for all students, clearly the educational stakes for URM students can be positioned as having less to do with "added" benefits and more to do with discrimination or equal access and opportunity. Thus, consideration of campus diversity should extend beyond a narrow educational rationale focus (Chang, 2002, 2005).

In conclusion, it is becoming increasingly clear that the quality of undergraduate education is appreciably enhanced by diversity-related efforts on colleges and universities. Those efforts appear to improve students' experiences and learning by cultivating key behaviors and knowledge and by providing a unique educational context. As we are now discovering, the effects associated with racial diversity are even more far-reaching because there are promising contextual effects that are independent of student-level engagement. Our findings suggest that organizational congruence and consistency make an appreciable difference in the educational process. Given this, the weakening of some diversity-related efforts, such as race-conscious programming and policies, will likely have a negative effect on an institution's organizational cohesiveness to address and support diversity, reducing its overall capacity to realize those related educational benefits for students. The issue concerning whether or not racial diversity adds value in higher education seems to be well settled in educational research. What is much less clear is whether or not future policy shifts will either improve or constrain the range of tools that institutions can utilize to maximize the educational benefits associated with diversity.

Indeed, the policy arena associated with those practices is rapidly shifting. In November of 2006, Michigan voters passed an initiative that banned public institutions from using affirmative-action programs that considered race, gender, color, ethnicity, or national origin for public employment, education, or contracting purposes. The language of this initiative resembles California's Proposition 209, which was passed in 1996. Also, the U.S. Supreme Court ruled in June 2007 that two separate voluntary school integration plans used in Seattle and Louisville, which considered students' race in admissions, were unconstitutional. The Supreme Court, however, did not overturn a prior ruling regarding the University of Michigan's law school, which allows for a narrow use of race in making admissions decisions in higher education. Even so, Justice Sandra Day O'Connor, who wrote the majority opinion in that 2003 ruling, does not believe that within 25 years of that decision, "racial preferences" will be necessary to further the educational interests that were upheld by the Court. Yet the findings from this study suggest that the elimination of race-conscious practices will likely have a detrimental effect on an institution's capacity to maximize those educational interests. More research, however, is needed to uncover the finer details regarding educational context, which will provide a clearer understanding of what institutions can actually do to apply diversity as an educational tool that supports student learning and development. After all, it appears that each campus, and not the courts, will in the end have the most control over and impact on whether and how those widely held educational interests will be realized.

APPENDIX A

List of Control Variables
(surveyed in 1994 unless noted otherwise)

Student Characteristics

Gender: Coded as 0 = male and 1 = female.

Race: Coded as five dummy variables indicating race of student (African American, Native American, Asian American, Latino, and White); 0 = no and 1 = yes.

Parental education: Mother's education and father's education coded on an 8-point scale from 1 = both have grammar school or less to 8 = both have graduate degrees.

High school GPA: Coded on a continuous scale from 1.0 = D to 4.0 = A or A+.

Lives on campus: Coded as 0 = no and 1 = yes.

Part-time job on campus (1998): Coded as 0 = not marked and 1 = marked.

Level of involvement (1998): Coded as 0 = not marked and 1 = marked (standardized).
    Index of student responses on three items about whether or not they joined a
        Fraternity or sorority
        Student government
        Racial-ethnic organization

Pretest for self-efficacy (standardized): Coded on a 5-point scale from 1 = lowest 10% to 5 = highest 10%. Index (α = .686) of self-rating comparing with the average person the student's age on the following traits (1994):
        Drive to achieve
        Self-confidence (intellectual)
        Competitiveness
        Academic ability
        Writing ability

Pretest for general academic skills (standardized): Coded on a 5-point scale from 1 = lowest 10% to 5 = highest 10%. Index (α = .510) of self-rating comparing with the average person the student's age on the following traits:
        Academic ability
        Writing ability

Pretest for racial-cultural engagement (standardized): Coded on a 4-point scale from 1 = not important to 4 = essential. Index (α = .528) of student responses on two items about the importance of
        Promoting racial understanding
        Helping others who are in difficulty

Curricular diversity (standardized) (1998): Coded as 0 = not marked and 1 = marked. Index of student responses on three items about whether or not they have participated in the following activities since entering college:
        Taken an ethnic studies course
        Attended a racial-cultural awareness workshop
        Participated in an ethnic-racial student organization

Cross-racial interaction (standardized) (1998): Coded on a 3-point scale from 1 = not at all to 3 = frequently. Index (α = .791) of student responses to the item, At the college you entered as a freshman, indicate how often you
        Interacted with someone of a different racial-ethnic group in class
        Studied with someone from a different racial-ethnic group
        Dined with someone from a different racial-ethnic group
        Dated someone from a different racial-ethnic group
        Socialized with someone from a different racial-ethnic group

Institutional Characteristics

Control: Coded as 0 = public and 1 = private.

Selectivity: Average SAT Verbal and SAT Math scores of entering freshmen.

Size: Number of full-time undergraduate students enrolled at the institution.

% of underrepresented minority students: % Latino + % Black + % Native American.

APPENDIX B

Descriptive Statistics for All Variables

Variable	Minimum	Maximum	Mean	Standard Deviation
Student-level variables (N = 20,178 students)				
Gender: Female (0 = male and 1 = female)	0.00	1.00	0.63	0.48
American Indian (0 = no and 1 = yes)	0.00	1.00	0.01	0.11
Asian American (0 = no and 1 = yes)	0.00	1.00	0.04	0.20
African American (0 = no and 1 = yes)	0.00	1.00	0.02	0.15
Latino/Latina (0 = no and 1 = yes)	0.00	1.00	0.03	0.17
Parental education (1 = grammar school to 8 = graduate degrees)	1.00	8.00	5.56	1.62
High school GPA (1 = D to 4 = A or A+)	1.00	4.00	3.50	0.45
Lived on campus in fall 1994 (0 = no and 1 = yes)	0.00	1.00	0.92	0.28
Had a part-time job on campus (0 = no and 1 = yes)	0.00	1.00	0.64	0.48
Level of campus involvement (standardized)	−0.77	3.64	0.00	1.00
Pretest for Factor 1: Self-Efficacy (standardized)	−4.46	2.28	0.00	1.00
Pretest for Factor 2: General Academic Skills (standardized)	−4.36	1.95	0.00	1.00
Pretest for Factor 3: Racial-Cultural Engagement (standardized)	−2.32	2.12	0.00	1.00
Curricular diversity (standardized)	−0.99	2.22	0.00	1.00
CRI (standardized)	−2.24	2.20	0.00	1.00
Factor 1: Self-Efficacy (5 = lowest 10% to 25 = highest 10%)	5.00	25.00	19.36	2.76
Factor 2: General Academic Skills (2 = lowest 10% to 10 = highest 10%)	4.00	20.00	17.20	1.83
Factor 3: Racial-Cultural Engagement (2 = not important to 8 = essential)	2.00	10.00	7.55	1.36
Institution-level variables (N = 236 institutions)				
Size (natural log of the number of full-time undergraduates)	5.95	10.35	7.64	0.90
Selectivity (average SAT Verbal + SAT Math of freshman)	756.00	1410.00	991.77	123.87
Institutional control: Private (0 = public and 1 = private)	0.00	1.00	0.84	0.36
% URM students	0.00	51.00	8.77	6.64
AVG: Gender: Female	0.00	1.00	0.65	0.16
AVG: American Indian	0.00	0.32	0.02	0.03
AVG: Asian American	0.00	0.44	0.04	0.06
AVG: African American	0.00	0.21	0.03	0.04

(continued)

APPENDIX B (cont.)

Variable	Minimum	Maximum	Mean	Standard Deviation
AVG: Latino	0.00	0.21	0.03	0.04
AVG: Parental education	3.79	6.86	5.41	0.63
AVG: High school GPA	2.89	3.93	3.47	0.20
AVG: Lived on campus in fall 1994	0.01	1.00	0.90	0.15
AVG: Had a part-time job on campus	0.00	0.96	0.65	0.17
AVG: Level of involvement	−0.61	1.15	0.01	0.36
AVG: Pretest for Factor 1	−0.94	1.14	−0.05	0.34
AVG: Pretest for Factor 2	−1.02	1.08	−0.04	0.36
AVG: Pretest for Factor 3	−0.75	0.61	0.01	0.22
AVG: Curricular diversity	−0.92	1.00	−0.01	0.39
AVG: CRI	−0.91	1.29	0.07	0.42
AVG: Factor 1: Self-Efficacy	17.52	21.91	19.33	0.73
AVG: Factor 2: General Academic Skills	15.91	18.76	17.14	0.43
AVG: Factor 3: Racial Cultural Engagement	6.80	8.69	7.64	0.32

Note. GPA = grade point average; CRI = cross-racial interaction; URM = underrepresented minority; AVG = average.

Notes

The authors wish to thank Michael H. Seltzer and three anonymous reviewers from the American Educational Research Journal for their insightful feedback and invaluable assistance in the writing of this manuscript.

1. We excluded students who had missing data or marked other on race (506 students) or planned residence for fall 1994 (52 students). We also excluded 2-year institutions (12 students), historically Black colleges and universities (313 students), institutions with fewer than 15 respondents (168 students), and institutions with missing data on the number of full-time undergraduate enrollment or selectivity (422 students). For the remainder of the sample, we replaced missing data on variables with the mean of the respondent's race.
2. Slope homogeneity was tested by examining the estimated institution-level variances for the random curricular diversity slope and the random cross-racial interaction slope using the following rationale:

   Curricular diversity slope: $H_0: \text{Var}(u_{1j}) = \text{Var}(\beta_{1j}) = 0;$

   and

   Cross-racial interaction slope: $H_0: \text{Var}(u_{2j}) = \text{Var}(\beta_{2j}) = 0.$

   If the null hypothesis is rejected, it implies variation among institutions in the effect of curricular diversity and/or cross-racial interaction (CRI) on the outcome. For the measures of self-efficacy, $\chi^2(\text{df} = 235) = 266.54$, general academic skills, $\chi^2(\text{df} = 235) = 249.57$, and racial-cultural engagement, $\chi^2(\text{df} = 235) = 230.67$, all three chi-square tests for the curricular diversity slope were nonsignificant ($p > .05$), suggesting that the effect of curricular diversity on all three outcomes does not seem to vary across institutions. Given this, the variances of the curricular diversity slopes for all three outcomes were specified as zero. For the measures of self-efficacy, $\chi^2(\text{df} = 235) = 250.89$, and racial-cultural engagement, $\chi^2(\text{df} = 235) = 243.46$, the chi-square tests for the CRI slope were nonsignificant ($p > .05$), suggesting that the effect of CRI on these two outcomes does not seem to vary across institutions. Thus, the variances of the CRI slopes for these two outcomes were specified as zero. Conversely, the variance for the CRI slope was specified as random for the general academic skills measure because its effect varied significantly across institutions, $\chi^2(\text{df} = 235) = 279.62$, $p < .05$.
3. Since there was no identical pretest for curricular diversity or CRI, we used an index of two items: the importance of promoting racial understanding and view that racial discrimination is no longer a problem (reverse coded).
4. The intraclass correlation (ρ) is computed by the following formula: $\rho = \tau_{00}/(\tau_{00} + \sigma^2)$.
5. The proportion reduction in variance, or variance explained, at the student level (within institutions) is calculated as

$$\frac{\sigma^2(\text{unconditional model}) - \sigma^2(\text{conditional model})}{\sigma^2(\text{unconditional model})}$$

The proportion reduction in variance, or variance explained, at the institution level (between institutions) is similarly calculated as

$$\frac{\tau_{00}(\text{unconditional model}) - \tau_{00}(\text{conditional model})}{\tau_{00}(\text{unconditional model})}$$

6. It is also quite plausible that increased structural diversity may give rise to campuses' being obligated to offer more diversity-related courses and/or activities. The correlation between percentage of underrepresented minority students and average level of curricular diversity is small ($r = .12$, $p > .05$). Thus, while this relationship seems plausible, our findings provide no support for this hypothesis.

References

Alger, J. R. (1997). The educational value of diversity. *Academe, 83,* 20–23.

antonio, a. l. (2001). The role of interracial interaction in the development of leadership skills and cultural knowledge and understanding. *Research in Higher Education, 42,* 593–617.

antonio, a. l. (2002). Faculty of color reconsidered: Reassessing contributions to scholarship. *Journal of Higher Education, 73,* 582–602.

antonio, a. l., Chang, M. J., Hakuta, K., Kenny, D. A., Levin, S., & Milem, J. F. (2004). Effects of racial diversity on complex thinking in college students. *Psychological Science, 15,* 507–510.

antonio, a. l., & Muñiz, M. M. (2007). The sociology of diversity. In P. J. Gumport (Ed.), *Sociology of higher education* (pp. 266–294). Baltimore: Johns Hopkins University Press.

Astin, A. W. (1993a). Diversity and multiculturalism on the campus: How are students affected? *Change, 23,* 44–49.

Astin, A. W. (1993b). What matters in college? *Four critical years revisited.* San Francisco: Jossey-Bass.

Berger, J. B. (2000). Organizational behavior at colleges and student outcomes: A new perspective on college impact. *Review of Higher Education, 23,* 177–198.

Bowen, W. G., & Bok, D. (1998). *The shape of the river: Long-term consequences of considering race in college and university admissions.* Princeton, NJ: Princeton University Press.

Brown, T. L. (2000). Gender differences in African American students' satisfaction with college. *Journal of College Student Development, 41,* 479–487.

Chang, M. J. (2001). Is it more than about getting along? The broader educational relevance of reducing students' racial biases. *Journal of College Student Development, 42,* 93–105.

Chang, M. J. (2002). Preservation or transformation: Where's the real educational discourse on diversity? *Review of Higher Education, 25,* 125–140.

Chang, M. J. (2005). Reconsidering the diversity rationale. *Liberal Education, 91,* 6–13.

Chang, M. J., Astin, A. W., & Kim, D. (2004). Cross-racial interaction among undergraduates: Some causes and consequences. *Research in Higher Education, 45,* 527–551.

Chang, M. J., Denson, N., Sáenz, V., & Misa, K. (2006). The educational benefits of sustaining cross-racial interaction among undergraduates. *Journal of Higher Education, 77,* 430–455.

Clark, B. R., Heist, P., McConnell, T. R., Trow, M. A., & Yonge, G. (1972). *Students and colleges: Interaction and change.* Berkeley, CA: Center for Research and Development in Higher Education.

Erikson, E. (1946). Ego development and historical change. *Psychoanalytic Study of the Child, 2,* 359–396.

Erikson, E. (1956). The problem of ego identity. *Journal of American Psychoanalytic Association, 4,* 56–121.

Espenshade, T. J., & Chung, C. Y. (2005). The opportunity cost of admission preferences at elite universities. *Social Science Quarterly, 86*(2), 293–305.

Grutter, et al. v. Bollinger, et al., 539 U.S. (2003).

Gurin, P. (1999). Expert report: "Gratz et al. v. Bollinger, et al." No. 97-75321 (E.D. Mich.); "Grutter, et al. v. Bollinger, et al." No. 97-75928 (E.D. Mich.). *Equity and Excellence in Education, 32*(2), 36–62.

Gurin, P., Dey, E. L., Hurtado, S., & Gurin, G. (2002). Diversity and higher education: Theory and impact on educational outcomes. *Harvard Educational Review, 72,* 330–366.

Hu, S., & Kuh, G. D. (2003). Diversity experiences and college student learning and personal development. *Journal of College Student Development, 44,* 320–334.

Hurtado, S. (2001). Linking diversity and educational purpose: How diversity affects the classroom environment and student development. In G. Orfield (Ed.), *Diversity challenged: Legal crisis and new evidence* (pp. 187–203). Cambridge, MA: Harvard Publishing Group.

Hurtado, S. (2005). The next generation of diversity and intergroup relations research. *Journal of Social Issues, 61,* 595–610.

Hurtado, S., Milem, J., Clayton-Pederson, A. R., & Allen, W. R. (1998). Enhancing campus climates for racial/ethnic diversity: Educational policy and practice. *Review of Higher Education, 21,* 279–302.

Lopez, G. E. (2004). Interethnic contact, curriculum, and attitudes in the first year of college. *Journal of Social Issues, 60,* 75–94.

Nelson Laird, T. F. (2005). College students' experiences with diversity and their effects on academic self-confidence, social agency, and disposition toward critical thinking. *Research in Higher Education, 46,* 365–387.

Nelson Laird, T. F., Engberg, M. E., & Hurtado, S. (2005). Modeling accentuation effects: Enrolling in a diversity course and the importance of social action engagement. *Journal of Higher Education, 76,* 448–476.

Pascarella, E. T. (2001). Using student self-reported gains to estimate college impact: A cautionary tale. *Journal of College Student Development, 42,* 488–492.

Pascarella, E. T., Palmer, B., Moye, M., & Pierson, C. T. (2001). Do diversity experiences influence the development of critical thinking? *Journal of College Student Development, 42,* 257–271.

Pascarella, E. T., & Terenzini, P. T. (1991). *How college affects students.* San Francisco: Jossey-Bass.

Pascarella, E. T., & Terenzini, P. T. (2005). *How college affects students: A third decade of research.* San Francisco: Jossey-Bass.

Piaget, J. (1985). *The equilibrium of cognitive structures: The central problem of intellectual development.* Chicago: University of Chicago Press. (Original work published 1975)

Pike, G. R. (1995). The relationship between self-reports of college experiences and achievement test scores. *Research in Higher Education, 36,* 1–21.

Pike, G. R., & Kuh, G. D. (2006). Relationships among structural diversity, informal peer interactions and perceptions of the campus environment. *Review of Higher Education, 29,* 425–450.

Raudenbush, S. W, & Bryk, A. S. (1986). A hierarchical model for studying school effects. *Sociology of Education, 59,* 1–17.

Raudenbush, S. W., & Bryk, A. S. (2002). *Hierarchical linear models: Applications and data analysis methods* (2nd ed.). Thousand Oaks, CA: Sage.

Richardson, R. C., & Skinner, E. F. (1990). Adapting to diversity: Organizational influences on student achievement. *Journal of Higher Education, 61,* 485–511.

Rothman, S., Lipset, S. M., & Nevitte, N. (2002). Does enrollment diversity improve university education? *International Journal of Public Opinion Research, 15,* 8–26.

Schneider, B., Carnoy, M., Kilpatrick, J., Schmidt, W. H., & Shavelson, R. J. (2007). *Estimating causal effects using experimental and observational designs* (Report from the governing board of the American Educational Research Association Grants Program). Washington, DC: American Educational Research Association.

Springer, L., Palmer, B., Terenzini, P. T., Pascarella, E. T., & Nora, A. (1996). Attitudes toward campus diversity: Participation in a racial or cultural awareness workshop. *Review of Higher Education, 20,* 53–68.

Terenzini, P. T., Cabrera, A. F., Colbeck, C. L., Bjorklund, S. A., & Parente, J. M. (2001). Racial and ethnic diversity in the classroom: Does it promote student learning? *Journal of Higher Education, 72,* 509–531.

Umbach, P. D., & Kuh, G. D. (2006). Student experiences with diversity at liberal arts colleges: Another claim for distinctiveness. *Journal of Higher Education, 77,* 169–192.

Wells, A., Duran, J., & White, T. (in press). Refusing to leave desegregation behind: From graduates of racially diverse schools to the Supreme Court. *Teachers College Record, 110*(12).

Zúñiga, X., Williams, E. A., & Berger, J. B. (2005). Action-oriented democratic outcomes: The impact of student involvement with campus diversity. *Journal of College Student Development, 46,* 660–678.

CHAPTER 15
ENHANCING CAMPUS CLIMATES FOR RACIAL/ETHNIC DIVERSITY: EDUCATIONAL POLICY AND PRACTICE

SYLVIA HURTADO, JEFFREY F. MILEM, ALMA R. CLAYTON-PEDERSEN, AND WALTER R. ALLEN

Probably few policy areas of higher education have received more recent attention than the issue of race on campus. Evidence appears in policies and programs related to college admissions, financial aid, affirmative action, discrimination and harassment, and desegregation. Yet, at the same time, probably no area of campus life has been so devoid of policy initiatives as the racial climate at individual institutions. Until recently, there has been no common framework for understanding the campus racial climate in a way that helps develop policies and practices that can be used to enhance the campus climate.

We pose four possible explanations for this phenomenon. First, higher education leaders and higher education institutions have taken the laissez-faire approach that people will (should) work things out interactively and that it is wrong to intervene too closely in student interactions (Horowitz, 1987). The second explanation involves ambiguity in the role that colleges and universities perform as agents of socialization. Administrators and faculty recognize that students bring with them to college a sense of identity and purpose shaped by their parents, their communities, their religions, etc., and that these influences are critically important to students' growth and development. The quandary lies in just how much of a resocializing agent higher education institutions wish to be. Higher education has not decided whether it should merely reflect our society or whether it should try to consciously shape the society. Third, while research findings document the important role that faculty serve as the "designated socializing agents" in higher education (Feldman & Newcomb, 1969, p. 227), policy initiatives that address faculty attitudes and behaviors have been implemented only with great hesitation and caution. Until now, it seems that only the most problematic discriminatory behaviors of faculty have been addressed. Finally, the situation has been exacerbated by neglect. A rich history of research on issues that affect the campus racial climate has existed for some time. However, this research has not always been valued by the higher education community. A study analyzing the major paradigms used in manuscripts published in "major" higher education journals found that fewer than 2% used paradigms that addressed issues of race from a critical perspective with the goal of producing meaningful change (Milam, 1989).

Attorneys, policy-makers, and institutional leaders across the country are searching for research evidence that demonstrates the benefits of diversity and documents persistent discrimination and inequality in higher education. Perhaps at no other time in our history have higher education scholars had the opportunity to provide evidence of the educational outcomes of diversity in a way that puts the benefits of diversity at the center of the educational enterprise. The purpose of this paper is to illustrate how research on issues related to campus racial climate can be used to enhance educational policy and practice. Both classic and contemporary research can inform national policy and debates surrounding affirmative action and other policies to create diverse learning environments (Hurtado, Milem, Clayton-Pedersen, & Allen, in press). What is needed are vehicles that translate higher education research into thoughtful policies incorporating the goal of educating diverse students. While such vehicles, or "translation documents," can be written in any number of higher education policy arenas, this paper focuses on the critical need for sustaining progress in educating diverse students.

We conducted an extensive multidisciplinary analysis of the research literature on the sources and outcomes of campus racial climate and developed a framework for understanding and describing the campus climate. It is our hope that policy-makers, institutional leaders, and scholars of higher education will find this framework useful as they seek to create comfortable, diverse environments for learning and socializing that facilitate the intellectual and social development of all students.

A Framework for Understanding Campus Climate

Considerable research on various racial/ethnic students in higher education addresses an array of cognitive and affective outcomes and group differences in educational attainments (Durán, 1983; Pascarella & Terenzini, 1991; Sedlacek, 1987). While these earlier research syntheses represent scholarly work on the achievement of various racial/ethnic groups, they contain almost no specific references to the institutional climate's potential influence on diversity. Some literature refers to the climate as important but "intangible." Recently, both qualitative and quantitative researchers have provided greater definition for this "intangible" quality by examining how students, faculty, and administrators perceive the institutional climate for racial/ethnic diversity, their experiences with campus diversity, and their own attitudes and interactions with different racial/ethnic groups. Multi-institutional studies have also shown, using a variety of measures, that the climate for diversity varies substantially from one institutional context to another (El-Khawas, 1989; Gilliard, 1996; Hurtado, 1992; Peterson, Blackburn, Gamson, Arce, Davenport, & Mingle, 1978).

This manuscript provides a framework for understanding four dimensions of the campus climate and a conceptual handle for understanding elements of the environment that were once thought too complex to comprehend. This framework was first introduced in a study of the climate for Latino students (Hurtado, 1994) and further developed in a synthesis of research done for practitioners (Hurtado, Milem, Clayton-Pedersen, & Allen, in press). It makes concrete observations of institutions and individuals. It also defines areas where research has been conducted and, more importantly, where practical or programmatic solutions can be targeted.

Most institutions, when considering diversity on campus, tend to focus on increasing the numbers of racial/ethnic students. While this area of institutional effort is important, the four-part framework underscores other elements that also require attention, defining key areas upon which to focus diversity efforts. The studies we reviewed contain specific references to these various dimensions of the climate, describe the climate's impact on students from different racial/ethnic groups, and capture the experiences or unique perspectives of racial/ethnic groups that have historically been underrepresented in higher education.

Central to the conceptualization of a campus climate for diversity is the concept that students are educated in distinct racial contexts. These contexts in higher education are shaped by external and internal (institutional) forces. We represent the external components of climate as two domains: (a) the impact of governmental policy, programs, and initiatives and (b) the impact of sociohistorical forces on campus racial climate. Examples of the first include financial aid policies and programs, state and federal policy on affirmative action, court decisions on the desegregation of higher education, and the manner in which states provide for institutional differentiation within their state system of higher education. Sociohistoric forces influencing the climate for diversity on campus are events or issues in the larger society, nearly always originating outside the campus, that influence how people view racial diversity in society. They stimulate discussion or other activity within the campus. Obviously, these two domains influence each other. Tierney (1997) points out, "No policy can be isolated from the social arena in which it is enacted" (p. 177). While research literature documents the effect of governmental policy, programs, and initiatives (particularly in financial aid), there are fewer studies of the influence of sociohistorical forces on the campus racial climate.

The institutional context contains four dimensions resulting from educational programs and practices. They include an institution's historical legacy of inclusion or exclusion of various racial/ethnic groups, its structural diversity in terms of numerical representation of various racial/ethnic groups, the psychological climate of perceptions and attitudes between and among groups, and the behavioral climate dimension, characterized by intergroup relations on campus. We conceive the institutional climate as a product of these various elements.

It is important to note that these dimensions are connected, not discrete. For example, the historical vestiges of segregation have an impact on an institution's ability to improve its racial/ethnic student enrollments, and the underrepresentation of specific groups contributes to stereotypical attitudes among individuals within the learning and work environment that affect the psychological and behavioral climate. In short, while some institutions are now trying to take a "multi-layered" approach toward assessing diversity on their campuses and are developing programs to address the climate on campus, very few recognize the importance of the dynamics of these interrelated elements of the climate.

The Institutional Context Historical Legacy of Inclusion or Exclusion

In many ways, the historical vestiges of segregated schools and colleges continue to affect the climate for racial/ethnic diversity on college campuses. The best example is resistance to desegregation in communities and specific campus settings, the maintenance of old campus policies at predominantly White institutions that best serve a homogeneous population, and attitudes and behaviors that prevent interaction across race and ethnicity. Because they are embedded in the culture of a historically segregated environment, many campuses sustain long-standing, often unrecognized, benefits for particular student groups (Duster, 1993).

Desegregation policies in schools and colleges were designed to alter their racial/ethnic composition, improve educational opportunity, and ultimately, change the environments of our educational institutions. Research on the outcomes of desegregation suggests that individuals who attend desegregated schools and colleges accept desegregation as adults in other educational settings, occupations, and social situations. Moreover, White adults who attended desegregated schools have fewer racial stereotypes and less fear of hostile reactions in interracial settings (Braddock, 1980, 1985; Braddock, Crain, & McPartland, 1984; Braddock & Dawkins, 1981; Braddock & McPartland, 1982, 1989; Green, 1982; Scott & McPartland, 1982).

While some campuses have a history of admitting and graduating students of color since their founding days, most predominantly White institutions (PWIs) have a history of limited access and exclusion (Thelin, 1985). A college's historical legacy of exclusion can determine the prevailing climate and influence current practices (Hurtado, 1992). Various institutional case studies document the impact of the historical context on the climate for diversity and on attempts to create a supportive climate for students of color (Peterson et al., 1978; Richardson & Skinner, 1991). Researchers found that success in creating supportive campus environments often depends on an institution's initial response to the entrance of students of color. Among important factors were the institutional philosophy of education for students of color, commitment to affirmative action, institutional intent for minority-specific programs, and attention to the psychological climate and intergroup relations on campus (Peterson et al., 1978). Higher education has had a long history of resistance to desegregation. The need for legal pressures and extended litigation to require institutions to accept their obligation to serve equitably a more diverse group of students has conveyed not only the message of institutional resistance but, in some cases, outright hostility toward people of diverse backgrounds.

Historically Black colleges and universities (HBCUs) and American Indian colleges (AICs) have historic commitments to serve populations previously excluded from higher education. These students continue to face seemingly intractable problems at PWIs. In recent years, due to dramatic changes in Latino enrollment, Hispanic-serving institutions (HSIs) have also begun to emphasize their commitment to educating Latino students. Today, as before, HBCUs, AICs, and HSIs not only represent alternative choices for students but also include attention to the cultural and academic development of these students and their communities as part of their mission.

Research that has examined differences in outcomes for African American students who have attended HBCUs as compared to students who have attended PWIs suggest that HBCUs provide more social and psychological support, higher levels of satisfaction and sense of community, and a greater likelihood that students will persist and complete their degrees (Allen, 1992; Allen, Epps, & Haniff, 1991; R. Davis, 1991; Jackson & Swan, 1991; Pascarella, Smart, Ethington, & Nettles, 1987). Recent findings from the National Study of Student Learning indicate that HBCUs also provide educational environments that support their students' intellectual development (Pascarella, Whitt, Nora, Edison, Hagedorn, Terenzini, 1996).

However, most racially and ethnically diverse students are educated in predominantly White environments (Carter & Wilson, 1993); therefore, PWIs's responses to desegregation are key in defining the campus racial climate. A positive response requires a clear definition of desegregation and strategic planning by the institution (Stewart, 1991). Further, the goals of desegregation plans must be precisely articulated with the objective of increasing overall representation of the historically excluded group.

Implications for Policy and Practice

Colleges and universities cannot change their past histories of exclusion nor should they deny that they exist. However, they can take steps to insure that diversity becomes a central value of their educational enterprise. Campus leaders should not assume that members of their community (particularly incoming students) know these histories, nor should they assume that teaching about these histories will lead to dissatisfaction. By being clear about an institution's past history of exclusion and the detrimental impact that this history has had on the campus, colleges and universities may garner broader support for their efforts to become more diverse through affirmative action programs and other programs and services designed to improve the climate for diversity. Moreover, acknowledging a past history of exclusion implies an institutional willingness to actively shed its exclusionary past. Such efforts may be even more effective if they are coupled with a clearly articulated vision for a more inclusive future.

In assessing the influence of the campus's history, leaders must consider whether "embedded benefits" may still exist on their campus. Institutions with a history of exclusion are likely to have evolved in ways that disproportionately benefit some group. For example, at many PWIs, fraternities and sororities have been a part of campus life much longer than people of color. Predominantly White fraternities and sororities frequently have houses that provide members with a place to meet or to live that are centrally located on campus or directly adjacent to the campus while the Greek system is deeply involved in daily campus activities, politics, socials, etc. In contrast, African American fraternities and sororities at these institutions seldom have been able to accumulate similar benefits for their members. The likelihood of finding the same quality of houses in equally convenient locations is quite low. In fact, students in these organizations may struggle to find places that they can meet on or near some campuses. Research shows that these organizations are critically important to the students who join them, but African American fraternities and sororities frequently seem less central than their White counterparts in daily campus activities, politics, and socials. As campus leaders thoughtfully consider their histories of exclusion, they are likely to find many more examples.

The success of legislation and litigation regarding desegregation in higher education has been mixed at best (Williams, 1988). In the prevailing climate, the federal government is taking a somewhat passive role and deferring to states. Even where the willingness to pursue desegregation exists, the capacity for most states to regulate their colleges and universities (particularly their flagship institutions) has been limited (Williams, 1988). Hence, efforts to maintain a commitment to desegregation and equality of opportunity in higher education are most likely to succeed at the campus level with provisions for support at the state level. Desegregating predominantly White institutions is particularly important in states and communities where high-school segregation has continued; as a result, college may be the first chance for many students to encounter and interact with someone of different race or ethnicity.

According to the Southern Education Foundation (1995), HBCUs and PWIs are the result of "purposeful, state-imposed segregation," hence "no set of institutions has any more right than another to survive. The burden of desegregation should not fall exclusively or disproportionately on HBCUs" (p. xix). To require this effort would be unfair and unwise. E. B. Davis (1993) explains: "Institutions that retain a specifically black identity will not easily be able to reach the level of integration which reflects the population. They are being challenged to change their very character, while historically White schools are being asked only to broaden access" (p. 523). HBCUs serve an essential role in the higher education system by providing educational environments that facilitate positive social, psychological, and intellectual outcomes for students who attend them. Hence, they must be maintained. Moreover, PWIs can learn much from HBCUs, AICs, and HSIs about enhancing their environments to insure the success of students of color on campus.

Structural Diversity and Its Impact on Students

Given recent assaults on affirmative action in states like California and judicial rulings like that in Hopwood, it is critically important to understand how changes in the enrollment of racial/ethnic students (or the lack thereof) transform into educational benefits for students. Research supports the concept that increasing the structural diversity of an institution is an important initial step toward improving the climate. First, environments with highly skewed distributions of students shape the dynamics of social interaction (Kanter, 1977). Campuses with high proportions of White students provide limited opportunities for interaction across race/ethnicity barriers and limit student learning experiences with socially and culturally diverse groups (Hurtado, Dey, & Treviño, 1994). Second, in environments that lack diverse populations, underrepresented groups are viewed as tokens. Tokenism contributes to the heightened visibility of the underrepresented group, exaggeration of group differences, and the distortion of images to fit existing stereotypes (Kanter, 1977). The sheer fact that racial and ethnic students remain minorities in majority White environments contributes to their social stigma (Steele, 1992) and can produce minority status stress (Prillerman, Myers, & Smedley, 1989; Smedley, Myers, & Harrell, 1993). Third, an institution's stance on increasing the representation of diverse racial/ethnic groups communicates whether maintaining a multicultural environment is a high institutional priority. For example, African American, Chicano, and White students tended to report that commitment to diversity was a high institutional priority on campuses with relatively high percentages of African American and Latino students (Hurtado, 1990).

Loo and Rolison (1986) conclude that sufficient racial/ethnic enrollments can give potential recruits the impression that the campus is hospitable: "No matter how outstanding the academic institution, ethnic minority students can feel alienated if their ethnic representation on campus is small" (p. 72). However, increasing the numbers of students of color on campus is not free from problems. The racial/ethnic restructuring of student enrollments can trigger conflict and resistance among groups. It can also create a need for institutional changes more substantial than first envisioned. Resulting changes affect both the academic and social life of the institution, resulting in, for example, the development of ethnic studies programs, diverse student organizations, specific academic support programs, and multicultural programming (Muñoz, 1989; Peterson et al., 1978; Treviño, 1992).

Increases in diverse student enrollment, however, have also become problematic for the White majority and racial/ethnic minority groups. Race relations theorists hypothesize that the larger the relative size of the minority group, the more likely it is that there will be minority/majority conflict over limited resources (Blalock, 1967). On campuses where Asian American enrollments have increased substantially, Asian American students have reported more personal experiences of discrimination than any other group (Asian Pacific, 1990). White students tend to perceive racial tension on predominantly White campuses with relatively high African American enrollments (Hurtado, 1992). However, results from this study also show that, when students feel that they are valued and that faculty and administrators are devoted to their development, they are less likely to report racial/ethnic tension on campus. This finding suggests that campuses can minimize racial tension and competition among groups by creating more "student-centered" environments.

Chang (1996) found that maximizing cross-racial interaction and encouraging ongoing discussions about race are educational practices that benefit all students. However, when minority enrollments increased without implementing these activities, students of color reported less overall satisfaction with their college experience (Chang, 1996). Thus, increasing only the structural diversity of an institution without considering the influence of each of the other dimensions of the campus racial climate is likely to produce problems for students at these institutions.

Implications for Policy and Practice

Clearly, one important step toward improving the campus climate for diversity is to increase the representation of people of color on campus. Hence, institutional and government policy must insure that access to college is available to all members of our society. Admissions practices and financial aid policies are two areas in which changes can be made that will have prompt, positive effects.

Some critics have suggested that college and graduate/professional admissions policies and practices place too much emphasis on standardized test scores and not enough on evidence of previous achievement such as high school or college grade point averages and a student's drive to achieve (Frierson, 1991; Guanier, 1997). Guanier (1997) has suggested that college and graduate/ professional school admission committees decide on a minimum acceptable score, then hold a lottery to draw the entering class from the pool of candidates meeting that criterion. Students who offer qualities considered valuable to the institution would have their names entered more than once to increase the likelihood that they would be selected. "These could be students who have overcome adversity, who have particular skills and credentials, who have outstanding academic records, or who have special and worthy career aspirations" (Guanier, 1997, p. 60).

Another approach to college admissions can be found in a proposal offered in response to the Bakke decision (Astin, 1985; Astin, Fuller, & Green, 1978). The authors reported that standardized tests presented a significant obstacle for students from historically disadvantaged backgrounds and that the negative impact of these tests increases dramatically as the selection ratio (number of applicants compared to the number of students admitted) increases at institutions. They suggested the use of a "disadvantagement index" derived from parental income, father's educational level, and mother's educational level. This index assumes that affluent parents are more likely to provide their children with greater access to educational opportunities and are more likely to live in communities where local schools are better funded and have more educational resources.

Neither proposal is likely to provide a single best answer about reforming the college admissions process to insure that diverse people are appropriately represented. Indeed, in the case of the disadvantagement index, critics might argue that class is an insufficient proxy for race (Tierney, 1997). However, in discussing the relative merits of such approaches, a discussion might begin on how college admissions policies and programs can be reformed to insure appropriate levels of structural diversity.

Without a doubt, state and federal financial aid policies have increased the diversity of college enrollments. Researchers of student financial aid have found that financial aid generally does what it was designed to do: It increases access to higher education by increasing the probability that students will attend college (St. John 1991a; Stampen & Fenske, 1988). While all forms of aid are positively associated with the decision to attend college when all students are considered, not all forms of aid are equally effective for students from historically disadvantaged backgrounds. Aid packages with loans are less consistently significant in facilitating access for minority applicants than for White applicants (St. John, 1991a), and Black, Latino, and American Indian students borrow considerably less than White or Asian students (Stampen, 1985).

Maintaining appropriate forms of financial aid at the state, federal, and institutional levels is critical in increasing the diversity of student enrollments. However, federal funding has not kept pace with increases in tuition in recent years (Orfield, 1992). Recent federal policies related to financial aid still disadvantage poor families from various racial/ethnic groups, thus reducing equity and college access for them (Olivas, 1986; Orfield, 1992). The expanded availability of and extended eligibility for loan dollars (and the decreased availability of grant and work study funds) has increased access for students from middle-income families while restricting access for students from low-income backgrounds. A key component of any long-term and short-term response to these trends should involve substantial increases in federal student grant funding, rather than an increased emphasis on loans (Astin, 1982; St. John, 1991b). Moreover, additional investment in financial aid programs makes good fiscal sense. Funding federal financial aid programs provides a substantial return on investment of public funds (St. John & Masten, 1990).

Recent research on the impact of financial aid provides an example of how external factors (governmental policy, programs, and initiatives) influence the campus climate for diversity. Campuses must find ways to counteract the negative consequences of changes in financial aid programs for students from historically disadvantaged backgrounds. If schools are sincere in their effort to attract more diverse students, they should change institutional aid policies so that they offer as much aid as possible in grants. Moreover, institutional leaders should work with state and federal policy-makers for appropriate levels of funding for financial aid and put this money into the aid programs that are most helpful to students from historically disadvantaged backgrounds—i.e., grants and work study programs.

Campus leaders and policy-makers should not expect to substantively improve the campus racial climate by increasing only the structural diversity of institutions. In fact, problems are likely to arise without improvements in other aspects of campus climate. Increased structural diversity will likely fail in achieving its goals unless accompanied by efforts to make institutions more "student-centered" in approaches to teaching and learning (Hurtado, 1992) and by regular and ongoing opportunities for students to communicate and interact cross-racially (Chang, 1996).

The Psychological Dimension of Climate and Its Impact on Students

The psychological dimension of the campus racial climate involves individuals' views of group relations, institutional responses to diversity, perceptions of discrimination or racial conflict, and attitudes toward those from other racial/ethnic backgrounds than one's own. It is important to note that more recent studies show that racially and ethnically diverse administrators, students, and faculty tend to view the campus climate differently. Thus, an individual's position and power within the organization and his or her status as "insider" or "outsider" strongly influence attitudes (Collins, 1986). In other words, who you are and where you are positioned in an institution will affect how you experience and view the institution. For example, Loo and Rolison (1986) found that 68 percent of White students thought their university was generally supportive of minority students; only 28 percent of the African American and Chicano students expressed the same opinion. Cabrera and Nora (1994) found that students of color were more sensitive to different forms of prejudice and discrimination; White students were less likely to perceive nuances. Variations within ethnic groups also occur, depending on the student's background and sense of ethnic identity. For example, one study found that American Indian students who closely held to American Indian values were likely to report more negative racial encounters in college than other students (Huffman, 1991). These perceptual differences of the college experience are significant, for perception is both a product of the environment and potential determinant of future interactions and outcomes (Astin, 1968; Tierney, 1987). As past and contemporary research reveals, these differing perceptions and experiences have real consequences for individuals.

General student perceptions of discrimination have a significant and negative effect on African American students' grades (Nettles, 1988; Prillerman et al., 1989; Smedley et al., 1993). First-year students who felt that they were singled out or treated differently in the classroom reported a higher sense of alienation at the end of their freshman year (Cabrera & Nora, 1994). While significant for all racial/ethnic groups, this form of discrimination was particularly detrimental to African Americans. A longitudinal study of highly talented Latino students found that perceptions of racial tension between groups on campus in the first year had a consistently negative effect on academic and psychological adjustment in subsequent college years (Hurtado, Carter, & Spuler, 1996). The study also found that while reports of overt instances of personal harassment/discrimination did not significantly affect academic and personal-emotional adjustment, they diminished Latino students' feelings of attachment to the institution. Another study of freshman minority students found that perceptions of discrimination affected their academic and social experiences but not their persistence in college (Nora & Cabrera, 1996). It may be that, although academically confident students of color continue to feel marginalized, they learn how to deal with discrimination (Tracey & Sedlacek, 1985).

However, even students of color who persist through graduation may feel high levels of alienation: one study found less satisfaction and more social alienation among African American and Asian American students who stayed at the institution as compared to those who left the university, presumably for better environments (Bennett & Okinaka, 1990). Introducing ways for students to report and seek redress for negative experiences is important, but campuses must also be aware that many psychological aspects of the college climate go unreported. A study of California State institutions revealed that Asian Pacific Americans often do not use formal grievance procedures when they experience discrimination or harassment (Asian Pacific, 1994). Native American students confirmed that perceptions of racial hostility were strongly associated with feelings of isolation, but the effect on their attitudes toward college or grade point average was not decisively significant (Lin, LaCounte, & Eder, 1988).

In a multi-campus study, Gilliard (1996) found that the most significant climate measure for Black students was their perceptions of racial discrimination by college administrators. She also found that White students' sense of belonging was negatively affected by a poor racial climate but was positively tied to having non-White friends and to perceptions that the campus accepted and respected African American students. Similarly, Nora and Cabrera (1996) found that White students' persistence in college was both directly and indirectly affected by perceptions of discrimination. These studies show that White students are also affected by the climate for racial/ethnic diversity.

Research on the impact of peer groups and other reference groups is helpful in understanding another important aspect of the psychological dimension of climate on campus. Peer groups influence students' attitudes and behavior through the norms that they communicate to their members. While faculty play an important role in the educational development of students, most researchers believe that student peer groups are principally responsible for socialization (Chickering, 1969; Feldman & Newcomb, 1969). This finding does not minimize the role of faculty; rather, it suggests that their normative influence will be amplified or attenuated by the interactions students have with their peers. While peer groups clearly have the greatest impact in the undergraduate socialization process, recent research on the impact of college on students' racial attitudes, cultural awareness/acceptance, and social/political attitudes suggests that faculty may have a larger, more important role than traditionally believed (Hurtado, 1990, 1992; Milem, 1992, 1994, 1998).

Implications for Policy and Practice

Institutional leaders can significantly strengthen the psychological climate on their campuses by purposefully becoming deliberate agents of socialization. They can begin by designing and implementing systematic and comprehensive educational programs to help all members of the campus community to identify and confront the stereotypes and myths that people have about those who are different from them. While much of what is known about the development and reduction of prejudice and bias comes from the research of college and university faculty, many businesses and organizations in the private sector have shown a greater willingness to apply these findings in the hope of strengthening their organizational effectiveness. If these activities provide opportunities for cross-racial interaction, the magnitude of difference in perceptions of the racial climate between White students and students of color on campus is likely to be dramatically reduced (Pascarella et al., 1996).

Because perceptions of discrimination have consequences for all students, institutions should do all that they can to insure that students perceive the institutional climate as fair and just. Hence, institutions must have clearly stated policies and procedures to help the campus community confront and resolve incidents of harassment and discrimination. These policies and procedures should include formal processes for resolving conflicts or disputes that involve representatives from all members of the campus community (students, faculty, staff).

As we discussed earlier, there will almost certainly be significant differences in perceptions of the climate based on the experience and position of the person being asked. Campus leaders should insure that the perspectives of all members of the campus community be considered in decision-making processes. Hence, institutions must implement regular and on-going assessments of the campus climate for diversity.

Research findings clearly document the important role of ethnic student organizations and other student support services for students of color on predominantly White campuses. Hence, campuses must insure that these services and organizations have enough staff, funding, and resources to serve students successfully.

An emerging body of research on mentoring suggests that academe poorly socializes graduate students of color into the culture of academic departments. Students of color who pursue research on issues relevant to their cultural/ethnic background frequently report difficulty in finding faculty who encourage and support their work. This faculty indifference probably influences negatively student perceptions of the climate of the institution and may have a detrimental effect on their graduate student experience (Nealy, 1996; Turner & Thompson, 1993; Willie, Grady, & Hope, 1991). Institutional leaders can address these concerns by providing formal mentoring programs where students are matched with faculty who will support them and their work as emerging scholars.

The research in social psychology and higher education has suggested for some time that peer groups are critical in students' educational experience. However, institutions of higher education have not done all that they can to incorporate these groups into the formal educational process. Rather than leaving cross-racial interactions among students to chance, educators should make peer groups a deliberate and positive part of the educational process in colleges and universities.

Recent research also suggests that faculty serve a more important role in influencing students' attitudes and values than had been previously thought. It is time to shift the debate from whether faculty can (or should) be "objective" to how to give faculty support and guidance in becoming aware of their biases and the effect of these biases on their students.

The Behavioral Dimension of Climate and Its Impact on Students

The behavioral dimension of the institutional climate consists of (a) actual reports of general social interaction, (b) interaction between and among individuals from different racial/ethnic backgrounds, and (c) the nature of intergroup relations on campus. Student involvement plays a central role in undergraduates' successful educational experience; it enhances cognitive and affective student outcomes (Astin 1988, 1991, 1993; Kuh, Schuh, Whitt, Andreas, Lyons, Strange, Krehbiel, & MacKay, 1991; Pascarella & Terenzini, 1991) and retention (Tinto 1987, 1993). "Involving colleges" foster high expectations for student performance, minimize status distinctions, and have an unwavering commitment to multiculturalism (Kuh et al., 1991).

The prevailing contemporary view is that campus race relations are poor, social interaction is low, and students from different racial/ethnic groups are segregating themselves from other groups (Altbach & Lomotey, 1991; Bunzel, 1992). To be sure, incidents of overt racism and harassment occurred with greater frequency at the end of the 1980s and received much press coverage (Farrell & Jones, 1988). However, several research studies based on students' interactions and relations on campus paint a different picture. White students interpreted ethnic group clustering as racial segregation, while minority students viewed this behavior as cultural support within a larger unsupportive environment (Loo & Rolison, 1986). Chicano, Asian American, and African American students reported widespread and frequent interaction across race/ethnicity in various informal situations (i.e., dining, roommates, dating, socializing), but White students were least likely to report any of these activities as interracial (Hurtado, Dey, & Treviño, 1994). Although African Americans and Asian Americans reported more frequent racial/ethnic harassment (32% and 30% respectively), such experiences did not significantly diminish interaction across race/ethnicity for these groups.

The absence of interracial contact clearly influences students' views toward others, support for campus initiatives, and educational outcomes. White students who had the least social interaction with someone of a different background were less likely to hold positive attitudes toward multiculturalism on campus (Globetti, Globetti, Brown, & Smith, 1993). Conversely, White students who had socialized with someone of another race, had discussed racial/ethnic issues with other students, or had attended racial/cultural awareness workshops were more likely to value the goal of promoting racial understanding (Milem, 1992, 1994, 1998). Another study revealed that socializing across race and discussing racial/ethnic issues have a positive effect on students' retention, overall satisfaction with college, intellectual self-concept, and social self-concept (Chang, 1996). After studying the complex dynamics of interaction on the U.C. Berkeley campus, where dramatic changes in racial/ethnic enrollments have occurred, Duster (1993) suggested continued support for strong ethnic identities and affiliations as well as institutional encouragement for multiracial contacts.

Although some suggest that racial/ethnic student organizations and minority programs contribute to campus segregation, a series of studies refutes this perspective. These studies have empirically demonstrated that students join racial/student organizations because they are identity enhancing and that such increased identity comfort may lead to a greater interest in both cultural and cross-cultural activities (Treviño, 1992; Mitchell & Dell, 1992). Treviño (1992) found that members of racial/ethnic student organizations were more likely to participate in racial/cultural awareness workshops. Students in such organizations also report more frequent informal interactions across race/ethnicity (Hurtado, Dey, & Treviño, 1994). In addition, Gilliard (1996) found that participation in racially focused cultural activities and support programs (e.g., Black Student Union, minority peer support services) was correlated with African Americans' higher social involvement, informal social interactions with faculty, and higher use of general support services.

Implications for Policy and Practice

Research on the behavioral dimension of racial climate suggests a wide range of beneficial practices for students. While institutions cannot change their pasts, they can clearly articulate to all members of the community the expectation that interracial dialogue and interaction are highly valued on campus. They should try to provide students with opportunities for cross-racial interaction whenever possible—both in and out of the classroom. This interaction should be structured so that it will be positive for participants. The contact should be regular, on-going, and viewed as equal in status by all participants. Finally, the contact should occur in an environment characterized by cooperation and not competition (Allport, 1954).

Faculty can facilitate positive interaction in the classroom by insuring that racial/ethnic diversity is part of the course content. Moreover, faculty can promote interaction across racial/ethnic groups and student achievement. Cooperative learning activities, inside and outside of the classroom, increase interaction across race/ethnicity and lead to intergroup friendships (Slavin, 1985). When students work cooperatively on course content, they learn more about one another as well as about the specific content areas. Faculty members should also consider how to modify their classroom practices to reduce competition in the classroom. Finally, given the important role of faculty contact (in and out of the classroom), institutions should provide abundant opportunities for all faculty-student contact in and out of the classroom. Given the academic reward structure at many institutions, institutional leaders may need to provide incentives to encourage faculty to engage students in this way.

Cross-race interactions can be also enhanced by the programs and activities of multicultural centers. These centers frequently house the ethnic student organizations that are critical to the educational success of the students they represent. Given the importance of these organizations in affirming a sense of identity for students and in their role of encouraging students to become involved in other aspects of campus life, campus leaders should vigorously support these organizations for all students, communicating their importance as essential educational resources. Such an approach should help overcome the problem that, while multicultural centers are frequently the center of activity and support for students of color, White students are less likely to be involved in these centers' programs and activities.

Finally, research in race relations indicates that increased structural diversity is usually accompanied by increased levels of conflict. However, conflict should not be viewed as a destabilizing force in higher education institutions. Parker Palmer (1987) suggests that conflict is an essential component of meaningful communities, which he defines "as a capacity for relatedness within individuals—relatedness not only to people but to events in history, to nature, to world of ideas, and yes, to things of the spirit" (p. 24). In communities that are not perceived as supportive, conflict is likely viewed as a threat to be avoided. Hence, it is essential that institutions provide ways for members of the campus community to successfully understand and resolve conflict. Then conflict can become a stimulus for creativity and community-building. Dialogue groups can provide both a structure and process for addressing the intergroup dynamics of multiculturalism within the learning environment. Activities for the learning process include the opportunity to break down barriers, challenge the ignorance inside and outside oneself, create new insights, forge new connections and identities, and finally, build coalitions to work toward a common goal (Zúñiga & Nagda, 1992). The issue of group conflict and social attitudes surrounding communities of difference addressed in dialogue groups are "not easily resolvable as long as the lack of adequate structures and processes for intergroup interactions in the college community maintains the invisible, but psychologically real walls that separate different groups" (Zúñiga and Nagda, 1992, p. 251).

From Research to Policy and Practice: Strategies for Improving Campus Diversity

Recent research on the campus climate for diversity has enabled campuses to better understand institutions and their impact on students, student responses to climate issues, and relationships that develop among diverse students and faculty. While many institutions are still contending with issues of diversifying their campus enrollments, more campuses need information to help them address the psychological and behavioral dimensions of the climate. At national higher education conferences, more individuals are talking about improving the climate and are sharing practices that work. The empirical evidence and policy recommendations provided here will help institutional administrators and program planners use a wealth of research, about both specific institutions and national samples of students and institutions. In addition, many institutions are undertaking assessments of their climate for diversity to understand better their own institutional contexts. While a wealth of knowledge is now available and institutions are better informed as they begin self-examinations, designing an action plan that will significantly improve the quality of experiences for undergraduates is perhaps the next important challenge in the process.

Campuses are complex social systems defined by the relationships between the people, bureaucratic procedures, structural arrangements, institutional goals and values, traditions, and larger socio-historical environments. Therefore, any effort to redesign campuses with the goal of improving the climate for racial and cultural diversity must be comprehensive and long term. Institutions change slowly. It is the nature of a stable system of higher education. Therefore, the success of efforts to achieve institutional change will rely on leadership, firm commitment, adequate resources, collaboration, monitoring, and long-range planning.

Institutional change can be implemented at several levels. Most important is the structural level. An institution should increase at all levels the number of previously excluded and underrepresented racial/ethnic minorities (i.e., students, faculty, staff, administrators). Ideally minorities should be represented on the campus in proportionate numbers. While efforts to increase the representation of minorities on campus and to remove barriers to their participation are crucial, these steps alone are not sufficient to achieve the goal of improving the climate for diversity.

Beyond the observable make-up of the students and faculty are the attitudinal and behavioral characteristics of how particular groups of individuals "feel" about and relate to one another. How does the campus "feel" to minority individuals (e.g., Do they feel welcome? Do they sense hostility? Do they feel valued?). How does the campus respond to racially and culturally different groups (e.g., Does the campus strive to change to incorporate these students or does the campus communicate that adaptation is the job of only the minority students? Does the campus genuinely value diversity?).

In short, two sets of issues are important when considering the success of efforts to improve the campus racial climate: (a) How diverse does the campus look in its representation of different cultural groups? and (b) To what extent do campus operations demonstrate that racial and ethnic diversity is an essential value?

References

Allen, W. R. (1992). The color of success: African-American college student outcomes at predominantly white and historically black public colleges and universities. *Harvard Educational Review, 62*(1), 26–44.

Allen, W. R., Epps, E. G., & Haniff, N. Z. (Eds). (1991). *College in Black and White: African American students in predominantly White and in historically Black public universities.* Albany: State University of New York Press.

Allport, G. W. (1954). *The nature of prejudice.* Reading, MA: Addison-Wesley.

Altbach, P. G., & Lomotey, K. (Eds.). (1991). *The racial crisis in American higher education.* Albany: State University of New York Press.

Asian Pacific American Education Advisory Committee. (1990). *Enriching California's future: Asian Pacific Americans in the CSU.* Long Beach, CA: Office of the Chancellor, The California State University.

Asian Pacific American Education Advisory Committee. (1994). *Asian Pacific Americans in the California State University: A follow-up report.* Long Beach, CA: Office of the Chancellor, The California State University.

Astin, A. W. (1968). *The college environment.* Washington, DC: American Council on Education.

Astin, A. W. (1982). *Minorities in American higher education.* San Francisco: Jossey-Bass.

Astin, A. W. (1985). *Achieving educational excellence.* San Francisco: Jossey-Bass.

Astin, A. W. (1988). Student involvement: A developmental theory for higher education. *Journal of College Student Personnel, 25*(4), 297–308.

Astin, A. W. (1991). *Assessment for excellence: The philosophy and practice of assessment and evaluation in higher education.* New York: Macmillan.

Astin, A. W. (1993). *What matters in college: Four critical years revisited.* San Francisco: Jossey-Bass.

Astin, A. W., Fuller, B., & Green, K. C. (1978). *Admitting and assisting students after Bakke.* New Directions for Higher Education, No. 23. San Francisco: Jossey-Bass.

Bennett, C., & Okinaka, A. M. (1990, March). Factors related to persistence among Asian, Black, Hispanic, and White undergraduates at a predominantly White university: Comparison between first and fourth year cohorts. *Urban Review, 22*(1), 33–60.

Blalock, J. M. (1967). *Toward a theory of minority-group relations.* New York: Wiley.

Braddock, J. H. (1980). The perpetuation of segregation across levels of education: A behavioral assessment of the contact hypothesis. *Sociology of Education, 53,* 178–186.

Braddock, J. H. (1985). School desegregation and Black assimilation. *Journal of Social Issues, 41*(3), 9–22.

Braddock, J. H., Crain, R. L., & McPartland, J. M. (1984, December). A long-term view of school desegregation: Some recent studies of graduates as adults. *Phi Delta Kappan,* 259–264.

Braddock, J. H., & Dawkins, M. (1981). Predicting achievement in higher education. *Journal of Negro Education, 50,* 319–327.

Braddock, J. H., & McPartland, J. M. (1982). Assessing school desegregation effects: New directions in research. In A. C. Kerckhoff (Ed.) & R. C. Corwin (Guest Ed.), *Research in Sociology of Education and Socialization, Vol. 3* (pp. 259–292) . Greenwich, CT: JAI.

Braddock, J. H., & McPartland, J. M. (1989). Social-psychological processes that perpetuate racial segregation: The relationship between school and employment desegregation. *Journal of Black Studies, 19*(3), 267–289.

Bunzel, J. H. (1992). *Race Relations on Campus: Stanford Students Speak.* Stanford, CA: Stanford Alumni Association.

Cabrera, A. F., & Nora, A. (1994). College student perceptions of prejudice and discrimination and their feelings of alienation: A construct validation approach. *Review of Education/Pedagogy/Cultural Studies, 16*(3–4), 387–409.

Carter, D. J., & Wilson, R. (1993). *Minorities in higher education: Eleventh annual status report.* Washington DC: American Council on Education.

Chang, M. J. (1996). *Racial diversity in higher education: Does a racially mixed student population affect educational outcomes?* Unpublished doctoral dissertation, University of California, Los Angeles.

Chickering, A. W. (1969). *Education and identity.* San Francisco: Jossey-Bass.

Collins, P. H. (1986). Learning from the outsider within: The sociological significance of Black feminist thought. *Social Problems, 33*(6), 514–532.

Davis, E. B. (1993). Desegregation in higher education: Twenty-five years of controversy from Geier to Ayers. *Journal of Law and Education, 22*(4), 519–524.

Davis, R. (1991). Social support networks and undergraduate student academic-success-related outcomes: A comparison of Black students on Black and White campuses. In W. R. Allen, E. G. Epps, & N. Z. Haniff (Eds.), *College in Black and White: African American students in predominantly White and in historically Black public universities* (pp. 143–57). Albany: SUNY Press.

Durán, R. P. (1983). *Hispanics' education and background: Predictors of college achievement.* New York: College Board Publications.

Duster, T. (1993). The diversity of California at Berkeley: An emerging reformulation of "competence" in an increasingly multicultural world. In B. W. Thompson and Sangeeta Tyagi (Eds.), *Beyond a dream deferred: Multicultural education and the politics of excellence* (pp. 231–255). Minneapolis, MN: University of Minnesota Press.

El-Khawas, E. (1989). *Campus Trends, 1989.* Higher Education Panel Reports, No. 78. Washington, DC: American Council on Education.

Farrell, W. C., Jr., & Jones, C. K. (1988). Recent racial incidents in higher education: A preliminary perspective. *Urban Review, 20*(3), 211–233.

Feldman, K. A., & Newcomb, T. M. (1969). *The impact of college on students, Vol. 1.* San Francisco: Jossey-Bass.

Frierson, H. T. (1991). Intervention can make a difference: The impact on standardized tests and classroom performance. In W. R. Allen, E. G. Epps, & N. Z. Haniff (Eds.), *College in Black and White: African American Students in predominantly White and in historically Black public universities* (pp. 225–238). Albany: SUNY Press.

Gilliard, M. D. (1996). *Racial climate and institutional support factors affecting success in predominantly White Institutions: An examination of African American and White student experiences.* Unpublished doctoral dissertation, University of Michigan.

Globetti, E. C., Globetti, G., Brown, C. L., & Smith, R. E. (1993). Social interaction and multiculturalism. *NASPA Journal, 30*(3), 209–218.

Green, K. C. (1982). *The impact of neighborhood and secondary school integration on educational achievement and occupational attainment of college-bound Blacks.* Unpublished doctoral dissertation, University of California, Los Angeles.

Guanier, L. (1997, August 7). The real bias in higher education. *Black Issues in Higher Education,* p. 60.

Horowitz, H. L. (1987). *Campus life: Undergraduate cultures from the end of the eighteenth century to the present.* Chicago: University of Chicago.

Huffman, T. E. (1991). The experiences, perceptions, and consequences of campus racism among Northern Plains Indians. *Journal of American Indian Education, 30*(2), 25–34.

Hurtado, S. (1990). *Campus racial climates and educational outcomes.* Unpublished doctoral dissertation, University of California, Los Angeles. Ann Arbor: University Microfilms International, No. 9111328.

Hurtado, S. (1992). The campus racial climate: Contexts for conflict. *The Journal of Higher Education, 63*(5), 539–569.

Hurtado, S. (1994). The institutional climate for talented Latino students. *Research in Higher Education, 35*(1), 21–41.

Hurtado, S., Dey, E., & Treviño, J. (1994). *Exclusion or self-segregation? Interaction across racial/ethnic groups on college campuses.* Paper presented at the American Educational Research Association conference, New Orleans.

Hurtado, S., Carter, D. F., & Spuler, A. (1996). Latino student transition to college. *Research in Higher Education, 37*(2), 135–157.

Hurtado, S., Milem, J. F., Clayton-Pedersen, A. R., & Allen, W. R. (in press). *Enacting diverse learning environments: Improving the campus climate for racial/ethnic diversity.* ASHE/ERIC Higher Education Report Series.

Jackson, K. W., & Swan, L. A. (1991). Institutional and individual factors affecting Black undergraduate student performance: Campus race and student gender. In W. R. Allen, E. G. Epps, & N. Z. Haniff (Eds.), *College in Black and White: African American students in predominantly White and in historically Black public universities* (pp. 127–141). Albany: SUNY Press.

Kanter, R. M. (1977). Some effects of proportions on group life: Skewed sex ratios and responses to token women. *American Journal of Sociology, 82,* 965–989.

Kuh, G., Schuh, J. S., Whitt, E. J., Andreas, R. E., Lyons, J. W., Strange, C. C., Krehbiel, L. E., & MacKay, K. A. (1991). *Involving colleges: Successful approaches to fostering student learning and personal development outside the classroom.* San Francisco: Jossey-Bass.

Lin, R., LaCounte, D., and Eder, J. (1988). A study of Native American students in a predominantly White college. *Journal of American Indian Education, 27*(3), 8–15.

Loo, C. M., & Rolison, G. (1986). Alienation of ethnic minority students at a predominately White university. *Journal of Higher Education, 57,* 58–77.

Milam, J. H. (1989). The presence of paradigms in the core higher education journal literature. *Research in Higher Education, 32*(6), 651–668.

Milem, J. F. (1992). *The impact of college on students' racial attitudes and levels of racial awareness.* Unpublished doctoral dissertation, UCLA. Ann Arbor: University Microforms International (UMI), No. 9301968.

Milem, J. F. (1994). College, students, and racial understanding. *Thought and Action, 9*(2), 51–92.

Milem, J. F. (1998). Attitude change in college students: Examining the effect of college peer groups and faculty normative groups. *Journal of Higher Education, 69*(2), 117–140.

Mitchell, S. L., & Dell, D. M. (1992). The relationship between Black students' racial identity attitude and participation in campus organizations. *Journal of College Student Development, 33,* 39–43.

Muñoz, C. (1989). *Youth, identity, and power in the Chicano movement.* New York: Verso.

Nealy, C. (1996). *The musing of an at-risk student.* Paper presented at the annual meeting of the American Educational Research Association, New York.

Nettles, M. (Ed.). (1988). *Toward Black undergraduate student equality in American higher education.* Westport, CT: Greenwood Press.

Nora, A., & Cabrera, A. F. (1996). The role of perceptions of prejudice and discrimination on the adjustment of minority students to college. *Journal of Higher Education, 67*(2), 119–148.

Olivas, M. A. (1986). The retreat from access. *Academe, 72*(6), 16–18.

Orfield, G. (1992). Money, equity, and college access. *Harvard Educational Review, 62*(3), 337–372.

Palmer, P. J. (1987). Community, conflict, and ways of knowing. *Change, 19*(5), 20–25.

Pascarella, E. T., & Terenzini, P. T. (1991). *How college affects students: Findings and insights from twenty years of research.* San Francisco: Jossey-Bass.

Pascarella, E. T., Smart, J. C., Ethington, C., & Nettles, M. (1987). The influence of college on self-concept: A consideration of race and gender differences. *American Educational Research Journal, 24,* 49–77.

Pascarella, E. T., Whitt, E. J., Nora, A., Edison, M., Hagedorn, L. S., & Terenzini, P. T. (1996). What have we learned from the first year of the national study of student learning? *Journal of College Student Development, 37*(2), 182–192.

Peterson, M. W., Blackburn, R. T., Gamson, Z. F., Arce, C. H., Davenport, R. W., & Mingle, J. R. (1978). *Black students on White campuses: The impacts of increased Blacks enrollments.* Ann Arbor: Institute for Social Research, University of Michigan.

Prillerman, S. L., Myers, H. F., & Smedley, B. D. (1989). Stress, well-being, and academic achievement in college. In G. L. Berry and J. K. Asamen (Eds.), *Black students: Psychosocial issues and academic achievement* (pp. 198–217). Newbury Park, CA: Sage.

Richardson, R., & Skinner, E. (1991). *Achieving diversity.* Washington, DC: ACE/Macmillan.

Scott, R. R., & McPartland, J. M. (1982). Desegregation as national policy: Correlates of racial attitudes. *American Educational Research Journal, 19*(3), 397–414.

Sedlacek, W. (1987). Black students on White campuses: 20 years of research. *Journal of College Student Personnel, 28*(6) 484–95.

Slavin, R. E. (1985). Cooperative learning: Applying contact theory in desegregated schools. *Journal of Social Issues, 41*(1), 45–62.

Smedley, B. D., Myers, H. F., & Harrell, S. P. (1993). Minority-status stresses and the college adjustment of ethnic minority freshmen. *Journal of Higher Education, 64*(4), 434–452.

Southern Education Foundation. (1995). *Redeeming the American promise: Report of the panel on educational opportunity and postsecondary desegregation.* Atlanta: Southern Education Foundation.

St. John, E. P. (1991a). The impact of student financial aid: A review of recent research. *Journal of Student Financial Aid, 21*(1), 18–32.

St. John, E. P. (1991b). What really influences minority attendance? Sequential analyses of the high school and beyond sophomore cohort. *Research in Higher Education, 32*(2), 141–158.

St. John, E. P., & Masten, C. L. (1990). Return on investment in student financial aid: An assessment for the high school class of 1972. *Journal of Student Financial Aid, 20*(3), 4–23.

Stampen, J. O. (1985). *Student aid and public higher education: Recent changes.* Washington, DC: American Association of State Colleges and Universities.

Stampen, J. O., & Fenske, R. H. (1988). The impact of financial aid on ethnic minorities. *Review of Higher Education, 11*(4), 337–353.

Steele, C. M. (1992, April). Race and the schooling of Black Americans. *Atlantic Monthly,* 68–78.

Stewart, J. B. (1991). Planning for cultural diversity: A case study. In H. E. Cheatham (Ed.), *Cultural Pluralism on Campus* (pp. 161–191). N.p.: American College Personnel Association.

Thelin, J. (1985). Beyond the background music: Historical research on admissions and access in higher education. In John C. Smart (Ed.), *Higher Education Handbook of Theory and Research, Vol. 1.* (pp. 349–380). New York: Agathon.

Tierney, W. G. (1997). The parameters of affirmative action: Equity and excellence in the academy. *Review of Educational Research, 67*(2), 165–196.

Tinto, V. (1987). *Leaving college: Rethinking the causes and cures of student attrition* (1st ed.) Chicago: University of Chicago Press.

Tinto, V. (1993). *Leaving college: Rethinking the causes and cures of student attrition* (2nd ed.). Chicago: University of Chicago Press.

Turner, C., & Thompson, J. (1993). Socializing women doctoral students: Minority and majority experiences. *The Review of Higher Education, 16,* 355–370.

Tracey, T. J., & Sedlacek, W. E. (1985). The relationship of noncognitive variables to academic success: A longitudinal comparison by race. *Journal of College Student Personnel, 26,* 405–410.

Treviño, J. G. (1992). *Participating in ethnic/racial student organizations.* Unpublished doctoral dissertation, University of California, Los Angeles.

Williams, John B., III. (1988). Title VI regulation of higher education. In J. B. Williams (Ed.), *Desegregating America's Colleges and Universities* (pp. 3–53). New York: Teachers College Press.

Willie, C., Grady, M., & Hope, R. (1991). *African-Americans and the doctoral experience: Implications for policy.* New York: Teachers College.

Zúñiga, X., & Nagda, B. A. (1992). Dialogue groups: An innovative approach to multicultural learning. In David Schoem (Ed.), *Multicultural teaching at the university* (pp. 233–248). New York: Praeger.

PART III

FACULTY

JENNY J. LEE, ASSOCIATE EDITOR

While there has been a slight increase in the proportion of faculty of color over time, they remain significantly underrepresented at postsecondary institutions in the U.S. (U.S. Department of Education, 2009). Many colleges and universities have steadily increased the enrollment of racial/ethnic minority students, but the hiring of a diverse faculty has not kept pace. The lack of faculty diversity becomes even more pronounced when one considers rates of underrepresentation in particular fields and in senior tenured ranks. Simply focusing on aggregate numbers of minority faculty masks their dismal representation and often isolating experiences at predominantly white institutions (PWIs).

In reviewing significant pieces of literature on the topic, the major issues concerning underrepresented racial minority (URM) faculty have not changed much over the past few decades. Tokenism, negative stereotypes, low expectations, and marginalization are just some of the challenges that continually cause difficulties for URM faculty at PWIs. While discrimination remains, its specific forms today are less overt than in the past. For example, simultaneously having empathy for the unique challenges that URM faculty face, while doubting their abilities to succeed in teaching and research roles is characteristic of what Stassen (1995) called "aversive racism" and "racial ambivalence" among White faculty. Chapters in this section focus on these and other experiential realities for faculty of color at PWIs.

In Chapter 16, Caroline Sotello Viernes Turner, Juan Carlos González, and J. Luke Wood review 20 years of literature (from 1988-2007) on faculty of color. Their work is situated in departmental, institutional, and national contexts, and includes a synthesis of 252 publications that offer much evidence of the persistence and pervasiveness of racism experienced by faculty in postsecondary settings in which they are underrepresented. Turner, González, and Wood engage the work of numerous scholars who have brought to light different ways of knowing and challenged myths about the recruitment, retention, and lived experiences of faculty of color. Other areas that have received attention include the scholarly contributions of URM faculty, their resiliency at PWIs, salary and promotion inequities, and mentoring. In Chapter 17, Christine A. Stanley enables faculty of color to speak for themselves and give voice to many of the experiences that other researchers have reported in the literature. Stanley's chapter is based on a qualitative study of American Indian, Asian, Asian American, Latina/o, Native Pacific Islander, and South African faculty who represented a variety of institutions, disciplines, and academic ranks. Her chapter is replete with rich, descriptive accounts of how these professors navigated and negotiated racial complexities within their institutions.

Using Critical Race Theory as a framework, Lori D. Patton and Christopher C. Catching offer in Chapter 18 a narrative of African American faculty who teach in student affairs graduate programs. While Turner, González, and Wood present a synthesis of the literature and Stanley furnishes self-reported qualitative insights into the experiences of faculty of color, Patton and Catching report findings that are complementary, but do so in a different fashion. Their chapter includes a critical race counterstory with "composite characters" that are based on actual interviews they conducted with 13 African American faculty at different institutions. This approach makes visual the racism, differential treatment, and constant invalidation that many faculty of color face in environments where the overwhelming majority of their colleagues are White.

Teaching and research activities among URM faculty have received considerable attention in the literature, so too have the demands and complexities of their service work. As Stanley acknowledges in her chapter, diversity-related service activities constitute a considerable proportion of URM faculty time, yet remain undervalued in tenure and promotion processes. Similarly, Iglesias and his colleagues (2002) explain that because URM faculty tend to be approached for campus diversity initiatives, to support students of color, and for diverse representation on committees, they are more likely to be pressured into service activities than are their White colleagues. While most scholars discuss diversity-related service activities as a detriment towards tenure and promotion, Benjamin Baez argues in Chapter 19 that such work has the potential to redefine the very structures that hinder faculty success. Beyond individual interests, diversity-related service can be used as a vehicle to advance social justice and contribute to academic and social change, he maintains. Moreover, Baez found that service provided a platform through which URM faculty could strategically fight oppression and institutionalized racism.

As Moreno, Smith, Clayton-Pedersen, Parker, and Teraguchi (2009) point out, there has been a "revolving door" of URM faculty at many colleges and universities in the U.S. This is partially explained by the absence of other faculty of color upon whom one can rely for support, validation, shared diversity-related service work, and the occasional debriefing of racist encounters. In other words, URM faculty sometimes leave PWIs because of the isolation associated with being the lone representative (or one of few) from their racial group in the department, college, or school. Scholars have critically examined the conditions of faculty recruitment and hiring. While Cole and Barber (2003) attribute rates of underrepresentation to an insufficient pipeline (meaning, there are too few URMs earning Ph.D.s and competing in the academic job market), other researchers (e.g., Olivas, 1994; Springer, 2002) have refuted the small pool argument by showing there are enough qualified URM doctoral degree recipients to change the diversity of faculty hired for professorships in various disciplines.

Tuitt, Sagaria, and Turner (2007) examined the national recruitment context of the labor market and legal landscape. With the tightening labor market, some presume that hiring URM faculty is too expensive due to overstated bidding wars. Also, the passage of anti-affirmative action legislation in several states has signaled to institutions nationwide that it is no longer safe to consider race in faculty hiring. Daryl G. Smith, Caroline Sotello Viernes Turner, Nana Osei-Kofi, and Sandra Richards challenge these and other misconceptions in Chapter 20. They found that over 70 percent of URM faculty in their study were hired with a diversity indicator in the job description or via a special hire intervention. In other words, targeted efforts are still required to attract URM faculty to PWIs. Smith and her colleagues identify other strategies that were employed to diversify the faculty.

Despite the magnitude of the challenges I have described, many URM faculty share many positive experiences that tend to be overshadowed by their negative experiences and overlooked by researchers. In Chapter 21, Caroline Sotello Viernes Turner reports that women of color often stay in faculty positions for the intellectual challenge, freedom to pursue their research interests, and opportunities to promote change and understanding around racial issues. In fact, most of the women Turner interviewed indicated that they planned to stay in academia despite perceptions of and experiences with "chilly climates." While such resilience does not minimize the racism that many URMs experience or pardon longstanding discriminatory practices, the commitment of these faculty to persevere and contribute to their college campuses and the larger academic community, despite the many barriers they encountered, should be recognized. As Paul D. Umbach reveals in Chapter 22, these faculty contribute much to undergraduate education by interacting with students (not just students of color) at higher rates and by employing a broader range of pedagogical techniques than do their White counterparts. Interestingly, Umbach found that increased numbers of URM faculty resulted in an increased use of effective educational practices among faculty members overall.

Conclusion

As Turner, González, and Wood note in their chapter, much research on faculty of color has been conducted and published over the past two decades. In my review of the recommended literature from top diversity scholars in the field, some areas that remain remarkably (and somewhat surprisingly) underexplored include intersections of race with sexual orientation, religion, and other aspects of faculty diversity. Also, discussions of racial and ethnic diversity continue to be largely focused on faculty born in the U.S., despite a significant presence of those hired from overseas (especially in the STEM fields). The research on college faculty with respect to race and ethnicity demonstrate that equity and diversity are still viable concerns in the academy. Despite an impressive number of publications on the topic, faculty of color remain underrepresented at most postsecondary institutions, including community colleges (Harvey & Valadez, 1994). Many continue to struggle with securing faculty employment as well as obtaining tenure and promotions. Consequently, URM faculty remain among the lower academic ranks and altogether absent in some disciplines. Meanwhile, they contribute to the diversity of perspectives that is so critical for scholarly engagement and enhancing student learning (antonio, 2002). While the value of a diverse faculty is largely unquestioned throughout the literature, the proportion of URMs and their positionality at most higher education institutions remain troubling. Many scholars have sought to represent the voices of faculty of color, yet these voices remain seemingly unheard by White colleagues, deans, and senior-level postsecondary administrators (e.g., provosts and presidents). Such stagnation signifies that racism is still very real, though harder to detect.

References

antonio, a. l. (2002). Faculty of color reconsidered: Reassessing contributions to scholarship. *The Journal of Higher Education, 73*(5), 582–602.

Cole, S., & Barber, E. (2003). *Increasing faculty diversity: The occupational choices of high-achieving minority students.* Cambridge: Harvard University Press.

Harvey, W. B., & Valadez, J. (Eds.). (1994). *Creating and maintaining a diverse faculty. New Directions for Community Colleges* (No. 87). San Francisco: Jossey-Bass.

Iglesias, E. M., Durako, J. A., Carbado, D. W., Montoya, M. E., Olivas, M. A. Perschbacher, R. R., Scherer, D. D., & Schultz, V. (2002). Labor and employment in the academy: A critical look at the ivory tower. *Employee Rights and Employee Policy Journal, 6,* 129–188.

Moreno, J. F., Smith, D. G., Clayton-Pedersen, A. R., Parker, S., & Teraguchi, D. H. (2009). *The revolving door for underrepresented minority faculty in higher education.* San Francisco: James Irvine Foundation.

Olivas, M. A. (1994). The education of Latino lawyers: An essay on crop cultivation. *Chicano-Latino Law Review, 14,* 117–138.

Springer, A. (2002). *How to diversify faculty: The current legal landscape.* Washington, DC: American Association of University Professors.

Stassen, M. L. A. (1995). White faculty members and racial diversity: A theory and its implications. *The Review of Higher Education, 18*(4), 361–391.

Tuitt F. A., Sagaria, M. D., & Turner, C. S. V. (2007). Signals and strategies in hiring faculty of color. In J. Smart (Ed.), *Higher education: Handbook of theory and research* (Vol. XXII, pp. 497–535). New York: Springer.

U.S. Department of Education. (2009). *Digest of education statistics, 2008.* Washington, DC: National Center for Education Statistics.

CHAPTER 16
FACULTY OF COLOR IN ACADEME: WHAT 20 YEARS OF LITERATURE TELLS US

CAROLINE SOTELLO VIERNES TURNER

JUAN CARLOS GONZÁLEZ

J. LUKE WOOD

To better prepare students for an increasingly diverse society, campuses across the country remain engaged in efforts to diversify the racial and ethnic makeup of their faculties. However, faculty of color remain seriously underrepresented, making up 17% of total full-time faculty. In the past 20 years, more than 300 authors have addressed the status and experience of faculty of color in academe. From 1988 to 2007, there was a continued rise in publications addressing the issue of the low representation of faculty of color. This chapter presents a literature review and synthesis of 252 publications, with the goal of informing scholars and practitioners of the current state of the field. Themes emerging from these publications and an interpretive model through which findings can be viewed are presented. The analysis, with a focus on the departmental, institutional, and national contexts, documents supports, challenges, and recommendations to address barriers and build on successes within these 3 contexts. The authors hope that this chapter informs researchers and practitioners as they continue their work to understand and promote the increased representation of faculty of color.

The increasing demographic diversity in the U.S. population begun in the past century continues into this century. The new millennium also brings a heightened awareness of the importance of global and national understanding of cross-cultural perspectives. Such trends and transitions contribute to the shaping of American higher education. Efforts toward faculty racial and ethnic diversity are fueled by the increasing diversity of the student body (Cook & Córdova, 2006; Cora-Bramble, 2006), compelling arguments about the need to prepare all students for a diverse society (antonio, 2002; C. A. Stanley, 2006; Umbach, 2006), continuing evidence that a diverse faculty is important to the success of a diverse student body (Hagedorn, Chi, Cepeda, & McLain (2007), evidence that a diverse faculty assists in the recruitment of students of color to higher education (Alger & Carrasco, 1997; antonio, 2000), and the contributions of diverse faculties to the engagement of new scholarship (Alger, 1999; Christian-Smith & Kellor, 1999; A. M. Padilla, 1994; Turner, 2000; Urrieta & Méndez Benavídez, 2007) and approaches to teaching (antonio, 2000; M. Garcia, 2000; Pineda, 1998; Turner, 2000; Umbach, 2006; Vargas, 2002).

To better prepare students for an increasingly diverse society, campuses across the country are engaged in efforts to diversify the racial and ethnic makeup of their faculties. These efforts are perhaps the least successful of campus diversity initiatives as faculty of color remain underrepresented and their achievements in the academy almost invisible. According to *The Chronicle of Higher Education Almanac* ("Number of Full-Time Faculty Members," 2007–2008), in 2005 faculty of color made up only 17% of total full-time faculty, with 7.5% Asian, 5.5% Black, 3.5% Hispanic, and 0.5% American Indian. When figures reported for the full professor rank are examined, we see that fewer than 12% of full professors in the United States were people of color: 6.5% Asian, 3% Black, 2% Hispanic, and 0.3% American Indian. For female faculty of color, the numbers are even more dismal: In 2005, only 1% of full professors were Black, 1% Asian, 0.6% Hispanic, and 0.1% American Indian.

According to Bland, Meurer, and Maldonado (1995) and Patterson, Thorne, Canam, and Jillings (2001), literature analyses and syntheses are important as a means of periodically bringing coherence to a research area, contributing new knowledge revealed by integrating single studies, and informing scholars and practitioners of the state of the field. From 1988 to 2007, more than 300 scholars published 211 studies and produced 41 doctoral dissertations related to the underrepresentation of faculty of color. We found it inspirational that so many scholars have written about issues pertaining to faculty of color in the past 2 decades. This chapter reviews and synthesizes these studies with the goal of informing scholars and practitioners of the current state of the field. During this process, we developed an interpretive framework to present common elements across publications.

We hope that this analysis will highlight critical information for practitioners and researchers as they attempt to further understand the departmental, institutional, and national processes to create, attract, and sustain a diverse professoriate.

TABLE 1

Review of Literature Related to Faculty of Color, by Type of Publication, in 5-Year Increments

5-year Increment	Journal Articles	Dissertations	Books	Reports	Book Chapters	Total
2003–2007	86	15	9	9	5	124
1998–2002	25	11	15	6	7	64
1993–1997	12	14	8	9	4	47
1988–1992	7	1	2	3	4	17
Total	130	41	34	27	20	252

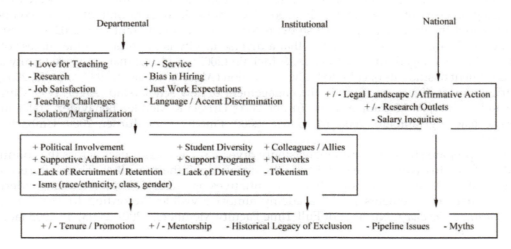

Figure 1 Supports (+) and challenges (−) within and across departmental, institutional, and national contexts.

Method

Our search for and collection of academic resources related to faculty of color began in 2005. We began collecting, annotating, and synthesizing resources from various academic databases for the years spanning 1988 to 2005. This produced more than 160 resources, including books, journal articles, book chapters, conference papers, Web sites, and videotapes. In 2007, searches for new material that had been written about faculty of color from 2004 to 2007 produced about 117 new references.

As a result of the plethora of publication and resource types included in both the 2005 and the 2007 searches and because of space constraints, we decided to focus our analysis on journal articles, books, dissertations, reports, and book chapters, eliminating conference papers, video resources, and Web sites. Even then, we had 252 pieces of literature to include in our analysis. Table 1 shows our search results in 5-year increments.

Google Scholar (accessible at http://www.scholar.google.com), a comprehensive academic search engine, was our major source for identifying, collecting, and checking references. This search engine is able to perform exhaustive searches of all academic work—from the easy-to-find academic articles to the hard-to-locate book chapters. According to Google Scholar (2007), articles in the academic search engine are sorted "the way researchers do, weighing the full text of each article, the author, the publication in which the article appears, and how often the piece has been cited in other scholarly literature." Supplementary article and report searches were conducted through (a) Education Resources Information Center (ERIC), (b) Blackwell Synergy, (c) Journal Storage (JSTOR), (d) Informaworld, (e) the Wilson Index, (f) Ebscohost Electronic Journal Service, (g) Wiley Interscience, (h) Project Muse, (i) the Springer Collection, (j) Questia Online Libraries, (k) Galegroup, (1) PsycINFO, and (m) the Sage Publications Collection. Dissertation searches were performed through Proquest Digital Dissertations. Additional book resources were identified through the Missouri Education and Research Libraries Information Network (MERLIN) and through the Arizona State University, Tempe, Campus Library Catalog. Our search keywords encompassed the following terms: *African American faculty, Black faculty, Native American faculty, Indian*

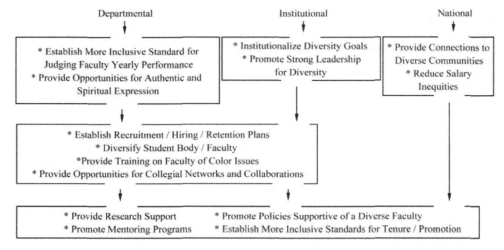

Figure 2   Recommendations for departmental, institutional, and national contexts.

TABLE 2

+ Love for Teaching

Hill-Brisbane & Dingus (2007) Turner (2003)	C. A. Stanley (2007a)	Turner & Myers (2000)

faculty, Indigenous faculty, Asian faculty, Asian American faculty, Hispanic faculty, Latino faculty, Latina faculty, Chicano faculty, Chicana faculty, women of color faculty, underrepresented minority faculty, and *minority faculty.*

After all references were collected and annotated, we began our analysis. All resources were reviewed with attention to their (a) research purpose, (b) research questions, (c) methodology, (d) theoretical framework, (e) findings, (f) recommendations, and (g) conclusions. We then identified emerging themes from the literature individually and cross-checked them in a team discussion. Then, themes were distilled and pictorially depicted using Inspiration (Inspiration, 2007), a software program used to develop, map, and organize themes in a visual treelike format. This analytical process produced about 230 tree branches, with each branch representing a different idea found in the literature about the experience of faculty of color. Inside each tree branch, each author and year of publication were included, so as to thicken the branches of the issues most addressed in the literature. The complete analysis is too complex to show here. A conceptualization of it is shown in Figures 1 and 2.

Framework for Analysis

Publications by more than 300 scholars, including 252 journal articles, dissertations, reports, books, and book chapters, are analyzed here. Figure 1 captures the richness of the themes emerging from this extant literature. Factors that positively (represented with a plus sign) or negatively (represented with a minus sign) affected the workplace experience of faculty of color are pictured here from three contexts: (a) the departmental, (b) the institutional, and (c) the national. In Figure 1, when boxes cut across various contexts, this means that faculty of color were affected positively or

TABLE 3

+ / − Service

Aguirre (2005)	Gregory (2001)	Skachkova (2007)
Aguirre & Martinez (1993)	Hamlet (1999)	E. Smith (1992)
Alemán & Renn (2002)	Hill-Brisbane & Dingus (2007)	C. A. Stanley (2007a)
Alexander-Snow & Johnson (1999)	W. J. Johnson (1996)	Takara (2006)
Arnold (2006)	Jones (2002)	Tierney & Rhoads (1993)
Baez (2002)	Loder et al. (2007)	Tomlinson (2006)
Bensimon et al. (2000)	McKenzie (2002)	Turner et al. (1996)
Bradley (2005)	Moule (2005)	Turner & Myers (2000)
Brayboy (2003)	Niemann (1999)	Urrieta & Méndez Benavídez (2007)
Brown et al. (2007)	Niemann (2003)	Valladares (2007)
Chesler et al. (2005)	A. M. Padilla (1994)	Vasquez et al. (2006)
Cowan (2006)	Rains (1995)	Whetsel-Ribeau (2007)
	Sámano (2007)	Wong & Bainer (1991)

TABLE 4

− Research

Aguirre (2005)	M. García (2000)	D. G. Smith et al. (2004)
Aguirre et al. (1993)	Gregory (2001)	C. A. Stanley (2007a, 2007b)
Benjamin (1997)	Hamlet (1999)	Takara (2006)
Bradley (2005)	Louis (2007)	Thompson & Dey (1998)
De la luz Reyes & Halcón (1988)	Niemann (2003)	Turner (2002a)
Delgado Bernal & Villalpando (2002)	Pepion (1993)	Turner & Myers (2000)
Fenelon (2003)	Rendón (2000)	B. N. Williams & Williams (2006)

negatively across contexts. Although elements in the departmental context, where working relationships among peers are most intense, are critical to the work life experience of faculty of color, as explicated in the literature included in this study, the importance of a positive and welcoming institutional and national context cannot be denied. The national context is made up of professional organizations and journals that are receptive to the research of the individual faculty member, the off-campus climate, and the legal landscape, including the impact of challenges to affirmative action on the experience of faculty of color. According to the literature, elements such as lack of diversity cut across the departmental and institutional contexts, and mentorship crosses all contexts: national, institutional, and departmental.

Emerging Themes: Supports and Challenges

In this section, themes identified across publications are listed below within departmental, institutional, and national contexts. Paragraphs briefly describing the various themes introduce each subsection. Words italicized within a paragraph denote themes that are listed within each introductory paragraph along with the relevant references where elaboration on the theme can be found. At least three references had to cite the factor listed to be included in Figure 1. Tables 2–10 relate to the framework presented in Figure 1. References for publications documenting each theme are presented alphabetically in three columns, starting from the top left and ending on the bottom right.

Departmental Context

Within the departmental context, faculty of color *love of teaching* was noted as a primary reason for their persistence in academe. However, undervaluation of their *research* interests, approaches, and theoretical frameworks and challenges to their credentials and intellect in the *classroom* contribute to their *dissatisfaction with their professorial roles*. In addition, *isolation*, perceived biases in the *hiring process*, *unrealistic expectations* of doing their work and being *representatives of their racial/ethnic group*,

TABLE 5

– Job Satisfaction

Aguirre (2000)	Kauper (1991)	E. Smith (1992)
Astin et al. (1997)	Laden & Hagedorn (2000)	D. G. Smith et al. (2004)
Blackburn & Lawrence (1995)	Morell-Thon (1998)	Tack & Patitu (1992)
Chused (1988)	Niemann (2003)	Thompson & Dey (1998)
Flowers (2005)	Niemann & Dovidio (2005)	Turner & Myers (2000)
Holcomb-McCoy & Addison-Bradley (2005)	Olivas (1988)	Van Ummersen (2005)
Isaac & Boyer (2007)	Peterson-Hickey (1998)	Whetsel-Ribeau (2007)
Jones (2002)	Ponjuan (2005)	Witt (1990)
	Rains (1995)	

TABLE 6

– Teaching Challenges

Aguirre (2000, 2005)	Johnsrud & Sadao (1998)	Sampaio (2006)
Bradley (2005)	Kauper (1991)	Skachkova (2007)
Brayboy (2003)	Marbley (2007)	G. Smith & Anderson (2005)
Hassouneh (2006)	Saavedra & Saavedra (2007)	C. A. Stanley (2006)
Hendrix (2007)		

and *accent discrimination* are noted negatives described in the literature. Although *service* can be detrimental to faculty of color as they progress toward tenure and promotion, it can also be what provides inspiration and passion as they fulfill their desire to serve in response to the needs of their communities. In fact, according to Baez (2000), service "may set the stage for a critical agency that resists and redefines academic structures that hinder faculty success" (p. 363).

Bridging Departmental and Institutional Contexts

Several themes described within the departmental context were also noted within an institutional context. Although we know that professional *networks, colleagues, and allies* can exist in all three contexts pictured here, the literature reviewed spoke about these factors primarily within the depart-

TABLE 7

— Isolation and Marginalization

Aguirre (2000, 2005)	Ginorio (1995)	Rendón (1996)
Aguirre & Martinez (1993)	C. M. Gonzalez (2002)	Reyes (2005)
Alemán & Renn (2002)	M. C. González (1995)	Sadao (2003)
Alexander-Snow & Johnson (1999)	Hamlet (1999)	J. W. Smith & Calasanti (2005)
Awe (2001)	Hune (1998)	C. A. Stanley (2006, 2007a)
Baez (2003)	Hune & Chan (1997)	Takara (2006)
Benjamin (1997)	K. W. Jackson (1991)	Thompson & Dey (1998)
Brayboy (2003)	Jacobs et al. (2002)	Tomlinson (2006)
Burden et al. (2005)	B. J. Johnson & Pichon (2007)	Townsend-Johnson (2006)
Carmen (1999)	Maher & Tetreault (2007)	Turner (2002b, 2003)
Chused (1988)	McKenzie (2002)	Turner et al. (1996)
Clark (2006)	Moses (1989)	Turner & Myers (1997, 2000)
Cowan (2006)	Niemann (1999)	TuSmith & Reddy (2002)
Cuádraz (1992)	R. V. Padilla & Chávez Chavez (1995)	Valladares (2007)
De la luz Reyes & Halcón (1988)	Pollard (2006)	Van Ummersen (2005)
Essien (2003)	Rains (1995)	Whetsel-Ribeau (2007)
		Wong & Bainer (1991)

TABLE 8

— Bias in Hiring

Alemán & Renn (2002)	Delgado-Romero et al. (2007)	Owino (2000)
Brayboy (2003)	W. J. Johnson (1996, D. R. Johnson, 2006)	Reyes & Ríos (2005)
Brown et al. (2007)	Johnston (1997)	Slater (1999)
Chapman (2001)	Kayes (2006)	D. G. Smith (2000)
Chesler et al. (2005)	Maturana (2005)	D. G. Smith et al. (2004)
Chused (1988)	Mickelson & Oliver (1991)	C. A. Stanley (2006)
Clark (2006)	Niemann (1999)	Tuitt et al. (2007)
De la luz Reyes & Halcón (1988)	Olivas (1988)	Turner & Myers (2000)

TABLE 9

— Unjust Work Expectations

Aguirre & Martinez (1993)	Johnsrud & Sadao (1998)	A. M. Padilla (1994)
Baez (2000, 2002)	Jones (2002)	Porter (2007)
Bensimon et al. (2000)	Loder et al. (2007)	Rains (1995)
Bradley (2005)	McLean (2007)	Sámano (2007)
Brayboy (2003)	R. Mitchell & Rosiek (2006)	Sampaio (2006)

mental and institutional context. These factors, coupled with the presence of *student diversity, faculty research/teaching/ professional development support programs, a political* understanding of the importance of sharing accomplishments with those who might provide departmental and institutional opportunities for advancement, and a *supportive administration* contribute to the creation of a positive departmental and institutional work environment. However, *lack of campus student/faculty diversity* and being the *token* person of color coupled with a perceived *lack of departmental/institutional effort to recruit,* hire, and *retain* faculty of color contribute negatively to the experience of faculty of color. In addition, the literature widely documents the negative, interlocking workplace effects *of racism, classism, and sexism.* (See Tables 11–20.)

National Context

In a national context, the processes of hiring and retaining faculty of color are influenced by the legal landscape, notably national debates on affirmative action and its application. Often, failure to systematically implement *affirmative action* policies is described as a contributing factor to the underrepresentation of minority faculty. The Supreme Court ruling in *Grutter v. Bollinger* (2003) provides the most recent judicial addition to the affirmative action debate. In this case, the court ruled that maintaining diversity in postsecondary institutions among students was a compelling interest for using race as a factor in university admissions. The court cited the need to prepare students for an increasingly diverse global society as a cause (in part) of this decision. Although this case was specific to the usage of diversity in student admissions processes, "many elements of the decisions lend support to the faculty diversity legal debate" (Springer, 2002, pp. 5). Thus, this case has begun to shift the sentiment of some scholars who see this decision as an important step toward enacting policies that aid

TABLE 10

− Language/Accent Discrimination

Alemán & Renn (2002)	McLean (2007)	Saavedra & Saavedra (2007)
Guang-Lea & Louis (2006)	Nevarez & Borunda (2004)	Turner & Myers (2000)

TABLE 11

+ Networks

Baez (1997)	J. C. González (2007a, 2007b)	A. M. Padilla (1994)
Essien (2003)	Hill-Brisbane & Dingus (2007)	Turner & Myers (2000)
Frierson (1990)	Lasalle (1995)	

TABLE 12

+ Student Diversity

antonio (2003)	Frierson (1990)	Guiffrida (2005)

TABLE 13

+ Colleagues/Allies

Baez (1997)	Hill-Brisbane & Dingus (2007)	C. A. Stanley (2006)
Buttner et al. (2007)	Marbley (2007)	Turner & Myers (2000)
Frierson (1990)	A. M. Padilla (1994)	

TABLE 14

+ Support Programs

Daley et al. (2006)	Moradi & Neimeyer (2005)	Segura (2003)
Gooden et al. (1994)	R. V. Padilla & Chávez Chavez (1995)	D. G. Smith et al. (2004)
Kosoko-Lasaki et al. (2006)	Piercy et al. (2005)	Soto-Greene et al. (2005)
Medina & Luna (2000)	Segovia (1994)	Waitzkin et al. (2006)
		Yager et al. (2007)

TABLE 15

+ Political Involvement

De la luz Reyes & Halcón (1988)	McKenzie (2002)	R. V. Padilla & Chávez Chavez (1995)
C. González (2007)		

TABLE 16

+ Supportive Administrative Leadership

Buttner et al. (2007)	Marbley (2007)	C. A. Stanley (2006)
C. González (2007)	Morris (2000)	C. A. Stanley & Lincoln (2005)
MacLachlan (2006)	Sámano (2007)	

TABLE 17

− Lack of Diversity

Aguirre (2000)	Hune (1998)	Opp & Gosetti (2002)
Alemán & Renn (2002)	Hune & Chan (1997)	Owino (2000)
Alger et al. (2000)	Hurtado et al. (1999)	Peoples (2004)
antonio (2003)	J. F. L. Jackson & Phelps (2004)	Perna (2003)
Arnold (2006)	Jacobs et al. (2002)	Perna et al. (2007)
Benjamin (1997)	Kirkpatrick (2001)	Ponjuan (2005)
Beutel & Nelson (2006)	Knowles & Harleston (1997)	Rai & Critzer (2000)
Bradley (2005)	Lindsay (1991)	Reyes & Ríos (2005)
Chesler et al. (2005)	Maher & Tetreault (2007)	E. Smith (1992)
Cole & Barber (2003)	MacLachlan (2006)	P. W. Smith et al. (2002)
Cook & Córdova (2006)	Maturana (2005)	C. A. Stanley (2007a)
Carnes et al. (2005)	Milem & Astin (1993)	Takara (2006)
Cora-Bramble (2006)	Millett & Nettles (2006)	Thompson & Dey (1998)
Cowan (2006)	Mitchell & Lassiter (2006)	Tierney & Rhoads (1993)
Essien (2003)	Moody (1988)	Turner et al. (2002)
Fenelon (2003)	Myers & Turner (2001, 2004)	Turner & Myers (1997)
Frierson (1990)	Nelson et al. (2007)	TuSmith & Reddy (2002)
J. C. González (2007b)	Nevarez & Borunda (2004)	Vasquez et al. (2006)
Gregory (2001)	Niemann (2003)	Witt (1990)
Greiner & Girardi (2007)	Nieves-Squires (1991)	Wong & Bainer (1991)
Holland (1995)	Olivas (1988)	

faculty diversification efforts. However, others have expressed fear that the programs and policies they currently have in place to support faculty diversity will cause their institution to be vulnerable to lawsuits. On the basis of marked increases in the number of publications regarding faculty of color since the *Grutter* decision, the ruling may have contributed to an increase of articles regarding faculty of color in academe (see Table 1). Another national theme that emerged from the literature was *research as an outlet* for faculty of color. Scholars described the challenges faculty of color face because of the illegitimization of their research and methodologies in academic culture, scholarly journals, disciplinary associations, professional networks, and funding entities. For example, Stanley (2007b), in her article "When Counter Narratives Meet Master Narratives in the Journal Editorial-Review Process," described her experiences with the editorial review process and called on "journal editors

TABLE 18

— Lack of Recruitment/Retention

Adams & Bargerhuff (2005)	K. Johnson (2003)	C. A. Stanley (2006, 2007a)
Aguirre (2000)	Kayes (2006)	J. M. Stanley et al. (2007)
Alemán & Renn (2002)	Maher & Tetreault (2007)	Subervi & Cantrell (2007)
Alex-Assenoh et al. (2005)	Marbley (2007)	Tierney & Rhoads (1993)
Carmen (1999)	Mickelson & Oliver (1991)	Townsend-Johnson (2006)
Clark (2006)	Morris (2000)	Turner (2003)
Cora-Bramble (2006)	Moss (2000)	Turner et al. (1996)
Cowan (2006)	Nelson et al. (2007)	Turner & Taylor (2002)
Cross (1994)	Niemann (1999)	TuSmith & Reddy (2002)
Daley et al. (2006)	Opp & Smith (1994)	Vasquez et al. (2006)
Delgado-Romero et al. (2007)	Price et al. (2005)	Whetsel-Ribeau (2007)
Hall (2006)	Pura (1993)	

TABLE 19

— Isms (Race/Ethnicity, Class, Gender, Sexual Orientation)

Aguirre (2000)	A. García (2005)	Olivas (1988)
Aguirre et al. (1993)	Ginorio (1995)	R. V. Padilla &
Akins (1997)	C. M. Gonzalez (2002)	Chávez Chavez (1995)
Alemán & Renn (2002)	J. C. González (2007b)	Rai & Critzer (2000)
Alexander-Snow &	Gregory (1995, 2001)	Saavedra & Saavedra (2007)
Johnson (1999)	Gumataotao-Lowe (1995)	Slater (1999)
Arnold (2006)	Hall (2006)	P. W. Smith et al. (2002)
Baez (1997)	Hamlet (1999)	Stanley (2006, 2007a)
Benjamin (1997)	Harris (2007)	Stein (1994)
Bower (2002)	Holcomb-McCoy &	Takara (2006)
Bradley (2005)	Addison-Bradley (2005)	Tomlinson (2006)
Brayboy (2003)	Horton (2000)	Turner (2002b, 2003)
Brown et al. (2007)	Hune (1998)	Turner & Myers (1997, 2000)
Carmen (1999)	Hurtado et al. (1999)	TuSmith & Reddy (2002)
Carr et al. (2007)	K. W. Jackson (1991)	Valladares (2007)
Chesler et al. (2005)	Jacobs et al. (2002)	Vasquez et al. (2006)
Cuádraz (1993)	W. J. Johnson (1996)	Wheeler (1996)
Delgado-Romero et al. (2007)	K. Johnson (2003)	Witt (1990)
De la luz Reyes & Halcón (1988)	Johnsrud & Sadao (1998)	Whetsel-Ribeau (2007)
Essien (2003)	Mickelson & Oliver (1991)	Wong & Bainer (1991)
Fenelon (2003)	Niemann (1999, 2003)	

and reviewers to examine their roles as disciplinary gatekeepers and to break the cycle of master narratives in educational research in the editorial review process" (p. 14). Additionally, national studies of *salary inequities* focus on the effect of pay on the representation of diverse faculty and variance in salary by race, ethnicity, and institutional type. (See Tables 21–23.)

Bridging Departmental, Institutional, and National Contexts

Across departmental, institutional, and national settings, the literature identifies major barriers to the tenure and promotion of faculty of color, such as negative student evaluations, undervaluation of research, and unwritten rules and policies regarding the tenure process. Conversely, the integration of policies that recognize contributions to diversity is an important step toward rethinking standards for hiring and *tenure and promotion* processes. For example, in 2004, the University of California system adopted Academic Personnel Policy No. 210 ("Section II: Appointment and Promotion," 2002), which states that "teaching, research, professional and public service contributions that promote diversity and equal opportunity are to be encouraged and given recognition in the evaluation of the candidate's qualifications" (p. 4) for appointment and promotion. This policy, which was revised and placed into effect in 2005, can serve as a model for other institutions seeking to place value on faculty contributions to diversity efforts when determining hiring, tenure, and promotion decisions. On one hand, faculty who were not successful in the tenure process often lacked *mentorship* to aid their incorporation into academia. On the other hand, scholarship on successful faculty revealed that mentorship was a critical support to their professional success. The *historical literature* on faculty of color indicates that underrepresentation, segregation, and exclusion are still prevalent in the educational system. These concerns, coupled with *pipeline* issues and pervasive *myths* in the recruitment and hiring process, maintain a lack of diversity in the professoriate. (See Tables 24–28.)

TABLE 20

− Tokenism

Aguirre (2000)	De la luz Reyes & Halcón (1988)	Niemann (2003)
Aguirre et al. (1993)	Fairbanks (2005)	Rains (1995)
Alemán & Renn (2002)	C. M. Gonzalez (2002)	Sámano (2007)
Alexander-Snow & Johnson (1999)	Guang-Lea & Louis (2006)	Segura (2003)
Bradley (2005)	Marbley (2007)	Skachkova (2007)
Brayboy (2003)	Medina & Luna (2000)	Takara (2006)
Chused (1988)	Niemann (1999)	Turner & Myers (2000)

TABLE 21

± Legal Landscape/Affirmative Action

Alemán & Renn (2002)	Hamlet (1999)	Slater (1999)
Alexander-Snow & Johnson (1999)	Jacobs et al. (2002)	E. Smith (1992)
Alger (1999, 2000)	Maher & Tetreault (2007)	P. W. Smith et al. (2002)
Ashraf & Shabbir (2006)	Maturana (2005)	Springer (2004)
Baez (2002)	Myers & Turner (2001)	Takara (2006)
Basri et al. (2007)	Nevarez & Borunda (2004)	Tomlinson (2006)
Blackshire-Belay (1998)	Niemann (1999, 2003)	Turner et al. (1996)
Brown et al. (2007)	Niemann & Dovidio (2005)	Turner (2003)
Chesler et al. (2005)	Peoples (2004)	Turner & Myers (1997)
Cowan (2006)	Rai & Critzer (2000)	Turner & Taylor (2002)
Delgado-Romero et al. (2007)	Sánchez (2007)	Vasquez et al. (2006)
Guang-Lea & Louis (2006)	Skachkova (2007)	Witt (1990)

TABLE 22

± Research Outlets

Alemán & Renn (2002)	Moule (2005)	Stanley (2007b)
Alexander-Snow & Johnson (1999)	A. M. Padilla (1994)	Turner (2000)
Louis (2007)	Reyes & Ríos (2005)	Turner & Myers (2000)

TABLE 23

− Salary Inequities

Alemán & Renn (2002)	Renzulli et al. (2006)	Witt (1990)
Myers & Turner (2001)	Toutkoushian et al. (2007)	

TABLE 24

± Tenure/Promotion

Alemán & Renn (2002)	Hune & Chan (1997)	Sampaio (2006)
Akins (1997)	Jacobs et al. (2002)	Slater (1999)
Baez (1997, 2002)	C. Johnson (2001)	P. A. Smith & Shoho (2007)
Basri et al. (2007)	B. J. Johnson & Harvey (2002)	Stanley (2006, 2007a)
Bensimon & Tierney (1996)	Jones (2001, 2002)	Thompson & Dey (1998)
Blackshire-Belay (1998)	Laden & Hagedorn (2000)	Tierney & Rhoads (1993)
Brown et al. (2007)	Maher & Tetreault (2007)	Townsend-Johnson (2006)
Chesler et al. (2005)	Marbley (2007)	Turner et al. (1996)
Cowan (2006)	Morell-Thon (1998)	Turner & Myers (2000)
Fenelon (2003)	Niemann (1999, 2003)	Turner & Taylor (2002)
Gregory (2001)	Pepion (1993)	TuSmith & Reddy (2002)
Guang-Lea & Louis (2006)	Perez (2001)	Valladares (2007)
Harris (2007)	Perna (2003)	Whetsel-Ribeau (2007)
Hassouneh (2006)	Perna et al. (2007)	Witt (1990)
Hendricks (1996)	Ponjuan (2005)	B. N. Williams & Williams (2006)
Hendrix (2007)	Rai & Critzer (2000)	Wong & Bainer (1991)

TABLE 25

± Mentorship

Alex-Assenoh et al. (2005)	Hendricks (1996)	C. A. Stanley (2006, 2007a)
Arnold (2006)	Holland (1995)	J. M. Stanley et al. (2007)
Barnett et al. (2003)	Johnsrud (1994)	Tierney & Rhoads (1993)
Blackshire-Belay (1998)	Kosoko-Lasaki et al. (2006)	Turner et al. (1996)
Burden et al. (2005)	Lewellen-Williams et al. (2006)	Turner & Thompson (1993)
Chesler et al. (2005)	Millett & Nettles (2006)	Turner & Myers (1997)
Daley et al. (2006)	Moss (2000)	Turner & Myers (2000)
Dixon-Reeves (2003)	Nelson et al. (2007)	Vasquez et al. (2006)
Frierson (1990)	Nevarez & Borunda (2004)	Waitzkin et al. (2006)
A. García (2000)	A. M. Padilla (1994)	D. A. Williams & Williams (2006)
C. M. Gonzalez (2002)	Peterson-Hickey (1998)	Yager et al. (2007)
Gregory (2001)		

Although campus climate is a major factor noted in the literature on faculty of color (Alemán & Renn, 2002; Bradley, 2005; Ginorio, 1995; Guang-Lea & Louis, 2006; Holcomb-McCoy & Addison-Bradley, 2005; Horton, 2000; Hurtado, Milem, Clayton-Pedersen, & Allen, 1999; Jacobs, Cintrón, & Canton, 2002; Niemann, 2003; Niemann & Dovidio, 2005; Piercy et al., 2005; Price et al., 2005; Pon-juan, 2005; Stanley, 2006; Whetsel-Ribeau, 2007), it is not included as a separate category in Figure 1. Our reasoning is that campus climate is an all-encompassing term that includes many of the supports and challenges already addressed in our model.

Emerging Themes: Recommendations

Figure 2 represents the major recommendations derived from the literature that address challenges presented in Figure 1. Similar to Figure 1, Figure 2 differentiates among three contexts—departmental, institutional, and national. Some recommendations are pictured as cutting across multiple contexts because they are applicable in each of them. For example, as in Figure 1, in Figure 2, a recommendation that cuts across all three contexts is *promote mentoring programs*.

Themes identified across publications are listed below within departmental, institutional, and national contexts. Listed after each theme are the references in which elaboration on the theme can be found. At least three references had to cite the factor listed for it to be included here.

Departmental Context Recommendations

Although most recommendations noted in the literature cited here applied to the departmental context, they were not exclusive to this context. According to the literature, departments need to *diversify their processes for how they judged faculty* pre- and post-tenure. The literature described new and/or alternative ways of thinking, teaching, writing, and just being an academic brought to higher education by current faculty of color. Their new approaches to research, teaching, and service are, in many cases, in conflict with traditional approaches leading to poor evaluations and lack of publications. This means that in a *publish or perish* environment based on traditional ways of knowing, many faculty of color may be at a disadvantage (see Table 29). Second, as the faculty diversifies and brings to the academy different ways of knowing, it is important that they are given the opportunity for individual expression—*authentic and spiritual*. The literature in this area

TABLE 26

— Pipeline Issues

Alemán & Renn (2002)	B. J. Johnson & Pichon (2007)	Nelson et al. (2007)
Chesler et al. (2005)	Jordan (2006)	P. W. Smith et al. (2002)
Cross (1994)	Lindsay (1991)	J. M. Stanley et al. (2007)
Hernández & Davis (2001)	Moody (1988)	Turner & Myers (1997, 2000)
Jacobs et al. (2002)	Myers & Turner (2001, 2004)	Turner & Taylor (2002)
K. Johnson (2003)		

TABLE 27

— Historical Legacy of Exclusion

Aguirre et al. (1993)	W. J. Johnson (1996)	Slater (1999)
Castellanos & Jones (2003)	Lindsay (1991)	E. Smith (1992)
Chesler et al. (2005)	Maher & Tetreault (2007)	Turner & Taylor (2002)
Gregory (2001)	Moody (2004)	Weems (2003)
Hurtado et al. (1999)	Rai & Critzer (2000)	

is growing and indicates the need for departments to recognize the underlying messages conveyed to faculty of color that devalue their research and writing in an oppressive fashion (see Table 30). For example, Louis (2007) urged scholars to accept, as legitimate ways of knowing, "knowledge systems that do not necessarily conform to Western academic standards." Additionally, departments should recognize that some scholars may believe that "the spiritual aspect of life is as important to the search for knowledge as is the physical" (p. 134).

Institutional Context Recommendations

D. A. Williams and Wade-Golden (2006) defined chief diversity officers (CDOs) as "the 'face' of diversity efforts [that] carry formal administrative titles like vice provost, vice chancellor, associate provost, vice president, assistant provost, dean, or special assistant to the president for multicultural, international, equity, diversity, and inclusion" (p. 1). Furthermore, D. A. Williams and Wade-Golden (2007) stated that "today's CDOs are often seen as change agents who are appointed to create an environment that is inclusive and supportive of all members of the institution in order to maximize both human and institutional capital" (p. iii). As institutions begin to recognize the importance of the role of the CDO to diversifying the faculty, it is critical to understand that although they may be centrally responsible, they should not be solely responsible for this important work. As the roles of CDOs increase and become more defined, it is important that that they continue their work to *institutionalize diversity goals* and to *promote strong campus leadership* that advocates for faculty diversification (see Tables 31 and 32). The following citations present work in support of the types of institutional factors important to the goal of increasing the racial and ethnic representation of faculty of color.

Departmental and Institutional Contexts Recommendations

The literature reviewed in this study underscores the importance of having *departmental and institutional plans* that systematically promote progress toward the *goal of diversifying the faculty*. Part of the plan should also include training to increase knowledge and sensitivity of all campus staff, faculty, and higher level administrators on issues facing faculty of color in the workplace. The alignment of diversity efforts at both levels of the organization is critical for progress to take place. In

TABLE 28

— Myths

Assensoh (2003)	Kayes (2006)	D. G. Smith et al. (1996)
Chapman (2001)	Maturana (2005)	C. A. Stanley (2007a)
Cho (2002)	Morris (2000)	Townsend-Johnson (2006)
Hune (1998)	Peoples (2004)	Turner et al. (1996)
K. Johnson (2003)	Pura (1993)	Turner & Myers (2000)
D. R. Johnson (2006)	D. G. Smith (2000)	Wong & Bainer (1991)

TABLE 29

Establish More Inclusive Standards for Judging Faculty Yearly Performance

Bensimon & Tierney (1996)	Louis (2007)	Rains (1995)
Bensimon et al. (2000)	Moule (2005)	C. A. Stanley (2006, 2007a, 2007b)
Cooper & Stevens (2002)	Pepion (1993)	Turner & Taylor (2002)
Hayden (1997)	Perez (2001)	Urrieta & Méndez Benavídez (2007)
Jones (2002)		

addition, the literature suggests that *increasing the campus presence of students and faculty of color* may lead to a synergy that supports the retention and development of both groups as well as attracting others. A more diverse environment has the potential to alleviate isolation for people of color on campus. As colleges and universities become diverse, it will also be important for students, staff, faculty, and administrators to be provided with *training on the issues faced by faculty of color*. Another recommendation emerging from this study, which can build scholarly community at the departmental and institutional levels, is deliberate efforts to provide opportunities for *collegial networking and cross-disciplinary collaborations* (see Tables 33–36).

National Context Recommendations

To achieve success in the recruitment and retention of faculty of color, communities of color and institutions of higher education must create relationships with one another, recognizing the importance of increased faculty racial and ethnic diversity and working in collaboration to achieve this goal. With regard to the hiring of Latino faculty, C. González (2007) stated that "the Hispanic community must establish a strong working relationship with institutions of higher learning and use power in a measured and sustained way" (p. 159) to encourage faculty diversification. Likewise, institutions must establish and maintain *connections to diverse communities* in support of the service and incorporation needs of faculty of color. Additionally, institutions must begin to address and reduce *salary inequities* between majority and minority faculties. (See Tables 37 and 38.) Pay inequities invalidate and devalue the contributions of diverse faculties and increase the likelihood that they will reject position offers or leave institutions early. Furthermore, disparities in the allocation of research space, graduate student research support, and funding for conference participation must be viewed as an extension of salary inequity issues. These funding inequities should be addressed for incoming and current faculty of color through policies that promote equity.

Departmental, Institutional, and National Contexts Recommendations

Recommendations cutting across all three contexts include the critical need for *research support* for faculty of color, particularly for nontenured faculty (see Table 39). Support can come from departmental, institutional, or national sources, including federal, state, professional organization, and foundation funding. However, although research support can be in the form of funding, it may also include opportunities to participate in nationwide workshops and seminars designed to assist junior faculty of color in the grant-getting and publication processes. The best of these programs would em-

TABLE 30

Provide Opportunities for Authentic and Spiritual Expression

Astin & Astin (1999)	Jones (2000)	Rendón (2000)
Guang-Lea & Louis (2006)	Louis (2007)	C. A. Stanley (2007b)
Hall (2006)		

TABLE 31

Institutionalize Diversity Goals

Alicea-Lugo (1998)	Guang-Lea & Louis (2006)	Sánchez (2007)
Brayboy (2003)	Harvey & Valadez (1994)	Sámano (2007)
Chapman (2001)	W. J. Johnson (1996)	C. A. Stanley (2007b)
Colby & Foote (1995)	Johnston (1997)	Tack & Patitu (1992)
Cowan (2006)	Maturana (2005)	

phasize collaborative and not hierarchical professional socialization. Having mentors along their career path is a leading factor contributing to the growth and development of faculty of color. Because mentorship is so critical, programs providing *opportunities for mentorship* should be made available at the departmental, institutional, and national levels. Such connections within all contexts, including internationally, play an important role in the development of faculty and in the promotion and tenure process. In addition, having different rubrics for evaluating tenure and promotion worthiness are mentioned in the literature. For example, value should be placed, during tenure and promotion evaluations, on contributions to diversity efforts and for faculty outreach to diverse on-campus communities, off-campus local communities, and diverse national communities. Also, emerging from the literature are recommendations to promote policies supportive of a diverse faculty (see Table 40). Included among these factors are the need to level the field with regard to inequitable pay for faculty of color and women employed in minority-serving institutions when compared with salaries paid in predominantly White institutions. Renzulli, Grant, and Kathuria (2006) referred to this phenomenon as "economic subordination" (p. 507). Overarching policies that create multilevel pathways to the professoriate and continue to support careers are also reported as important for implementation across contexts. Finally, practices that promote the building of scholarly and collaborative communities as opposed to individualism and competitiveness are recommended. (See Tables 41 and 42.)

Spanning 2 Decades: Methodological Approaches and the Study of Faculty of Color

Between 1988 and 2007, a number of publications on faculty of color were conceptual in nature. In addition, a cursory analysis of empirical research conducted during this time frame revealed the

TABLE 32

Promote Strong Leadership for Diversity

Alexander-Snow & Johnson (1999)	Maturana (2005)	C. A. Stanley & Lincoln (2005)
Arnold (2006)	Opp & Gosetti (2002)	Toutkoushian et al. (2007)
Buttner et al. (2007)	Price et al. (2005)	Whetsel-Ribeau (2007)
Fox (2005)	Sámano (2007)	Wong & Bainer (1991)
MacLachlan (2006)	C. A. Stanley (2006, 2007a)	

TABLE 33

Establish Recruitment/Hiring/Retention Plans

Alger (1999)	Hayden (1997)	Opp & Smith (1994)
Bowser et al. (1993)	Johnston (1997)	Peoples (2004)
Chapman (2001)	Jones (2001)	Peterson-Hickey (1998)
Colby & Foote (1995)	Kauper (1991)	Plata (1996)
Chused (1988)	Kayes (2006)	Pura (1993)
Clark-Louque (1996)	Kirkpatrick (2001)	Sámano (2007)
Cooper & Stevens (2002)	Light (1994)	C. A. Stanley (2007a)
Cross & Slater (2002)	Mickelson & Oliver (1991)	J. M. Stanley et al. (2007)
Delgado-Romero et al. (2007)	Moody (1988)	Stein (1994)
C. González (2007)	Moreno et al. (2006)	Tippeconnic & McKinney (2003)
J. C. González (2007a)	Morris (2000)	Turner (2002a)
Granger (1993)	Moss (2000)	Wong & Bainer (1991)
Harvey & Valadez (1994)	Opp & Gosetti (2002)	

preferred usage of the following research methodologies: (a) interviews, (b) surveys and question-naires, (c) large data sets, and (d) a combination of multiple qualitative methods (document analysis, interviews, and observations). An examination of the preferred research methodologies used during this period (divided into 5-year periods) is provided, as well as some citations relevant to these approaches.

Between 1988 and 1992, the preferred data collection approaches to the study of faculty of color in academe appeared to be surveys and questionnaires (Chused, 1988; Nieves-Squires, 1991; E. Smith, 1992) and (to a lesser extent) interviews—sometimes used in conjunction with other methods (Kauper, 1991; Nieves-Squires, 1991). Various forms of data collection were used by other researchers, such as auto-ethnographic narratives (Cuádraz, 1992), historical analysis (Lindsay, 1991), and the usage of large data sets (Mickelson & Oliver, 1991).

From 1993 to 1997, the primary data collection methods used were surveys (Aguirre, Martinez, & Hernández, 1993; Clark-Louque, 1996; Hendricks, 1996; Holland, 1995; Johnston, 1997), interviews (Baez, 1997; Cuádraz, 1993; D. R. Johnson, 1996; Knowles & Harleston, 1997; Lasalle, 1995; Turner & Thompson, 1993), and some combination of qualitative methods (i.e., archival and document analysis in conjunction with interviews and/or observations; Hayden, 1997; Pepion, 1993; Pura, 1993; Rains, 1995). Also used to a lesser degree were historical analysis (Gregory, 1995) and the analysis of large data sets (Akins, 1997; Milem & Astin, 1993).

From 1988 to 2002, the use of interviews as the primary form of data collection appeared to be preferred (Astin & Astin, 1999; Baez, 2000; Carmen, 1999; Morell-Thon, 1998; Peterson-Hickey, 1998; Pérez, 2001; Turner, 2002b). However, interviews were often combined with observations (Gonzalez, 2002; C. Johnson, 2001; Morris, 2000; Thomas & Hollenshead, 2001) and large data set analyses (Myers & Turner, 2001; Turner & Myers, 2000). Also, the use of large data sets seemed to increase during this period (antonio, 2002; Opp & Gosetti, 2002; Owino, 2000; Thompson & Dey, 1998). Additional publications indicate the continued use of surveys and questionnaires (Awe, 2001; Chapman, 2001; Hernández & Davis, 2001), narratives (Jacobs, Cintrón, & Canton, 2002; Medina & Luna, 2000), and historical analysis (Gregory, 2001).

Publications from 2003 to 2007 illustrate that researchers used interviews (Burden, Harrison, & Hodge, 2005; Carr, Palepu, Szalacha, Caswell, & Inui, 2007; J. C. González, 2007a, 2007b; McLean, 2007; Skachkova, 2007; Urrieta & Méndez Benavídez, 2007; B. N. Williams & Williams, 2006), analysis of large data sets (Ashraf & Shabbir, 2006; Isaac & Boyer, 2007; Perna, 2003; Perna, Gerald, Baum, &

TABLE 34

Diversify Student Body/Faculty

Adams & Bargerhuff (2005)	C. González (2007)	Morris (2000)
Alex-Assensoh (2003)	J. C. González (2007a)	Myers & Turner (2001)
antonio (2002, 2003)	Guang-Lea & Louis (2006)	Price et al. (2005)
Barnett et al. (2003)	Kauper (1991)	Pura (1993)
Fox (2005)	Kirkpatrick (2001)	Sánchez (2007)
Frierson (1990)		

TABLE 35

Provide Training on Faculty-of-Color Issues

Adams & Bargerhuff (2005)	Plata (1996)	Whetsel-Ribeau (2007)
Peoples (2004)	Sámano (2007)	Wong & Bainer (1991)
Pineda (1998)	C. A. Stanley (2006, 2007a)	

Milem, 2007; Porter, 2007; Toutkoushian, Bellas, & Moore, 2007), and surveys and questionnaires (Hagedorn, Chi, Cepeda, & McLain, 2007; Holcomb-McCoy & Addison-Bradley, 2005; Stanley, 2007a, 2007b; Subervi & Cantrell, 2007; Umbach, 2006). Also, historical research approaches (Weems, 2003) and narrative data analysis (Sámano, 2007; Stanley, 2006) were used during this period (although to a lesser degree). Authors also published studies that used a combination of qualitative research methods (interviews, observations, and document analysis; Hill-Brisbane & Dingus, 2007).

Table 43 shows a fairly consistent use by researchers of similar methodological approaches to examine the status of faculty of color throughout the 20-year time period.

Spanning 2 Decades: Issues Examined in the Study of Faculty of Color

Findings from our examination of publications included in this study (i.e., journal articles, dissertations, books, reports, and book chapters) document that the total number of publications on faculty of color has visibly increased over each 5-year period examined (1988–1992, 1993–1997, 1998–2002, and 2003–2007). The largest total publication increase occurred during the 2003–2007 period (see Table 1). This increase may be linked to the 2003 *Grutter v. Bollinger* Supreme Court decision, although there is no evidence to prove this link. In general, most of the publications during the time periods examined were journal articles, except from 1993 to 1997 when more dissertations were produced.

Several publications on faculty of color from 1988 to 1992 focused on the intersection of race and ethnicity and gender (Chused, 1988; Cuádraz, 1992; Lindsay, 1991; Moses, 1989; Nieves-Squires, 1991; Tack & Patitu, 1992; Witt, 1990). Also heavily researched was the lack of diversity in the academy (Frierson, 1990; Lindsay, 1991; C. D. Moody, 1988; Olivas, 1988; E. Smith, 1992) and job satisfaction (Chused, 1988; Tack & Patitu, 1992; Turner & Myers, 2000; Witt, 1990). During this time span, some publications focused on faculty of color career decisions (Kauper, 1991) and occupational stress (E. Smith, 1992).

Scholarly publications from 1993 to 1997 focused on (a) the socialization process for faculty of color (Bensimon & Tierney, 1996; Lasalle, 1995; Tierney & Rhoads, 1993; Turner & Thompson, 1993); (b) lack of faculty diversity (Benjamin, 1997; Holland, 1995; Milem & Astin, 1993; Tierney & Rhoads, 1993); (c) strategies for faculty racial/ethnic diversification (Colby & Foote, 1995; Knowles & Harleston, 1997; Light, 1994; Opp & Smith, 1994; Plata, 1996; Pura, 1993; D. G. Smith, Wolf, &

TABLE 36

Provide Opportunities for Collegial Networks and Collaborations

Alexander-Snow & Johnson (1999)	W. J. Johnson (1996)	Stein (1994)
Baez (1997)	B. J. Johnson & Harvey (2002)	Thomas & Hollenshead (2001)
Bowser et al. (1993)	MacLachlan (2006)	Turner & Myers (1997)
Butner et al. (2000)	Moses (1989)	Valladares (2007)
Essien (2003)	A. M. Padilla (1994)	Wong & Bainer (1991)
Gregory (2001)	Plata (1996)	

TABLE 37

Provide Connections to Diverse Community

C. González (2007)	Gregory (2001)	Turner & Thompson (1993)
J. C. González (2007a, 2007b)	Sámano (2007)	Urrieta & Méndez Benavídez (2007)
K. P. Gonzalez & Padilla (2007)	J. M. Stanley et al. (2007)	

Busenberg, 1996); (d) isms (with regard to race/ethnicity, class, gender, and sexual orientation; Aguirre et al., 1993; Akins, 1997; Ginorio, 1995; W. J. Johnson, 1996); (e) tenure and promotion issues (Akins, 1997; Pepion, 1993; Tierney & Rhoads, 1993); and (f) isolation and marginalization in the academy (Aguirre & Martinez, 1993; Benjamin, 1997; Hune & Chan, 1997; Padilla & Chávez Chavez, 1995; Rendón, 1996). Additionally, literature demonstrating the importance of faculty and academic administrator mentorship in support of the retention of faculty of color and the attraction of students to faculty careers was addressed (Holland, 1995; Johnsrud, 1994; Padilla, 1994; Segovia, 1994; Wheeler, 1996).

From 1998 to 2002, there was a continuation of literature documenting the intersection of race/ethnicity and gender among faculty (Aguirre, 2000; Alemán & Renn, 2002; Moss, 2000; Opp & Gosetti, 2002; Owino, 2000; Perna, 2003; Rai & Critzer, 2000; Turner, 2000, 2002b). This literature was accompanied by publications on specific female faculty of color groups such as African American women (Hamlet, 1999; McKenzie, 2002; Thomas & Hollenshead, 2001), Latinas (Alicea-Lugo, 1998; Medina & Luna, 2000), and Asian women (Hune, 1998). Some publications on African American male faculty were also evident during this period (Jones, 2000, 2002).

During this time frame, research on faculty of color also focused on (a) stress and coping (Butner, Burley, & Marbley, 2000; Thomas & Hollenshead, 2001; Thompson & Dey, 1998), (b) job satisfaction (Laden & Hagedorn, 2000; Morell-Thon, 1998), (c) myths (Cho, 2002; D. G. Smith, 2000), (d) different ways of knowing (A. W. Astin & Astin, 1999; Rendón, 2000), (e) service (Baez, 2000; Hamlet, 1999; McKenzie, 2002; Turner & Myers, 2000), (f) lack of diversity in the academy (Aguirre, 2000; Hune, 1998; Owino, 2000; Thompson & Dey, 1998), (g) recruitment and retention concerns (Carmen, 1999; Morris, 2000; Moss, 2000; Niemann, 1999), (h) isms (with regard to race/ethnicity, class, gender, and sexual orientation; Gonzalez, 2002; Horton, 2000; Rai & Critzer, 2000; Slater, 1999), (i) tokenism (Aguirre, 2000; Medina & Luna, 2000; Niemann, 1999), (j) bias in hiring (Chapman, 2001; Slater, 1999; D. G. Smith, 2000), (k) tenure and promotion issues (Blackshire-Belay 1998; Niemann, 1999; TuSmith & Reddy, 2002), (l) isolation and marginalization (Alemán & Renn, 2002; Awe, 2001; Hamlet, 1999), and (m) affirmative action and legal issues (Alexander-Snow & Johnson, 1999; Alger, 1999; Turner & Taylor, 2002). Additionally, two guidebooks specific to the recruitment and retention of faculty of color emerged, one that focused on the search committee process (Turner, 2002a) and the other designed to aid faculty of color to succeed in the academy (M. García, 2000).

From 2003 to 2007, emergent issues from the published literature reflected an interest in faculty of color and (a) their unique scholarly contributions (Fenelon, 2003; Louis, 2007; Tippeconnic & McKinney, 2003; Urrieta & Méndez Benavídez, 2007), (b) their perceptions of teaching and use of critical and alternative pedagogy (Hassouneh, 2006; McLean, 2007; Saavedra & Saavedra, 2007;

TABLE 38

Reduce Salary Inequities

Myers & Turner (2001)	Renzulli et al. (2006)	Toutkoushian et al. (2007)

TABLE 39

Provide Research Support

Alex-Assenoh et al. (2005)	J. C. González (2007a, 2007b)	Turner (2003)
Bradley (2005)	Louis (2007)	Turner & Myers (1997, 2000)
Dixon-Reeves (2003)	C. A. Stanley (2006)	Wong & Bainer (1991)
Fox (2005)	J. M. Stanley et al. (2007)	

Sampaio, 2006; G. Smith & Anderson, 2005), (c) job satisfaction (Flowers, 2005; Holcomb-McCoy & Addison-Bradley, 2005; Isaac & Boyer, 2007; Niemann & Dovidio, 2005; Ponjuan, 2005), (d) resiliency (Cora-Bramble, 2006; J. C. González, 2007a, 2007b), (e) lack of diverse faculty representation (Essien, 2003; Fenelon, 2003; Myers & Turner, 2004; Ponjuan, 2005), (f) service (Bradley, 2005; Brayboy, 2003; Skachkova, 2007; Urrieta & Méndez Benavídez, 2007), (g) recruitment and retention concerns (Clark, 2006; K. Johnson, 2003; Kayes, 2006; Turner, 2003), (h) isms (with regard to race/ethnicity, class, gender, and sexual orientation; Holcomb & Addison-Bradley, 2005; Stanley, 2007a; Valladares, 2007), (i) tokenism (Bradley, 2005; Fairbanks, 2005; Sámano, 2007; Segura, 2003), (j) bias in hiring (Maturana, 2005; Reyes & Ríos, 2005; Stanley, 2006), (k) tenure and promotion issues (Cowan, 2006; Perna, 2003; Sampaio, 2006), (l) isolation and marginalization (B. J. Johnson & Pichon, 2007; Reyes, 2005; Tomlinson, 2006; Townsend-Johnson, 2006), and (m) affirmative action and legal issues (Ashraf & Shabbir, 2006; Springer, 2004; Takara, 2006).

The predominant research emphasis during this time frame was scholarship on mentoring (Alex-Assenoh et al., 2005; Barnett, Gibson, & Black, 2003; Dixon-Reeves, 2003; Kosoko-Lasaki, Sonnino, & Voytko, 2006; Lewellen-Williams et al., 2006; C. A. Stanley & Lincoln, 2005; J. M. Stanley, Capers, & Berlin, 2007; Waitzkin, Yager, Parker, & Duran, 2006; Yager, Waitzkin, Parker, & Duran, 2007). Additionally, two interrelated fields experienced a growth in scholarly attention: (a) research on faculty and graduates of color in the science, technology, engineering, and mathematics fields (MacLachlan, 2006; Millett & Nettles, 2006; Nelson, Brammer, & Rhoads, 2007) and (b) literature on faculty of color in the health fields (Burden et al., 2005; Carnes, Handelsman, & Sheridan, 2005; Carr et al., 2007; Daley, Wingard, & Reznik, 2006; D. A. Mitchell & Lassiter, 2006; Soto-Greene, Sanchez, Churrango, & Salas-Lopez, 2005; Yager, Waitzkin, Parker, & Duran, 2007).

Table 44 indicates that some issues emerging from the published literature examined in this study appeared to remain somewhat constant, whereas others were added over different time periods. Scholarly interest in the intersection of gender with racial/ethnic diversity among the faculty, mentorship, job satisfaction, isms (with regard to race/ethnicity, class, gender, and sexual orientation), tenure and promotion, isolation and marginalization, and lack of diversity in the academy appear to hold researchers' attention over the 20-year span. Additions that stood out during 1998–2002 are respect for different ways of knowing and myths surrounding concerns related to the recruitment and retention of faculty of color. Additional issues receiving attention from 2003 to 2007 are scholarly contributions made by a diverse professoriate, resiliency, and experiences of faculty of color in science, technology, engineering, mathematics, and health fields.

Further Research

Further work is needed to capture insights from other sources. Even though we compiled and analyzed a comprehensive list of publications for this chapter, as stated earlier conference papers, videotapes, and Web sites, although identified, were excluded in the analysis provided here. It is also likely that we have not captured all existing publications on this subject. However, the works presented

TABLE 40

Promote Policies Supportive of a Diverse Faculty

Adams & Bargerhuff (2005)	J. C. González (2007a)	Renzulli et al. (2006)
Arnold (2006)	Granger (1993)	Sámano (2007)
Astin (1992)	Guang-Lea & Louis (2006)	Stanley (2007a)
Bowser et al. (1993)	W. J. Johnson (1996)	J. M. Stanley et al. (2007)
Bradley (2005)	Moody (1988)	Vasquez et al. (2006)
Chapman (2001)	Niemann (1999)	Wong & Bainer (1991)
Fox (2005)		

here likely represent the major themes on faculty diversity to be captured in journal articles, books, dissertations, reports, and book chapters written over the past 20 years.

However, our analysis has identified major gaps in the literature. First, most publications located and examined here focus on faculty of color within public 4-year university settings. As a result, more work examining faculty of color within community college, technical college, private college, for-profit college, minority-serving institutions, and faith-based campus environments needs to be conducted. Second, there is almost nothing written on issues related to faculty of color and the intersection of race/ethnicity and sexual orientation. Delgado-Romero, Manlove, Manlove, and Hernandez (2007) stated that "one aspect of Latino/a faculty experience that is virtually absent from the research literature is the experience of Latino/a lesbian, gay, bisexual, and transgendered (L-LGBT) faculty" (p. 43). Third, most of the literature analyzed here underscores the value of mentoring within departmental, institutional, and national contexts. Further work on the importance of such connections within an international context can be undertaken as these colleagues are critical to faculty development as well as in the promotion and tenure process. In fact, more comparative studies on faculty of color within a global context would be a welcome addition to the extant literature. Fourth, although our study showed that the literature, in general, reflected emerging themes across institutional types and racial/ethnic affiliation, more work needs to be done to examine sets of issues that are unique or specific to various racial/ethnic groups and to faculty women of color. For example, Turner and Myers (2000) began to identify themes that are specific to faculty by racial/ethnic affiliation and gender. Fifth, although several themes, such as mentorship, have been shown to support the recruitment and retention of faculty of color, more work needs to be done on how such factors can be implemented nationwide to contribute to the resolution of the critical problem examined in this chapter. Finally, empirical research needs to be conducted on the critical, emerging institutional role of the executive-level campus diversity officer, the CDO, and his or her impact on diversifying the faculty.

TABLE 41

Promote Mentoring Programs

Alexander-Snow & Johnson (1999)	Kosoko-Lasaki et al. (2006)	J. M. Stanley et al. (2007)
Alex-Assenoh et al. (2005)	Lewellen-Williams et al. (2006)	C. A. Stanley & Lincoln (2005)
Arnold (2006)	Moss (2000)	Stein (1994)
Barnett et al. (2003)	A. M. Padilla (1994)	Tippeconnic & McKinney (2003)
Bradley (2005)	Piercy et al. (2005)	Turner & Myers (1997)
Dixon-Reeves (2003)	Sámano (2007)	Waitzkin et al. (2006)
W. J. Johnson (1996)	Soto-Greene et al. (2005)	Wong & Bainer (1991)
Johnsrud (1994)	C. A. Stanley (2006, 2007a)	Yager et al. (2007)
Kirkpatrick (2001)		

TABLE 42

Establish More Inclusive Standards for Tenure and Promotion

Alexander-Snow & Johnson (1999)	Jones (2002)	C. A. Stanley (2006, 2007a, 2007b)
Bensimon & Tierney (1996)	Moule (2005)	Turner & Taylor (2002)
Bensimon et al. (2000)	Pepion (1993)	Louis (2007)
Cooper & Stevens (2002)	Perez (2001)	Urrieta & Méndez Benavídez (2007)
Fenelon (2003)	Rains (1995)	Wong & Bainer (1991)
Hayden (1997)		

Implications

This review and synthesis of extant literature on faculty of color has implications for policy-makers, administrators, faculty, and graduate students. In essence, this analysis highlights the complexity of the faculty of color experience in higher education by providing an integration of single studies conducted over an extensive time period and by presenting themes derived from these studies. In addition, the literature collected for this study addresses supports, challenges, and recommendations that cut across departmental, institutional, and national contexts. Those involved in making policies and decisions may find this analysis useful in understanding the interrelated factors affecting faculty of color hiring and persistence. For example, transcending context and time frame, mentoring is a factor described in the literature as critical to the persistence of faculty of color.

In conclusion, challenges afford opportunities. All involved in higher education have an opportunity to support others as they encounter the challenges presented in this chapter. According to our analysis, these challenges remain over time and appear to be pervasive in the social fabric of the academy. We must dissipate these barriers by helping faculty, staff, and students understand the nature of the barriers across contexts, as discussed in the literature, that impede the progress of potential and current faculty of color. By understanding challenges, supports, and recommendations described across single studies, there is an opportunity to develop strategies applicable in the contexts described here (departmental, institutional, and national) that can contribute to the creation of a more welcoming and affirming academic environment for faculty of color.

TABLE 43

Methodological Approaches and the Study of Faculty of Color

5-year Increment	Methodological Approach
1988–1992	Interviews, surveys/questionnaires
1993–1997	Interviews, multiple qualitative methods,[a] surveys/questionnaires
1998–2002	Interviews, surveys/questionnaires, large data set(s), observations/interviews
2003–2007	Interviews, surveys/questionnaires, large data set(s)

[a] Multiple qualitative methods: archival/document analysis combined with the usage of interviews and/or observations.

TABLE 44

Emerging Issues

5-year Increment	Emerging Issues
1988–1992	Intersection of gender, lack of diversity, job satisfaction
1993–1997	Socialization process, strategies for diversification, mentorship, lack of diversity, isms, tenure & promotion, isolation/marginalization
1998–2002	Intersection of gender, different ways of knowing, stress & coping, job satisfaction, myths, service
	Lack of diversity, recruitment & retention, isms, tokenism, bias in hiring, tenure & promotion, isolation/marginalization, affirmative action/legal issues
2003–2007	Scholarly contributions, teaching & pedagogy, job satisfaction, resiliency, mentorship, STEM fields
	Health fields, service, lack of diversity, recruitment & retention, isms, tokenism
	Bias in hiring, isolation/marginalization, tenure & promotion
	Affirmative action/legal issues

References

Asterisks denote references included in the literature review/synthesis.

*Adams, K., & Bargerhuff, M. E. (2005). Dialogue and action: Addressing recruitment of diverse faculty in one Midwestern university's college of education and human services. *Education, 125,* 539–545.

*Aguirre, A. (2000). Women and minority faculty in the academic workplace: Recruitment, retention, and academic culture. *ASHE-ERIC Higher Education Report, 27*(6).

*Aguirre, A. (2005). The personal narrative as academic storytelling: A Chicano's search for presence and voice in academe. *International Journal of Qualitative Studies in Education, 18,* 147–163.

*Aguirre, A., & Martinez, R. O. (1993). *Chicanos in higher education: Issues and dilemmas for the 21st century* (ASHE-ERIC Higher Education Report No. 3). Washington, DC: ERIC Clearinghouse on Higher Education, George Washington University, in cooperation with the Association for the Study of Higher Education.

*Aguirre, A., Martinez, R., & Hernández, A. (1993). Majority and minority faculty perceptions in academe. *Research in Higher Education, 34,* 371–385.

*Akins, D. (1997). *The economics of tenure: Understanding the effects of ethnicity, status and discipline on faculty attitude, workload and productivity.* Unpublished doctoral dissertation, University of Southern California.

*Alemán, A. M. M., & Renn, K. A. (Eds.). (2002). *Women in higher education: An encyclopedia.* Santa Barbara, CA: ABC-CLIO.

*Alexander-Snow, M., & Johnson, B. J. (1999). Perspectives from faculty of color. In R. J. Menges (Ed.), *Faculty in new jobs: A guide to settling in, becoming established, and building institutional support* (pp. 88–117). San Francisco: Jossey-Bass.

*Alex-Assensoh, Y. (2003). Race in the academy: Moving beyond diversity and toward the incorporation of faculty of color in predominately white colleges and universities. *Journal of Black Studies, 34,* 12–27.

*Alex-Assenoh, Y. M., Givens, T., Golden, K., Hutchings, V. L., Wallace, S. L., & Whitby, K. J. (2005). Mentoring and African-American political scientists. *Political Science and Politics, 38,* 283–285.

*Alger, J. R. (1999). When color-blind is color-bland: Ensuring faculty diversity in higher education. *Stanford Law & Policy Review, 10,* 191–204.

*Alger, J. R. (2000). How to recruit and promote minority faculty: Start by playing fair. *Black Issues in Higher Education, 17,* 160–163.

Alger, J. R., & Carrasco, G. P. (1997, August). *The role of faculty in achieving and retaining a diverse student population.* Paper presented at the AACRAO Policy Summit, Denver, CO.

*Alger, J. R., Chapa, J., Gudeman, R. H., Marin, P., Maruyama, G., Milem, J. F., et al. (2000). *Does diversity make a difference? Three research studies on diversity in college classrooms.* Washington, DC: American Council on Education & the American Association of University Professors.

*Alicea-Lugo, B. (1998). Salsa y adobo: Latino/Latina contributions to theological education. *Union Seminary Quarterly Review, 52,* 129–144.

antonio, a. l. (2000). Faculty of color and scholarship transformed: New arguments for diversifying faculty. *Diverse Digest, 3*(2), 6–7.

*antonio, a. l. (2002). Faculty of color reconsidered: Reassessing contributions to scholarship. *Journal of Higher Education, 73,* 582–602.

*antonio, a. l. (2003). Diverse student bodies, diverse faculties: The success or failure of ambitions to diversify faculty can depend on the diversity of student bodies. *Academe, 89*(6). Retrieved January 6, 2008, from http://www.aaup.org/AAUP/pubsres/academe/2003/ND/Feat/anto.htm?PF=1

*Arnold, J. (2006). *Moving beyond access: Institutionalizing best practices for the inclusion of underrepresented faculty and administrators.* Unpublished doctoral dissertation, University of Pennsylvania, Philadelphia.

*Ashraf, J., & Shabbir, T. (2006). Are there racial differences in faculty salaries? *Journal of Economics and Finance, 30,* 306–316.

*Assensoh, A. B. (2003). Trouble in the promised land: African American studies programs and the challenges of incorporation. *Journal of Black Studies, 34,* 52–62.

*Astin, A. W. (1992). The unrealized potential of American higher education. *Innovative Higher Education, 17,* 95–114.

*Astin, A. W., & Astin, H. S. (1999). *Meaning and spirituality in the lives of college faculty: A study of values, authenticity, and stress.* Los Angeles: University of California, Higher Education Research Institute.

*Astin, H. S., antonio, a. l., Cress, C. M., & Astin, A. W. (1997). *Race and ethnicity in the American professoriate, 1995–1996.* Los Angeles: University of California, Higher Education Research Institute.

*Awe, C. (2001). *The socialization of junior tenure-track faculty members in research universities.* Unpublished doctoral dissertation, University of Illinois, Urbana–Champaign.

*Baez, B. (1997). *How faculty of color construct the promotion and tenure process.* Unpublished doctoral dissertation, Syracuse University.

*Baez, B. (2000). Race-related service and faculty of color: Conceptualizing critical agency in academe. *Higher Education, 39,* 363–391.

*Baez, B. (2002). *Affirmative action, hate speech, and tenure: Narratives about race, law, and the academy.* Independence, KY: Routledge Falmer.

*Baez, B. (2003). Outsiders within? *Academe, 89*(4). Retrieved January 6, 2008, from http://www.aaup.org/AAUP/pubsres/academe/2003/JA/Feat/baez.htm

*Barnett, E., Gibson, M., & Black, P. (2003). Proactive steps to successfully recruit, retain, and mentor minority educators: Issues in education. *Journal of Early Education and Family Review, 10*(3), 18–28.

*Basri, G., Boechat, M. I., Island, E., Ledesma, M., Oakley, J., Pitts, L., et al. (2007). *Study group on university diversity: Overview report to the regents.* Oakland: Office of the President, University of California. Retrieved January 8, 2008, from http://www.universityofcalifornia.edu/news/2007/diversityreport0907.pdf

*Benjamin, L. (Ed.). (1997). *Black women in the academy: Promises and perils.* Gainesville: University Press of Florida.

*Bensimon, E. M., & Tierney, W. G. (1996). *Promotion and tenure: Community and socialization in academe.* Albany: State University of New York Press.

*Bensimon, E. M., Ward, K., & Sanders, K. (2000). *The department chair's role in developing new faculty into teachers and scholars.* Boston: Anker.

*Beutel, A. M., & Nelson, D. J. (2006). The gender and race-ethnicity of faculty in top social science research departments. *Social Science Journal, 43,* 111–125.

*Blackburn, R. T., & Lawrence, J. H. (1995). *Faculty at work: Motivation, expectation, satisfaction.* Baltimore: Johns Hopkins University Press.

*Blackshire-Belay, C. (1998). Under attack: The status of minority faculty members in the academy. *Academe, 84*(4), 30–36.

Bland, C. J., Meurer, L., & Maldonado, G. (1995). A systematic approach to conducting a non-statistical meta-analysis of research literature. *Academic Medicine, 70,* 642–653.

*Bower, B. L. (2002). Campus life for faculty of color: Still strangers after all these years? *New Directions for Community Colleges, 118,* 79–88.

*Bowser, B. P., Auletta, G. S., & Jones, T. (1993). *Confronting diversity issues on campus.* Newbury Park, CA: Sage.

*Bradley, C. (2005). The career experiences of African American women faculty: Implications for counselor education programs. *College Student Journal, 39,* 518–527.

*Brayboy, B. M. J. (2003). The implementation of diversity in predominantly White colleges and universities. *Journal of Black Studies, 34,* 72–86.

*Brown, O. G., Hinton, K. G., & Howard-Hamilton, M. (Eds.). (2007). *Unleashing suppressed voices on college campuses: Diversity issues in higher education.* New York: Peter Lang.

*Burden, J. W., Harrison, L., & Hodge, S. R. (2005). Perceptions of African American faculty in kinesiology-based programs at predominantly White American institutions of higher education. *Research Quarterly for Exercise and Sport, 76,* 224–237.

*Butner, B. K., Burley, H., & Marbley, A. F. (2000). Coping with the unexpected: Black faculty at predominantly White institutions. *Journal of Black Studies, 30,* 453–462.

*Buttner, E., Holly, L., Kevin, B., & Billings-Harris, L. (2007). Impact of leader racial attitude on ratings of causes and solutions for an employee of color shortage. *Journal of Business Ethics, 73,* 129–144.

*Carmen, F. (1999). *In their own voice: The experiences of counselor educators of color in academe.* Unpublished doctoral dissertation, University of New Mexico.

*Carnes, M., Handelsman, J., & Sheridan, J. (2005). Diversity in academic medicine: The stages of change model. *Journal of Women's Health, 14,* 471–475.

*Carr, P. L., Palepu, A., Szalacha, L., Caswell, C., & Inui, T. (2007). "Flying below the radar": A qualitative study of minority experience and management of discrimination in academic medicine. *Medical Education, 41,* 601–609.

*Castellanos, J., & Jones, L. (Eds.). (2003). *The majority in the minority: Expanding the representation of Latina/o faculty, administrators and students in higher education.* Herndon, VA: Stylus.

*Chapman, B. G. (2001). *Minority faculty recruitment in community colleges: Commitment, attitudes, beliefs, and perceptions of chief academic officers.* Unpublished doctoral dissertation, University of Texas at Austin.

*Chesler, M. A., Lewis, A., & Crowfoot, J. (2005). *Challenging racism in higher education: Promoting justice.* Lanham, MD: Rowman & Littlefield.

*Cho, S. (2002). Confronting the myths: Asian Pacific American faculty in higher education. In C. S. V. Turner, a. l. antonio, M. García, B. Laden, A. Nora, & C. Presley (Eds.), *Racial & ethnic diversity in higher education* (2nd ed.; pp. 169–184). Boston: Pearson Custom.

Christian-Smith, L. K., & Kellor, K. S. (Eds.). (1999). *Everyday knowledge and uncommon truths: Women of the academy.* Boulder, CO: Westview Press.

*Chused, R. H. (1988). The hiring and retention of minorities and women on American law school faculties. *University of Pennsylvania Law Review, 137,* 537–569.

*Clark, R. L. (2006). *Recruitment and retention of faculty of color in Oklahoma.* Unpublished doctoral dissertation, Oklahoma State University.

*Clark-Louque, A. R. (1996). *The participation of minorities in higher education.* Unpublished doctoral dissertation, Pepperdine University.

*Colby, A., & Foote, E. (1995). *Creating and maintaining a diverse faculty* (ERIC Document Reproduction Service No. Ed. 386 261). Los Angeles: ERIC Clearinghouse for Community Colleges. Retrieved January 6, 2008, from http://www.ericdigests.org/1996–2/diverse.html

*Cole, S., & Barber, E. G. (2003). *Increasing faculty diversity: The occupational choices of high-achieving minority students.* Cambridge, MA: Harvard University Press.

*Cook, B. J., & Córdova, D. I. (2006). *Minorities in higher education 2006: Twenty-second annual status report.* Washington, DC: American Council on Education.

*Cooper, J. E., & Stevens, D. D. (Eds.). (2002). *Tenure in the sacred grove: Issues and strategies for women and minority faculty.* Albany: State University of New York Press.

*Cora-Bramble, D. (2006). Minority faculty recruitment, retention and advancement: Applications of a resilience–based theoretical framework. *Journal of Health Care for the Poor and Underserved, 17,* 251–255.

*Cowan, L. Y. (2006). *An examination of policies and programs used to increase ethnic and racial diversity among faculty at research universities.* Unpublished doctoral dissertation, University of Illinois at Urbana–Champaign.

*Cross, T. (1994). Black faculty at Harvard: Does the pipeline defense hold water? *Journal of Blacks in Higher Education, 4,* 42–46.

*Cross, T., & Slater, R. (2002). A short list of colleges and universities that are taking measures to increase their number of Black faculty. *Journal of Blacks in Higher Education, 36,* 99–103.

*Cuádraz, G. H. (1992). Experiences of multiple marginality: A case of Chicana scholarship women. *Journal of the Association of Mexican American Educators, Inc, 12,* 31–43.

*Cuádraz, G. H. (1993). *Meritocracy (un)challenged: The making of a Chicano and Chicana professoriate and professional class.* Unpublished doctoral dissertation, University of California, Berkeley.

*Daley, S., Wingard, D. L., & Reznik, V. (2006). Improving the retention of underrepresented minority faculty in academic medicine. *Journal of the National Medical Association, 98,* 1435–1440.

*De la luz Reyes, M., & Halcón, J. J. (1988). Racism in academia: The old wolf revisited. *Harvard Education Review, 58,* 299–314.

*Delgado Bernal, D., & Villalpando, O. (2002). The apartheid of knowledge in the academy: The struggle over "legitimate" knowledge for faculty of color. *Equity & Excellence in Education, 35,* 169–180.

*Delgado-Romero, E. A., Manlove, A. N., Manlove, J. D., & Hernandez, C. A. (2007). Controversial issues in the recruitment and retention of Latino/a faculty. *Journal of Hispanic Higher Education, 6,* 34–51.

*Dixon-Reeves, R. (2003). Mentoring as a precursor to incorporation: An assessment of the mentoring experience of recently minted Ph.D.s. *Journal of Black Studies, 34,* 12–27.

*Essien, V. (2003). Visible and invisible barriers to the incorporation of faculty of color in predominantly White law schools. *Journal of Black Studies, 34,* 63–71.

*Fairbanks, A. R. (2005). *Walking in two worlds: Making professional transitions between native and non-native worlds.* Unpublished doctoral dissertation, University of Minnesota, Minneapolis.

*Fenelon, J. (2003). Race, research, and tenure: Institutional credibility and the incorporation of African, Latino, and American Indian faculty. *Journal of Black Studies, 34,* 87–100.

*Flowers, L. A. (2005). Job satisfaction differentials among African American faculty at 2-year and 4-year institutions. *Community College Journal of Research and Practice, 29,* 317–328.

*Fox, M. J. T. (2005). Voices from within: Native American faculty and staff on campus. *New Directions for Student Services, 109*(1), 49–59.

*Frierson, Jr., H. T. (1990). The situation of Black educational researchers: Continuation of a crisis. *Educational Researcher, 19*(2), 12–17.

*García, A. (2005). Counter stories of race and gender: Situating experiences of Latinas in the academy. *Latino Studies, 3,* 261–273.

*García, M. (Ed.). (2000). *Succeeding in an academic career: A guide for faculty of color.* Westport, CT: Greenwood Press.

*Ginorio, A. B. (1995). *Warming the climate for women in academic science.* Washington, DC: Association of American Colleges & Universities.

*González, C. M. (2002). *The Latina/o faculty: A perilous journey to the ivory tower in higher education.* Unpublished doctoral dissertation, Arizona State University, Tempe.

*González, C. (2007). Building sustainable power: Latino scholars and academic leadership positions at U.S. institutions of higher learning. *Journal of Hispanic Higher Education, 6,* 157–162.

*González, J. C. (2007a). Expanding our thinking of resiliency from K–12 to higher education: Resolute experiences of academic Latinas. In D. M. Davis (Ed.), *Resiliency reconsidered: Policy implications of the resiliency movement* (pp. 103–122). Charlotte, NC: Information Age.

*González, J. C. (2007b). Surviving the doctorate and thriving as faculty: Latina junior faculty reflecting on their doctoral studies experiences. *Equity & Excellence in Education, 40,* 291–300.

*Gonzalez, K. P., & Padilla, R. V. (2007). *Doing the public good: Latina/o scholars engage civic participation.* Sterling, VA: Stylus.

*González, M. C. (1995). In search of the voice I always had. In R. V. Padilla & R. Chávez Chavez (Eds.), *The leaning ivory tower: Latino professors in American universities* (pp. 77–90). Albany: State University of New York Press.

Gooden, J. S., Leary, P. A., & Childress, R. B. (1994). Initiating minorities into the professoriate: One school's model. *Innovative Higher Education, 18,* 243–253.

Google Scholar. (2007). *About Google Scholar.* Accessed on January 7, 2008, from http://scholar.google.com/intl/en/scholar/about.html

*Granger, M. W. (1993). A review of the literature on the status of women and minorities in higher education. *Journal of School Leadership, 3,* 121–135.

*Gregory, S. (1995). *Black women in the academy: The secrets to success and achievement.* New York: University Press of America.

*Gregory, S. T. (2001). Black faculty women in the academy: History, status, and future. *Journal of Negro Education, 70,* 124–138.

*Greiner, K., & Girardi, A. G. (2007). *Student and faculty ethnic diversity report* (Eric Reproduction Document Number 495714). Des Moines, IA: Iowa College Student Aid Commission. Retrieved December 23, 2007, from http://www.eric.ed.gov/ERICDocs/data/ericdocs2sql/content_storage_01/0000019b/80/28/03/f9.pdf

Grutter v. Bollinger. (2003). 539 U.S. 306.

*Guang-Lea, L., & Louis, J. (2006). Successful multicultural campus: Free from prejudice toward minority professors. *Multicultural Education, 14*(1), 27–30.

*Guiffrida, D. (2005). Othermothering as a framework for understanding African American students' definitions of student-centered faculty. *Journal of Higher Education, 76,* 701–723. Retrieved January 6, 2008, from https://dspace.lib.rochester.edu/retrieve/7328/ bs0.pdf

*Gumataotao-Lowe, C. S. N. (1995). *Institutional racism in higher education: Perceptions of people of color.* Unpublished doctoral dissertation, University of Washington.

*Hagedorn, L. S., Chi, W. Y., Cepeda, R. M., & McLain, M. (2007). An investigation of critical mass: The role of Latino representation in the success of urban community college students. *Research in Higher Education, 4,* 73–91.

*Hall, D. M. (2006). *Keeping hope alive: Retention of faculty of color at traditionally White four-year colleges and universities.* Unpublished doctoral dissertation, Illinois State University.

*Hamlet, J. D. (1999). Giving the sistuhs their due: The lived experiences of African American women in academia. In T. McDonald & T. Ford-Ahmed (Eds.), *Nature of a sistuh: Black women's lived experiences in contemporary culture* (pp. 11–26). Durham, NC: Carolina Academic Press.

*Harris, T. M. (2007). Black feminist thought and cultural contracts: Understanding the intersection and negotiation of racial, gendered, and professional identities in the academy. *New Directions for Teaching and Learning, 110*, 55–64.

*Harvey, W. B., & Valadez, J. (Eds.). (1994). Creating and maintaining a diverse faculty [Special issue]. *New Directions for Community Colleges, 22*(3). Retrieved January 6, 2008, from http://www.eric.ed.gov/ERICDocs/data/ericdocs2sql/content_storage_01/0000019b/80/13/72/82.pdf

*Hassouneh, D. (2006). Anti-racist pedagogy: Challenges faced by faculty of color in predominantly White schools of nursing. *Journal of Nursing Education, 45*, 255–262.

*Hayden, R. E. (1997). *Faculty affirmative action: A case study of underrepresented faculty at the University of California, Irvine.* Unpublished doctoral dissertation, University of California, Irvine.

*Hendricks, F. M. (1996). *Career experiences of Black women faculty at research I universities.* Unpublished doctoral dissertation, University of Missouri–Columbia.

*Hendrix, K. G. (2007). "She must be trippin": The secret of disrespect from students of color toward faculty of color. *New Directions for Teaching and Learning, 110*, 85–96.

*Hernández, E. I., & Davis, K. G. (2001). The national survey of Hispanic theological education. *Journal of Hispanic/Latino Theology, 8*, 37–58.

*Hill-Brisbane, D. A., & Dingus, J. E. (2007). Black women teacher educators: Creating enduring afriographies as leaders and change makers. *Advancing Women in Leadership, 22*(1). Retrieved December 30, 2007, from http://www.advancing-women.com/awl/winter2007/Hill.htm

*Holcomb-McCoy, C., & Addison-Bradley, C. (2005). African American counselor educators' job satisfaction and perceptions of departmental racial climate. *Counselor Education and Supervision, 45*(1), 2–15.

*Holland, G. (1995). *The effects of mentoring experiences on the retention of African-American faculty at four-year colleges and universities.* Unpublished doctoral dissertation, Illinois State University.

*Horton, H. W. (2000). Perspectives on the current status of the racial climate relative to students, staff, and faculty of color at predominantly White colleges/universities in America. *Equity & Excellence in Education, 33*(3), 35–37.

*Hune, S. (1998). *Asian Pacific American women in higher education: Claiming visibility and voice.* Washington, DC: Association of American Colleges & Universities.

*Hune, S., & Chan, K. S. (1997). *Special focus: Asian Pacific American demographic and educational trends: Fifteenth annual status report.* Washington, DC: American Council on Education.

*Hurtado, S., Milem, J., Clayton-Pedersen, A., & Allen, W. (1999). *Enacting diverse learning environments: Improving the climate for racial/ethnic diversity in higher education* (ASHE-ERIC Higher Education Report No. 26–8). Washington, DC: George Washington University, School of Education & Human Development.

Inspiration Software. (2007). Available at http://www.inspiration.com/

*Isaac, E. P., & Boyer, P. G. (2007). Voices of urban and rural community college minority faculty: Satisfaction and opinions. *Community College Journal of Research and Practice, 31*, 359–369.

Jackson, J. F. L., & Phelps, L. A. (2004). Diversity in the two-year college academic workforce. *New Directions for Community Colleges, 127*, 79–88.

*Jackson, K. W. (1991). Black faculty in academia. In P. G. Altbach & K. Lomotey (Eds.), *The racial crisis in American higher education* (pp. 135–148). Albany: State University of New York Press.

*Jacobs, L., Cintrón, J., & Canton, C. E. (2002). *The politics of survival in academia: Narratives of inequity, resilience, and success.* Lanham, MD: Rowman & Littlefield.

*Johnson, B. J., & Harvey, W. (2002). The socialization of Black college faculty: Implications for policy and practice. *Review of Higher Education, 25*, 297–314.

*Johnson, B. J., & Pichon, H. (2007). The status of African American faculty in the academy: Where do we go from here? In J. F. L. Jackson (Ed.) *Strengthening the African American educational pipeline: Informing research, policy, and practice* (pp. 97–114). Albany: State University of New York Press.

*Johnson, C. (2001). *The tenure process and five minority faculty members.* Unpublished doctoral dissertation, University of Nebraska–Lincoln.

*Johnson, D. R. (2006). *The hiring process: The Black experience in a community college search committee.* Unpublished doctoral dissertation, University of Texas at Austin.

*Johnson, K. (2003). *Encouraging the heart: How three University of California institutions responded to minority faculty recruitment after the implementation of Proposition 209.* Unpublished doctoral dissertation, Pepperdine University.

*Johnson, W. J. (1996). *A qualitative study of the factors affecting the recruitment and retention of African American faculty in Minnesota community colleges.* Unpublished doctoral dissertation, University of Minnesota, Twin Cities Campus.

*Johnsrud, L. K. (1994). Enabling the success of junior faculty women through mentoring. In M. A. Wunsch (Ed.), *Mentoring revisited: Making an impact on individuals and institutions* (pp. 53–64). San Francisco: Jossey-Bass.

*Johnsrud, L. K., & Sadao, K. C. (1998). The common experience of "otherness": Ethnic and racial minority faculty. *Review of Higher Education, 21,* 315–342.

*Johnston, G. H. (1997). *Piecing together the "mosaic called diversity": One community college's on-going experience with hiring a more diverse faculty.* Unpublished doctoral dissertation, University of Illinois at Urbana–Champaign.

*Jones, L. (Ed.). (2000). *Brothers of the academy: Up and coming Black scholars earning our way in higher education.* Sterling, VA: Stylus.

*Jones, L. (Ed.). (2001). *Retaining African Americans in higher education: Challenging paradigms for retaining students, faculty and administrators.* Herndon, VA: Stylus.

*Jones, L. (Ed.). (2002). *Making it on broken promises: African American male scholars confront the culture of higher education.* Herndon, VA: Stylus.

*Jordan, D. (2006). *Sisters in science: Conversations with Black women scientists about race, gender, and their passion for science.* West Lafayette, IN: Purdue University Press.

*Kauper, M. W. (1991). *Factors which influence the career decisions of minority faculty at a predominately White liberal arts institution: A case study.* Unpublished doctoral dissertation, Indiana University Bloomington.

*Kayes, P. E. (2006). New paradigms for diversifying faculty and staff in higher education: Uncovering cultural biases in the search and hiring process. *Multicultural Education, 14,* 65–69.

*Kirkpatrick, L. (2001). *Multicultural strategies for community colleges: Expanding faculty diversity.* Washington, DC: ERIC Clearinghouse for Community Colleges.

*Knowles, M. F., & Harleston, B. W. (1997). *Achieving diversity in the professoriate: Challenges and opportunities.* Washington, DC: American Council on Education.

*Kosoko-Lasaki, O., Sonnino, R. E., & Voytko, M. L. (2006). Mentoring for women and underrepresented minority faculty and students: Experience at two institutions of higher education. *Journal of the National Medical Association, 98,* 1449–1459.

*Laden, B. V., & Hagedorn, L. S. (2000). Job satisfaction among faculty of color in academe: Individual survivors or institutional transformers? *New Directions for Institutional Research, 27*(1), 57–66.

*Lasalle, L. A. (1995). *Racing the professoriate: The socialization of faculty of color.* Unpublished doctoral dissertation, Pennsylvania State University, State College.

*Lewellen-Williams, C., Johnson, V. A., Deloney, L. A., Thomas, B. R., Goyol, A., & Henry-Tillman, R. (2006). The pod: A new model for mentoring underrepresented minority faculty. *Academic Medicine, 81,* 275–279.

*Light, P. (1994). "Not like us": Removing the barriers to recruiting minority faculty. *Journal of Policy Analysis and Management, 13,* 164–180.

*Lindsay, B. (1991). Public and higher education policies influencing African-American women. In G. P. Kelly, & S. Slaughter (Eds.), *Women's higher education in comparative perspective* (pp. 85–102). Boston: Kluwer Academic.

*Loder, T. L., Sims, M. J., Collins, L., Brooks, M., Voltz, D., Calhoun, C., & Coker, A. D. (2007). On becoming and being faculty-leaders in urban education and also being African-American . . . Seems promising. *Advancing Women in Leadership Online Journal, 22*(1). Retrieved January 8, 2008, from http://www.advancingwomen .com/awl/winter2007/Loder.htm

*Louis, R. (2007). Can you hear us now? Voices from the margin: Using indigenous methodologies in geographic research. *Geographic Research, 45,* 130–139.

*MacLachlan, A. J. (2006). *Developing graduate students of color for the professoriate in science, technology, engineering and mathematics (STEM).* Berkeley, CA: Center for Studies in Higher Education. Retrieved December 24, 2007, from http://eric.ed.gov/ERICDocs/data/ericdocs2sql/content_storage_01/0000019b/80/29/de/c7.pdf

*Maher, F. A., & Tetreault, M. K. T. (2007). *Privilege and diversity in the academy.* New York: Routledge.

*Marbley, A. F. (2007). Finding my voice: An African-American female professor at a predominantly White university. *Advancing Women in Leadership Online Journal, 22.* Retrieved January 11, 2008, from http://www.advancingwomen.com/awl/winter2007/finding_my_voice.htm

*Maturana, I. M. (2005). *Factors in the search process that contribute to the recruitment and hiring of faculty of color.* Unpublished doctoral dissertation, University of Massachusetts at Boston.

*McKenzie, M. M. (2002). Labor above and beyond the call: A Black woman scholar in the academy. In S. Harley & The Black Women and Work Collective (Eds.), *Sister circle: Black women and work* (pp. 231–253). New Brunswick, NJ: Rutgers University Press.

*McLean, C. A. (2007). Establishing credibility in the multicultural classroom: When the instructor speaks with an accent. *New Directions for Teaching and Learning, 110,* 15–24.

*Medina, C., & Luna, G. (2000). Narratives from Latina professors in higher education. *Anthropology & Education Quarterly, 31,* 47–66.

*Mickelson, R. A., & Oliver, M. L. (1991). Making the short list: Black candidates and the faculty recruitment process. In P. A. Altbach & K. Lomotey (Eds.), *The racial crisis in American higher education* (pp. 149–166). Albany: State University of New York Press.

*Milem, J. F., & Astin, H. S. (1993). The changing composition of the faculty: What does it really mean for diversity? *Change, 25*(2), 21–27.

*Millett, C. M., & Nettles, M. T. (2006). Expanding and cultivating the Hispanic STEM doctoral workforce: Research on doctoral student experiences. *Journal of Hispanic Higher Education, 5,* 258–287.

*Mitchell, D. A., & Lassiter, S. (2006). Addressing health care disparities and increasing workforce diversity: The next step for the dental, medical, and public health professions. *American Journal of Public Health, 96,* 2093–2097.

*Mitchell, R., & Rosiek, J. (2006). Professor as embodied racial signifier: A case study of the significance of race in a university classroom. *Review of Education, Pedagogy and Cultural Studies, 28,* 395–409.

*Moody, C. D. (1988). Strategies for improving the representation of minority faculty in research universities. *Peabody Journal of Education, 66*(1), 77–90.

*Moody, J. (2004). *Faculty diversity: Problems and solutions.* New York: Routledge.

*Moradi, B., & Neimeyer, G. J. (2005). Diversity in the ivory White tower: A longitudinal look at faculty race/ethnicity in counseling psychology academic training programs. *Counseling Psychologist, 33,* 655–675.

*Morell-Thon, C. (1998). *Job satisfaction of Hispanic faculty in higher education.* Unpublished doctoral dissertation, University of Virginia.

*Moreno, J. F., Smith, D. G., Clayton-Pedersen, A. R., Parker, S., & Teraguchi, D. H. (2006). *The revolving door for underrepresented minority faculty in higher education: An analysis from the campus diversity initiative.* Washington, DC: Association of American Colleges & Universities.

*Morris, C. A. (2000). *Strategies for recruitment and retention of faculty of color in community colleges.* Unpublished doctoral dissertation, University of Texas at Austin.

*Moses, Y. T. (1989). *Black women in academe: Issues and strategies.* Washington, DC: Association of American Colleges & Universities.

*Moss, L. E. T. (2000). *Recruitment, retention, and mentoring of female and minority faculty in higher education.* Unpublished doctoral dissertation, Arkansas State University.

*Moule, J. (2005). Implementing a social justice perspective in teacher education: Invisible burden for faculty of color. *Teacher Education Quarterly, 32*(4), 23–42.

*Myers, S. L., Jr., & Turner, C. S. V. (2001). Affirmative action retrenchment and labor market outcomes for African-American faculty. In B. Lindsay & M. J. Justiz (Eds.), *The quest for equity in higher education: Toward new paradigms in an evolving affirmative action era* (pp. 63–98). Albany: State University of New York Press.

*Myers, S. L., Jr., & Turner, C. S. V. (2004). The effects of Ph.D. supply on minority faculty representation. *American Economic Review, 94,* 296–301.

*Nelson, D. J., Brammer, C. N., & Rhoads, H. (2007). *A national analysis of minorities in science and engineering faculties at research universities.* Arlington, VA: National Science Foundation. Retrieved January 10, 2008, from http://cheminfo.chem.ou.edu/~djn/diversity/Faculty_Tables_FY07/07Report.pdf

*Nevarez, C., & Borunda, R. (2004). *Faculty of color: Contesting the last frontier.* Sacramento, CA: Serna Center. Retrieved December 3, 2007, from http://www.csus.edu/sernacenter/assets/scholar_reports/nevarez_borunda.pdf

*Niemann, Y. F. (1999). The making of a token: A case study of stereotype threat, stigma, racism, and tokenism in academe. *Frontiers: A Journal of Women Studies, 20,* 111–134.

*Niemann, Y. F. (2003). The psychology of tokenism: Psychosocial realities of faculty of color. In G. Bernal., J. E. Trimble, A. K. Burlew, & F. T. L. Leong (Eds.), *Handbook of racial and ethnic minority psychology* (pp. 100–118). Thousand Oaks, CA: Sage.

*Niemann, Y. F., & Dovidio, J. F. (2005). Affirmative action and job satisfaction: Understanding underlying processes. *Journal of Social Issues, 61,* 507–523.

*Nieves-Squires, S. (1991). *Hispanic women: Making their presence on campus less tenuous.* Washington, DC: Association of American Colleges and Universities.

Number of full-time faculty members by sex, rank, and racial and ethnic group, fall 2005. (2007–2008). In *Chronicle of higher education: The 2007–08 almanac* (Vol. 54, p. 24). Retrieved January 9, 2007, from http://chronicle.com/weekly/almanac/2007/nation/0102402.htm

*Olivas, M. A. (1988). Latino faculty at the border: Increasing numbers key to more Hispanic access. *Change, 20*(3), 6–9.

*Opp, R. D., & Gosetti, P. P. (2002). Women full-time faculty of color in 2-year colleges: A trend and predictive analysis. *Community College Journal of Research and Practice, 26,* 609–627.

*Opp, R., & Smith, A. (1994). Effective strategies for enhancing minority faculty recruitment. *Community College Journal of Research and Practice, 18,* 147–163.

*Owino, A. Z. (2000). *An investigation of the hiring trends of women and minority faculty in institutions of higher learning.* Unpublished doctoral dissertation, Pennsylvania State University, State College.

*Padilla, A. M. (1994). Ethnic minority scholars, research, and mentoring: Current and future issues. *Educational Researcher, 23*(4), 24–27.

*Padilla, R. V., & Chávez Chavez, R. (1995). *The leaning ivory tower: Latino professors in American universities.* Albany: State University of New York Press.

Patterson, B. L., Thorne, S. E., Canam, C., & Jillings, C. (2001). *Meta-study of qualitative health research: A practical guide to meta-analysis and meta-synthesis.* Thousand Oaks, CA: Sage.

*Peoples, III, R. (2004). *Recruitment of minority faculty: A comparison of attitudes, beliefs, perceptions, commitments, and strategies of Texas administrators in selected community colleges.* Unpublished doctoral dissertation, Baylor University.

*Pepion, K. (1993). *Ideologies of excellence: Issues in the evaluation, promotion, and tenure of minority faculty.* Unpublished doctoral dissertation, University of Arizona.

*Pérez, E. T. (2001). *Negotiating tenure and promotion: An examination of legitimate scholarship productions, academic ambassadors and institutional dislocation of Latina/o professors in the midwest.* Unpublished doctoral dissertation, University of Nebraska.

*Perna, L. W. (2003). The status of women and minorities among community college faculty. *Research in Higher Education, 44,* 205–240.

*Perna, L., Gerald, D., Baum, E., & Milem, J. (2007). The status of equity for Black faculty and administrators in public higher education in the south. *Research in Higher Education, 48,* 193–228.

*Peterson-Hickey, M. M. (1998). *American Indian faculty experiences: Culture as a challenge and source of strength.* Unpublished doctoral dissertation, University of Minnesota, Twin Cities Campus.

*Piercy, F., Giddings, V., Allen, K., Dixon, B., Meszaros, P., & Joest, K. (2005). Improving campus climate to support faculty diversity and retention: A pilot program for new faculty. *Innovative Higher Education, 30*(1), 53–66.

*Pineda, A. M. (1998). The place of Hispanic theology in a theological curriculum. In P. Casarella & R. Gómez (Eds.), *El cuerpo de Cristo: The Hispanic presence in the U.S. Catholic Church* (pp. 134–154). New York: Crossroads.

*Plata, M. (1996). Retaining ethnic minority faculty at institutions of higher education. *Journal of Instructional Psychology, 23,* 221–227.

*Pollard, D. S. (2006). Women of color and research. In D. S. Pollard & O. M. Welch (Eds.), *From center to margins: The importance of self-definition in research* (pp. 7–20). Albany: State University of New York Press.

*Ponjuan, L. (2005). *Understanding the work lives of faculty of color: Job satisfaction, perception of climate, and intention to leave.* Unpublished doctoral dissertation, University of Michigan.

*Porter, S. R. (2007). A closer look at faculty service: What affects participation on committees? *Journal of Higher Education, 78,* 523–541.

*Price, E. G., Gozu, A., Kern, D. E., Power, N. R., Wand, G. S., Golden, S., & Cooper, L. A. (2005). The role of cultural diversity climate in recruitment, promotion, and retention of faculty in academic medicine. *Journal of General Internal Medicine, 20,* 565–571.

*Pura, R. L. (1993). *An analysis of the minority faculty recruitment strategies at a community college in an urban environment: A case study.* Unpublished doctoral dissertation, University of Texas at Austin.

*Rai, K. B., & Critzer, J. W. (2000). *Affirmative action and the university: Race, ethnicity, and gender in higher education employment.* Lincoln: University of Nebraska Press.

*Rains, F. V. (1995). *Views from within: Women faculty of color in a research university.* Unpublished doctoral dissertation, Indiana University Bloomington.

*Rendón, L. (1996). From the barrio to the academy: Revelations of a Mexican American "scholarship girl." In C. S. V. Turner, M. García, A. Nora, & L. I. Rendón (Eds.), *Racial & ethnic diversity in higher education* (pp. 281–287). Boston: Pearson.

*Rendón, L. I. (2000). Academics of the heart: Maintaining body, soul, and spirit. In M. García (Ed.), *Succeeding in an academic career: A guide for faculty of color* (pp. 141–154). Westport, CT: Greenwood Press.

*Renzulli, L. A., Grant, L., & Kathuria, S. (2006). Race, gender, and the wage gap: Comparing faculty salaries in predominantly White and historically Black colleges and universities. *Gender and Society, 20,* 491–510.

*Reyes, X. A. (2005). Dissonance in the academy: Reflections of a Latina professor. *Latino Studies, 3,* 274–279.

*Reyes, X. A., & Ríos, D. I. (2005). Dialoguing the Latina experiences in higher education. *Journal of Hispanic Higher Education, 4,* 377–391.

*Saavedra, D. E., & Saavedra, M. L. (2007). Women of color teaching students of color: Creating an effective classroom climate through caring, challenging, and consulting. *New Directions for Teaching and Learning, 110,* 73–83.

*Sadao, K. C. (2003). Living in two worlds: Success and the bicultural faculty of color. *Review of Higher Education, 26,* 397–418.

*Sámano, M. L. (2007). *Respecting one's abilities, or (post) colonial tokenism?: Narrative testimonios of faculty of color working in predominantly White community colleges.* Unpublished doctoral dissertation, Oregon State University. Retrieved January 6, 2008, from http://ir.library.oregonstate.edu/dspace/bitstream/1957/5011/1/Samano_Dissertation.pdf

*Sampaio, A. (2006). Women of color teaching political science: Examining the intersections of race, gender, and course material in the classroom. *Political Science and Politics, 39,* 917–922.

*Sánchez, R. M. (2007). *Best practices for recruiting and hiring a diverse workforce: Appendix d-diversity and position descriptions.* Pullman, WA: Washington State University, Center for Human Rights. Retrieved January 8, 2008, from http://www.chr.wsu.edu/Content/Documents/chr/best%20practices%20booklet%209–07%20(2).pdf

Section II: Appointment and promotion. (2002). In University of California academic personnel manual (pp. APM 200–APM 420). Oakland: University of California, Human Resources. Retrieved January 8, 2008, from http://www.ucop.edu/acadadv/acadpers/apm/apm-210.pdf

*Segovia, F. F. (1994). Theological education and scholarship as struggle: The life of racial/ethnic minorities in the profession. *Journal of Hispanic/Latino Theology, 2(2),* 5–25.

*Segura, D. A. (2003). Navigating between two worlds: The labyrinth of Chicana intellectual production in the academy. *Journal of Black Studies, 34,* 28–51.

*Skachkova, P. (2007). Academic careers of immigrant women professors in the U.S. *Higher Education, 53,* 697–738.

*Slater, R. B. (1999). The first Black faculty members at the nation's highest-ranked universities. *Journal of Blacks in Higher Education, 22,* 97–106.

*Smith, D. G. (2000). How to diversify the faculty. *Academe, 86(5),* 48–52. Retrieved January 6, 2008, from http://www.aaup.org/AAUP/pubsres/academe/2000/SO/Feat/smit.htm?PF=1

*Smith, D. G., Turner, C. S. V., Osefi-Kofi, N., & Richards, S. (2004). Interrupting the usual: Successful strategies for hiring diverse faculty. *Journal of Higher Education, 75,* 133–160.

*Smith, D. G., Wolf, L. E., & Busenberg, B. E. (1996). *Achieving faculty diversity: Debunking the myths.* Washington, DC: Association of American Colleges & Universities.

*Smith, E. (1992). *A comparative study of occupation stress in African American and White university faculty.* Lewiston, NY: Edwin Mellen Press.

*Smith, G., & Anderson, K. J. (2005). Students' ratings of professors: The teaching style contingency for Latino/a professors. *Journal of Latinos and Education, 4,* 115–136.

*Smith, J. W., & Calasanti, T. (2005). The influences of gender, race and ethnicity on workplace experiences of institutional and social isolation: An exploratory study of university faculty. *Sociological Spectrum, 25,* 307–334.

*Smith, P. A., & Shoho, A. R. (2007). Higher education trust, rank and race: A conceptual and empirical analysis. *Innovative Higher Education, 32,* 125–138.

*Smith, P. W., Altbach, P. G., & Lomotey, K. (Eds.). (2002). *The racial crisis in American higher education: Continuing challenges for the twenty-first century.* Albany: State University of New York Press.

*Soto-Greene, M. L., Sanchez, J., Churrango, J., & Salas-Lopez, D. (2005). Latino faculty development in U.S. medical schools: A Hispanic center of excellence perspective. *Journal of Hispanic Higher Education, 4,* 366–376.

*Springer, A. (2002). *How to diversify faculty: The current legal landscape.* Washington, DC: American Association of University Professors.

*Springer, A. D. (2004). Legal Watch: Faculty diversity in a brave new world. *Academe, 90*(4). Retrieved January 6, 2008, from http://www.aaup.org/AAUP/pubsres/academe/2004/JA/Col/lw.htm?PF=1

*Stanley, C. A. (2006). Coloring the academic landscape: Faculty of color breaking the silence in predominantly White colleges and universities. *American Educational Research Journal, 43,* 701–736.

*Stanley, C. A. (Ed.). (2007a). *Faculty of color: Teaching in predominantly White colleges and universities.* Bolton, MA: Anker.

*Stanley, C. A. (2007b). When counter narratives meet master narratives in the journal editorial-review process. *Educational Researcher, 36*(1), 14–24.

*Stanley, C. A., & Lincoln, Y. S. (2005). Cross-race faculty mentoring. *Change, 37*(2), 44–50.

*Stanley, J. M., Capers, C. F., & Berlin, L. E. (2007). Changing the face of nursing faculty: Minority faculty recruitment and retention. *Journal of Professional Nursing, 23,* 253–261.

*Stein, W. (1994). The survival of American Indian faculty: Thought and action. *National Education Association Higher Education Journal, 10,* 101–114.

*Subervi, F., & Cantrell, T. H. (2007). Assessing efforts and policies related to the recruitment and retention of minority faculty at accredited and non-accredited journalism and mass communication programs. *Journalism and Mass Communication Educator, 62*(1), 27–46.

*Tack, M., & Patitu, C. L. (1992). *Faculty job satisfaction: Women and minorities in peril* (ASHE-ERIC Higher Education Report No. 4). Washington, DC: George Washington University, School of Education & Human Development.

*Takara, K. W. (2006). A view from the academic edge: One Black woman who is dancing as fast as she can. *Du Bois Review, 3,* 463–470.

*Thomas, G. D., & Hollenshead, C. (2001). Resisting from the margins: The coping strategies of Black women and other women of color faculty members at a research university. *Journal of Negro Education, 70,* 166–175.

*Thompson, C. J., & Dey, E. L. (1998). Pushed to the margins: Sources of stress for African American college and university faculty. *Journal of Higher Education, 69,* 324–345.

*Tierney, W. G., & Rhoads, R. A. (1993). *Faculty socialization as cultural process: A mirror of institutional commitment* (ASHE-ERIC Higher Education Report No. 93–6). Washington, DC: George Washington University, School of Education & Human Development.

*Tippeconnic, III, J. W., & McKinney, S. (2003). Native faculty: Scholarship and development. In M. K. P. Ah Nee-Benham & W. J. Stein (Eds.), *The renaissance of American Indian higher education: Capturing the dream* (pp. 241–256). Mahwah, NJ: Erlbaum.

*Tomlinson, L. L. (2006). *Listening to faculty of color: Diverse experiences on a predominately White campus.* Unpublished doctoral dissertation, Illinois State University.

*Toutkoushian, R. K., Bellas, M. L., & Moore, J. V. (2007). The interaction effects of gender, race, and marital status on faculty salaries. *Journal of Higher Education, 78,* 572–601.

*Townsend-Johnson, L. (2006). *African-American women faculty teaching at institutions of higher-learning in the Pacific Northwest: Challenges, dilemmas, and sustainability.* Unpublished doctoral dissertation, Oregon State University.

*Tuitt, F. A., Sagaria, M. D., & Turner, C. S. V. (2007). Signals and strategies in hiring faculty of color. *Higher Education Handbook of Theory and Research, 22,* 497–535.

*Turner, C. S. V. (2000). New faces, new knowledge: As women and minorities join the faculty, they bring intellectual diversity in pedagogy and in scholarship. *Academe, 86*(5), 34–37.

*Turner, C. S. V. (2002a). *Diversifying the faculty: A guidebook for search committees* (2nd ed.). Washington, DC: Association of American Colleges & Universities.

*Turner, C. S. V. (2002b). Women of color in academe: Living with multiple marginality. *Journal of Higher Education, 73,* 74–93.

*Turner, C. S. V. (2003). Incorporation and marginalization in the academy: From border toward center for faculty of color? *Journal of Black Studies, 34,* 112–125.

Turner, C. S. V. (2006, September 29). Before starting a faculty search, take a good look at the search committee. *Chronicle of Higher Education*, pp. B32, B34.

*Turner, C. S. V., antonio, a. l., García, M., Laden, B. V., Nora, A., & Presley, C. L. (Eds.). (2002). *Racial & ethnic diversity in higher education* (2nd ed.). Boston: Pearson Custom.

*Turner, C. S. V., García, M., Nora, A., & Rendón, L. I. (Eds.). (1996). *Racial & ethnic diversity in higher education*. Needham Heights, MA: Simon & Schuster Custom.

*Turner, C. S. V., & Myers, S. L., Jr. (1997). Faculty diversity and affirmative action. In M. García (Ed.), *Affirmative action's testament of hope: Strategies for a new era in higher education* (pp. 131–148). Albany: State University of New York Press.

*Turner, C. S. V., & Myers, S. L., Jr. (2000). *Faculty of color in academe: Bittersweet success*. Boston: Allyn & Bacon.

*Turner, C. S. V., & Taylor, D. V. (2002). *Keeping our faculties: Addressing the recruitment and retention of faculty of color* (Position paper). Minneapolis: University of Minnesota, Office of the Associate Vice President for Multicultural & Academic Affairs. Retrieved January 6, 2008, from http://www.oma.umn.edu/kof/pdf/kofposition.pdf

*Turner, C. S. V., & Thompson, J. R. (1993). Socialization experiences of minority and majority women doctoral students: Implications for faculty recruitment and retention. *Review of Higher Education, 16*, 355–370.

*TuSmith, B., & Reddy, M. T. (Eds.). (2002). *Race in the college classroom: Pedagogy and politics*. Piscataway, NJ: Rutgers University Press.

Umbach, P. D. (2006). The contribution of faculty of color to undergraduate education. *Research in Higher Education, 47*, 317–345.

*Urrieta, L. Jr., & Méndez Benavídez, L. (2007). Community commitment and activist scholarship: Chicana/o professors and the practice of consciousness. *Journal of Hispanic Higher Education, 6*, 222–236.

*Valladares, S. E. (2007). *Challenges in the tenure process: The experiences of faculty of color who conduct social science, race-based academic work*. Unpublished doctoral dissertation, University of California, Los Angeles.

*Van Ummersen, C. A. (2005). No talent left behind. *Change, 37*(6), 26–31.

Vargas, L. (Ed.). (2002). *Women faculty of color in the White classroom: Narratives on the pedagogical implications of teacher diversity*. New York: Peter Lang.

*Vasquez, M. J. T., Lott, B., García-Vásquez, E., Grant, S. K., Iwamasa, G. Y., Molina, L., et al. (2006). Personal reflections: Barriers and strategies in increasing diversity in psychology. *American Psychologist, 61*, 157–172.

*Waitzkin, H., Yager, J., Parker, T., & Duran, B. (2006). Mentoring partnerships for minority faculty and graduate students in mental health services research. *Academic Psychiatry, 30*, 205–217.

*Weems, R. E., Jr. (2003). The incorporation of Black faculty at predominantly White institutions: A historical and contemporary perspective. *Journal of Black Studies, 34*, 101–111.

*Wheeler, B. G. (1996). True and false: The first in a series of reports from a study of theological school faculty. *Auburn Studies*. Retrieved January 6, 2008, from http://www.auburnsem.org/study/publications_details.asp?nsectionid=2&pageid=3&pubid=4

*Whetsel-Ribeau, P. (2007). *Retention of faculty of color as it relates to their perceptions of the academic climate at four-year predominately White public universities in Ohio*. Unpublished doctoral dissertation, Bowling Green State University.

*Williams, B. N., & Williams, S. M. (2006). Perceptions of African American male junior faculty on promotion and tenure: Implications for community building and social capital. *Teachers College Record, 108*, 287–315.

Williams, D. A., & Wade-Golden, K. C. (2006, April 18). What is a chief diversity officer? *Inside Higher Ed*. Retrieved January 10, 2008, from http://www.insidehighered.com/workplace/2006/04/18/williams

Williams, D. A., & Wade-Golden, K. C. (2007). *The chief diversity officer: A primer for college and university presidents*. Washington, DC: American Council on Education.

*Witt, S. L. (1990). *The pursuit of race and gender equity in American academe*. New York: Praeger.

*Wong, T. M., & Bainer, D. (1991). Ethnic-minority faculty in evangelical Christian colleges: Models in search of an identity. In D. J. Lee., A. L. Nieves., & H. L. Allen (Eds.), *Ethnic-minorities and evangelical Christian colleges* (pp. 239–258). Lanham, MD: University Press of America.

*Yager, J., Waitzkin, H., Parker, T., & Duran, B. (2007). Educating, training, and mentoring minority faculty and other trainees in mental health services research. *Academic Psychiatry, 31*, 146–151.

CHAPTER 17

COLORING THE ACADEMIC LANDSCAPE: FACULTY OF COLOR BREAKING THE SILENCE IN PREDOMINANTLY WHITE COLLEGES AND UNIVERSITIES

CHRISTINE A. STANLEY

This chapter, based on a larger, autoethnographic qualitative research project, focuses on the first-hand experiences of 27 faculty of color teaching in predominantly White colleges and universities. The 27 faculty represented a variety of institutions, disciplines, academic titles, and ranks. They identified themselves as African American, American Indian, Asian, Asian American, Latina/o, Native Pacific Islander, and South African. This chapter reports on the predominant themes of the narratives shared by these faculty of color: teaching, mentoring, collegiality, identity, service, and racism. These themes, consonant with findings from the research literature, can be used to offer suggestions and recommendations for the recruitment and retention of faculty of color in higher education.

It is not difference which immobilizes us, but silence. And there are so many silences to be broken. (Audre Lorde, 1984, p. 44)

There seems to be a growing conspiracy of silence surrounding the experiences of faculty of color teaching in predominantly White colleges and universities. For many faculty of color, who reside throughout the academic landscape, their silenced state is a burdensome cycle that is rarely broken. Only rarely are they asked to speak candidly about their experiences so that we can learn how to develop effective recruitment and retention strategies for diversifying higher education faculties. Many of their White colleagues, too, seem silent even though few are afraid to speak truth to power or stand up for faculty of color when they observe behaviors that are racist, sexist, xenophobic, or homophobic. Why is this, I have often wondered? I posed this nagging question to Joe Feagin, a sociologist and a White antiracist scholar, during a distinguished lecture he gave titled "Black Students Still Face Racism: White Colleges and Universities." His response, without a pause, was "because it costs White folks" (Feagin, 2004). When members of the dominant group speak up, it has tremendous impact because the dynamics of power, positionality, and authority are attributes that can only serve to deepen dialogues and influence policy and decision making on diversity and social justice in our colleges and universities. Conversely, when members of the targeted group speak up, the cost for us is enormous because these same dynamics are not yet equitable. We become at risk for a number of reasons, but a reason that often undergirds the silence is the lack of a critical mass of faculty of color in higher education.

When the silence is broken and faculty of color do choose to speak, many of us are not yet prepared to listen to the narratives. Even more problematic, we often remain unsure what to do with these data. African Americans, Asian Americans, Latina/os, and Native Americans constitute between 20% and 25% of the U.S. population. However, they represent 13.4% of the faculty at degree-granting institutions of higher education (National Center for Education Statistics, 2000). A review of the literature indicates that there are very few publications that focus on the experiences of these individuals in predominantly White colleges and universities (Aguirre, 2000; Alfred, 2001; Banks, 1984; Bowie, 1995; Essien, 2003; Fenelon, 2003; Harvey, 1991, 1994; Johnsrud & Sadao, 1998; Stanley, Porter, Simpson, & Ouellett, 2003; Stein, 1996; Thomas & Hollenshead, 2001; Turner, 2003). According to Blackburn, Wenzel, and Bieber (1994), "higher education institutions, as well as national research centers, need to focus on the experiences of faculty of color if we hope to understand the work environments needed to support creative talents" (p. 280).

In 2002, after 15 years of observing their classrooms, reading the literature, and participating in individual and group consultations about their teaching experiences, it became apparent to me that faculty of color were experiencing the classroom in ways that were unlike those of their majority, White colleagues. After conducting and publishing some preliminary research on African American faculty, particularly faculty at two predominantly White research universities in the South (Stanley et al., 2003), I embarked on another research project. I edited a book, *Faculty of Color: Teaching in Predominantly White Colleges and Universities*, that featured the voices of 27 faculty of color across the country who crafted narratives about their experiences on predominantly White campuses (Stanley, 2006). For many, their narratives have been made to feel silenced for far too long. After reading a draft of this manuscript my colleague, Susan Lynham, a White South African, shared an African proverb with me that captures the importance of individual narratives in breaking silences: "Until lions have their own 'story tellers,' tales of a lion hunt will always glorify the hunter."

The narratives, containing both positive and negative experiences in academia, can serve as tuning forks for faculty and administrators at predominantly White colleges and universities. The purpose of this work is to share the themes from these narratives as well as offer recommendations for individuals and institutions working to recruit and retain faculty of color in higher education. I begin by providing an overview of key issues raised in the literature. I then discuss the methodology, the authors, the theoretical framework, and the data analysis; highlight some of the salient themes from the narratives; and conclude by offering recommendations and implications for further study as well as for institutional change.

Overview of the Literature

The literature on faculty of color teaching in predominantly White colleges and universities seems to be concentrated around four broad, interlocking, yet distinct themes: campus life and climate, tenure and promotion, discrimination, and teaching. It is difficult, as becomes evident in the paragraphs to follow, to separate these themes. National research on faculty of color in predominantly White colleges and universities is rare. One can speculate several reasons why this is the case. First, they represent a small number of overall full-time faculty; second, many scholars of color refrain from participating in such studies because their numbers are so small that they are easily identifiable; third, prior to the 1960s, they were not viewed as an important focus of research; and, finally, these studies are often conducted by faculty of color, and many majority White faculty do not believe that these individuals can be objective when researching their own community. Therefore, research on the experiences of faculty of color is sometimes viewed by traditional, often White scholars as lacking in rigor.

Furthermore, and even more problematic, a belief exists that this research can be validated only with a comparison group of White faculty. The presumption is that we continue to see these issues as binary and that the standard for normality and comparison is White. The sections to follow illustrate that the themes of campus life and climate, tenure and promotion, teaching, and discrimination are critical to our understanding of the experiences of faculty of color in higher education. It is time that we look at the factors contributing to the silence of these individuals and how we can learn from this silence to effectively recruit and retain more diverse faculties.

Campus Life and Climate

Campus life and climate are discussed here in regard to the degree to which faculty of color are comfortable with the culture, habits, decisions, practices, and policies that are part of the academic environment (Aguirre, 2000; Alfred, 2001; Essien, 2003; Harvey, 1991, 1994; Thomas & Hollenshead, 2001; Turner, 2003). Terms such as "marginality," "alienation," "isolation," and "invisibility" are often used in the literature to describe the campus climate for faculty of color as well as their experiences with university life. A subtheme of the general theme of campus life and climate is the phenomenon described by many faculty of color as living in "two worlds," described by some of these individuals as the constant tension of being pulled between their ethnic culture and the university culture (Johnsrud & Sadao, 1998; Sadao, 2003; Segura, 2003). Many have developed coping strategies as a result. One such strategy is "code switching"—the ability to apply "parts of their separate value systems to different situations as appropriate" (Sadao, 2003, p. 410). Studies indicate that faculty of color experience higher levels of occupational stress than White faculty (Bronstein, 1993; Ruffins, 1997; Smith & Witt, 1996). They are "always in the spotlight" (Turner & Myers, 2000) and perceive that they have to "work twice as hard to be treated as equal" (Laden & Hagedorn, 2000). Stress is attributed to teaching, research, and service activities, with the latter two areas being more negatively affected by the nature and perceived load of the activities. For example, many faculty of color spend a great deal of time mentoring students of color. They engage in mentoring because they view this service activity as a way to give back to the community and a chance to effect positive change as role models. Some are looked upon as experts in matters of diversity.

Although many hesitate to serve the university and local communities as "diversity experts," they do so because they know that if they do not, the diversity voice gets lost at the table. Some see this as a natural opportunity to open new lines of research or to use their research to effect change and influence decision making. Ironically, many are sought after only when there is a specific call for diversity—to represent their group and to provide the diversity perspective. It is rare when they are sought after to serve on committees with much larger and what could be considered as more prestigious charges, such as those that affect university policy, governance, finance, curriculum development, and research. Even more troubling is that when they come up for tenure or promotion, these very activities are not given serious weight in the process.

Tenure and Promotion

The process of coming up for tenure is characterized as "hazing" by many faculty of color (Ruffins, 1997). Stories abound in the literature about the hidden or unwritten versus written rules about tenure and promotion. Research on faculty productivity and rate of publication is limited (antonio, 2002; Blackburn et al., 1994; Freeman, 1978). We often hear that faculty of color are not as productive as majority, White faculty, although available research comparing the publication performance of minority and majority faculty indicates no significant differences (Blackburn et al., 1994). In fact, according to Blackburn et al. (1994), the productivity argument needs to be substantiated with more research. In their study of faculty status among African Americans in U.S. higher education, Allen, Epps, Guillory, Suh, and Bonous-Hammarth (2000) stated that we must be cautious of such studies because of the vast difference in the total number of African American faculty and the total number of White faculty on predominantly White campuses.

One particular area of contention in the tenure and promotion literature is the research agendas pursued by some faculty of color and whether these agendas are rewarded in tenure and promotion processes. For example, many faculty of color engage in research that benefits communities of color. Affirmative action, diversity and student outcomes, institutional climate, and culture and ethnicity are just a few of the areas that, without a doubt, benefit most higher education institutions, but research on these topics is not always rewarded in the academy. Furthermore, such research is often viewed as "risky" and not mainstream. This clearly puts faculty of color at a disadvantage in the tenure and promotion process, wherein the most value is often placed on mainstream research. Many continue to feel the anguish of discrimination when behaviors and attitudes on the part of majority White colleagues, students, and staff point to racism, sexism, xenophobia, "Islam phobia," and homophobia.

Many faculty of color lament the fact that they have received very little or no mentoring from senior faculty colleagues. For the ones who have benefited from mentoring, there is no doubt that this experience has enabled their success (Stanley & Lincoln, 2005). Specifically, productive mentor-protégé relationships have been shown to lead to improvements in teaching performance and research productivity (Tillman, 2001). Cross-race faculty mentoring is also helpful for enhancing faculty relationships and administrative skills (Stanley & Lincoln, 2005). Some faculty of color report that they have had to look beyond senior faculty in their department to find mentors elsewhere (Thomas & Hollenshead, 2001). There is some literature emerging on mentoring faculty of color (Frierson, 1997, 1998; Singh & Stoloff, 2003; Tillman, 2001; Verdugo, 1995), but more work needs to be done to ascertain the nature and effectiveness of mentoring relationships.

Discrimination

The wounds of covert and overt racism, sexism, xenophobia, and homophobia run deep for many faculty of color. Discrimination cuts across many areas of the academy such as teaching, research, service, and overall experiences with the campus community. Women faculty of color face additional challenges, including discrimination related to gender as well as race—the double bind syndrome (Alfred, 2001; Bowie, 1995; Bronstein, Rothblum, & Solomon, 1993; Gregory, 2001; Opp & Gosetti, 2002; Phelps, 1995; Singh, Robinson, & Williams-Green, 1995; Thomas & Hollenshead, 2001; Turner, 2002). Female faculty of color are likely to be more engaged in teaching, advising, and committee-related activities than White male or female faculty, and they are often excluded from collaborative research with colleagues (Gregory, 2001).

Many women faculty of color report that they had to sacrifice family and nonacademic commitments for some years while working to establish a career or refrain from participating in these commitments for fear of not achieving tenure and promotion (Turner, 2002). The commitment to community that is honored by many African American, Native American, and Chicano faculty, in particular, is a constant source of frustration (Cross, 1996; de la Luz Reyes & Halcon, 1996; Stein, 1996; Turner, 2002). Many find solace in and among safe spaces such as their family, church, community, and allies who work to develop or understand their experiences in academia.

There is virtually no empirical research on the experiences of women administrators of color in predominantly White colleges and universities (Turner, 2002). This should not come as a surprise, because the numbers of these women are even sparser when one looks at the representation of faculty of color as a whole. The literature on women administrators of color (Chliwniak, 1997; DiCroce, 1995; Gorena, 1996; Opp & Gosetti, 2002; Poplin Gosetti & Opp, 2000; Ramey, 1995; Singh et al., 1995; Warner, 1995) indicates that their experiences are similar to those of women faculty. However, they experience even greater feelings of isolation, lower satisfaction with their professional lives, and more negative treatment by majority White colleagues.

Teaching

Empirical research on the teaching experiences of faculty of color in predominantly White colleges and universities is limited (McGowan, 2000; Stanley et al., 2003). The research that exists on the teaching experiences of faculty of color is largely found in the K–12 setting (see Delpit, 1993; Foster, 1990, 1991, 1994, 1995, 1997; Ladson-Billings & Henry, 1990). Many faculty of color report experiences in as well as outside of the classroom that include challenges to their authority and expertise, negative behaviors and attitudes of students, and complaints being made to senior faculty and administrators about their teaching (Bower, 2002; McGowan, 2000; Stanley et al., 2003; Vargas, 2002). Several studies show that many faculty of color believe they are negatively affected by student evaluations of their teaching (Bower, 2002; Delgado Bernal & Villalpando, 2002; McGowan, 2000; Stanley et al., 2003; Tusmith & Reddy, 2002; Vargas, 2002). In particular, studies indicate that some of the negative comments seem to be directed at faculty of color who work to be inclusive in their teaching efforts (McGowan, 2000; Stanley et al., 2003; Vargas, 2002).

Faculty of color who teach multicultural courses or work to incorporate a multicultural perspective into their courses often face resistance from White students (Stanley et al., 2003; Vargas, 2002). One illustration of such resistance was offered in the narrative of an American Indian faculty member who stated that when she used the example of tribal values to teach about social inequity, students would challenge her in class, expecting her to provide examples using nonmainstream norms (Vargas, 2002). Similar experiences from other faculty of color have been reported in other studies (Stanley et al., 2003).

McGowan (2000), in a study of African American faculty, noted that classroom challenges appear to be age and gender dependent. For example, African American women faculty who are 35 years of age or younger appear to face greater challenges from White female students in their 20s, while those who are 40 years old or older appear to face greater challenges from students in nontraditional age groups. African American male faculty appear to face greater challenges from White male students than African American women faculty.

Methodology

The narrative data included here were derived from a larger qualitative study focusing on the experiences of faculty of color teaching in predominantly White colleges and universities. The quotations and narratives are drawn from *Faculty of Color: Teaching in Predominantly White Colleges and Universities* (Stanley, 2006). The principal goal of the book was to address the need for faculty of color to provide ongoing narratives of their experiences so that predominantly White colleges and universities hiring faculty of color can understand the multiple forms of discrimination, bias, segregation, and unconscious racism these individuals encounter as a part of their daily institutional work.

The narratives were autoethnographic, with chapters solicited from the authors on their personal experiences teaching in predominantly White institutions. Autoethnography is an autobiographical genre of writing that, according to Ellis and Bochner (2000), "make[s] the researcher's own experiences a topic of investigation in [their] own right" (p. 733). Autoethnographers "ask their readers to feel the truth of their stories and to become co-participants, engaging in storyline[s] morally, emotionally, aesthetically, and intellectually" (p. 745). I wanted the contributing authors to frame their experiences in their own terms and within their own personal frames of meaning and experience. I had no previous knowledge of whether or not they used reflexive journaling before they wrote their chapters. I asked the respondents to reflect on two questions as they wrote their chapters: (a) How would you describe your experiences teaching in a predominantly White institution? and (b) What recommendations would you offer to faculty of color and administrators based on these experiences?

The 27 contributing authors were solicited via the snowball sampling technique (Lincoln & Guba, 1985). I relied on referrals through my association with the Professional and Organizational Development Network in Higher Education as well as from participants who recommended others for the book. Autoethnography allowed for contextualization in that it afforded faculty of color an opportunity to relate their life stories, thoughts, feelings, values, and beliefs as they pertained to their experiences as faculty on predominantly White campuses. In addition, it allowed an opportunity for these contributing authors to share personal accounts of their experiences with the majority culture and to express how, in many cases, they have been made to feel "othered" in academia.

About the Contributing Authors

The 27 contributing authors are from the disciplines of business, dentistry, education, engineering, ethnic studies, health education, political science, public policy, psychology, sociology, and speech, language, and hearing science. Two hold the title of lecturer, 7 are assistant professors, 13 are associate professors, and 5 are full professors. In addition, 5 are currently serving in an administrative role such as department chair or assistant dean. Many are the recipients of prestigious university, disciplinary, and national awards such as National Science Foundation career and young investigator awards, awards recognizing outstanding faculty members, college and university distinguished teaching and service awards, and fellowships. Twenty-five of the contributing authors are from research-extensive universities, while 2 are from liberal arts colleges.

The contributing authors also represent an array of social and cultural identities. For example, authors identified themselves as African, African American, American Indian, Asian, Asian American,

Black, Chamorro, Indian, Jamaican, Jewish, Latina/o, Mexican American, Muslim, Native Pacific Islander, Puerto Rican, and South African. Gay and lesbian were also used as self-identifiers.

Theoretical Framework

I used critical race theory as a theoretical framework in my effort to present and break the often silenced narratives of faculty of color in a way that positions them as authentic and understood for what they are. Critical race theory "challenges the experiences of Whites as the normative standard and grounds its conceptual framework in the distinctive experiences of people of color" (Taylor, 1998, p. 122). The origins of critical race theory date to the 1970s, when it was used in legal scholarship in response to the paucity of progress made by civil rights litigation in producing meaningful reform (Taylor, 1998, p. 122). Critical race theory scholars (Bell, 1994; Crenshaw, Gotanda, Peller, & Thomas, 1995; Delgado, 1995; Lawrence, 1991; Matsuda, Lawrence, Delgado, & Crenshaw, 1993) argue that "one powerful way to challenge the dominant mindset of society—the shared stereotypes, beliefs, and understandings—is the telling of stories. Stories can not only challenge the status quo, but they can help build consensus and create a shared, common understanding" (Taylor, 1998, p. 122).

I argue, in the context of the 24 narratives shared by the 27 contributing authors (African American, American Indian, Asian American, and Latina/o) in *Faculty of Color*, that specific themes emerged showing that critical race theory is paramount to our understanding of individual, institutional, and societal racism, sexism, xenophobia, and homophobia. Furthermore, if we ignore the narratives of faculty of color and do not listen to and learn from their experiences to effect institutional change in meaningful ways, this could have a profound impact on the recruitment and retention of faculty of color in higher education.

The Narratives and Data Analysis

The contributors were asked to write about their experiences teaching on a predominantly White campus. I emphasized that they could focus on either a specific issue or a variety of issues for their chapter, however, they were instructed to keep in mind that the primary audience for the book would be senior administrators in higher education institutions, such as presidents, chancellors, provosts, deans, and department chairs. The secondary audience is faculty, particularly future faculty of color. I also encouraged the authors to share any recommendations or suggestions for change based on their experiences.

The data analysis was carried out through the qualitative research methods of content and narrative analysis. Specifically, I read through the 24 chapters looking for themes that were consistent across the narratives. I discovered that the themes were remarkably similar to the issues raised in the overview of the literature; however, the experiences were shared with more depth and detail and far more clarity. Each experience provides an opportunity for analysis of what it means to be different or an outsider in academia. There were no issues specific to race, gender, or ethnicity. For example, a particularly strong theme was classroom teaching. African American faculty reported similar experiences in the classroom, as did Latino and American Indian faculty. However, for some faculty, identity issues such as sexual orientation, nationality, and religion were more salient to their experiences than race or ethnicity. The themes revealed as significant in analyses across the 24 narratives were as follows: teaching, mentoring, collegiality, identity, service, and racism.

Teaching

The first and strongest theme that came through a reading of the narratives was teaching. Many of the contributing authors wrote about their experiences with teaching and specifically the challenges they faced in as well as outside of the classroom. These challenges included problematic student attitudes and behaviors and questioning of their authority and credibility in the classroom. One of the contributors illustrated these challenges very clearly in her narrative.

On my first day of teaching, I walked into the large auditorium-style classroom and sensed the surprise of the students in seeing that I was a Black female. The male students sometimes would try to show that I did not know my material. For example, after I had explained a point in class, a male student would attempt to explain the point again in a manner that suggested my explanation was incorrect. From the tone of the student and the timing of the comment, I felt he was trying to demonstrate that I, this Black woman professor, was not knowledgeable. (African American full professor, electrical engineering)

Another contributor wrote about similar experiences in his classroom.

I like to think I have come a long way in facilitating demographic space. . . . A few years ago, a Euro-American male student seemingly promoted and celebrated the critical material on racial oppression presented in class by me and others nearly every class session. Eventually, it became obvious to others that this student wanted to hear himself speak and condescendingly mocked minority voices by overusing and overemphasizing phrases like "Right on, right on!" "I'm down!" and "The Man!" with a sarcastic smirk on his face. . . . These are only a few instances of verbosity patterned throughout my classes. (Native Pacific Islander [specifically Chamorro] assistant professor, sociology)

Some faculty of color went further and addressed the challenges they encountered while working to incorporate diversity issues in their course content. Those who adhered to a social justice teaching philosophy found that students were often resistant to hearing about diversity. This type of resistance can take many forms. For example, some students share their dissatisfaction on student evaluations and in public venues such as the Internet and student newspapers. One of the contributing authors shared an except written by an undergraduate White student for the university student newspaper about the course he had taken with this professor:

I am concerned that students who enroll in what they think is a course in political science and government know they are really signing up for a course in racial sensitivity. This type of deceptive advertising is nothing new to [the university]. If you sign up for an English course you are more likely to be required to attend a gay/lesbian teach-in. As an undergraduate I was less interested in what my professors thought about social topics and more interested in learning something about the course described in my catalog. I am fascinated that not only do professors have the extra class time to insert these ancillary topics, they seem to be the primary focus for the semester. Perhaps a fair approach would be creation of a department for these professors and be open and honest about their intent. This way students would not be ambushed. I realized this sounds terribly insensitive, but grant me [the] latitude of diversity of thought you expect for yourselves. (African American assistant professor, political science)

Another contributor, an assistant professor of education who is of American Indian background, teaches a course required of all preservice teachers as part of the licensure process. In his narrative, he shared the challenges he faced teaching students to be critical thinkers and to question the accuracy of what they read in textbooks. He wrote:

We push our students to consider how textbooks are written and revised based on censorship imposed from publishing executives, adoption boards, school administrators, parent groups, or other concerned citizens. . . . In the end, what we are asking is that they be open to hearing an alternative version of history, one that may be unsettling and that might force them to rethink their ideas about what it means to be "American." What is most important is that we do this knowing that our presence in the front of the room is held suspect. White students have been taught that when people who look like us speak dangerous and unpopular truths, we have hidden agendas. We are not to be trusted. When we assert ourselves we run the risk of being discredited by students emboldened by their anger. The challenge then becomes not only leading the students from point A to B but also leaving the room unharmed with our sense of integrity intact. (American Indian assistant professor, education)

The narratives of the contributing authors reveal that faculty of color enjoy teaching despite the challenges described in these excerpts. Many made it clear that teaching is one of the reasons why they decided on the professoriate. One author, an associate professor who is African American, wrote about her "journey of discovering the joy of teaching." I should also point out that many faculty of color were able to rely on senior colleagues who they felt mentored them about the challenges they faced when teaching. One particular author stated this point poignantly: "I had a mentor, a White female, who gave much of her time to listen and advise me during the difficult times of my early years. . . . She was the person who helped me change my habit of initially thinking people's responses were because of who I was" (Stanley, 2006, p. 118).

Teaching is clearly a complex activity. However, the level of complexity is heightened when individuals perceive that race factors into teaching. Many of our students do not get an opportunity to interact with and learn from a diverse faculty. Excerpts from these narratives illustrate that race matters in the classroom. Many faculty of color perceive that students treat them differently than they treat their White colleagues. When individuals experience this treatment, it can take a toll on their psyche, often forcing them to question whether it is due to race or not. As these narratives suggest, faculty of color encounter challenges related to authority, credibility, and validity in terms of multicultural course content. These challenges should be acknowledged, confronted, and supported. If we hope to prepare students to live and function in an increasingly diverse, global, and complex world, then we have to examine the dynamics of the teaching and learning process and the intersection of this process with those of us on the faculty who do not look or think like the majority members of our culture and society.

Mentoring

The second theme across the narratives was mentoring. Many faculty of color described mentors who helped shaped them as scholars in the academy. Mentors helped them with teaching and research and how to be good citizens, which for many enabled them to develop a presence of leadership in their field. Some faculty of color benefited from cross-race mentoring, while others described same-race mentoring experiences. The gender of the mentor did not seem to matter; many shared their experiences with mentors who were both female and male. Some emphasized that they had mentors outside their discipline and home institution. In addition, many relied on a specific mentor for a particular situation. It was clear from reading the narratives that mentoring had an impact on the professional lives of faculty of color. For example, one contributor offered the following advice to future and current faculty of color:

> I often reach back to a traditional value that many Latinos hold dear, the idea of community or "familia." Even where the number of Latinos or faculty of color is slim, seek out a diverse network of committed teachers. They not only provide you with an extra set of eyes and ears for the classroom; they can also provide you with the type of honest feedback both you and your students require to succeed. While senior White faculty cannot address all the dilemmas encountered by Latinos, many have successfully navigated troublesome classroom waters. You owe it to yourself to avail yourself of their considerable knowledge and experience. Everyone talks a good talk about diversity. Look to those colleagues (White as well as colleagues of color) who are doing the work and walking the talk. (Latino associate professor, education)

Another contributing author had an unusual career trajectory. She wrote about her experiences working at the National Research Council (NRC) and how a mentor facilitated her transition from a nonacademic position to the professoriate.

> My work at the NRC enhanced my professional development. It was at the NRC that I developed a research interest in human resource issues in the science and engineering workforce focusing on underrepresented groups—African Americans, Hispanics, and non-Hispanic White women. The executive director of my NRC unit actively encouraged my scholarly activities—including publishing. He understood academe and did everything he could to facilitate my return to the classroom. He was extraordinary. . . . Actively seek out mentors whether or not they are assigned. One can have more than one mentor at a given point in time. It is unrealistic to expect one person to be able to give advice on all aspects and phases of one's career. Mentors can be in one's home institution (but not necessarily in the same department) and/or can be in one's discipline or research area at another institution. (African American associate professor, public policy)

One of the contributors wrote about how conflicting messages received from a mentor during her third-year review almost cost her promotion and tenure.

Unlike many of my colleagues who had mentors in the academy who showed them the ropes, I was on my own. I often felt I was swimming upstream, barely able to keep my head above water. The moment of truth was the end of my third year, before my fourth-year review. Two weeks before my annual review meeting, I had met with my chairperson for my evaluation and was told that I was making adequate progress. At the annual review meeting I sat around the table with five White males, who comprised the promotion and tenure committee, and my chairperson, a White female. The committee proceeded to tell me that my teaching and service were excellent but that my scholarship was questionable, and they were not confident I would make tenure. One faculty member shared with me that one of the articles I wrote dealing with diversity had minimal significance and did not contribute to the diversity literature. This faculty member's area of research was not diversity. In the meeting, the chairperson, who two weeks prior assured me that I was on the right path, said absolutely nothing. . . . I met with my chairperson the next day to ask her about the conflicting messages I received. Her comment was, "Well, next year we'll see if you will be staying, or applying to a teaching university." (African American associate professor, school psychology)

Some faculty of color described experiences with mentors that were mixed. For example, one contributor described her experience in a mentoring program with an assigned mentor as well as other mentoring relationships she had worked to establish.

Upon my arrival at the university I elected to participate in a mentoring program offered by the university. I was assigned a mentor—a woman in the sciences, albeit a different college, who had already achieved the rank of full professor. During our few encounters, she admitted that I already knew more than she could possibly teach me. My true mentoring would come from an external network that I strategically created for myself. Networking was an invaluable tool during my first three years [at the university]. I found people who would nurture, collaborate, and provide me with feedback I needed to improve my research, teaching, and progress. I approached African American faculty members I already knew in my discipline, leading scholars that I met at conferences as well as administrators within my university system and other colleges and universities throughout the country. (African American associate professor, industrial and management systems engineering)

Many of us in the academy have come to know and understand that mentoring can be a crucial strategy for success. However, there are still some of us who adhere to the "sink or swim" mentality of mentoring. Furthermore, many of us believe that we achieved success without mentoring, so why should we spend our time and energy on an activity that sends the implicit message that someone needs help? After all, if one needs help, it means that one is lacking what it takes to succeed. Or we simply mentor the way we have been mentored, which is often based on a "one size fits all" model. Faculty come in all shapes and sizes, with different values, goals, beliefs, and needs. A "one size fits all" model is problematic for faculty of color, particularly when they look around and do not see many people like them represented among the senior faculty and administrative ranks. As is clear from their narratives, faculty of color often believe that cultivation of formal and informal networks makes a difference in their professional development. Mentoring remains one of the key attributes for the continued recruitment and retention of faculty of color at predominantly White colleges and universities.

Collegiality

The third theme was collegiality. Several faculty of color wrote about the relationships they had with their university colleagues. Some of these experiences were positive, while others were not. In the case of many faculty of color, their experiences with their majority White colleagues were either a major factor that enabled their success in academia or the tipping point that contributed to their decision to leave and move on to another institution. Collegiality is a nebulous concept in the college and university environment. One is never quite sure how to interpret the implicit and explicit rules that surround the metamessages in academia. Therefore, many faculty of color are often forced to examine these rules through various lenses, including race, ethnicity, nationality, sexual orientation, religion, and age. One of the contributors wrote the following to illustrate this point and how the energy spent on working to interpret these messages contributed to occupational stress.

I found the academic culture largely impervious to "border crossing." Decoding ambiguous messages from various institutional levels, especially the department level, represented an immediate challenge compounded by the need to ascertain a trustworthy colleague I could consult to assure I was decoding information as accurately as possible. A senior department colleague frequently reminded me that only thirty percent of tenure-line faculty were awarded tenure at our institution. I did not know how to decode this message. While the message may have been intended to inform, its effect was to incrementally ratchet up my stress level. (American Indian associate professor, educational leadership and policy analysis)

One contributor described his experiences with visibility and invisibility on the university campus and how these experiences affected collegiality.

At another occasion, one of my colleagues was honored with a university-wide award. Embarrassingly, only I and one other member of my department attended the event. The next day, the dean promptly called the department chairperson, chastising the department for their absence while praising, by name, the *one* faculty member that was present. The only person of color at this event, sitting right in front, next to the colleague now publicly named, I was present but not seen, noticed perhaps, but not remembered. It does not even help to attend university events for mercenary tenure and promotion capital when the colored corporeal yields such diminished returns. (African [South African] assistant professor, psychology)

Another contributing author, now located at a liberal arts college, described her experiences with collegiality at her previous institution.

At the time I joined the college, I was the only African American woman in the department of over forty colleagues. . . . The majority of the faculty had offices on the eighteenth floor. My office was on the nineteenth floor. It was also located down a little alcove off the main hallway. Many students—and some faculty—had difficulty finding me. It was tiny. It was dark. It had no windows. . . . I was one of four women, one of two African Americans. The other women had straight long hair; I wore my hair in a short, natural style. I was twenty-eight and my colleagues were primarily in their forties and older. I did not wear a suit, preferring to wear dress pants and a sweater or blouse. I was different. I did not fit the mold. Not fitting that mold meant that peers treated me differently. I wasn't like the others. I was "Other." (African American associate professor, psychology)

For many faculty of color, collegiality also meant having to prove and "overprove" their presence and worth in the academy. One contributing author who self-identified as Muslim shared the following in her narrative.

Unlike passing comments, misconceptions were the hardest obstacles to overcome because they put me at an uneven playing field. In every aspect of my career, I had to start by working harder to gain the respect and trust of my colleagues, students, patients, and staff. It seems that I am seen first as minority and second as a dentist, teacher, and researcher. My merits were not the only factor being judged. Over time, trust has been gained, relations have been built, and opportunities have been opened. However, all this required me first overcoming the barrier that existed based on my status as a unique minority. (Middle Eastern [Jordan] assistant professor, dentistry)

Finally, one contributor wrote about her experiences with collegiality in the context of prevailing American cultural norms and values.

Collegiality is seen as necessary for faculty evaluations, and collegiality means the particular American personality type that is valued. Shyness and reserve are not appreciated, instead one has to be extroverted, outgoing, and friendly with an open and forthcoming style of communicating even with strangers. . . . If I do not talk or volunteer some general comments and observations at a faculty gathering I am seen as not very friendly or interested in participating. I am more familiar with Indian small talk and English banter, and therefore, I am sometimes at a loss when there are pressures to be collegial on campus with my American colleagues. (Indian associate professor, psychology)

Colleges and universities expend a tremendous amount of energy espousing collegiality. Sometimes we act as if the proverbial state of being collegial is a common understanding to us all. In fact, at many colleges and universities, the word "collegial" is often synonymous with faculty. A common presumption is that all faculty are collegial. In addition, faculty are often held to certain expectations concerning what the requirements are for collegiality. These expectations are sometimes stated; in other instances they are not, leaving many faculty to figure them out on their own, sometimes at great cost. Some of these requirements can take the form of expressed presence at faculty meetings and campus events and unexpressed presence at social department and college gatherings. Regardless of the situation, faculty of color perceive that they are held to higher expectations and that they are not acknowledged when they make an effort to respond to the requirements in place.

Identity

The fourth theme was identity. Faculty of color described how they were perceived in terms of attributes salient to their gender, race, ethnicity, nationality, sexual orientation, religion, culture, and socioeconomic status. Negotiation of one's identity in the academic setting is a continuous process. Our social and cultural identities are complex. How we choose to identify ourselves in terms of the attributes just mentioned, for example, is important to our understanding of worldviews, values, and beliefs. In essence, it is difficult to separate our individual identities from the group memberships we hold and to grasp how our identities are constructed in relation to others and the cultures in which we are implanted (Epstein, 1987; Vygotsky, 1978). Many of the contributors wrote about their identities and how they intersected with their experiences on a predominantly White campus. One contributor described her experiences with "stepping out of the closet" as they related to her identity as a lesbian woman in the academy.

> I recall working closely with one colleague on a paper we were authoring together. During our meeting, I was talking—not complaining—about the work I had to do at home. My colleague said, "you need a wife." While I thought the comment was amusing (and yet insulting to the feminist in me), I chose not to view that as an opening for outing myself. I faced the common awkward interactions that many closeted gays and lesbians face when confronted with the seemingly innocuous question, "How was your weekend?" Fortunately, I had few close ties, so the question did not come up that often, but when it did, I had to figure out whether to talk about the "guy" I was dating, or say nothing, or say the truth. (African American associate professor, psychology)

Another contributor wrote about her identification as a Hispanic woman and her "other" self-identities.

> People look at me in disbelief when I tell them that I am Mexican. They wonder how a person with fair skin and a German name could call herself Hispanic. Individuals who are interested in my explanation will hear what follows. I am a Mexican citizen, born and raised in Tijuana, Mexico. . . . I have fair skin—my skin color is nowhere in the continuum of brown. After more than 15 years in the United States, I have lost my "foreigner" accent. People have a difficult time believing that my native language is Spanish. For survival reasons, my German-Jewish grandparents had to move from Germany in 1938. My parents were born in Mexico and I am part of the generation that followed. (Hispanic assistant professor, school psychology)

One of the contributing authors, a dentist who grew up in Jordan, wrote about her experiences as a Muslim woman in academia and how instrumental these experiences came to be for her, particularly in the aftermath of September 11, 2001.

> It is easy for people to make the connection that a woman wearing a hijab (head cover) is a Muslim. It is not easy for them to make the connection that an educated young woman with the advantages of western society would choose to cover herself in a manner reflective of her religion. Comments such as, "Aren't you hot in that?" or "You always wear that!" are a constant in my personal and professional life. At times reactions have been as extreme as a patient refusing my care based solely on my appearance and when I had to argue my way into the school affiliated hospital's operating room just because I had my head cover. It seems odd to me for a demand that I take off my head cover when we are allowed to go in with scrubs. . . . And with the wound of September 11 still fresh, the picture becomes dimmer. Now I am also a threat! (Middle Eastern [Jordan] assistant professor, dentistry)

Another contributing author described and defended his identity as a Pacific Islander in the following manner:

> I have been fiercely aware of the presence of racism as a minority in the United States throughout my life. . . . I became conscious of my combined invisibility and otherness as an "honorary Latino" and "oriental with a Spanish surname." For instance, I recall a conversation with a Euro-American's female classmate about childbirth and childrearing. Somehow, the conversation shifted to the fertility and procreation of Latinos. My classmate remarked, "You Hispanic men are so fertile. . . ." I attempted to clarify myself as a Pacific Islander and Chamorro, not to distance myself from the racialized stigma and distortion of machismo imposed on Latinos, but to avoid homogenization and to clarify my Spanish surname in the context of the Spanish colonization of Guam. (Native Pacific Islander [Chamorro] assistant professor, sociology)

Still another contributor, an Indian woman, did not identify with the term "faculty of color" but, rather, identified herself "as an Indian, a member of a cultural/national group." She went on to explain her struggle with the use of "faculty of color."

> The issue it raises for me is the construction of identity with skin color as opposed to identification with one's cultural group, which is a more natural, spontaneous identification process that comes from early membership within a family group, linguistic group, etc. There are many possible group identities, but shared skin color as a group identity is not a very salient one psychologically except in cases where it has been imposed from outside as a means of oppression. (Indian associate professor, psychology)

As a Jamaican woman who identifies with the term "Black" rather than African American, I, too, struggle with how groups of people perceived to be the same in skin color hue are often grouped together as "African American." In my own narrative, I shared the following experiences.

> The predominant culture shock that I have had to face (and I am still facing) living in the American culture is the assumption made by European Americans that all dark skinned people are alike and of one origin. I also face the assumption made by African Americans that as a Black woman, who was born and raised in another country, I could not understand the various systems of oppression in the United States. It is assumed that I have not experienced any of the "isms" (racism, sexism, classism) because I am a cultural outsider—an immigrant minority. . . . European Americans also position me as "different." To some, I am a bit of an enigma, because I do not conform to the many stereotypes and mental models that they hold about African Americans—I am always being compared to "them." (Jamaican professor, higher education administration)

Identity is a significant component of one's existence. We no longer live in a society where "Please check the box that best describes your race and/or ethnicity" is sufficient to describe one's identity. Identity is much more complex. In fact, as the narratives illustrate, faculty of color, like most faculty members, represent multiple social and cultural identities. For example, a Muslim woman faculty member faces many challenges as well as stereotypes in a university environment. In addition, depending on the situation, xenophobia may trump gender in her perception of the issue that is most relevant to her experience. Therefore, we should not make inferences based on inadequate data from visible and invisible differences. Identity presents a unique opportunity to participate in and learn from cross-racial, cross-cultural, cross-gender, cross-nationality, and cross-sexual orientation dialogues. It also provides an opportunity to model diversity and social justice—attributes that are important in achieving a more diverse student body and faculty.

Service

The fifth theme was service. Faculty of color described service activities that included the following: (a) mentoring students of color, (b) serving on university and national recruitment and retention committees focusing on diversity, (c) helping local communities in their educational efforts, (d) mentoring faculty of color, and (e) educating majority White faculty, administrators, students, and staff about diversity. The service activities that they engage in should not be ignored. Similar to what has been reported in the literature, the narratives continue to illustrate that faculty of color are often burdened with heavy service loads, specifically the need to use their scholarly expertise and experience to give something back to the community. In addition, participation in service activities, regardless of the rationale, is often not rewarded in merit and personnel decisions. In fact, for many, it involves a risk of not being promoted or tenured. The contributing authors shared their experiences with service at the university, state, local community, and national levels.

> I, and I suspect many other faculty, view their professional lives in the context of pre- and post-tenure. For most, working toward tenure is a grueling process, particularly in research universities where tenure decisions are based largely on number, quality, and type of research products favored by the faculty member's particular field. . . . Providing service to my tribal nation presented another challenge to my progress toward tenure. Service to tribes and tribal communities is recognized in the scholarly literature to compromise the successful progress of American Indian faculty to tenure [Stein, 1994, cited in Stanley, 2006]. Prior to my faculty appointment, I had been appointed by the Cherokee Nation Tribal Council to fulfill a major responsibility requiring an approximate time commitment of three years. Through strong verbal support, the dean endorsed my work with the Nation. (American Indian associate professor, educational leadership and policy analysis)

One contributor wrote about her experiences with service as a faculty member and during her years in her administrative role as an assistant dean.

> The demands of being a Black female faculty at a majority institution sometimes can be quite overwhelming. In addition to the usual teaching and research activities that all faculty perform, we also tend to perform more service because the small number of Black faculty means we are picked often for committees that need diverse representation, and become the "safe" person [to whom] underrepresented minority students turn to discuss their climate issues. . . . I overcame my feelings of isolation through certain university service activities. Even though senior faculty cautioned me against doing much service at the pre-tenure stage, it was my way of finding the "community" I needed. (African American full professor, electrical engineering)

Another contributor wrote about his struggles between heeding advice on not becoming too involved with service activities and knowing when to respond to invitations, particularly from senior colleagues. He described how he handled one particular situation:

> During Martin Luther King, Jr., week, I was asked to join two other senior colleagues in a campus forum on reparations. While reparations do fall under the much broader topic of my primary research, Black Politics, it is by no means an area for which I possess expertise. However, despite advice from colleagues to not get bogged down into [many] service activities, I found it impossible to turn down a request made by a senior colleague (and former chair). In preparing for this event, I found myself allocating at least two weeks of research time. This just happened to occur at the beginning of the spring semester, during a time that I was preparing a new course (first time taught by me). Additionally, I had also taken on the daunting responsibility of reading and evaluating a manuscript for a book publisher. . . . The moral of the story is to "just say no!" . . . As one scholar/activist once stated, "these problems will be here while you are living, as well as when you are dead." (African American assistant professor, political science)

Still another contributor described his experiences with service using the analogy of a forest and its relation to the constant dichotomy of being invisible and visible at the same time in an academic community.

> But then, the faculty of color—the colored faculty—speaks up, even demands to be heard. And now s/he becomes recognized—all too well. The pendulum seemingly swings right over to the next side, from Black guy no one knows to Black guy everyone knows (in the dual analogies of the forest undergrowth that gets stepped on, and the tallest trees that get cut down first, neither position sits all that comfortably in the politics of tenure and promotion). From the expectation that you don't have a voice, you now become a celebrity voice, a celebrity of color, to be sure, but a celebrity no less. Every university committee wants you in their band, every graduation ceremony has you walking next to the university president, every promotional flyer and glossy university magazine has you posing with chalk and tie in front of a rapt classroom, and your opinion is sought on all matters of difference without ever acknowledging yours. (African [South African] assistant professor, psychology)

One of the contributing authors found that his participation in service activities not only enabled the academic development of students of color but also bolstered White students' confidence in engaging with diversity and social justice issues in higher education.

> When you are one of a handful of faculty of color on campus, students of all colors often gravitate to you. Mentoring students is a privilege, but it's not always a picnic in the park. . . . They come to my office to express a range of concerns, from feeling like academic frauds to encountering other faculty who they experience as racially insensitive to advising on projects addressing diversity. The flip side of the dilemma of building trust and addressing the suspicions of the students of color is addressing the concerns and suspicions of the White students. Over the years, I have seen them wonder, "Will he cater to the students of color?" or "Will he lower academic standards?" . . . I have found White students are also hungry for advising time. Perhaps due to the lack of faculty of color, it's unusual for White students to be able to engage . . . with an older person of color truthfully and thoughtfully over their issues and concerns about diversity. A faculty of color can provide them with . . . new windows into the world, but also new mirrors upon which to reflect back their Whiteness. (Latino associate professor, education)

Similar to the situation with collegiality, faculty in general receive mixed messages about expectations for being a good citizen. For faculty of color, service activities often contribute to the development of their community and create avenues from which to build a research agenda. For others, service activities help to alleviate isolation and enhance a sense of community on campus. These narratives suggest that there is a delicate balance between being a good citizen and knowing how and when to be strategic so that service activities enhance one's scholarly agenda. There are no easy answers here. Faculty of color are often at a crossroads: One the one hand, they are recruited to diversify the faculty and further the university's diversity agenda (because of perceived or real expertise), and, on the other hand, they often engage in these activities only to be told that they are of little value in merit and personnel decisions. Participation in service activities remains a critical area to which many faculty of color fall prey, and it is often a component that costs them greatly when they are being evaluated for promotion or tenure.

Racism

The sixth and final theme was experiences with racism. In particular, the contributing authors wrote about two forms of racism that affected them: institutional racism and individual racism. They described incidents that pointed to policies and practices that disadvantaged them on the basis of their racial group, nationality, gender, or sexual orientation. Many found ways to continue their scholarly pursuits despite these overt or covert experiences.

> African American professors are confronted with institutional racism on a daily basis. Some of my students have challenged my credentials in and outside of the classroom and have had the audacity to question my appointment at a "superior" institution of higher learning. Often, majority students view me as an "affirmative action hire," just as they view minority students as being at a university because of their race or ethnicity rather than because of their intellectual abilities. In addition, parents have emailed and called me to question my knowledge, teaching skills, and grading scheme. I have actually had a parent tell me, "My husband is an M.D., and he read his daughter's paper, and she should have received an A. Are you sure you know how to write and teach?" I wonder, if I were a White male tenured faculty member, would I have been approached like this? (African American associate professor, health and kinesiology)

One contributor characterized her experiences with racism as being associated with a system of oppression.

> As do all institutions of higher education, the university I joined reflects the majority culture. Historically excluded from the academy, minority faculty have been admitted as guests within the majority culture's house, . . . expected to "honor their hosts' customs without question, . . . keep out of certain rooms . . . and . . . always be on their best behavior" [Turner, 2000, p. 85, cited in Stanley, 2006]. Minority faculty are subject to the expectation that they will think and act as do their White colleagues. Such statements and expectations have the isolating and alienating effect of objectifying an individual's personhood, a tiresome experience common to many mixed blood people. (American Indian associate professor, educational leadership and policy analysis)

Majority White faculty often say that faculty of color are quick to "play the race card." In fact, some will even go further and refute racism when it is called into question, saying that faculty of color are too sensitive and that all faculty members encounter many of the experiences described here. One of the contributing authors addressed this particular point in his narrative:

> While I recognize that these are burdens and challenges that all persons face, the overwhelming fact of continuing racial segregation in the United States adds extra dimensions to the journey for racialized ethnics. And while many of my White colleagues do indeed struggle mightily with their class status in relation to their faculty position at a college or university, I more often commiserate with my minority colleagues about the additional pressures that inhere in the very real attachments and commitments to the racialized ethnic communities that have produced us, wherever we find them. I feel this all too keenly as an African American faculty member in an Ethnic Studies department at what many Colorado residents refer to, with what I sometimes take as a barely repressed sense of pride, as one of the Whitest schools in the country. (African American instructor, ethnic studies)

One author wrote about his experiences with institutional racism during the time he was interviewing for a faculty position.

> Upon interviewing for the position, a recurring theme was the department's desire to be "sensitive to diversity." Now given that the department was already represented in terms of gender, that a variety of faith traditions were represented by the faculty, that the faculty enjoyed representation in terms of sexual orientation, and that at least two members came from decidedly working class backgrounds, I read the meaning of the departmental "sensitivity to diversity" as code for the wish to employ a faculty person of color. I say "code" because beyond a wish to appoint a qualified, "diverse" faculty person, it was never mentioned that what it meant, really, was a person of color. A senior member of the department commented: "While we'd like to diversify our department, we will make an appointment on merit, and will look for the best candidate," a statement that illustrates the discursive ambiguity and unease with naming race. Moreover, particular conceptions of merit often erase the pedagogical and human richness (merit) that diversity brings to bear on the educational enterprise. (African [South African] assistant professor, psychology)

Many White faculty succumb to this "encoding" behavior, in part because of the way nondiscrimination law is written and in part because they are seemingly uncomfortable talking about issues of race and ethnicity. Rather than open engagement in a dialogue and a willingness to learn, this leads to a "dancing act" around these issues that can be perceived, as in this case, as a lack of commitment to valuing diversity. This particular incident demonstrates that institutions rarely engage in authentic conversations about how diversity plays into merit. The current conception of merit, particularly at research universities, is far too narrow and permits faculty to encode perceptions of diversity. For example, a current measure used in evaluating research quality (for purposes of promotion, tenure, and merit) is number of articles published in highly refereed or top-tier journals in one's discipline. This practice is based on a socially constructed norm that benefits, in most instances, majority White faculty.

Diversity in and of itself has merit. What is becoming clearer, however, is that we have not yet found a means to weigh or count diversity. On the one hand, we are perfectly comfortable if, for example, an African American male professor does mainstream research and publishes in a top-tier journal. On the other hand, if a Latina woman does research that benefits her community and it is published in a journal that is not highly ranked or does not appear on the Social Sciences Citation Index, her work is often discounted as lacking in rigor. The preceding narrative suggests that this is a prime opportunity to discuss the value and merit of having diverse voices on the faculty and the implications in terms of shaping research, teaching, curriculum development, student learning outcome goals, and the overall department's vision for the future.

There is a tendency for some majority White faculty, particularly those who believe that they are "in tune" with diversity issues, to banter with faculty of color in ways that suggest that they are "one of us." Sometimes these behaviors and attitudes are not only condescending but racist. One author spoke to this point specifically:

> Only four years ago, while walking with another colleague of color to a faculty meeting, a colleague said in jest, "This side of the hallway sure is looking darker lately." My colleague and I exchange[d] glances with each other. This same colleague observe[d] the noticeable exchange and trie[d] to make light of the comment. "You ladies know I was just kidding, don't you?" (Black associate professor, higher education administration)

Many of the contributing authors wrote about their experiences with another form of racism: xenophobia. One author described one of several experiences with xenophobia as an Indian woman faculty member in the United States.

> I remember when doing my psychology internship at a major New York hospital that my natural impulse was to talk about my being from India, and to refer to myself as an Indian. . . . Instead, I was met with a wall of silence as if I had broken an unspoken taboo of never calling attention to your own or other people's difference. I slowly over the years began to understand some of the underlying attitudes here—that it is not polite to notice difference because being different means that you are inevitably deficient in some way. I remember that in the same hospital, when we all had to bring some eats for a departmental party, I was told that there was concern about what kind of cheese I would bring since who knew what kinds of cheese Indians ate. (Indian associate professor, psychology)

Another contributor wrote about her experiences as a Muslim woman and the perceptions that came with her religious identity when she sought to enter into conversations about terrorism in the United States.

> I remember watching the news with my colleagues when the first tower fell with a gloomy feeling taking over all of us when I heard the comment, "maybe you should go home." Despite the fact that the comment possibly came from a good intention for my own safety, it sure made me feel viewed as responsible for what we were watching. It was almost as if I would not be allowed to mourn with the rest because others assumed people like me were to blame. In addition to being deprived my right to mourn, there was a sense of loss of my right of speech. . . . With the media playing a major role in people's perceptions of Muslims, I was constantly looked upon as if I was liable for what was happening and therefore was not entitled to my opinions. (Middle Eastern [Jordan] assistant professor, dentistry)

Institutional racism is usually entrenched in an institution's history and is systemic and habitual. African Americans, Latina/os, American Indians, Asian Americans, those born and raised in another culture, and gay, lesbian, bisexual, and transgender individuals live daily with the effects of institutional and individual racism. Institutional racism occurs, for example, when administrators do not support faculty members when their academic credentials are called into question for a grade they assigned to a student. Individual racism occurs when a faculty member is not confronted for using a euphemism to describe the color of a hallway in the presence of two African American colleagues. Institutional racism is often subtle to the majority White culture and rarely acknowledged publicly. Many institutions value diversity, but they often do not look deep enough to ascertain how habitual policies and practices work to disadvantage certain social, racial, or cultural groups. This is one of the key arguments made in critical race theory. Individual racism, for example, is often invisible to the majority White culture and brings with it a defensive posture when it is confronted.

Some of us believe that the academy is truly a meritocracy and culturally neutral. However, critical race theory shows that understanding truth and merit means challenging concepts that are socially constructed to reflect and benefit the majority White culture. Furthermore, critical race theorists advocate that sharing experiences provides people of color with a "unique voice" to inform through their narratives (Bell, 1994; Crenshaw et al., 1995; Delgado, 1995; Lawrence, 1991; Matsuda et al., 1993). The excerpts from the narratives, which illustrate the themes of teaching, mentoring, collegiality, identity, service, and racism, suggest that unless we acknowledge the experiences of faculty of color as authentic and challenge behaviors and attitudes that are disparaging, the status quo will be maintained. We will have perpetuated and maintained the power, influence, and well-being of one group over another. One might ask "Why didn't these faculty members stand up for themselves? I certainly would have." The answer is simply "because speaking truth to power assumes many things." Among the assumptions we often forget are that there is an equal playing field, there will be no risk associated with engaging in the conflict, and, even more important, we will be heard and supported by our majority White colleagues when we break the silence.

Conclusion and Recommendations

Although their narratives were crafted on silence, all of the contributing authors expressed that the process of writing them was both cathartic and therapeutic. The excerpts presented here to illustrate each of the themes identified suggest some important ways in which colleges and universities can work to recruit and retain a more diverse faculty. In my review of the literature, I came across a descriptive study that explored gender-, race-, and ethnicity-specific differences on teaching, research, and service productivity measures among 665 tenured engineering faculty members at 19 research-intensive institutions (Jackson, 2004). Although the study was limited to engineering faculty, its argument—"that the story is not in the numbers"—was a fitting commentary on what I learned from reading the narratives of the contributing faculty of color. Individual stories are important. They provide qualitative data about oneself as part of a group or culture and help us understand and counter oppression. More important, they can lead to a better understanding of the experiences of faculty of color at predominantly White colleges and universities. This is the essence of critical race theory.

We can both learn from and break the silence on the experiences of faculty of color teaching at predominantly White colleges and universities. As indicated earlier, I asked all of the authors to offer recommendations based on their individual experiences. As I combed through the recommendations offered across the themes of teaching, mentoring, collegiality, identity, service, and racism, it became clear that most of them had strong implications for faculty and administrator development. In the Appendix, I present these recommendations according to the six themes identified. I do so with the hope that they will spark further dialogue and lead to the development of more effective strategies to recruit and retain faculty in our colleges and universities.

Appendix

Recommendations

Teaching

Recommendations for Faculty of Color

- Faculty of color should continue to advocate for themselves and educate White faculty and university administrators about the challenges involved in teaching in a predominantly White college or university campus when one is not the majority. This might be helpful for retention if White faculty, administrators, and students have a better understanding of what faculty of color can contribute to the teaching and learning of diversity and what it requires to do this well.

- Faculty of color should explore with administrators whether working to incorporate diversity and social justice issues in courses and curricula will place them at risk in regard to promotion and tenure, merit, or reappointment. Faculty of color are more likely than White faculty to develop and teach multicultural courses designed to better prepare our students to live and function in an increasingly diverse and global society. Therefore, when personnel decisions are made (e.g., annual performance reviews, promotion or tenure), these efforts should be taken into account.

- Faculty of color should encourage White colleagues and allies to teach or team teach multicultural courses. Teaching across racial identities as well as other social and cultural identities can only serve to deepen the discourse on diversity and social justice. In addition, when our students are able to observe and learn from faculty who team teach such courses, we will have modeled cross-cultural understanding.

Recommendations for Administrators

- Administrators should recognize that teaching multicultural courses might require additional investments of time and energy, increasing the workload of those who teach these courses. Therefore, it would be beneficial if expectations for personnel decisions such as promotion and tenure and merit pay were adjusted to account for these efforts.

- Administrators should survey all faculty, especially faculty of color, about their classroom teaching experiences and use the results of these data to inform policy and decision making. The teaching experiences of faculty should be made public. Through the creation of forums and other faculty development programs, for example, White faculty and students could be made aware of the obstacles faced by as well as the unique roles faculty of color could play in enhancing diversity in college classrooms.

- Administrators should support in financial ways faculty pursuit of social justice learning and teaching opportunities. Providing resources through departmental and college professional development funds so that faculty can attend conferences, symposiums, institutes, and retreats can help deepen the dialogue on diversity and social justice in faculty recruitment and course and curriculum development.

Mentoring

Recommendations for Faculty of Color

- Faculty of color should have mentors on as well as off campus. Mentors can come from within or outside one's discipline or research area. Successful mentoring relationships are long term and based on a variety of variables, including trust and a willingness to help others succeed. Cross-race mentoring relationships can be helpful in enhancing awareness about diversity and social justice and offer faculty of color opportunities to break the silence. One should not hesitate to terminate a mentor-protégé relationship if it is not working well.

- Faculty of color should take advantage of professional development opportunities offered by the institution. Grant writing and writing for publication workshops, for example, are ways to meet other faculty of color and university administrators across the campus. In addition, they can lay the groundwork for cultivating potential networks for interdisciplinary and cross-disciplinary collaborations.

- Faculty of color should engage in networking with professionals in their field of study. Networking venues such as conferences, symposiums, national committees, journal editorial review boards, research foundations, and the like are examples of places where faculty learn about opportunities that can help advance their careers.

- Faculty of color should study the political makeup and culture of their department to identify the "powerbrokers." Powerbrokers are usually senior faculty who are productive scholars, have been in the department for some time, and are respected by others. Spend time with these powerbrokers. They can help you get things done in the department, be research consultants for your ideas, and point out the landmines at your institution.

- Faculty of color should expect most people to think they receive special treatment because of their social or cultural group membership. This is the nature of being perceived as "different." You should try not to concern yourself with what others think and never hold the attitude that you received something because of who you are. Holding on to this attitude will only serve to weigh on your psyche and lead to occupational stress. Believe that you earned everything you received because of hard work and determination.

Recommendations for Administrators

- Administrators should reward and learn from senior faculty who are proven mentors. Although the mentor-protégé relationship is highly individual, one can learn from these relationships through the sharing of best practices. Faculty professional development programs such as new faculty orientations and orientations for administrators such as department chairs and deans, for example, are ways to encourage these important dialogues so that effective faculty mentoring programs can be established.

- Administrators should recognize that many faculty of color feel isolated and marginalized on a predominantly White campus. For example, some faculty of color are the only ones of their race or ethnicity in their department. One way to alleviate isolation and marginalization is cluster hires—the recruitment and subsequent hire of more than one faculty member from a particular social and cultural group in a department. It is a proven, productive, and responsible way to build a climate of collegiality, trust, and belonging for those who are often located on the margins of an institution.

- Administrators should work to nominate, support, and mentor faculty of color for leadership development opportunities and positions. The administrative leadership positions at predominantly White colleges and universities are disproportionately held by White males. If we hope to develop and model successful faculty mentoring relationships and build a diverse faculty and student body, administrative positions at our colleges and universities must be held to similar scrutiny.

Collegiality

Recommendations for Faculty of Color

- Faculty of color should work to know the culture of their department and institution. Departments and institutions have visible structures and processes, espoused values, and basic underlying assumptions about collegiality. These expectations are not always communicated or transparent; therefore, it is to the advantage of faculty of color to ask senior faculty and administrators about them so that they can make informed choices.

- Faculty of color should work to know the written and unwritten rules, practices, and customs relevant to promotion and tenure in departments, colleges, and universities. They should know what is expected and, more important, the benchmarks used to assess progress. For example, many faculty of color are hired into split appointments and promised resources upon arrival at the university only to later not have these commitments honored. Negotiations such as these, at the time of hire, should be in written form.

Recommendations for Administrators

- Administrators should work to ensure that there is a genuine interest in recruiting and retaining faculty of color. Furthermore, if diversity is an institutional priority, then espoused words should be consistent with one's actions. For example, it should be a criterion for performance evaluations of department chairs and deans.

- Administrators should regularly assess the extent to which the climate of the institution facilitates or inhibits faculty productivity. These assessment measures could include faculty focus groups, surveys, and work-life satisfaction questionnaires. The results of these efforts should include the extent to which faculty, students, and staff encourage or discourage faculty from underrepresented groups.

- College and universities should have a high-ranking administrator on campus who understands research on and best practices for the recruitment and retention of a diverse faculty. This person should have the institutional power and resources necessary to influence and create programs and policies to enhance opportunities for diversity on campus.

- Administrators should encourage collegiality and community building among all faculty by providing opportunities for faculty to network and meet colleagues. Faculty professional programs and informal social gatherings such as orientations, retreats, award ceremonies, graduation ceremonies, convocations, and the like are examples of events that create a sense of community and decrease isolation and marginalization.

- Administrators should meet with faculty of color when they are informed that other universities are trying to recruit them away from the institution. It is highly probable that other universities will approach a faculty member of color who is performing well. This occurs during as well as after the tenure years. Listening to the reasons why faculty of color are considering such offers and providing opportunities for counteroffers help to alleviate mixed messages and, more important, send the message that they are valuable to the university community.

Identity

Recommendations for Faculty of Color

- Faculty of color should strive to be true to themselves and not sacrifice their beliefs or identity just to fit in or assimilate. They should anticipate that the perception of being viewed as "different" often means that one will be misunderstood and judged. People assume that faculty of color are alike—hence the expectation that one can speak with authority on behalf of one's race, culture, ethnicity, or nationality. However, when these instances occur, they are an opportune way to dispel stereotypes, myths, and educate others about the value and richness of diversity in a college or university community.

Recommendations for Administrators

- Administrators should work to expand their understanding of the definition of diversity. Discussions on diversity must move beyond race, gender, and ethnicity if we hope to achieve social justice. Diversity also includes religion, class, sexual orientation, nationality, and physical and mental ability. This is not a recommendation to be "politically correct"; rather, it is an acknowledgment of the fact that the demographics of our society and nation are changing. Institutions are asked to prepare graduates to enter an increasingly diverse and complex global workforce. This is an inherent component of the mission of many institutions in higher education. Therefore, every effort should be made to ensure that our language is inclusive so that everyone feels valued in our nation's colleges and universities.

Service

Recommendations for Faculty of Color

- Faculty of color should work to develop strategies for responding to increased requests to serve on committees. There is a tendency for faculty, administrators, and students to ask faculty of color (because of real or perceived expertise) to serve on committees with a focus on diversity. Diversity is everyone's responsibility. Therefore, it is necessary that faculty of color be strategic about these requests and learn to prioritize. The aim is to maintain balance and focus so that one does not lose sight of other priorities that will also demand one's time.

- Faculty of color should actively participate in disciplinary professional associations and organizations by submitting, for example, conference papers and poster sessions. These activities heighten one's professional visibility and increase the range of one's professional networks. These activities are invaluable to promotion and tenure.

- Faculty of color should be cautious about taking on an administrative role before they are promoted or tenured. The career trajectory for many faculty of color is often not the same as that for majority White faculty. For example, it is not uncommon for faculty of color, because of their talent or expertise, to be approached to serve in administrative positions while they are on the tenure track. A primary reason for this is that the numbers of faculty of color in the tenured and tenure track ranks are so small. In addition, they are expected to maintain the same level of scholarly productivity in these positions as if they were still in their faculty role full time. Therefore, it is recommended that if faculty of color take on an administrative position before tenure or while working toward promotion, they ensure that the details of the appointment are in writing and the expectations are clear so that they can make realistic progress toward these goals.

Recommendations for Administrators

- Administrators should not assume that because an individual belongs to a certain racial, ethnic, nationality, or other social or cultural group, he or she is the best person to serve as an official or unofficial spokesperson for that group on a committee. Many faculty of color are approached to serve on committees related to diversity with far more intensity than other committees. This sends the message that this is their only area of expertise and the only area of value they can bring to the academic community.

- Administrators such as department chairs and deans should act as "buffers" and protect faculty of color from becoming involved in representing the department or college on committees. If administrators take an active buffering role, it will help faculty of color focus on the things they need to do to achieve tenure or promotion. Furthermore, if they are asked to serve because of their expertise, such efforts should be accounted for in personnel decisions and steps should be taken to appropriately adjust their teaching and research loads for this participation.

Racism

Recommendations for Faculty of Color

- Faculty of color should expect racism, sexism, homophobia, anti-Semitism, misogyny, "Islam phobia," and xenophobia to persist in academia as long as the playing field remains unequal. There are many White faculty who are strong allies for diversity and social justice. It is imperative that faculty of color work to find who they are and talk to them about their experiences. Faculty of color and their allies could work together to deepen diversity dialogues on campus. This is yet another opportunity to model social justice for the university community.

Recommendations for Administrators

- Administrators should require all institutional leaders to have appropriate diversity training that will equip them to lead in an academic environment that espouses diversity. This training should include but not be limited to identity development, critical race theory, levels and forms of oppression, multicultural organizational development theory, the cycle of socialization, race relations theory, and conflict management. A deep examination of these theories and their implications for practice in an academic setting is critical for the professional development of administrators and, ultimately, the goal of building a diverse academic community.

- Administrators should always be positioned to frame institutional diversity with a commitment to excellence. There is a common perception in academia that diversity does not equate to excellence. For example, faculty of color are often told that they are "affirmative action hires" or "diversity hires." These labels, regardless of the intention, come with a certain stigma. Furthermore, they are filtered down to the students and the remainder of the academic community in a disparaging way. This puts faculty of color at a disadvantage and forces them to be in a constant mode of working to "prove" themselves and always question whether a pejorative behavior or attitude directed toward them is due to their race, ethnicity, gender, nationality, religion, or sexual orientation.

- Administrators should develop appropriate guidelines for faculty search committees. Faculty search committees are not always equipped with strategies on how to diversify the applicant pool. For example, many of us are not aware of how our cognitive schemas work to disenfranchise certain groups. We tend to want to hire people who are most like us and who we think will best "fit" within the departmental culture. Faculty search committees need to be engaged early on in the process about diversity and what this means in the context of the department and the position they are seeking to fill. Such conversations engage everyone in a dialogue about the entire process so that every effort is made to bring in candidates who may not normally have been given a chance to apply.

- Administrators should recognize that recruitment and retention are not mutually exclusive and that a commitment to hiring a diverse faculty is also a commitment to retaining a diverse faculty. Retention begins immediately after the time of hire. Colleges and universities should develop strategies for retention once the recruitment phase is complete. These strategies could include mentoring, following through on promises and commitments made during the hiring process, and discussing expectations regarding teaching, research, and service.

- Administrators such as department chairs and deans should conduct periodic surveys gathering data on students' evaluations of teachers to determine whether racism exists in classrooms. These surveys could include comparisons of faculty members across similar disciplines to assess positive and negative student comments. The results of these efforts could be used to develop faculty development initiatives designed to help all faculty understand the perspectives of their students.

- Administrators should provide faculty of color with opportunities to offer feedback on how they perceive the campus environment. This feedback could be gathered through surveys, focus groups, or committee task forces. The results should then be appropriately used to effect change in faculty policies and procedures.

- Administrators should develop data management systems for accountability in terms of faculty diversity. Data on date of hire, rank, tenure track status, race and ethnicity, retention, attrition, and exit interviews, for example, could serve to help improve the climate for diversity. In addition, these data systems should be monitored to determine the rate of progress and, if possible, identify barriers to institutional growth and development.

- Administrators should understand that the advantages and disadvantages associated with various systems of privilege (e.g., White, Christian, sexual orientation, gender, class) are usually accorded to groups on the basis of their access to power and resources, which can work to disempower other groups that are marginalized in society and academia. Understanding and engaging in dialogues about the nature and effects of systems of privilege can decrease institutional racism and help to create an academic landscape that is more reflective of the diversity of our society.

Notes

This chapter is based on an autoethnographic qualitative study of the first-hand experiences of faculty of color teaching in predominantly White colleges and universities. The goal is to promote deeper dialogues on and offer recommendations for the recruitment and retention of faculty of color in higher education.

The excerpts included here are from *Faculty of Color: Teaching in Predominantly White Colleges and Universities*, Anker Publishing Company, 2006. Copyright 2006 by the Anker Publishing Company. Reprinted with permission.

References

Aguirre, A. (2000). Women and minority faculty in the academic workplace: Recruitment, retention, and academic culture. San Francisco: Jossey-Bass.

Alfred, M. V. (2001). Reconceptualizing marginality from the margins: Perspectives of African American tenured female faculty at a White research university. *Western Journal of Black Studies, 25*, 1–11.

Allen, W. R., Epps, E. G., Guillory, E. A., Suh, S. A., & Bonous-Hammarth, M. (2000). The Black academic: Faculty status among African-Americans in U.S. higher education. *Journal of Negro Education, 69*, 112–127.

antonio, a. l. (2002). Faculty of color revisited: Reassessing contributions to scholarship. *Journal of Higher Education, 73*, 582–602.

Banks, W. (1984). Afro-Americans in the university. *American Behavioral Scientist, 27*, 325–338.

Bell, D. (1994). *Confronting authority: Reflections of an ardent protester*. Boston: Beacon Press.

Blackburn, R., Wenzel, S., & Bieber, J. P. (1994). Minority vs. majority faculty publication performance: A research note. *Review of Higher Education, 17,* 217–282.

Bower, B. L. (2002, Summer). Campus life for faculty of color: Still strangers after all these years? *New Directions for Community Colleges,* pp. 79–87.

Bowie, M. M. (1995). African American female faculty at large research universities: Their need for information. *Innovative Higher Education, 19,* 269–276.

Bronstein, P. (1993). Challenges, rewards, and costs for feminists and minority scholars. In J. Gainen & R. Boice (Eds.), *Building a diverse faculty* (pp. 61–70). San Francisco: Jossey-Bass.

Bronstein, P., Rothblum, E. D., & Solomon, S. E. (1993). *Ivy halls and glass walls: Barriers to academic careers for women and ethnic minorities.* San Francisco: Jossey-Bass.

Chliwniak, L. (1997). *Higher education leadership: Analyzing the gender gap.* Washington, DC: George Washington University.

Crenshaw, K., Gotanda, N., Peller, G., & Thomas, K. (1995). *Critical race theory: The key writings that formed the movement.* New York: New Press.

Cross, W. T. (1996). Pathway to the professoriate: The American Indian pipeline. In C. Turner, M. Garcia, A. Nora, & L. Rendon (Eds.), *Racial and ethnic diversity in higher education* (pp. 327–336). Needham Heights, MA: Simon & Schuster.

de la Luz Reyes, M., & Halcon, J. J. (1996). Racism in academia: The old wolf revisited. In C. Turner, M. Garcia, A. Nora, & L. Rendon (Eds.), *Racial and ethnic diversity in higher education* (pp. 337–348). Needham Heights, MA: Simon & Schuster.

Delgado, R. (Ed.). (1995). *Critical race theory: The cutting edge.* Philadelphia: Temple University Press.

Delgado Bernal, D., & Villalpando, O. (2002). An apartheid of knowledge in academia: The struggle over the "legitimate" knowledge of faculty of color. *Equity and Excellence in Education, 35,* 169–180.

Delpit, L. (1993). The silenced dialogue: Power and pedagogy in educating other people's children. In M. Fine & L. Weis (Eds.), *Beyond silenced voices: Class, race, and gender in the United States.* New York: State University of New York Press.

DiCroce, D. M. (1995). Women and the community college presidency: Challenges and possibilities. In B. K. Townsend (Ed.), *Gender and power in the community college* (pp. 79–88). San Francisco: Jossey-Bass.

Ellis, C., & Bochner, A. P. (2000). Authoethnography, personal narrative, reflexivity: Researcher as subject. In N. Denzin & Y. S. Lincoln (Eds.), *The handbook of qualitative research* (2nd ed., pp. 733–768). Thousand Oaks, CA: Sage.

Epstein, S. (1987). Gay politics, ethnic identity: The limits of social constructionism. *Socialist Review, 17*(3–4), 9–54.

Essien, V. (2003). Visible and invisible barriers to the incorporation of faculty of color in predominantly White law schools. *Journal of Black Studies, 34,* 63–71.

Feagin, J. (2004). *Black students still face racism: White colleges and universities.* College Station: Texas A&M University.

Fenelon, J. (2003). Race, research, and tenure: Institutional credibility and the incorporation of African, Latino, and American Indian faculty. *Journal of Black Studies, 34,* 87–100.

Foster, M. (1990). The politics of race: Through African-American teachers' eyes. *Journal of Education, 172,* 123–141.

Foster, M. (1991). "Just to find way": Case studies of the lives and practices of exemplary Black high school teachers. In M. Foster (Ed.), *Readings on equal education: Qualitative investigations in schools and schooling* (Vol. 11, pp. 273–309). New York: AMS Press.

Foster, M. (1994). Effective Black teachers: A literature review. In E. R. Hollins, J. E. King, & W. C. Hayman (Eds.), *Teaching diverse populations: Formulating a knowledge base* (pp. 225–241). Albany: State University of New York Press.

Foster, M. (1995). African American teachers and culturally relevant pedagogy. In J. Banks & C. A. McGee Banks (Eds.), *Handbook of research on multicultural education* (pp. 570–581). New York: Macmillan.

Foster, M. (1997). *Black teachers on teaching.* New York: New Press.

Freeman, R. B. (1978). Discrimination in the academic workplace. In T. Sowell (Ed.), *American ethnic groups* (pp. 167–202). Washington, DC: Urban Institute.

Frierson, H. T., Jr. (Ed.). (1997). *Diversity in higher education: Vol. 1. Mentoring and diversity in higher education.* Greenwich, CT: JAI Press.

Frierson, H. T., Jr. (Ed.). (1998). *Diversity in higher education: Vol. 2. Examining mentor-protégé experiences.* Stamford, CT: JAI Press.

Gorena, M. (1996, April). *Hispanic women in higher education administration: Factors that positively influence or hinder advancement to leadership positions.* Paper presented at the annual meeting of the American Educational Research Association, New York, NY.

Gregory, S. (2001). Black faculty women in the academy: History, status and future. *Journal of Negro Education, 70,* 124–134.

Harvey, W. B. (1991). Faculty responsibility and tolerance. *Thought and Action, 7,* 115–136.

Harvey, W. B. (1994, Fall). African American faculty in community colleges: Why they aren't there. *New Directions for Community Colleges,* pp. 19–25.

Jackson, J. (2004). The story is not in the numbers: Academic socialization and diversifying the faculty. *NWSA Journal, 16,* 172–185.

Johnsrud, L. K., & Sadao, K. C. (1998). The common experience of "otherness:" Ethnic and racial minority faculty. *Review of Higher Education, 21,* 315–342.

Laden, B. V., & Hagedorn, L. S. (2000, Spring). Job satisfaction among faculty of color in academe: Individual survivors or institutional transformers? *New Directions for Institutional Research,* pp. 57–66.

Ladson-Billings, G., & Henry, A. (1990). Blurring the borders: Voices of African liberatory pedagogy in the United States and Canada. *Journal of Education, 172,* 72–88.

Lawrence, C. (1991). The word and the river: Pedagogy as scholarship and struggle. *Southern California Law Review, 65,* 2231–2298.

Lincoln, Y. S., & Guba, E. G. (1985). *Naturalistic inquiry.* Beverly Hills, CA: Sage.

Lorde, A. (1984). *Sister outsider.* Freedom, CA: Crossing Press.

Matsuda, M., Lawrence, C., Delgado, R., & Crenshaw, K. (1993). *Words that wound: Critical race theory, assaultive speech, and the first amendment.* Boulder, CO: Westview Press.

McGowan, J. M. (2000, Winter). African-American faculty classroom teaching experiences in predominantly White colleges and universities. *Multicultural Education,* pp. 19–22.

National Center for Education Statistics. (2000). *Digest of education statistics, 2000.* Washington, DC: U.S. Department of Education, Office of Educational Research and Improvement.

Opp, R. D., & Gosetti, P. P. (2002). Women full-time faculty of color in 2-year colleges: A trend and predictive analysis. *Community College Journal of Research and Practice, 26,* 609–627.

Phelps, R. E. (1995). What's in a number? Implications for African American female faculty at predominantly White colleges and universities. *Innovative Higher Education, 19,* 255–268.

Poplin Gosetti, P., & Opp, R. D. (2000, April). *Women administrators in higher education: A trend analysis of IPEDS data by institutional characteristics.* Paper presented at the annual meeting of the American Educational Research Association, New Orleans, LA.

Ramey, F. H. (1995). Obstacles faced by African American women administrators in higher education: How they cope. *Western Journal of Black Studies, 19,* 113–119.

Ruffins, P. (1997). The fall of the house of tenure: Special report. Careers in higher education. *Black Issues in Higher Education, 14,* 18–26.

Sadao, K. C. (2003). Living in two worlds: Success and bicultural faculty of color. *Review of Higher Education, 26,* 397–418.

Segura, D. A. (2003). Navigating between two worlds. The labyrinth of Chicana intellectual production in the academy. *Journal of Black Studies, 34,* 28–51.

Singh, D. K., & Stoloff, D. L. (2003, January). *Mentoring faculty of color.* Paper presented at the annual meeting of the American Association of Colleges for Teacher Education, New Orleans, LA.

Singh, K., Robinson, A., & Williams-Green, J. (1995). Differences in perceptions of African American women and men faculty and administrators. *Journal of Negro Education, 64,* 401–408.

Smith, E., & Witt, S. L. (1996). A comparative study of occupational stress among African American and White university faculty: A research note. In C. Turner, M. Garcia, A. Nora, & L. Rendon (Eds.), *Racial and ethnic diversity in higher education* (pp. 381–389). Needham Heights, MA: Simon & Schuster.

Stanley, C. A. (Ed.). (2006). *Faculty of color: Teaching in predominantly White colleges and universities.* Bolton, MA: Anker.

Stanley, C. A., & Lincoln, Y. S. (2005). Cross-race faculty mentoring. *Change, 37*(2), 44–50.

Stanley, C. A., Porter, M. E., Simpson, N. J., & Ouellett, M. L. (2003). A case study of the teaching experiences of African American faculty at two predominantly White research universities. *Journal on Excellence in College Teaching, 14*, 151–178.

Stein, W. (1994). The survival of American Indian faculty. *Thought and Action, 10*, 101–115.

Stein, W. (1996). The survival of American Indian faculty. In C. Turner, M. Garcia, A. Nora, & L. Rendon (Eds.), *Racial and ethnic diversity in higher education* (pp. 390–397). Needham Heights, MA: Simon & Schuster.

Taylor, E. (1998, Spring). A primer on critical race theory: Who are the critical race theorists and what are they saying? *Journal of Blacks in Higher Education*, pp. 122–124.

Thomas, G. D., & Hollenshead, C. (2001). Resisting from the margins: The coping strategies of Black women and other women of color faculty members at a research university. *Journal of Negro Education, 70*, 166–175.

Tillman, L. C. (2001). Mentoring African American faculty in predominantly White institutions. *Research in Higher Education, 42*, 295–325.

Turner, C. (2002). Women of color in academe. *Journal of Higher Education, 73*, 74–93.

Turner, C. (2003). Incorporation and marginalization in the academy: From border toward center for faculty of color? *Journal of Black Studies, 34*, 112–125.

Turner, C., & Myers, S. L., Jr. (2000). *Faculty of color in academe: Bittersweet success*. Needham Heights, MA: Allyn & Bacon.

Tusmith, B., & Reddy, M. T. (Eds.). (2002). *Race in the college classroom: Pedagogy and politics*. New Brunswick, NJ: Rutgers University Press.

Vargas, L. (Ed.). (2002). *Women faculty of color in the White classroom*. New York: Peter Lang.

Verdugo, R. R. (1995). Racial stratification and the use of Hispanic faculty as role models. *Journal of Higher Education, 66*, 669–685.

Vygotsky, L. (1978). *Mind in society*. Cambridge, MA: Harvard University Press.

Warner, L. S. (1995). A study of American Indian females in higher educational administration. *Initiatives, 56*(4), 11–17.

CHAPTER 18
'TEACHING WHILE BLACK': NARRATIVES OF AFRICAN AMERICAN STUDENT AFFAIRS FACULTY

LORI D. PATTON AND CHRISTOPHER CATCHING

African American faculty have historically been underrepresented within predominantly white institutions (PWIs) and deal with academic isolation, marginalization of their scholarship, and racial hostility. Little is known about the experiences of African American faculty who teach in student affairs graduate programs. The purpose of this study was to focus on their experiences through examination and utilization of their personal counter-narratives. This paper highlights the racial profiling that often shapes their experiences. We employ a qualitative critical race analysis that utilizes counterstorytelling as method to elucidate the experiences of the 13 African American faculty participants in our study.

Introduction

Our worlds comprise and are constructed around stories. Our lived experiences are transmitted through stories, which in turn story our lives. Connelly and Clandinin (1990) indicated, 'people by nature lead storied lives and tell stories of those lives' (2). Stories are especially relevant for outgroups, or individuals whose experiences have been relegated to the margins of society. 'An outgroup creates its own stories, which circulate within the group as a kind of counter-reality' (Delgado 1989). Through qualitative research, narrative inquiry in particular, such stories become the phenomenon of research (Connelly and Clandinin 1990). The study presented herein focuses on the lived experiences of an outgroup. We present a powerful example of how the lives of African American student affairs faculty are storied and how their narratives can be used to disrupt majoritarian stories of the academy. To do so, we relied on the larger societal story of racial profiling. Tomaskovic-Devey, Mason, and Zingraff (2004) described 'driving while black' as 'the practice of targeting drivers of color, especially African Americans, for unwarranted traffic law enforcement' (4). The story of 'driving while black' comprises three erroneous assumptions that allow police officers to single out African Americans based upon their location. The first assumption points to racism within the larger law enforcement system, which dictates expectations regarding 'who belongs and where they belong' (Meehan and Ponder 309). The second is that African Americans should remain within their communities or rather out of suburban neighborhoods. Meehan and Ponder (2002) argued, 'when driving through suburban communities, they [African Americans] are profiled because they are presumed to be "out of place"' (407). The third assumption, and perhaps most salient, is that African Americans should not be where they do not belong, that is, in white (codeword: suburban) residential neighborhoods.

We applied the 'driving while black' phenomenon as a metaphor to analyze the personal narratives of African American student affairs faculty. Hence we use the phrase 'teaching while black', coined by Frank Tuitt who first used the phrase to describe the racial profiling of African American scholars. African Americans and faculty of color in general often experience racial profiling, are presumed to be 'out of place' in the academy, and are subjected to assumptions regarding *whether* and *where* they belong.

Overview of the Literature

The relative absence of African American faculty has been a pervasive issue in higher education (Allen, Epps, and Guillory 2000; US Department of Education 2008). At present, 78% of the 675,624 full-time instructional faculty at degree-granting institutions are White and non-Hispanic. Faculty of color represented just 16.5% of the full-time faculty at degree-granting institutions— .004% (3340) American Indian or Alaskan Native, 7.6% (53,661) Asian/Pacific Islander, 3.55% (24,975) Hispanic/Latino, and 5.5% (37,930) Black/African American. Further, African American faculty constitute just 4% (12,886 of 307,636) of tenured faculty (associate professor level and above) compared to White colleagues who comprise 84% (258,443) of tenured faculty at these institutions. The presence of African American scholars within predominantly white institutions (PWIs) that are renowned for their resources, profitable social networks, large endowments, and high levels of prestige has typically been low and continues to decline (Constantine et al. 2008; Samuel and Wane 2005).

The absence of these scholars within PWIs reinforces false stereotypes that African Americans cannot or do not succeed in higher education (Smith 2004), inhibits an institution's ability to recruit and retain newer African American faculty (Blackwell 1989; Holland 1993; Witt 1990), and limits the number of same-race mentors for African American students, which is central to their academic success (Grant-Thompson and Atkinson 1997; Hickson 2002; Patton 2009). The absence of these scholars within the tenured ranks greatly restricts their capacity to be involved with politically relevant coalitions that push for the development of institutional policies to address diversity and equity issues on campus (Assensoh 2003). Moreover, their demographical absence contributes to feelings of isolation. They are invisible among the largely White professoriate, yet 'hyper-visible' when their presence is needed to serve as the 'diversity' voice (Stanley 2006; Thomas and Hollenshead 2001; Turner and Myers 2000). African American faculty also feel they must work twice as hard as White colleagues, which may induce significant stress (Johnson-Bailey 1999; Laden and Hagedorn 2000; Smith and Witt 1996).

There is a growing body of research that examines the gender dynamics among faculty of color. The vast majority focus primarily on African American women who comprise approximately 51% of African American faculty and 2.7% of the total full-time faculty at degree-granting institutions. These scholars often endure the effects of racism and sexism simultaneously (Allison 2008; Harris 2007; Patitu and Hinton 2003; Thomas and Hollenshead 2001; Turner 2002; Zamani 2003); are stereotyped as loud, aggressive, and bitchy (Weitz and Gordon 1993); and earn lower salaries than their White colleagues and male counterparts (Guillory 2001). African American male scholars, experience little or no senior-level African American male faculty mentors, lack knowledge regarding 'rules of the game', lack respect for their research and scholarship, receive resistance from White male students, and are expected to be intellectually inferior (Harrison 2000; Heggins 2004; Williams and Williams 2006).

In the classroom, African American faculty report that their authority and knowledge is challenged by students (Bower 2002; Stanley et al. 2003; Vargas 2002). Focus group interview findings with 10 African American faculty at a large PWI indicated that White students were more ready to '(1) critique their classroom effectiveness, (2) challenge their authority, (3) have a lower level of respect, and (4) report their concerns and critiques to the professor or to his or her superior' (McGowan 2000, 21). African American faculty also experience resistance from students regarding issues of diversity in the form of students' critiquing the validity of their work (McGowan 2000), sharing their dissatisfaction on course evaluations (Bower 2002; McGowan 2000; Stanley et al. 2003; Tusmith and Reddy 2002; Vargas 2002), expressing dissent through public venues such as the Internet or student newspapers (Stanley 2006), or utilizing silence and color-blind ideologies to resist the intellectual efforts of African American faculty (Williams and Evans-Winters 2005).

There are very few empirical analyses that examine the experiences of African American faculty in disciplines within the Graduate Schools of Education (GSEs) (Constantine et al. 2008; Smith 2004; William and Evans-Winters 2005), and none chronicling faculty of color in student affairs graduate programs, which prepare future practitioners, teachers, and scholars to facilitate the holistic development of postsecondary learners and pursue careers in higher education as administrators and leaders. The purpose of this study was to contribute to the non-existent knowledge about African American tenure-track faculty within student affairs graduate programs at PWIs. Using a critical race theoretical framework, we utilize counterstorytelling as a method to elucidate their experiences and offer implications for research and practice.

Critical Race Theory

The conceptual and methodological framework for this study is critical race theory (CRT), a movement of scholars committed to examining, challenging, and transforming the manner in which race, racism, and power operate to maintain systems of White supremacy. CRT emerged in the legal field but has since been used to understand racist policies and practices within education. According to Solórzano and Yosso (2001), CRT in education acknowledges the centrality of race and racism in society and is committed to challenging dominant ideologies such as colorblindness, objectivity, and race neutrality. CRT scholars situate race, racism, and power in historical and transdisciplinary contexts to promote social justice strategies that dismantle systems of oppression while simultaneously empowering oppressed groups (Solórzano and Yosso 2001).

The validation of the experiential knowledge of people of color is a major tenet of CRT and most applicable to this study. This 'voice-of-color thesis' presumes that due to their diverse histories and racially oppressive experiences, people of color possess knowledge that allows them to discuss race and racism with White people who are less likely to have those experiences (Delgado and Stefancic 2001). Nuanced understandings of their racial realities are shared through storytelling, interviews, life histories, chronicles, and narratives (see Bell 1987; Delgado 1989).

Race is particularly prevalent in the stories that we are told and ultimately retell. One type is the majoritarian story. Love (2004) described majoritarian stories as 'the description of events as told by members of dominant/majority groups, accompanied by the values and beliefs that justify the actions taken by dominants to insure their dominant position' (229). Those in positions of dominance create and tell majoritarian stories to continually be reminded of their dominance over marginalized groups and to fashion a shared, but subverted reality among other dominant group members to maintain their superiority as normal (Delgado 1989).

'If there are narratives that reinforce and reproduce dominant cultural perceptions, then narratives also have the possibility of revealing gaps in those same perceptions' (Williams 2004, 168). Solórzano and Yosso (2002) defined counterstories 'as a method of telling the stories of those people whose experiences are not often told (i.e. those on the margins of society)' (32). Counterstorytelling is a strategy of telling stories *and* an analytical tool for examining stories (Solórzano and Yosso 2001, 2002). They are important because they use race as a filter to deconstruct and contradict majoritarian stories, promote community building, challenge dominant thinking, and introduce alternative realities for those on societal margins (Solórzano and Yosso 2002).

Counterstorytelling as Method

Counterstories are not fictional, but instead grounded in actual life experiences. They can be presented in the form of a composite narrative in which the author uses a variety of data sources that when combined tell the experiences of marginalized communities. In this particular type of counterstory, composite characters are created and contextually located to allow the participants' experiences with racism and other intersecting identities to be foregrounded.

Solórzano and Yosso (2002) recommend a particular method for creating counterstories, grounded in theoretical sensitivity and cultural intuition. Theoretical sensitivity, introduced by Strauss and Corbin (1990), involves the process whereby researchers tap into the subtle nuances of making meaning of data by exercising particular sensitivity to their own experiences as well as those of the study participants. As researchers, we approached this study with particular sensitivity given our own experiences in the classroom. The first author is a tenure-track faculty member and the second is a student affairs practitioner-scholar with a sizeable amount of teaching experiences. We both identify as African American and have research experiences and interests that focus on African Americans in higher education. Our own experiences coupled with our knowledge of the literature contributed significantly to the sensitivity we practiced in approaching our data collection and analysis. Cultural intuition stems from Delgado Bernal's (1998) work on Chicana feminist epistemologies in which she extends Strauss and Corbin's idea of theoretical sensitivity. What distinguishes cultural intuition from theoretical sensitivity is that it expands beyond experiences on a personal level and acknowledges a more holistic process inclusive of communal experiences, knowledge, and memory. Moreover, cultural intuition is practiced in data analysis as a collaborative sensemaking process between the participants' and the researcher (Delgado Bernal 1998). Both theoretical sensitivity and cultural intuition stem from four main sources: existing literature, diverse sources of data, personal experiences, and professional experiences.

To construct the counterstory, we began by combing the current literature focusing on faculty of color broadly and African Americans specifically. Particular themes in the literature such as the impact of the campus climate, experiences related to teaching, the challenges of tenure and promotion, and gendered racism emerged to provide a backdrop. The literature also provided us with a guide for how we approached collection of our primary data. Invitations were sent to 24 African American student affairs faculty across the country at all levels, of which 13 agreed to write a narrative describing their experiences. They were provided with flexibility to story their own experiences and exercised sole authority with regard to the length and content of their individual narratives. However, they were asked to address aspects of teaching, research, service, and departmental perceptions and provided with optional prompts ('How would you describe your research agenda?'; 'How would you describe your teaching experiences?'; and 'In what ways do your identities (race, gender, sexuality, etc.) shape your experiences as a faculty member') that could be used to construct their narratives. Once all narratives were submitted, the lead author conducted the analysis, which involved reading each narrative individually and identifying key situations that shaped how participants viewed themselves in their faculty roles. The second reading was comprised of noting how their experiences were either supported by or missing from the literature. In the third round of analysis, both authors engaged in a series of conversations regarding the participants' experiences. We also reflected on our experiences as student affairs educators and the varied voices of colleagues who helped shape our meaning making with regard to the profession.

Upon completion of the data analysis, the lead author engaged in 'compositing' or the process of developing composite characters to construct a critical race counterstory. Compositing is an essential procedure to studies such as the one presented herein because it protects the identities of individuals within populations who might otherwise be easily identified if the information was presented thematically using direct quotes from participants. There are so few African American faculty in student affairs programs writ large; thus, composite characters were developed to illuminate the voices of participants without placing them at risk given the politics of the academy shared earlier. Compositing is also helpful in bringing similar themes that arose across narratives together to present a more cogent picture of the participants' experiences, while simultaneously allowing unique experiences to unfold. Compositing provides space for symbolism in scholarly writing and foregrounds our use of metaphor (teaching while black) to bring forth an enriched and alternative reality for the readers. The symbolism is also prominent in composite character development. The protagonist characters in the counterstory not only represent the stories of 13 African American faculty, they also have larger social meanings in relation to the operation of race and racism in society and its disproportionate impact on racially oppressed groups. Conversely, the antagonistic character not only reflects individual, localized thinking and behaviors among beneficiaries of systemic racial dominance but also alludes to how such elements typically play out in academic settings and beyond the academy.

In this counterstory, readers are invited into the lives of composite characters that explicate the hegemonic and overlapping nature of race, racism, and power. The characters were intentionally designed to contextualize the experiences of African American faculty in a student affairs setting and to represent individuals, much like ourselves who have experienced the 'teaching while black' phenomenon. Through their dialogical exchange, the findings of the data are illuminated, and readers will notice the prominent themes related to teaching experiences that emerged from the narratives including lack of respect, defending credentials, having their teaching questioned, and challenges with diversity courses.

A Critical Race Counterstory

For the past decade at the annual student affairs conference, faculty members have participated in a mentoring program designed to foster relationships between senior faculty and junior faculty. Ronald and Danielle, the youngest and only African American tenure-track student affairs faculty in their respective programs, wave to one another from across the room. The students whom they teach are 85–90% White. Although they had heard about one another and crossed paths early on, they officially met at a CRT in education conference a few months back. Ronald is in his third year of teaching, while Danielle is in her fourth. They had been selected to participate in the mentoring program and assigned to work with Ann Bailey. Ann, a senior faculty member, has been teaching for years and is excited to have an opportunity to serve as a mentor, especially to two African Americans. Ann approaches Ronald and Danielle:

> Hello. I can't tell you how nice it is to meet you. I want to learn about you. I am especially interested in your teaching experiences. I realize that research is very important to your tenure and promotion, but often teaching falls by the wayside. I hope to impart my wisdom in a way that will be helpful to you. Should we run out of time, we will continue our discussion at our next meeting, two days from now. How does that sound?

Ronald and Danielle equally express their excitement about the mentoring opportunity and agree with Ann, who inquires, 'So, I know we're going to focus on teaching but how are your overall experiences thus far?'

Danielle begins:

> Overall, things are okay, but let me clarify. I enjoy the pursuit of my research interests and teaching. However, it's not always easy. I've had experiences that caused me to reflect upon why I remain a faculty member. On the surface everything seems fine, but immediately beneath the surface, there's a lot of racism that I contend with. Oftentimes, it seems like a game that I have to play to get tenure. By this I mean that the rules for tenure, as you know Ann, are quite ambiguous and seemingly fluid. Therefore, I often feel as if I need to work twice as hard. After participating in several workshops on tenure and promotion and reading the university tenure policies, it seems like there are a lot of hidden rules and mixed messages. Not too much of 'this', a whole lot of 'that'. You work really hard to accomplish these things and find that your white colleague down the hall who has less of 'this' and 'that' got tenure. As an African American scholar, I never feel as if I can afford to have less of anything. So I'm in this system of hidden and coded language that I'm learning to understand but feel less comfortable about everyday. And don't let me get started on the teaching piece. I have much to say where that's concerned. As far as my teaching goes, I have four courses that include, theory, diverse issues, intro to student affairs, and the practicum experience.

'I'm experiencing a similar situation Danielle', Ronald interjects:

> I also teach the diversity course in my program as well as college environments, and the administration course. I'm working in a pretty decent department and feel really good about my decision to pursue faculty life. However, there are some situations that have forced me to really examine how my race shapes my experience. The CRT literature that I've been reading has made a significant impact on how I analyze my experiences in a student affairs graduate program.

'Danielle, I see you nodding in agreement. Can one of you expound on CRT. I'm not sure I understand to what you are referring'. Ronald states:

> Sure Ann. CRT stands for critical race theory. CRT is a movement of scholars as well as an oppositional framework that interrogates and challenges the status quo of systemic, racist ideologies, behaviors, and beliefs that continuously benefit dominant groups, while further marginalizing those who

fall outside the dominant group. Specifically, CRT is concerned with the relationships between race, racism, and power as well as how race intersects with other oppressed identities and is committed to working toward social justice. I really appreciate this framework because it gives voice to people of color and provides a language through which we can articulate and interpret our experiences, while also challenging dominant, white, hegemonic systems that are treated as 'normal' This is probably more than you wanted to know about CRT, but it really is worth exploring.

Danielle adds:

Ann, since you wanted to focus on teaching in this conversation, I can give you an example of how CRT has helped me better understand the racial dynamics of my life as a faculty member. It's fairly common in my department, and I'm sure it goes the same in yours, for students to address faculty by their first names. However, on several occasions, often inside the classroom, students will refer to me using my first name, but will refer to the senior colleagues in my department, all of whom are white, using their titles.

Ann notes, 'well, that happens all the time. You're right in that students often pick and choose how they will address professors. I'm not sure I understand what this has to do with race'.

Don't get me wrong Ann. I don't need to be referred to as 'Dr.' if that's the culture, but it's awfully rude for a student to call me Danielle in one breathe and then in the next refer to my white colleagues as 'Dr. so and so'. I believe race comes in because I'm not being extended the same respect as my colleagues. I also think that my gender and age play a major role in why students approach me in this fashion.

Ronald adds, 'Right Danielle. I totally understand the microaggressions you've mentioned'. Danielle goes further:

Microaggressions are pretty common in my experiences. During my first week in my position, a white male faculty member assumed I was a graduate student. I thought to myself sarcastically 'Of course, there's no way the department would hire a young, Black woman to teach in the program'. When I told him I was a new faculty member he proceeded to look at me in disbelief, telling me, 'You're too pretty to be a professor'. So immediately I saw my age, race, gender and physical appearance converging all at once. I could have screamed, but I'm too pretty to do that!

The group laughs and Danielle continues:

I remember one situation where a white male student would bring his computer to class and each time I said something, he would Google it on the internet. He would read what he found and then add to what I was teaching and even attempted to correct me once or twice. The funny thing about it is that he thought he was 'helping' me. I remember thinking about his assumption that *I needed* help in the first place. He was not confident in my abilities as an instructor. This type of challenge by students is particularly common and when I call students on their behavior, I'm perceived as having an attitude.

Ann adds:

Oh yes, students in our graduate programs are often excited to learn new information. I appreciate being challenged in class. It has made me a stronger teacher. I know how such situations may seem unpleasant now, but you should just use them as teachable moments and try to avoid being defensive. (Danielle pauses . . . She is now skeptical of Ann's advice)

Ronald begins to share some of his experiences:

Teachable moments [pause, sigh] indeed they are. I think what I learn most is that there are certain things I can expect in the classroom when it comes to being an African American faculty member. I expect to be challenged in class. I expect students to have arbitrary criteria that will be used to judge whether or not I am a suitable teacher. I know that I will have to 'pass' some informal test of competency that they construct as a valid measure of my abilities. I expect to receive a great deal of resistance in the diversity course I teach, mainly because students don't want me to perceive them as racist. I expect to work really hard on my facial expressions, body language, and tone of voice because when I do challenge students, I know the possibility of it being perceived as a personal attack on them. I expect that at the end of each semester, my course evaluations won't be as strong as they could be. They will be okay or even good, but laced with comments that will certainly reflect negatively during my tenure review process. 'He focuses too much on diversity issues', 'Too much of his perspective pervades the course discussion' and 'He inhibits students' comfort level in engaging diversity topics.

I know this story all too well. This all reminds me of a conference presentation I attended some years ago when a colleague used the phrase 'teaching while black' to describe a sort of racial profiling that happens in the classroom. He too suggested that African American faculty, by virtue of their race, are subjected to unwarranted attacks on their credibility. As each new cohort enters my classroom, I am prepared to present my credentials and prove my credibility. But it doesn't stop there. The students have to assess my teaching before I receive my 'pass'. I can't tell you the number of times where students, especially older White men in our doctoral program, have challenged my authority in the classroom or took subtle shots at my credibility. When I see them coming from semester to semester, I already know the 'unspoken assumption' is that the skill sets I bring to the academy are substandard.

Ann is intrigued. She follows up, 'Ronald it's interesting that you say that these types of challenges are going on. Clearly, you wouldn't have been hired if you didn't have the qualifications to teach right? Or at least that's how I see it. What do you think *you* could be doing to possibly offset these challenges?'

Danielle raises her right hand [index finger pointing up] and says:

Ann, let me respond to that question. The answer is *nothing*. There is nothing that Ronald or me, or any other African American professor can do. Resolving the issue with our credibility in the classroom does not rest with us. I think the way your question is framed assumes that the situation is our fault or our responsibility to resolve. I have attended teaching workshops, observed classrooms and have had my courses observed. These things have helped for sure but the reality is that when I enter the classroom a dominant script has been written that says I'm not good enough and I don't deserve to be there. I feel out of place, but if I think really, really hard, I can convince myself that surely every faculty member has to go through the same melodrama at some point or another. However, that is not the reality of the situation. My white colleagues don't deal with these types of situations nearly as much. They don't have to prove anything because their script says that they are credible before they even speak one word. I sometimes feel as if I spend a majority of my time explaining my credentials when instead it could be spent disseminating knowledge about the subject matter at hand. I have to work twice as hard on my teaching, all the while knowing that there are few extrinsic rewards that will follow. The result is that on many occasions, I feel frustrated, exhausted, and drained mentally, physically, spiritually and emotionally.

Ann expresses:

You two are giving me a lot to think about. I certainly don't want to blame you for what goes on in the classroom, but I want to impress upon you that as the instructor, you have to take responsibility for what goes on since you will be largely held accountable. Now I know that both of you teach the diversity course in your programs. I too have taught that type of course and understand some of the challenges. Some students enter student affairs programs having little to no experiences working with diverse student populations. What I have found is that with those courses you have to establish a level of trust. If you're patient with them in the learning process, they eventually come around, but it takes time and patience.

Danielle responds:

Indeed, it does take time. It's just that I have to first prove to them that I understand the process before they trust that I know how to guide and mentor them through it. When I provide feedback on assignments, there's always at least one student who disagrees with my assessment. Or perhaps they want to keep meeting to discuss their expectations of me or inform me that something I said upset them in class the week prior. When I reflect on all of this, I remind myself that it is part of playing the game, but wonder instead if the game is playing me. A key strategy for me is to rely on mentors and trusted friends to provide me with support and allow me to vent when I need to. They also offer suggestions for handling these difficult situations. I don't have what I would call mentors in my department. I remain in communication with African American faculty in similar programs across the country to get the support I need.

Ronald follows by stating:

In my experience the same is true. At other times however, the students are enamored with me. They are not used to seeing an African American faculty member, let alone a male. I often find them staring at me in awe as if they're thinking, 'How the hell did he get here?' So while I have dealt with some of what Danielle is sharing, there again is a gender-race intersection at work. Ann, it makes me think back to the statement you made earlier about being hired because I'm qualified. I sometimes wonder if I was hired because I'm like an anomaly in the academy. There's so few African American men that perhaps they just had to get 'one'. For example, when prospective students visit the program, it's essential that they meet me. If I'm not around during prospective visit days, it is *absolutely* noticed. As far as my diversity course goes, I feel as if I'm very patient with the students, but I often tow the line. I challenge the students in their thinking but am aware that pushing them too far will lead to negative repercussions. I guess one good thing is that my race brings a certain level of credibility in the classroom when it comes to discussing racial issues. By relating my own experiences to some of the materials, they see my teaching as more authentic. What has been key for me is identifying counter-spaces in which I can vent and share my experiences, while also gaining a sense of validation and accomplishment for the work that I continue to do. Unfortunately, I have not found many white scholars willing to serve as mentors. Sometimes I think that might be best because many of them simply just don't get it.

Ann responds:

Well, you both have certainly given me an earful. It was important for me to hear your perspectives. I just wish that I could give you more concrete advice. It seems that much of your experiences are filtered through a racial lens. That lens is definitely important, but it may also be necessary for you to consider alternative lenses that can shed light on your experiences as well as engage in continuous reflection about how you approach teaching. In my many years of teaching I have consistently sought methods to improve. Not all of them have worked, but I learn from each and every experience [she pauses]. My, how the time flies. I look forward to seeing you later this week at which time I want to provide some insights on research and departmental politics. Until then . . .

Ann exits the room. Ronald and Danielle sit in quiet contemplation about the time they just wasted, both realizing that this likely would be their last meeting with Ann.

Discussion and Implications of Our Counterstory

There are a number of noteworthy observations that stem from this counterstory, which was presented through the composite characters of Danielle, Ronald, and Ann. However, it is critically important for readers to understand that this story is less about these characters and more about the 13 African American student affairs faculty members that wrote the narratives necessary to construct this counterstory. First, this counterstory makes a significant contribution in validating existing research studies, many of which were mentioned in our literature review, that have highlighted the experiences of faculty of color. For example, both scholars faced oppressive experiences in the classroom where the majority of their students were White. These experiences, consistent with the literature, included having to prove their credibility, and garnering less respect from students (Thomas and Hollenshead 2001; Turner 2002; Turner and Myers 2000). In some cases, the students described in the counterstory resisted discussions of diversity by evaluating their instructors negatively at the end of the course (Bower 2002; McGowan 2000; Stanley et al. 2003; Tusmith and Reddy 2002; Vargas 2002). The students further resisted their assessments by perceiving any constructive criticism as a personal attack. This is indicative of how cross-racial communication is often misread prompting the emergence of stereotypes that construct African Americans as more aggressive and posing a threat to White people.

While the narrative focused on teaching, the experiences of the characters demonstrated that issues related to teaching extend beyond the boundaries of the classroom. African American faculty face a multitude of barriers, such as lack of mentors (Thomas and Hollenshead 2001) and trying to assess the 'rules of the game'. The scholars depicted in the counter-narrative shared a common experience with those discussed in the aforementioned research. They understood the requirements for tenure but understood that tenure was awarded in differential ways according to race. In order to resist some of the obstacles, they relied on mentors in student affairs programs across the country. In one way, CRT has served as a liberatory framework for both scholars, giving them a lens and language to confront racism in their professional lives (Solórzano and Yosso 2002). By having a mentoring connection with other faculty across student affairs programs, they resisted the racism that they felt on their campuses as African American faculty (Butner, Burley, and Marbley 2000). This supports the literature presented earlier in that there are too few same-race, same-gender mentors available broadly speaking, but also among student affairs graduate programs.

The counterstory also alluded to the role of differential effects of gender in the experiences of Ronald and Danielle. Danielle experienced a form of gendered racism when a White colleague challenged the reality of her being hired because he perceived her as a young, attractive, African American woman (Pope and Joseph 1997; Turner 2002). Immediately, her different identities converged in ways that challenged her viability as a faculty member. Her identities also converged in the classroom where her credibility was often questioned.

While Ronald noted that he had unique experiences that made him 'hyper-visible' to his students due to the lack of African American male faculty at the university (Thomas and Hollenshead 2001; Turner and Myers 2000), his physical presence was being objectified and commoditized. Farley (1997) poignantly detailed the use of the black body as a fetish object. He stated, 'Race is the preeminent pleasure of our time. Whiteness is not a color; it is a way of feeling pleasure in and about one's body. The black body is needed to fulfill this desire for race pleasure' (1). In essence, there are so few African American male faculty that they are deemed a rare commodity; one which every academic department must have. Underlying the desire to hire an African American male, or as Ronald noted 'to get one' is interest-convergence. Bell's (1995) interest-convergence theory, simply stated, is that Whites will only agree to advances for African Americans when their interests are also promoted. Thus, Ronald's department benefited from having him there because he represented 'diversity' or at least a departmental commitment to recruiting diverse faculty. His presence could also be beneficial in recruiting students of color to his graduate program. Ronald recognized the costs and benefits of being an African American faculty member leveraging his identity as a source of credibility and using it to authenticate his teaching (Alfred 2001; Allison 2008; Harris 2007).

Another observation that deserves mention is the nature of the dialog that ensued between Ronald, Danielle, and Ann. As they discussed their experiences and shared their stories with Ann, she offered very little substantive feedback. To be sure, much of what Ann discussed represented the types of microaggressions that White faculty often commit unconsciously. Microaggressions are subtle, covert racial attacks that are often subconscious in nature. White people make such comments without realizing how they may be perceived as insulting and racist. Microaggressions do not go away. Instead, they accumulate and become integrated into a person's collective memory (Delgado and Stefancic 2001; Smith, Allen, and Danley 2007; Solórzano, Ceja, and Yosso 2000). At several different points in the conversation, Ann committed microaggressions. For example, rather than thinking critically about the differential treatment that Danielle speaks of when students address her, Ann fails to acknowledge the relevance of race to the situation. Ann later encourages Danielle and Ronald to view their classroom challenges as teachable moments, again avoiding the obvious role of racism in their experiences and suggesting that all teachers have such challenges. Ann's third microaggression involves placing the onus on Ronald to offset the situations he encounters in class. Ann's response suggests that Ronald should be accountable for changing racist behaviors in his class and that somehow he is the cause for these issues, rather than offering helpful feedback for how the White students he teaches should own their behavior. Finally, Ann exits the conversation with Danielle and Ronald by suggesting that perhaps they should try to view their experiences through a lens other than race. Ann's statement was used to promote the minimization of racism (Bonilla-Silva 2006). Her overall approach ultimately resembled nothing close to the mentoring from which Danielle and Ronald might have benefited.

Not only did Ann represent much of what participants noted about the White colleagues with whom they work, a deeper examination of her character reveals that in many ways her behavior resembled the historical 'Miss Anne' often represented in Black literary works as deceptively appearing to be well intentioned, innocent, gentile, and untouchable (Thomas 1973). Historically, 'Miss Anne' represented 'the mistress of a plantation house and its slaves. Put on a pedestal by white men for her virtue, she derived her power from her position as wife, daughter, mother, and sister to the white slave owner; to maintain this power, she willingly deferred to her husband in all things' (Edomondson and Nkomo 2003, 240). The Ann in our counterstory brings many of these characteristics to light, particularly given her excitement about having the opportunity to work with faculty of color. Ann appears to be an altruistic, benevolent, and genuine person who has Ronald and Danielle's best interest at heart. However, as the meeting unfolds, we learn that her actions are nothing more than an unwarranted attempt of racial profiling in the academy. The undercurrents in much of what Ann shares suggest that Danielle and Ronald 'do not belong' in the academy due to their inability to view things beyond a racial lens, their lack of patience, and their failure to understand that their situations are not unique and are shared by faculty writ large. Ann's behavior helps maintain the status quo, fails to challenge dominant racist paradigms, and ignores the contextual role of race in the experiences of Ronald and Danielle. Even more troubling is that when she received push back from Danielle, she continued the conversation with an oblivious mindset. She listened to them discuss racism, but for her, racism was something that was 'out there' rather than something that she was actively practicing. Ann's behaviors are symptomatic of a larger issue in the academy in that faculty of color have a difficult time finding mentors who 'get it' and whom they can trust to offer sound advice and guidance when needed.

Implications

Ladson-Billings (1998) asked, 'What is critical theory and what's it doing in a nice field like education?' We further extend her question to consider what role CRT might have in a nice profession like higher education and student affairs. Given the challenges expressed by the study participants through our composite characters, Danielle and Ronald, perhaps the field of student affairs is not as nice as some believe. Danielle and Ronald experienced a great deal which often led to feelings of frustration, disappointment, exhaustion, and anger, factors symptomatic of racial battle fatigue or 'the constant physiological, psychological, cultural, and emotional coping with racial microaggressions in less-than-ideal and racially hostile or unsupportive environments (campus or otherwise)' (Smith, Allen, and Danley 2007).

Recruiting and retaining African American faculty in student affairs programs is essential to preparing future practitioners for a dynamic and diverse student population. Student affairs graduate programs that prepare faculty can assist in increasing the number of African Americans in the profession by developing intentional programs to recruit potential African American faculty. Such programs should be facilitated with the understanding that these faculty will be recruited because of a true departmental commitment to diverse perspectives. Thus, the end goal should not be about recruiting one faculty of color, but to consistently identify ways to recruit additional faculty, and also to incorporate diverse perspectives into the curriculum. One approach would be to encourage more African American graduate students to consider tenure-track faculty positions as a professional option. This can be accomplished through the provision of intentional research and publishing opportunities during the students' masters and doctoral graduate programs. Another approach is for student affairs graduate programs to intentionally develop partnerships with practitioners on their campuses to create opportunities for research collaboration on practical issues as well as the encouragement and training to publish. This might cultivate the interest of talented African American practitioners to consider pursuing student affairs faculty as a career option. Student affairs graduate programs should also consider reexamining the extent to which African American and faculty of color in general are supported and engage serious questions such as: (1) Are we doing everything in our power to support this person? (2) Have we constructed a safe and trusting mentoring space? (3) Do we assume that this person is the only one who can teach a diversity class? and (4) If we continue as we are, will we be able to realistically retain this faculty member?

The absence of a critical mass of African American faculty in higher education is an enduring reality. That being said, student affairs professional associations can also assist by constructing intentional mentoring programs that connect junior African American faculty with senior faculty who are committed to the professional success of these scholars regardless of their racial or gender background. In particular, White male faculty can be key allies in this effort. Recruiting these scholars as mentors and providing the necessary support for their success can counter some of the marginality that African American faculty face by broadening the pool of potential mentors considerably.

References

Alfred, M.V. 2001. Expanding theories of career development: Adding the voices of African American women in the white academy. *Adult Education Quarterly* 51, no. 2: 108–27.

Allen, W.R., E.G. Epps, and E.A. Guillory. 2000. The Black academic: Faculty status among African Americans in US higher education. *Journal of Negro Education* 69, nos. 1/2: 112–27.

Allison, D.C. 2008. Free to be me? Black professors, white institutions. *Journal of Black Studies* 38, no. 4: 641–62.

Assensoh, A.B. 2003. Trouble in the promised land: African American studies programs and the challenges of incorporation. *Journal of Black Studies* 34, no 1: 52–62.

Bell, D. 1987. *And we are not saved.* New York: Basic Books.

Blackwell, J. 1989. 'Mentoring': An action strategy for increasing minority faculty. *Academe* 75, no. 1: 8–14.

Bonilla-Silva, E. 2006. *Color-blind racism and the persistence of racial inequality in the United States.* 2nd ed. Lanham: Rowman & Littlefield.

Bower, B.L. 2002. Campus life for faculty of color: Still strangers after all these years? In *Community college faculty: Characteristics, practices, and challenges,* ed. C. Outcalt, 79–88. San Francisco: Jossey Bass.

Butner, B.K., H. Burley, and A.F. Marbley. 2000. Coping with the unexpected: Black faculty at predominantly white institutions. *Journal of Black Studies* 30, no. 3: 453–62.

Connelly, M., and J. Clandinin. 1990. Stories of experience and narrative inquiry. *Educational Researcher* 19, no. 5: 2–14.

Constantine, M.G., L. Smith, R.M. Redington, and D. Owens. 2008. Racial microaggressions against black counseling and counseling psychology faculty: A central challenge in the multicultural counseling movement. *Journal of Counseling and Development* 86, no. 3: 348–55.

Delgado, R. 1989. Storytelling for oppositionists and others: A plea for narrative. *Michigan Law Review* 87, no. 8: 2411–41.

Delgado, R., and J. Stefancic. 2001. *Critical race theory: An introduction.* New York: New York University Press.

Delgado Bernal, D. 1998. Using a Chicana feminist epistemology in educational research. *Harvard Educational Review* 68, no. 4: 555–82.

Edomondson, E.L.J., and S.M. Nkomo. 2003. *Our separate ways: Black and White women and the struggle for professional identity.* Cambridge: Harvard Business Press.

Farley, A.P. 1997. Black body as fetish object. *Oregon Law Review* 76: 457–535. LexisNexis Academic database http://bert.lib.indiana.edu:2093/us/Inacademic/mungo/ (accessed May 17, 2009).

Grant-Thompson, S.K., and D.R. Atkinson. 1997. Cross-cultural mentor effectiveness and African American male students. *Journal of Black Psychology* 23, no. 2: 120–34.

Guillory, E. 2001. The black professoriate: Explaining the salary gap for African American female professors. *Race, Ethnicity and Education* 4, no. 3: 129–48.

Harris, T.M. 2007. Black feminist thought and cultural contracts: Understanding the intersection and negotiation of racial, gendered, and professional identities in the academy. In *Neither white nor male: Female faculty of color,* ed. K.G. Hendrix, 55–64. San Francisco: Jossey-Bass.

Harrison, C.K. 2000. Black male images in athletics. In *Brothers of the academy: Up and coming Black scholars earning our way in higher education,* ed. L. Jones, 277–86. Virginia: Stylus.

Heggins, W.L. 2004. Preparing African American males for the professoriate: Issues and challenges. *Western Journal of Black Studies* 28, no. 2: 354–64.

Hickson, M.G. 2002. What role does the race of professors have on the retention of students attending historically black colleges and universities? *Education* 123, no. 1: 186–9.

Holland, J.W. 1993. Relationships between African-American doctoral students and their major advisors. Paper presented at the annual meeting of the American Educational Research Association, April, in Atlanta, GA (ERIC Document Reproduction Service No. ED 359915).

Johnson-Bailey, J. 1999. The ties that bind and the shackles that separate: Race, gender, class, and color in a research process. *International Journal of Qualitative Studies in Education* 12, no. 6: 660–71.

Ladson-Billings, G. 1998. Just what is critical race theory and what's it doing in a nice field like education? *International Journal of Qualitative Studies in Education* 11, no. 1: 7–24.

Laden, B.V., and L.S. Hagedorn. 2000. Job satisfaction among faculty of color in academe: Individual survivors or institutional transformers? In *What contributes to job satisfaction among faculty and staff*, ed. L.S. Hagedorn, 57–66. San Francisco: Jossey-Bass.

Love, B.J. 2004. Brown plus 50 counter-storytelling: A critical race theory analysis of the 'majoritarian achievement gap' story. *Equity & Excellence in Education* 37: 227–46.

McGowan, J.M. 2000. African-American faculty classroom teaching experiences in predominantly white colleges and universities. *Multicultural Education* 8, no. 2: 19–22.

Meehan, A.J., and M.C. Ponder. 2002. Race and place: The ecology of racial profiling African American motorists. *Justice Quarterly* 19, no. 3: 399–430.

Patitu, C.L., and K.G. Hinton. 2003. The experiences of African American women faculty and administrators in higher education: Has anything changed? In *Meeting the needs of African American women*, ed. M. Howard-Hamilton, 79–93. San Francisco: Jossey-Bass.

Patton, L.D. 2009. My sister's keeper: A qualitative examination of significant mentoring relationships among African American women in graduate and professional schools. *Journal of Higher Education* 80, no. 5: 510–37.

Pope, J., and J. Joseph. 1997. Student harassment of female faculty of African descent in the academy. In *Black women in the academy: Promises and perils*, ed. L. Benjamin, 252–60. Gainesville: The University Press of Florida.

Samuel, E., and N. Wane. 2005. 'Unsettling relations': Racism and sexism experienced by faculty of color in a predominantly white Canadian university. *Journal of Negro Education* 74, no. 1: 76–87.

Smith, E., and S.L. Witt. 1996. A comparative study of occupational stress among African American and White university faculty: A research note. In *Racial and ethnic diversity in higher education*, ed. C. Turner, M. Garcia, A. Nora, and L. Rendon, 381–9. Needham Heights, MA: Simon & Schuster.

Smith, S. 2004. Insider and outsider status: An African American perspective. In *Embracing and enhancing the margins of adult education*, ed. M. Wise and M. Glowacki-Dudka, 57–65. San Francisco: Jossey Bass.

Smith, W.A., W.R. Allen, and L.L. Danley. 2007. Assume the position . . . you fit the description: Psychosocial experiences and racial battle fatigue among African American male college students. *American Behavioral Scientist* 51, no. 4: 551–78.

Solórzano, D., M. Ceja, and T. Yosso. 2000. Critical race theory, racial microaggressions, and campus racial climate: The experiences of African American college students. *Journal of Negro Education* 69, nos. 1–2: 60–73.

Solórzano, D., and T. Yosso. 2001. Critical race and LatCrit theory and method: Counter-storytelling: Chicana and Chicano graduate school experiences. *International Journal of Qualitative Studies in Education* 14, no. 4: 471–95.

Solórzano, D., and T. Yosso. 2002. Critical race methodology: Counter-storytelling as an analytical framework for education research. *Qualitative Inquiry* 8, no. 1: 23–44.

Stanley, C.A. 2006. Coloring the academic landscape: Faculty of color breaking the silence in predominantly White colleges and universities. *American Educational Research Journal* 43, no. 4: 701–36.

Stanley, C.A., M.E. Porter, M. Simpson, and M.L. Ouellett. 2003. A case study of the teaching experiences of African American faculty at two predominantly white research universities. *Journal on Excellence in College Teaching* 14, no. 1: 151–78.

Strauss, A., and J. Corbin. 1990. *Basics of qualitative research: Grounded theory procedures and techniques.* Newbury Park, CA: Sage.

Thomas, G.D., and C. Hollenshead. 2001. Resisting from the margins: The coping strategies of black women and other women of color faculty members at a research university. *Journal of Negro Education* 70, no. 3: 166–75.

Thomas, M. 1973. An overview of Miss Anne: White women as seen by black playwrights. Doctoral diss., Florida State University, 1973. Abstract in Dissertation Abstracts International, 34/06, AAT 7330297.

Tomaskovic-Devey, D., D. Mason, and M. Zingraff. 2004. Looking for the driving while black phenomena: Conceptualizing racial bias processes and their associated distributions. *Police Quarterly* 7, no. 1: 3–29.

Turner, C. 2002. Women of color in academe. *Journal of Higher Education* 73: 74–93.

Turner, C.V., and S.L. Myers. 2000. *Faculty of color in academe: Bittersweet success.* Needham Heights, MA: Allyn and Bacon.

Tusmith, B., and M.T. Reddy, eds. 2002. *Race in the college classroom: Pedagogy and politics.* New Brunswick, NJ: Rutgers University Press.

U.S. Department of Education, National Center for Educational Statistics. 2008. *Digest of Educational Statistics* http://nces.ed.gov/programs/digest/d08/tables/dt08_249.asp (accessed November 25, 2008).

Vargas, L. ed. 2002. *Women faculty of color in the White classroom.* New York: Peter Lang

Weitz, R., and L. Gordon. 1993. Images of Black women among Anglo college students. *Sex Roles* 28, nos. 1–2: 19–34.

Williams, B.T. 2004. The truth in the tale: Race and 'counterstorytelling' in the classroom. *Journal of Adolescent & Adult Literacy* 48, no. 2: 164–9.

Williams, B.N., and S.N. Williams. 2006. Perceptions of African American male junior faculty on promotion and tenure: Implications for community building and social capital. *Teachers College Record* 108, no. 2: 287–315.

Williams, D.G., and V. Evans-Winters. 2005. The burden of teaching teachers: Memoirs of race discourse in teacher education. *Urban Review* 37, no. 3: 201–19.

Witt, S. 1990. *The pursuit of race and gender equity in American academe.* New York: Praeger.

Zamani, E.M. 2003. African American women in higher education. In *Meeting the needs of African American women,* ed. M. Howard-Hamilton, 5–18. San Francisco: Jossey-Bass.

CHAPTER 19
RACE-RELATED SERVICE AND FACULTY OF COLOR: CONCEPTUALIZING CRITICAL AGENCY IN ACADEME

BENJAMIN BAEZ

Based on a qualitative study of sixteen faculty of color at a private research university, this chapter argues that service, though significantly presenting obstacles to the promotion and retention of faculty of color, actually may set the stage for a critical agency that resists and redefines academic structures that hinder faculty success. The construct of 'service,' therefore, presents the opportunity for theorizing the interplay of human agency and social structures. The chapter suggests that faculty may seek to redefine oppressive structures through service, thus, exercising an agency that emerges from the very structures that constrain it. Faculty of color, in particular, may engage in service to promote the success of racial minorities in the academy and elsewhere. Thus, service, especially that which seeks to further social justice, contributes to the redefinition of the academy and society at large.

At most institutions, and at research universities in particular, service is the least important criterion for advancement (Blackburn and Lawrence 1995; Centra 1993; Jarvis 1991). Yet, paradoxically, service, broadly defined, is necessary for the functioning of institutions of higher education, and it might especially be important for promoting (and ensuring) shared governance. Thus, all faculty members struggle to balance service with the other promotion and tenure criteria. Faculty of color, however, struggle with this balance in particular ways given that they are offered more opportunities due to their high visibility, the belief that they present diverse perspectives, and the mentoring they are regarded by others as providing to students of color (Menges and Exum 1983). Consequently, faculty of color's opportunity for advancement likely is reduced significantly by excessive service demands.

Given the institutional need for service, and its potential consequences to individual faculty members, service often is conceptualized in the research literature as a structural "problem" of the promotion and tenure process (see, e.g., Exum 1983). I argue, however, that conceptualizing service as "problematic" negates the role of critical agency in resisting and redefining institutional structures. I suggest as well that rather than framing service as a "problem," scholars should question the institutional practices and views of merit that devalues an important part of faculty work. I do not intend to argue that service is more important than the other promotion and tenure criteria; instead, I suggest that scholars question the underlying assumptions that ensure that service is deemed inherently less valuable than those other criteria.

I intend in this paper to provoke readers to think differently about some of the "givens" of the promotion and tenure process. The paper does not feign objectivity; it intends to contribute to the dialectic surrounding notions of justice in the academy. Specifically, I argue for the recognition of a critical agency which uses service to redefine institutional structures, and in this regard service is important and valuable when it furthers social justice. In making this argument, I question the suggestion by many scholars that institutions loosen their demands for service. Such suggestions negate work that seeks to improve the subordinated status of people of color. The demand should be, therefore, not for a loosening of service requirements but for the justification of the institutional structures and norms that ensure that faculty members are evaluated in particular ways that maintain those structures and norms.

I start the paper with a brief discussion of service and how it is deemed problematic for faculty, particularly faculty of color. I then describe a study I conducted that highlighted the importance of service for faculty of color. I use this study, not so much to "prove" that faculty of color deem race-related service important, but to highlight the possibility that the prevailing conceptualizations of merit, justice, and faculty work might benefit from a theoretical elaboration of structure and agency. The body of the paper consists of the study's findings and my elaboration of critical agency in initiating social change. Finally, I provide suggestions for resisting institutional structures.

Service and Faculty Evaluation

I define "service" broadly, following generally Blackburn and Lawrence's (1995) definition of service as the "CATCHALL [sic] name for everything that is neither teaching, research, nor scholarship" (p. 222). Blackburn and Lawrence indicated that there are two types of service. The first is "internal" service, which is defined as:

> Performing "for the good of the organization" . . . Meeting with a board committee, speaking to an alumni association gathering, arranging a visiting-lecturer series, sponsoring a student organization, entertaining advisees at your home—almost anything that casts the college in a favorable light among its many constituencies falls under the heading of what we call "internal" service (p. 222).

The second type is "external" service, and it includes the functions and activities professors perform outside their college or university, particularly paid consulting, "pro bono" work (i.e., service with remuneration), and professional service (i.e., service given to a disciplinary specialty). Service includes, therefore, administrative tasks, institutional and community activities, and professional activities. Implied in this definition are those activities that can not easily be evaluated,[1] such as mentoring students, developing and participating in support groups and networks, and so forth.

The faculty at most institutions is evaluated on three criteria: scholarship, teaching, and service. Each criterion weighs differently depending on the institutional-type or mission of a college or university (Jarvis 1991; Tierney and Bensimon 1996). Many institutions, especially research universities, place greater value on scholarship than on the other criteria (Blackburn and Lawrence 1995). Non-research universities stress teaching (Jarvis 1991). But these generalities obscure important contentions about faculty work. As Altbach (1994) asserted "One of the main debates of this decade concerns the appropriate balance between teaching and research in academe—a debate that goes to the role of the university as an institution and is critical for the academic profession" (p. 235).

Service often is left out of this debate. If it is mentioned at all, it is framed as problematic for faculty. This "problem-perspective" is understandable, given the institutional practices that place greater emphasis on the other promotion and tenure criteria (Blackburn and Lawrence 1995; Centra 1993; Jarvis 1991; Tierney and Bensimon 1996). The research literature indicates that service is expected of all faculty members at most institutions of higher education but rarely is valued highly by promotion and tenure processes that actually punish faculty members for doing too much of it. Jarvis (1991), for example, explained that many junior faculty members are exploited by being assigned too much responsibility too early, hindering their publishing and teaching effectiveness. Consequently, a number of scholars claim that faculty members see service as taking time away from other preferred roles and activities (See, e.g., Blackburn and Lawrence 1995; Centra 1993).

There are some characterizations of faculty work in the research literature that frame these concerns in broader ways than merely whether institutions should give greater weight to teaching, service, or research. Boyer (1990), for example, argued in *Scholarship Reconsidered* that scholarship includes a wide range of activities, and he indicated that the scholarship of "application" may include the use of research in service activities that seek to solve social problems. He probably would contend, however, that this scholarship somehow must be "published" either through conventional means in books, journals, or monographs, or through, for example, presentations at professional and community associations. The follow-up to Boyer's study, *Scholarship Assessed* (Glassick et al. 1997), in stressing the need for standards of evaluation, substantiation, and documentation, illustrates that Boyer does not stray too far from privileging traditional notions of merit which emphasize the public dissemination of knowledge. Furthermore, as Davis and Chandler (1998) explained, Boyer's work supports the prevailing faculty reward system, which will privilege research and teaching over service given the arrangements and structures that are served by traditional faculty evaluation (e.g., entrepreneurship). Yet, in providing an alterative to traditional notions of scholarship, Boyer's work and its follow-up may be read as supporting a definition of merit that accounts for service that promotes social justice.

At any rate, service is made problematic in the research literature in two ways. First, since service is expected of all faculty members, and it usually is given little weight in faculty evaluation, it hinders scholarship and teaching effectiveness (e.g., Jarvis 1991). Second, because it is commonly understood that at research universities (at least) scholarship and teaching are valued more than service, faculty members feel burdened by service (See, e.g., Blackburn and Lawrence 1995; Jarvis 1991). Furthermore, the negative consequences of service are deemed to result either from the abuse of institutional authority or, structurally, as a necessary but unimportant (or undervalued) condition of faculty work. These conceptualizations are prevalent in the research literature about faculty of color.

Service and Faculty of Color

Banks (1984), in an often-cited article, argued that rather than being encouraged to focus on their "academic work," many Black professors were "sucked into a plethora of activities often unrelated to their competence and interests. . . . Scholarly work had to be accomplished in combination with the extra-academic responsibilities hoisted onto their shoulders and consciences" (p. 327). In distinguishing "academic work" from other activities, Banks recognizes, of course, that scholarship and teaching are important, and other activities can involve the "misuse of Black scholars." Such assertions, however, although appropriately recognizing the consequences of service, have three pitfalls: (a) they fail to challenge the bases for those consequences, (b) they fail to acknowledge that service may benefit faculty of color by furthering personal and political goals, and (c) they fail to recognize the importance of critical agency in initiating social change.

It can not be disputed by anyone that faculty of color have more difficulties with service than White faculty members (Exum et al. 1984; Garza 1987; Johnsrud and Des Jarlais 1994; Tierney and Bensimon 1996; Tierney and Rhoads 1993). Much of this literature emphasizes the institutional demands for service, particularly minority-related service (See, e.g., Blackwell 1988; Menges and Exum 1983; Turner et al. 1997). Service, these studies seem to indicate, involve institutional abuse of faculty of color because it rarely is weighed favorably in promotion and tenure decisions. Consequently, some studies indicate that faculty of color are vulnerable to the "revolving door" phenomenon (e.g., Blackwell 1988) or to the racism associated with the "typecasting syndrome" (e.g., Reyes and Halcon 1988).

Tierney and Bensimon (1996) provided a persuasive elaboration of the problem of service. They argued that institutional and personal expectations for service lead to "cultural taxation." Tierney and Bensimon explained that minority faculty are burdened by an *obligation* to serve the needs of their racial and ethnic groups. This obligation manifests itself in unreasonable institutional demands for service and the expectation (which bears significantly during faculty evaluation) that faculty of color will perform such service. Furthermore, cultural taxation, Tierney and Bensimon contended, includes the "commodification of race or ethnicity to make an institution look good" (p. 117). In other words, institutions overuse its few faculty of color in order to portray a commitment to diversity. For Tierney and Bensimon, the burden of relieving cultural taxation is on the institution: it is responsible for ensuring that information about promotion and tenure is disseminated freely to faculty of color, and for creating an "ethos of inclusiveness" in its environment (p. 117).

The focus on institutional demands for service, however, does not adequately explain the complexity of the issue. There is some evidence that faculty of color may engage (perhaps, even prefer) service to the other promotion and tenure criteria because they see significant personal or social benefits (See, e.g., Cuadraz 1997; Johnsrud 1993; Padilla and Chavez 1997; Pollard 1990). This research indicates that faculty of color are especially competent, and interested, in minority-related service (e.g., sitting on institutional committees, mentoring students of color). Furthermore, as Exum (1983) indicated, although service responsibilities burden faculty of color, institutions need the participation of these faculty members on committees. Service, therefore, may be important for both the faculty member and institution because it (a) increases the diversity of perspectives (Menges and Exum 1983); (b) ensures sensitivity to the needs of people of color (Tack and Patitu 1992); and (c) may be personally rewarding to faculty of color (Johnsrud 1993). In this regard, the problem is deemed not necessarily as one of institutional abuse, but as a structural barrier to faculty advancement.

In summary, the research literature privileges an understanding of the "problem of service" as resulting from institutional or structural constraints. This literature indicates either that (1) institutional structures create the problem of service, thus, it advocates the reduction of institutional demands (see, e.g., Banks 1984) or the development of special resources (e.g., mentors) to deal with the problem (see, e.g., Blackwell 1988; Tack and Patitu 1992); or (2) faculty members are unable (because of accumulative disadvantages) to understand institutional structures, thus, it provides advice for effective negotiation of those barriers (See, e.g., McKay 1988; Padilla and Chavez 1995). In both cases, the literature provides recommendations for helping faculty of color cope with the conflicting demands of the promotion and tenure process. The literature, however, neither criticizes the practices and norms that create the conflicting demands in the first place, nor acknowledges the role of agency in understanding faculty of color in White institutions. Using data from a study of faculty of color, I will argue that faculty of color do face serious constraints regarding service, but service sets the stage for a critical agency that presents the possibility of resisting and redefining those constraints.

Methods

The concerns raised in this paper arose from a qualitative study of faculty of color, in which I sought to understand how they constructed the promotion and tenure process. I conducted interviews between September 1994 and October 1995 with 16 faculty of color (8 tenured, 8 untenured) at a large, historically and predominantly White, private Carnegie Research II university in a moderate-sized city in the Northeastern part of the United States. The institution was a prestigious research university, with selective student and faculty recruitment processes. It ranked nationally within the top 40 of American institutions of higher education (U.S. News and World Report, 1995). Students and faculty were recruited nationally and internationally. The university had over ten-thousand undergraduate students, three-thousand graduate students, and nine-hundred full-time faculty (the latter number includes full-time tenured, tenure-track, and non-tenure-track faculty, but does not include part-time or adjunct faculty). The university was primarily residential, with the bulk of its student-body consisting of traditionally-aged college students. It had thirteen schools and colleges, numerous departments and programs, and granted undergraduate and graduate degrees in most academic disciplines and professions.

The faculty was evaluated on teaching, service, and scholarly achievement; scholarship was defined primarily through research and publications. During the period of the interviews, the institution's officers discussed giving more weight to teaching and service than in the past. They discussed this, for example, in the 1994 yearly presidential report to the community (which was published in the institution's newspaper), in a "town" meeting I attended, in the 1995 chief academic officer's address to the faculty, and through other avenues (e.g., the school newspaper, college of education and departmental faculty meetings I attended). The culture of the institution was such, however, that without an adequate number of publications no faculty member—no matter how well regarded in teaching and service—could expect to be positively considered for tenure. The few examples proffered by the administration as evidence of its commitment to teaching and service seemed mostly to be tenured faculty members who were promoted to full professor on the basis of excellent teaching evaluations and professional service (but who still published). At any rate, the faculty (as evidenced

TABLE 1

Breakdown by Gender, Rank, and Race

Rank	Gender	Race			Totals
		African American	Asian American	Latino/a	
Full Professor	Male	1 T	—	1 T	2
	Female	2 T	—	—	2
Associate Professor	Male	1 T	—	1 T	2
	Female	2 T	—	—	3
		1 N	—	—	(2 T)
Assistant Professor	Male	1 N	1 N	—	2
	Female	3 N	2 N	—	5
Totals		11	3	2	16
		(6 T)	(0 T)	(2 T)	(8 T)

Total = 16; T = tenured; N = non-tenured.

from remarks made in public, at faculty meetings, in school newspapers, and in interviews for this study) apparently agreed that the administration's rhetoric did not match what actually happened in the faculty reward system.

The faculty, staff, and students at the university were predominantly White, accounting for approximately 87 percent of full-time students and 87 percent of full-time faculty. Men represented 68% (621) and women 32% (290) of the 1995 faculty. Faculty of color accounted for 13% (118) of the faculty (these figures include full-time non-tenure-track positions). Men of color made up 9% (83) of the faculty, 13% of the male faculty, and 70% of the faculty of color population. Women of color accounted for 4% (35) of the faculty, 12% of the female faculty, and 30% of faculty of color. Women of color, however, were over-represented in this study's sample (10–6). The reason for this was that the snowballing technique was used to identify most of the participants in this study, and the faculty members tended to refer me to women. The extent to which the faculty members were involved in institutional governance may have had something to do with the over-representation of women in this study. The women in this study appeared to be more involved than the men in institutional activities (e.g., the Black and Latino faculty association), and so these women were easily identifiable to other faculty of color.

There were two selection criteria for this study: (1) the faculty members had to be tenured or on the tenure track; and (2) they had to be members of a traditionally underrepresented racial or ethnic group. Of the faculty members in this study, four were tenured full professors; four were tenured associate professors; two were untenured associate professors; and six were untenured assistant professors (see Table 1 for a breakdown of my sample by rank, gender, and race). Of the untenured faculty members, one Asian American woman was denied tenure and was appealing at the time of the interview, and one Asian American man had resigned and was completing the year (he believed that he was not going to be recommended for tenure by his colleagues). Of the other untenured faculty, one woman was preparing for the tenure review; two (1 woman and 1 man) had completed their third-year reviews; and three women were preparing for their third-year reviews.

The racial and gender make-up of the sample was: eight African American women; three African American men; two Asian American women; one Asian American man; and two Latino men (see Table 1). I attempted, but was unable, to obtain interviews with Latina professors. There were only seven Latina faculty members in the institution and only three were on the tenure-track—all were untenured. The three Latinas who qualified for this sample could not be reached in time to complete the study. There were no Native American professors at the institution who qualified for this study (in fact, there was only one non-tenure-track Native American woman in the institution).

TABLE 2

Breakdown by Race, Tenure Status, and Discipline

Race	Tenure Status	Discipline										
		Anthropology	Business	Counseling	History	Law	Nursing	Political Science	Psychology	Social Work	Sociology	Totals
African American	tenured	—	—	1W	1M	1W	—	—	1W	1W	1M	6 (4 W)
	non-tenured	—	1 M 1 W	—	—	1 W	1W	—	—	—	1W	5 (4 W)
Asian American	tenured	—	—	—	—	—	—	—	—	—	—	0
	non-tenured	—	—	—	1 W	1 W	—	1 M 1 W	—	—	—	3 (2 W)
Latino/a	tenured	1 M	—	—	—	—	—	—	—	1 M	—	2 (0 W)
	non-tenured	—	—	—	—	—	—	—	—	—	—	0
Totals		1 (0 W)	2 (1 W)	1 (1 W)	1 (0 W)	3 (3 W)	1 (1 W)	2 (1 W)	1 (1 W)	2 (1 W)	2 (1 W)	16 (8 W)

Total = 16; M = Man, W = Woman.

My sample represented 10 academic and professional disciplines: anthropology, business, counseling, history, law, nursing, political science, psychology, social work, and sociology (see Table 2 for a breakdown of my sample by race, tenure status, and discipline). Except for anthropology and counseling (where each faculty member was one of two faculty of color), the faculty members in this study accounted for all the racial or ethnic minorities in their departments (see Table 2).

Except for the first faculty member (who was interviewed twice so that she could respond to emerging themes), I interviewed each faculty member once in his or her office. The interviews averaged one and a half hours. I used an open-ended, semi-structured format and asked the participants to talk about their promotion and tenure experiences. As the study progressed, I asked the faculty members to respond to some of the emerging themes in the study. I analyzed and coded the data using Strauss' (1987) qualitative analysis method. This method involves raising questions and providing provisional answers, organizing the data into manageable units, looking for core concepts, labeling them, and attempting to understand the relationship among core concepts (Strauss 1987). The themes discussed in this chapter arose from careful coding and analysis of the interview transcripts, from the participants' responses to emerging issues, from discussions with colleagues, and from a review of the relevant literature.

The Significance of Race-Related Service

Service was a salient concern for all but two of the faculty members; the tenured African American man in sociology and the untenured Asian American woman in political science did not mention service in the interview (unless otherwise noted, the rest of the paper does not include them in the discussion). Although the rest of the faculty members knew they were evaluated on more important criteria (i.e., important for the institution), service took on significance in their day-to-day activities. This was as true for the five men as it was for the nine women. Apparently, gender was not related to the significance of service in this study, and so I do not elaborate on gender differences in this paper. Gender was significant, however, in other studies (see, e.g., Tierney and Bensimon 1996).

The Burden of Service

The faculty members, as expected, distinguished between internal and external service. For example, an untenured African American woman law professor described her current service activities, which she had indicated were typical for law professors:

> I'm on three faculty committees, and they all have different amounts of work that's required. But at least two of them require a great deal of work, the Faculty Governance Committee and the Curriculum Committee. Both of those committees this year require a lot of work, so that takes up a considerable amount of time. And then I am on some national committees, and the work there really depends on what's going on at the time. I might have to do reports or participate in some decision making. Sometimes it's by conference call, sometimes I have to travel to meetings and that kind of thing. I've been invited to speak at different places. It takes a lot of time to do these things.

According to this faculty member, she spent a great deal of her time doing service, but given the law profession's commitment to service, this may not be unusual. The other two law professors spoke similarly about service, and all three law professors indicated that service was an important and highly valued (but not as important as scholarship or teaching) criterion for promotion and tenure. The law professors' perceptions that service was valued in promotion and tenure, however, were not supported by the other faculty members, even in other professional studies (e.g., counseling, nursing, and social work). No other faculty member indicated that service was valued significantly in faculty evaluation. It may be, therefore, that law is unique in valuing service, or this finding may apply only to the particular law school in this study during the time of the interviews.

Despite the law professors' beliefs that service was important, they understood that too much service would seriously reduce their chances to attain tenure. Any kind of service activity necessarily meant the faculty members spent less time on scholarship and research. Their understanding of the demands on their time for service matched what was explained in the research literature; for example, that service can lead to cultural taxation (Tierney and Bensimon 1996). Because the faculty members knew that fulfilling these responsibilities took too much time away from research, they felt burdened by service expectations. As the untenured African American woman in business explained, "Service is the downfall of most faculty of color. They are pulled in so many directions for service that frequently their research is not as high a priority." In this study, the burdens of service required that the faculty members become very possessive of their time. They talked often about having to "control" their time or "be selective" when deciding which activities warranted their commitments.

My study revealed a distinction between tenured and untenured faculty members regarding the burdens felt due to service. The tenured faculty members were more likely than the untenured faculty to believe that individuals had *some* control over their time. The untenured faculty members, on the other hand, were somewhat more ambivalent about what they attributed as the reasons for their burdens. For example, this untenured woman in business explained how she negotiated the demands for service:

> I had to use my department head as an excuse to say no [to service requests]. When in fact, part of what I negotiated coming in here was the right to say no for two and a half years with no backlash—political backlash. In other words, hands off. And most institutions who are really committed to your survival will give you that.

This business professor, who was in her third year of service, indicated that she had "negotiated" the "right to say no." But she believed as well that the institutions who are committed to faculty of color "will give you" that right. She expressed to me prior to these comments that she had not published enough to attain tenure, mostly because she was heavily involved in service. She attributed her lack of scholarly production both to herself and to the institution, particularly her department. The business professor's sentiments contrasted with those of the tenured professor in history, who expressed little sympathy for those faculty members who spend too much time on service. He explained that promotion and tenure committees will not care about why a faculty member engages in too much service; they will judge that faculty member on the basis of his or her scholarship (and perhaps teaching). Thus, this history professor believed that if faculty of color do not focus on scholarship, they will have to "bear the consequences."

The history professor's sentiments were not completely supported by the other tenured faculty members, who recognized that it was difficult for untenured faculty members to refuse to participate in service activities (even this history professor explained that it was difficult for him to say no to others who requested his participation in institutional and community activities). His comments, however, indicate that tenured faculty of color have negotiated effectively the demands required of them, and the untenured faculty members could not be certain at the time of the interviews that they did so as well. It was understandable, therefore, that the tenured faculty members felt they had more control over their situations than the untenured faculty.

The Importance of Race-Related Service

The 14 faculty members who talked about service expressed a distinction between "general service" and "race-related work." General service included community, institutional, and professional activities that all faculty members are expected to perform (e.g., curriculum committees, program development, reviewing journal manuscripts, etc.) but that had little direct connection to race, diversity, or social justice. Race-related service, however, was any community, institutional, or professional activity perceived by the faculty members as benefitting their racial or ethnic communities. Race-related service presented for them the most difficult challenges because they felt compelled or driven to participate in activities they believed would benefit their racial or ethnic communities. This was true even for the history professor who believed that faculty of color had to "bear the consequences" of spending too much time on service. He decided often to choose race-related service over other types of activities.

To illustrate this compulsion toward race-related service, consider the comments of the Latino full professor in social work, who after telling me that he had to carefully control his time, explained why he chose to engage in race-related service and research:

Faculty of color's circumstances are quite different from other people in that if you have any social consciousness, and any identification with your respective ethnic or racial group, you are going to want to help in some way, through your discipline or otherwise.

Race-related service was perceived as providing political benefits to the faculty members' respective racial or ethnic communities. But such service seemed to have personal benefits as well. For example, the untenured assistant professor in sociology explained why her work with African-American women faculty and graduate students at the University were important to her:

My regular meetings with these people have really offered me a great cultural outlet and spiritual support. We need these groups to support each other. That kind of support fosters an environment that's going to be conducive for a person of color to thrive. And it allows us to maintain a critical mass, and that is really important.

Consider as well these comments from another untenured associate professor in nursing, who explained how her community work with other nurses of color allowed her to deal with political ("minority issues in the health community") and personal issues ("I need these other voices"):

I have a support group made up of black women nurses who work in the community. And next week, Thursday, Friday and Saturday, we will meet—we meet quarterly. We talk about minority issues in the health community. They're very important to me, these other voices. Because the question is, are you the only [Black] voice where you work? Is this just your experience? When I tell them what's happening in my school, I want to know if I'm crazy, because that's how I'm made to feel. I need these other voices. So this community activity is one of the places where I talk about these issues.

Race-related work, therefore, may provide an opportunity for interpersonal support, which was important for these few faculty of color at a predominant White institution. And although race-related service was particularly important for the untenured faculty members, it was significant for the tenured ones as well. For example, the tenured African American woman in counseling explained why she often works hard at forming networks and support groups at the institution and elsewhere:

You know, I benefit a lot, or I have benefitted a lot, because of my broad network. I know administrators. I know full professors. I know presidents of universities. I know scholars all over the country. And when I have decisions to make, I'll call them. And I'll ask what they think about such and such. And they say, "Well that's not even worth worrying about;" or, "You should be doing this, or have you thought about this." Because there's many people with a lot of wisdom. It's very difficult to maneuver academia by yourself. And they can save you from many mistakes and a lot of grief. And much of it they've experienced themselves. My network is multi-colored, multi-faceted. And I have a very strong support network in my home and in my academic circles. I know people in small colleges, historically Black colleges, Southern colleges, Northern colleges, Western colleges, all over the world.

The finding that race-related work has personal or political benefit was corroborated by the research literature. For example, Turner et al. (1997) stressed the importance of networks and support groups for retaining faculty of color (see also Tierney and Bensimon 1996).

The finding that race-related service is important for faculty of color may not be surprising to many, but its significance should not be underestimated by anyone. Consider the comments of these three faculty members, who did not feel connected to other faculty of color, and who were having difficulties in their departments. The first faculty member believed that her chances for tenure were "problematic." The other two faculty members did not attain tenure:

I think, consciously, and I think in terms of verbal communication, [my colleagues] are extremely supportive. I think, unconsciously, and given the structure and the system, not very much at all. It's up to me (untenured African American woman, third year, business—preparing for her third-year review).

I got here—nobody knew I was here. [pause] It was raining, and [my wife and I] had to go around town from hotel to hotel after a drive in the car from [another state], trying to find a place. And then, we're sitting in our apartment and had no furniture and stuff—and we don't know anyone. All I'm doing is I'm teaching courses. Nobody is checking out to see whether or not we're alive, whether we have things to do in the evening, whether we met people in the department, whether—there's just no humanity here (untenured Asian American man, sixth year, political science—resigned before our interview).

> I was very collegial with my colleagues. I got along well with them. I didn't think there was a problem until this tenure thing came up. I didn't realize I was hated (untenured Asian American woman, sixth year, political science—denied tenure before our interview).

These three faculty members, especially the two Asian American professors, did not feel connected to other faculty of color. The business faculty member engaged in a great deal of service with students and the community, but she felt isolated from other faculty of color. The Asian American man similarly engaged in a great deal of service but not with other faculty of color. The Asian American woman was one of two faculty members who did not mention service during the interview.[2] These comments illustrate the extreme isolation perceived by those faculty members who do not feel connected to other faculty of color. Unfortunately, there is little opportunity for faculty of color to meet others like them in their departments (only law had more than two faculty of color), and, therefore, race-related service may provide the only opportunities for faculty of color to meet others for support.

The finding that faculty of color might feel compelled to engage in race-related work for personal and political reasons must be tempered by the comments of a few of the faculty members in this study. Not all of the faculty members felt strongly about race-related work. As mentioned previously, two faculty members did not discuss service at all in the interviews (this does not mean, of course, that they did not have feelings about this issue). And the Latino tenured professor in anthropology expressed being insulted when he realized during his third-year review that he was expected to join the "faculty-staff minority association":

> [We appointed a new department chair before my third-year evaluation. In anthropology there is no committee for this review.] And [the chair] gave me my review, and it said that I had worked on this thing, and I was working on a book manuscript, and the teaching is good. And it said that I had "not been involved in the faculty-staff minority association." And I looked at that, and I thought, hell, what is this? And I said "this is racist. What you're doing is you're saying here that because of my skin color I'm supposed be involved in some voluntary organization?" And I swear I didn't make this up—I actually said this. I said, "if I were Irish—because remember this is in March—if I were Irish, would you put down that I didn't march in the St. Patrick's Day Parade?" She got really flustered. So she changed it around. And it later said, "as a minority faculty, Peter should be careful not to become too involved in organizations." And I kicked myself because I had been so embarrassed for her that I had given back the piece of paper. When I said I won't sign this—because you're supposed to sign off on it, and I said I wouldn't—I should have realized, my God, that I should have kept that review for blackmail. Because this is illegal. On that piece of paper, she's saying "I've seen you as a person of color, and I'm treating you differently." So, essentially, the message was the same as a derogatory name, it just wasn't as threatening.

This anthropology professor obviously resisted being victimized by what Reyes and Halcon (1988) called the racism of the "typecasting syndrome," or by what Tierney and Bensimon (1996) argued is one of the effects of "cultural taxation." He did, however, perform service for his ethnic community (e.g., he mentored his students of color, and he worked with the Latino community), but he was careful about dissociating this service from his ethnic identity. These comments illustrate, therefore, that although race-related service may be important to the most of faculty of color, it poses a risk that they will be typecasted as preferring such service to other types of activities (or other types of service).

The notion of *preference* should be explored further in these types of studies. It is important to note that in this study, the burdens perceived by the faculty members were as likely to be present regardless of whether the service was "race-related" or not. Although a few of the faculty members (five) indicated that they enjoyed race-related work more than any other type of activity, the importance of the finding about race-related work is *not* that the faculty members *preferred* such work, but that they perceived it as *more important* than other types of activities. This is not to say that the notion of preference is unsupportable; it means only that the assumption of preference should be examined in these types of studies.

Nevertheless, generally, the faculty members in this study clearly expressed that race-related work was important to them. This importance stemmed from the belief that this type of service (a) helped them cope with difficulties encountered in their workplaces [e.g., "I want to know if I'm crazy" (nursing professor), or "It offered me a cultural outlet" (the woman in sociology)]; and (b) benefitted their racial communities [e.g., "you're going to want to help out in some way" (the tenured man in social work)]. There might be, therefore, an inextricable link between race-related service and personal and political goals. In the next sections, I explore this link in more depth.

Race-Related Service and Coping

All except five faculty members talked about coping with isolating and alienating work environments by engaging in race-related service. This finding was not surprising, and it confirmed what sociologists contended about participation in ethnic institutions, rituals, and practices: such participation allows racial and ethnic groups to cope with hostile environments (See, e.g., Hutnik 1991; Lal 1995; Porter and Washington 1993). Eleven faculty members in this study participated in race-related service in order to cope with problems encountered in their departments and colleges, especially the problem of isolation. Few departments had more than a few faculty of color, and in this study only law had more than two such faculty members. Isolation was particularly difficult for the untenured faculty members (all but the law professors discussed feeling isolated), a problem that Boice (1993) and Tierney and Bensimon (1996) also found prevalent in their research.

Isolation is encountered by many faculty members (see, e.g., Tierney and Bensimon 1996), not just faculty of color; it may be an inherent consequence of conventional ways of performing faculty work. But isolation may strike faculty of color in particularly problematic ways given their under-representation at most institutions. These faculty members, therefore, must make an effort to find the kind of "ethnic participation" referred to by sociologists and that White faculty members may take for granted.

Furthermore, this kind of isolation (i.e., from others of one's racial or ethnic group) may be felt by tenured faculty as well. In this study, five tenured faculty members indicated feeling isolated from other faculty of color. For example, consider the comments of the Latino full professor in social work, who explained why he was working to form a Latino support group at the University:

> The reason is because I would like to see some kind of mutual support group for Latinos, which we don't have now. So that we know about one another; or know when somebody is down; or know how to help out. I think with the growing number of Latinos in this Country, this University is so far behind that it needs to move very quickly in making sure that there are Latinos throughout the University, including at the highest levels of the administration. All the way down. Right now, Latinos are concentrated in janitorial or custodial positions.

In this study, tenure status did not seem significant to perceptions of isolation. While White colleagues might be supportive, the faculty members usually sought other faculty of color (even those who were not members of their own ethnic or racial group) to cope with such isolation. This latter point was not surprising. As Hutnik (1991) explained, racial and ethnic minority individuals seek out others like them because they share a common culture, a common history, or a common tradition.

Furthermore, for the faculty members in this study, race-related service provided more than an opportunity to meet others with similar backgrounds, it offered them the opportunity to be *validated*. As the nursing faculty member indicated about her community work with other nurses of color, "When I tell them what's happening [in my school], I want to know if I'm crazy, because that's how I'm made to feel." This study confirmed, therefore, what Alperson (1975) indicated about racial minorities: that they often seek the support of other minorities in order to confirm and validate experiences of exclusion and to share the common experience of rage and pain engendered by such exclusion.

Race-Related Work and Political Change

The primary (and most common) reason given by the faculty members (all but two) in this study for the significance of race-related service was to represent and advance the interests of traditionally-subordinated social groups (all except three participants expressed this reason). They felt they were speaking for, and representing, those who could not do so for themselves. Despite feeling the burdens of service, the faculty members felt obligated to, and responsible for, their racial or ethnic groups. As a result, they engaged in activities within the academy and outside of the academy they felt benefitted their respective communities.

The faculty members' activities "within the academy" included participation in institutional committees addressing the retention of students of color, hate speech, affirmative action, ethnic studies departments, and teacher training. In their disciplines, the faculty members engaged in race-related work as well (e.g., heading up minority caucuses, or, for one faculty member, involvement in a national task force dealing with racism). This race-related work was perceived as extremely important for ensuring that their institution and disciplines address the needs of racial and ethnic minorities (as well as other traditionally-subordinated social groups). To illustrate this point, consider the comments of the nursing professor, who discussed why she felt it essential to become involved in the promotion and tenure committee of her college:

> In my second year here, I asked to be a member of the Promotion and Tenure Committee. It is one of the unique things about this University that you don't have to be tenured to be on the Promotion and Tenure Committee. Having found this out through my network with the minority faculty here, I made it my business to be asked to be on the Committee. There was a little resistance because they needed someone to do the work. So I've had the opportunity to be on the Committee, which was revising the promotion and tenure policies. And so I was able to talk about diversity issues.

None of the faculty members expressing this concern took for granted that their White colleagues would be similarly concerned about "diversity issues." As a result, they felt responsible for these issues, a responsibility which placed on them additional burdens but also provided them with a significant sense of accomplishment if their goals were achieved.

"Outside of the academy" the faculty members engaged often in work they believed benefitted their communities and promoted social justice. These activities included community work dealing with low income people (e.g., homelessness and hunger), police brutality, prisoners' rights, teenage pregnancy, urban public schools, and hate crimes. A tenured full professor in law, who specialized in communications law, for example, stated: "I am involved in work that addresses such questions as "What about children of color? How do decisions about pay per view affect communities of color in terms of that service?" " This faculty member indicated that she tied her service work with her scholarship; in other words, she wrote about these issues so that she could have credibility when she participated in such activities, and her involvement in these activities gave her the data she needed to write about those issues. Another law professor, an untenured African American woman, directly connected her service work with her teaching:

> You know the stuff that's going on at the jail [in this city], which prompted the Justice Department to investigate the county jail [police brutality of prisoners, particularly Black inmates]. We thought, myself and another professor here who works in the law clinic, that these are important issues. This was a unique opportunity to create a forum to provide some information not only about the conditions at the jail, but to tie that into the larger lessons that we're doing in the classroom. So we developed that. That kind of thing is important. You know, it's the way you view the role [as a faculty woman of color], and the kinds of things you do, and whether you try to bring those issues to the Law School.

Race-related work, therefore, gave the faculty members the opportunity to be engaged in political activism on behalf of traditionally-marginalized groups. The untenured African American law professor referred to her involvement in such service and "bringing these issues to the law school" as a matter of "social justice."

The law profession might be conducive to this understanding of one's faculty role. The untenured law professor argued explicitly that service allows law professors to become parts of the "larger debates in society":

> Service is not a difficult standard to meet because most of us would do those things anyway. It's part of why we want to do lawyering [sic] before we get into teaching. And we continue those aspects of our professional lives in academia, those activities that allow us to do things that are of interest to us—women in law types of things—that you may not have the opportunity to do within the law school. You know, there's a whole big world of lawyers and organizations doing things that interest you. Service actually encourages you to get out there and be a part of the larger debates in society.

For this faculty member, it was her commitment to service that led her into the classroom. Seven other faculty members expressed the same sentiment, so it might be inappropriate to suggest that the law professor's perceptions are limited solely to her profession. But the finding that faculty of color might choose academe to serve their communities provides a counter-argument to those offered by scholars claiming that faculty have other preferred roles and activities (See, e.g., Banks 1984; Blackburn and Lawrence 1995; Centra 1993; Jarvis 1991).

Furthermore, and perhaps more significant, is the finding that the faculty members linked service with teaching and research in a particularly important way. The law professor, for example, suggested that linking her activist service with her teaching was "social justice." The African American woman in sociology similarly indicated that she saw herself as a "scholar-activist" because she engaged in race-related research and service. This study corroborated, therefore, what a few scholars have implied about such service: it may provide evidence of political or social activism by faculty members (e.g., Cuadraz 1997).

By choosing to engage in race-related service despite understanding the risks of doing so, the faculty members were exercising an agency that appeared to contest the predominant definitions of faculty work. In other words, they knew that their institution required conformity with prevailing notions of merit, but they felt also that their work forced their colleagues to rethink (if not accept) its importance in creating social change. And, just as significant, some of the faculty members tied race-related service to their scholarship or teaching, thus, presenting themselves to their colleagues and students not as detached researchers and teachers but as "scholar activists," deeply engaged in initiating social change. Race-related service, and the agency that supports it, therefore, might set the stage for the contestation of institutional structures and roles, and the notions of merit ensured by them. The rest of the paper elaborates further on the notion of agency and social change.

Race-Related Service and Agency

It would be naive to deny that service demands, regardless of type, impose on faculty of color additional burdens not imposed on their White counterparts. Because service requires faculty of color to resolve difficult role-conflicts (e.g., between service and research roles; between racial minority and faculty roles), it can be, as this study's untenured woman in business explained, "the downfall of most faculty of color." Conversely, perhaps it would be naive as well to conceptualize service only in terms of institutional demands without accounting for agency in faculty of color's experiences. The research literature, even when it recognizes that faculty of color might prefer to engage in service over the other activities (e.g., Aguirre 1987; Johnsrud 1993), stresses institutional structures and de-emphasizes human agency. For example, Aguirre (1987) argued that the academy's organizational logic transforms faculty of color's participation in service into personal expectation. Aguirre seems to argue that there can be no agency that does not result from the structures of the academy.

Most of the faculty members in my study (all but four), and particularly the tenured faculty members (seven), however, suggested a soft kind of indeterminism in talking about their experiences. In other words, they often blamed themselves (or blamed others) for the negative consequences of decisions, or they attributed their actions to personal "choices," "mistakes," and so forth. The presence of this "blaming" was especially true in their discussion of service. The tenured professor in history, for example, explained that faculty of color's decisions to engage in service activities were "choices" that had "consequences":

> Those of us who sit in judgement on tenure and promotion will say, "Well, people don't realize that they've got some choices—hard choices to make. Are you going to accommodate the students in this way? Are you going to perform these off campus duties and responsibilities? Or are you going to do some research and writing, and become known off the campus in the general American academic field?" That's a decision that most would say each individual would have make for him or herself. And if people don't make the right one, then they have to bear the consequences.

As I indicated previously, no other tenured faculty spoke with such tone, but they did privilege an understanding of "choice" in discussing how faculty of color negotiate the promotion and tenure process. In addition to the word "choice," the faculty members used language that connoted a kind of "free will," and that academe (and the institution) could somehow be "negotiated." For example, the untenured African American professor in law explained regarding demands from students of color that *"You have to keep control over your time. . . . If I didn't keep some control over that situation, then I could spend all of my day talking to students outside of class."* The untenured woman in business stated, also about student demands, "The first year that I was here, I told people to pretend that I wasn't here—in terms of students and student groups' needs. *I was totally unavailable,* and I was extremely productive [in terms of scholarship]. This year *I made myself available,* and I have suffered." The other untenured professor in business stated in regards to departmental committee work, *"I got involved* in things that were for the school's benefit, but were not necessarily for my own. . . . *But that was a choice I made.* I don't put that off on anybody else." The tenured male professor in social work explained in regard to excessive service demands, *"You have a couple of choices.* You either stop doing these activities and concentrate on tenure and promotion. Or *you can do them over and above everything else* that is required for tenure. But you can not do them instead of what is required for tenure and promotion." All this language reveals that the faculty members perceived as *negotiable* the structural constraints that characterized their experiences as faculty of color in White institutions (e.g., excessive service demands, merit defined as scholarship). My study illustrates, therefore, that the structure/agency conflict is much more complex and contentious than is accounted for in the literature.

Any elaboration of a notion of agency, however, must recognize that faculty "choices" are not easy to make, and many faculty members do not make the "right" choices. Furthermore, and most important, such elaboration must account for the constraints imposed by social structures, which are there, obdurate, and seriously restrict individuals' ability to exercise "free will." The research literature's emphasis on institutional structures in explaining the challenges faced by faculty of color, however, fails to account for the "temporal" nature of social structures; that is, social structures must be repeated by individuals to ensure their efficacy (Butler 1997). In other words, as Giddens (1987) explained in different words, institutional structures results from "patterns of social activity reproduced across time and space" (p. 11). Paradoxically, social structures are created by an agency that is constrained by those structures. Thus, although the language in these interviews implies "free will," one must account in theorizing about the experiences of faculty of color the interplay between agency and social structures.

I put forward another view of agency that does not privilege the rationalist discourse of "free will." It is theoretical, and, thus, it is subject to application and evaluation. In the rest of this paper, I speculate on the complex link between structure, resistance, power, and agency in order to provoke readers into thinking differently about faculty of color and the promotion and tenure process. Using as illustration the notions of race-related service I discussed previously, I redefine agency, not as free will, but as *actions that are possible within the context of disciplinary power.* I borrow Gramsci's (1971) notion of "critical" agency as "purposeful" (or "deliberate" or "designed") action that resists hegemonic practices which ensure and justify the social domination of some individuals by others. In other words, "social-justice" service, for lack of a better term, arguably considered "the downfall of faculty of color," might resist institutional structures, and in resisting those structures presents the possibility of redefining them.

An understanding of the power of social structures is important in order to adequately recognize the "problem" of service for faculty of color. Blauner (1972) argued that racial oppression is institutionalized in processes that "maintain domination—control of whites over nonwhites—[because these processes] are built into the major institutions. These institutions either exclude or restrict the participation of racial groups by procedures that have become conventional, part of the bureaucratic system of rules and regulations" (pp. 9–10). Blauner, obviously, emphasizes social structures, explaining how they oppress individuals and constrain agency. Power, therefore, is, according to Blauner, not so much possessed by Whites, as it is embedded in social structures. Referring back to academe, power might be re-conceptualized, not as possessed by White faculty members, administrators, and promotion and tenure committees who intentionally reject any definition of merit that does not privilege scholarship, but is embedded (and disguised) in the structures of the promotion and tenure process—in the rules, practices, norms, and discourses which privilege certain behaviors over others.

Incorporating too static a notion of these structures, however, prevents understanding how human agency can subvert the power of structures. As indicated previously, the power of social structures has a "temporal life," thus, agency is constrained but not determined in advance. That is, because structures do not take place once and for all (they are "temporal"), they must be repeated by individuals to reconsolidate their power and efficacy (Butler 1997). Structures, therefore, remain structures only through their being reinstated as such, and because they must be reinstated to remain efficient, they are vulnerable to subversion and redefinition. Perhaps, from the repetition of institutional structures in higher education there emerges the possibility of a critical agency from the "margins of power," to borrow Butler's words (1997, p. 156). In other words, race-related (or social-justice) service, might provide the context for the kind of agency that subverts institutional structures.

The agency discussed here, however, can be overemphasized; that is, it can not be deemed to transcend power. Critical agency must be viewed within the context of disciplinary power. Foucault (1977) lends further understanding to this notion of agency. He argued that power can not be conceptualized merely as the prerogative of states, institutions, or classes of individuals. Foucault argued that power is "disciplinary" and its effects are normalization (pp. 200–201). Power is ensured by the "disciplinary mechanisms" embedded in structures, practices, and relationships (power is everywhere), and these mechanisms observe and regulate individuals. The effectiveness of disciplinary mechanisms lies in the fact that individuals know they are being observed, and behave appropriately. For example, the emphasis on scholarship in faculty evaluation might be a disciplinary mechanism that observes faculty (to determine which faculty warrant a reward) and regulates them (by providing an "objective" basis for punishing those faculty members who refuse to conform); scholarship, then, allows faculty to discipline themselves and each other through faculty evaluation committees. Power, though diffuse, scattered, and invisible, regulates behavior so pervasively and silently that individuals internalize its normalizing-effects and then regulate themselves. As Foucault (1980) argued, power is everywhere local, in the minute details of everyday life (p. 60).

Any understanding of the power of human agency or social structure should be understood within the context of disciplinary power. In other words, disciplinary power provides the "coercion" that constitutes the agency that creates and repeats social structures. Thus, for example, the discourse of academic merit, and its realization in institutional practices, might be the "discipline" that reinforces the structures of the promotion and tenure process. But human agency, as Butler (1997) suggested is constrained, but not determined in advance of social structures. Thus, resistance is possible, but perhaps only "locally." Resistance to power, for Foucault (1980) was "anti-disciplinarian" (i.e., the assertion of counter-mechanisms, potentially repressive, of course, but also potentially politically liberating). While disciplinary power "in general" might be impossible to resist because it permeates social relationships and practices, any particular disciplinary mechanism is subject to resistance and subversion. And, thus, resistance is always most effective when localized. That is, local struggles are the sites of confrontation with power. Resistance in academe, therefore, likely begins with individuals in departments who reject "common sense" to subvert what is deemed an oppressive social practice. Scholars should focus attention to the local sites of tension between structure and agency.

Neither Butler nor Foucault would negate the structural oppression explained by Blauner; they recognized, however, that social structures have temporal (Butler) and disciplinary (Foucault) bases. Although structures might be reinforced by "disciplinary mechanisms," those mechanisms can be stripped of their hegemonic power. Thus, the elaboration of structure in the research literature about faculty of color and service should be redefined as the instances of struggles between agency and structure—between power and its resistance. These struggles may provide the settings for the *possibility* of, per Butler, the agency that emerges from the margins of power, or, per Foucault, the local struggle at the site of confrontation with power. Therefore, while racism, institutional prerogatives, conventions of promotion and tenure, and traditional notions of merit all constrain faculty of color's choices, they might exercise a critical agency that resists these forces (not always effectively, of course), but in doing so, they make *possible* the subversion and redefinition of these structures.

Agency and Resistance in Higher Education

Despite pointing the benefits of service, much of the research literature emphasizes the problem of service (i.e., its obstacles to faculty advancement). Yet, when framing service as a problem for faculty members, many scholars fail to address the ethical questions raised by institutions (and the individuals who act on their behalf) which demand from faculty that which they know will not be rewarded. More important, the "problem perspective" reinforces prevailing notions of merit that work against faculty of color. This perspective does not question, for example, the economic and disciplinary coercion that ensures that service (a large part of faculty work) is deemed less valuable than the other promotion and tenure criteria. Faculty of color, of course, must be concerned with the consequences of service, but they also should be aware of those disciplinary mechanisms which impose obstacles to the kinds of political actions that will resist those mechanisms.

The prevailing discourse of merit does not account for how service, specifically that which may be called "social-justice" service (e.g., race-related work), presents the possibility of redefining existing structural barriers for traditionally-subordinated groups. I argued in this paper that such service sets the stage for critical agency. Without such agency, traditionally-subordinated groups will never share equally in society's resources, and social institutions will continue to maintain advantages for Whites and males. If it is accepted that the greatest obstacle in this society for the successful inclusion of people of color is racism (or sexism), especially that which is embedded in the apparently neutral policies, practices, and norms of social institutions, then race-related work must be seen as breaking down that obstacle. The discourse of service, by focusing on its negative aspects, belittles all faculty members, but especially faculty of color, who may use service to redefine themselves as scholars *and* activists, and to connect them to their racial communities in important ways.

My argument takes a "local" perspective to social change, and the suggestions provided below are directed at faculty scholars. I do not underestimate the power of institutional change "from above;" that is, through administrative decrees, as I indicated previously in this paper is emphasized by much of the research literature. But I hope that this paper is read as providing an understanding of how individual faculty members, who ignore "common sense" in order to engage in work that seeks to initiate political change, contribute to the resistance and, potentially, redefinition of social structures.

While it is prudent always to point out the detrimental aspects of service for all faculty members, given prevailing definitions of faculty work, scholars might pay attention as well to the kinds of discourses, and their realization in institutional practices, that devalues it (e.g., the privilege given to scholarship). Rather than exerting too much effort to encourage institutions to loosen their demands for service, an inclusive strategy might be to highlight how institutional change occurs "from the ground up." With this in mind, I offer three suggestions for resisting oppressive institutional structures.

First, scholars must focus on how faculty members repeat institutional structures that constrain the choices of other faculty. Foucault (1977) pointed out how disciplinary power produces self-regulating practices, norms, and discourses. Faculty, who most make up the academic community, constitute and are constituted by these practices, norms, and discourses. Faculty, through promotion and tenure committees, place emphasis on scholarship, partly because this promotes prestige but also because individual merit is defined primarily through publications. These faculty committees, therefore, often do the "dirty work" for institutions, and so it is inappropriate to "blame" solely the *institution* for the difficulties encountered by faculty of color. In other words, scholars should explore how faculty members "discipline themselves."

Second, scholars should emphasize both the positive and negative aspects of service for faculty, institutions, and society. There has been much discussion in the literature about the importance of teaching (e.g., Boyer 1990). Service, especially when it helps to eliminate barriers preventing some groups from fully participating in society's resources, also should be considered important. Faculty scholars should recast the discourse of service, as has been recently the case with teaching, by highlighting its positive and important political benefits, including the possibility for critical agency it presents.

Finally, scholars should offer critical perspectives on faculty evaluation. They should, for example, expose the underlying assumptions and power arrangements in the discourse of individual merit. While this kind of exposure is difficult (since these assumptions and power arrangements are hidden), the focus might be on the "effects" of traditional notions of merit (and other academic conventions). In the meantime, scholars should advocate the expansion of the definition of merit. As Tierney and Bensimon (1996) indicated about much of the promotion and tenure process, merit is a social construction, one that can be redefined in a less hegemonic way.

I do not suggest the substitution of one view of merit for another. And I do not contend that the academy should ignore scholarship (or teaching). All of the promotion and tenure criteria may be important in their own right. And scholarship and teaching, as with service, provide contexts for political activism and critical agency. Furthermore, some faculty of color may not want to engage in a great deal of service, choosing instead to concentrate on the other criteria. My point is that a limited view of merit can have hegemonic effects, and so I advocate for an expanded view of merit that accounts for important politically-activist work and that rewards those faculty members—regardless of race or ethnic background—who engage in this work. An expanded view of merit benefits everyone.

Notes

1. Service in general is difficult to evaluate (Blackburn and Lawrence 1995; Centra 1993), but especially, as Tierney and Bensimon (1996, pp. 27–32) indicated, because it is defined differently at each institution.
2. Ironically, the two Asian American professors were in the same department but each disliked (and, consequently, did not support) the other, though both failed to attain tenure. I can not go much more into detail about this relationship because to do so may compromise the promise of anonymity I gave each of them. It might be important to note here, however, that gender has a significant bearing on the support faculty of color can provide to others.

References

Aguirre, A. (1987). 'An interpretive analysis of Chicano faculty in academe', *The Social Science Journal* 24(1), 71–81.

Alperson, E.D. (1975). 'The minority woman in academe', *Professional Psychology* 6(3), 252–256.

Altbach, P.G. (1994). 'Problems and possibilities: The American academic profession', in Altbach, P.G., Berdahl, R.O. and Gumport, P.J. (eds.), *Higher Education in America* (3d ed.). Amherst, NY: Prometheus Books, pp. 225–247.

Banks, W.M. (1984). 'Afro-American scholars in the university: Roles and conflicts', *American Behavioral Scientist* 27(3), 325–338.

Blackburn, R.T. and Lawrence, J.H. (1995). *Faculty at Work: Motivation, Expectation, Satisfaction.* Baltimore: The John Hopkins University Press.

Blackwell, J.E. (1988). 'Faculty issues: The impact on minorities', *The Review of Higher Education* 11(4), 417–434.

Blauner, R. (1972). *Racial Oppression in America.* New York: Harper & Row Publishers.

Boice, R. (1993). 'New faculty involvement for women and minorities', *Research in Higher Education* 34(3), 291–341.

Boyer, E. (1990). *Scholarship Reconsidered: Priorities of the Professoriate.* Princeton, NJ: Carnegie Foundation for the Advancement of Teaching.

Butler, J. (1997). *Excitable Speech: A Politics of the Performative.* New York: Routledge.

Centra, J.A. (1993). *Reflective Faculty Evaluation: Enhancing Teaching and Determining Faculty Effectiveness.* San Francisco: Jossey-Bass Publishers.

Cuadraz, G.H. (1997). 'The Chicana/o generation and the Horatio Alger myth', *Thought and Action: The NEA Higher Education Journal* 13(1), 103–120.

Davis, W.E. and Chandler, T.J.L. (1998). 'Beyond Boyer's *Scholarship Reconsidered:* Fundamental change in the university and the socioeconomic systems', *Journal of Higher Education* 69(1), 23–64.

Exum, W.H. (1983). 'Climbing the crystal stair: Values, affirmative action, and minority faculty', *Social Problems* 30(4), 383–399.

Exum, W.H., Menges, R.J., Watkins, B. and Berglund, P. (1984). 'Making it at the top: Women and minority faculty in the academic labor market', *American Behavioral Scientist* 27(3), 301–323.

Foucault, M. (1977). *Discipline and Punish: The Birth of the Prison.* New York: Vintage Books.

Foucault, M. (1980). *Power/Knowledge: Selected Interviews & Other Writings 1972–1977.* New York: Pantheon Books.

Garza, H. (1987). 'The barrioization of Hispanic faculty', *Educational Record* 68/69(4/1), 122–124.

Giddens, A. (1987). *Sociology.* New York: Harcourt Brace Javanovich.

Glassick, C.E., Huber, M.T. and Maeroff, G.I. (1997). *Scholarship Assessed: Evaluation of the Professoriate.* San Francisco: Jossey-Bass Publishers.

Gramsci, A. (1971). *Selections from the Prison Notebooks.* London: Lawrence & Wishart.

Hutnik, N. (1991). *Ethnic Minority Identity: A Social Psychological Perspective.* New York: Oxford University Press.

Jarvis, D.K. (1991). *Junior Faculty Development: A Handbook.* New York: The Modern Language Association of America.

Johnsrud, L.K. (1993). 'Women and minority faculty experiences: Defining and responding to diverse realities', *New Directions for Teaching and Learning* 53(Spring 1993), 3–16.

Johnsrud, L.K. and Des Jarlais, C.D. (1994). 'Barriers to tenure for women and minorities', *The Review of Higher Education* 17(4), 335–353.

Lal, B.B. (1955). 'Symbolic interaction theories', *American Behavioral Scientist* 38(3), 421–441.

Menges, R.J. and Exum, W.H. (1983). 'Barriers to the progress of women and minority faculty', *Journal of Higher Education* 54(2), 123–144.

McKay, N.Y. (1988). 'Minority faculty in [mainstream White] academia', in Deneef, A.L., Goodwin, C.D. and McCrate, E.S. (eds.), *The Academic's Handbook* Durham, NC: Duke University Press. pp. 46–60.

Padilla, R.V. and Chavez, R.C. (eds.) (1995). *The Leaning Ivory Tower: Latino Professors in American Universities.* Albany, NY: State University of New York Press.

Pollard, D.S. (1990). 'Black women, interpersonal support, and institutional change', in Antler, J. and Biklen, S.K. (eds.), *Changing Education: Women as Radicals and Conservators.* Albany, NY: State University of New York Press, pp. 257–276.

Porter, J.R. and Washington, R.E. (1993). 'Minority identity and self-esteem', in Blake, J. and Hagen, J. (eds.), *Annual Review of Sociology* 19. Palo Alto, CA: Annual Reviews, Inc. pp. 139–161.

Reyes, M.D.L. and Halcon, J.J. (1988). 'Racism in academia: The old wolf revisited', *Harvard Educational Review* 58(3), 299–314.

Strauss, A.L. (1987). *Qualitative Analysis for Social Scientists.* New York: Cambridge University Press.

Tack, M.W. and Patitu, C.L. (1992). 'Faculty job satisfaction: Women and minorities in peril', *ASHE-ERIC Higher Education Reports* 4. Washington, D.C.: Association for the Study of Higher Education.

Tierney, W.G. and Bensimon, E.M. (1996). *Promotion and Tenure: Community and Socialization in Academe.* Albany, NY: State University of New York Press.

Tierney, W.G. and Rhoads, R.A. (1993). 'Enhancing promotion, tenure and beyond: Faculty socialization as a cultural process', *ASHE-ERIC Higher Education Reports* 6. Washington, D.C.: Association for the Study of Higher Education.

Turner, C.S.V., Myers, S.L. and Creswell, J.W. (1997). 'Bittersweet success: Faculty of color in academe', *Paper Presented at the Annual Meeting of the Association for the Study of Higher Education,* October, Albuquerque, New Mexico.

U.S. News and World Report (1995). *America's Best Colleges.*

CHAPTER 20
INTERRUPTING THE USUAL: SUCCESSFUL STRATEGIES FOR HIRING DIVERSE FACULTY

DARYL G. SMITH, CAROLINE S. TURNER,
NANA OSEI-KOFI, AND SANDRA RICHARDS

Introduction

Across the country, hundreds of campuses are engaged in efforts to diversify their faculties ethnically/racially, in response to both internal and external pressures. While fueled by numerous arguments related to the increasing diversity of their student body and the need to prepare all students for a diverse society, the reality is that perhaps the least successful of all the many diversity initiatives on campuses are those in the area of faculty diversity. Despite years of affirmative action policies, faculty of color continue to be underrepresented in higher education (Astin, antonio, Cress, & Astin, 1997; Blackshire-Belay, 1998; Harvey, 2001; Pavel, Swisher, & Ward, 1994; Trower & Chait, 2002; Turner & Myers, 2000; Wilson, 1995a,b).

In response to this reality, the current literature offers numerous explanations for the low representation of faculty of color in the academy, coupled with suggestions for improving this condition. While increasing attention is being paid to the condition of Asian-American faculty, the bulk of the research today has focused on historically underrepresented African-American, Latino/a, and American Indian faculty. However, few studies to date stem from empirical work that considers the *conditions* under which appointments are made that contribute to a diverse faculty. Given the significance of hiring processes and practices in achieving a diverse faculty, this study examines the departmental search committee process and those conditions that lead to hiring diverse faculty in terms of race/ethnicity and gender.

Specifically, this study examines whether specific interventions account for the hiring of diverse faculty above and beyond hiring done in academic areas specifically focused on race and ethnicity. Using data from approximately 700 searches, we investigate the hypothesis that at institutions with predominantly White populations, hiring of faculty from underrepresented groups (African-Americans, Latina/os, and American Indians) occurs when at least one of the following three *designated* conditions are met: (1) The job description used to recruit faculty members explicitly engages diversity at the department or subfield level: (2) An institutional "special hire" strategy, such as waiver of a search, target of opportunity hire, or spousal hire, is used; (3) The search is conducted by an ethnically/racially diverse search committee.

Brief Review of the Literature

A large part of the literature on faculty diversity suggests that the lack of faculty of color stems from the relatively few, particularly underrepresented, students of color earning doctorates (Adams, 1988; Bowen & Schuster, 1986; Bowen & Sosa, 1989; Clotfelter, Ehrenberg, Getz, & Sigfried, 1991; CPEC, 1990; Myers & Turner, 1995; National Center for Educational Statistics, 1992; Norrell & Gill, 1991; Ottinger, Sikula, & Washington, 1993; Schuster, 1992; Solórzano, 1993; Thurgood & Clarke, 1995). For example, Linda J. Sax, director of a research program that oversees the

Higher Education Research Institute (HERI) national faculty survey, explains the decline in proportional minority faculty representation in the 1998–1999 survey by saying, "There hasn't been much of an increase in minority doctoral recipients over the same period—they're still only 12 percent of the Ph.D.'s" (Magner, 1999, p. A18). Viewing the issue of doctorates awarded in relationship to gains in faculty hires from the same relational premise, Aguirre (2000), examining data from 1980 to 1993, suggests that the relationship between doctoral attainment pools and faculty hiring numbers are in some cases (though not always) positively related. The use of the pool argument to explain the lack of diverse faculty is often asserted by administrators and faculty. For example, commenting on the institution's lack of progress in hiring African Americans, former president of Harvard University, Neil Rudenstine, stated that "we have to keep going back to the still really unfortunate problem of the fact that only two percent of Ph.D.s in the United States—if you exclude clinical psychology and education—awarded annually are to African Americans, and that's just a tiny number of people" (Roach, 1999, p. 37).

This limited pipeline argument is also expressed at the community college level where minority faculty constitute an even smaller percentage of full-time faculty than at four-year institutions. A survey of beliefs on recruitment of minority faculty held by Chief Academic Officers (CAO) at two-year colleges reveals that 59% of White CAOs (versus 38% of their counterparts of color) believe faculty of color are not available in technical fields, and 49% of White CAOs (versus 32% of their counterparts of color) believe that minority faculty are not available in arts and science fields (Opp, 1994).

The concern about the pipeline for future faculty is a legitimate one. Nevertheless, using the situation of Latinos in law schools as an example of the larger academic community, Olivas submits that the pipeline rationale can be deceptive. Viewing higher education as the consumer, in this case of Latino law faculty, he points out that the consumer is also the producer of the product sought after. He asks "why it is schools do not see their responsibility to recruit and graduate more Latino lawyers?" (1994, p. 131). Olivas goes on to argue that even if graduation rates are considered low, the number of graduates over time produces a pool more than capable of altering the dismally low numbers of Latino lawyers currently employed as faculty in the academy. Furthermore, Trower and Chait (2002) point out that even in fields with more scholars of color, such as education and psychology, the faculty is not diverse.

Because of pipeline issues and because of the continued limits in the labor market for faculty (Busenberg & Smith, 1997; Schuster, 1995), many assume that there is a "bidding war" in which faculty of color are sought after over "traditional" White male faculty (Mooney, 1989; White, 1989, 1992; Yale, 1990). In this context, "ordinary" institutions believe they are not comparably rich enough, located well enough, or prestigious enough to attract the few candidates who are in such high demand (El-Khawas, 1990; Harvey & Scott-Jones, 1985; Wilson, 1995a). A report from a prestigious research institution about their diversity efforts typifies this belief, wherein the institution claims that "although a concerted effort has been made, small candidate pools and intense competition between top universities has made growth in faculty members extremely difficult" (Smith, Wolf, & Busenberg, 1996, p. 3).

Contrary to this belief, faculty, postdoctoral fellows, and administrators of color deny that the typical hiring experience of minority scholars is one of bidding wars (Carter & O'Brien, 1993; Almost, 1994; Bronstein, Rothblum, & Solomon, 1993; Collins, 1990; Collins & Johnson, 1990; Cross, 1994; de la Luz Reyes & Halcon, 1991; Delgado, Stefancic, & Lindsley, 2000; El-Khawas, 1988; Garza, 1988, 1992; Menges & Exum, 1983; Michelson & Oliver, 1991; Moore, 1988; Smith, 1989; Staples, 1984; Turner, 1999; Washington & Harvey, 1989; Wilson, 1987, 1995a,b).

A recent national empirical study was designed to test the competing beliefs about faculty diversity (Smith et al., 1996). The study, examining the employment experiences of scholars who had recently earned doctorates with funding from three prestigious fellowship programs, found that the underrepresented scholars of color, even in this group, were not highly sought after, and that the bidding wars were vastly overstated. Moreover, the majority of the scientists in this study (54%)—all underrepresented scholars of color—were not pursued for faculty positions by academic institutions. In another study addressing supply and demand arguments, Olivas (1994), in a study of Latino law school faculties, concludes that the credentials of Latino/a law school faculty exceed that of their White counterparts. Olivas suggests "For most schools, white candidates with good (but not sterling) credentials are routinely considered and hired, while the high-demand/low-supply mythology about minorities persists . . ." (1994, p. 133).

While it is clear that there are a number of factors involved in the issue of diversifying faculty, the literature reports that, in order to achieve greater success, search processes must change. Turner and Myers (2000) suggest, for example, that the absence of aggressive hiring strategies may contribute to the underrepresentation of faculty of color. Many agree that it is at the departmental level that most policy decisions about hiring are made. There is, indeed, considerable power at the departmental level. Department heads and senior faculty develop recruitment plans and decide what constitutes "quality," including how scholarly productivity" is measured, how publications and research are credited, and the areas of scholarship to be emphasized (Busenberg & Smith, 1997; de la Luz Reyes & Halcon, 1991; Gainen & Boice, 1993; Pepion, 1993; Swoboda, 1993; Turner & Myers, 1997; Turner, 2002; West, 2000).

In relationship to the power dynamic, de la Luz Reyes and Halcon state "The qualifications of minorities alone are almost irrelevant [in the hiring process, instead] personal and political preferences, prejudices and fears of majority faculty and inaction of administrators play a larger role in the final decisions reached" (1991, p. 179). Similarly, Busenberg and Smith question the system of meritocracy upon which hiring decisions are supposedly made, pointing out that "informal systems of preference still mold much of American life, and take marked importance over merit" (1997, p. 170). Others have echoed these concerns (e.g., Merritt & Resken, 1997; McGinley, 1997).

Suggestions for strategies that emerge from the literature take aim at both attitudinal and structural barriers, including recommendations to involve administrators in maintaining a stronger institutional commitment to diversity, urging faculty to become involved in programs that address diversity issues, and strengthening the support for scholars of color who are prepared to enter the faculty ranks. Additional suggestions include the use of job descriptions that are relevant to institutional diversity along with institutional interventions, such as target of opportunity hires and incentive programs (Caldwell-Colbert et al., 1996; Light, 1994; Opp and Smith, 1994; Smith et al., 1996; Turner, 1999, 2002).

As previously expressed, despite these various suggestions to improve the processes by which faculty are hired, few researchers have empirically addressed the question of whether searches using such strategies yield results in relationship to faculty diversity that differ from the outcomes of "regular" searches. The present study was designed to answer this question for a limited but important sample of institutions and to develop a protocol that could be used in other studies. Hiring in ethnic studies departments would be expected to yield hiring of faculty of color. Carefully constructing a job description represents a potential intervention that links hiring to the academic program. Strategies that allow a department to bypass the usual search process or that alter the composition of search committees could be employed by any field or subfield.

Methodology

Three large elite public research universities—each of which are member institutions of the Association of American Universities (AAU)—agreed to participate as partners in this study. Because of the nature of the study, the names of the institutions, as well as all information about individuals, were kept confidential. In the end, data were compiled on 689 searches.

Each campus was asked to include all faculty hires during the period from 1995 to 1998 and to provide the following information: (a) job description; (b) discipline of the appointment; (c) race/ethnicity and gender of faculty hire; (d) race/ethnicity and gender composition of the search committee; (e) any special initiatives, funding sources, or interventions that were used in the search; and (f) the institution from which the successful candidate came (Ph.D. institution and previous place of employment, where applicable). The data had to be developed search-by-search from campus records, affirmative action documents, and school-based records. As predicted, not all data were available in every case (particularly the composition of the search committee).

In the case of one campus, all searches during the time frame under study were included, with the exceptions of medicine, classics, philosophy, political science, microbiology and molecular genetics. These exceptions were due to an inability to gather data in time to meet the completion date of the study.

Variables

The following variables were used in the study:

Job description. For quantitative purposes, job descriptions were classified according to whether they contained requirements related to diversity in the subject matter or expertise of the faculty member. Job descriptions that contained requirements relating to diversity were categorized according to how the association to diversity was made. The categories used were "department indicates diversity," "subfield within department indicates diversity," and "other salient job qualification indicates diversity." The operational definitions were as follows:

1. *Department indicates diversity* refers to Ethnic Studies programs, i.e., African-American Studies, Asian-American Studies, American Indian Studies, and Chicano/Latino/a Studies;

2. *Subfield within a department indicates diversity* covers areas such as African-American literature within an English department or race relations within a sociology department;

3. *Other salient job qualification indicates diversity* is exemplified by a call for applicants, for example, who "engender a climate that values and uses diversity in all its forms to enliven and make more inclusive the work of the organization" and with "experience in community outreach in multi-cultural settings."

Each of these was given scores of one for "yes" and two for "no."

The discipline. Positions were classified by disciplines and fields. Interdisciplinary hires and joint appointments were also noted.

The composition of the search committee. The racial/ethnic and gender composition of the search committee was described and then categorized according to whether at least one member of the search committee was from an underrepresented group.

Special hire. Any intervention strategies that bypassed normal search processes were indicated. These included spousal hires, targeted hires for fields, and incentive funds of some sort.

Race/ethnicity and gender of the faculty hire. Ethnic and gender categories were used for this study according to the classification used by the campus. While the focus of the study was on historically underrepresented African-American, Latino/a, and American Indian faculty, patterns for Asian-American and White faculty along with gender were also investigated.

Institution from which the person came. The name and pre-2001 Carnegie classification of the Ph.D. granting institution and, where available and applicable, the prior institution of hires were noted.

Flexibility. Job descriptions were coded according to whether they had some flexibility in the areas of specialty sought. Those that were not highly specific were coded as flexible (yes = 1), those that were specific were coded as not flexible (no = 2).

Diversity in the final pool. Where available, we coded the data to indicate whether there was diversity in the final pool, that is, whether an underrepresented faculty candidate (an African American, Latino/a, American Indian), or an Asian-American candidate was included.

Analysis

The data were analyzed both quantitatively and qualitatively to see if any patterns emerged. In particular, the analysis tested the hypothesis that when underrepresented faculty of color are hired, (a) the field or department into which they are hired will be more likely related to race and ethnicity or (b) a proactive intervention strategy will have been employed—significantly more often than when White men or women are hired. In addition, OLS stepwise multiple regression was employed to validate what variable or combination of variables best predicted the presence or absence of a "diversity hire." Following several readings of the entire portfolio for each hire, additional observations about field specific issues and search committee issues were also analyzed. A meeting of all principals and representatives from the campuses further validated the results of the data.

Although narrative data were not available for each search case, some portfolios included information in addition to what was requested. Where available, this information was analyzed. For instance, curriculum vitas and letters of support written on behalf of candidates for exceptional hire searches provided information about the unique qualities brought by diverse faculty members and specific reasons for using "exceptional hire" as an intervention strategy. While case studies of the search process would be very useful in future research, the data in the study provided some information from a qualitative perspective.

The data for the three institutions were pooled after analysis suggested similar overall findings in each.

Reliability

Interrater reliability was used for both the categorization system developed in the matrix and for determination of "flexibility." A subsample of every tenth search was tested using interrater reliability between two coders, and 98% agreement was obtained on the coding protocol.

Results

Hiring Conditions

Table 1 summarizes the search results for the three campuses by condition and by race/ethnicity of the faculty member hired. Of the 689 searches completed during the three-year period of the study, 3% of those hired were African American, 6% were Latino/a, 1% were American Indian, 16% were Asian American, and 74% were White.

Using job descriptions to investigate the types of strategies/conditions used for faculty hiring, each search was coded according to whether (a) the department indicated diversity; (b) a subfield within a department indicated diversity; (c) diversity was salient in other desired job qualifications; or (d) a special hire was invoked. In addition, the data also noted where both a special hire was made and the job contained a diversity indicator.

Table 2 summarizes the conditions for the three campuses combined and the percentage of special hires within each race/ethnic category. Figure 1 presents a visual representation of the results for the hiring of all underrepresented faculty combined. Of these faculty hires, 71% were hired with a diversity indicator or special-hire intervention—24% using diversity in the job description, 24% special hires, and 23% a combination of special hire and diversity indicator.

TABLE 1

Faculty Hires for 1995–1998

	AA[1]	LA[2]	AI[3]	ASA[4]	W[5]	Totals
Department indicates diversity	2	5	2		2	11
Subfield within department indicates diversity	3	2		10	25	40
Other desired job qualification indicates diversity	3			3	33	39
Special hire	6	8	3	5	51	73
Special hire & department diversity	2	1	1		2	6
Special hire & subfield indicates diversity	3	2		2	1	7
Special hire & other indicator of diversity					2	2
Position with no diversity indicator	3	24		89	395	511
Totals	22	42	6	108	511	689
	(3%)	(6%)	(1%)	(16%)	(74%)	(100%)

[1]African-American; [2]Latino/a; [3]American Indian; [4]Asian-American; [5]White.

African Americans were hired almost entirely under the designated conditions expected (86%), divided among special hires, job descriptions, and diversity departments (see Figure 2 and Table 2). All American Indians were hired as a result of diversity indicators or special hires: 50% were special hires; 33% were hired with diversity indicated in the job description; and, 17% were special hires for positions in which diversity was indicated (see Figure 3).

TABLE 2

Conditions Under Which Racial/Ethnic Group Hired

Condition	AA	LA	AI	ASA	W
Diversity in position/job description	36% (8)	17% (7)	33% (2)	12% (13)	12% (60)
Special hire	27% (6)	19% (8)	50% (3)	5% (5)	10% (51)
Diversity in position/job description & special hire	23% (5)	7% (3)	17% (1)	1% (1)	1% (5)
Totals	86% (19)	43% (18)	100% (6)	18% (19)	23% (116)

	Underrepresented	ASA	W
Special hires/total hires of group	37% (43)	6% (19)	11% (116)

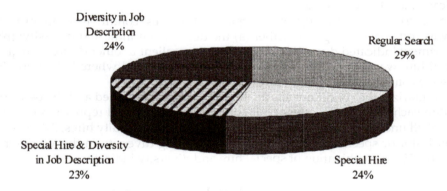

Figure 1   Hiring Patterns—Underrepresented Hires.

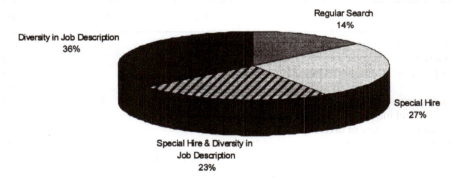

Figure 2   Hiring Patterns for African Americans.

For Latino/as the results showed a broader range of hiring circumstances, although 43% were hired outside of regular searches (See Table 2 and Figure 4). Because the initial definition of diversity indicators did not include such fields as Spanish or Latin American studies, the data were reanalyzed to see how many Latino/as were hired in these areas as well. This analysis revealed that an additional 14% of Latino/as would be included in hires resulting from a diversity indicator in the job description. Broadening the definition in this way would have brought the total percentage of Latino/as hired using a diversity indicator or special hire to 57%.

In the case of Asian Americans 18% were hired with a diversity indicator or special hire (see Table 2 and Figure 5). As with Latino/as, broadening the definition of diversity indicators to include Asian languages and international areas would result in an additional 7% of Asian Americans defined as hired under these conditions, bringing the total to 25%.

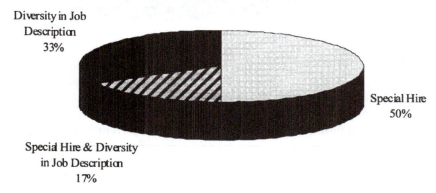

Figure 3   Hiring Patterns for American Indians.

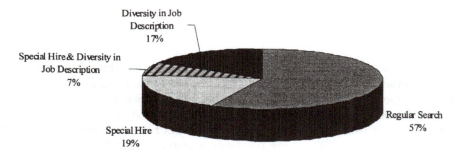

Figure 4   Hiring Patterns for Latino/as.

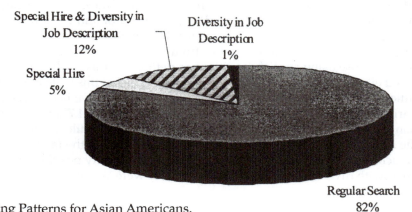

Figure 5   Hiring Patterns for Asian Americans.

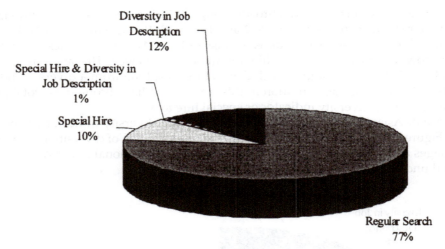

Figure 6   Hiring Patterns for Whites.

TABLE 3

Percentage of Positions Filled by Faculty from Underrepresented Groups

	%	(n)
Department indicates diversity	82%	(9)
Subfield within department indicates diversity	13%	(5)
Other desired job qualification indicates diversity	8%	(3)
Position with no diversity indicator	5%	(27)
Special hire	30%	(26)

A total of 23% of Whites were hired under the designated conditions, with 12% hired for positions indicating diversity and 11% hired as special hires (see Table 2, Figure 6).

Another way to view the data is to look at the hiring patterns within each of the conditions we have studied. For the positions where the department indicated diversity, 82% of those hired were underrepresented faculty (see Table 3 and Figure 7). Whites filled the remaining 18% of positions meeting this description. Only 13% of the positions where a subfield indicated diversity went to underrepresented faculty. Of the remaining 87% hired for positions meeting this description, 62% were White and 25% were Asian American. Special hiring represented an important intervention in securing underrepresented faculty, as it was utilized in 30% of the cases. A meager 5% of regular hires, that is to say hires for positions without a diversity indicator and without the use of a special hire, resulted in the hiring of an underrepresented faculty member.

Table 4 shows the ethnic distribution of hires from all searches, that is to say those employing regular searches and those using special conditions as defined by this study. Of the total number of searches, 26% used either diversity indicators or special hires. What this table illustrates is that without these conditions, the ethnic composition of the faculty would have been quite different. In the proposed scenario, only .6% of faculty would be African American, 4.7% would be Latino/a, 0% American Indian, 17% Asian American, and 77% White. However, while interventions or diversity indicators made a significant difference in the ethnic composition of the faculty, especially for underrepresented faculty, Whites maintained an overwhelming majority position throughout. Indeed, 65% of those hired with diversity indicators or special hires were White.

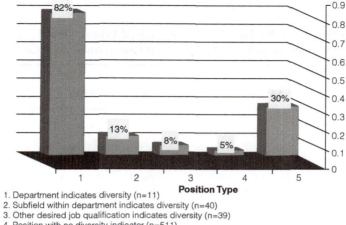

1. Department indicates diversity (n=11)
2. Subfield within department indicates diversity (n=40)
3. Other desired job qualification indicates diversity (n=39)
4. Position with no diversity indicator (n=511)
5. Special hire (n=38)

Figure 7   Percentage of Positions Filled by Faculty from Underrepresented Groups by Position Type.

TABLE 4

Faculty Diversity Profile for Regular Searches and Those Hired with Designated Conditions[1]

	No Designated Conditions	Total Hires	Designated Conditions
African American	.6% (3)	3% (22)	11% (19)
Latino	4.7% (24)	6% (42)	10% (18)
American Indian	0% (0)	1% (6)	3% (6)
Asian American	17% (89)	16% (108)	11% (19)
White	77% (395)	74% (511)	65% (116)
Total n	511	689	178

[1]Designated conditions include diversity indicators and/or special hires (see methods)

Search Committee Composition

We had some data on the composition of search committees from 419 (61%) of the searches. Table 5 summarizes the data for searches in which at least one member of the committee was an underrepresented faculty member. Of the 10 searches that resulted in the hiring of an African American and where we had search data, 40% (4) of the committees had at least one underrepresented faculty member. For Latinos/as, this number was 48% (11), for Asian Americans, 12% (8) and for Whites, 21% (69). Because there was so little diversity on the search committees, the findings here are merely suggestive that diversity on the search committee may increase the likelihood of a diverse hire.

An OLS multiple regression analysis was used (see Table 6) to verify findings from the descriptive data and to see what variables served as the best predictors for the hiring of underrepresented faculty (Berry & Feldman, 1985). Three variables entered significantly at the .01 level or below. These were diversity (Beta = .3), special hire (Beta = .2), and sub-field indicates diversity (Beta = .1).

TABLE 5

Percentage of Racial Ethnic Group Hired When There Is at Least One Member of an Underrepresented Group on Search Committee

Racial/Ethnic Group of Faculty Hire	AA	LA	AI	ASA	W	Unknown	Total
Was there a member of an underrepresented group on search committee?							
Yes	40% (4)	48% (11)	50% (1)	12% (8)	21% (69)		93
No	60% (6)	52% (12)	50% (1)	88% (61)	79% (257)		337
Total	100% (10)	100% (23)	100% (2)	100% (69)	100% (326)		430
Missing data (n) (No information on search committee composition)	12	19	4	39	185	1	260
Overall total (n)	22	42	6	108	511	1	690

TABLE 6

Results of the Regression Analysis for Predicting Underrepresented Faculty Hires

	Underrepresented Hire		
	Unstandardized Coefficient	Standardized Coefficient	Sig
Department indicates diversity	.627	.322	*
Special hire	.197	.218	*
Subfield indicates diversity	.122	.102	*
Other indicator of diversity	6.546E-03	.005	
Underrepresented member on search committee	5.715E-02	.065	
(Constant)	.308	—	
R^2	.18		
Adjusted R^2	.18		
N	690		

*$p < 0.01$

The variables entering account for almost 20% of the variance, thus supporting the hypothesis that intervention strategies are important in the hiring of underrepresented faculty.

Diversity in the Finalist Pool

From two institutions, we had information on the ethnic composition of finalists. Table 7 summarizes those data. Out of 267 searches where we had finalist information, 146 (55%) of the final pools included people of color. Of these, 18 (12%) resulted in the appointment of an underrepresented person of color, 44 (30%) resulted in the hiring of an Asian-American faculty member, and 84 (58%) resulted in the hiring of a white faculty member. Thus, diversity in the finalist pool served to increase somewhat the likelihood of hiring a person of color though a majority are still white.

TABLE 7

Effects of Diversity in the Finalist Pool on Final Hire

	Totals
Regular searches with finalist pool data available	N = 267
Finalist pools with no diversity	45% (121)
Finalist pools with diversity	55% (146)
Finalist pools with diversity resulting in the hire of a faculty member from an underrepresented group	12% (18)
Finalist pools with diversity resulting in the hire of an Asian faculty member	30% (44)
Finalist pools with diversity resulting in the hire of a White faculty member	58% (84)

Gender

The intervention strategies and hiring patterns by gender and race/ethnicity are displayed in Table 8. For the sample as a whole, 69% were men and 31% were women. This general relationship holds for each racial/ethnic group, though 59% of African Americans and only one-third of the American Indians hired were men. For each racial/ethnic group, with the exception of American Indians, more women were hired with diversity indicators or intervention strategies than were men. Indeed, all African-American women, 62% of Latinas, 100% of American Indians, 37% of Asian-American women, and 36% of White women were hired under these conditions in comparison to 77%, 34%, 100%, 8%, 17% respectively for men. These conditions were important conditions for hiring women across all groups as well as for hiring underrepresented faculty of color.

Doctoral Institutions

Because a key question often asked (even if presumptuous) is whether the candidates who come from underrepresented groups are somehow "less qualified," we did look at the doctoral granting institutions for the faculty by race ethnicity. The data were coded by an earlier version of Carnegie classifications that made distinctions between Research I, Research II, and Doctoral Granting Institutions. The data, as shown in Table 9, clearly reveal no differences. Virtually all those hired had received their degrees at Research I institutions regardless of ethnicity. Indeed, an inspection of the actual institutions by name, reveal degrees from the top tier of research universities in virtually all cases.

Rank

Similarly, the disaggregated data by race ethnicity and rank of appointment (Table 16) show that about two-thirds of all appointments were at the rank of Assistant Professor. At the same time, 23% of African Americans, 27% of Latinos/as, 25% of Whites were hired at the rank of Full Professor. Asian Americans were more likely to be hired at the Assistant Professor level than the other groups (75%) and fewer at the level of Full Professor (14%).

Fields

While most of the hiring of underrepresented faculty was in fields directly related to diversity, patterns varied for hiring in science and math, management/business, and other professional areas. Only two African Americans were hired in engineering, none in science or math, and only two in law. Three African Americans were hired in education and six in professional schools (nursing, landscape ecology, urban planning, public health, and journalism). For Latino/as, 12 (29%) were

TABLE 8

Hiring Patterns by Race/Ethnicity and Gender

Condition	AA		LA		AI		ASA		W		Total	
	M	F	M	F	M	F	M	F	M	F	M	F
Diversity	5	3	4	3	1	1	3	10	33	27	46	44
Special hire	3	3	6	2	1	2	3	2	25	26	38	35
Diversity & special hire	2	3	0	3	0	1	0	1	3	2	5	10
Total of gender with designated conditions	10	9	10	8	2	4	6	13	61	55	89	89
% of gender with designated conditions[1]	77%	100%	34%	62%	100%	100%	8%	37%	17%	36%	18%	42%
Total regular hires	3	0	19	5	0	0	67	22	299	96	388	123
% regular hires	23%	0%	64%	38%	0%	0%	92%	63%	83%	64%	82%	58%
Total overall hires	13	9	29	13	2	4	73	35	360	151	477	212
% of overall hires	59%	41%	69%	31%	33%	67%	68%	32%	70%	30%	69%	31%
% with designated conditions[1]	52%	48%	56%	44%	33%	67%	32%	68%	53%	47%	50%	50%

[1]Designated conditions include searches using diversity indicators and/or special hires

TABLE 9

Race/Ethnicity of Faculty Hire by Carnegie Classification of PhD Institution[1]

	Research University I	Research University II	Doctoral University I	Doctoral University II	Non-U.S. Degree	Other Terminal Degree	Total
African American	94% (15)		6% (1)				16
Latino	75% (21)	7% (2)		4% (1)	7% (2)	7% (2)	28
American Indian	67% (2)			33% (1)			3
Asian American	90% (79)	1% (1)		2% (2)	6% (5)	1% (1)	88
White	89% (372)	1% (3)	1% (3)	1% (3)	7% (30)	1% (5)	416
Total	89% (489)	1% (6)	1% (4)	1% (6)	7% (38)	1% (8)	551

[1]138 Unknown

TABLE 10

Race/Ethnicity of Faculty Hire By Rank

	Professor	Associate Professor	Assistant Professor	Total
African American	23% (5)	14% (3)	64% (14)	22
Latino	27% (11)	12% (5)	61% (25)	41
American Indian	17% (1)	17% (1)	67% (4)	6
Asian American	14% (15)	11% (12)	75% (81)	108
White	25% (128)	11% (56)	64% (326)	510
Total	23% (160)	11% (77)	66% (450)	687

hired in science and math, though it should be noted that one campus accounted for seven of these 12 hires. Management/business hired five (12%), education hired two, and law hired one. For Asian Americans, 48 were hired in math, science, or engineering (44%), 16 (15%) in management/business (mostly quantitative areas), two in education and one in public health. Whites were distributed throughout all fields. Of the 510 hired, 32% (n = 165) were in math, science, or engineering, 4% were in law (n = 22), 6% in health (n = 29), 4% in education (n = 21), and 8% in business (n = 40). The emphasis of Asian American hiring in science and business, mostly quantitative fields, and the lack of hiring of African Americans in these fields is apparent.

The conclusion apparent from this analysis is that intentional hires in the form of diversity indicators or interventions do make a difference. Regular searches in fields unrelated to diversity will not yield diverse hires. Moreover, it was clear from the data, that departments often used special hires to broaden the scope of hiring as an enhancement of the search process. In a number of cases, a special hire was used when a promising candidate did not emerge as a choice from a "regular" search but was discovered by the search committee through that process. For example, at one institution an exceptional hire search was used to advance the departmental goal of increasing diversity among faculty after the usual search did not yield a diverse hire. A statement quoted in the letter of support articulates this goal more fully:

> Senior faculty are of a single race. It is imperative in today's world to provide students with faculty that reflects, at least in some degree the ethnic diversity of the families they study and one day hope to serve . . . infusion of new blood is essential to the future vigor and robustness of the department.

Beyond the obvious need to continue support for the graduate and undergraduate programs of the department, they will bring the new perspectives and scholarly priorities that will keep the department alive and current.

In this particular case, unanimous support was given by the departmental faculty in the hiring of an African-American female into a tenure-track, Assistant Professor position. Within the letter of support, faculty outlined the ways in which the hire would promote the department's diversity goals. The letter stated, "This exceptional hire will impact the academic priorities of [Name of department] in the following ways:

- Provide a crucial element of diversity among an all Caucasian faculty;
- Allow for further diversity in the curriculum and the department research programs, responding to the needs and demands of our graduate and undergraduate students;
- Assist in the recruitment and retention of graduate and undergraduate students of color;
- Numerous opportunities for federal grants earmarked for faculty of color will increase the likelihood of external funding."

Such qualitative data support the hypothesis that institutional interventions or diversity indicators can be important strategies in the hiring of diverse faculty. This example also demonstrates the ways in which the rationale for hiring involves substantive scholarly, institutional, and pedagogical reasons. In many cases, we observed that the department itself took the initiative to put forth the candidate. This suggests that these conditions become important tools for department faculty as additions to search committee options and approaches.

Discussion

This study was designed to investigate the hypothesis that the use of diversity indicators or special-hiring interventions will explain the bulk of the hiring to the faculty of underrepresented faculty of color. The results of the analysis of 689 searches from three large public research universities give strong support to this hypothesis. Analysis of study data indicates that successful hires of underrepresented faculty of color at these predominantly White institutions are most likely to occur when a job description contains an educational or scholarly link to the study of race or ethnicity and/or when an institutional intervention strategy that bypasses or enhances the traditional search process is used. Additional data suggested a modest impact when finalist pools contain some diversity.

While hiring faculty for ethnic studies departments yields the most reliable hiring of underrepresented faculty of color, this does not represent a potential intervention strategy as such unless an institution is willing to have most of its diversity located in ethnic studies programs. The potential for marginalization and restriction of scholarly range is significant enough to suggest that overreliance on these searches to secure faculty diversity is a mistake. Indeed, such an approach would not be interrupting the usual but rather would be relying on the usual. Introducing a diversity indicator in the job description, however, does create the potential for expanding the role of diversity in faculty searches throughout the institution. Even in science searches, adding an explicit criterion in the job description for experience and success in working with diverse groups of students has significant potential to broaden the qualities being considered. Our data suggest that this strategy in the sciences is rarely considered. Reliance on diversity indicators in the job description to increase the likelihood that faculty of color will be considered and hired requires that program considerations be introduced.

While diversity indicators accounted for a significant portion of the hiring of underrepresented faculty of color, special hiring was equally important. Significantly, departments often took advantage of institutional resources to make a case for a "special hire" of talented individuals who were identified through the search process. While not precisely fitting an existing job description, they were otherwise well suited to strengthen the department. This is important because it suggests that such individuals might have had department support (an important factor for long-term success). This will be an important area for future research.

Study results indicate that the "special hire" interventions (a process circumventing the regular search process) prove to be a powerful strategy, coupled with the use of position description diversity indicators, in the hiring of faculty from all racial/ethnic backgrounds. However, the combination of diversity indicators and special hires is absolutely critical in the hiring of African-American and American Indian faculty. Fully half of African-American faculty and American Indian faculty were hired as special hires. Asian-American and White faculty hires were almost always hired through regular searches although they were in some instances hired through special hires and when diversity indicators were specified. The difference was that Asian-American and White faculty were hired with *and* without the use of specific conditions that were the focus of the study.

Overall, Asian American faculty are represented in greater percentages in this hiring cohort than African Americans, Latino/as, and American Indians. Indeed, there are legitimate challenges faced by Asian Americans in higher education. For instance, contrary to the common misconception that Asian Americans are well represented in faculty ranks, a closer look shows that they are hired primarily into fields such as science, engineering, medicine, and Asian language departments and are less commonly found in the social sciences and humanities. Nakanishi (1993), Hune and Chan (1997), and Cho (1996) argue that academic pipeline issues are still critical to achieving greater representation of Asian Americans at all levels of higher education and throughout a range of disciplines. Furthermore, the myth of the "model minority" still informs much of the public perception and attitudes toward Asian Americans. These challenges are also confounded by the fact that many who are perceived as Asian Americans are actually foreign nationals who received degrees abroad.

Thus, it is important for campuses to pay close attention to the diversity of faculty throughout fields and disaggregated by racial/ethnic group. Overall numbers of faculty of color might well increase because of the addition of Asian-American faculty in specified fields. Underrepresented faculty of color could well be declining at the same time.

While we had hoped to examine the effect of search committee composition on faculty hiring, for the most part search committees examined here had little or no racial/ethnic diversity. Almost all search committees were entirely White with little diversity on any of the committees except in ethnic studies areas. Thus, while the literature points to the importance of search committee racial/ethnic composition, outcomes as a result of diverse search committees could not be adequately analyzed.

Moreover, with the recent surge of lawsuits challenging affirmative action, it is important to note that the approaches described in this study were largely directed to the notion of bringing the scholarship of diversity to searches as opposed to only representative diversity, making these interventions a much more robust strategy from a legal perspective. In this context, it is also important to note that 65% of those who benefited from special-hire interventions were White.

Study Limitations

While study results paint a compelling scenario of successful departmental and institutional search processes, study results are limited in scope.

First, this study was conducted at three large, elite public research universities. Further research within other contexts (small liberal arts, private universities, community colleges, and so on) need to be undertaken in order to determine whether hiring patterns and practices are similar to those found in this study.

Second, while the data provided on each successful search pointed to important and revealing results, detailed case studies would shed more light on the particular circumstances under which a faculty of color hire was made. For example, what role did individual search committee members play in determining the outcome of the process? What exactly was the role of the search committee in the process in contrast to other institutional personnel? Did the search committee make the final decision? What are differences in successful search processes by department within the same institution?

Third, there are factors that complicate the interpretation of data for both Latino/a faculty hires and Asian-American faculty hires. First, study data do not report the various ethnic affiliations within these groupings. For example, an examination of the presence of Filipino/a or Chicano/a/ Mexican-American faculty hires may uncover more of a dependence on hiring interventions for these subgroups. Second, both Latino/a and Asian-American scholars can be hired in language departments (for example, to teach Spanish) and Latin American or East Asian Studies programs. Such departmental affiliations were not counted as diversity indicators in this study, though the additional analyses suggested their importance. Such affiliations, when they are the primary source of hiring, underscore the risk of marginalization.

Implications for Institutional Policy and Practice

Notwithstanding study limitations, results from data presented here can provide direction for further research as well as direction for further successes in the hiring of underrepresented faculty.

Continued support and use of strategies that work. Study results suggest that intentional hiring strategies will be required to promote success in the hiring of most underrepresented faculty outside of ethnic studies departments. Such practices are referred to in the following ways: exceptional hires, search waivers, spousal hires, special-hire intervention, expanded job descriptions, modification of usual search requirements to meet program needs, shortened search process (truncated process), cluster hiring, or out-of-cycle hiring. Special hiring will remain significant as long as searches result in hiring faculty of color only in expected fields. Significantly, such strategies yield hiring across all racial/ethnic groups, suggesting that it would not violate current restrictions in the use of affirmative action. Institutions can continue to support and use such strategies. However, an important caution should be noted. Because faculty success is dependent on department support and mentoring, continued research is needed to look at the success of faculty appointed with such interventions. In this study, some of the qualitative data suggested that special hires were made with enthusiastic support of the department and with high regard for the scholarly contribution of the person hired. This may not always be the case and could jeopardize faculty success.

Evaluation and Monitoring of Successful Departmental and Campus Practices

Institutions themselves can also assess "why" and "how" such strategies worked, particularly for faculty of color. This study indicates different results by discipline. Departments and fields with diversity indicators continue to be the most likely places for hiring of underrepresented faculty of color, while science and math fields are hiring Asian-American faculty through the use of regular searches. Over time, this could result in distorted and potentially stereotypical placements. In future studies, it would be interesting to closely examine those practices in the context of successful diversification of faculty within departments that traditionally have not been diverse. Such knowledge can inform all campus hiring processes. Each institution can craft and characterize its interventions in ways that are congruent with its department and campus environment.

Understand Organizational Processes for Success

Understanding the organizational processes that result in the use of intervention strategies and successful faculty hiring is critical for defining institutional practice and the role of academic administrators.

Question the Usual

Particularly for African-American and American Indian faculty, study results point to the importance of examining and changing how regular search and hiring processes are conducted. The search process will, no doubt, remain at the center of faculty hiring. Indeed, in this study, search committees were often central to recommendations for special hires. Modifications in search practices can be explored to expand the applicant pool, to require active recruiting, and to link job descriptions to educational requirements.

In conclusion, while one cannot deny that some progress has been made in the diversification of higher education faculty, much remains to be done. In spite of the special-hire interventions and the use of diversity indicators in position descriptions, racial/ethnic diversity among the total faculty hires in this study is still low. However, as the results attest, advances can be made with the implementation of strategic interventions. At every step, however, interrupting the usual will no doubt be required.

References

Aguirre, A. (2000). *Women and Minority Faculty in the Academic Workplace: Recruitment, Retention, and Academic Culture.* ASHE-ERIC Higher Education Report, Volume 27, Number 6. S.F. Jossey Bass.

Adams, H. G. (1988). *Tomorrow's professoriate: Insuring minority participation through talent development today.* Paper presented at the Engineering Deans Council Student Pipeline Workshop, American Society for Engineering Education, Washington, DC (ERIC Document Reproduction Service No. ED 291 273).

Almost no blacks in the natural sciences at the nation's highest ranked universities. (1994/1995). *The Journal of Blacks in Higher Education, 6,* 14–16.

Astin, H. S., antonio, a. l., Cress, C. M., & Astin, A. W. (1997). *Race and ethnicity in the American professoriate, 1995–96.* Los Angeles: Higher Education Research Institute, Graduate School of Education & Information Studies.

Berry, W. D. & Feldman, S. 1985. *Multiple regression in practice.* Newbury Park, CA: Sage.

Blackshire-Belay, C. A. (1998). The status of minority faculty members in the academy. *Academe, 84* (4), 30–36.

Bowen, H. R., & Schuster, J. H. (1986). *American professors: A national resource imperiled.* Fair Lawn, NJ: Oxford University Press.

Bowen, W. G., & Sosa, J. A. (1989). *Prospects for faculty in the arts and sciences: A study of factors affecting demand and supply, 1987–2012.* Princeton: Princeton University Press.

Bronstein, P., Rothblum, E. D., & Solomon, S. E. (1993). Ivy halls and glass walls: Barriers to academic careers for women and ethnic minorities. *New Directions for Teaching and Learning 53,* 17–31.

Busenberg, B. E., & Smith. D. G. (1997). Affirmative action and beyond: The woman's perspective. In M. Garcia (Ed.). *Affirmative action's testament of hope: Strategies for a new era in higher education* (pp. 149–180). Albany: State University of New York.

Caldwell-Colbert, A.T. et al. (1996). *How to recruit and hire ethnic minority faculty.* Commission on Ethnic Minority Recruitment, retention, and training in Psychology, Workgroup on Faculty Recruitment and Retention. Washington, DC: American Psychological Association.

California Postsecondary Education Commission. (1990). *Planning for a new faculty: Issues for the twenty-first century* (Report 90–20). Sacramento, CA: Author (ERIC Document Reproduction Service No. ED 329 204).

Carter, D. J., & O'Brien, E. M. (1993). Employment and hiring patterns for faculty of color. *Research Briefs, 4* (6). Washington, DC: Division of Policy Analysis and Research, American Council on Education.

Cho, S. (1996). Confronting the myths: Asian Pacific American faculty in higher education. Ninth Annual APAHE Conference Proceedings, 31–56. March, San Francisco, CA.

Clotfelter, C. T., Ehrenberg, R. G., Getz, M., & Siegfried, J. J. (Eds.) (1991). *Economic challenges in higher education.* Chicago: University of Chicago Press.

Collins, M. (1990). Enrollment, recruitment, and retention of minority faculty and staff in institutions of higher education. *Action in Teacher Education, 12* (3), 57–62.

Collins R. W., & Johnson, J. A. (1990). One institutions success in increasing the number of minority faculty: A provost's perspective. *Peabody Journal of Education, 66* (1), 71–76.

Cross, T. (1994). Black faculty at Harvard: Does the pipeline defense hold water? *The Journal of Blacks in Higher Education, 4,* 42–46.

de la Luz Reyes, M., & Halcon, J. J. (1991). Practices of the academy. Barriers to access for Chicano academics. In P. G. Altbach & K. Lomotey (Eds.), *The racial crisis in American higher education* (pp. 167–186). Albany, NY: State University of New York Press.

Delgado, R., Stefancic, J., & Lindsley, J. N. (2000). Symposium: Race and the Law at the turn of the century: California's racial history and constitutional rationales for race-conscious decision making in Higher Education, 47 *UCLA Law Review* 1521.

El-Khawas, E. (1988). *Campus trends, 1988.* Washington, DC: American Council on Education. (ERIC Document Reproduction Service No. ED 351 902).

El-Khawas, E. (1990). Campus trends, 1990. *Higher education panel report, 80.* Washington, DC: American Council on Education. (ERIC Document Reproduction Service No. ED 322 846).

Gainen, J., & Boice, R. (Eds.). (1993). *Building a diverse faculty.* San Francisco: Jossey-Bass, Inc.

Garza, H. (1988). The barrioization of Hispanic faculty. *Educational Record, 68* (4), 122–24.

Garza, H. (1992). Academic power, discourse, and legitimacy: Minority scholars in U.S. universities. In M. Romero & C. Candelaria (Eds.), *Community empowerment and Chicano scholarship,* 35–52. Proceedings of the 1987 National Association for Chicano Studies, Riverside, CA.

Harvey, W. B., & Scott-Jones, D. (1985). We can't find any: The elusiveness of black faculty members in American higher education. *Issues in Education, 3,* 68–76.

Harvey, W. B. (2001) *Minorities in Higher Education: Eighteenth Annual Report.* Washington, D.C.: American Council on Education.

Hune, S., & K. S. Chan. (1997). Special Focus: Asian Pacific American Demographic and Educational Trends. In *15th Annual Status Report on Minorities in Higher Education.* Washington, D.C.: American Council on Education.

Light, P. (1994). Diversity in the faculty "not like us": Moving barriers to minority recruitment. *Journal of Policy Analysis and Management, 13* (1), 163–186.

Magner, D. K. (1994). Duke tries again. *The Chronicle of Higher Education, 40* (24), A23.

Magner, D. K. (1999). The graying professoriate. *Chronicle of Higher Education, 46* (2), A18–21.

McGinley, A.C. (1997). The emerging cronyism defense and affirmative action: A critical perspective on the distinction between colorblind and race conscious decision making under Title VII, *39 Arizona Law Review 1003.*

Menges, R. J., & Exum, W. H. (1983). Barriers to the progress of women and minority faculty. *Journal of Higher Education, 54* (2), 122–143.

Merritt, D. J., & Resken, B. F. (1997). Sex, race and credentials: The truth about affirmative action in law faculty hiring, *97 Columbia Law Review 199,* 206–230.

Mickelson, R. A., & Oliver, M. L. (1991). Making the short list: Black candidates and the faculty recruitment process. In P. G. Altbach & K. Lomotey (Eds.), *The racial crisis in American higher education* (pp. 149–166). Albany, NY: Suny Press.

Mooney, C. J. (1989). Affirmative action goals, coupled with tiny number of minority Ph.D.s set off faculty recruiting frenzy. *The Chronicle of Higher Education 35* (47), A1, A10–A11.

Moore, W., Jr. (1988). Black faculty in White colleges: A dream deferred. *Educational Record,* 117–121.

Myers, S. L., Jr., & Turner, C. S. V. (1995). *Minority faculty development project* (Prepublication Report). Minneapolis: Midwestern Higher Education Commission.

Nakanishi, D. T. (1993). Asian Pacific Americans in higher education: Faculty and administrative representation and tenure. In J. Gainen & R. Boice (Eds.), *New Directions for Teaching and Learning, 53,* 51–59.

National Center for Education Statistics. (1992). *Digest of Educational Statistics.* Washington, DC: Author.

Norrell, S. A., & Gill, J. I. (1991). *Bringing into focus the factors affecting faculty supply and demand: A primer for higher education and state policy makers.* Boulder: Western Interstate Commission for Higher Education. (ERIC Document Reproduction Service No. ED 370–471).

Olivas, M. A. (1994). The education of Latino lawyers: An essay on crop cultivation. *Chicano-Latino Law Review, 14,* 117–138.

Opp, R. D. (1994). Minority versus White administrators' perceptions of the recruitment and retention of minority faculty in two-year colleges. *Journal of Applied Research in the Community College, 1* (2), 85–99.

Opp, R. D., & Smith, A. (1994). Effective strategies for enhancing minority faculty recruitment. *Community College Journal of Research and Practice, 10,* 147.

Ottinger, C., Sikula, R., & Washington, C. (1993). Production of minority doctorates. *Research Briefs, 4* (8). Washington, DC: Division of Policy Analysis and Research, American Council on Education.

Pavel, M., Swisher, K., & Ward, M. (1994). Special focus: American Indian and Alaska Native demographic and educational trends. *Minorities in higher education, 13,* 33–56.

Pepion, K. (1993). *Ideologies of excellence: Issue in the evaluation, promotion, and tenure of minority faculty.* Unpublished doctoral dissertation, University of Arizona.

Roach, R. (1999). Blacks in crimson. *Black Issues in Higher Education, 15* (25), 32–37.

Schuster, J. H. (1992). Academic labor markets. In B. R. Clark & G. R. Neave (Eds.), *The encyclopedia of higher education, 3* (pp. 1537–1547). Oxford: Pergamon Press.

Schuster, J. H. (1995). Whither the faculty? The changing academic labor market. *Educational Record, 76* (4), 28–33.

Smith, D. G. (1989). The challenge of diversity: Involvement or alienation in the academy? *ASHE-ERIC Report No. 5.* Washington, DC: School of Education and Human Development, The George Washington University.

Smith, D. G., Wolf, L. E., & Busenberg, B. E. (1996). *Achieving faculty diversity: Debunking the myths*. Washington, DC: Association of American Colleges and Universities.

Solórzano, D. G. (1993). *The road to the doctorate for California's Chicanas and Chicanos: A study of Ford Foundation minority fellows*. Berkeley: The Regents of the University of California. (ERIC Document Reproduction Service No. ED 374–941).

Staples, R. (1984). Racial ideology and intellectual racism: Blacks in academia. *Black Scholar, 15*, 2–17.

Swoboda, M. J. (1993). Hiring women and minorities. In R .H. Stein & S. J. Trachtenberg (Eds.), *The art of hiring in America's colleges and universities* (pp. 123–136). Buffalo: Prometheus Books.

Thurgood, D. H., & Clarke, J. E. (1995). *Doctorate recipients from United States universities. Summary report 1993*. Washington, DC: Doctorate Records Project, National Research Council.

Trower, C. A., & Chait, R. P. (2002). Faculty Diversity: Too little for too long. *Harvard Magazine*, March–April, pp. 33ff.

Turner, C. S. V. (1999). Addressing the recruitment and retention of faculty of color in higher education: Promoting business as unusual. In *Keeping our faculties: Symposium proceedings for plenary sessions* (pp. 1–42). University of Minnesota: Office of the Associate Vice President for Multicultural and Academic Affairs.

Turner, C. S. V. (2002). *Diversifying the faculty: A guidebook for search committees*. Washington, DC: American Association of Colleges and Universities

Turner, C. S., & Myers, S. L. (1997). Faculty diversity and affirmative action. In M. Garcia (Ed.), *Affirmative action's testament of hope: Strategies for a new era in higher education* (pp. 131–148). Albany: State University of New York Press.

Turner, C. S., & Myers, S. L., Jr. (2000). *Faculty of color in Academe: Bittersweet success*. Des Moines, IA: Longwood Division, Allyn and Bacon.

Washington, V., & Harvey, W. (1989). Affirmative rhetoric, negative action: African American and Hispanic faculty at predominantly White institutions. *ASHE-ERIC Report No. 2*. Washington, DC: School of Education and Human Development, The George Washington University.

West. M. E. (2000). Faculty women's struggle for equality at the University of California. *UCLA Women's Law Journal, 10*(2), 259–319.

White, J. A. (1989). The engineering faculty pipeline: An NSF perspective. *Engineering Education, 79* (5), 547–49.

White, P. E. (1992). *Women and minorities in science and engineering: An update*. Washington, DC: National Science Foundation.

Wilson, R. (1987). Recruitment and retention of minority faculty and staff. *AAHE Bulletin, 41* (38), 11–14.

Wilson, R. (1995a). Hiring of black scholars stalls at some major universities. *The Chronicle of Higher Education*, A16.

Wilson, R. (1995b). *Affirmative action: Yesterday, today, and beyond*. Washington DC American Council on Education.

Yale University. (1990). Report on the committee on recruitment and retention of minority group members on the faculty at Yale. *Minerva, 28*, (2), 217–47.

CHAPTER 21
WOMEN OF COLOR IN ACADEME
LIVING WITH MULTIPLE MARGINALITY

CAROLINE SOTELLO VIERNES TURNER

Introduction

I recall a personal example of how multiple social identities may shape one's opportunities in higher education. As a woman of color from a "no collar" class (I come from a farm labor background), when first exploring graduate school options I was discouraged from applying to a master's level program in business by an admissions officer. The admissions officer stated that I would not fit. I was a woman, a minority, a single parent, I had a background in the public sector, and I had some but not enough math background. This would make it nearly impossible for me to succeed as others in the program fit another and opposite profile. Although all of this may be true, it did not occur to the admissions officer that this might not be an appropriate state of affairs for student enrollment in the program. It was merely accepted as the way things are and should remain. I remember being struck by the many ways I could be defined as not "fitting" and, therefore, not encouraged and, more than likely, not admitted. I was so easily "defined out" rather than "defined in."

I am now a faculty member at a major research university. My current work focuses on the experiences of faculty of color in higher education. While pursuing this work, I have had many opportunities to interview, converse with, and read about the lives of other faculty women of color. Many continue to speak, although in different ways, about the experience of multiple marginality and being defined out. The following quotations from the literature give insight into the lives of faculty women of color, including my own.

Lived Contradiction

I am struck by my lived contradiction: To be a professor is to be an *anglo*; to be a *latina* is not to be an *anglo*. So how can I be both a Latina and a professor? To be a Latina professor, I conclude, means to be unlike *and* like me. Que locura! What madness! . . . As Latina professors, we are newcomers to a world defined and controlled by discourses that do not address our realities, that do not affirm our intellectual contributions, that do not seriously examine our worlds. Can I be both Latina and professor without compromise? (Ana M. Martinez Aleman in Padilla & Chavez, 1995, pp. 74–75)

Ambiguous Empowerment

Readers who have listened to any group of professional women talk about their work experiences will likely find these stories familiar. Like other successful women who work in male and white-dominated professions, women superintendents have much to say about the way they managed to get into such positions despite the anomaly of their gender or race, how they developed confidence in their competence and authority, and what they have accomplished by exercising their professional power. They also talk about various forms of gender and race inequality that structure the profession and how they respond to discriminatory treatment . . . I study these familiar stories in order to understand how professional women make sense of their—their ambiguous empowerment—in the context of contemporary American culture. (Chase, 1995, p. x)

The narrative data presented here portray the lives of faculty women of color as filled with lived contradictions and ambiguous empowerment. Chase's (1995) "ambiguous empowerment" based on the lives of women school superintendents also applies to the experiences of faculty women of color. Although faculty women of color have obtained academic positions, even when tenured they often confront situations that limit their authority and, as they address these situations, drain their energy. For example, in an interview[1] a woman of color who is a full professor and chair of her department observes:

I'm the department chair, . . . and I meet with a lot of people who don't know me—you know, prospective students and their parents. And I know that their first reaction to me is that I'm an Asian American woman, not that I'm a scientist or that I'm competent.

Statements by faculty women of color typically relay such observations. Unfortunately, the lives of faculty women of color are often invisible, hidden within studies that look at the experiences of women faculty and within studies that examine the lives of faculty of color. Women of color fit both categories, experience multiple marginality, and their stories are often masked within these contexts.[2] This chapter seeks to redress such shortcomings by presenting experiences expressed by faculty women of color in interviews conducted by the author and in statements published in the higher education literature. At times I include personal observations. I conclude with a set of recommendations to increase the positive experiences for faculty women of color.

How Do Proportions Count?

To begin, it is informative to discuss the importance and implications of representation or lack of representation within organizations. Kanter's theory of proportions (1977) first made me aware of the potential effects of marginality on social interactions and mobility in a corporate setting. Briefly, Kanter describes the effect of being a "token." She states that the numerical distribution of men and women in the upper reaches of the corporation provide different interaction contexts for those in the majority versus those in the minority (p. 206). For example, women in the minority (in very small proportion) inhabit a context characterized by the following:

- Being more visible and on display
- Feeling more pressure to conform, to make fewer mistakes
- Becoming socially invisible, not to stand out
- Finding it harder to gain credibility
- Being more isolated and peripheral
- Being more likely to be excluded from informal peer networks, having limited sources of power through alliances
- Having fewer opportunities to be sponsored
- Facing misperceptions of their identity and role in the organization
- Being stereotyped
- Facing more personal stress

Those in the majority (in very high proportion) face the opposite social context. They are seen as one of the group, preferred for sponsorship by others inhabiting higher level positions (pp. 248–249).

Although Kanter's work articulates the social situation for "tokens" quite well, she primarily speaks to the situation of White women in an organizational setting. Kanter's argument suggests that those who differ from the norm within the corporate hierarchy encounter a cycle of cumulative disadvantage, whereas those who fit the norm experience a cycle of cumulative advantage. Her theories imply that the more ways in which one differs from the "norm," the more social interactions will be affected within multiple contexts. Situations in which a woman of color might experience marginality are multiplied depending on her marginal status within various contexts. Often it is difficult to tell whether race or gender stereotyping is operating. When asked if she experienced any barriers, one woman of color in academe, quoted in Hune (1998), responded: "The answer is yes. I think for me personally, it's hard to know if it's because I am a woman or because I am Asian, or both" (p. 11). In a conversation with me, another faculty member stated: "Dealing with the senior, [mostly white] males in my department has been a huge challenge. . . . I don't know if they tend to discount my contributions because I'm new, female, Latina, young, or what. Perhaps a combination of all of the above." Rains (1999) calls attention to the complexities that daily pervade the experiences of many women of color in the academy (p. 152).

Cho (1996) sheds light on the complexities of defining parity. Her work describes bias suffered by Asian Pacific Americans in the academic workplace even though the perception is that they are well represented and, therefore, successful. She contends the following: (1) numbers showing over-parity in some fields or disciplines mask related under-parity in other fields; (2) over-parity status at the entry level does not mean over-parity status higher up on the promotion ladder; and (3) inferences drawn from an aggregated over-parity status serve to make invisible the varied needs of a heterogeneous population (p. 34). Cho's work made me realize that drawing a statistical picture of numerical "inclusion" without reflecting on the context of that inclusion and "quality of life" factors paints an incomplete portrait.

Representation and the Creation of Campus Climate

Studies by Harvey (1991) and Spann (1990) further illuminate the importance and complexity of representation in the development of the campus climates within which faculty women of color work. According to Harvey, "campus climate" is a "term used to describe the culture, habits, decisions, practices, and policies that make up campus life. The degree to which the climate is hospitable determines the 'comfort factor' for African Americans and other nonwhite persons on campus" (p. 128). In defining the chilly climate within an academic setting, Spann gives voice to discussions by her study respondents (referred to as panelists):

> Panelists defined climate as the quality of respect and support accorded to women and minorities on individual campuses and in individual departments. They believed that climates were created by institutions and could be measured in specific ways, . . . by the number of women and minority faculty members at junior and senior levels, . . . by the social distance between majority and minority group faculty and administrators, . . . by the equitability of work assignments. (p. 1)

Spann's study implies that nontraditional faculty representation within different locations (i.e. junior and senior faculty status as well as administrative positions) in the organization determines, in large part, what her respondents describe as campus climate. Providing support for the impact of social distance argument, Etzkowitz, Kemelgor, and Uzzi (2000) stress that the existence of a "critical mass" (i.e., at least 15% of women in an organization) to address tokenism will not fully address the situation of the minority in an organization. They state that "the precise number is less important than the nature of the response the new minority receives from the majority" (p. 107).

Representation and Distribution: Demographic Data

The Chronicle of Higher Education Almanac (2001) reports that the total of full-time faculty members, including instructor and lecturer, is 568,719, of which 204,794 (36%) are women. Of the total women, 29,546 (14%) are women of color. Table 1 shows the underrepresentation of women of color in the professoriate by rank and racial/ethnic breakdown.

Similar patterns are reported for the Instructor and Lecturer categories, with women of color represented in small numbers in each academic rank. Contrary to the "model minority" myth, women in the Asian category are not the most represented of the faculty women of color. Hune and Chan (1997) note that Asian Pacific American (APA) men represent three-quarters of all APA faculty,

TABLE 1

Full-Time Women in the Professoriate by Rank, Race/Ethnicity 1997

Women Faculty by Race/Ethnicity	Rank		
	Full Professor	**Associate Professor**	**Assistant Professor**
Total Women	32,353	43,522	57,354
American Indian	92	145	285
Asian	1,243	1,633	3,113
Black	1,924	2,674	4,288
Hispanic	767	1,088	1,753
White	28,107	37,586	46,385

Source: *The Chronicle of Higher Education Almanac,* 2001.

and that APAs have the largest gender gap of any racial/ethnic group (p. 57). In the main, faculty women of color primarily occupy the junior, untenured ranks whereas men of color occupy the more senior, tenured ranks. For more information on within group patterns, see Carter and Wilson (1997). The American Council on Education (ACE) data also report lower tenure rates for women of color in tenure-track positions (Wilds, 2000, p. 101).[3]

Interviews with Faculty Women of Color

In this section I draw from and elaborate on interviews with 64 faculty members of color to analyze the consequences of underrepresentation for women faculty of color.[4] Four Asian Pacific American females, fifteen African American females, four Native American females, and eight Latinas were interviewed. Most of these women occupy tenured positions; some are high-level academic administrators.[5] They spoke about the interlocking effects of race and gender bias in the academic workplace.

Manifestation of Interlocking Race and Gender Bias

In general, faculty of color describe racial and ethnic bias in ways that overlap with the concerns raised by women.[6] Yet the interlocking effects of gender and race compound the pressures of the workplace environment for faculty women of color. They perceive that being both minority and female hampers their success as faculty members.[7] This respondent talks about being defined out of consideration for an administrative position because she is an Asian female.

> A [university administrative] position opened up and there were a lot of names mentioned—it was clear that an active [internal] person would be named. I would hear on the grapevine 'so-and-so's' name. . . . I felt that if I were a white male, my name would have been out there. I mean I am sure of that. But it never was and, you know, . . . there is no question in my mind that race and gender influenced that.[8]

Challenges from Academic Old Boy Networks

Although noted in the literature, I uncovered only indirect mention of challenges from academic old boy networks in the interviews. One American Indian woman alludes to this situation in her comment: "This is hard to believe—for a long time I was the only woman of color on this faculty—for years. . . . This campus is very, very white. Almost all of the Indian faculty have been men." Montero-Sieburth (1996) similarly states that Latina professors must overcome more obstacles to gain support for academic advancement, because they are farther removed from the academic old-boy network than Latino or White female counterparts. Although instances of mentorship across and within racial/ethnic and gender groups exists, scarce resources such as tenured faculty positions and chairs of Chicano studies programs can pit Latinas against Latinos. In a similar vein, hooks (1991) states that scholars writing about Black intellectual life focus solely on the lives and works of Black men, ignoring and devaluing the scholarship of Black women intellectuals.

Themes that emerge from the study interviews include: (1) feeling isolated and underrespected; (2) salience of race over gender; (3) being underemployed and overused by departments and/or institutions; (4) being torn between family, community, and career; and (5) being challenged by students. I describe these themes below.

Feeling Isolated and Underrespected

One professor expresses the isolation and the added pressure to perform as a woman of color:

> I have to think about the fact that black females or any female in the field of [name] that has been predominantly a white male profession, has a problem. Many [white] females in the college complain about the fact that up until recently . . . we had never had a full professor in [department name]. It's changing, but it's not changing fast. And then you add to that being the black female who has to be superwoman.

Focusing more on slots filled rather than on expertise or potential programmatic contributions are reported by this newly hired faculty member:

> This one dean . . . was writing down all the federal slots that I would fit in as far as hiring. . . . And he says, "Okay, you're a woman, you're over fifty-five, you're an American Indian," and then he looks at me and grins. He said, "Do you have a handicap?" . . . These schools have to fulfill these guidelines and in getting me they can check a lot of boxes.

Salience of Race over Gender

Despite shared gender discrimination, women faculty of color cannot always expect support from their white female colleagues. A sense that white women have fared and are faring better than are women or men of color exists. This perception speaks to the salience of race over gender. An American Indian woman notes: "Even the white females they've hired still have a problem with minority students and minority perspectives. This is particularly true in [discipline]. It is really dominated by Western European notions."

Montero-Sieburth (1996) points out that "being female does not necessarily guarantee the sympathy of mainstream women toward them nor does it offer entry into mainstream academic domains" (p. 84). She quotes one Latina professor commenting on an experience with White female researchers: "I was always singled out when we needed to present research about underserved communities or make statements about the Latino population; otherwise, my research was ignored" (p. 84).

Gains made by white women resulting from affirmative action are not reflected for women of color. A report by the Women's Environment and Development Organization entitled *Women's Equality: An Unfinished Agenda* (2000) supports this perception:

> Although all women benefit from affirmative action, white women have been the major beneficiaries in the areas of education, contracting and employment. Indeed, white women have progressed to such a significant degree in the area of education that the challenge of affirmative action is no longer in college admissions but in graduate schools and in such areas as engineering and science for which the numbers of women are woefully small. . . . However, affirmative action is still a vital necessity in higher education for women of color, particularly African American and Latino women, whose numbers still lag in undergraduate admissions and in all levels of graduate and professional schools. (www.wedo.org/book.txt)

However, as stated previously, statistical representation is not entirely revealing of the quality of inclusion or equitable distribution in higher education even for white women in the academy. Within the higher education literature (i.e., Glazer-Raymo, 1999), exclusion and the "glass ceiling" phenomenon are well documented as affecting all women. Nonetheless, such statistics fuel the perception that white women, not women of color, have been the primary benefactors of affirmative action.

Being Underemployed and Overused by Departments and/or Institutions

Unlike White male faculty members, women of color say they are expected to handle minority and gender affairs, representing two constituencies. An American Indian female faculty member states:

> Issues of pedagogy and cultural diversity and gender are not the province of just women or just faculty of color. I think that happens too often and that puts the faculty of color person or woman on the spot, to kind of convince or persuade—be this change agent. . . . The faculty members feel the added pressure, but are caught in a 'Catch-22' because minority issues are also important to them.

Mitchell (1994) notes that the small numbers of faculty women of color compels them to serve simultaneously as a role model for their profession, race, and gender: "The accountability and time demands that the female ethnic professor encounters are especially pressing, given the fact that minority women occupy even fewer positions than minority men"[9] (p. 387). In retrospect, this African American woman, who did not attain tenure in her first university states: "I am a female and African American. . . . I was doing a lot of things in terms of serving on this board, serving on that board, being faculty adviser for one of the professional fraternities." A Latina notes: "When you are one of three or four Latinos and being a woman, almost every committee wants you to be on it. It gives you opportunities, at the same time, I think, you are expected to do a lot of things not expected of other faculty."

These quotes bring attention to the apparent contradiction and "double whammy" faced by women of color. On the one hand, there is too little opportunity and support for the work that is valued (research) (Fairweather, 1996); on the other hand, there is too much demand for work that is not rewarded (committee work, student club advisor, etc.). In most instances, service does not lead to tenure or to prestigious positions related to committee service, such as administration. Junior faculty members are particularly at risk. Institutional reward systems can deny tenure and security of employment to those who spend more time on service than on research and scholarship, even when the service is assigned to meet institutional needs.

Being Torn Between Family, Community, and Career

Many faculty women of color speak about being "psychologically divided between home and career" or between community and career. They seemingly have two choices: sacrifice family and community commitments for several years to focus almost exclusively on their careers, or honor nonwork commitments, an essential part of their identity, at the risk of not earning tenure. Although policies to accommodate faculty needs for maternity and family leave and childcare are becoming common, little attention has been paid in the academy to minority faculty's desire to contribute actively to their racial or ethnic community (for further discussion see Townsend & Turner, 2000). For example, for many Native Americans, including faculty members (Stein, 1996), "the social value and preeminent goal in life . . . is the survival of the Indian people" (Cross, 1996, p. 335). Similarly, some Chicano faculty "maintain a strong affiliation with their community and feel a strong sense of responsibility to improve the status of other Chicanos in the larger community" (de la Luz Reyes & Halcon, 1988/1996, p. 145; see also Rendon, 1992/1996). For most African American faculty, ties with the Black community are extremely important partly because of "the African heritage of communalism" (Gregory, 1995, p. 7).

Being Challenged by Students

Faculty women of color perceive that they are more likely to have their authority challenged by students than are White male professors.[10] As examples, consider the following:

If a white male professor says something that's wrong in class, my observation is that even if the students perceive that it's wrong, they may say something outside of class, but they hesitate to challenge a 50+ white male professor. They feel quite comfortable challenging an African American woman in class.

Regarding interaction with students, there's a different expectation for us when we walk in as a minority, they automatically assume that we know less than our colleagues in the same department. . . . It doesn't matter whether it's undergraduate level or graduate level. . . . They challenge females more. . . . So, I wear dark, tailored suits and I am very well prepared. They don't hire us unless we're prepared anyway, but students think we are here because of our color.

Many women faculty of color are called on to advise students of color and others studying in similar fields. Because of their scarcity, faculty women of color can face great out-of-class instructional loads. One junior faculty member of color describes her experience as teacher/mentor:

As teacher/mentor, the main issue has been balancing. When I first arrived, I was overwhelmed by the amounts of students who came to me to ask for guidance (not always in so many words)—mostly women of color, feeling like most other faculty did not acknowledge their existence. It is difficult to balance this with the research and publication pressures, and course preparation.

Another female faculty member states:

It is hard to say no, especially on minority issues, when there are so few people. . . . I realize how few people are available [to address these issues]. . . . I sit on 53 doctoral committees. Doctoral students take a lot of time for the dissertation process. I turned down being chair of one doctoral student's committee and she nearly cried. She was a good student studying multicultural issues, but I can't chair these committees. I'll wind up spending all my time correcting dissertations and not doing my own writing.

Andrews (1993) describes this situation as an "emotional drain":

The Black woman professor is often called upon to serve as mentor, mother, and counselor in addition to educator in these settings. The consequences of these multifaceted role expectations by students are compounded by the existence of similar demands placed upon Black women by colleagues and administrators. . . . If we consider the fact that Black women often also have these same expectations to meet at home, it is abundantly clear that in many cases something has to give. (p. 190)

Cruz (1995) summarizes her reaction to such experiences: "It was not simply that my colleagues and students made me feel different; it was that my difference was equated with inferiority" (In Padilla & Chavez, 1995, p. 93).

Increasing Positive Experiences for Faculty Women of Color

In this section I make recommendations to assure the affirmation, validation, and valuation of contributions faculty women of color bring to the academy.

Validate Service and Teaching

Gregory (1995) recommends the transformation of tenure and promotion criteria by exploring ways to expand the definition of scholarly activity and to place more importance on teaching, service, and curriculum development activities. Baez (2000) stresses that scholars must condemn higher education practices and norms that produce such conflicting situations with differential rewards for faculty of color, especially for minority scholars dedicated to race-based service. Baez contends that "service, though significantly presenting obstacles to the promotion and retention of faculty of color, actually may set the stage for a critical agency that resists and redefines academic structures that hinder faculty success" (p. 363). If service is seen as addressing social justice issues, it can be a source of pride and validation for many minority faculty. It gives them much needed connection with communities of color within and outside of the academy as a whole, which can translate into supportive networks for the individual providing the service. Baez reminds us of the importance and relevance of such service. The key is finding ways to validate it, not to discourage faculty women of color from engaging in it.

Promote Networking and Mentoring

Networking and mentoring are mentioned many times by faculty women of color as key components of individual and group success and progress. Aleman (2000) and Cuadraz and Pierce (1994) identify participation in formal and informal networks as critical to their persistence in academe. Ladson-Billings (1997) speaks about the importance of finding intellectual peers "interested in the issues of race and racism in the same way I was" (p. 57). This Asian American faculty member describes one of her networking/mentoring activities:

> I know a woman who's Chinese. She's in the [name of department] so we have no overlap in the field, but I and another woman in my college who's in computer science have sort of taken it upon ourselves to keep her from getting isolated. We're not even in her college, but we have lunch with her—I like her a lot, so she's become my friend, but we started this by just trying to keep her from being so isolated over there in the [name of department]. I feel so strongly about trying to combat isolation. . . . It's sort of hard because we have families but [it is important to our persistence].

Colleges and universities can facilitate opportunities for faculty women of color to get together. For example, colleges can host social gatherings and academic activities targeted at promoting networking among its faculty women of color. Such activities could include: providing seed money for collaborative research of interest to women of color across disciplines, hold national or local conferences with the intent of bringing together faculty women of color, and host open forums that showcase research conducted by faculty women of color.

Provide Professional Development Sensitive to Campus Political Dynamics

Colleges and universities can provide professional development experiences that assist a new faculty woman of color to overcome challenges of multiple marginality. One example from my own experience is the participation in a teaching development program provided at the University of Minnesota. Participants in this program worked in small groups guided by senior faculty members who were recipients of university teaching awards. In my view, the best mentor teachers grasped the need for faculty members to understand the technical side of teaching as well as the classroom dynamics that can take place when a person of color or a woman steps in front of students who expect a White male teacher. Such mentor teachers can help newer faculty to see and address power relationships that may develop in a classroom that challenge the authority and credibility of a woman of color. Mentor teachers can also encourage new faculty members to accept their leadership role as the professor. Participating in such a program can foster understanding of group dynamics in the classroom. It can affirm different styles of teaching, such as fostering collaborative and small-group work. These programs can be used to inform not only faculty women of color but the rest of the campus community as well.

Break the Conspiracy of Silence

Programs like the one described above can help to uncover the challenges faculty women of color may face in the classroom and on campus generally. Ng (1997) stresses that whether we belong to minority groups or not, educators must "break the conspiracy of silence that has ensured the perpetuation of racism, sexism, and other forms of marginalization and exclusion in the university" (p. 367). In order to address the conflicting and anxiety provoking situations as described in this chapter, academic administrators and policymakers must acknowledge and come to understand the racial and gender composition of their departments and the effects such composition has on the success or failure of faculty women of color.

Promote a Welcoming Environment

Most faculty women of color contend that a healthy, supportive, rewarding, inclusive environment is good for everyone. Kanter (1977) and others reveal that one crucial component in producing such an environment *is to increase the representation of women of color across the campus*—as students, administrators, and faculty. This representation must also be reflected across student (undergraduate, graduate) and professional ranks (for example, across the faculty ranks of assistant, associate, and full professor). However, Harvey (1991) and others remind us of the critical importance of *developing a campus culture that values and welcomes the contributions made by faculty women of color* to the academic enterprise; that is, acknowledging that the inclusion of faculty women of color contributes to the academy as a whole. Cole (2000) emphasizes this point by stating that diversity—in the people, the ideas, the theories and the perspectives, and experiences and the pedagogy in American higher education—is crucial to a quality education (p. 2). Such support promotes a comfort level that can increase productivity at work and persistence on campus.

Accommodate Conflicts of Commitments

Townsend and Turner (2000) state that institutional leaders must address the challenges and better accommodate conflicts of commitments described by faculty women of color to ensure that these faculty members will stay at their institutions. Specific steps include the following:

1. Identify and acknowledge institutional norms and policies that place women faculty of color at a disadvantage resulting from their family and community commitments.

2. Once these norms and policies are identified, promote the development of new ones that will support rather than punish community and family involvement. Such changes will benefit all faculty who take on a nurturing and supportive role in their communities and families.

3. Include women of color in the identification of problems and solutions.

4. Examine initiatives used by private corporations rated as "family friendly" and evaluate them in light of their appropriateness for a higher education setting.

Internal Rewards and Satisfactions: Contributing to the Reshaping of the Academy

Although confronted by unique pressures, interviews and conversations with faculty women of color reveal the many satisfactions that attract them to and keep them in academia. Foremost among their reasons for becoming faculty members are the intellectual challenge, freedom to pursue research interests, and the opportunity to promote racial/ethnic understanding. The most commonly articulated personal rewards include: satisfaction with teaching, supportive working relationships, and sense of accomplishment. Contributions to scholarship and new knowledge are also important. I will focus here on the desire of faculty women of color to contribute to the reshaping of the academy as described by faculty women of color themselves.

A Sense of Accomplishment

A female American Indian faculty member enthusiastically describes one accomplishment contributing to organizational change and multiculturalism on her campus: "We initiated an endowment to establish an endowed chair for American Indian education, and we managed after years of advocacy to get well over a million dollars for that chair. So the chair was finally established. . . . It will be forever more."

Aligning Service with Research

Consistent with Baez, I have chosen to consider myself a scholar advocate to alleviate some of the tension between service and research. I conduct research to illuminate issues of access and equity for racial/ethnic groups in higher education. As a direct result of this work, I serve racial/ethnic communities in higher education, professional organizations, and the university with which I am affiliated. I have the opportunity to address students as well as administration and faculty audiences who are interested in implementing diversity within academe. Graduate students and faculty of color, at times, come up to me and say that my work provides validation and support for the work in which they are engaged. From this experience, such service, tightly connected with research, confers needed energy, revitalization, and life meaning for my work. Closely aligning the many tasks in academe has helped to sustain my persistence in the field.

Alignment with Communities of Color and Gender

Professor bell hooks, in a 1995 interview for *The Times Higher Education Supplement,* states that "assimilation, touted as an answer to racial divisions, is dehumanizing; it requires eradication of one's blackness so that a white self can come into being" (Griffiths, 1995, p. 20). Doing work that closely aligns oneself to communities of color and gender may provide a way to maintain a sense of self as a woman of color. Delgado-Gaitan (1997) describes this process as a kind of dance: "My life has been a 'TINKLING' dance in which I have hopped between two clanking bamboo sticks, skillfully avoiding getting a foot severed as I jumped in and out. I have searched to find the space that is a synthesis of my worlds, . . . the 'borderland' or meeting ground that synthesizes my identity, experience, feelings, beliefs, and dreams" (p. 37).

Contributions to New Knowledge

Johnetta Cole (2000) asserts that "education promotes critical reflection and stimulates efforts for social change" (p.1). Turner (2000a) and Neumann and Peterson (1997) describe faculty women of color as important contributors to new knowledge in academe. The contributions of one faculty woman of color[11] led to the development of research and teaching in areas such as the history of African American women. Many faculty women of color see themselves as reflecting and projecting their realities in the work that they do. As professors they bring their experience and knowledge into campus dialogues in the classroom, in the literature, and in their communities. Faculty women of color provide guidance and support for young women of color who are their students or who are their colleagues in the professoriate. They advocate for the admission of talented women of color into the student and faculty bodies. Their presence encourages others to pursue individual educational goals. Such contributions by faculty women of color are described in the following quote:

> The academy is shaped by many social forces. More women of color are defining and redefining their roles within it. New ways of thinking about teaching and research have provided spaces for women scholars to challenge old assumptions about what it means to be in the academy. While both the women's movement and black [ethnic] studies movement have helped increase the parameters of academic work, new paradigms emerging from black women's scholarship provide me with a liberatory lens through which to view and construct my scholarly life.[12] The academy and my scholarly life need not be in conflict with the community and cultural work I do (and intend to do). (Ladson-Billings, 1997, p. 66)

Conclusion

Over the last decade, I have interviewed many women of color who are undergraduate students, graduate students, and who are faculty members. Many of these individuals feel that to succeed in academe requires them to leave themselves, who they are, at the door of graduate education and the tenure process. This loss would be a tragedy for both current and future faculty women of color. Acknowledging who we are and how that affects our approaches to research as well as what we find of scholarly interest may result in a more viable work environment for women faculty of color now and in the future:

> Each person brings a unique cultural background to their experience. Who you are shapes the types of questions you ask, the kinds of issues which interest you, and the ways in which you go about seeking

solutions. . . . Although doctoral student and faculty socialization processes are very strong, we must not lose ourselves in the process of fitting in. . . . [Also, as demonstrated here,] the backgrounds [faculty women of color] bring to academia need not take a back seat. . . . They can be placed in the foreground of our work. (Turner, 2000b, p. 133)

By bringing ourselves through the door and supporting others in doing so as well, we can define ourselves in and claim unambiguous empowerment, creating discourses that address our realities, affirm our intellectual contributions, and seriously examine our worlds.

Notes

1. Throughout this text I use quotations to exemplify issues discussed. Quotations from interviews are observations made by faculty women of color who participated in a study conducted by the author and Samuel L. Myers, Jr. (2000).
2. Even though common themes are noted in this essay, it is also important to acknowledge that all women of color are not the same and that institutions should not expect them to behave as such. Furthermore, women of color have a range of interests and ways in which they choose to contribute to the academy.
3. Numbers of full-time faculty in higher education are also noted in the latest American Council on Education (ACE) Status Report (Wilds, 2000, p. 98). These numbers show that women of color comprise 14% of the professoriate, the same percent as reported in *The Chronicle of Higher Education Almanac* for Fall, 1997. Of the total full-time faculty (538,023) in 1995, 187,267 (35%) were women; 26,247 of the women were women of color (14%). These data show that across ranks and tenure status the proportion of full-time women faculty of color is low.
4. See Turner and Myers (2000) for a detailed description of the study design.
5. Respondents were located in the biological and physical sciences as well as in the social sciences, humanities, and education. Interviews solicited views on reasons for pursuing an academic career, the pathways that led them to the current position, professional development experiences, experiences as faculty members, general experiences in the academic workplace, future plans and expectations with regard to leaving academia, and recommendations for improving the recruitment and retention of faculty of color.
6. Respondents of color in the Turner and Myers study (2000) reveal that they face covert and overt forms of racial and ethnic bias. Manifestations of bias described by faculty respondents include: (1) Denial of tenure or promotion due to race/ethnicity; (2) being expected to work harder than whites; (3) having their color/ethnicity given more attention than their credentials; (4) being treated like a token; (5) lack of support or validation of research on minority issues; (6) being expected to handle minority affairs; (7) too few minorities on campus.
7. Similar results are reflected in *Through My Lens*, a video production by Women of Color in the Academy Project at the University of Michigan (Aparicio, 1999). One featured participant speaks of the intersection of race and gender in the academy: "I think that the university is committed but oftentimes has a hard time understanding the position of women of color, certainly understanding how color, how culture and race, make an impact on one's career is a challenge. And then, understanding how being a woman impacts one's career is a challenge as well."
8. In the literature, Ideta and Cooper (1999) note that "Asian women leaders seem to live in the confines of paradoxes. As Asian females they struggle in organizations which define leaders as primarily male and White. . . . Behaviors which are typical of leaders (displays of power, authority, and fortitude) are considered atypical for women and doubly atypical for Asian women . . . expected to be compliant and subservient in their behavior" (p. 141).
9. Padilla (1994) refers to being expected to handle minority affairs as "cultural taxation," "the obligation to show good citizenship toward the institution by serving its needs for ethnic representation on committees, or to demonstrate knowledge and commitment to a cultural group, which may even bring accolades to the institution but which is not usually rewarded by the institution on whose behalf the service was performed" (p. 26). He goes on to state that as long as people of color are scarce, such expectations will continue to be the norm.
10. One White male professor quoted in *Silences as weapons: Challenges of a Black professor teaching white students* (Ladson-Billings, 1996, p. 78) states that students will perceive him as objective, scholarly, and disinterested when teaching issues related to class, race, and gender. On the other hand, minority females

teaching in these areas are often seen as self-interested, bitter, and espousing political agendas. His observations mirror comments made by women of color about their classroom experiences (see Committee on Women in Psychology and American Psychological Association Committee, *Surviving and Thriving in Academia: A Guide for Women and Ethnic Minorities*, 1998).

11. For the story of Darlene Clark Hine see *Shattering the Silences* (Nelson & Pillett, 1997), a highly acclaimed PBS Documentary. The video portrays the lives of eight scholars of color in the humanities and social sciences, illustrating how they transformed and were transformed by their respective disciplines and institutions. These scholars bring new research questions and fresh perspectives to the academic enterprise.

12. One of the examples Ladson-Billings provides her reader is the influence the work of Patricia Hill Collins (1991) has had on her work. She states that Collins provides a theoretical and conceptual platform on which she rests her methodology. Collins asserts that knowledge claims must be grounded in individual character, values, and ethics. She further contends that "individuals who have lived through the experiences about which they claim to be experts are more believable and credible than those who have merely read or thought about such experience" (p. 209).

References

Aleman, A. M. (1995). Actuando. In R. Padilla & R. Chavez (Eds.), *The leaning ivory tower: Latino professors in American universities* (pp. 67–76). Albany: State University of New York Press.

Aleman, A. M. (2000). Race talks: Undergraduate women of color and female friendships. *Review of Higher Education, 23,* 133–152.

Andrews, A. R. (1993). Balancing personal and professional. In J. James & R. Farmer (Eds.), *Spirit, space, and survival: African American women in (White) academe.* New York: Routledge.

Aparicio, F. R. (1999). Through my lens: A video project about women of color faculty at the University of Michigan. *Feminist Studies, 25,* 119–130.

Baez, B. (2000). Race-related service and faculty of color: Conceptualizing critical agency in academe. *Higher Education, 39,* 363–391.

Carter, D. J., & Wilson, R. (1997). *Minorities in higher education: Fifteenth annual status report.* Washington DC: American Council on Education.

Chase, S. E. (1995). *Ambiguous empowerment: The work narratives of women school superintendents.* Amherst: The University of Massachusetts Press.

Cho, S. (1996). Confronting the Myths: Asian Pacific American faculty in higher education. *Ninth Annual APAHE Conference Proceedings* (pp. 31–56). San Francisco: APAHE.

Cole, J. (2000). Social change requires academic women's leadership. *Women in Higher Education, 9* (6), 1–2.

Collins, P. H. (1991). *Black feminist thought: Knowledge, consciousness, and the politics of empowerment.* New York: Routledge.

Committee on Women in Psychology and APA Commission on Ethnic Minority Recruitment, Retention, and Training in Psychology. (1998). *Surviving and thriving in academia: A guide for women and ethnic minorities.* Washington, DC: American Psychological Association.

Cross, W. T. (1996). Pathway to the professoriate: The American Indian faculty pipeline. In C. Turner, M. Garcia, A. Nora, & L. I. Rendon (Eds.), *Racial and ethnic diversity in higher education* (pp. 327–336). Needham Heights, MA: Simon & Schuster Custom Publishing.

Cruz, D. M. (1995). Struggling with the labels that mark my identity. In R. Padilla & R. Chavez (Eds.), *The leaning ivory tower: Latino professors in American universities* (pp. 91–100). Albany: State University of New York Press.

Cuadraz, G. H., & Pierce, J. L. (1994). From scholarship girls to scholarship women: Surviving the contradictions of class and race in academe. *Explorations in Ethnic Studies, 17,* 21–44.

De la Luz Reyes, M., & Halcon, J. J. (1988/1996). Racism in academia: The old wolf revisited. In C. Turner, M. Garcia, A. Nora, & L. I. Rendon (Eds.), *Racial and ethnic diversity in higher education* (pp. 337–348). Needham Heights, MA: Simon & Schuster Custom Publishing.

Delgado-Gaitan, C. (1997). Dismantling borders. In A. Neumann and P. Peterson (Eds.). *Learning from our lives: Women, research, and autobiography in education* (pp. 37–51). New York: Teachers College, Columbia University.

Etzkowitz, H., Kemelgor, C., & Uzzi, B. (2000). *Athena unbound: The advancement of women in science and technology.* New York: Cambridge University Press.

Fairweather, J. (1996). *Faculty work and the public trust.* Boston: Allyn & Bacon.

Glazer-Raymo, J. (1999). *Shattering the myths: Women in academe.* Baltimore, MD: The Johns Hopkins University Press.

Gregory, S. (1995). *Black women in the academy: The secrets to success and achievement.* New York: University Press of America.

Griffiths, S. (1995). A class sister act. *The Times Higher Education Supplement, 1197,* 20.

Harvey, W. B. (1991). Faculty responsibility and tolerance. *Thought and Action, 7,* 115–136.

hooks, b. (1991). *Breaking bread: Insurgent Black intellectual life.* Boston, MA: South End Press.

Hune, S. (1998). *Asian Pacific American women in higher education: Claiming visibility and voice.* Washington, DC: Association of American Colleges and Universities.

Hune, S., & Chan, K. S. (1997). Special focus: Asian Pacific American demographic and educational trends. In D. J. Carter & R. Wilson (Eds.), *Minorities in higher education: Fifteenth annual status report* (pp. 39–67). Washington DC: American Council on Education.

Ideta, L. M., & Cooper, J. E. (1999). Asian women leaders of higher education: Stories of strength and self-discovery. In L. Christian-Smith & K. Kellor (Eds.), *Everyday knowledge and uncommon truths: Women of the academy* (pp. 129–146). Boulder, CO: Westview Press.

Kanter, R. M. (1977). *Men and women of the corporation.* New York: Basic Books.

Ladson-Billings, G. (1996). Silences as weapons: Challenges of a Black professor teaching white students. *Theory into Practice, 35*(2), 79–85.

Ladson-Billings, G. (1997). For colored girls who have considered suicide when the academy's not enough: Reflections of an African American woman scholar. In A. Neumann & P. Peterson (Eds.), *Learning from our lives: Women, research, and autobiography in education* (pp. 52–70). New York: Teachers College, Columbia University.

Mitchell, J. (1994). Visible, vulnerable, and viable: Emerging perspectives of a minority professor. In K. Feldman & M. Paulsen (Eds.), *Teaching and learning in the college classroom* (pp. 383–390). Needham Heights, MA: Simon & Schuster Custom Publishing.

Montero-Sieburth, M. (1996). Beyond affirmative action: An inquiry into the experiences on Latinas in academia. *New England Journal of Public Policy, 2,* 65–98.

Nelson, S., & Pillett, G. (Producers). (1997). *Shattering the silence: Minority professors break into the ivory tower.* Public Broadcasting Service.

Neumann, A., & Peterson, P. L. (1997). *Learning from our lives: Women, research, and autobiography in education.* New York: Teachers College, Columbia University.

Ng, R. (1997). A woman out of control: Deconstructing sexism and racism in the university. In J. Glazer-Raymo, B. Townsend, & B. Ropers-Huliman (Eds.). *Women in higher education: A feminist perspective* (pp. 360–370). Boston, MA: Pearson Custom Publishing.

Padilla, A. M. (1994). Ethnic minority scholars, research, and mentoring: Current and future issues. *Educational Researcher, 23*(4), 24–27.

Padilla, R. V., & Chavez, R. C. (1995). *The leaning ivory tower: Latino professors in American universities.* Albany State University of New York Press.

Rains, F. V. (1999). Dancing on the sharp edge of the sword: Women faculty of color in white academe. In L. Christian-Smith & K. Kellor (Eds.), *Everyday knowledge and uncommon truths: Women of the academy* (pp. 147–174). Boulder, CO: Westview Press.

Rendon, L. I. (1992/1996). From the barrio to the academy: Revelations of a Mexican American "scholarship girl." In C. Turner, M. Garcia, A. Nora, & L. I. Rendon (Eds.), *Racial and ethnic diversity in higher education* (pp. 281–287). Needham Heights, MA: Simon & Schuster Custom Publishing.

Spann, J. (1990). *Retaining and promoting minority faculty members: Problems and possibilities.* Madison: The University of Wisconsin System.

Stein, W. (1996). The survival of American Indian faculty. In C. Turner, M. Garcia, A. Nora, & L. I. Rendon (Eds.), *Racial and ethnic diversity in higher education* (pp. 390–397). Needham Heights, MA: Simon & Schuster Custom Publishing.

The Chronicle of Higher Education Almanac. (2001). Volume *48,* Number 1. Washington, DC.

Townsend, B., & Turner, C. (2000, March 27). *Reshaping the academy to accommodate conflicts of commitment: Then what?* Paper presented at the Shaping a National Agenda for Women in Higher Education conference. Minneapolis, MN.

Turner, C. S. V. (2000a). New faces, new knowledge. *Academe, 86,* pp. 34–37.

Turner, C. S. V. (2000b). Defining success: Promotion and tenure—Planning for each career stage and beyond. In M. Garcia (Ed.), *Succeeding in an academic career: A guide for faculty of color* (pp. 111–140). Westport, CT: Greenwood Press.

Turner, C. S. V., & Myers, Jr. S. L. (2000). *Faculty of color in academe: Bittersweet success.* Needham Heights, MA: Allyn and Bacon.

University of Michigan. (1999). *Through my lens.* Ann Arbor, MI: The Women of Color in the Academy Project, sponsored by the Center for the Education of Women and the Women's Studies Program, The University of Michigan.

Wilds, D. J. (2000). *Minorities in higher education: Seventeenth annual status report.* Washington, DC: American Council on Education, Office of Minorities in Higher Education.

Women's Environment and Development Organization. (2000). *Women's equality 1995–2000: An unfinished agenda.* Retrieved December 2000 from www.wedo.org/book.txt. New York: Women's Environment and Development Organization.

CHAPTER 22
THE CONTRIBUTION OF FACULTY OF COLOR TO UNDERGRADUATE EDUCATION

PAUL D. UMBACH

Using data from a national study of 13,499 faculty at 134 colleges and universities, this study explores the impact of faculty of color on undergraduate education. This study finds compelling evidence to suggest that faculty of color do provide an important contribution to undergraduate education in two ways. First, faculty of color employ a broader range of pedagogical techniques and interact more frequently with students than their White counterparts. Second, greater structural diversity among faculty leads to an increased use of effective educational practices.

By all accounts, the United States is becoming an increasingly pluralistic society. According to recent estimates, people of color now make up approximately 31% of the United States population. Experts predict that by the middle of the century, Whites will make up less than half the population in the United States (Cole and Barber, 2003). Many have argued that higher education plays an important role in preparing students to live and work in this increasingly diverse society (Gurin, 1999; Milem and Hakuta, 2000; Rudenstine, 1996; Smith and Schonfeld, 2000).

Some have suggested that the diversification of college faculty is an important component of preparing students to be citizens in a pluralistic society (Cole and Barber, 2003; Hurtado, 2001; Smith, 1989). Although affirmative action has been portrayed as a way to increase the number of faculty of color in higher education, it has done little to increase their representation in the faculty (Aguirre, 2000; Higgerson and Higgerson, 1991; Johnsrud and Sadao, 1998). In fact, even with the rapid increases in diversity in America, the diversity of faculty changed very little in the last 30 years (Perna, 2001; Trower and Chait, 2002). What implications does the lack of diversity among college faculty have on students preparing to live and work in an increasingly diverse society?

At the same time that the United States is becoming more diverse, colleges and universities find they must defend themselves against attacks on affirmative action. In response to lawsuits brought against affirmative action in college admissions, many have argued that diversity is a "compelling interest" in that it enhances higher education through the benefits it brings to individual students (Astone and Nunez-Wormack, 1990; Duster, 1993; Hurtado et al., 1998; Liu, 1998; Smith and Associates, 1997; Tierney, 1993). In a climate where affirmative action is under increased scrutiny, it is important that researchers extend this line of inquiry to all levels of higher education. One avenue that is beginning to emerge is the impact that diverse faculty have on student experiences.

Research suggests that a racially diverse faculty has many benefits for colleges and for society. One of the most compelling arguments for diversification of college faculty relates to the important contribution made by faculty of color in the education of undergraduates. Diversification of faculty increases the variation of perspectives and approaches creating a richer learning environment for students (Smith, 1989). Hurtado (2001) argues that institutions with higher proportion of faculty of color are more likely to incorporate a wider range of pedagogical techniques. While the body of evidence is growing, some have suggested that contribution faculty of color make to the undergraduate experience remains "in the realm of conjecture rather than empirically demonstrated facts" (Cole and Barber, 2003, p. 3).

Purpose and Research Questions

Given the limited evidence on the impact of faculty diversity on undergraduate education, the purpose of this study is to explore the relationship between the background of faculty and the ways in which they involve students in and out of the classroom. More specifically, this study asks the following questions:

1. Do faculty of color engage students in ways that are significantly different than their White counterparts?

2. Do structural factors, such as diversity of an institution's faculty, relate to the ways in which faculty engage students in and out of the classroom?

Review of the Literature

Background

Relative to the rapid changes in the diversity of undergraduates, the racial diversity of college faculty has changed little over the last two decades. In 1983, faculty of color represented only 9% of all college faculty. In 1997, that number increased to only 13% (Carter and Wilson, 1997). The Department of Education (Snyder and Hoffman, 2003) estimates that approximately 14% (5% African American, 5% Asian Pacific American, 3%, Latino/a, and .4% Native American) of all U.S. faculty are faculty of color. At the same time, the representation of students of color among all U.S undergraduates is 28%.

Researchers offer several explanations for the low numbers of minorities among the faculty ranks. Some have argued that too few people of color are in the pool of PhDs (Cole and Barber, 2003; Mickelson and Oliver, 1991; Turner, Myers, and Creswell, 1999), while others have suggested disproportionate tenure rates and pre-tenure departure rates (Menges and Exum, 1983). Many (Astin et al., 1997; De la Luz Reyes and Halcon, 1991; Turner, 2003; Turner and Myers, 2000; Turner et al., 1999) have pointed to racial and ethnic bias in the workplace as impediments the professional progress of faculty of color. Still others cite social isolation and lack of mentoring (Blackwell, 1989; Turner et al., 1999) and a devaluation of their work on issues related to race and ethnicity (Aguirre, 2000; Milem and Astin, 1993).

Although the causes of under-representation of faculty of color have been the focus of much research, the study of "the value of faculty of color to higher education has not been subject to the same volume of research and debate" (antonio, 2002, p. 583). The limited amount of research available on the impact of faculty of color can be divided into two categories: benefits to students and benefits to institutions. Faculty diversity appears to have several positive impacts on students. Among the most important, faculty of color create a comfortable environment and provide support and mentoring for students of color (Cole and Barber, 2003; Smith, 1989). Students of color look to faculty who they believe will be able to understand them. Faculty of color are best able to understand their special problems and provide them with the encouragement they need to succeed (Cole and Barber, 2003). Academic performance and career aspirations are enhanced when students of color have minority faculty who serve as role models for them (Cole and Barber, 2003; Hurtado et al., 1999; Smith, 1989).

Others have argued that faculty provide diverse perspectives in the classroom (Smith, 1989), yet few studies have found empirical evidence to support this claim (antonio, 2002). Although the empirical evidence is limited, it has been argued that faculty of color bring a wide range of pedagogical techniques and introduce new perspectives in the classroom in ways that enhance student learning (Cole and Barber, 2003; Hurtado, 2001; Smith, 1989). Fairweather (1996) suggests that, among junior faculty, minorities are somewhat more committed to teaching than Whites. The same does not hold true for senior faculty. Others have found the relationship between race/ethnicity and pedagogy is mixed. antonio (2002) found that faculty of color held more holistic goals for undergraduates than did White faculty. These goals include items such as helping students to develop their person values, moral character, and self-understanding. However, the same study did not find any pedagogical differences between White faculty and faculty of color.

From an organizational perspective, faculty diversity can have several benefits as well. A racially diverse faculty demonstrates the commitment the institution has to diversity (Hurtado et al., 1998, 1999; Smith, 1989). In a society that is coming increasingly more diverse, symbols of commitment to diversity are critical. Students have come to expect representation of minorities among the faculty to be roughly proportionate of the representation of students from these minority groups (Cole and Barber, 2003).

As with the benefits students gain from faculty diversity, the evidence of the impact faculty diversity has on organizational effectiveness is limited. Astin (1993) provides support of the impact such an institutional commitment has on student learning. Emphasis on institutional diversity, signaled by the representation of minorities among students and faculty, is positively related to student growth in cultural awareness. Diversity emphasis has positive indirect effects on student satisfaction with student life and the overall college experience.

Conceptual Framework

This study is framed by Weick's (1979) application of Ashby's theory of requisite variety (Ashby, 1956; Conant and Ashby, 1970). Ashby argues that every effective regulator or control system of a system must be a model of environment in which it operates. A control system is better able to compensate for disturbances if it has a variety of options from which to choose. Weick uses the work of Ashby to argue that the success of an organization is dependent on obtaining diversity within an organization that is as great as the diversity in the environment in which it exists. This diversity is essential for the organization to understand and respond to changes in the environment. A lack of variety or diversity prohibits an organization from having different perspectives and often produces failure or an inability to adapt.

Underlying Weick's application of the theory of requisite variety is an assumption about the interaction of individuals and organizations. Individuals bring diverse perspectives or variety to an organization. In turn, this variety allows for organizations to function effectively and respond to environmental variety. The structural diversity of faculty, defined in this study as the representation of people of color on an institution's faculty, may also serve as a symbol of the commitment or emphasis that institution places on diversity. Symbols are particularly important in loosely coupled systems where efforts are often uncoordinated (Weick, 1976). A symbol, such as high minority representation among faculty, can help individuals make sense of organizational goals and focus attention on institutional values (Weick, 1982).

The application of requisite variety to the study of faculty diversity is underscored by the work of Smith. She argues that "diversification of faculty is likely to contribute to what is taught, how it is taught, and what is important to learn, contributions that are vital to the institution" (Smith, 1989, pp. 56–57). A greater representation of faculty of color increases the likelihood that institutions will change to meet the needs of an increasingly diverse society. As a result, institutions will be more successful in educating all of their students.

One measure of this success, is the extent to which institutions engage students in effective educational practices that lead to student learning. Research shows that engagement in educationally purposeful activities contributes to high levels of learning and personal development (Pascarella and Terenzini, 1991, 2005). Astin's (1993) model of inputs-environments-outcomes assesses the impacts that various institutional practices and environmental experiences (e.g., faculty-student contact, pedagogical techniques) has on student outcomes (e.g., student engagement and student learning). Astin argues that student involvement (e.g., involvement with student peer groups and involvement with faculty) enhances almost all aspects of learning and academic performance. Moreover, the amount of time and physical and psychological energy that students invest influences their development (Astin, 1993).

Chickering and Gamson (1987) outline seven effective educational practices predicted to influence the quality of students' learning and their educational experiences. Four of the principles advanced by

Chickering and Gamson address faculty behaviors and characteristics and are directly relevant to the current study: encouraging cooperation among students, encouraging active learning, communicating high expectations, encouraging contact between students and faculty, and including diverse perspectives in the classroom.

Therefore, I offer two hypotheses for this study. First, I hypothesize that faculty of color bring important perspectives to their work with students, therefore they are more likely than their White colleagues to engage students in a broad range of effective educational practices. Second, faculty on campuses where faculty of color are well represented more frequently engage in effective educational practices than faculty from less diverse campuses.

Data and Methods

The sample of faculty used in this study comes from a survey administered at 137 colleges and universities in spring 2003. Full-time and part-time faculty members who taught at least one undergraduate course in the 2002–2003 academic year are included in the data set. The instrument was designed to measure faculty expectations for student engagement in educational practices that are known to be linked with high levels of learning and development (Astin, 1993; Kuh, 2001; Pascarella and Terenzini, 1991, 2005). Additionally, the instrument examined how faculty members structure their classroom and out-of-class work. Approximately 43%, or 14,336 faculty members, completed the survey. Three historically black colleges and universities were removed from the sample, leaving 13,499 faculty from 134 institutions. Of those faculty, approximately 8% of the faculty who responded were faculty of color (3% African American, 3% Asian Pacific American, 1% Latino/a, 1%, Native American, 1% Multi-racial or other).

I construct four composites (See Appendix for a full listing of items included in the constructs) to represent pedagogy and engagement of students in educational practices that have been linked to increases in student learning (Astin, 1993; Kuh, 2001; Pascarella and Terenzini, 1991, 2005). I include each as a dependent variable in my models. *Interactions with students* is a nine-item construct (alpha = .72) that includes items such as the percentage of students with whom faculty talk about career plans or discuss ideas from readings or classes outside of class, and the amount of time spent advising students. *Active and collaborative learning techniques* is a 10-item construct (alpha = .78) that represents the extent to which faculty employ techniques that actively engage students and allow them to work together. Included in the construct are measures of the importance faculty place on having students work with others outside of class, students discuss ideas or readings from class with others outside of class. Additional measures also include the percent of class time spent on discussion, small group activities, and student presentations. *Diversity-related activities* is a three-item construct (alpha = .82) that represents the frequency with which faculty members utilize diversity in classroom instruction (e.g., include class discussions or writing assignments that include diverse perspectives, students have serious conversations in your course with students of a different race or ethnicity than their own). *Higher order thinking activities* is a seven item construct (alpha = .78) that represents the importance and frequency with which faculty engage student in activities such as applying theories or concepts, analyzing the basic elements of an idea, making judgments about the value of information, and putting together ideas or concepts from different courses when completing assignments or during class discussions.

Models

This study employs hierarchical linear modeling (HLM) to examine institutional and individual characteristics related to the outcomes of interest. Implicit in the research questions posed is a data structure where faculty are nested within colleges and universities. Very often researchers build individual-level regression models where they include institution-level characteristics. This technique is considered by many as inappropriate when examining complex data at multiple levels (Heck and Thomas, 2000; Luke, 2004). In fact, it is quite possible that this strategy will result in inaccurate parameter estimates (Ethington, 1997; Heck and Thomas, 2000; Luke, 2004; Raudenbush and Bryk, 2002). Using HLM overcomes the problems associated with complex multilevel data by simultaneously estimating equations for both individual and institutional effects.

The multilevel analyses for this study were run in several steps. First, I create a model with no predictor variables. The intercept for this model, often called the null model or one-way ANOVA model, is allowed to vary, thereby partitioning the variance within and between institutions. Equation 1 displays the null model,

$$Y_{ij} = \beta_{0j} + r_{ij} \tag{1}$$

where Y_{ij} is the dependent variable, and β_{0j} is the institution mean for college j, and r_{ij} is the deviation from the institution mean for faculty ij. The results of the null model are used to estimate the proportion of variance that exists between and within colleges. Table 1 presents the variance components. The proportion of variance between institutions ranges from .04 for higher order cognitive activities to .13 for diversity related activities. Although only one exceeds .10, the variance between institutions for the other three measures is not trivial, and warrants further investigation. Additionally, for this study, it is conceptually important to understand the organizational effects (e.g., structural diversity of faculty) that significantly relate to the dependent measures used in this study.

The second step of the modeling procedure is the creation of the within institution models (also know as the level-1 models or the individual level models). The within institution models are entered in two separate blocks. Table 2 presents the descriptive statistics and descriptions of the independent variables included in the analyses. Researchers (Fairweather, 1996; Finkelstein, Seal, and Schuster, 1998; Milem, 2001; Statham, Richardson, and Cook, 1991; Umbach and Wawrzynski, 2005, in press) have found gender to be a strong predictor of faculty teaching behaviors. Others have found that younger people are more innovative and more likely to take risks (Mulkay, 1972). Therefore, the first block or the demographic model (Model 1 in Tables 3–6), includes controls for age and gender along with race/ethnicity.

$$
\begin{aligned}
Y_{ij} = \beta_{0j} &+ \beta1(\text{AfricanAm}) + \beta2(\text{Latino}) + \beta3(\text{APA}) + \beta4(\text{NativeAm}) \\
&+ \beta5(\text{other}) + \beta6(\text{female}) + \quad + \beta7(\text{age}) + r_{ij}
\end{aligned} \tag{2}
$$

For Eq. (2), the j subscripts indicate individual institutions, and the i subscripts indicate individual students. Because I allow the intercept to vary by institution, a separate equation for each institution is created. In other words, each β_{0j} has a j subscript to indicate the intercept for institution j. Therefore, each faculty member's score can be determined as a deviation from their institution average (β_{0j}), a deviation from this average based on their individual characteristics (β_1 to β_7), and error (r_{ij}).

Several factors related to a faculty member's career also may affect the ways in which they engage students in and out of the classroom. I include these factors as controls in the second block (Model 2 in Tables 3–6). Equation (3) displays the model with demographic and career variables included. Junior faculty are more likely to adopt collaborative activities in their teaching (Statham et al., 1991),

TABLE 1

Variance Components of Dependent Variable

	Interactions with Students	Active and Collaborative Techniques	Higher Order Cognitive Activities	Diversity-Related Activities
Total variance	0.945	0.938	0.944	0.959
Variance within institutions	0.899	0.879	0.906	0.832
Variance between institutions	0.047	0.059	0.038	0.127
Proportion between institutions	0.049	0.063	0.040	0.132

TABLE 2

Descriptive Statistics for Variables Included in Models

Independent Variable	Mean	Standard Deviation	Variable Description
Institutional Characteristics			
Doctoral Research-Extensive	0.07	0.25	Carnegie classification; 1 = DRU-EXT, 0 = all others
Doctoral Research-Intensive	0.10	0.31	Carnegie classification; 1 = DRU-INT, 0 = all others
Master's I and II	0.44	0.50	Carnegie classification; 1 = MA, 0 = all others
Baccalaureate-Liberal Arts[a]	0.17	0.38	Carnegie classification; 1 = BAC-LA, 0 = all others
Baccalaureate-General	0.18	0.38	Carnegie classification; 1 = BAC-GEN, 0 = all others
Other institution type	0.04	0.19	Carnegie classification; 1 = Other, 0 = all others
Private	0.56	0.50	1 = private, 2 = public
Selectivity[b]	3.18	1.01	1 = noncompetitive, 2 = less competitive, 3 = competitive, 4 = very competitive, 5 = highly competitive, 6 = most competitive
Size [c,d]	5.02	5.59	Undergraduate headcount in thousands
Diversity[e]—1st quartile[a]	0.25	0.44	First quartile of proportion of faculty of color
Diversity—2nd quartile	0.25	0.44	Second quartile of proportion of faculty of color (cutpoint = 0.051)
Diversity—3rd quartile	0.25	0.44	Third quartile of proportion of faculty of color (cutpoint = 0.082)
Diversity—4th quartile	0.25	0.44	Fourth quartile of proportion of faculty of color (cutpoint = 0.131)
Individual Characteristics			
African American	0.02	0.13	1 = African American, 0 = all others
Latino/a	0.01	0.07	1 = Latino/a, 0 = all others
Asian Pacific American	0.03	0.16	1 = Asian Pacific American, 0 = all others
Native American	0.00	0.07	1 = Native American, 0 = all others
Other race	0.01	0.26	1 = Other race/ethnicity, 0 = all others

(continued)

399

TABLE 2 (Cont.)

Independent Variable	Mean	Standard Deviation	Variable Description
White[a]	0.88	0.63	1 = White, 0 = all others
Female	0.44	0.50	1 = female, 0 = male
Age[c]	48.98	11.11	Age in years
Years teaching[c]	16.04	10.97	Years teaching in higher education
Full Professor	0.24	0.42	Rank, 1 = full professor, 0 = all others
Associate professor	0.23	0.42	Rank, 1 = associate professor, 0 = all others
Assistant professor	0.25	0.44	Rank, 1 = assistant professor, 0 = all others
Other rank	0.22	0.41	Rank, 1 = instructor, lecturer, other 0 = all others
Part-time	0.15	0.36	1 = part-time status, 0 = full-time status
Realistic discipline	0.01	0.09	Holland discipline, 1 = realistic, 0 = all others
Investigative discipline	0.36	0.48	Holland discipline, 1 = investigative, 0 = all others
Artistic discipline	0.17	0.37	Holland discipline, 1 = artistic, 0 = all others
Conventional discipline	0.01	0.12	Holland discipline, 1 = conventional, 0 = all others
Enterprising discipline	0.19	0.39	Holland discipline, 1 = enterprising, 0 = all others
Social discipline[a]	0.08	0.27	Holland discipline, 1 = social, 0 = all others
Other discipline	0.19	0.39	Holland discipline, 1 = other, 0 = all others

[a] Serves as reference group in models.
[b] Source: 2003 Barron's College Guide.
[c] Standardized (mean = 0 and standard deviation = 1) before entering into models.
[d] Source: IPEDS Fall Enrollment Data 2000–2001.
[e] Source: IPEDS Fall Staff Data 1997–1998.

400

TABLE 3

HLM Results[a]: Faculty Interactions with Students

	Model 1 Demographic Model	Model 2 Career Model	Model 3 Institutional Model
Intercept	0.062**	0.052**	0.064***
Institutional Characteristics			
Doctoral research-extensive			−0.113
Doctoral research-intensive			−0.133
Master's I and II			−0.125+
Baccalaureate-General			−0.165*
Other institution type			−0.163+
Private			0.094*
Selectivity			−0.019
Size			−0.065**
Diversity—2nd quartile			−0.077
Diversity—3rd quartile			−0.015
Diversity—4th quartile			−0.067
Individual Characteristics			
African American	0.268**	0.244**	0.256**
Latino/a	0.134	0.128	0.133
Asian Pacific American	0.076	0.044	0.049
Native American	0.505***	0.479**	0.482**
Other race	0.090*	0.095*	0.098*
Female	0.212***	0.201***	0.200***
Age	0.029**	0.024*	0.025*
Years teaching		−0.022*	−0.023*
Associate professor		0.081**	0.079**
Assistant professor		−0.008	−0.010
Other rank		−0.031	−0.025
Part-time		−0.376***	−0.379***
Realistic discipline		0.200	0.209
Investigative discipline		−0.320***	−0.320***
Artistic discipline		−0.146**	−0.148**
Conventional discipline		−0.422***	−0.421***
Enterprising discipline		−0.175***	−0.175***
Other discipline		0.048	0.051
Variance Components			
Variance between institutions	0.043***	0.038***	0.023***
Variance between explained	8.0%	23.4%	98.9%
Variance within institutions	0.886	0.850	0.850
Variance within explained	1.5%	5.7%	5.7%
Reliability	0.754	0.738	0.645

[a]Coefficients are presented as effect sizes. + $p<.10$,*$p<.05$,**$p<.01$,***$p<.001$. Given the relatively small sample size at level 2 ($N = 134$), alpha level set at .10.

TABLE 4

HLM Results[a]: Active and Collaborative Learning Techniques

	Model 1 Demographic Model	Model 2 Career Model	Model 3 Institutional Model
Intercept	0.031	0.033	0.042*
Institutional Characteristics			
Doctoral research-extensive			−0.183+
Doctoral research-intensive			−0.150*
Master's I and II			−0.133*
Baccalaureate-General			−0.101
Other institution type			−0.184
Private			0.171**
Selectivity			−0.069**
Size			−0.016
Diversity—2nd quartile			0.069
Diversity—3rd quartile			0.092
Diversity—4th quartile			0.060
Individual Characteristics			
African American	0.536***	0.491***	0.496***
Latino/a	0.562***	0.545***	0.551***
Asian Pacific American	0.164**	0.152**	0.156**
Native American	0.471***	0.430***	0.431**
Other race	0.230***	0.219***	0.222***
Female	0.413***	0.359***	0.358***
Age	0.015+	0.054***	0.054***
Years teaching		−0.052***	−0.052***
Associate professor		0.045+	0.043+
Assistant professor		0.062*	0.060*
Other rank		0.093*	0.096*
Part-time		−0.057+	−0.061+
Realistic discipline		0.405*	0.415*
Investigative discipline		−0.216**	−0.214**
Artistic discipline		0.001	0.000
Conventional discipline		−0.376**	−0.373**
Enterprising discipline		−0.013	−0.012
Other discipline		0.251***	0.254***
Variance Components			
Variance between institutions	0.046***	0.042***	0.030***
Variance between explained	26.9%	41.4%	97.0%
Variance within institutions	0.829	0.796	0.796
Variance within explained	6.0%	10.4%	10.4%
Reliability	0.777	0.771	0.706

[a]Coefficients are presented as effect sizes. $+ p<.10, *p<.05, **p<.01, ***p<.001$. Given the relatively small sample size at level 2 ($N = 134$), alpha level set at .10.

are more innovative (Mulkay, 1972), and spend more time and effort on teaching (Fairweather, 1996; Finkelstein et al., 1998). Therefore, rank and years teaching in higher education are included in the models as controls for experience.

$$
\begin{aligned}
Y_{ij} = \beta_{0j} &+ \beta_1(\text{AfricanAm}) + \beta_2(\text{Latino}) + \beta_3(\text{APA}) + \beta_4(\text{NativeAm}) \\
&+ \beta_5(\text{other}) + \beta_6(\text{female}) + \beta_7(\text{age}) + \beta_8(\text{yrsteach}) \\
&+ \beta_9(\text{associate}) + \beta_{10}(\text{assistant}) + \beta_{11}(\text{other}) + \beta_{12}(\text{parttime}) \\
&+ \beta_{13}(\text{realistic}) + \beta_{14}(\text{investigative}) + \beta_{15}(\text{artistic}) + \beta_{16}(\text{conventl}) \\
&+ \beta_{17}(\text{enterprise}) + \beta_{18}(\text{other}) + r_{ij}
\end{aligned}
\tag{3}
$$

Part-time status is also a predictor of teaching behaviors; thus, I include part-time status in the models. Some assert that the reliance on part-time appointments negatively impacts undergraduate education (Benjamin, 1998, 1998, 2002). Others, however, have suggested that part-time faculty are as effective, and in some cases more effective, in delivering instruction when compared with their tenured or tenure-track counterparts (Baldwin and Chronister, 2001; Chronister and Baldwin, 1999; Gappa and Leslie, 1993; Roueche, Rouche, and Milliron, 1995).

Finally, included in the models are variables representing academic discipline of appointment. A long line of research establishes the differential impacts of academic fields on college students (Feldman and Newcomb, 1969; Pascarella and Terenzini, 1991, 2005). Researchers have applied typologies developed by Biglan (1973, 1973) and Holland (Holland, 1966, 1985) to understand differences between faculty. Smart, Feldman, and Ethington (2000) use Holland's typology in a study of faculty and find disciplinary differences in goals for undergraduate education and teaching foci. They classify faculty into one of six types: realistic (e.g, electrical engineering, mechanical engineering), investigative (e.g., biology, mathematics), artistic (e.g., arts, English), social (e.g., science, nursing), enterprising (e.g., business, journalism), and conventional (e.g., accounting). Previous research (Milem and Umbach, 2003; Milem, Umbach, & Liang, 2004; Smart et al., 2000; Umbach & Milem, 2004) suggests that faculty in social disciplines would be the most likely to engage students in effective educational practices.

The final step in the modeling process is the specification of the between institution model (also known as the level-2 or institution level model). Institution type is a strong predictor how faculty engage students in and out of the classroom. Many find a relationship between institutional characteristics such as Carnegie classification, sector (public/private), and selectivity, and teaching behaviors (Fairweather, 1996; Umbach and Wawrzynski, 2005) and student engagement (Kuh, 2001, 2003; Kuh and Hu, 2001). Included in the level two models are controls for Carnegie classification, sector, selectivity (Barron's), size (undergraduate headcount), as well as structural diversity of the faculty (entered as quartiles).

$$
\begin{aligned}
\beta_{0j} = \gamma_{00} &+ \gamma_{01}(\text{DRUEXT}) + \gamma_{02}(\text{DRUINT}) + \gamma_{03}(\text{MA}) + \gamma_{04}(\text{BACGEN}) \\
&+ \gamma_{05}(\text{OTHERCARN}) + \gamma_{06}(\text{PRIVATE}) + \gamma_{07}(\text{SELECTIVITY}) \\
&+ \gamma_{08}\text{SIZE}_j + \gamma_{09}(\text{2ndquart}) + \gamma_{10}(\text{3rdquart}) + \gamma_{11}(\text{4thquart}) + u_{0j}
\end{aligned}
\tag{4}
$$

To aid in the interpretation of the model results, I calculate effect sizes for all of the coefficients (Rosenthal and Rosnow, 1991). An effect size is the proportion of a standard deviation change in the dependent variable as a result of a one-unit change in an independent variable. All continuous independent measures and dependent are standardized measures prior to entry into the models, so the unstandardized coefficients represent effect sizes. It has been suggested that an effect size of .10 or less to reflect a trivial difference, between .10 and .30 small, between .30 and .50 moderate, and greater than .50 large (Rosenthal and Rosnow, 1991).

TABLE 5

HLM Results[a]: Higher Order Cognitive Activities

	Model 1 Demographic Model	Model 2 Career Model	Model 3 Institutional Model
Intercept	0.006	−0.001	0.003
Institutional Characteristics			
Doctoral research-extensive			−0.127
Doctoral research-intensive			−0.082
Master's I and II			−0.108+
Baccalaureate-General			−0.094
Other institution type			0.062
Private			0.108*
Selectivity			−0.042+
Size			0.009
Diversity—2nd quartile			0.101+
Diversity—3rd quartile			0.117*
Diversity—4th quartile			0.158**
Individual Characteristics			
African American	0.333***	0.314***	0.308***
Latino/a	0.381***	0.407***	0.402***
Asian Pacific American	0.281***	0.274***	0.272***
Native American	0.173	0.171	0.171
Other race	0.185***	0.189***	0.187*
Female	0.163***	0.152***	0.151***
Age	0.025**	0.028**	0.028**
Years teaching		−0.028*	−0.028*
Associate professor		0.036	0.036
Assistant professor		0.019	0.019
Other rank		−0.187***	−0.185***
Part-time		0.000	−0.004
Realistic discipline		0.243*	0.244*
Investigative discipline		−0.252***	−0.253***
Artistic discipline		−0.024	−0.029
Conventional discipline		−0.322**	−0.321**
Enterprising discipline		0.007	0.006
Other discipline		0.000	−0.001
Variance Components			
Variance between institutions	0.032***	0.032***	0.029***
Variance between explained	18.6%	17.9%	30.0%
Variance within institutions	0.895	0.874	0.874
Variance within explained	9.3%	13.9%	13.9%
Reliability	0.695	0.701	0.682

[a]Coefficients are presented as effect sizes. + $p<.10$,*$p<.05$,**$p<.01$,***$p<.001$. Given the relatively small sample size at level 2 ($N = 134$), alpha level set at .10.

TABLE 6

HLM Results[a]: Diversity Related Activities

	Model 1 Demographic Model	Model 2 Career Model	Model 3 Institutional Model
Intercept	0.044	0.038	0.041+
Institutional Characteristics			
Doctoral research-extensive			−0.302*
Doctoral research-intensive			−0.313**
Master's I and II			−0.299**
Baccalaureate-General			−0.345**
Other institution type			−0.463*
Private			0.257***
Selectivity			−0.128***
Size			0.027
Diversity—2nd quartile			0.103
Diversity—3rd quartile			0.174*
Diversity—4th quartile			0.374***
Individual Characteristics			
African American	0.338***	0.330***	0.321***
Latino/a	0.337**	0.368**	0.360**
Asian Pacific American	−0.132*	−0.100+	−0.101+
Native American	0.435***	0.419***	0.416***
Other race	0.203***	0.206***	0.203***
Female	0.311***	0.260***	0.259***
Age	0.044***	0.039**	0.040**
Years teaching		−0.005	−0.005
Associate professor		−0.002	−0.002
Assistant professor		0.037	0.004
Other rank		0.009	0.010
Part-time		−0.051*	−0.053***
Realistic discipline		−0.505***	−0.503***
Investigative discipline		−0.578***	−0.578***
Artistic discipline		−0.098*	−0.099**
Conventional discipline		−0.965***	−0.965***
Enterprising discipline		−0.113**	−0.113**
Other discipline		−0.262***	−0.263***
Variance Components			
Variance between institutions	0.112***	0.108***	0.071***
Variance between explained	12.9%	17.6%	79.6%
Variance within institutions	0.803	0.752	0.752
Variance within explained	3.6%	10.7%	10.6%
Reliability	0.892	0.895	0.850

[a]Coefficients are presented as effect sizes. $+ p<.10, *p<.05, **p<.01, ***p<.001$. Given the relatively small sample size at level 2 ($N = 134$), alpha level set at .10.

Results

Faculty Interactions with Students

Table 3 presents the model estimates for faculty interactions with students. The demographic model indicates that African American and Native American faculty more frequently interact with students than White faculty. These effects remain relatively stable, even after all other controls are introduced into the model. Women faculty members also interact with students more than their male counterparts. Age is significantly positively related with interactions with students, but the effect size is trivial.

Some differences also appear in the career model. Part-time faculty interact less with students than their full-time peers. Faculty in social and realistic disciplines are more likely than all other faculty interact with students. While statistically significant, the effects of years teaching and rank on interactions with students are trivial.

Model 3 includes estimates from the level-2 models. In general, faculty at Baccalaureate-Liberal Arts Colleges interact with students more than faculty at other colleges. The effect size differences between institution types are small, but not nontrivial. Additionally, institutional size is negatively related to interactions with students and private is positively related to interactions with students; however these effects are trivial. Contrary to the hypothesis posed in this study, the structural diversity of faculty is not statistically significantly related to faculty interactions with students.

Active and Collaborative Learning Techniques

Table 4 displays the coefficients for the models of active and collaborative learning techniques. Faculty of color (from all racial/ethnic groups) employ active and collaborative learning techniques with greater frequency than White faculty. Even after all controls are included, the effects for faculty of color are quite substantial. Except for Asian Pacific Americans and Others, the effect sizes exceed .40 (for Latinos/as the effect size exceeds .50). Women also employ these techniques with greater frequency than men.

The only substantive differences observed among the career variables are seen between disciplinary groups. Realistic faculty are the most likely to use active a collaborative techniques in instruction. Investigative and conventional faculty are the least likely to employ active and collaborative learning techniques in the classroom.

Except for Baccalaureate-General institutions, faculty at Liberal Arts Colleges, on average, are more likely to use active and collaborative learning techniques in the classroom. Faculty at private colleges use these techniques with greater frequency than their public college counterparts. No significant relationship exists between the structural diversity of faculty on a campus and the use of active and collaborative techniques.

Higher Order Cognitive Activities

Except for Native American faculty, faculty of color emphasize higher order cognitive experiences more than White faculty (See Table 5). Even in the fully controlled model, the effect sizes for all racial ethnic groups are noteworthy, ranging from .187 to .402. Women also engage students in higher order cognitive activities more frequently than men.

The models suggest statistically significant and substantive differences between disciplines in the use of higher order activities. Investigative and conventional faculty are the least likely to emphasize higher order thinking activities in their classes. Realistic faculty are the most likely to emphasizes these activities.

Institution type, as represented by Carnegie classification, has little relationship with faculty emphasis on higher order cognitive activities. Faculty at Master's institutions use higher order activities less frequently than faculty at Liberal Arts Colleges. Private college faculty are more likely than public college faculty to use these activities in their instruction. The structural diversity variables are positively related to institutional average faculty use of higher order activities. The coefficients for the diversity quartile variables suggest a positive linear relationship between faculty structural diversity and the outcome of interest. In other words, the greater the diversity among faculty the higher the frequency of use of higher order cognitive activities on a campus.

Diversity Related Activities

Table 6 presents the coefficients from the diversity related activities model. Except for Asian Pacific Americans, faculty of color more frequently engage students in diversity related activities than White faculty, even after all controls are included in the model. For African Americans, Native Americans, and Latinos/as, the effect sizes all exceed .3. Asian Pacific American faculty are slightly less likely than Whites to emphasize diversity in their classes. On average, women use diversity in their classes with greater frequency than men.

Discipline is an important predictor of faculty use of diversity in the classroom. Social faculty use diversity related activities more frequently than any other faculty. Conventional, realistic, and investigative faculty are less likely to use diversity in classroom instruction.

The institutional model suggests a number of significant differences between institutions. Faculty at Liberal Arts Colleges, on average, use diversity related activities in instruction more frequently than faculty at other institution types. The effects here are worthy of note, ranging from .30 to .46. Additionally, private college faculty are more likely to use diversity than are public college faculty. Selectivity relates negatively with the faculty use of diversity in the classroom.

Finally, the structural diversity of faculty is positively related to the use of diversity related activities on a campus. As with the higher order activities model, the diversity model results suggest a positive linear relationship between the diversity of an institution's faculty and the use of diversity in the classroom. A closer look at the diversity quartile coefficients suggests a marked difference between campuses with a highly structurally diverse faculty (the highest quartile) and campuses with few faculty of color.

Summary

Hypothesis 1: Faculty of color employ a broader range of pedagogical techniques compared with their White counterparts. Faculty of color scored higher than Whites for nearly every dependent variable. In only a few cases did a minority faculty group, on average, score similar to White faculty. Only one time did a minority faculty group score lower than Whites (Asian Pacific Americans and the use of diversity related activities). Additionally, in most cases, the effect sizes for the different racial ethnic groups exceeded .10, a threshold that many consider to be worthy of examination. In fact, many of the effect sizes exceeded .30 and some were greater than .50. Effect sizes of this magnitude suggest that faculty of color do offer an important contribution to undergraduate student learning and engagement.

Hypothesis 2: Faculty on campuses where faculty of color are well represented more frequently engage students in effective educational practices than faculty from less diverse campuses. In addition to testing racial/ethnic differences, this study sought to determine whether a large proportion of faculty of color on a campus creates a context for learning that offers additional benefits to students. For the models of higher order cognitive activities and diversity related activities, the greater the diversity of faculty on a campus, the higher the levels of faculty involvement. Given that, the results suggest that greater structural diversity leads to an increased use of effective educational practices.

Limitations

This study is limited five ways. First, the study may be biased by convenience sampling. Because institutions volunteered to participate in the study, it is difficult to say the sample is fully representative of American higher education. Although a close examination comparing the sample of institutions to the population suggests adequate representation by Carnegie classification, sector, and region, it is possible that the sample is different than the population in ways that cannot be captured quantitatively. However, it is important to note that this is possibly the largest data set that includes a very detailed accounting of faculty attitudes, instructional techniques, and work patterns in and out of the classroom.

Second, like many studies that use secondary data analysis to conduct research, these data are limited in the inclusion of some controls that may have an impact on the outcomes. Most notable is the exclusion of a variable for highest degree earned. While the effect of degree is possibly ameliorated by the inclusion of disciplinary affiliation, rank, and institutional type, it is possible that its exclusion may have a confounding effect on the study.

Third, the intraclass correlations, or the amount of variation explained by institutional membership, are somewhat low ranging from 0.04 to 0.13. In other words, most of the variance between faculty (96% to 87%) lies within institutions rather than between institutions. Therefore, any assertions made about organizational effects should not be overstated. However, because models of behaviors and attitudes often explain very little of the variance between individuals, the conclusions drawn here should not be disregarded as trivial. In fact, the models presented in this study explain nearly all of the between institution variance for three of the four models and approximately one third of the variance for the fourth. Additionally, the models explain acceptable levels of within institution variance.

Fourth, the limited variability of the structural diversity measure of faculty presents a possible limitation in the study. For three quarters of the institutions in the sample, faculty of color made up approximately 13% or less of their entire faculty. In fact, only half had more than 8% faculty of color. In terms of modeling, truncated variance of this kind presents unique challenges. My solution was to convert the structural diversity measure into quartiles and include them in the models as dummy-coded variables.

Discussion and Implications

The findings of this study provide empirical evidence that suggests that faculty of color offer a significant contribution to undergraduate student learning and involvement. The variety they bring to colleges and universities appears to be significant. Faculty of color more frequently engage students in practices that research (Astin, 1993; Kuh, 2001; Pascarella and Terenzini, 1991, 2005) suggests leads to greater learning among undergraduates. Even after controlling for a number of individual and institutional characteristics, faculty of color were more likely to interact with students, to employ active learning and collaborative learning techniques, to create environments that increase diverse interactions, and to emphasize higher-order thinking activities in the classroom.

Research offers some possible explanations for the positive behaviors of faculty of color. One quite obvious explanation is that faculty of color come from diverse and varying backgrounds that translate into unique perspectives and pedagogical techniques in the college classroom (Aguirre, 2000; Harlow, 2003; Hurtado et al., 1999; Turner and Myers, 2000). Quite simply, faculty of color offer a broader range of perspectives "to what is taught, how it is taught, and why it is important to learn" (Smith, 1989, p. 57).

Another possible explanation is that faculty of color believe they need to work harder to prove they are as good as their White colleagues (Aguirre, 2000; De la Luz Reyes and Halcón, 1991; Harlow, 2003; Rakow, 1991; Turner and Myers, 2000). A long line of inquiry into status characteristics theory (for detailed descriptions see Berger et al., 1977; Berger, Rosenholtz, and Zelditch, 1980) provides further insight into the performance of faculty of color. A status characteristic is "a characteristic around which differences in cognitions, and evaluations of individuals or social types of them come to be organized" (Berger et al., 1977, p. 5). Among the characteristics around which individuals become organized is race, where people of color typically have less status or power than Whites. Although an individual's status may be irrelevant to a task, persons of high status are considered more competent. For faculty of color, a conflict arises as a result of their racial status and their faculty status; therefore, they must work especially hard to prove that they deserve their high-status position (Cohen, 1982; Harlow, 2003). This study offers some evidence to support this assertion.

This study also provides some evidence to support Weick's (1976) application of the theory of requisite variety, and its impact on organizational functioning. In general, on campuses with diversity that more closely matches the diversity of American society, faculty employ a broader range of instructional techniques. Faculty on diverse campuses are more likely than faculty on racially homogenous campuses to emphasize higher order cognitive activities and diversity in their instruction. The structural diversity of faculty has an effect on instruction at an institution regardless of the individual race/ethnicity of a faculty member. In other words, a White member of a very diverse faculty is more likely than a White peer at a homogenous institution to emphasize higher order cognitive activities and use diversity in their instruction. It would seem the diversity of faculty acts as a symbol of an institution's commitment to diversity; therefore, creating a context or culture where diversity is highly valued. This symbol allows faculty to make sense (Weick, 1979) of the institutional environment and institutional priorities. In turn, faculty act in a way that is compatible with institutional goals and priorities related to diversity.

This study also provides further insight into and support of other research related to faculty use of effective instructional practices. Academic discipline plays an important role in the use of effective instructional practices. The findings from this study and others (Milem and Umbach, 2003; Milem et al., 2004; Umbach and Milem, 2004) suggest that social, and to a lesser extent artistic, major environments are more likely to engage students in effective educational practices, in particular diversity related activities. Our findings of the positive effect of women faculty parallel research that indicates women are more committed to teaching (Fairweather, 1996) and have a greater repertoire of teaching techniques than men (Finkelstein et al., 1998; Harlow, 2003).

Faculty behaviors also vary significantly by institution type. As other research suggests (Umbach and Wawrzynski, 2005), faculty at Liberal Arts Colleges create a unique learning environment for students by engaging them in effective educational practices. Perhaps this study also explains why students at liberal arts colleges, despite low structural diversity, are more likely to interact across race than their peers at other institution types (Umbach and Kuh, in press). Additional research exploring the experiences of faculty at liberal arts colleges would be instructive.

The findings of this study inform policy and practice in several ways. Given evidence of the positive impact that faculty of color have on undergraduate education, the diversification of faculty should be a compelling interest for colleges and universities. The recruitment and retention of faculty of color are important goals for campuses that wish to offer a positive learning environment for their students. Although evidence suggests that it has not been terribly effective in diversifying faculty, continuing affirmative action in the hiring practices of college faculty may be one important component in diversifying the faculty ranks.

In addition to considering race/ethnicity in the hiring of faculty, it also is important to consider the pipeline into the faculty ranks. While there may be a supply problem, the challenges that face people of color may be systemic. Trower and Chait (2002, p. 33) suggest that "even if the pipeline were awash with women and minorities, a fundamental challenge would remain: the pipeline empties into territory women and faculty of color too often experience as uninviting, un-accommodating, and unappealing." Many qualified students of color forgo graduate school because of the climate of higher education or drop out in the middle of their graduate work. Still others decide to pursue other career options after earning their doctoral degree because of the uninviting nature of colleges and universities. Programs that offer educational and social support to students of color at both the graduate and undergraduate level are important.

The unique challenges that face new faculty of color as they become socialized in the academic workplace poses a barrier to their retention (Tierney and Bensimon, 1996). Reports of social isolation are not uncommon among young scholars of color (Aguirre, 2000; De la Luz Reyes and Halcón, 1991). Without adequate socialization, faculty of color are prevented from participating fully in the academic workplace. Highly structured mentoring programs and minority postdoctoral scholarships may serve as possible tools to socialize faculty of color.

Conclusion

While this study presents some compelling evidence of the effect of diverse of faculty, the representation of people of color in the faculty ranks continues to be quite small. In fact, for this study, institutions considered the most diverse only had 13% faculty of color. While small in numbers, the impact that these faculty have on undergraduate education appears to be significant. The perspectives that faculty of color offer is critical to the success colleges and universities as work to prepare students to live in an increasingly pluralistic society.

Constructs and Items	Responses
Interactions with students (Alpha = .72)	
Discuss grades or assignments with you	None, 1–24%, 25–49%, 50–74%, 75% or higher
Talk about career plans with you	None, 1–24%, 25–49%, 50–74%, 75% or higher
Discuss ideas from readings or classes with you outside of class	None, 1–24%, 25–49%, 50–74%, 75% or higher
Use e-mail to communicate with you	None, 1–24%, 25–49%, 50–74%, 75% or higher
Working with students on activities other than course work (committees, organizations, student life activities, orientation, intramurals, etc)	Hours/week: 0, 1–4, 5–8, 13–16, 17–20, 21–30, more than 30
Other interactions with students outside of the classroom	Hours/week: 0,1–4,5–8, 13–16, 17–20, 21–30, more than 30
Advising undergraduate students	Hours/week: 0,1–4,5–8, 13–16, 17–20, 21–30, more than 30
Working with undergraduates on research	Hours/week: 0,1–4,5–8, 13–16, 17–20, 21–30, more than 30
Supervising internships or other field experiences	Hours/week: 0,1–4,5–8, 13–16, 17–20, 21–30, more than 30
Active and Collaborative Learning Techniques (Alpha = .78)	
Working effectively with others	Very much, quite a bit, some, very little
Work with other students on projects during class	Very important, important, somewhat important, not important
Work with classmates outside of class to prepare class assignments	Very important, important, somewhat important, not important
Tutor or teach other students (paid or voluntary)	Very important, important, somewhat important, not important
Discuss ideas or readings from class with others outside of class (other students, faculty members, coworkers, etc.)	Very important, important, somewhat important, not important
Ask questions in class or contribute to class discussions	None, 1–24%, 25–49%, 50–74%, 75% or higher
Teacher-student shared responsibility (seminar, discussion, etc.)	% of class time: 0, 1–9, 10–19, 20–29, 30–39, 40–49, 75 or more
Student presentations	% of class time: 0, 1–9, 10–19, 20–29, 30–39, 40–49, 75 or more

410

Item	Response options
Small group activities	% of class time: 0, 1–9, 10–19, 20–29, 30–39, 40–49, 75 or more
In-class writing	% of class time: 0, 1–9, 10–19, 20–29, 30–39, 40–49, 75 or more
Diversity-related activities (Alpha = .82)	
Have serious conversations in your course with students who are very different from them in terms of their religious beliefs, political opinions, or personal values	Very often, often, sometimes, never
Have class discussions or writing assignments that include diverse perspectives (different races, religions, genders, political beliefs, etc.)	Very often, often, sometimes, never
Have serious conversations in your course with students of a different race or ethnicity than their own	Very often, often, sometimes, never
Higher order cognitive activities (Alpha = .78)	
Thinking critically and analytically	Very much, quite a bit, some, very little
Synthesizing and organizing ideas, information, or experiences into new, more complex interpretations and relationships	Very much, quite a bit, some, very little
Solving complex real-world problems	Very much, quite a bit, some, very little
Making judgments about the value of information, arguments or methods such as examining how others gathered and interpreted data and assessing the soundness of their conclusions	Very much, quite a bit, some, very little
Applying theories or concepts to practical problems or in new situations	Very much, quite a bit, some, very little
Analyzing the basic elements of an idea, experience or theory, such as examining a particular case or situation in depth, and considering its components	Very much, quite a bit, some, very little
Put together ideas or concepts from different courses when completing assignments or during class discussions	Very important, important, somewhat important, not important

References

Aguirre, A. (2000). *Women and Minority Faculty in the Academic Workplace: Recruitment, Retention, and Academic Culture,* Jossey-Bass, San Francisco, CA.

antonio, a. l. (2002). Faculty of color reconsidered: Reassessing contributions to scholarship. *The Journal of Higher Education* 73(5): 582–602.

Ashby, W. R. (1956). *An Introduction to Cybernetics,* Chapman and Hall, London.

Astin, A. W. (1993). *What Matters in College: Four Critical Years Revisited,* Jossey-Bass, San Francisco, CA.

Astin, H. S., antonio, a. l., Cress, C. M., and Astin, A. W. (1997). *Race and Ethnicity in the American Professoriate, 1995–1996,* Higher Education Research Institute, Los Angeles, CA.

Astone, B., and Nunez-Wormack, E. (1990). *Pursuing Diversity: Recruiting College Minority Students,* George Washington University, Washington, DC.

Baldwin, R., and Chronister, J. (2001). *Teaching without Tenure: Practices and Policies for a New Era,* Johns Hopkins University Press, Baltimore, MD.

Benjamin, E. (1998). Declining faculty availability to students is the problem—but tenure is not the explanation. *American Behavioral Scientist* 41(5): 716–735.

Benjamin, E. (1998). Variations in the characteristics of part-time faculty by general fields of instruction and research. In: Leslie, D. W. (ed.): *The Growing use of Part-time Faculty: Understanding the Causes and effects,* Jossey-Bass, San Francisco, pp. 45–59.

Benjamin, E. (2002). How over-reliance on contingent appointments diminishes faculty involvement in student learning. *Peer Review* 5(1): 4–10.

Berger, J. M., Fisek, M. H., Norman, R. Z., and Zelditch, M. J. (1977). *Status Characteristics and Social Interaction,* Elsevier, New York, NY.

Berger, J. M., Rosenholtz, S. J., and Zelditch, M. J. (1980). Status organizing processes. *Annual Review of Sociology* 6: 479–508.

Biglan, A. (1973). The characteristics of subject matter in different academic areas. *Journal of Applied Psychology* 57(3): 195–203.

Biglan, A. (1973). Relationships between subject matter characteristics and the structure and output of university departments. *Journal of Applied Psychology* 51(3): 204–213.

Blackwell, J. E. (1989). Mentoring: An action strategy for increasing minority faculty. *Academe* 75(5): 8–14.

Carter, D. J., and Wilson, R. (1997). *Fifteenth Annual Status Report on Minorities in Higher Education,* American Council on Education, Washington, DC.

Chickering, A. W., and Gamson, Z. F. (1987). Seven principles for good practice in undergraduate education. *AAHE Bulletin* 39(7): 3–7.

Chronister, J., and Baldwin, R. (1999). Marginal or mainstream? Full-time faculty of the tenure track. *Liberal Education* 85(4): 16–23.

Cohen, E. G. (1982). Expectation states and interracial interaction in school settings. *Annual Review of Sociology* 8: 209–235.

Cole, S., and Barber, E. (2003). *Increasing Faculty Diversity: The Occupational Choices of High-achieving Minority Students,* Harvard University Press, Cambridge, MA.

Conant, R. C., and Ashby, W. R. (1970). Every good regulator of a system must be a model of that system. *International Journal of Systems Science* 1(2): 89–97.

De la Luz Reyes, M., and Halcón, J. J. (1991). Practices of the academy: Barriers to access for Chicano academics. In: Altbach, P. G., and Lomotey, K. (eds.), *The Racial Crisis in American Higher Education,* SUNY Press, Albany, NY, pp. 167–186.

Duster, T. (1993). The diversity of California at Berkeley: An emerging reformulation of "competence" in a multicultural world. In: Thompson, B. W., and Tyagi, S. (eds.), *Beyond a Dream Deferred: Multicultural Education and the Politics of Excellence,* University of Minnesota Press, Minneapolis, MN, pp. 143–157.

Ethington, C. A. (1997). A hierarchical linear modeling approach to studying college effects. In: Smart, J. (ed.), *Higher Education: Handbook of Theory and Research, Vol. 12,* Agathon, New York, pp. 165–194.

Fairweather, J. S. (1996). *Faculty Work and Public Trust: Restoring the Value of Teaching and Public Service in American Academic Life,* Allyn and Bacon, Boston, MA.

Feldman, K. A., and Newcomb, T. M. (1969). *The Impact of College on Students,* Jossey-Bass, San Francisco.

Finkelstein, M. J., Seal, R. K., and Schuster, J. H. (1998). *The New Academic Generation: A Profession in Transformation*, The Johns Hopkins University Press, Baltimore, MD.

Gappa, J. M., and Leslie, D. W. (1993). *The Invisible Faculty: Improving the Status of Part-timers in Higher Education*, Jossey-Bass, San Francisco, CA.

Gurin, P. (1999). Expert report of Patricia Gurin. In: Mich. (ed.), *The compelling need for diversity in higher education, Gratz et al. V. Bollinger et al., No. 97–75237 and Grutter et al. V. Bollinger et al. No. 97–75928*. Ann Arbor, MI: The University of Michigan.

Harlow, R. (2003). "Race doesn't matter, but . . .": The effect of race on professors' experiences and emotion management in the undergraduate classroom. *Social Psychology Quarterly* 66(4): 348–363.

Heck, R. H., and Thomas, S. L. (2000). *An Introduction to Multilevel Modeling Techniques*, Lawrence Erlbaum Associates, Mahwah, NJ.

Higgerson, M., and Higgerson, R. (1991). Affirmative action guidelines: Do they impede progress? *CUPA Journal* 42(4): 11–14.

Holland, J. L. (1966). *The Psychology of Vocational Choice*, Blaisdell, Waltham, MA.

Holland, J. L. (1985). *Making Vocational Choices*, Prentice-Hall, Englewood Cliffs, NJ.

Hurtado, S. (2001). Linking diversity and educational purpose: How diversity affects the classroom environment and student development. In: Orfield, G., and Kurlaender, M. (eds.), *Diversity Challenged: Evidence on the Impact of Affirmative Action*, Harvard University Press, Cambridge, MA, pp. 187–203.

Hurtado, S., Milem, J., Clayton-Pedersen, A., and Allen, W. (1998). Enacting campus climates for racial/ethnic diversity through educational policy and practice. *The Review of Higher Education* 21(3): 279–302.

Hurtado, S., Milem, J., Clayton-Pedersen, A., and Allen, W. (1999). *Enacting Diverse Learning Environments: Improving the Climate for Racial/ethnic Diversity in Higher Education*, The George Washington University, Washington, DC.

Johnsrud, L., and Sadao, K. (1998). The common experience of otherness: Ethnic and racial minority faculty. *Review of Higher Education* 21(4): 315–342.

Kuh, G. D. (2001). Assessing what really matters to student learning: Inside the national survey of student engagement. *Change* 33(3): 10–17, 66.

Kuh, G. D. (2003). What we're learning about student engagement from NSSE. *Change* 35(2): 24–32.

Kuh, G. D., and Hu, S. P. (2001). The effects of student-faculty interaction in the 1990s. *Review of Higher Education* 24(3): 309–332.

Liu, G. (1998). Affirmative action in higher education: The diversity rationale and the compelling interest test. *Harvard Civil Rights-Civil Liberties Law Review* 33: 381–442.

Luke, D. A. (2004). *Multilevel Modeling*, Sage Publications, Thousand Oaks, CA.

Menges, R. J., and Exum, W. H. (1983). Barriers to the progress of women and minority faculty. *The Journal of Higher Education* 54: 123–144.

Mickelson, M. L., and Oliver, M. L. (1991). Making the short list: Black candidates and the faculty recruitment process. In: Altbach, P. G., and Lomotey, K. (eds.), *The Racial Crisis in American Higher Education*, SUNY Press, Albany, NY.

Milem, J. F. (2001). Diversity is not enough: How campus climate and faculty teaching methods affect student outcomes. In: Orfield, G. (eds.), *Diversity Challenged: Legal Crisis and New Evidence*, Harvard Education Publishing Group, Cambridge, MA, pp. 233–249.

Milem, J. F., and Astin, H. S. (1993). The changing composition of faculty: What does it really mean for diversity?. *Change* 25(2): 21–27.

Milem, J. F., and Hakuta, K. (2000). The benefits of racial and ethnic diversity in higher education. In: Wilds, D. (ed.), *Minorities in Higher Education: Seventeenth Annual Status Report*, American Council on Education, Washington, DC, pp. 39–67.

Milem, J. F., and Umbach, P. D. (2003). Examining the perpetuation hypothesis: The influence of pre-college factors on students' predispositions regarding diversity activities in college. *Journal of College Student Development* 44(5): 611–624.

Milem, J. F., Umbach, P. D., and Liang, C. (2004). Exploring the perpetuation hypothesis: The role of college and universities in desegregating society. *Journal of College Student Development* 45(6): 688–700.

Mulkay, M. (1972). *The Social Process of Innovation: A Study in the Sociology of Science*, Macmillan Press, London.

Pascarella, E. T., and Terenzini, P. T. (1991). *How College Affects Students: Findings and Insights from 20 Years of Research*, Jossey-Bass, San Francisco.

Pascarella, E. T., and Terenzini, P. T. (2005). *How College Affects Students: A Third Decade of Research,* Jossey-Bass, San Francisco.

Perna, L. (2001). Sex and race differences in faculty tenure and promotion. *Research in Higher Education* 42(5): 541–567.

Rakow, L. (1991). Gender and race in the classroom: Teaching way out of line. *Feminist Teacher* 6: 10–13.

Raudenbush, S. W., and Bryk, A. S. (2002). *Hierarchical Linear Models: Applications and Data Analysis Methods,* Sage Publications, Thousand Oaks, CA.

Rosenthal, R., and Rosnow, R. L. (1991). *Essentials of Behavioral Research: Methods and Data Analysis,* 2nd ed. McGraw-Hill, New York.

Roueche, J. E., Rouche, S. D., and Milliron, M. D. (1995). *Strangers in their Own Land: Part-time Faculty in American Community Colleges,* Community College Press, Washington, DC.

Rudenstine, N. (1996). The uses of diversity. *Harvard Magazine* 4: 48–62.

Smart, J. C., Feldman, K. A., and Ethington, C. A. (2000). *Academic Disciplines: Holland's Theory and the Study of College Students and Faculty,* Vanderbilt University Press, Nashville, TN.

Smith, D. G. (1989). *The Challenge of Diversity: Involvement or Alienation in the Academy,* The George Washington University, Washington, DC.

Smith, D. G., and Associates, (1997). *Diversity Works: The Emerging Picture of How Students Benefit,* American Association of Colleges and Universities, Washington, DC.

Smith, D. G., and Schonfeld, (2000). The benefits of diversity: What the research tells us. *About Campus* 5(5): 16–23.

Snyder, T. D., and Hoffman, C. M. (2003). *Digest of Education Statistics 2002,* U.S. Department of Education, National Center for Education Statistics., Washington, DC.

Statham, A., Richardson, L., and Cook, J. (1991). *Gender and University Teaching: A Negotiated Difference,* SUNY Press, Albany, NY.

Tierney, W. G. (1993). *Building Communities of difference: Higher Education in the Twenty-first Century,* Bergin & Garvey, Westport, CT.

Tierney, W. G., and Bensimon, E. M. (1996). *Promotion and Tenure: Community and Socialization in Academe,* SUNY Press, Albany, NY.

Trower, C. A., and Chait, R. (2002). Faculty diversity: Too little for too long. *Harvard Magazine* 104(4): 33.

Turner, C. S. (2003). Incorporation and marginalization in the academy: From border toward center for faculty of color. *Journal of Black Studies* 34(1): 112–125.

Turner, C. S., and Myers, S. L. J. (2000). *Faculty of Color in Academe: Bittersweet Success,* Allyn & Bacon, Needham Heights, MA.

Turner, C. S., Myers, S. L. J., and Creswell, J. W. (1999). Exploring underrepresentation: The case of faculty of color in the Midwest. *The Journal of Higher Education* 70(1): 27–59.

Umbach, P. D., and Kuh, G. D. (in press). Student experiences with diversity at liberal arts colleges: Another claim for distinctiveness. *The Journal of Higher Education.*

Umbach, P. D., and Milem, J. F. (2004). Applying Holland's typology to the study of differences in student views about diversity. *Research in Higher Education* 45(6): 625–649.

Umbach, P. D., and Wawrzynski, M. R. (2005). Faculty do matter: The role of college faculty in student learning and engagement. *Research in Higher Education* 46(2): 153–184.

Weick, K. E. (1976). Educational organizations as loosely coupled systems. *Administrative Science Quarterly* 21(1): 1–19.

Weick, K. E. (1979). *The Social Psychology of Organizing,* McGraw-Hill, New York, NY.

Weick, K. E. (1982). Administering education in loosely coupled schools. *Phi Delta Kappan* 63(10): 673–676.

PART IV

CURRICULUM, TEACHING, AND LEARNING

CAROLINE SOTELLO VIERNES TURNER AND STEPHEN JOHN QUAYE, ASSOCIATE EDITORS

Since the publication of the second edition of the *ASHE Reader on Racial and Ethnic Diversity in Higher Education* (Turner et al., 2002), a growing body of research on the benefits of diversity in educational contexts has emerged. This literature addresses the role of structured contact and intentional dialogues in improving student learning outcomes, such as critical thinking skills (Pascarella & Terenzini, 2005), academic and social self-confidence (Chang, 1999), and comfort with racial/ethnic differences (Chang, Witt, Jones, & Hakuta, 2003). This line of research has spawned further examinations of efficacious practices that serve to engage learners in addressing racial issues through teaching, learning, and curricular strategies. The eight chapters in this section are exemplars of this research. In this preface, we summarize four themes across the selections: (1) racial/ethnic diversity and classroom experiences; (2) racial/ethnic diversity in specific disciplines; (3) racial/ethnic diversity and the curriculum; and (4) racial/ethnic diversity, student learning, and applications beyond the classroom.

Racial/Ethnic Diversity and Classroom Experiences

In Chapter 23, Bryan McKinley Jones Brayboy focuses on an under-examined population within college and university settings: American Indian students. He uses data from an ethnographic study of American Indian students attending Ivy League institutions to examine their experiences with professors and peers in their courses. Many quantitative studies of students' perceptions fail to include American Indian students due to the lack of sufficient sample sizes needed to demonstrate significant effects. Thus, qualitative inquiry is best suited to understand the nature and meaning of their experiences in the classroom. Brayboy's study exemplifies the advantages of such inquiry through an in-depth ethnographic analysis of three American Indian students: Debbie, Tom, and Heather.

Debbie's story concentrated on her invisibility within the classroom environment and challenges in contending with professors who reinforced stereotypes about American Indians. For example, one anthropology professor incorrectly "characterized her tribe as having a primitive clan system and a fairly easy language." Given the power imbalances between herself and the professor as well as her desire to maintain her cultural integrity and values of respecting elders, she chose not to challenge her professor's remarks. Brayboy highlights the cultural mismatch that occurred between faculty members and American Indian students. Tom's story also reflected experiences of isolation and invisibility. In the midst of feeling like he needed to assimilate to the dominant norms of the institution, Tom developed strategies for maintaining his cultural integrity in this environment such as "spending the majority of his time outside of class in his dorm room."

Finally, similar to Debbie and Tom, Heather also dealt with feelings of isolation, assimilation, and lack of cultural sensitivity in her courses. However, she found proactive ways of interacting with her professors that maintained her cultural values, and ultimately led to her achievement and success. By organizing questions in advance of meetings with professors during their office hours, she demonstrated her interest in the course and preparedness. Each of the vignettes provided by Brayboy underscores creative responses by American Indian students for succeeding in the classroom environment without forfeiting their cultural values. Ultimately, Brayboy illuminates within-group differences in American Indian students and their responses for contending with invisibility and stereotypes in the classroom. He contends, however, that "the differences in cultures are so vast that it becomes clear that the dilemmas cannot be easily answered or rectified."

In Chapter 24, Beverly Daniel Tatum addresses one of the most difficult issues that students face in college classrooms: how to talk openly about racism and learn about racial/ethnic differences. Tatum's description of her process of teaching a class, The Psychology of Racism, revealed both the challenges and outcomes of her pedagogical efforts. She found that students were typically resistant to talking about racial issues due to the continued taboo nature of race, prior socialization to regard the U.S. as a socially just society, and believing that they were not prejudiced or racist. After describing these sources of resistance in greater detail, Tatum foregrounds racial identity development theory "as a framework for understanding students' psychological responses to race-related context and the student resistance that can result as well as some strategies for overcoming this resistance." She underscores the various stages through which students of color and White students in her courses progressed. Students moved from a denial of racism and lack of awareness of their racial identities to conflict or dissonance that prompted them to explore racial issues. Progressing through these stages, students began to associate with other members of their own racial/ethnic groups in order to engage in deeper self-exploration, and then moved to a willingness to interact across racial/ethnic differences with their peers.

Although this was the general pattern of racial identity development among students, Tatum points out the nuances involved in this process. For example, students may not move from one stage to another along a linear path, but may move back and forth and revisit earlier stages. Tatum provides several implications for teaching about race and racism in one's courses including fostering a safe climate to promote discussion of racial issues and finding avenues for students to consider themselves change agents. She concludes the chapter by noting how educators can create more comfortable classroom and campus environments by making a serious commitment to providing learning opportunities that heighten awareness of racism and how the lives of White students and students of color are affected by racism.

In Chapter 25, C. Alejandra Elenes uses Chicana feminist transformative pedagogies to connect with students through decentering hegemonic practices and norms about Whiteness in the classroom. Embracing a self-reflexive approach, she explores the dynamics between herself and students in the classroom, as they discussed race, gender, and class issues. Her pedagogical beliefs were predicated on the assumption that race, class, gender, and other social identities can be seen as intersecting and that groups should not be viewed as monolithic. Consequently, she stressed the importance of forming relationships with learners that were grounded in mutuality, decentering of authority, and awareness of one's positionality. Although she advocated for the creation of a democratic classroom that included multiple perspectives, Elenes was careful to indicate that not all viewpoints were equally valid. Those that perpetuated oppression and aimed to maintain social inequalities should be challenged and reconceptualized, she argued. Drawing on classroom interactions with students and course evaluations, she reveals in the chapter how students of different racial/ethnic and gender identities perceived the treatment of racial issues in her course.

In Chapter 26, Patrick T. Terenzini, Alberto F. Cabrera, Carol L. Colbeck, Stefani A. Bjorklund, and John A. Parente ask the question: "Does racial and ethnic diversity in the classroom promote student learning?" Inviting students to complete the *Classroom Activities and Outcomes Survey*, the authors set out to answer the aforementioned question. In the process, they concluded that: "Portions of the evidence do, however, support claims about the educational benefits of racially or ethnically diverse classrooms. Level of classroom diversity was related at small—but statistically significant—levels to students' reported gains in both their problem-solving and their group skills." This finding is important in considering the implications of increased racial/ethnic diversity in the classroom and its effects on student learning.

Racial/Ethnic Diversity in Specific Disciplines

In Chapter 27, Richard Tapia and Cynthia Johnson focus on disciplines where racial/ethnic minority students remain underrepresented. Much attention has been devoted to studying the achievement of racial/ethnic minority students in Science, Technology, Engineering, and Mathematics (STEM) fields. Tapia and Johnson's chapter addresses the importance of increasing the representation of racial/ethnic minority students in STEM fields and offer innovative strategies for doing so. The authors detail the prejudice and racism with which these students contend in the classroom, and discuss the lack of effective mentoring by professors based on racial/ethnic differences and lack of understanding about the unique needs of these students. Thus, students of color in STEM fields reported being regarded as affirmative action admits, needing to represent their entire racial/ethnic group in class discussions, and enduring low expectations for their achievement from professors. Tapia and Johnson note that faculty expressions of colorblindness or commentary regarding the insignificance of race exacerbated feelings of isolation and tokenism among minority students. The authors elaborate on how effective mentoring could increase the representation and success of racial/ethnic minority students in STEM fields, but a lack of sustained institutional change often makes this mentoring difficult. The authors conclude that effective models have been developed to support STEM education among racial/ethnic minority students and that faculty and administrators should seek out and utilize these models.

Racial/Ethnic Diversity and the Curriculum

Although it might appear that curricula have remained unchanged despite the increased diversity of the U.S. population and postsecondary student enrollments, Sheila Slaughter challenges this notion in Chapter 28. She situates her analysis on curriculum change borne out of social movements, not as a result of increased enrollments among racial/ethnic minority students. She insists that faculty and administrators did not change curricula to be more emblematic of the experiences of students of color until students demanded that they do so through protests and other forms of activism. As a result of these movements, fields such as Ethnic Studies and Women's Studies emerged.

Another theme presented in Slaughter's chapter is the notion of objective, value-free individual faculty members as the purveyor of knowledge through the curricula used in their courses. Rather, Slaughter suggests that this dominant narrative masks how racial/ethnic, class, and gender differences affected the creation and dissemination of curricula. Her argument is that those wishing to think about curricula as tied to student learning needed to develop alternative conceptions of the ways in which curricula were tied to racial/ethnic minority students. According to Slaughter, this position meant thinking of how curricula were negotiated between professors and students. Slaughter's final argument centers on the connection between curricula and organizations, such as corporations, the government, and foundations. By paying attention to how curricula were tied to organizations, she argues, faculty could find ways to better link curricula to the diverse needs of students of color beyond the classroom setting. This argument is reminiscent of one of Tapia and Johnson's observation that STEM disciplines are tied to the corporations that hire their graduates.

Matthew J. Mayhew, Heidi E. Grunwald, and Eric L. Dey note in Chapter 29 what students deem important elements in creating a positive classroom climate for diversity. Using survey responses from 544 undergraduates at a large, predominantly White university in the Midwest, the authors found that positive climates for diversity were informed by students' pre-college interactions with diverse peers and by the incorporation of diversity-related issues into the curriculum. They maintain that faculty represent a critical element in enacting institutional commitments to diversity: "If the institution wants to be perceived by students as a community that welcomes diversity, it needs to include diversity in its curriculum." According to Mayhew, Grunwald, and Dey, although co-curricular experiences related to diversity are important, in order for students to achieve the outcomes associated with cross-racial engagement, the curriculum seems to be the most important area to which educators should devote attention.

Racial/Ethnic Diversity and Student Learning Beyond the Classroom

The final chapter in this section helps readers consider how to support students in applying what they learn about racial/ethnic issues in their courses to life beyond the classroom. Sam Marullo used service-learning to teach about racial/ethnic relations. Specifically, he developed a study to compare two courses focused on addressing racial and ethnic relations after noticing that students often had difficulty connecting racial concepts and theories taught in class to practical experiences outside the classroom environment. One course was grounded in service-learning pedagogy, requiring the introduction of the community into the learning process. The other was a lecture-discussion course with some experiential exercises. When compared to his experiential learning course, Marullo demonstrates the strength of service-learning as those students showed "improved learning in the areas of citizenship, empowerment, diversity awareness, leadership, moral development, and their ability to understand structural causes of social problems." While noting the added time needed to locate relevant community service sites for students, he recommends incorporating service-learning into one's courses given the value-added outcomes students glean from this experience.

Conclusion

Collectively, the eight chapters in this section address the tokenism experienced by students of color in the classroom; the need for structured, sustained spaces to engage in racial dialogues; the importance of self-reflexivity among faculty; and finding ways to help students connect classroom learning about racial issues beyond the classroom. The chapters also point to the importance of understanding racial/ethnic minority students' lived experiences within learning contexts that are based on their perspectives. Readers should be cautiously encouraged by the strides made in examining racial diversity in teaching and curricula. However, the same challenge continues to persist: how to respond effectively to the continued presence of racial/ethnic diversity in postsecondary institutions in ways that encourage healthy dialogues, reflection, and action.

References

Chang, M. J. (1999). Does racial diversity matter?: The educational impact of a racially diverse undergraduate population. *Journal of College Student Development, 40*(4), 377–395.

Chang, M. J., Witt, D., Jones, J., & Hakuta, K. (Eds.). (2003). *Compelling interest: Examining the evidence on racial dynamics in colleges and universities.* Stanford, CA: Stanford University Press.

Pascarella, E. T., & Terenzini, P. T. (2005). *How college affects students, Volume 2: A third decade of research.* San Francisco: Jossey-Bass.

Turner, C. S. V., antonio, a. l., García, M., Laden, B. V., Nora, A., & Presley, C. L. (Eds.). (2002). *Racial and ethnic diversity in higher education. ASHE Reader Series.* (2nd ed.). Boston, MA: Pearson.

CHAPTER 23
HIDING IN THE IVY: AMERICAN INDIAN STUDENTS AND VISIBILITY IN ELITE EDUCATIONAL SETTINGS

BRYAN MCKINLEY JONES BRAYBOY

In this chapter, Bryan McKinley Jones Brayboy explores how the experiences of Tom, Debbie, and Heather, three Native American students attending Ivy League universities in the 1990s, reflect larger societal beliefs and statements about the perceived place of Native Americans in higher education and U.S. society. Brayboy posits that Native Americans are visible in these institutions in ways that contribute to their marginalization, surveillance, and oppression. In response, the three Native American students exercise strategies that make them invisible to the largely White communities in which they attend school. These strategies help to preserve the students' sense of cultural integrity, but further serve to marginalize them on campus. At times, the students in the study make themselves visible to emphasize that they are a voice in the campus community. Brayboy argues that these strategies, while possibly confusing to the layperson, make sense if viewed from the perspective of the students preserving their cultural integrity.

On many of the days that I spent with Debbie, an American Indian woman from the Southwest, we met at a place not far from her apartment around 8:00 in the morning for coffee, a bagel, and a cup of yogurt.[1] After breakfast, we went to her class in the university museum. Although Debbie lived on the same street and only seven blocks from the museum, she did not go to class using the most direct route. Rather than walk down the street to the museum, Debbie turned away from the street (a main campus thoroughfare) after only two blocks and walked behind a large health institution. She negotiated the hidden alleys and tricky turns that traveled through and between buildings, emerging on the other side of the hospital. From there she slid down another alley and entered the museum from the rear. She took the stairs rather than the elevator, where she rarely met another soul. Although she might occasionally encounter physical plant workers and delivery people, her communication with them was minimal.

The first time I accompanied Debbie on this walk, I was amazed at her knowledge of these buildings and their intricate layouts, and the fact that there was a back door to the museum accessible to students. I was even more impressed by her decision to take this circuitous route, which took forty-five minutes, rather than the more efficient 15-minute walk directly down the street between her room and the museum. It was not long before I began to recognize the value she placed on avoiding contact with other students. When I asked Debbie why she chose such a route, she said she needed to go out of her way to not see anyone who knew her or might look at her like she is "from another planet." To those from the larger student population at this university, her behavior might seem strange. To some American Indians, however, her choice makes sense and can be interpreted as one way of acting in a culturally appropriate manner and maintaining her cultural integrity (Deyhle, 1995). By discovering and using the route she did, Debbie demonstrated her ability to "fly under the radar screen" and to make herself less visible to others on campus, actions that had strategic purposes and allowed her to interact minimally with others throughout her day.

In order to be a "good" Indian and a "good" student simultaneously, Debbie employed strategies that allowed her some control over how visible (or invisible) she would be to others in the institution. The fact that Debbie had some control over the amount of distance between herself and others (i.e., her degree of visibility) remains a major finding of my original study (Brayboy, 1999) and a challenge to many theories of accommodation, assimilation, and resistance (e.g., Fordham & Ogbu, 1986; Ogbu, 1987; Tinto, 1993).[2]

In this chapter, I explore the ways in which the situations, views, and actions of American Indian students attending Ivy League universities in the late 1990s reflect larger societal beliefs and practices about the perceived "place" and status of American Indians in U.S. society. I examine the experiences and hardships that three American Indian students encountered at two prestigious Ivy League institutions in order to understand the nature and challenges of their everyday lives. I argue that American Indian students are both visible and invisible on such campuses in ways that contribute to their marginalization, oppression, and surveillance. By surveillance, I refer to being closely watched in a way that controls one's identity and actions (Phelan, 1995; Vizenor, 1998).

Surveillance can take multiple forms, such as White peers asking American Indian students if they can "clean up the mess in the classroom" (mistaking them for housekeeping staff), or White students questioning American Indian students' admission status with statements like, "You are American Indian? Wow, you must have really benefited from affirmative action. You must have gotten in everywhere." Surveillance can also occur when White peers place American Indian students in the role of either the romantic "Other" (e.g., with comments like, "Can you talk to us about what it took for you to be here, having grown up on the reservation?") or as a savage who is "intimidating" because a student is quiet and reserved. As a result, American Indian students use strategies to make themselves less visible to the dominant population, thus minimizing the surveillance and oppression they experience on a daily basis. I conclude that, although the use of such strategies does not eradicate the marginal status of American Indian students in school communities, the strategies make sense when viewed through the lens of cultural integrity (Deyhle, 1995).

Cultural integrity refers to a set of beliefs, and actions directly linked to these beliefs, that are shared by a group of people. The beliefs are free from outside influences and are "distinct and independent tradition[s]" (Deyhle, 1995, p. 28). Individuals who participated in this study described this notion of cultural integrity in terms of their "Indianness" or "those things that make me [and others] Indian or tribal." These students used strategies that helped them maintain a connection with their cultural and tribal backgrounds, and thus preserved their individual and group identities within an uncomfortable and often oppressive context. It also allowed them to succeed academically: each student graduated from his or her university and achieved a minimum grade point average of 3.2.

Doing a Fancy Dance: Methods and Methodology

The data I present come out of a larger two-year ethnographic study that relied on participant observation, interviews, focus groups, and institutional documents to examine the experiences of seven American Indian students attending two Ivy League institutions. I attended class, studied, ate, and socialized with these students. I also accompanied each of the students to their family homes during semester and summer breaks. In the original study, I focused on the academic, social, financial, cultural, psychological, and political costs and benefits of being academically successful for these individuals. I became increasingly interested in the ways that the students in the study developed strategies for maintaining their cultural sense of self (what they called their Indianness) while simultaneously thriving academically. In other words, the students found ways to be both good Indians and good students.

It is important to note that my role as a researcher and an Indigenous person is complicated in the reporting of Heather's, Tom's, and Debbie's experiences. I offer my analysis from both viewpoints in this text.[3] I also hold graduate degrees from an Ivy League university, so my analysis in this chapter is professional, cultural, and experiential. I understand what it means to be an Indigenous person and have a grasp of the demands to be both a good Indian and a good student. My analysis, then, is multilayered and has a range and variation in its conclusions. I use knowledge as an Indigenous person to explore the personal implications of (in)visibility, and my knowledge as an Ivy-educated person to analyze the larger structural implications of the in(visibility).

I have decided to use the terms *visibility* and *invisibility* in my analysis of space management and issues of cultural integrity because they capture the dynamic and complicated nature of the American Indian students' relationship to the institution and the actors in it.[4] By using these terms, I capture the ways two seemingly opposing states are intimately related, explain the complicated role of individual agency, and describe the ways individuals respond to issues of marginalization and surveillance. For the students in this study, their visibility and invisibility simultaneously create and are created by processes of marginalization, exclusion, assimilation, and oppression. By focusing on the policies and practices of the institution in relation to American Indian students' (in)visibility, this work contributes to an understanding of the dynamic relationship between historical structures or processes and the everyday experiences of individual actors (Holland & Lave, 2001).

Specifically, I examine the following three questions. One, in what ways do these students make themselves (in)visible in educational settings and spaces and to what ends? Two, in what ways do institutions and their agents make American Indian students (in)visible in educational settings and spaces, and to what end? Three, what is the relationship among (in)visibility, marginalization, surveillance, and cultural integrity?

Visibility, Marginalization, Surveillance, and Cultural Integrity

Owens (2001) has argued that American Indians must hide behind the masks created by White America in order to be the Indian that Whites want to see. Shanley (2001) argues similarly that America loves its Indians as long as they are hidden from view. I would extend this argument to U.S. institutions of higher education—see King and Springwood (1996) and Spindel (2000) for examples that document the use of Native Americans as team mascots. On the other hand, postcolonial literature frequently argues that visibility—often in the form of voice and perspective—is one important vehicle for addressing processes of marginalization and the silencing of underrepresented, marginalized, colonized peoples (e.g., Fanon, 1967; Grossberg, 1997; Hall, 1991). Like Phelan (1995), however, I am not totally convinced that invisibility is always negative and visibility is inherently positive. hooks (1990) makes a similar point when she calls for the margins to serve as sites of resistance and affirmation, rather than simply as wastelands of passivity and destruction.[5] That is, individuals can be powerful and resistant when they are hidden. In this chapter I argue that avoiding surveillance can—like being in the margins—be a source of strength.

Phelan (1995) also argues that the binary distinction between the power of visibility and the impotence of invisibility is misrepresentative. She notes that there is real power in remaining unmarked and that there are serious limitations to visual representations as a political goal. In the September 11 aftermath, for example, Muslims became marked as visible Others. This was complicated further by the visions that many Americans had of what a Middle Easterner or Muslim looked like. For example, in Salt Lake City, Utah, a man tried to set on fire a restaurant owned by East Indian Punjabis (Cantera, 2001). In this case, the man's (false) image of a Muslim was more important than whether the owners of the restaurant were actually Muslim. In this way, visibility—real or imagined—offered serious limitations for the restaurant owners and for the man who tried to set it on fire.[6]

Phelan (1995) also argues that visibility becomes a trap when it summons surveillance by the law (or, I would argue, by anyone holding power), voyeurism, fetishism, and the colonialist appetite for possession. For American Indians, this means that being watched or located as a noble savage or romantic Other, being fetishized, or being identified as someone from the past is constricting and paralyzing. Vizenor (1994, 1998) specifically discusses the surveillance of Indigenous people through their visibility as the invented Other. He notes that the image of the Indian produced by the dominant society is "treacherous and elusive in histories [that] become the real without a referent to an actual tribal remembrance" (p. 8). Vizenor also argues that the image of the Indian is invented and does not exist within tribal communities, but has been created by Whites in dominant society to fulfill their need to create and own a "real Indian" that they can control and manipulate.

The need for control and manipulation by members of dominant society influences their creation of an image that is visible and that suits their own agenda. Still other Indigenous scholars (Almeida, 1997; Kaomea, 2000, 2001) have noted the role of invisibility and visibility among Indigenous peoples, observing that Indians are beloved (or romanticized) when they fit a particular image but loathed when they fit another. There are few images of American Indian people that fall somewhere in between.

I do not mean to suggest that American Indians do not have a sense of what their Indianness means to them. My point is that this image often contradicts what the media, larger society, and non-Native individuals hold for American Indian people. In this study and in previous work, I found that Indians were seen variously by their classmates, administrations, and institutions as romantic Others, welfare mongers, whiners who need to get over past injuries, affirmative action babies, and noble savages (Brayboy, 1999). In contrast, the American Indian individuals viewed themselves as viable citizens contributing to the dominant society and to their tribal nations, as well as individuals capable of both honoring their cultural and spiritual ways and being admitted to Phi Beta Kappa at elite institutions of higher education.

In a race- and color-conscious society, it is inevitable that race and color are issues for the students in this study. Almost all of them concluded that the cost of being visible was rarely mitigated by the benefits associated with that visibility. It is worth mentioning that individuals cannot always control their visibility. They become visible because of their physical appearances as well as by their words and actions. The examples of Debbie, Tom, and Heather illustrate that the ways individuals become visible are based marginally on the ways they present themselves and more substantially on the background, experiences, and visions of the seer, as well as the context in which they are being seen. The same individuals are seen differently, depending on who is seeing them and when. They also view themselves differently, based on the context and situation. The co-construction of self, how students view themselves, how they are viewed by others, and the importance of the context becomes complex, complicated, and varied.

Although being a visible American Indian does not necessarily have to be problematic, it currently is, due to the racialized nature of social relations in the United States and the history of colonization of the Americas with its accompanying oppression of Indigenous peoples. Owens' (2001) idea that present-day American Indians must hide behind a mask created by White America refers to the unfortunate reality that members of dominant groups in the United States often have inaccurate perceptions of the norms, traditions, and values of American Indians. These inaccurate perceptions lead to harmful stereotyping, a lack of understanding, and behavior motivated by racist views and assumptions. Marginalized from and misunderstood by the larger society, American Indians are constantly under surveillance. Other researchers have discussed the simultaneous "presence" and "absence" of colonized Indigenous peoples and other disenfranchised groups in the United States in terms of invisibility:

> In the case of indigenous peoples, migrants, women, and working-class students, the historical movement has been from an outright namelessness and invisibility to an inclusion in public discourses and human sciences as colonized, deficit human subjects. This ontology of simultaneous presence and absence continues. Cultural imperialism involves a paradoxical state where the colonized are rendered invisible and marked as different, at once both absent and present. (Young, cited in Luke, 1995–1996, p. 38)

Tom, Debbie, and Heather are simultaneously visible and invisible, marked and absent. Their visibility as American Indians and members of formerly colonized groups and their need to preserve their cultural integrity motivate their desire to make themselves as invisible or visible as possible within certain contexts.

An American Indian may choose to make him- or herself less visible as a way to avoid romanticization, marginalization, and surveillance, while actively maintaining their sense of cultural integrity or Indianness. Striving for invisibility (a state that can never be entirely reached), individuals may behave in ways that make them less noticeable to others, which becomes a strategic response to oppression and surveillance. In this way, invisibility can be a conscious choice and an active state with certain beneficial results. For at least two of the individuals in this study, this was true. At the same time, however, there are certain costs associated with invisibility and visibility. Below, I examine visibility and invisibility as strategic responses to oppressive circumstances, the ways these strategic responses enabled individuals to maintain cultural integrity, and the immediate short-term costs associated with invisibility.

The Context: Prospect and Sherwood Universities

Prospect and Sherwood[7] are Ivy League universities that pride themselves on being selective institutions and among the best of the best. Sherwood is the smaller of the two. It has a structure congruent with its relatively small size, which is characterized by small, seminar-like classes with a faculty to student ratio of roughly 15 to 1. While there are a few professional schools within this university, it emphasizes its undergraduate liberal arts and humanities curriculum, which offers students an opportunity to read and write extensively. Many of the classes focus on close examinations of text, and writing is an integral part of the entire curriculum. Most students have a sophomore, junior, and senior writing project. The town culture revolves around university activities, and local businesses rely on the student body for their livelihood.

Prospect is larger than Sherwood and has a substantial number of professional schools and larger classes. With almost twice as many students as Sherwood, many of Prospect's classes are held in large lecture halls, and undergraduate students have more of an opportunity for professional specialization. Reading and writing are, of course, important here, but the emphasis is not as great as at Sherwood.

The Actors: Debbie, Tom, and Heather

Debbie, who attends Prospect, is from the Southwest. She was born and raised on a reservation and speaks the language of her tribal nation. Debbie has attended schools both on and off the reservation, and during high school and summer breaks from Prospect, she has worked in the town that borders her reservation. She has long black hair the color of her eyes, and her skin is deep brown. She usually dresses in jeans, and t-shirts (or sweatshirts), and sneakers.

Debbie chose to attend Prospect because she "wanted to do something for [her tribe]":

> I can be a role model for girls, you know, and also I think we need someone to study what I study. . . .
> I had never been out East and never lived in a city. . . . I wanted to try that and see what it was like.

She enrolled in an undergraduate program that she hoped would allow her to address problems encountered by her tribal nation.

Tom, a student at Sherwood, is also from the Southwest. Like Debbie, he was born and raised on his tribe's reservation, and he speaks the language of his tribal nation. He attended the local reservation schools, and he told me that one summer he had "lived on twelve dollars a month." His black hair is cut to the middle of his back. His eyes, like his hair and the boots he often wears, are dark and his skin is a rich brown. I never saw him dressed in anything except jeans and a t-shirt, although during winter months he would wear a jacket, and once I saw him with a sweatshirt over his t-shirt. Explaining why he chose to attend Sherwood, Tom discussed the importance for his community of his earning a credential from such a prestigious institution:

> It is a recognizable name. I knew I wanted to go here or to [another Ivy League university] and I liked
> it here better. . . . I knew that if I could make it here, I would be able to go back home and do my part.
> I feel like I need to go back and do that . . . to just do whatever they want me to do.

During this conversation, Tom told me he missed home and intended to return there as soon as possible. When I met Tom, he was enrolled in an undergraduate program that gave him the flexibility to pursue many areas of work. He was acquiring a liberal arts education in the truest sense.

Heather, who also attends Sherwood, is from a western tribe. She grew up on the fringes of her tribe's reservation, and is not fluent in her tribal nation's heritage language, although she understands much of it and can speak it a little. Her hair is long and black, her eyes are brown, and she dresses according to the occasion. Heather is a chameleon, changing her appearance to fit the context and situation. She looks equally at home in jeans and sneakers or a formal dress. She attended public schools in the city bordering her reservation. She matriculated at Sherwood because she believed that:

> [Sherwood] can provide me with a foundation to pursue my goals. The name of [Sherwood] means a lot and I think it will help. . . . Having a law degree will allow me to help [my tribe] in our struggles with the government and [the local city]. . . . I've always wanted to be able to do this work and help us and others. . . . I would like to have a firm one day that services only Indian clients.

Heather majored in a field that allowed her to read widely and focus on topics that were pertinent to preparation for both law school and the issues facing her tribe. She later attended law school and now works on her reservation for her tribal nation.

In this chapter, I examine data gathered from these three students during my earlier study. Data gathered from other students in the study also highlight the issues of marginalization, surveillance, (in)visibility, and cultural integrity, but I am able to provide a rich account of the experiences of only three individuals.[8] Although these data are not generalizable, they are illuminating in that they represent the situations and difficulties encountered by a number of American Indian students attending Ivy League institutions.

Debbie's Story: Invisible Strategies and Hidden Hurts

Returning to the opening vignette about Debbie, I examine some of the factors that may have influenced her decision to take such a circuitous route to her classroom in the museum. I asked her about what appeared to me to be confusing behavior, and she explained the complicated rationale behind her actions:

> I go that way for a lot of reasons. Mostly because I don't want to see anyone or anything. I can do my own thing; it's less noisy and people can't stare at me. I don't like it when people stare at me and a lot of people here do that. It's like they have never seen an Indian, or whatever they think I am, before. I mind my own business and leave people alone and hope they'll leave me alone. I don't want to have to look at people or talk to them either. . . . Back home, many people understand me; no one minds my business or stares at me. They leave me alone and I leave them alone unless it's family. . . . I also don't want to see someone I know because I'll have to stop and talk to them. I have an obligation to talk to my friends and I need to go to class. . . . Then I end up coming to class and everyone looks at me, because they are all on time most of the time. It's hard, you know. . . . Plus people who have seen me before when I spoke when I first got here will want to talk to me about their work on the reservation or hang out and talk to me about stuff. It's easier for me to just avoid them.

This statement is loaded with reasons why some American Indian students might want to be less visible in certain contexts. Taking her circuitous route, Debbie was seen by only a few people who saw her regularly, as opposed to great numbers of unfamiliar students. She felt ignored, which did not bother her. However, while walking down the street among other students, Debbie felt that people were staring at her, which made her uncomfortable. Although the university is tucked in the middle of a diverse residential area, the student body itself is predominantly White. Many students at Prospect assumed people of color were from the local area (which was largely African American and poor), and thus constructed as problematic. The university itself is like a fortress where "outsiders" (e.g., the local African American population) are viewed suspiciously and with disdain.[9] Debbie was aware of these dynamics, as people stared at her as if she were an "outsider" too. Student or not, she felt like an outsider because she looked much different from everyone else. For these reasons, Debbie chose to minimize her contact with other students at Prospect and hoped this would make her less visible.

Once in the museum, we found ourselves sitting in an undergraduate anthropology class called "Indigenous Peoples of the Americas." The class was interesting and was taught by a White male professor. It was a survey course that covered as many tribes as possible during the semester. On one occasion, the professor's actions highlighted the problems associated with teaching a class about topics that are not the instructor's area of expertise. I was sitting next to Debbie during a lecture when the professor described her tribe and its characteristics. He characterized her tribe as having a primitive clan system and a fairly easy language. Contrary to his description, the clan system of this tribe is complex and difficult for outsiders to understand. In addition, the language of her tribe is extremely difficult to understand and learn.[10]

I watched Debbie as she sat patiently through the lecture, and we left the classroom as soon as it was over. One of her classmates, another Indigenous person, asked her, "Why didn't you tell that [#$@!***] that he is an idiot? You should have called him on that. Your language is so hard to learn, and the clan system is so damn hard. I should have said something." Debbie said nothing at the time but later told me that she "felt like jumping out of [her] skin" as the professor was speaking. When I asked why she had not said anything and how she felt about what happened in class, she paused for a few minutes, which seemed to me like hours. She finally responded:

> I was always taught to respect my elders. He is my elder, and I must respect him. What he said is not right, but it is not my place to correct him. He will learn. . . . I could not say anything to him.

In essence, she told me the professor represented someone who deserved her respect even if he was insulting her. Debbie told me she was always taught to be "nonconfrontational" and that it was easier for her to just let it go. Debbie's interactions in this particular class also highlight an entirely different form of invisibility she encountered. By not speaking up in class, she illustrated a real sense of loyalty to her cultural background and the maintenance of her cultural integrity or Indianness. This contrasts with the academically appropriate action, which might have been to educate the professor and the one hundred students in the class. This is a strategy Debbie employs for a larger cause: she and her elders recognize the power of a degree from an Ivy League university. They have made a choice for her to engage in schooling for the long-term good and not to get caught up in issues that may impact her psychically.

This situation begs the question of where students like Debbie go to "decompress" after a class like this. That is, where are American Indian students finding a safe space to talk about the day's events and the assaults (intentional and not) on their cultural beings? Implicit in this story is a critique of the institution and the professor for teaching information that is not only wrong, but also problematic for a student. It also highlights the ways that visibility leads to marginalization. Debbie is made visible when the professor misrepresents characteristics of her tribal nation in the classroom. If he had fairly and accurately represented her tribal nation, that visibility could have been empowering and given her a sense of pride in the midst of an institution that was often harsh when she was made visible, but the moment was lost.

Debbie's decision to not draw attention to herself during the lecture illustrates her ability to maintain her traditional values by respecting her elder while simultaneously engaging in the "untraditional" act of getting a degree from an elite institution of higher education. Her participation in the class allowed her to "buy in" to the system of higher education, but she did this while maintaining her identity as an Indigenous person.

On the other hand, if Debbie had spoken up, she might have enlightened others in the classroom, including the professor, and her participation could have led to a lively and interesting discussion. If she opted for this approach, Debbie could have made herself visible in a way that is appropriate according to rules of classroom participation. But she plays by a different set of rules, which makes her perception and participation different from many of the other students in the classroom and at the university. In order to be able to evaluate Debbie's classroom participation, others must readjust their perceptions to better understand why she does what she does.[11] The costs associated with being visible in and out of class for American Indian students help to explain why they may choose to make themselves less visible to others.

Part of Debbie's avoidance of others is rooted in her cultural beliefs. Her avoidance of attention is not uncommon among Indigenous people; other researchers have found that many Native American Indian students are hesitant to receive any attention (Collier, 1973; Deyhle, 1995; Dumont, 1972; Erickson & Mohatt, 1982; Foley, 1996; Lipka & Ilustik; 1995; Macias, 1987; Philips, 1972, 1983; Suina & Smolkin, 1994). Another part of her avoidance strategies result from her experiences with students at

Prospect. At the time this study was conducted, many applicants (and later students) at these elite institutions, in order to illustrate a diversity of experiences, would pay to work on a reservation and be around Indigenous people.[12] On several occasions, Debbie would meet White mainstream students who had "spent time building houses" on her reservation as part of a summer service project. Many of these students would try to speak some of her heritage language to her and engage her in conversations about life on the reservation. These students would also tell her either how beautiful the country was or wonder how she ever survived in such a "backward place." Each instance placed undue attention on her as an Indigenous person and highlighted other ways that visibility leads to fetishism or romanticism. The fact that Debbie's behavior was based on both her cultural background and experiences at Prospect complicate the analysis of this issue. In essence, this reiterates the point that context and situation are important.

Visibility in terms of skin color and other marked characteristics led to surveillance on a daily basis for students like Debbie. Other students occasionally asked Debbie why she had been admitted to Prospect. For example, while we ate together at an on-campus dining area, people sometimes asked us if we were "Indians." They especially asked about Debbie, because she looked like a traditional Indian—she had long, straight black hair and deep brown eyes and skin. At the time I had wavy hair cut to my shoulders, and my eyes, like my skin, are dark brown. We would tell students that we were not Indians, but rather American Indians or Native Americans, or tell them our tribal affiliation.[13] They would continue to ask questions and eventually say something like, "Oh, you must have gotten in everywhere as a Native American" or "You don't have to pay tuition to go here, huh?" Implicit in such statements is a belief and discourse that many American Indian students in elite institutions are admitted because of their ethnic background. The qualities that American Indians bring to these educational institutions and their abilities to fully engage in the intellectual process are often disregarded.[14]

Inherent in Debbie's interactions with such students is a notion that some students receive preferential treatment from the university based on their skin color or cultural status. Preferential treatment occurs with many individuals at Prospect and Sherwood based on their status as athletes (most of whom are White), veterans, and children of alumni and/or large donors to the universities. Still, much of the thinking and public discourse appears to be arguing that everyone should be judged on their individual merit.

After having fellow students assume she was a "special admit" so often, Debbie began to say less and less about herself and to limit her interactions with other students. She once told me, "I just don't deal anymore. I try to just do my work and hang out with the people who understand me. You know, it's all good, but sometimes I just don't want to deal." Rather than being seen as an active, viable part of the university community, Debbie's visibility as an American Indian student had put her in a place of deficiency or an unearned special status. Once again, visibility becomes a trap in which students are held up for surveillance that is unfair and rooted in problematic conceptions of what Indians are supposed to be.

While the university has provided Debbie with a number of opportunities, her experiences have been laden with racist undertones and innuendoes. Foley (1996) captures the motives behind her efforts to become invisible when he writes, "Silence is this political retreat into a separate cultural space and identity far from the white world" (p. 88). In other words, Debbie chose to be silent and to withdraw in order to find a more comfortable and positive space for herself in the midst of misinformation about her tribe, attacks on her abilities, and other harmful stereotypical images.

Tom's Story: Slowly and Brutally Erasing the Visible Indian

It was a cold winter day as I walked through the chilled air to the dining hall where I was meeting Tom. I found him sitting at a formica-topped rectangular table. Tom was sitting by himself, eating, with empty chairs on either side of him. Beyond the empty chairs were several groups of students. I had noticed on other occasions that he was eating alone; when he did eat with others, it was with a friend from town or a member of the American Indian student group. In class, a similar phenomenon occurred. He would sit at a table in a seminar and all of the seats around him would fill up, except for those directly next to him. The late stragglers would be forced to sit next to him or opt to sit behind the seminar table.

During the two years I spent time with him, isolation or lack of interaction was the norm for Tom. In one of our first informal interviews, he said to me, "I don't feel like I exist here. I feel like I am invisible." Initially I thought this was the frustration of a student in a new environment making sense of his time away from home. At the end of the first year, however, he contemplated not returning to Sherwood for a number of reasons. Perhaps the most prominent reason was the fact that he did not seem to fit the mold of students at Sherwood and the interactional norms or the guiding rules of interaction between and among individuals; he clearly was not an active part of the Sherwood community. As a result, he worked at becoming less and less visible by limiting his interactions with non-Indian students and by focusing on his work. On the day before he left to go home after his first year, he said to me, "I don't know if people know I exist here." He did return, but over the next twenty months he said he felt increasingly invisible. Although people knew he existed, that existence was characterized by surveillance, marginalization, and ostracism. The next pages outline the ways he suffered from mistreatment.

Tom told me that he came to Sherwood because an admissions officer told him that Tom had "something to offer Sherwood." About a month after my initial meeting with Tom, he asked a pretty woman with light red hair and green eyes why she and others did not talk to him. She looked at him and responded, "I'm intimidated by you." When he asked her what he had done to make her feel this way, she said he was always so quiet and no one was really sure what to make of him.

Tom's behavior had real costs that are reminiscent of those encountered by the Indigenous people in Foley's (1996) study, which addressed the issue of the "silent Indian" (p. 79) with respect to Meskwaki youth. The teens in his study chose to be silent as a way of coping with the stresses of school and in order to intimidate teachers, get out of schoolwork, and rebel in classrooms. He writes, "The price for heroic retreat into silence may be lost in future educational opportunities. . . . In their cultural milieu, it is often the honorable way of handling the garrulous, aggressive whites" (p. 78). The students in Foley's study, it appears, were forced by "garrulous, aggressive whites" to choose from a number of options—the "ways of the school" and those of their home culture. The costs of either choice are heavy; the former asks them to override their own culture, while the latter leads to "lost . . . future educational opportunities." The heavy choices illustrate one kind of brutal bargain that students are asked to make at institutions like Prospect and Sherwood. This bargain essentially asks American Indian students to assimilate, accommodate on others' terms, or suffer marginalization. Any of these "choices" requires these students to give up significant pieces of who they are. Many White students are not required to make such bargains; instead, they enjoy a certain amount of privilege (McIntosh, 1995). In Tom's case, his everyday mode of interaction did not meet the norms at Sherwood and he was therefore cast as an intimidating person. In these instances, Tom's identity as an American Indian has become visible to his peers who attached negative meanings to behavior and actions that would be considered valuable personal attributes among members of his tribe.[15] But at Sherwood, the way he was constructed as an Indian "other" became a liability for him.

After three years at Sherwood, Tom ultimately adopted strategies similar to those used by Debbie, although his differed in that invisibility was a reactive tool of survival, rather than a proactive, strategic response. I visited him one gray fall day when the leaves were changing from green to rich yellows, oranges, and reds. After having coffee, he said to me, "Life at Sherwood outside of my room does not exist anymore. It might, but I am not a part of it. I don't go out anymore." These words were hauntingly familiar to the ones that Debbie had said to me a few years before. During three and a half years at an institution of higher education, Tom had been reduced to spending the majority of his time outside of class in his dorm room. At the heart of this transformation in how he socialized was the tension between being *forced* to assimilate into the norms of the institution or spend the majority of his "free" time in his room, and his ability to *choose* what he did in his spare time. But this was more than simply an either/or argument or a case in which Tom's choices were limited by the institution. Rather than limit his options to those offered by the institution, he found another outlet. Tom told me when I asked him if he literally spent all of his spare time in his room:

Not really all of it. You know, I hang out up town with the Townies [people from the local town who do not attend the university] and enjoy them. . . . I like them because they are real people and we connect on a level that most of the people at [Sherwood] don't like or understand. I want to be a musician in my spare time and they [the Townies] don't have a problem with that. It's cool and I get a chance to get out of my room. . . . Sometimes they come to my room, but it is always easier for me to go out than for them to come in.

Rather than be completely isolated in his room by the prevailing culture at Sherwood, Tom found a way to maintain his cultural integrity. This form of invisibility is directly tied to the surveillance (e.g., being called "intimidating") and marginalization (e.g., being continually shunned in class and the dining halls) he experienced with his Sherwood peers. His adaptive response highlights some of the negative consequences of visibility; he is not a part of the Sherwood community and his absence hurts everyone. He had a set of friends completely outside of the university setting who had a connection with him. His love of music and the fact that he writes and plays it gave him a freedom to have another social outlet. This social outlet, along with his desire to "contribute to my tribe's betterment" and a need to "prove all those people wrong," were the primary reasons for Tom to stay through until graduation.

The social costs of being in an environment in which differences are devalued are tremendous. I reflected on how resigned Tom was to biding his time until graduation. The outgoing nature that marked his first years in college had been replaced by a hardened resolve to survive and get by.[16] I believe that Tom's attitude much more closely resembled Debbie's after the realities of social interaction were presented to him. The beliefs and values with which these students entered the institution were crucial to the ways in which they interacted with others. Because of their Indianness and systems of belief that are different from the university norm, Tom and Debbie were outsiders looking into the system. Even if they had decided to try to integrate (as Tom did) and were accepted by their peers, they were tied to their belief systems and culture. Interestingly, Tom and Debbie began with intentions, beliefs, and ideas that were quite different, but they exited in similar positions. A constant for both of these students was attendance at an elite institution of higher education and a desire to successfully complete the degree requirements so that they could return home and help their tribe.

Tom's interactions with others continued to be influenced by feelings of intimidation, a lack of understanding, and an unwillingness to embrace difference. Certainly, Tom could have chosen to become more overtly talkative, cut his hair, and act more like those around him in order to make other students "feel comfortable" or less "intimidated," but he chose not to. He understood the costs associated with such adaptation and assimilation, telling me, "I can never truly be one of them [White students]. . . . Look at me. I'm [Indian] and I would never cut my hair or change who I am. I can't . . . and if I could, I wouldn't do it anyway. Besides, [White society and students] won't ever let me fully be like them." At the same time, he found the pain and discomfort associated with his visibility to be extremely undesirable. As a result, Tom opted to make himself as invisible as possible and retreated into silence to do so, thus choosing the lesser of two evils. His silence makes him simultaneously visible (because he's different and thus noticeable and intimidating) and invisible (not an active contributor to conversation, class, etc.). He once told me, "I'm just going to do my thing and hang out . . . enjoy my music and wait for the day to get out of here." This quote highlights another sense of the heroic retreat into silence previously referenced by Foley (1996). In the end, Tom's desire to assist his community outweighed the great personal difficulties he encountered in his everyday existence at Sherwood.

I want to return to the experience that eventually inspired Tom to make himself less visible. It is a sad and traumatic one, because it is based on his experiences with people who clearly do not understand what they are doing or seeing or simply do not care. For Tom, his hair and shoulders were sacred parts of his body. He did not expect anyone to touch them or to come into contact with them at any time. He told me the story of how his sense of "personal and spiritual space" was violated by various students at Sherwood:

During my freshman year, someone touched my hair and shoulders at a party. By doing this they were being disrespectful and I did not like it. I slapped the guy's hand away and told him not to do it again . . . that it was disrespectful. . . . This guy was obviously drunk. People here get drunk and feel like they can do anything. . . . So he did it again and again. Finally, I hit him. This made him stop, but it also made everyone around me uneasy because people don't deal with things that way here. I had to defend myself and he was being [disrespectful].

This interaction happened the first week in which all students were back from summer break, and returning and new students were attending a party hosted by a social group. It was unclear if this person simply wanted to touch Tom's hair (not an uncommon occurrence during the time I spent with Tom) or if he had another motivation. Whatever the reason, Tom made it clear to the student that he did not want his hair touched. Much of this is tied to an idea of "sacred space" that should not be crossed. This particular individual failed to heed Tom's warning and a fight ensued. How much of this was about a lack of respect? How much about a lack of understanding? Couldn't Tom just realize that he was in a different place with a different set of rules and "loosen up"?

In terms of how Tom dealt with the situation, I can imagine some people arguing that Tom should adapt and adjust to the situation. An argument of this type is based on a clear misunderstanding of the issues. Touching his hair would be no different than someone invading a personal, sacred space for another person. Invading an American Indian's spiritual space and disrespecting his religious beliefs represents an assault not only on his culture, but also on him as an individual (Locust, 1998). In this case, Tom's visibility and how someone else was constructing his visibility were largely negative. He was placed in a position of defending himself and the ideas and beliefs that he holds sacred to his disadvantage. Because the religious aspects are misunderstood and/or devalued, the institution and its agents simply branded Tom as a "troublemaker" rather than a defender of principles.

Phelan (1995) argues that visibility may lead to a colonialist appetite for desire. In the cases where Tom's sacred spaces were invaded even though he objected, it appears that the students at Sherwood may have believed that they owned the Indian or that his desires to be left unmolested were invalid because of his status as an Indigenous person. On other occasions, while I walked through campus with Tom, men would say to him, "I'm going to cut your hair" or "Don't let me catch you at night, I'll cut your hair, you little Indian." I was always amazed that the groups of students who did this were capable of doing so without ever breaking stride or looking directly at Tom. The other men and women in the group would laugh loudly as they continued walking. It was infuriating; it also illustrates the manner in which the students acted as if they owned Tom.[17] These examples highlight the fact that visibility leads to surveillance, and marginalization speeds the process toward invisibility. The choice to become invisible also highlights the brutal bargain established between the university and the Indigenous student who wants to maintain ties to his home culture. Tom could either sacrifice his spiritual beliefs in order to fit into the system, or he could actively seek to be invisible in order to maintain his cultural integrity in a hostile, unwelcome environment. The choices offered to Tom were limited and constricting. Tom chose to deal with these incidents in a manner that made sense to him at the time.

Adding to the notion that these institutions serve as oppressive structures, the institutions and their administrative agents played an active role in making students feel as if their cultural beliefs were not valued. Tom had little faith that Sherwood would address his cultural and spiritual needs. Much of his distrust arose from an incident that involved another American Indian student at Sherwood, a woman who was a member of a tribe from the plains of the United States. After a number of weeks of living in the dorm, she discovered that the remains of former Sherwood students and alumni were buried within the grounds of the dorm. She had, unknowingly, walked past the gravesites daily. When it was brought to her attention, she realized she could not continue to stay in the dorms, for it was against her spiritual and cultural beliefs to live in an area with the dead.

She appealed to the dean of residence and asked to be moved from the dormitory to another on-campus residential space. Because the time had passed for moving requests, the dean would not allow this student to move. When she persisted, the dean asked her to write "an essay" on her reasons for wanting to move and "provide justification" for the move. To complicate this display of cultural insensitivity, the student was required to write and complete the essay within a three-hour time slot. The student refused to abide by this, believing the act to be a violation of her religious freedom. Word of the conflict quickly spread to a vice president of the university, who intervened on behalf of the student and moved her within a few hours.

This vignette highlights a somewhat different notion of invisibility of Indigenous students in troublesome ways. Essentially, the administrator asked the student to justify her religious and cultural beliefs in a way that was not consistent with many other students' beliefs. The administrator who asked for the essay highlights a deep misunderstanding of American Indian spiritual beliefs. In and of itself, ignorance is not necessarily problematic; however, in this case, because of the manner in which the incident was initially handled, the visibility of the student's belief system became illegitimate and was held up for surveillance and judgment. Whatever the reasoning behind the action (or, in this case, inaction), the results were devastating to Tom and the other Indigenous students who were aware of the problem with the dean of residence. Clearly, actions like this from the administration (and hence, by the institution) influence the ways students act or behave, and directly influence the choices that they make.

Heather: The Good, the Bad, and the Ugly of Visibility

Heather's experiences highlight the ways that strategic visibility can lead to both positive and negative results. On a warm day in early April, I accompanied Heather to office hours. I saw the way Heather used office hours to demonstrate to her professor that she understood the material; this allowed her to be strategic in terms of maintaining her cultural integrity. The office we entered was large and contained antique furniture. Books and papers were scattered on the floor in piles, and the professor's desk had a layer of books and papers that, to my eye, was about eight inches high.

Heather introduced me to her professor and told him that I was "studying Native American students in college . . . and he is a friend of mine." She asked permission for me to stay while they talked so that I could know what she does when she is not in class. The professor asked me about my findings and about my own graduate work. The three of us chuckled as we discussed the past basketball season and results of the games between some of the Ivy League teams. The professor told me to "sit wherever you can find a spot" and turned his attention to Heather. I found a small chair in the corner and, after removing a pile of books and paper, sat down. At this point, Heather, as she would tell me later, "went to work." She was organized with questions and had a clear direction to guide the conversation. She explained to me later:

> I learned from Sara [her American Indian friend who was a senior when Heather was a first-year student] to be organized when you go into these meetings. The prof thinks you are always this organized and is more willing to help someone who seems focused than someone who does not. I keep telling other people [other Indigenous students] this, but no one wants to listen. . . . Anyway, I have a plan when I go in and they [professors] give me so much back.

Heather's planning highlights how social networks can be used to disrupt reproduction of inequality in educational institutions (Stanton-Salazar, 1997). Heather is also clearly building on the work of others to maintain her cultural integrity in a creative and strategic manner. She successfully illustrates one way she was able to be a "good student" and a "good Indian" simultaneously.

Heather provided the professor with a sheet listing her questions. She offered an overview of the questions and methodically went through each one. Before beginning a conversation, Heather "let the professor know that I'm not fishing for answers" by telling him what her own understanding of the issue or topic was. In this case, they were discussing John Rawls' book *A Theory of Justice*. The professor would nod and say things like, "um . . . hmm . . . very good, but you may also want to think about what Rawls' argument of the greater good might mean for you as a young woman in today's society." He later added, "Remember that I am also going to ask you about the connections between Rawls and Kant. . . . We talked about that in class." By the end of her meeting with the professor, Heather had her questions answered and the professor had given her "a strong clue" about what was going to be on the upcoming exam. I found myself making notes about how to take better advantage of my own time with my professors. Heather showed me that she could use her visibility as a meticulous student to succeed academically without losing her cultural integrity.

I later asked her about her strategies for using office hours, and why she did not ask these questions in class. She responded, "I think about my profs in ways similar to—not exactly the same—but similar to elders in my own community. They just know so much, and I have a lot to learn." She continued later, saying,

> I would never dream of bothering or interrupting an elder, but having some quiet time when I know [the professor] is there to answer questions makes it easier. . . . The other thing is that [Sara] reminded me that I need to have good letters of recommendation to go to [law school], and stopping in on a regular basis, being organized and all, means that I make an impression.

Heather used her time with her professor to work toward academic success. That she was advised to do this by another American Indian student is important. Citing Boissevain, Stanton-Salazar (1997) writes,

> Personal access to many valued resources and opportunities in society—by way of social networks—occurs through the messy business of commanding, negotiating, and managing many diverse (and sometimes conflicting) social relationships and personalities, and which usually entails skillfully negotiating the rules and constraints underlying the social acts of help-seeking and help-giving. (p. 4)

Heather is "skillfully negotiating" social (and academic) relationships to help her maintain what many have thought were conflicting goals: being a "good Indian" and a "good student." Clearly, these two descriptors need not be in conflict; Heather does both well.

She summed it up by telling me that her professor "knows who I am and that I think about this. I'm able to do this without feeling like I'm showing off for anyone." She demonstrated in a private setting that she understood the material; the intimacy of the setting allowed her to maintain fidelity to her own cultural norms and values regarding interaction in public places. In this way, she is using visibility as a strategic form of activism and advocacy; that is, she is able to be visible to her professor, maintain a sense of her Indianness, and advocate for her "participation" grade. Interestingly, the participation happens outside of a formal class setting and in a one-on-one arena. This is very much in keeping with her own beliefs regarding interactions, as it highlights other research about American Indians (Deyhle, 1995; Erickson & Mohatt, 1982; McCarty, 2001; Philips, 1983). Her visibility, however, was not always positive; in fact, an incident the prior fall illustrated ways that visibility can become a trap and be hurtful to some American Indian students.

One Columbus Day, I attended a small "awareness day" organized by the Indigenous group at one of the campuses. The activity took place in a prominent spot in the middle of campus, where many students had to pass in order to get to the gym, dining halls, and the undergraduate library. As Heather spoke about the injustices of the past and the ways Indigenous people have been mistreated, a group of students walked by, and one of the young men shouted, "Go back to the reservation or get with the program, lady. Stop whining about the past and get on with it. Wa-hoo-wah!" Such comments ignore larger historical issues and how they continue to affect individuals' lives in profound ways.

This incident highlights the fact that Indigenous people who are active and serve as advocates may be made invisible by their peers because they do not fit the mold of what an American Indian should be, or they may be made visible in pejorative, destructive ways. In ways described by Owens (2001) and Shanley (2001), Heather has stepped from behind the mask and no longer represents a romantic picture or that of the noble savage. She clearly highlights the fact that visibility, when used strategically, can have positive consequences; yet visibility can also be constructed as problematic because it leads to surveillance and to her peers telling her to "stop whining." Ultimately, context matters in terms of how visibility or invisibility is constructed.

Debbie, Tom, and Heather: Showing the Intricacies of (In)Visibility

What is especially interesting about the three stories outlined above is the way visibility and invisibility are interrelated. Debbie, Heather, and Tom have cultural backgrounds and physical characteristics that stand out in certain situations, particularly at institutions full of members of dominant groups (e.g., the power-holding, mostly upper-middle-class White populations at Ivy League universities). In this way, the appearance and behavior of American Indian students like Heather, Debbie, and Tom are "marked," and thus visible.

The experiences of American Indian students like these are typically either ignored or misrepresented by university policies and practices that privilege the dominant group's experiences, norms of interacting and behaving, and perspectives. As a result, American Indian students are left to choose between the lesser of two evils: retreating into the silence and invisibility that are more comfortable, or challenging inaccurate representations and sharing information about what "real" Indians are, and thus becoming more visible. This can be an uncomfortable position for students like Debbie, Tom, and Heather, who are interested in maintaining some degree of cultural integrity. Unfortunately, even extreme silence (because it is so different) is visible, while true identities remain unknown or invisible.

There is clearly a range and variation in the experiences of American Indian students, who often are portrayed as a group of people who have uniform experiences. Tom and Debbie grew up on reservations 100 miles apart, and their experiences were significantly different. Heather's reservation was located within a day's drive of Tom's and Debbie's. Tom believed that he had something to offer Sherwood, and that the college had something to offer him as well. He believed in a reciprocal relationship, yet his peers continually rejected his entrance into their world. He was, in a sense, an unwelcome guest. Like those of many institutions of higher education, Sherwood's publications and recruitment efforts offer an image of community and diversity, but in reality, the institution is as exclusive for its members as it is for those applying for membership.

On the other hand, Debbie decided she did not want to be a part of the Prospect experience almost immediately after arriving on campus, when it became clear to her that she was different from many other members of her class. She became as invisible as she could within the structure of the institution. She recognized that her life, her belief systems, and her very presence at this elite institution would be questioned, but she resolved not to change how she lived in spite of the pressure many young people feel to belong. She found a way to stay connected to her cultural norms and mores in the face of an institutional culture that was oppositional to her own. She was, and continues to be, grounded in her culture.

Her experiences and ties to her own culture, as well as her will to succeed academically, complicated Debbie's experiences at Prospect. In a discussion of why she decided to become mostly invisible, Debbie pointed out the ways that her efforts to remain invisible to her peers are tied to her attempts to maintain cultural integrity: "Sticking out is not a good thing. I am part of a community, and to draw attention to myself as an individual would not be looked upon favorably. . . . I've never thought about it; it's just that way." Debbie also declined offers to speak in class and other educational/social arenas about her experiences as a tribal person. While she could have made some extra money by doing so, she believed that this would not be an appropriate way to act as an Indigenous person. There were strong tensions between what the institution requested from her and what she felt she was able and willing to give.

Heather chose to be an active part of Sherwood's American Indian community. She worked hard at being visible in appropriate ways. Her use of office hours highlights the fact that she could be a "good" student and a "good" Indian simultaneously. Rather than acting inappropriately in class (e.g., by drawing attention to herself), she simply employed another structural part of higher education—office hours—to illustrate her knowledge and ability to the professor.

Debbie, Tom, and Heather illustrate the dangers of assuming that two members from the same group will have similar experiences. Both Tom and Debbie worked at making themselves invisible as a strategy for dealing with the oppressive aspects of their experiences, and both eventually chose to isolate themselves and become as invisible as possible, although for very different reasons. Heather made herself visible in a strategic manner that allowed her to maintain her cultural integrity *and* excel academically. She did not isolate herself, although she did retreat in the face of racism perpetuated by her college peers.

The three students' experiences are tied, in part, to Owens's (2001) and Shanley's (2001) arguments around visible Indians. Americans from the United States want an Indian as long as she or he fits behind the mask that dominant society has constructed for her or him. Those Indigenous people who do not fit into the mask are either not seen, or they are seen in mostly negative and pejorative ways. Because the environment was different and at times hostile toward these students, they worked to achieve invisibility, or in Heather's case, controlled visibility. In Tom's case, the process of making himself invisible resulted from a rejection by others based on his physical appearance, his quiet nature, and his beliefs that were antithetical and foreign to students at Sherwood. Debbie simply worked toward invisibility because of her fears of encountering situations like those faced by Tom. Heather's visibility was made problematic by the group of men who suggested she go "back to the reservation."

Debbie, Tom, and Heather have struggled with the negative consequences of visibility as American Indian students at Ivy League universities. When they are visible, it is often for negative or stereotypical reasons (e.g., as an affirmative action admit or an intimidating person). Debbie, Tom, and Heather are quiet, and for the most part keep to themselves. According to their cultural norms and backgrounds, calling attention to oneself is unhealthy and undesirable. Debbie said:

> I work hard at being anonymous. I keep my head down, don't make eye contact, and I don't talk in class. This is not the place for me to do this and the other [students] here do plenty of talking. I was taught to deflect attention, not seek it.

Heather provides an example of the ways that American Indian students at Sherwood and Prospect were often selectively made visible during Native American Month (or at a Columbus Day event) or when a new movie about Indigenous peoples was released. Suddenly, individuals who were excluded and ignored from the larger campus conversations that related to all students became highly visible, and the consequences were difficult. These students, because there are so few at Prospect and Sherwood, are made visible by their very presence, and their lives are romanticized or relegated to images of the past. In almost every case visibility serves to educate a few, and serves as the exotic "Other" for many.

Ollie, Ollie, In Come Free: Concluding Remarks on (In)Visibility

In this chapter, I explain the strategic uses of (in)visibility to illustrate that these three individuals were able to manipulate certain campus structures to their benefit. Whether an out-of-the-way route to class or a strategic use of office hours, their choices highlight thoughtful, complicated responses to oppressive institutional structures. However, it is also clear that they were not always able to control how, and in what ways, they were made (in)visible. The power of the institutions and their agents to define the identities of American Indians illustrates the individuals' lack of control. Ultimately, these students' experiences show that visibility can lead to surveillance, marginalization, and ostracism, while simultaneously having positive consequences that are directly related to strategic forms of activism, advocacy, and the maintenance of cultural integrity. Invisibility serves to assist some students in "flying under the radar" in order to maintain their cultural integrity, but it can also have damaging influences on students regarding marginalization.

This chapter is largely based on how individuals position themselves in relation to others and how the institution and its agents position them. Evading surveillance is necessitated by a hostile environment that forces individuals to make a brutal bargain. The bargain requires American Indian students to be visible—and therefore romanticized, fetishized, watched, or seen in pejorative ways, co-opted by individuals who still see American Indians as static figures from the past or as more romantic versions of the noble savage, or hidden from view. The brutal bargain encountered by these students is largely rooted in their visibility as members of groups that are fixed in the past or as individuals asked simply to adapt and change without a full understanding of the consequences of these actions. Other underrepresented and majority students face dilemmas, but I believe they are distinctly different because the numbers for Native American Indians at both universities represented in this study are miniscule. Additionally, the differences in cultures are so vast that it becomes clear that the dilemmas cannot be easily answered or rectified.

The individuals in this chapter were made visible and marginalized in ways that are problematic and, in response, actively made themselves invisible in order to maintain their cultural integrity.

Still others made themselves visible in order to illustrate their abilities to a professor without being overtly active in class. In this case, visibility is a strategic form of activism that illustrates that American Indians are not only present, but are capable, viable members of the university community.

The students in this study have backgrounds and qualities that stand out in certain contexts, particularly at Ivy League universities where the power holding, mostly upper-middle-class populations predominate. In this environment, the actions and behaviors of American Indian students are "marked" and thus noticeable. Such students are simultaneously visible and invisible to their peers; their differences (e.g., silences) are visible, while their true identities are invisible.

Ultimately, Tom, Debbie, and Heather highlight the power of (in)visibility for marginalized students in institutions of higher education. How do we—as academics, policymakers, students, and teachers—examine and help resolve the tensions these students face in their lives in a fair and equitable manner?

Notes

1. Throughout this chapter I use the terms *American Indian, Indigenous,* and *Native American* interchangeably.
2. In the original study, I found that students were able to be both "good" Indians and "good" students simultaneously. They did so by enacting strategies that allowed them both to maintain their cultural integrity and to meet the requirements of the university. Before I began the original study, I believed that the "action" would be in the classroom; at the conclusion of the ethnography, however, I found that the most important actions and strategies were enacted or formed outside of the classroom.
3. I am an enrolled member of the Lumbee-Cheraw tribe from North Carolina.
4. I draw on the work of Ellison (1994), Kaomea (2000, 2001), Phelan (1995), and Shanley (2001) to address notions of visibility and invisibility, although I aim to extend the ways they have used these terms.
5. I am not necessarily arguing here against representation or having a voice; rather, my intention is to examine the ways that both visibility and invisibility are manifested in the lives of the subaltern.
6. Incidentally, the local community was outraged, and the would-be arsonist was sentenced to five years in prison. Inebriated at the time of the attempted arson, he apologized for his behavior.
7. The names of both the institutions and the individuals that appear in this chapter are pseudonyms. I have consulted with the individuals and with the cultural affairs offices of their tribal nations. In every case, the individuals and the tribal nations asked me to change certain identifying traits so that they would be anonymous. One individual told me, "I'm not important in this, the story that is being told is important. It could happen to any of us." Additionally, an elder in one of the communities told me, "Tell your story, and make sure that [readers] understand how hard it is for us to do this work. We don't want people to know who we are when it comes to how we are doing our business." Although I believe the analysis could be richer given the knowledge about their tribal nations, I follow my own sense of what is "right," including my agreements with the tribal nations. Additionally, Lomawaima (2000) has outlined the importance of working with tribal communities when research interfaces with the community and its members.
8. I do not claim that these students' experiences are generalizable, although their demographics do represent many of the students at these institutions. Due to space constraints in this chapter, I only focus on three of the original seven students in the larger study. It is important to note that at Sherwood there were twenty-one undergraduate American Indian students, and at Prospect the number was twenty-two. I culled these numbers from a list generated by the registrar's office. Importantly, I contacted each of the students who self-identified as American Indian. Of the original forty-three at both institutions, twelve were willing to talk to me. The other thirty-one students were fairly represented by one student I met. After being unable to get him to return my phone calls and e-mails, I knocked on his dorm room door. He answered and told me that he had no interest in participating in the study. When I asked him about his tribal affiliation, he looked me in the eye and said, "My grandmother was Cherokee, and I thought it would help me get in here. It did . . . it served its purpose, and I have no interest in your group or any other Indian group." At the end of his sentence, he politely slammed the door in my face. Others have written eloquently about ethnic fraud among American Indians and the implications on campus (e.g., see Grande, 2000; Guerrero, 1996; Machamer, 1997; Pavel, Sanchez, Pueble, & Machamer, 1994).
9. There were numerous editorials and articles in the student newspaper around an idea of constructing a 12-foot-high fence around the perimeter of campus. While the idea never was implemented, there were places on campus where large brick columns were constructed with wrought iron gates attached. The gates were closed and locked each morning at 2 a.m. Interestingly, these locked gates directly faced the

side of campus closest to the local community. Prospect struggled with its image of a "safe" campus and they employed one of the largest police forces in the state. More recently, the university has offered generous benefits to its employees (the majority of whom are White) who buy houses in the local neighborhoods. These benefits and the individuals who have taken advantage of them have forced lifelong residents out of the area and driven house prices up.

10. In fairness to the professor, he has gotten much better. A student confronted him about his treatment of cultural groups. He decided to stop simply reading books and to talk to people who know something about the tribes he was discussing. More importantly, a fidelity to good, correct information exists in his present courses.

11. I have wondered if there were gender issues at work here. While I never asked Debbie if she believed this was an issue, I believe it was not in the same way it may have been for a woman in another setting or culture. I base this opinion on my observations of Debbie at home and outside of class. When I traveled home with her, I saw that she engaged in interactions with others in very much the same ways as her brothers. She carried firewood, cooked, worked on cars, and did many of the things they did. Outside of classrooms, she played basketball and volleyball at the university gym. Often, she was the only woman on the court. She had, by the time I visited her at the gym, earned respect from the young men for her abilities. The very fact that she ventured over to the courts is a testament to her confidence in her abilities (she can play!) and her sense that gender barriers do not directly influence her perceptions in the same ways they may other women's.

12. I worked and consulted in the admissions offices on both campuses, reading applications, assisting applicants in getting interviews, and recruiting American Indian students. The admissions staff would regularly joke with me when they read the application of a non-Indigenous applicant who did this work. Invariably, the applicant would discuss this work in their personal statement and application.

13. We would refer to each other or other Indigenous people as "Indians" but felt fairly protective of outsiders referring to us in this manner.

14. This analysis oversimplifies the issue. Clearly, there are admissions policies in place to assist Native Americans in getting admitted to college, but once there, students are forced to do the work of everyone else. Ironically, it is the children of alumni at institutions of higher education who receive the most preferential treatment in admissions. The fact that this issue is not highlighted in public discussion of affirmative action while racially based measures are illustrates the way that students of color are marked and made visible in pejorative and damaging ways.

15. Some of the attributes include being extremely quiet, soft spoken, and contemplative; in keeping with his style, Tom rarely made eye contact with others.

16. By outgoing I mean someone who is interested in getting to know other people. Remember in the previous pages that a woman referred to Tom as "quiet." I believe that outgoing means different things to different people and is contextual. Outgoing at a sales representatives conference would look much different than outgoing at a powwow.

17. White people who have read this manuscript in draft form have, almost without fail, asked me, "Why didn't he go to the dean or legal authorities about this treatment. . . . Isn't there something he could do?" At the time these acts were being committed, I similarly wondered where Tom's protection resided in the institution. I thought very much about a marginalized student's safe space and where (or if) that exists on campus. I believe that, for the African American students on these campuses, there was a "safe space" in theme-related housing that celebrated African Americans. A space like this does not exist for any of the Native American Indian students on either campus. I understand that the idea of a safe space is problematic on many fronts. For those who do not hold membership to the marginalized group, this appears to be self-segregating. For members of the marginalized group, there are concerns that the institution recognize that the environment is harsh enough to provide students with a "safe space." Additionally, the groups argue that safe spaces are not always so safe, as housing of the sort described here often come under attack from the outside. Finally, feeling completely comfortable in an environment that is often unfriendly, insensitive, and foreign is difficult. The safe space only allows a brief respite from the tensions of everyday life in these institutions.

References

Almeida, D. (1997). The hidden half: A history of Native American women's education. *Harvard Educational Review, 67*, 757–771.

Boissevain, J. (1974). *Friends of friends: Networks, manipulators and coalitions.* Oxford, Eng.: Basil Blackwell.

Brayboy, B. M. (1999). *Climbing the ivy: Examining the experiences of academically successful Native American Indian students in two Ivy League universities.* Unpublished doctoral dissertation, University of Pennsylvania.

Cantera, K. (2001, September 27). Utah man charged with hate crime; Feds: Accused arsonist targeted Pakistani family. *Salt Lake Tribune*, p. D3.

Collier, J., Jr. (1973). *Alaskan Eskimo education: A film analysis of cultural confrontation in the schools.* New York: Holt, Rinehart & Winston.

Deyhle, D. (1995). Navajo youth and Anglo racism: Cultural integrity and resistance. *Harvard Educational Review, 65*, 403–444.

Dumont, R. V., Jr. (1972). Learning English and how to be silent: Studies in Sioux and Cherokee classrooms. In C. Cazden, V. John, & D. Hymes (Eds.), *Functions of language in the classroom* (pp. 334–369). New York: Teachers College Press.

Ellison, R. (1994). *The invisible man.* New York: Vintage Books.

Erickson, F., & Mohatt, G. (1982). Cultural organization of participation structures in two classrooms of Indian students. In G. Spindler (Ed.), *Doing the ethnography of schooling* (pp. 132–174). New York: Holt, Rinehart & Winston.

Fanon, F. (1965). *The wretched of the earth.* New York: Grove Press.

Fanon, F. (1967). *Black skin, white masks.* New York: Grove Press.

Foley, D. (1996). The silent Indian as a cultural production. In A. Levinson, D. Foley, & D. Holland (Eds.), *The cultural production of the educated person* (pp. 79–91). Albany: State University of New York Press.

Fordham, S., & Ogbu, J. (1986). Black students' school success: Coping with the "burden of 'acting white.'" *Urban Review, 18*, 176–206.

Grande, S. (2000). American Indian geographies of identity and power: At the crossroads of Indigena and Mestizaje. *Harvard Educational Review, 70*, 467–498.

Grossberg, L. (1997). Identity and cultural studies: Is that all there is? In S. Hall & P. DuGay (Eds.), *Questions of cultural identity* (pp. 87–107). Thousand Oaks, CA: Sage.

Guerrero, M. A. J. (1996). Academic apartheid: American Indian studies and "multiculturalism." In A. Gordon & C. Newfield (Eds.), *Mapping multiculturalism* (pp. 49–63). Minneapolis: University of Minnesota Press.

Hall, S. (1991). Ethnicity: Identity and difference. *Radical America, 23*, 9–20.

Hay, J., Grossberg, L., & Wartella, E. (Eds.). (1996). *The audience and its landscape.* Boulder, CO: Westview Press.

Holland, D., & Lave, J. (2001). History in person: An introduction. In D. Holland & J. Lave (Eds.), *History in person: Enduring struggles, contentious practice, intimate identities* (pp. 3–33). Santa Fe: School of American Research Press.

hooks, b. (1990). *Yearning, race, gender, and cultural politics.* Boston: South End Press.

Kaomea, J. (2000). A curriculum of Aloha? Colonialism and tourism in Hawai'i's elementary textbooks. *Curriculum Inquiry, 30*, 319–344.

Kaomea, J. L. (2001). Pointed noses and yellow hair: Deconstructing children's writing on race and ethnicity in Hawai'i. In J. A. Jipson & R. T. Johnson (Eds.), *Resistance and representation: Rethinking childhood education* (pp. 67–82). New York: Peter Lang.

King, C. R., & Springwood, C. F. (1996). *Team spirits: The Native American mascots controversy.* Lincoln: University of Nebraska Press.

Lipka, J., & Ilutsik, E. (1995). Negotiated change: Yup'ik perspectives on indigenous schooling. *Bilingual Research Journal, 19*, 195–207.

Locust, C. (1998). Wounding the spirit: Discrimination and traditional American Indian belief systems. In T. Beauboef-Lafontant & D. Smith Augustine (Eds.), *Facing racism in education* (2nd ed., pp. 5–21). Cambridge, MA: Harvard Educational Review.

Lomawaima, K. T. (2000). Tribal sovereigns: Reframing research in American Indian education. *Harvard Educational Review, 70*, 1–21.

Luke, A. (1995–1996). Text and discourse in education: An introduction to critical discourse analysis. *Review of Research in Education, 21*, 3–48.

Machamer, A. M. (1997). Ethnic fraud in the university: Serious implications for American Indian education. *Native Bruin, 2*, 1–2.

Macias, J. (1987). The hidden curriculum of Papago teachers: American Indian strategies for mitigating cultural discontinuity in early schooling. In G. Spindler & L. Spindler (Eds.), *Interpretive ethnography of education at home and abroad* (pp. 365–380). Hillsdale, NJ: Erlbaum.

McCarty, T. L. (2001). *A place to be Navajo: The struggle for self-determination in Indigenous schooling.* Mahwah, NJ: Lawrence Erlbaum Associates.

McIntosh, P. (1995). White privilege and male privilege. In M. L. Anderson & P. H. Collins (Eds.), *Race, class, and gender* (pp. 76–87). Belmont, CA: Wadsworth.

Ogbu, J. (1987). Variability in minority school achievement: A problem in search of an explanation. *Anthropology and Education Quarterly, 18,* 312–334.

Owens, L. (2001). As if an Indian were really an Indian: Native American voices and postcolonial theory. In G. Bataille (Ed.), *Native American representations: First encounters, distorted images, and literary appropriations* (pp. 11–24). Lincoln: University of Nebraska Press.

Pavel, D. M., Sanchez, T., Pueble, F., & Machamer, A. (1994). Ethnic fraud, native peoples, and higher education. *Thought and Action: The NEA Journal of Higher Education, 10,* 91–100.

Phelan, P. (1995). *Unmarked: The politics of performance.* New York: Routledge.

Philips, S. (1972). Participant structures and communicative competence: Warm Springs children in community and classroom. In C. Cazden, V. John, & D. Hymes (Eds.), *Functions of language in the classroom* (pp. 370–392). New York: Teachers College Press.

Philips, S. (1983). *The invisible culture: Communication in classroom and on the Warm Springs Indian reservation.* New York: Longman.

Shanley, K. (2001). The Indians America loves to love and read: American Indian identity and cultural appropriation. In G. Bataille (Ed.), *Native American representations: First encounters, distorted images, and literary appropriations* (pp. 26–49). Lincoln: University of Nebraska Press.

Spindel, C. (2000). *Dancing at halftime: Sports and the controversy over American Indian mascots.* New York: New York University Press.

Stanton-Salazar, R. D. (1997). A social capital framework for understanding the socialization of racial minority children and youths. *Harvard Educational Review, 67,* 1–40.

Suina, J., & Smolkin, L. B. (1994). From natal culture to school culture to dominant society culture: Supporting transitions for Pueblo Indian students. In P. Grenfield & R. Cocking (Eds.), *Cross-cultural roots of minority child development* (pp. 115–130). Hillsdale, NJ: Erlbaum.

Tinto, V. (1993). *Leaving college: Rethinking the causes and cures of student attrition* (2nd ed.). Chicago: University of Chicago Press.

Vizenor, G. (1994). *Manifest manners: Postindian warriors of survivance.* Hanover, NH: University Press of New England.

Vizenor, G. (1998). *Fugitive poses: Native American Indian scenes of absence and presence.* Lincoln: University of Nebraska Press.

Wilkins, D. E., & Lomawaima, K. T. (2001). *Uneven ground: American Indian sovereignty and federal law.* Norman: University of Oklahoma Press.

Young, I. M. (1990). *Justice and the politics of difference.* Princeton, NJ: Princeton University Press.

CHAPTER 24

TALKING ABOUT RACE, LEARNING ABOUT RACISM: THE APPLICATION OF RACIAL IDENTITY DEVELOPMENT THEORY IN THE CLASSROOM

BEVERLY DANIEL TATUM

The inclusion of race-related content in college courses often generates emotional responses in students that range from guilt and shame to anger and despair. The discomfort associated with these emotions can lead students to resist the learning process. Based on her experience teaching a course on the psychology of racism and an application of racial identity development theory, Beverly Daniel Tatum identifies three major sources of student resistance to talking about race and learning about racism, as well as some strategies for overcoming this resistance.

As many educational institutions struggle to become more multicultural in terms of their students, faculty, and staff, they also begin to examine issues of cultural representation within their curriculum. This examination has evoked a growing number of courses that give specific consideration to the effect of variables such as race, class, and gender on human experience—an important trend that is reflected and supported by the increasing availability of resource manuals for the modification of course content (Bronstein & Quina, 1988; Hull, Scott, & Smith, 1982; Schuster & Van Dyne, 1985).

Unfortunately, less attention has been given to the issues of process that inevitably emerge in the classroom when attention is focused on race, class, and/or gender. It is very difficult to talk about these concepts in a meaningful way without also talking and learning about racism, classism, and sexism.[1] The introduction of these issues of oppression often generates powerful emotional responses in students that range from guilt and shame to anger and despair. If not addressed, these emotional responses can result in student resistance to oppression-related content areas. Such resistance can ultimately interfere with the cognitive understanding and mastery of the material. This resistance and potential interference is particularly common when specifically addressing issues of race and racism. Yet, when students are given the opportunity to explore race-related material in a classroom where both their affective and intellectual responses are acknowledged and addressed, their level of understanding is greatly enhanced.

This chapter seeks to provide a framework for understanding students' psychological responses to race-related content and the student resistance that can result, as well as some strategies for overcoming this resistance. It is informed by more than a decade of experience as an African-American woman engaged in teaching an undergraduate course on the psychology of racism, by thematic analyses of student journals and essays written for the racism class, and by an understanding and application of racial identity development theory (Helms, 1990).

Setting the Context

As a clinical psychologist with a research interest in racial identity development among African-American youth raised in predominantly White communities, I began teaching about racism quite fortuitously. In 1980, while I was a part-time lecturer in the Black Studies department of a large public university, I was invited to teach a course called Group Exploration of Racism (Black Studies 2). A requirement for Black Studies majors, the course had to be offered, yet the instructor who regularly taught the course was no longer affiliated with the institution. Armed with a folder full of handouts, old syllabi that the previous instructor left behind, a copy of *White Awareness: Handbook for Anti-racism Training* (Katz, 1978), and my own clinical skills as a group facilitator, I constructed a course that seemed to meet the goals already outlined in the course catalogue. Designed "to provide students with an understanding of the psychological causes and emotional reality of racism as it appears in everyday life," the course incorporated the use of lectures, readings, simulation exercises, group research projects, and extensive class discussion to help students explore the psychological impact of racism on both the oppressor and the oppressed.

Though my first efforts were tentative, the results were powerful. The students in my class, most of whom were White, repeatedly described the course in their evaluations as one of the most valuable educational experiences of their college careers. I was convinced that helping students understand the ways in which racism operates in their own lives, and what they could do about it, was a social responsibility that I should accept. The freedom to institute the course in the curriculum of the psychology departments in which I would eventually teach became a personal condition of employment. I have successfully introduced the course in each new educational setting I have been in since leaving that university.

Since 1980, I have taught the course (now called the Psychology of Racism) eighteen times, at three different institutions. Although each of these schools is very different—a large public university, a small state college, and a private, elite women's college—the challenges of teaching about racism in each setting have been more similar than different.

In all of the settings, class size has been limited to thirty students (averaging twenty-four). Though typically predominantly White and female (even in coeducational settings), the class makeup has always been mixed in terms of both race and gender. The students of color who have taken the course include Asians and Latinos/as, but most frequently the students of color have been Black. Though most students have described themselves as middle class, all socioeconomic backgrounds (ranging from very poor to very wealthy) have been represented over the years.

The course has necessarily evolved in response to my own deepening awareness of the psychological legacy of racism and my expanding awareness of other forms of oppression, although the basic format has remained the same. Our weekly three-hour class meeting is held in a room with movable chairs, arranged in a circle. The physical structure communicates an important premise of the course—that I expect the students to speak with each other as well as with me.

My other expectations (timely completion of assignments, regular class attendance) are clearly communicated in our first class meeting, along with the assumptions and guidelines for discussion that I rely upon to guide our work together. Because the assumptions and guidelines are so central to the process of talking and learning about racism, it may be useful to outline them here.

Working Assumptions

1. Racism, defined as a "system of advantage based on race" (see Wellman, 1977), is a pervasive aspect of U.S. socialization. It is virtually impossible to live in U.S. contemporary society and not be exposed to some aspect of the personal, cultural, and/or institutional manifestations of racism in our society. It is also assumed that, as a result, all of us have received some misinformation about those groups disadvantaged by racism.

2. Prejudice, defined as a "preconceived judgment or opinion, often based on limited information," is clearly distinguished from racism (see Katz, 1978). I assume that all of us may have prejudices as a result of the various cultural stereotypes to which we have been exposed. Even when these preconceived ideas have positive associations (such as "Asian students are good in math"), they have negative effects because they deny a person's individuality. These attitudes may influence the individual behaviors of people of color as well as of Whites, and may affect intergroup as well as intragroup interaction. However, a distinction must be made between the negative racial attitudes held by individuals of color and White individuals, because it is only the attitudes of Whites that routinely carry with them the social power inherent in the systematic cultural reinforcement and institutionalization of those racial prejudices. To distinguish the prejudices of students of color from the racism of White students is *not* to say that the former is acceptable and the latter is not; both are clearly problematic. The distinction is important, however, to identify the power differential between members of dominant and subordinate groups.

3. In the context of U.S. society, the system of advantage clearly operates to benefit Whites as a group. However, it is assumed that racism, like other forms of oppression, hurts members of the privileged group as well as those targeted by racism. While the impact of racism on Whites is clearly different from its impact on people of color, racism has negative ramifications for everyone. For example, some White students might remember the pain of having lost important relationships because Black friends were not allowed to visit their homes. Others may express sadness at having been denied access to a broad range of experiences because of social segregation. These individuals often attribute the discomfort or fear they now experience in racially mixed settings to the cultural limitations of their youth.

4. Because of the prejudice and racism inherent in our environments when we were children, I assume that we cannot be blamed for learning what we were taught (intentionally or unintentionally). Yet as adults, we have a responsibility to try to identify and interrupt the cycle of oppression. When we recognize that we have been misinformed, we have a responsibility to seek out more accurate information and to adjust our behavior accordingly.

5. It is assumed that change, both individual and institutional, is possible. Understanding and unlearning prejudice and racism is a lifelong process that may have begun prior to enrolling in this class, and which will surely continue after the course is over. Each of us may be at a different point in that process, and I assume that we will have mutual respect for each other, regardless of where we perceive one another to be.

To facilitate further our work together, I ask students to honor the following guidelines for our discussion. Specifically, I ask students to demonstrate their respect for one another by honoring the confidentiality of the group. So that students may feel free to ask potentially awkward or embarrassing questions, or share race-related experiences, I ask that students refrain from making personal attributions when discussing the course content with their friends. I also discourage the use of "zaps," overt or covert put-downs often used as comic relief when someone is feeling anxious about the content of the discussion. Finally, students are asked to speak from their own experience, to say, for example, "I think . . ." or "In my experience, I have found . . ." rather than generalizing their experience to others, as in "People say . . .".

Many students are reassured by the climate of safety that is created by these guidelines and find comfort in the nonblaming assumptions I outline for the class. Nevertheless, my experience has been that most students, regardless of their class and ethnic background, still find racism a difficult topic to discuss, as is revealed by these journal comments written after the first class meeting (all names are pseudonyms):

> The class is called Psychology of Racism, the atmosphere is friendly and open, yet I feel very closed in. I feel guilt and doubt well up inside of me. (Tiffany, a White woman)

> Class has started on a good note thus far. The class seems rather large and disturbs me. In a class of this nature, I expect there will be many painful and emotional moments. (Linda, an Asian woman)

I am a little nervous that as one of the few students of color in the class people are going to be looking at me for answers, or whatever other reasons. The thought of this inhibits me a great deal. (Louise, an African-American woman)

I had never thought about my social position as being totally dominant. There wasn't one area in which I wasn't in the dominant group. . . . I first felt embarrassed. . . . Through association alone I felt in many ways responsible for the unequal condition existing in the world. This made me feel like shrinking in a hole in a class where I was surrounded by 27 women and 2 men, one of whom was Black and the other was Jewish. I felt that all these people would be justified in venting their anger upon me. After a short period, I realized that no one in the room was attacking or even blaming me for the conditions that exist. (Carl, a White man)

Even though most of my students voluntarily enroll in the course as an elective, their anxiety and subsequent resistance to learning about racism quickly emerge.

Sources of Resistance

In predominantly White college classrooms, I have experienced at least three major sources of student resistance to talking and learning about race and racism. They can be readily identified as the following:

1. Race is considered a taboo topic for discussion, especially in racially mixed settings.
2. Many students, regardless of racial-group membership, have been socialized to think of the United States as a just society.
3. Many students, particularly White students, initially deny any personal prejudice, recognizing the impact of racism on other people's lives, but failing to acknowledge its impact on their own.

Race as Taboo Topic

The first source of resistance, race as a taboo topic, is an essential obstacle to overcome if class discussion is to begin at all. Although many students are interested in the topic, they are often most interested in hearing other people talk about it, afraid to break the taboo themselves.

One source of this self-consciousness can be seen in the early childhood experiences of many students. It is known that children as young as three notice racial differences (see Phinney & Rotheram, 1987). Certainly preschoolers talk about what they see. Unfortunately, they often do so in ways that make adults uncomfortable. Imagine the following scenario: A White child in a public place points to a dark-skinned African-American child and says loudly, "Why is that boy Black?" The embarrassed parent quickly responds, "Sh! Don't say that." The child is only attempting to make sense of a new observation (Derman-Sparks, Higa, & Sparks, 1980), yet the parent's attempt to silence the perplexed child sends a message that this observation is not okay to talk about. White children quickly become aware that their questions about race raise adult anxiety, and as a result, they learn not to ask the questions.

When asked to reflect on their earliest race-related memories and the feelings associated with them, both White students and students of color often report feelings of confusion, anxiety, and/or fear. Students of color often have early memories of name-calling or other negative interactions with other children, and sometimes with adults. They also report having had questions that went both unasked and unanswered. In addition, many students have had uncomfortable interchanges around race-related topics as adults. When asked at the beginning of the semester, "How many of you have had difficult, perhaps heated conversations with someone on a race-related topic?", routinely almost everyone in the class raises his or her hand. It should come as no surprise then that students often approach the topic of race and/or racism with both curiosity and trepidation.

The Myth of the Meritocracy

The second source of student resistance to be discussed here is rooted in students' belief that the United States is a just society, a meritocracy where individual efforts are fairly rewarded. While some students (particularly students of color) may already have become disillusioned with that notion of the United States, the majority of my students who have experienced at least the personal success of college acceptance still have faith in this notion. To the extent that these students acknowledge that racism exists, they tend to view it as an individual phenomenon, rooted in the attitudes of the "Archie Bunkers" of the world or located only in particular parts of the country.

After several class meetings, Karen, a White woman, acknowledged this attitude in her journal:

> At one point in my life—the beginning of this class—I actually perceived America to be a relatively racist free society. I thought that the people who were racist or subjected to racist stereotypes were found only in small pockets of the U.S., such as the South. As I've come to realize, racism (or at least racially orientated stereotypes) is rampant.

An understanding of racism as a system of advantage presents a serious challenge to the notion of the United States as a just society where rewards are based solely on one's merit. Such a challenge often creates discomfort in students. The old adage "ignorance is bliss" seems to hold true in this case; students are not necessarily eager to recognize the painful reality of racism.

One common response to the discomfort is to engage in denial of what they are learning. White students in particular may question the accuracy or currency of statistical information regarding the prevalence of discrimination (housing, employment, access to health care, and so on). More qualitative data, such as autobiographical accounts of experiences with racism, may be challenged on the basis of their subjectivity.

It should be pointed out that the basic assumption that the United States is a just society for all is only one of many basic assumptions that might be challenged in the learning process. Another example can be seen in an interchange between two White students following a discussion about cultural racism, in which the omission or distortion of historical information about people of color was offered as an example of the cultural transmission of racism.

"Yeah, I just found out that Cleopatra was actually a Black woman."

"What?"

The first student went on to explain her newly learned information. Finally, the second student exclaimed in disbelief, "That can't be true. Cleopatra was beautiful!" This new information and her own deeply ingrained assumptions about who is beautiful and who is not were too incongruous to allow her to assimilate the information at that moment.

If outright denial of information is not possible, then withdrawal may be. Physical withdrawal in the form of absenteeism is one possible result; it is for precisely this reason that class attendance is mandatory. The reduction in the completion of reading and/or written assignments is another form of withdrawal. I have found this response to be so common that I now alert students to this possibility at the beginning of the semester. Knowing that this response is a common one seems to help students stay engaged, even when they experience the desire to withdraw.

Following an absence in the fifth week of the semester, one White student wrote, "I think I've hit the point you talked about, the point where you don't want to hear any more about racism. I sometimes begin to get the feeling we are all hypersensitive." (Two weeks later she wrote, "Class is getting better. I think I am beginning to get over my hump.")

Perhaps not surprisingly, this response can be found in both White students and students of color. Students of color often enter a discussion of racism with some awareness of the issue, based on personal experiences. However, even these students find that they did not have a full understanding of the widespread impact of racism in our society. For students who are targeted by racism, an increased awareness of the impact in and on their lives is painful, and often generates anger.

Four weeks into the semester, Louise, an African-American woman, wrote in her journal about her own heightened sensitivity:

Many times in class I feel uncomfortable when White students use the term Black because even if they aren't aware of it they say it with all or at least a lot of the negative connotations they've been taught goes along with Black. Sometimes it just causes a stinging feeling inside of me. Sometimes I get real tired of hearing White people talk about the conditions of Black people. I think it's an important thing for them to talk about, but still I don't always like being around when they do it. I also get tired of hearing them talk about how hard it is for them, though I understand it, and most times I am very willing to listen and be open, but sometimes I can't. Right now I can't.

For White students, advantaged by racism, a heightened awareness of it often generates painful feelings of guilt. The following responses are typical:

After reading the article about privilege, I felt very guilty. (Rachel, a White woman)

Questions of racism are so full of anger and pain. When I think of all the pain White people have caused people of color, I get a feeling of guilt. How could someone like myself care so much about the color of someone's skin that they would do them harm? (Terri, a White woman)

White students also sometimes express a sense of betrayal when they realize the gaps in their own education about racism. After seeing the first episode of the documentary series *Eyes on the Prize*, Chris, a White man, wrote:

I never knew it was really that bad just 35 years ago. Why didn't I learn this in elementary or high school? Could it be that the White people of America want to forget this injustice? . . . I will never forget that movie for as long as I live. It was like a big slap in the face.

Barbara, a White woman, also felt anger and embarrassment in response to her own previous lack of information about the internment of Japanese Americans during World War II. She wrote:

I feel so stupid because I never even knew that these existed. I never knew that the Japanese were treated so poorly. I am becoming angry and upset about all of the things that I do not know. I have been so sheltered. My parents never wanted to let me know about the bad things that have happened in the world. After I saw the movie (*Mitsuye and Nellie*), I even called them up to ask them why they never told me this. . . . I am angry at them too for not teaching me and exposing me to the complete picture of my country.

Avoiding the subject matter is one way to avoid these uncomfortable feelings.

"I'm Not Racist, But . . ."

A third source of student resistance (particularly among White students) is the initial denial of any personal connection to racism. When asked why they have decided to enroll in a course on racism, White students typically explain their interest in the topic with such disclaimers as, "I'm not racist myself, but I know people who are, and I want to understand them better."

Because of their position as the targets of racism, students of color do not typically focus on their own prejudices or lack of them. Instead they usually express a desire to understand why racism exists, and how they have been affected by it.

However, as all students gain a better grasp of what racism is and its many manifestations in U.S. society, they inevitably start to recognize its legacy within themselves. Beliefs, attitudes, and actions based on racial stereotypes begin to be remembered and are newly observed by White students. Students of color as well often recognize negative attitudes they may have internalized about their own racial group or that they have believed about others. Those who previously thought themselves immune to the effects of growing up in a racist society often find themselves reliving uncomfortable feelings of guilt or anger.

After taping her own responses to a questionnaire on racial attitudes, Barbara, a White woman previously quoted, wrote:

I always want to think of myself as open to all races. Yet when I did the interview to myself, I found that I did respond differently to the same questions about different races. No one could ever have told me that I would have. I would have denied it. But I found that I did respond differently even though I didn't want to. This really upset me. I was angry with myself because I thought I was not prejudiced and yet the stereotypes that I had created had an impact on the answers that I gave even though I didn't want it to happen.

The new self-awareness, represented here by Barbara's journal entry, changes the classroom dynamic. One common result is that some White students, once perhaps active participants in class discussion, now hesitate to continue their participation for fear that their newly recognized racism will be revealed to others.

Today I did feel guilty, and like I had to watch what I was saying (make it good enough), I guess to prove I'm really not prejudiced. From the conversations the first day, I guess this is a normal enough reaction, but I certainly never expected it in me. (Joanne, a White woman)

This withdrawal on the part of White students is often paralleled by an increase in participation by students of color who are seeking an outlet for what are often feelings of anger. The withdrawal of some previously vocal White students from the classroom exchange, however, is sometimes interpreted by students of color as indifference. This perceived indifference often serves to fuel the anger and frustration that many students of color experience, as awareness of their own oppression is heightened. For example, Robert, an African-American man, wrote:

I really wish the White students would talk more. When I read these articles, it makes me so mad and I really want to know what the White kids think. Don't they care?

Sonia, a Latina, described the classroom tension from another perspective:

I would like to comment that at many points in the discussions I have felt uncomfortable and sometimes even angry with people. I guess I am at the stage where I am tired of listening to Whites feel guilty and watch their eyes fill up with tears. I do understand that everyone is at their own stage of development and I even tell myself every Tuesday that these people have come to this class by choice. Some days I am just more tolerant than others. . . . It takes courage to say things in that room with so many women of color present. It also takes courage for the women of color to say things about Whites.

What seems to be happening in the classroom at such moments is a collision of developmental processes that can be inherently useful for the racial identity development of the individuals involved. Nevertheless, the interaction may be perceived as problematic to instructors and students who are unfamiliar with the process. Although space does not allow for an exhaustive discussion of racial identity development theory, a brief explication of it here will provide additional clarity regarding the classroom dynamics when issues of race are discussed. It will also provide a theoretical framework for the strategies for dealing with student resistance that will be discussed at the conclusion of this chapter.

Stages of Racial Identity Development

Racial identity and racial identity development theory are defined by Janet Helms (1990) as

a sense of group or collective identity based on one's *perception* that he or she shares a common racial heritage with a particular racial group . . . racial identity development theory concerns the psychological implications of racial-group membership, that is belief systems that evolve in reaction to perceived differential racial-group membership. (p. 3)

It is assumed that in a society where racial-group membership is emphasized, the development of a racial identity will occur in some form in everyone. Given the dominant/subordinate relationship of Whites and people of color in this society, however, it is not surprising that this developmental process will unfold in different ways. For purposes of this discussion, William Cross's (1971, 1978) model of Black identity development will be described along with Helms's (1990) model of White racial identity development theory. While the identity development of other students (Asian, Latino/a, Native American) is not included in this particular theoretical formulation, there is evidence to suggest that the process for these oppressed groups is similar to that described for African

Americans (Highlen, et al., 1988; Phinney, 1990).[2] In each case, it is assumed that a positive sense of one's self as a member of one's group (which is not based on any assumed superiority) is important for psychological health.

Black Racial Identity Development

According to Cross's (1971, 1978, 1991) model of Black racial identity development, there are five stages in the process, identified as Preencounter, Encounter, Immersion/Emersion, Internalization, and Internalization-Commitment. In the first stage of Preencounter, the African American has absorbed many of the beliefs and values of the dominant White culture, including the notion that "White is right" and "Black is wrong." Though the internalization of negative Black stereotypes may be outside of his or her conscious awareness, the individual seeks to assimilate and be accepted by Whites, and actively or passively distances him/herself from other Blacks.[3]

Louise, an African-American woman previously quoted, captured the essence of this stage in the following description of herself at an earlier time:

> For a long time it seemed as if I didn't remember my background, and I guess in some ways I didn't. I was never taught to be proud of my African heritage. Like we talked about in class, I went through a very long stage of identifying with my oppressors. Wanting to be like, live like, and be accepted by them. Even to the point of hating my own race and myself for being a part of it. Now I am ashamed that I ever was ashamed. I lost so much of myself in my denial of and refusal to accept my people.

In order to maintain psychological comfort at this stage of development, Helms writes:

> The person must maintain the fiction that race and racial indoctrination have nothing to do with how he or she lives life. It is probably the case that the Preencounter person is bombarded on a regular basis with information that he or she cannot really be a member of the "in" racial group, but relies on denial to selectively screen such information from awareness. (1990, p. 23)

This de-emphasis on one's racial-group membership may allow the individual to think that race has not been or will not be a relevant factor in one's own achievement, and may contribute to the belief in a U.S. meritocracy that is often a part of a Preencounter worldview.

Movement into the Encounter phase is typically precipitated by an event or series of events that forces the individual to acknowledge the impact of racism in one's life. For example, instances of social rejection by White friends or colleagues (or reading new personally relevant information about racism) may lead the individual to the conclusion that many Whites will not view him or her as an equal. Faced with the reality that he or she cannot truly be White, the individual is forced to focus on his or her identity as a member of a group targeted by racism.

Brenda, a Korean-American student, described her own experience of this process as a result of her participation in the racism course:

> I feel that because of this class, I have become much more aware of racism that exists around. Because of my awareness of racism, I am now bothered by acts and behaviors that might not have bothered me in the past. Before when racial comments were said around me I would somehow ignore it and pretend that nothing was said. By ignoring comments such as these, I was protecting myself. It became sort of a defense mechanism. I never realized I did this, until I was confronted with stories that were found in our reading, by other people of color, who also ignored comments that bothered them. In realizing that there is racism out in the world and that there are comments concerning race that are directed towards me, I feel as if I have reached the first step. I also think I have reached the second step, because I am now bothered and irritated by such comments. I no longer ignore them, but now confront them.

The Immersion/Emersion stage is characterized by the simultaneous desire to surround oneself with visible symbols of one's racial identity and an active avoidance of symbols of Whiteness. As Thomas Parham describes, "At this stage, everything of value in life must be Black or relevant to Blackness. This stage is also characterized by a tendency to denigrate White people, simultaneously glorifying Black people. . . ." (1989, p. 190). The previously described anger that emerges in class among African-American students and other students of color in the process of learning about racism may be seen as part of the transition through these stages.

As individuals enter the Immersion stage, they actively seek out opportunities to explore aspects of their own history and culture with the support of peers from their own racial background. Typically, White-focused anger dissipates during this phase because so much of the person's energy is directed toward his or her own group- and self-exploration. The result of this exploration is an emerging security in a newly defined and affirmed sense of self.

Sharon, another African-American woman, described herself at the beginning of the semester as angry, seemingly in the Encounter stage of development. She wrote after our class meeting:

> Another point that I must put down is that before I entered class today I was angry about the way Black people have been treated in this country. I don't think I will easily overcome that and I basically feel justified in my feelings.

At the end of the semester, Sharon had joined with two other Black students in the class to work on their final class project. She observed that the three of them had planned their project to focus on Black people specifically, suggesting movement into the Immersion stage of racial identity development. She wrote:

> We are concerned about the well-being of our own people. They cannot be well if they have this pinned-up hatred for their own people. This internalized racism is something that we all felt, at various times, needed to be talked about. This semester it has really been important to me, and I believe Gordon [a Black classmate], too.

The emergence from this stage marks the beginning of Internalization. Secure in one's own sense of racial identity, there is less need to assert the "Blacker than thou" attitude often characteristic of the Immersion stage (Parham, 1989). In general, "pro-Black attitudes become more expansive, open, and less defensive" (Cross, 1971, p. 24). While still maintaining his or her connections with Black peers, the internalized individual is willing to establish meaningful relationships with Whites who acknowledge and are respectful of his or her self-definition. The individual is also ready to build coalitions with members of other oppressed groups. At the end of the semester, Brenda, a Korean American, concluded that she had in fact internalized a positive sense of racial identity. The process she described parallels the stages described by Cross:

> I have been aware for a long time that I am Korean. But through this class I am beginning to really become aware of my race. I am beginning to find out that White people can be accepting of me and at the same time accept me as a Korean.

> I grew up wanting to be accepted and ended up almost denying my race and culture. I don't think I did this consciously, but the denial did occur. As I grew older, I realized that I was different. I became for the first time, friends with other Koreans. I realized I had much in common with them. This was when I went through my "Korean friend" stage. I began to enjoy being friends with Koreans more than I did with Caucasians.

> Well, ultimately, through many years of growing up, I am pretty much in focus about who I am and who my friends are. I knew before I took this class that there were people not of color that were understanding of my differences. In our class, I feel that everyone is trying to sincerely find the answer of abolishing racism. I knew people like this existed, but it's nice to meet with them weekly.

Cross suggests that there are few psychological differences between the fourth stage, Internalization, and the fifth stage, Internalization-Commitment. However, those at the fifth stage have found ways to translate their "personal sense of Blackness into a plan of action or a general sense of commitment" to the concerns of Blacks as a group, which is sustained over time (Cross, 1991, p. 220). Whether at the fourth or fifth stage, the process of Internalization allows the individual, anchored in a positive sense of racial identity, both to proactively perceive and transcend race. Blackness becomes "the point of departure for discovering the universe of ideas, cultures and experiences beyond blackness in place of mistaking blackness as the universe itself" (Cross, Parham, & Helms, 1991, p. 330).

Though the process of racial identity development has been presented here in linear form, in fact it is probably more accurate to think of it in a spiral form. Often a person may move from one stage to the next, only to revisit an earlier stage as the result of new encounter experiences (Parham, 1989), though the later experience of the stage may be different from the original experience. The image that students often find helpful in understanding this concept of recycling through the stages is that of a spiral staircase. As a person ascends a spiral staircase, she may stop and look down at a spot below. When she reaches the next level, she may look down and see the same spot, but the vantage point has changed.[4]

White Racial Identity Development

The transformations experienced by those targeted by racism are often paralleled by those of White students. Helms (1990) describes the evolution of a positive White racial identity as involving both the abandonment of racism and the development of a nonracist White identity. In order to do the latter,

> he or she must accept his or her own Whiteness, the cultural implications of being White, and define a view of Self as a racial being that does not depend on the perceived superiority of one racial group over another. (p. 49)

She identifies six stages in her model of White racial identity development: Contact, Disintegration, Reintegration, Pseudo-Independent, Immersion/Emersion, and Autonomy.

The Contact stage is characterized by a lack of awareness of cultural and institutional racism, and of one's own White privilege. Peggy McIntosh (1989) writes eloquently about her own experience of this state of being:

> As a white person, I realized I had been taught about racism as something which puts others at a disadvantage, but had been taught not to see one of its corollary aspects, white privilege, which puts me at an advantage. . . . I was taught to see racism only in individual acts of meanness, not in invisible systems conferring dominance on my group. (p. 10)

In addition, the Contact stage often includes naive curiosity about or fear of people of color, based on stereotypes learned from friends, family, or the media. These stereotypes represent the framework in use when a person at this stage of development makes a comment such as, "You don't act like a Black person" (Helms, 1990, p. 57).

Those Whites whose lives are structured so as to limit their interaction with people of color, as well as their awareness of racial issues, may remain at this stage indefinitely. However, certain kinds of experiences (increased interaction with people of color or exposure to new information about racism) may lead to a new understanding that cultural and institutional racism exist. This new understanding marks the beginning of the Disintegration stage.

At this stage, the bliss of ignorance or lack of awareness is replaced by the discomfort of guilt, shame, and sometimes anger at the recognition of one's own advantage because of being White and the acknowledgement of the role of Whites in the maintenance of a racist system. Attempts to reduce discomfort may include denial (convincing oneself that racism doesn't really exist, or if it does, it is the fault of its victims).

For example, Tom, a White male student, responded with some frustration in his journal to a classmate's observation that the fact that she had never read any books by Black authors in any of her high school or college English classes was an example of cultural racism. He wrote, "It's not my fault that Blacks don't write books."

After viewing a film in which a psychologist used examples of Black children's drawings to illustrate the potentially damaging effect of negative cultural messages on a Black child's developing self-esteem, David, another White male student, wrote:

> I found it interesting the way Black children drew themselves without arms. The psychologist said this is saying that the child feels unable to control his environment. It can't be because the child has notions and beliefs already about being Black. It must be built in or hereditary due to the past history of the Blacks. I don't believe it's cognitive but more biological due to a long past history of repression and being put down.

Though Tom's and David's explanations seem quite problematic, they can be understood in the context of racial identity development theory as a way of reducing their cognitive dissonance upon learning this new race-related information. As was discussed earlier, withdrawal (accomplished by avoiding contact with people of color and the topic of racism) is another strategy for dealing with the discomfort experienced at this stage. Many of the previously described responses of White students to race-related content are characteristic of the transition from the Contact to the Disintegration stage of development.

Helms (1990) describes another response to the discomfort of Disintegration, which involves attempts to change significant others' attitudes toward African Americans and other people of color. However, as she points out,

> due to the racial naivete with which this approach may be undertaken and the person's ambivalent racial identification, this dissonance-reducing strategy is likely to be met with rejection by Whites as well as Blacks. (p. 59)

In fact, this response is also frequently observed among White students who have an opportunity to talk with friends and family during holiday visits. Suddenly they are noticing the racist content of jokes or comments of their friends and relatives and will try to confront them, often only to find that their efforts are, at best, ignored or dismissed as a "phase," or, at worst, greeted with open hostility.

Carl, a White male previously quoted, wrote at length about this dilemma:

> I realized that it was possible to simply go through life totally oblivious to the entire situation or, even if one realizes it, one can totally repress it. It is easy to fade into the woodwork, run with the rest of society, and never have to deal with these problems. So many people I know from home are like this. They have simply accepted what society has taught them with little, if any, question. My father is a prime example of this. . . . It has caused much friction in our relationship, and he often tells me as a father he has failed in raising me correctly. Most of my high school friends will never deal with these issues and propagate them on to their own children. It's easy to see how the cycle continues. I don't think I could ever justify within myself simply turning my back on the problem. I finally realized that my position in all of these dominant groups gives me power to make change occur. . . . It is an unfortunate result often though that I feel alienated from friends and family. It's often played off as a mere stage that I'm going through. I obviously can't tell if it's merely a stage, but I know that they say this to take the attention off of the truth of what I'm saying. By belittling me, they take the power out of my argument. It's very depressing that being compassionate and considerate are seen as only phases that people go through. I don't want it to be a phase for me, but as obvious as this may sound, I look at my environment and often wonder how it will not be.

The societal pressure to accept the status quo may lead the individual from Disintegration to Reintegration. At this point the desire to be accepted by one's own racial group, in which the overt or covert belief in White superiority is so prevalent, may lead to a reshaping of the person's belief system to be more congruent with an acceptance of racism. The guilt and anxiety associated with Disintegration may be redirected in the form of fear and anger directed toward people of color (particularly Blacks), who are now blamed as the source of discomfort.

Connie, a White woman of Italian ancestry, in many ways exemplified the progression from the Contact stage to Reintegration, a process she herself described seven weeks into the semester. After reading about the stages of White identity development, she wrote:

> I think mostly I can find myself in the disintegration stage of development. . . . There was a time when I never considered myself a color. I never described myself as a "White, Italian female" until I got to college and noticed that people of color always described themselves by their color/race. While taking this class, I have begun to understand that being White makes a difference. I never thought about it before but there are many privileges to being White. In my personal life, I cannot say that I have ever felt that I have had the advantage over a Black person, but I am aware that my race has the advantage.
>
> I am feeling really guilty lately about that. I find myself thinking: "I didn't mean to be White, I really didn't mean it." I am starting to feel angry towards my race for ever using this advantage towards personal gains. But at the same time I resent the minority groups. I mean, it's not our fault that society

has deemed us "superior." I don't feel any better than a Black person. But it really doesn't matter because I am a member of the dominant race. . . . I can't help it . . . and I sometimes get angry and feel like I'm being attacked.

I guess my anger toward a minority group would enter me into the next stage of Reintegration, where I am once again starting to blame the victim. This is all very trying for me and it has been on my mind a lot. I really would like to be able to reach the last stage, autonomy, where I can accept being White without hostility and anger. That is really hard to do.

Helms (1990) suggests that it is relatively easy for Whites to become stuck at the Reintegration stage of development, particularly if avoidance of people of color is possible. However, if there is a catalyst for continued self-examination, the person "begins to question her or his previous definition of Whiteness and the justifiability of racism in any of its forms. . . ." (p. 61). In my experience, continued participation in a course on racism provides the catalyst for this deeper self-examination.

This process was again exemplified by Connie. At the end of the semester, she listened to her own taped interview of her racial attitudes that she had recorded at the beginning of the semester. She wrote:

Oh wow! I could not believe some of the things that I said. I was obviously in different stages of the White identity development. As I listened and got more and more disgusted with myself when I was at the Reintegration stage, I tried to remind myself that these are stages that all (most) White people go through when dealing with notions of racism. I can remember clearly the resentment I had for people of color. I feel the one thing I enjoyed from listening to my interview was noticing how much I have changed. I think I am finally out of the Reintegration stage. I am beginning to make a conscious effort to seek out information about people of color and accept their criticism. . . . I still feel guilty about the feeling I had about people of color and I always feel bad about being privileged as a result of racism. But I am glad that I have reached what I feel is the Pseudo-Independent stage of White identity development.

The information-seeking that Connie describes often marks the onset of the Pseudo-Independent stage. At this stage, the individual is abandoning beliefs in White superiority, but may still behave in ways that unintentionally perpetuate the system. Looking to those targeted by racism to help him or her understand racism, the White person often tries to disavow his or her own Whiteness through active affiliation with Blacks, for example. The individual experiences a sense of alienation from other Whites who have not yet begun to examine their own racism, yet may also experience rejection from Blacks or other people of color who are suspicious of his or her motives. Students of color moving from the Encounter to the Immersion phase of their own racial identity development may be particularly unreceptive to the White person's attempts to connect with them.

Uncomfortable with his or her own Whiteness, yet unable to be truly anything else, the individual may begin searching for a new, more comfortable way to be White. This search is characteristic of the Immersion/Emersion stage of development. Just as the Black student seeks to redefine positively what it means to be of African ancestry in the United States through immersion in accurate information about one's culture and history, the White individual seeks to replace racially related myths and stereotypes with accurate information about what it means and has meant to be White in U.S. society (Helms, 1990). Learning about Whites who have been antiracist allies to people of color is a very important part of this process.

After reading articles written by antiracist activists describing their own process of unlearning racism, White students often comment on how helpful it is to know that others have experienced similar feelings and have found ways to resist the racism in their environments.[5] For example, Joanne, a White woman who initially experienced a lot of guilt, wrote:

This article helped me out in many ways. I've been feeling helpless and frustrated. I know there are all these terrible things going on and I want to be able to do something. . . . Anyway this article helped me realize, again, that others feel this way, and gave me some positive ideas to resolve my dominant class guilt and shame.

Finally, reading the biographies and autobiographies of White individuals who have embarked on a similar process of identity development (such as Barnard, 1987) provides White students with important models for change.

Learning about White antiracists can also provide students of color with a sense of hope that they can have White allies. After hearing a White antiracist activist address the class, Sonia, a Latina who had written about her impatience with expressions of White guilt, wrote:

> I don't know when I have been more impressed by anyone. She filled me with hope for the future. She made me believe that there are good people in the world and that Whites suffer too and want to change things.

For White students, the internalization of a newly defined sense of oneself as White is the primary task of the Autonomy stage. The positive feelings associated with this redefinition energize the person's efforts to confront racism and oppression in his or her daily life. Alliances with people of color can be more easily forged at this stage of development than previously because the person's antiracist behaviors and attitudes will be more consistently expressed. While Autonomy might be described as "racial self-actualization, . . . it is best to think of it as an ongoing process . . . wherein the person is continually open to new information and new ways of thinking about racial and cultural variables" (Helms, 1990, p. 66).

Annette, a White woman, described herself in the Autonomy stage, but talked at length about the circular process she felt she had been engaged in during the semester:

> If people as racist as C. P. Ellis (a former Klansman) can change, I think anyone can change. If that makes me idealistic, fine. I do not think my expecting society to change is naive anymore because I now *know* exactly what I want. To be naive means a lack of knowledge that allows me to accept myself both as a White person and as an idealist. This class showed me that these two are not mutually exclusive but are an integral part of me that I cannot deny. I realize now that through most of this class I was trying to deny both of them.
>
> While I was not accepting society's racism, I was accepting society's telling me as a White person, there was nothing I could do to change racism. So, I told myself I was being naive and tried to suppress my desire to change society. This is what made me so frustrated—while I saw society's racism through examples in the readings and the media, I kept telling myself there was nothing I could do. Listening to my tape, I think I was already in the Autonomy stage when I started this class. I then seemed to decide that being White, I also had to be racist which is when I became frustrated and went back to the Disintegration stage. I was frustrated because I was not only telling myself there was nothing I could do but I also was assuming society's racism was my own which made me feel like I did not want to be White. Actually, it was not being White that I was disavowing but being racist. I think I have now returned to the Autonomy stage and am much more secure in my position there. I accept my Whiteness now as just a part of me as is my idealism. I will no longer disavow these characteristics as I have realized I can be proud of both of them. In turn, I can now truly accept other people for their unique characteristics and not by the labels society has given them as I can accept myself that way.
>
> While I thought the main ideas that I learned in this class were that White people need to be educated to end racism and everyone should be treated as human beings, I really had already incorporated these ideas into my thoughts. What I learned from this class is being White does not mean being racist and being idealistic does not mean being naive. I really did not have to form new ideas about people of color; I had to form them about myself—and I did.

Implications for Classroom Teaching

Although movement through all the stages of racial identity development will not necessarily occur for each student within the course of a semester (or even four years of college), it is certainly common to witness beginning transformations in classes with race-related content. An awareness of the existence of this process has helped me to implement strategies to facilitate positive student development, as well as to improve interracial dialogue within the classroom.

Four strategies for reducing student resistance and promoting student development that I have found useful are the following:

1. the creation of a safe classroom atmosphere by establishing clear guidelines for discussion;
2. the creation of opportunities for self-generated knowledge;

3. the provision of an appropriate developmental model that students can use as a framework for understanding their own process;

4. the exploration of strategies to empower students as change agents.

Creating a Safe Climate

As was discussed earlier, making the classroom a safe space for discussion is essential for overcoming students' fears about breaking the race taboo, and will also reduce later anxieties about exposing one's own internalized racism. Establishing the guidelines of confidentiality, mutual respect, "no zaps," and speaking from one's own experience on the first day of class is a necessary step in the process.

Students respond very positively to these ground rules, and do try to honor them. While the rules do not totally eliminate anxiety, they clearly communicate to students that there is a safety net for the discussion. Students are also encouraged to direct their comments and questions to each other rather than always focusing their attention on me as the instructor, and to learn each other's names rather than referring to each other as "he," "she," or "the person in the red sweater" when responding to each other.[6]

The Power of Self-Generated Knowledge

The creation of opportunities for self-generated knowledge on the part of students is a powerful tool for reducing the initial stage of denial that many students experience. While it may seem easy for some students to challenge the validity of what they read or what the instructor says, it is harder to deny what they have seen with their own eyes. Students can be given hands-on assignments outside of class to facilitate this process.

For example, after reading *Portraits of White Racism* (Wellman, 1977), some students expressed the belief that the attitudes expressed by the White interviewees in the book were no longer commonly held attitudes. Students were then asked to use the same interview protocol used in the book (with some revision) to interview a White adult of their choice. When students reported on these interviews in class, their own observation of the similarity between those they had interviewed and those they had read about was more convincing than anything I might have said.

After doing her interview, Patty, a usually quiet White student, wrote:

> I think I learned a lot from it and that I'm finally getting a better grip on the idea of racism. I think that was why I participated so much in class. I really felt like I knew what I was talking about.

Other examples of creating opportunities for self-generated knowledge include assigning students the task of visiting grocery stores in neighborhoods of differing racial composition to compare the cost and quality of goods and services available at the two locations, and to observe the interactions between the shoppers and the store personnel. For White students, one of the most powerful assignments of this type has been to go apartment hunting with an African-American student and to experience housing discrimination firsthand. While one concern with such an assignment is the effect it will have on the student(s) of color involved, I have found that those Black students who choose this assignment rather than another are typically eager to have their White classmates experience the reality of racism, and thus participate quite willingly in the process.

Naming the Problem

The emotional responses that students have to talking and learning about racism are quite predictable and related to their own racial identity development. Unfortunately, students typically do not know this; thus they consider their own guilt, shame, embarrassment, or anger an uncomfortable experience that they alone are having. Informing students at the beginning of the semester that these feelings may be part of the learning process is ethically necessary (in the sense of informed consent), and helps to normalize the students' experience. Knowing in advance that a desire to withdraw from classroom discussion or not to complete assignments is a common response helps students to remain engaged when they reach that point. As Alice, a White woman, wrote at the end of the semester:

> You were so right in saying in the beginning how we would grow tired of racism (I did in October) but then it would get so good! I have *loved* the class once I passed that point.

In addition, sharing the model of racial identity development with students gives them a useful framework for understanding each other's processes as well as their own. This cognitive framework does not necessarily prevent the collision of developmental processes previously described, but it does allow students to be less frightened by it when it occurs. If, for example, White students understand the stages of racial identity development for students of color, they are less likely to personalize or feel threatened by an African-American student's anger.

Connie, a White student who initially expressed a lot of resentment at the way students of color tended to congregate in the college cafeteria, was much more understanding of this behavior after she learned about racial identity development theory. She wrote:

> I learned a lot from reading the article about the stages of development in the model of oppressed people. As a White person going through my stages of identity development, I do not take time to think about the struggle people of color go through to reach a stage of complete understanding. I am glad that I know about the stages because now I can understand people of color's behavior in certain situations. For example, when people of color stay to themselves and appear to be in a clique, it is not because they are being rude as I originally thought. Rather they are engaged perhaps in the Immersion stage.

Mary, another White student, wrote:

> I found the entire Cross model of racial identity development very enlightening. I knew that there were stages of racial identity development before I entered this class. I did not know what they were, or what they really entailed. After reading through this article I found myself saying, "Oh. That explains why she reacted this way to this incident instead of how she would have a year ago." Clearly this person has entered a different stage and is working through different problems from a new viewpoint. Thankfully, the model provides a degree of hope that people will not always be angry, and will not always be separatists, etc. Although I'm not really sure about that.

Conversely, when students of color understand the stages of White racial identity development, they can be more tolerant or appreciative of a White student's struggle with guilt, for example. After reading about the stages of White identity development, Sonia, a Latina previously quoted, wrote:

> This article was the one that made me feel that my own prejudices were showing. I never knew that Whites went through an identity development of their own.

She later told me outside of class that she found it much easier to listen to some of the things White students said because she could understand their potentially offensive comments as part of a developmental stage.

Sharon, an African-American woman, also found that an understanding of the respective stages of racial identity development helped her to understand some of the interactions she had had with White students since coming to college. She wrote:

> There is a lot of clash that occurs between Black and White people at college which is best explained by their respective stages of development. Unfortunately schools have not helped to alleviate these problems earlier in life.

In a course on the psychology of racism, it is easy to build in the provision of this information as part of the course content. For instructors teaching courses with race-related content in other fields, it may seem less natural to do so. However, the inclusion of articles on racial identity development and/or class discussion of these issues in conjunction with the other strategies that have been suggested can improve student receptivity to the course content in important ways, making it a very useful investment of class time. Because the stages describe kinds of behavior that many people have commonly observed in themselves, as well as in their own intraracial and interracial interactions, my experience has been that most students grasp the basic conceptual framework fairly easily, even if they do not have a background in psychology.

Empowering Students as Change Agents

Heightening students' awareness of racism without also developing an awareness of the possibility of change is a prescription for despair. I consider it unethical to do one without the other. Exploring strategies to empower students as change agents is thus a necessary part of the process of talking about race and learning about racism. As was previously mentioned, students find it very helpful to read about and hear from individuals who have been effective change agents. Newspaper and magazine articles, as well as biographical or autobiographical essays or book excerpts, are often important sources for this information.

I also ask students to work in small groups to develop an action plan of their own for interrupting racism. While I do not consider it appropriate to require students to engage in antiracist activity (since I believe this should be a personal choice the student makes for him/herself), students are required to think about the possibility. Guidelines are provided (see Katz, 1978), and the plans that they develop over several weeks are presented at the end of the semester. Students are generally impressed with each other's good ideas, and, in fact, they often do go on to implement their projects.

Joanne, a White student who initially struggled with feelings of guilt, wrote:

> I thought that hearing others' ideas for action plans was interesting and informative. It really helps me realize (reminds me) the many choices and avenues there are once I decided to be an ally. Not only did I develop my own concrete way to be an ally, I have found many other ways that I, as a college student, can be an active anti-racist. It was really empowering.

Another way all students can be empowered is by offering them the opportunity to consciously observe their own development. The taped exercise to which some of the previously quoted students have referred is an example of one way to provide this opportunity. At the beginning of the semester, students are given an interview guide with many open-ended questions concerning racial attitudes and opinions. They are asked to interview themselves on tape as a way of recording their own ideas for future reference. Though the tapes are collected, students are assured that no one (including me) will listen to them. The tapes are returned near the end of the semester, and students are asked to listen to their own tapes and use their understanding of racial identity development to discuss it in essay form.

The resulting essays are often remarkable and underscore the psychological importance of giving students the chance to examine racial issues in the classroom. The following was written by Elaine, a White woman:

> Another common theme that was apparent in the tape was that, for the most part, I was aware of my own ignorance and was embarrassed because of it. I wanted to know more about the oppression of people in the country so that I could do something about it. Since I have been here, I have begun to be actively resistant to racism. I have been able to confront my grandparents and some old friends from high school when they make racist comments. Taking this psychology of racism class is another step toward active resistance to racism. I am trying to educate myself so that I have a knowledge base to work from.
>
> When the tape was made, I was just beginning to be active and just beginning to be educated. I think I am now starting to move into the redefinition stage. I am starting to feel ok about being White. Some of my guilt is dissipating, and I do not feel as ignorant as I used to be. I think I have an understanding of racism; how it effects [sic] myself, and how it effects this country. Because of this I think I can be more active in doing something about it.

In the words of Louise, a Black female student:

> One of the greatest things I learned from this semester in general is that the world is not only Black and White, nor is the United States. I learned a lot about my own erasure of many American ethnic groups. . . . I am in the (immersion) stage of my identity development. I think I am also dangling a little in the (encounter) stage. I say this because a lot of my energies are still directed toward White people. I began writing a poem two days ago and it was directed to White racism. However, I have also become more Black-identified. I am reaching to the strength in Afro-American heritage. I am learning more about the heritage and history of Afro-American culture. Knowledge = strength and strength = power.

While some students are clearly more self-reflective and articulate about their own process than others, most students experience the opportunity to talk and learn about these issues as a transforming process. In my experience, even those students who are frustrated by aspects of the course find themselves changed by it. One such student wrote in her final journal entry:

> What I felt to be a major hindrance to me was the amount of people. Despite the philosophy, I really never felt at ease enough to speak openly about the feelings I have and kind of watched the class pull farther and farther apart as the semester went on. . . . I think that it was your attitude that kept me intrigued by the topics we were studying despite my frustrations with the class time. I really feel as though I made some significant moves in my understanding of other people's positions in our world as well as of my feelings of racism, and I feel very good about them. I feel like this class has moved me in the right direction. I'm on a roll I think, because I've been introduced to so much.

Facilitating student development in this way is a challenging and complex task, but the results are clearly worth the effort.

Implications for the Institution

What are the institutional implications for an understanding of racial identity development theory beyond the classroom? How can this framework be used to address the pressing issues of increasing diversity and decreasing racial tensions on college campuses? How can providing opportunities in the curriculum to talk about race and learn about racism affect the recruitment and retention of students of color specifically, especially when the majority of the students enrolled are White?

The fact is, educating White students about race and racism changes attitudes in ways that go beyond the classroom boundaries. As White students move through their own stages of identity development, they take their friends with them by engaging them in dialogue. They share the articles they have read with roommates, and involve them in their projects. An example of this involvement can be seen in the following journal entry, written by Larry, a White man:

> Here it is our fifth week of class and more and more I am becoming aware of the racism around me. Our second project made things clearer, because while watching T.V. I picked up many kinds of discrimination and stereotyping. Since the project was over, I still find myself watching these shows and picking up bits and pieces every show I watch. Even my friends will be watching a show and they will say, "Hey, Larry, put that in your paper." Since they know I am taking this class, they are looking out for these things. They are also watching what they say around me for fear that I will use them as an example. For example, one of my friends has this fascination with making fun of Jewish people. Before I would listen to his comments and take them in stride, but now I confront him about his comments.

The heightened awareness of the White students enrolled in the class has a ripple effect in their peer group, which helps to create a climate in which students of color and other targeted groups (Jewish students, for example) might feel more comfortable. It is likely that White students who have had the opportunity to learn about racism in a supportive atmosphere will be better able to be allies to students of color in extracurricular settings, like student government meetings and other organizational settings, where students of color often feel isolated and unheard.

At the same time, students of color who have had the opportunity to examine the ways in which racism may have affected their own lives are able to give voice to their own experience, and to validate it rather than be demoralized by it. An understanding of internalized oppression can help students of color recognize the ways in which they may have unknowingly participated in their own victimization, or the victimization of others. They may be able to move beyond victimization to empowerment, and share their learning with others, as Sharon, a previously quoted Black woman, planned to do.

Campus communities with an understanding of racial identity development could become more supportive of special-interest groups, such as the Black Student Union or the Asian Student Alliance, because they would recognize them not as "separatist" but as important outlets for students of color who may be at the Encounter or Immersion stage of racial identity development. Not only could speakers of color be sought out to add diversity to campus programming, but Whites who had made a commitment to unlearning their own racism could be offered as models to those White students looking for new ways to understand their own Whiteness, and to students of color looking for allies.

It has become painfully clear on many college campuses across the United States that we cannot have successfully multiracial campuses without talking about race and learning about racism. Providing a forum where this discussion can take place safely over a semester, a time period that allows personal and group development to unfold in ways that day-long or weekend programs do not, may be among the most proactive learning opportunities an institution can provide.

Notes

1. A similar point could be made about other issues of oppression, such as anti-Semitism, homophobia and heterosexism, ageism, and so on.
2. While similar models of racial identity development exist, Cross and Helms are referenced here because they are among the most frequently cited writers on Black racial identity development and on White racial identity development, respectively. For a discussion of the commonalities between these and other identity development models, see Phinney (1989, 1990) and Helms (1990).
3. Both Parham (1989) and Phinney (1989) suggest that a preference for the dominant group is not always a characteristic of this stage. For example, children raised in households and communities with explicitly positive Afrocentric attitudes may absorb a pro-Black perspective, which then serves as the starting point for their own exploration of racial identity.
4. After being introduced to this model and Helms's model of White identity development, students are encouraged to think about how the models might apply to their own experience or the experiences of people they know. As is reflected in the cited journal entries, some students resonate to the theories quite readily, easily seeing their own process of growth reflected in them. Other students are sometimes puzzled because they feel as though their own process varies from these models, and may ask if it is possible to "skip" a particular stage, for example. Such questions provide a useful departure point for discussing the limitations of stage theories in general, and the potential variations in experience that make questions of racial identity development so complex.
5. Examples of useful articles include essays by McIntosh (1988), Lester (1987), and Braden (1987). Each of these combines autobiographical material, as well as a conceptual framework for understanding some aspect of racism that students find very helpful. Bowser and Hunt's (1981) edited book, *Impacts of Racism on Whites*, though less autobiographical in nature, is also a valuable resource.
6. Class size has a direct bearing on my ability to create safety in the classroom. Dividing the class into pairs or small groups of five or six students to discuss initial reactions to a particular article or film helps to increase participation, both in the small groups and later in the large group discussions.

References

Barnard, H. F. (Ed.). (1987). *Outside the magic circle: The autobiography of Virginia Foster Durr*. New York: Simon & Schuster. (Originally published in 1985 by University of Alabama Press)

Bowser, B. P., & Hunt, R. G. (1981). *Impacts of racism on whites*. Beverly Hills: Sage.

Braden, A. (1987, April-May). Undoing racism: Lessons for the peace movement. *The Nonviolent Activist*, pp. 3–6.

Bronstein, P. A., & Quina, K. (Eds.). (1988). *Teaching a psychology of people: Resources for gender and sociocultural awareness*. Washington, DC: American Psychological Association.

Cross, W. E., Jr. (1971). The Negro to black conversion experience: Toward a psychology of black liberation. *Black World, 20*(9), 13–27.

Cross, W. E., Jr. (1978). The Cross and Thomas models of psychological nigrescence. *Journal of Black Psychology, 5*(1), 13–19.

Cross, W. E., Jr. (1991). *Shades of black: Diversity in African-American identity*. Philadelphia: Temple University Press.

Cross, W. E., Jr., Parham, T. A., & Helms, J. E. (1991). The stages of black identity development: Nigrescence models. In R. Jones (Ed.), *Black psychology* (3rd ed., pp. 319–338). San Francisco: Cobb and Henry.

Derman-Sparks, L., Higa, C. T., & Sparks, B. (1980). Children, race and racism: How race awareness develops. *Interracial Books for Children Bulletin, 11*(3/4), 3–15.

Helms, J. E. (Ed.). (1990). *Black and white racial identity: Theory, research and practice.* Westport, CT: Greenwood Press.

Highlen, P. S., Reynolds, A. L., Adams, E. M., Hanley, T. C., Myers, L. J., Cox, C., & Speight, S. (1988, August 13). *Self-identity development model of oppressed people: Inclusive model for all?* Paper presented at the American Psychological Association Convention, Atlanta, GA.

Hull, G. T., Scott, P. B., & Smith, B. (Eds.). (1982). *All the women are white, all the blacks are men, but some of us are brave: Black women's studies.* Old Westbury, NY: Feminist Press.

Katz, J. H. (1978). *White awareness: Handbook for anti-racism training.* Norman: University of Oklahoma Press.

Lester, J. (1987). *What happens to the mythmakers when the myths are found to be untrue?* Unpublished paper, Equity Institute, Emeryville, CA.

McIntosh, P. (1988). *White privilege and male privilege: A personal account of coming to see correspondences through work in women's studies.* Working paper, Wellesley College Center for Research on Women, Wellesley, MA.

McIntosh, P. (1989, July/August). White privilege: Unpacking the invisible knapsack. *Peace and Freedom,* pp. 10–12.

Parham, T. A. (1989). Cycles of psychological nigrescence. *The Counseling Psychologist, 17*(2), 187–226.

Phinney, J. (1989). Stages of ethnic identity in minority group adolescents. *Journal of Early Adolescence, 9,* 34–39.

Phinney, J. (1990). Ethnic identity in adolescents and adults: Review of research. *Psychological Bulletin, 108*(3), 499–514.

Phinney, J. S., & Rotheram, M. J. (Eds.). (1987). *Children's ethnic socialization: Pluralism and development.* Newbury Park, CA: Sage.

Schuster, M. R., & Van Dyne, S. R. (Eds.). (1985). *Women's place in the academy: Transforming the liberal arts curriculum.* Totowa, NJ: Rowman & Allanheld.

Wellman, D. (1977). *Portraits of white racism.* New York: Cambridge University Press.

CHAPTER 25
TRANSFORMANDO FRONTERAS: *CHICANA FEMINIST TRANSFORMATIVE PEDAGOGIES*

C. ALEJANDRA ELENES

In this paper, C. Alejandra Elenes proposes ways to implement the goals of border/transformative pedagogies in classroom practices in order to deal with the multiplicity of ideologies present in educational settings. The theorization and discussion presented is based on the sometimes tense relationships between Chicana faculty and White women students. Border/transformative pedagogy incorporates as social practices the construction of knowledge(s) capable of analyzing conflicts over meaning. This pedagogy is concerned with the elimination of racial, gender, class, and sexual orientation hierarchies by decentralizing hegemonic practices that places at the center of cultural practices a homogeneous belief in US society that has marginalized the cultural practices of people of color, women, and gays and lesbians. Thus, it can be viewed as liberatory by students who agree with those goals, and oppressive for students with more conservative leanings. Based on Gloria Anzaldúa's conceptualization of mestiza consciousness, border/transformative pedagogies propose ways in which we can enact a practice where students and teachers participate, and that tries to undo dualistic thinking. Thus, this paper, which is based on classroom observations and analysis of student evaluations, is self-reflexive. Particular emphasis is placed on finding ways to be able to bring multiple ideologies and points of view to classroom discussion in ways that productive discourse is enabled. The discussion also centers on the contradictions present in classrooms that seek to be liberatory to the goals of democracy. Finally, the paper discusses ways in which women of color faculty can deal with racism existing in many contemporary educational settings.

Introduction

My vision of education and teaching centers on social justice and constructing counternarratives that offer alternatives to contemporary hegemonic discourses of race, class, gender, and sexuality. My efforts are to open educational spaces where multicultural democracy can be enacted. This philosophy can be described as a multicultural liberal arts perspective that is more concerned with constructing knowledge and critical thinking than with so-called "pragmatic" and/or vocational education. I also claim to engage in a democratic practice "where everyone feels a responsibility to contribute" (hooks, 1994, p. 39). However, at times my educational views and practices bring me at odds with my educational philosophy, given that I have many students who view their education in very different ways. Not only do many undergraduates believe in their education as technical and pragmatic, i.e., as a means to get a better-paid job, but also several students do not see the need for, or do not agree politically with, multicultural education.[1] Thus, much of my discussion here focuses on the tensions between Chicana faculty and students in terms of the problems that multiple subjectivity/positionality brings to pedagogical discussions when efforts to democratize education might seem to be more autocratic than democratic. There is a paradoxical position entailed in having the goal of teaching for change and transformation when students are not interested in such changes or presume that teachers are the conduits for students' consciousness (Ellsworth, 1989; Lather, 1991; Gore, 1993).

This paper examines observations of my classroom dynamics and students' comments—in class and on teacher evaluations. As such, much of my discussion here is self-reflexive. I am basing most of my comments on a "Race, Class and Gender" course that I teach in a Women's Studies Department. I teach this course at an upper division campus that forms part of a three-campus "geographically distributed" university. The majority of students are returning adults, and most of them are female. Indeed a considerable number of the women's studies students are women in their 40s and 50s who interrupted their educational paths for a variety of reasons including marriage and family responsibilities. There are a few students who decided to return to college to start new careers.

Demographically most of the women's studies students share similar characteristics: They are white, female, lower middle and working class, single parents, and heterosexual. Chicana, African-American, and Native American students are also mostly single mothers, of working-class origin and the first generation attending college. Most self-identified lesbians are women of color. Nevertheless, even the White students who share many demographic characteristics differ in significant ways: in their political ideologies (i.e., outlook of national politics and party affiliation), the ways in which they understand how gender is constructed and women's position in society, and in feminist politics. For example, currently most of the White students in my classes have difficulty dealing with race and/or have clearly articulated conservative ideologies. This, unfortunately, has created a division among Whites and students of color as well as faculty of color.[2]

"Race, Class, and Gender"[3] forms part of the core courses that every women's studies major, minor, and certificate must take. (It is also cross-listed with sociology and social and behavioral studies). Unlike its development in women's studies programs developed in the 1970s and 1980s, this course has been part of the core since the inception of the department. This is due in part to the relative youth of the program and the university, given that the major was approved in the early 1990s. But, more importantly, it is part of the core because it is consistent with the philosophy of the department. "Race, Class and Gender" is not the only course that addresses race, class, gender, and sexuality issues, nor the only one that has a focus on women of color. For example, the introductory course "Women in Contemporary Society" also analyzes the aforementioned intersections. In order not to duplicate the efforts from "Women in Contemporary Society" but to build on the foundations it offers, I redesigned "Race, Class and Gender" following a cultural studies perspective. It is an interdisciplinary course that analyzes how culture in the US has been transformed as a result of the feminist, civil rights, and gay and lesbian movements. We approach this by combining history, sociology, literature, cultural studies, education, and anthropological perspectives. However, because of the history of exclusionary practices in women's studies, the course focuses on four groupings of women of color: African-American, Asian-American, Latinas, and Native American. The main "textbooks" and readings reflect this. Included in the readings are theories of racial formation and the social construction of whiteness; the tensions between predominantly white feminist theory and that developed by women of color; and critiques of male-centric class theories. The class format includes whole-and small-group discussion, lecture, and extensive use of videos. In order to provide context to understand the significance of the intersection of race, class, and gender, I provide a historical overview of people of color in the US.

The pedagogical issues I discuss in this paper deal with the ways in which border/transformative pedagogy can be implemented in order to find ways to deal with the multiplicity of ideologies present in the classroom, such that democratic practices can be enacted. Additionally, my theorization and discussion is based on the sometimes tense relationship between Chicana faculty and White women students.

Border/Transformative Pedagogy

Most of my research and thinking on pedagogy has looked at Chicana/o cultural productions as part of those narratives that offer an alternative to the official (educational and/or social) scripts for Chicanas/os (Elenes, 1999). I have named these practices border/transformative pedagogies, which "can draw from Chicana/o aesthetic experiences that deconstruct the notion of a unified subject and essentialist notions of culture" (Elenes, 1997, p. 373). Border/transformative pedagogies involve cultural politics that incorporate as social practices the construction of knowledge(s) capable of analyzing conflicts over meanings. As such they offer a cultural critique of material conditions of subaltern communities that invoke politics of change to transform society in order to become truly democratic. I claim these pedagogical practices as border or borderlands because they blur many distinctions artificially created in cultural productions and classroom practices: mainly the incorporation of the everyday cultural practices as a source for the construction of knowledge outside the officially sanctioned space for such a creation, as well as transcending disciplinary boundaries. Border/transformative pedagogy is also concerned with the elimination of racial, gender, class, and sexual orientation hierarchies by decentralizing hegemonic practices that place at the center of cultural practices a homogenous belief in US society that has marginalized the cultural practices of people of color, women, and gays and lesbians. The "Border" part of the term refers to the multiple boundaries along race, class, gender, sexuality, and age differences that have been built by dominant hierarchical discourses, and efforts to resist these forms of domination. It refers, as well, to oppositional politics that try to alter existing power relations. Thus, it is a transformative practice that seeks to change the conditions that limit and undervalue marginalized identities and cultures. It offers an alternative vision of society, culture, and education. As a discourse, then, it can be viewed as oppressive for those students who do not want to be "liberated" or do not see any reason for liberal or progressive politics, and seen as liberatory by those students who engage in progressive and/or leftist politics.

For the most part, my theorization of border/transformative pedagogy centers around the struggles of the Chicana/o community, particularly material conditions that keep Chicanas working in the fields, garment industry, and service sector, as well as the limited educational opportunities they encounter in US society. Border/transformative pedagogy also connects the limitations of social mobility of Chicanas with essentialist definitions of Chicana/o identity. As part of borderlands discourses it engages in a discussion of the social conditions of subjects with hybrid identities (Elenes, 1997). A particular characteristic of borderlands discourse is that it refutes dualistic, essentialist, and oversimplified thinking. Chicana/o border pedagogy seeks to construct theoretical and political movements based on an understanding of a multiplicity of constructions of identity markers, dominant ideologies, and modes of resistance. That is, it refuses to work with neat dualistic axes of domination and resistance where dominant and dominated are always already clearly identified (Elenes, 1997). In my early theoretical discussions I proposed that in order to accomplish this it is necessary to take into consideration the many discontinuities within Chicana/o subjectivity (see Elenes, 1997). Given that one of the goals of border/transformative pedagogy is to undo dualistic thinking, it is necessary to understand that all identities must be viewed as flexible. That is, students and teachers cannot be viewed in monolithic terms.

Mestiza Consciousness: Epistemology and Pedagogy

The pedagogical issues and problems that I am raising here come from my experiences as a woman of color teaching counternarratives to predominantly white and/or conservative students. I have been very cognizant from the beginning of my academic career that the way students and colleagues perceived me was based on my race, class, gender, and sexuality. I am *mexicana*/Chicana. I was born and raised in Mexico in a bilingual/bicultural home. My father is Mexican and my mother Anglo-German. I have always traveled and transversed borders. After a short time in the US, and as I became involved with the Chicana/o community, I soon understood the struggle of people of Latin American descent and embraced the Chicana/o movement for liberation. I have, thus, identified myself as a *Chicana*[4] as a result of my politics, not from the experience of growing up Mexican American in the US. Like many other Chicanas, I bring this cultural and political perspective into my teaching.

My coming into Chicana/o politics is an engagement in what Gloria Anzaldúa (1987) call *mestiza consciousness*. Anzaldúa opened up the way in which Chicano identity was constructed by the Chicano movement: from a static definition to one that is characterized by plurality and flexibility. Specifically, Anzaldúa proposed that we could not speak of Chicana/o liberation when we continued to reproduce forms of oppression such as racism (negating the Indian and African), sexism, classism, and homophobia. Anzaldúa, then, proposed a politics of liberation that moved beyond nationalistic discourses based on dialectical oppositions between oppressors and oppressed.

As such Anzaldúa's project, because it is grounded in the material conditions of Chicanas/os, forms part of a Chicana feminist epistemology. It is constructed by experiences of exploitation and marginalization, and analysis of such unequal social positioning. Chéla Sandoval (1991) calls it "oppositional consciousness," which, like Anzaldúa's project, is based on a flexible model. Mestiza consciousness refers to the ability of an individual subject to understand her position in a world that undervalues subaltern communities and how she uses this knowledge to transform society. It is an ability to construct "theories" from personal experience.

Sandoval (1998) proposes that "mestizaje as method" is a set of principles based on *la facultad*. For Gloria Anzaldúa *la facultad* is the "capacity to see in surface phenomena the meaning of deeper realities, to see the deep structure below the surface" (p. 38). It is an ability of seeing or understanding developed by those in the margins. It is a survival tactic, a vision, developed from "below" based on experiences of oppression. However, this is not a static form of consciousness, or even a construction of a Truth. Rather, as Sandoval proposes, mestizaje as method requires:

> . . . differential movement through, over, and within any dominant system of resistance, identity, race, gender, sex, class, or national meanings: The differential strategy is directed, but it is also a "diasporic/immigration" in consciousness and politics enacted to ensure that ethical commitment to egalitarian social relations enters into the everyday, political sphere of culture. (p. 360)

As Dolores Delgado Bernal (this issue) asserts, Chicana feminist pedagogy is partially shaped by Chicana/o cultural practices manifested in *corridos*, storytelling, and behavior. Moreover, we can extend Delgado Bernal's (1998) contention that there is a connection between a researcher's methods and his/her epistemological standpoint to pedagogy as well. Although it is not always clearly articulated (or perhaps even conscious), pedagogical orientation and epistemology are also connected. What texts will be used, classroom dynamics, content of the course, assignments, and methods of evaluation are all connected with the teacher's own epistemology and ontology. Indeed, the teacher, not the students, sets the political perspectives that are "valued" in the classroom.[5]

Moving to the Same Side of the River

Gloria Anzaldúa's (1987) conceptualization of *mestiza consciousness* seeks to undo dualistic thinking in a variety of discursive practices such as identity formation, and feminist and ethnic/racial oppositional movements. This line of thought, then, includes social and political transformation. Thus she proposes that in order to transform existing unequal social relations it is necessary for all parties to participate in this new form of consciousness, exemplified when she proposes that "it is not enough to stand on the opposite river bank, shouting questions, challenging patriarchal white conventions. A counterstance locks one into a duel of oppressor and oppressed; locked in mortal combat, like the cop and the criminal, both are reduced to a common denominator of violence" (p. 78). My pedagogical efforts are to try to get us all to the "same side of the river" or, at least, to agree that there is a river (e.g., racism, discrimination, double standards, etc.).

Most of us have a tendency to fall back into the "comfortable" territory where the world gets divided into an "us" vs. "them": teacher/student, male/female, white/nonwhite. Sometimes we do this because we do not have, or cannot find, another language by which to express our feelings and thoughts; other times because we work on preconceived perceptions of who we are according to social position. Whatever the reasons for our slippage, I find myself constantly engaged in a process where first I must continuously be self-reflective of my own participation in dualistic thinking. And students do point it out. As one student wrote[6] in a course evaluation, "I felt there was no balance in the presentations. I took the course to learn about the issues, but I felt that opposing viewpoints could not be articulated." In a similar vein, another student pointed out "I think there should be more articulation of other viewpoints which would enrichen [*sic*] everyone's experience." Given such comments, I keep working to find ways in which we can learn to communicate in the classroom, where we can find a "common language" through which multiple and even contradictory discourses can be discussed, respected, and understood. I do this with the acknowledgement that oftentimes, even a mere articulation of different points of view is perceived by students as not being able to express their opinions. If we are to move to the "same side of river" we[7] must constantly negotiate the tensions that emerge in the classroom as a result of the multiplicity of identities and ideologies present.

Working with Multiple Ideologies and Opinions

There are two pedagogical problems here: (1) the recognition that there are multiple perspectives present in the classroom; (2) some of these perspectives can reproduce forms of oppression. That is, while a democratic classroom is one where all perspectives are welcome, a course that studies the effects of race, class, gender, and sexuality oppression recognizes that there are ideologies that are oppressive. Thus, taking a liberal stance that accepts all discourse as equal might leave racism, sexism, classism, and homophobia unchallenged. A simplistic answer to this problem is to accept all viewpoints. However, that is at odds with the goals of progressive and transformative pedagogy. There are opinions and discourses that are hurtful and that aim at maintaining social inequalities. White supremacist ideologies and the acceptance of rape for example are harmful. Thus, they cannot be presented in the classroom as just one of many ideas present within a discursive field; these are ideologies that must be challenged in order to create a democratic society. But there are other issues at stake as well. Not only are there discourses that should not be acceptable within a classroom; it is also important to learn to distinguish between discourse and opinion. Often, students bring to classroom discussion ideas that they have based on their personal opinions, which are not necessarily based on any type of knowledge or even a coherent set of well thought out arguments. These ideas can range from their own popular culture beliefs to mimicking dominant ideology.[8]

I have found that the best way to avoid dualistic or "commonsensical" thinking is by moving the discussion outside the ideological realm to a philosophical standpoint. By outside the ideological realm what I mean is to elevate the conversation from personal opinion based on "common sense" logic to a discussion of the philosophical principles involved in certain ideologies. In this sense, I am taking an Althusserian understanding of ideology when he proposes that the developmental principle motor of an ideology is found outside the particular ideology: "its author as a concrete individual and the actual history reflected in this individual development according to the complex ties between the individual and this history" (Althusser, 1970, p. 63). And, as Eagleton (1991) proposes, for Althusser ideology "is a particular organization of signifying practices which goes to constitute human beings as social subjects, and which produces the lived relations by which such subjects are connected to the dominant relations of production in a society" (p. 18). Ideologies, perspectives, and opinions are based, in part, on an individual's own history. While it is important to encourage students to use their own personal experience to understand and make sense of the world, students should not stay within the narrow confines of experience. A goal of transformative pedagogy is to enable students to expand their horizons. Although I do not necessarily agree that ideology refers exclusively to the ideas of dominant groups in a society, I do find that in my classroom practices many students accept dominant ideologies as basic commonsensical Truths. We cannot avoid the mystifying power of certain ideologies. One of the efforts of transformative pedagogy is to enable students to demystify their own ideologies, whether on the left or the right.

Therefore, more than rejecting ideology per se, what I propose is to use a philosophical approach to analyze and critique beliefs, to get to know how they are conceptualized and formulated. I, then, distinguish ideology from philosophy in that the latter offers a process of reflection and understanding of where certain ideologies and opinions come from. My intentions are not to avoid ideological discussions, or for students not to express their own opinion. Rather, what I seek for in a democratic classroom is for all (this includes myself) to be cognizant of where our ideas and opinions come from. How is it that we know and understand how we are formulating our opinions? How do we arrive at certain conceptualizations of the world? Through this process of self-scrutiny we avoid simply speaking from an unfounded point of view. For example, when we discuss Welfare policies I try to extend the definition and purpose of Welfare and taxation. As an alternative to the arguments about who is deserving of government subsidies, the discussion moves to the purpose of distribution of resources and how a society might decide who receives such benefits. Instead of only discussing the issues regarding whether welfare families deserve their grants or not, I try to move the discussion to a philosophical discussion of the role of the Welfare State and government.

A key aspect of this pedagogy is to avoid trying to convince people to change their minds (although it would be nice!). Rather, what "moving to the same side of the river" means is to elevate the discussion to a "common language" of the philosophical arguments on any particular issue. I do not mean to find a common ground of agreement and consensus. Rather what I seek to do is to learn how to communicate our own position by being able to name what this position might be. The purpose of this is to dilute any notion that there is one exclusive Truth, denaturalizing the hegemony of dominant discourses. In order to avoid the dualistic counterstances, it is necessary to learn to understand and respect the adversary (Nadesan & Elenes, 1998). For example, White female students often complain about minority students receiving scholarships based on race. More often than not, the complaint centers on the unfairness of having scholarships based on group characteristics (i.e., race) and not on "merit." I have pointed out to some of the complaining students that there are scholarships for women and then asked them if they are willing to apply to those. Usually they say yes. I point out that scholarships for women also fall under the category of group characteristic, and if indeed they do not philosophically believe in such programs they should not apply. After all, there are men who are needy and excluded from those scholarships. My efforts here are to point to inconsistencies in arguments based more on exclusionary practices than philosophical standpoints. By naming our opinions, and knowing that there are other viewpoints, we can learn to discuss the philosophies at an abstract and not a personal level. And this can lead us to the same side of the river.

Aren't We All Women? Racism in Women's Studies

In this section, I want to discuss how the concept of mestiza consciousness can serve as a framework to negotiate and survive oppressive formations that we encounter in classrooms, especially within a conservative climate within the US that is trying to deny the significance of race, class, gender, and sexuality in the formation of identities of students and teachers. Particularly, I am addressing the problematics that Chicana and other women of color encounter when dealing with racism in the classroom. The frustrations that we are encountering in college classrooms are the result of a multitude of contradictory discourses and ideologies that push us all in opposite directions. Classroom dynamics have become a contortionist battleground where all these different ideologies try to get center stage, or at least, claim its ground. I start with two similar quotes from students in course evaluations.

> To paraphrase Sojourner Truth: "Ain't I a color, too?"
>
> I guess not, at least not according to the Women's Studies department. . . . Since I am neither Black nor Asian, Hispanic nor Native American, I don't count. Because I am white, euro-american woman, my history, my culture, my art and literature don't rate attention in the course called "Race, Class and Gender."
>
> . . . "Race, Class, and Gender" is described in the syllabus as addressing "the intersections of race, ethnicity, class, gender, sexual orientation, age et cetera in the lives of women of color in the US." Well, excuse me, but don't white euro-american women (who probably don't rate capital letters like Hispanics and Blacks) have race and gender? Aren't there poor white euro-american women, and aren't they oppressed by classism as poor Blacks and Asians are, even if not in exactly the same way? Aren't white euro-american lesbians discriminated against? Doesn't ageism affect all women, of all colors, all ethnicities, all classes, in one way or another?
>
> I honestly thought that when I enrolled in this course, I'd be in an environment where educated, enlightened women and men would be practicing a higher level of egalitarianism than in the general population. Instead, I've found what I can only call reverse discrimination. (Adeline[9])

> [the instructor] appears to give a BIASED point of view. There was a lot of putting down anglo/white [sic] people. All semester this happened. Not all whites treat people bad. I'm tired of reading about "LATINOS". . . . (emphasis in the original) (Anonymous student)

Adeline's and the anonymous student's words are paradigmatic of the tensions that exist in women's studies between Whites and women of color. If anything, as soon as women of color become professors engaged in area studies (i.e., ethnic and women's studies) and/or challenge existing theoretical and methodological paradigms in traditional disciplines they have expressed the difficulties of doing their job in a system that continues to be racist, sexist, classist, and homophobic (hooks, 1994; Ng, 1997; Reyes, 1997; Sandoval, 1990; Utall, 1990; Williams, 1991). Even at the beginning of the new millennium, the subject of women's studies and feminism is still contested. For years the tensions among whites and feminists of color have centered on issues of race, exclusionary practices, and the tendency to generalize the experience of white middle-class women as normative. The appropriation of the rubric "woman" by white feminists, according to Chicana feminist theorist Norma Alarcón (1990b) "leaves many a woman in this country having to call herself otherwise, i.e., 'woman of color', which is equally 'meaningless' without further specification" (p. 362). Indeed, more than a hundred years after Sojourner Truth dared to claim the subject position "woman" by rhetorically asking, "Ain't I a Woman?" the tendency to monopolize "woman" as white is still operating within feminist circles. While women's studies has struggled to ease the tensions occasioned by such appropriation, the problematic is still present in many college classrooms, creating a pedagogical dilemma that needs to be addressed. This is particularly the case in classrooms where discussions of multiple markers of difference (i.e., race, class, gender, and sexual orientation) are central. There are still many feminists who are continuing to enact the theoretical position that views women's oppression exclusively through the axis of gender. This position, additionally, looks at oppressive formation in static terms. That is, it does not accept that we can all move from a position of oppressed to oppressor. Thus these women find it difficult to deal with racism and homophobia within feminist circles.

Additionally, as faculty of color are entering women's studies as "full citizens," there is a new form of racism that is emerging. A new "logic" has emerged that argues that exclusionary practices are coming from women of color's insistence on rethinking the narrow confines of the subject of feminism. What is happening in my classrooms (as in many other women's studies classrooms) is that the mere mention of race and racism is seen as racist discourse. In this rearticulation of the meaning of racism, the perception is that women of color and lesbians are not marginalized anymore. When the struggles to deal with differences among women are seen as "reverse racism," feminists are situating themselves within a neo-conservative discourse of color blindness. To me, this represents a desire to return to a time and place where White women were the central subject of feminism and women's studies, as well as the universalization of their experiences to all women. Adeline's words, an ironic appropriation of Truth, represent the efforts to return women's studies where White women would take central space. For her and Anonymous a curriculum that centralized race, class, and gender, and one that presents a global perspective, is problematic because White/Euro-American women must share that central stage with Other women. Women's studies curriculums in general, and "Race, Class and Gender" in particular, are not marginalizing White women, but are decentralizing the hegemony and universalization of Whiteness. If Women's Studies continued to tokenize only women of color, these tensions would not exist.

Adeline and Anonymous's words are troubling because they take a dialectical oppositional stand where discussions of racial differences can only occur as mutually exclusive. That is, for both Adeline and Anonymous any of the discussions we had in "Race, Class and Gender" meant that the experiences of Euro-American or White women were erased. Consciously or unconsciously both students are invoking neoconservatism and the universalization and normativity of Whiteness. There is an odd logic at play here when studying one group means the erasure of another. It is one thing to generalize from one's own experience and another to scrutinize how multiple markers of oppression affect one's social position. Naming one's position in the world is not the same as erasing others' existence. Instead of making connections between multiple and interlocking systems of oppression and privilege where these students could have explored their own subject position within the social order, they could see only "reverse racism."

These positions are not new as there is plenty of evidence that many faculty of color get similar statements in their evaluations (e.g., Nieto, 1998; Ng, 1997; Reyes, 1997).[10] And, although no doubt racism is behind the students' view, I want to discuss ways in which we can deal with this polarization. Gloria Romero's (1991) point that "Race, class and gender—when intertwined—do not necessarily make for pleasant polite discourse, and [the] need to allow for that" (p. 215) is a starting point for discussion. These tensions have surfaced when the normative space of women's studies is altered. Although an integral component of the course is to study the social construction of whiteness, it is not always possible in one semester for students to self-reflect on many years of conditioning. I do not advocate "giving in" to these views but I do think that it is important to think about how we can construct communication practices that lead toward the dismantling of the "us" versus "them" mentality and the ensuing racism that is enacted. We are asking students to become border crossers when they are not ready, willing, and able. Although we need to continue pushing toward that goal, we do need to take into account that crossing those borders might take more than a semester.

Relational Theory of Difference

The main strategy I have started to implement is to be much clearer on how race, class, and gender theories have advanced in the last years. We read Patricia Hill Collins's (1998) book *Fighting Words,* where she discusses how the emerging paradigm of intersectionality of race, class, and gender "problematizes [the] entire process of group construction. As a heuristic devise, intersectionality references the ability of social phenomena such as race, class, and gender to mutually construct one another" (p. 205). That is, recent theoretical discussion has advanced the understanding of race, class, and gender as interlocking systems of oppression and privilege.

In order to adequately account for multiple subject positions encountered in contemporary classrooms a relational theory of difference is necessary (Yarbro-Bejarano, 1999). According to Yvonne Yarbro-Bejarano, a relational theory of difference examines "the formation of identity in the dynamic interpenetration of gender, race, sexuality, class and nation" (p. 340). Quoting Stuart Hall, Yarbro-Bejarano argues that this theory is similar to new conceptualizations of ethnicity in cultural studies that incorporate "recognition of the extraordinary diversity of subject position" (pp. 340–341). By not accepting a construction of identity based on only one social category, Yarbro-Bejarano demonstrates that "no representation of sexuality or desire is free of racialization (even in the absence of people of colour)" (p. 341). Yet this is a position that is still not accepted in women's studies and by some feminist theorists, and is exemplified in Yarbro-Bejarano's critique of Theresa de Lauretis and Judith Butler's "articulated position against the relational paradigm" (p. 341). Adeline's words are also a manifestation of the reluctance of many women to see their oppression in more than the axis of gender.

This reconceptualization helps understand better the similarities and differences among women. For example, I continue to use Angela Davis's (1981) essay "Racism, Birth Control and Reproductive Rights" to study reproductive rights and women of color. Although the article is almost 20 years old, the issues Davis presents are still pertinent. In class we update the essay to contemporary reproductive technologies. I used to start class discussion by lecturing on Malthusian and Eugenics ideologies and how they have influenced reproductive rights policies in the US. I changed my approach to discuss how these policies have affected all women, not only women of color. The limitations on reproductive choices for women of color have also resulted in curtailing White middle class women's personal decisions. Our discussion centered on how defining people of color as inferior (and thus the need to limit their ability to have children) also affects White women in that society has decided it is they who should have children. Soon White women were talking about their experiences of how their reproductive choices had been limited by racism. This time the conversation was one of solidarity, and not in any polarizing way. This way our classroom discussion centered more on the issues rather than on feelings of exclusion and alienation. I did not change classroom practices in order to appease racist attitudes; rather, my intention was to avoid as much as possible any type of polarization that results in reproduced racist hierarchical practices. White women were able to see that what seemed to be someone else's problem was indeed theirs as well. And, if all women were to be able to make their own reproductive choices we all needed to know the history of birth control in the US and that we all needed to work together to improve the limited choices that all women have right now.

Multiple Identities

Part of the understanding of different points of view is to recognize how identities are constructed and constituted through multiple markers of difference. As Connolly (1991) reminds us, "identity and difference are bound together. It may be impossible to reconstitute the relation to the second without confounding the experience of the first" (p. 44). In learning how to communicate across differences, I bring to the classroom texts that address the complexities and contradictions of identity. Two particular videos I show in class, Marlon Riggs's *Black Is . . . Black Ain't* and Pratibha Parmar's *A Place of Rage,* and Chandra Talpade Mohanty's (1997) essay "Defining genealogies: Feminist reflections on being South Asian in North America" are used as illustrations of the complexity of identity formations. As we work out how to communicate across our differences, the videos serve as a place by which to explore the meanings of multiple identities. In this sense, *Black Is . . . Black Ain't* and Mohanty's essay are helpful because they both delve into the ways in which identity is constructed by social forces not always of our own making. Marlon Riggs explores the way in which African-Americans have been historically stereotyped in the US. But he argues that essentialists' definitions of blackness imposed by African-Americans are equally devastating, especially for gays and lesbians, and feminists.

A Place of Rage also provides excellent examples of the problematic of narrow definition of identity. This video accomplished this by making connections with other forms of oppression, and exploring a range of African-American women's feminist interventions in contemporary social issues such as women in prisons, police brutality, nationalism, drug abuse, and domestic violence.

In order to not leave this conceptualization of identity at a theoretical level, we discuss two different readings that deal with how these constructions of identity affect the everyday lives of women of color. Lisa Lowe's (1997) essay "Work, immigration, gender and Asian 'American' women" discusses identity formation among Asian immigrant garment workers in California. Mónica Russel y Rodríguez (1997) article "(En)Countering domestic violence, complicity, and definitions of Chicana womanhood" offers an anthropological reading, via Chicana cultural studies theories, of definitions of womanhood and domestic violence. Interestingly, during a summer session a student pointed out that the underlying theme of most of the videos previewed in class was identity formation.

Conclusion

I conclude this paper with another anecdote—this time a positive one. During one of the few gay and lesbian rallies on my campus, a White gay former student of mine spoke of how a women's studies course he had taken had helped him open his eyes and make connections between different forms of oppression. I was surprised by his words because during the semester he had struggled with the feminist content of the course. This story is a reminder that whatever it is that we do in the classroom can impact students beyond the semester they are in our classes. It took this particular student more than a semester to make the connection I was struggling to make but the point is that eventually he did.

In this paper, I have presented ways in which pedagogical practices can change in order to accommodate the multiplicity of ideologies present in a classroom. Most of my discussion centered on the relationship between Chicana faculty and White women, and the tensions that these relationships present for feminist pedagogies. Even though I strongly believe and acknowledge that racism is what creates these tensions, in my experience it is more productive to look at how certain philosophical positions let us out of the impasse that racism presents rather than dwell on it. As Gloria Anzaldúa (1990) reminded us, "to call a text or a methodology under discussion in a classroom or conference 'racist', or to call a white person on her or his Racism, is to let loose a stink bomb" (p. xix). My experience in the classroom and in political organizing has been that whenever I confront racism head on, the changes I have been looking for do not occur. On the contrary, we hit a dead-end. We need to find ways to make this recognition not less painful but more productive. Similarly, Grossberg (1997) proposes that cultural studies does not say or start its analysis on what we already know. As I have demonstrated in this paper, there is plenty of evidence of racism in the classroom. The point, then, is to look at ways in which we can name that racism and its practices without throwing the "stink bomb" that limits any form of productive discourse. My strategy has been to move the discussion from the merits (or lack) of any particular issue to an analysis of how certain philosophies are implicit in the creation of forms of oppression.

Much of the problem we have in contemporary classroom discussion is that students enter classrooms with their minds made up about what feminism is, or what perspectives are expected of them in ethnic studies. Most of us also work on preconceived notions of how certain people act (i.e., feminists), and how they will deal with those who are different from them. It is our job as teachers who are preparing a workforce to deal with a diverse environment to enable students to learn to be self-reflexive of their own ideologies, preconceived notions, and stereotypes. This is not an easy task. If we all learn how to be flexible, to name our own ideologies, and to question the assumptions we take for granted, we might move into a more democratic society. However, one course cannot do this by itself. Colleges and universities need to take this as a holistic approach in the teaching of diversity and critical-thinking skills. And most especially, this task cannot be the exclusive or main responsibility of faculty of color.

Gloria Anzaldúa's mestiza consciousness can help us all—Chicanas/os and nonChicanas/os—learn to deal with differences in a productive way. Her conceptualization and my notions of border/transformative pedagogy are not intended to reproduce forms of oppression, or to sanitize classroom practices. On the contrary, this methodology offers ways in which we can all bring our different, contradictory, and oppositional points of view for discussion. In contemporary classroom settings, we need to learn to present our views in ways that do not personally attack those who might disagree with us. A democratic society is one where everybody believes that they can contribute to discourse; the same applies in a classroom setting.

Notes

An earlier version of this paper was presented at the American Educational Research Association, New Orleans, LA April 25, 2000. Under draft form no portion of this paper can be quoted without the written permission of the author.

1. I must point out that I do not believe that multicultural and pragmatic education are at odds with each other. Rather, I think this is a false dichotomy. Moreover, there is enough evidence that competences in dealing with diverse populations are skills that many employers are looking for.

2. I want to point out that these differences have not always plagued the program. Indeed, during my tenure in this department most White students have embraced antiracist and antihomophobic struggles.

3. Although the course is titled "Race, Class and Gender" I have always added sexuality to the three dynamics. I am not sure why sexuality is not included in the name. Perhaps it is a reflection of the internalized homophobia that still plagues many Women's Studies Departments, including my own. Or it could be the result of living in such a conservative state as Arizona. After all, in the last year women elected officials moved to close Women's Studies Departments in the whole state because we are teaching lesbianism. And, last fall, one legislator proposed to change the name to Lesbian Studies so there was truth in advertising not knowing that such field of study exists.

4. The term and identification Chicana has come to be associated with a political self-identification. As Norma Alarcón (1990a) claims, "the name Chicana, in the present, is the name of resistance that enables cultural and political points of departure and thinking through the multiple migrations and dislocations of women of 'Mexican' descent. The name Chicana is not a name that women (or men) are born to or with, as is often the case with 'Mexican', but rather it is consciously and critically assumed . . ."(p. 250). Moreover, Francisca González (this issue) proposes that Chicana is "a political ethnic term referring to Mexican American, Central American and South American women residing in the US who share indigenous ancestry, memory, culture, and are conscious of patriarchy, colonization, and racialized-political structural realities" (fn. 1).

5. For example, when I teach, even though I tell students that all viewpoints are welcome to the discussion, this is not always the case. (And students do point this up in class discussion and through the evaluations.) There are several topics that bring this to light, such as immigration. When discussing immigration issues, the perspective that is "valued" or hegemonic in the classroom is pro-immigrant. Students find it difficult to articulate conservative standpoints. It is not impossible for students to express different points of view from mine. Indeed, many students have been able to bring their viewpoints to classroom discussion and to write papers and get good grades.

6. I decided not to assign pseudonyms to students' course evaluations because these are anonymous. I don't even know the gender of students whose statements I am quoting in this paper. That is why I use the vague terminology "student".

7 By "we" I mean the students and myself.

8. This is another contradictory point. *Mestiza consciousness* is constructed, in part, by the experiences of Chicana women and it could be argued that it is an ideological position. I do not want to argue that students should not bring their own experience to the classroom, or their ideological beliefs. What I am proposing is to be cognizant of the philosophical foundations of a particular way of thinking, and argue from a perspective that is based on some fundamental knowledge. That is, to move away from "this is the ways things are or ought to be" to "this is how I suggest things can be, and why."

9. Because this student identified her gender, I gave her a pseudonym.

10. Additionally, when I presented an earlier version of this paper at the American Educational Research Association conference in New Orleans, April 25, 2000, many audience members nodded their heads as I gave these examples. Several people shared similar experiences during the question-and-answer period.

References

Alarcón, N. (1990a). Chicana feminism: In the tracks of "the" Native woman. *Cultural Studies, 4,* 248–256.

Alarcón, N. (1990b). The theoretical subject(s) of *This bridge called my back* and Anglo-American feminism. In G. Anzaldúa (Ed.), *Making face, making soul: Haciendo caras* (pp. 356–369). San Francisco: Aunt Lute.

Althusser, L. (1970). *For Marx* (B. Brewster, Trans.). New York: Vintage Books.

Anzaldúa, G. (1987). *Borderlands/la frontera: The new mestiza.* San Francisco: Aunt Lute.

Anzaldúa, G. (1990). Haciendo caras, una entrada: An introduction by Gloria Anzaldúa. In G. Anzaldúa (Ed.) *Making face, making soul: Haciendo caras* (pp. xv–xxviii). San Francisco: Aunt Lute.

Collins, P. H. (1998). *Fighting words: Black women and the search for justice.* Minneapolis: University of Minnesota Press.

Connolly, W. E. (1991). *Identity/difference.* London: Cornell University Press.

Davis, A. (1981). *Women, race and class.* New York: Vintage Books.

Delgado Bernal, D. (1998). Using a Chicana feminist epistemology in educational research. *Harvard Educational Review, 68*(4), 555–582.

Delgado Bernal, D. (2000). *Learning and living pedagogies of the home: The mestiza consciousness of Chicana students.* Unpublished manuscript.

Eagleton, T. (1991). *Ideology: An introduction.* London and New York: Verso.

Elenes, C. A. (1997). Reclaiming the borderlands: Chicana/o identity, difference, and critical pedagogy. *Educational Theory, 47*(3), 359–375.

Elenes, C. A. (1999). Toward the construction of Chicana/o identity: Borderlands and the educational discourses. In A. Sosa-Riddell, M. J. Hernández, & L. San Miguel (Eds.), *Expanding raza world views: sexuality and regionalism* (pp. 8–25). National Association for Chicana and Chicano Studies.

Ellsworth, E. (1989). Why doesn't this feel empowering? Working through the repressive myths of critical pedagogy. *Harvard Educational Review, 59,* 297–324.

Ellsworth, E. (1996). Situated response-ability to student papers. *Theory into Practice, 35*(2), 138–143.

González, F. (2000). Haciendo que hacer: *Cultivating a Mestiza worldview and academic achievement: Braiding cultural knowledge into educational research, policy, and practice.* Unpublished manuscript.

Gore, J. (1993). *The struggle for pedagogies: Critical and feminist discourses and the regimes of truth.* New York: Routledge.

Grossberg, L. (1997). *Bringing it all back home: essays on cultural studies.* Durham: Duke University Press.

hooks, b. (1994). *Teaching to transgress: Education as the practice of freedom.* New York: Routledge.

Lather, P. (1991). *Getting smart: Feminist research and pedagogy with/in the postmodern.* New York: Routledge.

Lowe, L. (1997). Work, immigration, gender and Asian "American" women. In E. H. Kim, L. A. Villaneuva, & Asian Women United of California (Eds.), *Making More Waves: New Writings by Asian American Women* (pp. 269–277). Boston: Beacon Press.

Mohanty, C. T. (1997). Defining genealogies: Feminist reflections on being South Asian in North America. In E. H. Kim, L. A. Villaneuva, & Asian Women United of California (Eds.) *Making more waves* (pp. 119–127). Boston: Beacon Press.

Nadesan, M. H., & Elenes, C. A. (1998). Chantal Mouffe: pedagogy for democratic citizenship. In M. Peters (Eds.), *Naming the multiple: poststructuralism and education* (pp. 245–263). Wesport, CT: Bergin & Garvey.

Ng, R. (1997). A woman out of control: Deconstructing sexism and racism in the university. In S. De Castell, & M. Bryson (Eds.). *Radical Interventions: Identity, politics and difference/s in educational praxis* (pp. 39–57). Albany: SUNY Press.

Nieto, S. (1998). From claiming hegemony to sharing space: Creating community in multicultural courses. In R. Chávez Chávez, & J. O'Donnell (Eds.), *Speaking the unpleasant: The politics of (non) engagement in the multicultural education terrain* (pp. 16–31). Albany: SUNY Press.

Parmar, P. (Producer/Director). (1991). *A place of rage.* New York: Women Make Movies.

Reyes, M. L. (1997). Chicanas in academe: An endangered species. In S. de Castell, & M. Bryson (Eds.), *Radical Interventions: Identity, politics, and difference/s in educational praxis* (pp. 15–37). Albany: SUNY Press.

Riggs, M. (Producer/Director). (1995). *Black is . . . black ain't: a personal journey through black identity.* San Francisco: California Newsreel.

Russel y Rodríguez, M. (1997). (En)Countering domestic violence, complicity, and definitions of Chicana womanhood. *Voces: A Journal of Chicana/Latina Studies, 1*(2), 104–141.

Sandoval, C. (1990). A report on the 1981 National Women's Studies Association conference. In G. Anzaldúa (Ed.), *Making face, making soul: Haciendo caras* (pp. 55–71). San Francisco: Aunt Lute.

Sandoval, C. (1991). U.S. Third World feminism: The theory and method of oppositional consciousness in the postmodern world. *Genders, 10,* 1–24.

Sandoval, C. (1998). Mestizaje as method: feminists-of-color challenge the canon. In C. Trujillo (Ed.), *Living Chicana theory* (pp. 352–370). Berkeley: Third Women Press.

Utall, L. (1990). Inclusion without influence: the continuing tokenism of women of color. In G. Anzaldúa (Ed.), *Making face, making soul: Haciendo cras* (pp. 42–45). San Francisco: Aunt Lute.

Williams, P. (1991). *The alchemy of race and rights.* Cambridge, MA: Harvard University Press.

Yarbro-Bejarano, Y. (1999). Sexuality and Chicana/o Studies: Toward a theoretical paradigm for the twenty-first century. *Cultural Studies, 13,* 335–345.

CHAPTER 26
RACIAL AND ETHNIC DIVERSITY IN THE CLASSROOM
DOES IT PROMOTE STUDENT LEARNING?

PATRICK T. TERENZINI, ALBERTO F. CABRERA, CAROL L. COLBECK,
STEFANI A. BJORKLUND, AND JOHN M. PARENTE

Since passage of the Civil Rights Act of 1964 and the Higher Education Act of 1965, America's colleges and universities have struggled to increase the racial and ethnic diversity of their students and faculty members, and "affirmative action" has become the policy-of-choice to achieve that heterogeneity. These policies, however, are now at the center of an intense national debate. The current legal foundation for affirmative action policies rests on the 1978 *Regents of the University of California v. Bakke* case, in which Justice William Powell argued that race could be considered among the factors on which admissions decisions were based. More recently, however, the U.S. Court of Appeals for the Fifth Circuit, in the 1996 *Hopwood v. State of Texas* case, found Powell's argument wanting. Court decisions turning affirmative action policies aside have been accompanied by state referenda, legislation, and related actions banning or sharply reducing race-sensitive admissions or hiring in California, Florida, Louisiana, Maine, Massachusetts, Michigan, Mississippi, New Hampshire, Rhode Island, and Puerto Rico (Healy, 1998a, 1998b, 1999).

In response, educators and others have advanced educational arguments supporting affirmative action, claiming that a diverse student body is more educationally effective than a more homogeneous one. Harvard University President Neil Rudenstine claims that the "fundamental rationale for student diversity in higher education [is] its educational value" (Rudenstine, 1999, p. 1). Lee Bollinger, Rudenstine's counterpart at the University of Michigan, has asserted, "A classroom that does not have a significant representation from members of different races produces an impoverished discussion" (Schmidt, 1998, p. A32). These two presidents are not alone in their beliefs. A statement published by the Association of American Universities and endorsed by the presidents of 62 research universities stated: "We speak first and foremost as educators. We believe that our students benefit significantly from education that takes place within a diverse setting" ("On the Importance of Diversity in University Admissions," *The New York Times*, April 24, 1997, p. A27).

Studies of the impact of diversity on student educational outcomes tend to approach the ways students encounter "diversity" in any of three ways. A small group of studies treat students' contacts with "diversity" largely as a function of the numerical or proportional racial/ethnic or gender mix of students on a campus (e.g., Chang, 1996, 1999a; Kanter, 1977; Sax, 1996). Gurin (1999) and Hurtado, Milem, Clayton-Pedersen, and Allen (1999) refer to this numerical or proportional "mix" of students as "structural diversity." Whether such diversity is a *sufficient* condition to promote student educational outcomes, however, is far from clear.

A second, considerably larger set of studies take some modicum of structural diversity as a given and operationalize students' encounters with diversity using the frequency or nature of their reported interactions with peers who are racially/ethnically different from themselves. In these studies, which might be labeled "*in situ* diversity studies," encountering diversity is viewed as part of the normal processes and functioning of campus life or of a campus's racial/ethnic and gender climate (e.g., antonio, 1998; Astin, 1993; Cabrera, Nora, Terenzini, Pascarella, & Hagedorn, 1999; Davis, 1994; Gurin, 1999; Pascarella, Edison, Nora, Hagedorn, & Terenzini, 1996; Whitt, Edison, Pascarella, Nora, & Terenzini, 1999).

A third set of studies examines institutionally structured and purposeful programmatic efforts to help students engage racial/ethnic and/or gender "diversity" in the form of both ideas and people. This category includes studies of the influences of coursework and the curriculum (e.g., Astin, 1993; Chang, 1999b; Cohen, 1994; Cohen, Bianchini, Cossey, Holthuis, Morphew, & Whitcomb, 1997; Hurtado, 1999; MacPhee, Kreutzer, & Fritz, 1994; Palmer, 1999), and participation in racial or multicultural awareness workshops (e.g., Antony, 1993; Astin, 1993; Springer, Palmer, Terenzini, Pascarella, & Nora, 1996; Vilalpando, 1994), as well as various other forms of institutional programming intended to enhance the diversity of a campus or the educational consequences of engaging "diversity" in one form or another (see Musil, Garcia, Moses, & Smith, 1995; Rendon & Hope, 1996; Sedlacek, 1995). Appel, Cartwright, Smith, and Wolf (1996), Smith (1989), and Hurtado et al. (1999) provide useful reviews of this literature.

These various approaches have been used to examine the effects of diversity on a broad array of student educational outcomes. The evidence is almost uniformly consistent in indicating that students in a racial/ethnically or gender-diverse community, or engaged in a diversity-related activity, reap a wide array of positive educational benefits. "Diversity" in its various forms has been linked to such outcomes as higher minority student retention (e.g., Bowen & Bok, 1998; Chang, 1996, 1999a), greater cognitive development (e.g., Adams & Zhou-McGovern, 1994; Cohen, 1994; Cohen, et al., 1997; Hurtado, 1999; MacPhee et al., 1994; Sax, 1996), and positive gains on a wide-range of measures of interpersonal and psychosocial developmental changes, including increased openness to diversity and challenge (Pascarella, et al., 1996), greater racial/cultural knowledge and understanding and commitment to social justice (antonio, 1998; Astin, 1993; Chang, 1999b; Milem, 1994; Palmer, 1999; Springer, et al., 1996), more positive academic and social self-concepts (Astin, 1993; Chang, 1996; Sax, 1996), more complex civic-related attitudes and values, and greater involvement in civic and community-service behaviors (Astin, 1993; Milem, 1994; Hurtado, 1999). (Chang [1998] and Milem [1999] provide excellent reviews of this literature.)

As noted above, however, only a relative handful of studies (e.g., Chang, 1996, 1999a; Sax, 1996) have specifically examined whether *the racial/ethnic or gender composition* of the students on a campus, in an academic major, or in a classroom (i.e., structural diversity) has the educational benefits claimed by Rudenstine, Bollinger, and others. Sax found that the proportion of women in an academic major field had no impact on students' cognitive or affective development. Chang's analyses reveal a good bit of the complexity of the relation between structural diversity, student interactions and experiences, and educational outcomes. He found that a campus's racial heterogeneity had an effect on learning outcomes through its influence on students' diversity-related experiences, specifically, socializing with peers from different racial/ethnic backgrounds and discussing racial/ethnic issues. Whether the degree of racial diversity of a campus or classroom has a *direct* effect on learning outcomes, however, remains an open question. The scarcity of information on the educational benefits of the structural diversity on a campus or in its classrooms is regrettable because it is the sort of evidence the courts appear to be requiring if they are to support race-sensitive admissions policies.

In addition to the shortage of information on the role of structural diversity, most studies examine diversity's influence on various dimensions of students' psychosocial development, including (but not limited to) racial/ethnic attitudes and values, academic and social self-concepts, civic behaviors, and racial/ethnic awareness and knowledge. Far fewer studies (e.g., Cohen, 1994; Cohen, et al., 1997; MacPhee et al., 1994; Slavin, 1995) explore the influence of diversity in the classroom or in other small groups on students' development of academic or intellectual knowledge and skills.

This study attempted to contribute to the knowledge base by exploring the influence of structural diversity in the classroom on students' development of academic and intellectual skills. The study put to an empirical test Bollinger's claim that racially/ethnically homogeneous classrooms produce "an impoverished" educational experience (Schmidt, 1998, p. A32). The study was designed to evaluate whether and to what extent (if any) the racial/ethnic diversity of the students in a classroom is related to student learning, specifically, to gains in students' problem-solving skills and their abilities to work in groups. In addition, this study sought to extend Chang's (1996, 1999a) work indicating that structural diversity was associated with more frequent, diversity-related experiences which, in turn, were related to educational outcomes. This study examines both the direct effect of classroom diversity on academic/intellectual outcomes and whether any effects of classroom diversity may be moderated by the extent to which active and collaborative instructional approaches are used in the course.

Methods

Conceptual Underpinnings

In this study, we assume that the development of students' course-related skills are shaped by students' precourse characteristics, the instructional practices encountered in the classroom, and the racial/ethnic diversity of the classroom. Students' precourse characteristics are assumed to be temporally prior to both classroom diversity and instructional methods in their effects on learning outcomes. Our primary focus is on the influence of varying levels of classroom diversity on students' learning outcome *above and beyond the effects of other variables that may also influence learning* (e.g., students' precourse characteristics and the pedagogical methods adopted by instructors).

Sample and Data Collection

This study was part of an evaluation of the National Science Foundation-funded Engineering Coalition of Schools for Excellence in Education and Leadership (ECSEL). ECSEL comprises seven colleges of engineering: City College of New York, Howard University, the Massachusetts Institute of Technology, Morgan State University, Pennsylvania State University, the University of Maryland, and the University of Washington. Among other goals, ECSEL seeks to promote the use of design groups, or engineering teams, throughout the undergraduate curriculum in helping students learn to solve unstructured engineering problems. The original data collection was intended to evaluate the extent to which the active and collaborative learning activities inherent in group-based engineering design promoted student learning when compared with more traditional approaches to teaching (e.g., lecture and discussion).

The base sample consists of 1,258 engineering students enrolled at all 7 ECSEL institutions who completed the Classroom Activities and Outcomes Survey (described below). Participating courses and students were not randomly selected. The local ECSEL evaluator on each campus was asked to identify as many "ECSEL" courses (in which design was being taught using active and collaborative learning techniques) as feasible, as well as (for comparative purposes) several "non-ECSEL" courses with educational goals similar to those of the ECSEL courses. In the non-ECSEL courses, traditional lecture and discussion techniques were the primary mode of instruction.

Survey forms were administered in 49 classrooms. Of these, 29 were ECSEL classes, and 20 were non-ECSEL classes. Of the 1,258 students, 936 (74%) were enrolled in an ECSEL course while 322 (26%) were in non-ECSEL courses. Because of the nonrandom nature of the data collection, 46% of the students were enrolled at the University of Maryland, 21% at the University of Washington, and 13% at The Pennsylvania State University. The remaining 20% were distributed approximately evenly across the City College of New York, Howard University, Morgan State University, and MIT. The analyses reported here are based on the responses of 680 white students (58% of the sample) and 488 students of color. In the overall sample, 180 respondents (15.4%) were African Americans, 234 (20.0%) were Asian Americans, 64 (5.5%) were Latino/as, and 10 (0.9%) were Native Americans. Students were approximately evenly distributed across class years, with 57% in lower-division courses and 43% in upper-division courses. No significant differences in this distribution were identified between ECSEL and non-ECSEL course students. While the total database for this study contained the original 1,258 students, the n's for the several analyses described below varied between 962 and 1,194 because of missing data. Because of the relatively large number of cases with missing data on some variables, it was decided to drop those cases from analyses rather than use mean replacement.

Instrument and Variables

The data for this study come from the Classroom Activities and Outcomes Survey, a pencil-and-paper, multiple-choice questionnaire completed at the end of a course. The instrument has three sections. The first gathers information on students' personal and academic backgrounds and demographic characteristics. The second section asks about the characteristics and activities of the course in which the students were enrolled when completing the questionnaire. The final section asks students about the extent to which they believe they have made progress in various learning and skill development areas *as a result of taking that particular course*. (A copy of the Classroom Activities and Outcomes Survey is available from the first author at <ptt2@psu.edu>.)

Control variables. Background characteristics controlled in this study included gender (coded: 1 = male, 0 = female), race/ethnicity (coded: 1 = nonminority, 0 = minority; group *n*'s did not permit disaggregation of race/ethnicity into more discrete categories), and high school academic achievement (combined SAT scores).

Independent variables. The second section of The Classroom Activities and Outcomes Survey asks students to report how often during the course they or their instructor engaged in each of 26 classroom activities. Respondents use a 4-point scale, where 1 = never, 2 = occasionally, 3 = often, and 4 = very often/almost always. The items comprising this section were drawn from the research literature on effective instructional practices and activities.

A principal components factor analysis of these 26 items (with varimax rotation) produced 5 factors. This solution, accounting for 62.2% of the variance in the correlation matrix, is shown in Table 1. Three of the five factors related to specific instructional practices. Collaborative Learning consists of 7 practices that reflect the interdependence among students required by working in groups. The Instructor Interaction and Feedback factor included 5 practices that fostered frequent, supportive communication between faculty and students. The 3-item Clarity and Organization factor reflects instructors' use of clear explanations and an integrated course structure. The fourth and fifth factors contained 2 and 4 items, respectively, reflecting students' perceptions of fairness in the treatment of minorities and women in the classroom by the faculty member (the Faculty Climate scale) and by other students (the Peer Climate scale). As can be seen at the bottom of the table, the internal consistency reliabilities (Cronbach's alpha) for these scales were generally high, ranging from 0.77 to 0.89. The classroom climate measures were excluded from the set of independent variables to provide a more precise estimation of the effects of classroom diversity on learning unconfounded by students' perceptions of racial or gender dynamics in the classroom, which might, in themselves, affect learning. In affirmative action cases, moreover, the courts' interest has been specifically in the educational contributions (if any) of the racial/ethnic composition of the learning setting.

Classroom diversity, the independent variable of principal interest in this study, was operationalized using a "diversity index" created by dividing the number of students who reported their racial/ethnic identity to be non-white by the total number of students in the class. Because two ECSEL institutions are Historically Black Universities, the diversity index was calculated so that classrooms with a diversity "mix" approaching 50% were considered the most diverse. Classrooms with a percentage of students of color lower than 50% (or, in the case of HBCU classrooms, greater than 50%) were considered to be less diverse. For example, a classroom in which all students were white *or* all were students of color was considered to have no diversity.

A preliminary examination indicated that the distribution of the diversity index was curvilinear (i.e., as classroom diversity increased, the nature of the effect on reported learning gains changed). In order to examine the nature and effects of this nonlinear relation more easily, the diversity index was used to develop five categories of "classroom diversity." Table 2 shows the five categories, the ranges of the classroom diversity levels within each category, and the number and percentage of students who were in classes falling within each category. For example, about 40% of the students were in courses characterized as "medium" diversity classrooms. This category contains students in predominantly white courses in which 33–38% of the total enrollment were students of color *as well as* students in predominantly minority-student courses in which 33–38% of all the students were white. The categories were formed using natural breaks in the multi-modal frequency distribution.

TABLE 1

Factor Structures for Classroom Practice Items

Items	Collaborative Learning	Instructor Interaction & Feedback	Clarity & Organization	Faculty Climate	Peer Climate
	Factor Loadings				
Discuss ideas with classmates	0.822				
Work cooperatively with students	0.739				
Opportunities to work in groups	0.753				
Get feedback from classmates	0.753				
Students teach & learn from one another	0.679				
Interact with classmates outside of class	0.650				
Require participation in class	0.589				
Interact with instructor as part of the course		0.780			
Interact with instructor outside of class		0.741			
Instructor gives *detailed* feedback		0.713			
Instructor gives *frequent* feedback		0.689			
Guided student learning versus lecturing		0.578			
Assignments/activities clearly explained			0.767		
Assignments/presentations clearly related			0.722		
Instructor makes clear expectations for activities			0.677		
Instructor treats minorities the same as whites				0.913	
Instructor treats women the same as men				0.901	
In groups, some males treat women differently					0.876
Some male students treat women differently					0.869
Some white students treat minorities differently					0.865
In groups, some whites treat minorities differently					0.809
Internal Consistency Reliability (Alpha)	0.88	0.83	0.77	0.86	0.89

TABLE 2

Classroom Diversity Categories, Intervals, and Number and Percentage of Students in Each Group

Categories	Classroom Diversity Intervals	Students n	Students %
No diversity	0% or 100%	142	11.3%
Low diversity	6–19%	184	14.7
Medium-low diversity	22–30	185	14.7
Medium diversity	33–38	500	39.7
High diversity	40–50	247	19.6
TOTALS		1,258	100.0%

With the exception of the "medium" diversity category, which is the largest group, respondents were distributed relatively evenly across the five categories.

Dependent variables. The third part of the Classroom Activities and Outcomes Survey asks students to report the progress they believe they have made in 27 areas *as a result of the course for which they were completing the survey form.* Progress is reported on a 1-to-4 scale, where 1 = none, 2 = slight,

3 = moderate, and 4 = a great deal. These items were drawn primarily (but not exclusively) from a series of Delphi studies by Jones and her colleagues (Jones, 1994; Jones, et al., 1994) intended to develop consensus among faculty members, research specialists, academic administrators, and employers on definitions and components of "critical thinking" and "problem solving."

A principal components factor analysis (with varimax rotation) of the 27 skill development items yielded three factors: Problem-Solving Skills (12 items), Group Functioning Skills (7 items), and Occupational Awareness (4 items). This three-factor solution explained 64.6% of the total item variance and produced scales with internal consistency reliabilities ranging from 0.81 to 0.93. The composition of these factors is given in Table 3. Because of the interest in this study in students' skill development, the Occupational Awareness scale was excluded from further analyses.

For both the Classroom Activities and Skill Development Outcome factors, scales were created by summing students' responses on a factor's component items and then dividing by the number of items the factor contains.

TABLE 3

Factor Structures for Learning Outcome Items

Items	Factor Loadings		
	Group Skills	Problem-Solving Skills	Occupational Awareness
Developing ways to resolve conflict & reach agreement	0.779		
Being aware of feelings of members in group	0.841		
Listening to the ideas of others with open mind	0.829		
Working on collaborative projects as member of a team	0.815		
Organizing information to aid comprehension	0.679		
Asking probing questions that clarify facts, concepts	0.606		
Developing alternatives that combine best from previous work	0.618		
Ability to do design		0.578	
Solve an unstructured problem		0.697	
Identify knowledge, resources, & people to solve problem		0.666	
Evaluate arguments & evidence of competing alternatives		0.675	
Apply an abstract concept or idea to a real problem		0.735	
Divide problems into manageable components		0.744	
Clearly describe a problem orally		0.679	
Clearly describe a problem in writing		0.667	
Develop several methods to solve unstructured problem		0.732	
Identify tasks needed to solve an unstructured problem		0.752	
Visualize what the product of a design project would look like		0.584	
Weigh the pros/cons of possible solutions to a problem		0.623	
Understanding what engineers do			0.754
Understanding language of design			0.721
Understanding engineering has a nontechnical side			0.710
Understanding of the process of design			0.703
Internal Consistency Reliability (Alpha)	0.926	0.943	0.813

Analytical Methods

Ordinary least-squares multiple regression analyses were used in a series of hierarchical analyses. First, to determine whether the diversity of the classrooms had *any* association with learning outcomes, each of the two dependent variables (self-reported gains in problem-solving and group skills) was regressed on four of the five levels of classroom diversity (students in courses with no diversity constituted the reference group). Second, reported gains in problem-solving and group skills were again regressed on classroom diversity after controlling for students' race/ethnicity, gender, and academic ability. Third, each learning outcome was regressed hierarchically on: (1) students' race/ethnicity, gender, and ability, (2) the three scales reflecting the instructional methods used in the classroom (collaborative learning, instructor interaction and feedback, and course clarity and organization), and (3) four levels of classroom diversity.

Finally, the influence of classroom diversity may well be contextual, that is, conditional (or dependent) on the degree to which students interact with one another in course-related activities. For example, interpersonal contacts among students in low diversity courses may well have a different effect on learning than similar contacts in medium- or high-diversity classrooms. To evaluate the extent to which classroom diversity's effects may vary depending on the instructional methods used, a set of four cross-product interaction terms was created by cross-multiplying each of the four levels of classroom diversity (low through high) by students' scores on the Collaborative Learning scale. These interaction terms were then entered as a set into an OLS regression (one for each dependent variable) after students' precourse characteristics, instructional methods, and the four diversity levels had been entered as main effects variables.

Results

Table 4 reports the means and standard deviations for each group's reported gains in problem-solving and group skill development, although the relations among (and magnitudes of the differences between) the group means for both outcomes are more easily seen in Figures 1 and 2. The basic patterns of the relations between classroom diversity and reported learning are the same for both problem-solving and group skill development. As can be seen in both figures, and with students in "no diversity" classrooms as the reference group, the reported gains drop to their lowest among students in "low diversity" classrooms, although those drops are not statistically significant (as indicated by the "n.s." between the data points). The trend line then climbs through the mean for "low-medium" diversity classrooms, peaking among students in "medium" diversity classes, only to fall again for students in "high diversity" courses. The magnitudes of the differences between the various diversity levels are similar and relatively small. Only the differences between medium-level course means and (with one exception) all other group means are statistically significant (based on pair-wise Scheffé *post hoc* comparisons). (The exception is that for the problem-solving outcome, students in medium diversity classrooms report gains at approximately the same level as do students in classrooms with no diversity.)

The results of each of the three phases of the analyses are reported in Table 5. Consistent with the analyses underlying Figures 1 and 2, the first-phase regressions (with levels of classroom diversity as the only predictors) indicate that classroom diversity is, indeed, related to students' self-reported development of both their problem-solving and group skills. While statistically significant ($p < 0.001$), however, the overall relation in both analyses is small (adjusted R^2s of 0.02 and 0.05 for the problem-solving and group skill models, respectively). The beta weights indicate that (relative to the reference group: students in classes with no diversity) low classroom diversity is negatively related to students' development of both problem-solving and group skills at statistically significant levels. In the regression on group skills, moreover, both low and medium-low levels of classroom diversity are significantly and negatively related to reported gains. It is worth noting that in the group skills model, the beta weights for both medium and high levels of diversity (0.07 and -0.09, respectively) approach traditional levels of statistical significance ($p < 0.17$ and $p < 0.07$, respectively), with

TABLE 4

Means and Standard Deviations on Learning Outcomes by Level of Classroom Diversity (*n* = 1,199)

Classroom Diversity Level	Problem-Solving Skills		Group Skills	
	Mean	SD	Mean	SD
No diversity	2.82	0.75	2.81	0.88
Low diversity	2.68	0.68	2.57	0.83
Medium-low diversity	2.77	0.63	2.71	0.81
Medium diversity	2.96	0.64	3.05	0.64
High diversity	2.77	0.67	2.72	0.83
TOTALS	2.84	0.67	2.84	0.78

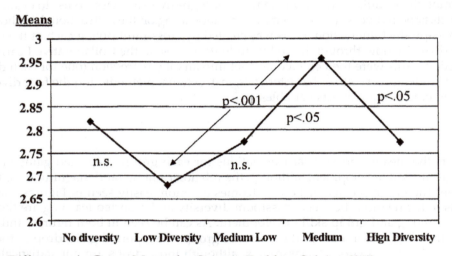

Figure 1   Differences in Group Means for Gains in Problem-Solving Skills.

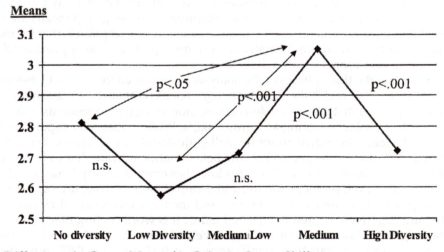

Figure 2   Differences in Group Means for Gains in Group Skills.

TABLE 5

Results of the Three Phases of Regression Analyses

Independent Variables	Problem-Solving Skills		Group Skills	
	Adj. R^2	Betas	Adj. R^2	Betas
Classroom Diversity Only	0.02***		0.05***	
Low diversity		−0.12**		−0.16***
Medium-low diversity		−0.05		−0.09*
Medium diversity		0.04		0.07
High diversity		−0.04		−0.09
Precourse Characteristics				
and Classroom Diversity	0.02***		0.05***	
Gender		0.03		−0.05
Race/ethnicity		−0.04		−0.00
Ability (SATs)		−0.03		−0.02
Low diversity		−0.13**		−0.15***
Medium-low diversity		−0.06		−0.08
Medium diversity		0.03		0.09
High diversity		−0.04		−0.08
Precourse Characteristics, Classroom				
Activities, and Classroom Diversity	0.34***		0.34***	
Gender		0.04		−0.02
Race/ethnicity		−0.01		0.03
Ability		−0.07*		−0.08**
Collaborative learning		0.28***		0.41***
Instructor interaction		0.32***		0.20***
Clarity & organization		0.13***		0.08**
Low diversity		0.00		−0.01
Medium-low diversity		−0.01		−0.01
Medium diversity		0.06		0.09
High diversity		0.04		0.00

*$p < 0.05$.   **$p < 0.01$.   ***$p < 0.001$.

medium diversity positively related to reported group skill learning gains, while a high level of diversity is negatively related to students' reported gains.

In the second phase analyses (reported in the middle portion of Table 4), despite the addition of controls for students' race/ethnicity, gender, and academic ability, the association between classroom diversity and both learning outcomes persists relatively unchanged. The adjusted R^2s remain low and, indeed, are identical (within rounding error) to those in the first-phase models. Again, low levels of classroom diversity (relative to no diversity at all) were negatively related to gains in both problem-solving and group skills at statistically significant levels. The pattern of the signs of the beta weights also remained unchanged, suggesting that medium-low and high levels of classroom diversity may be negatively related to reported learning gains, while medium levels of diversity appear to have a positive effect on learning. None of these weights, however, reached the traditional standard of statistical significance. In the group skills model, however, the weights for medium-low, medium, and high levels of classroom diversity did approach the traditional criterion of statistical significance ($p < 0.08$, 0.11, and 0.13, respectively). In sum, gender, race/ethnicity, and academic ability appear to have no statistically significant effect on the learning reported by students in this study, while the evidence continues to suggest that classroom diversity may be a factor (possibly both positive and negative).

In the third phase of the analyses, with students' precourse characteristics and the three classroom activity scales included as control variables, the adjusted R^2 values climb substantially to 0.34

for both problem-solving and group skills. The sharp rise in the R^2 was predictable. Both the research literature and common sense would lead one to expect the addition of three scales reflecting what goes on in a classroom to be powerful predictors of how much students think they have learned. Indeed, one might reasonably expect these close-to-the-action predictors to eliminate what the earlier regressions have suggested is the relatively small contribution of classroom diversity to learning gains. Such expectations were largely—but not completely—borne out. As can be seen in the bottom portion of Table 4, none of the beta weights for the various levels of classroom diversity reached statistical significance. Classroom diversity, as a factor in student learning, however, did not disappear entirely. In the model predicting reported gains in problem-solving skills, the diversity index, when treated as a *continuous* variable (rather than being treated as dichotomous categories), produced a beta weight of 0.045. Although small relative to the weights of the three classroom activity scales, the diversity index weight remained statistically significant ($p < 0.05$). Similarly, in the group skills model, the beta weight for medium levels of diversity (0.09) was statistically significant at $p < 0.067$, only narrowly failing to meet the conventional $p < 0.05$ standard. Thus, these findings indicate that what happens in a classroom (e.g., the degree to which students engage in active and collaborative learning activities, their interactions with instructors and peers, and the level of clarity and organization in the classroom) are clearly more powerful influences on students' reported learning gains than is the level of the classroom's structural diversity. Nonetheless, classroom diversity, *despite* the presence of these more proximal and powerful influences, continued to have a measurable influence on student learning (albeit a small and statistically marginal one by conventional standards).

Finally, entry of the set of four diversity-by-collaborative learning scale interaction terms produced no appreciable increase in the value of R^2 for either the problem-solving or group skills models. Thus, the data in this study suggest that the effects of the level of classroom diversity on students' reported skill-development gains are general rather than conditional (or dependent) on the use of collaborative learning approaches in the course.

Limitations

This study has several limitations. First, although the sample is multi-institutional and contains a broad range of engineering schools, the seven institutions that participated in the study were not randomly selected. Thus, to an unknown degree, these institutions may not be representative of the national mix of engineering schools or, indeed, of all four-year universities. Similarly, the classes and students invited to participate in the study were not randomly selected. Although local evaluators were urged to sample ECSEL and non-ECSEL courses from across their institution's college of engineering's class levels, the resulting samples may not be representative of the course or student populations (engineering or otherwise) on each campus. Moreover, the number of classes and students participating vary widely across the participating institutions. Thus, generalizations to other institutions' engineering classes and students must be made cautiously. With regard to sampling, however, the study has two distinct assets when compared to most studies of classroom effects on student learning: its multi-institutional design and its relatively large sample of both courses and students.

Second, the influences of gender and academic ability are probably underestimated in this study due to the relative homogeneity of engineering students on these campuses with respect to these variables. By and large, the participants in this study were male (73%) and academically very able (mean combined SATs of 1,241).

Third, while problem-solving and group skills are basic educational outcomes of most engineering (and general education) programs, they are certainly not the only dimensions along which future engineers (or students in general) develop academically and intellectually during their undergraduate programs. Moreover, alternative conceptualizations and operationalizations of "problem-solving" and "group" skills have been advanced, and the results of this study might have been somewhat different had other conceptualizations and/or measures of each skill been used, or if other, entirely different learning outcomes had been the foci of this study.

Fourth, the measurements of skill development in this study are based on students' self-reports rather than on more objective measures of student learning (e.g., standardized tests). Recent research suggests, however, that self-report measures of learning can be used to appraise gains in cognitive skills. Pike (1995) found self-reported measures of educational gains to be as valid as objective measures to the extent that the self-report measures reflect the content of the learning outcome under consideration. As noted earlier, the items reflecting the learning outcomes studied in this research came primarily (albeit not exclusively) from a national study of the beliefs of faculty members, researchers, administrators, and employers about what component abilities make up those skills (Jones, 1994; Jones, et al., 1994). Similarly, Anaya (1999), after examining a representative sample of students who took the Graduate Record Examinations in 1989, concluded that self-reported measures of gains in cognitive skills are valid proxies of cognitive skills as measured by the verbal and math components of the GRE. Moreover, while standardized measures have some advantages over self-reports, they also come with limitations of their own for classroom use, including availability, length, cost, and relevance to specific courses. The self-report instrument used in this study was designed specifically to gather course-level information and to be easy and inexpensive to use. One must, nonetheless, acknowledge the trade-offs being made.

Fifth, the study's design and database are cross-sectional. The concept of learning "gains" or skill "development" implies change over time. Moreover, the impact of course- (or campus-) diversity may also vary over time. A longitudinal design would provide a more rigorous test of whether classroom diversity is related to learning. It is worth noting in this regard, however, that the relations identified between classroom diversity and reported learning gains persisted in the presence of controls for selected precourse student characteristics (gender, race/ethnicity, and high-school academic achievement) and remained marginally significant even in the presence of psychometrically sound measures of classroom activities designed to promote learning. These latter measures, as one might expect, were clearly more powerful forces for student learning, but they failed to completely eradicate evidence that classroom diversity may also be involved.

Sixth, for reasons explained earlier relating to the apparent curvilinear effect of classroom diversity on reported learning gains, this study operationalized classroom diversity as four, dummy-coded levels, rather than as a single, continuous variable. Subsequent use of these dummy-coded variables in statistical interaction terms to examine whether classroom diversity might have a different effect depending on the degree of interpersonal contact among students in the course provides a relatively low-power test of the possible, conditional effects of diversity on learning. Future studies should examine more rigorously the possibility of such "contextual" effects. The structural diversity in a classroom (and elsewhere) may, indeed, have a general effect (i.e., one that is about the same, regardless of classroom activities), rather than "conditional" or "contextual" (i.e., one in which the magnitude of the effect varies depending on the setting), but for theoretical, practical, and policy reasons, that relation should be validated.

Seventh, this study examined the influence of different levels of classroom diversity only in relation to the effect of no classroom diversity at all. Some levels of diversity, independent of the kinds of pedagogies adopted, may be more or less, positively or negatively, related to learning gains. This study shed no light on these questions, and future research on the matter is strongly encouraged.

Finally, students develop their problem-solving and group skills over time and at varying rates. This study is limited by the fact that changes in these skill areas were examined after only one course. The *cumulative* changes in these areas that can be attributed to the racial/ethnic diversity in these and subsequent courses throughout students' academic programs, as well as in their out-of-class encounters with racially and ethnically diverse individuals, may be more extensive than what is reported here. Indeed, one might also hypothesize that the overall institutional climate for diversity is a more powerful force for learning than is the level of diversity in individual classrooms. Chang's (1996, 1999a) work supports this proposition, but it offers no insight into the relative influence of campus- vs. classroom-level diversity. Because this study was unable to control for campus-level diversity climate, the hypothesis that the campus climate is the dominant force remains a plausible alternative to the interpretation of the findings in this study. It is worth noting, however, that the phrasing of the survey items consistently reminded students that they were being asked to describe the activities going on in a specific course and to report learning gains associated specifically with that course. Moreover, Cabrera and Nora (1994) report findings consistent across racial/ethnic groups that students' sense of institutional alienation is shaped more powerfully by their in-class experiences than by their perceptions of the general campus climate.

Conclusions and Implications

Since the passage of the Civil Rights Act of 1964 and the Higher Education Act of 1965, America's colleges and universities have struggled to provide equal access to applicants of all races and ethnicities. Affirmative Action, based on racially and ethnically sensitive admissions decision making, has been the policy of choice in trying to achieve equality of access and racially and ethnically diverse student bodies.

Widely adopted as it has been, however, affirmative action has become increasingly controversial. Reliance on race-sensitive admissions received the support of the U.S. Supreme Court in the 1978 *University of California v. Bakke* decision, when Justice William Powell, writing for the majority, argued that race could be one of the factors on which admissions decisions were based. The *Bakke* decision came under fire, however, in the 1996 *Hopwood v. Texas* case when the U.S. Court of Appeals for the Fifth Circuit rejected arguments supporting the University of Texas' use of race-sensitive admissions to its law school. That ruling was subsequently extended to all admissions activities in Texas' public higher education systems, and it has shaped referenda or legislative actions in a number of other states nationwide.

In response, representatives of colleges and universities have argued that affirmative action is necessary to maintain racially and ethnically diverse student bodies and that the practice is defensible on educational, if not legal, grounds. Diverse student bodies and classrooms, the argument goes, are more educationally effective than are less- or non-diverse ones. Lee Bollinger, president of the University of Michigan, for example, has asserted, "A classroom that does not have a significant representation from members of different races produces an impoverished discussion" (Schmidt, 1998, p. A32).

A growing body of research has lent support to this argument, although the evidence is far from conclusive. A significant segment of this literature focuses on the effects of a campus's racial/ethnic climate on students' racial/ethnic attitudes or learning. These studies are generally consistent in finding that a "warmer" climate is related to students' willingness to socialize and discuss racial issues and to greater tolerance and appreciation for diverse populations. A second segment of the diversity research has examined the effectiveness of specific, programmatic initiatives (e.g., cultural awareness workshops and diversity course requirements) intended to promote greater tolerance and understanding among racially and ethnically diverse students. Like the campus climate research, this body of evidence generally supports the effectiveness of such programmatic interventions.

Few studies, however, specifically examine whether the racial/ethnic composition of a campus or classroom—the so-called "structural diversity" of these settings—has a measurable impact on student learning. This study explored precisely that question with respect to the racial/ethnic composition of individual classrooms, as well as whether the effects of structural diversity might be mediated by the kinds of instructional methods in use in the classroom. The findings of this study hardly constitute a ringing endorsement of Bollinger's claim that "a classroom that does not have a significant representation from members of different races produces an impoverished discussion" (Schmidt, 1998, p. A32). Portions of the evidence do, however, support claims about the educational benefits of racially or ethnically diverse classrooms. Level of classroom diversity was related at small—but statistically significant—levels to students' reported gains in both their problem-solving and their group skills. Moreover, those relations persisted even in the presence of controls for students' race/ethnicity, gender, and academic ability. In the most rigorous tests applied in this study, both students' precourse characteristics (including ability) and three scales reflecting the instructional practices in use in the course were controlled, the level of classroom diversity *continued* to show a positive, if small, statistically marginal relation to reported learning gains. In a regression on students' reported gains in problem-solving skills, a continuous measure of classroom diversity had a small, but statistically significant, positive effect (beta $= 0.045$, $p < 0.05$). In a similar regression on students' reported gains in their group skills, being in a "medium diversity" classroom was positively related to reported gains net of other student characteristics, instructional methods, and other levels of classroom diversity. This effect failed, but only narrowly ($p < 0.07$), to meet the conventional standard for statistical significance. These findings indicate quite clearly that what happens in a course is far-and-away a more powerful predictor of learning outcomes than is the level of classroom diversity. Nonetheless, the persistence of diversity's influence *despite* the presence of more powerful predictors is, we believe, substantively noteworthy and relevant to the policy question this study seeks to illuminate.

The evidence also suggests that the relation between the racial/ethnic composition of a classroom and students' learning gains may not be a simple, linear one. The evidence quite consistently indicates that "medium" levels of classroom diversity (i.e., approximately in the 30–40% range) are positively, if not always significantly, related to students' reports of learning gains. At the most rudimentary level of analysis, however, the data also suggest the possibility that low or high levels of classroom diversity *may* be negatively related to learning gains. Analyses examining the effects of only classroom diversity level, or of diversity level while controlling for students' race/ethnicity, gender, and ability, produced some marginal evidence of statistically significant but negative effects among students in classrooms with low or high levels of diversity (compared to no diversity at all). These negative relations, however, were not supported when measures of the instructional practices in use in these classrooms entered the analyses. Entry of a set of interaction terms (reflecting whether the effects of various levels of diversity varied depending on the extent to which collaborative learning activities were used in the classroom) produced no appreciable increase in the value of the R^2 for either model. This finding suggests that any effects of structural diversity appear to be general and not conditional on the instructional methods in use in the classroom. That conclusion, however, warrants further validation. Similarly, future research should examine more precisely than was possible here the levels at which classroom diversity becomes a salient positive or negative force in shaping students' learning.

At best, the findings in this study suggest a small, if statistically significant, link between the level of racial/ethnic diversity in a classroom and students' reports of increases in their problem-solving and group skills. The relatively consistent and positive salience of medium levels of classroom diversity is the most supportive evidence for arguments that classroom diversity has positive, educational effects on student learning. That evidence, however, is far from conclusive.

The findings of this study are all the more suggestive when one considers that the relation between diversity and student learning is at least modestly detectable *in individual classrooms*. One might reasonably speculate that, if the beneficial effects of racial/ethnic diversity are apparent in *individual* classrooms, then those effects may well be substantially magnified in the aggregate, when accumulated across the courses students take and across their out-of-class experiences in racially/ethnically diverse settings.

Should subsequent studies of the effects of the racial/ethnic composition of classrooms and other campus settings bear out the relations suggested in this research, then much of the current cloudiness in the legal and policy worlds concerning the educational effectiveness of diverse settings may be clarified. Arguments for affirmative action and race-sensitive admissions that assert the educational effectiveness of such policies will rest on substantially firmer empirical ground, and campus, state, and federal policies permitting or encouraging race/ethnicity-sensitive admissions will also rest on firmer empirical ground.

References

Adams, M., & Zhou-McGovern, Y. (1994, April). *The sociomoral development of undergraduates in a "social diversity" course*. Paper presented at the meeting of the American Educational Research Association, New Orleans, LA.

Anaya, G. (1999). College impact on student learning: Comparing the use of self-reported gains, standardized test scores, and college grades. *Research in Higher Education, 40*, 499–527.

antonio, a. l. (1998). *The impact of friendship groups in a multicultural university*. Unpublished doctoral dissertation, University of California, Los Angeles.

Antony, J. (1993, November). *Can we all get along? How college impacts students' sense of promoting racial understanding.* Paper presented at the meeting of the Association for the Study of Higher Education, Pittsburgh, PA.

Appel, M., Cartwright, D., Smith, D. G., & Wolf, L. E. (1996). *The impact of diversity on students: A preliminary review of the research literature.* Washington, DC: Association of American Colleges and Universities.

Astin, A. W. (1993). *What matters in college? Four critical years revisited.* San Francisco: Jossey-Bass.

Bowen, W. G., & Bok, D. (1998). *The shape of the river: Long-term consequences of considering race in college and university admissions.* Princeton, NJ: Princeton University Press.

Cabrera, A. F., & Nora, A. (1994). College students' perceptions of prejudice and discrimination and their feelings of alienation: A construct validation approach. *Review of Education, Pedagogy, Cultural Studies, 16,* 387–409.

Cabrera, A. F., Nora, A., Terenzini, P. T., Pascarella, E. T., & Hagedorn, L. S. (1999). Campus racial climate and the adjustment of students to college: A comparison between white students and African-American students. *Journal of Higher Education, 70,* 134–160.

Chang, M. J. (1996). *Racial diversity in higher education: Does a racially mixed student population affect educational outcomes?* Unpublished doctoral dissertation, University of California, Los Angeles.

Chang, M. J. (1998). *An examination of conceptual and empirical linkages between diversity initiatives and student learning in higher education.* Unpublished manuscript prepared for the American Council on Education's Symposium and Working Research Meeting on Diversity and Affirmative Action, Arlington, VA, January 1999.

Chang, M. J. (1999a). Does racial diversity matter? The educational impact of a racially diverse undergraduate population. *Journal of College Student Development, 40,* 377–395.

Chang, M. J. (1999b, November). *The impact of an undergraduate diversity requirement on students' level of racial prejudice.* Paper presented at the meeting of the Association for the Study of Higher Education, San Antonio, TX.

Cohen, E. G. (1994). *Designing group work: Strategies for heterogeneous classrooms* (2nd ed.). New York: Teachers College Press.

Cohen, E. G., Bianchini, J. A., Cossey, R., Holthuis, N. C., Morphew, C. C., & Whitcomb, J. A. (1997). What did students learn? (1982–1994). In E. G. Cohen & R. A. Lotan (Eds.), *Working for equity in heterogeneous classrooms.* New York: Teachers College Press.

Davis, J. E. (1994). College in black and white: Campus environment and academic achievement of African American males. *Journal of Negro Education, 63,* 620–633.

Gurin, P. (1999). Empirical results from the analyses conducted for this litigation. From *Expert report of Patricia Gurin: Gratz, et al., v. Bollinger, et al., No. 97–75321* (E.D. Mich.), *Grutter, et al. v. Bollinger, et al., No. 97–75928* (E.D. Mich.). http://www.umich.edu/~urel/admissions/legal/expert/empir.html

Healy, P. (1998a, November). Advocates of more money for colleges win key gubernatorial races. *Chronicle of Higher Education,* pp. A29–A30.

Healy, P. (1998b, December). U.S. Appeals Court ruling may imperil university defenses of affirmative action. *Chronicle of Higher Education,* pp. A30–A31.

Healy, P. (1999, March). University of Massachusetts limits racial preferences, despite vow to increase minority enrollment. *Chronicle of Higher Education,* pp. A30–A31.

Hurtado, S. (1999). Linking diversity and educational purpose: How the diversity of the faculty and student body impacts the classroom environment and student development. In G. Orfield (Ed.), *Diversity challenged: Legal crisis and new evidence.* Cambridge, MA: Harvard Publishing Group.

Hurtado, S., Milem, J., Clayton-Pedersen, A., & Allen, W. (1999). *Enacting diverse learning environments: Improving the climate for racial/ethnic diversity in higher education.* (ASHE-ERIC Higher Education Report, Vol. 26, No. 8). Washington, DC: The George Washington University, Graduate School of Education and Human Development.

Jones, E. A. (1994). *Goals inventories.* University Park, PA: The Pennsylvania State University, Center for the Study of Higher Education, National Center on Postsecondary Teaching, Learning, and Assessment.

Jones, E. A., with Hoffman, S., Moore, L. M., Ratcliff, G., Tibbetts, B., & Click, B. A. (1994). *Essential skills in writing, speech and listening, and critical thinking: Perspectives of faculty, employers, and policy makers.* University Park, PA: The Pennsylvania State University, Center for the Study of Higher Education, National Center on Postsecondary Teaching, Learning, and Assessment.

Kanter, R. M. (1977). Some effects of proportions on group life: Skewed sex ratios and responses to token women. *American Journal of Sociology, 82,* 965–990.

MacPhee, D., Kreutzer, J. C., & Fritz, J. J. (1994). Infusing a diversity perspective into human development courses. *Child Development, 65,* 699–715.

Milem, J. F. (1994). College, students, and racial understanding. *Thought & Action, 9,* 51–92.

Milem, J. F. (1999). The educational benefits of diversity: Evidence from multiple sectors. In M. Chang, D. Witt, J. Jones, & K. Hakuta (Eds.), *Compelling interest: Examining the evidence on racial dynamics in higher education.* Report of the AERA Panel on Racial Dynamics in Colleges and Universities. Palo Alto, CA: Stanford University Center for Comparative Studies in Race and Ethnicity. (Prepublication copy, available at http://www.stanford.edu/~hakuta/RaceInHigherEducation.html.)

Musil, C., Garcia, M., Moses, Y., & Smith, D. (1995). *Diversity in higher education: A work in progress.* Washington, DC: Association of American Colleges and Universities.

Palmer, E. A. (1999). *An analysis of a diversity requirement: The effects of course characteristics on students' racial attitudes, gender attitudes, and self-perceived learning.* Unpublished doctoral dissertation, The Pennsylvania State University, University Park, PA.

Pascarella, E. T., Edison, M., Nora, A., Hagedorn, L. S., & Terenzini, P. T. (1996). Influences on students' openness to diversity and challenge in the first year of college. *Journal of Higher Education, 67,* 174–195.

Pike, G. R. (1995). The relationship between self-reports of college experiences and achievement test scores. *Research in Higher Education, 36,* 1–22.

Rendon, L. I., & Hope, R. (1996). *Educating a new majority.* San Francisco: Jossey-Bass.

Rudenstine, N. L. (1999). *Why a diverse student body is so important.* http://www.inform.umd.edu/diversity_web/Profiles/divdbase/harvard/ilsc.html

Sax, L. J. (1996). The dynamics of "tokenism:" How college students are affected by the proportion of women in their major. *Research in Higher Education, 37,* 389–425.

Schmidt, P. (1998, October). University of Michigan prepared to defend admissions policy in court. *Chronicle of Higher Education,* p. A32.

Sedlacek, W. (1995). *Improving racial and ethnic diversity and campus climate at four-year independent Midwest colleges: An evaluation report of the Lilly endowment Grant Program.* College Park, MD: University of Maryland—College Park.

Slavin, R. (1995). Cooperative learning groups and intergroup relations. In J. A. Banks & C. A. McGee Banks (Eds.), *Handbook of research on multicultural education.* New York: MacMillan.

Smith, D. G. (1989). *The challenge of diversity: Involvement or alienation in the academy?* (ASHE-ERIC Higher Education Reports, No. 5). Washington, DC: George Washington University Press.

Springer, L., Palmer, B., Terenzini, P. T., Pascarella, E. T., & Nora, A. (1996). Attitudes toward campus diversity: Participation in a racial or cultural awareness workshop. *Review of Higher Education, 20,* 53–68.

Vilalpando, O. (1994, November). *Comparing effects of multiculturalism and diversity on minority and white students' satisfaction with college.* Paper presented at the meeting of the Association for the Study of Higher Education, Tucson, AZ. (ERIC Document Reproduction Service No. ED 375 721)

Whitt, E. J., Edison, M., Pascarella, E. T., Nora, A., & Terenzini, P. T. (1999). Women's perceptions of a "chilly" climate and cognitive outcomes in college: Additional evidence. *Journal of College Student Development, 40,* 163–177.

CHAPTER 27
MINORITY STUDENTS IN SCIENCE AND MATH
WHAT UNIVERSITIES STILL DO NOT UNDERSTAND ABOUT RACE IN AMERICA

RICHARD TAPIA AND CYNTHIA JOHNSON

Why do so few Hispanics and African Americans enter science, technology, engineering, and mathematics (STEM) fields, which are essential to the economic and social health of the nation? Simply put, the educational system grows increasingly unresponsive to America's Hispanic and black populations as the degree stakes go up. Borrowing the pipeline analogy, the STEM faculty pipeline is just the last, smallest-diameter section of a system that eliminates large numbers of Hispanic and black students all along the way while providing little support to those who try to stay the course. Some universities are beginning to complain not only of a shortage of candidates for faculty positions in the sciences and engineering but also of a shortfall of graduate students, a situation mirrored in industry, where the demands for a technically skilled workforce are increasingly difficult to meet. With their strong market orientation, business and industry are asking for a diverse workforce to meet the needs of a diverse population; the university case for diversity is less straightforward, to say the least. Among other things, universities work for diversity so that students study in an environment that prepares them for life after graduation. But universities are academic institutions, with an increasingly strong orientation toward research. They want strong students with a good academic foundation. When it comes to admissions, university STEM faculty still strongly favor rank-ordering systems of students based on test scores and tend to rate underrepresented minority candidates below white men in ability and potential. Women have made considerable inroads, but their situation is only marginally better than that of underrepresented people of color.

American education is on two separate trajectories serving two populations, one of which is growing rapidly. In the next fifty years, the Hispanic population is projected to reach 102.6 million (U.S. Census 2004). As educators we need to learn how to reach minority students unless we intend to shut ourselves off from what will soon be half of the population. We might think about the K–12 teachers' refrain, "You teach the kids you get."

Dwindling numbers in the STEM workforce pipeline generally and in the STEM academic pipeline in particular is not a new problem. In the past, the solution to a shortage of academic candidates was to bring in talent from overseas; the United States has reaped enormous benefits from the importation of talent. It is difficult to imagine U.S. technology in the middle decades of the twentieth century without the scientists who fled Adolf Hitler, or those who immigrated to this country for a variety of other reasons. In past decades we have also imported considerable numbers of faculty members of color. And of course, the United States is fortunate in that many international students remain in this country after completing their education here.

The importation solution is becoming a less viable option, however, as other countries strive to keep their talent at home and/or bring scholars back from the United States when they have completed their graduate work here. And just as it is becoming more difficult to import and keep international talent, the United States is requiring far larger numbers of scientists and engineers than ever before. Like other nations, we are increasingly dependent on technology and the foundational disciplines that produce it. Better technology is, in fact, a result of better science, not just more technology.

Yet another consideration as we face this deficit is that science and technology continue to develop in complexity. Whereas in the past many people obtained adequate job training for careers in technology through high school or vocational training programs, society now depends on universities to produce this labor force. And we should not forget that our country also needs large numbers of K–12 teachers with a strong science background.

So we have a shortage, and the old solution is no longer viable, or adequate to our needs. But we do have resources—the untapped talent of minority Americans. This should mean we have the answer to the problem: welcoming large numbers of minority students into STEM education. But this is not happening. In fact, we now have a problem of demand as well as a problem of supply. Black and Hispanic students not only drop out of higher education in STEM fields at a significant rate, but many are opting out of science and math long before they go to college by avoiding these subjects in high school. While there is growing awareness that the United States stands to lose its competitive edge in science and technology (sectors critical to the health of the economy) if we do not produce more scientists and engineers, foreign students—not U.S. minority students—are still suggested as the solution. There seems to be little real concern that the United States might be wasting valuable resources of its own. Indeed, black and Hispanic minorities are viewed as having little to offer to science, mathematics, and technology.

In 2004, there were 73,327 African American undergraduate students enrolled at four-year, Title IV (using the 2000 Carnegie Classification of Institutes of Higher Education system) degree-granting institutions in biological/life sciences, mathematics, physical sciences, and engineering. The corresponding number for Hispanics was 55,725, and for Native Americans, 10,987.[1] The combined population of these groups was 83.5 million people. The number of these minority students who will complete the undergraduate degree is even smaller, for attrition from the university as well as from the scientific and technical disciplines is a serious problem for these population groups.[2]

By itself, then, the underrepresentation of minorities in the STEM fields—which leads to their underrepresentation in the critical technical workforce—represents a tremendous waste of talent, the scale of which is increasing as minority populations grow. But there are also repercussions for universities themselves if they do not reach and teach far larger numbers of minority students: they stand to lose support on many fronts—political, social, and financial. As we have noted above, universities have been active in civil rights advocacy and, to a lesser extent, support for equal opportunity and affirmative action policies; nonetheless, things have changed very little within higher education itself—especially graduate education and faculty composition. Universities are out of step with other key sectors of our society.

To understand the current situation in higher education, we have to look at the education process as a whole for underrepresented minorities. When we do, we see that there are problems all along the way, from elementary schoolchildren who think they can't learn math to high school seniors counseled into "soft" disciplines and away from science. But the greatest problem that minority students face in higher education is poor preparation at all prior levels of schooling.

Much has been said and written about the plight of U.S. public education. The problems that beset our schools have especially serious consequences for minority students, who are nearly always enrolled in public education and whose families are among the most vulnerable sector of the population. Parental levels of education still tend to be proportionately low among Hispanic and African American families when compared to white families. This means more than parents not being able to help students with their homework, although that, too, is a problem. It also means that Hispanic and black parents cannot successfully guide their children through the educational process—especially postsecondary education.

Many minority families are simply not acquainted with higher education, its language, its processes, its demands, or its advantages. They are not aware of the far greater opportunities open to students with baccalaureate degrees, much less the career options for those with PhDs. They are not aware of what has to be done to prepare for college—from selecting the right courses in high school to signing up to take the Scholastic Aptitude Test. Recent immigrants from Mexico have been schooled in a very different system, one in which parents participate little to not at all; these students and their parents may be limited by weak English language capabilities. An apt analogy for not only many Hispanic but also many African American students is to think of higher education as a foreign land, where the lifestyle and language are different—and in fact they are, from matriculation and dormitories to commencement. All in all, many minority parents are not able to give their children informed support through the trials of education—trials that all students experience but that may be devastating in their consequences for these students, as Bowen and Bok point out in their 1998 study of minorities in higher education.[3]

Although many public K–12 schools are extending their social mission and providing extensive services to students and parents, from tutoring to food programs, their resources are limited and demands are increasing. The burdens on urban schools are particularly heavy. These institutions are typically viewed as unattractive work environments, where challenges are great and rewards few. Consequently, they face daunting problems in staffing alone. Recruiting good teachers is a challenge for these schools, as is teacher burnout.

Communities under stress, parents with few if any resources, overworked teachers, and underfunded schools have a hard time producing good scholars. So do teachers ill-prepared or unqualified to teach the subjects they are assigned—a problem in U.S. schools generally. Increasingly, U.S. students are not competitive with students from overseas at all levels. Foreign students who enter our universities continue to expose (by comparison) the deficits in the academic preparation of many of our students, majority and minority alike.[4]

Ironically, although universities and politicians are quick to point out the inadequacies of K–12 teachers and schools for their part in the poor performance of students, similar performance issues in the academy are rarely ascribed to professors and universities.

Further complicating the situation for poorly prepared students going into STEM fields is the importance of mathematics in these disciplines. A weak math background is hard to correct because of the cumulative nature of mathematics. Lack of a good foundation in math, then, puts students at risk not only in math courses but in all of science and engineering. No matter what a student's level of talent, it is nearly impossible to succeed in a doctoral program in mathematics or a math-based field without excellent preparation, and excellent preparation is not the norm for most underrepresented minorities. Other skills less directly (but still significantly) related to professional achievement (e.g., writing, the development of an argument, understanding research methods) are also likely to be poorly developed in minority students who have not had a good K–12 education.

Educational deficits, then, loom large as a problem for Hispanic and African American minority students. Unfortunately, attempts to remedy these deficits, such as support programs or "catch-up" courses, often stigmatize the students enrolled in them. If not carefully designed and implemented—and sometimes in spite of careful design and implementation—these programs are typically viewed as remedial, and that is a sore point for minority students. The programs may even engender negative feelings by majority students who perceive this assistance as a form of favoritism extended to minorities.[5]

Hispanics and African Americans are, in fact, caught between a rock and a hard place when they try to compensate for their poor preparation. If these programs were designed to bring majority Americans up to the level of their international peers, would they "taint" participants in the same way that programs designed to help minority students have tended to do, or would they be viewed as "enrichment"? If programs designed for minorities are viewed differently, it may be explained by the fact that minorities are viewed differently.

Although progress has arguably been made toward a less racist society in the United States over the last fifty years, minorities still must cope with forms of bias and prejudice. One of the most pernicious of these in the academic environment is low expectations of success—a serious obstacle to academic achievement. Although it is good to be able to say that today's minority students very seldom complain of outright racism on campus,[6] the issue of low expectations is perhaps more acute at the university level than in K–12 education; so, also, is the specter of affirmative action—still. Minority students express both anger and hurt at the implication that they have been admitted to the university as an act of charity and have not earned the right to be there, for that is the attitude they sense in others.

A third set of problems exists for these students, and they are arguably the most difficult to address because they deal with the beliefs minority students carry within them. More than fifty years after *Brown v. Board of Education of Topeka,* the minority internalization of the experience of race in the United States is still a challenge to the well-being of black and Hispanic students on our campuses.

Race is on the minds of Hispanic, African American, and Native American students—and Asian students, for that matter—a great deal of the time. They think about how they are perceived as minorities, not how they are perceived as students or individuals. Indeed, a minority student often feels that she leads two lives—one personal and unique, the other as a representative of her race. For Hispanics and African Americans, failure carries the perceived risk of failing for *all* Hispanics or *all* African Americans. It is not difficult to see how the assumption of this symbolic role may adversely affect performance—especially the risk taking that is so important in creative research. Minority students most emphatically do not want to "let their race down," and this is a source of inner conflict as they reconcile the demands of their work with their need not to place themselves in jeopardy.

University faculty may find this deep, constant awareness of race on the part of minorities hard to comprehend—unless they are minorities themselves, of course. Indeed, one frequently hears faculty say, "I do not care what color my students are," presumably thinking that the issue of race has been laid to rest. Telling a minority student that race does not matter means little. Minority youth will identify forms of bias that people in the majority do not observe; they may, in fact, sometimes believe there is prejudice where none exists. But their feelings are, in the words of sociologist W. I. Thomas, "real in their consequences." These feelings and their consequences thus cannot be dismissed out of hand.

It is not hard to understand, then, why moving into the upper reaches of academe in the STEM fields has been beyond the reach of all but a few. The fact that comparatively few minorities undertake science and math—and in a climate of skepticism about their abilities based on performance on standardized tests—contrives to create a negative environment, or at least one that does not enable them to feel that they belong (as other students do even at the undergraduate level). Not surprisingly, they may doubt their chances of success. When they overcome these reservations sufficiently to venture into graduate education, their advantages—unique perspectives on problem-solving honed through life experience, distinctive forms of creativity, the potential to serve as role models to other minority students, and their interest in fields where science and human problems intersect, to name only a few—may be undervalued. At the same time, their probability of failure is exaggerated. They are evaluated by standards developed for a different student population; they find few peers; and there are not many people, including faculty, who understand their challenges and want to talk about them. There is not much energy in evidence on our campuses when it comes to minority underrepresentation issues, in spite of the expansion of programs focused on diversity.

Overturning segregation laws was not sufficient in and of itself to establish equality; affirmative action programs were created with the purpose of continuing the process of achieving a level playing field. The same optimism, naïveté, and expectation of rapid results that greeted the end of legal segregation also surrounded the early years of affirmative action. But while the ending of legal segregation and the creation of affirmative action programs were the sine qua non of equality, they were nonetheless only the first of many steps needed to complete the long process of righting very old wrongs and creating equal opportunity for all Americans. However, when progress seemed slow (or in some cases virtually nonexistent), frustration grew, fueling a backlash. That backlash continues.[7]

Cultural change is a slow process. More than fifty years have passed since the great social upheavals of the early civil rights movement; it has been more than thirty years since the creation of the first affirmative action programs. We are now in what could be called a third stage of the civil rights movement, working through the problems that are deeply rooted in our society and in the races and ethnicities of which it is composed. What better place to do this work than in the university? It is not at all clear, however, that universities are doing the work necessary to bring U.S. minorities into the economic mainstream—at least where this involves science and technology—or if indeed such universities are even able to meet this challenge.

There are, of course, departments with a good climate for minorities, and there are minority students thriving in excellent programs throughout the country, but all too often these situations are serendipitous—depending, for example, on a department chair, faculty member, or supportive dean who works successfully with minority students. There is no assurance that the next chair, adviser, or dean will show the same level of interest or provide the same level of support. In addition, there may be no model for institutionalizing effective programs; unless initiatives are properly institutionalized they merely become a drain on faculty time and energy, dying out as a professor, adviser, or dean burns out. Without institutional change, there will be no lasting improvement in the climate for minority students.

Institutionalizing change is challenging in an academic setting. Faculty both need and demand considerable autonomy and tend to resist top-down management. There may in fact be not only considerable resistance to change but no good organizational model for change or effective leadership as institutions contemplate a different role with regard to the student population in our country or reevaluate long held beliefs about student aptitudes and the mission of the academy.[8] But this is not to say that universities cannot or do not change, even in the way they view themselves; witness the recent trend of institutions identifying themselves as *research universities* or *urban research universities* rather than simply universities. Institutes, centers, and consortia at which faculty work with other faculty and less often with students are proliferating, and new facilities house these enterprises. Outreach initiatives and mentoring programs—increasingly directed by staff, and seldom by faculty— proliferate as well, yet the line between K–12 and university education remains clearly drawn.

Universities grow, change, and redefine themselves. Demands on faculty increasingly emphasize research, expertise in getting funding, and scholarly publication. The subordination of teaching (and the skills it requires) to research and its benefits is by now an old story on most university campuses. This shift has had serious repercussions for underrepresented minority students, for whom mentoring has particular significance. Of the many ways in which top administration officials could change the climate for African Americans and Hispanics, one of the most effective would be to put more emphasis on teaching, and to reward both good teaching and successful mentoring—especially in the tenure process.

Although colleges were mainly for the elite from colonial times through the early years of the twentieth century, the nation's leaders showed considerable wisdom and foresight in also establishing some specialized institutions to meet teacher training needs or serve other populations of students, as in the case of agricultural and technical schools. It might also be worthwhile to note the dramatic gesture of Columbia University in the early years of the twentieth century, when it removed the Latin requirement in order to serve a growing and different population of students.[9]

The second era for universities in America began with the GI Bill; as a result of this legislation, education became the great equalizer in our society. The GIs returning from World War II sixty years ago brought a very different kind of life experience to university classrooms; many of them were significantly different from the youth who matriculated in the late nineteenth and early twentieth centuries. These former soldiers most likely would not have earned a degree without the stimulus and assistance the government provided.

The inclusion of large numbers of students who have a cultural and racial history that defines them in a very different way from the students of the past would create a third era in U.S. education. In many ways, this shift in campus demographics, if it occurs, will parallel the changes that the introduction of the GI Bill produced, or what happened when Columbia decided to serve the immigrant population. As the students of the 1940s did, great numbers of Hispanic and African American students will transform the landscape on our campuses, especially in disciplines on which the nation's economy depends.

Clearly, then, when we ask why there are so few minorities on university faculties in the STEM fields, we are beginning at the end. The problems begin with the all-too-often substandard early education of minority students, and they do not end there. Many of the challenges these students face are also to be found in America's universities. These challenges may not be as obvious as the clear deficiencies in K–12 education, and indeed most are not. The ambivalent relationship that exists between America's largest minority populations and the STEM disciplines in universities has its roots in how universities define themselves and view their role in society; how faculty members describe themselves and their professional responsibilities; academic institutional competition that affects the choices made by administrators and department chairs; and universities' ability to assess potential and nurture talent in students significantly different from those of the past. At present most universities are majority enclaves, and majorities do not experience race in the same ways that minorities do—not emotionally, not personally, not intellectually. Is there, finally, anything positive to say?

Although we do not have systems in place to address all of these issues in a coherent manner, and there are certainly no solutions that work in every case for specific challenges in educating and supporting Hispanic and black students as well as we do other students, we have collected a good deal of information about what it takes to recruit, retain, and graduate minority scientists, engineers, and mathematicians. Good models have been developed by faculty at a number of institutions,[10] and these models generally include:

- new approaches to assessment and re-evaluation of the use of standardized tests in evaluating performance
- strong mentoring and advising, from matriculation of undergraduates through early career development
- establishing a critical mass of minority students in order to counter feelings of isolation
- building community and creating support networks; in fields where student numbers are exceptionally low, it is helpful to create these communities across departmental lines
- development of a departmental mission statement and/or plan to ensure faculty commitment to the success of underrepresented minority students
- programs to help students overcome deficiencies in preparation that are designed with care so that participants are not stigmatized

In addition to these components of successful models, we would add that for minority students, points of transition are especially critical. One of the most critical points—especially as we consider increasing the number of faculty of color in the sciences—is the transition to graduate school. All models should emphasize support at points of change from one academic setting to the next.

The transition from undergraduate school to a graduate program poses challenges to most if not all students. Yet while minority students increasingly have friends or relatives who have undergraduate degrees, PhD programs and careers for PhD holders may still largely constitute unknowns. In fact, for many if not most minority students, the transition from undergraduate school to graduate education is nearly as significant an adjustment as going from high school to college. Like most undergraduates, they may talk of "going on" for a master's degree or PhD as if they were going from a hypothetical grade 16 to grade 17. It is important for students to understand the difference between undergraduate and graduate education—a distinction made in no uncertain terms by faculty.

Graduate study is intense, because it is difficult and because there is no "relief" from it—days are not broken up by a variety of courses and activities as they are in undergraduate school. And graduate school can often be characterized by isolation; the relative solitude of graduate study is exacerbated for underrepresented minorities by the fact that graduate minority populations in the STEM fields are generally small. It is not unusual for an African American or Hispanic student to be the only minority student in a department. Minority students repeatedly cite racial isolation as a problem, a good illustration of how universities are failing to put into practice what we have learned about supporting minority students. While it is important to do further research to increase our understanding of minority issues in general and student attrition versus persistence in particular, most universities would do better now to shore up mentoring and student support programs than to create yet another task force. After a certain point in time, doing further research on minority student issues begins to look like an avoidance tactic, or at best a lack of leadership. As has been noted herein, good models exist, and it is time to use them.

University presidents have influence and power both within their institutions and beyond as public intellectuals, and it is difficult to make substantial changes in higher education without the leadership of these presidents. With support and direction by university administration and accountability built into the process at every level there could be many more success stories for Hispanic and black students. But universities are also highly decentralized places. In spite of all that a president can do, without comprehensive buy-in (particularly at the departmental level) there will be no real change in how universities support minority student education and view faculty composition.

Decisions on admissions, recruitment, testing, hiring, and tenure—activities that lie at the heart of the academic enterprise—are largely and in some cases almost exclusively controlled by academic departments. Indeed, we learn much about the interpersonal skills and goals of faculty by observing their behavior in departments.

The university as a whole may have any number of policies on equal opportunity hiring, discrimination, and so forth, but the individual department is the site where policies are or are not implemented. Initiatives such as the development of a more effective mentoring program or the creation of a student support group must be implemented at the departmental level. We need these sorts of middle-range activities, and the department is the crucial middle ground between administration and classroom.

The talents that individual professors bring to the tasks of advising or sponsoring student support groups, which are of course essentially social activities, are critical to the success of these programs. They often require not only interpersonal skills that span a difference in age, but also the ability to communicate effectively across cultural lines. Of course, not all educators are good communicators. Teaching in one's area of specialization is different from talking across racial and ethnic divides. But an awareness of the need to establish a dialogue goes a long way toward creating that dialogue, and it is an important first step.

We hear about diversity every day on our campuses. Universities have been successful with diversity in the sense that they work hard at showing openness to all types of people, and this is certainly the way things should be on a campus. But this kind of diversity is not the antidote to minority underrepresentation. It is easier to create a diverse campus, with people from many religions, nations, and ethnicities, than it is to successfully integrate large numbers of U.S.-born minorities into higher education. Without significant numbers of Hispanics, Native Americans, and African Americans, our universities are diverse in letter but not in spirit. The problem of underrepresentation was behind the drive to create a diverse university, but underrepresentation itself has slipped below the radar. Hiring a professor from Buenos Aires is not a diversity achievement; hiring a Chicano from East Los Angeles is. Hiring one black professor and giving him six titles is a new form of tokenism; it does not change the composition of the faculty. Black faculty clustered in African studies programs and Hispanics clustered in Chicano studies programs, but with neither represented in the STEM fields, is not a good model for minority representation on campus.

In the United States we like things to happen quickly; we are known for that—all of us, minorities included, for we are alike in many ways. Achieving racial fairness, however, takes time. It calls for profound change in everyone involved in the process, including minority students themselves. Perhaps the frustratingly slow pace of change accounts for the fact that in the past few years there has seemed to be less energy in the drive to deal with underrepresentation and to create a university that mirrors our society more accurately from a demographic standpoint, especially in the fields that drive the economy. But we cannot afford to lose, or not regain, our momentum. When one-third of this country's population remains on the outskirts of science and technology in the university, what does it say about the university and its understanding of human potential?

The challenges are there, but so are the accomplishments. We have learned a great deal about what works; now it is time to put that knowledge to work. Until we see far greater numbers of minorities enrolled in higher education, embarking on graduate study, and represented on our faculties in not only the humanities and the arts but also the STEM fields, diversity will be mere window dressing and universities will have little to do with the world beyond the campus. It would be hard to estimate the harm that will continue to be done to the minority population and to our nation if that should happen.

Notes

1. Source: Commission on Professionals in Science and Technology, data derived from U.S. Department of Education, National Center for Education Statistics; unpublished data.
2. For an interesting look at the problem of attrition, see Alexander et al. 1998.
3. One of these trials for graduate students can be the adviser-student relationship. Over the years many students have suffered under a demanding professor whose goal seems to be to drive off as many students as possible. The old model required students to say "How high?" when the professor commanded "Jump." Many of today's faculty members can give examples of these tough masters and the paces they themselves were put through as graduate students. Unfortunately, academic hazing to weed out the weak still exists, and for minority students this kind of behavior can be unbearable. Hazing is no picnic even without the element of race, and many students have been made miserable or chosen to drop out because of it. Add to this the element of racial difference (for most STEM faculty are, to this day, white) and we have recipe for disaster.
4. To be fair, the caliber of students who come to the United States may not be typical for their countries of origin. These students are competing with *our* best, however, and performing very well. They do not need developmental work.
5. One solution offered is to direct minority students into minority-serving institutions, those that offer a nurturing environment. Many minority families have a long and happy relationship with historically black colleges and universities (HBCUs) in particular. However, for students who anticipate joining the faculty of a major university in one of the STEM fields, the HBCU or Hispanic-serving institutions is not the best choice. The limited access to good research laboratories, among other things, hampers candidates from these institutions in the highly competitive STEM fields. There are many good reasons to choose a minority-serving institution, but students and parents need to be realistic about the likely long-term effect of this decision on an academic career.
6. This observation is based on interviews conducted with students at Rice University in 2006.
7. See Chubin and Malcom 2006.
8. For an example of how quickly the atmosphere becomes "unfriendly" in the face of change in spite of what we have learned about the unreliability of standardized tests in predicting the academic success of women and minorities, teaching faculty strongly uphold the use of standardized tests—a prime example of the irresistible force changing demographics meeting the immovable university. When standards are invoked, albeit tactfully and indirectly, as a reason for the small numbers of minorities in STEM education, we soon alienate the minority community.
9. See Lewis 2006, 50.
10. A highly effective program has been developed at the University of Iowa under the direction of David Manderscheid; Freeman Hrabowski has had good results with the Meyerhoff Scholars Program at the University of Maryland–Baltimore County; and Richard Tapia's programs at Rice University have achieved notable success, producing half of the nation's Hispanic female PhD holders in mathematics. See also Castillo-Chavez and Castillo-Garsow, this volume.

References

Alexander, Benjamin, Julie Foertsch, Dianne Bowcock, and Steve Kosciuk. 1998. *Minority Undergraduate Retention at UW–Madison: A Report on the Factors Influencing the Persistence of Today's Minority Undergraduates.* LEAD Center, University of Wisconsin–Madison.

Chubin, Daryl E., and Shirley M. Malcom. 2006. "The New Backlash on Campus." *College and University Journal* 81, no. 4: 65–68.

Lewis, Harry R. 2006. *Excellence without a Soul: How a Great University Forgot Eduction.* New York: PublicAffairs.

CHAPTER 28
CLASS, RACE AND GENDER AND THE CONSTRUCTION OF POST-SECONDARY CURRICULA IN THE UNITED STATES: SOCIAL MOVEMENT, PROFESSIONALIZATION AND POLITICAL ECONOMIC THEORIES OF CURRICULAR CHANGE

SHEILA SLAUGHTER

In this paper I briefly consider what I see as the standard conceptions of curricular formation in US post-secondary education: demographic (faculty and institutional responses to changes in student populations); faculty as professional and scholarly actors who shape curricula according to the logic of their fields or disciplines; faculty and institutions responding to broad technological and economic changes. I suggest variations in these standard interpretations that attend to social movements, class structures and political and economic forces. When I use social movement theory, I draw on Foucault and give special attention to professorial 'pleasures of analysis'. When I examine the political econ-omy of higher education, I draw on the rich literature that addresses funding patterns and power structures in business and industry, and US government mission agencies with an interest in higher education. I point out how these theories might provide us with a more complete understanding of curricular formation in post-secondary education.

In the 1990s, post-secondary education curricula in the USA are increasingly contested. General ed-ucation, beset with controversies over 'political correctness' and 'the canon', is perhaps most in the public eye, given media attention to the backlash against women and minorities (Bloom 1987, Hirsch 1987, D'Sousa 1991, Faludi 1991). But questions are also being raised in state and national public policy discourse about the value of various specialized and professional fields. These restruc-turing and cost-cutting narratives are ostensibly driven by the need to contain rapidly escalating post-secondary costs. Although the restructuring and cost-cutting discourse is usually not dis-cussed as central to curricular formation, these processes dramatically affect the shape of curricula, redefining majors and minors, and disciplines and fields of study when specialized programmes and departments are cut (Gumport 1993, Kerlin and Dunlap 1993, Slaughter 1993a). The media de-bate over the canon and the public policy discourse about restructuring and cost-cutting rarely in-tersect, but, taken together, they suggest increasing concern about post-secondary curricula by groups external to the academy.

Although public controversies over general education and restructuring have moved post-secondary curricula into public consciousness, most American scholars of the post-secondary cur-riculum continue to write about curricular formation and change as if it were internal to community colleges, colleges and universities. This literature rarely considers the role in curricular formation played by groups, associations and organizations external to the academy, nor does it treat scholarly and professional associations as having any interests other than the advancement of knowledge.

492

When scholars of post-secondary education do treat curricular formation or change, as Tierney (1990: 41) notes, they generally take the positions that '(1) the curriculum is ahistorical, (2) participants such as teachers and students do not create the curricula, and (3) the models are ideologically neutral'. Or, as Conrad and Pratt (1983) note, the scholarly literature on curricular change focuses on rational, linear models of decision-making.[1]

The scholarly literature on post-secondary curricula that appears in American higher education journals tends to treat formation or change as: demographic, i.e. a faculty and institutional response to changes in student population (Levine 1989, 1993a, Haworth and Conrad 1990, Adelman 1992); a largely undefined institutional process by which significant knowledge is preserved and balanced by new knowledge judiciously introduced after being tested by peer review (Sawhill 1980, Gaff 1991, Arthurs 1993); an unspecified societal and institutional process through which skills—science and engineering in the late nineteenth century, computing, writing, higher-order thinking skills in the late twentieth century—are somehow aligned in a very general way with large shifts in the economy, such as the industrial revolution and the development of national markets in the late nineteenth century and the information and computer revolutions and the development of global markets in the late twentieth century (Rudy 1960, Rudolph 1977, Levine 1993a). Even when relations between curricula and the world external to academe are addressed, scholars usually focus on abstract models or very broad connections, not locating or closely examining mechanisms of mediation.[2]

The unquestioned assumption underlying these scholars' conception is that faculty, sometimes aided by administrators, create curricula. Faculty are the first, if not the sole, and appropriate authors of curricula. Faculty experts are seen as generating curricula through research, scholarship, sometimes through service, and as disseminating it to students through teaching. Faculty are viewed as modifying or altering the curricula when student populations change, or perhaps when the structure of the labour market changes, although the processes and mechanisms of change are undefined. Administrators are seen as keeping the needs of the institution as a whole in view, as correcting any imbalances, and as attending to transdisciplinary needs (such as writing across the curriculum) and sometimes, general education (Conrad 1990, Gaff 1990, Mayhew et al. 1990). Occasionally there is mention of faculty politics, sometimes talk of faculty self-interest as playing a part in curricular formation, and often obligatory discussion of the problems the major/discipline structure creates for general education and interdisciplinary curricula, but the ways in which these play out in concrete instances of curricular formation are seldom explored.

Generally, I find the conceptions of curricular formation outlined by scholars of higher education incomplete, if only due to the lack of clarity about specific mechanisms and processes. I think that higher education curricular scholarship has not paid sufficient attention to social movements, the political imperatives of the professional class or to the influence of external entities. Indeed, I will argue that class, race and gender politics, as manifested through the multiple linkages between higher education, the disciplines and external organizations, tell us as much about curricular formation as does examination of internal processes.

In making my case, the theories on which I primarily draw are social movement theory, monopoly or power theories of professionalism, leavened with postmodern interest in the ways that information and ideology are shaped by social narratives, and post-Marxist theory, enlivened by post-structuralist skepticism about grand narratives. I see social movement theory as providing a collective and political explanation for the way that various fields or specialties enter the university, from science and social science in the last quarter of the nineteenth century (Ben-David 1964, Oberschall 1972, Noble 1977) to women's studies, African-American and Latino studies in the last quarter of the twentieth (Evans 1979, DuBois et al. 1985, Acuna 1988, Echols 1989, Altbach and Lomotey 1991, Davis 1991). I extend social movement theory, making the case that continued connections with clients, sponsors and advocacy groups external to the university are central to the maintenance of the status, prestige, funding, popularity and sometimes even the existence of specific curricula.

I see professionalization theory as providing the central modern narrative explaining the success of various curricula (Greenwood 1957, Etzioni 1969, Moore 1970). Although the modern, functionalist narrative is still dominant, power or monopolist professionalization theory destabilized that narrative in ways that created space for alternative, multi-causal narratives about knowledge and curricular formation (Larson 1977, Starr 1982, Friedson 1986). (In turn, a neo-functionalist critique of power/monopolist theorists is now emerging [Abbott 1990, Brint 1994]). Postmodern accounts of professionals rely less on science journal writing as the central legitimate genre and more on complex, dense, incomplete, provocative narratives (Williams 1977, Foucault 1978, Keller 1985, Harding 1986), sometimes even on experiential, fictional and science fiction approaches to the systematic ordering of professional experience (Haraway 1989, Williams 1991, Matsudi 1993). I read these new narratives—with their emphasis on created subjectivities of author and audience, on voice, inclusion and exclusion—as pointing to the part played by faculty as members of a professional class in constructing particular knowledge and genre conventions that simultaneously maintain and destabilize university curricula, but usually sustain professorial privilege.

The post-Marxist approach points to the role that professionals' class position plays in their theorizing and offers insights into the way that the political economy figures in curriculum construction. Post-Marxism, like neo-Marxism, continues a critique of oligopolistic capitalism, but sees class structures as fluid, pays greater attention to a state as distinct from capital, to human agency, to ideology and to social constructionism and has ceased posing some form of centralized socialism as the inevitable and only viable alternative to capitalism. In other words, post-Marxism has become somewhat post-structural, moving away from all encompassing explanations, deterministic approaches and structuralism of the left, while continuing to examine the power of capitalism and the myriad manifestations of class conflict. On the one hand, post-Marxist theory points to the continued and complex interaction between the military, federal mission agencies, civilian technology policy and large corporations in sustaining high prestige science and engineering curricula in the university (Kevles 1978, Dickson 1984, Noble 1984, Winks 1987, Barrow 1990, Slaughter 1990). On the other hand, post-Marxist theory underscores the connections between low prestige fields and the class, race and gender of their faculty and students as well as the relation of these curricula to (perceived) social welfare functions of the state (Slaughter 1993a).

To recapitulate and summarize, in this paper I will briefly consider what I see as the standard conceptions of curricular formation: demographic, a faculty and institutional response to changes in student population; faculty as authors of the scholarly and professional curricula, which flow from research tested by peer review and balanced by institutional concern for preservation and breadth of knowledge; undefined societal and institutional processes through which skills—science and engineering in the late nineteenth century; computing, writing, higher-order thinking skills in the late twentieth century—are somehow aligned in a very general way with large shifts in the economy. I will suggest variations in these standard interpretations that attend to social movements, class structures and political economic forces and point out how these variations might provide us with a more complete understanding of curricular formation.

Demographics and Curricula

The demographic explanation of curricula sees curricular change as faculty and institutional response to changes in the student population (Rudy 1960, Rudolph 1977, Conrad and Haworth 1990).[3] As Haworth and Conrad (1990: 4, 9) state:

> The ethnic composition of American society has diversified markedly over the past decade, a trend expected to continue well into the twenty-first century. By 1996, for example, it is expected that one out of every three 15- to 24-year-olds will be a member of a minority group.... A chorus of new voices has recently been heard in the academy. These stakeholders—although expressing diverse points of view—have a single shared perspective in common: the belief that knowledge, as it is currently understood in the undergraduate curriculum, is partial, incomplete, and distorted. Calling for an end to the exclusive dominance of the traditional canon in the undergraduate curriculum, these scholars have argued for an expansion of curricular borders in higher education to include various cultural and theoretical perspectives.

Certainly demographic explanations account for a great deal of curricular change in American universities, but I see these explanations as inadequate precisely for those groups that Haworth and

Conrad see as the crux of the demographic argument. Conrad and Haworth (1990), Adelman (1992) and Levine (1993a) see curricula changing to meet the needs of the new groups and populations that have become stakeholders. Contrarily, I see faculty and administrators as making little effort to accommodate the curricular interests of these groups until student and community activists forced new knowledge created by them into the curricula. In other words, the curricula were changed not through faculty and institutional response to demographic change, but through social movements originating outside the American university.

In the early 1960s, African-American college students were overwhelmingly concentrated in segregated institutions (Trent 1991). Black studies programmes did not exist at the colleges that would come to be known as historically Black institutions nor at white institutions. In the 1960s, the civil rights movement led to the Black Power and student movements and together they radicalized community and student groups who pressed for increased access to white institutions for Black students and for curricula that addressed their historical experience (McAdam 1988). These social movements provided the impetus for the formation of 500 Black Studies programmes by 1971 (Altbach 1991). Contrary to demographic explanations of curricula, examination of the history of African-Americans suggests that African-American students were not automatically nor easily included in post-secondary education as their numbers increased. Disruptive, popular social movements were the keys to access and to the creation of curricula that spoke to the lives of a group previously excluded from higher education.

Similarly, curricula that had anarchist, Marxian or socialist content were not a part of the postwar American academy. McCarthyism ruthlessly expunged Left curricula, often through public hearings that branded dissident faculty as traitors and spies, cost them their jobs and kept them from employment in other colleges and universities (Shrecker 1986). Tolerance for left-of-centre activity was not great; the largest numbers of faculty fired in the 1950s were dismissed for their support of Henry Wallace (Lewis 1988). Not until faculty who had participated in the civil rights and student movements entered academe did anarchist, Marxian, socialist or third world liberation (now postcolonialist) curricula reappear.

Like African-American studies, women's studies followed social movements into the academy. The two points in time when the percentage of women increased most dramatically were in 1920, as first-wave feminists (1890–1920) succeeded in winning the vote, and in 1980, after the women's liberation movement or second wave feminism (1968–1975) opened new fields to women. In 1920, women were 47.3 per cent of all college students; in 1980, they were 51.8 per cent. In 1950, in the absence of a strong women's movement and in the presence of a powerful, conservative celebration of family values and domesticity, the percentage of women enrolled in college dipped to 30.2 per cent (Solomon 1985).

Despite women being at least 30 per cent of all college students from 1880 forward, women's studies did not become part of the curricula. Instead, the turn-of-the-century academy responded to the ever-increasing numbers of women with informally but forcefully gender-segregated curricula (Rosenberg 1982). Despite the many women in the general curricula and over the protests of women faculty, women who enrolled in economics were shunted into home economics, in sociology into social work, in psychiatry into psychology and counseling (Rosenberg 1982, Abbott 1990). Women were routinely directed to fields associated with women's work, such as education and nursing. Women's intellectual work was separated into spheres separate from men, mirroring the division of labour in the wider society (Welter 1966, Cott 1975, Smith-Rosenberg 1975, Rosenberg 1982, Rossiter 1982). If women enrolled in non-gender segregated fields in the humanities or social science, their primary goal was assumed to be finding a husband, their secondary goal educating themselves to better educate their families, and a tertiary goal the development of career skills that could be applied to women's work, such as teaching, so they could better support their families in the event of their husbands' deaths. Epistemologically, the universal person, the central subject of academic social and scientific inquiry, the active agent in history and diplomacy, was still male, despite the ever increasing numbers of women in post-secondary education.

By 1970, women constituted approximately 41.9 per cent of the student population, but women by and large had not been incorporated into the curricula. Even the literature on students in post-secondary education considered only males when exploring moral and psychological development patterns (Perry 1970, Kohlberg 1981). Not until 1982, when Carol Gilligan wrote *In a Different Voice* was the moral development of women considered, let alone investigated, as something that could possibly differ from men's.

What created the conditions that made women's studies possible? I see the necessary catalyst as the development of a radical feminist movement organized around an analysis of society that saw gender as the central and salient divide (Echols 1989). This analysis, fueled by the civil rights and student movements, was developed outside the purview of faculty and administrators, and moved into the academy only after demands and protests by participants in the women's liberation movement. Until women organized around gender as a fertile field for inquiry, the academy—faculty and institution—remained blind to gender as a problematic, as a major division that informed personal, political, social and cultural life.[4]

The civil rights movement, the student movement and the women's movement were not the only 1960s social movements to shape curricula. The Chicano movement, as embodied in La Raza (Acuna 1988, Shorris 1992), the Native American movement, as embodied in the American Indian Movement, as well as lesbian and gay social movements all began outside the university (D'Emilio 1983, Bensimon 1992, Kennedy and Davis 1993) and entered the academy as students, who became movement participants, demonstrated on campuses demanding that curricula and programmes treating a wider scope of human experience be developed. Programmes and specific curricula were dedicated to exploring the history, culture and multiple contributions to society made by these groups. Simultaneously, efforts were made to integrate knowledge about previously marginalized groups into the curricula (Aiken *et al.* 1988) and to require that students who were not members of these groups take at least one or two courses that treated the experience of non-white male, non-middle class persons (Adelman 1992). Curricula were broadened in response to direct action by social movements and by modest institutional response to these movements.

As many commentators have observed, the reaction to the social movements of the 1960s was the organization of a conservative political movement that sought to reverse or at least contain changes stemming from the social movements of the 1960s. Neo-conservatives made their debut in American higher education through a spate of widely reviewed and well-publicized books, such as Bloom's *Closing of the American Mind* (1987), Hirsch's *Cultural Literacy* (1987), D'Sousa's *Illiberal Education* (1991). These books, which were not written by scholars of curricula in higher education, attacked almost all changes in the curriculum that challenged what their authors construed as the heritage of Western civilization. Unlike the members of the social movements of the 1960s, neo-conservative academics are largely professional and upper-middle class, white and male, and lacking close connections to grassroots conservative movements. Although there are many populist conservative movements—the Moral Majority and Right to Life, for example—the work of Bloom, Hirsch and D'Sousa was not grounded in or nourished by this grassroots activism. Rather, the attack against curricular changes that stemmed from the social movements of the 1960s was sponsored by a number of foundations with an extremely conservative fiscal agenda, specifically the Coors Foundation, the John M. Olin and Smith-Richardson foundations, the Sara Scaife Foundation, the Institute for Educational Affairs, the Bradley Foundation and the Heritage Foundation (Diamond 1992, Weisberg 1992). The relations of these organizations and agencies to grassroots conservative movements are problematic and uncertain. The audience for conservative public intellectuals such as Bloom and Hirsch has not been the moral majority, but the National Academy of Scholars, an organization of senior professors committed to pre-1960s notions of what constitutes knowledge.[5]

The neo-conservatives' narrative of curricular change is very different from that of the participants of the social movements of the 1960s. In the main, they tell a tale of science and civilization being pushed out of the post-secondary curriculum by required courses on race, gender and non-Western societies demanded by new types of students unable to deal with the rigours of the traditional curriculum. Appropriating popular democratic narratives of heroic social struggle by underdogs against tyrannical elites, the neo-conservatives portray themselves as bravely confronting the mass of students and tenured radicals in the name of academic standards, values and excellence. As many commentators have pointed out, this narrative is an inversion of the material situation on most campuses, where few minority students are present, where women are still heavily concentrated in fields according to traditional gender patterns, where white, male professors still hold most senior faculty positions, where undergraduates are at most required to take one class that deals with race, gender and non-Western societies, and where 80 per cent of the students still take Western civilization courses (Adelman 1992, Levine 1993b).

Just as curriculum change was a product of social movements, so opposition to curriculum change is a social movement, albeit funded and led by participants with greater access to power and privilege than was the case with the social movements of the 1960s. The past 25 years underscores the part played by social movements in curriculum change, whether these are social movements of the left or right.[6] However, the current debates over political correctness and the post-secondary curriculum distort understanding of the process of curriculum formation in at least two ways. First, they suggest that politicization of the curriculum is a recent phenomenon, a notion that fosters the fantasy that it is possible to retreat to the *status quo ante,* when knowledge was pristine. Second, the current debates about the curriculum focus almost exclusively on the humanities and social sciences, intimating that hard, rigorous or real science is above the fray, beyond reinterpretation. These often unstated suppositions are a distortion because the curriculum has always been contested, although the degree of struggle varies, and science itself entered the curriculum as a social movement.

According to historians and sociologists of science, such as Max Weber (1958), Joseph Ben-David (1964), and Daniel Kevles (1978) science was a social movement, inextricably intertwined with the struggle of the rising European, Protestant bourgeoisie against the Catholic aristocracy, and, in the USA, a rising professional middle class struggling to find a place between the urban, industrial proletariat and the emerging corporate capitalist class (Williams 1966, Bledstein 1977, Silva and Slaughter 1984, Perkin 1989). As these scholars note, science (whether physical or social) was organized outside the academy, in Europe in organizations like the Royal Societies, and in the USA in associations such as the American Statistical Society, the American Physical Society, and the American Social Science Association. In the USA science was only incorporated in colleges and universities after pressure by complex and often shifting coalitions of professionals, aspiring professionals, university managers, businessmen and philanthropists. At its peak, science as a social movement in the USA was embodied by the Progressive movement, which celebrated all things scientific, from physics to management (Noble 1977, Kevles 1978). Without the Progressive movement and the myriad secondary associations that championed science, the penetration of science into the post-secondary curriculum might have been more successfully constrained by a coalition of clergy, humanists, moral philosophers and landed gentry committed to a relatively static vision of the higher learning, one that saw knowledge as furniture for the mind (Veysey 1965).

Although often seen as a force for reform, Progressivism has been convincingly re-interpreted as a somewhat conservative social movement that empowered a fledgling middle class, particularly the professional middle class (Kolko 1967, Bledstein 1977). Often professionals housed in emerging graduate and professional schools used their claims to expertise connected directly to developing curricula to discredit populist and working class participation in policy making. For example, books about economics topped the non-fiction best seller lists in the last quarter of the nineteenth century and the literate but non-degreed populace contributed theoretically as well as empirically to public debate on national economic policy. However, professors with doctorates (often from German universities) deployed their expertise against the non-degreed in lecture halls, the Chatauqua circuit and the popular press, most usually speaking against the single-tax, utopian and Christian Socialism and any solutions to economic problems that involved direct redistribution of wealth (Silva and Slaughter 1984). Political scientists aligned themselves with middle-class reformers in organizations like the National Municipal League to institute reforms such as city-wide, non-partisan ballots that effectively undercut the power of immigrant party organizations rooted in urban neighbourhoods. Engineers used their degrees to capture supervisory authority from skilled workers and to assert managerial power over factory processes through Taylorism, also known as scientific management (Noble 1977). Allopathic physicians based in university medical schools were able to defeat curative claims made by homeopaths, midwives and hydrotherapists who had not studied the Flexner/Carnegie standardized curriculum (Starr 1982).

Science was able to enter the university curriculum at least in part because it was a broad social movement. Science was not limited to a handful of physical science disciplines, but had proponents in the social sciences, medicine, engineering, agriculture and education. Science was an expression of middle-class claims to professional authority, a way of staking out space between the industrial proletariat and corporate capitalism. Specialized curricula that led to credentials with a university imprimatur were building blocks of expertise and authority. Science was a social movement that established the legitimacy of the professional class.

In portraying science as a social movement, I do not want to discount or undermine all truth-claims of science. I do want to point out that science is an intersection of a variety of narratives, many of which are competitive and have implications that go far beyond the college classroom. Curriculum theorists need to move away from narratives that tell a simple tale of depersonalized, disembodied science entering the university because it successfully demonstrated superior explanatory power, and examine the complex interplay of shifting coalitions of professionals, aspiring professionals, reformers, university managers, businessmen and philanthropists. Such an examination might reveal that the social movements of the 1960s are probably not an exception to normal patterns of curricular formation, but closer to a rule.

In speaking about the importance of social movements to curriculum formation, I do not want to discount demographics. Demographics, understood as student demand for particular courses of study, may provide us with a broad map of curricular development in the twentieth century. However there are a number of cases, besides African-American studies and women's studies, which demographics do not explain. For example, agriculture was once a high demand field reflecting the employment patterns of large numbers of the population. Presently less than two per cent of the population is engaged in farm work, earned bachelor's degrees in agriculture fell from 2.4 per cent of all degrees in 1979–80 to 1.2 per cent in 1989–90, but colleges of agriculture continue to flourish (US Department of Education 1991: Table 236).

Even when demographics and curricula coincide, this intersection offers only a correlation, not an explanation. I have suggested that external forces, such as social movements, together with social locations and identities (for example, social class and gender) come together to shape curricula in complex but quite specific and knowable ways. If we can understand these patterns, we might better act to change curricula.

Faculty as the Authors of Curricula

Most formal curricula that undergraduates encounter at American public research or comprehensive universities (where approximately 75 per cent of all students are educated) are in the major or minor, or courses preparatory to the major or minor. Typically, undergraduates take from 30–40 credit hours in the major, from 12–24 hours in the minor (which is prelude to another field's major), between 40–50 hours of general education, and between 25–30 hours of electives, for a total of 125–130 hours. A good deal of the general education curricula and most of the minor are open to all undergraduates but are designed to introduce students to the major or specialty. Even if general education is construed to include one or two courses that concentrate on race, class, gender or non-Western civilizations, students seldom take more than four hours of such courses, and even then the material is often presented as the prelude to specialization in majors such as women's studies, cultural studies, Asian or area studies. Given the centrality of the major, even with regard to general education courses, the debate over the canon is something of a red herring. The great majority of the curricula are in or shaped by the imperatives of the major.

To understand curricular formation, we need to look at the disciplines and their local manifestations, departments. What faculty consider appropriate for their curricula are shaped by their discipline and department; specialization is paramount. Course offerings are determined not by what meets broad student needs, but by blocks, units or sequences of information that faculty see as inducting students into particular fields.

The close ties between discipline, department and curricula are suggested by the model syllabi supplied as a service by most American scholarly or learned associations. The associations of disciplines poll members who teach introductory courses, then construct course outlines by sorting and synthesizing the results into an officially sanctioned curriculum. In recent years, learned and scholarly associations have sometimes sponsored special interest groups or sections that deal with the teaching of a field or specialty, but curricula and teaching are subordinate to the discipline.

The narratives that leaders and historians of the several disciplines tell about curricular formation pay more attention to research than teaching. According to these narratives, knowledge makes its way into the curricula as part of a lengthy but rational and linear process. Researchers discover new knowledge which is incorporated into peer-reviewed journals, then into textbooks, and finally appears as curricula in the classroom. Scholarly research and peer review are at the heart of the process.

Introductory textbook writing, a central vehicle for curricula, is profitable but not privileged, and is often not considered when faculty come up for tenure and promotion. The same is true of the edited books and readers often used at the graduate level. The content of the discipline, which forms the basis of the curricula, is shaped by scholar-researchers, allegedly exploring the frontiers of knowledge, pushing back the boundaries of the unknown, and reporting their exploits in journals sanctioned by the disciplines. The scholars, not the textbook authors or the instructors of introductory courses, ultimately determine the shape of the field. In this narrative, the only negative is the inevitable time lag between research findings and their appearance in curricula and classroom.

In the learned disciplines' curricular formation narratives, new knowledge—knowledge that is markedly different—is always recognized through the peer review process, if such knowledge is meritorious. Narratives that privilege the peer review process and the authority of the community of scholars seldom speak to the politics of knowledge. They rarely acknowledge that knowledge that is different is sometimes rejected or given short shrift by the associations, occasionally resulting in the formation of new associations (Kuhn 1962, Silva and Slaughter 1984). They do not speak to the political caucuses or special interest groups (SIGs) that formed within associations, as was the case in social science and education associations in the late 1960s and early 1970s, to bring together scholars doing research that used Marxist or feminist theory, or the caucuses' and SIGs' struggles to create programmatic space for material on class, race, gender, ethnicity and sexual identity (Bloland and Bloland 1974). Why are curricular formation narratives so often silent about the difficulties experienced by proponents of knowledge that is unconventional? Perhaps a closer look at the more popular professorial narratives of curricular formation will help us understand the hold they have on the academic imagination, why they leave little room for alternative accounts of curricula.

The most powerful narrative sustaining the position of research faculty as the authors of curricula is the tale of the expert/scholar/scientist/hero, embodied in late nineteenth and early twentieth century works of fiction such as Sinclair Lewis's *Arrowsmith,* Ibsen's *Enemy of the People,* or C. P. Snow's *The New Men.* In this story, physical, biological and social scientists develop knowledge purified by the scientific method, truth that is value-free, non-partisan, unassailable by political forces. Usually this knowledge is linear, sequential, cumulative, and ultimately non-contradictory, therefore easily packaged into academic disciplines and presented to students and the public as expertise. So powerful is the need for incontrovertible knowledge that some sociologists make the curious case that knowledge about which there is greatest consensus is most scientific, and therefore has highest prestige (Lodahl and Gordon 1972).

A related narrative is a story about unruly special interests being subdued, if not tamed, by informed, if not enlightened, policy makers. In this tale, experts (their self-interest tempered by professional altruism) mobilize discipline-based knowledge to develop social policy that serves the public interest. Informed policy makers, drawing on this scientific expertise, are able to see the good of the whole, determine the proper course of action, and sometimes are able to overcome powerful special interests. In the biological sciences, the embodiment of this narrative was the rise of germ theory, followed by public health campaigns that led to the dramatic reduction of disease; polio is perhaps the paramount example. In the social sciences, Franklin D. Roosevelt's Brain Trust exemplifies this narrative. The Brain Trust, which consisted primarily of economists such as Rexford Guy Tugwell and Adolph Berle, developed policies that led to the social programmes and economic experiments that mitigated the impact of the Great Depression. For the story to have an ending that allows the protagonists (social, physical and biological scientists) to live happily ever after, the narrative requires the populace to recognize the wisdom of scientifically informed policymakers, to validate science as the final arbiter of public decision-making (Silva and Slaughter 1984).

In recent years, the authors of these narratives recognized that scientific knowledge evolved more slowly than expected and that mistakes were made. But scientists have not interrogated concepts of universality, falsifiability and testability (Ricci 1984). Instead, they strive to make such concepts more encompassing, sometimes including, for example, gender, race, ethnicity, perhaps even social class, in their accounts of social organization. Similarly, physical and biological scientists have recognized that the impact of radiation, the effects of certain drugs, the environmental repercussions of some forms of chemistry, had disastrous consequences, but have not given up their search for technological solutions to problems in the material world. Even though increasing numbers of problems plague the physical and social sciences, mainstream narratives of science continue to tell stories about the expert/scholar/scientists' search for truth readily encapsulated in better social policy and technology. The only concession these narratives make to intractable problems that defy easy technical solutions is to portray an even more arduous search for ever more perfect knowledge. The narratives never entertain the possibility of rethinking the way science is constructed.

These narratives place disembodied knowledge at centre stage, so we see neither the persons who organize knowledge nor the ways that the structures of organized knowledge articulate with the political economy. Absent is the author of the curricula, the faculty. Or, if present, the faculty are the servants of science and scholarship, not persons with gender preferences, class interests, economic concerns and political passions, or at least positions. Although faculty are not obviously in the text, our unnamed presence is taken for granted, because when all is said and done, we are the hero/expert/scholar/scientists, the authors of curricula. The stories obliquely but powerfully confirm our control of knowledge and our authority over the curriculum. The narratives command the allegiance of faculty because even those of us who question and challenge them believe, in some recess of our soul, that our knowledge has exceptional value.

Although the hero-expert and policy-maker narratives are the tales academics most frequently tell about themselves, alternative accounts of the development of knowledge, expertise, and ultimately, curricula, have always been available. For example, the work of Chomsky (1967), Gouldner (1970), Noble (1977, 1984), Latour and Woolgar (1979), Ricci (1984), Silva and Slaughter (1984), Keller (1985), Harding (1986), Haraway (1989), Traweek (1988), Rhoades and Slaughter (1991a, b), Slaughter (1990), Leslie (1993) and others attempts to destabilize narratives of objective, value-free physical and social science. These narratives do not have a popular, sometimes not even an easily recognizable, story-line. Initially, they were most often told by radicals and neo-Marxists, and at least they had villains: corporate capitalists working in concert with state agents and agencies (frequently faculty and research universities) to turn physical and biological science toward profit and empire and social science toward social control. Feminists told stories about science that linked profit and control to gender. As other alternatives to the expert/scholar/hero narrative began to be told by postmodernists, post-structuralists, and post-Marxists, the villains became harder to discern. Indeed, these accounts often name the university as institutional villain, with the only possibility for heroism held forth in the person of the former object of study, a minority or woman, now an organic or public intellectual with a voice and a degree (Gramsci 1988, Matsudi 1993, West 1993), a hero/heroine whom I read as an overly-theorized, retro version of the teacher/scholar as political actor (Bowles and Gintis 1976).

These alternative narratives of curricula lack the appeal of the expert/scholar/scientist narrative for a variety of reasons. Alternative narratives are often dense, complex, mystifying—not only because of the author's prose, but because they defy narrative conventions of academic genres, especially when they focus on what mainstream scholars see as particularistic characteristics, such as race and gender. The plots of the alternative narratives are unfamiliar, even threatening, with their concern for giving voice to the unprivileged and under-represented, and their location of stories in the domestic realm, the private sphere. These narratives do not confirm our authority in the classroom. Instead, they suggest that construction of curricula involves more than choosing the best materials and point to our complicity in existing power arrangements as well as our self-defeating participation in defining knowledge that undermines our best intentions.

A problem I have with both mainstream and alternative narratives of curricula and knowledge is that very often these phenomena are situated in very simple organizational landscape.[7] When

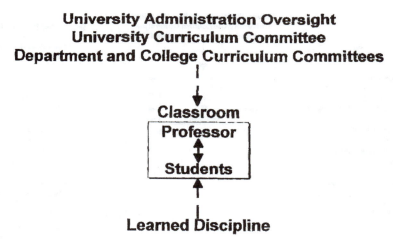

Figure 1 Conventional views of social construction of curriculum.

mainstream and alternative authors deal with curricular formation, they usually focus on a classroom or series of classrooms in a single institution, where the major interaction takes place between students and professor. The students perhaps have ties to student government, the professor's ties are to the department, where decisions about how to present the specialty are made, and, via the department to faculty committees that deal with general education (figure 1). Perhaps there is some administrative oversight. Even when authors focus on enactment or social construction of curricula, these negotiations occur primarily between students and professor, and are generally studied only at the classroom or institutional level (Tierney 1990). Few scholars examine the ways curricula are negotiated beyond the classroom and the institution. If external organizations are considered at all, the focus is usually on the discipline, and not on the many ties disciplines have to other organizations.

The organizational structures that shape the curricula enacted in classrooms are much more complex than those depicted in figure 1. The organizations that mould curricular formation for the disciplines, thereby strongly influencing the major, the department, and ultimately concrete course offerings, are multiple and powerful (figures 2 and 3). Students and professors are located at a dense intersection of organizations, most of which the students are not aware of, many to which professors give only intermittent and cursory attention. Although students are often unaware of these linkages, the organizations in figures 2 and 3 are part of negotiations in the classroom, because they outline the limits of disciplinary and institutional flexibility. Even when professors do not attend to these organizations, they are usually aware of them, and perhaps influenced by them, because the organizations confer expertise and authority, structure opportunity within institutions and fields, and bestow coveted rewards, such as grants, contracts, prizes, positions on boards, and the like.

The disciplines, many of which were established during the last quarter of the nineteenth century, have socially constructed the boundaries of various fields, and *enforced* those boundaries through hosts of secondary associations and ties to the state and various sectors of the economy. Indeed, the very term discipline suggests habits of work, boundaries of fields, and punishment should work habits be abandoned or boundaries infringed. Sometimes claims to knowledge and curricula are legally mandated through certification and licensure, particularly in professional schools. More often claims to knowledge and curricula are informally but forcefully upheld through processes such as accreditation, ratings, rankings, promotion and tenure.

Social construction of the curricula occurs not only in the classroom and discipline, but in a great variety of other organizational settings. The flexibility of students and professors gathered in a classroom is quite limited, if they want to be considered legitimate by the institution and the variety of other organizations that impinge on their classroom. If they do not care about legitimacy, and the rewards that come with legitimacy, then they have a great deal of flexibility—but their career trajectories are not likely to lead them to positions of power and influence in the external organizations

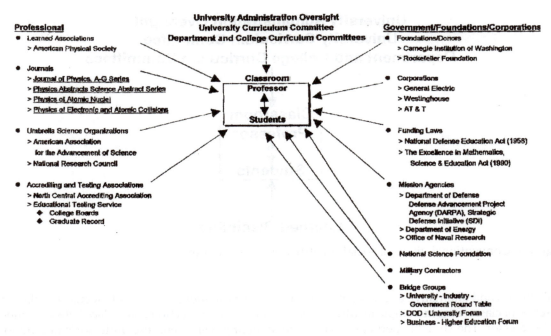

Figure 2 Social construction of physics curriculum.

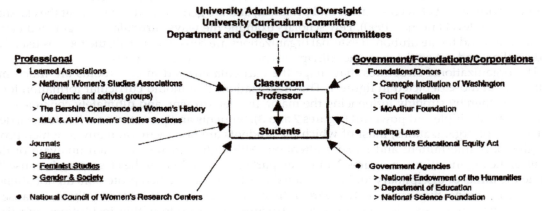

Figure 3 Social construction of women's studies.

that shape their chosen fields. In other words, they, as individuals or as a small group, can embrace liberating curricula, but the institution as a whole or post-secondary education as a sector is unlikely to make similar commitments.

Specialized knowledge is above all organized. The work of an isolated scholar, even a great work, is unlikely to become central to an audience of experts if its author does not share in their community. Scholarship (expertise) is developed in communities, even though the communities are dispersed or convene only occasionally. The myth of the solitary scholar, labouring long years in the library over her manuscript, is analogous to narratives of the individual expert/scientist/scholar making discoveries that revolutionize science in a lonely laboratory. The plots of science and scholarship narratives resonate with many other American stories of individual success, from Horatio Alger to the movie, *Personal Best*. They are professional stories with roots in an earlier era that celebrated the solo practitioner, autonomous and self-reliant. The individual is foregrounded, making invisible multiple organizational services and structures as well as the many people who inhabit them and contribute to academics' success. These stories are often unconnected to the actual career trajectories of late twentieth century scholars. These tales distort the lived experience of academic lives, which are spent in complex and increasingly bureaucratic organizations that are tightly linked to broad sets of local, state and national organizations. Because our narratives of academe, science, and scholarship do not make the negotiation of bureaucratic culture and adroit manoeuvering among multiple organizations part of narrative conventions, we do not see how organizations and the interests that inform them shape academic careers and university curricula.

For example, when we think of American economists, the name from the Progressive era that is usually mentioned is Thorstein Veblen; his books are still in print, even available in paperback, while most of his contemporaries are not. But Veblen was not part of organized academic networks, received few honours, was offered no offices in scholarly associations until so late in his career that he rejected them. He did not participate regularly in organized scholarly activities and was regarded by his contemporaries as a womanizer, a deviant, an outsider. His separation from the scholarly community influenced his career. Initially, he could not find a job, and, after losing his position at the University of Chicago because of his extramarital activities, he was academically downwardly mobile, despite the outstanding quality of his work. As one biographer put it, 'he had no talent for promotion or organization' (*Dictionary of American Biography* p. 244). E. R. A. Seligman, Veblen's Progressive era contemporary, is a name not nearly so easily recognized. Although he wrote many books and papers, few are currently in print. In his day, he was widely known as the 'dean of American economists', and was much more widely known and more successful' than Veblen. He was a leader in most of the organizations that shaped the academic and social landscape of economists and professors: the American Economic Association, the National Tax Association, the League of Nations Committee on Economics and Finance, the Transportation Conference, the Committee of Fifteen, the Bureau of Municipal Research, the Society for Ethical Culture, the Educational Alliance, the National League on Urban Conditions among Negroes, the National Civic Association, and the American Association of University Professors. He was editor-in-chief of the *Encyclopaedia of the Social Sciences*. As one biographer said, 'Seligman played a prominent role in almost every important issue of economic or social reform that arose in his day' (*Dictionary of American Biography*, p. 608). In other words, organizational labour may be as important as scholarly work for a contemporary career.

Because narratives of scholarly success do not foreground the dense and complex organizational landscape, they rarely speak to the great differences in power and resources between scholarly associations, nor do they explore the relationship between these differences and institutional perceptions of curricular legitimacy. Each discipline spawns a list of organizations like those in figures 2 and 3, organizations that link the discipline to other secondary associations, to the state and the economy, although the density under headings such as corporations, mission agencies and the like, varies dramatically by field. Generally, those fields associated with the rise of the graduate school in the last quarter of the nineteenth century, and those fields able to position themselves close to the market during the twentieth century are those with the curricula most highly valued by the institution. Established associations with multiple connections on the right side of figures 2 and 3, particularly to career opportunities, the corporate sector, and the federal government hold pride of place in research universities. The agencies and organizations on the right side are associated with resources, prestige and power in the wider society as well as in the academy. (Because the right side of the chart does not include dollar amounts for research in the disciplines, the disparity between physics and women studies is grossly underestimated.)

New fields that promote new curricula—women's studies, African-American studies, Latino studies, gay and lesbian studies—often do not see the importance of the organizations on the right side of figures 2 and 3 because they have listened so long to often-told narratives of science, professionalization and scholarly success. Even though scholars in new fields may understand that established narratives do not serve them well, they nonetheless attempt to tell similar stories for their new fields, to construct similar organizational landscapes. So members of new fields, aspiring to find a secure niche in the university, piece together the obvious accoutrements of academic organization listed on the left side of figures 2 and 3: learned associations with annual meetings; heavily footnoted, peer-refereed journals; programmes or perhaps departments; and finally, graduate programmes, the better to reproduce themselves. In their quest for legitimacy, scholars in new fields trying to create curricula very often defeat their initial ends by reproducing the signs, symbols and structures that perforce put distance between themselves and their communities, between their heartfelt passion and its expression, between a quest for social justice and its realization. Although the faculty in new fields may acquire some trappings of academic legitimacy, they are unlikely to achieve the status and prestige of established or resource-rich disciplines. Institutional denial of curricular legitimacy stems not so much from racism, sexism or homophobia, although these may play a part, as from institutional commitment to those fields and departments with tight resource-rich links to the right side of figures 2 and 3.

Although external organizations shape the status of disciplines, learned associations and their members are not without agency. The multitude of professional organizations is a vehicle of middle class solidarity. They are simultaneously professional and class organizations. Professional associations serve the middle class in much the same way that unions serve(d) factory and, now, service workers. But narratives of the expert/scholar/scientist render almost invisible the connection between social class, professional career, and association/membership mobilization of state power and private sector opportunity on behalf of the professional class. For example, learned and professional associations are sometimes able to keep salaries high, as is the case with the American Medical Association, do not pay taxes, indirectly subsidize the work of members, often maintain journals that are indirectly supported by professors' research and writing time, frequently act as political lobbies, making the case for more funds for various professional causes to legislatures and bureaucrats, and win government support for a variety of research, outreach and service projects, all furthering academics' careers.

Faculty in new or aspiring fields, particularly those that incorporate the previously unaccepted and under-represented in the academy, do not seem to understand that scholarly credibility depends as much on organizations and relationships beyond the disciplines and external to the university as those that are internal, as much on the field's ability to secure and maintain upper-middle class status for its membership as on commitment to truth. Although peer review, autonomy and the individual quest for truth are foregrounded in academic narratives, the background is equally important. Unless communities of scholars intersect with external demand in high salaried professions and with resource-rich organizations, they are unlikely to be preferred, even though they may be tolerated. To some degree, the stories that academic scientists tell about the disinterested search for truth are simultaneously stories that are deeply believed, talismans against dependence, and devices for securing a modicum of autonomy. Very often faculty in new fields do not comprehend the polyvalent properties of these stories. They do not see that scholarly legitimacy requires abandoning advocacy (Furner 1975) for the previously unaccepted and currently underrepresented, that the only acceptable advocacy is for the existing order (Silva and Slaughter 1984).

Finally, we often overlook our personal and pleasurable participation in power relations that give form to the class character of higher education. As Foucault (1978)[8] reminds us, professors are primary actors in the 'norming' that gives form to the disembodied power relations of postmodern society. Every time we select students, grade, evaluate masters' theses, dissertations, junior colleagues and peers, we are 'norming'. A large and unexamined part of our everyday work consists of passing judgement on others. Our daily decisions shape the lives of students and colleagues with whom we interact, and are fed by our research and scholarship, the source of our 'pleasures of analysis'. When we do research, we engage in discursive practices that shape the narratives that constrain our lives as well as the lives of others, establish norms that multiply, magnify and finally contain deviance, build data sets that measure, calibrate and set up surveillance of the most hidden aspects of our subjects' lives. The perversity of our pleasure is manifest in our participation in the maintenance of hierarchy, narrow concepts of excellence, the violent side of academic practice that labels, fails and rejects. This is a narrative that faculty, regardless of discipline, do not want to examine closely.

Curricula and the Market

Mainstream theories of curricular formation that focus on the market very often portray students rather than faculty members as agents of change (Rudy 1960, Rudolph 1977, Levine 1993a). According to these theorists, students are rational economic actors. As they enter college, students assess their possibilities in the job market and choose curricula accordingly. Because students respond to changes in the professional job market, curricular emphases change. In the early 1980s, students moved away from disciplines popular in the 1960s and 1970s—sociology, history, the humanities, education—and into fields such as business, engineering and computer science to find positions in fields fairly directly attached to the market in an economy of (induced) scarcity. Students and faculty were also credited with developing and broadening new majors, such as media arts and communications, which drew on new skills and new technologies that articulated with the economy of an information society. Faculty and administrators were seen as working together to bring particular skills—computers, higher-order thinking skills, writing, mathematics—to students across curricula, skills that better fit students for the rigours of the current marketplace. In this conception of curricular formation, students' choices as rational economic actors together with faculty and institutional responsiveness to these choices are the keys to change.

Although this conception of the relation of curricula and the market is not without merit, I find it somewhat disingenuous. According to this account, curricula and the market are related, but not in any way that would compromise the autonomy, integrity, or authority of faculty as authors of curricula. Missing from this picture is any direct linkage between curricula and political economy, linkage that might suggest that segments of the curricula serve power rather than the student or the public good. There are numerous accounts of curricula and histories of various fields that suggest a much greater dependence on the economy than mainstream narratives of cooperation between students, institutions and faculty suggest. The alternative accounts are written from radical, neo-Marxist and resource dependency perspectives (Greenberg 1967, Noble 1976, 1984, Melman 1982, Slaughter and Silva 1983a, b, Dickson 1984, Leslie 1993, Slaughter and Leslie in press). These critiques range from the very abstract—for example, the humanities as preserving and valorizing the language of upper class discourse—to the quite concrete—for example, biotechnology developing as an opportunity structure for entrepreneurial faculty or large pharmaceutical companies, using public research funding for private profit (Rifkin 1983, Kenny 1986). (See right side of figure 2 for examples of the relationship between the political economy and physics.)

In most cases, alternative accounts of the relationship of curricula and fields to the market stress the close ties between these fields and specific sectors of the political economy, especially the monopoly capital or oligopilistic sector and to mission agencies that have close ties to the monopoly sector (Domhoff 1970, 1978, O'Connor 1973, Braverman 1975). For example, numerous scholarly studies detail the close relationship between the military and medical industrial-academic complexes. Some studies stress the ties between university departments of science and engineering, the Department of Defense and defence industries, such as aerospace, computers and electronics (Melman 1982, Dickson 1984, Noble 1984, Markusen and Yudkin 1992, Leslie 1993). Other studies stress the ties between university departments of chemistry, bioscience, pharmacy and the medical technology industries (Ehrenreich and Ehrenreich 1970, Starr 1982, Navarro 1994). These studies usually demonstrate benefits to faculty, institution and industry that would compromise the integrity of a university that claims even a modicum of autonomy. They trace the movement of faculty between corporations and universities, detail lucrative consulting and spin-off arrangements as well as formation of curricula that directly serve mission agencies and corporations (Forman 1987, Leslie 1993). Moreover, the accounts stress that these practices are not the exception but the rule, an 'iron triangle' of shared interests between department/institution, mission agencies and industries that together account for the bulk of academic science funding.

Ironically, the physical and biological sciences, which have the closest links to corporations and mission agencies, are those that make the most emphatic claims to objectivity. As Anderson (1990: 135) notes, 'Of all the disciplines, the natural and physical sciences have the closest connections to political and economic structures, yet they make the strongest claims to academic neutrality'. Perhaps objectivity is in part an effort to distance these fields from sponsors and patrons, strengthening the brittle professional autonomy of scientists.

Although studies of the relationships between physical and biological science departments, mission agencies and large corporations are most numerous, a significant body of literature ties the social sciences to corporate and government activity. Some studies link the development of engineering and administration together, describing these fields' efforts to increase productivity by close surveillance of labour, often through time-and-motion studies that provided management with control over almost every physical movement made by workers (Baritz 1960, Larson 1977, Noble 1977). Other studies document the relationship of fields such as area studies to Cold War politics or detail the effects of Central Intelligence Agency funding on fields, such as agriculture, in which international development policies shaped by US concerns with the global balance of power and the export of agribusiness models and chemicals strongly influenced curriculum. Still others link some social science programmes to efforts to control popular insurgencies in third world countries to better preserve investments and markets (Rowen 1971, Horowitz 1974, 1975). A large body of literature in education and social work speaks to ways in which curricula in these fields instruct students in methods designed to socially control the wayward, deviant and underprivileged who do not share the values and habits of the larger society (Piven and Cloward 1977, Apple 1979, Kunzel 1994).

Most of the close links between academic programmes and departments and industries and government agencies are at the graduate level. However, they greatly affect undergraduate curricular formation. As noted in the previous section, research at the frontiers of knowledge, where graduate students work with faculty to pioneer new territory in science, ultimately drives curricula in the major, the vehicle for most undergraduate education.

Materialist theories, whether of the radical, Marxian or resource dependency variety, suggest tight links between corporate capital, state agencies and academic programmes, especially academic programmes in the sciences, engineering, and agriculture. In many ways, accounts of direct connections between curricula and political economy could be understood as fleshing out mainstream narratives about students linking higher education to the market through rational curricular choices. But, as we noted in the previous section, narratives of curricular formation generally deny direct linkages, perhaps because such ties do not fit with the dominant narrative of science as objective, disinterested, and value-free. Direct ties between curricula and external, well-resourced organizations raise the possibility of academic knowledge as the servant of power, ministering to special interests at odds with the public good, creating a facade of expertise that shields the benefits knowledge brings to a variety of élites. Even worse, were curricula developed to cement our ties with external groups, nonacademics would become the co-authors of curricula, reducing, if not undermining, the autonomy, authority and integrity of science.

Historically ties between higher education and corporations were mediated by the mission agencies, with the Departments of Defense and Energy administering contracts that called for university–industry cooperation. In the 1980s and 1990s, university fiscal crises, state budgetary short-falls and the rise of conservative social movements that promote and valorize entrepreneurial activity in the non-profit as well as the profit sector have created conditions that link university and corporations very directly with regard to research (Etzkowitz 1983, 1989, Blumenthal *et al.* 1986, Louis *et al.* 1989, Slaughter 1990, Rhoades and Slaughter 1991a, b). If faculty research is a primary ingredient of curricula, then current course offerings may have increasingly direct links to corporate needs. University administrators, faculty active in entrepreneurial research, and funding agency staff have recently begun telling narratives of science that speak about 'generic' and 'precompetitive' research that directly meets the product development needs of a wide variety of corporations without giving any specific businesses or services a distinct advantage (Wells and Bradshaw 1992). The story-tellers are trying to create narratives that make possible faculty research activity that better meets the development needs of corporations, without making a heavy commitment to applied and contract research that would compromise faculty claims to disinterested, objective knowledge.

At present, narratives about the relationship of curricula to the market are highly dichotomized. Generally, the narratives tell stories about students making rational curricular choices that will lead them to lucrative and/or rewarding careers and faculty/institutional efforts to meet student demand, or, conversely, relate tales of curricula shaped by faculty who are agents of corporations or power élites that pursue their own agendas at the expense of the public interest. Although both narratives are probably accurate accounts of curricular formation for some fields or segments of some fields, neither plausibly explains curricular formation generally. Unless we develop a variety of narratives that cover a range of possible relationships between the curricula and markets, we are unlikely to be able to escape, meet or partially accommodate powerful market forces.

Conclusion

I have tried to broaden curricular formation theory with social movement theory, power and monopoly theories of professionalism, leavened with postmodernist interest in the ways that information and ideology are shaped by social narratives and post-Marxist theory, enlivened by post-structuralist interest at looking beyond grand narratives. Generally, I have tried to make the case that curricular formation theory, as it stands, is incomplete and provides only a partial picture of the forces that shape the content of our classrooms. A richer understanding of the complex and multiple forces that shape the content we select for our courses and the ways we enact curricula may better enable us to appreciate the problems involved in changing curricula.

Social movement theory tells us that the presence of new and different students is not necessarily enough to trigger meaningful change in post-secondary education curricula. New fields, from the sciences to ethnic studies, depended on social movements to introduce new curricula. The most successful curricula, if we take success to mean securing a high-prestige, highly resourced place in the university, are curricula that continue to have close ties to their sponsors and patrons. On this point, I differ with theorists such as Ben-David (1964), Oberschall (1972), Furner (1975), and Ross (1991) who argue that institutionalization in the university, which provides distance from social movements and sponsors as well as room for autonomy and scope for objectivity, is the key to legitimacy. On the contrary, I think that the most successful disciplines are those that have maintained close ties to their sponsors and continue to cultivate corporate and/or middle class constituencies. The illustrative cases are the physical and biological sciences. Whether mediated through government mission agencies, or through consulting and advisory boards, scientists remain deeply involved with corporations that hire their graduates and use their research to develop products. They were supported by social movements incorporated in bipartisan party politics: the Cold War and the commitment to national defence, various hygiene movements and the commitment to eradicate some forms of disease (Slaughter and Rhoades in press).

The intersection of social movement theory and curricular formation theory argues that new fields of study—African-American studies, women's studies, Latino studies, Native American studies—should remain closely connected to the social movements from which they arose. The caveat is that many of these movements are not middle class, and the successful formula for building curricula seems to be the construction of knowledge embedded in middle-class social movements. Of all the hyphenated fields, women's studies, with cross-class constituents and strong support in some sectors of the middle class, seems to have become most entrenched in the academy, albeit not without major difficulties.

Monopoly or power theories of professionalization intersect curricular formation theory instead that sees faculty as authors of curricula by pointing out that faculty have social class positions and allegiances. These theories deconstruct professionalization narratives that disembody knowledge and try to locate knowledge in concrete persons embedded in organizational structures. They inform us that the most meritorious knowledge is unlikely to be discovered and rewarded unless its authors participate in organized communities of scholars. Moreover, knowledge that is markedly different from the scholarly and scientific genres and narrative conventions common to established organizations of researchers is not likely to be considered seriously. Alternative organizations offer some possibilities for developing new knowledge, but separate organizations run the risk of marginalization. If legitimacy, rather than space for exploration, is a key issue for creators of new knowledge, they have to do more than sustain their contributions to curricula with work underwritten by their state or institutional lines and dues from their members: they need to connect with resource-rich organizations embedded in the economy. Of course, such a connection might mean undermining the commitment of these authors of curricula to the social movements that sustained and nourished them.

Post-Marxist theory informs the curricular formation literature by reminding us that students are not always the main link between curricula and market. Post-Marxist theory points to the direct ties between curricula in some fields and mission agencies, corporations and the state. In these instances, the ties are usually tight enough that the external groups are coauthors, perhaps even first authors of the curricula. These connections undermine faculty claims to autonomy, authority, integrity, objectivity and the many other virtues associated with professionalism. Although most fields have discernible connections to markets, ranging from degrees and certification to forums with regional and national business persons who hire their graduates, many are not involved so directly as the physical and biological sciences, agricultural business and law schools. Even within these schools, not all professors are directly involved with corporate and state sponsors trying to build particular products and achieve specific missions. Nor is involvement in the economy and state necessarily bad. However, direct association with resource-rich mission agencies and corporations does provide the engaged fields with privileges unavailable to others. We need to move past the dichotomous debate on external relations (basic/applied, autonomous/dependent) to a deeper and more realistic discussion of how curricula are related and should be related to agencies and organizations outside the university.

The process of curricular formation is complex and defies easy theoretical treatment, but is knowable. For example, this paper suggests that the contemporary debate over the canon, while important and worthy of our energies, is probably not the momentous curricular contest of the day. Given that the major, department and discipline, not general education, are the building blocks of curricula, restructuring of post-secondary education that involves department mergers and closings is probably the arena where the most far-reaching curricular decisions are currently being made.

Notes

1. African-American Studies, women's studies, Latino studies and queer studies do deal with the role played by social movements in the formation of their curricula, but these fields are usually treated in the diversity literature, a literature separate from the curriculum literature. The two literatures are usually not brought together, perhaps because they are written by different authors and speak to different audiences. The higher education curriculum literature is for the most part written by scholars in the field of higher education and addressed to institutional managers seeking to plan how to distribute courses to students, culminating in a degree. The diversity literature is largely written by persons who benefited from the social movements of the 1960s—women, minorities, gays and lesbians—and addressed to faculty and students who seek to at least maintain and perhaps broaden the knowledge and legitimacy of new communities within the academy. See, for example, DuBois and Ruiz (1990), Aufderheide (1992), McLaughlin and Tierney (1993), Matsudi (1993), Thompson and Tygai (1993), Tokarczyk and Fay (1993), West (1993).
2. The notable exceptions to this treatment of curricula formation occur with regard to the role of the federal government. The work of post-secondary curricula scholars tends to view the role of the federal government as having 'turned from a helping hand to a clenched fist' (Mayville 1980) through legislation and regulation. This conception of the federal government sees the state as monolithic and authoritarian, and sees post-secondary education, whether public or private, as separate from or other than the state, a disingenuous and inaccurate conception that pits 'us' (non-state) against 'them' (state) and argues that post-secondary institutions, often formally part of the state sector, should receive state and federal monies without oversight or standard accountability procedures (Berdahl 1978, Mayville 1980). This argument is self-serving, aimed at preserving the autonomy of post-secondary education. For an account of the state and higher education that goes beyond a limited conception of the state as regulator, see Rhoades and Slaughter (1991b).
3. In recent years, feminist and critical theorists within higher education have begun to challenge the demographic explanation of curriculum that dominates the higher educational literature on curricula change. See, for example, Gumport (1988, 1990), Tierney (1990), Bensimon (1992), and Glazer et al. (1993).
4. Parenthetically, I think the entry of second-wave feminism into the academy prepared the ground for postmodernism and post-structuralism. The feminist analysis of difference was essential to breaking

down customary structures of thought. The feminists' attack on mainstream theory and their refusal to put social structure, function or class before gender undermined many standard explanations of social organizations and social change. Women filled this expanded academic space with new theories that gendered science (subverting standard narratives of the physical universe and discovery), that undermined positivist conceptions of subjectivity and voice (greatly increasing the territory for social construction), and, perhaps most importantly, that re-opened questions about sexualities, by speaking to heterosexuality as a historically specific institution that privileged males (Firestone 1970, Millet 1970, Rich 1976, 1979).

These new theoretical trends infused the humanities in the 1980s, but in many cases, their feminist origins were obscured in gendered citation politics that, interacting with deconstructionism, privileged French male theorists. Postmodernists and post-structuralists always genuflect to Foucault (1975, 1980), Derrida (1988), or Lacan (Ragland-Sullivan et al. 1991), rarely to Firestone, Rich, or Millet. Women's studies participated in the theorizing that swept the humanities and eventually began to enter the social sciences, legitimizing gender as a category of analysis and, to a degree, women's studies as a field, but the radical, militant, activist women's liberation movement and early feminist thought was smothered as women's studies became more entrenched in academe.

5. Although liberal foundations such as the Brookings Institution funded some support activities of the 1960s social movements, as well as some public intellectuals, for example, Gunnar Myrdal and Jonathan Cole, they usually did not fund direct action movements. The CIA and the FBI did contribute to a number of direct action movements, but with the goal of controlling, manipulating and eventually exterminating them, rather than contributing to their growth (Horowitz 1974, 1975).

6. In response to social movements on the right, new books by scholars critical of these movements are now coming out. Examples are L. C. Soley's (1994) *Leasing the Ivory Tower: The Corporate Takeover of Academia*, N. Hamilton's (1994) *Zealotry and Academic Freedom*, and J. K. Wilson's (1995) *The Myth of Political Correctness: The Conservative Attack on Higher Education.*

7. A number of authors who write about the disciplines take a more complex approach to the organization of knowledge—for example, Noble (1977), Kelves (1978), Silva and Slaughter (1984), Ricci (1984), Forman (1987), and Haraway (1989)—but for the most part these authors do not move from the discipline to the curricula as experienced by students in the classroom.

8. Although I generally find Foucault's (1978) notion of power too diffuse, turning our attention away from factions and class segments that hold disproportionate amounts of power, I think his concept of disembodied power that permeates society brilliant and particularly illuminating for faculty. His concept concentrates not on the relation of faculty to power Èlites and the upper class, but on the pleasures faculty derive from analysis, pleasures which give them power over students and colleagues and the educated middle class. In this analytical scheme, there is no need to connect all professors to structures of power; we are part of the structures of power because research and analysis are a form of power.

References

Abbott, A. (1988) *The System of Professions: An Essay in the Division of Expert Labor* (Chicago: University of Chicago Press).

Acuna, R. (1988) *Occupied America: A History of Chicanos* (New York: Harper & Row).

Adelman, C. (1992) *Tourists in Our Own Land: Cultural Literacies and the College Curriculum* (Washington: US Department of Education).

Aiken, S. H., Anderson, K., Dinnerstein, M., Lensink, J. N. and MacCorquodale, P. (1988) (eds) *Changing our Minds: Feminist Transformations of Knowledge* (Albany: State University of New York Press).

Altbach, P. G. (1991) The racial dilemma. In P. G. Altbach and K. Lomotey (eds), *The Racial Crisis in American Higher Education* (Albany: State University of New York Press), 3–17.

Altbach, P. G. and Lomotey, K. (eds) (1991) *The Racial Crisis in American Higher Education* (Albany: State University of New York Press).

Anderson, M. L. (1990) Changing curriculum in higher education. In C. F. Conrad and J. G. Haworth (eds), *Curriculum in Transition: Perspectives on the Undergraduate Experience* (Needham Heights, MA: Ginn), 119–144.

Apple, M. W. (1979) *Ideology and Curriculum* (London: Routledge & Kegan Paul).

Arthurs, A. (1993) The humanities in the 1990s. In A. Levine (ed.), *The Higher Learning in America: 1980–2000* (Baltimore: Johns Hopkins University Press), 259–272.

Aufderheide, P. (ed.) (1992) *Beyond PC: Toward a Politics of Understanding* (St. Paul, MN: Graywolf).

Baritz, L. (1960) *The Servants of Power: A History of the Use of Social Science in American Industry* (Freeport, CT.: Wesleyan University Press).

Barrow, C. W. (1990) *Universities and the Capitalist State: Corporate Liberalism and the Reconstruction of American Higher Education, 1894–1928* (Madison: University of Wisconsin Press).

Ben-David, J. (1964) The scientific role: the conditions of its establishment in Europe. *Minerva*, 4(1): 15–54.

Bensimon, E. M. (1992) Lesbian existence: the challenge to normative constructions of the academy. *Journal of Education*, 173 (3): 98–113.

Berdahl, R. O. (1978) *Statewide Coordination and Governance of Postsecondary Education: Quality, Costs and Accountability* (ERIC ED 202 388).

Bledstein, B. J. (1977) *The Culture of Professionalism* (New York: Norton).

Bloland, H. J. and Bloland, S. M. (1974) *American Learned Societies in Transition: The Impact of Dissent and Recession* (New York: McGraw-Hill).

Bloom, A. (1987) *The Closing of the American Mind* (New York: Simon and Schuster).

Blumenthal, D., Gluck, M. and Seashore, L. K. (1986) University–industry relationships in biotechnology: implications for the university. *Science*, 232 (June 13): 1361–66.

Bowles, S. and Gintis, H. (1976) *Schooling in Capitalist America: Educational Reform and the Contradictions of Economic Life* (New York: Basic).

Braverman, H. (1975) *Labor and Monopoly Capital: The Degradation of Work in the Twentieth Century* (New York: Monthly Review Press).

Brint, S. (1994) *In an Age of Experts: The Changing Role of Professionals in Politics and Public Life* (Princeton: Princeton University Press).

Chomsky, N. (1967) *American Power and the New Mandarins* (New York: Vintage).

Conrad, C. F. (1990) A grounded theory of academic change. In C. F. Conrad and J. G. Haworth (eds), *Curriculum in Transition: Perspectives on the Undergraduate Experience* (Needham Heights, MA: Ginn), 337–50.

Conrad, C. F. and Pratt, A. M. (1983) Making decisions about the curriculum: from metaphor to model. *Journal of Higher Education*, 54 (1): 16–30.

Conrad, C. F. and Haworth, J. G. (1990) (eds) *Curriculum in Transition: Perspectives on the Undergraduate Experience* (Needham Heights, MA: Ginn).

Cott, N. (1975) *The Bonds of Womanhood: Women's Sphere in New England, 1780–1835* (New Haven: Yale University Press).

Davis, F. (1991) *Moving the Mountain: The Women's Movement in America since 1960* (New York: Simon and Schuster).

D'Emilio, J. (1983) *Sexual Politics, Sexual Communities: The Making of a Homosexual Minority in the U.S.* (Chicago: University of Chicago Press).

Derrida, J. (1988) *The New Modernism: Deconstructionist Tendencies in Art* (New York: St. Martin's Press).

Diamond, S. (1992) The funding of the nas. In P. Aufderheide (ed.), *Beyond PC: Toward a Politics of Understanding* (St. Paul, Minn.: Graywolf), 89–96.

Dickson, D. (1984) *The New Politics of Science* (New York: Pantheon).

Domhoff, W. (1970) *The Higher Circles: The Governing Class in America* (New York: Random House).

D'Sousa, D. (1991) *Illiberal Education: The Politics of Race and Sex on Campus* (New York: Free Press).

DuBois, E. C., Kelly, G. P., Kennedy, E. L., Korsmeyer, C. W. and Robinson, L. S. (1985) *Feminist Scholarship: Kindling in the Groves of Academe* (Urbana: University of Illinois Press).

DuBois, E. C. and Ruiz, V. L. (1990) (eds) *Unequal Sisters: A Multicultural Reader in U.S. Women's History* (New York: Routledge).

Echols, A. (1989) *Daring to Be Bad: Radical Feminism in America, 1967–1975* (Minneapolis: University of Minnesota Press).

Ehrenreich, J. and Ehrenreich, B. (1970) *The American Health Empire* (New York: Random House).

Etzkowitz, H. (1983) Entrepreneurial science and entrepreneurial universities in American academic science. *Minerva*, 21 (2): 198–233.

Etzkowitz, H. (1989) Entrepreneurial science in the academy: a case of the transformation of norms. *Social Problems*, 36 (1): 14–29.

Evans, S. M. (1979) *Personal Politics: The Roots of Women's Liberation in the Civil Rights Movement and the New Left* (New York: Knopf).

Faludi, S. (1991) *Backlash: The Undeclared War Against American Women* (New York: Anchor Doubleday).

Firestone, S. (1970) *The Dialectic of Sex: The Case for Feminist Revolution* (New York: Morrow).

Forman, P. (1987) Behind quantum electronics: national security as basis for physical research in the United States: Part 1. *Historical Studies in the Physical and Biological Sciences,* 18 (1): 149–229.

Foucault, M. (1978) *Discipline and Punish: The Birth of the Prison* (New York: Pantheon).

Foucault, M. (1990) *The History of Sexuality: An Introduction,* Vol. 1 (New York: Random House).

Friedson, E. (1986) *Professional Powers: A Study of the Institutionalization of Formal Knowledge* (Chicago: University of Chicago Press).

Furner, M. O. (1975) *Advocacy and Objectivity: A Crisis in the Professionalization of American Social Science, 1865–1905* (Lexington: University Press of Kentucky).

Gaff, J. G. (1990) Emerging curricular patterns. In C. F. Conrad and J. G. Haworth (eds), *Curriculum in Transition: Perspectives on the Undergraduate Experience* (Needham Heights, MA: Ginn), 205–24.

Gaff, J. G. (1991) *New Life for the College Curriculum: Assessing Achievements and Further Progress in the Reform of General Education* (San Francisco: Jossey-Bass).

Gilligan, C. (1982) *In a Different Voice: Psychological Theory and Women's Development* (Cambridge; MA: Harvard University Press).

Glazer, J. S., Bensimon, E. M. and Townsend, B. K. (eds) (1993) *Women in Higher Education: A Feminist Perspective* (Needham Heights, MA: Ginn).

Gouldner, A. W. (1970) *The Coming Crisis of Western Sociology* (New York: Basic Books).

Gramsci, A. (1988) *An Antonio Gramsci Reader: Selected Writings, 1916–1935,* D. Forgacs, ed. (New York: Schocken).

Greenburg, D. (1967) *The Politics of Pure Science* (New York: New American Library).

Gumport, P. J. (1988) Curricula as signposts of cultural change. *Review of Higher Education,* 12 (1): 49–62.

Gumport, P. J. (1990) Feminist scholarship as a vocation. *Higher Education,* 20 (3): 231–43.

Gumport, P. (1993) The contested terrain of academic program reduction. *Journal of Higher Education,* 64 (3): 283–311.

Hamilton, N. (1995) *Zealotry and Academic Freedom* (New Brunswick, NJ: Transaction).

Haraway, D. (1989) *Primate Visions: Gender, Race and Nature in the World of Modern Science* (New York: Routledge).

Harding, S. G. (1986) *The Science Question in Feminism* (Ithaca: Cornell University Press).

Haworth, J. G. and Conrad, C. F. (1990) Curricular transformations: traditional and emerging voices in the academy. In C. F. Conrad and J. G. Haworth (eds), *Curriculum in Transition: Perspectives on the Undergraduate Experience* (Needham Heights, MA: Ginn), 3–19.

Hirsch, E. D. (1987) *Cultural Literacy* (Boston: Houghton-Mifflin).

Horowitz, I. L. (1974) *The Rise and Fall of Project Camelot: Studies in the Relationship Between Social Science and Practical Policy* (rev. edn) (Cambridge, MA: MIT Press).

Horowitz, I. L. (ed.) (1975) *The Use and Abuse of Social Science: Behavioral Research and Policy Making* (New Brunswick, NJ: Transaction).

Howard, T. and Rifkin, J. (1977) *Who Should Play God? The Artificial Creation of Life and What it Means for the Future of the Human Race* (New York: Delacorte).

Keller, E. F. (1985) *Reflections on Gender and Science* (New Haven: Yale University Press).

Kennedy, E. and Davis, M. (1993) *Boots of Leather, Slippers of Gold: The History of a Lesbian Community* (New York: Routledge).

Kenney, M. (1986) *Biotechnology: The University-Industrial Complex* (New Haven: Yale University Press).

Kerlin, S. and Dunlap, D. (1993) For richer, for poorer: faculty morale in periods of austerity and retrenchment. *Journal of Higher Education,* 64 (3), 348–377.

Kevles, D. J. (1978) *The Physicists* (New York: Knopf).

Kohlberg, L. (1981) *Essays on Moral Development* (San Francisco: Harper and Row).

Kolko, G. (1967) *The Triumph of Conservatism: A Reinterpretation of American History* (Chicago: Quadrangle).

Kuhn, T. (1962) *The Structure of Scientific Revolutions* (Chicago: University of Chicago Press).

Kunzel, R. (1994) *Fallen Women, Problem Girls: Unmarried Mothers and the Professionalization of Social Work* (New Haven: Yale University Press).

Larson, M. S. (1977) *The Rise of Professionalism: A Sociological Analysis* (Berkeley: University of California Press).

Latour, B. and Woolgar, S. (1979) *Laboratory Life: The Social Construction of Scientific Facts* (Beverly Hills: Sage).

Leslie, S. W. (1993) *The Cold War and American Science: The Military–industrial–academic Complex at MIT and Stanford* (New York: Columbia University Press).

Levine, A. (1989) *Shaping Higher Education's Future* (San Francisco: Jossey-Bass).

Levine, A. (ed.) (1993a) *The Higher Learning in America: 1980–2000* (Baltimore: Johns Hopkins University Press).

Levine, A. (1993b) Diversity on campus. In A. Levine (ed.), *The Higher Learning in America: 1980–2000* (Baltimore: Johns Hopkins University Press), 333–43.

Lewis, L. S. (1988) *Cold War on Campus: A Study of the Politics of Organizational Control* (New Brunswick, NJ: Transaction Books).

Lodahl, J. B. and Gordon, G. (1972) The structure of scientific fields and the functioning of university graduate departments. *American Sociological Review,* 37 (1): 57–62.

Louis, K. S., Blumenthal, D., Gluck, M. and Stoto, M. A. (1989) Entrepreneurs in academe: an explanation of behaviors among life scientists. *Administrative Science Quarterly,* 34 (1): 110–31.

McAdam, D. (1988) *Freedom Summer* (New York: Oxford University Press, 1988).

McLaughlin, D. and Tierney, W. G. (eds) (1993) *Naming Silenced Lives: Personal Narratives and the Process of Educational Change* (New York: Routledge).

Markusen, A. and Yudkin, J. (1992) *Dismantling the Cold War Economy* (New York: Basic Books).

Matsudi, M. J. (1993) *Words That Wound: Critical Race Theory, Assaultive Speech, and the First Amendment* (Boulder, CO: Westview Press).

Mayhew, L., Wick, D. and Hoffman, M. J. (1990) Beyond breadth: general education in the research university. In C. F. Conrad and J. G. Haworth (eds), *Curriculum in Transition: Perspectives on the Undergraduate experience* (Needham Heights, MA: Ginn), 367–82.

Mayville, W. V. (1980) *Federal Influence on Higher Education Curriculum* Research Report No. 1. (Washington: American Association for Higher Education).

Melman, S. (1982) *Profits without Production* (New York: Knopf).

Millet, K. (1970) *Sexual Politics* (Garden City: Doubleday).

Navarro, V. (1994) *The Politics of Health Policy: The U.S. Reforms, 1980–1994* (Oxford: Blackwell).

Noble, D. F. (1976) *America by Design: Science, Technology and the Rise of Corporate Capitalism* (New York: Knopf).

Noble, D. F. (1984) *Forces of Production: A Social History of Industrial Automation* (New York: Knopf).

Oberschall, A. (1972) The institutionalization of American sociology. In A. Oberschall (ed.), *The Establishment of Empirical Sociology: Studies in Continuity, Discontinuity, and Institutionalization* (New York: Harper & Row), 187–251.

O'Connor, J. (1973) *The Fiscal Crisis of the State* (New York: St. Martin's).

Perkin, H. J. (1989) *The Rise of Professional Societies in England since 1880* (London: Routledge).

Perry, W. G. (1970) *Forms of Intellectual and Ethical Development in the College Years: A Scheme* (New York: Holt, Rhinehart & Winston).

Piven, F. F. and Cloward, R. A. (1977) *Poor People's Movements: Why They Succeed, How They Fail* (New York: Pantheon).

Ragland-Sullivan, E., Lacan, J. W. and Bracher, M. (1991) *Lacan and the Subject of Language* (New York: Routledge).

Rhoades, G. D. and Slaughter, S. (1991a) Professors, administrators, and patents: the negotiation of technology transfer. *Sociology of Education,* 64 (2): 65–78.

Rhoades, G. D. and Slaughter, S. (1991b) The public interest and professional labor: research universities. In W. G. Tierney (ed.), *Culture and Ideology in Higher Education: Advancing a Critical Agenda* (New York: Praeger), 187–211.

Ricci, D. M. (1984) *The Tragedy of American Political Science: Politics, Scholarship and Democracy* (New Haven: Yale University Press).

Rich, A. C. (1976) *Of Women Born: Motherhood as an Institution* (New York: Norton).

Rich, A. C. (1979) *On Lies, Secrets and Silence: Selected Prose* (New York: Norton).

Rifkin, J. (1983) *Algeny* (New York: Viking).

Rosenberg, R. (1982) *Beyond Separate Spheres: Intellectual Roots of Modern Feminism* (New Haven: Yale University Press).

Ross, D. (1991) *The Origins of American Social Science* (Cambridge: Cambridge University Press).

Rossiter, M. W. (1982) *Women Scientists in America: Struggles and Strategies to 1940* (Baltimore: Johns Hopkins University Press).

Rowen, J. (1971) Politics of university research. In P. G. Altbach, Laufer, R. S. and McVey, S. (eds), *Academic Supermarkets* (San Francisco: Jossey-Bass), 121–34.

Rudolph, F. (1977) *Curriculum: A History of the American Undergraduate Course of Study since 1636* (San Francisco: Jossey-Bass).

Rudy, W. (1960) *The Evolving Liberal Arts Curriculum: A Historical Review of Basic Themes* (New York: Bureau of Publications, Teachers College, Columbia University).

Sawhill, J. C. (1980) New models for general education. In American Association for Higher Education, *Current Issues in Higher Education* Report No. 4. (Washington, AAHE).

Schrecker, E. W. (1986) *No Ivory Tower: McCarthyism and the Universities* (New York: Oxford University Press).

Shorris, E. (1992) *Latinos: An Autobiography of a People* (New York: Norton).

Silva, E. T. and Slaughter, S. (1984) *Serving Power: The Making of the American Social Science Expert* (Westport, CT: Greenwood).

Slaughter, S. (1990) *The Higher Learning and High Technology: Dynamics of Higher Education Policy Formation* (Albany: State University of New York Press).

Slaughter, S. (1993a) Retrenchment in the 1980s: the politics of prestige and gender. *Journal of Higher Education,* 64 (3): 250–82.

Slaughter, S. (1993b) Beyond basic science: research university presidents' narratives of science policy. *Science, Technology and Human Values,* 18 (3): 278–302.

Slaughter, S. and Leslie, L. (in press) *Academic Capitalism: Politics, Policies and the Entrepreneurial University* (Baltimore: Johns Hopkins Press).

Slaughter, S. and Rhoades, G. (in press) The emergence of a competitiveness research and development policy coalition and the commercialization of academic science and technology. *Science, Technology and Human Values.*

Slaughter, S. and Silva, E. T. (1983a) Making hegemony problematic for the professoriate: power, knowledge and the concurrent centre in America's higher learning. *Educational Theory,* 33 (2): 79–90.

Slaughter, S. and Silva, E. T. (1983b) Service and the dynamics of developing fields: the social sciences and higher education studies. *Journal of Higher Education,* 54 (5): 481–99.

Smith-Rosenberg, C. (1975) The female world of love and ritual: relations between women in nineteenth century America. *Signs,* 1 (1): 1–29.

Solomon, B. M. (1985) *In the Company of Educated Women: A History of Women in Higher Education in America* (New Haven: Yale University Press).

Starr, P. (1982) *The Social Transformation of American Medicine* (New York: Basic Books).

Thompson, B. W. and Tyagi, S. (eds) (1993) *Beyond a Dream Deferred: Multicultural Education and the Politics of Excellence.* (Minneapolis: University of Minnesota Press).

Tierney, W. G. (1990) Cultural politics and the curriculum in post-secondary education. In C. F. Conrad and J. G. Haworth (eds), *Curriculum in Transition: Perspectives on the Undergraduate Experience* (Needham Heights, MA: Ginn), 39–54.

Tokarczyk, M. M. and Fay, E. A. (eds) (1993) *Working Class Women in the Academy: Laborers in the Knowledge Factory* (Amherst: University of Massachusetts Press).

Traweek, S. (1988) *Beamtimes and Lifetimes: The World of High Energy Physicists* (Cambridge, MA: Harvard University Press).

Trent, W. T. (1991) Student affirmative action in higher education: addressing underrepresentation. In P. G. Altbach and K. Lomotey (eds), *The Racial Crisis in American Higher Education* (Albany: State University of New York Press), 107–32.

U.S. Department of Education, National Center for Education Statistics (1991) *Digest of Education Statistics* NCES 91–697 (Washington: Department of Education, Office of Educational Research and Improvement).

Veysey, L. R. (1965) *The Emergence of the American University* (Chicago: University of Chicago Press).

Weber, Max (1958) *The Protestant Ethic and the Spirit of Capitalism* (New York: Scribner).

Weisberg, J. (1992) NAS: who are these guys, anyway? In P. Aufderheide (ed.) *Beyond PC: Toward a Politics of Understanding* (St. Paul MN: Graywolf), 80–88.

Wells, W. and Bradshaw, R. E. (1992) *A Report on Science and Technology in the Clinton Administration: Recommendations for Transition Planning* (Washington: National Science Foundation).

Welter, B. (1966) The cult of true womanhood: 1820–1860. *American Quarterly*, 18 (Summer): 151–74.

West, C. (1993) *Beyond Eurocentrism and Multiculturalism: Prophetic Thought in Postmodern Times, Prophetic Reflection, Notes on Race and Power in America* (Monroe, ME: Common Courage Press).

Williams, P. J. (1991) *The Alchemy of Race and Rights: Diary of a Law Professor* (Cambridge, MA: Harvard University Press).

Williams, R. (1977) *Marxism and Literature* (Oxford: Oxford University Press).

Williams, W. A. (1966) *Contours of American History* (Chicago: Quadrangle).

Wilson, J. K. (1995) *The Myth of Political Correctness: The Conservative Attack on Higher Education* (Durham: Duke University Press).

Winks, R. W. (1987) *Cloak and Gown: Scholars in the Secret War* (New York: Morrow).

CHAPTER 29

CURRICULUM MATTERS: CREATING A POSITIVE CLIMATE FOR DIVERSITY FROM THE STUDENT PERSPECTIVE

MATTHEW J. MAYHEW, HEIDI E. GRUNWALD, AND ERIC L. DEY

The purpose of this chapter is to identify the factors that predict students' perceptions of their institution's success in achieving a positive climate for diversity. This study examines a sample of 544 students at a large, public, predominantly White Mid-Western institution. Results show that students' perceptions of the institution's ability to achieve a positive climate for diversity is a reflection of students' pre-college interactions with diverse peers and the institution's ability to incorporate diversity-related issues into its curriculum. Results also indicate that these perceptions differ by race and gender. Implications for institutional researchers are discussed.

Introduction

Diversity concerns continue to enjoy a good deal of attention on college campuses due, in part, to recent Supreme Court rulings associated with the use of affirmative action in college admissions processes. One decisive element in the thinking of the Supreme Court in this case, is the body of research documenting the educational value of a diverse campus climate and its role in positively affecting student-learning outcomes (Gurin, Dey, Hurtado, and Gurin, 2002; Hurtado, 1996, 2001; Gurin, 1999). As a result, many institutions have initiated system-wide reform efforts to improve the extent to which both classes and co-curricular activities address knowledge about diverse groups and issues of diversity on campus (Gurin, 1999). To ensure the success of these reform efforts, campus leaders have scrambled to understand the variety of factors that contribute to creating a positive climate for diversity on campus (Hurtado, Milem, Clayton-Pedersen and Allen, 1998). Institutional researchers have been charged with the difficult tasks of identifying these factors, understanding how these factors work together to achieve a positive climate for diversity, and making sense of these factors in ways that enable administrators to act with a given campus community.

Part of the process involved with identifying and making sense of the factors that contribute to creating a positive climate for diversity on a particular campus involves understanding the distinctive complexities and constituents of that campus (Hurtado and Dey, 1997). However, the majority of empirical efforts that investigate issues of climates for diversity solicit information from samples of thousands of students and faculty from across multiple institutional types and controls (Astin, 1993a; Chang, 2001; Hurtado, 1993, 2001; Hurtado et al., 1995; Milem, 1998, 2001; Villalpando, 1994). While informative, the utility of these research efforts and subsequently the accessibility of their findings may be lost as a means of informing administrators to make effective and meaningful change within their distinctive institutional contexts.

This study provides a unique contribution to research that considers how different factors influence students' perceptions of their campus as having achieved a positive climate for diversity. This study is the first to investigate students' perceptions of the institution as having achieved a positive

515

climate for diversity as a collegiate outcome. Second, data for this study were recently collected in January of 2002; although recently published, much of the data analyzed for existing research in this area was collected over 10 years ago. Finally, this study is grounded in the context of a single institution. As such, we have the ability to use institutional figures to weight data so that the percentages of women and students of color match those reported by the institution. In addition, we can make more meaningful interpretations of our findings by providing a description of the institution's context beyond institutional type and control; such a description provides insight into students' "distinct racial contexts" (Hurtado et al., 1998, p. 282).

The purpose of this paper is twofold: to identify the multiplicity of factors that create a positive climate for diversity at a large, public, predominantly White institution and to demonstrate how these factors predict this campus' success in achieving a positive climate for diversity. To this end, this study examines the beliefs, experiences, and perceptions of 544 undergraduate students. First, we perform a factor analysis on 65 items designed to capture the essence of the institution's climate for diversity on campus. Next, through linear regression modeling, we examine how these factors predict students' perceptions of the institution's success in achieving a positive campus climate for diversity. Our hope is that the results of this study will not only contribute to the emergent literature on diversity, but that they will be of some value to researchers interested in institutional management as institutions strive to engage in system-wide reform efforts relating to diversity initiatives.

Theoretical Overview

Institutional climate is a term that organizational theorists use to describe "the current common patterns of important dimensions of organizational life or its members' perceptions of and attitudes towards those dimensions" (Peterson and Spencer, 1990, p. 173). The current study is interested in dimensions of campus life that are related to the institution's success in achieving positive climate for diversity and how students' perceptions of these dimensions vary as a function of their race, gender, and pre-college interactions with diverse peers.

What do we mean by a "positive climate for diversity"? Hurtado et al. (1998) describe an institution's climate for diversity using four dimensions of campus life that have a substantial impact on issues related to diversity. These include a campus' historical legacy of inclusions or exclusion of various racial or ethnic groups, its structural diversity (i.e., the numerical and proportional representation of diverse groups on campus), its psychological climate (i.e., perceptions, attitudes, and beliefs about diversity) and its behavioral climate (i.e., how different racial and ethnic groups interact on campus). The extent to which these four dimensions makes diverse students feel comfortable as welcome and belonging members of the campus community is the extent to which a campus has achieved a positive climate for diversity (Hurtado and Carter, 1997; Loo and Rolison, 1986; Mackay and Kuh, 1994; McClelland and Auster, 1990; Pascarella, Edison, Nora, Hagedorn, and Terenzini, 1996). As Green (1989) notes,

> Campus climate embraces the culture, habits, decision, practices and policies that make up campus life. It is the sum total of the daily environment, and central to the 'comfort factor' that minority students, faculty, and staff, and administrators feel on campus. Students and other members of the campus community who feel unwelcome or alienated from the mainstream of campus life and unlikely to remain. If they do remain, they are unlikely to be successful (p. 113).

For the purposes of this study, we want to extend this understanding of "positive climate for diversity" to include more than the institution's success in making students of color feel comfortable and welcomed by their campus community; we want also to understand this "comfort factor" as it relates to students in the gay and lesbian community. For this reason, we operationalized the outcome for this study, students' perceptions of their institutions' success in achieving a positive climate for diversity, as a factor consisting of three items, this institution has achieved a positive climate for diversity, students are treated fairly here regardless of their racial/ethnic background, and gay and lesbian students are accepted and respected at this university.

Literature Review

Student perceptions of their institution and its climate are important for providing a framework for understanding and interpreting institutional events (Hurtado et al., 1998). Jessor (1981) argues how perceptions act like filters that function by attaching meaning to the experiences of institutional participants, while simultaneously emphasizing a concern for the perspectives of the institution's constituents. Peterson and White (1992) add that perceptions of the climate can be viewed as implicit models and mini-theories that describe the ways in which particular institutions operate. In terms of understanding an institution's climate for diversity, perceptions reflect important elements of how students experience the institution; as (Hurtado et al., 1998) note "perception is both a product of the environment and a potential determinant of future interactions and outcomes" (p. 290).

As "a potential determinant of future interactions and outcomes," student perceptions of the institutional climate for diversity are often measured and analyzed in an effort to provide information on the "E" in Astin's Input–Environment–Output model, a conceptual framework that provides a guiding rubric for assessing collegiate contexts in the absence of true experimental designs (Astin, 1993b). For example, Hurtado and others (1995) examined the how interactions across different races and ethnicities and level of academic and social involvement predicted students' perceived academic ability level; for this study, two perceptual measures of the racial climate (i.e., to what extent did students feel they experienced discrimination on campus and to what extent did they feel their tolerance for other increased during college) were examined as possible determinants of the outcome under investigation. In addition, Milem (1998) investigated how student peer groups and faculty referent groups influence students' sociopolitical attitudes; the peer group construct and the faculty referent construct were created from a series of perceptual measures designed to capture both peer and faculty normative environments. These examples demonstrate how student perception variables are often positioned as conceptual mediators that help to explain how pre-college environments and student characteristics influence outcomes related to student learning, engagement, development and attitudes. The current study uses three perception-based factors as conceptual mediators (i.e., perceptions of the institution's commitment to diversity, perceptions of interactions with diverse faculty, and perceptions of efforts to incorporate diversity-related course learning into the curriculum) to determine students' perceptions of their institutions as having achieved a positive climate for diversity.

As a "product of the environment," student perceptions have often served as the outcome of interest for many research efforts interested in understanding how diverse educational environments shape student experiences. For example, Hurtado (1993) investigated how high achieving Latino college students perceived the receptivity of their institutions to a Latino presence on campus; she used perceptions of racial and ethnic tensions on campus as one of her two outcomes of interest. In addition, Villalpando (1994) and Chang (2001) examined the effects of an institution's emphasis on diversity as a determinant of student satisfaction. Interestingly, studies that position perception-based variables as outcomes in their own right frequently use these measures as conceptual proxies for the institution's ability to create a positive climate for diversity on campus; most measure one dimension of an institution's climate for diversity and then make inferences as to how this dimension reflects the institution's ability to achieve a positive climate for diversity. This study marks a departure from using proxies for outcomes related to the institution's ability to achieve a positive climate for diversity by modeling a perceptual-based outcome with high face and context validity, namely, the institutions' success in achieving a positive climate for diversity.

Whether they serve as products of the environment or as determinants of future interactions and outcomes, student perceptual variables have been used in a variety of different ways to measure elements of institutional climates for diversity. The current study uses student perception variables as both determinants (i.e., perceptions of the institution's commitment to diversity, perceptions of interactions with diverse faculty, and perceptions of efforts to incorporate diversity-related course learning into the curriculum) and as the outcome describing the institution's climate for diversity (i.e., perceptions of the institutions' success in achieving a positive climate for diversity). To date, none of the literature has used student perceptions of the institution as having achieved a positive climate for diversity as an outcome in its own right; however, a number of studies have informed our understanding of the factors that contribute to explaining student perceptions of other diversity-related issues on campus.

Research suggests that student perceptions related to issues of diversity on campus vary by gender (Hurtado, Engberg, Ponjuan, and Landreman, 2002; Whitt, Edison, Pascarella, Terenzini, and Nora, 2001), race (Ancis, Sedlacek, and Mohr, 2000; Cabrera and Nora, 1994; Hurtado, 1993; Loo and Rolison, 1986; Oliver, Rodriguez, and Mickelson, 1985; Patterson, Sedlacek, and Perry, 1984; Villalpando, 1994; Whitt et al., 2001) and students' pre-college experiences with diversity (Hurtado et al., 2002). For example, in their 1992–1995 study of 3331 students from 18 four-year colleges and universities, Whitt et al. (2001) found that women were more open to diversity than men before beginning college and were also significantly more likely than men to change in the direction of greater openness to diversity during college. Similarly, Ancis et al. (2000) found that when compared to White students, African American students reported significantly more racial ethnic conflict on campus, pressure to conform to stereotypes, and less equitable treatment by faculty, staff, and teaching assistants.

In terms of pre-college experiences with diversity, Hurtado et al. (2002) found that pre-college experiences with diversity (i.e., racial composition of friends, interaction with people of different racial or ethnic backgrounds, etc.) and gender significantly predicted three democratic outcomes, measured by factors comprised of student perception variables (i.e., ability to see multiple perspectives, the belief that conflict enhances diversity, and the perception of importance of social action engagement). Although findings from these studies do not speak directly to how students perceive their institutions as having achieved a positive climate for diversity, they underscore the importance of understanding how students of color and females may perceive their institution's climate for diversity differently than whites and males. These findings are supported by Hurtado et al. (1998) assertion that "racially and ethnically diverse administrators, students, and faculty tend to view the campus climate differently" (p. 289).

Perceptions of the institution's climate for diversity vary as a function of gender, race, and precollege interactions with diverse peers. The pervasiveness of these findings throughout the literature serves as the foundation for two of the research hypotheses developed for this study. First, we expect that students' perceptions of their campus as having achieved a positive climate for diversity will vary by gender, race, and previous interaction with diverse peers. Specifically, we expect that females and students of color will have more negative perceptions of their institutions' success in achieving a positive climate for diversity than either males or white students. In addition, we expect that race and gender will interact with different contexts and experiences with diversity on campus to predict students' perceptions of their institutions as having achieved a positive climate for diversity. For this reason, we include a series of interaction terms as a block of variables used to predict the institution's success in achieving a positive climate for diversity. We turn now to a discussion of these diversity-related contexts and experiences.

A considerable amount of research has investigated the role of diversity-related contexts and experiences in influencing student perceptions and outcomes related to diversity. Examples of such contexts and experiences include: overall beliefs about diversity (Ancis et al., 2000; Cabrera and Nora, 1994), perceptions of institutional commitment to diversity (Astin, 1993a; Villalpando, 1994), opportunities for interaction with diverse peers (Chang, 2001; Hurtado, 2001; Hurtado et al., 2002; Pascarella et al., 1996), perceptions of interactions with diverse faculty (Hurtado, 2001; Villalpando, 1994; Cabrera and Nora, 1994), involvement in co-curricular activities (Hurtado et al., 2002; Mackay and Kuh, 1994), and perceptions of and participation in diversity-related course learning (Adams and Zhou-McGovern, 1990, 1994; Astin, 1993a; Chang, 2002a; Hurtado, Mayhew, and Enberg, 2003; Katz, 2001 (Unpublished Thesis); Villalpando, 1994). Each of these seven contexts and experiences contribute to explaining significant proportions of the variance in outcomes related to a campus' ability to achieve a positive climate for diversity. For this reason, we selected iterations of the same seven environmental constructs for use in this study.

Conceptual Framework

Figure 1 presents the conceptual framework used for this study. We adapted Astin's (1993b) Inputs–Environments–Outputs model to organize the constructs used in this study. Here, the inputs construct refers to student characteristics and pre-college experiences with diversity that contribute to their experiences with diversity on campus and that influence their perceptions of their institution as having achieved a positive climate for diversity. The environments construct include factors that measure overall beliefs about diversity, perceptions of institutional commitments toward diversity, interaction with diverse peers, interaction with diverse faculty, level of involvement in co-curricular activities, participation in curricular-based diversity courses, and perceptions of diversity-related course learning as integrated in the curriculum. These factors are analyzed as one block of variables because we did not want to imply causality or directionality between them. The interaction terms construct refers to the interaction terms created for race and gender with every other variable in the model. Figure 1 presents only those interaction terms that reached statistical significance. The outcome for this analysis is student perceptions of the institution as having achieved a positive climate for diversity.

Research Questions

The conceptual framework guides the research questions developed for this study. The overarching research question is: what factors influence student perceptions of their institution as having achieved a positive climate for diversity? More specifically, we seek to answer the following sub-questions:

1. What student pre-college characteristics and pre-college interactions with diverse peers predict student perceptions of the institution as having achieved a positive climate for diversity?

2. What diversity-related environments and experiences (overall beliefs about campus diversity, perceptions of the institution's commitment to diversity, interaction with diverse peers, perceptions of interactions with diverse faculty, perceptions of curricular diversity, participation in curricular-based diversity courses, and level of involvement in co-curricular activities) influence student perceptions of their institution as having achieved a positive diversity climate?

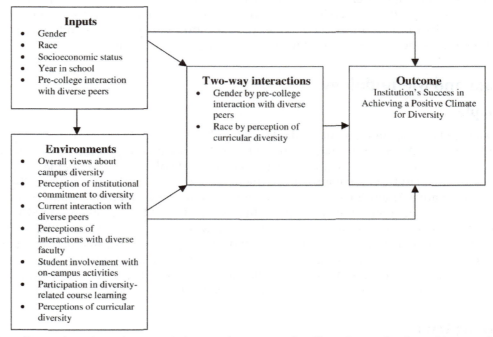

Figure 1   The effects of student characteristics, environments for diversity, and selected interactions on the institution's success in achieving a positive climate for diversity.

3. How do these diversity-related environments and experiences interact with race and gender to predict the institution's ability to achieve a positive climate for diversity?

University Context

This university is a predominantly White, public university in the Midwest. Historically, this university has struggled with creating an environment that welcomes and appreciates diversity. In the university president's words,

> There are those in our own community who are unable to enjoy a life free from hateful words and deeds. There are those in our own community who have been denied basic opportunities that others take for granted. Our challenge as a university community is to face up to these problems, to deal with them forthrightly, to do our part to make the great American dream a reality for all her peoples. We meet this challenge by making certain our own house is in order.

In an effort to make certain that the "house was in order," the university instituted a comprehensive university plan for strengthening its diversification efforts; this plan was distributed to faculty and staff in the fall of 1998. The plan institutionalized diversity initiatives, including the integration of diversity-related course learning into the existing curriculum, the creation of co-curricular programs and events designed to increase diversity awareness and sensitivity, and the recruitment of minority faculty and students.

A series of curricular and co-curricular diversity-related initiatives have been created. Curricular initiatives include: a new core requirement that students enroll in at least one course with a diversity focus, providing numerous courses that focus on diversity throughout the curriculum, and a new major and minor in "Black World Studies." Examples of co-curricular initiatives include a center for the study of Black culture and learning and the provision of financial and infrastructure support for new student organizations, ranging from an association of Latin and American students to a disability awareness club.

In addition, the university has made significant strides in recruiting students and faculty of color. Over the course of the past 6 years, diverse student enrollment has increased 26%. Diverse faculty recruitment efforts follow similar patterns: from 61 minority faculty members in 1992 to 97 in 2002. Although this university has not yet reached its goals with regard to increasing the structural diversity of the campus, it continues to brainstorm new programs and initiatives with the intention of creating a more welcoming and diverse campus community.

Data and Methodology

Sample

A sample of 3000 undergraduate students was randomly selected from 14,413 at a large, Midwestern, predominantly White, public university. Of the 3000 students solicited for participation in the study, 544 returned useable surveys; this yielded a response rate of 18.1%. The sample consisted of 70% females and 24% students of color (African American = 9.8%; Asian/Pacific = 6.8%; Hispanic/Latino = 5.0%; and Native American = 1.5%). Nearly 6% of students did not provide information on their race or ethnicity. Student respondents reported that nearly 85% of their mothers and 87% of their fathers had attended college. Institutional percentages show that the 544 students in this sample overrepresented females and students of color, at 55% and 10% respectively. Because gender and race appear in the literature as critically important variables for consideration in any models designed to predict outcomes related to diversity-related issues, the data were weighted so that the percentages of women and students of color matched percentages reported by the institution.

Missing Data

Due to the relatively low response rate, we performed mean substitution imputations for missing data on all continuous independent variables that made up the factors used in the model. For the dependent variables that comprised the criterion identified for use in this study, we did not impute data. Also, we did not impute data for categorical variables.

Instrument

The survey instrument used for this study was adopted from a diversity climate survey that was developed at the Higher Education Research Institute (HERI) at University of California at Los Angeles. HERI's survey was adapted from a diversity climate survey previously developed at University of California at Berkeley.

The survey questions have been tested over time and continue to hold content validity. Cronbach's alpha was used as a measure of reliability for a factor analysis designed to test how well the questions on the survey measured the particular constructs of the survey (e.g., experience with diversity, etc.); alpha levels for this instrument indicated that the survey was well within the limits of acceptable reliability.

In addition, the survey was adapted to reflect diversity-related concerns indigenous to this university. For example, a series of items were designed to measure the climate for diversity of the city in which the university is situated; students were asked to indicate the degree to which they agreed with statements like, "XXX is a diverse community," and "XXX is a safe (i.e., crime-free) community."

Moreover, in order to measure the different kinds of diversity represented on campus, questions were specifically asked about racial/ethnic diversity, religious diversity, LGBT diversity, and gender diversity. The survey also included some open-ended items.

Variables

In order to reduce the number of variables used in the regression model, exploratory factor analyses were conducted using principle axis factoring and orthogonal rotation methods for the independent variables. When necessary, certain items were reverse coded for ease in interpretation. Variables selected for the factor analysis were standardized due to differing scales of measurement for individual variables; factors with eigenvalues greater than 1 were included in the model. Factor loadings that contained a score of at least .35 or higher were used in the development of subsequent summated scales. Internal validity for each of these scales was moderate, with Cronbach's alpha reliabilities ranging from .60 to .90; see Table 1.

Dependent Variable

One of these factors, "institution's success in achieving a positive climate for diversity," served as the criterion for the multiple regression analysis. This factor was created from three individual items: students are treated fairly here regardless of their racial/ethnic background, gay and lesbian students are accepted and respected, and this university has achieved a positive climate for diversity. Cronbach's alpha for this factor was .60.

Independent Variable

Three blocks of independent variables were used to predict the variance in the criterion factor, institution's success in achieving a positive climate for diversity.

The first block of predicting variables included student demographics, such as sex, race, socioeconomic status (from here on, SES), year in school (i.e., first-year, sophomore, junior, senior), and a factor constituting precollege interactions with diverse peers. Race was coded white students and students of color due to the small sample sizes of the students of color subgroups. SES was computed as a summative index of mother and father's education.

The second block of variables included seven factors: overall beliefs about campus diversity, perceptions of the institution's commitment to diversity, interaction with diverse peers, perceptions of interactions with diverse faculty, perceptions of curricular diversity, participation in curricular-based diversity courses, and level of involvement in co-curricular activities. See Table 1 for factor loadings, individual items, and reliabilities.

TABLE 1

Items, Factor Loadings, and Reliabilities for Dependent and Independent Variables

Factor and Survey Items	Factor Loading	Alpha
DEPENDENT VARIABLE		
Positive climate for diversity[a]		.60
This institution has achieved a positive climate for diversity	.83	
Students are treated fairly here regardless of their racial/ethnic background	.65	
Gay and lesbian students are accepted and respected	.63	
INDEPENDENT VARIABLES		
Pre-college interaction with diverse peers[c]		.79
The neighborhood where you grew up	.84	
The high school you attended	.79	
Your friends in general	.78	
Overall views about campus diversity[a]		.78
Emphasizing diversity leads to campus disunity	.71	
One problem with pursuing diversity goal is admission of too many unprepared students	.71	
Affirmative action leads to the hiring of less qualified faculty and staff	.67	
Institution is placing too much emphasis on achieving diversity at expense of enhancing prestige	.65	
Student perceptions of institutional commitment to diversity[b]		.87
Creating a diverse multicultural environment on campus	.82	
Developing among students and faculty an appreciation for a multicultural society	.76	
Increasing the representation of minorities in the faculty and administration	.75	
Recruiting more minority students	.75	
Increasing an understanding of a multicultural society	.72	
Current interaction with diverse peers[d]		.82
Socialized with someone from a different racial/ethnic group	.86	
Studied with someone from a different racial/ethnic group	.74	
Dined with someone from a different racial/ethnic group	.73	
Student perceptions about interactions with diverse faculty[a]	.84	
Faculty who are race/ethnically similar to me address issues of greater relevance to me	.81	
I get more personal attention from faculty who are racially/ethnically similar to me	.76	
Student involvement in campus activities		.56
Been a member of a campus group/club[e]	.64	
Attended a cultural event[e]	.60	
Participated in ethnic or cross-cultural activities and organizations[c]	.59	
Served in a leadership role in the university[c]	.47	
Participation in diversity-related course learning[e]		.63
Taken a course related to women's studies	.69	
Taken a course addressing gay/lesbian issues	.66	
Student perceptions about curricular diversity[a]		.62
Many courses include minority group perspectives	.77	
Non-dominant cultures are emphasized in the curriculum	.68	
The emphasis on Western Civilization and non-dominant cultures is balanced in the curriculum	.60	

[a]Four-point scale: From Strongly disagree = 1 to Strongly agree = 4.
[b]Four-point scale: From Not a priority = 1 to Highest priority = 4.
[c]Five-point scale: From All or nearly all white = 1 to All or nearly all non-white = 5.
[d]Three-point scale: From Never = 1 to Frequently = 3.
[e]Two-point scale: From No = 1 to Yes = 1.

The third block of variables included for consideration in the full model consisted of a series of two-way interactions. Interaction terms were computed for race, sex and each of the factors developed for this study.

Analyses

Descriptive and exploratory analyses for all variables and factors were performed. This was done for two reasons: to determine the relationship between each predicting variable and the criterion and to check for significant relationships between predicting variables. Frequencies and cross-tabulations were used to examine subgroup phenomena (e.g., previous interaction with diverse peers by race/ethnicity and on-campus interaction with diverse peers by race/ethnicity). Descriptive analyses of the dependent variable, this institution has achieved a positive climate for diversity, indicated that this factor was normally distributed and shared linear relationships to each predicting variable. Residual diagnostic analyses confirmed that all assumptions of linear regression (i.e., normality, linearity, independence and homogeneity) were met.

A series of multiple linear regression analyses were performed to predict the criterion, this institution has achieved a positive climate for diversity. The first model included student demographics and precollege interactions with diverse peers. The second model included student demographics and the seven environmental factors. The third model included student demographics, the seven factors and all possible two-way interactions with race, sex and each of the eight factors (the seven environmental factors and the one factor measuring students' precollege interaction with diverse peers). Demographic variables and environmental factors were retained in each model as control variables, however, in an effort to improve the parsimony of the model, interactions that did not significantly contribute to explaining the variability in the criterion were excluded from consideration in the final model.

Based on these results, we performed a second series of regressions for white and students of color and men and women, respectively. These regressions helped us identify consistent predictors of the institution's success in achieving a positive climate for diversity across the different subgroups. There were not, however, sufficient samples size to run regressions for the intersection of these four groups (e.g., female students of color, male students of color, etc.).

Results

Analysis One

Student demographics (sex, race, SES, year in school) and previous interaction with diverse peers collectively explained a significant 4% of the variance in students' perceptions of their institution as having achieved a positive campus climate for diversity. Of these variables, year in school and previous interactions with diverse peers were statistically significant. When compared to first-year students, sophomores (b ¼ :13, $p < :05$) were significantly less likely to perceive their institutions as having achieved a positive climate for diversity. Students with more pre-college interactions with diverse peers (b ¼ :14, $p < :01$) were less likely to perceive their institutions as having succeeded in creating a positive climate for diversity. See Table 2 for unstandardized and standardized regression coefficients for each model.

The second block of variables, environments for diversity, collectively explained a significant 19% of the variance in students' perceptions of their institutions as having achieved a positive campus climate for diversity. After the second block of variables was entered into the model, none of the student demographic variables, including pre-college interactions with diverse peers, reached statistical significance.

Five of the seven predictors that comprised the environmental construct reached statistical significance. Students' perceptions of curricular diversity (b ¼ :28, $p < :01$) was the strongest environmental predictor; students who were more likely to perceive their curriculum to be diverse were significantly more likely to perceive that their institutions had succeeded in achieving a positive

TABLE 2

Weighted Regression Models Predicting Students' Perceptions of Institutional Success of Achieving a Positive Climate for Diversity

	Model 1			Model 2			Model 3		
	B	SE B	b	B	SE B	b	B	SE B	b
Student Demographics									
Constant	).40	.28		).51	.27		)3.25	.64	
Female	.02	.06	.02	.12	.06	.08	1.93	.39	1.21**
Students of color	).15	.11	).07	.06	.11	.03	.08	.11	.03
SES	).01	.02	).03	).003	.01	.01	).004	.01	.01
Sophomore (first year)	).21	.11	).13*	.08	.10	.05	.04	.10	.02
Junior (first year)	).17	.10	.11	.04	.10	.03	.01	.10	.01
Senior (first year)	).19	.10	.13	.04	.10	.03	.01	.09	.01
Pre-college interaction with diverse peers	).15	.05	).14**	).09	.05	.08	.30	.07	).27**
Environments for Diversity									
Overall views about campus diversity				.12	.04	.12**	.12	.04	.13**
Perception of institutional commitment to diversity				.04	.04	.04	).04	.04	.05
Current interaction with diverse peers				.04	.04	.05	.04	.04	.05
Perceptions of interaction with diverse faculty				.09	.03	).11**	).07	.03	).09*
Student involvement with on-campus activities				.12	.05	).12**	.11	.05	).10*
Participation in diversity-related course learning				.13	.04	).15**	.13	.04	).15**
Perception of curricular diversity				.28	.04	.28**	.24	.04	.25**
Two-way Interactions									
Female X pre-college interaction with diverse peers							.43	.09	1.35**
Students of Color X perception of curricular diversity							.24	.13	).09*
Model Statistics	Adj. R² = .04**			Adj. R² = .19**			Adj. R² = .23**		

Note: Parentheses indicate reference group used for comparison.
*p < .05, **p < .01.

climate for diversity. The next strongest predictor was participation in diversity-related course learning (b ¼ :15, $p <$:01). Students who participated in more courses related to understanding marginalized groups were less likely to perceive that their institutions had achieved a positive climate for diversity. Next followed students' overall views about campus diversity (b ¼ :12, $p <$:01) and students' involvement with on-campus activities (b ¼ :12, $p <$:05); the less involved a student, the more likely he or she is to perceive their institutions as being successful in achieving a positive climate for diversity. The final significant predictor among this block of variables was student perceptions of their interactions with diverse faculty (b ¼ :11, $p <$:01). This finding suggests that students who perceived their interaction with diverse faculty to be less relevant and less supportive were more likely to perceive that their institution had achieved a positive climate for diversity.

The third and final model included all of the demographic variables, pre-college interactions with diverse peers, the seven environmental variables and 2 two-way interactions between these variables. Adding these interaction terms to the model significantly contributed an additional 4% of the overall variance in the criterion.

Two interactions were statistically significant. Overall, students with more pre-college interactions with diverse peers were less likely to perceive their institutions as having succeeded in creating a positive climate for diversity. This effect is different for men than it is for women. When compared with females with few pre-college interactions with diverse peers, females reporting a greater number of pre-college interactions with diverse peers were more likely to perceive that the campus had achieved a positive climate for diversity. For men, the opposite is true. Males reporting more pre-college interactions with diverse peers had more negative perceptions of their institution's ability to achieve a positive climate for diversity than did men with fewer pre-college interactions with diverse peers.

The second significant interaction was race by perception of curricular diversity, which was significant ($p <$:05). On average, holding all other variables constant, students who perceived that the curriculum reflected diversity were more likely to perceive that the institution had achieved a positive climate for diversity. This effect was stronger for students of color than for white students. Students of color who perceived the curriculum to be less integrated with diversity-related content were less likely to perceive their campus as having achieved a positive campus climate for diversity than white students who perceived the curriculum to be less integrated with diversity-related content. Students of color who perceived the curriculum to be more highly integrated with diversity-related content were more likely to perceive their campus as having achieved a positive climate for diversity than white students with the same perceptions of a highly integrated diverse curriculum.

After adding this block of variables, gender and pre-college interactions with diverse peers reached statistical significance. Perceptions of curricular diversity, participation in course-related diversity learning, overall views about campus diversity, student involvement with on-campus activities and perceptions of interactions with diverse faculty remained statistically significant.

Analysis Two

We performed a second series of regressions for white students and students of color and men and women, respectively. For male students, the model explained a significant 22% of the variance in the criterion. For females, the model explained a significant 19%. For white students, the model explained a significant 14%. For students of color, the model explained a significant 13%. Here, we want to note that after weighting, the sample size for students of color was reduced to 52 total cases; any findings reported for this group must be interpreted with caution. See Table 3 for the patterns across subgroups.

In terms of student demographics, for males, students with more precollege interactions with diverse peers were less likely to perceive their institutions as having succeeded in creating a positive climate for diversity (b ¼ :27, $p <$:01).

Of the seven environmental factors, only perception of curricular diversity was a positive significant predictor of a perceived positive campus climate for diversity across all subgroups. This effect was strongest for students of color (b ¼ :39, $p <$:01) and women (b ¼ :33, $p <$:01). The effects for

TABLE 3

Comparison of Regression Models Predicting Students' Perceptions of the Institution's Positive Climate for Diversity for Students of Color, White Students, Men and Women, Respectively

	Race		Gender	
	Students of Color[a] b (n 5 52)	White b (n 5 477)	Men b (n 5 235)	Women b (n 5 293)
Student Demographics				
Female	.14	.07		
Student of color			.03	).02
SES	.03	).02	).09	.06
Sophomore	).14	).04	.08	).13
Junior	).09	).01	.06	).08
Senior	).14	.001	.08	).10
Pre-college interactions with diverse peers	).03	).08	).27**	.11
Environments for Diversity				
Overall views about campus diversity	.05	.13**	.15*	.12*
Perception of institutional commitment to diversity	.12	.04	.01	.10
Current interaction with diverse peers	).03	.06	.10	.01
Perceptions of interaction with div/same faculty	).11	).09*	).09	).08
Student involvement with on-campus activities	).11	).11*	).18**	).01
Participation in diversity related course learning	).15	).16**	).09	).19**
Perception of curricular diversity	.39**	.26**	.20**	.33**
Model Statistics	Adj. R² = .13*	Adj. R² = .14**	Adj. R² = .22**	Adj. R² = .19**

[a] After weighting, the sample size for students of color was reduced to 52 total cases. Findings from this model should be interpreted with caution.
*p < .05, **p < .01.

white students (b ¼ :26, $p < :01$) and males (b ¼ :20, $p < :01$) were weaker, but still statistically significant. In addition, one other environmental predictor, overall views about campus diversity, was a positive predictor for three student subgroups, namely men (b ¼ :15, $p < :05$), white students (b ¼ :13, $p < :01$), and women (b ¼ :12, $p < :05$), but not students of color.

Three environmental predictors shared negative relationships with perceptions of the institution as having achieved a positive campus climate for diversity. For white students (b ¼ :16, $p < :01$) and women (b ¼ :19, $p < :01$), participating in diversity-related course learning had negative effects on their perceptions of the campus as having achieved a positive climate for diversity. In addition, white students (b ¼ :11, $p < :01$) who perceived their interaction with diverse faculty to be less relevant and less supportive were more likely to perceive that their institution had achieved a positive climate for diversity.

For males (b ¼ :18, $p < :01$) and white students (b ¼ :11, $p < :05$), student involvement with on-campus activities had negative effects on their perceptions of the institution as having achieved a positive climate for diversity.

Limitations

There are several limitations to this study. First is the low response rate of 18% for the students sampled for this study. We realize that this is much lower than the normally acceptable convention of 30–40%. To compensate for the low response rate, we have weighted the data to match the institutional percentages for males, females, students of color and white students. After weighting, the small subgroup size of student of color likely had an effect on the statistical power of the respective statistical analyses.

Another limitation to the study is the marginal reliability coefficients for the criterion and several of the independent predictors. For example, Cronbach's alpha for the criterion was .60. Nunnelly (1978) has stated that alphas should be at least .70. Given the content validity of the measures in question, we decided to proceed with the analytical strategy developed for this study. We think that the small sample size and sampling variability contributed to sampling errors that decreased the factor reliabilities.

Discussion and Conclusion

Creating a supportive climate for diversity may seem to many to be an ephemeral goal, both in terms of external pressure to move in that direction and the longevity of any successful efforts at achieving the same. Nevertheless, these findings provide specific guidance for moving toward a positive climate from the perspective of undergraduates, including the need to have a publicly visible institutional commitment toward diversity goals and obvious reinforcement of these kinds of messages as embodied in the curriculum. The recent Supreme Court rulings about the role of affirmative action in college admissions and the recognized importance that campus diversity has for the growth and development of all students has served to reinforce the general trend toward emphasizing diversity. Of course, the particular history of a campus and the experiences that students bring with them to the campus are important contributors to institutional dynamics, suggesting the need for additional campus-based studies of this kind.

Taken together, the results of our analyses suggest that student experiences related to diversity do have an influence on the perception of an institution having achieved a positive campus climate, but that these effects are not always straightforward. While students are to varying degrees enveloped in experiences that are diversity related, including many not directly tied to institutional action (e.g., interaction with diverse peers), these experiences do not automatically produce perceptions of a positive climate. Rather, when students are exposed to diversity they tend to develop a more critical perspective about the ways in which their campuses support and foster a positive climate for diversity, as opposed to simply accepting that their institutions have positive institutional climates.

One aspect where this is particularly clear is in the influence of curriculum and how faculty practice reinforces diversity goals. This finding holds true for all subgroups but most effectively for students of color. In terms of formal and public commitment, an institution's ability to achieve a positive climate for diversity is indeed reflected by the faculty's commitment to incorporate diversity-related issues into their academic agenda. Within its very definition, an institution's curriculum functions to communicate "a college's or program's mission, or collective expression of what is important for students to learn" (Stark and Lattuca, 1997, p. 7). In other words, the curriculum reflects the institution's priorities, especially for students of color. In terms of diversity, the magnitude of an institution's commitment to diversity is measured by its willingness to integrate different racial and ethnic perspectives into its curricular initiatives. In short, if the institution wants to be perceived by students as a community that welcomes diversity, it needs to include diversity within its curriculum.

Earlier research has also shown this to be important on a number of different dimensions, including the classroom environment (Smith, Gerbick, Figueroa, Watkins, Levitan, Moore, Merchant, Beliak, and Figueroa, 1997) and the general influence of the curriculum as an important environmental attribute in studying outcomes related to diversity (Gurin, Dey, Hurtado, and Gurin, 2002). Co-curricular activities are, of course, important as well, but do not have the same symbolic power of a college's curriculum, to demonstrate an institution's commitment to diversity.

In some ways, these results present institutions and their leaders and faculty with an ironic challenge. By moving forward and providing students with opportunities to have diversity experiences, the more experienced students develop greater expectations for their institutions to honestly embrace diversity and create a positive campus climate with respect to diversity. Public relations efforts intended to create the surface illusion of a positive climate for diversity would appear to be destined for difficulty, unless accompanied by movement toward genuine institutional transformation (Chang, 2002b).

Institutional stakeholders (faculty, administrators and institutional researchers) need to keep track of many pieces of the institutional puzzle when they are attempting to boost the student perceptions of having achieved a positive campus climate for diversity. Nine constructs were identified in this study as potential determinants of student perceptions of having achieved a positive campus climate for diversity; among these were student demographics, pre-college interactions with diverse peers, overall beliefs about the campus diversity, perceptions of institutional commitments toward diversity, current interaction with diverse peers, interactions with diverse faculty, perceptions of diversity as reflected in the curriculum, participation in diversity courses and level of involvement in co-curricular activities. We urge researchers to continue to examine the multiplicity of factors that have the potential to enrich our understanding of diversity climates. Doing so will help institutional stakeholders make more informed decisions about creating welcoming environments for all campus constituencies.

References

Adams, M., and Zhou-McGovern, Y. (1994). The sociomoral development of undergraduates in a "social diversity" course: developmental theory, research, and instructional applications. Paper presented at the Annual Meeting of the American Educational Research Association. New Orleans, LA.

Adams, M., and Zhou-McGovern, Y. (1990). Some cognitive developmental characteristics of social diversity education. Paper presented at the Annual Meeting of the American Educational Research Association. Boston, MA.

Ancis, J. R., Sedlacek, W. E., and Mohr, J. J. (2000). Student perceptions of campus cultural climate by race. *Journal of Counseling and Development 78:* 180–185.

Astin, A. (1993a). *What Matters in College: Four Critical Years Revisited.* San Francisco: Jossey-Bass.

Astin, A. (1993b). *Assessment for Excellence.* American Council on Education. The Oryx Press.

Cabrera, A. G., and Nora, A. (1994). College student perceptions of prejudice and discrimination and their feelings of alienation: A construct validation approach. *Review of Education/Pedagogy/Cultural Studies 16(34):* 387–409.

Chang, M. (2001). The positive educational effects of racial diversity on campus. In: Orfield, G. (ed.), *Diversity Challenged: Evidence on the Impact of Affirmative Action.* Education Publishing Group, Cambridge, Harvard, pp. 175–186.

Chang, M. (2002a). The impact of an undergraduate diversity course requirement on students' racial views and attitudes. *The Journal of General Education 51(1):* 21–42.

Chang, M. J. (2002b). Preservation or transformation: Where's the real educational discourse on diversity? *The Review of Higher Education 25(2):* 125–140.

Green, M. (ed.) (1989). *Minorities on campus: A handbook for enhancing diversity.* Washington, DC: American Council on Education.

Gurin, P. (1999). Expert report of Patricia Gurin. In: *The Compelling Need for Diversity in Higher Education.* Gratz et al. v. Bollinger et al. No. 97-75231 (E.D. Mich.) and Grutter et al. v. Bollinger et al. No. 97-75928 (E.D. Mich). Ann Arbor, Michigan: The University of Michigan, pp. 99–234.

Gurin, P., Dey, E. L., Hurtado, S., and Gurin, G. (2002). Diversity and higher education: Theory and impact on student outcomes. *Harvard Educational Review 72(3):* 330–366.

Hurtado, S. (1993). The Institutional Climate for Diversity: The Climate for Talented Latino Students. Paper presented at the Association for Institutional Research (33rd, Chicago, IL, May 16–19, 1993). Eric Digest, ED 360 930.

Hurtado, S. (1996). How diversity affects teaching and learning: A climate for inclusion and a positive effect on learning outcomes. *Educational Record 77(4):* 27–29.

Hurtado, S. (2001). Linking diversity and educational purpose: How diversity affects the classroom environment and student development. In Orfield, G. (ed.), *Diversity Challenged: Evidence on the Impact of Affirmative Action.* Education Publishing Group, Cambridge, Harvard, pp. 187–203.

Hurtado, S., and Carter, D. F. (1997). Effects of college transition and perceptions of campus racial climate on Latino College Students' sense of belonging. *Sociology of Education 70(4):* 324–345.

Hurtado, S., and Dey, E. L. (1997). Achieving the goals of multiculturalism and diversity. In: Peterson M., Dill D., Mets L., and Associates (eds.), *Planning and Management for a Changing Environment.* Jossey-Bass, San Francisco, pp. 405–431.

Hurtado, S., Engberg, M. E., Ponjuan, L., and Landreman, L. (2002). Students' precollege preparation for participation in a diverse democracy. *Research in Higher Education 43(2):* 163–186.

Hurtado, S., Mayhew, M. J., and Engberg, M. E. (2003). Diversity in the Classroom and Students' Moral Reasoning. Paper presented at the Association for the Study of Higher Education. OR, November, 18–20. Portland.

Hurtado, S., Milem, J., Clayton-Pedersen, A., and Allen, W. (1998). Enacting Diverse Learning Environments: Improving the Climate for Racial/Ethnic Diversity in Higher Education. ASHE-ERIC Higher Education Report Volume 16, No. 8. Washington D.C: Graduate School of Education and Human Development, The George Washington University.

Hurtado, S., and others. (1995). Social Interaction on Campus: Differences Among Self-perceived Ability Groups. Paper presented at the Association for Institutional Research (35th, Boston, MA, May 28–31, 1995). ERIC Digest, ED 387 014.

Jessor, R. (1981). The perceived environment in psychological theory and research. In: Mangnusson D. (ed.), *Toward a Psychology of Situations: An Interactional Perspective.* Hillsdale NJ: Lawrence Erlbaum Associates.

Loo, C. M., and Rolison, G. (1986). Alienation of ethnic minority students at a predominantly White university. *The Journal of Higher Education 57:* 58–77.

Mackay, K. A., and Kuh, G. D. (1994). A comparison of students effort and educational gains of Caucasian and African-American students at predominantly White liberal arts colleges. *Journal of College Student Development 35:* 217–223.

McClelland, K. E., and Auster, C. J. (1990). Public platitudes and hidden tensions: Racial climates at predominantly White liberal arts colleges. *Journal of Higher Education 61:* 607–642.

Milem, J. P. (1998). Attitude change in college students: Examining the effect of college peer groups and faculty normative groups. *The Journal of Higher Education 69(2):* 117–140.

Milem, J. P. (2001). Increasing diversity benefits: How campus climate and teaching methods affects student outcomes. In Orfield G. (ed.), *Diversity challenged: Evidence on the impact of Affirmative Action.* Education Publishing Group, Cambridge, Harvard., pp. 233–249.

Nunnelly, J. C. (1978). *Psychometric Theory.* 2nd ed. New York: McGraw Hill.

Oliver, M. L., Rodriguez, C. J., and Mickelson, R. A. (1985). Brown and Black in White: The social adjustment and academic performance of Chicano and Black students in a predominantly White university. *The Urban Review: Issues and Ideas in Public Education 17:* 3–24.

Pascarella, E. T., Edison, M., Nora, A., Hagedorn, L. S., and Terenzini, P. T. (1996). Influences on students' openness to diversity and challenge in the first year of college. *Journal of Higher Education 67(2):* 174–195.

Patterson, A. M., Sedlacek, W. E., and Perry, F. W. (1984). Perceptions of Blacks and Hispanics in two campus environments. *Journal of College Student Personnel 25:* 513–518.

Peterson, M. W., and Spencer, M. G. (1990). Understanding academic culture and climate. In: Peterson M. W., Chaffee E. E., and White T. H. (ed.), *ASHE Reader on Organization and Governance in Higher Education.* 4th ed. Simon and Schuster Custom Publishing, Needham Heights, MA. pp.140–152. (Reprinted from New Directions for Institutional Research, no. 68, 1990).

Peterson, M. W., and White, T. H. (1992). Faculty and administrator perceptions of their environments: Different view or different model of organization? *Research in Higher Education 33(2):* 177–204.

Smith, D. G., Gerbick, G. L., Figueroa, M. A., Watkins, G. H., Levitan, T., Moore, L. C., Merchant, P. A., Beliak, H. D., and Figueroa, B. (1997). *Diversity Works: The Emerging Picture of How Students Benefit.* Washington, DC: American Colleges and Universities. ERIC Digest, ED 416797.

Stark, J. S., and Lattuca, L. R. (1997). *Shaping the college curriculum: Academic plans in action.* Needham Heights, MA: Allyn & Bacon.

Villalpando, O. (1994). Comparing the Effects of Multiculturalism and Diversity on Minority and White Students' Satisfaction with College. Paper presented at the Association for the Study of Higher Education. Tuscon AZ.

Whitt, E. J., Edison, M. I., Pascarella, E. T., Terenzini, P. T., and Nora, A. (2001). Influences on students' openness to diversity and challenge in the second and third year of college. *The Journal of Higher Education 72(2):* 172–204.

CHAPTER 30
BRINGING HOME DIVERSITY: A SERVICE-LEARNING APPROACH TO TEACHING RACE AND ETHNIC RELATIONS

SAM MARULLO

In this chapter, I test claims about students' development and sociological learning by comparing two classes of students enrolled in a Race and Ethnic Relations course—one section that took the course as a service-learning course and another that took it as a lecture-discussion course with some required experiential exercises. Change in students' development over the course of the semester is examined in the areas of citizenship, empowerment, diversity awareness, leadership, moral development, and rejection of individualistic explanations of social problems. Based on results from changes in survey responses, service-learning pedagogy appears to have an advantage over experiential learning with respect to students' development in these six areas. Students enrolled in the service-learning section of Race and Ethnic Relations engaged in service-learning projects by either: (1) working as an intern at an appropriate site; (2) working on a group project—either working with a Latino agency to survey the community's health care needs, or compiling a curriculum for an educational initiative in a housing project, or testing local financial institutions to determine whether they were discriminating against Hispanics with respect to their fees for money-wiring services; or (3) working on a large, ongoing violence-prevention project.

A number of authors assert that service-learning enriches students' learning, not only regarding the content of the course, but also in matters such as diversity, citizenship, empowerment, leadership, and values development (Cohen and Kinsey 1994; Enos 1998; Hedin 1989; Hesser 1995; Marullo 1996; Miller 1994). However, these claims have been based largely on professors' observations and anecdotal evidence. To skeptics, such claims might not carry much weight. Unfortunately, the field of evaluation research on service-learning is fairly new and quite underdeveloped in terms of empirical studies of students' learning outcomes (for exceptions, see Batchelder and Root 1994; Boss 1994; Miller 1994; and Olney and Grande 1995). In this chapter, I test claims about students' development and sociological learning by comparing two classes of students enrolled in my Race and Ethnic Relations course. One section took the course as a service-learning course and another took it as a lecture-discussion course with some required experiential exercises. I used a survey instrument, developed by Giles and Eyler (1994), to compare students' responses to a number of questions concerning citizenship, empowerment, diversity awareness, leadership, moral development, and rejection of individualistic explanations of social problems. Through this stringent experimental test of the value of service-learning, the results reported here contribute to the nascent body of research that demonstrates the comparative strengths of service-learning pedagogy.

Over the past 10 years, I have taught 14 sections of Race and Ethnic Relations at Georgetown University. When I first started teaching this course, I used a traditional lecture/discussion format. However, I found that students were too interested in the topic to sit through lectures, and they preferred to discuss race issues. Oftentimes, these discussions were quite heated and well-reasoned. Yet, the students did not seem to be comprehending the sociological theory and concepts because they tended not to incorporate them into their discussion. Or, worse, they would spout off an uninformed opinion or repeat a commonly held misconception about racial matters, while inappropriately using a statement they had read in the assigned reading materials as support for their claim. I was looking for a means of maintaining lively classroom discussions that would utilize readings and allow students to demonstrate an understanding of the sociological theory and concepts. I hoped to inspire them to read the material more carefully so that they could understand the reality of race relations and the effects of racial inequality. My goal was to enable them to apply the sociological concepts and theories to their everyday understandings of racial issues in the United States. However, too many of the students did not have enough interracial experiences to apply the course readings.

I first turned to experiential exercises as a means of enabling students to overcome, or at least challenge, their racial stereotypes and misperceptions. I had students pair up with a person of a different race, ethnicity, or nationality than themselves and interview each other, accompany each other to social activities on campus, and travel off campus to engage in cultural activities in the city. Although a few students resisted or resented such assignments at first, primarily due to social awkwardness or additional time and scheduling difficulties required to complete the assignments, they eventually loved the experience. They would talk and write enthusiastically about the activities they had undertaken with their partners and how these exercises helped them to overcome their misperceptions of the other. They almost always thanked me for placing them in a situation that enabled them to grow by engaging in activities that they would otherwise never have undertaken. Thus, the experiential activities were beneficial in terms of enabling students to confront and challenge some of their pre-existing beliefs and to better develop their skills in engaging in cross-racial/ethnic dialogue.

However, the students were still unable to place these interactions in a larger social context. Although they understood how individuals' perceptions differed based on their past experiences, they still had problems understanding the structural inequalities of race. Furthermore, since most of my students came from economically comfortable backgrounds, including many students of color, they still were unable to experience much of the "real world" of racial inequality in their social and cultural adventures with their partners. It was about this time that I discovered service-learning and began to realize its potential for placing students in "real world" situations where race and class matter. As a sociologist, I feel that our most important contribution to undergraduate liberal arts education is to enable students to understand that ascribed statuses such as race and sex have the effect of changing the opportunity afforded individuals. Service learning—whereby students engage in community service activities related explicitly to their course work and deliberately apply course material to their service work—could be the vehicle to expose students to racial inequality and enable them to process their readings and common experiences in a multiracial group context.

As I first began to experiment with service learning, I employed group service projects as an alternative to the social and cultural partner exercises. This enabled mixed racial or ethnic groups to engage in a project that exposed them to the devastating effects of racial segregation, poverty, discrimination, failing schools, and economic disinvestment, while still allowing them to work together. I felt that these projects were more valuable than the partnered exercises because of their beneficial impact on the community, and also in terms of the students' learning. Such a comparison between students who engaged in the partnered experiential exercises and the group service-learning exercises was inconclusive, however, because of the self-selective nature of the students choosing the exercises they would undertake. I found that more students with higher grade point averages tended to select the service-learning option.[1] This prompted me to undertake a natural experiment the next time that I taught two sections of Race and Ethnic Relations. In one section, I had all students undertake service-learning projects whereas the other section engaged in the partnered social and cultural exercises. This would control any self-selection bias and enable a better observation of the additional value (if any) of service learning.

In the spring semester of 1996, I offered two sections of Race and Ethnic Relations. Each section contained approximately 40 students (the maximum class size). Their selection of one section over the other was "random," based on their schedules and the university's priority system for selection into over-subscribed courses.[2] In order to eliminate self-selection bias, I did not indicate in the registration materials or in the course catalogue that the two sections would differ in any way. I did not even determine which section would be the service-learning section until I flipped a coin on the first day of class. Students were not allowed to switch sections, although they could withdraw from the course without sanction during the first 10 days of the semester (according to university policy). Only three students dropped out of the service-learning section and two students dropped the nonservice-learning section. They were replaced by students on the original class waiting lists. I did not tell students that the two sections differed until after they had taken the pretest questionnaire on the third day of class.[3] The race and gender composition of both sections was roughly the same, with females comprising roughly 60 percent of both sections and a race/ethnic mix of roughly 40 percent white, 35 percent African American, 15 percent Latino/a, and the remaining 10 percent Asian and others. For the purpose of this experiment, I felt that the two sections were well matched and students "randomly" assigned.

Service-Learning Pedagogy and Sociology

Service learning is the term used to describe curricular efforts to link community service to course work. It is an academic program that enables students to gain academic credit by participating in organized service activity that meets identified community needs. Students reflect on their service so that it furthers their understanding of course material (Bringle and Hatcher 1995). When service learning is done properly, it should provide students with an increased awareness of civic responsibility, it should promote their moral development, and it should help them analyze and explain the causes and consequences of the social problems with which they are involved (Honnet and Poulsen 1989; Levison 1990). The key principles underlying service learning are: (1) students' service activities in the community are integrated into the course work through assignments, exercises, discussion, and writing; (2) the needs and attempted remedies are defined by a partnership among university and community actors in order to benefit those in the community with fewer life chances; and (3) students undertake a process of observation, action, analysis, and reflection that demonstrates their educational development (Honnet and Poulsen 1989; Marullo, Lance, and Schwarz 1999).

Sociology's critical contribution to an intellectually rigorous service-learning program is that it can provide students with a conceptual understanding of the underlying structural causes of social problems, distinguishing them from individual problems or deficiencies (Marullo 1998). All too often, students see social problems as the result of individual's failures, poor choices, or simply "bad luck." Sociology adds to students' understanding of social problems by demonstrating that individual's life chances are structured, whereby those with higher status along particular dimensions such as race, social class, and education, have greater abilities to "succeed" or acquire greater societal rewards through socially acceptable means. Conversely, the individuals that students meet during the course of their service projects may have few resources and little ability to alter their circumstances due to the consolidation of their "poverties" along many social dimensions. Although students hear the "hard luck stories" of the people they work with in the community, they are also able to see that social conditions differentially affect entire classes of people.[4]

Since sociology is the science of social interactions, group dynamics, and institutional and structural relations, it is quite obvious that students learn sociological theories and concepts better when they observe such interactions firsthand (Chesler 1993; Cotter et al. 1995; Miller 1994; Porter and Schwartz 1993; Shumer 1994). In contrast to the natural sciences, the social sciences do not have a formal laboratory for applying their claims or findings to "real life" circumstances. Our laboratory to apply, test, and evaluate our sociological claims about social relations is the larger society. Because of the nature of our discipline, we are particularly well suited for service learning. Dating back to the earliest Chicago School studies, the city and the community have served as the laboratory for sociological research (Enos 1998). For as long as there has been a discipline, sociology faculty members have sent students into the field to do ethnographies and participant research. The service-learning pedagogical claim that "the real world is a crucible to test our theories" is second nature to us (Shulman 1991). Evaluation studies, community power studies, organizational studies, and studies of social movements and community organizing—with their large bodies of knowledge and longstanding research traditions—can be carried over to service-learning initiatives. Sociological theories of social problems, race relations, poverty, and urban problems help service-learning students understand the problems they attempt to address through their service work. Conversely, working on such problems helps students learn sociological theories and concepts (Enos 1998).

Service-learning assignments enable students to take the claims they read and hear in their sociology courses and test them against the reality they observe at their service sites. This experience not only enables them to understand the material they are reading, but also helps them to place their own life experiences in a broader context by providing a comparative base of a different reality (Cohen and Kinsey 1994; Miller 1994). Especially for the more affluent students at a private liberal arts college, but also for university students in general, awareness of the living conditions of the poor is quite an educational experience.[5] It is not merely exposure, however, that brings to life the concepts and theories that we teach about in our lectures and that the students read about in their texts. Through discussion and readings on participatory observation research, students become aware of their observer status, and I try to encourage them to be systematic and deliberate in making their observations. Through the writing and reflection exercises that accompany their service (papers, journals, field notes, and guided writing), students must apply the theories and concepts to the social interactions they observe and participate in at their site.[6] (Although I planned to devote roughly three-fourths of class time to discussing readings and one-fourth to applications to their service projects, the actual ratio was probably closer to a 60-40 split between reading and application focus during class.) To paraphrase Shulman, we learn not by doing, but by *thinking* about what we are doing (1991).

Service-learning programs expose students to differences among people along class, race, ethnicity, gender, age, sexual orientation, religion, and other social dimensions. This exposure has the potential of simply reinforcing stereotypes and prejudices and perhaps even sparking conflict across these divisions. Appendix A summarizes this problem and some of the other potential problems that may arise as students enter the community to engage in service. Faculty members must be sensitive to these matters and address them directly as they arise. Appendix A also provides some methods of addressing these challenges.

We know from social psychological research on race relations that positive inter-group relations are most likely to emerge when people are placed in contexts in which they can work together for a common good (Allport 1954). Service-learning programs promote such positive interactions and provide a supportive context for their development and interpretation (Berry 1990; Permaul 1993). Because most housing in the United States is allocated along racial and class lines, most of our students grow up in fairly homogeneous neighborhoods, segregated typically by race and class. Service-learning experiences are likely to expose students to a wide range of class, race and ethnic, and other social statuses in the community with which they are likely to have had little previous contact. Similarly, by working in groups, the diversity of the student body itself can play a role in helping our students to appreciate and become familiar with differences. Working toward a common goal is the best way to create mutually respectful and egalitarian views (Barber 1991). Furthermore, most college students are still experiencing the challenge of discovering and defining their own identity, so exposure to different types of people helps in this identity formation and teaches respect for others. Most educational institutions have made a commitment to educating for a culturally diverse world. Aparicio and Jose-Kampfner discuss the effectiveness and value of service learning in preparing teachers for teaching in a multicultural classroom (1995). From the university's point of view, having students and faculty members work with community partners is not only a good way to diversify the educators and role models with whom our students work, but it is also an effective mechanism for improving university-community relations.

In my Race and Ethnic Relations classes, my students work on group service or research projects with community organizations. These projects are built on having diversity in each group and creating group incentives and reward structures that encourage cooperation.[7] In addition, students work with community organization leaders—more likely in our case to be women and/or people of color—in developing the projects and learning about the organization's and the community's goals. This design helps students gain a greater awareness of diversity, overcome some of their preconceived notions about others, and practice the skills of communicating and interacting in a diverse context. In their report on teaching a class about HIV/AIDS, Porter and Schwartz report that students' anxieties about working with people with HIV/AIDS and with organizations based in the gay and lesbian community dissipate throughout the semester (1993). Similarly, my students' journals often relate their anxieties at the beginning of the semester about working with "others" with whom they are not very familiar. Yet by the end of the semester, they often comment on their new familiarity with the environment that they once perceived as "foreign."

The Service-Learning Context

Georgetown University utilizes three primary models to integrate community service into a course: the Service-Learning Credit Option (at some institutions known as the "Fourth Credit Option"), the service-learning project, and the intensive service-learning seminar. I will describe each of these briefly, before detailing some of the projects undertaken by the students in the service-learning section of my Race and Ethnic Relations class. The university as a whole is fairly supportive of community service, especially as an extracurricular activity, as indicated by the large community service center within student affairs that supports roughly one-fourth of the undergraduate student body's active, regular engagement in service groups or projects.

The most widespread method of incorporating service learning into a class at Georgetown University is through the Service-Learning Credit Option. Seventy-five to 100 students voluntarily add this option to one of their courses each semester and over 30 percent of the faculty members have sponsored at least one Service-Learning Credit Option. Through this method, students can undertake an individual community service activity—completing at least 40 hours of service during the semester—in conjunction with virtually any course where the professor approves of the student's service-learning contract describing how she or he will integrate the service activity with the course material. This is often accomplished by the student writing a paper or keeping an analytical journal where she or he applies course material to her or his volunteer activities. Although this may significantly enrich the student's understanding of the course material, this service-learning credit model barely impacts the community (because the student volunteers for a limited number of hours for just one semester) and the class (since only a few students may be so engaged and they are probably serving in different locations). Another drawback of this model of service learning is that the faculty member must do more work (reading students' papers or journals, keeping track of the service site, etc.) with little payoff for the rest of the students or the course as a whole. (See Appendix B for a comparison of the strengths and weaknesses of these three models in terms of their impact on the student, the faculty member, the class, and the community.)

At the other end of the continuum, the intensive service-learning course has an enormous impact on all of the students in class and on the very design and conduct of the course (see Appendix B, column three). The university has approximately 12 of these courses across six departments (five listed or cross-listed in sociology). Only a couple are offered each semester. These courses are built around all students in the class undertaking community service. Students complete at least 40 and as many as 120 hours of service during the semester. Readings are selected with reference to the type of service work done in the course. Class discussions explicitly draw on students' experiences. Their writing is based on data or observations made during the course of their service activity. This type of course can support a wide range of service work. In addition to direct service, students can develop research projects or engage in advocacy work or policy analysis on behalf of those in need.[8] The service work and the impact on students tend to be much more powerful in such courses, as is their impact on the community. The drawbacks of this type of course include the limited number of courses that can incorporate service work and the increased amount of work required of the faculty member due to the need for closer monitoring of the field work and building ongoing relations with community partners to sustain such activities. (See Appendix B, column three, for a summary of my assessment of the impacts of the intensive service-learning seminar.)

The third model of incorporating students' service projects into the course as a required component or as an alternative to more traditional term papers best suits my goals for the Race and Ethnic Relations course. This model, described below, enables students to work (in diverse groups) on a collective project (their research report) that meets a need defined by the community. The class meets for the usual three hours of contact time each week, with a few sessions devoted to group organizing, planning, and site work, and the students must work at least 25 hours throughout the semester at the service site. At the end of the semester, I require students to present a version of their research project to the host community organization and solicit feedback, thereby strengthening students' accountability to the community. Readings and class discussions can be applied to a small number of service sites, about which all students acquire at least a minimal level of familiarity. We have perhaps two dozen courses across the campus that fit this model. (See Appendix B, second column, for a summary of this model's impacts on the students, classroom, faculty members, and community.)

Race and Ethnic Relations as a Service-Learning Course

In the service-learning section of my Race and Ethnic Relations course, students selected from three options: working as an intern at an appropriate site for approximately five hours per week (8 students), working in a group on a project for an average of three hours per week for the semester (three groups, 18 students), or working on a large, ongoing violence-prevention project for roughly three hours per week (15 students). The first option, working as an intern, resembled the Service-Learning Credit Option because each of the eight students selected a different organization as their site, and each engaged in fairly different activities. For example, one student interned with the Mexican American Legal Defense Fund, undertaking background research on legal cases; another interned with TransAfrica, following developments in South Africa's transition from apartheid to democracy and writing briefing papers for the staff; and a third interned at a Black-Jewish dialogue organization, helping to train high school students on diversity and learning the history of Black-Jewish alliances during the Civil Rights era.

The three group projects arose out of my ongoing relations with community groups and their major concerns at the time. These included: (1) working with a Latino coalition organization to survey the Latino community's health care needs; (2) compiling a curriculum for an educational initiative in a housing project to serve the adults' needs for acquiring their G.E.D.s and obtaining vocational training; and (3) testing local financial institutions to determine whether they were discriminating against Hispanics with respect to their fees for money-wiring services.[9] Each of these projects was discussed prior to the semester with community organization staff members, and they agreed to the broad outline of the research process in advance. The community organization staff assumed much of the day-to-day oversight of students' involvement on the project, although I met with students and staff on several occasions during the semester. The fourth project, a community-based violence prevention initiative, was (and remains) a project in which I was directly involved with the community. Students had to work with the youth leadership council to establish mentoring relations with the teens in the community who were receiving leadership training.[10] This training was a precursor to the conflict resolution and peer mediation training that has since been developed for the community youth. I explained each of these four projects to students at the beginning of the semester, and they stated their preferences for the project on which they wanted to work. The student teams were well balanced in terms of race, gender, and past community experience. Thus, all students in the service-learning section were engaged in community service, primarily of the project type. Meanwhile, students in the nonservice-learning section were engaged in experiential learning, as defined by the partnered social and cultural exercises described earlier. This would test whether service-learning pedagogy would produce more positive outcomes than the experiential-learning pedagogy.[11] In particular, I wanted to test whether the service-learning students would demonstrate greater development than the nonservice-learning students in the areas of citizenship, empowerment, diversity awareness, leadership, moral development, and attribution of structural causality.

Methodology and Results

I gave students in both sections pretest and posttest surveys.[12] The 20-page survey contained over 400 attitude and behavior questions—primarily five-point Likert items with responses ranging from "strongly disagree" to "strongly agree." The survey instrument was adapted from Eyler and Giles' national study of service-learning programs, funded by the Fund for Innovation in Post-Secondary Education.[13] I examined specific items on the survey to determine the impact of service learning with respect to students' responses in the areas of: citizenship, empowerment, diversity awareness, leadership, moral development, and attribution of structural rather than individual causality for social problems. Four to six questions on the survey related to each particular concept. The overall hypothesis in this study is that the service-learning students would benefit more in each of these areas—citizenship, empowerment, diversity awareness, leadership, moral development, and attribution of structural rather than individual causality for social problems—than the nonservice-learning students. Given the fairly small sample size of approximately 40 students per section, it was not surprising to find a large number of items that did not show any significant differences between the two groups.[14] However, the differences discussed below did show changes in the hypothesized direction over the course of the semester. Most of these changes were significantly greater for the service-learning section than for the nonservice-learning section.[15]

Citizenship. Two citizenship items indicated significantly greater increases for the service-learning students than for the control group. They were: voting in local elections and fighting for what one believes in. Items showing significantly greater increases for the service-learning group compared to the nonservice-learning group are italicized in Table 1. Both sets of students "strongly agreed" that they discussed political issues with friends at the end of the semester more often than at the beginning of the semester (not italicized in Table 1). The local voting differences are important, I believe, since a mayoral primary election occurred during the semester, and the service-learning students were more likely to have voted in it. In contrast, there was no change and no difference reported in the national election voting rates (results not shown).

Empowerment. Students in the service-learning section were significantly more likely to report an increase in their rate of participation in community affairs than the nonservice-learning students. Both groups reported an increase in their participation in advocacy or action groups, but the difference between the two groups was not significant. For the remaining empowerment items (not shown here), students were asked their beliefs about the importance of people's involvement in the community and the importance of their own role in solving community problems. Neither of these attitude items showed any changes over time or differences between the classes.

Diversity awareness. Students in the service-learning section were more likely to increase their agreement with the statement that they "try to understand things from their friends' point of view." They were also more likely to show an increase in their claims that they respect the views of others. In addition, the nonservice-learning students demonstrated an increased likelihood to claim that they make up their minds right away (which I took to be a negative indicator), compared to the service-learning students who showed no change over the semester. All three of these differences are significant in the direction of the service-learning class showing greater increases in diversity awareness than the nonservice-learning class.

Leadership. Of the four items that asked the students about their leadership abilities, only one showed a significant increase for the service-learning students relative to the nonservice-learning students. Service-learning students felt that they were more able to lead a group at the end of the semester than at the beginning. The importance of assuming leadership in general, their belief in the importance of becoming a community leader, and the role of community service in enhancing their leadership abilities did not show any changes over time or any differences between the two groups (results not shown). Given their actual experience in groups during the semester, this difference seems logical. The nonservice-learning students worked in pairs rather than in small groups. The lack of other differences might be explained by students' previous leadership positions or their already high level assessments of the importance of leadership.

TABLE 1

Outcome Differences in Students' Self Assessment

	Time One		Change by Time Two	
	SL	Not SL	SL	Not SL
Citizenship				
*Vote in state and local elections**	2.63	2.65	+.43	−.47[a]
Discuss political issues with my friends	3.83	3.63	+.22	+.26[b]
I fight for what I believe in	3.89	3.58	+.42	−.05[a]
Empowerment				
Participating in community affairs	3.06	3.22	+.33	−.05[a]
Participate in advocacy or action groups	1.61	1.84	+.41	+.42[b]
Diversity awareness				
I usually make up my mind right away	2.61	2.58	−.05	+.42[a]
Try to understand things from friends' point of view	3.61	4.05	+.50	+.21[a]
Respecting the views of others	3.78	4.26[c]	+.44	−.08[a]
Leadership				
Ability to lead a group	3.44	3.42	+.22	−.16[a]
Moral development				
Ability to see consequences of actions	3.89	4.16	+.30	−.25[a]
Feeling responsible for others	3.56	4.00[c]	+.20	−.22[a]
Structural rather than individual causality				
Problems that cause people to need services are often beyond their control	3.50	3.53	+.32	+.20[b]
People have only themselves to blame for needing services	2.00	1.79	−.32	−.21[b]
Individuals control whether they are poor or wealthy	2.33	2.37	−.36	−.13[a]

[a]Change between time 1 and time 2 is significantly greater for SL than non-SL students at .05 level (one tail).
[b]Change is significant for both SL and non-SL students at .05 level (one tail), but the difference between the two groups is not significant.
[c]Significant difference (p < .05) at time one.
*Items showing significantly greater increases for the service-learning group compared to the nonservice-learning group are italicized.

Moral development. The service-learning students showed significantly greater increases in their claims regarding their ability to see the consequences of their own actions and in their perceived responsibility for others. The nonservice-learning students' feelings of responsibility for others decreased during the semester.

Structural versus individual causes of social problems. I consider this final area to be most important, given the value I place on sociology as a discipline that enables students to understand structural inequality and serves as an antidote to the larger culture's victim-blaming explanations for poverty. Students in both sections showed an increased sensitivity to the claim that individuals who need services suffer from problems that are often beyond their control. They also showed a decreased acceptance of the claim that individuals have only themselves to blame for needing services. Thus, students in both sections absorbed the key lesson that I sought to convey. The one item that showed a significant difference between the two groups is that the service-learning students became even less likely to believe the claim that individuals control whether they are poor or wealthy, compared to the nonservice-learning students who showed a smaller likelihood to accept this claim.

Altogether, 14 items indicated a significant change in students' beliefs from the beginning to the end of the semester. Four of these items demonstrated a change for both sections in the direction of beneficial learning in the areas of citizenship, empowerment, and structural understanding of social problems. Ten of the items, at least one in each area, demonstrated the additional beneficial development of students in the service-learning section as compared to students in the experiential-learning section. Thus, service-learning pedagogy appears to have an advantage over experiential learning with respect to students' development in these six areas. In the following section, we turn to students' evaluations and course grades to discern other differences between the two sections.

Students' Feedback

Finally, I used students' course evaluations and grades to attain additional indicators of the educational value of the two pedagogies (see Table 2). The results are a bit more complex, but nevertheless present a positive assessment of the service-learning pedagogy. When students were asked their opinion of the "special learning exercises"—specified as the service-learning projects or the partnered intercultural and social activities—the service-learning students were substantially more likely to respond with "excellent" or "above average" evaluations (63%) than were the experiential-exercise students (42% responding "excellent" or "above average"). The service-learning students also were more likely to find the class presentations stimulating and were likely to claim that they learned more in the course as compared to the experiential-learning students.

Despite these more favorable student assessments of the service-learning section, the experiential-learning students felt more challenged and gave me a better overall evaluation. I can only speculate on reasons for these results. My greater familiarity with the experiential exercises may have enabled me to push students further into applying the sociological insights contained in them. In the service-learning courses, I tended to be more supportive, less critical, and less certain of my expectations of them. The additional time demanded of the service-learning student also may have influenced their greater self-assessed learning and the value of their service project. My greater level of experience with the experiential-learning course, and perhaps even the higher "fun content" of these exercises, may explain the difference in students' overall instructor evaluations.

With respect to students' grades, there were no differences in the mean midterm grades. Service-learning students earned slightly higher grades on the final exams.[16] I also graded the service-learning students' class participation higher, which reflected my sense throughout the semester that class discussions were livelier and tended to take on the harder issues more often. Overall, given the higher grades for the service-learning students on their final exams, their course participation, and their project grades, they received slightly higher overall course grades.

I selected some quotes from student evaluations to summarize, in their words, the benefits of the service-learning model. Although I did not ask students to compare this course—with its major component being a service-learning project—to others they had taken, a large number did focus on the project and make implicit comparisons. A sample of their comments reflects students' assessments that their conceptual learning was enhanced, that they understood the meaning of diversity, and that they worked hard in the class:

Conceptual
The service-learning associated with this class was very important to promote understanding of the subject material. I learned a lot from the group work.

The community service projects were an asset to the class. They provided a practical basis from which to discuss and better understand the textbook materials.

I was heavily involved in the service project. [This] is the best way to experience what the course is about.

Diversity
I think the community service helped us see hands-on interaction with different races. I think it helped break down some barriers that might have been initially present.

The course was great! My classmates were from so many different backgrounds that I was constantly getting different perspectives on things. The service-learning project was a great asset.

The service-learning part of the course was good because it made you become involved. It should be required so that all groups on this campus can get to learn about each other and have an open dialogue.

TABLE 2

Aggregate Differences Between Service-Learning and Nonservice-Learning Sections Based on Student Course Evaluations

	SL	Non-SL
Percent of students responding high/outstanding on:		
Value of special learning exercises*	63	42
Class presentations stimulating	69	30
Instructor challenged me*	44	64
How much learned in course	67	60
Overall instructor evaluation	60	73
Percent based on student grades		
Midterm average grade	83.3	83.2
Final exam average grade	89.5	88.1
Class participation grade	93.3	90.0
Course average	89.9	87.8

*$p < .05$ for difference in students' responses

(Complaints of) Greater Time Commitment
The course should come with more credit. I really did a lot of work on it.

My involvement in the course was high only because it was required that we do community service.

I did a lot of outside work for this class. But it was worth it and it was fun!

Conclusions

Although diversity is very popular in higher education today, sociology has long been the discipline (along with anthropology) that has studied diversity, encouraged understanding of differences, and promoted respect for other cultures. Clearly, we have much to offer our colleagues in the design of service-learning programs and our students in the way that we teach our courses on race and ethnicity, social class and stratification, gender, and other social inequalities (Marullo 1998). In addition to teaching the theories and research on social differences, we are in a position to demonstrate them through service learning. We can also model the findings in the way that we set up our group projects, both in terms of students' internal group dynamics and externally in the way that we deal with our community partners.

The experimental design reported on here demonstrates the strength of service learning relative to experiential learning in terms of students' improved learning in the areas of citizenship, empowerment, diversity awareness, leadership, moral development, and their ability to understand structural causes of social problems. We need further research to test these findings on students' enhanced learning across a wider range of courses and disciplines. Within the discipline, we need additional studies comparing students' learning of concepts, theories, and their applications resulting from a range of pedagogies. In the short run, however, the results provided here and my classroom experience of teaching over a dozen service-learning courses convinces me that this pedagogy is at least as powerful as other teaching styles. My suspicion is that the service-learning students will remember the material they have learned in the course for a good deal longer than the students in my more traditional courses. These experiences may be more likely to inform their behavior in their communities later in life. These suspicions suggest that a longitudinal type of research is also needed to test for such long-term effects.

However, these greater benefits do not come without additional costs. In terms of my time, the preparation for the service-learning class required additional work: setting up the projects with community representatives prior to the beginning of the semester, meeting with students in groups outside of class time, meeting and/or talking with community representatives during the semester, and managing the research projects.[17] However, the value of the projects, students' greater interest in the course, the livelier class discussions, and the value of their group reports for the community, made me feel like the additional time, effort, and aggravation was worthwhile. (The aggravations came from my continuously high expectations of what the students could accomplish and their actual efforts and performances that did not meet these expectations.) In the past four semesters since I taught these two sections, far more students who were engaged in the service-learning projects have talked to me (in casual conversations on campus) to inform me of how well they remember the project and/or to tell me about the community work they have been doing since then.

Overall, despite the challenges being stacked *against* finding differences between the experiential-learning and the service-learning sections—small numbers, less well-developed service-learning projects, and overall homogeneity of the students involved—the service-learning course provided enhanced learning and greater student development than the experiential-learning course. For me, as a teacher, the powerful impact this experience has on students justifies the greater amount of required work. It is most gratifying to see students continuing to work as volunteers in the communities in which they undertook their service-learning projects.

In professional terms, I have found it beneficial to create a research agenda that supports and enables me to continue this work in the community. In my case, I have used my background and interest in social movements research to enable me to study community organizing efforts and thereby integrate my service-learning teaching with my research agenda and my own professional service to the community. However, making such a shift can be a risk to one's career advancement, depending on how the university evaluates this work (i.e., in terms of merit review and rank and tenure decisions). Pursuing such work may require embarking on a mission to change the institution's agenda by developing a group of allied faculty members and administrators who value service-learning pedagogy and understand the greater time commitments entailed and the greater contingent nature of achieving desired outcomes in the community. National organizations such as the American Association for Higher Education and the Campus Compact, funders such as FIPSE and the Pew Foundation, and the American Sociological Association support and advocate the institutional changes needed to sustain service-learning pedagogy. Service-learning pedagogy requires the introduction of the community into the learning process comprised typically of only faculty members and students. Such a change alters not only the classroom dynamics, but also challenges the institution's means of evaluating the teaching process.[18] If we are doing this work correctly, we are also changing the nature of the university's relationship to the community in a larger sense by defining a partnership engaged in solving the community's problems by mobilizing some the university's resources to that end. From the microlevel effects of changing individual student's understanding of diversity to the middle-range impact of altering the power relations in the community to the macrolevel effect of altering the goals of higher education institutions to address social problems and changing their relationship to the surrounding community, service learning has powerful transformative potential.

APPENDIX A

Potential Problems and Some Suggested Solutions

Problem	Suggested Responses
Stereotypes and prejudices reinforced	Challenge the stereotypes, even if only subtle evidence is presented; challenge students to be explicit about assumptions; defuse the language of "the other;" create and/or highlight experiences contrary to their stereotypes.
Students "dis" community members	Foster respect for partners; raise questions about and explain constraints, resources, and challenges faced by the community; role model a respectful relationship with community partners; explain how particular comments or actions are disrespectful.

APPENDIX A (cont.)

Problem	Suggested Responses
Students do not want to work in diverse student groupings	Assign groups (allowing for students to state preferences) that ensure diversity.
Students lack social and interpersonal skills to work together	Explicitly discuss "rules" and expectations of working in groups; develop a work plan to which all group members agree; address the need for skills and language development in this area.
Intragroup discord	Create outcome/product for common good; create incentives for integrated work by the group; use student-peer evaluations; develop a work plan with tasks delegated and deadlines enumerated clearly; develop and announce mediation procedure.
Group versus community discord	Maintain communication channels with partners and with student groups; have site supervisors participate in course evaluation of students.

APPENDIX B

Three Models of Service Learning in Undergraduate Sociology Courses

Effect	Service-Learning Credit (Introduction Sociology, Social Problems)	Group Projects in Course (Race and Ethnic Relations, Contemporary City)	Intensive SL Seminar (Social Movements, Community Involvement)
Impact on Community			
Service delivery	good for one-on-one, good for administrative work	good for participatory action research project	direct service discouraged, administrative work possible
Social change	minimal potential	limited component as part of larger campaign	advocacy work, research, or project well supported
Impact on Student			
Course concepts	journals/papers good for applications	in-depth, complex interactions become visible	complex systems, social change, and empowerment
Skills/intellectual	problem-solving, empathy, conflict resolution	group dynamics, problem-solving, conflict resolution	commitment to activism, advocate for oppressed
Impact on Classroom			
Discussion	hard to incorporate, occasional cases to illustrate point	easier to incorporate, some shared understanding of projects	topics selected apply across all sites
Assigned material	minimal ability to select readings that will fit all sites and course	difficult to select readings that fit across project sites, case studies used	theoretical, practical and case studies apply across sites
Impact on Faculty			
Student interactions	rich via journals, but requires much time	good for small group interactions, requires extra time	intense one-on-one, requires much time with each student
Community interactions	minimal, can be done through volunteer center	requires fair amount of coordination with site supervisors	requires fair amount of communication with site supervisors

Notes

1. I can only speculate as to the reasons that students with higher grade point averages self-selected the service-learning activities. Students with higher grade point averages may be more likely to be involved in community service, and this option would seem to require less additional work on their part.

2. Seniority in school and major status are considered in determining students' priority for admittance into a course. The "older" students and sociology majors are given higher priority for admittance into this sociology elective than those in lower grades and nonsociology majors.

3. The reading lists for the two sections were basically the same, including Gonzales (1993) as the basic course text and readings from Anderson (1990), Baca Zinn and Dill (1994), Blassingame (1979), King (1963), Steinberg (1995), and West (1993). The service-learning groups were given additional information describing the service organization with which they worked, such as brochures or annual reports. Since teaching this course, Sage has published a very accessible research handbook (Stringer 1996) that I have used in another service-learning course and would highly recommend as a supplemental methods primer. The syllabus and other course materials are available for examination on my website, under my biography *www.georgetown.edu/outreach/vps*.

4. Students often experience this as two different "breakthroughs" or "aha!" moments. The first comes when they realize that the people they serve are, in many ways, "just like me" and that something like this "could happen to me too." The second breakthrough occurs among the financially well-off students when they realize that they have a great number of resources and safety nets in place that are likely to prevent them from ever finding themselves in such a position.

5. It also challenges students to move beyond the initial shock, anger, and guilt reactions they are likely to experience in observing such desperate conditions, which may contribute to a sense of hopelessness and futility. The challenge lies in exploring with students the steps they can take to act on their desires to alleviate the suffering of the disadvantaged and move them to a point where they believe they can become agents of change.

6. In all my service-learning classes, I have students write at least one short paper that advocates or represents the point of view of the person(s) receiving assistance. This not only helps them to acquire the ability to empathize with others, but, sociologically, it helps them to see the influence of one's location in a social context on one's life chances.

7. My incentives to encourage group cooperation include: having the group meet together with me, outside of class time, to develop their project and fairly divide roles among themselves, all of which are spelled out, with timelines attached, in a group work plan; having the group project receive a single grade, which makes them all accountable for the project; and creating a peer evaluation procedure that enables each student to grade the quality and quantity of work done by each of the other students in the group, which can lead to a raising or lowering of a student's grade.

8. This differs in emphasis from an internship in that the service-learning community work focuses more on course content rather than professional (skills) development, and there is more emphasis on reflection and analysis based on the site work.

9. The Latino Economic Development Corporation (LEDC) was interested in establishing a credit union, since the community was underserved by commercial banks. They were particularly concerned with the large fees charged by the banks and other financial institutions to wire money abroad, since a large portion of the D.C. Latino community sends money to relatives in their country of origin. My students (mostly "Anglo") worked with similarly aged Hispanic testers—trained by LEDC staff—to determine whether the fees sought for wiring money to El Salvador, Mexico, and Colombia were different for Spanish-speaking testers versus English-speaking testers. They found significant differences, which were cited in the LEDC's proposal to the District's banking committee as part of the rationale for licensing a new credit union.

10. This entailed one group meeting per week and a one-to-one meeting each week between each Georgetown University student and teen partner, each lasting roughly one and one-half hours. The group meetings were built around a leadership development curriculum, whereas the one-to-one meetings ranged from homework assistance tutoring, to planned outings, to unstructured "hanging out."

11. Making this an even more difficult test for the service-learning pedagogy was the fact that I had done the experiential exercises for several years prior to this semester, refining them and improving my own ability to incorporate their experiences into classroom discussion. I developed and modified the service-learning projects "on-the-fly" as the semester progressed, forcing us to scale back our overly ambitious plans as the course proceeded.

12. Some students received a "placebo" survey rather than the pretest, so as to be able to determine if a testing effect existed. There were no significant differences at time two between students who received the real survey and those who received the placebo survey at time one.

13. I am most grateful to Dwight Giles and Janet Eyler for sharing their research instruments and providing assistance regarding their methodology while their own research was still in progress. For some of their preliminary results, see Eyler, Giles, and Braxton (1997).

14. Other factors mitigating against finding significant differences are: the relative homogeneity of the overall Georgetown University undergraduate student body, those self-selecting into an elective Race and Ethnic Relations course, and students' fairly widespread involvement in community service prior to this course. Roughly two-thirds of both sections claimed to have undertaken community service in high school.

15. However, it should be noted that although there are 14 significant differences cited in Table 1, 40 items were considered for inclusion in this analysis.

16. I graded the midterm and final exams without knowledge of students' name or section affiliation. The exams were identical for three-fourths of the material covered, with one-fourth being based on their projects.

17. On average, each of the three projects required additional meeting time as follows: (1) four hours prior to the semester (two meetings at two hours each) to set up the broad outline of the project; (2) four hours during the early part of the semester to meet with the teams and community representative to detail the project and work plan; and (3) two hours for closing/wrap-up meeting. Additional time, roughly four hours per project, was needed for: phone calls to set up meetings, travel time, preparing materials about the projects for students, and preparing and sending correspondence (thank you letters, site supervisor evaluation forms, and cover memos).

18. At Georgetown, we have undertaken a number of steps to engage faculty members in service learning, including: summer faculty development institutes, ongoing workshops, stipends and grants for developing service-learning courses, competitive grants to support community-based research projects, providing infrastructure support through the university's volunteer center, and creating a faculty center for the study and support of community service. For a description of these initiatives, please refer to the web site for the Georgetown University Volunteer and Public Service Center, *www.georgetown.edu/outreach/vps* and select "service learning."

References

Allport, Gordon. 1954. *The Nature of Prejudice.* Cambridge, MA: Addison-Wesley.

Anderson, Elijah. 1990. *Streetwise: Race, Class, and Change in an Urban Community.* Chicago, IL: University of Chicago Press.

Aparicio, Frances and Christina Jose-Kampfner. 1995. "Language, Culture, and Violence in the Educational Crisis of U.S. Latino/as: Two Courses for Intervention." *Michigan Journal of Community Service Learning* 2(Fall):95–104.

Baca Zinn, Maxine and Bonnie Thornton Dill. 1994. *Women of Color in U.S. Society.* Philadelphia, PA: Temple University Press.

Barber, Benjamin. 1991. "A Mandate for Liberty: Requiring Education-Based Community Service." *The Responsive Community* 1(2): 46–55.

Batchelder, Thomas and Susan Root. 1994. "Effects of an Undergraduate Program to Integrate Academic Learning and Service: Cognitive, Prosocial, and Identity Outcomes." *Journal of Adolescence* 17:341–55.

Berry, Howard. 1990. "Service-Learning in International and Intercultural Settings." Pp. 311–13 in *Combining Service and Learning,* edited by Jane Kendall and Associates. Raleigh, NC: National Society for Internships and Experiential Education.

Blassingame, John. 1979. *The Slave Community: Plantation Life in the Antebellum South,* revised ed. New York: Oxford University Press.

Boss, Judith. 1994. "The Effect of Community Service Work on the Moral Development of College Ethics Students." *Journal of Moral Education* 23(2):183–98.

Bringle, Robert and Julie Hatcher. 1995. "A Service-Learning Curriculum for Faculty." *Michigan Journal of Community Service Learning* 2(Fall):112–22.

Chesler, Mark. 1993. "Community Service Learning as Innovation in the University." Pp. 27–40 in *Praxis I: A Faculty Casebook on Community Service Learning,* edited by J. Howard. Ann Arbor, MI: OCSL Press, University of Michigan.

Cohen, Jeremy and Dennis Kinsey. 1994. " 'Doing Good' and Scholarship: A Service Learning Study." *Journalism Educator* 48(4):4–14.

Cotter, David, Morten Ender, Pam Gindoff, and Brenda Kowalewski. 1995. "Integrating Community Service into Introductory College Courses." *Journal of College Student Development* 36(1):87–103.

Enos, Sandra. 1998. "Service-Learning Roots in the Chicago School." In *Sociology and Service-Learning,* edited by James Ostrow, Garry Hesser, and Sandra Enos. Washington, DC: American Association of Higher Education.

Eyler, Janet, Dwight Giles, and John Braxton. 1997. "The Impact of Service-Learning on College Students." *Michigan Journal of Community Service Learning* 4(Fall):5–15.

Giles, Dwight and Janet Eyler. 1994. "The Impact of a College Community Service Laboratory on Students' Personal, Social, and Cognitive Outcomes." *Journal of Adolescence* 17: 327–39.

Gonzales, Juan, Jr. 1993. *Racial and Ethnic Groups in America.* Dubuque, IA: Kendall/Hunt Publishing Group.

Hedin, Diane. 1989. "The Power of Community Service," *Academy of Political Science Proceedings* 37:210–13.

Hesser, Garry. 1995. "Faculty Assessment of Student Learning: Outcomes Attributed to Service-Learning and Evidence of Changes in Faculty Attitudes about Experiential Education." *Michigan Journal of Community Service Learning* 2(Fall):33–42.

Honnet, Ellen Porter and Susan J. Poulsen. 1989. "Principles of Good Practice for Combining Service and Learning." Racine, WI: Wingspread Special Report, the Johnson Foundation.

King, Martin Luther, Jr. 1963. *Why We Can't Wait.* New York: Mentor.

Levison, Lee. 1990. "Choose Engagement over Exposure." Pp. 68–75 in *Combining Service and Learning,* edited by Jane Kendall and Associates. Raleigh, NC: National Society for Internships and Experiential Education.

Marullo, Sam. 1996. "The Service-Learning Movement in Higher Education: An Academic Response to Troubled Times." *Sociological Imagination* 33(2):117–37.

———. 1998. "Sociology's Essential Role: Promoting Critical Analysis in Service-Learning." In *Sociology and Service-Learning,* edited by James Ostrow, Garry Hesser, and Sandra Enos. Washington, DC: American Association of Higher Education.

Marullo, Sam, Mark Lance, and Henry Schwarz, 1999. "Study, Act, Reflect, Analyze: Service-Learning and the Justice and Peace Studies Program at Georgetown." In *Peace Studies and Service-Learning,* edited by Robin Crews and Kathleen Weigert. Washington, DC: American Association of Higher Education.

Miller, Jerry. 1994. "Linking Traditional and Service-Learning Courses: Outcome Evaluations Utilizing Two Pedagogically Distinct Models." *Michigan Journal of University Service Learning* 1(Fall):29–36.

Olney, Cynthia and Steve Grande. 1995. "Validation of a Scale to Measure Development of Social Responsibility." *Michigan Journal of Community Service Learning* 2(Fall):43–53.

Permaul, Jane S. 1993. "Community Service and Intercultural Education." Pp. 83–88 in *Rethinking Tradition,* edited by T. Kupiec. Providence, RI: Education Commission for the States and The Campus Compact.

Porter, Judith and Lisa Schwartz. 1993. "Experiential Service-Based Learning: An Integrated HIV/AIDS Education Model for College Campuses." *Teaching Sociology* 21:409–15.

Shulman, Lee. 1991. "Professing the Liberal Arts." Presented at the Institute on Integrating Service with Academic Study, July 22, Stanford University.

Shumer, Robert. 1994. "Community-Based Learning: Humanizing Education." *Journal of Adolescence* 17:357–67.

Steinberg, Stephen. 1995. *Turning Back: The Retreat from Racial Justice in American Thought and Policy.* Boston, MA: Beacon.

Stringer, Ernest. 1996. *Action Research: A Handbook for Practitioners.* Thousand Oaks, CA: Sage.

West, Cornel. 1993. *Race Matters.* New York: Vintage.

PART V

ORGANIZATIONS, LEADERSHIP, AND GOVERNANCE

JAMES T. MINOR AND ALMA R. CLAYTON-PEDERSEN, ASSOCIATE EDITORS

Colleges and universities in the U.S. have changed drastically over the last two decades. Yet, the nation's social consciousness concerning race in higher education remains unclear—even in the face of the 2008 historic election of the first person of color as president. These realities make this is a particularly interesting time to study the intersection of diversity, leadership, and governance in higher education. The chapters in this section offer some of the latest theoretical reasoning and critical analyses concerning issues of race and equity in higher education. These institutional and system-level investigations offer concrete approaches to bridge theory with practice to significantly advance institutional efforts related to diversity, access, and degree attainment for underrepresented students. We begin by setting the context for how race and governance intersect.

For decades, policymakers and higher education leaders have undertaken a wide range of initiatives to increase college access for minority students. But unfortunately, college leaders, to a large extent, ignored the need to prepare their campuses to foster the success of new entrants—governance structures and leadership capacities to address diversity remain virtually unchanged. After more than a half century of effort and a multitude of diversity initiatives, higher education finds itself at a critical crossroad. There is increasing recognition that U.S. colleges cannot afford to continue business as usual, yet they are not equipped to effectively address the rapid changes taking place. The nation is demanding greater access and attainment for diverse populations and more accountability for providing a quality learning experience.

There is an emerging consensus among policymakers and higher education leaders about the necessity of increasing the quantity and quality of college degrees conferred. Increasing the attainment of the population is now seen as critical to the nation's economic and democratic vitality, and thus an imperative that must be aggressively tackled. To accomplish these ambitious goals, serious and concerted effort must be aimed at improving college access and success among racial and ethnic minority groups. Equally important is how colleges and universities are organized to meet these challenges and the capacity of leaders to move institutions in new directions. The reality is that America's fastest growing populations are among those least likely to complete a college degree.

Leadership, socioeconomic conditions, public will, and necessity create ideal conditions for achieving the nation's longstanding diversity and equity goals. Not since President Lyndon B. Johnson's administration has there been such a significant infusion of federal resources aimed at improving access to college. And never before has there been such attention and resources dedicated to address the quality of the education students receive. This agenda, which calls for greater college access and increased rates of attainment, demands that colleges and universities make sizable advances and strategic moves. Some institutions, however, may squander this opportunity because of leadership *unwillingness* (not capacity) and their inability to align decision making bodies in ways to strategically pursue and actualize equity goals.

Although the last decade marks a period of more sophisticated institution and system-level efforts to address diversity and equity (i.e., developing strategic plans, hiring chief diversity officers, and establishing ethnic advocacy groups), progress has been slow relative to the scale of the challenge. Notwithstanding these efforts, campus leaders have largely neglected to examine how higher education institutions function to achieve their espoused diversity missions, how to develop the leadership to achieve the diversity elements of its mission, or how to respond effectively to rapid demographic shifts in the student population.

Higher education theorists (e.g., Birnbaum, 1988) claim that the behaviors of colleges and universities are best understood by using multiple frames to interpret complex phenomena—bureaucratic, political, collegial, and organized anarchy, for example. These frames have been used primarily to understand incomprehensible and contradictory activities on campuses and in postsecondary education systems. The study of higher education has moved well beyond using organizational theory merely to frame college and university behavior. Scholars now invoke a wider array of theoretical constructs to solve problems and lend alternative perspectives to examining contemporary challenges such as racism and racial equity.

Two significant changes are noteworthy for readers as they approach the seven chapters in this section. First is what we call the "professionalization" of higher education administrators. In the last two decades, the operation of colleges and universities has required individuals with more specialization to manage increasingly complex functions of the campus. Fundraising, government relations, marketing, health services, and facilities management are only a few of the areas that have become more specialized. Decision making in colleges and universities is still as diffuse, political, and culture bound as ever. However, specialization is required now because decision making must happen more rapidly and address significantly more intricate issues. Consequently, leadership practices, governing structures, and constituents' influence in decision making have a significant impact on the institutional effectiveness of any initiative and at all functional levels. The question of how to effectively organize decision making bodies to accomplish institutional goals is worthy of consistent and rigorous examination, particularly around questions of racial diversity and minority student access and success.

The second important change concerns public opinion about race and its place in U.S. higher education. History reminds us how the nation's moral ambiguity plays out on college campuses. Higher education has been an arena for segregation, integration, legal mandates, affirmative action, and propositions to end them. For the last 30 years, debates about race and equity in higher education have centered on issues of social justice, remediation for past discrimination, and the law. There is sufficient evidence to indicate the lack of progress made, despite valiant efforts, across multiple domains like diversifying the faculty or improving the representation of racial minorities enrolled in graduate and professional programs. Social justice arguments for diversity have been met not only with philosophical resistance, but also structural barriers that have impeded progress, institutionally and systemically. We believe the direction of these conversations is moving away from social justice precepts toward those with economic tenor, but with equally important consequences.

We argue that a new imperative has emerged that adds a different dimension to diversity and equity discourse. The number of Americans with postsecondary degrees is now more directly linked to the economic and social wellbeing of the nation. Additionally, there is consensus among some that increasing the percentage of U.S. citizens with college degrees is necessary to sustain current workforce needs and for the development of new industries to strengthen global competitiveness. This need to educate a greater percentage of Americans will prove difficult without addressing current enrollment and degree attainment gaps among racial minorities. The movement to expand higher education access will require new governance structures, innovative leadership, and a different set of organizational behaviors. This context calls for new thinking about who higher education decisions makers are, how they govern, and the effectiveness of their practices.

Scholars of governance, leadership and organizational change are concerned with developing more sophisticated understandings of how universities function and, to some degree, how to make them function better. The challenge is making sense of diverse institutions that are fluid organizations in a constantly changing sociopolitical context. Institutional action taken to achieve diversity remains one of the most important and challenging issues that higher education must address. The extent to which campus leaders understand how the working parts of an organization cooperate, contradict, or neutralize efforts towards intended equity goals will influence the effectiveness of actions taken. Chapters in this section address the challenge of translating how emerging theoretical frameworks can be used to craft policies and enact practices that help institutions enact their varied missions and enable the nation to achieve its diversity goals.

In Chapter 31, Estela Mara Bensimon confronts the way institutions collect and use data to understand student outcomes, how college leaders perceive the causes of inequity, and how a deficient model of thinking about students of color influences institutional action and decision making processes. Her cognitive frames provide a way of identifying the organizational mindsets that enhance or impede progress in achieving equitable outcomes. She offers institutional leaders an alternative frame to more accurately interpret data about how well minority students are performing compared to their majority counterparts, and how this new knowledge can inform policy and practice. Like Bensimon, Susan VanDeventer Iverson identifies in Chapter 32 various diversity paradigms and explains how they influence the development of institutional strategies to address racial diversity issues. Through a critical analysis of the language used in institutional diversity plans, Iverson explores how the representation of people of color reproduces inequity. She provides ample evidence of how diversity plans adopt particular frames to define the problem. She concludes that reframing the problem—and offering space to interrogate assumptions about the nature of the diversity challenges—will likely produce different, more effective options for institutional action.

In Chapter 33, Patricia Marin and Stella M. Flores address larger systemic issues concerning how colleges might preserve and use what autonomy remains to improve student diversity. This autonomy is afforded to higher education leaders by the court's deference to the academic freedom of colleges and universities to narrowly define for themselves the dimensions of a quality education. This places the issue of diversity in tension with the traditional governance considerations that attempt to balance institutional autonomy against accountability to external constituents to achieve a complex set of goals. Marin and Flores call for institutional leaders to be courageous and seize this moment to increase racial diversity and success for diverse student populations.

Using various theoretical lenses, Adrianna J. Kezar examines in Chapter 34 how diversity politics play out at colleges and universities. By applying these frames to interview data from a cross-section of presidents, she offers insights into how various political negotiation strategies may be more effective for different institutional sectors. In the chapter that follows, Alfredo G. de los Santos, Jr. and Irene Vega offer a rich description and baseline data about Hispanic chief executive officers in higher education, by sector and by institutional type. At the nexus of these two chapters is the question of whether negotiating the politics of diversity as a president is significantly different based on the ethnic identity of the leader or the institutional type.

In Chapter 36, Bridget R. McCurtis, Jerlando F. L. Jackson, and Elizabeth O'Callaghan offer a critical analysis of professional develop opportunities for leaders of color in the academy, specifically in top administrative positions. The authors underscore the need to systemically attend to the racial and ethnic composition of higher education leaders and improve the ways in which they are developed. They provide a comprehensive model for leadership development for people of color that involves creating context-specific curriculum, instituting formal mentoring opportunities, addressing the cost of these efforts to participants, and establishing national networks. Their model has both policy and practical implications for institutions and national higher education associations that provide professional development opportunities.

In the final chapter, James T. Minor illustrates how governance and leadership practices vary by institutional context. Minority-Serving Institutions (MSIs) have distinct missions of providing access to minority students and fostering unique environments that strengthen their academic and social self-concepts, increase their sense of belonging, facilitate the productive development of their racial identities, and ultimately support their college completion. Minor offers important roadmaps for understanding governance and leadership practices specific to MSIs. Rarely have scholars considered institutional practices from the perspective that an MSI could be susceptible to racism vis-à-vis the broader higher education context. Situated specifically in a Historically Black University context, Minor questions whether traditional tenets of academic governance are appropriate or useful for determining the quality of decision making at MSIs.

Conclusion

Taken together, these chapters provide readers with a comprehensive understanding of both persistent and new challenges concerning racial diversity in American higher education. The authors value what is already known about leadership, academic governance, and organizational change, but balance this knowledge against contemporary diversity trends and priorities. They also offer practical insights to inform decision making and action to achieve institutional and national goals for diversity. These chapters also illuminate the impact of institutional policies, leadership practices, and governance decisions on college access and success for racial/ethnic minority students.

Reference

Birnbaum, R. (1988). *How colleges work: The cybernetics of academic organization and leadership.* San Francisco: Jossey-Bass.

CHAPTER 31
CLOSING THE ACHIEVEMENT GAP IN HIGHER EDUCATION: AN ORGANIZATIONAL LEARNING PERSPECTIVE

ESTELA MARA BENSIMON

In this chapter I address one of the most urgent and intractable problems in higher education—inequality in educational outcomes for historically under-served groups—from the perspective of organizational learning theory. Historically, in the higher education research community, the study of minority students has been primarily through the lens of student development theories. (In this chapter, I use the terms *minority* and *underrepresented* interchangeably to refer to racial and ethnic groups that are experiencing the greatest achievement gaps as measured by traditional educational indicators such as attainment of the bachelor's degree: Puerto Ricans, Mexican Americans, African Americans, Native Americans, Native Hawaiians, and others.) I propose that the theory and processes of organizational learning can help researchers and practitioners understand and address the structural and cultural obstacles that prevent colleges and universities from producing equitable educational outcomes. Organization learning, in both theory and practice, is particularly effective in making the invisible visible and the undiscussable discussable, two conditions that aptly describe the status of race-and ethnic-based unequal outcomes on most campuses.

Among the many factors that contribute to the invisibility of unequal college outcomes for underrepresented minorities, an obvious one is that the disaggregation of student outcome data by race and ethnicity (and by gender within racial and ethnic categories) is not an institutionalized practice. Institutional practices develop from and reflect the shared cognitive frames of institutional participants. Cognitive frames, also known as mental maps, represent "the rules or reasoning" that govern how individuals interpret situations and how they design and implement their actions (Argyris, 1991). Organizational learning theory can help us understand the nature of cognitive frames and the ways in which some reveal patterns of unequal outcomes, while others hide them. If patterns of inequality are invisible, they will not be discussed, and if institutional participants do not have a reason or opportunity to talk about unequal outcomes, the problem will not be addressed directly.

I am concerned here with a particular kind of organizational learning problem: the persistence of unequal educational outcomes for racial and ethnic groups with a history of past discrimination in postsecondary education. I view inequality in educational outcomes as a learning problem of institutional actors—faculty members, administrators, counselors, and others—rather than as a learning problem of students, the more typical interpretation (Garmoran and others, 2003). The problem of unequal outcomes resides within individuals, in the cognitive frames that govern their attitudes, beliefs, values, and actions. Similarly, the reduction of inequalities also lies within individuals, specifically, in their capacity to develop equity as their cognitive frame. That is, individuals whose institutional roles can influence whether students are successful or not need to learn cognitive processes that enable

The study on which this chapter is based, "Designing and Implementing a Diversity Scorecard to Improve Institutional Effectiveness for Underserved Minority Students," is funded by the James Irvine Foundation. The findings and opinions here are solely those of the author and do not reflect the position or priorities of the foundation.

them to think about the situation of underrepresented students and their outcomes through the lens of equity. To put it simply, faculty members, counselors, and institutional leaders need to become equity minded. However, even if they were to consider the educational status of underrepresented students within their own institutions or departments (reflection on the educational outcomes of minorities is not a routine practice in most institutions of higher education), institutional actors are more predisposed to do so from the standpoint of diversity or deficit. Institutional actors are more likely to view diversity as a generalized characteristic of institutions and be blind to the particular circumstances of the racial and ethnic groups that constitute diversity. Or if they are or become aware of the educational status of specific racial/ethnic groups within their own campuses and departments, they are more likely to make stereotypical attributions, such as associating deficit with blacks and Hispanics and achievement with whites and Asians.

The Role of Individuals in Organizational Learning

The key concepts in regard to individuals are that (1) learning is done by individuals who are members of an organizational entity such as a college or university, an administrative division, an academic department, or a research team; (2) individuals inquire into a problem collectively, on behalf of an organizational entity (Huber, 1991); and (3) organizational culture and structures can promote or inhibit individual learning (Argyris and Schön, 1996; Kezar, Glenn, Lester, and Nakamoto, 2004).

Contrary to the dominant belief that the solution to unequal educational outcomes lies in a new program or technique, somewhere out there, that has been validated as a "best practice," I (along with my colleagues at the Center for Urban Education) believe that institutional actors, as a consequence of their beliefs, expectations, values, and practices, create or perpetuate unequal outcomes and that the possibility for reversing inequalities depends on individual learning that holds the potential for bringing about self-change. That is, individuals—the ways in which they teach, think students learn, and connect with students, and the assumptions they make about students based on their race or ethnicity—can create the problem of unequal outcomes. Such individuals, if placed in situations where they learn the ways in which their own thinking creates or accentuates inequities, can also learn new ways of thinking that are more equity minded. Individually and collectively, campus members can be the creators of the conditions that result in unequal or equitable outcomes.

What Is a Cognitive Frame?

I use the concept of cognitive frame to describe the interpretive frameworks through which individuals make sense of phenomena. A cognitive frame is the way in which an individual understands a situation. Cognitive frames represent conceptual maps and determine what questions may be asked, what information is collected, how problems are defined, and what action should be taken (Bensimon, 1989; Bensimon and Neumann, 1993; Neumann, 1989; Neumann and Bensimon, 1990). Understanding cognitive frames is important because at the same time that frames make some things visible, they also function as cognitive blinders in that whatever is out of frame may be imperceptible (Bensimon, 1990).

Over time, individuals develop cognitive frames that represent implicit sense-making theories to help them interpret why things are as they are. Cognitive frames are reflections of how individuals think; they represent the cognitive "rules or reasoning" they use to design and implement their actions" (Argyris, 1991). Cognitive frames are important because they help us understand the ways in which individuals can manufacture inequality, as well as reduce it.

The Cognitive Frames of Diversity, Deficit, and Equity

Briefly, when individuals are guided by diversity as their cognitive frame (see Bensimon, Hao, and Bustillos, forthcoming, for a more expanded discussion of the three cognitive frames), they focus their attention on demographic characteristics of the student body, and view diversity in terms of interracial contact and human relations. Diversity is also viewed as an institutional characteristic that promotes learning outcomes and better prepares students for an increasingly diverse workforce and society. For example, the Supreme Court's ruling in favor of the University of Michigan's consideration of race as a criterion for admission to the law school is based on the premise that universities have a "compelling interest in attaining a diverse student body" because diversity yields educational benefits, promotes cross-racial understanding, and so forth (*Grutter v. Bollinger*, 2003).

Individuals with a deficit cognitive frame may value diversity and have positive attitudes toward increasing minority student participation in higher education, but they are inclined to attribute differences in educational outcomes for black, Hispanic, and Native American students, such as lower rates of retention or degree completion, to cultural stereotypes, inadequate socialization, or lack of motivation and initiative on the part of the students. The deficit cognitive frame is expressed in disapproving attributions such as complaining that "minority students" do not take advantage of the tutorial and academic support services the institution makes available. It can also be conveyed in well-meaning but pessimistic attributions, such as concluding that students cannot be expected to overcome the disadvantages of poverty and undepreparation; therefore, unequal outcomes are to be expected. Attributions framed by a deficit perspective imply that the academic difficulties of minority students are either self-inflicted or a natural outcome of socioeconomic and educational background. Essentially, from a deficit perspective, unequal outcomes are a problem without a solution.

Diversity-minded individuals are attuned to demographic differences; for example, they will comment on how diverse the student population is or how it lacks diversity, but more likely than not, they will be blind to the fact that the very students whose presence makes campus diversity possible are themselves experiencing unequal educational outcomes. In contrast, individuals whose beliefs and actions are guided by the deficit cognitive frame may be cognizant that their student body is diverse, and they may also be cognizant that there are racial disparities in educational outcomes, but they are impervious to the fact that they attribute the problem to the students and fail to take into account their own roles in the creation or solution of unequal outcomes. In sum, diversity-minded individuals may embrace diversity but not take into account racial achievement patterns (Pollock, 2001), and deficit-minded individuals take note of racial achievement patterns but treat them as "natural" in the light of the individuals' cultural, socioeconomic, and educational backgrounds.

Individuals who are guided by the equity cognitive frame focus intentionally on the educational results or outcomes of black, Hispanic, and Native American students. They are color conscious in an affirmative sense. For example, they are more prone to notice and question patterns of educational outcomes, and they are also more likely to view inequalities in the context of a history of exclusion, discrimination, and educational apartheid. Most important, equity-minded individuals are far more likely to understand that the beliefs, expectations, and actions of individuals influence whether minority group students are construed as being capable or incapable. Table 1 compares the three cognitive frames on four dimensions: orientation, discourse, strategy, and guiding questions.

In most institutions of higher education, the discourses of deficit and diversity are more likely to be heard than the discourse of equity. But the kinds of personal and institutional changes needed to eliminate the achievement gap are more likely to originate from equity thinking, which raises the following questions: In what ways can equity thinking be encouraged? In what ways might we shift individuals' cognitive frames from deficit and diversity toward equity? More to the point, what kinds of structures and processes might produce individual and collective learning that brings about equity thinking? In the section that follows, I offer ways of considering these questions, but with a caveat. Given the intractability of the problem of racial inequity in the United States, it would be foolhardy to claim a solution. Instead, what I offer is a way of thinking about the problem, one that is grounded in the theory of organization learning.

Equity Thinking Requires Double-Loop Learning

Argyris and Schön (1996) differentiate between two types of learning: single loop and double loop. Single-loop learners are prone to externalize problems by attributing them to forces and circumstances that are beyond their control and to resort to compensatory strategies as the treatment for problems that are perceived as dysfunctions. In single-loop learning, the focus is on reestablishing stability and normality by enacting corrections and eliminating errors. Solutions that come from single-loop learning focus on the external manifestations of the problem and leave internal values, norms, and beliefs intact—hence, the label *single loop*.

TABLE 1

Diversity, Deficit, and Equity Cognitive Frames Compared on Four Dimensions

	Diversity Cognitive Frame	Deficit Cognitive Frame	Equity Cognitive Frame
Orientation	Focus on the representation of differences (for example, gender, race, ethnicity, sexual orientation, religion, and so on) in the student body	Focus on stereotypical characteristics associated with the culture of disadvantage and poverty	Focus on institutional practices and the production of unequal educational outcomes for minority group students
Discourse	Celebrating diversity, crossracial relationships, and color-blindness, enhancing access, cognitive and social benefits of having a diverse student body	Lack of preparation, motivation, study skills, blaming students and/or their backgrounds	Institutional responsibility for student outcomes, the manifestation of institutionalized racism, color-conscious, awareness of racialized practices and their differential consequences, awareness of white privilege
Strategies	Workshops, sensitivity training, exposing whites to the "other," diversifying the curriculum, creating inter-cultural centers	Compensatory educational programs, remedial courses, special programs, all focused onfixing the student	Changing institutions, developing institutional accountability of equitable educational outcomes, changing individuals' cognitive frames

For example, individuals who have a deficit cognitive frame turn the focus of unequal outcomes away from their own attitudes, beliefs, and behaviors to those of the students. They externalize the problem and by so doing bring their "own learning to a grinding halt" (Argyris, 1991, p. 7). To put it simply, they fail to see how changes in their own attitudes, beliefs, and practices could reverse unequal outcomes.

Double-loop learning focuses attention on the root causes of a problem and the changes that need to be made in the attitudes, values, beliefs, and practices of individuals to bring about enduring results (Bauman, 2002). Looking inward is the capacity to reflect on how practices (also beliefs and expectations) at the individual and institutional levels produce racial inequalities. In particular, according to Argyris (1991), individuals "must learn how the very way they go about defining and solving problems can be a source of the problems in its own right" (p. 2).

Simply put, the difference between single-loop and double-loop learning is that in the former, change is at a surface level, whereas in the latter, the change is in underlying norms, beliefs, and principles (Coburn, 2003). Thus, bringing about a cognitive shift from diversity to equity or from deficit to equity involves double-loop learning.

The development of equity as a cognitive frame is a double-loop learning problem because it requires the willingness of individuals (1) to make the disaggregating of data on student outcomes by race/ethnicity and gender a routine and necessary practice to self-assess progress toward equity in educational outcomes; (2) identify equity in educational outcomes as an essential indicator of institutional performance and quality; and (3) assume responsibility for the elimination of unequal results.

Inquiry as a Method of Developing New Cognitive Frames

Bringing about a cognitive shift in individuals whose dominant frames are diversity or deficit requires an approach that enables them to see, on their own and as concretely as possible, racial and ethnic patterns in educational outcomes. Over the past three years, researchers at the University of Southern California's Center for Urban Education have been experimenting with such an approach. This approach, which is described in detail in other publications (Bensimon, 2004; Bensimon, Polkinghorne, Bauman, and Vallejo, 2004; www.usc.edu/dept/education/CUE), is designed to create or intensify awareness of equity or inequity by organizing campus members, such as professors, counselors, and deans, into inquiry teams that have been dubbed *evidence teams* because their role is to collect data on student outcomes disaggregated by race and ethnicity and analyze them. Their purpose is to hold a mirror up to their institution that reflects clearly and unambiguously the status of underrepresented students with respect to basic educational outcomes. Through inquiry, it is expected that individuals will learn of the nature of racial patterns in educational outcomes. By "learning," I mean noticing and seeing—that is, developing an awareness that racial and ethnic patterns of inequalities exist. By "equity," I mean that the outcomes of minority group students should more closely reflect their representation in the student body (for a more technical definition, see Bensimon, Hao, and Bustillos, forthcoming). Some individuals lack complete awareness, while others have a generalized sense of them; thus, for some individuals, there is a need to develop initial awareness, and for others there is a need to intensify their awareness. The challenge is how to develop or intensify equity-oriented awareness.

The critical importance of learning new or intensified awareness is exemplified by some of the initial reactions of individuals who were appointed by their presidents to serve on campus evidence teams. For example, a dean whose president had appointed him as the leader of the campus's evidence team told us on our first meeting, "We are 100 percent diverse. The Equity Scorecard may be relevant for other institutions like yours [meaning the University of Southern California], but we don't need to do that [disaggregate]; we know what it will look like . . . for us there are no differences by ethnicity." Clearly, this individual was aware of diversity as an institutional characteristic and could not entertain the possibility that within the diversity of the student body, some racial or ethnic groups may have been experiencing more equitable educational outcomes than others.

However, it is possible that through a process of inquiry, a diversity-minded individual such as this dean can learn to think from the perspective of equity. As it happens, this individual's cognitive frame evidenced a shift toward equity. In addition, members of the evidence teams whose dominant cognitive frame was diversity initially failed to see the need for disaggregating the data, a necessary condition for double-loop learning. Although disaggregating of data is not a guarantee of double-loop learning or equity thinking, it is a necessary step.

Other individuals were generally aware of unequal results, and the inquiry process was a catalyst for intensifying it and giving the individual the impetus to act more assertively to bring about change. For example, an individual, after having seen data on outcomes disaggregated by race and ethnicity, said, "I had always felt and had a pretty good sense of the situation of minority students, but then for the first time started looking at the data, and it was just overwhelming. So, [seeing the data] has really had a tremendous impact" (unpublished field notes, Center for Urban Education).

Although most institutions routinely disaggregate enrollment data, they rarely disaggregate data on more finely grained indicators of outcomes. When the evidence teams were asked to do this, these were some of the reactions we heard:

"We track financial aid, but we don't usually disaggregate it by ethnicity and types of awards."

"No one has ever asked us to disaggregate data by ethnicity and gender, and by program and academic preparation."

"I [chair of a humanities discipline] never asked [the institutional researcher] to disaggregate the data for my department. . . . I didn't have a reason."

In sum, disaggregated data serve as the medium through which individuals learn about unequal outcomes on behalf of their campuses. The way in which data are displayed and discussed can intensify learning, confirm or refute untested hypotheses, challenge preconceived ideas, motivate further inquiry, and provide the impetus for change.

Becoming Equity Minded

For practitioners to realize the enormity of the problem of unequal outcomes, they have to see hard evidence for themselves. This is accomplished by scrutinizing the data, asking questions that have suddenly come to mind, and discovering patterns of student conditions that had been concealed before the data were examined. Thus, to bring about new or intensified awareness of unequal results, evidence team members are directly involved in collecting student data, talking about the information, and using it to create equity measures and benchmarks to put into an institutional self-assessment tool known as the Equity Scorecard. The scorecard provides four concurrent perspectives on institutional performance in terms of equity in educational outcomes: access, retention, institutional receptivity, and excellence. The responsibility of the evidence teams was to create indicators of equity for each of the four perspectives. (The measures are available at http://www.usc.edu/dept/education/CUE/projects/ds/diversityscorecard.html.)

Typically institutional researchers are responsible for gathering and analyzing data, and their findings are disseminated primarily to administrators in written reports. In order to bring the members of the evidence teams in close proximity to the problem of unequal outcomes, they are assigned the role of researchers and have the responsibility for developing and interpreting the needed equity indicators. This heightens their awareness of the issues. Faculty members and others may be generally aware that there are disparities in educational outcomes, but persuading individuals to reflect on how their own practices may be contributing to the problem is another matter. They must learn to look at the particulars of the problem within their own context.

Shifting from Diversity and Deficit to an Equity Cognitive Frame

To illustrate the process of individuals' becoming more equity-minded, I introduce two individuals, whom I refer to as Carter and Stone, both actual members of evidence teams whose language during the course of the project changed noticeably from diversity and deficit to equity. I focus on these two individuals because their initial attitude toward the project was one of skepticism and lack of enthusiasm and because it was clear that for both of them, the concept of equity in educational outcomes was new and suspect. I will describe their cognitive frames before they saw any data disaggregated by race and ethnicity and after their team began to examine and talk about disaggregated data. These descriptions are based on field notes that describe what these individuals said in the context of their participation in their campus evidence team.

Carter is the dean that I referred to earlier whose initial reaction to the Equity Scorecard was that since the campus was so diverse, it would not be very useful and that he doubted what could be learned from the process of disaggregating data. Carter was a dean at a community college that was predominantly Hispanic and also had a large number of immigrants of all races and ethnicities from nations around the world. On our first meeting with this team, Carter, despite not having seen any data, was quick to say, "We are like the UN, so for us, there is not going to be any difference by ethnicity. In fact, by the very nature of the student population, what we are likely to find is that it is all bad" regardless of the students' ethnicity or racial background. The cognitive frames that are identifiable in this brief excerpt are diversity ("we are like the UN") and deficit ("the outcomes will be bad for all").

In subsequent meetings, when the team began to look at actual outcomes data that unequivocally showed Hispanics and blacks faring much worse than whites on just about every measure of educational outcomes, Carter's language began to change. Examining a printout showing grades earned in math courses broken down by race and ethnicity and seeing dramatic differences, he said, "I just think that there's going to be some nonpedagogical explanation, a racist explanation for lack of a better term." On the same day as he looked at data on student performance in gateway courses into the majors, he suddenly exclaimed, "Goddamit! Look at Business. There is a much higher success rate for whites than for the other groups. I bet that the reason for this is that some professors encourage particular students [high-achieving white immigrant ethnic groups] to take their course sections and give them better grades."

The point in this brief example is not whether this individual was right or wrong in attributing the inequalities he was seeing for the first time to racism. What matters is that Carter, on becoming aware of unequal outcomes, began to see the problem in ways that he had not previously considered. Rather than talking about diversity or suggesting that the differences in outcomes were a reflection of student deficits, he was considering the possibility that differences in outcomes might be attributable to individuals' unconscious practices or to institutional practices that unintentionally create circumstances that result in inequalities.

Like Carter, Stone is also in a college that is predominantly Hispanic and black, except that it is a four-year college. Before seeing data disaggregated by race and ethnicity, Stone's cognitive frame was clearly identifiable as diversity and deficit. At the outset of the project, he protested that "the Equity Scorecard focuses on remediating wrongs instead of celebrating differences." He said he would much rather "focus on how diversity is encouraged, celebrated, and welcomed" (diversity cognitive frame). At another meeting but before any data had been reviewed, he expressed a concern about the "low enrollment of Asians and whites among the first-time freshmen" and said that maybe they should be more concerned "with the dynamic of white flight" rather than with equity in outcomes (deficit cognitive frame). While this individual exhibited both diversity and deficit thinking, it was clear that deficit was his dominant cognitive frame. For example, on seeing data that Hispanics were graduating at a higher rate than whites, he commented that this was an "atypical" finding because it went against his expectation that Hispanics would do less well than whites.

After several months, this team finally began to look at disaggregated data, and once they did, Stone's language changed noticeably. For example, in looking at data that showed large gaps in the outcomes for African American students in mathematics, he said to the others on the team, "I am profoundly affected by the performance of African Americans." Had this statement been made by someone who had been identified as having an equity cognitive frame, it would not have attracted our attention. However, since up to this point Carter had been resistant to the equity-oriented aspects of the project and on different occasions had made comments that reflected a deficit perspective, being "profoundly" affected represented a departure from his usual way of thinking. I am not suggesting that simply because Stone admitted to being "profoundly affected by the performance of African Americans," he had experienced a sudden and dramatic shift in cognitive frames. Rather, his statement hinted at a possible change that we should watch for.

Indeed, subsequent statements demonstrated that he was undergoing a cognitive shift. For example, when one of his colleagues on the team mentioned how much had been learned by disaggregating data by race and ethnicity, Stone experienced an Aha! moment. He suddenly realized that the collaborative process of examining data served the purpose of "raising consciousness about disparities among different groups." "We almost do a disservice by not looking at equity as a focal point," he said. At another meeting, he spoke about the results of a faculty survey: "We conducted a faculty survey, and one item that was rated very high was the potential of our students." "But in conversations with faculty," it was disturbing for him to discover that despite espousing a belief in the students' potential, "they disparage their academic quality."

After this team began to examine data disaggregated by race and ethnicity and started discussing the clear-cut patterns of inequality that were revealed, Stone's language shifted from diversity and deficit toward equity. The language of deficit that had been prevalent in the first year of the project was gradually replaced by discourse that reflected a growing awareness of racism and inconsistencies in what faculty espouse at an abstract level as opposed to their actual perceptions when they speak about students from particular groups.

Do these brief illustrations suggest that individuals who reflected changes in their language and interpretations become equity minded? That is, do these subtle changes in language indicate that these individuals had changed and therefore were more likely to examine their own practices? Were they now ready to spearhead change within their own institutions? At this juncture in our work, it is premature to suggest that the learning evidenced in the shifts in interpretation will systematically translate into significant and large-scale changes. In addition, I cannot rule out that Carter and Stone will not revert to diversity or deficit thinking. Ultimately what is important is whether individuals like Carter and Stone consistently act from an equity frame of mind so that it spreads throughout the institution and becomes a shared way of thinking and acting. It would be foolhardy for me to assert that this goal has been achieved. Nevertheless, our work underscores that in order to move toward the reversal of unequal higher educational outcomes, individuals who occupy positions of power and authority, like Carter and Stone, or like me and the other authors of this volume, we all need to learn to think from the standpoint of equity. Unless that happens, we are not likely to even get started.

Conclusion

After four years of listening to and interpreting the conversations of the individuals who form the teams in the Equity Scorecard project, I believe that organizational learning, at the local level, by individuals who are closest to the problem may have a greater impact in reversing inequality in higher education than the numerous diversity-oriented interventions developed throughout the 1980s and 1990s. The illustrations I have shared provide a glimpse into the power of organizational learning to bring about changes in the cognitive frames of individuals. In essence, "the knowledge production itself may become the form of mobilization" that induces individuals to make the cognitive shift (Gaventa and Cornwall, 2001, p. 76) that leads to change from within the self outward to the institution.

References

Argyris, C. "Teaching Smart People How to Learn." *Reflections,* 1991, *4*(2), 4–15.

Argyris, C. "Good Communication That Blocks Learning." In C. Argyris (ed.), *On Organizational Learning.* Boston: Harvard Business Review Press, 1994.

Argyris, C., and Schön, D. A. *Organizational Learning II: Theory, Method, and Practice.* Reading, Mass.: Addison-Wesley, 1996.

Bauman, G. L. "Developing a Culture of Evidence: Using Institutional Data to Identify Inequitable Educational Outcomes." Unpublished doctoral dissertation, University of Southern California, 2002.

Bensimon, E., and Neumann, A. *Redesigning Collegiate Leadership.* Baltimore, Md.: Johns Hopkins University Press, 1993.

Bensimon, E. M. "The Meaning of 'Good Presidential Leadership': A Frame Analysis." *Review of Higher Education,* 1989, *12*(2), 107–123.

Bensimon, E. M. "Viewing the Presidency: Perceptual Congruence Between Presidents and Leaders on Their Campuses." *Leadership Quarterly,* 1990, *1*(2), 71–90.

Bensimon, E. M. "The Diversity Scorecard: A Learning Approach to Institutional Change." *Change,* 2004, *36*(1), 45–52.

Bensimon, E. M. *Equality in Fact, Equality in Results: A Matter of Institutional Accountability.* Washington D.C.: American Council on Education, 2005.

Bensimon, E. M., Hao, L., and Bustillos, L. T. "Measuring the State of Equity in Higher Education." In P. Gandara, G. Orfield, and C. Horn (eds.), Leveraging Promise and Expanding Opportunity in Higher Education. Albany: State University of New York Press, forthcoming.

Bensimon, E. M., Polkinghorne, D. E., Bauman, G. L., and Vallejo, E. "Research That Makes a Difference." *Journal of Higher Education,* 2004, *75*(1), 104–126.

Coburn, C. E. "Rethinking Scale: Moving Beyond Numbers to Deep and Lasting Change." *Educational Researcher,* 2003, *32*(6), 3–12.

Gaventa, J., and Cornwall, A. "Power and Knowledge." In P. Reason and H. Bradbury (eds.), *Handbook of Action Research.* Thousand Oaks, Calif.: Sage, 2001.

Grutter v. Bollinger, 539 U.S. 306, 2003.

Huber, G. P. "Organizational Learning: The Contributing Processes and the Literatures." *Organization Science,* 1991, *2*(1), 88–115.

Kezar, A., Glenn, W., Lester, J., and Nakamoto, J. *Institutional Contexts and Equitable Educational Outcomes: Empowered to Learn.* University of Southern California: Center for Urban Education, 2004.

Kim, D. "The Link Between Individual and Organizational Learning." *Sloan Management Review,* 1993, *35*(1), 37–50.

Neumann, A. "Strategic Leadership: The Changing Orientations of College Presidents." *Review of Higher Education,* 1989, *12*(2), 137–151.

Neumann, A., and Bensimon, E. M. "Constructing the Presidency: College Presidents' Images of Their Leadership Roles, a Comparative Study." *Journal of Higher Education,* 1990, *61*(6), 678–701.

Pollock, M. "How the Question We Ask Most About Race in Education Is the Very Question We Most Suppress." *Educational Researcher,* 2001, *30*(9), 2–12.

Stanton-Salazar, R. *Manufacturing Hope and Despair: The School and Kin Support Networks of U.S.-Mexican Youth.* New York: Teachers College Press, 2001.

CHAPTER 32

CAMOUFLAGING POWER AND PRIVILEGE: A CRITICAL RACE ANALYSIS OF UNIVERSITY DIVERSITY POLICIES

SUSAN VANDEVENTER IVERSON

A 2006 report released by the Education Trust, *Engines of Inequality: Diminishing Equity in the Nation's Premier Public Universities*, decries how public universities, namely, flagship and other "research extensive" institutions, contribute to serious inequities in higher education (Gerald & Haycock, 2006). This report, similar to many others, continues to elevate inequity and diversity on the agendas of most educational practitioners and scholars today. Typically, senior administrators assemble Diversity Councils to document issues related to diversity (e.g., attrition of minority students and faculty, concerns about "chilly" campus climate, exclusionary policies and practices) and to propose recommendations for change. These special committees compile their findings in diversity action plans—official university policy documents that serve as a primary means by which postsecondary institutions formally advance and influence policy for building diverse, inclusive campus communities.

Although recommendations, initiatives, and strategies proliferate, many segments of the national population continue to be grossly underrepresented on campus, and equity in education remains a much-sought-after goal (Morfin, Perez, Parker, Lynn, & Arrona, 2006). The scholarly literature on the impact and effects of diversity in higher education is growing; however, relatively little research exists investigating institutional policies (e.g., diversity action plans) and their role as a solution to social problems on college and university campuses. Iverson (2005), in her analysis of diversity action plans issued at 20 U.S. land-grant universities, investigated how discourses generated by these reports framed diversity in higher education. The findings suggest that the discursive representation of people of color in these policies is neither natural nor neutral. Rather, this representation is embedded in "the hegemonic system of White supremacy" (DeCuir & Dixson, 2004, p. 27). As Evelyn Hu-DeHart (2000) argues, "the diversity project as we know it on our campuses is complicit in perpetuating the racial order as historically constructed" (p. 42).

In this chapter, I use critical race theory (CRT) as an analytic framework through which to examine the relative subordination of people of color in university settings and how racial inequality may be reproduced through educational policies. In a recent examination of university diversity action plans, Iverson's use of policy discourse analysis illuminated the discursive framing of diversity and the cultural realities (re)produced for people of color through discourse. CRT adds to this analysis by illuminating the use of Whiteness as a standard in policy against which to measure the progress and success of people of color and exposes the inherent racism in diversity policies.

Conceptual Framework

Critical Race Theory

CRT originated in the 1970s from the work of legal scholars to contest the absence of attention to race in the courts and in law; however, its use and influence has extended to other disciplines. Ladson-Billings and Tate (1995) are credited with introducing CRT to education and its use as a powerful theoretical and analytical framework within educational research. This chapter extends this application by using CRT as an analytic lens through which to examine how educational policy may deploy dominant discourses that perpetuate racial inequality.

My use of CRT acknowledges the existence of racism in policy discourses and analyzes the deficit-based beliefs about people of color (Ladson-Billings, 2000; Solórzano & Yosso, 2001b; Villalpando, 2003). This chapter uses as its point of analysis an investigation of diversity policies that sought to understand how these documents frame diversity and what reality is produced by diversity action plans (Iverson, 2005). Diversity action plans typically describe people of color as outsiders to the university, disadvantaged and at risk before and after entering higher education, and in this discursive framing, propose strategies aimed at individuals to compensate for deficiencies (Iverson, 2005). A CRT framework challenges "dominant ideology that supports deficit theorizing" prevalent in educational administration and policies (Solórzano & Yosso, 2002, p. 156). Furthermore, the use of CRT as an analytic lens challenges preconceived notions of race and confirms that scholars and practitioners must listen to those who experience racism, sexism, and classism to counter the dominant discourses circulating in educational policies (Delgado Bernal & Villalpando, 2002).

CRT can expose forms of racial inequality in educational policy, assumed to be neutral or objective in diversity action plans, and challenge assumptions that White racial experience is and should serve as the normative standard for progress and success in higher education (Ladson-Billings, 1998, 2000; Lopez & Parker, 2003; Lynn & Adams, 2002; Parker, 2003; Villalpando, 2003; Yosso, 2002). University administrators, faculty, and students drafting diversity action plans are ordering and constituting the cultural reality for people of color on campus through the ways in which they write about diversity. Who has the power to shape the perception about the logic and worth of diversity action plans is an important consideration as well as the ways knowledge is used to reproduce racial inequalities (Delgado Bernal & Villalpando, 2002).

Policy Analysis

A variety of approaches to the study of policy exist. The dominant, conventional—sometimes called rational—approach to policy analysis views policy making principally as a process of problem solving; it involves "description, explanation, and prediction of issues" (Hawkesworth, 1988, p. 2). Policy makers employ formulaic steps in policy making, and value decisions are assumed to be "relatively straightforward" and are "clearly formulated in advance," meaning the problem that the policy seeks to resolve is accepted as an unquestioned, objective fact, and attention is instead focused on identifying solutions to the given problem (Bacchi, 1999, p. 18).

Critiques of conventional approaches to policy analysis (Bacchi, 1999; Ball, 1990; Marshall, 1999, 2000; Scheurich, 1994) posit that such policy approaches are guided by a technical-rational evaluation of what makes effective policy—meaning they want to offer ways of "doing it better" (Bacchi, 1999, p. 20)—and serve to legitimize some socially constructed norm of behavior that functions to categorize people, things, and ideas. Policy problems, studied using rational approaches, are typically uncritically accepted, naturalized in the individual, and ignore the social construction of the policy problem (Allan, 2003; Bacchi, 1999; Baez, 2002; Scheurich, 1994). From this perspective, policy implies consensus and risks "ignoring and creating silences on the contradictions of lived experience and social ideals" (Ball, 1990, p. 139). Such approaches to policy making and analysis often fail to examine underlying and often taken-for-granted assumptions about solutions embedded within how a problem is represented and the implications for these representations (Allan, 2003; Bacchi, 1999; Baez, 2002).

Blending critical approaches to policy analysis with methods of textual analysis invites researchers to focus on silences and exclusions, giving voice to those at the margins (Baez, 2002; Revilla & Asato, 2002; Roe, 1994). Specifically, the use of CRT elucidates the ways in which Whites are primary beneficiaries of policy initiatives intended to serve historically disadvantaged and underrepresented populations (e.g., affirmation action; see Ladson-Billings, 1998). A CRT perspective on policy goes further than the rational approach in its attention to discourses that normalize some institutional practices and marginalize others (Baez, 2002; Bell, 2003; Ladson-Billings, 2000; Solórzano, Villalpando, & Oseguera, 2005; Solórzano & Yosso, 2002; Yosso, 2002). CRT approaches to policy analysis help to raise important questions about the control and production of knowledge and the ways that policy can be used to empower individuals to act on/in their environment to challenge dominant ideology (Aleman, 2006; Ladson-Billings, 1998, 2005; Lopez, 2003; Morfin et al., 2006; Parker, 2003).

Discourse

In the study that serves as the point of analysis in this chapter, Iverson (2005) investigated discursive practices shaping diversity in university diversity action plans. As such, diversity was examined as a subject of discourse. Discourse is a term often used but without simple definition. For the purposes of this study, discourse is "larger than language, more than words" (Bacchi, 1999, p. 40); it is about what can be said and who can speak, when, and with what authority (Ball, 1990). Discourse refers to "the way in which language, or, more broadly, bodies of knowledge . . . define the terrain and consequently complicate attempts at change" (Bacchi, 1999, p. 40). Thus, knowledge is inextricably linked with power.

Discourse enables us to give meaning to the world and act to transform it; "through language [written and spoken words], we actively construct our experience" (Wilkinson & Kitzinger, 1995, p. 35; also Mills, 1997). Language, then, is not simply descriptive or a reflection of the world; it "doesn't just mirror reality; it actively shapes the way we perceive and understand it" (Fischer & Forester, 1993, cited in Hajer & Wagenaar, 2003, p. 14). Thus, the discursive practices set forth in educational policy "have a profound influence on the way that individuals act and think" (Mills, 1997, p. 62).

Applied to this inquiry, the study of discourse (discourse analysis) includes the examination of text, its relationship to the social context in which it is constructed, and why, out of all the possible things that could be articulated, only certain statements and ideas are made visible or heard (Allan, 2003; Ball, 1990). Thus, a critical analysis of the discursive practices in diversity action plans illuminates "the ways in which arguments are structured and objects and subjects are constituted in language" (Bacchi, 1999, pp. 40-41). Furthermore, individual identities are shaped through discourse—"the place where our sense of ourselves . . . is *constructed*" (Weedon, 1997, p. 21).

Method

The data presented here are from an analysis of 21 diversity action plans issued at 20 U.S. land-grant universities[1] from 1999-2004 (see Table 1). I conducted a search of the Web site for each "1862 land-grant"[2] institution in each of the 50 states; I used the search function and keywords *diversity* and *diversity plan*. Every university, of the 50 screened, possessed diversity-related content (e.g., multicultural student affairs, faculty committee on diversity in the curriculum, diversity workshops). Most of the universities have one or more diversity-related groups[3] committed to one or more of the following concerns: recruitment and retention of underrepresented populations, curriculum change, and campus climate. I sought those universities that had a diversity committee, charged by a senior administrator (president, provost), that had at least one diversity action plan[4] generated within the past 5 years (1999-2004). My Web search was complemented with numerous e-mail exchanges and phone conversations with academic and administrative personnel to discern which universities had policies that met the sampling criteria and to collect any documents not accessible via the Web. The search yielded a data sample of 21 reports from 20 institutions.

This investigation (Iverson, 2005) used the method of policy discourse analysis to investigate university diversity policies to understand how these documents frame diversity and what reality is produced by diversity action plans. A hybrid methodology, policy discourse analysis focuses on written documents; it is a strategy for examining policy discourses and the ways they come together to make particular perspectives more prominent than others (Allan, 2003). The use of assumptive concepts in language may limit a policy's effectiveness and actually reinscribe the very problem the

TABLE 1

Sample

State	Institution	Diversity Action Plan(s)
Alabama	Auburn University	Strategic Diversity Plan, 2004
Arizona	University of Arizona	Diversity Action Plan, 2003–2004
Arkansas	University of Arkansas	Diversity Plan, 2002–2005
California	University of California, Berkeley	Report of the Chancellor's Advisory Committee on Diversity, 2000
Connecticut	University of Connecticut	Diversity Action Plan, 2002
Georgia	University of Georgia	Institutional Diversity Strategic Plan, 2002–2005
Idaho	University of Idaho	Diversity and Human Rights at the University of Idaho: Comprehensive Plan for Action and Accountability, 2004
Illinois	University of Illinois at Urbana–Champaign	Final Report of the Diversity Initiatives Planning Committee, 2002
Maine	University of Maine	Diversity Action Plan, 1999, 2003–2005
Maryland	University of Maryland, College Park	Report and Recommendations of the President's Diversity Panel, 2000
Nebraska	University of Nebraska, Lincoln	Comprehensive Diversity Plan, 1999 (revised draft)
Nevada	University of Nevada, Reno	Strategic Plan for Diversity Initiatives, 2002
New York	Cornell University	*The Cornell University Story: A Holistic Approach to Diversity and Inclusiveness*, 2004
North Carolina	North Carolina State University	Diversity Initiative, 1999 (revised and final)
Ohio	The Ohio State University	Diversity Action Plan, 2000
Oklahoma	Oklahoma State University	Institutional Diversity Strategic Plan, 2003
Pennsylvania	Pennsylvania State University	Framework to foster diversity, 2004–2009
Texas	Texas A&M University	Report by the President's Ad Hoc Committee on Diversity and Globalization, 2002
Virginia	Virginia Tech	Diversity Strategic Plan, 2000–2005
Wisconsin	University of Wisconsin, Madison	Plan 2008: The Campus Diversity Plan (1999)

policy seeks to alleviate (Allan, 2003; Bacchi, 1999; Stein, 2004). A university's diversity action plan may construct a world for racial minorities that disqualifies them from participation, even as it strives to include them as full participants.

To examine the discursive framing of diversity in diversity action plans, the following questions guided this study:

- What are the predominant images of diversity in diversity action plans?
- How are problems related to diversity represented in diversity action plans?
- How are solutions related to diversity problems represented in diversity action plans?
- What discourses are employed to shape these images, problems, and solutions?

The process of data analysis was informed by established methods of coding and categorizing to identify broad themes and predominant images of diversity (Marshall & Rossman, 1999; Miles & Huberman, 1994). The first phase of the analysis involved deductive coding in reply to the research questions. Through the use of NVivo, computer software designed for qualitative data analysis, I conducted line-by-line analysis of each report to identify and code images of diversity, the problems related to diversity described in diversity action plans, and the proposed solutions to these problems. Once all of the documents were coded, I used NVivo to generate reports for each category—

images, problems, and solutions—across all diversity action plans; these reports were then analyzed using both deductive and inductive processes, which served as the second phase of coding. These codes were then clustered according to common themes to generate image categories and identify identity positions that emerged from these images. All 21 documents then were reanalyzed inductively, listening for silences (Pollock, 2004; Stein, 2004) and with a focus on what is taken for granted or accepted as given, and analyzed deductively, using the following research question as a guide: What discourses are employed to shape the predominant images? In this phase of the analytic process, I also examined the identity positions that emerged in Phase 1 of the analysis to identify discourses that were most prominent in constituting these positions.

The Discursive Representation of Diversity in Educational Policy

The goal of the investigation was to understand how university diversity policies frame ideas about diversity and what realities are produced by the discourses carried in these documents. Analysis revealed four predominant discourses shaping images of people of color: access, disadvantage, marketplace, and democracy.[5] These discourses construct images of people of color as outsiders, at-risk victims, commodities, and change agents. In this chapter, I argue that these discursive representations (re)produce a relative subordination of people of color and reinscribe a racially neutral conception of educational policies—even in policies that have as their focal point diversity in general and race in particular. Next, I examine these discursive themes through a CRT lens.

Discourse of Access

The discourse of access, along with three discursive strands (entrée, representation, and affirmation), coalesces to produce a reality where people of color are outsiders. As described in the diversity action plans, barriers and obstacles routinely limit access, retention, and advancement of people of color. Most arenas of the university—in fact, the institution itself—are characterized as inaccessible. Diversity action plans propose to "feed the educational pipeline" to open access, to "widen the net," and to eliminate barriers and obstacles to increase the "presence" and "prevalence" of people of color who "remain hardly noticeable." The emphasis in diversity action plans is on opening access for people of color, supporting their entrance to and participation in the university, and increasing numbers of people of color to achieve "critical masses." Once inside the university, diversity action plans shift their focus to affirming and welcoming the presence of marginalized groups. This insider/outsider binary also is visible through characterizations of people of color as different from a majority and different from both other members of historically disadvantaged groups who remain outside the institution and from some people of color who have achieved insider status. I will elaborate on each of these observations.

Insider/Outsider: Whiteness as Criteria. Diversity policies use a majority (White and male) as the standard against which to measure minority progress and success, as illustrated by this data quote: "Close the gap in educational achievement, by bringing retention and graduation rates for students of color in line with those of the student body as a whole" (University of Wisconsin, 1999). Similarly, another report observes that African American and Hispanic students have a lower graduation rate than do White students and recommends the development of "a plan to reduce the disparity in graduation rates between White and minority students" (Ohio State University, 2000). The majority, represented as the norm—White, male, and/or middle class—serves to signal the ways in which people of color are outsiders, as shown in the following quote: "a significant disparity in graduation rates persists between undergraduate students of color and White students" (Pennsylvania State University, 2004). These characterizations construct a White, middle-class standard against which others are judged (hooks, 1994; Yosso, 2002).

A CRT analysis interrogates the unquestioned use of a White, male majority experience as criteria against which to measure the progress and success of people of color. This standard reifies a

"Eurocentric epistemological perspective based on White privilege and 'American democratic' ideals of meritocracy, objectivity, and individuality" (Delgado Bernal & Villalpando, 2002, p. 171). CRT challenges claims by universities of "color-blindness, race neutrality, and equal opportunity" and reveals these as "camouflage for the self-interest, power, and privilege of dominant groups" (Villalpando, 2003, p. 623). CRT contests the "race neutral" movement in higher education that supports "the normalizing of White student behavior as 'standard'" (Nebeker, 1998, p. 27). CRT invites a destabilizing of the structures and conditions that privilege some and systematically disadvantage others, disrupting the hierarchy and status quo (Solórzano et al., 2005).

Insider/Outsider: Difference Within Groups. The discourse of access also produces difference within racial minority groups as it works to produce sameness in relation to a White, male experience situated as the norm. The discourse of access (re)produces a standard of eligibility that accords an elite status to people of color who achieve insider status; this representation is evident through descriptions of people of color who are desired and targeted (and ultimately included) as "high achieving," "high profile," "high performing," and "promising." For instance, one report recommends the following: "Identify *high performing* [italics added] people of color, women and members of other under-represented groups in staff positions and develop a professional development track for them" (Auburn University, 2004). Another document recommends, "Emphasize retaining and promoting *high quality* [italics added] faculty and staff members from underrepresented groups" (Pennsylvania State University, 2004). Still another report recommends using fellowships to attract "*talented* [italics added] junior faculty of color" (University of Wisconsin, 1999). Finally, one policy describes a program targeted at and designed to recruit "*talented* women and minority graduates . . . back to the campus when they have achieved *scholarly distinction*" (University of California at Berkeley, 2000, italics added).

By attributing insider status to one's elevated placement on a hierarchy of achievement, reports denote that not all people of color are eligible (capable) of gaining insider status, further marking those who gain insider status as different. This framing is linked to assumptions of deficiency that I will discuss later; however, it also veils the standardization of White, male, middle-class culture. CRT reveals the racism that is "well disguised in the rhetoric of shared 'normative' values" (Yosso, 2005, p. 74). CRT elucidates the ways in which specific forms of knowledge, skills, and abilities are valued over others, namely, the cultural capital possessed by privileged groups in society (Yosso, 2005). Thus, only the exemplary or elite people of color are the eligible candidates and the target of diversity efforts; therefore, only some people of color—those who "pass"—qualify (to compete) for insider status.

Insider/Outsider: Difference Among Groups. Finally, diversity action plans situate some people of color as outsiders among other historically disadvantaged groups, namely, describing Asian Americans as an exception to institutional diversity challenges. As observed by one report, the success of Asian Americans in moving from outsider to insider status skews the university's diversity numbers.

> The university continues to face major challenges in the recruitment and hiring of faculty of color. For fall 1997, faculty of color (all ranks) constituted only 10% (220) of the legal faculty (2,171). . . . *When Asian American faculty are left out of our count* [italics added], the number drops to 4% (100). (University of Wisconsin, 1999)

Another report suggests a similar assessment through its attention to only two racial-ethnic groups: "Although there has been some increase in the representation of minorities at the university, by all accounts net increases in the employment of Black and Latino faculty have been minimal in 8 years" (University of Connecticut, 2002). Still another document observes that what appears to be diversity in the international student population is largely attributed to students from Asian countries; thus, issues of diversity remain. This report notes, "There are issues of diversity within the international student population. Although 115 countries are represented in Texas A&M's international student population, 55% of these students come from only three Asian countries: India, China, and Korea" (Texas A&M University, 2002). Finally, another report, in a comprehensive summary report of their climate assessment, implies that their diversity concerns do not include Asian Americans: "The responses of Asian faculty members on many items did not differ significantly from White responses" (Virginia Tech University, 2000).

CRT illuminates how these characterizations reinforce stereotypes and perceptions of Asian Americans as the "successful or model minority" and, consequently, Asian Americans are "excluded altogether from racial discourse on educational issues because it is believed that there is no need to address their educational needs or issues" (Teranishi, 2002, p. 144). Furthermore, the homogenization of a heterogeneous racial group (e.g., Asian Americans) erases the variation within identity categories and depicts different social and institutional experiences as monolithic "issues of diversity" (Ibarra, 2001; Teranishi, 2002; Walker-Moffat, 1995; Yanow, 2003).

Discourse of Disadvantage

The discourse of disadvantage is characterized in diversity action plans by descriptions of people of color as at risk before entering institutions of higher education and remaining at risk once a member of the university—at risk for educational failure, for being victims of hate crime, discrimination, harassment, nonpromotion, no advancement, no tenure, among other things. This portrayal is echoed by the U.S. Department of Education's (1994) estimate that at-risk students make up anywhere from 20% to 40% of the U.S. student population (also Freeman, 1998). The Department of Education elaborates that the vast majority of at-risk students are poor and reside in the inner city, rural areas, or on Indian reservations, and many have limited English proficiency.

Before entering the university, people of color are typically described in the diversity action plans as deficient. One report states that "disadvantaged and underprepared students" need "college preparatory and remedial courses" (University of Maine, 2003). Another report recommends, "Expand efforts with targeted middle and high schools to better prepare students for college [and] expand outreach efforts to parents of potential students from underrepresented groups" (University of Arizona, 2003). Yet another document suggests, "Enhance the academic summer program and introduce underrepresented, low-income youth to transportation career options" (University of Nebraska, 1999).

Looking through a CRT lens enables a critique of this discursive framing of diversity as disadvantaged and deficient. Yosso (2005) notes that "deficit thinking takes the position that minority students and families are at fault for poor academic performance because (a) students enter school without the normative cultural knowledge and skills and (b) parents neither value nor support their child's education" (p. 75). This construction of the problem focuses on the identification of individuals' deficiencies, such as inadequate preparation or skills, and the need to develop programs and services to compensate for deficiencies (e.g., leadership and professional development, mentoring, academic support services, financial aid). The underlying assumption from this deficit perspective is that people of color "need to change to conform to this already effective and equitable system" (Yosso, 2005, p. 75; Solórzano & Yosso, 2001b). Framed in this way, the playing field should be level for people of color who acquire the necessary skills and resources, risk will be reduced, and people of color will be more likely to succeed in higher education. This discourse situates people of color as vulnerable and at risk both inside and outside the institution and dependent on the university and its programs to compensate for these deficiencies. This discursive framing of diversity fails to critically examine the "systemic factors that perpetuate deficit thinking and reproduce educational inequities" for people of color (Garcia & Guerra, 2004, p. 155).

Using CRT as an analytic lens also illuminates the presence of stressful events and conditions—both before and during attendance at college—that place students of color at risk of poor performance and attrition (Solórzano, Ceja, & Yosso, 2000). Throughout the diversity action plans, people of color are described as at risk for being victims of discrimination, harassment, intimidation, bias incidents, hate crimes, unfair treatment, silencing, isolation, and abuse. One report reveals that "on-campus African American faculty members perceived the climate for diversity, particularly outside their departments, as racist, and they were deeply skeptical of the university's commitment to diversity in general and to the success of faculty members and students of color," later adding that "approximately one third of all graduate students had heard derogatory comments or read insulting materials concerning racial/ethnic minorities, nonheterosexuals, and individuals from Appalachia" (Virginia Tech University, 2000). Discriminatory acts, sometimes more euphemistically referred to as "potential problems (including hate crimes)" (University of Maryland, 2000), "climate issues" (North Carolina State University, 1999), or "obstacles" (University of Idaho, 2004), are described in most diversity action plans.

Although harassment and discrimination are viewed in the policies with dismay and concern, no exclamation of surprise exists, suggesting that racism is accepted as pervasive and commonplace. Rather than address the source of the problem—subtle and overt acts of discrimination—the policies suggest support services: "Create mechanisms to support and protect students who bring allegations of gender, sexual and racial discrimination in order to lessen their vulnerability, fears of reprisals and harassment" (Ohio State University, 2000) and "identify problem areas where women, persons of color, and gays and lesbians are not welcome, safe, and respected, and/or fairly compensated" (University of Maryland, 2000). Furthermore, numerous diversity action plans recommend creating ombuds services and implementing diversity awareness programming and sensitivity training.

Employing a CRT analysis explores the ways in which such support services and multicultural programming have (or have not) challenged and changed harassing behavior and discriminatory practices (DeCuir & Dixson, 2004). The discourse of disadvantage constitutes people of color as at-risk victims and focuses attention on their needs, challenges, fears, and inability to remain safe (Allan, 2003; Ladson-Billings, 1998; Pollock, 2004). Through frequent use of passive voice, for example, "Black staff receive inconsistent and unfair treatment" (University of California at Berkeley, 2000), the documents gave little attention to the source of discrimination. The bodies of people of color are inscribed as "always already" victims of oppression (Heberle, 1996). CRT exposes the "permanence of racism" in U.S. society and calls for an exploration of an institutional culture that allows individuals to feel comfortable in producing racist words and actions (DeCuir & Dixson, 2004) and an environment that supports a negative racial climate and harbors the "threat of possibly being judged and treated stereotypically" (Solórzano et al., 2000, p. 62). Rather than engage in provocative thinking about the inherent contradictions between goals of equity and fair treatment and the individual lived realities of discrimination and harassment, universities celebrate diversity concomitantly with developing strategies to help people of color feel safe (Ladson-Billings, 1998). Presented in this way, the origins of and systems that perpetuate discrimination are uninterrogated, and advantage remains camouflaged (Ladson-Billings & Tate, 1995).

Marketplace Discourse

Diversity action plans describe higher education as a "highly competitive market"; fierce competition exists in the recruitment of diverse individuals, and institutions strategize about how to maintain a competitive edge in response to "rapidly changing market conditions" and "a new demographic reality" in an increasingly global marketplace. Furthermore, in response to external pressures, diversity action plans describe the need for students to have exposure to multicultural perspectives to compete and understand the concerns of a global workforce. These characterizations in the reports are made visible by a marketplace discourse.

Diversity (and by implication people of color) is described in the policies as essential—"a key ingredient"—for achieving and maintaining a competitive edge. For instance, one document states that "internal and external constituencies both expect to see *visible signs of commitment to diversity* reflected in the institution's leadership," adding that "major American businesses have made clear that the skills needed in today's *increasingly global marketplace* can only be developed through exposure to widely diverse people, cultures, ideas, and viewpoints" (Pennsylvania State University, 2004, italics added). Academic initiatives (e.g., developing Area Studies programs, creating international programs, and diversifying the curriculum) often are recommended for universities to respond to market demand.

Diversity action plans assert that "diversity increases educational possibilities" and, to capitalize on diversity, the reports recommend to "make effective use of all our citizens" and "take full advantage of educational benefits of diversity." Furthermore, diversity action plans demand "effectively managing and leveraging diversity" to "promote the value and benefits of diversity" in and by the institution to maintain (or gain) a competitive edge and to achieve prominence in the academic marketplace. These characterizations are made visible by the marketplace discourse that produces people of color as a commodity that (who) has value to the university.

Analysis identified diversity (people of color) as useful (e.g., the university can use diversity to advance its reputation). Numerous diversity action plans describe the use of diversity in promotional materials to market the university's commitment to diversity and the "value and benefits of diversity." Cognizant of this use value, many diversity action plans also propose the "diversification of academic offerings" to "appeal to a wider audience." An aspect of CRT is its illumination of "interest convergence"—that "Whites will tolerate and advance the interests of people of color only when they promote the self-interests of Whites" (Lopez, 2003, p. 84).

People of color, discursively shaped as a commodity, also have exchange value or economic value. This exchange value is most evident in linkages in diversity action plans between the acquisition of diverse individuals and subsequent financial gains. For instance, this point is exemplified in one report that notes "increasing diversity" is "directly tied" to "expenditures of federal monies" (Auburn University, 2004). The exchange value of the diverse individual also is apparent in descriptions of the relationship between diversity and a university's reputation, status, and ultimate standing in the market. Thus, the university who successfully acquires this commodity (diversity) enjoys elevated status in the marketplace and benefits from enhanced purchasing power to acquire other/ more diverse individuals as well as related commodities (e.g., area studies programs).

A central tenet of CRT is the notion of race as property, and specifically that "Whiteness can be considered a property interest" (Harris, in DeCuir & Dixson, 2004, p. 28). Ladson-Billings and Tate (1995) note that U.S. history is replete with race-based struggles over property—a commodity—and that "the ability to define, possess, and own property has been a central figure in America" (p. 53). Yet, they add, the centrality of property can be disguised as individual rights and civil rights and entangles democratic ideals with capitalistic pursuits. Descriptions of "area studies" (e.g., Black studies, ethnic studies) in diversity policies provide a useful illustration. These interdisciplinary, academic programs hold the promise to transform curriculum, redesign the criteria for evaluating scholarship in tenure and promotion decisions, and "engender fundamental structural change" (Hu-DeHart, 2000, p. 41). One report proclaims, "The strength of the Institute for Ethnic Studies and the Women's Studies Program *manifests the University's commitment* to racial and gender diversity" (University of Nebraska, 1999, italics added). However, recommendations to realize the transformative promise of these programs include proposals for "cluster hiring," "shared visiting positions," "joint recruiting strategies," and "better coordination of priorities"—constraints imposed by limited funding to these programs. CRT reveals that the change-making potential of "area studies" and the broader, liberatory goals of the diversity action plans collapse under the greater weight of the marketplace discourse. This tension will be explored further later in this chapter.

Analysis informed by CRT reveals the racism embedded in representations of people of color as commodities—their being "objectified as property" (Ladson-Billing & Tate, 1995, p. 53). Furthermore, it is important to consider the question "Who benefits?" from the commodification of diversity. The CRT concept of reputation as property (Ladson-Billing & Tate, 1995) elucidates that universities benefit—the strategic use of this commodity enables universities to acquire or maintain a competitive edge in the market. As one policy considers,

> Those universities recognized in national rankings as among the best in the country are generally more diverse in their faculty, staff and student body than is Auburn. We must at least consider the possibility that their diversity contributes to the high regard that people have for these institutions. . . . Achieving prominence in the absence of diversity is just as improbable in academics as it is in athletics. (Auburn University, 2004)

In addition, CRT illuminates "interest convergence"—a university opens access to others knowing a more diverse faculty, staff, and student body will enhance its reputation (DeCuir & Dixson, 2004). Notably, however, a few diversity policies cite concerns about a perceived overemphasis on diversity and that an increase in diversity could compromise institutional reputation and undermine one's standing in the market. For instance, one report remarks,

> For many on the Berkeley campus, "diversity" is perceived as a compromise with academic excellence or a "trade-off" between academic rigor and political correctness. . . . Efforts to promote diversity at the expense of this norm [scholarly distinction], we believe, will be deeply resisted by the faculty and have little effect. (University of California at Berkeley, 2000)

Thus, using CRT as an analytic lens illuminates racist beliefs of "the 'contaminating' influence of Blackness" and justifies the absolute right to exclude some, constitutes others as outsiders, and situates still others as "intruders who have been granted special permission to be there" (Ladson-Billing & Tate, 1995, p. 60). This discursive framing of diversity is in tension with a discourse of democracy.

Discourse of Democracy

Analysis of diversity action plans revealed institutional calls for "inclusion and opportunity"; "civic responsibility"; "commitment to freedom, equity, and reason"; "deliberative dialogue"; and professed a "moral imperative" for "justice, fairness, and equal access" and social equality and respect for the individual within a community. These characterizations in the policies are made visible by a discourse of democracy, which emerges as an alternative to and challenges the constitutive power of the dominant marketplace discourse and shapes an image of change-agent, an identity status for individuals and institutions to inhabit. "Working together," "the right thing to do," "collaborative spirit," "alliance," and "grassroots action" are evidence of change-making potential that exists within the individual, a collective, and an institution.

"Shared democratic values" are exemplified by calls for equality. In large part, the purpose for diversity planning and policy development is to address intergroup disparities. Thus, inequality is described by diversity action plans as a significant impediment to the realization of democratic ideals. The policies recognize "that previous discrimination . . . has foreclosed economic opportunity" and cite the need to "redress historical inequities that continue to plague our nation"; the reports further express concern "about the real hardships imposed on some families" by current policies that produce "clear inequity."

Equality as a concept has been a cornerstone of democracy, yet this concept has been contested throughout history and this struggle is evident in the diversity action plans. A solution to inequality, not unique to land-grant universities, is the use of law to ensure equal treatment; more specifically, taking affirmative action and using equal opportunity laws. As one diversity action plan succinctly states, "Affirmative action is a tool used to facilitate equal opportunity" (University of Idaho, 2004; Virginia Tech University, 2000). However, the use of this tool often is characterized as a problem by the policies: Explicitly stated in two documents that appended climate survey results in their diversity action plans, some faculty, staff, and students associate the use of affirmative action with a reduction in standards. CRT illuminates the ways in which the permanence of racism in institutional practices, such as affirmative action, privileges Whites and Whiteness and sustains exclusionary procedures (DeCuir & Dixson, 2004; Ladson-Billings, 1998; Ladson-Billing & Tate, 1995). Furthermore, CRT critiques the objectivity, neutrality, and color blindness professed in liberal legal ideology, an ideology that ensures only incremental and superficial change (Dixson & Rousseau, 2005). Finally, CRT invites counterstorytelling that can "sound an alarm" about equal opportunity initiatives that are more bureaucratic activities than assurances of equity (Aguirre, 2000).

In their calls for "the academy [to] remain free to educate all the nation, opening doors of opportunity to all our fellow citizens" (Pennsylvania State University, 2004), diversity policies identify "rigorous dialogue" as essential for the realization of democratic ideals. For instance, one report asserts the need for "critical institutional dialogue which will forge the agenda for change" (North Carolina State University, 1999). Diversity action plans further emphasize the need for intergroup dialogue. Scholars attest to the need for and benefits of cross-difference dialogue (Boler, 2004; Bonnell & Hunt, 1999; Nieto, 1999; Tierney, 1992). Yet these policy recommendations to facilitate dialogue are situated in opposition to or in the shadow of calls for expert hierarchy and centralized decision making. Although the intentions in the use of dialogue are democratic—facilitate a robust exchange of ideas—CRT illuminates that the mechanisms by which to do this (presidential commissions, town hall meetings) are elitist by definition. Furthermore, CRT exposes and critiques "normalized dialogues that perpetuate racial stereotypes" (DeCuir & Dixson, 2004, p. 27). The intergroup dialogue programs proposed in diversity action plans typically "skirt the very problem which multicultural education seeks to address: WHITE RACISM" (McCarthy, cited in Nebeker, 1998, p. 27). CRT's counterstorytelling amplifies narratives of racially marginalized students, documenting their exclusion, challenging prevailing notions of race neutrality in education, and illuminating the "ways some have had to compromise their race to survive" (Parker, 1998, p. 49; also Aguirre, 2000).

The policy recommendation to facilitate dialogue may be a well-intentioned masquerade of counterstorytelling; however, the dominance of the marketplace discourse undermines the promise of dialogue and the change-making possibilities of the discourse of democracy. The change agent is situated as a resource to be exploited for what is "good" and "common" and "shared" and "normal" (Carlson & Apple, 1998, p. 13). Diversity action plans profess "the 'rightness' of democracy while ignoring the structural inequality of capitalism" (Ladson-Billings & Tate, 1995, p. 52) evident in the marketplace discourse.

Implications for Practice

The goal of this research is to enable individuals engaged in the policy-making process (e.g., drafting diversity action plans) to be more aware of the discursive effects of their efforts to inform change and achieve equity in U.S. higher education. The findings of this study offer a particular perspective that invite an opportunity for thinking differently about diversity policies and the discourses carried by them. I will offer a few suggestions for how educational administrators might engage new possibilities for thinking to improve practice. Specifically, I will discuss the potential (a) for the use of counterstorytelling to amplify experiential knowledge and stories other than the dominant (institutional) one, (b) to facilitate dialogue for the purpose of understanding each other and our stories, and (c) for the strategic deployment of discourse to reframe the conception of the problem and facilitate discursive shifts.

Counterstorytelling

Diversity action plans are authored by institutional agents, faculty, administrators, and experts, all engaged in a policy-making process that is at times guided by contracted consultants; these diversity policies tell only one (part of the) story. A key tenet of CRT is the centrality of experiential knowledge, amplified through stories and counterstories told by people of color (DeCuir & Dixson, 2004; Dixson & Rousseau, 2005; Solórzano & Yosso, 2001a; Villalpando, 2004). Although an exploration of the diversity-planning process quickly reveals multiple stories, the university's narrative, disseminated through institutional policy (and the university newswire), is the dominant story; it can appear to be the only story and "looks ordinary and natural" (Delgado, 1995, p. xiv). Practitioners, then, are challenged with identifying and amplifying the many perspectives on campus diversity. I will draw on one university's story to illuminate policy silences and suggest alternatives.

One diversity action plan described in its background and introduction that its diversity-planning efforts originated with a resolution by the Board of Trustees in 1996, which led to the generation of an initial plan in 1998 and the publication of a second diversity action plan in 2004; it also provided a demographic profile of the university and contextualized its commitment to diversity and equity with numerous references to the U.S. Supreme Court's 2003 landmark decisions "affirming the significance of diversity on college campuses" (Pennsylvania State University, 2004). Absent in the university policy was any description of the ongoing hate crimes and harassment that elevated student concern to outrage,[6] resulting in student activism and ultimately a sit-in demanding the administration take a more aggressive stance in improving race relations. The *Intercom*, Penn State's electronic news service, reported that "University administrators and members of the student Black Caucus came together to endorse a broad diversity plan for the institution" (Mountz, 2001)—this story makes visible the student Black Caucus but fails to illuminate the demands they made. A third-party source, *The Daily Texan*, reported, "For 10 days last spring semester, almost 100 students protested the way Pennsylvania State University handles racism by sleeping on the floor of the HUB-Robeson Center [student union]" (Swift, 2001). This third-party source, and a "history of hate at Penn State" published on a student organization (Black Caucus) Web site, reveal a very different story than was conveyed through policy. The university policy filters out and censors the racial reality.

Thus, the university, through educational policy, conveys a whitewashed version that appears to be the only truth. However, the use of CRT's counterstorytelling can amplify other voices and additional sources of knowledge; it can tell "another story of a highly racialized social order: a story where social institutions and practices serve the interest of White individuals" (Chaisson, 2004; Lopez, 2003, p. 85). Practitioners involved in diversity-planning efforts can use their role and charge to uncover counterstories (similar to the one reported in *The Daily Texan* and accessible on the student Black Caucus Web site); they also can identify informants from the campus from whom to gain access to new/additional information. Practitioners then can amplify these stories as an act of transparency. A cacophony of stories holds the potential to disrupt (erase) the "normative supremacy of Whiteness" (Valdes, Culp, & Harris, 2002, p. 3).

Facilitate Dialogue

The counterstories, uncovered by practitioners, also can be used to facilitate cross-difference dialogue. Scholars attest to the need for and benefits of such dialogues (Boler, 2004; Bonnell & Hunt, 1999; Tierney, 1992). These are not tolerant, sensitive, affirming, homogenizing dialogues but rather are "dangerous discourses" (Nieto, 1999) that will likely generate "moments of discomfort, feelings experienced as we hover on the threshold between certainty and uncertainty, knowing and unknowing as we step out of familiar and into unfamiliar story lines" (Huber, Murphy, & Clandinin, 2003, p. 359). Educational administrators and policy makers are challenged to provide "free spaces" (Phelan, 1994, p. 88) in which people can share individual histories and expectations and connect multiple communities. Furthermore, policy-making groups are encouraged to engage discussion of not just difference but also of privilege and power (Johnson, 2005). This should not divert attention from the material realities of oppression and disadvantage but extend discussion to include awareness of the privileging conditions that construct both discriminatory and empowering realities for individuals.

Strategic Deployment of Discourse

Another potential strategy for change is to reframe the problem. Generally, institutions approach educational policy making as a process of problem solving and thus every policy proposal contains within it problems representations and an explicit or implicit diagnosis of the problem (Bacchi, 1999). How the problem is framed determines the range of solutions available; in turn, it also conceals from view an array of options that could emerge from alternate conceptions of the problem. Awareness calls for an interrogation of the assumptions that ground the construction of the policy problem—the "assumptions about the causes of the 'problem'" (Bacchi, 1999, p. 109; Lopez, 2003).

What does it mean to initiate an interrogation of assumptions? Practitioners are challenged to consider how the articulation of solutions in policy corresponds with the stated problems. For instance, in this investigation, the problems made visible by a discourse of discrimination are harassment, bias, racism, sexism, and homophobia; solutions include to offer support services to those who are victims, deliver training and education, and facilitate intergroup dialogue. These solutions are important but fail to sufficiently address the source of the problem: the individuals or systems that are discriminatory, racist, sexist, and homophobic. Examining the (in)congruence between problems and solutions articulated in policy, coupled with an awareness of the discursive construction of diversity, can provide a different lens through which to view diversity. Such a "cognitive shift" (Bensimon, 2005) may inspire discussions about different solutions and deploy the tactical use of discourse.

Practitioners, then, have the potential to influence discursive shifts. Notably, individuals do not "stand outside of discourse and choose when, where, and how to take up particular discourses to produce some intended and predictable effect" (Allan, 2003, p. 65). Thus, policy makers cannot write discourse into a policy recommendation to produce different effects; they cannot simply rewrite policy by finding and replacing certain words with others, such as searching a document for *disadvantage* and replacing it with *equality* to shift from a deficit to an equity focus. However, practitioners can be more informed and critical of the ways in which policy documents are discursively constituted and inspire opportunities for different discourses to be taken up. For instance, as noted above, the marketplace discourse undermines the change-making potential of the discourse of democracy. Diversity councils could take up strategies made visible by a discourse of democracy to facilitate difficult dialogues, suspend a rush to affirm and unite across difference, and lean into conflict and dissonance. However, one must be cautious: As CRT illuminates, embedded within the discourse of democracy is an emphasis on inclusion, unity, and tolerance that privileges the "harmful fictions" of meritocracy, neutrality, and equality for all (Valdes et al., 2002, p. 3). CRT elucidates the inherent racism in the liberal ideology of this democratic discourse.

Conclusion

This chapter demonstrates the utility of CRT as an analytic lens through which to view the discursive construction of people of color in educational diversity policies and illuminates how well-intentioned attempts to create a more inclusive campus may unwittingly reinforce practices that support exclusion and inequality. CRT as a theoretical framework can enhance practitioners' and scholars' understanding about how racial inequality is (re)produced through educational policies, specifically, diversity action plans, and how existing policies and practices may reinscribe the problems they seek to address.

The use of CRT as an analytic lens theorizes that "the racial experiences of racial minority groups are subordinate relative to White racial experience" (Lazos Vargas, cited in Lopez & Parker, 2003, p. 1). Diversity action plans, as discussed above, use White racial (and male, middle-class) experience as a standard against which to measure racial minority groups' progress and success in higher education. I reject the assumption that this majority standard is guided by objective or disinterested criteria; instead, I assume that the White, male majority standard is contingent and contextual and seek to make visible the normative power of the practices and processes to which others must conform. Although the aim is to create and support a community inclusive and affirming of difference, the dominant discourses circulating in and through diversity action plans reinforce conformity to a taken-for-granted standard. To realize the professed goals of access and equity, diversity-planning needs to be informed by theory "based on 'difference' rather than on 'sameness'" (Bensimon, 1995, p. 608). CRT offers such a theoretical framework for practitioners and scholars to analyze and critique "rules, norms, standards, and assumptions that appear 'neutral' but which systematically disadvantage or 'subordinate' racial minorities" (Lazos Vargas, cited in Lopez & Parker, 2003, p. 1).

In sum, those who produce and implement policy documents that will address racial inequities can be more informed and critical of the ways in which such documents are discursively constituted. A CRT analysis of the assumptions embedded in existing practices and how these may maintain existing racial inequities can "begin the process of naming and dismantling racism" in educational practice and policy making (Lopez, 2003, p. 87). CRT affords practitioners and scholars an opportunity to unveil the web of power and privilege that privileges some knowledge over others, constructs normative standards, and simultaneously conceals this practice. Furthermore, the "strategic deployment of discourse" (Allan, 2003) can lead to meaningful conversations about racial inequality, enabling policy makers to disrupt the status quo and destabilize the regulatory tendencies of dominant discourses.

Notes

1. Although sampling from land-grant universities enabled the collection of data from a consistent institutional type, this does not mean that these institutions are all the same. They are significantly different in size, control, culture, demographics, and geography. However, land-grant universities hold status in the higher education community; their classification as research or doctoral institutions meets "the prestige standard by which most colleges judge their progress" and positions them, symbolically and in actuality, as a benchmark for other institutions on a local, regional, and national level (Fairweather & Beach, 2002, p. 99). Furthermore, the missions of the 1862 land grants—"the peoples' colleges" (Campbell, 1995, p. 26)—are consistent with the professed values and beliefs articulated in diversity action plans; these institutions are explicitly seeking to create an environment where people of diverse backgrounds and economic classes can flourish and contribute in the classroom and the workplace. Thus, land-grant universities hold the potential to emerge as a social force in higher education's response to the public concern of diversity.

2. The designation of "1862 land grant" derives from legislation passed in 1862—Morrill Land Grant Act—that awarded land grants to states and were extended to more institutions as present state boundaries were defined. Typically, references to land-grant universities do not include this designator (1862); however, it is important to acknowledge and differentiate between the 1890 land grants and the 1994 land grants. For a complete list of land-grant universities in the United States, see *The 105 Land-Grant Colleges and Universities* available from http:// www.nasulgc.org/publications/Land_Grant/Schools.htm.

3. These diversity-related groups include President's Council on Disabilities: President's Commission on Women: President's Commission on the Status of Gay, Lesbian, Bisexual, and Transgender (GLBT) Issues: and Provost's Committee on the Status of People of Color.

4. Although committees and reports have various titles, I was seeking plans that addressed diversity in the broadest sense. This parameter excluded reports generated by other committees charged by senior administrators, for example, commission on women, disabilities.

5. For a complete description of these findings, see Iverson (2005).

6. A search of electronic media reveals bias incidents and hate crimes directed at Penn State students dating back to 1996. In addition, The Black Caucus, a student organization, published a "history of hate at Penn State" on their Web site detailing incidents since 2000 (see http://www.clubs.psu.edu/up/blackcaucusweb).

References

Aguirre, A. (2000). Academic storytelling: A critical race theory story of affirmative action. *Sociological Perspectives, 43*(2), 319-339.

Aleman, E., Jr. (2006). Is Robin Hood the "Prince of Thieves" or a pathway to equity? Applying critical race theory to school finance political discourse. *Educational Policy, 20*(1), 113-142.

Allan, E. J. (2003). Constructing women's status: Policy discourses of university women's commission policy reports. *Harvard Educational Review, 73*(1), 44-72.

Bacchi, C. L. (1999). *Women, policy and politics: The construction of policy problems.* Thousand Oaks, CA: Sage.

Baez, B. (2002). *Affirmative action, hate speech, and tenure: Narratives about race, law, and the academy.* New York: Routledge.

Ball, S. J. (Ed.). (1990). *Foucault and education: Disciplines and knowledge.* New York: Routledge.

Bell, L. A. (2003). Telling tales: What stories can teach us about racism. *Race Ethnicity and Education, 6*(1), 3-28.

Bensimon, E. M. (1995). Total quality management in the academy: A rebellious reading. *Harvard Educational Review, 65*(4), 593-611.

Bensimon, E. M. (2005). Closing the achievement gap in higher education: An organizational learning perspective. *New Directions for Higher Education, 131,* 99-111.

Boler, M. (Ed.). (2004). *Democratic dialogue in education: Troubling speech, disturbing silence.* New York: Peter Lang.

Bonnell, V. E., & Hunt, L. (Eds.). (1999). *Beyond the cultural turn: New directions in the study of society and culture.* Los Angeles: University of California Press.

Campbell, J. R. (1995). *Reclaiming a lost heritage: Land-grant and other higher education initiatives for the twenty-first century.* Ames: Iowa State University Press.

Carlson, D., & Apple, M. W. (Eds.). (1998). *Power/knowledge/pedagogy: The meaning of democratic education in unsettling times.* Boulder, CO: Westview.

Chaisson, R. L. (2004). A crack in the door: Critical race theory in practice at a predominantly white institution. *Teaching Sociology, 32,* 345-357.

DeCuir, J. T., & Dixson, A. D. (2004). "So when it comes out, they aren't that surprised that it is there": Using critical race theory as a tool of analysis of race and racism in education. *Educational Researcher, 33*(5), 26-31.

Delgado, R. (1995). *Critical race theory: The cutting edge.* Philadelphia: Temple University Press.

Delgado Bernal, D., & Villalpando, O. (2002). An apartheid of knowledge in academia: The struggle over the "legitimate" knowledge of faculty of color. *Equity and Excellence in Education, 35*(2), 169-180.

Dixson, A. D., & Rousseau, C. K. (2005). And we are still not saved: Critical race theory in education 10 years later. *Race Ethnicity and Education, 8*(1), 7-27.

Fairweather, J. S., & Beach, A. L. (2002). Variations in faculty work at research universities: Implications for state and institutional policy. *Review of Higher Education, 26*(1), 97-115.

Freeman, K. (Ed.). (1998). *African American culture and heritage in higher education research and practice.* Westport, CT: Praeger.

Garcia, S. B., & Guerra, P. L. (2004). Deconstructing deficit thinking: Working with educators to create more equitable learning environments. *Education and Urban Society, 36*(2), 150-168.

Gerald, D., & Haycock, K. (2006). *Engines of inequality: Diminishing equity in the nation's premier public universities.* Washington, DC: The Education Trust. Retrieved February 18, 2007, from http://www2.edtrust.org/NR/rdonlyres/F755E80E-9431-45AF-B28E-653C612D503D/0/ EnginesofInequality.pdf

Hajer, M. A., & Wagenaar, H. (Eds.). (2003). *Deliberative policy analysis: Understanding governance in the network society.* New York: Cambridge University Press.

Hawkesworth, M. E. (1988). *Theoretical issues in policy analysis.* Albany: State University of New York Press.

Heberle, R. (1996). Deconstructive strategies and the movement against sexual violence. *Hypatia, 11*(4), 63-76.

hooks, b. (1994). *Teaching to transgress: Education as the practice of freedom.* New York: Routledge.

Huber, J., Murphy, M. S., & Clandinin, D. J. (2003). Creating communities of cultural imagination: Negotiating a curriculum of diversity. *Curriculum Inquiry, 33*(4), 343-362.

Hu-DeHart, E. (2000). The diversity project: Institutionalizing multiculturalism or managing differences? *Academe, 86*(5), 39-42.

Ibarra, R. A. (2001). *Beyond affirmative action: Reframing the context of higher education.* Madison: University of Wisconsin Press.

Iverson, S. V. (2005). *A policy discourse analysis of U.S. land-grant university diversity action plans.* Unpublished doctoral dissertation, University of Maine.

Johnson, A. (2005). *Privilege, power and difference* (2nd ed.). New York: McGraw-Hill.

Ladson-Billings, G. (1998). Just what is critical race theory and what's it doing in a nice field like education? *International Journal of Qualitative Studies in Education, 11*(1), 7-24. Ladson-Billings, G. (2000). Racialized discourses and ethnic epistemologies. In N. Denzin &

Y. Lincoln (Eds.), *Handbook of qualitative research* (2nd ed., pp. 257-277). Thousand Oaks, CA: Sage.

Ladson-Billings, G. (2005). The evolving role of critical race theory in educational scholarship. *Race Ethnicity and Education, 8*(1), 115-119.

Ladson-Billings, G., & Tate, W. E., IV. (1995). Toward a critical race theory of education. *Teachers College Record, 97*(1), 47-68.

Lopez, G. R. (2003). The (racially neutral) politics of education: A critical race theory perspective. *Educational Administration Quarterly, 39*(1), 68-94.

Lopez, G. R., & Parker, L. (Eds.). (2003). *Interrogating racism in qualitative research methodology.* New York: Peter Lang.

Lynn, M., & Adams, M. (2002). Introductory overview to the special issue critical race theory and education: Recent developments in the field. *Equity and Excellence in Education, 35*(2), 87-92.

Marshall, C. (1999). Researching the margins: Feminist critical policy analysis. *Educational Policy, 13*(1), 59-77.

Marshall, C. (2000). Policy discourse analysis: Negotiating gender equity. *Journal of Education Policy, 15*(2), 125-156.

Marshall, C., & Rossman, G. B. (1999). *Designing qualitative research* (3rd ed.). Thousand Oaks, CA: Sage.

Miles, M., & Huberman, A. M. (1994). *Qualitative data analysis: An expanded sourcebook of new methods* (2nd ed.). Thousand Oaks, CA: Sage.

Mills, S. (1997). *Discourse.* New York: Routledge.

Morfin, O. J., Perez, V. H., Parker, L., Lynn, M., & Arrona, J. (2006). Hiding the politically obvious: A critical race theory preview of diversity as racial neutrality in higher education. *Educational Policy, 20*(1), 249-270.

Mountz, A. (2001, May 10). Broad diversity plan put into place. *Penn State Intercom.* Retrieved September 26, 2006, from http://www.psu.edu/ur/archives/intercom_2001/May10/diversity.html

Nebeker, K. C. (1998). Critical race theory: A White graduate student's struggle with this growing area of scholarship. *Qualitative Studies in Education, 11*(1), 25-41.

Nieto, S. (1999). *The light in their eyes: Creating multicultural learning communities.* New York: Teachers College Press.

Parker, L. (1998). "Race is . . . race ain't": An exploration of the utility of critical race theory in qualitative research in education. *Qualitative Studies in Education, 11*(1), 43-55.

Parker, L. (2003). Critical race theory and its implications for methodology and policy analysis in higher education desegregation. In G. R. Lopez & L. Parker (Eds.), *Interrogating racism in qualitative research methodology* (pp. 145-173). New York: Peter Lang.

Phelan, S. (1994). *Getting specific: Postmodern lesbian politics.* Minneapolis: University of Minnesota Press.

Pollock, M. (2004). *Colormute: Race talk dilemmas in an American school.* Princeton, NJ: Princeton University Press.

Revilla, A. T., & Asato, J. (2002). The implementation of Proposition 227 in California schools: A critical analysis of the effect on teacher beliefs and classroom practices. *Equity and Excellence in Education, 35*(2), 108-118.

Roe, E. (1994). *Narrative policy analysis: Theory and practice.* Durham, NC: Duke University Press.

Scheurich, J. J. (1994). Policy archaeology: A new policy studies methodology. *Journal of Education Policy, 9*(4), 297-316.

Solórzano, D. G., Ceja, M., & Yosso, T. J. (2000). Critical race theory, racial microaggressions, and campus racial climate: The experiences of African American college students. *Journal of Negro Education, 69*(1/2), 60-73.

Solórzano, D. G., Villalpando, O., & Oseguera, L. (2005). Educational inequities and Latina/o undergraduate students in the United States: A critical race analysis of their educational progress. *Journal of Hispanic Higher Education, 4*(3), 272-294.

Solórzano, D. G., & Yosso, T. J. (2001a). Critical race and LatCrit theory and method: Counter-storytelling. *Qualitative Studies in Education, 14*(4), 471-495.

Solórzano, D. G., & Yosso, T. J. (2001b). From racial stereotyping and deficit discourse toward a critical race theory in teacher education. *Multicultural Education, 9*(1), 2-8.

Solórzano, D. G., & Yosso, T. J. (2002). A critical race counterstory of race, racism, and affirmative action. *Equity and Excellence in Education, 35*(2), 155-168.

Stein, S. J. (2004). *The culture of education policy.* New York: Teachers College Press.

Swift, T. (2001, June 26). Penn State student group holds sit-in to protest school's handling of alleged racist incident. *The Daily Texan, 101*(166). Retrieved September 26, 2006, from http://tspweb02.tsp.utexas.edu/webarchive/06-26-01/2001062606_s01_Penn.html

Teranishi, R. T. (2002). Asian Pacific Americans and critical race theory: An examination of school racial climate. *Equity and Excellence in Education, 35*(2), 144-154.

Tierney, W. G. (1992). *Official encouragement, institutional discouragement: Minorities in academe—The Native American experience.* Norwood, NJ: Ablex.

U.S. Department of Education. (1994). *Improving possibilities for students placed at risk.* Washington, DC: Author. Retrieved April 1, 2005, from http://www.ed.gov/bulletin/winter1994/atrisk.html

Valdes, F., Culp, J. M., & Harris, A. P. (Eds.). (2002). *Crossroads, directions, and a new critical race theory.* Philadelphia: Temple University Press.

Villalpando, O. (2003). Self-segregation or self-preservation? A critical race theory and Latina/o critical theory analysis of a study of Chicana/o college students. *International Journal of Qualitative Studies in Education, 16*(5), 619-646.

Villalpando, O. (2004). Practical considerations of critical race theory and Latino critical theory for Latino college students. *New Directions for Student Services, 105*, 41-50.

Walker-Moffat, W. (1995). *The other side of the Asian American success story.* San Francisco: Jossey-Bass.

Weedon, C. (1997). *Feminist practice and poststructuralist theory* (2nd ed.). Oxford, UK: Blackwell.

Wilkinson, S., & Kitzinger, C. (Eds.). (1995). *Feminism and discourse: Psychological perspectives*. Thousand Oaks, CA: Sage.

Yanow, D. (2003). *Constructing "race" and "ethnicity" in America: Category-making in public policy and administration*. Armonk, NY: M. E. Sharpe.

Yosso, T. J. (2002). Toward a critical race curriculum. *Equity and Excellence in Education, 35*(2), 93-107.

Yosso, T. J. (2005). Whose culture has capital? A critical race theory discussion of community cultural wealth. *Race Ethnicity and Education, 8*(1), 69-91.

CHAPTER 33
UNDERSTANDING LEADERSHIP STRATEGIES FOR ADDRESSING THE POLITICS OF DIVERSITY

ADRIANNA KEZAR

A group of students conducts a sit-in because they perceive students of color are getting special advantages.

Members of the African American business community ask to meet with the campus president about the decline in the number of African Americans on campus.

An alumni group calls for a special meeting with the board of trustees to discuss its concerns with the diversity agenda being developed on campus.

A staff member posts a critical letter on a highly visible blog about the diversity initiative.

Each of these scenarios represents the type of politics that campus leaders face as they engage in the work of moving a diversity agenda forward and trying to create an inclusive campus environment. While you see these stories of campus politics commonly reported in the *Chronicle of Higher Education*, little research has examined how leaders address these complicated political situations that arise on campuses across the country. This study endeavored to examine the role of presidents in advancing a diversity agenda and focused on examining the type of political situations that emerge, particularly strategies that college presidents use to negotiate these politics.[1] While higher education leaders have addressed campus climate and concerns about equity for many years, since the 1980s it has become more commonplace to speak about campuses having a diversity agenda. The *Chronicle of Higher Education* regularly showcases stories about leaders advancing diversity agendas—for example, the University of Michigan, Penn State University, and the University of California at Los Angeles including ways they are trying to increase the diversity of their students, faculty, and staff and provide a better environment so that they are retained. Diversity initiatives have several broad goals, including developing an understanding of diversity; infusing attention to differences by race, sexual orientations, and gender; and creating greater equity and parity in the experience and outcomes of individuals from diverse backgrounds (Hale, 2004; Hurtado et al., 1999; Musil, Garcia, Hudgins, Nettles, Sedlacek, & Smith, 1999; Smith, 1989). An initiative can emerge from the top down, with the president or other leaders in positions of authority, or it can emerge bottom up from faculty and staff to eventually become integrated into the overall institutional agenda. A brief review of presidential leadership and its role in advancing diversity agendas and politics will help to set the context for this chapter.

Presidents play many important roles to help advance a diversity agenda—roles that most other leaders cannot play because they do not have the authority or leverage that is critical to institutionalization (Birnbaum, 1992; Fisher, 1984). For example, presidents help to create institutional commitment by relating a diversity agenda to the institutional mission or by including diversity in strategic planning and budget processes or establishing rewards and incentives (Hurtado et al., 1999; McGovern, Foster, & Ward, 2002; Musil et al., 1999; Smith, 1989; Smith & Wolf-Wendel, 2005). Presidents also help to create ownership by obtaining board support, hosting campuswide dialogues, and establishing commissions and committees. They even get involved in specific initiatives such as transforming the curriculum, measuring progress, and evaluating and creating accountability (Hurtado et al., 1999; Smith & Wolf-Wendel, 2005). Some authors, in fact, suggest that leadership is perhaps the most important factor in ensuring institutional transformation and institutionalizing a diversity agenda (Hurtado et al., 1999; Kezar, 2007; Kezar & Eckel, 2005; Tierney, 1991, 1993).

While leadership has been demonstrated to be particularly important, few studies have delved into the challenges that leaders face as they take on what can be perceived, on many campuses, as a controversial topic. Research has provided leaders with a variety of strategies to help move a diversity agenda forward and to overcome common barriers, but there is limited exploration of the politics surrounding the issue (Davis, 2002; Hale, 2004; Milem, Chang, & antonio, 2005; Musil et al., 1999; Smith, 1989).[2] Other literature documents the political landscape and dynamics that leaders face but offers no suggestions for addressing the politics (Beckham, 2000; Bensimon, 1992; Humphreys, 1997; Rhoads, 1998). This often leaves leaders in a precarious position: They know strategies that have worked to create change and some strategies for overcoming barriers (such as role modeling or rewards), but they are left helpless when faced with significant political resistance. I was interested in exploring in a systematic and empirical way the politics of diversity and how leaders face trenchant resistance based on differing interests and values.

Politics is typically defined as how people use power within a social setting, gain status, or maintain distinctive interests (Bolman & Deal, 1997; Clark, 1983). The critical elements within this definition are that politics involves the way people define their interests or concerns and that it is natural for different individuals and groups to have different interests. Politics relates to the way that people try to assert their particular interests and the way they use power and strategies to assert their interests. A set of White faculty might write a letter to the academic senate about declining standards in hiring faculty. In this situation, the interest group is a set of White faculty, and the way they are exerting power is through writing down their concerns and sending them to a powerful group on campus with whom they believe they have influence. They have defined their interests as declining standards in hiring faculty.

Given the importance of moving diversity agendas forward nationally and the lack of understanding about how to address the politics that almost always emerge when institutionalizing a diversity initiative, I examined the method by which presidents handled the politics related to moving a diversity agenda forward. I focused on college presidents because they are usually at the center of politics and because they are one of the most important leaders in efforts to institutionalizing diversity initiatives. In this chapter, I argue that political theories of change are a particularly important but underutilized perspective for understanding change related to diversity within the higher education environment. The overall study explores presidential leadership in moving a diversity agenda forward, including key strategies, presidential leadership style, institutional context and culture, and phases of institutionalization. I focus on the way presidents negotiated "the politics" of diversity and address two research questions: How and in what ways do presidents find that moving a diversity agenda forward is a political process, and what is the nature of the politics? What strategies do presidents use to negotiate a political environment and create change?

Theoretical Framework

This study is framed by political theories of change and leadership, which maintain a unique set of assumptions that are helpful for examining the politics that leaders face in implementing a diversity agenda (Baldridge, Curtis, Ecker, & Riley, 1977; Bolman & Deal, 1997; Clark, 1983; Gioia & Thomas, 1996; Hearn, 1996; Sporn, 1999). Political theories posit that there are different interest groups in organizations that fight over scarce resources and priorities. People do not operate in rational ways and will resist issues about which they have fears. Research in higher education has not focused on political barriers that often take on an irrational character, nor has research examined the ways in which leaders can negotiate these situations. Much of the literature on change focuses on technical strategies such as providing training to help individuals to work in new ways or creating strategic plans to help provide direction and new habits for people (Bauman, Bustillos, Bensimon, Brown, & Bartee, 2005; Milem, Chang, & antonio, 2005; Musil et al., 1999; Smith & Associates, 1997). While these are all important strategies for addressing resistance, these technical solutions often do not address the politics that emerge related to change issues such as diversity.[3]

In the next section, I attempt to demonstrate why political theories are a helpful lens for understanding change within the higher education environment regarding diversity initiatives.[4] I then describe the common strategies offered to leaders within political theories for negotiating conflict and resistance and for creating change. This literature was used to analyze and make sense of the data presented later in the chapter.

Higher Education as a Political Organization and Diversity as a Political Position

Research suggests that higher education is a particularly political environment and that conflict and resistance will be a major problem in creating change. One of the reasons that higher education is open to politics is that hierarchical authority is limited and shared governance is practiced widely (Birnbaum, 1988). Leaders typically do not mandate change, and persuasion and power have emerged in the place of authority (Birnbaum, 1988, 1992; Kezar, 2001). Studies of higher education as an organization demonstrate that it has many different interest groups. Faculty, staff, students, and administrators form separate subcultures with different value systems and often different institutional goals and purposes (Baldridge, 1971; Birnbaum, 1988; Kezar, 2001). Within these various interest groups or subcultures, there are also competing factions. Research has identified a variety of different student (different ethnicities, student organizations, majors), faculty (different disciplines and ranks), staff (support staff and middle-level management), and administrative (student and academic affairs) subcultures (Kuh & Whitt, 1988). Because of the multitude of differing subcultures representing varying interests and values, conflict and disagreement is more likely and commonplace. With so many different interest groups, there is no common direction or values. Existing groups defend the resources and power that they have, and new groups emerge trying to obtain resources and power, creating conflict. Clark describes this process in his book about academic institutions:

> The situation is like a seesaw, a long board on which reform supporting and reform opposing groups sit at different points in relation to the center of balance, far out towards the end or close to the center according to the extremity of their views. If all groups were equal in power, the seesaw's direction would depend on how many groups were located on either side of the balance, and particularly the intensity of their commitment. But some groups are genuine heavies in terms of power where others are lightweights. . . . when the heavies assert themselves, they can throw the weaker innovative groups off the seesaw, leaving them dangling uncomfortably in midair, or force them to declare that the game is over. (1983, pp. 225–226)

A variety of commentators have suggested that in recent years college campuses have become increasingly politicized based on the corporatization and commercialization of the higher education enterprise, resource constraint, and the growing encroachment of outside groups (Hearn, 1996; Kezar, 2001). There is growing separation between administrators and faculty; administrators are increasingly coming from outside academe and have been focused on reorganizing faculty work and roles, creating more tension and deeper divisions among interest groups. Faculty feel that administrators are becoming more managerial and believe that it is important for them to assert an academic perspective in the face of commercialization (Kezar, Chambers, & Burkhardt, 2005). Faculty groups are also increasingly divided between part-time and contract faculty (nontenured) and tenured faculty. Student groups and associations with distinct interests are rapidly growing on campus, creating even more progressive (environmental or multicultural) and conservative (campus Republicans, David Horowitz–sponsored organizations) subcultures. Boards are increasingly made up of members of the business community, and the number of board members that have an understanding of educational issues is decreasing as politics are instead playing a more prominent role in board appointments (Kezar, 2004). Unions have been growing, and collective bargaining is becoming more prevalent on campuses among graduate students, staff, and part-time faculty, drawing more politics to campus. Outside groups are also asserting their interests on campus more often. For example, activist trustees and groups/individuals that are critical of campus policies (such as David Horowitz) are growing and trying to assert their interests on campus. Resource constraints also make college campuses more political environments. Public support for higher education has waned in the last 15 years, and resources are limited on most college campuses. These are just a few examples of the types of changes that are creating a more political environment on campus. Each of these leads to trends that can affect diversity agendas. For example, resource constraints can result in disagreement over developing support programs for students of color that may not have occurred in flush financial times.

Colleges and universities are inherently political organizations, and many scholars argue that they are becoming more political over time (Gumport, 2000; Kezar et al., 2005). While this alone might make leaders consider the importance of political approaches for creating and negotiating change, the type of change initiative is also important to examine in evaluating the right framework for understanding how to navigate change (Kezar, 2001). Creating a campus that supports diverse students, faculty, and staff has been identified as a political issue (Gioia & Thomas, 1996). Faculty, staff, and students from dominant groups often perceive the development of specific programs for groups that have been traditionally underrepresented on campus as taking away resources and support from dominant groups. Traditionally underrepresented groups often do not have the power base that dominant groups have and need to create coalitions, alliances, and informal-influence processes. As a result, their interests are not represented, and enough resources are often not allocated and programs are not developed so that students, faculty, and staff from traditionally underrepresented groups can be successful. In addition, traditionally underrepresented groups may hold values that dominant groups do not share or understand. For example, traditionally underrepresented groups might want graduation ceremonies to be in two languages to embrace their culture. This clashing of interests and values creates conflict between the groups and resistance by the dominant group to changes suggested by the underrepresented group (Birnbaum, 1988).

Studies of the change process in higher education demonstrate that politics—comprised of conflict, resistance, and competing values—often thwart efforts at change (Kezar, 2001). Examining efforts of institutions to create change on a variety of initiatives, Gioia and Thomas (1996) demonstrated that if an issue is identified as political, then change is often not likely to occur. If leaders believed conflict would emerge, interest groups and factions were forming, competing interests were prevalent, and fighting over resources was likely on an issue, then they tended to shy away from the issue. Leaders are traditionally not well equipped to address politics, and it often prevents strategic change and subverts change processes. While practitioners shy away from issues that are labeled political, research from political theory suggests that political strategies can be extremely effective for overcoming these barriers to change (Bolman & Deal, 1997).

Strategies for Creating Change from Political Theory

In this section, I review some of the common strategies described in political theories of leadership related to negotiating conflict. These strategies were explored as themes in reviewing data collected from college presidents.[5] Bolman and Deal (1997) suggest that there are four main activities for political leaders: mapping the political terrain, coalition building and developing advocates/allies, persuasion, and bargaining and negotiating. I describe these four as well as two others identified in the literature—mediation and persistence. While these strategies are not used in any strict progression, certain strategies are more helpful at the beginning phase of politics (e.g., mapping the political terrain) and some are better as the politics become more advanced (negotiation).

Mapping the Political Terrain

Political leadership theories suggest that to be successful at change, leaders need to carefully assess the political landscape of their organization (Bolman & Deal, 1997). Bolman and Deal (1997) refer to this as "mapping the political terrain." They suggest that there are four main activities involved in such mapping: determining channels of communication, identifying principal agents of political influence, analyzing trends in mobilization, and anticipating strategies that others are likely to employ. Within a diversity initiative, this might mean identifying different interest groups and their opinions about the diversity initiative, examining whether any of these groups might mobilize based on their collective interests, trying to anticipate how they might resist the diversity initiative, and finding ways to become part of their communication network so that you understand more about their strategies and interest.

Coalition Building and Developing Advocates/Allies

Perhaps the most widely cited strategy for leaders is to create a power base (coalition) by gaining support from various interest groups—for example, African Americans, Hispanics, gays and lesbians (Baldridge, 1971; Baldridge et al., 1977; Bolman & Deal, 1997). Successful leaders negotiate the political climate by aligning with as many powerful interest groups as possible. Leaders need to speak effectively to individuals representing different interests and help them see commonalities. For example, a president might identify staff, students, administrators, and faculty of color and bring them together into a larger coalition, creating a power base around diversity.

In addition to creating a power base through interest groups' support, leaders are also encouraged to gain support from influential individuals such as a long-time faculty members, dedicated alumni, or local leaders who can become advocates or allies (Birnbaum, 1988; Bolman & Deal, 1997). These influential individuals tend to have the trust and attention of a variety of groups on campus, and they are the individuals that people check in with to clarify their own perspective. Usually seen as being fair and not maintaining a particular political position, these individuals vary by campus culture, so it is important for leaders to become familiar with these trusted opinion leaders. A vocal alumnus that supports the hiring of faculty of color and who is willing to bring in outside speakers from industry to discuss the issue can be a strong political tool.

Persuasion

Political leaders need to learn the skills of persuasion, helping people to understand different perspectives and values outside their own narrow interests (Bolman & Deal, 1997). As noted earlier, political processes involve competing values and interests. Successful leaders can reframe issues and help individuals from very different groups and subcultures to see the value of an idea—even one outside their own interests and values. Key persuasion tactics include storytelling, using symbols, appealing to expertise, and connecting the issue to something meaningful to the group (Bolman & Deal, 1997). For example, the leader of a campus might appeal to a campus mission of liberal learning and respect for different perspectives as a way to get dominant groups to engage in discussion about diversity. Obviously, understanding the logic of different interest groups also helps in being persuasive, and these tactics are linked.

Bargaining and Negotiation

Organizations would be deadlocked in interest groups if they did not have leaders who could bargain and negotiate to create compromises (Baldridge et al., 1977; Bolman & Deal, 1997). In recent years, political theories have focused on bargaining that is more principled and that attempts to make all parties feel that their interests are represented in some way in the decision. In addition, they emphasize creating a solution that is satisfactory for both parties and that usually differs from the solution of all parties involved. Thus, in recent years there has been a greater recognition that interest groups are interdependent—all of these individuals will remain within the organization, and creating decisions with which all parties agree is important to the long-term viability of the organization.

Political theories also highlight the importance of informal processes and behind-the-scenes deal making (Baldridge, 1971; Bolman & Deal, 1997). Often an interest group will not concede publicly to issues that are outside its agenda. However, research demonstrates that savvy political leaders negotiate and make compromises (Conrad, 1978). In behind-the-scenes deal making, the constituents' leaders compromise parts of their agendas in order to advance a mutual interest that they worked to identify. For example, the president, chair of faculty senate, head of the student government, and staff union representative might meet to think about ways to move the diversity agenda forward. The chair of the faculty senate might concede to new hiring processes if the curriculum is left up to the faculty. This would be one among many deals developed at that meeting. Informal processes and behind-the-scenes deal making have proven difficult to study in any detail because few people admit to this behavior (Hearn, 1996).

Mediation

A very different strategy to developing a coalition is to try to be a mediator (Bolman & Deal, 1997). Presidents may negotiate politics best if they try to stay outside of any particular interest groups and instead try to mediate between groups. While it is often difficult to be perceived as being outside of a particular interest, one way to stay more neutral is to understand and surround yourself with the logic of a variety of interest groups (Bolman & Deal, 1997). Savvy political leaders attempt to understand the varying values, beliefs, information, interests, and perceptions of reality among different groups (Bolman & Deal, 1997). This also provides leaders with the opportunity to negotiate and bargain, which is another important political strategy. Having advocates who support a leader can also help legitimize a leader as a mediator.

While leaders might sometimes be mediators, other times they need to know when to rely on other professional facilitators (Bolman & Deal, 1997). In order to break a deadlock that can occur when competing interests clash, outside facilitators or individuals who are considered unbiased are often needed. Leaders need to know when they need to step back and allow other people to lead discussions, bring groups together, and help facilitate decision-making. This strategy needs to be used sparingly or groups will perceive that leaders have limited or no authority or are not willing to make a commitment, which can end up compromising their long-term legitimacy (Kezar, 2001).

Persistence

Because many interest groups are changing and shifting (for example, students are graduating, staff turnover can be relatively high, etc.), an important political strategy can be persistence. Studies in higher education have shown that groups that advocate for change over the long run tend to get results (Baldridge et al., 1977; Cohen & March, 1974). Being willing to attend regular meetings, meet with administrative leaders, and be vocal on a regular basis are likely to create change. Persistence is marked by repetitively bringing up an idea and providing ways to implement it in all settings. In this way, the idea is just waiting for an opportunity to present itself.

In conclusion, political theories identify strategies that can be used by leaders to confront conflict and resistance. However, there is a limitation in this theory that this study hoped to overcome. The techniques offered by researchers using political theory are overly broad and do not provide the type of advice leaders need to negotiate a specific conflict—for example, implementing a diversity initiative. This study aimed to uncover specific strategies and examples to help presidents move diversity agendas forward.

Methodology

In order to understand the politics that leaders face in advancing their diversity agendas, the research team conducted "elite interviews" with 27 college presidents (Dexter, 1970; Holstein & Gubrium, 1995; Merton et al., 1990) because doing so enabled us to obtain information about a phenomenon that had not been pursued in earlier research.[6] Elite interviewing is a specific research methodology that evolved in disciplines such as sociology and political science (Dexter, 1970; Holstein & Gubrium, 1995). Based on the assumption that access to elites is often difficult and therefore key people that participate in a process are often not interviewed, it is characterized by the following qualities: Researchers conduct extensive analysis of documents and background work before conducting interviews; developing rapport is critical to obtaining information; the interview protocol is based on a combination of background research and literature; the interviewees are allowed more freedom to shape the direction of the interview because they are chosen for their expertise on the issues; and the interview sample selection is particularly important for ensuring that the phenomenon of interest is elucidated. This section focuses on sampling strategy, background research for the interviews, and strategy around access and rapport. The theoretical framework provided in the chapter is important to the methodology, and it informed the interview protocol and analysis.

Sample

Selection of interviewees is a particularly important part of the elite interviewing method, as the trustworthiness of the results is based on identifying individuals with significant experience and expertise (Holstein & Gubrium, 1995). The choice of interviewees was driven by three primary criteria related to expertise: (1) presidents who had significant presidential experience as defined above and who made significant progress advancing a diversity agenda (as identified by national experts on diversity in higher education); (2) presidents who represented different institutional types or sectors in a variety of settings (rural, urban, and suburban) and at different phases within their diversity agenda (early, middle, and late); and (3) presidents who had a reputation for being reflective about their leadership strategies.[7] To develop an initial list of participants, we asked organizations that are familiar with issues of diversity (such as the American Council on Education's Center for Advancement of Racial and Ethnic Equity and Office of Women in Higher Education) to nominate individuals based on these criteria and asked presidents to provide names of peers whom they respected on diversity-related issues. We allowed nominees and presidents to define diversity and a diversity agenda. Most embraced a broad definition of diversity that included race and ethnicity, gender, disability, sexual orientation, national origin, and the like. Both objective and subjective data (reputation) were used to identify presidents who had been successful advancing a diversity agenda. Objective criteria related to advancing the diversity agenda included but were not limited to the following (institutions did not have to meet all of these criteria): change in the mission of the institution to include diversity, a strategic plan focused on diversity, increase in the amount of funding for diversity related activities, increase in the number of programs related to diversity, hiring of key staff to support diversity, climate studies that suggested change in the campus environment, and so forth. Over 50 individuals were nominated, but only 32 presidents met our criteria of experience and having made progress. Five presidents declined to be interviewed because of a policy of not conducting interviews, in general, or because they felt they did not have time.

The final list of potential participants included individuals from every region of the country and from all higher education sectors. Many had held presidencies in different geographic regions and some at different types of institutions. Age, gender, race/ethnicity, and other criteria were not purposefully sampled, but an effort was made to ensure that a diverse set of individuals was included. It should be noted that the sample had close to 50% presidents of color. In addition, over one third of the presidents were women, so both the number of women presidents and presidents of color are in greater proportion to presidential demographics (Corrigan, 2003). Fourteen presidents were at predominantly White institutions, while eight were at institutions with a predominant number of minority students but a mix of various groups, as three were at Hispanic-serving institutions, one was at an HBCU, one was at a tribal-serving institution. Because the institutions sampled are so diverse, the nature of the politics was also wide-ranging. The nature of these politics are described at the beginning of the Results section.

Data Collection

The primary method of data collection was phone interviews because the individuals were geographically dispersed and extremely busy, making visits difficult. Ensuring rapport was extremely important because we wanted to create an environment in which individuals would share information about ways they have been successful in advancing a diversity agenda and strategies that failed, both of which might challenge traditional opinions (Holstein & Gubrium, 1995; Merriam, 1998; Seidman, 1991). Elites have limited time for interviews; therefore, it was critical to provide information and data to their staff up front so that the presidents could be briefed on the study and questions. Background information about the interviewees was gathered from Web sites, press releases, and through personal contacts. We conducted detailed analyses of institutional Web sites to identify information related to campus diversity agendas and requested documents from institutions. We conducted pre-interviews with key members of the presidents' staff and with informants on campus to garner information about the campuses, presidential leadership to advance diversity, and politics on campus (these interviews were not directly used as a source of data but to shape questions and provide contextual sensitivity for the interviewer). The interviewers attempted to establish an immediate connection with each interviewee, using the information gathered from Web sites and staff in order to garner their trust and interest in the study as quickly as possible before beginning the formal interview process. It should be noted that both researchers have done previous research on college presidents and were known by many of the presidents interviewed, helping with the development of rapport and increasing trustworthiness. Interviews averaged two hours in length and were tape-recorded. Presidents are usually unlikely to provide this amount of time to interviewers, but our interviewees were willing to based on the personal relationships with the researchers and their dedication to the topic of advancing diversity agendas. Extensive notes were also taken, and the interviews were transcribed verbatim.

An interview protocol was developed from the literature on diversity, organizational politics, and presidential leadership. The interview protocol focused on examining the main strategies and activities that presidents believed helped to advance their diversity agenda, the specific role of the presidents in advancing diversity on campus, the leadership style or approach they used, lessons they learned about leadership in advancing institutional diversity, how they handled situations of conflict and controversy, and how the campus context (region, student body, institutional phase, institutional demographic, institutional type, funding, mission) shaped the advancement of the diversity agenda and the politics they faced. Because this chapter is part of a larger study, the questions addressed are broader than only politics the leader faced, but this was a specific set of questions within the interviews. Questions related to politics included items such as: Did conflict emerge as you made progress on your diversity agenda? What kind of politics emerged? What strategies did you use to negotiate politics? Which strategies seem to work best? Why do you think they worked? Two researchers conducted the interviews using a common protocol, but the interviews would vary as elites were allowed to move the conversation in directions they felt were important.

Analysis

The interview data and documents were analyzed using Boyatzis's (1998) thematic analysis, a helpful technique that provides particular emphasis on how to identify codes and themes, how to carefully define codes/themes using examples, ways to use theory to create code definitions, and ways to use both deductive and inductive coding simultaneously. It differs from grounded theory analysis, for example, in emphasizing the importance of deductive and inductive codes (grounded theory focuses on inductive coding) and how to examine them at the same time. Essentially, with thematic analysis, the researcher begins with deductive codes from the theory to begin analysis, but the researcher remains open to other codes (inductive codes) that emerge while analyzing data. This approach to data analysis is helpful for studies that are deductive in nature—where prior or related research exists and where an existing theoretical framework is being used to analyze data.

Based on the research questions, analysis focused on strategies that leaders used to move the diversity agenda forward and to navigate politics. The political theoretical framework provided a variety of deductive themes to explore. Examples of deductive codes extrapolated from political theory include competing interest groups, competing goals, competing value systems, vying for resources, mapping the political terrain, persuasion, allies, persistence, coalitions, and mediators. Boyatzis's framework begins by using deductive analysis but also instructs the researcher to examine data for inductive or emerging themes, so the researcher read through the transcribed interviews for inductive themes. A variety of inductive codes emerged, including using data, learning from controversy, and public relations and showcasing success. Three different individuals coded the data and compared the strategies identified. The criteria used to identify themes/subcategories related to politics focused on (1) the number of different individuals who brought up the code/theme and (2) the amount of time they discussed the concept and level of significance they placed on a code/theme.

Trustworthiness and Limitations

With elite interviewing, some of the primary methods for trustworthiness include amount of background research, careful sampling procedures, and obtaining access to elites and building rapport—all of which were critical components of the study design. In addition to these techniques, member checks were conducted by sending summaries of key points, preliminary analysis, and possible quotations from the transcripts to each president. We provided them the opportunity to ensure that our interpretations matched what they had intended and said in interviews. We additionally ensured trustworthiness by having three different researchers review the interview transcripts for themes related to politics.

In terms of limitations, the data focused on the perceptions of college presidents about what political strategies are important to advancing a diversity agenda and helping diverse students succeed on their campuses. However, we do not know the extent to which these perceptions were shared with other key campus stakeholders, and perceptions of complex organizational phenomena may vary within the same organization (Pettigrew, 1995; Starbuck & Milliken, 1988). However, the focus of the study was on gaining insight into a particular set of influential individuals who, although widely acknowledged as essential to advancing meaningful change on campus, have not been examined empirically. Because the actions of leaders are difficult to link with organizational outcomes in higher education (Birnbaum, 1988), we speculate that the data obtained from diverse individuals leading different types of institutions would yield adequate confirming and disconfirming data to uncover important and common perceptions. What we offer are words of wisdom through experienced individuals who have worked hard for many years to create a successful environment for students from diverse backgrounds. We elected not to conduct case studies of each campus to explore the themes that presidents described in more detail because the focus was on presidential leadership, not on organizations and their change. Doing so would have added important depth and richness to this study, but traveling to 27 institutions was cost prohibitive. There is one caveat in terms of the implications of the research: Presidents typically yield more power than many other leaders on campus, and the results of the study are likely not generalizable to other leaders or at least need further study.

Results

Every president noted that they faced politics and that it was an inevitable part of this process, reinforcing the importance of the theoretical framework used to shape study. Presidents also revealed a set of approaches for negotiating the difficult politics that emerge while trying to create a more inclusive environment and institutionalize a diversity agenda. They describe how the strategies helped them maintain resilience in the face of significant challenges and that without using these strategies they certainly doubted whether presidents could be successful in moving diversity agendas forward. The six strategies mentioned by presidents as most important are (1) develop coalitions and advocates, (2) take the political pulse regularly, (3) anticipate resistance, (4) use data to neutralize politics and rationalize the process, (5) create public relations campaigns and showcase success, and (6) capitalize on controversy for learning and unearth interest groups. While distinctive campus cultures certainly affected the political climate and presidents noted that they had to carefully assess the unique political climate on campus, similar strategies emerged across campuses. Three strategies that emerged—creating coalitions, taking the political pulse, and anticipating resistance (both similar to mapping the political terrain)—were described in the Theoretical Framework section under political theories. However, three new strategies were identified: using data, creating public relations campaigns, and capitalizing on controversy for learning. The results are summarized in the Appendix. Before describing the focus of the results—the six strategies that emerged—I briefly describe the nature of politics that presidents faced, as this sets the stage for the strategies they used.

The Nature of Politics

Before describing the way that presidents negotiated politics, it is important to understand the range of politics they needed to negotiate. There were three main types of politics: (1) dominant groups resistant to a diversity agenda; (2) one traditionally underrepresented group questioning the diversity agenda or trying to narrow the scope of the diversity initiative; (3) conflict between two or more traditionally underrepresented groups.[8]

By far the most common politics that presidents had to negotiate was resistance by dominant groups to a diversity agenda (only five campuses did not describe this issue, usually based on being a single-serving institution—an HBCU or a predominantly minority-serving school). This involved alumni, students, faculty, administrators, and staff that questioned the need for a diversity agenda and that often actively mounted resistance to the change initiative. Sometimes the conflict and controversy did not emerge at the beginning of the diversity agenda, but the presidents encountered a backlash when students of color became successful or gays and lesbians were successful in obtaining health care. At the beginning, some dominant groups did not think the initiative would make a difference and did not actively fight the diversity initiative, but they became active later. This type of politics was more common on predominantly White campuses.

While the most common politics that presidents faced was resistance by dominant groups to the idea of changing the institution to embrace a diversity agenda, this is not the only type of politics they encountered. Presidents at nine institutions noted that from time to time faculty, students, and staff from a traditionally underrepresented group, for example Asians or Hispanics, will question what they think is favoring of another underrepresented group, such as African Americans, or a minority religious group might question gay and lesbian rights. In addition, presidents of color describe pressure from communities of color both on and off campus to promote their interests and agenda. For example, an Hispanic president is pressured by Hispanic parents to focus the diversity agenda only on that group or more heavily on that group. This type of politics occurred on both predominantly White campuses and at predominantly minority campuses.

Lastly, 14 presidents described conflict between two traditionally underrepresented groups on campus. They noted that this was more common on campuses that were farther along in their diversity agendas. On campuses that have more advanced diversity agendas, differing values and interests have often become more open, and often-overlooked inequities become visible. This created conflict between groups particularly among competing Asian groups and Hispanic groups and between African Americans and Africans. This was more likely to occur on campuses that had large compositions of individuals from various racial and ethnic backgrounds and religions.

Almost all of the presidents noted that it is important for leaders to be aware that politics take on a variety of forms. Most described that they were prepared for politics between dominant and nondominant groups but were more surprised by politics between and among underrepresented groups. While the strategies used did not differ significantly to address each of these sets of politics, some strategies described below are particularly important for certain types of politics. Differences in addressing different types of politics are highlighted in the discussion of strategies. I now turn to the various strategies that were used by presidents to navigate politics on their campus in service of advancing a diversity agenda.

Develop Coalitions and Advocates

Perhaps the most important strategy mentioned by presidents was developing an extensive network of supporters. Several groups were particularly critical, including the governing board, external community, legislators, and student groups. Most presidents suggested that it would not be wise to move forward with a diversity agenda if the board had not been cultivated first. While this can take time, the board is one of the only groups that can take on significant faculty resistance (including votes of no confidence) and can respond to parent or alumni complaints. Presidents often began by working with the board chair and using the chair to leverage support among the rest of the board. However, other presidents faced the dilemma that the board chair was not supportive of the diversity initiative, and so they approached other board members whom they were able to identify as sympathetic to such a cause. One president told the story of how important it is to get your board to advocate for the diversity agenda:

> I started with the board. I knew the campus was not particularly open to changing; I wasn't sure if they would be resistant. I sensed that if diversity was a priority for the board it would certainly make change easier. The board chair wasn't a particular advocate so I met with a couple of the other board members. Pretty soon, I was having one-on-ones with them, saying, "You know everybody else on the board seems to be really supportive of the initiative; I hope you are." And by the power of peer pressure, shortly the whole board was passing a resolution of the importance of diversity for the campus. But that took some time to make happen. But it became really important later on. As the initiative unrolled several faculty and alumni got together and started to mobilize against the initiative. The board took them on and diffused them immediately. I'm pretty sure I would not have been able to do it.

Another president describes the importance of the board:

> If I were to give advice to any new president, it would be, get your board to understand the importance of the agenda and your vision. And make sure that they can defend it on their own. Spend time really educating them about diversity. They are your best advocates and you don't have to be there and they can defend the campus perspective on diversity. And in my experience, you'll likely need that support at some point in time.

While presidents described the board as the most important ally, they also noted the significance of external supporters and the local community. Some institutions are located in urban areas or diverse environments where the community can be a rich source of support. However, in instances where the community is not particularly diverse, presidents sought other types of external support, such as business and industry, that are particularly interested in creating a more diverse work force. Sometimes presidents looked to government agencies at the local, regional, state, or even federal level (National Science Foundation, for example). Various government agencies are often advocates for diversity, as certain parts of the government have supported equity and civil rights. Leaders note that accreditation agencies and other voluntary groups can also provide a source of external support since some have included diversity in the accreditation standards. These are some of the external groups that presidents used to leverage support and that they would consult for support when resistance emerged. As with the board, presidents did not wait until a problem occurred to create these coalitions; instead, they began building the network of support as they began their diversity agenda. One president even created a formal advisory board or commission related to diversity that included a variety of external groups to connect these groups to the campus diversity agenda. Several presidents expressed how this external network was helpful for negotiating politics:

> I was having no luck getting the various schools and colleges to meet their goals—hiring faculty of color and changing the curriculum. In fact, I began to hear stories about resistance emerging. So things were going from bad to worse. That's when I decided I needed to bring in leaders from business and industry. When engineering companies tell the school of engineering that their faculty is too white, that their graduates are not diverse enough, and that their curriculum is outdated, that really makes a difference. After that, things started to change and the resistance subsided.

Another president explains how the community supported the institution's diversity agenda:

> There are a lot of faculty that were beginning to question our separate graduation ceremonies for different ethnic groups. They kept asking me why we needed this and saying it was a waste of money.

They kept pressing how we were under a tight budget crunch, which we were. So rather than try to argue with them, I invited them to the graduation ceremony and asked them to meet with members of the African American and Hispanic communities. I told a couple of the community members about the resistance I was facing from faculty. Well, needless to say, after they attended the ceremony and talked to these community members, they changed their minds. People in the community can be really convincing.

Presidents also suggested that students can be among the greatest supporters. While students do not have to kind of power that the board of trustees or external groups such as business and industry have, students have the "special power of being what the institution is all about." Sometimes faculty and staff that resist a diversity initiative believe it is being foisted on the campus by overzealous administrators. When they see that students support the initiative and it has a broad base of support across students, this can counter resistance. Several presidents told stories of how their strongest supporters and allies were students:

> There was a conservative group of faculty and staff on campus that was mounting a defense against the diversity initiative. They started to question the programs and scholarships. They were getting more and more vocal. There were also a group of students that felt I wasn't supporting them enough. Even though they were not resistant to the diversity initiative, they were challenging my legitimacy, which didn't help. Well, a group of students from my prior institution, without my knowledge, came to campus and defended me to students and argued in support of me to the campus community. It was just amazing and it worked.

Presidents suggested that it is important for leaders to meet with the student leaders of Black, Latino, and Hillel student associations. By having ongoing communication with these groups, they can be helpful when politics emerge.

Presidents also noted that it is important to keep local and regional legislators informed of campus activities and to continually advocate for the campus. Many different presidents had leveraged significant resources or political support needed to advance their diversity agendas through the support of legislators. A president sums up the lessons learned from this study about the importance of building coalitions and advocates:

> I have worked to build trust with different groups—African Americans, Hispanics, various religious groups, gays and lesbians. When I have been challenged by a particular group of students or faculty, others have emerged to defend me. You want others defending you. Ideally, the lesson is to build alliances and trust up front. Students can often be your best defenders, as they are considered legitimate by legislatures, alumni, and the community and do not seem self-interested.

This quotation also illustrates a key theme across the interviews; savvy presidents described how they needed to know when to step aside and allow a member of the campus community to support or advocate for the diversity initiative. It is not always best for the president to be the primary advocate and to confront conflict, resistance, and politics.

Take the Political Pulse Regularly (Mapping the Political Terrain)

In addition to creating allies and coalitions, presidents described the way that they needed to regularly assess the political environment. Presidents need to have informants throughout the campus to help them know how faculty, staff, and students are feeling about the diversity agenda. In addition, they needed informants off campus in the community. Several presidents talked about the importance of assessing the political climate:

> While I'm not really a political animal, I do recognize that I need to be aware of people who resist the direction we are going. Every couple months, I have a group of people that I talk with and get a sense for what the vibe is out there. Usually I don't learn a lot that's new; however, a couple times it's really helped me avoid being sideswiped.

A variety of presidents also described how they had forgotten to take the political pulse or stopped taking it as the agenda progressed. The story of one president who stopped taking the political pulse demonstrates some of the problems that emerge:

> I thought it was time that we start to examine some of the values held on campus. The campus was moving at such a slow pace and I thought that if I could get people to fundamentally rethink their values, we could start to change the curriculum and programming and hiring and admissions. So I issued some challenging concept papers and asked some campus groups to make some deep fundamental changes. A few people pulled me aside and said, "I'm really excited about the direction you're taking, but if I make changes you are asking for now there's going to be a serious backlash and were just not ready yet. Several people I have talked to will mount a resistance if you go forward with this." I really appreciated these insightful people telling me that I needed to get broader ownership first and mak[ing] me aware of the politics related to the actions I was taking.

Taking the political pulse was important for several reasons. First, presidents needed to know when it was time to tap allies for support. Allies are much more powerful when used at times of resistance; having allies talk all the time decreases their power and effectiveness. Second, presidents were able to identify if they were pushing the agenda too hard and too fast. By taking the pulse, they can see where they need to slow down again and gain more support. One president aptly captures this idea:

> You can't do good things if you're not there. Be careful about understanding the politics of the campus as you move forward. Look at your timing of things, your pacing of things, how people are reacting to your strategies. Make sure you're not running into a brick wall. This is a long-distance race. How can you put into play strategies that will, over the long haul, result in change? If you go head-on, and the environment is not ready for it and there's a pushback, you only serve to remove yourself from the environment you are trying to change.

Third, this approach also anticipates forms of resistance and facilitates developing an effective strategy to address resistance in a proactive rather than a reactive manner. A president describes how taking the political pulse helped anticipate resistance:

> We realized some members the African American community were upset because the number of Hispanic faculty, students, and staff was expanding and the African American presence shrinking. There were accusations we were not being supportive of African Americans. There could have been mounting disapproval of our diversity agenda. Right away, I set up a dialogue between African American students and community members and my administration. We sat down and looked at the data and realized it was due to demographic trends. But I took this as an opportunity to try to talk about ways we could ensure that African American students maintained a presence on campus. That could have exploded down the line.

Several presidents had established a human relations commission or presidential diversity task force that had the charge to assess the campus climate and monitor for politics. This group can take the political pulse of the campus in a systematic way and on an ongoing basis. The president from a campus that experienced a lot of conflict and politics describes how the human relations committee helped the campus move forward on its diversity initiative: "We found that we needed a group that was really monitoring how things were going related to diversity. If you don't have a group that is devoted to this, there's a good chance that you will miss something and the politics might spin out-of-control."

An important time for taking the political pulse is at the beginning of the presidency or the beginning of the diversity of agenda. Many presidents made a point to either have focus groups with people across campus to understand the various views about diversity or to host a retreat with leaders across campus. The president has an opportunity to identify people that might be allies as well as individuals who might set up countercoalitions or be barriers in the future. Outside facilitators were often brought to initial retreats or meetings to assist in getting more honest responses:

> That's where facilitation has become really important in our process. A facilitator asks questions that no one else can. You have to get people to speak their minds. You can't be politically naïve in any of this and believe people will be up front without some prodding. A skilled facilitator can get people to share things they normally would not.

In sum, taking the political pulse allows presidents to pace the initiative and defuse some of the politics; it also helps them develop a proactive strategy to address the inevitable politics.

Anticipate Resistance

Taking the political pulse assists presidents in anticipating resistance. However, presidents noted that there are some types of resistance that you can anticipate without taking a political pulse. Because the alumni of most institutions are predominantly White (even of the Hispanic-serving institutions, for example), they often see the changes happening on campus as no longer serving their interests and values. Many express concern that the institution is changing from the way it was when these alumni were students. Presidents noted that it is imperative to contact alumni at the beginning of the diversity initiative and to try to help them understand the changes taking place rather than ignore them or hope they support the new values. When possible, it is important to invite influential alumni to campus conversations, and it is certainly important to communicate to alumni through newsletters and other communication vehicles. The more informed the alumni are, the less likely they are to mount a resistance (in most cases). One president describes interaction with alumni and the problems of not anticipating resistance:

> When we began our diversity initiative, I started to get a lot of calls from angry alumni. I should have anticipated this. I tried to explain to them why we are moving in the direction that we are; some got it and some didn't. I would suggest that presidents anticipate this type of resistance and be more proactive. You can mount a better campaign up front.

While alumni were mentioned by almost all the presidents, the group that was mentioned next as resistant is the faculty, particularly regarding hiring faculty of color and curriculum revision. In fact, presidents noted that faculty seemed quite supportive of the diversity initiative as long as it related to students, but as soon as it began to focus on the issues closer to their identity, then they became increasingly resistant. Therefore, many presidents were surprised when the faculty who were initially supportive became resistant. In the words of one president:

> What's important is to remember that just because people are supportive at one point in time doesn't mean they'll always be supportive. In particular, faculty appeared to do a 180 once we began to talk about hiring faculty of color and the curriculum. That really slowed things down for a while, and in fact we haven't made much progress since.

Most presidents mentioned that they experienced difficulty in having faculty think about hiring practices in new ways. There are strong disciplinary norms about the definition of a "quality" faculty member that typically favor White male candidates. Presidents need to consider becoming more knowledgeable about strategies for diversifying the faculty and need to be ready to present data and evidence to combat typical criteria that often prohibit faculty from diverse backgrounds from being hired.

Presidents mentioned students as one of their greatest allies, but students can also be one of their greatest sources of resistance. In recent years, students have become much more powerful in their abilities to organize resistance. Several presidents mentioned student blogs and Web sites where student groups mounted campaigns against the diversity initiative. The power of e-mail makes it easy to contact people and create a network. A president describes how technology is used by students, in particular, to create resistance:

> One of the things I had to learn was the way that new technology changes the rules of the game. You need to be aware of student Web sites and blogs and how they're using them to stir things up. And the newspapers have taken hold of these as well for a source of information. Leaders need to be aware of these new information sources and realize that you have to respond to things quickly. You have to use your own technology and Web sites to provide counterperspectives and share information and you have to do this on a timely basis. Information is less under control than ever. This makes politics even more challenging.

Technology has emerged as a public forum to organize resistance to organizational change efforts among all the groups mentioned above. Staff, faculty, and alumni also use technology to personally attack members of the institutional advocates of diversity. The Internet has provided resisting groups with an instrument of empowerment that can be used to thwart change efforts.

Use Data to Neutralize Politics and Rationalize the Process (Persuasion)

Most presidents described how data can be used to diffuse harmful politics that can thwart diversity efforts. People often feel passionately about issues of diversity, and an emotional climate is created. While passion can facilitate change, it can also subvert transformation. The presidents described how they used data to neutralize politics and rationalize the process of change. They noted the importance of having an excellent institutional research (IR) director and examining the IR infrastructure to ensure that you are getting quality data. There are several different ways that presidents use data. First, they describe the importance of creating a culture of evidence for decision-making. One president describes his efforts to diffuse politics by creating a culture based on evidence:

> One day I literally stopped making decisions and refused to until data was presented. I said: "That is an urgent issue, but until I see data to support the issue, I cannot make a decision." They finally realized I was serious even though I had been saying this for a year. I just stopped making decisions.

This helps move people from basing decisions on assumptions, anecdotal evidence, and stereotypes to database decision-making practices. Presidents noted that "Politics are much more likely to thrive in a culture of stereotypes and misinformation than one based on data."

Many presidents described how their campuses operated from false assumptions or outdated notions about the campus. For example, some people believed a diversity agenda was not needed because the campuses were already diverse. One president showed faculty and staff that students of color were not succeeding and not graduating compared to their White counterparts, and the campus realized a diversity agenda was needed.

> I kept sitting faculty and staff groups down, and saying, look at this data. You don't think we have any problems, but our retention and graduation rates are horrible. Faculty of color keep leaving here. Then I ask them a set of questions and said, "I want you to be part of the solution." Faculty, in particular, really like this approach. Every time I've done that we've moved the campus farther ahead.

On another campus, faculty were unaware of the ways students had diversified and the range of backgrounds they came from. Once data were presented about the true range of backgrounds and ethnicities of students, the faculty and staff were much more open to programs and interventions aimed at these diverse groups. Presidents described that, before data was presented at these campuses, they were teeming with conflict and resistance.

As mentioned in this section on the nature of politics, some of the politics related to perceived inequities were between underrepresented racial and ethnic groups. Several presidents were pressured to support particular racial or ethnic groups that felt their needs were more important than those of other groups. Presidents were able to successfully defuse claims for favoring a particular ethnic group by providing data about the needs of other racial and ethnic groups. For example, presidents described pressures from the African American or Hispanic communities to focus on the needs of their particular groups, especially if the president was a member of that group. Presidents recounted that the challenge of diversity is typically conceptualized as a Black-White issue on most campuses. Providing data about the lack of success of other racial and ethnic groups is extremely important to supporting a broad diversity agenda. African American presidents were able to offer data about the low graduation rates of Hispanic students to African American communities and help them understand the necessity of programs for these students. In particular, there are many Asian groups that have experienced inequities and that are often overlooked in terms of their success. Campuses that had collected more detailed data on student backgrounds and had conducted qualitative research about the experience of Asians students, for example, had data to show that many Asian groups were struggling to be successful and could present the data to support programs aimed at these students.

In addition to data, presidents described the importance of "rationale" or logic to defuse politics. Presidents need to carefully think through the logic that supports diversity and make sure that it is communicated to all campus constituents as often as possible. Some leaders noted how having a clear and simple explanation about the importance of diversity makes it easier for supporters to advocate the message and more difficult for political adversaries to topple the diversity agenda. In the words of one president, "I've learned one powerful lesson in my three presidencies, the value of a simple idea or message and to repeat it consistently. They did that at the University of Michigan. And they've done it at other places." Presidents use different logic—from the benefits of diversity to learning, to the connection of diversity to a liberal arts education, to the importance of diversity for a global economy and multicultural work force. Presidents also described the power of asking questions and having people examine their own rationale. One of the presidents described the story of using questions to redirect conflict on his campus:

> Some White students came to my office and said they were really upset that Black students are doing so well academically in science. I said, "Well, our Asian students have always been at the top. Why is it that you've never been bothered by the fact that they do so well?" They sat there and they were really taken aback and it made them think.

By helping people to critically analyze the situation, many presidents moved past difficult political situations. They stressed the importance of not becoming defensive and instead emphasized the importance of a repeated simple message and humbly questioning other people's rationales.

Public Relations: Showcasing Success

Presidents mentioned the power of creating events, publications, and other avenues that helped demonstrate and make visible the success of diversity efforts on campus. It was noted as particularly important to include various constituent groups or stakeholders in the creation of such events and publications. One president described an event that he hosted to demonstrate the success of a Hispanic and African American leadership project and how it helped to subvert politics that were emerging on campus:

> I noticed there were groups on campus that were upset that funds were being set aside for our Hispanic and African-American leadership program. I decided to host this event and invited foundation officers and members of our corporate community as well as key constituents across campus. I demonstrated how students from our program were going on to be leaders in the local community and some of the changes they had made. We also showed the community service they had done. Not only did these groups praise us for the work we've done, but they provided us funding for more programs. That really stopped the grumbling on campus. If external groups think what you're doing is good, more people on campus are likely to think so too. But if it's not showcased, they often miss it.

Bringing back successful alumni was used as a strategy to showcase how the diversity agenda had successfully assisted certain students. Faculty and staff often forget the students after they leave, and the institutional impact is often forgotten or missed. One president comments on the strategy, "We bring back alumni, very intentionally, to give a talk, to celebrate their successes, to show how our institution has made a difference. I have received notes from faculty and staff who changed their perspective after hearing these talks."

Another president describes her work to obtain support for the diversity agenda by focusing on celebrating the institution's successes. In particular, this president describes the importance of data to demonstrating progress on a diversity initiative and for combating politics and dissent:

> I think we've gotten through politics by demonstrating results. When I've experienced flak from the state, I go up and show them how the programs have substantially changed our success with students of color. If alumni or faculty are concerned, I set up a meeting or event and present our positive results. So that's how I handle politics, by demonstrating results.

Other presidents experienced pressure from students and faculty of color for not doing enough to support them and for not moving fast enough on the agenda. A strategy for handling this political situation is that presidents recommended an honest review and presentation of data related to results and efforts. Presidents cautioned that unless the data shows that progress is not being made, it is important that they not change the pace of their diversity agenda to meet certain interest group needs, since doing so might compromise achieving the overall agenda. In most cases, data supported that campuses were moving forward and helped to answer questions and decrease conflict between the administration and these various racial and ethnic groups that hoped the agenda would move more quickly. One president describes this dilemma:

> We were getting a lot of heat from students of color that we weren't doing enough to support them. So we took this as an opportunity to look at what we were doing—maybe we weren't doing as much as we needed to do. We went to the students and showed them all that we were doing and the data on progress we had, and they were really impressed. They had no idea all the efforts going on and the progress. So this actually helped to get them more supportive of our agenda and allowed us to maintain the pace we thought made sense.

Capitalize on Controversy for Learning and Unearthing Interest Groups

While most presidents felt frustrated by the politics that emerged as they tried to support and/or implement a diversity initiative, they also recognized that some of the greatest progress on the diversity initiative was made by engaging the politics head on and by understanding different interest groups. Presidents described how they capitalized on the controversy (such as conflicting claims about the success or failure of certain groups, beliefs that certain groups were favored and given undue advantage, or differing values among groups) to create learning for the campus. They used situations of conflict that arose to engage people on campus in conversations. It is at times of great controversy that people tend to become more aware and break out of their routines, and it is at these times that they might be open to learning. Presidents recognized this potential and used the politics to create organizational learning.

Many presidents noted that the human relations commission or presidential diversity task force (noted earlier) was often the group that helped create dialogues or conversations that helped move from politics and conflict to learning for individuals and groups. These groups would create campuswide conversations where learning could occur. The over-arching philosophy of these groups was to humanize the conflict and to get people to talk and to learn from one another. The strategy is particularly important for combating politics between different underrepresented groups. Student protests and demonstrations are key opportunities for helping the campus to learn and grow. In the words of one president:

> The students are protesting; they have taken over the president's office. I realize this is a great opportunity for us to challenge the campus to rethink what's going on. They believe that affirmative action is lowering standards on campus. I invite them as well as the rest of the campus community to dialogue about this issue. Sure, there were some hard moments and one of the faculty presented a pretty racist paper that really angered a lot of groups on campus. But you can't shy away from these conversations. There is some real learning that occurred in the end, and it turned out to be a phenomenal success.

One of the presidents described the ways she used conflict between Christian, Muslim, and Jewish students and faculty to try to advance the campus understanding of diversity:

> Our Christian and Muslim student clubs were holding prayer services and advertising them across campus. A group of Jewish faculty became really concerned about the visibility of their advertising and were starting to question the line between church and state. Also, the gay and lesbian students were upset because the Christians and Muslims were praying for them to change their lifestyles. The faculty wanted me to set up some policy against what the Christian and Muslim students were doing. Instead, I said let's have a dialogue about religion on campus. This accomplished two important things. First, the Christian, Muslim, Jewish, and gay and lesbian groups began to get to know each other, which is very powerful. It is easy for one group to—from a distant place—to critique the other group. When they really get to know each other, then they have to think about their actions more. They also became much more respectful of each other's positions.

Controversy allows constituents to also see the common ground, which can help move a diversity agenda forward. By actively engaging the conflict, rather than ignoring it as leaders are often apt to do, presidents can use controversy as a teachable moment that helps build respect and understanding among different groups and that often creates greater commitment to the diversity initiatives. Presidents noted that campuses that have the most conflict are often the campuses that have made the most progress on their diversity agendas and that engagement of controversy was one of the issues that helped them progress.

By actively engaging conflict, leaders are also able to identify other interest groups and possible areas of conflict to anticipate for the future. One president who was on a campus that had been working on a diversity initiative for over 30 years describes the issue of conflict becoming more visible when you have been successful at moving at diversity agenda forward:

> One of the recent controversies helped us to identify some other groups on campus that are in conflict with each other. It used to be the Hispanic and Asian groups had competing interests, but now it's the native Mexicans versus the Spanish Mexicans. Controversy helps you to see what might be issues coming down the road and groups that are not included on campus.

By creatively engaging controversy, leaders also were able to effectively take the political pulse since these conversations often unearth differing interests of which they were unaware.

Personally Surviving Politics

Politics do not always stay focused on the campus and often turn inward on the presidents themselves. Several presidents mentioned that it is important for them to survive the politics, because "if you don't make it through and initiate these changes, then the important path that you came to the campus for will fall apart. And this will keep delaying the change; you have to survive." Some of the strategies described above help to defuse some of the personal focus of politics (particularly, having board support, establishing a human relations council, or creating coalitions and networks), but presidents also described the importance of developing internal strategies for navigating politics. Perhaps the most important strategy was keeping focused on their goal—their passion for helping students succeed. In fact, talking to students on an ongoing basis was one of the best ways to help presidents survive the difficult politics associated with moving a diversity agenda forward. One president's comments reflected what many said: "It's the students—they are what help me survive. When I hear their stories, when I see the changes we have made, I know I can take on the next battle. Presidents need to stay close to students; it really keeps you sane."

Many presidents also mention the importance of having a network outside of the institution. Moving a diversity agenda forward often alienates various groups on campus. A few presidents had trusted people on campus and been burned by sharing information with people whom they thought they could trust. Instead, presidents need a trusted set of individuals off campus to share information and to "blow off steam" from time to time. It is not wise for the president to share information with people on campus, and they need to identify people in their broader professional or personal network. In the words of one president, "I can pick up the phone and talk to whole series of people across the country. And they are there for me 24/7. That really helps. Presidents and other leaders need this type of support if they want to make it through the politics. Politics defeats people who do not sustain themselves." In general, presidents noted the importance of identifying strategies that made them resilient in the face of difficult politics.

Implications for Theory and Practice

This study offers several theoretical and practical implications. From a theoretical perspective, presidents agreed that a political framework for understanding change related to diversity is particularly important, mirroring earlier studies by Baldridge et al. (1977), Bolman and Deal, (1997), Clark (1983), Gioia and Thomas (1996), Hearn (1996), and Sporn (1999). While many leadership studies of diversity have examined the issue from scientific management or human relations/resource theories, this study supports the importance of conceptualizing this issue as a political one. This study also highlights the nature of politics that have not been previously described. For example, it highlights an often overlooked aspect of campus politics—the political relationship between underrepresented groups.

In addition, this study adds needed detail about the types of strategies that presidents can use to negotiate politics, which has both theoretical and practical insights. Political theories suggested the importance of creating coalitions; mapping the political terrain; bargaining, informal processes, and behind-the-scenes deal making; persuasion; the role of mediators; and the importance of persistence (Baldridge et al., 1977; Bolman & Deal, 1997; Clark, 1983; Gioia & Thomas, 1996; Hearn, 1996; Sporn, 1999). While many of these strategies proved important to presidents, other strategies were discovered that are not typically described in political theory, such as using data to neutralize politics, showcasing success, or capitalizing on controversy for learning and unearthing interest groups. These new strategies represent important new insights for leaders: data, learning, and demonstrating success are techniques that engage the conflict but also help overcome divisive politics related to diversity. Presidents noted that a typical problem in advancing a diversity agenda is for presidents to ignore conflict and to stay safely in the realm of vision and strategic planning. As long as leaders see politics and power as negative and try to ignore it, they prevent themselves from engaging in the creative aspect of politics and conflict that can help to create a new future on campus. While most of the presidents expressed that they did not enjoy politics and conflict, the successful leaders acknowledge that they needed to engage it.

In addition, the data provided detailed examples and stories for leaders to use rather than the generic advice of being persuasive or developing coalitions described in the Theoretical Framework section (Bolman & Deal, 1997). Instead, the study describes who are the important groups to develop coalitions with, how they can be used best, and why they are important—thus building on the work by Baldridge et al. (1977), Bolman and Deal (1997), and Hearn (1996). In particular, understanding the political terrain surrounding diversity issues is an important insight from the study which is only hinted at in Bolman and Deal (1997), for example. Being proactive in contacting alumni and knowing to watch student Web sites provides leaders with specific advice about how to tackle resistance against a diversity initiative. While a general set of strategies was identified across different institutional contexts, demographics, and types, the reader is cautioned that politics varied by campus culture—which is why taking the political pulse is such a critical finding and was reiterated by most presidents we spoke with.

Another important finding is that leaders need to be proactive in identifying ways to maintain resilience in the face of politics that threaten their survival. These presidents had witnessed other leaders who had not been successful negotiating the politics, and they were each particularly thoughtful about developing a strategy for personally surviving the politics. Over time they learned the importance of board support, campus coalitions, and keeping close to students.

Two interesting relationships that appear to emerge in the data should be the focus of future study. This study has identified a preliminary connection between the nature of the politics encountered and the type of political strategy used by leaders. In general, each strategy was used for all three types of politics (resistance by the dominant group, resistance by a traditionally underrepresented group, conflict between traditionally underrepresented groups), but leaders noted that certain strategies had more salience for certain forms of conflict. Each strategy reviewed was successful in negotiating resistance by dominant groups to a diversity agenda. Using data to neutralize politics, taking the political pulse, and developing coalitions and advocates were helpful when traditionally underrepresented groups questioned the diversity agenda or tried to narrow the scope of the initiative. Capitalizing on controversy for learning was noted as a particularly important strategy when conflict between two or more traditionally underrepresented groups emerged. In addition, there may be a relationship between the phase of the institution's initiative and the strategies used to negotiate politics. Institutions that are early in their diversity initiatives tend to focus more on developing coalitions, anticipating resistance, and using data and logic to rationalize the process,

APPENDIX

Type of Political Strategy Used by Presidents and Cited as Important Including Frequency

Type of Strategy	Number of Presidents Describing Strategy as Important
Develop coalitions	22
Take political pulse/anticipate resistance	17/14
Use data/rationalize process	15/12
Initiate public relations campaigns and showcase results	13
Capitalize on controversy for learning	14

which mirrors the progression of political strategies described in the Theoretical Framework section (Bolman & Deal, 1997; Kezar, 2001). As institutions progress, they tend to use public relations and showcasing success as well as capitalizing on controversy for learning more often. With progress, leaders can shift to other strategies that they found "easier" to use to address politics and can use fewer strategies. This finding suggests that leaders at early-phase institutions face an additional burden, meaning that they need to take greater care to personally sustain themselves and to be cognizant of the need to invoke a variety of strategies. Future studies should examine these issues in greater detail. In addition, presidents of different races likely face distinctive challenges related to politics. It appears, for example, that leaders of color may use data more often because it detracts from naysayers who believe that their commitment to diversity is personal rather than an institutional imperative. Leaders of color may also need to rely even more heavily on powerful external coalitions. While some of these issues emerged in the data, there was not enough detail and future research is necessary. These emergent findings about the impact of the race of the president are reviewed in Kezar and Eckel (2005).

Future studies should also examine the nature of politics in more detail, following up on trends identified in the study. The major focus of this study was on strategies that presidents used to negotiate politics. Detailed case studies related to the nature of politics around diversity initiatives would be extremely helpful. Often researchers focus on success stories and facilitators of change, neglecting barriers and politics. Case study research of problems encountered and a more detailed account of the nature of these problems would be an important next step in the search.

This study highlights the importance of making politics related to advancing a diversity agenda more visible so that the politics can be addressed by leaders on campus. By beginning to examine the nature of politics and the strategies that college presidents use to negotiate them, advocates for diversity initiatives can be better prepared to move their causes forward.

Notes

1. A diversity agenda or initiative as I am defining it and as defined by the presidents is multifaceted and attempts to integrate diversity into the structure, culture, and fabric of the institution—so that it is truly institutionalized (Curry, 1992). While I did not impose a definition of diversity, almost all presidents defined it broadly to include race, gender, sexual orientation, disability, class, and the government-designated protected classes and beyond. It is beyond the scope of this paper to examine how diversity and multiculturalism have evolved historically on college campuses, but it should be noted that campuses have wrestled with different definitions and approaches to diversity initiatives over the last 40 years. Definitions have expanded from focusing mostly on race to include broader definitions as different disenfranchised groups wanted to be recognized. Multiculturalism (a broader term that moved beyond race to gender, sexual orientation, etc.) rather than diversity was adopted by many campuses in the 1990s as a way of embracing a variety of oppressed groups. However, it should be noted that there is much disagreement over these terms and their precise definitions, particularly as they are used in practice.

2. In particular, the American Association of Colleges and Universities has developed a set of publications over the last 15 years that have attempted to help campuses advance diversity agendas. See Bauman et al. (2005), Milem et al. (2005), Musil et al. (1999), and Smith and Associates (1997). But these publications have focused less on leaders and their role in overcoming politics. This current chapter provides data to complement these important resources.

3. Two theories are typically used to understand the change process and barriers/resistance: human relations or resources theory and scientific management (Bolman & Deal, 1997). Human relations theory suggests that people resist change because they do not understand the issues properly and that, once trained, they will alter their behaviors. Scientific management theories indicate that people resist change because they are entrenched in certain routines. By providing strategic plans, a vision, and new ideas outside of their routines, employees will begin work differently. Within these theories, common strategies for addressing barriers to change include training, providing rewards, and restructuring. While these theories help understand resistance, they ignore politics—different interests and values that often underpin issues of diversity.

4. Politics and power are related concepts but are distinct phenomena. I chose to focus on politics since power has been examined in other studies of diversity—particularly from a critical theory perspective. Please see these publications for an understanding of the relationship of power to diversity initiatives (Astin & Leland, 1991; Kezar, Carducci, & Contreras-McGavin, 2006; Safarik, 2003; Tierney, 1991, 1993; Wolf-Wendel, Twombly, Tuttle, Ward, & Gaston-Gayles, 2004). I chose not to review the literature on power because it is so expansive, and I could not do justice to the concepts within the space of this chapter. However, it is important to note the relationship of these concepts and provide the reader with additional resources to follow up on this relationship.

5. I acknowledge that political issues need not only be handled through political strategies and leadership approaches. In fact, in other articles, I have discussed the importance of human relations strategies (Kezar & Eckel, forthcoming), in particular, for helping to prevent political issues from emerging at all. However, once political issues have emerged, I wondered whether political theories could help in providing guidance for leaders in how to negotiate these issues. In addition, since political strategies tend to be underconceptualized in relation to moving diversity agendas forward, I felt it particularly important to investigate this issue within the study.

6. In this section, I refer to a research team because the data was collected by two individuals and because my analysis was confirmed by the research team. However, in other sections I refer only to myself as author of this chapter. This methodology is also referenced in other papers related to this study.

7. An article focused on leadership strategies and phases is published separately (Kezar, 2007; see also Kezar et al., forthcoming).

8. While presidents described a variety of differing interest groups from different races, genders, religions, and sexual orientations, by far the most frequently mentioned differing interest related to race. This was followed by examples of sexual orientation and religion. It should also be noted that presidents described a broad diversity agenda that included race, gender, religion, sexual orientation, ability status, and the like. However, gender, for example, was almost never brought up in relation to politics.

References

Astin, H. S., & Leland, C. (1991). *Women of influence, women of vision*. San Francisco: Jossey-Bass.

Baldridge, J. (1971). *Power and conflict in the university*. New York: John Wiley.

Bauman, G., Bustillos, L., Bensimon, E., Brown, M. C., & Bartee, R. (2005). *Achieving equitable educational outcomes with all students: The institution's role and responsibilities*. Washington, DC: Association of American Colleges and Universities.

Beckham, E. (2000). *Diversity, democracy, and higher education: A view from three nations*. Washington, DC: Association of American Colleges and Universities.

Bensimon, E. (1992). *The normalization of diversity: Multicultural curricular change at urban university*. University Park, PA: National Center on Postsecondary Teaching, Learning, and Assessment.

Birnbaum, R. (1988). *How colleges work: The cybernetics of academic organization and leadership*. San Francisco: Jossey-Bass.

Birnbaum, R. (1992). *How leadership works*. San Francisco: Jossey-Bass.

Bolman, L. G., & Deal, T. E. (1997). *Reframing organizations: Artistry, choice, and leadership*. San Francisco: Jossey-Bass.

Boyatzis, R. (1998). *Transforming qualitative information*. Thousand Oaks, CA: Sage.

Clark, B. R. (1983). *The higher education system: Academic organization in cross-national perspective*. Berkeley: University of California Press. (ERIC Document Reproduction Service No. ED262687)

Cohen, M. D., & March, J. G. (1974). *Leadership and ambiguity: The American college president*. Boston: Harvard Business School Press.

Conrad, C. F. (1978). A grounded theory of academic change. *Sociology of Education, 51*, 101–112.

Corrigan, M. (2003). *The American college president*. Washington, DC: American Council on Education.

Curry, B. (1992). *Instituting enduring innovations: Achieving continuity of change in higher education* (ASHE-ERIC Higher Education Reports Series, No. 7). Washington, DC: George Washington University.

Davis, L. R. (2002). Racial diversity in higher education: Ingredients for success and failure. *The Journal of Applied Behavioral Science, 38*(2), 137–156.

Dexter, L. (1970). *Elite and specialized interviewing*. Evanston, IL: Northwestern University Press.

Fisher, J. G. (1984). *The power of the presidency*. New York: Macmillan.

Gioia, D. A., & Thomas, J. B. (1996). Identity, image, and issue interpretation: Sensemaking during strategic change in academia. *Administrative Science Quarterly, 41*, 370–403.

Gumport, P. (2000). Academic restructuring: Organizational change and institutional imperatives. *Higher Education, 39*, 67–91.

Hale, F. W. (Ed.). (2004). *What makes racial diversity work in higher education?* Sterling, VA: Stylus.

Hearn, J. C. (1996). Transforming U.S. higher education: An organizational perspective. *Innovative higher education, 21*(2), 141–154.

Holstein, J., & Gubrium, J. (1995). *The active interview*. Thousand Oaks, CA: Sage.

Humphreys, D. (1997). *General education and American commitments*. Washington, DC: Association of American Colleges and Universities.

Hurtado, S., et al. (1999). *Enacting diverse learning environments*. Washington, DC: ASHE-ERIC.

Kezar, A. (2001). *Understanding and facilitating organizational change in the 21st Century: Recent research and conceptualizations*. Washington, DC: ASHE-ERIC Higher Education Reports.

Kezar, A. (2004). Obtaining integrity?: Reviewing and examining the charter between higher education and society. *The Review of Higher Education, 27*(4), 429–459.

Kezar, A. (2007). Tools for a time and place: Phased leadership strategies for advancing campus diversity. *Review of Higher Education, 30*(4), 413–439.

Kezar, A., Carducci, R., & Contreras McGavin, M. (2006). *Rethinking the "L" word in higher education: The revolution on research in leadership*. San Francisco: Jossey-Bass.

Kezar, A., Chambers, T., & Burkhardt, J. (Eds.). (2005). *Higher education for the public good: Emerging voices from a national movement*. San Francisco: Jossey-Bass.

Kezar, A., & Eckel, P. (2005). *Important journeys: Presidents supporting students of color*. Washington, DC: American Council on Education.

Kezar, A., & Eckel, P. (forthcoming). Advancing diversity agendas on campus: Examining transactional and transformational presidential leadership styles. *International Journal of Leadership in Education*.

Kezar, A., Eckel, P., Contreras-McGavin, M., & Quaye, S. (forthcoming). Creating a web of support: An important leadership strategy for advancing campus diversity. *Higher Education*.

Kuh, G., & Whitt, E. (1988). *The invisible tapestry* (ASHE-ERIC Higher Education Report No. 1). Washington, DC: George Washington University.

McGovern, D., Foster, L, & Ward, K. (2002). College leadership: Learning from experience. *Journal of Leadership Studies, 8*(3), 29–41.

Merriam, S. (1998). *Qualitative research and case study applications in education*. San Francisco: Jossey-Bass.

Merton, R., Fiske, M., & Kendall, P. (1990). *The focused interview: A manual of problems and procedures* (2nd ed.). New York: The Free Press.

Milem, J., Chang, M., & antonio, a. (2005). *Making diversity work on campus: A research based perspective*. Washington, DC: Association of American Colleges and Universities.

Musil, C., Garcia, M., Hudgins, C., Nettles, M., Sedlacek, E., & Smith, D. (1999). *To form a more perfect union: Campus diversity initiatives*. Washington, DC: Association of American Colleges and Universities.

Pettigrew, A. M. (1995). Longitudinal field research on change: Theory and practice. In G. P. Huber & A. H. Van de Ven (Eds.), *Longitudinal field research methods: Studying processes of organizational change* (pp. 91–125). Thousand Oaks, CA: Sage.

Rhoads, R. (1998). Student protest and multicultural reform: Making sense of campus unrest in the 1990s. *Journal of Higher Education, 69*(6), 621–646.

Safarik, L. (2003). Feminist transformation in higher education: Discipline, structure, and institution. *The Review of Higher Education, 26*(4), 419–445.

Seidman, I. (1991). *Interviewing as qualitative research.* New York: Teacher's College Press.

Smith, D. (1989). *The challenge of diversity.* Washington, DC: ASHE-ERIC.

Smith, D., & Associates. (1997). *Diversity works: The emerging picture of how students benefit.* Washington, DC: Association of American College and Universities.

Smith, D., & Wolf-Wendel, L. (2005). *The challenge of diversity.* Washington, DC: ASHE-ERIC.

Sporn, B. (1999). *Adaptive university structures.* London: Jessica Kingsley.

Starbuck, W. H., & Milliken, F. J. (1988). Executive's perceptual filters: What they notice and how they make sense. In D. C. Hambrick (Ed.), *The executive effect: Concepts and methods for studying top managers* (pp. 35–65). Greenwich, CT: JAI Press.

Tierney, W. G. (1991). Advancing democracy: A critical interpretation of leadership. *Peabody Journal of Education, 66*(3), 157–175.

Tierney, W. G. (1993). *Building communities of difference: Higher education in the twenty-first century.* Westport, CT: Bergin & Garvey.

Wolf-Wendel, L. E., Twombly, S. B., Tuttle, K. N, Ward, K., & Gaston-Gayles, J. L. (2004). *Reflecting back, looking forward: Civil rights and student affairs.* Washington, DC: National Association of Student Personnel Administrators.

CHAPTER 34
DEVELOPING LEADERS OF COLOR IN HIGHER EDUCATION
CAN CONTEMPORARY PROGRAMS ADDRESS HISTORICAL EMPLOYMENT TRENDS?

BRIDGET R. MCCURTIS, JERLANDO F. L. JACKSON,
AND ELIZABETH M. O'CALLAGHAN

While the number of college students from diverse ethnic/racial backgrounds has steadily increased, the same level of diversity has not been achieved for those holding leadership roles in higher education (Harvey & Anderson, 2005), and certainly not for positions that traditionally lead to the college presidency (Jackson, 2004a). Bensimon and Tierney (1993) note that the "absence of diversity in the upper administrative echelon works against the creation of a multicultural campus" (p. 67). For instance, while there has been an overall decrease in participation in leadership positions for African Americans (Jackson, 2004a); interestingly, there has been a slight increase in African Americans' participation in executive-level positions (i.e., department chair and provost) at particular types of institutions (i.e., 2-year institutions). This growth in leadership diversity among certain institution types creates a unique opportunity for these campuses to realize the benefits of creating a multicultural environment.

In order to thrive in an increasingly competitive and diverse global market, institutions of higher education cannot leave leadership development for people of color to chance (León, 2005). Developing leaders of color requires special attention and focus because racism and inequities in the workplace are still a prevalent issue in the United States. In turn, discriminatory practices are often embedded in the social norms, structures, and practices of universities (Bensimon & Tierney, 1993; Coleman, 1998; Howard-Hamilton & Williams, 1996). Leadership development for people of color is an important and sometimes missing component of efforts to diversify the higher education workforce (Jackson, 2004b; Jackson & Daniels, 2007). However, recognizing the importance of a diverse workforce and focusing on specific cultural differences and needs is a hallmark of the leadership revolution.

This chapter seeks to move beyond the published literature on leadership within higher education and focus on leaders of color who make daily contributions to our campuses yet whose development is often ignored. In order to set the context for this chapter, we review national employment trends for leaders of color in higher education and summarize the literature on leaders of color. The main focus of this chapter is the identification and review of professional associations and leadership programs to develop current and future leaders of color, demonstrating how many are limited in their ability to appropriately prepare leaders of color. The chapter concludes by proposing a new model of leadership development for people of color, informed by an analysis of the literature and guided by the revolutionary leadership concepts such as context, culture, and collaboration.

TABLE 1

Distribution of Full-Time Administrators in Higher Education

Race/Ethnicity	1983	1993	2003	% Change
African Americans/Blacks	8,362	12,232	17,228	106%
Hispanics	2,040	3,580	7,006	243%
Asian American[a]	1,234	2,243	4,813	290%
American Indians[b]	430	726	1,064	147%
Whites	105,420	118,651	147,613	40%
Total	**117,486**	**137,432**	**177,724**	**51%**

Note. [a]Asian American includes Pacific Islanders. [b]American Indian includes Alaska Natives. Calculations are based on data from the U.S. Department of Education, National Center for Educational Statistics, Integrated Postsecondary Education Data System (IPEDS), Fall Staff Surveys.

National Employment Trends for Leaders of Color in Higher Education

National-level data highlight differences between people of color and their counterparts at various points in time.[1] The trends that emerge from the data help to form the core need for development of specific programs targeted for leaders of color as they increasingly become part of the leadership ranks. Data show that while advancements are discernible for these groups, they lag behind in terms of sufficient percentage growth to meet equitable levels in relation to their total percentage of the higher education leadership workforce.

Full-Time Administrators in Higher Education

Employment opportunities for full-time administrators in higher education increased significantly during the past two decades (see Table 1). Over a 20-year period (1983 to 2003), the number of full-time administrative positions in higher education increased 51%. Therefore, any ethnic/racial group with a percent change of less than 51% did not keep pace with the growth in the academic job market. Interestingly, while Whites remain the largest number of full-time higher education administrators, their numbers (40%) did not keep pace with the academic job market. Therefore, the majority of the new positions appear to have been filled with people of color. Among people of color, Asian Americans realized the largest percent increase (290%), more than doubling that of African Americans/Blacks who had the lowest percent increase (106%). It must be noted that while African Americans/Blacks had the lowest percent increase, they still are the largest group of color numerically. Next, Hispanics experienced a 243% increase in full-time higher education administrative positions, followed by American Indians with a 147% increase.

College and University Presidents

Employment opportunities for college and university presidents in higher education increased modestly during the past 10 years (see Table 2). Between 1995 and 2005, the number of college and university president positions in higher education increased 12%. Therefore, any ethnic/racial group with a percent change of less than 12% did not keep pace with the growth in the academic job market. Again, as with full-time higher education administrators, Whites remain the largest number of college and university presidents despite the fact that their increase (10%) did not keep pace with the academic job market. Therefore, the majority of the new positions appear to have been filled with people of color. Among people of color, Hispanics realized the largest percent increase (54%), more than doubling that of African Americans/Blacks who had the lowest percent increase (23%). Again, it must be noted that while African Americans/Blacks had the lowest percent increase, they still are the largest single group

TABLE 2

College and University Presidents

Race/Ethnicity	1995	2000	2005	% Change
African Americans/Blacks	171	175	211	23%
Hispanics	59	80	91	54%
Asian American[a]	35	37	45	29%
American Indians[b]	31	22	24	−23%
Whites	2,475	2,500	2,728	10%
Total	**12,771**	**2,814**	**3,099**	**12%**

Note. [a]Asian American includes Pacific Islanders. [b]American Indian includes Alaska Natives. Figures include presidents of regionally accredited, degree-granting institutions in the United States or its outlying areas (e.g., Puerto Rico). The term *president* is defined within the American Council on Education's Corporate Database as the president, chancellor, superintendent, executive director, campus dean, and so forth, including interim/acting president heading regionally accredited institutions, branches, and affiliates. From American Council on Education database. Data compiled in June 2006.

of people of color. Next, Asian Americans experienced a 29% increase in college and university president positions, and American Indians was the only group to experience a decrease (−23%).

These data present encouragement and cause for concern with regard to diversifying higher education leadership. The encouraging news is that people of color are increasingly assuming a share of the leadership positions in higher education. For example, the number of Asian American and Hispanic leaders shows great promise to continue growing at a rapid pace. These trends are particularly encouraging for full-time administrative staff, and less so for college and university presidents. A significant concern is that while the growth in leaders of color is encouraging, the pace would have to intensify in order to reduce their numerical distance from Whites. The slow steady growth and sometimes setbacks (decline for American Indians) for people of color in college and university president positions is another area of major concern.

Literature on Leaders of Color in Higher Education

To date, there is nascent literature that focuses specifically on leadership development for people of color in higher education. The most comprehensive volume is León's (2005) *Lessons in Leadership: Executive Leadership Programs for Advancing Diversity in Higher Education*. Considering that research on leaders of color in higher education is minimal, it is no surprise that there is a dearth of literature regarding people of color in leadership development programs (Jackson, 2000). Much of the literature on leaders of color focuses on recruitment and retention (e.g., Jackson, 2001) but not on the actual preparation of leaders. Nevertheless, professional growth and development have been conceptualized as a key component of retention and as a benchmark for campus diversity (Davis, 1994; Jackson, 2003; Jackson, 2004b). Of the research that has been identified, it is important to note that it tends to center predominantly on African Americans (women in particular), with little research on Hispanics/Latinos (Esquibel, 1992; Gorena, 1996; Haro, 1990; Martinez, 2005), Asian Americans (Fujimoto, 1996; Montez, 1998; Nakanishi, 1993), and American Indians (Kern-Foxworth, 2000; Lynch & Charleston, 1990; Swisher, 2001; Warner, 1995).

Research narratives from the qualitative tradition have demonstrated that people of color who have successfully risen to leadership positions have participated in leadership development programs at some point during their careers (Cavanaugh, 2007; Holmes, 2004; Jenifer, 2005; Thomas, 2005). The literature highlights the need for targeted leadership development but suggests many connections between racial/ethnic classification, gender, and institution type. Beyond identification of success stories from specific individuals, two distinct features emerged: (a) there is a specific focus on *women of color* in leadership, and (b) the presence of diverse leaders is predominantly at *2-year institutions and minority-serving institutions, primarily Historically Black Colleges and Universities (HBCUs).* Each of these features is discussed in greater depth below.

Women Leaders of Color

The literature surrounding people of color focused mostly on women of color in leadership roles (e.g., Holmes, 2004; Watson 2001). It has been speculated that this is because of the overwhelming historical underrepresentation of women in leadership positions in higher education, and the volume of literature with this focus is evidence of early efforts to remedy this fact (Jackson, 2001, 2006). For example, women in general tend to be concentrated in lower-level leadership positions, with women of color holding a small percentage of these positions (Berryman-Fink, Lemaster, & Nelson, 2003). While the role of leadership development programs for women of color must be stressed, it cannot be discussed outside of the context of other social obstacles, such as racism and sexism. The "dual burden" (Singh, Robinson & Williams-Greene, 1995), also known as a "double bind" of discrimination (Montez, 1998; Warner, 1995), illustrates the continued struggles that women of color face as they pursue and prepare for executive-level leadership roles in higher education (Wilson, 1989).

It should be noted that through program initiatives that provide targeted skill development and mentoring, some women have been successful in assuming leadership positions (Berryman-Fink et al., 2003) and navigating the pitfalls of sexism and racism. In addition to skill development, female participants in leadership development programs have reported increased self-esteem, self-worth, and self-confidence (Ebbers, Gallisath, Rockel, & Coyan, 2000). However, lest the picture for women of color in leadership be painted as rosy, it should be noted that increases in representation in senior-level leadership have not been consistent across all types of institutions, and the increase for women of color who take on executive leadership roles has been largely at 2-year institutions (Opp & Gosetti, 2000). This trend, which runs parallel to the overall increases in diversity at the upper level, highlights a fundamental distinction in the practice of leadership selection based on institutional type. The next section discusses this dynamic in detail.

Specific Institutional Types: Community Colleges and HBCUs

Institutional types have distinct cultures and practices that influence the kinds of leaders who are attracted to them and the scope of support provided to leaders by the institution. Community colleges and Minority-Serving Institutions (MSIs; Vaughan, 1996) particularly HBCUs, have traditionally enrolled large numbers of students of color and have been known to nurture people of color (Nichols, 2004). Literature points to HBCUs as the training ground for Black leaders, and select research has focused on creating leadership programs for Black administrators (Lauth, 2005; Zolner, 2005), and students (Glenn, 1997). In addition, research highlights leadership challenges (Manzo, 1996; Pluviose, 2006) and at times offers suggestions for success by examining the historical significance of HBCUs (Cheek, 1988) and the important social and societal implications (Jean-Marie, 2006).

Community colleges have been particularly focused on developing leaders of color and women compared to 4-year institutions (Pierce, Mahoney, & Kee, 1996). However, these institutions are still underprepared to facilitate the succession of diverse candidates to leadership roles because few individuals are prepared to step into those leadership roles (Zamani, 2003). Community colleges have focused on leadership development through professional associations dedicated to community college concerns, such as the American Association of Community Colleges (AACC), which serves as the primary advocacy group, and through programs connected to doctoral-granting institutions such as the community college leadership program at the University of Texas, Austin (Manzo, 1996; Phelan, 2005). Higher education would benefit greatly from a more robust understanding of the specific ways that community colleges and HBCUs cultivate and support leaders of color, as they may influence practice and help set leadership agendas for higher education at large. Consistent themes in the literature on leaders of color surrounding race, gender, and institutional type highlight the importance of considering culture and context in developing leaders of color. This is further underscored in the review of professional associations and leadership development programs.

Select Professional Associations and Higher Education Leadership Development Programs

At least two entities have played and continue to play a significant role in leadership development in higher education: (a) professional associations and (b) leadership development programs. Higher education professional associations have collectively defined core missions, visions, and values for higher education in general, as well as governing practices for various subspecialties. These associations have been proactive in setting standards for the field, as well as reactive in offering new and emerging efforts as higher education continues to change and diversify. Leadership development programs address the need to develop and train potential leaders who can most appropriately address the needs of students, administrators, and society today. This section begins with a discussion of various professional associations and leadership development programs. Next, a general discussion for each approach will be provided, followed by specific initiatives for people of color.

Professional Associations

Professional associations provide their prospective fields and professions with a governing body, guidelines, and most offer some form of targeted approach to advance the leadership capabilities of their members (Pierce et al., 1996). A multitude of associations and councils focus on higher education (see http://www.acenet.edu/Content/NavigationMenu/ProgramsServices/Leadership/Leadership_ACE.htm). However, often missing from general lists are several professional associations that pay particular attention to increasingly diverse needs of higher education constituents (see Table 3). Some focus on the needs of specialty subfields or professions within higher education, such as the American Association of Collegiate Registrars and Admissions Officers (AACRAO) and the American Association of University Professors (AAUP). While others focus by institutional type, such as liberal education (Association of American Colleges and Universities [AAC&U]); community colleges (American Association of Community Colleges [AACC]); and state colleges and universities (American Association of State Colleges and Universities [AASCU]). Still others focus on scholarly pursuits and research, such as the American Educational Research Association (AERA) and the Association for the Study of Higher Education (ASHE).

With the changing climate of higher education and the increase of diverse participants, it is important to have organizations that focus on special racial and ethnic populations, such as the American Association of Hispanics in Higher Education (AAHHE) and the Hispanic Association of Colleges and Universities (HACU), both committed to providing access and strengthening the understanding of Hispanics in college; those committed to HBCUs and predominantly Black institutions, such as the National Association for Equal Opportunity in Higher Education (NAFEO) and the National Association of Student Affairs Professionals (NASAP); as well as those committed to the American Indian experience, such as the American Indian Higher Education Consortium (AIHEC). Two in particular continue to focus on professional development for student affairs administrators: the National Association of Student Personnel Administrators (NASPA) and the American College Personnel Association (ACPA). Last, the American Council on Education (ACE) provides a unifying voice of all higher education public policy. Though not an exhaustive list, the aforementioned are representative of the varying types of organizations that share a common theme for the advancement of higher education. These organizations guide the field, are charged with developing leaders, and are most often associated with administering leadership programs.

Participation in professional associations is particularly beneficial for people of color because (a) participants have access to standard practices and are able to stay abreast of current topics and trends in higher education; (b) participation provides an opportunity for professionals to reenergize, retool, and receive recognition for their efforts; and (c) there is an opportunity to focus on a specialized area of the field. For example, NASPA offers knowledge to communities that disseminate information to targeted populations—African Americans, Hispanics, Latinos/Latinas, and Asian Pacific Islanders—and seminars such as the Multicultural Institute, which focuses on addressing critical

TABLE 3

Higher Education Organizations Focusing on Ethnic Minority Groups

Name	URL	Purpose
American Association of Blacks in Higher Education (AABHE)	http://www.blacksinhighered.org	Focus on leadership development for various constituents and collaborate with other ethnic minority groups to achieve this.
American Association of Hispanics in Higher Education (AAHHE)	http://aahhe.org/	Highlight achievements of Hispanics in the academy; identify professional opportunities to increase Hispanic faculty and focus on issues surrounding Hispanics in higher education.
American Indian Higher Education Consortium (AIHEC)	http://www.aihec.org/	Support tribal colleges to enhance American Indian education and to develop and maintain consistent standards for these colleges.
Hispanic Association of Colleges and Universities (HACU)	http://www.hacu.net	Provide Hispanic Serving Institutions (HSIs) with the necessary resources, professional development and legislative power to serve Hispanic students.
National Association for Student Affairs Professionals (NASAP)	http://www.nasap.net	Provide professional development, promote scholarly inquiry and foster a sense of unity among student affairs professionals devoted to the needs of minority students.
National Association for Equal Opportunity in Higher Education (NAFEO)	http://www.nafeo.org/	Provide a unifying voice to issues pertinent to Historically Black Colleges and Universities (HBCUs) and Predominantly Black Institutions (PBIs) and to provide support through advocacy for these organizations.

concerns of multicultural professionals and the constituents they serve (see www.naspa.org). These opportunities allow leaders of color to focus on issues that may be important to them professionally or personally while engaging in professional development. Though some leaders of color may not be part of the good old boy network on their campus, participation in professional organizations provides them with access to a national network.

Leadership Development Programs

Leadership development programs were traditionally formed to address pertinent higher education issues and to provide training opportunities for current and future leaders (Green, 1990; Montez, 1998). Perhaps the most well-known and comprehensive leadership development program that focuses on training college- and university-level leaders is the fellows program administered through ACE (Smith & Ross, 2005). An ACE fellows report stated that its participants preferred the specific leadership development and internship components of the program compared to other professional development and leader development programs (Cavanaugh, 2007). The finding that the internship is a significant benefit relates to the importance of skill development, observation, and exposure to new responsibilities happening through on-the-job-experience and is valuable in the leadership development process (Green, 1990).

ACE notwithstanding, an examination of six national leadership development programs, at various stages of a career trajectory in higher education (preentry, midlevel, and senior level), revealed various parallels within the group (see Table 4). Each program, though different in focus and time commitment, includes an intensive learning/seminar experience ranging from 2 days to 1 year, provides access to a national network of colleagues, stresses the importance of using formal or informal mentors, and provides a comprehensive and ongoing experience even after the completion of the program (Institute for Higher Education Policy, 2004; León, 2005; Thomas, 2005). What follows is a brief description of six leadership development programs by level.

Pre-entry Career

The NASPA Undergraduate Fellows Program (NUFP) is the only program of the six that focuses on development prior to beginning a professional career. NUFP, formerly known as the Minority Undergraduate Fellows Program (MUFP), was started in 1989 with the intent to increase the number of ethnic minority students interested in pursuing student affairs careers. In 2003 the participant population was expanded to continue to address increasing diversity on campus and to be more inclusive of other traditionally underrepresented students such as disabled, and lesbian, gay, bisexual, and transgender students. The NASPA fellows participate in a structured internship, a 4-day summer institute, and at least one conference coupled with a formal mentoring relationship. To gain admission, applicants must be supported by a mentor and have support of a senior-level administrator at the university. Financial and other professional support resources are provided by the program and the senior-level supporter at the host university (see http://www.naspa.org).

Mid-level Career

The Donna M. Bourassa Mid-Level Management Institute administered through the ACPA prepares midlevel professionals with 5 or more years of experience with the necessary skills to better understand increasingly complex and changing campus communities. The institute enhances development through a week-long curriculum of group seminars and discussions as well as promotes future discussions through a Listserv. This program serves to provide midlevel student affairs leaders with necessary professional development and does not focus on targeted populations. The application focuses solely on support documents from the applicant and does not require a recommendation and institutional support. Up to 50 applicants may compete for two scholarships of $245 to offset program costs (excluding transportation and travel). Early registration costs $525 for ACPA members or $645 for nonmembers (see http://www.myacpa.org).

The Higher Education Resource Services (HERS) Institutes for Women in Higher Education supports three residential programs that prepare mid- and senior-level female professionals to successfully deal with increasing diversity on campus and globalization by training more women administrators and faculty in management and governance. The Summer Institute for Women in Higher Education, sponsored by HERS and Bryn Mawr College offers 4 weeks of intense seminars and activities 6 days a week; the HERS Institute for Women in Higher Education Administration at Wellesley College offers 5 weekends of comprehensive seminars and activities; and the HERS Institute for Women in Higher Education Administration at the University of Denver offers a 6-day, full-time program followed by 2-day seminars during 3 separate weekends. The programs stress intensive seminars, a national network, and mentoring, including a connection to alumnae. To gain admission, applicants must submit an application and have support from a senior-level executive (specifically for the summer institute). Although the three programs operate at separate locations, have an individualized curriculum, and varied timeframes and costs, they all focus on preparing participants for institutional leadership and addressing diverse administrative needs in higher education (see http://www.hersnet.org).

TABLE 4

Comprehensive Leadership Development Programs for Pre-Entry, Mid- and Senior-Level Professionals

Name	Organization	Participants	Purpose	Length	Key Features	Cast
Pre-Entry						
NASPA Undergraduate Fellows (NUFP)	National Association of Student Personnel Administrators (NASPA)	Undergraduates interested in student affairs careers	To expose diverse undergraduates to careers in higher education	4 day summer institute—ongoing mentoring	Mentoring Internship Seminars Summers Institute National Network	Cost absorbed by NASPA and home institution
Mid-Level						
Donna M. Bourassa Mid-level Management Institute	American College Personnel Association (ACPA)	Mid level career—with 5+ years experience	Focus is on understanding the changing campus climate to further develop skills	5 days	Seminars National Network Mentoring	$525 for members/$625 for non-members with early registration
Higher Education Resource Services (HERS) Institutes	HERS Institute for Women in Higher Educ. Administration at the University of Denver	Mid- and upper-level female administrators	To enhance governance and management skills	6 day residential & 3 weekends	Mentoring Seminars National Network	$4675 for residents/$4175 for weekend commuters
	HERS Institute for Women in Higher Educ. Administration at Wellesley College	Mid- and upper-level female administrators	To enhance governance and management skills	5 inter-related weekends	Mentoring Seminars National Network	$3475 covers materials and meals
	Summer Institute for Women in Higher Educ. at Bryn Mawr College	Mid- and upper-level female administrators	To enhance governance and management skills	Approx. 4 weeks	Mentoring Seminars National Network	$6950 residential/$5950 commuter covers room & board and materials
Senior-Level						
ACE Fellows Program	American Council on Education (ACE)	Faculty or Admin. with institutional wide responsibilities	To prepare individuals with min. of 5 years experience with tools to become Admin. Leaders, i.e. Assist. Deans	up to 1 year	Mentoring Internship Seminars National Network	Split cost between nominating and host institution up to $10,000 each
Kellogg MSI Leadership Program (Consists of 3 separate programs)	AIHEC, HACU, and NAFEO Kellogg Leadership Fellows Program	Those interested in senior level and presidential posts in MSIs.	To prepare leaders of MSIs with the skills to become college leaders-Presidents	1 week institute, conference attendance	Mentoring Seminars National Network Conference	No cost to participants or mentors
Millennium Leadership Initiative (MLI)	American Association of State Colleges and Universities (AASCU)	State colleges and universities Senior admin.	To prepare underrepresented individuals for leadership in higher education	4 days	Mentoring Seminars National Network	$2500 members/$3500 non-member for room & board and materials

Senior-Level Career

The ACE Fellows Program prepares emerging leaders for institution-wide leadership roles through a year-long experience that includes seminars, mentoring, and on-the-job training through an internship. The ACE Fellows Program also stresses the national network and participation in national associations. This program is for all emerging leaders and does not have a specific focus on targeted populations. In addition to the application, participants must submit a recommendation from the chief administrative officer at the university, participate in an interview, and agree to participate in an internship up to 1 year in length. Fellows are responsible only for their living expenses during the internship, while the host and nominating institution split the cost of the $6,000 program fee and the additional professional development budget up to $14,000. In addition, the nominating institution agrees to maintain the participant's salary and benefits during the fellowship year (see http://www.acenet.edu).

The Kellogg MSI Leadership Fellows Program administers three separate programs: the American Indian Higher Education Consortium (AIHEC) Leadership Fellows Program, the Hispanic Association of Colleges and Universities (HACU) Leadership Fellows Program, and the National Association for Equal Opportunity (NAFEO) Kellogg Leadership Fellows Program. All of them are overseen by the Institute for Higher Education Policy, the Alliance for Equity in Higher Education, and supported by a 4-year grant of $6 million from the W. K. Kellogg Foundation. The collaborative programs provide week-long intensive seminars, mentoring, and other professional development elements to prepare a cohort of senior-level leaders for institution-wide leadership, with a particular focus on MSIs. All expenses for participation for mentors and fellows in the Kellogg MSI Leadership Fellows Program are covered by the program (see http://www.hacu.net).

The Millennium Leadership Project prepares senior-level administrators of color at state colleges and universities for the chief executive role through a 4-day professional institute and a year-long mentoring relationship with a president or chancellor. Universities identify participants and nominate them for participation. Member institutions have raised funds to support participation in the program. However, the cost of the program is $2,500 for member institutions and $3,500 for non-member institutions and includes meals, housing, and materials (see http://www.aascu.org).

Only one of these programs provides exposure and prepares potential college student leaders for careers in higher education, two others primarily support midlevel professionals, and three more provide opportunities for seasoned individuals with institution-wide responsibilities. These programs are further distinguished by one program focusing on women administrators (mid-senior level) and three focusing on ethnic minority populations. All but one of the programs for underrepresented populations focus on training senior-level leaders of color, while one is a preentry undergraduate exposure program. This is particularly interesting because Taliaferro and Montoya (1995) found that many leaders of color set their sights on positions as coordinators, directors, and vice presidents, but there do not seem to be targeted efforts to help individuals advance to or achieve mid-level positions.

Leadership programs for people of color have primarily been reactive responses to the growing number of students of color on campus (Harvey & Anderson, 2005) and an attempt to provide higher education with prepared and diverse leadership to address the increasingly complex political and social climate on campus (Thomas, 2005). For example, the Kellogg MSI fellows program was a pilot effort supported with a 4-year grant from the Kellogg Foundation in conjunction with the Alliance for Equity in Higher Education, HACU, AIHEC, and NAFEO, with the intent to address the needs of MSIs (Merisotis & Aveilhe, 2005). Of the leadership programs specifically designed to help leaders of color prepare for institution-wide responsibilities at MSIs, this is the one that concentrates on success at MSIs. This program has the explicit purpose of preparing leaders who work at MSIs, which have a distinct culture and face a unique set of challenges different from those at Predominantly White Institutions (PWIs). Considering that the majority of college presidents of color lead MSIs, it would seem reasonable for at least one of the three leadership programs to focus on those types of institutions (Jackson, 2004c). However, the experience for leaders of color at PWIs should not be minimized. It is important to note that all discussed mainstream national programs (i.e., ACE, HERS, and Donna M. Bourassa Management Institute) do address racial/ethnic diversity in the curriculum as a seminar, but it is not a driving objective of the program.

Discussion and Conclusion

There is great opportunity to diversify the higher education administrative workforce by providing exposure, experience, and support to an increasingly diverse group of higher education leaders. If we are to see diversity among those at the presidents' and vice presidents' ranks, it is crucial to provide developmental opportunities at various levels of the career trajectory. This development should include specific targeted efforts that focus on skill development, mentoring, and participation in a national network. A body of knowledge is emerging regarding leadership development for leaders of color, especially as it relates to their participation in leadership development programs and professional associations. As discussed in this chapter and elsewhere, affiliation with and participation in these programs has been beneficial for many people of color. Additionally, literature on leadership development has focused primarily on community colleges and gender. For the most part, leadership development options for people of color focus primarily on preparation for top-level positions (e.g., vice president and president). Therefore, in turn, support for leaders of color for entry to mid-level positions seems to be absent. Giving full consideration to all of this, there is clearly a need for more research on leadership development of leaders of color.

New Directions for Inquiry on Leaders of Color

When discussing leadership programs for people of color, researchers have generally asked: What are the different needs of senior-level people of color in the leadership role? (Lauth, 2005; León, 2005). One question that has gone unanswered is: Are the needs of senior-level leaders of color different from their majority counterparts? From the current review of the research, the answer appears to be yes and no. Based on the paucity of research on the experiences of those in leadership development programs the needs are not different as they relate to the diverse curricula that address such topics as financial management, strategy and planning, and the need for mentors. However, the needs are different when it comes to addressing specific issues that are associated with certain institution types or climates, and these are the needs that the people of color-centered programs tend to focus on (Merisotis & Aveilhe, 2005). The lack of leadership programs through the career life span leads to another unanswered question: How do leadership needs change for people of color at different stages of the *career trajectory*? Clearly, existing institutional, cultural, social, and political dynamics in the U.S. higher education system continue to be perpetuated through organizational structures that highlight multiple factors that have an impact on success for leaders of color (Chesler & Crowfoot, 2000).

Though some recognizable efforts exist through a few programs (e.g., the Kellogg MSI Leadership Fellows Program and the Millennium Leadership Project) that primarily focus on leaders of MSIs, there is a clear need for further consideration to be given to leaders of color who serve at PWIs. These individuals face a unique challenge on campuses where they are the minority within the campus community but especially in the upper-level leadership positions. Furthermore, a long-term comprehensive study on leaders of color in executive leadership positions who have participated in leadership programs is absent. There is an opportunity to use evaluation and research data to improve upon the implementation of existing leadership development programs at various career stages (e.g., pre-entry level, entry, and mid-level). A clear opportunity exists to provide leadership development at the pre-entry, entry, and mid-level stages where the bulk of leaders reside in the professional ranks and may never ascend to the senior-level position without appropriate guidance, development, and mentoring.

Barriers to Participation in Leadership Programs for Leaders of Color

Participation in leadership development programs is not as straightforward as identifying individuals who have the capacity for leadership. The pipeline is sometimes riddled with challenges as individuals try to ascend to leadership. As Jackson (2007) indicates, the pipeline is sometimes clogged by personal or professional attainment, cracked because of poor perceptions, leaky because of an inability to persist, noisy because internal and outside influences interfere with the goal, and frozen because of an inability to navigate through the circumstances of the institution. These metaphors emphasize the many internal and external impediments that exist as individuals move through their career. In addition to barriers in the structure of higher education, such as racial tension and feelings of tokenism and isolation, there are very real barriers and/or obstacles within the structure of these leadership programs that impede participation: lack of financial resources, support from senior-level executives, and time.

For those who do have access to and understand the value of participating in a structured leadership experience, financial constraints remain a significant reason why more individuals do not participate. Costs associated with the majority of the programs may prove to be a financial burden to the leader or the nominating institution. Most programs are costly for individuals to participate in and offer limited financial aid. One such example is the Summer Institute for Women in Higher Education at Bryn Mawr College at $6,950. The exception is the Kellogg MSI Leadership Fellows Program, which absorbs all costs of participation. Although the institution may assume some or all of the costs, the participant will inevitably incur some general living expenses from being away from home for an extended period of time.

Second, leadership programs expect the participants to have the support and buy-in from their universities. Many of the programs require the application to be accompanied by a recommendation from the chief executive officer, provost, president, or another senior-level leader. This requirement assumes that participants have a certain amount of cultural capital and exposure to these university leaders. This may be problematic for people of color who may not have had the opportunity to interface with senior-level leadership on campus, particularly because people of color tend to work in areas that are more student focused and take on such roles as advisor for a student organization and committee member for diversity issues. Additionally, leadership development may be perceived as an individual priority versus an institutional opportunity (Green, 1990).

Finally, time is a factor for the individual and the institution when determining if an employee is able to participate in a 2-day program or a more intense 26-day program. Personal priorities such as raising a family or serving as a caregiver for an elderly relative make attending a residential program virtually impossible for some. Since participants are considered leaders, their absences are surely to be felt on their campuses, and a short or long absence may adversely affect the day-to-day work schedule, particularly for smaller institutions. Therefore, personal circumstance can influence professional attainment. Ideally, leadership programs are valuable rigorous experiences that continue to help shape higher education and successful leaders. However, sometimes realistically they are difficult to partake in because of the concentrated amount of time required to participate.

Thus far, this chapter has provided insights into current employment and research trends on leaders of color, existing levels of intervention through leadership programs, noted gaps in career development efforts, and described some of the barriers to participation in these programs. As previously revealed, several key leadership programs have indicated that participation in mentor-mentee relationships, seminars, and a national network are crucial components to a successful leadership experience. An examination of the collective efforts and landscape of professional development for leaders of color indicates there is an opportunity to develop a program that will successfully prepare those individuals for leadership roles in higher education and address some of the barriers of financial resources, executive-level support, and time. A model of a leadership development program that can be implemented at various stages of the career trajectory and facilitated by associations that guide the profession follows.

Toward a Comprehensive Approach to Leadership Development for People of Color

To consider a true comprehensive approach to leadership, a few assumptions guide this program development. These assumptions are derived from the previous review of the literature, demonstrated success from existing leadership programs, an examination of what is missing from current leadership development efforts, and includes revolutionary leadership characteristics. First, and arguably most important, culture and context guide the leadership development process. In the model program, race, sex, institution type, and geographic cultural realities are considered throughout all key components of the program. Second, it is beneficial for leaders of color to interact with their White counterparts as part of a comprehensive approach to leadership development, but it is crucial that they interact with other leaders of color. Third, leadership development requires individual motivation, group support, and collaboration throughout each of the key components. Fourth, the most effective leadership development efforts involve buying in from the participant's home institution and support from a national professional association. Fifth, development of a leadership program should go beyond on-site programming and in-person interactions to include creative programming that includes the implementation of technology and flexible time schedules. These assumptions were used to establish a model for a comprehensive leadership development program designed for leaders of color. In order to provide a heuristic tool, this model is referred to as the Comprehensive Approach to Leadership Development for People of Color (CALD-PC). We must warn readers, CALD-PC is a dream leadership program that is national in scope. The following are its key components:

Program Curriculum/Seminars

All participants in CALD-PC will take part in a standard curriculum appropriate to the career level that covers general information and skills. For example, those at the midcareer level will engage in seminars that focus on managing a unit, gaining senior-level support, fiscal responsibility, and effecting change. In addition to participating in the standard curriculum, participants will choose educational tracks that focus specifically on the type of institution and institutional climate they are presently in or desire to work in. Therefore a participant from a midwestern PWI will participate in seminars that address some of the cultural, political, and racial themes particular to those types of environments. There will be opportunities to address some institutional climate idiosyncrasies through mentoring. Options for participating in content-focused components include a week-long residential experience, weekend and evening seminars, Web and video conferencing, and live online discussions. Because this is a national-level program, the on-site options will be duplicated in various regions of the country. Collectively, these experiences purposely stress collaboration with other CALD-PC peers but will include some individual activities. Attendees have the option to choose how they will fully participate in the experience but will have to complete a specific set of experiential requirements.

Though participants may choose components that meet their individual needs and lifestyle, they do not have the option to experience the program in isolation. CALD-PC is a national-level program, administered at various stages of the career trajectory, and therefore seminars and projects are designed to be interactive and require work with participants in various educational units, not just their own functional area. The CALD-PC programs at different career levels will run simultaneously or overlap to allow participants to engage in at least one seminar with a different career-level class. For example, senior-level and entry-level CALD-PC participants may take a seminar together on technology and its impact on university management/leadership. This encourages participants to see beyond the individual cohort they begin the program with, expand their perspective by interfacing with leaders at different career levels, and cultivate membership in a larger community of CALD-PC participants. Along with the curriculum, individuals will be expected to develop an individualized leadership development career plan they can reference and revise during and after the formalized leadership development program.

Mentoring

CALD-PC mentoring is seen as an ongoing exchange of ideas and experience with individuals and groups. Often we think of mentoring as only a one-on-one process. However, mentoring takes place in many forms, and attendees will have the opportunity to participate in one-on-one and group mentoring. One-on-one mentoring matches participants to leaders of color. It is not just important that leaders of color interface with other leaders of color but, specifically, leaders of color who work in similar institutional settings. For example, an aspiring dean at a Hispanic-Serving Institution (HSI) on the West Coast will be matched with or have access to a dean of color at a western HSI. This mentoring match complements the educational track the participant has chosen and provides real-life examples of experiences in that setting. However, group mentoring incorporates majority leaders into the process who are invested in developing leaders of color for their particular institutions. This is beneficial for the mentors, because they are able to share the mentoring load and have an opportunity to identify potential future talent for their institutions.

National Network

CALD-PC has built-in structural mechanisms that facilitate a national connection. This national network is composed of a consortium of national professional organizations that work together to create context and culturally relevant professional development experiences for leaders of color that meet the needs of an increasingly diverse field of higher education. This true national network reiterates shared purpose, ensures a diversity of resources, provides a preexisting support system, and places the responsibility of developing leaders of color on the field and not on one particular association. For CALD-PC the national network will facilitate a programmatic network that includes a shared database for participants, instructors, mentors, and those who desire to support but may have less of a formal role (e.g., a retired college president who may not take on a formal program role but is open to being listed as a resource); optional quarterly conference calls hosted by institutions of past participants; yearly skill refreshers or new information seminars; and 5-year reunions. Relationship building is ingrained in the culture of CALD-PC and facilitated through seminars and mentoring that provide individual attention as well as group development. To regenerate the experience and continue to develop future leaders, past participants are encouraged to stay involved through evolving roles, such as seminar instructor and mentor.

Administrative Components

Several administrative components that affect participation include the application process, funding, and program administration. These are discussed last because the greater focus for developing leaders of color appropriately lies in the curriculum, mentoring, and establishing a career-long network. However, these issues require equal attention by administrators and institutions because, as established previously, the administrative processes associated with participation in leadership programs can create barriers to participation for people of color.

An ideal CALD-PC application packet would include a minimum of three items. The first is two professional recommendation letters—one from a professional in a more senior position than the applicant to help establish work abilities and work ethic, and one from a professional peer to help establish the applicant's ability to work with others and the desire to participate in a peer-supported environment. While it is important to express leadership capabilities outside one's own self-description, this is best demonstrated by those who know the applicant well. The second is a demonstrated interest in leadership development determined through participation in other informal or formal leadership experiences, projects taken on, and positions held professionally or in a volunteer capacity. The third item is an essay that details the applicant's leadership and career goals. Though the application requires support from others through references, the focus for acceptance is individual merit and abilities.

One of the most crucial administrative aspects of successfully facilitating CALD-PC is funding. CALD-PC requires funding and support from a consortium of national-level professional associations, educational institutes, or foundations to administer the program and to offset the costs of participation, because ultimately the goal is for CALD-PC to offer full-experience scholarships to participants. However, CALD-PC will also offer other funding options to increase the diversity of participants and reduce finance as a barrier. Some of those options include a sliding pay scale based on need, or fund-raising opportunities for individuals and institutions. A new, unexplored option for funding might include an educational loan provided from a partner institution that will be forgiven based on the number of years a participant decides to work at that particular institution. While not currently in use in the leadership development setting, it is successful in other areas of advanced educational opportunity (e.g., AmeriCorps). In addition, CALD-PC works to lower the cost of administration through donations and in-kind gifts. For example, CALD-PC works with CALD-PC-friendly institutions that may or may not have employees participating in the program but have an expressed interest in developing leaders of color. Accordingly, it might be possible for CALD-PC to tap into resources of CALD-PC institutions (e.g., space to conduct seminars) to help run the program. This serves as a mutually rewarding relationship, because not only do the CALD-PC institutions become part of the national network, they are able to highlight their campuses while providing much needed resources.

To help visualize this proposed model, participation in a CALD-PC leadership development program resembles a wheel that moves the process of professional development forward (see Figure 1). The national and institutional supporters provide the structure and overall direction of the CALD-PC process. These organizations also provide financial resources, such as scholarships and forgivable loans, to help students participate, and in-kind donations, such as meeting space and materials, to help with the administration of the CALD-PC experience. The key program components of mentoring, curriculum/seminars, and national network provide the content and ongoing link to other participants. In essence, these key components are the core of the program and allow for participants to remain connected with CALD-PC after graduation in evolving roles (e.g., those who have participated in mentoring may one day become a mentor or may facilitate a seminar). As with any wheel, if there is a deficiency in it (e.g., a flat) or the resources are not fully employed, the wheel may continue to move forward, but it makes getting to the destination of leadership development

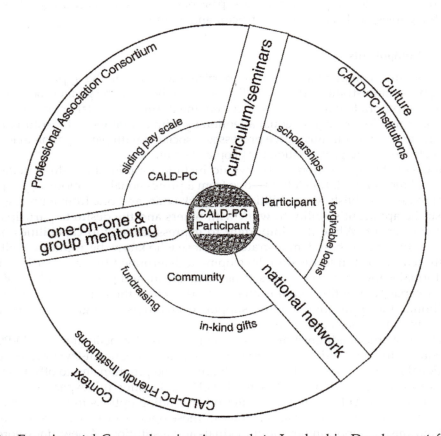

Figure 1 An Experimental Comprehensive Approach to Leadership Development for People of Color (CALD-PC).

more difficult. Therefore, participation in a leadership development program is not the only part but may play a significant role in the career development process. However, a true comprehensive approach to leadership development focuses not just on skill development but fully integrates into the curriculum the context and culture of institutions individuals lead (Kezar & Carducci, 2007).

In closing, institutions of higher education can no longer be silent about race within these unique organizations (Nkomo, 2000). With the increasing number for people of color joining the ranks of higher education, we must reconsider how, when, and why we engage in leadership development. Institutions of higher education that claim to embrace the value of diversity must put forth a sincere, pointed effort to increase the number of people of color in leadership positions. As well, key decision makers must work to acknowledge and affirm racial differences, and work to break down the misconceptions and stereotypes that impede productive developmental experiences and the inclusion of diverse groups. The higher education community has recognized through the efforts of leadership development programs that mentoring, networking, and skill development work. Now we have an opportunity to take a major step in this regard by developing more programs that meet the unique needs for leaders of color in various institutional settings, cultural climates, and geographic regions, while simultaneously recognizing the historical and cultural discriminatory practices that exist in society. Additionally, institutions that currently provide leadership programming would benefit from a firm understanding of the barriers and challenges that remain with regard to participation based on a traditional format. The future development and promotion for leaders of color demand that these barriers be removed or minimized in order to maximize participation from a more diverse participant pool.

Notes

1. Discussion of leadership positions included full-time administrators and college and university presidents. Data for this section were computed using two national data sets/sources: (a) the Integrated Post-secondary Educational Data Systems (IPEDS) and (b) the American Council on Education database on college and university presidents.

References

Bensimon, E., & Tierney, W. (1993). Shaping the multicultural college campus. *Education Digest, 59*(3), 67.

Berryman-Fink, C., Lemaster, B., & Nelson, K. (2003). The women's leadership program: A case study. *Liberal Education, 89*(1), 59–63.

Cavanaugh, C. (2007). *The ACE fellows program: The benefits and values to ACE fellows.* Pensacola, FL: American Council on Education.

Cheek, J. (1988). A leadership blueprint for equity and excellence in Black higher education. *Urban League Review, 11*(1/2), 18–27.

Chesler, M. A., & Crowfoot, J. (2000). An organizational analysis of racism in higher education. In M. C. Brown II (Ed.), *Organization and governance in higher education* (5th ed.; pp. 436–469). Boston, MA: Pearson.

Coleman, J. (1998, April). *Barriers to career advancement by African-American and Caucasian female administrators in Minnesota organizations: A perception or reality?* Paper presented at the annual meeting of the American Educational Research Association, San Diego, CA.

Davis, J. D. (Ed.). (1994). *Coloring the halls of ivy: Leadership & diversity in the academy.* Bolton, MA: Anker.

Ebbers, L. H., Gallisath, G., Rockel, V., & Coyan, M. (2000). The leadership institute for a new century: LINCing women and minorities into tomorrow's community college leadership roles. *Community College Journal of Research & Practice, 24*(5), 375–382.

Esquibel, A. (1992). *The career mobility of Chicano administrators in higher education: A fifty year replication study.* Boulder, CO: Western Interstate Commission for Higher Education.

Fujimoto, M. J. (1996). The community college presidency: An Asian Pacific American perspective. *New Directions for Community Colleges, 1996*(94), 47–56.

Glenn, G. (1997). Following the leaders: The establishment of leadership development centers in historically Black colleges and universities. *Black Issues in Higher Education, 14*(1), 22–25.

Gorena, M. (1996, April). *Hispanic women in higher education administration: Factors that positively influence or hinder advancement to leadership positions.* Paper presented at the annual meeting of the American Educational Research Association, New York.

Green, M. (1990). Investing in leadership. *Liberal Education, 76*(1), 6.

Haro, R. (1990). Latino and executive positions in higher education. *The Educational Record, 71*(3), p. 39–42.

Harvey, W. B., & Anderson, E. L. (2005, February). *Minorities in higher education twenty-first annual status report.* Washington, DC: American Council on Education.

Holmes, S. L. (2004). An overview of African American college presidents: A game of two steps forward, one step backward, and standing still. *The Journal of Negro Education, 73*(1), 21–39.

Howard-Hamilton, M. F., & Williams, V. A. (1996). *Assessing the environment for women of color in student affairs.* Paper prepared for Office of Affirmative Action, Florida University, Gainesville.

Institute for Higher Education Policy. (2004, August). *Leading the way to America's future: A monograph about the launch and implementation of the Kellogg MSI leadership fellows program, 2002–2004.* Washington, DC: Institute for Higher Education Policy.

Jackson, J. F. L. (2000). Administrators of color at predominantly White institutions. In L. Jones (Ed.), *Brothers of the academy: Up and coming African Americans earning our way in higher education!* (pp. 42–52). Sterling, VA: Stylus.

Jackson, J. F. L. (2001). A new test for diversity: Retaining African American administrators at predominantly White institutions. In L. Jones (Ed.), *Retaining African Americans in higher education: Challenging paradigms for retaining students, faculty, and administrators* (pp. 93–109). Sterling, VA: Stylus.

Jackson, J. F. L. (2003). Engaging, retaining and advancing African Americans in student affairs administration: An analysis of employment status. *NASAP Journal, 6*(1), 9–24.

Jackson, J. F. L. (2004a). Engaging, retaining, and advancing African Americans to executive-level positions: A descriptive and trend analysis of academic administrators in higher and postsecondary education. *Journal of Negro Education, 73*(1), 4–20.

Jackson, J. F. L. (2004b). An emerging engagement, retention, and advancement model for African American administrators at predominantly White institutions: The results of two delphi studies. In D. Cleveland (Ed.), *A long way to go: Conversations about race by African American faculty and graduate students in higher education* (pp. 211–222). New York: Peter Lang.

Jackson, J. F. L. (2004c). A crisis at the top: A national perspective [Editor's introduction]. In J. F. L. Jackson (Ed.), Top line: A status report on African American leadership in higher and postsecondary education [Special focused section]. *Journal of Negro Education, 73*(1), 1–3.

Jackson, J. F. L. (2006). Hiring practices of African American males in academic leadership positions at American colleges and universities: An employment trends and disparate impact analysis. *Teachers College Record, 108*(2), 316–338.

Jackson, J. F. L. (2007). Reconceptualizing the African American educational pipeline. In J. F. L. Jackson (Ed.), *Strengthening the African American pipeline: Informing research, policy and practice* (pp. 197–209). Albany, NY: SUNY Press.

Jackson, J. F. L., & Daniels, B. D. (2007). A national progress report of African Americans in the administrative workforce in higher education. In J. F. L. Jackson (Ed.), *Strengthening the educational pipeline for African Americans: Informing policy and practice* (pp. 115–137). Albany, NY: SUNY Press.

Jean-Marie, G. (2006). Welcoming the unwelcomed: A social justice imperative of African-American female leaders at historically Black colleges and universities. *Educational Foundations, 20*(1/2), 85–104.

Jenifer, F. G. (2005). *Minorities and women in higher education and the role mentoring plays in their advancement.* Austin, TX: Office of Academic Affairs, University of Texas System.

Kern-Foxworth, M. (2000). Beyond gender: The experience of women of color. In D. M. Smith (Ed.), *Women at work: Leadership for the next century.* (pp. 80–100). Upper Saddle River, NJ: Prentice Hall.

Kezar, A., & Carducci, R. (2007). Cultivating revolutionary educational leaders: Translating emerging theories into action. *Journal of Research on Leadership Education, 2*(1), 1–46.

Lauth, R. (2005). Handing one another along: The creation of AASCU's millennium leadership initiative. In D. J. León (Ed.), *Lessons in leadership: Executive leadership programs for advancing diversity in higher education* (pp. 151–171). New York: Elsevier/JAI Press.

León, D. J. (2005). Why leadership programs matter. In D. J. León (Ed.), *Lessons in leadership: Executive leadership programs for advancing diversity in higher education* (pp. 85–105). New York: Elsevier/JAI Press.

Lynch, P. D., & Charleston, M. (1990). The emergence of American Indian leadership in education. *Journal of American Indian Education, 29*(2), 1–10.

Manzo, K. (1996). Building leaders. Leadership development program important step for community college presidents. *Black Issues in Higher Education, 13*(17), 18.

Martinez, R. O. (2005). Latino demographic and institutional issues in higher education: Implications for leadership development. In D. J. León (Ed.), *Lessons in leadership: Executive leadership programs for advancing diversity in higher education* (pp. 85–105). New York: Elsevier/JAI Press.

Merisotis, J. P., & Aveilhe, K. (2005). The Kellogg MSI Leadership Fellows Program. In D. J. León (Ed.), *Lessons in leadership: Executive leadership programs for advancing diversity in higher education* (pp. 207–222). New York: Elsevier/JAI Press.

Montez, J. (1998). Asian/Pacific American women in higher education administration: Doubly bound, doubly scarce. *Issues in Policy, 9.* Pullman, WA: Washington State University.

Nakanishi, D. T. (1993). Asian Pacific Americans in higher education: Faculty and administrative representation and tenure. *New Directions for Teaching and Learning, 1993* (53), 51–59.

Nichols, J. (2004). Unique characteristics, leadership styles, and management of historically Black colleges and universities. *Innovative Higher Education, 28*(3), 219–229.

Nkomo, S. M. (2000). Race in organizations. In M. C. Brown II (Ed.), *Organization and governance in higher education* (5th ed., pp. 417–431). Boston, MA: Pearson.

Opp, R., & Gosetti, P. (2000). Equity for women administrators of color in two-year colleges: Progress and prospects. *Community College Journal of Research and Practice, 2,* 591–608.

Phelan, D. (2005). Crossing the generations: Learning to lead across the leadership life cycle. *Community College Journal of Research and Practice, 29*(9/10), 783–792.

Pierce, D. R., Mahoney, J. R., & Kee, A. M. (1996). Professional development resources for minority administrators. *New Directions for Community Colleges, 1996* (94), 81–92.

Pluviose, D. (2006). Hung out to dry. *Diverse: Issues in Higher Education, 23*(14), 22–25.

Singh, K., Robinson, A., & Williams-Greene, J. (1995). Differences in perceptions of African American women and men faculty and administrators. *The Journal of Negro Education, 64*(4), 401–408.

Smith, G. A., & Ross, M. (2005). American Council on Education Fellows Program: Celebrating 40 years of leadership development in higher education. In D. J. León (Ed.), *Lessons in leadership: Executive leadership programs for advancing diversity in higher education* (pp. 109–126). New York: Elsevier/JAI Press.

Swisher, K. G. (2001). Solid ground: Comment on "Shifting Sands: Reflections from the Field of Higher Education." *Anthropology & Education Quarterly, 32*(4), 502–506.

Taliaferro, B., & Montoya, A. (1995). *Faculty and administrators of color in the Pennsylvania state system of higher education: A status report.* (ERIC Document Reproduction Service No. ED381504).

Thomas, J. (2005). African American leadership in higher education. In D. J. León (Ed.), *Lessons in leadership: Executive leadership programs for advancing diversity in higher education* (pp. 85–105). New York: Elsevier/JAI Press.

Vaughan, G. B. (1996). Paradox and promise: Leadership and the neglected minority. *New Directions for Community Colleges, 1996* (94), 5–12.

Warner, L. S. (1995). A study of American Indian females in higher education administration. *Initiatives, 56*(4), pp. 11–17.

Watson, L. W. (2001). In their voices: A glimpse of African-American women administrators in higher education. *NASPA Journal, 4,* 7–16.

Wilson, R. (1989). Women of color in academic administration: Trends, progress, and barriers. *Sex Roles: A Journal of Research, 21,* 85–97.

Zamani, E. M. (2003). African American student affairs professionals in community college settings: A commentary for future research. *NASAP Journal, 6*(1), 91–103.

Zolner, J. P. (2005). The Harvard institutes for higher education. In D. J. León (Ed.), *Lessons in leadership: Executive leadership programs for advancing diversity in higher education* (pp. 127–147). New York: Elsevier/JAI Press.

Chapter 35
Hispanic Presidents and Chancellors of Institutions of Higher Education in the United States in 2001 and 2006

Alfredo G. de los Santos Jr. and Irene I. Vega

Abstract: This manuscript examines the number of Hispanic individuals who serve as presidents or chancellor and the type of institutions they serve. In 2001, only 13 states had institutions in which the president or chancellor was Latina/o. By 2006, that number had increased to 22. Both in 2001 and 2006, 61% of all Latina/o CEOs served in associate's degree institutions. Of the 180 Hispanic-serving institutions in the continental United States that were members of HACU in 2007, only 56, or 31%, had Latina/o CEOs.

Resumen: Este manuscrito examina el número de individuos hispanos que sirven como presidentes o rectores y el tipo de institución en el que sirven. En 2001 solo 13 estados tenían instituciones en las que un latina/o era presidente o rector. Para 2006 ese número había incrementado a 22. Ambos en 2001 y 2006, el 61% de todos los latinas/os CEOs servían en instituciones de grado asociado. De las 180 instituciones al servicio del hispano en los EUA que eran miembros de HACU en 2007 solo 56 o el 31% tenían individuos latinas/os como *CEOs.*

Even though Hispanic individuals represented 14.5% of the U.S. population in 2005 and projections of high school graduates show that Hispanic individuals will represent more than one fifth of the total graduates by 2017–2018, very few Hispanic individuals are presidents or chancellors of institutions of higher education.[1] In addition, the research literature shows that little scholarly attention has focused on Hispanic leaders in higher education. The earlier research literature dealt with Hispanic *administrators* or *leaders*, not with presidents or chancellors. The extant research on Hispanic presidents or chancellors is relatively recent; the earliest study was published in 1990. Very little is known about the number of Hispanic individuals who serve as president or chancellor, the type of institutions they serve, their gender, and so forth.

The Hispanic population in the United States increased from 34.5 million in 2000 to 41.5 million in 2005, making Hispanic individuals the largest minority in the country. This 21.4% increase was almost 4 times the rate of increase of the population as a whole, which increased by 5.4% during the same time period. In 2005, Hispanic individuals represented 14.5% of the total U.S. population of 288.4 million (Pew Hispanic Center, 2006). Thus, one of every seven persons in the country was Hispanic in 2005.

At middecade, California had a Hispanic population of 12,534,628 and was the state with the largest number of Hispanic individuals; Texas followed with a Hispanic population of 7,882,254. The state with the third largest Hispanic population in 2005 was Florida with 3,433,355 Hispanic individuals. The fourth and fifth states in terms of Hispanic populations were New York, with 3,026,286 Hispanic individuals and Illinois, with 1,807,908 Hispanic individuals. Arizona had the sixth largest Hispanic population (1,679,11) in 2005, followed by New Jersey as the seventh state, with 1,312,326 Hispanic individuals (Pew Hispanic Center, 2006).

The Western Interstate Commission for Higher Education (WICHE) has projected that by 2017–2018, 634,280 Hispanic individuals will graduate from the public high schools in the United States. Hispanic individuals will represent 21.2% of the total 2,886,193 total students projected to graduate from the public schools (WICHE, ACT, and The College Board, 2003). By 2018, one out of five high school graduates will be Hispanic.

Carnevale and Fry (1999) projected that the number of Latina/o students enrolling in college will increase from 1.4 million in 1995 to 2.5 million in 2015. This represents a 73% increase in twenty years. This same study projected that by 2015, Latinas/os will represent 15% of all undergraduates. Thus, one of every six undergraduates in 2015 will be Hispanic.

A majority of Latinas/os enrolled in institutions of higher education are enrolled in community colleges. According to the American Association of Community Colleges, approximately 55% of all Latina/o undergraduates enrolled in institutions of higher education are enrolled in community colleges (American Association of Community Colleges, 2006).

A small number of institutions which meet the definition of "Hispanic-serving institutions" (HSIs)[2] enroll more than 60% of all Latino students. The Hispanic Association of Colleges and Universities (HACU) reports that although its U.S. members represent only 10% of the total institutions of higher education, they enroll more than two thirds of all Hispanic college students (HACU, 2007a).

In 2003, a total of 7,006 Hispanic individuals were full-time administrators at institutions of higher education in the United States; they represented 3.9% of the total 178,443. The number of Hispanic full-time female administrators exceeded the number of Hispanic male full-time administrators, 3,847 to 3,159. Although Hispanic females outnumber Hispanic males as administrators, males outnumber females in the president or chancellor rank. That same year, a total of 91 Hispanic individuals were presidents or chancellors of institutions of higher education in the country—66 were male and 25 were female. The majority, or 48, of the Hispanic presidents or chancellors served in community colleges. Of these, 33 were male and 15 were female. Of the 42 Hispanic presidents or chancellors at 4-year colleges and universities, 33 were male and only 9 were female (Cook & Cordova, 2006).

Review of Literature—Hispanic Leaders in Higher Education

A review of the available literature shows that there has been little or no scholarly attention to Hispanic leaders in higher education. Furthermore, the mainstream research on Hispanic leaders in higher education has little salience for the president or chancellor of the institution because the focus has been on *administrators* or *leaders*. Martinez (2005) said that "there still is no discernable body of knowledge on the nature and dynamics about Latino leadership in higher education" (p. 17). Haro and Lara (2003) note that when the "professional literature is reviewed, there were but a handful of studies prepared on Latinos in leadership roles in American higher education" (p. 153). A few articles and some dissertations make up the body of literature on Hispanic presidents or chancellors of institutions of higher education in this country.

This brief review of the literature is divided into two parts: Hispanic administrators or leaders and Hispanic presidents or chancellors.

Hispanic Administrators and Leaders

The earliest scholarly study of Hispanic administrators or leaders found was Esquibel's (1977) dissertation on the Chicano administrators in colleges and universities in the Southwest. Esquibel surveyed Chicano administrators in 2-year colleges and 4-year colleges at the department chairperson level or higher, who were either tenured or on regular institutional funds, in five states: Arizona,

California, Colorado, New Mexico, and Texas. He found four factors as influential in their appointment: (a) political involvement and contacts; (b) pressures by Chicano students and community members for more Chicano administrators; (c) the Chicano concentration or ethnic composition of the respondent's institution and community; and (d) affirmative action plans and requirements.

Acevedo did a study 2 years later on the socialization of Mexican-American midlevel administrators in Texas institutions of higher education (Acevedo, 1979). Acevedo found that five factors affected their socialization: (a) limited prior socialization to the norms and values of the institution; (b) limited roles at the institutions, in many instances prescribed along ethnic concerns; (c) demands of ethnic constituencies to take their needs within the purview of the institution; (d) paucity of reference or peer group members important for direction on reference to institutional requirements; and (e) lack of institutional sponsors or mentors to serve as advocates or support system.

As reported by Martinez, some scholarly works on Latina/o leaders were published in the 1990s (Martinez, 2005). In the early 1990s, two important studies were done; one by Esquibel in 1992 and the other by Haro in 1995. The study by Esquibel (1992) was a replication of his 1977 dissertation 15 years earlier. He found that in addition to the four factors identified in his 1977 dissertation that influenced the appointment of Chicano administrators, three other factors were cited by the respondents to this survey: (a) new initiatives, such as training programs, workshops, and so forth; (b) emphasis the administrator placed on maintaining Chicano roots; and (c) advocates on the governing boards, screening committees, and search firms (Esquibel, 1992). In his 1995 study, Haro found that Latinas/os being interviewed for executive positions were held to a higher standard during the search process (Haro, 1995).

In addition, beginning in the 1990s, a few dissertations began to focus on Hispanic women in higher education administration. Gorena (1994) collected data from 68 participants in the United States using an instrument adapted from one used by the American Council on Education to survey women presidents in colleges and universities. Among her findings was a profile of the Latina senior higher education level administrator: a dean, Mexican-American, 45 years old, married, Catholic, and holding a doctorate. In a more recent study of the life experiences and professional challenges of Mexican-American female academic and student affairs administrators at four institutions in the University of Texas system, Silva (2003) found the female administrators also adjusted in cultural identity, grounded in family, with a strong work ethic and a passion to make a difference.

More recent works include Valverde's (2003) book on the adversity, challenges, and dilemmas faced by leaders of color in institutions of higher education, institutions that at times can be harsh. Leon's (2003, 2005) two recent books are important contributions to the literature on the development of Latina/o leaders in higher education.

Leon's 2003 book includes demographic information about Latinas/os in the 21st century, the transition of Latina/o students from high school to college, their experiences in urban community colleges, and options for them to enter graduate studies. In addition, faculty mentoring programs and the experience of Latina/o and academic leaders are described. Leon proposes a model for leadership development programs for Latinas/os.

The book that Leon edited in 2005 not only provides data about Latina/o demographics, but also includes a chapter on the experiences of presidents of color in higher education. The main part of the book describes not only the older, traditional programs of leadership development in higher education, but also newer programs designed to prepare the future leaders in higher education.

Hispanic Presidents and Chancellors

As noted above, the extant literature on Hispanic presidents or chancellors is quite limited. In addition, with the exception of a study by Haro, the focus of the majority of studies found focused on community college presidents. Last, these studies were done quite recently—the earliest one in 1990.

Ruiz did a study in 1990 on the leadership behavior and the identification of special problems as perceived by Hispanic community college presidents in the country. He found that family values, models, personal needs and values, and institutional values had extensive influence on the leadership philosophy and behavior of Hispanic community college presidents. In addition, the issue of ethnicity can cause role conflict for Hispanic presidents, thus adding additional responsibilities to their complex lives. Ruiz (1990) found that if Hispanic presidents do pursue ethnic concerns and are successful administrators, they must balance both ethnic and organizational matters.

In 1997, Mata did a multimethod study of the leadership development and functioning of 40 Latina/o community college presidents. Mata found that luck, making geographic moves, Latina/o consciousness, encouragement, and mentors led to the presidency. Lack of cultural capital, cultural barriers, and systemic barriers represented challenges to the presidents.

Two years later, Cipres (1999), in a study of Latina community college presidents in California, projected a profile of the participants: (a) is probably Catholic, (b) is married to a non-Hispanic male, (c) is bilingual and bicultural, and (d) is the first generation in her family to be college educated.

Rodriguez did a study in 2006 that explored the experiences, events, and circumstances that provided four Latinas/os the opportunity to become a president of a community college. More specifically, Rodriguez tried to recapture the individual experiences of the four Latino community college presidents who came from working class, immigrant families as they ascended to the presidency. Seven themes emerged from the study: (a) the influence of family, (b) a sense of struggle and resilience, (c) positive connections to schools and learning, (d) quality mentoring experiences, (e) participation in leadership development programs, (f) a strong commitment to public service, and (g) the impact of race, culture, and gender.

A total of two dissertations focused on individual Latinas: a president of a college of a multicollege district and a chancellor of a multicollege district. The first study, by Knowlton in 1993, focused on the influence of the gender and ethnicity on the leadership behavior of the Latina president of a college in a multicollege district and also attempted to determine if similar influences existed among eight other women who were presidents of community colleges in the United States. Knowlton found that all the Latina community college presidents were influenced by close family ties, their cultural identity, and emphasis on education by their parents. The presidents' leadership focused on increased collaborative decision making and a focus on developing a family or community on campus, often through celebrations and ceremonies, all based on a vision of a more inclusive institution that welcomed and valued the diverse student population served (Knowlton, 1993).

The other dissertation, based on Knowlton's study, focused on the only Latina chancellor to lead a multicollege district at the time. The author, Olga Flores (1999), found that the chancellor (a) was most influenced by elements of both the "traditional" and "nontraditional" familial environment at the institution, (b) had a perception that neither ethnicity or gender were barriers to her ascension to her position as CEO, (c) possessed specific leadership behaviors, and (d) validated the importance of traditional preparation for the position but also stressed the importance of nontraditional pathways.

Perhaps the latest study on Latino and other presidents of color focused on the question: Did the person experience bias while a sitting president (Haro, 2005)? If a president did experience bias, the focus then became the nature (ethnic, racial, gender) of the bias, and the frequency, location, source, and longevity of the bias (Haro, 2005). The author found that all the Latina/o presidents did in fact experience bias while they served as presidents, and he recommended ways to ameliorate it (Haro, 2005).

Statement of the Problem

Although some information about Hispanic *administrators* and *leaders* in higher education is available, little is known about Hispanic CEOs—presidents or chancellors—in the institutions of higher education in this country. Even though a few articles and some dissertations have been written about Hispanic presidents and chancellors, very little is known about the actual number of Latinos who serve in these positions, the type of institutions they serve, their gender, whether they serve at a HSI, and so forth.

Purpose of the Study

The purpose of the study was to provide baseline data on the number of Latina/o presidents and chancellors of institutions of higher education in the United States, using two data points, in 2001 and 2006, a 5-year period. More specifically, the study attempted to answer the following questions:

1. How many of the presidents or chancellors listed in the 2001 *Higher Education Directory* (Rodenhouse, 2001) and the 2006 *Higher Education Directory* (Burke, 2006) were Hispanic?
2. In how many states were the institutions of higher education with Latina/o CEOs located both in 2001 and 2006?
3. How many of the Hispanic presidents or chancellors in 2001 and 2006 were female? How many were male?
4. What was the gender, both in 2001 and 2006, of the Latina/o CEOs by institution type?
5. Using the Carnegie classification system,[3] in what type of institutions did the Latina/o presidents or chancellors serve, both in 2001 and 2006?
6. Which states had the most Hispanic presidents or chancellors in 2001 and 2006?
7. How many of the HSIs in 2007 had Hispanic presidents or chancellors? By state?

Method

The methodology used in this study was quite simple and direct. The authors reviewed the 2001 and 2006 *Higher Education Directories*, looked at all the institutions listed and noted the presidents or chancellors with Latina/o names, and made a list of all of them, by state. A matrix, in alphabetical order by state, was created that included the name of the institution, the name of the president or chancellor, and the institution's Carnegie classification (see the appendix).

The information in this matrix was used to determine the gender of each individual based on the CEO's first name. In a number of instances, where the authors were not sure whether a CEO was Hispanic, telephone calls were made to verify. The information in the matrix was also used to generate the four tables, that form the base of this chapter.

To determine how many of the institutions with Hispanic presidents or chancellors were HSIs, the list of institutions in the matrix was compared with the list of institutions that were members of the HACU in February 2007.

Limitations of the Study

This study had a number of limitations, the first one being that only the Hispanic presidents or chancellors listed in both the 2001 and 2006 *Higher Education Directories* were included. A second limitation is that the authors excluded private-for-profit institutions with an enrollment of less than 1,000 students.

The other limitation is that only institutions in the continental United States were included; institutions in Puerto Rico were excluded. Another limitation is that the authors made no attempt to differentiate between those who served as CEOs of a system of institutions or were CEOs of an institution that was part of a larger system. For example, the chancellor of a multicollege community college district was considered the same as the president of one of the institutions in that district.

Another limitation is that the list of HSIs used might not include all the institutions that meet the definitions of these institutions used by HACU. Not all institutions that meet the HACU definition are members of the association.

The final limitation is the authors' acquaintance with those presidents or chancellors whose last name is not Latina/o. It is possible that some presidents or chancellors with non-Latina/o names were not included because the authors did not know them.

Conversely, some non-Latina/o presidents or chancellors may have been included if they acquired a Hispanic surname through marriage.

Presentation of the Data: Latina/o CEOs in Institutions of Higher Education

The data in the four tables generated for this study are presented in the following sections and brief explanations and descriptions of the data in each table are provided.

Latina/o CEOs by State, by Institution Type

This section provides information about Latina/o CEOs in institutions of higher education in the United States both in 2001 and 2006, by state, by institution type, and gender (see Table 1).

As shown in Table 1, in 2001, only 13 states in the country had institutions of higher education in which the CEO was Latina/o. By 2006, the number of states with Latina/o CEOs had increased to 22. All the states in which Latina/o CEOs served in 2001 also had Latina/o CEOs in 2006. These states include Arizona, California, Colorado, Florida, Illinois, Louisiana, Michigan, Missouri, New Jersey, New Mexico, New York, Pennsylvania, and Texas.

The following states that did not have any Latina/o CEOs in 2001 had at least one Latina/o CEO in 2006: Alabama, Connecticut, Indiana, Maine, New Hampshire, Oklahoma, Oregon, Virginia, and Wisconsin.

Ten States with the Most Latina/o CEOs, 2001 and 2006

In this section, the 10 states with the most Latinas/os serving as CEOs in institutions of higher education in 2001 and 2006 will be described (see Table 2).

As shown in Table 2, in 2001, 85 of the 90 Latina/o CEOs served in the top 10 states. In 2006, 98 of the 112 Latina/o CEOs served in the top 10 states. Thus, in 2001, 94% of all Latina/o CEOs served in the top 10 states, compared to 88% in 2006.

It is interesting to know that three states—Illinois, New Jersey, and Pennsylvania with four Latina/o CEOs each—are included in the list of the top 10 states in 2006, when they were not listed in 2001. Colorado, which was the 7th state in 2001 with three Latina/o CEOs dropped to 10th in 2006 with two.

In 2001, California had the highest number of Latina/o CEOs, 35, which represented 39% of the total. In 2006, California still had the largest number of Latina/o CEOs, 35, which represented 32% of the total of 112.

Texas was the state both in 2001 and 2006 with the second largest number of Latina/o CEOs (see Table 2). In 2001, the 17 Latina/o CEOs in Texas represented 19% of the total. By 2006, the number of Latina/o CEOs in Texas had increased by 3, to 20, which represented 18% of the total.

The state with the third largest number of Latina/o CEOs, both in 2001 and 2006, was New Mexico, with eight in 2001 and nine in 2006. Florida was the state with the fourth largest number of Latina/o CEOs, with five in 2001 and eight in 2006.

In 2006, both Arizona and New York had six Latina/o CEOs. In 2001, New York was fifth, with six and Arizona was sixth with four.

In 2001, of the 85 Latina/o CEOs who served in the 10 top states, 64 were males and 21 were females. By 2006, the number of Latina female CEOs who served in the top 10 states increased to 38; the number of Latino male CEOs who served in the same states decreased by four, from 64 to 60.

TABLE 1

Latino CEOs of Institutions of Higher Education in the United States, 2001 and 2006, by State, by Institution Type

	Associate's			Baccalaureate			Master's			Specialized			Doctoral			N/A			Total		
	Total	M	F	Total	M	F	Total	M	F	Total	M	F	Total	M	F	Total	M	F	Total	M	F
2001																					
Arizona	3	2	1							1	1	0							4	3	1
California	24	12	12	1	1	0	4	4	0	1	0	1				5	5	0	35	22	13
Colorado	1	1	0				1	1	0	1	1	0							3	3	0
Florida	3	2	1							1	1	0	1	1	0				5	4	1
Illinois	1	1	0																1	1	0
Louisiana	2	2	0																2	2	0
Michigan	1	1	0				1	1	0										2	2	0
Missouri	1	1	0	1	1	0										1	1	0	3	3	0
New Jersey							1	1	0							1	1	0	2	2	0
New Mexico	6	6	0				1	1	0							1	1	0	8	8	0
New York	3	2	1	1	1	0	1	1	0	1	0	1							6	4	2
Pennsylvania										1	0	1	1	1	0				2	1	1
Texas	10	7	3	1	1	0	4	3	1				1	1	0	1	1	0	17	13	4
All states	55	37	18	4	4	0	13	12	1	6	3	3	3	3	0	9	9	0	90	68	22
2006																					
Alabama				1	1	0													1	1	0
Arizona	5	4	1				1	1	0										6	5	1
California	22	10	12	2	2	0	4	3	1	1	0	1	1	0	1	5	3	2	35	18	17
Colorado	2	1	1																2	1	1
Connecticut	1	1	0																1	1	0

	Associate's			Baccalaureate			Master's			Specialized			Doctoral			N/A			Total		
	Total	M	F	Total	M	F	Total	M	F	Total	M	F	Total	M	F	Total	M	F	Total	M	F
Florida	6	4	2							1	1	0	1	1	0				8	6	2
Illinois	3	0	3				1	1	0										4	1	3
Indiana	1	1	0																1	1	0
Louisiana	2	2	0																2	2	0
Maine	1	1	0																1	1	0
Michigan	1	1	0				1	1	0										2	2	0
Missouri				1	1	0													1	1	0
New Hampshire	1	1	0																1	1	0
New Jersey	1	0	1				1	1	0	2	1	1							4	2	2
New Mexico	6	3	3				1	1	0				2	2	0				9	6	3
New York	4	2	2	1	1	0	1	1	0										6	4	2
Oklahoma										1	1	0							1	1	0
Oregon	1	0	1																1	0	1
Pennsylvania	1	0	1				1	1	0	2	1	1							4	2	2
Texas	9	7	2	2	2	0	5	2	3	1	1	0	1	1	0	2	2	0	20	15	5
Virginia	1	1	0																1	1	0
Wisconsin													1	1	0				1	1	0
All states	69	40	29	6	6	0	16	12	4	8	5	3	6	5	1	7	5	2	112	73	39

TABLE 2

Ten States with the Most Latina/o CEOs of Institutions of Higher Education 2001 and 2006

	M	F	Total	% of All States Total[a]
2001				
1. California	22	13	35	39
2. Texas	13	4	17	19
3. New Mexico	8	0	8	9
4. Florida	4	1	5	6
5. New York	4	2	6	7
6. Arizona	3	1	4	4
7. Colorado	3	0	3	3
8. Missouri	3	0	3	3
9. Louisiana	2	0	2	2
10. Michigan	2	0	2	2
Top 10	64	21	85	94
All states	68	22	90	

	M	F	Total	% of All States Total[b]
2006				
1. California	18	17	35	32
2. Texas	15	5	20	18
3. New Mexico	6	3	9	8
4. Florida	6	2	8	7
5. Arizona	5	1	6	5
6. New York	4	2	6	5
7. New Jersey	2	2	4	4
8. Pennsylvania	2	2	4	4
9. Illinois	1	3	4	4
10. Colorado	1	1	2	2
Top 10	60	38	98	88
All states	73	39	112	

a. These figures reflect the percentage of the total number of Latina/o CEOs in the country (90).

b. These figures reflect the percentage of the total number of Latina/o CEOs in the country (112).

Latina/o CEOs by Institution Type and Gender

In this section, data will be presented about Latina/o CEOs by institution type and gender for both 2001 and 2006 (see Table 3).

In 2001, as shown in Table 3, 55 of the 90 Latina/o CEOs served in institutions that award associate's degrees—community colleges. This represented 61% of the total of 90. The next largest group of Latina/o CEOs—13 of them—served in master's degree granting institutions or 14% of the total. Only three Latina/o CEOs served at doctoral institutions, four at baccalaureate institutions, and six at specialized institutions.

By 2006, there was little change in the type of institutions in which Latina/o CEOs served: 61% in community colleges, 14% in master's granting institutions, and 5% in baccalaureate, 7% in specialized and 5% in doctoral institutions (see Table 3).

More than three fourths (76%) of all Latina/o CEOs in 2001 were males; a little less than one fourth (24%) were females (see Table 3). At baccalaureate and doctoral institutions, all the Hispanic CEOs were male; only one of the 13 Latina/o CEOs at master's institutions was female. Almost two

TABLE 3

Latina/o CEOs by Institution Type and Gender 2001 and 2006

	Associate's	Baccalaureate	Master's	Specialized	Doctoral	N/A	Total
2001							
% by institution type	61	4	14	7	3	1	90
# by institution type	55	4	13	6	3	9	90
# of male	37	4	12	3	3	9	68
# of female	18	0	1	3	0	0	22
% male	67	100	92	50	100	100	76
% female	33	0	8	50	0	0	24
2006							
% by institution type	61	5	14	7	5	6	100
# by institution type	69	6	16	8	6	7	112
# of male	40	6	12	5	5	5	73
# of female	29	0	4	3	1	2	39
% male	58	100	75	63	83	71	65
% female	42	0	25	37	17	29	35

thirds (61% or 37 of 55) of the Latina/o CEOs serving in associate's degree-granting institutions were male; more than one third (18 of 55, or 33%) were female.

In 2006, Latina CEOs had made some progress but they were still in the minority. Of the total 112 Latina/o CEOs in 2006, the 73 males represented 65% of the total; 39 females represented 35%. At community colleges, of the 69 Latina/o CEOs, the 40 males represented 58% of the total and the 29 females represented 42% of the total. Of the 16 Latina/o CEOs at master's institutions, the 12 males represented three fourths of the total whereas the 4 females represented one quarter. At doctoral institutions, the five Latino males represented 83% of the total of 6; the one female Latina CEO represented 17%. In 2006, there were no Latina female CEOs at baccalaureate institutions. At specialized institutions, five Latino male CEOs represented 63% of the total, whereas the three females represented 37%.

HSIs with Hispanic CEOs

In this section, information is provided regarding HSIs with Hispanic CEOs. The list of HSIs includes those institutions that met the definition of an HSI used by the HACU and were members of HACU in February 2007.[4] The HACU member institutions totaled 212 then, including 32 institutions in Puerto Rico. Because this study included only Hispanic CEOs in the continental United States, the 32 institutions in Puerto Rico were excluded. Thus, a total of 180 HACU-member institutions are included here. As can be seen in Table 4, the list is in alphabetical order by state and includes the name of the HSI in each state in which a Hispanic serves as president and the name of the president or chancellor. The total number of HSIs in each state is also indicated.

Of the total 180 HSIs located in the continental United States which were members of HACU in February 2007, only 56 had Latina/o CEOs or 31% of the total.

The state of California was the state with the largest number of HSIs served by a Latina/o CEO: 18 of the 64 HACU-member institutions, or 28% of the total number of HSIs. Texas was the state with the second largest number of HSIs served by a Latina/o CEO, with 16 of 43, or 37% of the total. The state with the third largest number of HSIs in which a Hispanic CEO served was Florida, 6 of 10, or 60%. New Mexico followed, with 5 of 18 HSIs; thus, 28% of the HSIs were led by Latina/o CEOs. In New York, 4 of the 12 HSIs that were HACU members were led by Latina/o CEOs. In Arizona, Latina/o CEOs served in three of the nine HSIs in the state. In some states with at least one HACU member institutions, no Latina/o CEO served: Connecticut, Kansas, Massachusetts, North Carolina, Pennsylvania, and Washington.

TABLE 4

Hispanic-Serving Institutions with Hispanic CEOs in 2006

Institution	CEO
Arizona	
Phoenix College	Ana Solley
Estrella Mountain Community College	Homero Lopez
Pima County Community College	Roy Flores
3 of 9	
California	
Allan Hancock College	Jose M. Ortiz
California State Polytechnic University, Pomona	J. Michael Ortiz
California State University, Monterey Bay	Diane Cordero de Noriega
Cerritos College	Noelia Vela
College of the Desert	Maria C. Sheenan
Crafton Hills Community College	Gloria Harrison
East Los Angeles College	Ernest Moreno
Kern Community College District	Sandra V. Serrano
Los Angeles Mission College	Adriana Barrera
Los Medanos College	Peter Garcia
Merced College	Benjamin T. Duran
National Hispanic University	David P. Lopez
San Joaquin Delta Community College	Raul Rodriguez
Santa Ana College	Erlinda Martinez
Southwestern College–Chula Vista	Norma Hernandez
Oxnard College	Lydia Ledesma—Reese
Rio Hondo College	Rose Marie Joyce
University of Riverside	France A. Cordova
18 of 64	
Colorado	
Community College of Denver	Christine Johnson
1 of 6	
Connecticut	
0 of 1	
Florida	
Broward Community College District Administrative Offices	Larry A. Calderon
Carlos Albizu University Miami	Salvador Santiago-Negron
Florida International University	Modesto A. Maidique
Miami Dade College District Administration	Eduardo Padron
Valencia Community College Osceola	Sylvia Zapico
Miami Dade College North Campus	Dr. Jose A. Vicente
6 of 10	
Illinois	
City Colleges of Chicago Richard J. Daley College	Sylvia Ramos
St. Augustine College	Zoila Z. Brennan
2 of 7	
Kansas	
0 of 1	
Massachusetts	
0 of 1	
New Jersey	
New Jersey City University	Carlos Hernandez
1 of 4	

Institution	CEO
New Mexico	
New Mexico Highlands University	Manny M. Aragon
New Mexico State University Doña Ana Branch Community College	Margie Huerta
New Mexico State University Grants	Felicia Casados
Northern New Mexico College	Jose Griego
University of New Mexico, Main Campus	Louis Caldera
5 of 18	
New York	
Boricua College	Victor G. Alicea
Borough of Manhattan Community College, City University of New York	Antonio Perez
Hostos Community College, City University of New York	Dolores M. Fernandez
Lehman College, City University of New York	Ricardo R. Fernandez
4 of 12	
North Carolina	
0 of 1	
Pennsylvania	
0 of 1	
Texas	
Baptist University of the Americas	Albert L. Reyes
Dallas County Community College District	Jesus (Jess) Carreon
Del Mar College	Carlos A. Garcia
Laredo Community College	Ramon Dovalina
Mountain View College	Felix A. Zamora
Our Lady of the Lake University	Teresa M. Pollack
Palo Alto College	Ana M. Guzman
Southwest Texas Junior College	Ismael Sosa
Texas A&M University Kingsville	Rumaldo Z. Juarez
University of Houston Downtown	Max Castillo
University of Texas at Brownsville and Texas Southmost College	Juliet V. Garcia
University of Texas San Antonio	Ricardo Romo
Galveston College	Elva Concha LeBlanc
University of Texas Health Science Center at San Antonio	Francisco C. Cigarroa
Texas State Technical College	J. Gilbert Leal
University of Texas Pan American	Blandina Cardenas
16 of 43	
Washington	
0 of 2	

Note: There are a total 212 Hispanic Association of Colleges and Universities (HACU) member institutions (including Puerto Rico). There are 180 HACU member institutions (excluding Puerto Rico). Of the institutions, 56 have Latina/o CEOs.

Findings and Conclusions

In this section, answers will be provided to the seven questions that guided this study. In addition, as appropriate, additional comments are added to elaborate on the answers.

1. How many of the presidents or chancellors listed in the *2001 Higher Education Directory* (Rodenhouse, 2001) and the *2006 Higher Education Directory* (Burke, 2006) were Hispanic?

In 2001, a total of 90 Latina/o CEOs served in institutions of higher education in the continental United States. By 2006, the number had increased to 112, an increase of 22. In effect, this is only a 12.4% increase.

2. In how many states were the institutions of higher education with Latina/o CEOs located both in 2001 and 2006?

Only 13 states had institutions of higher education in which the president or chancellor was Latina/o in 2001. By 2006, the number of states with Latina/o CEOs in at least one institution of higher education increased to 22.

All the states in which Latina/o CEOs served in 2001 also had Latina/o CEOs in 2006.

It is interesting to note that nine states which did not have any Latina/o CEOs in 2001 had at least one Latina/o CEO in 2006: Alabama, Connecticut, Indiana, Maine, New Hampshire, Oklahoma, Oregon, Virginia, and Wisconsin.

The increase of the number of states from 13 in 2001 to 22 in 2006 with at least one Latina/o CEO represents almost a 70% increase in 5 years. It is also important to note that Hispanic individuals are now serving as CEOs of institutions of higher education in states in geographical areas of the country where Latinos historically have not been a major presence. Hispanic individuals now serve in states in the deep South, the Northeast, the Northwest, and the Midwest.

3. How many of the Hispanic presidents or chancellors in 2001 and 2006 were female? How many were male?

Of the total 90 Latina/o CEOs who served in 2001, 68 were males and only 22 were females. Males represented 76% of the total in 2001. By 2006, the 73 male Latino CEOs presented 65% of the total and the 39 females represented 35% of the total. Clearly, both the number of Latinas serving as CEOs and the portion they present of the total of Latina/o CEOs increased.

4. What was the gender, both in 2001 and 2006, of the Latina/o CEOs by institution type?

In 2001, 37 of the 55 Latina/o CEOs who served in associate's degree institutions were males, or 67% of the total. By 2006, the 40 of the 69 Latina/o CEOs in associate's degree institutions were male, or 58% of the total. The 29 Latina CEOs in community colleges represented 42% of the total in 2006.

All the Hispanic CEOs who served in baccalaureate institutions both in 2001 and in 2006 were males. In 2001, 12 of the Latina/o CEOs who served in Master's institutions were male; only one was female. By 2006, the number of male Hispanic CEOs who served in Master's institutions had remained the same (12), but the number of females had increased to 4.

A total of three males and three female Hispanic CEOs served in specialized institutions in 2001. In 2006, the number of males increased to five and the number of females remained the same.

In 2001, only males (three) served in doctoral institutions. In 2006, five males and one female served in doctoral institutions.

5. Using the Carnegie classification system,[5] in what type of institutions did the Latina/o presidents/chancellors serve, both in 2001 and 2006?

In 2001, almost two thirds of all Latina/o CEOs (61%) served in associate's degree institutions or community colleges; 55 of the total of 90. In 2006, 69 of the 112 Latina/o CEOs served in community colleges, still 61% of the total.

The second largest number of Latina/o CEOs served in master's level institutions. In 2001, 13 Latina/o CEOs served in this type of institutions compared to 16 in 2006. The third largest number of Latina/o CEOs served in specialized institutions; 6 in 2001 and 8 in 2006.

6. Which states had the most Hispanic presidents or chancellors in 2001 and 2006?

Both in 2001 and 2006, California had the largest number of Latina/o CEOs: 35 in 2001 and 35 in 2006. Texas was the state with the second largest number of Latina/o CEOs with 17 in 2001 and 20 in 2006. New Mexico was next with 8 in 2001 and 9 in 2006. Florida was the state with fourth largest number of Latina/o CEOs: 5 in 2001 and 8 in 2006.

It in interesting to note that Illinois, New Jersey, and Pennsylvania with four Latina/o CEOs each were in the top 10 states in 2006. Neither was in the top 10 states in 2001.

7. How many of the HSIs in 2007 had Hispanic presidents or chancellors? By state?

The 180 HSIs in the continental United States that were members in February 2007 of the HACU were included in this study. Of this total, only 56 or 31%, had Latina/o CEOs.

California was the state with the largest number of HSIs with Latino CEOs, 18 of 64, or 28% of the HSIs in that state. Texas was the state with the second largest number of HSIs served by Latina/o CEOs, 16 of 43, or 37% of the total. Florida followed, with 6 of the 10 HSIs in the state.

In some states with at least one HSI, no Latina/o served: Connecticut, Kansas, Massachusetts, North Carolina, Pennsylvania, and Washington.

Recommendations for Future Research

As noted in the section on the review of the literature, little or no scholarly research has been done on Latina/o leadership in institutions of higher education. The research that focuses on Latina/o presidents/chancellors is even more limited. Thus, much more research is needed.

Perhaps someone should replicate for the third time the studies done by Esquibel in 1977 and 15 years later in 1992. It has been 15 years since this study was last done. In addition, 5 years hence, the data in this chapter should be updated; an article using the same questions based on the 2011 *Directory of Higher Education* should be written, using three data points, 2001, 2006, and 2011.

Further research is needed to compare the career paths for female and male Hispanic presidents and chancellors. Do female Hispanic CEOs have different career paths than do males? What is different? What is common?

Leon (2003) recommended a model for developing Latinas/os for leadership positions in institutions of higher education. Which of the leadership development programs which have served Latinas/os have been most successful? Is there a model that is most effective?

Do Latinas/os have longer or shorter tenure as CEOs in institutions of higher education than do non-Latinas/os? What are the factors that influence this?

Needless to say, many questions remain unanswered about Latina/o leaders and CEOs in institutions of higher education in the United States. These suggestions might begin to answer some of them.

APPENDIX

Latino CEOs of Institutions of Higher Education, 2001

Name	Carnegie Classification	Institution, City
Arizona		
Jim Lopez	Specialized–Theological	American Indian College of the Assemblies of God, Phoenix
Homero Lopez	Associate's	Estrella Mountain Community College, Avondale
Tessa Martinez Pollack	Associate's	Glendale Community College, Glendale
John Cordova	Associate's	South Mountain Community College, Phoenix
California		
Patricia A. Sandoval	Associate's	Antelope Valley College, Lancaster
Thomas A. Arciniega	Master's	California State University, Bakersfield
Gloria Harrison	Associate's	Crafton Hills College
Manuel A. Esteban	Master's .	California State University, Chico
Alexander Gonzalez	Master's	California State University, San Marcos
Ruben Arminana	Master's	Sonoma State University, Rohnert Park
Susan Cota	Associate's	Las Positas College, Livermore
William M. Vega	N/A	Coast Community College District Administration Offices, Costa Mesa
Kenneth D. Yglesias	Associate's	Golden West College, Huntington Beach
Martha G. Romero	Associate's	College of the Siskiyous, Weed
Raul Rodriguez	Associate's	Los Medanos College, Pittsburg

(continued)

APPENDIX (Cont.)

Name	Carnegie Classification	Institution, City
Leo E. Chavez	N/A	Foothill-De Anza Community College District System Office, Los Altos Hills
Omero Suarez	N/A	Grossmont-Cuyamaca Community College District, El Cajon
Sherrill L. Amador	Associate's	Cuyamaca College, El Cajon
Ted Martinez Jr.	Associate's	Grossmont College, El Cajon
Gilbert M. Dominguez	Associate's	Imperial Valley College, Imperial
Sandra V. Serrano	Associate's	Bakersfield College, Bakersfield
Ernest H. Moreno	Associate's	East Los Angeles College, Monterey Park
Adriana D. Barerra	Associate's	Los Angeles Mission College, Sylmar
Benjamin T. Duran	Associate's	Merced College, Merced
Roberto Cruz	Baccalaureate	National Hispanic University, San Jose
Edward Hernandez Jr.	N/A	Ranchero Santiago Community College District, Santa Ana
Rita Cepeda	Associate's	Santa Ana College
Jesus Carreon	Associate's	Rio Honda College, Whittier
Sharon Diaz	Specialized–health	Samuel Merritt College, Oakland
Sharon S. Caballero	Associate's	San Bernardino Valley College, San Bernardino
Augustine P. Gallego	N/A	San Diego Community College District Administration Offices, San Diego
David Agosto	Associate's	San Diego City College
Rosa G. Perez	Associate's	Cañada College, Redwood City
Piedad F. Robertson	Associate's	Santa Monica College
Kevin M. Ramirez	Associate's	Sierra College, Rocklin
Serafin A. Zasueta	Associate's	Southwestern College, Chula Vista
Steven F. Arvizu	Associate's	Oxnard College
Larry Calderon	Associate's	Ventura College
Maria C. Sheehan	Associate's	Modesto Junior College
Colorado		
Tito Guerrero III	Master's	University of Southern Colorado, Pueblo
Thomas Gonzalez	Associate's	Front Range Community College, Westminster
David Maldonado Jr.	Specialized–theological	Iliff School of Theology, Denver
Florida		
Salvador Santiago-Negron	Specialized	Carlos Albizu University–Miami Campus
Eduardo J. Padron	Associate's	Miami-Dade Community College, Miami
Jose Vicente	Associate's	Miami-Dade Community College, Inter-American Campus
Sylvia Zapico	Associate's	Valencia Community College, Osceola Campus
Modesto A. Maidique	Doctoral	Florida International University, Miami
Illinois		
Bruno Bondavalli	Associate's	St. Augustine College, Chicago
Louisiana		
William J. Nunez, III	Associate's	Louisiana State University at Eunice
Darrell Rodriquez	Associate's	Louisiana Technical College-Oakdale Campus
Michigan		
Juan O. Olivarez	Associate's	Grand Rapids Community College
Juan E. Mestas	Master's	University of Michigan–Flint
Missouri		
Julio S. Leon	Baccalaureate	Missouri Southern State College, Joplin
Gustavo R. Valdez Ortiz	Associate's	Saint Louis Community College at Florissant Valley, Saint Louis

Name	Carnegie Classification	Institution, City
Manuel T. Pacheco	N/A	University of Missouri System Administration, Columbia
New Jersey		
Carlos Hernandez	Master's	New Jersey City University, Jersey City
Harold L. Paz	N/A	UMDNJ–Robert Wood Johnson Medical School, Piscataway
New Mexico		
Lawrence Pino	Associate's	Luna Vocational Technical Institute, A Community College, Las Vegas
Selimo Rael	Master's	New Mexico Highlands University, Las Vegas
Daniel H. Lopez	Doctoral	New Mexico Institute of Mining and Technology, Socorro
Raul Ramirez	Associate's	New Mexico State University Dona Ana Branch, Las Cruces
Sigfredo Maestas	Associate's	Northern New Mexico Community College, Espanola
John Pacheco	Associate's	Santa Fe Community College
Carlos B. Ramirez	Associate's	University of New Mexico–Los Alamos
Augustine Martinez	Associate's	University of New Mexico–Taos
New York		
Victor G. Alicea	Baccalaureate	Boricua College, New York
Antonio Perez	Associate's	City University of New York Borough of Manhattan Community College
Ricardo R. Fernandez	Master's	City University of New York Herbert H. Lehman College, Bronx
Dolores M. Fernandez	Associate's	City University of New York Hostos Community College, Bronx
Eduardo J. Marti	Associate's	City University of New York Queensborough Community College, Bayside
Ileana Rodriguez	Specializes–theological	New York Theological Seminary, New York
Pennsylvania		
Roy Flores	N/A	Community College of Allegheny County College Office, Pittsburg
Happy C. Fernandez	Specialized–art, music, design	Moore College of Art and Design, Philadelphia
Texas		
Enrique Solis	Associate's	Palo Alto College, San Antonio
Ramon Dominquez	Associate's	El Paso Community College
Ruth Burgos-Sasscer	Associate's	Houston Community College
Ramon H. Dovalina	Associate's	Laredo Community College
Louis J. Rodriguez	Master's	Midwestern State University, Wichita Falls
Richard M. Sanchez	Associate's	Navarro College, Corsicana
Adena Williams Loston	Associate's	San Jacinto College South, Houston
Ismael Sosa	Associate's	Southwest Texas Junior College, Uvalde
Leonardo de la Garza	Associate's	Tarrant County College District, Fort Worth
Marc A. Cisneros	Doctoral	Texas A&M University–Kingsville
Juliet V. Garcia	Associate's	Texas Southmost College, Brownsville
William E. Segura	N/A	Texas State Technical College System Office, Waco
J. Gilbert Leal	Associate's	Texas State Technical College-Harlingen
Max Castillo	Baccalaureate	University of Houston–Downtown
Juliet V. Garcia	Master's	University of Texas at Brownsville
Miguel A. Nevarez	Master's	University of Texas–Pan American, Edinburg
Ricardo Romo	Master's	University of Texas at San Antonio
Lydia Ledesma-Reese	Associate's	Skagit Valley College, Mount Vernon

(continued)

APPENDIX (Cont.)

Latino CEOs of Institutions of Higher Education, 2006

Name	Carnegie Classification	Institution, City
Alabama		
Anthony L. Molina	Associate's	Trenholm State Technical College, Montgomery
Arizona		
Homero Lopez	Associate's	Estrella Mountain Community College, Avondale
Anna Solley	Associate's	Phoenix College
Roy Flores	Associate's	Pima County Community College, Tucson
Raul Ramirez	Associate's	Pima County Community College East Campus, Tucson
Richard Duran	Associate's	Pima County Community College Desert Vista Campus, Tucson
Angel Cabrera	Master's	Thunderbird, Garvin School of International Management, Glendale
California		
Jose M. Ortiz	Associate's	Allan Hancock College, Santa Maria
J. Michael Ortiz	Master's	California State Polytechnic University, Pomona
Diane Cordero de Noriega	Master's	California State University-Monterey Bay, Seaside
Alexander Gonzalez	Master's	California State University, Sacramento
Ruben Arminana	Master's	Sonoma State University, Rohnert Park
Noelia Vela	Associate's	Cerritos College, Norwalk
Susan Cota	N/A	Chabot-Las Positas Community College District, Pleasanton
Kenneth D. Yglesias	N/A	Coast Community College District Administration Offices, Costa Mesa
Peter Garcia	Associate's	Los Medanos College, Pittsburg
Omero Suarez	N/A	Grossmont-Cuyamaca Community College District, El Cajon
Ted Martinez, Jr.	Associate's	Grossmont College, El Cajon
Sandra V. Serrano	N/A	Kern Community College District, Bakersfield
Ernest H Moreno	Associate's	East Los Angeles College, Los Angeles
Adriana Barrera	Associate's	Los Angeles Mission College, Sylmar
Daniel A. Castro	Associate's	Los Angeles Trade-Tech College, Los Angeles
Francisco C. Rodriguez	Associate's	Cosumnes River College, Sacramento
Carlos Lopez	Baccalaureate	Menlo College, Atherton
Benjamin T. Duran	Associate's	Merced College
David P. Lopez	Baccalaureate	National Hispanic University, San Jose
Cecilia Cervantes	Associate's	College of Alameda, Alameda
Edward Hernandez, Jr.	N/A	Rancho Santiago Community College District, Santa Ana
Erlinda Martinez	Associate's	Santa Ana College
Juan Vasquez	Associate's	Santiago Canyon College, Orange
Sharon C. Diaz	Specialized–other health	Samuel Merritt College, Oakland
Rita Cepeda	Associate's	San Diego Mesa College, San Diego
Raul Rodriguez	Associate's	San Joaquin Delta College, Stockton
John B. Romo	Associate's	Santa Barbara City College
Norma L. Hernandez	Associate's	Southwestern College, Chula Vista
France A. Cordova	Doctoral	University of California, Riverside
Lydia Ledesma-Reese	Associate's	Oxnard College
Rosa Carlson	Associate's	Porterville College
Paulette Perfumo	Associate's	Solano Community College
Gloria Harrison	Associate's	Crafton Hills College
Victoria Muñoz Richart	Associate's	Mira Costa Community College
Maria C. Sheehan	Associate's	College of the Desert

(continued)

Name	Carnegie Classification	Institution, City
Colorado		
Christine Johnson	Associate's	Community College of Denver
Joseph Garcia	Associate's	Pikes Peak Community College, Colorado Springs
Connecticut		
Wilfredo Nieves	Associate's	Middlesex Community-Technical College, Middletown
Florida		
Modesto A. Maidique	Doctoral	Florida International University, Miami
Larry A. Calderon	Associate's	Broward Community College, Fort Lauderdale
Salvador Santiago-Negron	Specialized–other	Carlos Albizu University Miami Campus
Eduardo J. Padron	Associate's	Miami-Dade College, Miami
Jose Vicente	Associate's	Miami-Dade College, North
Rolando Montoya	Associate's	Miami-Dade College, Wolfson
Maria Vallejo	Associate's	Provost of Central Campus Palm Beach CC
Sylvia Zapico	Associate's	Richard J. Daley College
Illinois		
Sylvia Ramos	Associate's	City Colleges of Chicago Richard J. Daley College, Chicago
Patricia Granados	Associate's	Triton College, River Grove
Michael J. Vinciguerra	Master's	University of Saint Francis, Joliet
Zoila C. Brennan	Associate's	St. Augustine College
Indiana		
Jose G. Valtierra	Associate's	Ivy Tech Community College of Indiana-Northwest, Gary
Louisiana		
Darrell Rodriguez	Associate's	Louisiana Technical College Oakdale Campus, Oakdale
William J. Nunez. III	Associate's	Louisiana State University at Eunice
Maine		
James O. Ortiz	Associate's	Southern Maine Community College, South Portland
Michigan		
Juan R. Olivarez	Associate's	Grand Rapids Community College
Juan E. Mestas	Master's	University of Michigan–Flint
Missouri		
Julio S. Leon	Baccalaureate	Missouri Southern State University, Joplin
New Hampshire		
Peter L. Mora	Associate's	Atlantic Cape Community College, Mays Landing
New Jersey		
Joann La Perla-Morales	Associate's	Middlesex County College, Edison
Carlos Hernandez	Master's	New Jersey City University, Jersey City
Harold L. Paz	Specialized–medical	UMDNJ–Robert Wood Johnson Medical School, Piscataway
Sara Torres	Specialized–medical	UMDNJ–School of Nursing, Newark
New Mexico		
Leroy Sanchez	Associate's	Luna Community College, Las Vegas
Manny M. Aragon	Master's	New Mexico Highlands University, Las Vegas
Daniel H. Lopez	Doctoral	New Mexico Institute of Mining and Technology, Socorro
Margie C. Huerta	Associate's	New Mexico State University Dona Ana Branch, Las Cruces
Felicia Casados	Associate's	New Mexico State University Grants Branch, Grants
Jose Griego	Associate's	Northern New Mexico College, Espanola
Louis E. Caldera	Doctoral	University of New Mexico Main Campus, Albuquerque
Carlos B. Ramirez	Associate's	University of New Mexico–Los Alamos
Alicia F. Chavez	Associate's	University of New Mexico–Taos

(continued)

APPENDIX (Cont.)

Name	Carnegie Classification	Institution, City
New York		
Mildred Garcia	Associate's	Berkeley College, New York
Victor G. Alicea	Baccalaureate/ Associate's	Boricua College, New York
Antonio Perez	Associate's	City University of New York Borough of Manhattan Community College
Ricardo R. Fernandez	Master's	City University of New York Herbert H. Lehman College, Bronx
Dolores Fernandez	Associate's	Hostos Community College-City University of New York, Bronx
Eduardo J. Marti	Associate's	City University of New York Queensborough Community College, Bayside
Oklahoma		
John J. Fernandes	Specialized– medical	Oklahoma State University Center for Health Sciences College of Osteopathic Medicine, Tulsa
Oregon		
Rita B. Cavin	Associate's	Linn-Benton Community College
Pennsylvania		
Happy C. Fernandez	Specialized–art, music, design	Moore College of Art and Design, Philadelphia
F. Javier Cevallos	Master's	Kutztown University of Pennsylvania, Kutztown
Miguel Angel Corzo	Specialized–art, music, design	University of the Arts, Philadelphia
Cynthia Azari	Associate's	Butler County Community College
Texas		
Ana M. Guzman	Associate's	Palo Alto College, San Antonio
Jesus (Jess) Carreon	N/A	Dallas County Community College District Office
Felix A. Zamora	Associate's	Mountain View College, Dallas
Carlos A. Garcia	Associate's	Del Mar College, Corpus Christi
Elva Concha Le Blanc	Associate's	Galveston College
Fena Garza	Associate's	Houston Community College—Southeast Campus
Ramon H. Dovalina	Associate's	Laredo Community College
Richard M. Sanchez	Associate's	Navarro College, Corsicana
Teresa M. Pollack	Master's	Our Lady of the Lake University, San Antonio
Tito Guerrero	Master's	Stephen F. Austin State University, Nacogdoches
Leonardo De La Garza	Associate's	Tarrant County College District, Fort Worth
Michael Saenz	Associates	Tarrant County College District, Northeast Campus, Fort Worth
Rumaldo Z. Juarez	Doctoral	Texas A&M University–Kingsville
William E. Segura	N/A	Texas Sate Technical College System Office, Waco
J. Gilbert Leal	Associate's	Texas State Technical College Harlingen, Harlingen
Max Castillo	Baccalaureate	University of Houston–Downtown
Juliet V. Garcia	Master's	University of Texas at Brownsville
Blandina Cardenas	Master's	University of Texas–Pan America, Edinburg
Ricardo Romo	Master's	University of Texas at San Antonio
Francisco G. Cigarroa	Specialized– medical	University of Texas Health Science Center at San Antonio
Herlinda Glasscock	Associate's	North Lake College–Dallas County CC District
Albert Reyes	Baccalaureate	University of the Americas–Baptist University
Ismael Sosa	Associate's	Southwest Texas Jr. College
Virginia		
Terrence E. Suarez	Associate's	Mountain Empire Community College, Big Stone Gap
Wisconsin		
Carlos Santiago	Doctoral	University of Wisconsin–Milwaukee

Notes

1. The terms *Hispanic* and *Latino* are used interchangeably to identify people from the Caribbean, Central America, Cuba, Mexico, Puerto Rico, South America, Spain and other countries where Spanish is the primary language. In addition, the term *Chicano* is used because it was used in some of items cited. In addition, instead of using *president or chancellor* throughout, *CEO* is also used to mean the same thing: the chief executive officer of an institution.

2. A number of definitions of HSIs are available. In federal legislation, HSIs are defined as 2-and 4-year institutions of higher education at which Latinos constitute a minimum of 25% of the total undergraduate enrollment (see Public Law 102-325, as amended). In addition, a number of lists of HSIs are available. The Developing Hispanic-Serving Institutions program of the U.S. Department of Education—Title V of the Higher Education Act defines HSIs as nonprofit institutions that have at least 25% Hispanic full-time equivalent enrollment and, of the Hispanic student enrollment, at least 50% low income (U.S. Department of Education, 2007). According to Santiago (2006), the Developing HSI program office "produces a list of institutions that have been awarded program funds" (p. 8). Thus, this list does not represent all the institutions that meet this definition. The Office of Civil Rights in the U.S. Department of Education also maintains a list of HSIs, using IPEDs data. Santiago notes that although this list "uses the basic definition of HSIs in the legislation, more institutions are included than would meet the legislative definition of HSIs because it includes for-profit institutions, which are not included in the definition of HSIs in the HEA" (p. 8). The Hispanic Association of Colleges and Universities (HACU) defines HSIs as colleges, universities, and systems or districts in which total Hispanic enrollment constitutes a minimum of 25% of the total enrollment, including full-time and part-time students whether at the undergraduate or graduate levels (including professional schools) or both (head count, for-credit students) In February 2007, HACU listed 212 institutions that met this definition and were members (Hispanic Association of Colleges and Universities, 2007b). This list of 180 institutions was used in this study—the 212 institutions, minus the 32 institutions in Puerto Rico.

3. The Carnegie Classification of Institutions of Higher Education classified institutions based on their degree-granting activities in 1995-1996 through 1997-1998. The 2000 Carnegie Classification includes the following classifications: (a) doctoral or research universities, divided into two subcategories (extensive and intensive); (b) master's colleges and universities, subdivided into two categories (I and II), baccalaureate colleges, subdivided into three categories (liberal arts, general, and baccalaureate or associate's); (c) associate's colleges; (d) specialized institutions, subdivided into nine categories; and (e) tribal colleges and universities. In this study, only the broader general categories, not the subcategories, are used (see Carnegie Foundation for the Advancement of Teaching, 2001, pp. 1-2). The revised, updated classification was not available when the *2006 Higher Education Directory* went to press (Burke, 2006, p. xlix).

4. See Note 2 for more definitions of HSIs.

5. See Note 3.

References

Acevedo, B. A. (1979). *Socialization: The Mexican-American mid-level administrator in Texas institutions of higher education.* Unpublished doctoral dissertation, University of Texas at Austin.

American Association of Community Colleges. (2006). *Facts 2006: Community college facts at a glance.* Washington, DC: Author.

Burke, J. M. (Ed.). (2006). *2006 higher education directory.* Falls Church, VA: Higher Education Publications.

Carnegie Foundation for the Advancement of Teaching. (2001). *The Carnegie classification of institutions of higher education.* Menlo Park, CA: Author.

Carnevale, A. P., & Fry, R. A. (1999). *Crossing the great divide: Can we achieve equity when generation Y goes to college?* Princeton, NJ: Educational Testing Service.

Cipres, E. L. (1999). A case study of perceived characteristics and life events that enabled Latinas to become California community college presidents. *Dissertation Abstracts International, 61* (01), 36.

Cook, B. J., & Cordova, D. L. (2006). *Minorities in higher education: Twenty-second annual status report.* Washington, DC: American Council on Education.

Esquibel, A. (1977). *The Chicano administrator in colleges and universities in the Southwest.* Unpublished doctoral dissertation, University of New Mexico, Albuquerque.

Esquibel, A. (1992). *The career mobility of Chicano administrators in higher education: The Chicano administrator in colleges and universities of the Southwest—Fifteen year replication study.* Boulder, CO: Western Interstate Commission for Higher Education.

Flores, O. (1999). In an exquisite voice (en una voz exquisita): A case study of one Latina community college chancellor. *Dissertation Abstracts International, 60* (12), 4261.

Gorena, M. (1994). Hispanic women in higher education administration: Factors that positively influence or hinder advancement to leadership positions. *Dissertation Abstracts International, 55* (01), 52.

Haro, R. (1995). Held to a higher standard: Latino executive selection in higher education. In R. V. Padilla & R. C. Chavez (Eds.), *The leaning ivory tower: Latino professors in American universities* (pp. 189–208). Albany: State University of New York Press.

Haro, R. (2005). Experiences of presidents of color: When perceptions challenge reality. In D. Leon (Ed.), *Lessons in leadership: Executive leadership programs for advancing diversity in higher education* (pp. 57–83). New York: Elsevier/JAI. Haro, R., & Lara, J. F. (2003). Latinos and administrative positions in American Higher education. In J. Castellanos & L. Jones (Eds.), *The majority in the minority: Expanding the representation of Latina/o faculty, administrators and students in higher education* (pp. 153–175). Sterling, VA: Stylus.

Hispanic Association of Colleges and Universities. (2007a, February 16). *HACU 101: The Hispanic Association of Colleges and Universities.* Retrieved February 16, 2007, from http://www.hacu.net/ hacu/ HACU_1011_EN.asp?SnID=945587643

Hispanic Association of Colleges and Universities. (2007b, February 22). *2007 membership dues information.* Retrieved February 22, 2007, from http://www.hacu.net/hacu/Dues_EN.asp?SnID=945587643

Knowlton, L. M. (1993). Leadership in a different voice: An ethnographic study of a Latina chief executive officer in a California community college. *Dissertation Abstracts International, 53* (10), 3431.

Leon, D. J. (Ed.). (2003). *Latinos in higher education.* New York: Elsevier/JAI.

Leon, D. J. (Ed.). (2005). *Lessons in leadership: Executive leadership programs for advancing diversity in higher education.* New York: Elsevier/JAI.

Martinez, R. O. (2005). Latino demographic and institutional issues in higher education: Implications for leadership development. In D. J. Leon (Ed.), *Lessons in leadership: Executive leadership programs for advancing diversity in higher education* (pp. 17–55). New York: Elsevier/JAI.

Mata, D. N. (1997). A profile of Latino community college presidents: A multi-method study of leadership development and functioning. *Dissertation Abstracts International, 58* (10), 3817.

Pew Hispanic Center. (2006). *A statistical portrait of Hispanic individuals at mid-decade.* Washington, DC: Author.

Public Law 102-325 (20 U.S.C. 1059c), Section 302(d)(l), most recently amended December 30, 1993, in Section 2.7 of P.L. 1103.208.

Rodenhouse, M. P. (Ed.). (2001). *2001 higher education directory.* Falls Church, VA: Higher Education Publications.

Rodriguez, F. C. (2006). Immigrant lives and presidential dreams: Exploring the experiences of Latino community college presidents. *Dissertation Abstracts International, 67* (02).

Ruiz, A. (1990). A study of leadership behavior and the identification of special problems as perceived by Hispanic community college presidents throughout the United States. *Dissertation Abstracts International, 51* (12), 4003.

Santiago, D. A. (2006). *Inventing Hispanic-serving institutions (HSIs): The basics.* Washington, DC: Excelencia in Education.

Silva, S. (2003). A culture of success: An examination of the life experiences and professional challenges of Mexican-American female academic and student affairs administrators at four institutions in the University of Texas system. *Dissertation Abstracts International, 65* (03), 789.

U.S. Department of Education. (2007). *Developing Hispanic-serving institutions program—Title V. Definition of Hispanic-serving institutions.* Retrieved February 22, 2007, from http://www.ed .gov/programs/idueshsi/ definition.html

Valverde, L. A. (2003). *Leaders of color in higher education: Unrecognized triumphs in harsh institutions.* New York: Altamira. Western Interstate Commission for Higher Education, ACT, & the College Board. (2003). *Knocking at the college door: Projections of high school graduates by state, income and race/ethnicity, 1998–2018.* Denver, CO: Author.

Western Interstate Commission for Higher Education, ACT, & the College Board. (2003). *Knocking at the college door: Projections of high school graduates by state, income and race/ethnicity, 1998–2018.* Denver, CO: Author.

CHAPTER 36
DECISION MAKING IN HISTORICALLY BLACK COLLEGES AND UNIVERSITIES: DEFINING THE GOVERNANCE CONTEXT

JAMES T. MINOR

Decision-making practices at historically Black colleges and universities are the subject of healthy criticism. However, many conclusions are drawn in the absence of governance research on HBCUs. To better understand and evaluate the appropriateness of decision-making in these institutions, I use case study data to define three key contextual aspects of an HBCU that influence governance: (a) faculty traditions; (b) the paradox of mission; and (c) a racialized climate. Given these findings, I consider alternative theoretical frames to more accurately assess governance structures and decision-making practices in HBCUs.

At a time when affirmative action in higher education is under attack, considering the health of historically Black colleges and universities (HBCUs) is increasingly important (Brown & Freeman, 2004). Since their inception, these institutions have collectively championed access and opportunity for African Americans (Allen & Jewell, 2002). On a larger scale HBCUs serve an important educational, economic, and social function in America by sustaining a pipeline of educated African Americans (Brown & Davis, 2001). Additionally, African Americans who attend HBCUs demonstrate greater satisfaction with their college experience, academic achievement, and developmental gains when compared to those who attend predominately White institutions (Allen, 1992; Davis, 1991; Fleming, 1984). Although HBCUs represent just 3% of all institutions of higher education, they grant roughly 25% of baccalaureate degrees awarded to African Americans (Nettles & Perna, 1997).

Despite the accomplishments of HBCUs they are the subjects of considerable criticism within the higher education community. Presidents of historically Black colleges and universities are often accused of being autocratic and the mission of these institutions is said to compromise academic quality while upholding segregation (Hamilton, 2002). Moreover, financial instability, accreditation challenges, and questionable governance structures are constant quandaries associated with HBCUs.

However, the mission and plight of HBCUs situates them in distinctly different contexts that potentially affect campus decision-making and leadership practices (Drewry & Doermann, 2001). Decision-making contexts can be affected by structural, cultural, or situational distinctions that leaders of these institutions must take into account. If governance is the structure by which decisions are made determining the direction of a campus, then research on what affects decision making is important. While the distinctiveness of HBCUs is widely recognized, defining what contextual aspects potentially affect decision-making practices has not been a focal point of scholarship. As a way to understand the challenges associated with governance in HBCUs, this chapter utilizes a case study to define the decision-making context at one historically Black university. In doing so, those concerned with the status of HBCUs may be able to appraise leadership practices and institutional effectiveness. To begin, I frame the discussion by defining governance and decision making from the research literature. In the following sections, I outline the case study, define aspects of the decision-making context, and consider the ways governance is affected.

Defining Governance and Decision-Making

In higher education the phrase "shared governance" is often used to suggest collaborative management of an institution (Ramo, 1998). However, the phrase can connote multiple and sometimes conflicting ideas about how a campus should make decisions. In a recent national study, Tierney and Minor (2003) found that campus constituents define shared governance in three ways:

1. Collaborative—university constituents collectively make decisions about the direction of the campus.

2. Stratified—systems of governance where certain constituents make decisions according to decision type (e.g., faculty decide on curriculum and the administration determines policy and budgetary issues).

3. Consultative—governance structures in which the president reserves decision-making authority with the expectation that they consult with university constituents before making decisions.

As stated earlier, for many institutions shared governance remains an ambiguous phrase that can take on different meanings at various times (Hamilton, 1999; Keller, 2001). For this study, I define governance as the configuration of decision-making bodies (i.e., the structure that grants authority). The organization of governing bodies can vary significantly from campus to campus (Minor, 2003). Decision making then is considered the process by which those granted authority make determinations on issues under consideration. Also important to understanding governance is the context in which decisions are made (e.g., the political, academic, financial, social, cultural, and situational circumstances that can influence decision making). Decision-making environments are fluid and can, in some cases, influence decisions more than static structures.

Research on governance in higher education is limited (Kezar & Eckel, in press), and research on governance at HBCUs is virtually nonexistent. In the last two decades, a time when higher education has experienced drastic change, governance issues remain understudied. The role of adjunct professors in determining curriculum, for example, is a relatively new issue that challenges conventional governance structures. Decision making around technology and distance education is another concern worthy of investigation. Recent legal decisions on the issue of affirmative action will cause many campuses to reconsider admission policies. Perhaps the latest governance matter is the concern over academic freedom and privacy in the wake of the terrorist attacks in the United States. Since September 11, 2001, campuses are experiencing increased government influence over issues such as the availability of student information and financial aid. Each of these decisions invites the question of who should decide. In what area of decision making should faculty be involved? How much authority does the president have? What should be the role of the board? Answers to these questions will be different for each campus. While the majority of four-year colleges and universities will face similar issues irrespective of institutional status, each decision is made while taking into account a unique set of circumstances that can influence decision outcomes.

The handful of studies conducted on governance issues focuses almost exclusively on structural components or the involvement of faculty (Baldwin & Leslie, 2001; Longin, 2002; Ramo, 1998; Randall & Miller, 1999; Schuster, 1989). Structural perspectives alone do not fully explain governance activity. Fewer studies consider the context in which university decisions are made (Berdahl, 1991; Duderstadt, 2001; Gumport, 2000; Mingle, 2000). Taking into account social, political, and cultural perspectives in addition to structure provide a fuller picture of governance activity. More recently, scholars point to the changing landscape of higher education and the need to create governance structures that are more responsive (Benjamin & Carroll, 1999; Duderstadt, 2001; Ferren, Kennan, & Lerch, 2001). Because research on governance at HBCUs has been ignored, differences that exist between HBCUs and predominately White institutions, with respect to decision making, are not well documented.

Determining contextual differences that influence decision making or leadership practices are important when assessing institutional effectiveness. I argue that criticisms endured by HBCUs and their leaders have been made in the absence of contextual understanding that may shed a different light on the appropriateness of governance structures and decision-making practices used in these institutions. Unfortunately, scholarship on governance forces scholars, policymakers, and campus leaders to speculate about how well or poorly HBCUs are governed. The crux of this chapter sits at the intersection of research and practice. Before conclusions can be drawn about the effectiveness of decision-making practices in HBCUs there is a need to research the context in which governance activity takes place. In what has been classified as a distinctly different institutional setting, the question that focuses this study asks: What contextual factors come into play as campus leaders make decisions at HBCUs?

An Interpretive Approach to Developing a Case

As a theoretical guide for this study, I employ an interpretive perspective that considers intentions, circumstances, and actions to be novel and filled with multiple meaning (Denzin, 1988). This perspective is not predictive but rather seeks to make sense out of social interaction within a particular context (Glaser & Strauss, 1967). Given the paucity of research on governance within HBCUs, it is important to develop a fundamental understanding before theorizing about why particular challenges exist. Consequently, my approach to this research is devoted to interpretation and definition based on an analysis of interviews and a review of documents (Glesne & Peshkin, 1992; Yin, 1984). A case study method provides a useful means to explore what contextual factors might influence decision making within a particular institutional setting. Additionally, some scholars argue that taking into account the culture and traditions of an institution is an essential element to higher education research (Freeman, 1998; Tierney, 1988). An interpretive view is particularly useful for determining contextual factors that those within HBCUs deem important. This approach can also neutralize potential biases that come into play when precepts used to evaluate predominately White institutions are applied to HBCUs.

The case presented was part of a three-year research project on governance in higher education. The campus visit was conducted in a series of emblematic site visits to four-year institutions. Due to confidentiality agreements, the name of the institution and participants are not revealed. The pseudonym Urban State University is used for the campus and only the positions of participants are disclosed. Participants were purposively sampled with the help of "insiders" and selected according to criteria set by researchers (Glesne & Peshkin, 1992). To enhance trustworthiness of these data, participants included a cross-section of campus constituents that represent diverse views on campus governance and hold various positions within the institution. This study of decision-making context is couched within a larger frame that seeks to discern institutional aspects that influence campus governance. With that goal, participants, through a series of semistructured questions, were asked to consider campus governance while taking into account both internal and external factors that might influence decisions or decision makers.

During the site visit, I conducted hour-long interviews with 17 members of the campus. Included were the president, provost, past and present leaders of the faculty senate, department chairs, long-time faculty members, and newcomers. In addition to the interviews, I also collected governance related documents such as the faculty handbook, minutes from faculty senate meetings, strategic planning documents, and documents that define shared governance for the campus. To analyze these data, I used a grounded theory method that involves an inductive strategy to develop themes based on a constant comparison of these data (Glaser & Strauss, 1967).

Urban State University

Urban State (USU) was founded in the late 1800s as a small teachers college for Blacks by an American Baptist missionary group. For many years, the institution operated under religious influence with an excellent reputation for producing Black teachers. The southern state in which it resides began providing financial support for the institution in the mid-1900s, making it a public university. Today the student population at USU remains 95% Black. The university is classified as a research-intensive institution and is located in an urban setting. USU offers a range of undergraduate and graduate programs through eight schools and colleges. While the student population remains primarily African American, Urban State has an increasingly diverse collection of faculty, one third of whom are adjunct.

In the state, much has been made about appropriation disparities made by the legislature. The historically Black universities in the state have traditionally received significantly less support than predominately White institutions. USU is designated as the urban institution of the state but has traditionally lacked the resources to provide extensive graduate and professional programs. Still, USU maintains a moderately healthy institution; but, due to funding disparities, often has had contentious relations with its state government. Urban State maintains fidelity to its historical mission of providing access and quality education to African Americans. Through emphasis on teaching and student development, USU seeks to inspire positive social change in society through its students.

The governance structure is comprised of a governor-appointed Commissioner of Higher Education responsible for administering board policies. The 12-member Board of Trustees is appointed by the governor to staggered terms and governs all public institutions in the state. The president of Urban State was recently appointed by the board and in the last two years has selected a new provost who also serves as the vice president for academic affairs. Faculty governance at USU is troubled by internal conflicts, an ineffective committee structure, and a reputation for being dysfunctional. The relationship between the faculty senate and president has traditionally been litigious. The senate, for example, forwarded three votes of no confidence in the previous president. However, the current senate president and the administration have a fragile but working relationship. The senate is a deliberative body and their authority is limited to the forwarding of recommendations. Academic matters such as curriculum change are decided within committees located in individual colleges and program approval is granted by the board leaving the senate with little responsibility.

With new leadership and a surge of financial resources Urban State has recently undergone aggressive strategic planning with ambitions to expand and significantly strengthen academic programs. This includes improvements to the physical plant, improving faculty salaries, and investment in technological capabilities. There is also a clear institutional shift toward increased research capacity among faculty and an enhancement of graduate and professional programs. As plans for the campus move forward, what institutional circumstances, political forces, or cultural aspects will influence decision making?

The Function of Campus Governance

Although the governance structure at Urban State resembles that of many institutions, it is important to understand the relationship between internal constituencies (e.g., the president, senior administrators, and faculty). The level of authority and interaction between these bodies significantly influences the function of governance. As a way to understand governance at USU, I consider not only the structure but also the function of particular bodies and how they interact.

At USU, the president reserves final decision-making power, faculty authority is limited to making recommendations, and the board is seen as external but important. According to the immediate past president of the senate, "Faculty governance on this campus has meant a small group of familiar faculty who stay in the loop while the large majority walk around either uninterested or marginalized." The senate suffers from internal disputes that inhibit organized faculty participation. An engineering professor of two years remarked, "It seems to me that if the faculty could ever get past themselves they might be able to get something done." Additionally, faculty at USU teach a standard of four courses per semester and receive salaries well below the state and regional average. As a result, their participation in governance is often limited and cynical.

Shared governance is currently being reconsidered on the campus. In an attempt to improve faculty governance, the provost, after soliciting faculty input, presented a statement to define shared governance for the campus. The document implies a collaborative model stating that "shared governance means and requires full participation of the faculty, staff, and students on all matters that directly or indirectly affect the environment at the University." However, the meaning of "full participation" is vague and the declaration is confused. In the same paragraph the document states that "administrators will act upon such recommendations and provide timely rationale for any modification or rejection of input received," which suggests a more consultative model of decision making.

In addition to an ambiguous statement on shared governance, other internal challenges include faculty apathy, broken trust, and a lack of communication between the faculty and administrators. This is most often expressed through quarrels between the faculty and administration over access to information and inclusive decision making. According to a sociology professor, "The leadership in the senate is not well respected and it has a history of being confrontational so I think over the years a lot of faculty see that as their purpose." The senate lacks an agenda for the faculty which results in ineffective senate committees. When asked about the activity of the senate, one political science professor laughed saying, "I don't pay attention to the senate. They are essentially irrelevant to what happens on this campus."

"The nature of the faculty is to resign themselves to whatever decisions are made by the administration and then complain about them later," one faculty member remarked. The senate president stated, "For a long time the senate and administration have had a distrusting relationship. We sent up three votes of no confidence in the last president. The combination of distrust and disempowerment has led to the disenfranchisement of many faculty." Symbolic of faculty power, the votes of no confidence in the last president were virtually ineffective in his departure.

The new administration has aggressively sought to repair faculty relations by employing more open systems of decision making, but for now, the history of faculty-administrator relations supercedes those efforts. The provost, in an effort to support faculty governance despite the dysfunction of the senate, created alternative decision-making bodies to advance campus initiatives. "The provost goes out of his way to ensure that faculty are involved and there is the sense that the president is open," said one kinesiology professor. The provost explained:

> We [the new administration] know that faculty governance has been an issue in the past. This is part of the reason that I've gone overboard trying the revise documents that guide our process and trying to convince faculty that there is a place for them at the table.

Similarly, the president stated:

> I'm open to the voice of the faculty but I'm also disturbed that it is sometimes uninformed, irrational, and hostile. Faculty governance is something we're working on but we've got a ways to go before we get to the point where the faculty and administrators can come together and make decisions in the best interest of the campus without the past or personalities getting in the way.

In spite of such efforts there is a small contingent of faculty who are suspicious of the board's agenda and the new administration. Their suspicion is expressed by antagonistic questioning of the president during public events and regular correspondence with the board. "We are here to ensure this place [USU] is not run like a plantation as the board would have it," asserted the faculty leader of this group. This contingent regularly indicts the president and senior staff with claims that the campus is being run "irresponsibly" and at that the president is "too heavily influenced by the board." They have also made accusation of improprieties that range from illegal hiring practices to compromising the integrity of the university. Most faculty on the campus, when asked about this group, acknowledged their concerns but were disapproving of their tactics.

Like many institutions, the structure and function of governance at USU could be improved; however, it is operable. The president maintains control of campus and commands the respect from most USU constituents. The faculty quarrel about not having more authority, but run an ineffective senate. Additionally, the board is distant and maintains less than admirable relations with Urban State. According to an associate provost, "Over the years the board has not been a good friend; USU is viewed as the step-child." One faculty member suggested that "the president and everyone has been deceived and let down by our predominately White and conservative board." Many at Urban State expressed concerns about the lack of representation and advocacy on the board and they often related to funding disparities.

Combating External Perceptions

In addition to the internal governance challenges, Urban State faces a number of external and political forces that affect the institution. The majority of the participants (14 of 17) expressed a belief that USU, because of its status as an HBCU, is perceived as an inferior academic institution. This problem poses an internal challenge to uphold a positive institutional image to combat negative perceptions that exist. In fact, a significant portion of the USU strategic plan concerns "enhancing the image." When asked about external perceptions of the institution across the state, many participants expressed feelings of regret that "USU rarely receives the credit it deserves." Moreover, many felt as though the university is often unfairly depicted by the media which further perpetuates negative images of USU. Participants described the external challenges faced by the institution as undeserved and often motivated by race. A long-time faculty member in the School of Health Professions explained:

> As a White man involved in state politics, I'll sometimes have another White guy come up to me and say 'you know I hired a USU graduate and. . . .' have a negative comment attached not knowing that I work here. USU seems to get a bad rap in the state just because it's Black. I've worked at a number of other White institutions and have lived long enough to know that White graduates sometimes perform poorly also. Many times the ole southern racist ideal that Blacks are intellectually inferior plays into how the institution is handled by the state.

Another White professor recalled an incident she felt was unfairly being played out by the media. According to her, "If it can go wrong and it's bad, it's at Urban State, if you let the local paper and television stations tell it." She went on to say:

> A few years ago a student was stabbed on campus and it had little to do with USU per se. The incident happened on a Monday and the perpetrator was not a student. The stabbing was a result of an off-campus dispute that carried over from the weekend. That made front page news! In the same paper, it was reported that a student had been pushed over a balcony and killed in a football dorm at [a predominately White state institution] and that was on the third page of the sports section in an article about this big [she makes a hand gesture].

The associate dean of the School of Education insisted that the external challenges USU face have to do with its name:

> To many in higher education the title of "historically Black" still connotes a tradition of teaching colleges and second-rate education for Blacks who couldn't go to White schools. The idea of supporting an HBCU as the flagship research institution, in the minds of many, does not make sense. I think that the tradition and plight of the institution, not to mention that it's Black, prevents a lot of people from seeing it as a competitor with the White schools in the state.

The associate vice provost used a teaching parable to explain Urban State's external challenges:

> It's like when you teach any class, the assumption is that everyone has an A. That's the starting point and you have to do something substandard to receive a lower grade. I've been here for 36 years and it seems to me that USU, as far as the state and board are concerned, starts with an F and continuously has to prove that we're worthy of an A. To them, it's like our ice is not as cold.

A graduate student agreed that "there is a negative stereotype attached to USU." "I have attended [a predominately White institution in the state] and there is virtually no difference in instruction," she claimed.

Others pointed to the economic and political implications of state support for USU. Because the campus is located in the capitol city, which represents the only metropolitan area in the state, some suggest that USU poses a threat to White campuses. A biology professor explained:

> If the state supported USU like it does White institutions, we [Urban State] would flourish. We are located in the heart of the state and could be a major provider of graduate and professional education. That would make us a leading institution in [the state] and possibly over time, the premier institution in [the state].

The associate provost claimed:

> There seems to be a subtle jealously and fear of our capabilities. I have always felt that this has been part of the reason the board continues to deny us a law school, graduate programs in medicine, and adequate support.

Institutional Ethos

Because of Urban State's traditions, mission, and current governance context, its institutional culture is orientated toward resistance, social justice, and equality in education. Traditionally, the institution has operated from a deficit which many claim was perpetuated by the state. Still there is a sense of pride and resiliency associated with the survival of the institution and its accomplishments. Urban State, as an institution, symbolizes the ethos of many Black and ethnic communities in America. A student service administrator expressed this notion by stating, "We started with very little and have suffered blatant injustices in a time when education is supposed to be equal. In spite of that, [Urban State] has not only survived but thrived on far fewer resources than other campuses."

A political science professor of 23 years explained the culture of USU as having gone through phases:

> We [the institution] have just arrived at the point of charting a preferred future. For the last generation, we have been slowly moving between a culture of resistance and survival. Resistance meaning that we reject the notion that education for Blacks in this state should be limited or tracked for specific jobs such as teachers or industry workers. For many years, we've had to resist that notion as an institution. We went from that to a mode of survival. The institution, and I mean that collectively, had to make up its mind that it would survive while remaining true to the mission as an HBCU no matter the circumstances and no matter the funding received from the state. I would even argue that we attracted leadership that understood their duty to be surviving rather than advancing.

An academic counselor asserted, "In this state race will always play a part in everything we do as a Black institution." As a social parallel, many faculty, students, and staff accept the struggles the institution will face as a result of being predominately Black. A member of the faculty senate stated: "I know I could make more money by leaving but I'm committed to our students and this institution. If I leave I would play into the hands of the board and politicians to further denigrate USU."

"The state has under funded us [the institution] for years and denied us programs, but we haven't let that stop us from moving forward as an institution," a dean lamented. She went on to say:

> It's a shame that the unfair practice of funding higher education in this state has been allowed. But the social foundations of this country and particularly this state are such that prejudice on the basis of race guides actions and decision making.

USU culture acknowledges the history of discrimination and embraces the "uphill climb" or an "uneven playing field" as described by one communications professor. This climate significantly influences the culture of the institution.

Defining the Context

After describing institutional conditions, I now turn my attention to making sense of the governance context at Urban State. Based on the analysis of data from this case, I identify three contextual aspects believed to influence decision making in this institution: (a) faculty traditions; (b) the paradox of mission; and (c) a racialized climate. Certainly no single case will illuminate every detail of decision-making contexts. University decision making is dynamic and the context is made up of fluid circumstances and individuals. A new governor, university president, or legislation can significantly change the contextual dynamics. Aspects of the governance context described are thought to be more static features of the institution. Likewise, I recognize the diversity among HBCUs and the differences, for example, between public and private institutions. Defining aspects of the decision-making context at Urban State is intended to help develop a framework for better understating governance at HBCUs.

Faculty Committed to Teaching

Consonant with the tradition of Urban State, the majority of faculty are more dedicated to teaching than to research. With a standard teaching load of four courses per semester, the traditions of faculty governance resemble a management style where faculty are viewed as employees rather than specialized professionals responsible for making decisions concerning their discipline. This does not suggest that teaching faculty cannot be engaged participants in governance. Liberal arts colleges dispel such a notion. However, Urban State is a doctoral university with a significant number of faculty who do not conduct research. This creates a mismatch between the structure and culture of governance. The nature of faculty work at Urban State does, in some ways, contradict faculty involvement in decision making. A political science professor explained that "the majority of faculty are concerned with teaching classes and helping students."

Only in the last decade has Urban State focused on recruiting research-intensive faculty. Currently, 32% of the faculty have been employed at Urban State for more than 20 years and have enculturated the traditions of teaching. For years, resource shortages prevented the recruitment of research faculty and created a heavy reliance on adjunct faculty. The faculty senate was not founded until the late 1940s and has only recently become affiliated with the American Association of University Professors. Urban State does not have a strong tradition of faculty governance.

Teaching loads and low pay leave little time for service among USU faculty. Additionally, the faculty senate, an emblem of faculty governance, is riddled with internal conflict. On campuses where faculty governance is effective, faculty have formal authority, see themselves as responsible for improving institutional quality, and maintain collaborative relationships with the administration (Floyd, 1994; Minor, in press). The small cohort of USU professors who are engaged in governance are significantly younger research faculty who have worked at other campuses. These faculty also participate in venues outside the senate.

The leadership at USU is making efforts to establish a functional senate, but their current activity involves laying the foundation for participatory governance. The statement on shared governance is new representing the preliminary stage of establishing sound faculty governance. When asked about the challenges of the senate, the current president stated, "We [USU] need to establish a tradition of faculty governance which takes time. Campuses that have strong faculty governance have strong traditions." As the campus moves forward, there is an increased need for faculty governance, yet a teaching faculty, an ineffective senate, and traditions of strong leadership create challenges that require USU to reconsider traditional models of faculty participation. USU and other HBCUs with similar characteristics must recognize the tensions between teaching traditions and the requirements for effective participation in governance. The combination of these factors calls into question the application and usefulness of traditional governance practices for the effective involvement of HBCU faculty.

The Paradox of Mission

Traditionally, Urban State has been dedicated to providing higher education to African American students who were excluded from predominately White institutions. More recently, a large part of their mission has been providing access to higher education for African American students who might not otherwise gain admittance to four-year colleges. Access and student development has long been a part of the mission at Urban State. However, as the campus seeks to improve its academic reputation, maintaining fidelity to its mission presents a paradox. To achieve a better academic reputation, raising admission standards and increasing tuition are frequently considered, but such moves come at the cost of diminishing access. Additionally, the push to increase graduate and professional programs will attract an increasing number of White, international, and adult students.

As the institution changes, some USU constituents worry about what such a transformation means for the identity of the institution. "In my opinion the board has bought out the president to turn [Urban State] into a White campus," argued one professor. Another from the physical sciences claimed that "for years there has been a stand off with the state where they [the board] will leverage money for influence." The president also expressed the challenge to balance the traditions of Urban State with new initiatives that would improve academic quality. This paradox most recently has been manifested through administrative revisions to tenure and promotion polices that place more emphasis on research and less on teaching. The president explained: "There are a lot of times when I have to consider the history and traditions of this institution while trying to move it forward. A lot of people feel as though moving in certain directions compromises who we are."

The time-honored mission of Urban State and the current direction of the campus are not necessarily harmonious. Consequently, decision making on issues perceived to compromise the mission of the institution are strained and frequently contested. This has been the case even when decisions could potentially advance the campus. A great deal of contention, for example, surrounds the state's request for USU to recruit more White students in exchange for increased support.

A Racialized Climate

In much of the discussion with participants it was clear that race is seen as a salient feature that influences the decision-making context at Urban State. Members of the campus consider race to be a significant aspect of the institution's identity and culture. There is also an indication that those outside the institution often view the campus through racial lenses. Many of the racial undertones present in the larger society are also apparent at the institutional level. That is, Urban State as an institution is likely to experience similar prejudices and discrimination that an African American individual might experience in the larger society. The provost captured the notion when he stated:

> This institution is great in many ways and Black people recognize all the wonderful things about it through experience. Others who will never experience this university simply because it's Black and will never fully see its value. Even for Whites who do experience Urban State, preconceived notions about what an HBCU is can often ruin their experience before it takes place.

From a governance perspective, the infusion of race further complicates the decision-making context. In addition to the more standard challenges that governance presents, USU must contend with racial dynamics that influence internal and external decisions. The president while bemoaning this concept explained:

> There have been a few gifts that I've had to turn down and some partnerships that won't fly because we are a Black institution. The flip side has been that there are also a number of doors that have been closed because we're a Black school, so it works both ways.

The mission of the institution, its relationship with the state, and its future are all permeated by race. To assume that race does not affect decision making about the campus would be naïve. This notion is particularly important when considering external decision making at the local, state, and federal levels.

Understanding Decision Making in HBCUs

When considering decision making at HBCUs it is important to acknowledge that although historically Black institutions share many historical and cultural attributes, they are not all the same. The point is that institutional characteristics that HBCUs share can be used to help comprehend the context in which decisions are made. In the case of Urban State, a public institution, two important lessons can be learned. First, assessments about the soundness of governance at HBCUs are better made with an understanding of the context in which decisions are made. The teaching traditions of these institutions, the potential paradox their missions present, and the acknowledgement of a racialized climate are key to understanding governance and decision in this institutional sector. Policymakers and practitioners that have an understanding of the context are likely to view governance at HBCUs more accurately. Those without an understanding of the context are susceptible to making unqualified comparisons between HBCUs and predominately White institutions which usually renders HBCUs deficient. The consequences of such may be apparent in the seemingly negative or pitiful disposition many higher education leaders exhibit toward HBCUs.

To be clear, this perspective does not imply that governance at HBCUs is without problems. Governance at Urban State could benefit from structural reforms that empower the faculty senate, cultural shifts that enhance trust and communication, and a better articulation of what shared governance means. The purpose of this chapter is not to defend poor practice. Urban State, given their circumstances, could significantly improve governance and the processes of decision making. Instead, the purpose here has been to better understand the context in which decisions are made at HBCUs. Understanding the decision-making context can help higher education leaders and campus constituents more accurately assess the challenges associated with governance at HBCUs. For those outside these institutions, taking into account the context permits a fuller consideration of the challenges facing these institutions and offers insight about how they might be improved.

A second lesson that can be learned from this case concerns how HBCUs are studied. What criteria, concepts, or methods should be used to assess decision making at HBCUs? Historically Black colleges and universities are distinct institutions and cannot be compared to predominately White institutions without declarations that give significance to such distinction. Although many functional elements of teaching and learning are similar to other institutions, the historical foundations, cultural aspects, student population, and racialized climate in which USU operates clearly distinguishes them and potentially many other HBCUs from all other higher education sectors. Each of these factors can significantly influence governance and decision making. For these reasons, researchers must question the usefulness of applying conventional higher education theory and concepts in study of HBCU governance.

For scholars conducting higher education research, using a culturally sensitive approach is useful for studying governance. Governance research on colleges with strong religious affiliations where clergy serve as trustees, for example, would require an understanding on how religious traditions currently influence decision making. Many of the current hypotheses about the state of governance and decision making at HBCUs are void of appropriate methods or theoretical frameworks for studying this population of institutions and those who lead them. An increasing body of K–12 literature suggests *culturally sensitive methods* or *Afrocentric methods* that take into account historical, cultural, and contemporary experiences of African Americans as central to research paradigms (Kershaw, 1990; Tillman, 2002). These approaches can also be applied to higher education research. Delgado and Villalpando (2002) offer the following assertion:

> Higher education in the United States is founded on a Eurocentric epistemological perspective based on white privilege and 'American democratic' ideals of meritocracy, objectivity, and individuality. This epistemological perspective presumes that there is only one way of knowing and understanding the world, and it is the natural way of interpreting truth, knowledge, and reality. (p. 171)

Critical race theory, for instance, provides another alternative theoretical approach to governance research on HBCUs. Critical race theory, derived from the work of legal scholars, is now used in K–12 research as an analytic tool for understanding school inequality (Crenshaw, Gotanda, Peller, & Thomas, 1995; Ladson-Billings & Tate, 1995). This theory is based on the following assumptions: (a) race continues to be a significant factor in determining inequality in America; (b) racism is not a series of isolated acts but is endemic in American life; and (c) the intersection of race and property rights creates a tool for understanding social and school inequality (Ladson-Billings & Tate, 1995). Using race conscious theory conjointly with traditional higher education paradigms may be a useful approach to research on HBCUs. From this perspective research questions might concern how external perceptions of higher education leaders about the effectiveness of a "Black college" affect political aspects of governance. Research questions might also consider how cultural differences among American constituents within HBCUs influence decision-making processes. Are there significant differences in communications styles, decision-making traditions, or the charisma of leaders that influences governance?

Conclusion

The tenor of conversations about governance in HBCUs is often cynical. Critiques are highlighted by a number of articles that report violations of faculty rights, financial fragility, or contention between the faculty and the president. Scholarships on these institutions void of contextual understanding will continually, and in some cases erroneously, view HBCUs as troubled and underperforming. Those familiar with HBCUs intuitively know of the particular challenges faced by HBCUs but operate without a framework to express the effects of such differences. Leaders and supporters of HBCUs spend a significant amount of effort defending the virtue of their institutions. A more explicit understanding of the decision-making context compared to predominately White institutions would likely enhance their leadership abilities while at the same time enabling them to better articulate the challenges they face. This notion not only gives credence to distinct decision-making contexts but also helps understand and give credibility to discrete practices.

Many historically Black colleges and universities now face an important point in their history. Scores of teaching faculty will soon retire, the paradox of mission must be reconciled, and the courts are defining the place of race in higher education. This decade will likely prove crucial for many HBCUs. Those institutions able to effectively make decisions in response to their environment stand a much better chance at surviving and thriving; those that do not face a threat of extinction. While assessing their progress, it is important to consider how contextual factors influence decision making. Desegregation mandates, funding disparities, and racialized institutional perceptions are just a few that affect Urban State. As HBCUs seek to resituate themselves in the current environment of higher education, the ability to define the governance context is critical. Doing so will enhance decision making and institutional effectiveness while strengthening their defense against critics.

References

Allen, W. (1992). The color of success: African American college student outcomes at predominately White and historically Black colleges. *Harvard Educational Review, 62*, 26–44.

Allen, W., & Jewell, J. (2002). A backward glance forward: Past, present, future perspectives on historically Black colleges and universities. *Review of Higher Education, 25*(3), 241–261.

Baldwin, R., & Leslie, D. (2001). Rethinking the structure of shared governance. *Peer Review, 3*(3), 18–19.

Benjamin, R., & Carroll, S. (1999). The implications of the changes environment for governance in higher education. In W. G. Tierney (Ed.), *Responsive university: Restructuring for high performance* (pp. 92–119). Baltimore, MD: Johns Hopkins University Press.

Berdahl, R. O. (1991). Shared academic governance and external constraints. In M. W. Peterson, E. E. Chaffee, & T. H. White (Eds.), *Organization and academic governance in higher education.* (4th ed.; pp. 167–179). Needham Heights, MA: Ginn Press.

Brown, M. C., & Davis, J. E. (2001). The historically Black college as a social contract, social capital, and social equalizer. *Peabody Journal of Education, 76*(1), 31–49.

Brown, M.C., & Freeman, K. (2004). Black colleges: New perspectives on policy and practice. Westport, CT: Praeger Publishers.

Crenshaw, K., Gotanda, N., Peller, G., & Thomas, K. (Eds.). (1995). *Critical race theory: The key writings that formed the movement.* New York: The New Press.

Davis, R. B. (1991). Social support networks and undergraduate student academic success-related outcomes: A comparison of Black students on Black and White campuses. In W. R. Allen, E. Epps, & N. Hanniff (Eds.), *College in Black and White: African American students in predominately White and in historically Black universities* (pp. 143–157). New York: State University of New York Press.

Delgado, D. & Villalpando, O. (2002). An apartheid of knowledge in academia: The struggle over the "legitimate" knowledge of faculty of color. *Equity and Excellence in Education, 35*(2), 169–180.

Denzin, N. (1988). *The research act* (rev. ed.). New York: McGraw-Hill.

Drewry, H. N., & Doermann, H. (2001). *Stand and prosper: Private Black colleges and their students.* Princeton, NJ: Princeton University Press.

Duderstadt, J. J. (2001). *A university for the 21st century*. Ann Arbor, ME: The University of Michigan Press.

Ferren, A., Kennan, W., & Lerch, S. (2001). Reconciling corporate and academic cultures. *Peer Review, 3*(3), 9–11.

Fleming, J. (1984). *Blacks in college*. San Francisco: Jossey-Bass.

Floyd, C. E. (1994). Faculty participation and shared governance. *The Review of Higher Education, 17*(2), 197–209.

Freeman, K. (Ed.). (1998). *African American culture and heritage in higher education research and practice*. Westport, CT: Praeger.

Glaser, B. G., & Strauss, A. L. (1967). *The discovery of grounded theory: Strategies for qualitative research*. Chicago: Aldine Publishing Co.

Glesne, C., & Peshkin, A. (1992). *Becoming a qualitative researcher*. White Plains, NY: Longman.

Gumport, P. J. (2000). Academic restructuring: Organizational change and institutional imperatives. *Higher Education* (Netherlands), *39*(1), 67–91.

Hamilton, K. (2002). When the campus becomes a battle ground: Shared governance can seem a distant dream when needs for faculty freedoms, speedy decisions clash. *Black Issues in Higher Education, 19*(14), 20–23.

Hamilton, N. (1999). Are we speaking the same language? Comparing AAUP & AGB. *Liberal Education, 8*(4), 24–31.

Keller, G. (2001). Governance: The remarkable ambiguity. In P. G. Altbach, P. Gumport, & B. Johnstone (Eds.), *In defense of higher education* (pp. 132–140). Baltimore, MD: Johns Hopkins University Press.

Kershaw, T. (1990). The emerging paradigm in Black studies. In T. Anderson, (Ed.), *Black studies. Theory, method, and cultural perspective* (pp. 16–24). Pullman, WA: Washington State University Press.

Kezar, A., & Eckel, P. (in press). Meeting today's governance challenges: A synthesis of the literature and examination of a future research agenda. *Journal of Higher Education*.

Ladson-Billings, G., & Tate, W. (1995). Toward a critical race theory of education. *Teachers College Record, 97*(1), 47–68.

Longin, T. C. (2002). Institutional governance: A call for collaborative decision-making in American higher education. In W. G. Berberet & L. A. McMillin (Eds.), *A new academic compact* (pp. 211–221). Bolton, MA: Anker Publishing Co.

Mingle, J. R. (2000). *Higher education's future in the "corporatized" economy* (Occasional Paper No. 44, September). Washington, DC: Association of Governing Boards of Universities and Colleges.

Minor, J. T. (in press). Four challenges for faculty senates. *Thought & Action*.

Minor, J. T. (2003). Assessing the senate: Critical issues considered. *American Behavioral Scientist, 46*(7), 960–977.

Nettles, M., & Perna, L. (1997). *The African American data book: Higher and adult education, Volume 1*. Fairfax, VA: The Frederick D. Patterson Research Institute of the College Fund/UNCF.

Ramo, K. J. (1998). *Assessing the faculty's role in shared governance: Implications of AAUP standards*. Washington, DC: American Association of University Professors.

Randall, K., & Miller, M. (1999). Putting it all together: Effective faculty governance. In M. T. Miller (Ed.), *Responsive academic decision-making: Involving faculty in higher education governance* (pp. 131–145). Stillwater, OK: New Forums Press.

Schuster, J. H. (1989). Governance and the changing faculty condition. In J. H. Schuster & L. H. Miller (Eds.), *Governing tomorrow's campus: Perspectives and agendas*. New York: MacMillan.

Tierney, W. G. (1988). Organizational culture in higher education: Defining the essentials. *Journal of Higher Education, 59*(1), 2–21.

Tierney, W. G., & Minor, J. T. (2003). *Challenges for governance: A national report*. (Available from The Center for Higher Education Policy Analysis, The University of Southern California, WPH 701, Los Angeles, CA 90089)

Tillman, L. (2002). Culturally sensitive research approaches: An African American perspective. *Educational Researcher, 31*(9), 3–12.

Yin, R. K. (1984). *Case study research: Design and methods*. Beverly Hills, CA: Sage.

CHAPTER 37
BAKKE AND STATE POLICY

EXERCISING INSTITUTIONAL AUTONOMY TO MAINTAIN A DIVERSE STUDENT BODY

PATRICIA MARIN AND STELLA M. FLORES

In *Regents of the University of California v. Bakke* (1978), the matter before the Court was the constitutionality of the admissions policy of the medical school at the University of California, Davis (UC Davis). Of the various rationales put forward to justify this admissions policy,[1] the only one acknowledged in Justice Lewis Powell's deciding opinion as a compelling state interest was "obtaining the educational benefits that flow from an ethnically diverse student body" (*Bakke*, 1978, p. 306).[2] Although Powell's opinion was the subject of debate for many years, his conclusion was decidedly affirmed in the *Gratz v. Bollinger* (2003) and *Grutter v. Bollinger* (2003) Supreme Court opinions.[3]

Although many recognize *Bakke* as the Supreme Court case that secured the "benefits of diversity" rationale for higher education, it is not as well known that Justice Powell supported this conclusion employing the principle of academic freedom (also known as institutional autonomy when referring to institutions). In his opinion, Justice Powell suggested that higher education institutions are unique and, therefore, must have the ability to make their own academic decisions. Providing a specific example, he explained,

> Academic freedom, though not a specifically enumerated constitutional right, long has been viewed as a special concern of the First Amendment. The freedom of a university to make its own judgments as to education includes the selection of its student body. (*Bakke*, 1978, p. 312)

Drawing from *Keyishian v. Board of Regents of the University of the State of New York* (1967), he further emphasized his point by acknowledging "our national commitment to the safeguarding of these freedoms within university communities" (*Bakke*, 1978, p. 312). Ultimately, he concluded that UC Davis "must be viewed as seeking to achieve a goal that is of paramount importance in the fulfillment of its mission" (p. 313). Twenty-five years later, Justice Sandra Day O'Connor, writing for the *Grutter* majority, supported Powell's conclusions and reinforced the importance of "giving a degree of deference to a university's academic decisions" (2003, p. 328)—what she refers to as "educational autonomy" (p. 329).

Although Justices Powell and O'Connor asserted that, because of academic freedom, an institution should be allowed to admit its own student body, this autonomy was not offered without restrictions. Of course, institutions are governed by more than just their own missions and academic freedom. For example, the *Grutter* Court talked about autonomy "within constitutionally prescribed limits" (2003, p. 328). In fact, an institution is governed and affected by a whole host of parameters including federal, state, and local laws and policies (Kaplin & Lee, 1995) that may work in concert with, or against, the goals of an institution. Abiding by all of these laws and policies, while remaining true to their institutional missions and their desired outcomes, therefore, can be quite a challenge for colleges and universities. As a result, campuses intentionally exercising institutional autonomy to create the diverse student body they have asserted is necessary to achieve their missions occurs in the larger context of supporting and competing external policy. This also contributes to and affects institutional decision making.

This chapter considers some of the external limits on an institution's academic freedom and what colleges and universities have to or can do to creatively exercise their autonomy, within these existing parameters, to admit a diverse student body as per *Bakke*. In doing so, we ask the question: what affect can state policy have on an institution's ability to admit a diverse student body as afforded in *Bakke*? To begin this examination, we provide a brief discussion of academic freedom, particularly defining the concept of institutional autonomy. Then we examine how the law can affect an institution's academic freedom, focusing on state policy because of its central role in public higher education (McGuinness, 1994). In the next section we provide two examples of current state policies that directly hinder or enhance an institution's ability to achieve a diverse student body. We follow by providing two examples of state policies that may indirectly support or interfere with an institution's implementation of diversity goals.[4] In the final section, we discuss why the intersection of institutional autonomy and state policy continues to be relevant to campuses and their decision making. In the current climate that is generally hostile to race-conscious policies, we argue that institutions interested in reaping the benefits of a diverse student body must act intentionally to successfully achieve their institutional missions.

Academic Freedom

Academic freedom, considered "a safeguard essential to the aims of the university and to the welfare of those who work within it" (Bok, 1982, p. 20), refers "to the custom and practice, and the ideal, by which faculties may best flourish in their work as teachers and researchers" (Kaplin & Lee, 1995, p. 299). Although a more specific definition is elusive (Kaplin & Lee, 1995), higher education most often uses the 1940 Statement of Principles on Academic Freedom and Tenure, developed by the Association of American University Professors (AAUP) and the American Association of Colleges and Universities (AAC&U), to explain this unique concept (Springer, 2006). The 1940 Statement of Principles indicates,

> Teachers are entitled to full freedom in research and in the publication of the results. . . . Teachers are entitled to freedom in the classroom in discussing their subject. . . . When [teachers] speak or write as citizens, they should be free from institutional censorship or discipline. (AAUP & AAC&U, 2006, p. 3)

In addition to its relevance for individual faculty members, academic freedom also has meaning at the institutional level.

Institutional Academic Freedom

Sweezy v. New Hampshire, a 1957 Supreme Court decision,[5] provides "the basis for the academic freedom of institutions" (Euben, 2002, n.p.). Institutional academic freedom, similar to individual academic freedom, is considered a First Amendment right by the Court (Euben, 2002). Most often quoted in this matter is Justice Felix Frankfurter's concurring opinion in *Sweezy*.[6] In writing about "the dependence of a free society on free universities," he indicates, "This means the exclusion of governmental intervention in the intellectual life of a university" (1957, p. 262). Expanding on this notion, he quotes from a statement of South African scholars who at that time were fighting for open universities:

> It is the business of a university to provide that atmosphere which is most conducive to speculation, experiment, and creation. It is an atmosphere in which there prevail "the four essential freedoms" of a university—to determine for itself on academic grounds who may teach, what may be taught, how it shall be taught, and who may be admitted to study. (p. 263)

Overall Justice Frankfurter believed that "political power must abstain from intrusion into this activity of [academic] freedom, pursued in the interest of wise government and the people's well-being, except for reasons that are exigent and obviously compelling" (1957, p. 262). Guided by the Supreme Court, the AAUP "has concluded that institutions have academic freedom when a challenged decision involves educational or academic policy and functions (as opposed to other nonacademic decisions)" (Euben, 2002, n.p.). Therefore, the educational aspects of college and university decision making, such as faculty hiring and academic requirements, fall under the umbrella of institutional autonomy. Nevertheless, this autonomy is not without limits, mainly as a result of government intervention. The chapter now turns to this issue.

State Action Intersects with Institutional Autonomy

Scholars have argued that "if a college or university is effectively to define its goals and select or invent the means of attaining them, it must have a high degree of substantive autonomy" (Berdahl & McConnell, 1994, p. 56). Because of the public interest in higher education, especially public higher education, however, we are witnessing increasing involvement in the matters of colleges and universities by both the federal and state governments (Berdahl & McConnell, 1994). Sometimes this involvement provides added support to an institution as it attempts to successfully reach particular goals; other times this involvement works against an institution's interests (Berdahl & McConnell, 1994). Derek Bok, former president of Harvard University, has argued, "Professors and administrators have both been losing some of their independence to the mounting requirements of the state," and "Universities find themselves subjected to a host of rules covering a long and growing list of campus activities" (Bok, 1982, p. 37).

It comes as no surprise that state action affects whether or not an institution meets its goals, especially as the public has become more aware of higher education institutions and their important role in society (Berdahl & McConnell, 1994; Bok, 1982; McGuinness, 1994). This has led to suggestions of strained relations between a state government and the public colleges and universities within the state (McGuinness, 1994). Given a steady erosion of institutional autonomy (Berdahl & McConnell, 1994), then, it is important to have a general understanding of these "external sources of law" (Kaplin & Lee, 1995, p. 13) and how they relate to each other and to an institution's autonomy.[7] Although a detailed discussion of these "external sources of law" is beyond the scope of this chapter, we provide relevant highlights and focus on the *Bakke* Supreme Court case and its intersection with state policy.

The U.S. Constitution "is the highest legal authority that exists" (Kaplin & Lee, 1995, p. 13). As such, any law that conflicts with it is "subject to invalidation by the courts" (Kaplin & Lee, 1995, p. 13), including provisions in any state constitution, considered the highest legal authority in a state, or any state statute or law. Although many laws affect higher education without specifically addressing matters of education (e.g., fair hiring practices, anti-discrimination laws, etc.), we are most interested in examples of state policy that focus directly on colleges and universities.

Although governmental bodies at all levels may enact legislation specifically related to higher education, the states provide most of these statutes (Kaplin & Lee, 1995). This is both because the U.S. Constitution does not provide specifically for higher education and the Tenth Amendment reserves powers not delegated to the federal government to the states (Gladieux, Hauptman, & Knapp, 1994). As such, higher education is considered the responsibility of the states (Kaplin & Lee, 1995). Under this context, "federal law establishes a 'floor' upon which state law may, in appropriate circumstances, 'build' " (Coleman, Palmer, Sanghavi, & Winnick, 2007, p. 4). Specifically related to *Bakke,* then, the Supreme Court decision does not *"mandate or require* that higher education institutions use race or ethnicity in their admissions programs. Rather, [it] *permit*[s] institutions to use race and ethnicity in limited ways in admissions decisions" (Coleman et al., 2007, p. 4). This lack of mandate, for example, then, allows for "state constitutional, statutory, or regulatory provisions that forbid the use of race or ethnicity in public higher education" (2007, p. 4). In such situations, institutions that want to assert their institutional autonomy to determine "who may be admitted to study" (*Sweezy,* 1957, p. 263) would be prohibited from implementing a race-conscious admissions plan. This is only one example of how external laws and policies can limit the ability of colleges and universities to completely self-govern.

Ultimately, the goal must be "to decide how government and universities can work in harmony so that higher education will be able to make its greatest contribution" (Bok, 1982, p. 39).[8] The challenge in accomplishing this relationship, in part, lies in acknowledging the importance of institutional autonomy, recognizing the role of the states in developing higher education policy that addresses and protects local interests and needs, and establishing the requisite balance between the two. With this in mind, we now discuss two examples of instances where state policy intersected, either positively or negatively, with an institution's ability to recruit and enroll a diverse student body in efforts to fulfill its educational mission.

Considering State-Level Policy

A range of state-level policies can affect an institution's ability to determine "who may be admitted to study" and, thereby, affect the admission of a racially/ethnically diverse student body. Although some are clearly written to directly address higher education admissions decisions and may affect the enrollment outcomes of a student body, other state policies do not have as specific a connection. Yet, these latter public policies, by their design, also may have the power to alter enrollment outcomes. Further, although some policies are race-conscious or specifically bar the use of race, others do not address issues of race specifically but still may affect racial/ethnic outcomes.

In this section, we detail examples of state admissions-specific policies that can directly affect the racial/ethnic diversity of an institution's student body. Those we consider to have direct effects on student body diversity by either attempting to prevent the loss of racial and ethnic representation in college admissions or barring the consideration of race/ethnicity in decision making include (1) the Top Ten Percent Plan in Texas, a state legislative initiative that grants automatic admission to the top 10% of a graduating class in any Texas high school to public colleges and universities in the state, and (2) Proposition 209 in California, the voter referendum that banned the use of race in admissions, employment, and financial aid decisions by public state entities.

State Policies with Direct Effects on Student Body Diversity

Public postsecondary institutions in Texas and California have each experienced limitations on their autonomy to admit a diverse student body through distinct legal and policy mechanisms. In Texas, a federal court ruling banned the use of race and ethnicity in college admissions in states in the Fifth Circuit Court of Appeals (Texas, Louisiana, and Mississippi).[9] In California, a voter-approved constitutional amendment banned the use of race/ethnicity in college admissions. What these states similarly demonstrate, however, is the use of institution-level action as a response to those external limitations on autonomy to admit and retain a diverse student body. Texas, in seeking to uphold the ability to achieve the educational benefits of student body diversity outcomes as outlined in *Bakke*, used legislative action via the Texas Top Ten Percent Plan, supported and supplemented by institutional-level university investment in programmatic and publicity efforts, to counteract federal limits on institutional autonomy. California has employed multiple methods to counteract state imposed limits on institutional autonomy over admissions decisions as a result of Proposition 209. These include a University of California system initiative modeled after the Texas percent plan and supported by California state leaders—Eligibility in Local Context (ELC)—and significant state investment in college outreach to underserved areas with low college enrollment rates. We discuss each of these examples, in turn, below.

Texas' Top Ten Percent Plan

Institutional autonomy in Texas was limited by the *Hopwood v. Texas* (1996) decision—a federal court ruling barring the use of race/ethnicity in college admissions in the Fifth Circuit. As a result, state policymakers in Texas (with the support of academics and community members), concerned about the potential loss of underrepresented students in the state's public higher education institutions, legislated an admissions bill that would counteract such losses in racial and ethnic diversity. House Bill 508, known as the Top Ten Percent Plan, guarantees admission to the top 10% of a high school graduating class to any public higher education institution in the state. The automatic admissions plan was designed as a viable option to replace the loss of the use of affirmative action in the state (Montejano, 1998) and was written acknowledging the educational benefits of diversity expressed in *Bakke*. For

Texas, this meant that there were benefits to admitting a pool of students from various geographic areas across the state because that also represented various racial, ethnic, and income groups; the plan has been successful largely because of demographic distribution (Tienda & Niu, 2004).

Legislative action to replace the loss of affirmative action in Texas, however, was not the only tool designed to meet this goal of achieving a racially diverse student body. Instead, for example, the University of Texas at Austin, followed by Texas A&M University, supplemented the state automatic admissions plan at their respective institutions with specific scholarship and retention programming designed to attract a diverse student body (Horn & Flores, 2003). The Longhorn Opportunity Scholarship (LOS) available at the University of Texas at Austin targeted low-income students in the top 10% of their high school graduating class in schools that had low rates of college enrollment at the University of Texas (Horn & Flores, 2003). LOS students were further supported by retention services once they enrolled on campus. Texas' other flagship institution also initiated a similar scholarship program, although without specific income requirements. In sum, each institution designed particular scholarship and retention programs connected to the state percent plan but particular to their contexts and recruitment needs.

By the time the *Bakke* principles were reaffirmed in *Grutter*, enrollment by almost all underrepresented racial and ethnic groups, which initially saw declines, had risen to near pre-*Hopwood* levels at the University of Texas at Austin. The same was not true at Texas A&M, however, signaling different levels of institutional involvement and success with recruiting and admitting a diverse student body (Chapa & Horn, 2007). Rising enrollment of racial and ethnic minorities at the University of Texas at Austin before the reinstatement of affirmative action has been attributed to the strategic implementation of an institutional-level response coordinated with state legislation post-*Hopwood* (Domina, 2007; Horn & Flores, 2003). Selective institutions in Texas, therefore, used their autonomy to directly link programmatic services likely to recruit a diverse student body with state policy (the Top Ten Percent Plan) to offset the Fifth Circuit's retraction of affirmative action and enhance the implementation of the state-mandated percent plan. Texas presents a distinct and successful story regarding the assertion of academic freedom via institutional-level responses to maintain the ability to admit a diverse student body.

California's Proposition 209

California, through Proposition 209, was the first state to specifically use state policy to ban the use of race, sex, color, ethnicity, and national origin for all public education, employment, and public contracting decisions, including college admissions (Chavez, 1998; Coleman et al., 2007; Pusser, 2004). The new state constitutional amendment was a result of a voter referendum instigated after the University of California system's Board of Regents voted on resolutions—SP-1 and SP-2—to prohibit the use of race in college admissions, employment, and contracting (Horn & Flores, 2003). Although these were not institutional-level decisions but, rather, university system initiatives, the vote approving SP-1 and SP-2 represented the decision of the UC system's governing board; all institutions in the public state system were obliged to abide. In 2000, the UC Board of Regents voted to repeal SP-1 and SP-2, although the vote was considered largely symbolic because Proposition 209 had already been in place for 3 years and the regent vote would have no effect on this state law (Pusser, 2004).

Proposition 209, the most formal, longest standing, and permanent state action on higher education admissions, offers a second example of the complex relationship between state policy and college and university institutional autonomy. Before Proposition 209, the California state constitution provided language directing universities to admit classes that reflected the gender, racial, and ethnic diversity of the state (Pusser, 2004), a provision that coincided with the goals of the institutions. Actually, despite the regents' vote on SP-1 and SP-2, some members of the university faculty and administration, including UC System President Richard Atkinson, had opposed SP-1 and SP-2 and continued to voice support for diversity-enhancing initiatives (Pusser, 2004). Regardless of the extent to which they opposed bans on race-conscious initiatives and wanted to preserve their institutional autonomy regarding admissions decisions, public universities' actions were legally limited.

Once Proposition 209 became official state policy that governed all public college and university systems, the implications for college access for particular student groups became more pronounced. As a remedy to the restrictive state law, state and university leadership at that time (e.g., Governor Gray Davis and UC President Atkinson) offered an alternative UC system admissions plan called "Eligibility in Local Context" to address potential losses in student body diversity (Ball, 2000). In 1999, this new admissions plan was passed by an overwhelming majority of the members of the UC Board of Regents, the same group that voted to dismantle the use of race in college admissions, with the intention of mitigating some of the loss of racial and ethnic diversity resulting from Proposition 209 (Pusser, 2004).

ELC differed from the Texas initiative in that it only allowed admission to those graduating in the top 4% of any high school graduating class in California to the UC system (and not the institution of choice). However, the plan was designed with the intention of evaluating a student based on the opportunities afforded by his or her local high school context (Student Academic Services, 2002). Other requirements specific to California's ELC not present in the initial Texas percent plan included required high school course taking and recommendations to take the range of required UC tests to become UC-eligible (University of California, 2003). In general, the plan was designed to identify students who were within reach of achieving UC eligibility the summer after their junior year of high school so that individual UC campuses could make concerted efforts to advise students regarding their course-taking patterns as well as remain connected throughout the college application process.

Another attempt to mitigate the potential decline in minority enrollment after Proposition 209 became investment in college outreach programs through state-mandated legislative funding. Legislative action in this circumstance involved carefully targeted and, initially, generous budgetary commitments that included funding for K–12 outreach, university and K–12 partnerships, and the creation of summer training academies (Pusser, 2004). Although funding proposals for college outreach were as much as six times the amount of any funds spent on these activities before the 1995 passing of SP-1 and SP-2 (Ristine, 2000), this form of response proved to be temporary and vulnerable. Conflict between other state economy needs and changing gubernatorial administrations led to significant decreases in state support for this remedy (Schevitz, 2004). In California, therefore, we see that attempts to exercise institutional autonomy did not have lasting state support. As a result, these efforts have not proven a strong counterbalance to the state constitutional law banning race-conscious admissions.

Data reflecting the policy implementations of SP-1, Proposition 209, and ELC do not tell a tale of full recovery. By 2003, underrepresented minority enrollment at the UC system-level had dropped significantly from 1995 enrollment levels. In fact, the UC system saw its most dismal level of underrepresented minority enrollment upon the implementation of Proposition 209 in 1998. Enrollment overall began a climb upon the implementation of various outreach programs, but the trends at the individual campus level could not boast much, if any, steady increases. Although the UC system showed some recovery by 2003 at the system level post-ELC, most campuses had not recovered to the 1995 levels of underrepresented minority applicants and enrollees (University of California, 2003). In any case, much of the gain could be simply a result of the growing proportion of underrepresented minority groups in California's pool of graduating high school seniors (Horn & Flores, 2003; University of California, 2003).

State Policies with Indirect Effects on Student Body Diversity

The Texas and California examples of how admission policies and limits on them can affect an institution's ability to achieve a diverse student body are fairly straightforward. It is not hard to understand how directly relevant admissions legislation is likely to affect admission outcomes. What may be less obvious is that non-admissions policies may also have an effect on student diversity. In these instances, the outcomes of state policy, rather than the policy itself, can have an effect on the institution. Examples are policies that serve as financial incentives to apply to and enroll in an institution including the following: (1) the HOPE Scholarship, a merit-based financial aid program in Georgia (one of at least 14 states to provide such an incentive), and (2) an in-state resident tuition (ISRT) policy, House Bill 1403, which provides an in-state resident tuition discount to high school graduates in Texas (one of 10 states that offers the discount). Further, although these policies are facially race-neutral, targeting students, whether by citizenship status or grade point average, is likely to have an effect on the racial and ethnic makeup of a student body.

The HOPE Scholarship

State merit-aid programs are examples of policies that have an indirect effect on the student body of institutions.[10] Although these scholarship programs do not dictate or limit institutional action, they affect institutions because of the funds provided to students, the criteria used to distribute those funds, and the choices students make in using the funds. As a result, different students may be accepting admission to colleges and universities in Georgia in different ways than in the past. Georgia's Helping Outstanding Students Educationally (HOPE) Scholarship is one example of such a state merit-aid program.

The Georgia HOPE Scholarship, instituted in 1993 and funded by state lottery revenue, is "the largest state-financed, merit-based aid program in the U.S." (Cornwell-Mustard HOPE Scholarship Page, 2007, n.p.), having disbursed more than $3.61 billion dollars to more than 1 million students.[11] It has served as the model for more than a dozen similar scholarships around the country (Heller & Marin, 2004). The Georgia program, the longest in existence, is also the most studied, thereby offering extensive information to examine the potential effects of such a financial aid incentive.

To be eligible for the HOPE Scholarship, a student must have Georgia residency and "have graduated from an eligible Georgia high school since 1993 with at least a 'B' (3.0 grade-point) average" (Cornwell-Mustard HOPE Scholarship Page, 2007, n.p.). The original program design included an eligibility income cap of $66,000 that was increased to $100,000 in the second year; the cap has now been eliminated altogether. HOPE Scholars can use the aid at either a public or private degree-granting institution.[12] Finally, to maintain the scholarship, students are required to have at least a 3.0 college GPA (Cornwell-Mustard HOPE Scholarship Page, 2007).

It seems hard to argue against a merit-based scholarship that provides financial support to students who have demonstrated some level of academic achievement as defined by the program's criteria, especially "given the popularity of these programs among middle-class citizens" (Doyle, 2006, p. 260). Yet, a closer examination of many of these scholarships has demonstrated that they tend to be awarded to those who would already attend higher education rather than to underrepresented students whose opportunity to attend college might be enhanced as a result of such a financial incentive (see Heller & Marin, 2002, 2004; Marin, 2002). As Dynarski (2004) notes, although the programs are facially race-neutral, these "scholarships flow disproportionately to white, non-Hispanic, upper-income students" (p. 68). Specifically examining the HOPE Scholarship, Dynarski found that it "has increased racial and ethnic gaps in college attendance in Georgia" (2004, p. 82). These results, though unintentional, are nevertheless significant for institutions interested in admitting and retaining a diverse student body. Further, these outcomes take on even greater importance for states where race-conscious policies are barred by state law or in states with low college attainment for its minority groups.

The use of state merit aid programs "represents one of the most pronounced policy shifts in higher education in the last 20 years" (Doyle, 2006, p. 259), with an increase in the proportion of all state aid going to merit-based programs and a simultaneous decrease in the proportion of all state aid funding need-based programs (Doyle, 2006). This type of massive state policy overhaul, especially given who tends to benefit from merit aid programs, must be examined in light of institutional goals to admit a diverse student body. For example, as per its mission, the University of Georgia (UGA) "seeks to foster the understanding of and respect for cultural differences necessary for an enlightened and educated citizenry. It further provides for cultural, ethnic, gender and racial diversity in the faculty, staff and student body" (University of Georgia, 2005, n.p.). As such, the institution, and others with the same interests, may need to exercise its institutional autonomy to implement policies and programs that would still allow it to achieve its goal of admitting a diverse student body.

In-State Resident Tuition Legislation

Another example of state policy gaining both prominence and controversy across the United States is that of in-state resident tuition (ISRT) legislation. These policies are designed to provide an in-state tuition discount to any student who graduates from a state's secondary school system and has lived in that state for a particular number of years. This includes undocumented immigrant students who meet these requirements. The legislation has, in effect, mirrored a proposed federal law that would allow undocumented immigrant high school graduates to pay in-state resident tuition, among other provisions. In addition to the tuition discount, the proposed federal act, called the Development, Relief, and Education for Alien Minors Act (DREAM), would allow undocumented students to begin the path toward obtaining U.S. citizenship and gaining legal employment if they go to college or serve in the U.S. military (Olivas, 2004). The state versions, however, are limited in scope because they cannot override federal immigration law and are, therefore, in the form of a basic tuition discount. ISRT legislation grants undocumented immigrant students, as well as any other student who moves to an ISRT state, the same in-state resident tuition discount as legal residents, if they meet specific residency and graduation requirements (Olivas, 2004). As out-of-state rates are significantly higher than in-state rates, the tuition discount is particularly significant for students who do not qualify for federal aid because of citizenship status (Olivas, 2004).

ISRT policies are controversial in nature because of those students they are likely to serve—undocumented high school graduates of a racial/ethnic minority status. Most undocumented individuals in the United States are of Latin American origin, and a number of the states with tuition legislation represent regions of the country with the highest number of Latino-origin individuals and undocumented immigrants (Passel, 2005; Passel, Van Hook, & Bean, 2004). As such, the likelihood that an individual benefiting from such a policy is of Latino origin is relatively high. Texas, which has the oldest ISRT policy in the nation, has documented the increase of students identified as ISRT policy-eligible from approximately 1,488 students in fall 2001 to almost 9,000 in fall 2005 (Texas Higher Education Coordinating Board, n.d.). Although in most cases community college entrance makes up most of the ISRT higher education enrollment, there was a steady increase in 4-year enrollment by this category of students from 2001 to 2005, a number of whom entered the University of Texas at Austin, one of the state's flagship institutions (Texas Higher Education Coordinating Board, n.d.).

This resulting trend represents a unique opportunity for colleges and universities to exercise their institutional autonomy with regard to how the outcomes of these state ISRT policies may contribute to a potential increase in the racial and economic diversity of their incoming students. Although the policies may not have been designed with *Bakke* principles in mind, the mission to provide access through a financial aid discount to students who likely cannot afford high tuition and are barred from all forms of federal financial aid likely yields an economically and racially diverse pool of students entering higher education.[13] In states where the tuition discount is available, institutions may use this policy mechanism as a diversity-enhancing tool and implement methods successful to their particular context to recruit and retain these students. As the pool of students likely to be undocumented will vary based on geographic region, some institutions may have to make more concerted efforts than will others. A number of institutions in Texas, for example, have partnered with local community, nonprofit, and religious organizations to publicize the rights afforded by the tuition legislation to immigrant families (Flores, 2007; Rincon, 2005). Such methods of creative partnerships may serve as a lesson to other institutions in states where the benefit is available but the take-up rate of the policy does not reflect the number of students who may be eligible.

State policy in this area, however, is not static; several states have had to adjust to legislative changes regarding the college access opportunities for undocumented immigrants. While 10 states to date have ISRT policies, Arizona, for example, through a voter referendum known as Proposition 300, has barred undocumented students from receiving any state financial aid benefits such as those accorded by an in-state resident tuition law (Redden, 2007). In addition, a number of other states with ISRT legislation have introduced bills to repeal any financial discounts supported by state funds and offered by these policies to undocumented students (Redden, 2007). Thus, although the discount was originally approved by various state legislatures around the country, it appears that voters in at least Arizona have taken active initiative to oppose this practice for a particular category of students—undocumented immigrants. As state reaction to this type of tuition legislation continues to unfold across the country, institutions should remain vigilant and creative about how to take advantage of policy windows of access for students who contribute to their overall mission of diversity.

Exercising Institutional Autonomy

Mounting state policy related to postsecondary education confirms the increasing interest the public has in higher education and the "right" to a college degree. As long as this interest remains, state policy will continue to intersect with institutional autonomy and colleges and universities will need to determine if, how, and when to exercise their academic freedom to achieve their institutional missions.

As a result of the defense of the University of Michigan undergraduate and law school admissions policies in the *Gratz* and *Grutter* cases, it became more evident than ever that higher education institutions believe, as affirmed in *Bakke*, that a racially/ethnically diverse student body is an essential component in achieving their educational missions. However, obtaining a diverse student body remains a matter of concern despite the 2003 upholding of *Bakke* in *Gratz* and *Grutter*. For example, three states to date—California, Washington, and Michigan—have barred the use of race/ethnicity in college admissions through referenda and campaigns are underway in five more states—Arizona, Colorado, Missouri, Nebraska, and Oklahoma—to have citizens vote on anti-affirmative action ballot measures in November 2008 (Schmidt, 2007). The affirmative action initiatives have also been increasingly associated with issues of illegal immigration, bringing any policies that may benefit immigrants in a state to even greater visibility (Schmidt, 2007). Of the five states with potential referenda votes, two—Oklahoma and Nebraska—have in-state resident tuition policies and Arizona already has implemented a ban on use of the state tuition discount for undocumented students.

Research has shown a drop in the percentage of racial and ethnic minority applications and enrollment in states that prohibit the use of race/ethnicity in college admission (Horn & Flores, 2003; Long, 2004). Although we have seen a partial recovery of underrepresented minority enrollment in some institutions where state-level policy has restricted the consideration of race, the rise has been only partially the result of alternative admissions plans such as a percent plan and these results vary even by institution within a state. Instead, lessons in California and Texas have shown that creativity in exercising institutional autonomy, which has included partnerships with external agents such as the legislature, is essential to enrolling and serving a diverse student body and attempting to reverse the negative trends caused by policies that prohibit the use of race/ethnicity in decision making.

With regard to policies that are not directly admissions-related but instead affect outcomes of student body enrollment by their design, it will be increasingly important for institutions to acknowledge and assess the indirect affects of these policies and to exercise their institutional autonomy to mitigate any negative effect on student diversity.

Conclusion

Institutions that believe in the *Bakke* principle that diversity is a compelling state interest must be prepared to exercise their institutional autonomy, sometimes creatively, to admit and retain a racially/ethnically diverse student body. Institutions cannot be passive, especially when state policy negatively affects their desired goals. Of course, this is a complex endeavor because institutions have multiple missions and many goals, and even these sometimes internally conflict (see Marin & Yun, 2005). Nevertheless, institutions must serve as policy evaluators, assessing the impact state policy will have on their interests, as well as policy actors, actively developing solutions to the challenges they face. Remaining committed to *Bakke* will increasingly require institutions to exercise their institutional autonomy to intentionally address obstacles to their diversity goals.

Notes

1. The other rationales presented by UC Davis but discounted by Justice Powell include reducing the scarcity of underrepresented minorities in both medical schools and the medical profession, addressing the effects of societal discrimination, and increasing the number of doctors who would practice in underserved communities.

2. Although Justice Powell supported this rationale, he did not support the specific admissions policy in question at UC Davis. Therefore, the admissions policy at Davis was deemed unconstitutional.

3. The 2007 *Parents Involved in Community Schools v. Seattle School District No. 1* and *Meredith v. Jefferson County Board of Education* cases involving voluntary elementary and secondary desegregation plans also left *Bakke* standing.

4. Because public universities are accountable to the state in ways that private universities are not (Berdahl & McConnell, 1994), our examples focus only on public institutions.

5. This Supreme Court case considered whether New Hampshire's attorney general could prosecute a professor for refusing to answer questions about a lecture delivered at the state university.

6. Concurring opinions generally agree with the decision of a court case, but usually provide alternative reasoning. Even though they are not binding in any way, they can have influence on future decisions, as is the case with Justice Frankfurter's concurring opinion in *Sweezy*, as well as in the public arena.

7. For a detailed explanation, see Kaplin and Lee (1995).

8. For a discussion of the moral disagreement present in the affirmative action debate, see Moses (2011).

9. At the time of the *Hopwood v. Texas* ruling, public colleges in Louisiana and Mississippi struggled to interpret the limits set by this Court decision because these states were under federal desegregation court orders (Healy, 1998).

10. These scholarship opportunities are generally available to any state resident who meets the established award criteria. Award criteria, based on measures of academic merit such as grade point average or test score, vary by state (Heller, 2002).

11. In addition to the HOPE Scholarship, the HOPE Program also includes the HOPE Grant, which does not have any merit requirements and can be used for nondegree programs at technical schools (Cornwell-Mustard HOPE Scholarship Page, 2007). This chapter does not discuss the HOPE Grant.

12. For HOPE scholars using their scholarship at degree-granting public institutions, "the program covers tuition, HOPE-approved mandatory fees and a book allowance. The value of the award is about $5,000 for the 2006–2007 academic year" (Cornwell-Mustard HOPE Scholarship Page, 2007, n.p.). Those students using their scholarships at private, degree-granting institutions receive $3,000 per academic year to use toward tuition (Cornwell-Mustard HOPE Scholarship Page, 2007).

13. One assessment limitation of this analysis is the lack of demographic data that include accurate and detailed citizenship status. No government agency in the United States, including public higher education institutions, collects data solely on undocumented immigrants (Passel, 2005). Therefore, directly studying how the role of citizenship status, by race/ethnicity, affects student diversity outcomes poses different and more complex challenges than does studying other higher education policies that affect racial and ethnic minorities.

References

Association of American University Professors (AAUP) & American Association of Colleges and Universities (AAC&U). (2006). *1940 statement of principles on academic freedom and tenure*. Washington, DC: AAUP.

Ball, H. (2000). *The* Bakke *case*. Lawrence: University of Kansas Press.

Berdahl, R. O., & McConnell, T. R. (1994). Autonomy and accountability: Some fundamental issues. In P. G. Altbach, R. O. Berdahl, & P. J. Gumport (Eds.), *Higher education in American society* (3rd ed., pp. 55–72). Amherst, NY: Prometheus Books.

Bok, D. (1982). *Beyond the ivory tower: Social responsibilities of the modern university*. Cambridge, MA: Harvard University Press.

Chapa, J., & Horn, C. L. (2007). Is anything race neutral? Comparing "race-neutral" admissions policies at the University of Texas and the University of California. In G. Orfield, P. Marin, S. M. Flores, & L. M. Garces (Eds.), *Charting the future of college affirmative action: Legal victories, continuing attacks, and new research* (pp. 157–172). Los Angeles: The Civil Rights Project at UCLA.

Chavez, L. (1998). *The color bind: California's battle to end affirmative action*. Berkeley: University of California Press.

Coleman, A. L., Palmer, S. R., Sanghavi, E., & Winnick, S. Y. (2007, March). *From federal law to state voter initiatives: Preserving higher education's authority to achieve the educational, economic, civic, and security benefits associated with a diverse student body.* New York: College Board.

Cornwell-Mustard HOPE Scholarship Page. (2007). *Georgia's HOPE scholarship.* Retrieved November 4, 2007, from http://www.terry.uga.edu/hope/gahope.html

Domina, T. (2007). Higher education policy as secondary school reform: Texas public high schools after *Hopwood. Educational Evaluation and Policy Analysis, 29*(3), 200–217.

Doyle, W. R. (2006). Adoption of merit-based student grant programs: An event history analysis. *Educational Evaluation and Policy Analysis, 28*(3), 259–285.

Dynarski, S. (2004). The new merit aid. In C. M. Hoxby (Ed.), *College choices: The economics of where to go, when to go, and how to pay for it* (pp. 63–97). Chicago: University of Chicago Press and the National Bureau of Economic Research.

Euben, D. R. (2002, May). *Academic freedom of individual professors and higher education institutions: The current legal landscape.* Washington, DC: AAUP. Retrieved November 17, 2007, from http://www.aaup.org/AAUP/protect/legal/topics/AF-profs-inst.htm

Flores, S. M. (2007). *The effect of in-state resident tuition policies on the college enrollment of undocumented Latino students in Texas and the United States.* Unpublished doctoral dissertation, Harvard University, Cambridge, MA.

Gladieux, L. E., Hauptman, A. M., & Knapp, L. G. (1994). The federal government and higher education. In P. G. Altbach, R. O. Berdahl, & P. J. Gumport (Eds.), *Higher education in American society* (3rd ed., pp. 125–154). Amherst, NY: Prometheus Books.

Gratz v. Bollinger, 539 U.S. 244 (2003).

Grutter v. Bollinger, 539 U.S. 306 (2003).

Healy, P. (1998, April 24). Affirmative action survives at colleges in some states covered by *Hopwood* ruling. *The Chronicle of Higher Education.* Retrieved December 5, 2007, from http://chronicle.com/che-data/articles.dir/art-44.dir/issue-33.dir/33a04201.htm

Heller, D. E. (2002). State merit scholarship programs: An introduction. In D. E. Heller & P. Marin (Eds.), *Who should we help? The negative social consequences of merit scholarships* (pp. 15–24). Cambridge, MA: The Civil Rights Project at Harvard University.

Heller, D. E., & Marin, P. (Eds.). (2002). *Who should we help? The negative social consequences of merit scholarships.* Cambridge, MA: The Civil Rights Project at Harvard University.

Heller, D. E., & Marin, P. (Eds.). (2004). *State merit scholarship programs and racial inequality.* Cambridge, MA: The Civil Rights Project at Harvard University.

Hopwood v. Texas, 78 F. 3d 932 (5th Cir.); *cert. denied,* 518 U.S. 1033 (1996).

Horn, C. L., & Flores, S. (2003). *Percent plans in college admissions: A comparative analysis of three states' experiences.* Cambridge, MA: The Civil Rights Project at Harvard University.

Kaplin, W. A., & Lee, B. A. (1995). *The law of higher education* (3rd ed.). San Francisco: Jossey-Bass.

Keyishian v. Board of Regents of the University of the State of New York, 385 U.S. 589 (1967).

Long, M. C. (2004). College applications and the effect of affirmative action. *Journal of Econometrics, 121,* 319–342.

Marin, P. (2002). Merit scholarships and the outlook for equal opportunity in higher education. In D. E. Heller & P. Marin (Eds.), *Who should we help? The negative social consequences of merit scholarships* (pp. 111–116). Cambridge, MA: The Civil Rights Project at Harvard University.

Marin, P., & Yun, J. T. (2005). From strict scrutiny to educational scrutiny: A new vision for higher education policy and research. In G. Orfield, P. Marin, & C. L. Horn (Eds.), *Higher education and the color line: College access, racial equity, and social change* (pp. 197–218). Cambridge, MA: Harvard Education Press.

McGuinness, A. C., Jr. (1994). The states and higher education. In P. G. Altbach, R. O. Berdahl, & P. J. Gumport (Eds.), *Higher education in American society* (3rd ed., pp. 155–180). Amherst, NY: Prometheus Books.

Meredith v. Jefferson County Board of Education, 127 S. Ct. 2738 (2007).

Montejano, D. (1998). On *Hopwood:* The continuing challenge. In N. Foley (Ed.), *Reflexiones 1997: New directions in Mexican American studies* (pp. 133–156). Austin, TX: CMAS Books.

Moses, M. S. (2011). Affirmative and the creation of more favorable contexts of choice. In S. R. Harper & J. F. L. Jackson (Eds.), *Introduction to American higher education* (pp. 427–453). New York: Routledge.

Olivas, M. A. (2004). IIRIRA, the Dream Act, and undocumented college student residency. *Journal of College and University Law, 30,* 435–464.

Parents Involved in Community Schools v. Seattle School District No. 1, 127 S. Ct. 2738 (2007).

Passel, J. S. (2005, March 21). *Estimates of the size and characteristics of the undocumented population* (Pew Hispanic Center). Retrieved September 1, 2005, from http://pewhispanic.org/reports/report.php?ReportID = 44

Passel, J. S., Van Hook, J., & Bean, F. D. (2004). *Estimates of the legal and unauthorized foreign-born population for the United States and selected states, based on Census 2000* (Report to the Census Bureau). Washington, DC: Urban Institute.

Pusser, B. (2004). *Burning down the house: Politics, governance, and affirmative action at the University of California.* New York: State University of New York Press.

Redden, E. (2007). An in-state tuition debate. *Inside Higher Education.* Retrieved March 1, 2007, from http://www.insidehighered.com/news/2007/02/28/immigration

Regents of the University of California v. Bakke, 438 U.S. 265 (1978).

Rincon, A. (2005). *Paying for their status: Undocumented immigrants and college access.* Unpublished doctoral dissertation, University of Texas at Austin, Austin, Texas.

Ristine, J. (2000, January 21). UC's efforts to boost minority admissions hit. *San Diego Union-Tribune,* p. A3.

Schevitz, T. (2004, January 27). College outreach imperiled: Budget ax may hit programs helping disadvantaged students. *San Francisco Chronicle,* p. A1.

Schmidt, P. (2007, October 19). 5 more states may curtail affirmative action: Ballot measures pushed by Ward Connerly are likely to win passage. *The Chronicle of Higher Education, 54*(8), p. A1.

Springer, A. (2006). Academic freedom of students and professors, and political discrimination. Washington, DC: AAUP. Retrieved November 17, 2007, from http://www.aaup.org/AAUP/protect/legal/topics/PolDivDiscrim.htm

Student Academic Services, Office of the President at the University of California. (2002, February). *Eligibility in Local Context program evaluation report.* Retrieved June 14, 2002, from http://www.ucop.edu/news/cr/report02.pdf

Sweezy v. New Hampshire, 354 U.S. 234 (1957).

Texas Higher Education Coordinating Board. (n.d.). *HB 1403 students, 2001–2004* [Data file]. Austin, TX: Author.

Tienda, M., & Niu, S. (2004). *Capitalizing on segregation, pretending neutrality: College admissions and the Texas Top 10 Percent law.* Retrieved August 22, 2005, from http://www.texastop10.princeton.edu/reports/forthcoming/capitalizing_on_segregation.pdf

University of California Office of the President. (2003, March). *Undergraduate access to the University of California after the elimination of race-conscious policies.* Retrieved December 5, 2007, from ucop.edu/outreach/aa_finalcx%202.pdf

The University of Georgia. (2005). *The mission of the University of Georgia.* Retrieved November 4, 2007, http://www.uga.edu/profile/mission.html

PART VI

POLICY, FINANCE, AND ECONOMICS

BRIDGET TERRY LONG AND STELLA M. FLORES, ASSOCIATE EDITORS

Chapters in this section relate to a series of issues in higher education policy, law, and finance. In recent years, race and ethnicity have been at the core of multiple debates within the postsecondary educational context. In terms of college access, admissions policies and preferences have been major topics of interest both in terms of traditional approaches to affirmative action as well as alternatives to such policies in the face of state bans. The treatment of undocumented students has also been an issue of debate as states consider whether to offer in-state tuition discounts to this population. More generally, changes in federal, state, and institutional financial aid have had significant repercussions on college enrollment and choice, especially for racial and ethnic minorities. Finally, the important role of community colleges for students of color underscores the need to better understand how well they are serving particular populations. This section covers these important topics.

College access is predicated on being admitted to an institution. While the bulk of postsecondary institutions are functionally non-selective, most attention is paid to the practices of selective colleges and universities. These institutions tend to have far more resources and are seen as the gatekeepers to lucrative careers, top graduate programs, and leadership positions. Viewed through the lens of economics, the number of slots at such institutions is a limited resource and debate has ensued about how best to distribute admission to various groups. The consideration of race as a factor in admissions has long been used by such institutions, and the 2003 Supreme Court decision in *Grutter v. Bollinger* reconfirmed for many institutions that certain race-sensitive practices are permissible. Yet racial affirmative action in higher education remains a hotly contested issue.

It is worth noting, however, that preferences are also used for other groups in selective admissions. In Chapter 38, Douglas S. Massey and Margarita Mooney highlight the role of preferences exercised for athletes and legacy candidates. They compare the impact of these "other large affirmative action programs" to the racial and ethnic preferences used in admissions. Using data on nearly 4,000 students at 28 elite colleges and universities, they examine the effects of affirmative action on the academic experiences of three groups: minority students, athletes, and legacies. They find that students of color who attended institutions that used greater preferences in admissions reported lower grades, but these students were less likely to drop out of college. Meanwhile, athlete and legacy candidates who attended such schools with stronger preferences were more likely to drop out, and legacy students who enjoyed a greater admissions bonus due to their status earned lower grades. This research underscores the fact that preferences in higher education are multifaceted, and although racial and ethnic preferences have garnered the most attention, preferences for other special groups are also strong. In fact, the preferences exercised for athletes and legacies may be more indicative of the concerns of affirmative action critics (i.e., those who argue in favor of mismatch theory and stereotype threat) than the preferences exercised in favor of race and ethnicity.

While the use of racial preferences remains currently permissible, there is a question of whether they will always be needed. Alan B. Krueger, Jesse Rothstein, and Sarah Turner quote Supreme Court Justice O'Connor in her opinion in *Grutter v. Bollinger*: "We expect that 25 years from now, the use of racial preferences will no longer be necessary." In Chapter 39, these authors evaluate the plausibility of this forecast by projecting the characteristics of the applicant pool to selective, elite institutions 25 years into the future. They expect that changes in the black-white relative distribution of income and a narrowing of the test score gap between Black and White students within family income groups will help to reduce the gap in academic qualifications among students by race. However, they conclude that such progress will not be enough to yield as much racial diversity in admissions decisions as is currently obtained with racial and ethnic preferences. Krueger, Rothstein, and Turner suggest that, to meet Justice O'Connor's expectation, far more would need to be done at the elementary and secondary school levels to drastically narrow the racial test score gap over the next quarter century.

As debates continue to ensue about affirmative action in higher education, one major question is whether there are alternative policies that would help ensure diversity in U.S. higher education. In the midst of the debate before the Supreme Court decision, the 1996 *Hopwood* decision in Texas imposed a ban on affirmative action at colleges and universities in states that are part of the 5th Circuit Court jurisdiction and not under desegregation court decrees. In Chapter 40, Mark C. Long and Marta Tienda describe the repercussions of that decision on the admissions practices of three Texas universities. They found that the schools complied with the Hopwood decision by eliminating the direct preferences given to Black and Hispanic applicants. However, they also found some evidence suggesting that universities adapted to the ban by placing weight on characteristics that are more prominent among underrepresented minority applicants. Yet, these new weights were insufficient to restore the share of Black and Hispanic applicants among admitted students. Findings reported in this chapter mirror much of the other research included in this section, which has found that none of the alternatives to racial affirmative action appear to do as well in maintaining diversity. Policies that have been more successful have tended to also include significant outreach, recruitment, and financial aid strategies.

Another population that has received increasing attention is undocumented students. Estimates indicate that there are approximately 6.3 million households with undocumented residents in the United States, and one-sixth of the undocumented population is under eighteen years of age. Core to current policy debates is whether this population should be eligible for in-state, discounted tuition rates. The discount to attend public colleges and universities at an in-state resident price is particularly significant to undocumented students because they do not qualify for federal aid to finance a postsecondary education. In 2001, Texas passed the first in-state resident tuition legislation targeted at undocumented high school graduates; ten other states have since passed similar legislation. Despite the considerable legal, policy, and electoral attention this issue has received, little empirical research has examined the effects of such policies on the enrollment rates of undocumented students.

Stella M. Flores provides one of the first such analyses in Chapter 41. Using data from the *Current Population Survey*, she finds that that foreign-born, noncitizen Latinos, which includes both undocumented as well as legal residents, were more likely to enroll in college in locations with an in-state resident tuition benefit in comparison to similar students in states without such legislation. The effects are particularly strong in Texas, but at the national level, in which states differ somewhat in terms of the length of residency and prior educational attainment requirements, the overall impact is also positive and statistically significant. These analyses have important implications for the current state and national policy context regarding educational opportunities for the undocumented population. Research on whether in-state tuition benefits work to increase college attendance among this population and the implications of increased educational attainment are timely, as legislators and voters debate whether to accept or resist such policies.

While in-state tuition discounts are important to undocumented students, affordability issues are central to the college choice decisions of almost all students. Financial aid has long played an essential role in enabling the attendance and persistence of students, especially racial/ethnic minorities and undergraduates from low-income families. There is an extensive body of literature documenting the important role of college price in access and choice decisions. For example, Long and Riley (2007) described how U.S. financial aid policy has shifted in recent years from focusing on the goal of increasing access for low-income students toward reducing the burden on middle- and upper-income families. They explained how loans, merit-based aid, and education tax breaks are increasingly replacing need-based aid. They also discussed how the declining role of need-based grants may disproportionately disadvantage students who are already underrepresented in higher education. Using a variety of data sources, Long and Riley documented the rise in unmet financial need over the past decade and showed that low-income students and students of color are especially likely to face substantial unmet need. In response to these trends, they called for a greater emphasis on need-based aid, especially grants, to reduce the role of cost as a barrier to college access.

Susan Dynarski focuses in Chapter 42 on the growth of merit-based aid at the state level. Nearly 20 states now have large, broad-based merit aid initiatives, with the typical program waiving tuition and fees at public colleges and universities within a student's home state. Dynarski examines how merit aid programs in seven states have affected schooling decisions, with particular attention on how the effects of such policies have varied by race and ethnicity. She found that the policies have generally increased the likelihood of college attendance and shifted students from community colleges towards four-year institutions. However, the distributional impact by race differs by state and likely depends on the particular design of the policy. For instance, in Georgia, the relatively stringent academic requirements and an original provision that did not allow Pell Grant recipients to get the full scholarship most likely resulted in the Georgia HOPE Scholarship widening racial gaps in college attendance. However, this pattern is atypical in comparison to the other states included in Dynarski's analyses.

In Chapter 43, Edward P. St. John, Britany Affolter-Caine, and Anna S. Chung consider the fact that the above noted trends in financial aid may need to be counterbalanced with race-conscious aid policies to address increasing racial inequality in college opportunity. However, due to legal resistance to race-conscious aid awards, the authors suggest that it is increasingly important to adapt other forms of aid to ensure racial and ethnic diversity in higher education. Their chapter examines how practitioners can respond to legal challenges to race-conscious aid and well as redesign merit and other targeted grant programs to improve diversity and expand opportunity. Moreover, St. John, Affolter-Caine, and Chung discuss how research on race-conscious aid can inform legal and policy agendas for improving diversity in higher education.

The final chapter in this section focuses on the role of community colleges. Minority and low-income students disproportionally rely on the community colleges as the primary portal for post-secondary entry due to academic and financial barriers that often prevent their attendance at a four-year institution. A majority of Latino students in higher education attend public, two-year colleges, and the proportions for Black and Asian students are above 40 percent. Many community college students intend to eventually transfer and attain a baccalaureate degree. However, as more data have become available, some question the viability of the transfer function and wonder whether students suffer a penalty for starting at two-year institutions. In Chapter 44, Bridget Terry Long and Michal Kurlaender examine this issue by comparing the outcomes of community college entrants to similar students who initially entered four-year institutions within the Ohio public higher education system. After accounting for the fact that community college students tend to have lower incomes and less academic preparation, the results suggest that students who initially begin at a community college were 14.5 percent less likely to complete a bachelor's degree within nine years. On the one hand, this estimate is much smaller than most reported in the literature, which fails to adequately adjust for the fact that community college students tend to come from more disadvantaged backgrounds. But on the other hand, the results underscore the need to improve system-wide institutional policies and programs that support community college students and help them transfer to four-year institutions.

Conclusion

To summarize, the seven chapters in this section offers multiple perspectives on policies that affect racial/ethnic minority students. These studies use rigorous research designs, strong data sources, and emphasize how research translates into credible, data-driven recommendations to transform U.S. higher education policy and practice. Together, they make clear how policies, the law, and economics separately and collectively work to determine which students are admitted to college, allowable criteria for their selection, the institutional choices they will have, longer-term consequences associated with their enrollment at particular colleges and universities, and options they are presented to finance their degrees. The chapters that follow provide detailed evidence of these and other considerations at institutional, state, and federal government levels with respect to racial and ethnic minority students.

Reference

Long, B. T., & Riley, E. (2007). Financial aid: A broken bridge to college access. *Harvard Educational Review, 77*(1), 39–63.

CHAPTER 38
THE EFFECTS OF AMERICA'S THREE AFFIRMATIVE ACTION PROGRAMS ON ACADEMIC PERFORMANCE

DOUGLAS S. MASSEY AND MAGARITA MOONEY

Although affirmative action programs for minority students form just one of several criteria for preferential admissions to American colleges and universities, little research has compared the impact of other large "affirmative actions" programs such as those for athletes and legacies. Using data from the National Longitudinal Survey of Freshmen (NLSF), a sample of nearly 4,000 students in 28 elite American colleges and universities, we develop models that test claims about the effects of affirmative action—namely mismatch hypothesis and stereotype threat—on college performance in three groups: minorities, athletes, and legacies. First, we estimate models predicting two direct and indirect effects suggested by stereotype threat: hours studied per week and the degree of psychological performance burden reported by students. Next we include these direct and indirect measures of stereotype threat and the mismatch hypothesis on grades earned through the end of sophomore year and the likelihood of leaving school by spring of junior year. We do not find strong evidence for the mismatch hypothesis as applied to minorities and athletes, although legacies who enjoyed a greater admissions bonus earned lower grades. Minorities attending institutions that practice greater affirmative action were less likely to drop out but did report lower grades. We also find that legacies and athletes who attend a school that practices institutional affirmative action are indeed more likely to drop out of school.

Affirmative action in favor of underrepresented minorities has been debated by scholars, the media, and the public for many years. Attention crested in 2003 with the Supreme Court's Bollinger decisions, which reaffirmed the constitutionality of using race as one factor, among several, in college admission decisions. Less controversial have been two other preferential admission programs also in widespread use, one granting an admissions bonus to applicants with athletic skills and the other conferring preferential treatment on the children of alumni, commonly known as "legacy admissions." Even less attention has focused on smaller preferential admissions programs having to do with region, class, and rural origin. As these various categories suggest, entry into selective institutions of higher education has never been decided purely on academic criteria—before or after minority affirmative action came into effect (Fetter 1995; Zwick 2002).

The term "affirmative action" comes from the legal requirement that institutional officials take concrete, identifiable, and positive (in other words, *affirmative*) steps to include historically excluded groups in their selection pools and to adopt mechanisms that enure their representation among those ultimately chosen (Skrentny 1996). We realize, of course, that legacy admissions and athletic recruitment originate from very different motivations, but here we label them as "affirmative" because they, too, bring non-academic criteria positively to bear in the admissions process. In attaching the label "affirmative action" to legacy and athletic admissions, we are being deliberately provocative in order to underscore the fact that minorities are not the only social group to benefit from a "thumb on the scale" in academic admissions.

The lack of popular or scholarly attention to America's two other major affirmative action programs does not stem from their small size. James L. Shulman and William G. Bowen (2001) document the huge importance of athletic affirmative action in college admissions and demonstrate that its influence is greatest in small liberal arts colleges. Among students entering institutions in the New England Small College Athletic Conference in 1995, for example, Bowen and Sarah A. Levin (2003:86) found that 24 percent of males and 17 percent of females were *recruited* athletes. According to their calculations, recruited athletes had roughly a 33-percentage point advantage over non-athletes in the admissions process.

A survey conducted by H. M. Breland and associates (1995) found that affirmative action for children of alumni is practiced widely at both public and private institutions. A recent survey by Daniel Golden (2003) found that 23 percent of freshmen enrolled at Notre Dame were the children of alumni, with corresponding figures of 14 percent at Penn, 13 percent at Harvard, 11 percent at Princeton, and 11 percent at the University of Virginia. The seemingly modest size of these percentages belies the fact that children of alumni constitute a relatively small share of all applicants to selective schools. When one controls for the number of applicants, the children of alumni are found to benefit from exceptionally high admission rates. According to William G. Bowen and Derek Bok (1998), legacies had a two to one admissions advantage over non-legacies. Cameron Howell and Sarah E. Turner (2004) document a similar advantage at the University of Virginia, where only 32 percent of regular applicants were admitted compared with 57 percent of alumni children. As a result, the freshman class of 2002 was 7 percent legacy, compared with 3 percent African American, even though the state is 20 percent black.

The preferential boost given to alumni children appears to be greatest at private institutions. The University of Pennsylvania is one of the few institutions brave enough to publish admissions data online. According to final tabulations for the Class of 2008, legacies accounted for 4.6 percent of applicants but made up 11.2 percent of admissions; and whereas the overall admission rate at Penn was 21 percent, it was 51 percent for the children of alumni, yielding an advantage of 2.4 to 1 (University of Pennsylvania 2005). In their study of three private research universities, Thomas J. Espenshade, Chang Y. Chung, and Joan L. Walling (2004) found that 50 percent of legacies were admitted compared with only 25 percent overall. By way of comparison, the authors learned that 49 percent of athletes were admitted, compared with 39 percent of African Americans and 32 percent of Latinos.

It is clear that the United States hosts three major programs of "affirmative action" that assign significant weight to membership in a social group. It is also clear that programs targeting athletes and alumni children are at least as large (in terms of numbers of people who benefit) as those favoring minorities. The foregoing statistics can be misleading, however, because they do not take into account the scholarly qualifications of different sets of applicants. Although in raw terms, athletes and legacies may both enjoy a 2 to 1 admissions advantage, it is quite possible that the former are relatively less qualified, while the latter are relatively more qualified, on average.

The only comprehensive study of all three affirmative action programs that has sought to control for variation in qualifications is that of Espenshade and associates (2004). They used special tabulations of admissions data to estimate models predicting the likelihood of admission using variables such as sex, citizenship, SAT score, high school GPA, race, athletic recruitment, and legacy status. Other things equal, they found that being African American instead of white translated into the equivalent of 230 extra SAT points on a 1600 point scale. For athletes the advantage was 200 points, and for legacies it was 160 points. Thus, when objective qualifications are held constant, being African American appears to be somewhat more powerful in achieving selective admission than athletic ability or alumni family origins. All three groups nonetheless receive a substantial premium in the entry sweepstakes compared with other applicants.

Despite the large size of America's three affirmative action programs, only minority affirmative action has been controversial. Critics have leveled three basic charges against race-sensitive admissions: (1) affirmative action constitutes reverse discrimination that lowers the odds of admission for other, better qualified non-minority students; (2) affirmative action creates a mismatch between the skills of minority students and the abilities required for success at selective institutions, setting up minorities for academic problems; and (3) affirmative action stigmatizes members of the target group as less than fully qualified, which results in demoralization and substandard performance by students in the favored group who may, in fact, be very well qualified.

The first criticism—that affirmative action constitutes reverse discrimination (see Glazer 1976)—has not stood up to empirical scrutiny. Studies show that minority affirmative action generally has small and insignificant effects on the admission prospects of white students (Dickens and Kane 1999; Wilson 1995). In legal terms, the Supreme Court recently held that using race, as one of *several* factors, in college admissions is indeed constitutional and allowable under federal law (see *Gratz v. Bollinger* 2003; *Grutter v. Bollinger* 2003). In light of this decision, and owing to a lack of appropriate data at our disposal, we will not consider the reverse discrimination hypothesis further in this paper.

The second hypothesis, which argues that affirmative action sets up minority students for failure by placing them in academic settings where they are under-prepared, has been called the mismatch hypothesis because it posits a disconnect between the skills minority students possess and those they need for success at competitive institutions of higher education (Sowell 2004; Thernstrom and Thernstrom 1999). Although this hypothesis makes intuitive sense, it has not been supported empirically (see Holzer and Neumark 2000; Kane 1998). Bowen and Bok (1998), for example, found that blacks who attended selective institutions were more likely to graduate than their counterparts at less selective institutions. Sigal Alon and Marta Tienda (2005) found that minority students generally thrive at selective institutions, whatever their origins.

In his assessment of minority affirmative action at U.S. law schools, Richard H. Sander (2004) argued that black students were substantially less qualified than whites and that, as a result, they clustered at the bottom of the class, dropped out at higher rates, and failed the bar more often. Based on these data, he concluded that affirmative action actually undermined the goal of producing black lawyers. The fact that blacks earn lower test scores, achieve lower grades, and graduate at lower rates is well-documented across all institutions, selective or not, but critics have argued that these facts alone provide no basis for concluding that affirmative action is causing academic problems (see Chambers et al. 2005).

A recent analysis of the academic effects of minority affirmative action programs at selective schools led Mary J. Fischer and Douglas S. Massey (forthcoming) to conclude that affirmative action did *not* set up minority students for unusual academic difficulties. They developed an index measuring the degree to which minority students were likely to have benefited from affirmative action and found that likely beneficiaries actually earned *higher* grades than other minority students, other things equal. That is, black and Hispanic students with SAT scores below the institutional average earned better grades than minority students generally, contradicting the mismatch hypothesis.

A third argument against affirmative action is that, at a collective level, it stigmatizes minority group members as intellectually inferior (see Thernstrom and Thernstrom 1999). We label this proposition the stereotype threat hypothesis because it claims that affirmative action underscores the belief—deeply ingrained in American culture—that minority students, especially African Americans, are less intelligent (a hypothesis originated by Steele 1992). In this case, affirmative action's exacerbation of racial stigma influences not only how white students view their minority peers, but also how minority students view themselves. Even proponents of affirmative action admit that heightening racial stigma is a possible negative consequence of affirmative action (Bowen and Bok 1998).

If white students believe that many of their black peers wouldn't be there were it not for a "lowering" of academic standards under affirmative action, and more importantly, if black students *perceive* whites to believe this (see Torres and Charles 2004), then affirmative action may indeed undermine minorities' academic performance by increasing the psychological burden they experience. Fischer and Massey (forthcoming) also addressed the issue of stereotype threat and found that affirmative action policies did, in fact, heighten the level of psychological threat to black students and contributed to their under-performance.

In the present study, we expand on this earlier work by measuring simultaneously the academic effects of all three of America's large affirmative action programs. Specifically, we estimate models to test whether skills mismatch and stereotype threat influence the academic performance of legacies and athletes as well as minorities. Presumably skills mismatch operates similarly for all three groups—to the extent that admissions standards are "relaxed" to recruit athletes or admit the children of alumni, then these students likewise are set up for academic difficulties. Moreover, if it is widely believed on campus that standards have been lowered to admit athletes and legacies, this belief could trigger mechanisms of stereotype threat similar to those experienced by minorities, emphasizing negative images about college athletes ("dumb jocks") and alumni children ("stupid rich kids").

Affirmative Action and Academic Performance

Measuring Affirmative Action

To gauge the effects of affirmative action on academic performance, one must rely on some operational measure by which students from extremely diverse backgrounds can be compared. For this reason, debates about the effects of affirmative action intersect with broader debates about the value and appropriateness of standardized tests in evaluating students for college admission (Lemann 1999; Owen 1999; Zwick 2002). Much attention has focused on the SAT, which has been shown to be an imperfect predictor of college performance, especially among minorities (Bowen and Bok 1998; Fleming 2002; Fleming and Garcia 1998). Despite vocal criticisms (see Gould 1981; Taylor 1980), the SAT remains a staple of the college admissions process, though it may be less important at selective private institutions, which generally cast a wider net in their search for meritorious students by taking into account a variety of skills, talents, and accomplishments in addition to grades and test scores (see Springer and Franck 2005; Steinberg 2002).

Wherever they apply, however, students and parents display an obsessive concern with SAT scores and this test continues to signify to the general public how well qualified a student is to attend a prestigious college, as evidenced by their prominence in the institutional ratings published annually by *U.S. News and World Report* (see U.S. News and World Report 2005). When critics of affirmative action speak out against race-sensitive admissions, the evidence they most often cite to document the "unfairness" of race-sensitive admissions are the large black-white test score gaps (see Jencks and Philips 1998; Thernstrom and Thernstrom 1999).

Perhaps for these reasons, when Espenshade and associates (2004) sought to quantify the admissions advantage granted to affirmatively targeted groups, they did so in terms of an SAT score "bonus." We also use SAT scores to measure affirmative action, not because they are ideal, but because they offer a practical method that can be applied across groups and schools, in addition to occupying center stage in the affirmative action debate. In essence, we take the critics at their word and reason that if admissions standards have indeed been "loosened" to facilitate the entry of a particular group of students—athletes, legacies, or minorities— then we expect to observe an SAT gap between the group in question and other students on campus. Whenever a targeted group's SAT scores lie below the institutional average, we assume it is because admissions officers have traded off low test scores against other criteria associated with a desire to recruit members of the group— the essence of affirmative action. The more group-specific criteria are applied, the less weight is given to SAT scores, and the larger the test-score gap.

Modeling Affirmative Action's Effects

As Fischer and Massey (forthcoming) pointed out, applying group-sensitive admissions policies yields gaps at both the individual and institutional level. Given the plethora of guides publishing institutional average SAT scores (see College Board 2005; Fiske, 2005; Meltzer et al. 2005; U.S. News and World Report 2005; Yale Daily News 2005), an individual from a targeted group with a low SAT score will most likely be aware that his or her score is below the usual level for the institution. In addition, whatever one's own SAT score might be, students in theory can observe a gap between members of a targeted group and students in general, either directly because the data are published (online or a in college guide) or indirectly because group differences in performance are apparent in classrooms and members of targeted groups concentrate in what are perceived to be "easy" classes.

Following Fischer and Massey (forthcoming), we define two measures of affirmative action that attempt to capture different pathways through which such policies may affect students' achievement. We hypothesize that individual and institutional affirmative action influence academic achievement in direct and indirect ways, yielding a more complicated model of the program's consequences than has been specified before. Our expanded conceptualization of the process by which affirmative action influences academic achievement is summarized in Figure 1.

For students entering a selective college or university, whether they themselves received an affirmative action benefit (measured by the gap between their SAT score and the school average) and whether their institution makes extensive use of affirmative action criteria (indicated by the gap between their group's average SAT score and students in general) are exogenous factors over which they have no control. They either received an individual admissions benefit or they did not, and they are entering a school that practices affirmative action for certain groups of students or does not. Of course, they don't know either fact with absolute certainty—they are simply making informed guesses based on knowledge of their own and their group's test scores.

Testing Stereotype Threat

In their study of stereotype threat among minority students, Massey and Fischer (2005) showed that negative stereotypes within minority student culture operate in two distinct ways to undermine academic performance. Stereotype internalization refers to the extent that group members come to believe, at least at some level, negative stereotypes about their own group. Stereotypes are internalized when they are wholly or partly adopted by the individual and incorporated into his or her social cognition (Fiske and Taylor 1991). If a student has internalized negative stereotypes about his or her group (fearing that a negative stereotype may, in fact, be true) it creates a painful psychological situation. If a student agrees that good grades indicate intelligence and works very hard to earn high marks, but nonetheless achieves low grades, then he or she confirms, at least to him or herself, the negative stereotype of group intellectual inferiority, a very painful psychological prospect for most people (see Steele 1992, 1997).

To reduce the implicit level of threat, members of stereotyped groups have been found to engage in a process of disidentification, in which academic achievement is simply removed from the domain of factors that determine self-esteem (Crocker and Major 1989; Crocker and Quinn 1998). In their analysis of stereotype threat, Massey and Fischer (2005) conceived of disidentification in terms of academic effort. They found that students who internalized negative stereotypes about their group's intellectual ability significantly reduced the hours they studied, which led to lower grades.

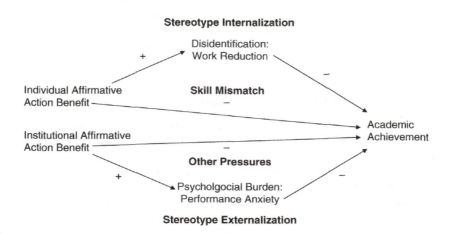

Figure 1   Conceptual Model of the Effect of Affirmative Action on Academic Performance.

Although the grades may have been low, the students were protected psychologically because they could tell themselves, "well, I didn't work that hard anyway." Poor performance is thus rationalized by limited work effort rather than by supposed group-specific deficiencies (Steele and Aronson 1995). Michael J. Lovaglia and associates (1998) suggest that stereotype threat and disidentification are not limited to minorities, but can work to undermine the performance of any group that is symbolically labeled as intellectually or morally suspect, such as athletes or legacy students.

The externalization of stereotypes occurs when minority members expect others to act on the basis of prejudicial notions in evaluating them (Massey and Fischer 2005). Most African Americans, for example, are well aware of negative stereotypes about black intellectual ability (Torres and Charles 2004). Indeed, growing up black in American society, it is nearly impossible *not* to learn about the stigma of black intellectual inferiority (Loury 2001). It is logical to assume, therefore, that many black students *expect* that white professors and students will draw on this stereotype in evaluating their performance on intellectual tasks.

Externalization creates a different kind of psychological burden compared with internalization because the stereotype is acknowledged publicly. Specifically, the expectation that others will draw on negative stereotypes in making evaluations increases performance anxiety to put extra pressure on students whenever they are called upon to demonstrate what they have learned and how well they can think. Students who believe that professors and other students are prejudiced against them come to feel as if they are carrying the entire group on their backs every time they are asked to perform. Massey and Fischer (2005) showed that students who saw out-group members as biased and prejudiced experienced a much higher performance burden because they viewed their performance as reflecting well or badly on the entire group, and that this psychological burden lowered grades significantly.

If the application of affirmative action policies leads to perceived differences between groups in terms of preparation or ability at a particular institution (as measured by average test-score gaps between group members and other students on campus), then the externalization of stereotypes will be exacerbated. Apparent differences between a group's SAT scores and those of other students only serve to underscore negative stereotypes about the group's intellectual ability. If students from the group fail to acquit themselves well, it reflects badly not only on themselves, but on all group members. They will have confirmed the negative stereotype not only to themselves, but to their professors and fellow students. As a result, when it comes time to perform on a test or assignment, they choke.

We do not argue that the potential for stereotype threat is equal for all three affirmatively targeted groups. The canard of black racial inferiority is no doubt far more vicious and deep-seated than stereotypes about dumb jocks or stupid rich kids, and minority status is far more visible to other students than being a recruited athlete or alumni child. Virtually all people of African ancestry, and most Latinos, are easily recognizable as minorities by other students and faculty on campus. Aside from unusually large males who play on the on the football or basketball teams, however, athletes are not necessarily recognizable by others, and legacies are even more difficult to identify. We thus expect minorities such as blacks and Latinos to be more vulnerable to stereotype threat than athletes or legacies.

Testing the Mismatch and Other Hypotheses

While the theory of stereotype threat argues that affirmative action affects performance indirectly through disidentification and performance burden, the skills mismatch hypothesis postulates a direct effect at the individual level. Members of targeted groups who benefit from a relaxing of admissions standards under affirmative action are set up for academic trouble later on because they are less prepared than other students for the rigors of competition on elite campuses. Holding constant the effect of stereotype threat, students who have benefited from affirmative action should achieve less academic success than other students, and the greater the divergence between their academic preparation (as captured by the SAT) and the institutional norm, the worse they are expected to do academically.

The direct effect of institutional-level affirmative action on academic performance has not been well theorized up to this point. In addition to whatever effects institutional affirmative action may have in undermining academic performance through stereotype externalization, it may also lead to other pressures that inhibit scholarly achievement. If a group is perceived to be on campus "illegitimately," such perceptions could produce a tense social atmosphere characterized by inter-group disputes that poison relations on campus and make life difficult for members of a targeted group, yielding social pressures that undermine academic performance. We label this the social subversion hypothesis because affirmative action is hypothesized to undermine the social legitimacy of group members on campus.

Data and Measures

Our data come from the National Longitudinal Survey of Freshmen (NLSF), a probability sample of students who entered 28 selective U.S. colleges and universities as freshmen in the fall of 1999. Some 35 schools were asked to participate in the study, including all of the institutions studied by Bowen and Bok (1998), plus the University of California at Berkeley. All but seven of the schools (Duke, Hamilton, Morehouse, Spelman, Vanderbilt, Wellesley, and Xavier) agreed and were able to participate, yielding an institutional response rate of 80 percent. This sample is ideal for our analysis precisely because it is comprised only of students from the most selective academic institutions. Affirmative action programs—whether geared toward minorities, athletes, or legacies—are only relevant if admissions are competitive, and the more competitive the competition the more relevant—and controversial—they become.

Among institutions that agreed to participate, NLSF investigators approached 4,573 randomly selected students and completed 3,924 face-to-face interviews, for an overall response rate of 86 percent (Massey et al. 2003). The baseline sample included 998 whites, 959 Asians, 916 Latinos, and 1,051 African Americans. The survey gathered extensive information about respondents prior to entering college and measured in some detail their attitudes, motivations, and perceptions. A detailed description of the sampling methodology and questionnaire and a list of the 28 institutions are presented in Massey and associates (2003).

The baseline survey was followed by a series of shorter telephone surveys designed to determine how respondents had fared since the first interview. Follow-up surveys were administered each spring from 2000 through 2003. Here we draw upon data compiled in the follow-up surveys of 2000 and 2001 when most respondents were finishing their freshman and sophomore years. The respective response rates for these waves were 96 percent and 90 percent. Whereas the independent variables used in the analyses are defined from the baseline survey, the intervening variables and the outcomes come from the freshman and sophomore follow-up surveys.

We sought to consider the effect of affirmative action on two academic outcomes. The first outcome considered is the cumulative GPA earned through the sophomore year. GPA was calculated from retrospective self-reports of courses taken and grades earned. A validation exercise performed by Massey and associates (2003) compared self-reported grades to those from official transcripts and found that student self-reports were accurate and reliable. The second outcome is whether the student left school by the end of the junior year (the spring of 2002). Leaving the institution in which a student matriculated as a freshman does not necessarily mean that a person dropped out of higher education entirely, but it nonetheless indicates something problematic about the student's presence at the institution (either social, financial, or academic). We defined school leaving as a dichotomous variable coded 1 if the student was not enrolled in the same institution during the spring of their junior year and 0 otherwise.

To measure affirmative action at the individual level, we computed the difference between the SAT score earned by a member of a targeted group and the institutional average, yielding three different individual level scores—one for legacies, one for athletes, and one for minorities. For group members with SAT scores that equaled or exceeded the school average, we coded the individual affirmative action score as 0. For those having scores below the institutional average, we coded the score as the absolute value of the deviation between that person's score and the school average. A value of 0 indicates that the student likely did not receive an affirmative action benefit, and a positive score means that some benefit may have accrued, with the size of the likely benefit roughly indicated by the size of the score. Because legacies, athletes, and minorities are subsets of the larger student population it is possible for all subgroup members to have SAT scores below the institutional average.

To measure affirmative action at the institutional level we took the difference between the average SAT score earned by a targeted group and all students at the college or university in question, once again yielding three scores—an institutional score for legacies, one for athletes, and one for minorities. As before, a score of 0 means that the targeted group likely received no average benefit at the aggregate level, and a positive score indicates the relative size of the benefit that was received. The larger the aggregate gap, the more an institution may be presumed to have used criteria other than SAT scores to determine admission for athletes, legacies, or minorities. The institutional affirmative action indices were assigned only to individuals belonging to the relevant group. Thus only minority students received an institutional score for minority affirmative action, only athletes received an institutional score for athletic affirmative action, and only the children of alumni get an institutional score for legacy affirmative action. All other students received a score of 0. Again, since each group constitutes a small subset of all students at each institution, it is possible for the group mean to lie below the institutional mean across all schools and groups.

We built on prior work by Massey and Fischer (2005) to define the two intervening variables described in Figure 1—academic effort and performance burden. Although all respondents provided a self-rating of their academic effort using a 0 to 100 scale (where 0 indicated no effort and 100 indicated maximum possible effort), this subjective rating was highly correlated with another, clearer, and more objective indicator: the number of hours per week spent studying. Students were asked to estimate the number of hours per week they spent studying, and given this variable's concrete meaning and straightforward interpretation, we employ it here (as did Massey and Fischer 2005).

Whereas Massey and Fischer (2005) measured performance burden using items that explicitly referenced the respondent's own racial/ethnic group, we selected items that were general and could apply to any student regardless of ethnicity. In order to maximize the number of items and increase the reliability of our index, we included items from waves 1, 2, and 3 (listed in the Appendix). From the wave 1 survey we included an item that asked respondents about their experience as seniors in high school:

> How self-conscious were you about the way that your teachers perceived you, with 0 meaning you were not conscious at all and 10 meaning that you were extremely sensitive to what they thought?

From waves 2 and 3 we included the following two items:

> Using the same 0 to 10 scale, where 0 indicates total disagreement and 10 indicates total agreement, how much do you agree or disagree with the following statements? (a) If I let my instructors know that I am having difficulty in class, they will think less of me. (b) If I let other students know that I am having difficulty in class, they will think less of me.

Finally, from wave 3 we used these items:

> Using the same 0 to 10 scale, where 0 indicates total disagreement and 10 indicates total agreement, how much do you agree or disagree with the following statements? (a) I don't want to look foolish or stupid in class. (b) If I don't do well, people will look down on others like me.

With nine items, each scored 0 to 10, the resulting composite scale has a theoretical range of 0 to 90, though in practice it varied only from 0 to 85. Across the entire sample the mean value of performance burden was 33.9 with a standard deviation of 13.6 and a Cronbach's alpha of 0.77, indicating a relatively high degree of reliability. Minorities and athletes generally experienced the greatest performance burden, with index values of 34.4 and 34.7, respectively, compared with 32.8 among legacies. Within each group, however, the reliability of measurement was roughly comparable, with alpha coefficients of 0.77 for minorities, 0.78 for legacies, and 0.72 for athletes. This index measures performance burden in a very general sense and it remains empirically to be determined whether and how this overall anxiety is affected by affirmative action.

In seeking to measure the direct and indirect effects of individual and institutional affirmative action, we hold constant a variety of social characteristics. Because demographic background has been shown to affect academic performance, we include controls for variables such gender (1 if male, 0 otherwise); whether the student grew up in an intact, two-parent family (1 for intact and 0 otherwise); and being of foreign origin (1 if the student had a foreign born parent and 0 otherwise). We also control for indicators of socioeconomic status such as parental education, which we measure by counting the number of college degrees held by parents. An undergraduate degree (BA, BS, AB) counts for one point, while an advanced degree (PhD, JD, MD) yields an additional point. Thus each parent contributes a maximum of two points, yielding a scale of 0 (neither parent went to college) and 4 (both parents have advanced degrees). Parental income is measured as a dichotomous variable coded 1 if the student reported that household income during the year prior to college was greater than or equal to $100,000, and 0 otherwise. Poverty status was measured with a dummy variable that equaled 1 if the respondent's family had ever been on welfare while growing up, and 0 otherwise.

We measured prior academic preparation for college using five indicators. First, we included self-reported SAT scores in the model. This question was asked in the third wave of data collection, so there are some cases that are missing this information due to non-participation in that wave (those who had dropped out by then couldn't report). There were also students who were present in wave 3, but who chose to not answer the question. Unit and item non-response leave us with 2,865 cases for analysis. In addition, because one cannot speak of affirmative action for minorities at Howard University, the only Historically Black College in our sample, the 60 students from Howard were dropped in this paper.

Another potentially important factor in predicting performance is whether or not the student attended a private school prior to coming to college. Attending private schools may be one method that parents living in less desirable neighborhoods can offset the negative impact of their immediate environment. If the student reported attending private school at age 6, age 13, and age 18, we coded the private school indicator as 1. The variable was coded 0 if the student attended public schools exclusively or for some of their schooling. We also include an indicator of advanced placement (AP) courses. Students were asked to list any AP courses that they took in high school. Based on this report, we created a count of the number of AP courses taken. Students also reported grades earned in major academic subjects during high school and from this roster of course grades, we computed a high school grade point average. Finally, students were asked to rate the overall quality of their high school, from poor (1) to excellent (4).

Following Massey et al. (2003) we control for a student's social and psychological preparation for college by measuring social distance from whites (presumably the normative population on elite campuses) and susceptibility to peer influence, along with standard indices of self-efficacy and self-esteem. Social distance from whites was measured using 0 to 10 closeness ratings with respect to five different targets: young white men, young white women, rich whites, middle class whites, and whites in general. The resulting scale had a range of 0 to 50 and a reliability of .898 (see Appendix B in Massey et al. 2003). We measured the degree to which respondents were susceptible to peer influence by coding the degree of agreement with statements pertaining to their high school years, such as "I thought and acted like others;" "I valued the same thing as others;" "I worried about what others thought of me;" and "I did things so that others would like me." Each of seven such items was coded 0 to 4 such that a higher score indicated less sensitivity to peer influence and more individual autonomy. The resulting index had a possible range of 0 to 28 and a Cronbach's alpha of .592.

The NLSF assessed psychological preparation using standard measures of self-esteem and self-efficacy developed by Morris Rosenberg and Roberta Simmons (1971). To measure self-esteem, the questionnaire asked respondents the degree to which they agreed or disagreed with ten statements about self-worth, such as "I am a person of worth equal to others;" "I have a number of good qualities;" and "I am inclined to feel I am a failure." Each item was coded 0 to 4 such that a higher value indicated a higher self-appraisal. Summing across all items yielded a scale with a potential range of 0 to 40 and a reliability of .855. The scale of self-efficacy was created from questions asking about agreement or disagreement with statements such as "I don't have control over the direction of my life" and "every time I try to get ahead something stops me." Six such items were coded 0 to 4 to yield a scale of self-efficacy that ranged from 0 to 24 and had an alpha of 0.69.

Finally, in response to helpful suggestions from reviewers we included several controls for institutional characteristics as well as student financial aid. The racial environment in each school is assessed by computing the percentage of same-race students for each student within each group at each campus. Following Massey and Fischer (2005) we also include an indicator of whether the number of minority faculty reported by students in their classes is above or below the median for the NLSF in general. Type of institution is represented by dummy variables indicating whether the institution is a public research institution or a private liberal arts college, with the reference category being a private research university. To assess a student's financial status, we note whether he or she received a grant or fellowship and whether or not he or she worked for pay during the freshman or sophomore year.

Explaining Study Effort and Performance Burden

Our comparison focuses on three groups that have been well documented to benefit from special consideration in the college admissions process: athletes, legacies, and minorities. For our purposes, athletes are those students who played for a varsity or junior varsity team in their freshman year; legacies are defined as students with at least one parent who attended the institution in question; and minorities include African Americans and Latinos but not Asians, who are over-represented at most selective schools.

In order to conserve space, we do not present a full table of means. Instead we simply highlight salient contrasts between the three groups on key variables. In terms of grades, legacies appear to do best, earning a GPA of 3.26 over the first two years of college, followed by athletes at 3.12, and minorities at 3.05. In terms of school leaving, athletes have the lowest departure rate (just 5 percent) through the junior year, followed by legacies (7 percent), and minorities (11 percent).

The critical exogenous predictors are the affirmative action indicators defined above. In general, athletes and minorities were most likely to be affirmative action beneficiaries under our operationalization. Whereas 70 percent of athletes and 77 percent of minorities evinced SAT scores below the institutional average, the figure was only 48 percent for legacy students. Among those members of targeted groups who appeared to benefit from affirmative action, athletes and minorities received roughly the same SAT bonus of 108 points, followed by legacies with 47 points. Thus, legacies were least likely to benefit from affirmative action and received the smallest bonus when they did so; minorities were 7 percent more likely to receive a benefit than athletes but both groups received a comparable benefit. At the institutional level, athletes received the largest bonus—93 SAT points—compared to 88 points for minorities and 23 points for legacies.

In Table 1 we show models used to estimate hours studied per week and the performance burden experienced by students on campus. Because the data are grouped by institution, we corrected for intra-group correlation in the estimation of standard errors. The top panel includes dummy variables indicating membership in the targeted groups, which are not mutually exclusive. It is possible, though statistically unlikely, that someone is simultaneously a legacy, a minority, and an athlete. Just seven respondents in the sample met all three criteria, but 159 of the 294 athletes were also minorities. The next two panels show the effect of the affirmative action benefit received by each of the three groups, first at the individual level and then at the institutional level. The remaining panels in the table show the effect of background factors we sought to control in assessing affirmative action's effects. Inspection of a correlation matrix revealed little colinearity between the various measures of affirmative action.

In the model predicting hours studied, we see that once all the variables are included in the model, most of the inter-group differences in study effort diminish to insignificance. The exception is minority students. Other things equal, they put in about 1.9 more hours per week of study effort. In terms of background variables, males study less than females and those with foreign born parents study more than those with native parents. Study time is unrelated to individual SAT scores, private school attendance, or overall school quality, but is strongly and positively predicted by the GPA earned in high school. Among social-psychological variables, social independence was positively related to study time: those who were more independent from peers tended to study more. Students at liberal arts colleges also studied more hours per week than those at other kinds of institutions.

TABLE 1

Effect of Three Affirmative Action Variables on Hours Studied per Week and Performance Burden Felt by Students in the NLSF

Independent Variables	Hours Studied per Week B	SE	Performance Burden B	SE
Key predictors				
Group status				
Minority	1.877*	0.845	0.854	0.858
Athlete	0.050	0.933	1.238	0.967
Legacy	0.829	1.684	1.127	1.019
Individual affirmative action				
Minority benefit	0.005	0.005	—	—
Athletic benefit	0.012	0.007	—	—
Legacy benefit	0.015	0.010	—	—
Institutional affirmative action				
Minority benefit	—	—	0.016	0.010
Athlete benefit	—	—	0.010*	0.004
Legacy benefit	—	—	0.011	0.009
Control variables				
Demographic background				
Male	1.782**	0.582	0.188	0.558
Intact family	0.919	0.596	0.564	0.683
Foreign parent	1.981**	0.573	1.565*	0.666
Socioeconomic background				
No. degrees held by parents	0.060	0.152	0.192	0.203
Family ever on welfare	0.820	0.871	1.854*	0.913
Income over $100K	0.172	0.543	1.529*	0.621
Academic preparation				
SAT combined	0.002	0.004	0.014***	0.003
Private school	0.255	0.875	1.321	0.770
No. AP courses taken	0.285	0.148	0.526**	0.153
High school GPA	7.116**	1.083	1.753	1.045
Self-rated school quality	0.193	0.464	0.719	0.412
Social-psychological preparation				
Social distance from whites	0.059	0.057	0.176***	0.054
Independence from peers	0.198**	0.065	0.676***	0.065
Self-efficacy	0.094	0.143	0.469***	0.124
Self-esteem	0.011	0.064	0.279***	0.066
Campus racial environment				
Percent students same race	0.010	0.013	0.031*	0.014
High no. minority professors	0.180	0.699	1.438*	0.553
Kind of institution				
Private research	—	—	—	—
Public research	1.684	1.447	1.362	0.714
Private liberal arts	2.718**	0.711	4.184***	1.071
Student financial status				
On grant or fellowship	0.297	0.519	0.434	0.614
Worked for pay	0.437	0.502	0.177	0.569
Constant	4.640	6.684	53.224***	5.027
R^2	0.070		0.145	
Number of cases	2,375		2,288	

Source: NLSF

*$p < .05$ **$p < .01$ ***$p < .001$(two-tailed tests)

Contrary to the stereotype threat hypothesis, we found no evidence that individual level affirmative action led to disidentification and reduced work effort among minority students. All of the estimated coefficients were statistically insignificant, leading us to conclude that the receipt of an affirmative action benefit by minorities and other preferred groups does not exacerbate the internalization of stereotypes to heighten stigma and produce disidentification with academic achievement.

Turning to the model predicting performance burden, we likewise ?nd no support for the hypothesized externalizing effects of stereotype threat. For minorities and legacies the coefficients are small and statistically insignificant, and for athletes the effect, though modest, is significant and negative. Although Massey and Fischer (2005) earlier found that minorities experienced a greater performance burden, using the more general measure developed here we find that once other factors are controlled, none of the affirmatively targeted experience a significant performance burden.

Beyond the effects of affirmative action, the estimated coefficients for our control variables indicate that the burden of academic performance is lowered by having a high SAT score and reporting high levels of self-esteem, self-efficacy, and social distance from whites, but the burden is raised by being of foreign origins and having taken advanced placement courses. Those students who report themselves as relatively more independent of peers also experience a higher psychological burden. Paradoxically, having more students of the same race or ethnicity on campus reduces performance burden whereas having more minority professors increases it. Students at liberal arts colleges generally feel less burdened than those at other institutions. Thus performance anxiety is predicted by a variety of individual and structural factors, but affirmative action is not one of them.

Determinants of Academic Achievement

Table 2 completes our estimation of the conceptual model by showing the effects of individual and institutional affirmative action on two indicators of academic success: GPA and the likelihood of leaving school. The equation predicting GPA was estimated using an ordinary least squares regression whereas predicting school leaving was estimated using maximum likelihood logistic regression, both corrected for clustering across institutions.

As can be seen, in terms of school leaving, the effects of affirmative action hypothesized by critics are generally not sustained. Neither of the two intervening variables (hours studied and performance burden) influence the odds of departure, rendering the indirect pathways shown in Figure 1 inoperative. In addition, once background characteristics are controlled, inter-group differences in school leaving dissolve into statistical insignificance and none of the individual indicators of affirmative action has a statistically detectable effect on the odds of departure either.

Likewise, we find no evidence that an institution's commitment to racial affirmative action raises the odds that a minority student will leave school. In this case, the lack of evidence stems not from a lack of statistically significant effects, but from a significant coefficient the sign opposite that hypothesized by affirmative action's critics. For minority students, attending a school where the application of affirmative action criteria have produced a large SAT gap between minorities and other students actually appears to lower the odds of leaving school.

Among athletes and legacy students, however, the critique is sustained. Attending an institution where these groups have lower average scores than others at the institutions does raise the odds that individual members of those groups decide to leave school, thus confirming the hypothesis of stereotype externalization. Holding these effects constant, the odds of school leaving are also strongly predicted by one indicator of academic preparation—SAT scores—as well as by a strong sense of self-efficacy, all of which decrease the likelihood of leaving school. Surprisingly, students at liberal arts colleges are more likely to leave school compared to others as are those students who received a grant or fellowship.

The statistical power of the independent variables is greater in the ordinary least squares model predicting GPA than in the logit model predicting school leaving (compare the respective R^2 values). Both performance burden and hours studied have significant effects on GPA in the expected direction, and the effect of hours studied is particularly strong, meaning that any indirect pathways going through it are potentially operative. Unfortunately, in Table 1 we have already demonstrated that affirmative

TABLE 2

Effect of Selected Variables on GPA Earned through Sophomore Year and the Odds of Leaving School among Students in the NLSF

Independent Variables	GPA through Sophomore Year		Left School	
	B	SE	B	SE
Intervening variables				
Hours studied	0.0026***	0.0006	0.0083	0.0071
Performance burden	0.0012*	0.0006	0.0106	0.0080
Key predictors				
Group status				
Minority	0.1282***	0.0258	0.0500	0.3070
Athlete	0.0405	0.0342	0.8013	0.4991
Legacy	0.0188	0.0375	0.1364	0.4361
Individual affirmative action				
Minority benefit	0.0001	0.0002	0.0002	0.0015
Athletic benefit	0.0001	0.0002	0.0030	0.0026
Legacy benefit	0.0008*	0.0004	0.0033	0.0047
Institutional affirmative action				
Minority benefit	0.0006*	0.0003	0.0061*	0.0032
Athlete benefit	0.0000	0.0001	0.0033**	0.0012
Legacy benefit	0.0003	0.0002	0.0060*	0.0027
Control variables				
Demographic background				
Male	0.0962***	0.0162	0.3306	0.1807
Intact family	0.0273	0.0207	0.0064	0.2100
Foreign parent	0.0073	0.0180	0.0036	0.2112
Socioeconomic background				
No. degrees held by parents	0.0269***	0.0054	0.0108	0.0655
Family ever on welfare	0.0114	0.0271	0.2344	0.3091
Income over $100K	0.0001	0.0179	0.2343	0.2077
Academic preparation				
Combined SAT score	0.0006***	0.0001	0.0023*	0.0010
Private school	0.0020	0.0191	0.2268	0.2633
No. AP courses taken	0.0025	0.0047	0.0892	0.0522
High school GPA	0.3562***	0.0315	0.2992	0.2796
Self-rated school quality	0.0407***	0.0108	0.1428	0.1340
Social-psychological preparation				
Social distance from whites	0.0010	0.0014	0.0126	0.0167
Independence from peers	0.0078***	0.0019	0.0303	0.0227
Self-efficacy	0.0042	0.0035	0.0776*	0.0382
Self-esteem	0.0042*	0.0019	0.0131	0.0210
Campus racial environment				
Percent students same race	0.0002	0.0004	0.0009	0.0051
High no. minority professors	0.0050	0.0155	0.1474	0.1827
Kind of institution				
Private research	—	—	—	—
Public research	0.0384	0.0213	0.3189	0.2480
Private liberal arts	0.0353	0.0298	1.5131**	0.3087
Student financial status				
On grant or fellowship	0.0084	0.0174	0.4275*	0.1975
Worked for pay	0.0127	0.0163	0.0071	0.1879
Constant	0.9280	0.1504	2.9901	1.6014
R^2	0.3244		0.077	
Number of cases	2,285		2,056	

Source: NLSF
*$p < .05$ **$p < .01$ ***$p < .001$ (two-tailed tests)

action has no significant effects on hours studied, so this indirect pathway contributes nothing to the determination of academic success. Table 1 also indicates that affirmative action is unrelated to performance burden, so despite the significant effect of performance burden on GPA, pathways through it are also inoperative.

At the individual level, there is little evidence that affirmative action itself has any direct effect on minority grade performance. For minorities as well as athletes, the coefficients in the third panel of Table 2 are small and statistically insignificant, thereby disconfirming the mismatch hypothesis. By granting these students an admissions bonus, colleges and universities do not appear to be setting them up for academic failure by placing them in situations where they are ill prepared to compete. Only among legacies does this story appear to hold: the greater the gap between an individual legacy student's SAT and the institutional average, the lower the grades earned.

At the institutional level, however, we do find some evidence of a negative effect of minority affirmative action as hypothesized under the social subversion hypothesis, though not for the other two groups. As indicated by the significant negative coefficient in the fourth panel of Table 1, the greater the gap on campus between minority SAT scores and those at the institution generally, the lower the grades earned by individual minority students at that institution. It appears that minority affirmative action as applied in the institutions under study does serve to undermine the perceived legitimacy of minority students' presence on elite campuses. Thus, institutions that grant a large SAT admissions bonus to underrepresented minorities may unwittingly undermine minority grade performance to the extent that non-minority students and professors view the presence of minority students on campus as undeserving and unearned, or seen as being there only because standards were "lowered" or "relaxed" to admit them.

Considering the control variables, we see that males earn significantly lower grades than females and that grade achievement is strongly and positively related to parents' education. The more college degrees held by a student's parents, the higher the GPA he or she earns in college. Grade attainment is also strongly and positively predicted by high SAT scores, the quality of the high school attended, and high grades earned there. College GPA is also positively predicted by greater self-esteem and independence from peers, but negatively predicted by attending a public research institution.

Even controlling for all the variables in the model, however, minority group members still earn lower grades than other students, suggesting the effect of other, unmeasured factors in determining grade performance. One such factor not considered here is the degree of school and neighborhood segregation experienced while growing up, which has been shown to have important strong consequences for minority achievement even after they come to inhabit a privileged niche in American society (see Charles, Massey and Dinwiddie 2004; Fischer and Massey 2005).

In response to the suggestion of a reviewer, we also tested for an interaction between institutional and individual level affirmative action in determining grades and school leaving among minorities. Perhaps individual affirmative action operated to undermine minority performance only in schools where it was extensively practiced at the institutional level. To consider this possibility we computed the average institutional affirmative action score for each school and divided them into high and low categories. Those schools in the high category had institutional affirmative action scores above the median and those in the low category had scores below the median. We then estimated the models in Table 2 separately for the high and low categories to test whether individual affirmative action had different effects depending on the degree to which schools practice affirmative action at the institutional level. We found no apparent difference in the effect of individual affirmative action for minorities on either grades or school leaving between the two categories.

Conclusions

In this analysis we sought to place affirmative action programs for athletes and the children of alumni on a par with the better-known and more controversial affirmative efforts undertaken to recruit underrepresented minorities. Our review of the literature revealed that all three programs are significant in size and yield a sizeable admissions bonus for members of the targeted groups. We used data from the NLSF to determine whether the detrimental effects of affirmative action hypothesized by critics might help to explain differentials in academic performance, specifying a structural equations model to test several specific hypotheses about group-specific performance. The mismatch hypothesis argues that affirmative action beneficiaries are set up for academic failure because they are less prepared than other students for scholarly competition at selective schools. The stereotype threat hypothesis argues that granting targeted groups an SAT admissions bonus underscores negative stereotypes about group intellectual abilities and thereby generates psychological pressures that compromise academic performance.

Our systematic analysis of the academic performance of affirmatively targeted groups found little support for the mismatch hypothesis. Other things equal, minorities and athletes who received an apparent SAT admissions bonus did not earn lower grades or leave school at higher rates than other students on campus. Affirmative action programs thus do not appear to set up either minorities or athletes for academic failure by dumping them unprepared into a very competitive academic environment. Ironically, the only evidence we find of a skills mismatch is for the children of alumni. The greater the gap between a legacy student's SAT and the institutional average SAT, the lower the grades he or she earned, though the effect size was modest.

Likewise, when we tested stereotype threat theory at the institutional level, we did not find that affirmative action increased the performance burden experienced by minority students. The only significant effect was for athletes and for them the effect of institutional affirmative action was negative, acting to reduce anxieties about academic performance. We found no evidence that affirmative action increased performance burden. Even though performance burden itself was associated with lower grades, affirmative action did not operate indirectly through it to affect academic performance.

In terms of the direct effects of institutional affirmative action, we did find that in schools where athletic affirmative action was widely practiced, athletes were more likely to leave the institution before graduation. We also found that in schools with a stronger commitment to legacy admissions, the children of alumni were more likely to drop out. With respect to minorities, however, we found opposite effects of institutional affirmative action when the outcome was grades earned versus school leaving. Contrary to expectations derived from the critics, the stronger an institution's apparent commitment to affirmative action, the lower the likelihood minority students would leave school. Consistent with their critique, however, the direct effect of institutional affirmative action on GPA was negative for minorities. We interpreted this as supporting the social subversion hypothesis, which argues that a large gap between minority students and others at an institution challenges the legitimacy of their presence on campus, thereby creating a social climate within which it is difficult to function effectively.

We do not expect these findings to settle the debate on affirmative action. We do hope, however, that they enable readers to place the issue of minority affirmative action in a broader context, viewing it as just one of several programs to target a subgroup of students affirmatively. Although athletes and legacy students, as well as minorities, may be granted a bonus in the admissions process, the worst fears of the critics of affirmative action do not seem to be realized. Whatever the effects of affirmative action in raising or lowering the odds of academic success, they are relatively minor compared with the influence of factors such as socioeconomic status and academic preparation. Greater attention should probably be paid to improving the access of poor children of all races to high-quality schooling than to arguing about the relatively small effects of affirmative action on academic achievement.

Appendix

Items in Scale of Performance Burden
From wave 1: How self-conscious were you about the way that your teachers perceived you, with 0 meaning you were not conscious at all and 10 meaning that you were extremely sensitive to what they thought?

0 not conscious at all .... 10 extremely sensitive

From waves 2 and 3: Using the same 0 to 10 scale, where 0 indicates total disagreement and 10 indicates total agreement, how much do you agree or disagree with the following statements?

If I let my instructors know that I am having difficulty in class, they will think less of me.

If I let other students know that I am having difficulty in class, they will think less of me.

From wave 3: Using the same 0 to 10 scale, where 0 indicates total disagreement and 10 indicates total agreement, how much do you agree or disagree with the following statements?

I don't want to look foolish or stupid in class.

If I don't do well, people will look down on others like me.

References

Alon, Sigal and Marta Tienda. 2005. "Assessing the 'Mismatch' Hypothesis: Differentials in College Graduation Rates by Institutional Selectivity." *Sociology of Education* 78:294–315.

Bowen, William G. and Derek Bok. 1998. *The Shape of the River: Long-Term Consequences of Considering Race in College and University Admissions*. Princeton, NJ: Princeton University Press.

Bowen, William G. and Sarah A. Levin. 2003. *Reclaiming the Game: College Sports and Educational Values*. Princeton, NJ: Princeton University Press.

Breland, H. M., J. Maxey, G. T. McLure, M. J. Valiga, M. A. Boatwright, and V. L. Ganley. 1995. *Challenges in College Admissions: A Report of a Survey of Undergraduate Admissions Policies, Practices, and Procedures*. Princeton, NJ: Educational Testing Service.

Chambers, David L., Timothy T. Clydesdale, William C. Kidder, and Richard O. Lempert. 2005. "The Real Impact of Eliminating Affirmative Action in American Law Schools: A Critique of Richard Sander's *Stanford Law Review* Study." *Stanford Law Review* 57(6):1855–98.

Charles, Camille Z., Douglas S. Massey, and Gniesha Dinwiddie. 2004. "The Continuing Consequences of Segregation." *Social Science Quarterly* 85:1353–74.

College Board. 2005. *The College Board College Handbook 2000: All-New 43rd Edition*. New York: College Board.

Crocker, Jennifer and Brenda Major. 1989. "Social Stigma and Self-Esteem: The Self-Protective Properties of Stigma." *Psychological Review* 96:608–30.

Crocker, Jennifer and Diane Quinn. 1998. "Racism and Self-Esteem." Pp. 169–87 in *Confronting Racism: The Problem and the Response*, edited by Jennifer Eberhardt and Susan T. Fiske. Thousand Oaks, CA: Sage Publications.

Dickens, William T. and Thomas J. Kane. 1999. "Racial Test Score Differences as Evidence of Reverse Discrimination: Less than Meets the Eye." *Industrial Relations* 38:331–63.

Espenshade, Thomas J., Chang Y. Chung, and Joan L. Walling. 2004. "Admission Preferences for Minority Studies, Athletes, and Legacies at Elite Universities." *Social Science Quarterly* 85:1422–46.

Fetter, Jean H. 1995. *Questions and Admissions: Reflections on 100,000 Admissions Decisions at Stanford*. Stanford, CA: Stanford University Press.

Fischer, Mary J. and Douglas S. Massey. 2005. "The Effect of Childhood Segregation on Minority Academic Performance at Selective Colleges." *Ethnic and Racial Studies* 29:1–26.

———. Forthcoming. "The Academic Effects of Affirmative Action in Higher Education." *Social Science Research*.

Fiske, Edward B. 2005. *Fiske Guide To Colleges 2006*. New York: Sourcebooks.

Fiske, Susan T. and Shelly E. Taylor. 1991. *Social Cognition*. New York: Mc-Graw Hill.

Fleming, Jacqueline. 2002. "Who Will Succeed in College? When the SAT Predicts Black Students' Performance." *The Review of Higher Education* 25:281–96.

Fleming, Jacqueline and Nancy Garcia. 1998. "Are Standardized Tests Fair to African Americans? Predictive Validity of the SAT in Black and White Colleges". *Journal of Higher Education* 69:471–95.

Glazer, Nathan. 1976. *Affirmative Discrimination: Ethnic Inequality and Public Policy*. New York: Basic Books.

Golden, Daniel. 2003. "Family Ties: Preference for Alumni Children in College Admission Draws Fire." *Wall Street Journal*, January 15, p. A1.

Gould, Stephen J. 1981. *The Mismeasure of Man*. New York: Norton.

Gratz v. Bollinger. 2003. 123 S. Ct. 2411.

Grutter v. Bollinger. 2003. 123 S. Ct. 2325.

Holzer, Harry and David Neumark. 2000. "Assessing Affirmative Action." *Journal of Economic Literature* 38:483–568.

Howell, Cameron and Sarah E. Turner. 2004. "Legacies in Black and White: The Racial Composition of the Legacy Pool." *Research in Higher Education* 45:325–51.

Jencks, Christopher and Meredith Philips. 1998. *The Black-White Test Score Gap*. Washington, DC: Brookings Institution.

Kane, Thomas J. 1998. "Racial and Ethnic Preferences in College Admissions." Pp. 431–56 in *The Black-White Test Score Gap*, edited by Christopher Jencks and Meredith Philips. Washington, DC: Brookings Institution.

Lemann, Nicholas. 1999. *The Big Test: The Secret History of the American Meritocracy*. New York: Farrar Straus Giroux.

Loury, Glenn C. 2001. *The Anatomy of Racial Inequality*. Cambridge, MA: Harvard University Press.

Lovaglia, Michael J., Jeffrey W. Lucas, Jeffrey A. Houser, Shane R. Thye, and Barry Markovsky. 1998. "Status Processes and Mental Ability Test Scores." *American Journal of Sociology* 104:195–228.

Massey, Douglas S., Camille Z. Charles, Garvey F. Lundy, and Mary J. Fischer. 2003. *Source of the River: The Social Origins of Freshmen at America's Selective Colleges and Universities*. Princeton, NJ: Princeton University Press.

Massey, Douglas S. and Mary J. Fischer. 2005. "Stereotype Threat and Academic Performance: New Data from the National Longitudinal Survey of Freshmen." *The DuBois Review: Social Science Research on Race* 2:45–68.

Meltzer, Tom, Christopher Maier, Carson Brown, Julie Doherty, Andrew Friedman, and Robert Franek. 2005. *Best 361 Colleges, 2006*. Princeton, NJ: Princeton Review.

Owen, David. 1999. *None of the Above, Revised : The Truth Behind the SATs*. Lanham, MD: Rowan and Littlefield.

Rosenberg, Morris and Roberta G. Simmons. 1971. *Black and White Self-Esteem: The Urban School Child*. Washington, DC: American Sociological Association.

Sander, Richard H. 2004. "A Systematic Analysis of Affirmative Action in American Law Schools." *Stanford Law Review* 47:367–483.

Shulman, James L. and William G. Bowen. 2001. *The Game of Life: College Sports and Educational Values*. Princeton, NJ: Princeton University Press.

Skrentny, John D. 1996. *The Ironies of Affirmative Action: Politics, Culture, and Justice in America*. Chicago: University of Chicago Press.

Sowell, Thomas. 2004. *Affirmative Action Around the World: An Empirical Study*. New Haven, CT: Yale University Press.

Springer, Sally P. and Marion R. Franck. 2005. *Admission Matters: What Students and Parents Need to Know About Getting Into College*. San Francisco: Jossey Bass.

Steele, Claude M. 1992. "Race and the Schooling of Black Americans." *The Atlantic Monthly* 269(4):68–78.

———. 1997. "A Threat in the Air: How Stereotypes Shape Intellectual Identity and Performance." *American Psychologist* 52:613–29.

Steele, Claude M. and Joshua Aronson. 1995. "Stereotype Treat and the Intellectual Test Performance of African Americans." *Journal of Personality and Social Psychology* 69:797–811.

Steinberg, Jacques. 2002. *The Gamekeepers: Inside the Admissions Process of a Premier College*. New York: Viking.

Taylor, Howard F. 1980. *The IQ Game: A Methodological Inquiry into the Heredity-Environment Controversy*. New Brunswick, NJ: Rutgers University Press.

Thernstrom, Stephen and Abigail Thernstrom. 1999. "Reflections on the Shape of the River." *UCLA Law Review* 46:1583–1631.

Torres, Kimberly C. and Camille Z. Charles. 2004. "Metastereotypes and the Black-White Divide: A Qualitative View of Race on an Elite College Campus." *The DuBois Review: Social Science Research on Race* 1:115–49.

University of Pennsylvania. 2005. Penn Admissions: Incoming Student Profile. Accessed June 26, 2005 (www.admissionsug.upenn.edu/applying/profile.php?).

U.S. News and World Report. 2005. *U.S. News Ultimate College Guide 2006*. New York: Sourcebook, Inc.

Wilson, John K. 1995. *The Myth of Political Correctness: The Conservative Attack on Higher Education*. Durham, NC: Duke University Press.

Yale Daily News. 2005. *The Insider's Guide to the Colleges, 2006*. 32d ed. New York: St. Martins.

Zwick, Rebecca. 2002. *Fair Game? The Use of Standardized Admissions Tests in Higher Education*. New York: Routledge.

CHAPTER 39
WAS JUSTICE O'CONNOR RIGHT?
RACE AND HIGHLY SELECTIVE COLLEGE
ADMISSIONS IN 25 YEARS

ALAN B. KRUEGER, JESSE ROTHSTEIN, AND SARAH TURNER

In her opinion in *Grutter v. Bollinger*, Justice Sandra Day O'Connor concluded that affirmative action in college admissions is justifiable, but not in perpetuity: "We expect that 25 years from now, the use of racial preferences will no longer be necessary to further the interest [in student body diversity] approved today."

The rate at which racial gaps in precollegiate academic achievement can plausibly be expected to erode is a matter of considerable uncertainty. In this essay, we attempt to evaluate the plausibility of Justice O'Connor's conjecture by projecting the racial composition of the 2025 elite college applicant pool. Our projections extrapolate past trends on two important margins: Gaps between the economic resources of black and white students' families, and narrowing of test score gaps between black and white students with similar family incomes. Just as the last decades have seen considerable narrowing of gaps on each margin, further progress can be expected over the next quarter century.

Our central question is whether this progress will plausibly be fast enough to validate Justice O'Connor's prediction. We are well aware of the hazards inherent in our exercise: No such distant projections can be definitive. Nevertheless, by relying on reasonable historical assumptions that are arguably optimistic, we develop a baseline case for assessing the likelihood of O'Connor's forecast.

We conclude that under reasonable assumptions, African American students will continue to be substantially underrepresented among the most qualified college applicants for the foreseeable future. The magnitude of the underrepresentation is likely to shrink—in our most optimistic simulation, somewhat over half of the gap that would be opened by the elimination of race preferences will be closed by the projected improvement in black achievement. Still, it seems unlikely that today's level of racial diversity will be achievable without some form of continuing affirmative action. If the Supreme Court follows through with O'Connor's stated intention to ban affirmative action in 25 years, and if colleges do not adjust in other ways (such as reducing the importance of numerical qualifications to admissions), we project substantial declines in the representation of African Americans among admitted students at selective institutions.

Our analysis proceeds from the assumption that the most likely future course will resemble past trends. Substantial changes in educational policy, in school effectiveness, and in income inequality would all have important effects on black test score distributions and on the admissions landscape.[1]

Recent Trends in Racial Inequality

Currently, racial gaps in precollegiate achievement are extremely large, and very few black students would be admitted to elite colleges under race-blind admissions rules. Figure 1a shows the distribution of SAT scores among black and white students in 2000. The black–white gap in mean scores is approximately 201 points, or almost exactly one standard deviation. More relevant is the top of the

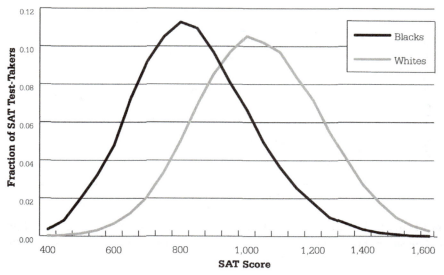

Figure 1a   SAT distributions among black and white test-takers, 2000.

Source: Authors' analysis of Test-Takers Database (an extract of SAT test-takers), 2000 cohort.

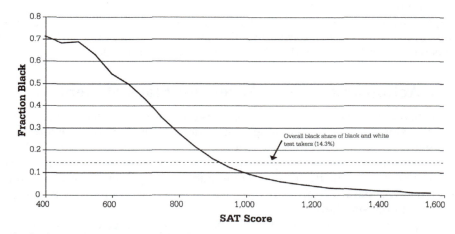

Figure 1b   Black share of black and white SAT test-takers, 2000.

distribution, as the selective schools that are our focus admit few students with scores below 1200. As shown in Figure 1b, only 4 percent of students who earn SAT scores of 1200 are black (as compared with 14.3 percent of all SAT test-takers), and the fraction is even lower for higher scores; only 2.4 percent of students with scores exceeding 1200 are black.[2]

Historically comparable data on SAT score distributions are not readily available, but Figure 2 shows black–white test score gaps on the National Assessment of Education Progress (NAEP) assessment since 1970. In that year, the average 17-year-old black student scored over 1.1 standard deviations below the average white student in reading. For reasons that are not well understood, this gap was stable in the 1970s, shrunk dramatically in the 1980s, and has grown somewhat since around 1990. Today, the black–white gap stands at about three quarters of a standard deviation in reading, and is even higher in math.

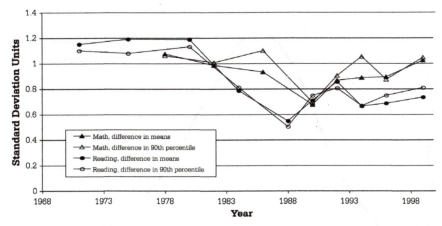

Figure 2 Trends in black–white gaps in student achievement at age 17, in standard deviation units.
Source: National Assessment of Educational Progress results (National Center for Education Statistics, 1999).

An obvious partial explanation for the persistence of the test score gap is the continuing gap in economic resources between black and white students' families. Black workers earn substantially less, on average, than do whites, though the differential has slowly narrowed. The earnings gap between black and white men was 38 percent in 1960 and 26 percent in 2000. This progress has been largely offset, however, by deterioration in black family structures, as single parenthood has risen and the number of children in two-earner families has consequently fallen. The gap in total family income between black and white children has hardly moved in three decades.

Affirmative Action and College Access for Black Students

The precise mechanics of selective college admissions are closely guarded secrets.[3] Still, by examining average admissions probabilities among groups defined by important determinants, like SAT scores, it is possible to get an idea of the current roles of race and academic qualifications in admissions. We focus on four groups of colleges and universities: most selective, highly selective, and moderately selective private institutions, and elite public universities.[4] It must be emphasized that these labels are relative characterizations; even the least selective group in our typology is extremely selective by any national standard.

Admissions profiles are shown in Figure 3. These show evidence of substantial affirmative action preferences, with black admissions rates exceeding those of white students with much higher SAT scores. Table 1 shows the current black share of admitted students in each group and our estimate of what it would be if black students were admitted according to the profiles seen for white applicants. With race-blind admissions, black representation at the four clusters of schools would fall by 70, 58, 46, and 55 percent, respectively.

Projections

Test Scores

Our projections of likely future improvement in the black relative test score distribution proceed in two stages. First, we estimate the degree to which black family income gains can be expected to close the test score gap shown in Figure 1. As SAT scores depend heavily on family income, predictable increases in black families' relative incomes will lead to increases in black students' relative scores. Second, we incorporate plausible reductions in the black–white gap in test scores among children with the same family incomes by extrapolating the trend in NAEP scores shown in

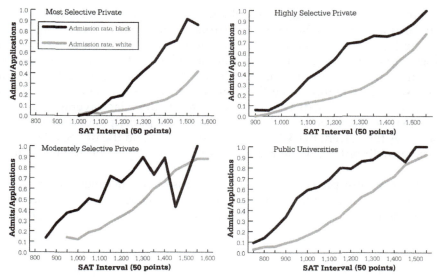

Figure 3   Admission rates by type of institution, SAT score, and race.

Source: Authors' calculations from the Expanded College and Beyond database.

TABLE 1

Black Share of Admitted Students at Elite Institutions, 2000, Actual and with Race-Blind Admission Rules

	Most Selective Colleges	Highly Selective Colleges	Moderately Selective Colleges	Public Universities
Actual	0.171	0.142	0.094	0.118
With race-blind admissions	0.051	0.060	0.051	0.053
Change with shift to race-blind admissions	−70 %	−58 %	−46 %	−55 %

Notes: "Most selective" is a composite of Harvard, Princeton, and Yale; "highly selective" is a composite of Columbia, the University of Pennsylvania, Swarthmore, and Williams; "moderately selective" is a composite of Barnard, Bowdoin, Middlebury, Oberlin, Pomona, and Wellesley; and "public" is a composite of the University of Virginia and Pennsylvania State.

Figure 2.[5] Reasonable people may differ in their projections of the likely rate of future convergence on either margin; our estimates are meant to indicate what sort of progress will be required to obtain desired admissions results.

Among families with children ages 15 to 17 in the 2000 census, black families had incomes 54 percent less than white families, on average. Estimates of the intergenerational transmission of incomes indicate that, on average, somewhere between 40 and 60 percent of the gap between a family's income and the mean income will be closed with each generation.[6] We take the center of this range, which implies that the black–white income gap will decline by half with each successive generation. This does a good job of fitting the black–white gap in male earnings in recent decades, which fell from 37 percent in 1969 to 19 percent in 1999.[7] As noted above, however, it overstates recent progress in family incomes, and our assumption that the gap on this margin will fall by half in the next quarter century is thus probably optimistic.

Halving the black–white gap in log family incomes will have disproportionate effects on the number of black families at the very high income levels from which elite college applicants are largely drawn. We estimate, for example, that the fraction of black families with incomes between $80,000 and $100,000 will increase by 69 percent (from 4.7 percent to 8.0 percent). Because children from families with higher incomes are more likely to take the SAT and more likely to earn high scores, increases in black family incomes will yield increases in the number of high-scoring black students. To quantify this, we assume that the "new" high-income black students will have test-taking rates and score distributions like those of current high-income black students. When we apply the projected future income distribution, we compute that black average scores will be about 19 points higher than they are today, and that the black SAT participation rate will rise by 0.7 percent. Figure 4a shows the current black SAT score distribution and the projected future distribution (labeled "income growth only"), while Figure 4b shows the impact on the fraction black at each SAT score.[8]

The way to interpret our projection is that we increase black families' incomes by the amount predicted from the narrowing of the black–white gap over a generation, while holding everything else—the distribution of white incomes and the distribution of test scores conditional on income

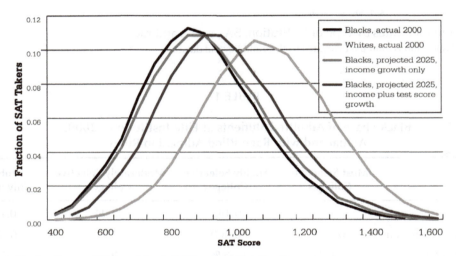

Figure 4a   Projections of future black SAT score distribution.

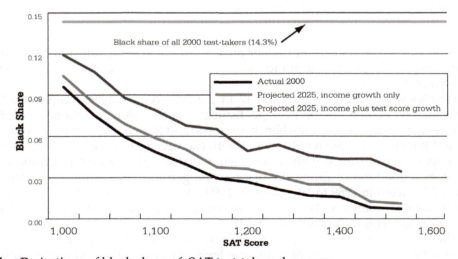

Figure 4b   Projections of black share of SAT test-takers, by score.

and race—constant. Of course, real income growth will raise both black and white incomes over the next quarter century, and black and white mean test scores may evolve in tandem. Absent changes in inequality, however, this will not affect the shape of the distribution. Our approach indexes black income and test score growth against that of whites, and we implicitly assume that admissions standards adjust to maintain each institution's selectivity.

Income is not the only source of potential changes in admissions qualifications, so the "income growth only" estimate in Figures 4a and 4b might be seen as a lower bound. An alternative includes some closing of the black–white test score gap within income groups. To make our projections, we assume that conditional-on-income test score gaps will close as much in the next 25 years as the unconditional gaps did over the last 25 years. The black–white gap in NAEP scores has shrunk by an average of about 1 percent of a standard deviation per year (with faster progress in reading and slower progress in math). If this average rate of progress continues for 25 years, we should see the racial gap in SAT scores fall by 50 points.

The final series in Figures 4a and 4b shows the combined impact of this and income convergence. This almost certainly overestimates the extent of black score growth over the next quarter century. As Figure 2 indicates, essentially all of the progress over the last 25 years in NAEP scores occurred in the 1980s, and the gap grew during the 1990s. It requires substantial optimism to believe that future progress will occur at the rate seen over the full NAEP period rather than the much slower rate seen recently, particularly as we are assuming that this progress will be in addition to that generated by income convergence.

Admissions Projections

Our interest is in how the projected changes in the relative distribution of the academic achievement (measured by test scores) of black and white students will alter the relative representation of black and white students among those likely to be admitted to selective colleges and universities under race-blind admission policies. Our income convergence estimate implies a 33 percent increase in the number of black students who score above 1200 (over today's low level); when we additionally apply NAEP trends, we project a 109 percent increase. Even under this counterfactual, however, the proportion of blacks scoring above 1200 will be about one-third of the corresponding proportion of whites, with more extreme underrepresentation at higher scores.

The next step is to convert the projected change in the SAT distribution to admissions rates. We model expected admissions to "composite" schools corresponding to each of our four clusters, rather than to the individual institutions.

To calculate expected admissions under each of our simulations, we simply multiply the projected number of test-takers at each SAT level by an estimated application rate to each type of school and then by an estimated admissions rate. Under the current regime both application rates and admissions rates differ by race. Under a race-neutral policy, blacks and whites with the same test scores would face the same probability of admission, conditional on application; we use observed white admissions rates (Figure 3) as a proxy for the race-blind admissions rule.[9]

A large shift in admissions probabilities would likely lead to responses in black students' decisions about where to apply. At each SAT score, black students are currently more likely than whites to apply to the most selective institutions. One might expect application rates to converge as admissions probabilities do. On the other hand, at least in the short run the elimination of race-conscious admission policies in Texas and California appears not to have altered the pattern of applications of high-achieving black students.[10] Our baseline estimates assume that race-specific application rates do not change, but we also consider a scenario in which black application rates come to resemble those of whites with similar scores.

Table 2 presents simulations based on the assumption that black application behavior remains as it is today. The first two rows repeat the actual black representation in 2000 and the simulated current race-blind representation from Table 1.[11] Row 3 applies the race-neutral admissions rule to the first counterfactual SAT distribution, assuming income convergence but no additional progress in test scores. This produces small gains in the representation of black students. Row 4 allows for projected

TABLE 2

Projected Black Share of Admitted Students at Elite Institutions in 2025

	Most Selective	Highly Selective	Moderately Selective	Public
	Black Share of Admits			
Actual, 2000				
Status quo admissions rules	0.171	0.142	0.094	0.118
Race-blind admissions rules	0.051	0.060	0.051	0.053
Projected, 2025, with race-blind admissions				
Income growth only	0.069	0.078	0.062	0.064
Income plus test score growth	0.118	0.117	0.087	0.088
	Share of Gap Closed			
Actual, 2000				
Race-blind admissions rules	0.000	0.000	0.000	0.000
Projected, 2025, with race-blind admissions				
Income growth only	0.153	0.214	0.254	0.169
Income plus test score growth	0.557	0.700	0.835	0.545

reductions in the black–white test score gap among students with the same family income, on top of the impact of expected income convergence. This has a substantial effect on black representation.

For each type of college, we measure the distance to be covered as the gap between the current representation of black students and that which would be seen with race-neutral admissions, as in Table 1. For each projection, we then compute the share of this distance that is actually covered. Income convergence alone closes only about one-fifth of the gap. *It appears that reasonable income convergence will not, on its own, allow for the abolition of affirmative action without severely affecting the representation of African American students at elite colleges.* Additional progress on test scores will be required. Our estimates show that past experience will not be sufficient, at least at the public and most selective institutions: Even in our optimistic projections, only half of the gap is closed. (At the highly and moderately selective institutions, progress is more impressive but still insufficient to reproduce today's racial diversity.)

The estimates in Table 2 are predicated on the assumption that black application behavior will not change in response to the elimination of race-based preferences. We have also conducted the analysis under the alternative assumption that black application rates will come to resemble those of whites with the same test scores. This is decidedly more pessimistic, as many more high-scoring whites than blacks opt not to apply to the most selective colleges. The impact of a shift to race-blind admissions would then be much more dramatic, and projected future black representation at elite colleges would fall far short of that seen today.[12]

Discussion

In an equal opportunity society, the effects of past discrimination on current generations will eventually asymptote to zero, though there is substantial uncertainty about the rate at which this might be expected to occur. In *Grutter v. Bollinger*, Justice O'Connor suggests rapid progress, enough so that the use of affirmative action to achieve diversity will be unnecessary within the next generation. Our simulations suggest that O'Conner's prediction is quite optimistic but not outside the realm of possibility.

We are most confident in predicting that economic progress alone will not yield as much racial diversity as is generated with today's race-sensitive admissions policies. Under plausible assumptions, black economic gains over the next quarter century can be expected to provide only about 17 percent of the incremental representation of African American students on elite college campuses that is provided by affirmative action today.

Our projections that also extrapolate past increases in black students' test scores relative to whites' are more hopeful. In this scenario, and if black college application behavior is assumed stable, we find that race-blind admissions policies may approach the black representation achieved by affirmative action, at least in some categories of colleges. This projection is likely overly optimistic: The last 25 years saw two distinct regimes, with rapidly closing black–white gaps in the first period and a widening gap since 1990. To extrapolate a linear trend a full quarter century into the future is to assume a dramatic turnaround from recent patterns and sustained growth over a long period. On the other hand, if we could somehow return to and sustain the rapid rate of progress seen in the 1980s, the future will be brighter than even our optimistic forecasts indicate.

As an indication of the difficulty of achieving racial diversity on highly selective college campuses without affirmative action, we have also considered the effects of a wholly implausible intervention producing the complete integration of the nation's secondary schools.[13] This, we estimate, would produce only a small fraction of the test score gains that would be needed to make Justice O'Connor's prediction a reality. Clearly, substantial progress in increasing black students' precollegiate performance is critical to any hope of eliminating the need for affirmative action within the next generation.

Absent such progress, a shift to race-blind admissions in 25 years would lead to substantial declines in black representation at the nation's most selective colleges and universities. Our simulations, crude as they are, lead us to agree with Justice Ruth Bader Ginsburg's concurring opinion in *Grutter*: "From today's vantage point, one may hope, but not firmly forecast, that over the next generation's span, progress toward nondiscrimination and genuinely equal opportunity will make it safe to sunset affirmative action."

Notes

1. There are several additional limitations to our study. First, we restrict our attention to black and white students. In light of the United States' distinct historical legacy of racial policies, the representation of African Americans in elite colleges is of unique interest; in any event, projections are hazardous for groups experiencing substantial continuing immigration. Second, we focus on selective institutions. Thus, we say little about aggregate college attainment trends, which primarily reflect outcomes at nonselective, open-access institutions. Third, we neglect aspects of the college pipeline other than the admissions decision itself. Though application and matriculation behavior will certainly change—perhaps even in response to the trends that we study—these are not our focus.

2. Here and elsewhere, the fraction refers to the black share of black and white students; students of other races are omitted from all computations.

3. Jerome Karabel, *The Chosen: The Hidden History of Admission and Exclusion at Harvard, Yale, and Princeton* (Boston: Houghton Mifflin, 2005).

4. William Bowen, Martin Kurzweil, and Eugene Tobin have generously provided us extracts from the Expanded College and Beyond (ECB) study of the 1995 admissions cycle that was assembled by the Andrew W. Mellon Foundation and used in their book, *Equity and Excellence in Higher Education* (Charlottesville, Va.: University of Virginia Press, 2005). The most selective private institutions are Harvard, Princeton, and Yale; the highly selective are Columbia, the University of Pennsylvania, Swarthmore, and Williams; and the moderately selective are Barnard, Bowdoin, Middlebury, Oberlin, Pomona, and Wellesley. Public universities are Pennsylvania State University and the University of Virginia. Confidentiality requirements prevent a more disaggregated presentation.

5. "Results Over Time—NAEP 1999 Long-Term Trend Summary Data Tables," National Center for Education Statistics (1999), http://nces.ed.gov/nationsreportcard/tables/Ltt1999/. For details of our methods and descriptions of the underlying data, interested readers are referred to Alan B. Krueger, Jesse Rothstein, and Sarah Turner, "Race, Income, and College in 25 Years: Evaluating Justice O'Connor's Conjecture," *American Law and Economics Review* (forthcoming).

6. As is conventional, we work with the logarithm of family income rather than the level; all figures in this paragraph refer to log incomes. Bhashkar Mazumder, "Earnings Mobility in the U.S.: A New Look at Intergenerational Mobility," mimeo (2000); Gary Solon, "Intergenerational Mobility in the Labor Market," in *Handbook of Labor Economics*, Vol. 3A (Orley Ashenfelter and David Card, eds), (1999): 1761–1800, Elsevier Science: Amsterdam; Laura Chadwick and Gary Solon, "Intergenerational Income Mobility Among Daughters," *American Economic Review* 92, No. 1. (March 2002): 335–344; Gary Solon, "Cross-Country Differences in Intergenerational Earnings Mobility," *Journal of Economic Perspectives* 16, No. 3 (Summer 2002): 59–66.

7. Alan B. Krueger, "The Supreme Court Finds the 'Mushball Middle' on Affirmative Action," *New York Times* (July 23, 2003): C2.

8. One disconnect between our simulation and the educational process is worth noting. Although the reasons why family income affects student performance on the SAT are unclear, it is quite likely that the entire stream of family income over a child's time at home is relevant, not just income in the year he or she takes the SAT. Unfortunately, we lack data on family income in earlier years. Many of the intergenerational convergence estimates in the literature apply to long run, not annual, income.

9. If application behavior is unchanged, the elimination of racial preferences will reduce the total number of admittees. As the share of students admitted under affirmative action is small, this effect is as well. Nevertheless, to the extent that colleges lower the race-blind admissions standards to compensate, we will very slightly overestimate the effect of affirmative action on black admission shares.

10. David Card and Alan Krueger, "Would the Elimination of Affirmative Action Affect Highly Qualified Minority Applicants? Evidence from California and Texas," *Industrial and Labor Relations Review* 58, No. 3 (April 2005): 416–434.

11 Note that our analysis focuses on the number of admissions offers to black and white students. A single student may be admitted to several schools but can accept only one offer. We do not attempt to project changes in matriculation decisions.

12. Krueger, Rothstein, and Turner, "Race, Income, and College in 25 Years."

13. David Card and Jesse Rothstein ("Racial Segregation and the Black–White Test Score Gap," National Bureau of Economic Research, Working Paper #12078 [May 2005]) show that racial segregation has a negative effect on black students' performance. We almost certainly overstate the benefits of integration by assuming that it would equalize the contribution of schools to black and white students' achievement (Krueger, Rothstein, and Turner, "Race, Income, and College in 25 Years"). That even this indicates substantially smaller test score gains than are assumed in our primary analysis serves to underscore the optimism inherent in the latter.

CHAPTER 40
WINNERS AND LOSERS: CHANGES IN TEXAS UNIVERSITY ADMISSIONS POST-HOPWOOD

MARK C. LONG

MARTA TIENDA

This chapter evaluates changes in racial and ethnic composition of three Texas universities following the ban on affirmative action imposed by the 1996 *Hopwood* decision. The authors estimate the extent to which universities practiced affirmative action before the ban and evaluate how officers at these universities responded by changing relative weights accorded to various applicant characteristics. After assessing whether changes in the relative weights favored minority applicants, the degree to which these new policies succeeded in maintaining minority shares at their pre-*Hopwood* levels is simulated. This chapter finds that these universities complied with the *Hopwood* ruling such that direct advantages given to Black and Hispanic applicants disappeared (and in some cases became disadvantages). Although there is some evidence that universities changed the weights they placed on applicant characteristics in ways that aided underrepresented minority applicants, these changes were insufficient to restore Black and Hispanic applicants' share of admitted students.

1. Introduction and Research Questions

During the past decade, several states have banned affirmative action in their public university admissions (including Texas, California, Florida, Washington, Georgia, and Michigan),[1] and ballot initiatives have been attempted in other states. In all of these states, the general public and policy makers have expressed concerns about the difficulty of maintaining minority enrollment at elite institutions while questioning the fairness of using race preferences in college admissions. Unlike public referenda and ballot initiatives, legal challenges transcend state jurisdictions when they invoke the Equal Protection Clause of the Fourteenth Amendment of the U.S. Constitution, as Cheryl Hopwood and her coplaintiffs did in their 1992 lawsuit against the University of Texas School of Law.[2]

In its July 1996 *Hopwood* decision, the Fifth Circuit Court of Appeals opined that the only legal justification for affirmative action is to rectify the present effects of past discrimination (Staff, 1997). The decision challenged the 1978 *Bakke* decision by asserting that the goal of achieving institutional diversity was not an acceptable rationale for considering race in admissions decisions.[3] Then Texas Attorney General Dan González interpreted the *Hopwood* decision as a ban not only on race-based admissions but also scholarships, financial aid, and retention and recruiting policies of all colleges and universities in the state (Barr, 2002). This ban was in force for the fall class of 1997, which registered appreciable declines in the representation of minority students at the state's public flagship institutions as well as University of Texas at Dallas and Texas Tech University (TTU; Barr, 2002).

Anticipating further declines in minority enrollment at public universities with selective admission policies, the Texas legislature passed H.B. 588, the "uniform admission law." H.B. 588 is popularly known as the top 10% law because it guarantees admission to any public university in the state to Texas high school seniors who graduate in the top 10% of their class. A lesser known, but nonetheless important, provision of the uniform admission law specifies 18 factors that universities should consider in admitting students who do not graduate in the top 10% of their high school class, including socioeconomic status, second language ability, and indications that the student overcame adversity.[4]

Although H.B. 588 was triggered by the judicial ban on the use of race in college admissions, authors and sponsors of the legislation sought to broaden college access and better represent the geographic, socioeconomic, and ethno-racial diversity of the state at all postsecondary institutions, but particularly the public flagships (Giovanola, 2005; Olivas, 2007). Both key author Irma Rangel and primary sponsor Gonzálo Barrientos appreciated that a handful of largely suburban Texas high schools sent disproportionate numbers of applicants to the University of Texas at Austin (UT) and Texas A&M University (TAMU) while hundreds of others never sent a single student.[5] In striving to design a race-neutral admission regime that rewarded merit, that was fair, and that could ensure a large, well-qualified pool of minority and economically disadvantaged applicants, there was little consideration of the carrying capacity of the state's public higher education system (Giovanola, 2005; Tienda & Sullivan, in press).[6] Passed in May 1997, the uniform admission law was fully in force for the fall 1998 admission cohort.

Some have argued that under an affirmative action ban colleges will have an incentive to employ admissions practices that partially ignore an applicant's "quality," thereby placing more emphasis on characteristics that are correlated with race/ethnicity (Chan & Eyster, 2003). Among the criteria explicitly named in H.B. 588 for college admission are several nontraditional factors that could be used as proxies for race/ethnicity in order to achieve institutional diversity.

Whether a change from an explicit consideration of race to the use of proxy indicators of minority group status can effectively increase minority college admission rates and whether the allowable proxies are as efficient as traditional race-sensitive admission criteria poses an empirical question with clear policy implications. Using unique administrative data from three Texas universities, this chapter will answer the following questions. First, to what extent was affirmative action practiced in the admissions decisions of Texas universities before the *Hopwood* decision?[7] Second, how did these universities change the weight they placed on various applicant characteristics, and did compliance with the *Hopwood* decision reduce or eliminate the direct or indirect weight placed on an applicant's race/ethnicity? Finally, did these universities add weight to characteristics that are correlated with an applicant's race/ethnicity in ways that advantage underrepresented minority applicants? Assuming that the answer to the last question is yes, we then conduct simulations that estimate the extent to which the policy responses were able to maintain minority students' share of admitted students.

Although there are some limitations on the available data that limit our analysis, we provide empirical evidence bearing on all of these questions. Specifically, for the first research question, we demonstrate that both Texas flagship public institutions (University of Texas at Austin and Texas A&M University) practiced affirmative action in the pre-*Hopwood* years. For the second and third questions, we find that both universities complied with the *Hopwood* decision by eliminating the direct admission advantages given to minority applicants, but they also changed the weights placed on other applicant characteristics in ways that favored Black and Hispanic applicants. However, these changes were not sufficient to restore minority representation to the level that would have occurred under the prior affirmative action policies.

Our analyses are based on data from Texas universities, but the results have broader policy implications because the use of race-sensitive admission criteria in college admissions remains a highly controversial issue and because of mounting evidence that class rank is a more powerful indicator of college success than standardized test scores (Alon & Tienda, 2007).[8] Following judicial and legislative bans on affirmative action, public universities in California, Florida, and Washington have used various strategies to increase minority representation on their campuses, including percentage plans and proxy indicators for race and ethnicity.

Three years after the passage of the California Civil Rights Initiative (Proposition 209) in 1996, which prohibited the explicit use of race, ethnicity, national origin, and sex in university admissions, the University of California (UC) Regents approved a policy that guarantees admission to one of the UC campuses to the top 4% of graduates in each California high school.[9] The University of California System issued additional guidelines for admission: For 25% to 50% of the freshmen admissions, decisions could consider "academic accomplishments in light of the applicant's life experiences and special circumstances."[10] Since 1999, the University of California has adopted a series of reforms that increase the consideration of nonacademic criteria and expanded its comprehensive review in the admissions process to all students (Chan & Eyster 2003; University of California, 2001a, 2001b). For example, in 2001, the class rank criterion was amended by the UC Regents to offer students who were not in the top 4% but were in the top 12.5% of their high school class admission to one of the UC campuses if they successfully completed first-and second-year requirements at a community college.

Changes in admission criteria implemented in Florida and Washington also allow for the consideration of nonacademic factors. Florida Governor Jeb Bush announced the "One Florida" policy in 1999, which simultaneously eliminated affirmative action in admissions and guaranteed admission to one of the state's public universities to the top 20% of graduates in each Florida high school. Subsequently the University of Florida added an essay requirement to its application and in the application–solicited information about students' "extracurricular activities, work history, whether they were raised by a single parent, etc." (Marin & Lee, 2003, p. 33). According to James (2002), the University of Florida also gives special consideration to "students who are poor, attended a low-performing high school, or whose parents didn't attend college" (p. A1).

With a 1998 ballot initiative (I-200) similar to California's Proposition 209, voters in the state of Washington prohibited the use of race and ethnicity in college admissions. Concerned about the potential drop in minority enrollment as experienced in Texas and California following the ban on affirmative action, admission officers at the University of Washington (UW) also modified their college admissions policies and recruitment strategies. UW added essays and solicited additional information in its application materials that could be used to signal ethnic group membership (McCormick, 2000). A broader survey of the efforts being attempted by these universities can be found in Long (2007).

Given that efforts to use proxy indicators for race/ethnicity are being implemented at public universities in all of the states that have eliminated preferential admissions, the results in this chapter have national importance as they are the first to show whether such efforts have succeeded in replacing traditional affirmative action in actual practice.[11]

2. Administrative Data

For this analysis, we use administrative records from three public Texas universities: University of Texas at Austin, Texas A&M University, and Texas Tech University. The time span of these records includes several years before and after the judicial ban on affirmative action.[12] *Barron's Profiles of American Colleges* (1996) classified UT as very competitive, TAMU as highly competitive, and TTU as competitive.[13] In the years for which we have admissions data, the average SAT scores of admitted students were 1,233 at UT, 1,182 at TAMU, and 1,094 at TTU.[14]

The administrative records, which contain a wealth of information about the applicant pool, have been transformed to machine readable format, standardized to the extent feasible, and verified for consistency.[15] Although specific data elements vary across the universities, the student records for all of the universities include test scores (e.g., SAT/ACT), class rank percentile, and high school identifiers that allow us to append high school characteristics to the applicant records. Unfortunately, the data generally lack information about students' high school coursework and their admission essays. We take special note of these data limitations in interpreting the results and provide a sensitivity analysis of the likely effects of omitted variable bias in the appendix. As we argue in the appendix, the likely effect of omitted variable bias is to produce slight underestimates of pre-*Hopwood* affirmative action at these universities. Moreover, it is important to note that the data used in this chapter are the most complete records available for these universities, and thus future work is unlikely to produce more definitive results.

3. Method

A convenient way to model a university's admissions process is to assume that the university "scores" each applicant (explicitly or implicitly) by assigning weights to individual applicant characteristics and then admits all students whose scores are above some threshold. Assuming that a normally distributed error is included in the applicant's score when the admissions decision is made naturally leads to a probit specification. Estimating the parameters of the specification will allow us to evaluate the relative weights placed on various applicant characteristics.[16] Using a probit regression, the following equation is estimated for student i applying to college j in year t:

$$\Pr(Admitted_{ijt}=1) = \Phi(\beta_0 + U_i\beta_{jt} + X_i\theta_{jt} + \varepsilon_{ijt}) \quad (1)$$

where U is a vector of race and ethnicity indicator variables, X is a vector of other applicant characteristics including measures of high school quality, and ε is a normally distributed error term.

Equation 1 is estimated separately for each college in each year. β_{jt} represents the added advantage (if any) given to racial and ethnic group applicants at college j in year t, controlling for other applicant characteristics. This method of identifying the degree of affirmative action in admissions has been used previously in several prior studies including Kane (1998b), Long (2004b), and Espenshade, Chung, and Walling (2004). Because these studies were based on cohorts of applicants in years prior to the elimination of affirmative action, their results can only suggest how such a policy change would affect admissions decisions. Notably, prior studies could not simulate whether and how universities might shift the weights placed on other applicant attributes. Estimating Equation 1 across successive cohorts of institution-specific applicants enables us to evaluate these policy responses directly. Specifically, three hypotheses are tested:

Hypothesis 1: $\beta_{jt} > 0$ for Black, Hispanic, and Native American applicants in the years prior to the *Hopwood* decision (i.e., the colleges practiced affirmative action in their admissions decisions).

Hypothesis 2: In the years prior to the *Hopwood* decision, β_{jt} is larger for the more selective colleges.

Hypothesis 3: $\beta_{jt} = 0$ in the years after the *Hopwood* decision (i.e., the colleges did not practice affirmative action in their admissions decisions).[17]

In addition, we test whether the universities changed the weights placed on applicant characteristics in such a way as to favor underrepresented minority applicants. To conduct this test, we simulate the admissions decisions that would have occurred in the absence of the *Hopwood* decision and the top 10% policy. This counter-factual estimation begins by estimating Equation 1 using all applicants from the years 1996 and earlier.[18] We then apply the resulting parameter estimates to each applicant and estimate his or her probability of admission.[19] A simulated class of admitted students is constructed by assuming that the university would accept the students with the highest probabilities of being accepted. We assume that university j would accept Z_{jt} students in year t, where Z_{jt} is set equal to the actual number of students accepted by university j in year t.[20] We then compare the composition of the simulated class to the students actually accepted to infer the net effect of the *Hopwood* decision, the top 10% policy, and any other changes to the university's admissions system.

Next, we estimate the consequences on the ethno-racial composition of admitted students of the judicial ban on affirmative action resulting from the *Hopwood* decision and the top 10% policy by holding the pre-*Hopwood* admission weights constant but setting the race-ethnicity coefficients to zero and admitting all in-state applicants who are in the top 10% of their high school class. By comparing the resulting composition of this simulated admission class to that of students who were actually accepted, we can infer the net effects of the university shifting the weights placed on applicant characteristics. These simulations permit us to evaluate the effectiveness of the changing admission policies in restoring minority applicants' share of the admitted class that would have existed in the absence of the *Hopwood* ban and the top 10% policy.[21]

It is important to note that our simulation takes the applicant pool as given. However, if the universities' applicant pools changed as a result of the *Hopwood* decision and the top 10% policy, then the universities might be prompted to change the weights placed on various applicant characteristics in response. However, as we show in the appendix, the composition of the applicant pools at these institutions did not substantially change.[22] Thus, we conclude that observed changes in the universities' processes of making admissions decisions mostly reflect their attempts to maintain minority enrollment rather than endogenous responses to changing applicant characteristics.

A related concern is that the changes in the universities' admissions policies for students not in the top 10% of their high school classes could be a function of their success in recruiting minority top 10% applicants. If minority top 10% applications rose, then we might not observe institutional responses in discretionary admission practices. In fact, the underrepresented minority share of top 10% applicants at UT-Austin rose from 20.9% to 22.5% and at Texas Tech from 19.1% to 20.1% but declined at Texas A&M from 18.2% to 16.2%. These changes in the ethnoracial composition of the applicant pool eligible for automatic admission might have had some modest effects on these universities' discretionary decisions, and the following results should be understood in this context.

4. Applicant Characteristics

Before turning to the statistical results, this section discusses various details of the data and the definitions used for several applicant characteristics. In the admissions probit regressions, we use each piece of information that is available for at least 20% of the applicants to university j in year t. Race and ethnicity variables are taken as labeled by the universities. The percentage of students with missing race/ethnicity is below 0.4% for each institution.[23] We treat students with missing race/ethnicity as if they were White, which renders our estimates of policy effects conservative.[24]

ACT test scores were converted into their equivalent SAT test score values using a conversion table provided by the College Board (Dorans, 2002), and for students who took both tests we use the higher of the two scores.[25] This conversion is valid for SAT scores after the College Board "recentered" scores upward in 1996, therefore we have recentered prior years' SAT scores prior to using this conversion.[26]

The statistical models include several variables to measure the type and quality of the applicants' high school, namely, whether the applicant's high school was a private, a *feeder*, a *Longhorn*, and/or *Century* high school. Feeder high schools are defined as the top 20 high schools based on the absolute number of students admitted to UT-Austin and Texas A&M in the year 2000, which yields a combined pool of 28 campuses due to considerable overlap between the sets (Tienda & Niu, 2004, 2006b). Longhorn high schools are defined as those ever targeted by the University of Texas for the Longhorn Opportunity Scholarships (LOS) for students who qualify for the admission guarantee. According to UT's Office of Student Financial Services (2005),

> These schools were included based on criteria that takes into account their students' historical under-representation, measured in terms of a significantly lower than average percentage of college entrance exams sent to The University by students from this particular school, and an average parental income of less than $35,000.

Century high schools are the LOS counterparts at Texas A&M, namely, campuses ever targeted for Century Scholarships for applicants who graduate in the top decile of their senior class. Finally, we include the average SAT/ACT score for the student's high school, converted into ACT-score equivalent points,[27] and the sum of the share taking the SAT and the share taking the ACT in the student's high school.[28]

Students with missing values for their SAT/ACT score, grade point average, class rank percentile, or their high school's average SAT/ACT score are assigned the average value for that characteristic among all applicants to university j in year t, and dummy variable flags indicating missing values are included for each of these characteristics. At TAMU, courses taken and participation in various extracurricular activities are taken from SAT surveys. If the SAT survey data are unavailable, each of these variables is set equal to zero and an indicator variable for missing SAT survey data is added. Students lacking high school identifiers are assumed not to attend a private, feeder, LOS, or Century high school or high school in the state of Texas. Missing data for advanced placement (AP) course testing are also set equal to zero.[29]

5. Results

5.1 University of Texas at Austin

Table 1 reports the admissions probit regression results for UT. To facilitate interpretation, rather than show the parameter estimates for Equation 1, we present marginal effects for each student attribute for a hypothetical applicant with mean characteristics. The first column of Table 1 presents estimates for all applicants between 1990 and 1996, which was before the *Hopwood* decision. During these years, the likelihood of admission for Black and Hispanic applicants was 13 to 14 percentage points higher than comparable non-Hispanic White applicants. Year-by-year, cohort-specific esti-

TABLE 1

University of Texas at Austin—Admission Probit Regression Results

Applicant Characteristic	Admission Entry Year			
	1990–1996	1990–1996	1997	1998–2003
Race/ethnicity				
Black	.132***	.309***	−.017	.070***
Hispanic	.142***	.302***	−.023*	.016*
Asian	−.007	−.028***	−.015	.047***
American Indian	−.032*	−.072**	−.042	−.043
Ethnic = International	.116***	.221***	−.069*	−.257***
U.S. citizen	.084***	.091***	.069**	.060***
Female	−.001	−.003	.046***	.052***
Test scores and class rank				
SAT/ACT (00s)	.152***	.286***	.127***	.153***
SAT/ACT = missing	−.681***	−.544***	−.776***	−.566***
Class rank percentile (0s)	.101***	.175***	.158***	.116***
Class rank percentile = missing	−.257***	−.384***	−.331***	−.203***
Top 10%	.079***	−.110***	−.223***	.166***
AP exams				
Took test	.141***	.258***	.137***	.348***
Passed math test			−.005	.171***
Passed science test			.050	.096***
Passed foreign language test			.028	.092***
Passed social science test			.010	.020
Passed other test			.096***	.011
High school characteristics				
SAT/ACT average score (in ACT points)	.007***	.017***	.006	.003
SAT/ACT average score = missing	−.241***	−.349***	−.205***	−.017
Percentage took SAT + percentage took ACT	.015	.051**	.039	.018
Percentage took SAT + percentage took ACT = missing	.013	.021	.004	.066***
Feeder	.007	.019	.014	.020
Longhorn Opportunity Scholarships	−.033***	−.050*	−.054	−.001
Century	.006	−.013	.034	.006
Private	.037**	.075**	.048	−.020
In-state	.096*	.079	−.040	.060***
Including in-state top 10% applicants?	Yes	No	No	No
Number of observations	103,548	72,074	10,592	72,552
McFadden's pseudo R^2	51.9%	46.8%	51.1%	37.4%
Joint significance of race-ethnicity variables (p value)	0.0%***	0.0%***	40.6%	0.0%***

Note. Table displays the marginal effect of each dependent variable for an applicant with mean characteristics. When multiple years are included in the regression, the specification also includes a vector of year of application dummy variables. Robust standard errors that are clustered at the high school level (and that are omitted here for space concerns) are available on request.
*p < .10. **p < .05. ***p < .01.

mates (not shown) also reveal consistently positive admission advantages for Black and Hispanic applicants before 1996; these range from 9 to 17 percentage points, with no obvious pre-*Hopwood* trends.[30] Under the affirmative action regime, the admission probability for Asian applicants was indistinguishable from White students. Surprisingly, American Indian applicants were 3 percentage points less likely to gain admission than comparable White students (this estimate, which is weakly significant, is based on 468 American Indian applicants).

The second column of Table 1 again focuses on applicants in the years 1990–1996 but excludes those who were in the top 10% of their Texas high school class.[31] Among this group of applicants, race/ethnicity was an even stronger factor in admission. Specifically, the admission likelihood for Hispanic and Black applicants was 30 to 31 percentage points higher than comparable non-Hispanic White applicants. This result is consistent with evidence that affirmative action largely involved students ranked in the second decile of their class because UT had a nearly de facto practice of admitting applicants who graduated in the top 10 decile of their high school class (Tienda, Alon, & Niu, in press).[32] Asian and American Indians were at disadvantages of 3 and 7 percentage points, respectively. The bottom row of Table 1, which shows the p value for the joint test of significance for group status, reveals that jointly, race and ethnicity was a highly significant determinant of an applicant's likelihood of admission during this period. These results accord with claims that UT practiced affirmative action for Black and Hispanic applicants in the years prior to the *Hopwood* decision (Texas Higher Education Coordinating Board, 1998).[33]

To comply with the judicial ban imposed by the *Hopwood* decision, UT immediately eliminated the admission advantages given to Black and Hispanic applicants. Among students who did not graduate in the top 10% of a Texas high school, the marginal effects on the likelihood of admission for Black and Hispanic applicants fell to –2 percentage points in 1997, the year the judicial ban on affirmative action was in force but before the uniform admission law went into effect. During the years 1998–2003, a period covered both by the judicial ban and the top 10% law, the marginal effects on the likelihood of being admitted in individual years ranged from +4 to +13 percentage points for Blacks and from –3 to +6 percentage points for Hispanics relative to comparable White applicants.[34] The last column of Table 1 shows that over this whole period Blacks and Hispanics enjoyed significant admission advantages of 7 and 2 percentage points, respectively. It is noteworthy that the magnitudes of the estimated advantages given to minority applicants in the years 1998–2003 were substantially smaller than the advantages given in the pre-*Hopwood* years. Moreover, in the year 2003, the treatment of Black and Hispanic youth strongly diverge, with Black applicants receiving a significant positive boost of 13 percentage points and Hispanic applicants receiving a significant 3 percentage point reduction in their likelihood of admission (relative to Whites not in the top 10%).[35]

It is crucial to underscore that these results *do not* necessarily imply that UT was using the applicant's race or ethnicity in making its admissions decisions. Rather, UT may have changed the weights it placed on other applicant characteristics that are not available to us (e.g., essays or high school coursework) or used the observed applicant characteristics in nonlinear or interactive ways (e.g., Class Rank × Took AP Exam, etc.) that favor Black and Hispanic students. The Office of Admissions at UT published criteria considered in admission since 1997, explicitly noting that in addition to the academic index based on the high school record (class rank, completion of the required curriculum, completion of additional academic units, and standardized test scores), students would be evaluated on a personal achievement index (PAI) that included scores on two essays, leadership and extracurricular activities, awards/honors, work experience, community service, and special circumstances (University of Texas at Austin, Office of Admissions, 2005). The latter includes both family and school socioeconomic status as well as home language, domestic responsibilities, and students' test scores relative to the average for their high school. In short, the PAI scores enabled admissions officers to take a "holistic approach" in reviewing applications.[36]

Although informative, the marginal effects cannot answer whether UT admission officers changed the weights accorded to observed applicant characteristics in ways that favored minority applicants. A few results are suggestive, however. First, the positive weight placed on an applicant's SAT/ACT test score declined by half post-*Hopwood*. Second, the admission advantages enjoyed by applicants from high schools with high average SAT/ACT scores disappeared in the post-*Hopwood* years.[37] Black and Hispanic students compose relatively small shares of the student bodies at affluent high schools with high average SAT scores (Tienda & Niu, 2006a).[38] Finally, attending a high school that was targeted for the Longhorn Opportunity Scholarships lowered applicants' likelihoods of admission in the years 1990–1996 but had an insignificant effect on their likelihood of admission in the post-*Hopwood* years. Likewise, attending a private high school, which had been a positive factor before 1997, became a nonsignificant factor in the post-*Hopwood* years. Each of these changes is likely to benefit minority applicants. The simulation presented in section 5.4 illustrates how these changes, along with other components of the admissions policy, altered the composition of the admitted class.

5.2 Texas A&M University

Table 2 reports the regression results for TAMU, which gave similar admission boosts to Black and Hispanic applicants as UT in the pre-*Hopwood* years. From 1992 to 1996, a Black or Hispanic applicant's admission probability was 12 to 13 percentage points higher than a comparable non-Hispanic White applicant at TAMU, with some annual variation. Cohort-specific estimates reveal that preferences for Black and Hispanic applicants rose from 8 to 10 percentage points in 1992 and 1993 to 15 to 18 percentage points in 1994 and 1995 and subsequently declined to 9 to 10 percentage points in 1996 (perhaps suggesting that TAMU responded in advance to the anticipated *Hopwood* ruling).[39] When restricted to applicants not in the top 10% of their Texas high school class, Black and Hispanic admission preferences were higher still, averaging 28 to 29 percentage points for the pre-*Hopwood* period, with considerable variation across years (23 to 26 percentage points in the years 1992 and 1993, 32 to 36 percentage points in 1994 and 1995, and 18 to 19 percentage points in 1996). The large fluctuation in the size of the admission boosts for Black and Hispanic students across years suggests that the university did not use preestablished quotas to make its decisions.[40]

From 1998 to 2002, Black and Hispanic applicants were slightly *less* likely to be accepted than comparable White youth, although this difference was insignificant. This average effect conceals substantial year-to-year fluctuations, however. The estimated penalty (boost) accorded to Black and Hispanic applicants, respectively, ranged from –8 to +11 and from –9 to +9 percentage points, with no clearly discernable trends.

Among applicants not in the top 10% of their Texas high school class, the admission probability for Asian Americans was 3 percentage points lower than comparable White applicants between 1992 and 1996. After the top 10% law was in force, this disadvantage widened to 14 percentage points. This admission disadvantage, which ranged from 6 to 19 percentage points over the post-*Hopwood* years, was statistically significant in each year. Again, it bears emphasizing that this result does not necessarily indicate that Texas A&M discriminated against Asian American applicants. Among Texas students who did not graduate in the top decile of their class, it is possible that TAMU considered other unobservable applicant characteristics or used the observed applicant characteristics in ways that favor White students.[41]

In every year during both the pre- and post-*Hopwood* periods, race and ethnicity were highly influential in determining the likelihood that an applicant to TAMU would be admitted, although the winners and losers differed by period and demographic group. By law, the university could not directly consider these ascribed characteristics in their admission decisions after 1996, therefore the apparent disadvantages experienced by Black, Hispanic, and Asian applicants likely reflect either the weight placed on other applicant characteristics that are not available in the administrative data or interactive combinations of the observed characteristics that favor White applicants. Whereas these results show that university admission officers did not place weights on *unobserved* applicant characteristics in ways that favored Black or Hispanic applicants after the judicial ban on affirmative action, it is both permissible and plausible that they changed the weights placed on *observed* applicant characteristics in a manner that boosted minority students' likelihood of admission. For example, when we restrict the sample to students not in the top 10% of their Texas high school class, we observe declining weight placed on the student's SAT/ACT and their high

TABLE 2

Texas A&M—Admission Probit Regression Results

Dependent Variable	Admission Entry Year			
	1990–1996	1990–1996	1997	1998–2003
Race/ethnicity				
Black	.124***	.286***	−.040	−.021
Hispanic	.132***	.280***	.014	−.013
Asian	−.014**	−.029**	−.110***	−.141***
American Indian	.008	.020	−.071	.039
Ethnic = Other	−.065***	−.102***	−.063**	−.078***
U.S. citizen	.062***	.113***	.085***	.071***
Female	−.006*	−.011*	.043***	−.011**
Test scores				
SAT/ACT (00s)	.102***	.183***	.122***	.125***
SAT/ACT = missing	−.224***	−.312***	−.334***	−.313***
Class rank percentile (0s)	.084***	.147***	.152***	.141***
Class rank percentile = missing	−.037***	−.074***	−.083***	−.126***
Top 10%	.100***	.026	.130***	.156***
Curriculum				
Took AP test	−.024***	−.043***	−.042***	.125***
Took 4 years of high school English	.001	.006	−.013	−.313
Took 2 years of high school foreign language	.026***	.032**	−.007	.141**
Took 3 years of high school math	.024***	.037**	.004	−.126
Took 2 years of high school science	−.042***	−.068***	−.042	.156***
Activities				
High school band	.015***	.030***	.032*	.002
High school athlete	.021***	.040***	.076***	.040***
High school drama			.009	.030***
High school student government	.016***	.031***	.074***	.071***
High school National Honor Society	.048***	.088***	.058***	.047***
High school yearbook	−.028***	−.041***	.050**	.010
High school hobby club	−.003	−.005	.004	.006
SAT survey data missing	.098***	.202***	.150***	.090***
High school characteristics				
SAT/ACT average score (in ACT points)	.005***	.010***	−.007	−.020***
SAT/ACT average score = missing	.041***	.071**	.082*	.177***
Percentage took SAT + percentage took ACT	.036***	.058**	−.045	−.025
Percentage took SAT + percentage took ACT = missing	−.012	−.026*	−.039	.042**
Feeder	.003	.010	−.011	.018
Longhorn Opportunity Scholarships	−.036***	−.055*	−.065	−.012
Century	.021	.050	.092*	.193***
Private	.022**	.046**	.018	−.005
In-state	.202***	.245***	.195***	.182***
Including in-state top 10% applicants?	Yes	No	No	No
Number of observations	69,691	46,701	10,016	52,525
McFadden's pseudo R^2	40.4%	30.5%	29.8%	24.7%
Joint significance of race-ethnicity variables (p value)	0.0%***	0.0%***	0.0%***	0.0%***

Note. Table displays the marginal effect of each dependent variable for an applicant with mean characteristics. When multiple years are included in the regression, the specification also includes a vector of year of application dummy variables. Robust standard errors that are clustered at the high school level (and that are omitted here for space concerns) are available on request.
*$p < .10$. **$p < .05$. ***$p < .01$.

school's average SAT/ACT score and increasing weight placed on attending a high school that was targeted for the Longhorn or Century scholarships. The effects of these changes are simulated in Section 5.4.

5.3 Texas Tech University

Apparently Texas Tech did not mirror UT-Austin and Texas A&M in giving sizeable admission boosts to Black and Hispanic applicants in the years before *Hopwood* (see Texas Higher Education Coordinating Board, 1998). In fact, as shown in Table 3, from 1991 through 1996 Black applicants were slightly less likely (–1 percentage points) to be accepted than comparable White applicants, whereas Hispanic applicants were slightly more likely to be accepted (+1 percentage points). Asian American applicants were significantly less likely to be accepted than comparable White applicants, by 9 percentage points.

TABLE 3

Texas Tech—Admission Probit Regression Results

	Admission Entry Year			
Dependent Variable	1991, 1993, 1995, 1996	1991, 1993, 1995, 1996	1997	1998–2003
Race/ethnicity				
Black	–.013	–.008	.030	–.105***
Hispanic	.013*	.024**	.032	–.046***
Asian	–.091***	–.084***	.024	–.067***
American Indian	–.033	–.055	.008	–.003
Ethnic = international	–.376***	–.408***	.085**	.158***
U.S. citizen	.001	.002	–.066**	.064***
Female	–.018***	–.026***	.030*	–.003
Test scores and class rank				
SAT/ACT (00s)	.012**	.022***	.105***	.123***
SAT/ACT = missing	–.286***	–.357***	–.963***	–.650***
Class rank percentile (0s)	.047***	.063***	.004	.065***
Class rank percentile = missing	–.844***	–.852***	–.627***	–.733***
Top 10%	–.026**	–.025*	.051*	–.169***
High school characteristics				
High school SAT/ACT average score (in ACT points)	.009***	.015***	–.004	.018***
High school SAT/ACT average score = missing	.005	–.001	.049	.035
Percentage took SAT + percentage took ACT	.013	.017	–.075	–.008
Percentage took SAT + percentage took ACT = missing	–.003	.008	.009	.001
Feeder high school	.014***	.017**	–.108***	–.024**
Longhorn Opportunity Scholarship high school	–.018	–.014	–.168**	–.134***
Century high school	–.017	–.007	–.102	–.020
Private high school	.021	.027	–.077*	–.009
In-state high school	.006	.012	.002	.003
Including in-state top 10% applicants?	Yes	No	No	No
Number of observations	25,509	20,892	6,046	50,661
McFadden's pseudo R2	51.3%	51.0%	84.8%	45.9%
Joint significance of race-ethnicity variables (p value)	0.0%***	0.0%***	85.1%	0.0%***

Note. Table displays the marginal effect of each dependent variable for an applicant with mean characteristics. When multiple years are included in the regression, the specification also includes a vector of year of application dummy variables. Robust standard errors that are clustered at the high school level (and that are omitted here for space concerns) are available on request.
*$p < .10$. **$p < .05$. ***$p < .01$.

This practice continued after the judicial ban on affirmative action. Between 1998 and 2003, Black, Hispanic, and Asian American applicants who did not qualify for automatic admission under the uniform admission law were significantly less likely to be accepted than comparable White applicants. Moreover, the admission disadvantages for Black applicants to TTU who did not graduate in the top decile of their Texas high school were even larger compared with pre-*Hopwood* levels, ranging from 9 to 12 percentage points over the period and statistically significant in each year. Likewise, beginning in 2000, Hispanic applicants witnessed a significant admission disadvantage relative to comparable White students, which ranged from 3 to 6 percentage points through 2003. Asian American applicants also were 4 to 8 percentage points less likely to be accepted at TTU than comparable White students who applied for admission between 1998 and 2003; however, the disadvantage was significant only in 2002. Thus, there does not appear to be any evidence that TTU's admission officers used unobserved applicant characteristics in ways that boosted the admissions probabilities of Black and Hispanic applicants when the ban on affirmative action was in force—rather, it appears that Texas Tech placed such applicants at a disadvantage post-*Hopwood*.

With respect to observable applicant characteristics, the results are mixed. On one hand, the positive weights placed on attending a feeder or private high school declined, which would tend to favor minority applicants. On the other hand, the weight placed on the student's SAT/ACT scores increased, and attending a Longhorn Opportunity High School became a disadvantage to the applicant. The following section evaluates the relative impact of changing admission policies on the ethno-racial composition of these three universities.

5.4 Simulated Effects of Hopwood, the Top 10% Policy, and University Responses

Because the weights assigned to several individual attributes appear to have changed at each of the three universities, we disaggregate the net impacts using a simulation exercise. The composition of the admitted class is simulated by computing the hypothetical probability of admission (as shown in Equation 1, with a standard normal error term added to $\beta_0 + U_i\beta_{jt} + X_i\theta_{jt}$) and "accepting" Z_t number of students with the highest probabilities of admission. Z_t is set equal to the number of students who were actually admitted by each institution in year t.[42,43]

Table 4 reports the shares of White, Black, Hispanic, and Asian students who would be admitted (with American Indian and International shares not shown) along with the mean SAT/ACT of admitted students. Each panel shows four counterfactuals:

A: Actual admit class = students actually admitted.

B: Predicted admit class with affirmative action (AA) = admitted students simulated by applying the estimated 1990–1996 admissions formula in each year.

C: Predicted admit class with AA ban = admitted students simulated by applying the estimated 1990–1996 admission formula but setting race–ethnicity coefficients to zero.[44]

D: Predicted admit class with AA ban and automatic top 10% = admitted students simulated by applying the estimated 1990–1996 admission formula but setting race–ethnicity coefficients to zero and admitting all in-state top 10% students.

Table 4 shows the simulation results. By comparing the distributions of admitted students between counterfactuals A and B (i.e., A – B), we obtain an estimate of the total effect of *Hopwood*, the top 10% policy, and other changes to the universities' admissions policies. For the years after 1997, this total effect can be decomposed into A – D and D – B, where D – B reveals the admission consequences of Hopwood and the top 10% law and A – D shows the effects of discretionary changes in the admissions policy implemented by each institution.

For UT, the row designating net effects of the policy change shows that the combined effects of *Hopwood* and the top 10% law shifted the composition of the admission class toward Whites and Asian Americans and away from Blacks and Hispanics. For Blacks and Hispanics, the net effect of these policy changes lowered their combined shares of admitted students from 19.8% to 17.7%. However, other changes in UT's admissions decisions offset some of these effects. The discretionary

TABLE 4

Effects of University Responses to *Hopwood* and the Top 10% Policy

Period and Place	Counterfactual	Percentage White	Percentage Black	Percentage Hispanic	Percentage Asian	SAT/ACT
University of Texas at Austin						
1990–1996: Pre-*Hopwood*	A: Actual admits	65.1	4.0	15.9	12.8	1,229
	B: Predicted admits	65.2	4.0	15.9	12.7	1,228
	C: AA ban	68.0	3.1	13.2	13.3	1,232
	D: AA ban + top 10%	67.2	3.2	14.0	13.4	1,228
1997: *Hopwood*	A: Actual admits	65.7	3.2	12.4	16.0	1,234
	B: Predicted admits	63.4	3.9	13.8	15.5	1,235
	C: AA ban	65.1	3.1	12.2	15.9	1,238
	Policy change (C – B)	1.7	–0.8	–1.6	0.4	3
	Discretionary (A – C)	0.6	0.1	0.2	0.1	–4
1998–2003: Top 10%	A: Actual admits	61.7	3.9	14.5	17.1	1,236
	B: Predicted admits	60.3	4.3	15.6	16.0	1,247
	C: AA ban	62.8	3.3	12.9	16.7	1,251
	D: AA ban + top 10%	61.7	3.7	14.0	16.6	1,244
	Policy change (D – B)	1.5	–0.6	–1.6	0.6	–3
	Discretionary (A – D)	–0.1	0.3	0.5	0.5	–8
Texas A&M						
1992–1996: Pre-*Hopwood*	A: Actual admits	73.4	5.1	14.6	5.9	1,172
	B: Predicted admits	73.4	5.1	14.6	5.9	1,172
	C: AA ban	76.8	3.9	12.0	6.3	1,175
	D: AA ban + top 10%	76.5	4.0	12.3	6.3	1,174
1997: *Hopwood*	A: Actual admits	75.1	3.7	11.5	6.7	1,185
	B: Predicted admits	72.3	4.7	13.1	6.9	1,188
	C: AA ban	75.1	3.5	10.9	7.3	1,191
	Policy change (C – B)	2.8	–1.1	–2.2	0.4	3
	Discretionary (A – C)	–0.1	0.1	0.6	–0.6	–6
1998–2002: Top 10%	A: Actual admits	76.8	3.4	11.2	6.5	1,187
	B: Predicted admits	74.1	4.2	13.0	6.8	1,194
	C: AA ban	77.2	3.1	10.4	7.2	1,197
	D: AA Ban + top 10%	76.9	3.2	10.7	7.2	1,195
	Policy change (D – B)	2.8	–1.0	–2.3	0.4	1
	Discretionary (A – D)	0.0	0.2	0.4	–0.7	–8
Texas Tech						
1991–1996: Pre-*Hopwood*	A: Actual admits	78.6	4.4	13.6	2.3	1,057
	B: Predicted admits	78.8	4.4	13.6	2.3	1,057
	C: AA ban	78.7	4.5	13.3	2.6	1,057
	D: AA ban + top 10%	78.5	4.5	13.4	2.6	1,057
1997: *Hopwood*	A: Actual admits	81.8	3.9	10.3	2.8	1,097
	B: Predicted admits	81.6	4.0	10.8	2.7	1,100
	C: AA ban	81.4	4.1	10.6	3.0	1,100
	Policy change (C – B)	–0.1	0.1	–0.2	0.2	0
	Discretionary (A – C)	0.4	–0.2	–0.3	–0.2	–3
1998–2003: Top 10%	A: Actual admits	80.3	3.5	11.4	3.3	1,106
	B: Predicted admits	79.2	4.2	12.7	3.1	1,094
	C: AA ban	79.0	4.3	12.4	3.4	1,094
	D: AA ban + top 10%	78.8	4.3	12.5	3.4	1,094
	Policy change (D – B)	–0.3	0.1	–0.2	0.4	1
	Discretionary (A – D)	1.5	–0.8	–1.1	–0.1	11

Note. Conterfactual: A: Actual admits = actually admitted. B: Predicted admits = simulated by applying the 1990–1996 admissions formula in each year. C: AA ban = simulated by applying the 1990–1996 admission formula but setting race–ethnicity coefficients to zero (i.e., automatic effect of *Hopwood*). D:AA ban + top 10% = simulated by applying the 1990–1996 admission formula but setting race–ethnicity coefficients to zero and admitting all in-state top 10% students (i.e., automatic effect of *Hopwood* and top 10% policy). Policy change (D – B) = effect of policy changes in the university's admissions required by *Hopwood* and the top 10% policy for the years after 1997. Discretionary (A – D) = net effect of discretionary changes in the university's admissions policy for the years after 1997.

changes in UT's admissions decisions shifted the composition of UT's admitted students toward Blacks, Hispanics, and Asian Americans and away from Whites. This policy response helped recover the combined share of admitted Black and Hispanic students to 18.4%. That is, UT's response produced a 33% rebound in Black and Hispanic students' combined share of admitted students, namely, (18.4% – 17.7%)/(19.8% – 17.7%).[45] Nonetheless, despite a reweighting of applicant characteristics in a legally compliant manner, the university was unable to maintain the share of Black and Hispanic students that would have been admitted under a regime that allowed explicit consideration of race.[46]

Finally, it is worth noting that the combined effects of *Hopwood*, the top 10% policy, and UT's response led to a modest 11-point *reduction* in the average SAT/ACT score of admitted students. Most of this decrease resulted from discretionary changes in the weights placed on other applicant characteristics by UT's admission officers rather than the mandatory policy changes. This result might be surprising to those who expect the elimination of affirmative action at selective institutions to substantially *raise* the average ability level of admitted students, and it challenges critics who might attribute the drop in average test scores to the top 10% law.

The second panel of Table 4 shows the collective effects of changes in TAMU's admission regime. As occurred at UT, the winners from the combined effects of *Hopwood* and the top 10% policy were White and Asian American applicants, whose share of the admission pool rose. Again, Blacks and Hispanics were the losers in the shuffle produced by the affirmative action ban and the top 10% law combined; the net effect of these policy changes was to lower their combined shares of admitted students from 17.2% to 13.9%. As occurred at UT, changes in the weights placed on other applicant characteristics by TAMU's admissions officials offset some of these losses. The discretionary changes in TAMU's admissions decisions increased Black and Hispanic students' combined share of admitted students to 14.5%. Thus, TAMU's discretionary response in admissions led to a 19% rebound in Black and Hispanic students' combined share of admitted students, namely, (14.5% – 13.9%)/(17.2% –13.9%).[47] Furthermore, the collective impact of changes in policy and weights assigned to applicant attributes produced a 7-point decline in the average SAT/ACT score of students admitted to TAMU, a drop due entirely to changes in the weights placed on applicant characteristics. Our results showing that the strategies to restore campus diversity pursued at UT and TAMU did not restore minority representation to the levels that would have occurred with traditional affirmative action are consistent with the findings in Bucks (2004) and Kain and O'Brien (2004).

The third panel of Table 4 presents the simulation results for Texas Tech. The policy change row shows the combined effects of TTU complying with both the *Hopwood* ruling and the top 10% law. For this simulation, compliance with the *Hopwood* ruling would require Texas Tech to eliminate pre-*Hopwood* admissions advantages for Hispanic applicants and disadvantages for Black and Asian American applicants. This simulation thus predicts a modest decline in the share of White and Hispanic students admitted, combined with increases in the shares of Black and Asian American students. The final row shows the effect of discretionary changes in TTU's admissions policy, which benefited White students and lowered other students' admission shares. On balance, there is no evidence that TTU sought to boost the admission prospects of Black and Hispanic students in the wake of the *Hopwood* decision. Finally, in contrast to the experiences of the two public flagships, the shift in admission regimes coupled with changes in the institution-specific admission system raised the average SAT/ACT score of students admitted to TTU by 11 points.

Figure 1 diagrams the net effects on the composition of admitted students of the *Hopwood* decision, the top 10% policy, and other discretionary changes in the admission decisions of these three universities. This figure corresponds to a plot of the difference between the "Actual Admits" and "Predicted Admits" under the admission regime that permitted affirmative action, but disaggregated by individual years. At all three universities, which differ appreciably in the selectivity of their admissions, White students were the clear winners in that their rising shares among the admitted were accompanied by corresponding declines for Black and Hispanic applicants. Not surprisingly, the impact of the change in admission regime was greatest at TAMU and UT, which gave admission boosts to minority applicants before the judicial ban imposed by the *Hopwood* decision. Using the simulation results shown in Table 4 and given the total numbers of students admitted in

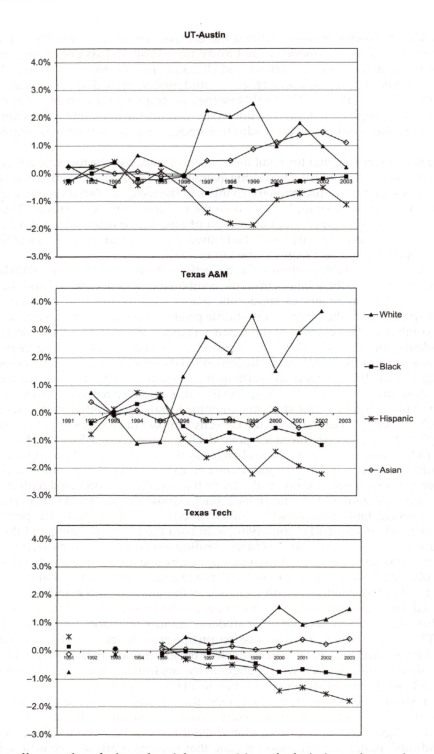

Figure 1   Net effect on the ethnic and racial composition of admission cohorts of *Hopwood*, the top 10% law, and allowable discretionary changes in university admission policies: University of Texas (UT) at Austin, Texas A&M, and Texas Tech University, 1991–2003.

Note. Deviations from zero in the years before 1997 reflect prediction errors.

the post-*Hopwood* years, we find that the combination of the policy and discretionary changes reduced the number of accepted Black and Hispanic applicants by 1,273 at UT (1997–2003), 1,794 at TAMU (1997–2002), and 906 at TTU (1997–2003).

6. Conclusion

Many studies of the change in Texas college admission regimes have concluded that the top 10% law is less efficient than affirmative action in achieving campus diversity, but none has explicitly quantified the differential impact over time and across institutions. Moreover, most evaluations of the relative success of the percentage plan in restoring campus diversity focuses on enrollment rather than admission. The top 10% law guarantees admissions to rank-eligible students, but it cannot similarly guarantee enrollment. Our focus on admission outcomes is more directly related to an evaluation of the law based on actual admission decisions at three of the largest public Texas universities. Using a unique administrative file to model the admission decision, we show that the *Hopwood* decision and the top 10% policy had sizable effects on the racial and ethnic composition of public universities in Texas—but the winners and losers differed across institutions and over time. We find evidence that the public flagships (UT-Austin and Texas A&M) offered significant advantages to Black and Hispanic applicants prior to the *Hopwood* decision. Both universities responded to changes in admission policies by shifting the weights they placed on applicant characteristics in ways that boosted the admissions probabilities of Black and Hispanic applicants. However, these efforts did not fully compensate for the effects of the *Hopwood* decision in lowering the odds of admission for Blacks and Hispanics. Public universities were unable (or did not sufficiently attempt) to proxy race and ethnicity using other applicant attributes, although UT's personal achievement index sought to weight extracurricular and extraordinary circumstances in its admission decisions in ways that could have boosted minority applicants' admission probabilities. Furthermore, the two flagships targeted fellowships to high schools with low college-going traditions. Although minority students composed large shares of the student body at the Longhorn and Century high schools, they are less likely than Whites to qualify for the admission guarantee and more likely to report financial barriers as reasons for not enrolling (Tienda & Niu, 2006a). This suggests the need for financial aid as a necessary adjunct to race-sensitive admission criteria as an ingredient for diversifying college campuses. Finally, we find no evidence that Texas Tech University gave substantial preferences to minority applicants in the pre- or post-*Hopwood* period, and changes in TTU's post-*Hopwood* admissions policy lowered the probability of acceptance for minority applicants.

Also unclear is whether public universities that did not use full file review could have used proxies in ways that allowed them to maintain campus diversity achieved before the *Hopwood* decision. For example, in the wake of *Hopwood* and Attorney General Morales's stringent interpretation of the decision, many Texas universities examined their admission policies. Staff (1997) reported that the University of Houston not only changed the numerical weights assigned to grade point averages and law school admission tests but also used "full file review" for two thirds of applicants compared with only 30% before the decision. However, simulations produced by Kane (1998a) suggest the folly of using proxies as a full substitute for race-based affirmative action; to maintain the same admissions rates for Black and Hispanic applicants, the new admissions rules imply that colleges in the top quintile of the SAT/ACT distribution would have to include a *lower* chance of admission for students with higher SAT scores! Thus, our findings showing only modest shifts in the weights used by these colleges in their admissions systems are highly plausible.

Minority applicants were the "winners" of the institutional responses by UT and Texas A&M. Despite their intentions in restoring and maintaining campus diversity however, these institutional efforts were unable to offset the deleterious effects of the judicial ban on affirmative action imposed by the *Hopwood* decision. In the end, minority applicants were the net "losers" of the changing admission regimes while Whites continued to maintain their admission advantage. This outcome is all the more remarkable in a state where Black and Hispanic students are rapidly moving toward being the majority of high school graduates.

Although instructive, the lessons from the Texas experience cannot necessarily be generalized to other states that differ in the ethno-racial composition of their college-age population, the distribution of postsecondary education institutions by public-private status, and the level of segregation of secondary schools. Texas is a large state with a college-age population that is more than half minority, where private institutions account for less than 10% of postsecondary enrollment, and where high schools are becoming more rather than less segregated. Few states fit this profile. Yet, diversification of the college-age population is not confined to Texas and most universities seek to garner the educational benefits that derive from a diverse student body, which the 2003 Supreme Court decision permits.[48] Although the *Grutter* decision narrowly *permits* consideration of race in college admissions, it does not translate into a constitutional *obligation*. States like California and Washington that imposed statutory bans on affirmative action cannot use race-based affirmative action without repealing the laws prohibiting race preferences, which means that they must seek alternative means to diversify their student bodies. Whether and under what circumstances a percentage plan can restore diversity to college campuses must be considered within the context of the demography of higher education and the contours of social inequality of each state.

Appendix

In this appendix, we evaluate two potential threats to the analysis: (a) omitted variable bias resulting from incomplete data considered in admissions decisions and (b) endogenous changes in the applicant pool.

Potential Omitted Variable Bias

The administrative data from these Texas universities do not include all of the variables that might have been available to the admissions committees. For example, the University of Texas (UT) data lack information about students' grade point averages, coursework, and participation in athletics, clubs, and community organizations. The omission of these variables might bias our estimates of pre-*Hopwood* affirmative action if such variables are correlated with the student's race (controlling for other included variables). To test the direction and magnitude of such bias, we use data from the National Education Longitudinal Study (NELS), which followed a 1988 cohort of eighth-grade students through 2000. Using these students' observed applications to 4-year colleges (from the third follow-up interviews conducted in 1994), we estimate the affirmative action boost using a specification similar to that subsequently used for UT based on a subset of institutions of comparable selectivity.[49] Table A1 reports these results.

The first column replicates the analysis using variables similar to those available in the UT administrative data. The marginal effect of being an underrepresented minority (i.e., Black, Hispanic, or Native American) is 15.1 percentage points.[50] This result closely mirrors the estimates we report for Blacks (13.2) and Hispanics (14.2) at UT during the pre-*Hopwood* period.[51] The second column shows estimates after including controls for parental income and education, variables that were considered by UT data after the *Hopwood* decision. NELS estimates reveal that the inclusion of parental socioeconomic status indicators raises the estimated affirmative action boost to 16.7 percentage points.

Columns 3 through 7 further illustrate how variables that are not available in the UT data but were likely available to UT's admissions officers may have influenced admissions decisions for underrepresented minority groups. Each group of omitted variables raises the estimated admission boost to underrepresented minority applicants, which suggests that the variables omitted in column 1 favored White and Asian American applicants, conditional on the included variables. When the full set of student attributes possibly considered in admissions decisions are included in the model (column 7), the estimated affirmative action boost is 20.8%. The results imply that our estimates based on variables available in the administrative databases are likely to be conservative. Thus, the simulation results discussed likely understate the decline in minority student's share of admitted students.

TABLE A1

Test of Omitted Variable Bias Using National Education Longitudinal Study (NELS) College Applicants

	Specification						
	1	2	3	4	5	6	7
Coefficient on underrepresented minority	0.151	0.167	0.207	0.196	0.175	0.160	0.208
Robust standard error	0.065	0.062	0.059	0.057	0.058	0.055	0.047
Controlling for:							
SAT/ACT score[a]	Y	Y	Y	Y	Y	Y	Y
Class rank percentile[a] and top 10% dummy	Y	Y	Y	Y	Y	Y	Y
AP test taken	Y	Y	Y	Y	Y	Y	Y
High school quality index	Y	Y	Y	Y	Y	Y	Y
Private high school dummy	Y	Y	Y	Y	Y	Y	Y
In-state applicant dummy	Y	Y	Y	Y	Y	Y	Y
Parent's highest education level dummies[a]	N	Y	Y	Y	Y	Y	Y
Parent's income[a]	N	Y	Y	Y	Y	Y	Y
High school GPA[a]	N	N	Y	N	N	N	Y
High school academic units[a]	N	N	N	Y	N	N	Y
High school varsity and nonvarsity athletics	N	N	N	N	Y	N	Y
High school participation in various activities and community service	N	N	N	N	N	Y	Y
Significantly different from full specification β_{URM} from column 7 (p value):	0.25	0.39	0.90	0.74	0.45	0.30	NA
Number of observations	1,013	1,013	1,013	1,013	1,013	1,013	1,013
McFadden's pseudo R^2	0.105	0.154	0.174	0.179	0.160	0.192	0.229

Note. URM = underrepresented minorities (Blacks, Hispanics/Mexicans, and Native Americans). The sample is restricted to (third follow-up) NELS applicants to 4-year colleges where the college's median freshman SAT score was between 1,160 and 1,300. NELS records data on up to two applications. If data are available on two of the student's applications, both applications are included in the regression. Standard errors are clustered based on the applicant's ID to account for students who have multiple applications in the data set. ACT scores are converted into SAT-equivalent units and the higher value is used when both are available. The high school quality index is constructed using the first principal component from a principal component analysis based on the following characteristics (sign of weights in parentheses): pupil–teacher ratio (–), daily attendance rate (+), percentage of students who drop out (–), percentage of students in college preparation program (+), and percentage of students who attend a 2-or 4-year college (+). Parent's highest education levels include no high school, high school dropout, high school graduate (or GED), some college, bachelor's degree, and graduate degree. Parent's income, which was recorded in NELS in 15 categorical ranges, was imputed using data from a 1% sample of the 1990 census, based on the average family income of those families who had a child present who was younger than 18 and income in the NELS income ranges. High school academic units include separate variables for the number of units taken in English, math, science, social studies, and foreign languages. High school varsity and nonvarsity athletics include separate dummy variables for 10th grade and 12th grade. Varsity athlete equals one if the student is a varsity athlete in any team or individual sport during that grade. Nonvarsity athlete equals one if the student was not a varsity athlete but was a nonvarsity athlete in any team or individual sport during that grade. High school participation includes: separate dummy variables for participation in 10th grade and 12th grade in band, play, musical, student government, and honor society; a count of the number of other clubs the student participated in during each grade; and a dummy variable indicating whether the student performed community service at least once per week during each grade.

a. This variable was set equal to zero if missing, and a missing variable indicator variable was also included.

Endogenous Changes in the Applicant Pool

The empirical analysis takes the applicant pool as a given. However, if the composition of applicant pool was altered by the *Hopwood* decision and the top 10% policy,[52] universities might change the weights attached to applicant characteristics in accordance with changes in the applicant pool. For example, an increase in the number of applications could allow the institution to become more selective, thus allowing for a change in the weights placed on SAT/ACT scores, and so on.

However, as Table A2 shows, the composition of the applicant pools to these institutions did not substantially change. The first panel of Table A2 shows that all of these institutions experienced substantial increases in their numbers of applications. In particular, the number of applicants nearly doubled after 1998 for Texas Tech University (TTU). These experiences correspond to a strong surge in the number of graduates from Texas high schools, which (at public high schools) rose from

TABLE A2

Changes in the Characteristics of Applicant Pools and Admitted Students

		Year of Application														
		1990	1991	1992	1993	1994	1995	1996	1997	1998	1999	2000	2001	2002	2003	Average
Number of applications	UT	14,887	14,230	14,106	14,648	14,217	14,831	16,624	14,571	16,100	17,363	17,425	16,727	18,662	20,502	16,064
	TAMU			12,787	13,325	14,039	14,623	14,899	14,914	13,258	14,453	16,769	16,679	17,281		14,821
	TTU		6,712	5,988	5,599	5,924	6,478	6,720	7,545	7,144	7,247	9,602	11,005	12,332	13,080	8,106
Share accepted	UT	70	73	69	69	72	71	66	78	66	63	75	75	76	53	69
	TAMU			75	79	73	75	75	78	87	75	66	69	68		74
	TTU		71	71	79	79	81	80	73	75	80	79	75	75	69	76
Average SAT/ACT score of admitted students	UT	1,202	1,204	1,222	1,227	1,237	1,250	1,259	1,234	1,241	1,235	1,226	1,233	1,228	1,257	1,233
	TAMU			1,169	1,164	1,172	1,180	1,186	1,185	1,182	1,187	1,189	1,189	1,190		1,182
	TTU		1,053	1,057	1,061	1,062	1,065	1,053	1,097	1,094	1,095	1,093	1,108	1,107	1,127	1,094
Share of applicants who are URMs	UT	20	20	19	20	20	19	19	18	18	20	19	19	20	21	19
	TAMU			17	17	18	19	19	17	16	16	15	16	16		17
	TTU		22	20	19	20	19	20	18	19	16	20	19	21	21	20
Share of URMs accepted	UT	75	75	74	75	72	71	65	71	61	58	75	76	76	52	69
	TAMU			80	88	87	89	76	72	80	68	68	67	63		76
	TTU		65	63	72	71	76	74	59	62	70	64	59	58	51	63
Yield rate	UT	53	52	52	52	54	54	50	58	56	59	62	58	56	60	56
	TAMU			58	60	59	55	57	53	63	62	60	58	58		53
	TTU		45	51	52	52	48	50	48	51	54	52	50	48	48	50
Yield rate for URMs	UT	51	50	48	50	50	50	46	55	54	58	62	54	52	62	53
	TAMU			48	52	52	49	46	45	54	52	49	50	51		50
	TTU		28	38	37	37	35	38	38	39	47	43	41	41	42	39

Source. Texas Higher Education Opportunity Project administrative data files. *Note.* UT = University of Texas at Austin. TAMU = Texas A&M University. TTU = Texas Tech University. URMs = underrepresented minorities (Blacks, Hispanics/Mexicans, and Native Americans).

172,480 in 1990 to 197,186 in 1998 to 238,111 in 2003 (Snyder & Hoffman, 1993, 2001; Snyder, Tan, & Hoffman, 2006). These universities largely accommodated higher demand by increasing the supply of available slots, as evident in the modest declines in the share admitted for each institution. Moreover, the average SAT/ACT score of admitted students rose 2% to 7% at these institutions, indicating only a modest increase in selectivity.

The bottom two panels show the changes for underrepresented minorities (URMs; i.e., Blacks, Hispanics, and Native Americans). For the most part, the shares of URM applicants changed only slightly—fluctuating between 16% to 22% at UT and TTU, and declining from 19% to 16% percent at Texas A&M (TAMU). The share of URMs who were accepted roughly parallels the changes in the overall shares accepted. Changes in the yield rates (i.e., the shares of admitted students who enrolled) were also parallel between URMs and all students at UT and TAMU. That is, the elimination of affirmative action did not provoke a radical change in URMs' propensity to enroll conditional on being admitted. At Texas Tech the overall yield rate declined modestly from 51% to 48% between 1998 and 2003, while the URM yield rate increased modestly from 39% to 42%. Thus, although endogenous shifts in the applicant pool have likely occurred, these changes are small enough to not substantially vitiate our subsequent analysis. We conduct a much more detailed analysis of the changes in the applicant pools in Long and Tienda (2008).

Notes

1. The judicial bans in Texas and Georgia were effectively overturned by the Supreme Court's 2003 *Grutter* decision.
2. The *Hopwood* lawsuit was filed against the University of Texas (UT) School of Law by four White plaintiffs (including Cheryl Hopwood) who were denied admission, claiming that less qualified minority candidates were admitted.
3. The *Hopwood* decision was the first successful legal challenge to the use of race-sensitive admissions criteria in college admissions since the 1978 *Bakke* decision, which rejected quotas but supported the value of diversity in achieving an institution's educational mission. There were only limited forecasts of the effects of eliminating affirmative action at the University of Texas Law School. The lower court concluded:

   > In 1992, the entering class would have included at most nine blacks and eighteen Mexican Americans, had the review of minorities been limited to those applicants in the presumptive admit and discretionary zones for white applicants. . . . These numbers reflect the maximum potential and assume no adverse effect on the number of applicants stemming from the abandonment of affirmative action. . . . In fact, the record in this case demonstrates that, without affirmative action, the perception of the law school as a "white" institution would be exacerbated, which would compound the difficulties of attracting top minority students. (*Hopwood v. State of Tex.*, 1994)

   Prior to the Fifth Circuit Court of Appeals ruling in the case, there were no estimates of the likely effect on undergraduate admissions, as the *Hopwood* case only dealt with the UT Law School's admissions policy.
4. The characteristics listed in H.B. 588 included the following:

   > (1) the applicant's academic record; (2) the socioeconomic background of the applicant, including the percentage by which the applicant's family is above or below any recognized measure of poverty, the applicant's household income, and the applicant's parents' level of education; (3) whether the applicant would be the first generation of the applicant's family to attend or graduate from an institution of higher education; (4) whether the applicant has bilingual proficiency; (5) the financial status of the applicant's school district; (6) the performance level of the applicant's school as determined by the school accountability criteria used by the Texas Education Agency; (7) the applicant's responsibilities while attending school, including whether the applicant has been employed, whether the applicant has helped to raise children, or other similar factors; (8) the applicant's region of residence; (9) whether the applicant is a resident of a rural or urban area or a resident of a central city or suburban area in the state; (10) the applicant's performance on standardized tests; (11) the applicant's performance on standardized tests in comparison with that of other students from similar socioeconomic

backgrounds; (12) whether the applicant attended any school while the school was under a court ordered desegregation plan; (13) the applicant's involvement in community activities; (14) the applicant's extracurricular activities; (15) the applicant's commitment to a particular field of study; (16) the applicant's personal interview; (17) the applicant's admission to a comparable accredited out of state institution; and (18) any other consideration the institution considers necessary to accomplish the institution's stated mission.

5. Additional information about joint authors, coauthors, sponsors, and cosponsors is available at http://www.legis.state.tx.us.

6. Whether higher rank thresholds were considered and subsequently rejected is unclear as these negotiations often took place behind the scenes. H.B. 588 allows institutional discretion to automatically admit the top quarter of applicants, but all public institutions were required to admit applicants who graduated in the top decile of their class. Staff (1997) described some of the unsuccessful house and senate bills crafted in response to the *Hopwood* decision.

7. We define *affirmative action* as the admission boost associated with race or Hispanic origin; empirically, affirmative action in admissions is identified via systematic race and ethnic differences in the likelihood of being admitted after controlling for all other applicant characteristics that are systematically related to the odds of acceptance. In this chapter, we are not estimating affirmative action in recruiting or financial aid.

8. The Michigan referendum (Proposition 2) banning affirmative action in college admissions (3 years after the Supreme Court decision allowed narrowly tailored consideration of race) attests to the continued salience of this issue for the general public.

9. California's automatic admission guarantee only kicks in if the student was not ranked high enough on a statewide academic index (based on standardized test scores, grades, and class rank, among other factors) to guarantee admission to the University of California system.

10. "These experiences and circumstances may include but are not limited to disabilities, low family income, first generation to attend college, need to work, disadvantaged social or educational environment, difficult personal and family situations or circumstances, refugee status, or veteran status." (University of California, 1996).

11. Long (2004b) predicted that replacing affirmative action with a top x% program (like the top 10% policy in Texas) will not restore minority representation. However, Long's simulation results are based on pre-*Hopwood* data and do not include any estimation of the institutional changes in other components of the admissions formulae.

12. The administrative data are available for University of Texas from 1990 to 2003, for Texas A&M University (TAMU) from 1992 to 2002, and for Texas Tech University (TTU) from 1991 to 2003.

13. The empirical results for these institutions may provide insights into the policy responses of similarly selective institutions in other states. For comparison purposes, note that *Barron's Profiles of American Colleges* (1996) gives the following selectivity ratings: UC-Berkeley (highly competitive +), UCLA (highly competitive), University of Florida (highly competitive), Florida State University (very competitive), and the University of Washington (very competitive).

14. ACT test scores were converted into their equivalent SAT test score and included in these averages.

15. These data were compiled by the Texas Higher Education Opportunity Project as part of a multiyear assessment of college-going behavior in Texas following the ban on affirmative action. Further information can be found at http://theop.princeton.edu/ index.html.

16. We are not able to estimate whether the student was "eligible" for admission (i.e., whether the student met the minimum qualifications for admission) as "eligibility" is not available in the administrative data. However, admission rates were relatively high in the pre-*Hopwood* period, even at the public flagships (between 60% to 80% of applicants were admitted at the universities included in our analyses; see Appendix Table 2).

17. Note that lack of data on student's high school coursework and admissions essays could bias the estimates of β_{jt} if coursework and essay quality is correlated with the student's race/ethnicity. As such, we exercise caution in interpreting the coefficients.

18. We add year of application dummy variables to the specification in Equation 1 to capture any year-to-year changes in the institution's degree of selectivity.

19. Student i's predicted probability of admission is set equal to $\Phi(\beta_0 + U_i\beta_{jt} + X_i\theta_{jt} + \varepsilon_{ijt})$, where ε_{ijt} is a randomly generated standard normal error term. If we did not add the error term to the predicted probability equation, the simulated admitted class would be biased in the direction of students with high SAT/ACT scores and other observed characteristics that raise the likelihood of admission. In essence,

the simulated class would place too much emphasis on the observed characteristics as no weight is placed on unobserved characteristics. Parameters for the probit model are estimated relative to the scale of the variance of the error term, which is normalized to equal one. Thus, the inclusion of a standard normal error term places the appropriate emphasis on observed and unobserved terms. Therefore, the inclusion of the error term produces simulated classes that nearly match the average observed characteristics of students actually admitted in the pre-*Hopwood* period.

20. This procedure implicitly assumes that the universities would opt to accept the same number of students under this counterfactual as they actually accepted. This assumption may not be correct if the yield rate (i.e., the share of admitted students who enroll) would be substantially altered by the change in the composition of admitted students. As we show in the appendix, the yield rates at these institutions were relatively constant.

21. The 2003 Supreme Court *Grutter* decision invalidated *Hopwood*. However, our study period occurs before this change.

22. In Long and Tienda (2008), we evaluate the changes in these applicant pools in much greater detail. The SAT/ACT and class rank distributions of applicants to UT-Austin and Texas A&M were largely unchanged. The SAT/ACT distribution of applicants to Texas Tech shifted in the direction of higher test scores for both minority and nonminority applicants. The share of Texas Tech's applicants who were in the top 10% of their high school class declined, particularly for nonminority applicants.

23. The 35 applicants (0.03%) classified as Other at Texas Tech are treated as White students, whereas the 2,060 applicants (1.3%) classified as Other at TAMU are treated as a separate ethnic group. The results for Texas Tech are virtually identical when we drop these 35 students.

24. For the most part, these institutional files do not contain other family characteristics. The exception is for UT, which began collecting data on parental education in 1996, income in 1997, and single-parent family status in 1998. (UT-Austin's admissions officers did not have this family information as data elements to be used in admission decisions in prior years; B. Walker, personal communication, June 18, 2007.) Single-parent family status was collected between 1998 and 2000 and is coded yes for 14% to 15% of applicants and missing for nearly all the rest. Although the use of such socioeconomic indicators in admissions was sanctioned by the uniform admissions law (as described in note 3), there is no clear evidence that UT actually used such indicators in its admissions decisions. The sets of categorical variables for parental education and parental income are jointly insignificant in every year, except 1997, during which the parent's education indicators were jointly significant. For 1997, there was a significant negative effect for having parent's highest education being a high school graduate and a significant positive effect for having parent's highest education being a college graduate, with insignificant effects for the other four indicators of parent's education. The single-parent family indicator variable was significant and negative for 1998, insignificant for 1999, and significant and positive for 2000. However, given the high rate of missing responses for this variable, these results should be taken with caution. Because these parental variables do not show any clear pattern of use in UT's admissions decisions, we have dropped them from the specification. Nonetheless, the results we present are robust to the inclusion of these variables, and the full results are available on request.

25. Although we have no evidence that these universities used the higher of the scores, such a procedure would be consistent in spirit with the findings of Vigdor and Clotfelter (2003), who noted that for students who take the SAT test multiple times, there is a "widespread policy stated by college admissions offices to use only the highest score . . . for purposes of ranking applicants, ignoring the scores from all other attempts" (p. 2). Consistent with this practice, the University of Michigan's point system, which was the subject of the Supreme Court's *Gratz* decision, used the higher value of the points assigned based on the student's SAT and ACT scores (see http://www.vpcomm.umich.edu/admissions/legal/gratz/gra-cert.html). Given these widespread practices, it seems reasonable to assume that these Texas universities used the higher value of the SAT and ACT score in making their admissions decisions.

26. The SAT scores at Texas Tech only include the sum of the math and verbal scores. As a result, we do not have a natural method for recentering the scores before 1996 (as SAT math and verbal scores were separately recentered by the College Board). To conduct the recentering, we began with the recentering conversion chart available from the College Board (1999). We summed the original math and verbal scores and summed the recentered math and verbal scores (effectively, this assumes that an SAT score of X is composed of a math score of $X/2$ and a verbal score of $X/2$). We then regressed the summed recentered scores on the summed original scores and these original scores squared and cubed. The regression results were then used to "recenter" the SAT scores for Texas Tech before 1996. We examined the sensitivity of the simulation results discussed in Section 5.4 by simulating the pre-*Hopwood* admission system using only the 1996 data (for which the recentering is not problematic). The results were relatively unchanged.

27. For every high school in the United States, including private schools, we obtained data on average SAT scores for the years 1994–2001 and average ACT scores for the years 1991, 1992, 1994, 1996, 1998, 2000, and 2004. Because our ACT data span a greater range of years, we converted all SAT scores into ACT equivalents. We used a linear regression of average SAT scores on average ACT scores for the years 1994, 1996, 1998, and 2000. (These regressions are weighted based on the minimum value of the number of test takers on either test.) For these years, we compute a weighted average of the high school's average SAT and average ACT scores, using the number of test takers on each test as weights. For the years 1995, 1997, 1999, and 2001, we use the previous year's regression parameters for the conversion of SAT scores into ACT equivalents. For years with missing values for the high school's average SAT/ACT score, we impute using the nearest available year and give preference to years in the same period (i.e., before and after the 1996 "recentering" of SAT scores).

28. These shares were determined by merging the SAT and ACT data sets discussed in the prior footnote with 11th-grade enrollment data from the U.S. Department of Education, Common Core of Data. For years with missing information on the shares taking either the SAT or ACT, we impute using the nearest available year.

29. The results are relatively robust to dropping observations with missing values.

30. These results are available upon request.

31. Because we omit in-state top 10% applicants, the coefficient on top 10% in the second, third, and fourth columns are identified based on out-of-state applicants who are in the top 10% of their class.

32. In the years 1990 to 1997, the percentage of top 10% students who were admitted ranged between 94% and 98%. The marginal effect of race/ethnicity on admission for students who were in the top 10% of their high school classes could not be large because these students were very likely to be admitted before H.B. 588 was enacted. Thus, when these students are excluded, the estimated marginal effect of race/ethnicity on the probability of admission rises. Rather than infer that UT had stronger preferences for minority applicants among the marginal applicants, our results could indicate a uniform preference for minority applicants relative to equally qualified nonminority applicants. However, this preference for minority applicants is irrelevant for students who are very likely to be admitted because of their high class rank.

33. The Texas Higher Education Coordinating Board indicated that affirmative action was mainly used by the public flagships with selective admissions, but private institutions also used race-sensitive criteria to diversify their campuses.

34. These estimates exclude the top 10% graduates from Texas high schools who were admitted automatically if they submitted a completed application. These individual year-by-year regression results are available on request.

35. In the immediate aftermath of the *Grutter* (2003) decision, UT-Austin announced plans to reintroduce the use of race and ethnicity in their admissions decisions for the fall 2004 applicants (UT-Austin, 2003b, 2003c) but subsequently agreed to delay the change until fall 2005 as required by law (UT-Austin, 2003a). The Texas education code requires that an institution publish in its admission catalogue a description of the factors considered in admission a year prior to their implementation.

36. Beginning with the entering class of 2005, race and ethnicity were added to the list of special circumstances.

37. It is possible that these declining weights placed on the student's SAT/ACT test score and their high schools' SAT/ACT scores could reflect increasing weight placed on unobserved student characteristics that are negatively correlated with these observed characteristics.

38. Correlations between average test scores and the percentage of the student body that is Black or Hispanic are consistently negative, ranging from −.24 to −.44; when both groups are combined, the correlation rises to −.53.

39. The first decision in the case, by Judge Sparks of the federal district court in Austin, Texas, was released on August 19, 1994 (Kain & O'Brien, 2004).

40. Between the years 1992 and 1995, the number of applications from Black and Hispanics increased, and the average SAT/ACT score of these minority applicants increased. Thus, the higher preferences given to Black and Hispanic applicants in the years 1994 and 1995 do not reflect an attempt by Texas A&M to offset declining pools of qualified minority applicants.

41. Asian students are highly likely to qualify for the admission guarantee and thus are well represented at the public flagships relative to their population share. For example, Tienda and Niu (2006a) showed that Asian students represented 4% of Texas high school graduates in 2002 but 10% of students who graduated in the top decile of their class.

42. For these simulations, we replace each applicant in the data set with 10 copies of that applicant's record prior to adding the random error term. This expansion of the data set was done to avoid producing misleading results that might have arisen due to small sample sizes of minority applicants.

43. These simulations take the applicant pool as a given. However, for each university, the difference between rows D and B for the pre-*Hopwood* years are fairly similar to the differences between rows D and B for the years 1998–2003, suggesting that the effects of *Hopwood* and the top 10% law would have been similar even if the applicant pools have changed. Thus, we do not believe that the changing composition of the applicant pool alters our central findings. A further discussion of changes in the applicant pools can be found in the appendix.

44. By setting the coefficient to zero, we implicitly assume that the distribution of characteristics excluded in the probit regressions (but observed by the admissions officers) are identical (on average) for students of differing races, which may not be the case. Alternatively, assuming that disadvantaged minority students have worse unobserved characteristics implies that the estimated race coefficient would be negative in an affirmative action–free world. As an alternative approach, we take the negative coefficients on "Black," "Hispanic," "Asian," and "American Indian" at Texas Tech in the years 1998–2003 to reflect the average value of the unobserved characteristics for these racial/ethnic groups (under the assumption that Texas Tech most closely resembles a campus that does not employ affirmative action in the top 10% period). We then scale these relative to the SAT/ACT coefficient at Texas Tech in this period. For example, the unobserved characteristics of the average Black applicant to Texas Tech are roughly equivalent to a 78point reduction in the student's SAT score (derived by dividing the coefficient associated with "Black" by the "SAT/ACT" point estimate). The comparable reductions would be 36 points for Hispanics, 51 points for Asians, and 3 points for American Indians. We apply these alternative simulated reductions to the SAT/ACT scores of applicants to each of the three universities and redo the simulation results shown in Table 4. These results are available from the authors. As one would expect, these results show larger adverse effects of the ban on affirmative action on Black and Hispanic students' shares of the simulated admitted class (i.e., lower shares in the C rows of Table 4) and correspondingly larger estimated effects of the universities' discretionary responses in raising Black and Hispanic students' shares (i.e., larger values in the A–C rows of Table 4). Therefore, the estimates we show in Table 4 could be considered lower-bound estimates of the effects of both affirmative action and the universities' responses. We would like to thank an anonymous referee for suggesting this approach.

45. Comparing rows C: AA ban and D: AA ban + top 10%, we find that the top 10% policy led to a rebound of 41%, namely, (17.7% – 16.2%)/(19.8% – 16.2%). This rebound is comparable to the findings in Long (2004b). Using national data holding applications constant, Long predicted that a top 10% policy would produce rebounds of 43%, 16%, and 10% for public colleges in the top decile, second decile, and second quintile of the freshman SAT score distribution, respectively. Comparing rows A: Actual admits and C: AA ban, we find that the combination of the top 10% policy and UT-Austin's reweighting of applicant characteristics led to a rebound of 61%, namely, (18.4% – 16.2%)/(19.8% – 16.2%).

46. The percentage of UT-Austin's admitted students who were Black fell only modestly from a pre-*Hopwood* level of 4.0% to 3.9%. However, if UT-Austin had maintained its pre-*Hopwood* admissions system, the Black student share would have been 4.3% based on the characteristics of the applicants in the top 10% years. UT-Austin's response produced a 44% rebound in Black students' share of admitted students, namely, (3.9% – 3.7%)/(4.3% – 3.7%), while the combined effect of the top 10% policy and UT-Austin's reweighting of applicant characteristics led to a rebound of 66%, namely, (3.9% – 3.3%)/(4.3% – 3.3%). For Hispanics, the rebounds were only modestly smaller: 29% and 59%, respectively.

47. The top 10% policy had a smaller effect on Black and Hispanic students' combined share at Texas A&M than at UT-Austin, with a rebound of only 12%, namely, (13.9% – 13.5%)/(17.2% – 13.5%). The combination of the top 10% policy and Texas A&M's reweighting of applicant characteristics led to a rebound of 29%, namely, (14.5% – 13.5%)/(17.2% – 13.5%).

48. *Grutter v. Bollinger* (2003).

49. These results are estimated based on National Education Longitudinal Study (NELS) students' applications to colleges whose median freshman SAT score was between 1,160 and 1,300. This range corresponds to UT, whose median freshman SAT score was 1,233. Roughly half of the NELS students' applications within this range were submitted to colleges with median SAT scores above 1,233, and roughly half were submitted to institutions with median SAT scores below this level. Similar results obtained in tests that used broader and narrower ranges (1,150 to 1,340, 1,170 to 1,280, 1,180 to 1,270, and 1,200 to 1,250).

50. Owing to small sample sizes, it was not possible to estimate the group-specific admission boost given to Black, Hispanic, and Native American applicants. However, Long (2004b) found insignificant differences in the degree of affirmative action given to Black and Hispanic applicants using NELS data.
51. The similarity of the results based on the NELS survey data and UT-Austin administrative data inspire confidence that the UT-Austin results reflect what should be expected at similarly selective institutions across the nation.
52. For discussion of such applicant responses, see Tienda, Cortes, and Niu (2003); Bucks (2004); Long (2004a); Kain and O'Brien (2004); Card and Krueger (2005); and Long and Tienda (2008).

References

Alon, S., & Tienda, M. (2007). Diversity, opportunity and the shifting meritocracy in higher education. *American Sociological Review, 72*, 487–511.

Barr, R. (2002). Top 10 percent policy: Higher education diversity after *Hopwood*. Austin: Texas House of Representatives, House Research Organization.

Barron's profiles of American colleges (21st ed.). (1996). Hauppauge, NY: Barron's Educational Series, Inc.

Bucks, B. K. (2004). *Legislating equal access in education and employment*. Unpublished doctoral dissertation, University of Wisconsin.

Card, D., & Krueger, A. B. (2005). Would the elimination of affirmative action affect highly qualified minority applicants? Evidence from California and Texas. *Industrial and Labor Relations Review, 58*, 416–434.

Chan, J., & Eyster, E. (2003). Does banning affirmative action lower college student quality? *American Economic Review, 93*, 858–872.

College Board. (1999). *The effects of SAT scale recentering on percentiles* (RS-05, May). NewYork: Author.

Dorans, N. J. (2002). *The recentering of SAT scales and its effects on score distributions and score interpretations* (Research Report No. 2002-11). New York: College Board.

Espenshade, T. J., Chung, C. Y., & Walling, J. L. (2004). Admission preferences for minority students, athletes, and legacies at elite universities. *Social Science Quarterly, 85*, 1422–1446.

Giovanola, A. (2005). *Irma Rangel*. Retrieved January 28, 2008, from http://womenslegalhistory.stanford.edu/papers05/Rangel_bio_Giovandola

Grutter v. Bollinger, 539 U.S. 306 (2003).

Hopwood v. State of Tex., 861 F.Supp. 551 W.D. Tex. (1994).

Hopwood v. Texas, 78 F.3d 932(5th Cir.), *cert. denied*, 518 U.S. 1033 (1996).

James, J. (2002, October 27). Florida governor stands by plan to boost minority enrollment at universities. *Miami Herald*, p. 1A.

Kain, J. F., & O'Brien, D. M. (2004). Hopwood *and the top 10 percent law: How they have affected the college enrollment decisions of Texas high school graduates*. Dallas: The Cecil and Ida Green Center for the Study of Science and Society, University of Texas at Dallas.

Kane, T. J. (1998a). Misconceptions in the debate over affirmative action. In G. Orfield & E. Miller (Eds.), *Chilling admissions: The affirmative action crisis and the search for alternatives* (pp. 17–32). Cambridge, MA: The Civil Rights Project, Harvard University, Harvard Education Publishing Group.

Kane, T. J. (1998b). Racial and ethnic preferences in college admissions. In C. Jencks & M. Phillips (Eds.), *The Black-White test score gap* (pp. 431–456). Washington, DC: Brookings Institution.

Long, M. C. (2004a). College applications and the effect of affirmative action. *Journal of Econometrics, 121*, 319–342.

Long, M. C. (2004b). Race and college admissions: An alternative to affirmative action. *Review of Economics and Statistics, 86*, 1020–1033.

Long, M. C. (2007). Affirmative action and its alternatives in public universities: What do we know? *Public Administration Review, 67*, 311–325.

Long, M. C., & Tienda, M. (2008, March). *Changes in Texas universities' applicant pools after the* Hopwood *decision*. Paper presented at the American Educational Research Association Conference, New York.

Marin, P., & Lee, E. K. (2003). *Appearance and reality in the Sunshine State: The Talented 20 Program in Florida*. Cambridge, MA: The Civil Rights Project at Harvard University.

McCormick, R. (2000, March 19). Race and the university: Why social justice leads to academic excellence [Editorial]. *The Seattle Times*.

Olivas, M. (2007, April 26). Don't scrap top 10% plans [Electronic version]. *Inside Higher Education*. Retrieved January 28, 2008, from http://www.insidehighered.com/layout/set/print/ views/2007/04/26/olivas

Regents of the University of California v. Bakke 438 U.S. 265 (1978).

Snyder, T. D., & Hoffman, C. M. (1993). *Digest of education statistics, 1992*. Washington, DC: Government Printing Office.

Snyder, T. D., & Hoffman, C. M. (2001). *Digest of education statistics, 2000* (NCES 2001-034). Washington, DC: Government Printing Office.

Snyder, T. D., Tan, A. G., & Hoffman, C. M. (2006). *Digest of education statistics, 2005* (NCES 2006-030). Washington, DC: Government Printing Office.

Staff, J. (1997). *Texas after* Hopwood: *Revisiting affirmative action*. Austin: Texas House of Representatives, House Research Organization.

Texas Higher Education Coordinating Board. (1998). *Report on the effects of the* Hopwood *decision on minority applications, offers, and enrollments at public institutions of higher education in Texas* (Report). Austin: Texas Higher Education Coordinating Board.

Tienda, M., Alon, S., & Niu, S. (in press). Affirmative action and the Texas top 10% admission law: Balancing equity and access to higher education. *Sociétés Contemporaines*.

Tienda, M., Cortes, K., & Niu, S. (2003). *College attendance and the Texas top 10 percent law: Permanent contagion or transitory promise?* Retrieved January 28, 2008, from http://www.texastop10.princeton.edu/reports/wp/college_attendance.pdf

Tienda, M., & Niu, S. (2004). Texas' 10-percent plan: The truth behind the numbers. *The Chronicle of Higher Education, 50*(20), B10.

Tienda, M., & Niu, S. (2006a). Capitalizing on segregation, pretending neutrality: College admissions and the Texas top 10% law. *American Law and Economics Review, 8*, 312–346.

Tienda, M., & Niu, S. (2006b). Flagships, feeders, and the Texas top 10% plan. *Journal of Higher Education, 77*, 712–739.

Tienda, M., & Sullivan, T. A. (in press). The promise and peril of the Texas uniform admission law. In M. Hall, M. Krislov, & D. L. Featherman (Eds.), *The next twenty-five years? Affirmative action and higher education in the United States and South Africa*. Ann Arbor: University of Michigan Press.

University of California. (1996). *Guidelines for implementation of university policy on undergraduate admissions*. Retrieved May 29, 2005, from http://www.ucop.edu/sas/admit/admitguide.htm

University of California. (2001a). *Comprehensive review*. Retrieved June 5, 2005, from http://www.ucop.edu/news/factsheets/2001/comprev.pdf

University of California. (2001b, May). *FACTS about the University of California*. Oakland: UC Office of the President, Office of Strategic Communications.

University of Texas at Austin, Office of Admissions. (2005). *Participating Texas high schools*. Retrieved June 4, 2005, from http://finaid.utexas.edu/sources/ scholarships/programs/los/hschools.html

University of Texas at Austin, Office of Public Affairs. (2003a). *Statement on reinstatement of affirmative action in admission*. Retrieved August 1, 2006, from www.utexas.edu/opa/news/03newsreleases/nr_200309/nr_affirmative030910.html

University of Texas at Austin, Office of Public Affairs. (2003b). *The University of Texas at Austin reacts to the Supreme Court's affirmative action decisions*. Retrieved August 1, 2006, from www.utexas.edu/opa/news/03newsreleases/nr_200306/nr_affirmativeaction030623.html

University of Texas at Austin, Office of Public Affairs. (2003c). *University's admission policy to include consideration of race*. Retrieved August 1, 2006, from www.utexas.edu/opa/news/03newsreleases/nr_200308/nr_admission030828.html

University of Texas at Austin, Office of Student Financial Services. (2005). *Implementation and results of the Texas Automatic Admission Law (HB588) at the University of Texas at Austin*. Retrieved February 27, 2007, from http://www .utexas.edu/student/admissions/research/HB588-Report7.pdf

Vigdor, J. L., & Clotfelter, C. T. (2003). Retaking the SAT. *Journal of Human Resources, 38*, 1–33.

CHAPTER 41
STATE DREAM ACTS: THE EFFECT OF IN-STATE RESIDENT TUITION POLICIES AND UNDOCUMENTED LATINO STUDENTS

STELLA M. FLORES

Introduction

In 1982, the U.S. Supreme Court struck down a 1975 Texas law that sought to deny undocumented immigrant children a free elementary and secondary public education by charging them tuition to attend state schools. This ruling, *Plyler v. Doe* (1982), addressed only the educational rights of students attending public primary and secondary schools, however, and did not address state or federal actions regarding the postsecondary opportunities of undocumented students (Olivas, 2004). Multiple generations of school-age students benefiting from the *Plyler* decision have since attended and graduated from U.S. public high schools.

Despite an absence of direction from the U.S. Supreme Court regarding these students' right to postsecondary schooling, action on this issue has not been lacking. Since the 1980s, a number of statutes have arisen in state legislatures attempting to address this gap in educational accessibility for students with uncertain citizenship status. Most notably, *Leticia A. v. Board of Regents of the University of California* (1985) gave undocumented students in California in-state tuition rates and state financial aid, but the ruling was overturned in 1990 (Olivas, 1995, 2004; Rincon, 2008). In addition, universities in New York, such as the City University of New York and the State University of New York, also made in-state tuition rates available to undocumented students through university administrative policies made in the 1980s (Olivas, 1995; Rincon, 2008).

While such examples indicate that the option of in-state resident tuition (ISRT) is not a new phenomenon, the configuration of the most recent such policies, 10 across the nation by 2006, is distinctive, given the federal era in which the legislation was passed. In 1996, the U.S. Congress passed the Illegal Immigration Reform and Immigrant Responsibility Act (IIRIRA) and the Personal Responsibility and Work Opportunity Reconciliation Act, which initiated a new policy context regarding benefits for undocumented immigrants (Kobach, 2007; Olivas, 2008). The IIRIRA law, for example, mandates:

> Unauthorized aliens, "shall not be eligible on the basis of residence within a State (or a political subdivision) for any postsecondary education benefit unless a citizen or national of the United States is eligible for such a benefit . . . without regard to whether the citizen or national is such a resident." (Feder, 2006, p. 1)

Nevertheless, a number of states have passed legislation aimed at making tuition benefits available to undocumented immigrants without violating the provisions of federal law (Feder, 2006). (For an alternative legal analysis about the legality of the in-state resident tuition policies as they relate to federal immigration law, see Kobach, 2007.) It was in this post-IIRIRA context that the first of 10 in-state resident tuition bills passed in Texas in 2001. The most recent bill passed in 2006 in Nebraska, which I excluded from this study due to data limitations.

The purpose of this study is to build on the legal, philosophical, and descriptive trend analyses of these policies to date. Specifically, the study estimates the responses of individuals likely to be undocumented to the various in-state resident tuition policies by applying an econometric methodology and, hence, is one of the first empirical efforts to investigate this impact, if there is any. It complements previous studies examining the impact of financial assistance on college enrollment.

The next section presents the research questions, describes recent research on in-state resident tuition policies, and justifies the current study as a next step in research analysis on this topic. The following section describes the criteria of the various in-state tuition policies across the United States. A fourth section describes the theoretical framework guiding this study and reviews the literature examining the impact of price and financial aid on the college access of Latinos and Latino (used interchangeably with "Hispanic") immigrant youth. The following section presents the research design, including data, analytic strategy, and threats to validity associated with the design's potential limitations. I next describe the estimated effect of the various in-state resident tuition policies on the college-enrollment odds of Latino foreign-born noncitizen (FBNC) students and discuss additional checks on the robustness of my results. The final section discusses the implications of this policy analysis research.

Background and Research Questions

In 2001, Texas became the first state to pass an in-state resident tuition policy benefiting undocumented students following passage of the 1996 IIRIRA law. In-state resident tuition policies allow out-of-state resident students to attend college at the same price as in-state resident students if they meet certain requirements. The tuition policies are not exclusively for undocumented students, although this group may be the most likely beneficiaries.

In 2003, a federal version of in-state resident tuition policies was introduced in the U.S. Congress. Called the Development, Relief, and Education for Alien Minors Act (DREAM Act), the federal policy was designed to allow, among the tuition discount provisions, undocumented students to get on the path toward citizenship and gain legal employment by going to college or serving in the U.S. military (National Immigration Law Center, 2006; Olivas, 2004). Although Congress has not passed any form of the DREAM Act to date, the terminology used in the original version of the proposed act has been adopted by researchers and media outlets across the country to describe the multiple in-state resident tuition policies (Immigrant Legal Resource Coalition, n.d.; Rincon, 2008; Taylor, 2006). Since 2001, nine other states have passed similar Dream Act legislation, including California, Utah, New York, Washington, Oklahoma, Illinois, Kansas, New Mexico, and Nebraska (Appendix A). In 2007, Oklahoma became the first state to retract its policy (Hebel, 2007).

The issue of whether ISRT policies increase the college-enrollment rates of undocumented immigrant high school graduates is particularly relevant, given the growing demographic significance of immigrants in the United States. In 2004, the Pew Hispanic Center reported that 11.3 million undocumented immigrants represent almost 30% of all foreign-born individuals living in the United States.[1] Three of the five states with the highest percentage of undocumented immigrants in the country (California, Texas, and Illinois) have a version of the in-state tuition policy. California has the largest percentage of undocumented immigrants, 24%, followed by Texas (14%), Florida (9%), New York (7%), Arizona (5%), Illinois (4%), New Jersey (4%), and North Carolina (3%) (Passel, 2005a).[2] The ages and education completion rates of undocumented high school students are also particularly important in assessing the pool of students likely to benefit from an ISRT policy. One-sixth of the undocumented population is under age 18. Furthermore, the Urban Institute estimates that 49% of "unauthorized youth" of all races and ethnicities do not complete high school, compared to 21% of their legal immigrant counterparts and 11% of native-born students in the United States (Passel, 2005b). Despite graduation rates below those of other categories of students, it is estimated that, by 2004, approximately 48% of the 65,000 undocumented students who graduated from high school attended some college (Passel, 2005b). How and what factors facilitated this college attendance, however, requires further exploration, and as such is the subject of this analysis.

This study examines whether students likely to be undocumented Latinos living in states that have an ISRT policy were more likely to enroll in college after the policy was implemented than their student counterparts in states without similar state legislation. The changes in tuition legislation brought about by the introduction of each ISRT policy—and in the context of the 1996 IIRIRA law—provide a unique opportunity to use quasi-experimental methods to investigate the impact of policies targeting undocumented students (Dynarski, 2003, 2004).

To investigate whether these tuition policies have had an impact on the college-enrollment rates of the estimated population of undocumented Latino students, I explore the following question: Did the introduction of instate resident tuition benefits to undocumented students in Texas, California, Utah, New York, Washington, Oklahoma, Illinois, Kansas, and New Mexico have an impact on their college participation rates, compared to similar students living in states without an in-state resident tuition policy?

To answer this question, I use a nationally representative dataset of individuals, the Current Population Survey's (CPS) Merged Outgoing Rotation Groups (MORG), to examine the college-enrollment rates of the estimated undocumented Latino population. This measure includes students who are classified as foreign-born noncitizens (FBNCs), an official citizenship category of the CPS. Citizenship status in the CPS MORGs is represented by the following categories: (a) native, born in the United States; (b) native, born in Puerto Rico or U.S. outlying areas; (c) native, born abroad of American parents; (d) foreign-born, U.S. citizen by naturalization; and (e) foreign-born and not a citizen of the United States—the primary category of interest for this study.

I use FBNCs as a proxy for the undocumented because the category includes only legal residents, residents without proper authorization to live in the United States, and refugees (humanitarian migrants), whom the census counts in the percentage of the foreign-born population without U.S. citizenship (U.S. Census, 2009). While the inclusion of legal residents and refugees is not ideal, this category provides the closest level of detail on the presence of undocumented immigrants of a government survey (Passel, 2005a; Passel, VanHook, & Bean, 2004). I discuss additional advantages and limitations of the dataset below.

I focus on immigrants of Latin American origin (i.e., Latinos) and do not include foreign-born individuals of Asian or African origin because Latinos (a) are the most likely to be undocumented, (b) comprise almost 85% of the total estimated undocumented population, (c) have historically lower citizenship rates than immigrants of Asian origin, and (d) have lower educational attainment rates than immigrants of Asian and African origin in the United States (Dixon, 2006; Erisman & Looney, 2007; Hagy & Staniec, 2002; Margon, 2004; Passel, 2005a). Of the estimated undocumented population, Asian-origin individuals comprise 9%, African and "other" comprise 4%, and Europeans and Canadians comprise 6%. In addition, individuals of Mexican origin, who comprise the majority (57%) of all foreign-born U.S. residents from Latin America, both dominate unauthorized immigration to the United States and "drive U.S. policy debates about international migration," legal or illegal (Bean & Lowell, 2007, p. 70).

Research on the undocumented, however, reaches beyond demographic accounts. An increasing volume of studies on college students in particular has emerged since the 1990s, particularly since 2001. For example, a number of researchers have contributed to the field of undocumented student access to postsecondary education, including legal analyses, descriptive policy briefs, congressional research reports, legislative and historical reviews, philosophical analyses of the concept of citizenship as it pertains to financial aid and educational attainment, and other analyses and journalistic accounts of the ISRT policies (Batalova & Fix, 2006; Castillo, 2007; Feder, 2006; Flores & Chapa, 2009; Olivas, 2004, 2007, 2008; Olivérez, Chavez, Soriano, & Tierney, 2006; Perry, 2006; Rincon, 2008). Olivas (1995, 2004, 2007, 2008, 2009), for example, has continued to document the legal context and conflicts surrounding the debates among postsecondary, state, and federal jurisdictions as they relate to undocumented individuals. Perry (2006) has addressed the philosophical conflicts and opportunities in definitions of membership and citizenship as they relate to this group of students, from the 1982 *Plyler v. Doe* decision to a more recent education policy context. Rincon (2008) documents the case history of the Texas policy in historical and legislative detail.

Others have begun to document enrollment trends based on state higher education reports or estimates of potentially eligible unauthorized students in the United States (Batalova & Fix, 2006; Gonzales, 2007; Texas Comptroller, 2006). Gonzales (2007), for example, documents results from a Texas Higher Education Coordinating Board study of the growth in the number of students enrolling in Texas colleges after passage of the ISRT policy, from 393 students in 2001 to 3,792 students in 2004. Although an impressive growth trend, a report from the Texas Comptroller (2006) notes that only 0.36% of students in Texas public colleges and universities paid in-state tuition as a result of this policy provision. Other states, including Kansas, New Mexico, Washington, and Utah, cite growth in undocumented student enrollment, although at much lower numbers (Gonzales, 2007). Finally, Batalova and Fix (2006), using U.S. census data, estimate the pool of unauthorized students who might benefit from national implementation of the DREAM Act.

This study improves on existing quantitative analyses by statistically modeling varying legal criteria of the in-state resident tuition laws while incorporating a control group to account for general enrollment trends that may be occurring over time regardless of the impact of the tuition policy. That is, while enrollment trends suggest an increase in student response due to the passage of the tuition policies, without further analysis it is not clear whether such growth trends are any different than they might have been without any such tuition policies. While not all colleges and universities allow undocumented students to attend college, some do, although under the category of international residents and at international student rates, which are considerably higher than in-state resident prices (Olivas, 1995). To estimate the impact on enrollment of the benefits accorded by the in-state resident tuition policies designed as of 2001, I use an econometric method known as differences-in-differences, which is commonly used in public policy analyses measuring policy interventions of this type (Dynarski, 2003, 2004; Kane, 1994).

Criteria of the In-State Resident Tuition Policies

As of 2006, 10 states (nine, excluding Nebraska) had passed in-state resident tuition polices targeted at undocumented students. While not exclusively for the undocumented, the 10 bills have three primary components in common. All require eligible students to have attended school in the state for a set number of years, to have graduated from high school or received a GED from that state, and to sign an affidavit declaring that they will apply for legal status as soon as they are eligible (National Immigration Law Center, 2006). While similar in primary eligibility criteria for the tuition benefit, each state's policy differs in terms of date enacted and other particular provisions. (See Appendix A.)

Finally, the tuition policies, while contested, have been deemed legal in many state legislatures based on the following reasoning: In-state residency is a state-determined benefit and "purely state benefits can be extended or withheld to undocumented students because tuition benefits and state residency determinations are properly designated as state classifications and may incorporate, but not determine immigrant status" (Olivas, 2008, p. 4). Nevertheless, the policies relating to undocumented students continue to remain controversial, and those of Kansas and California, for example, have been challenged in state and federal courts (Kobach, 2006; Olivas, 2009). Moreover, controversy over undocumented immigrant benefits has continued to extend beyond the context of education to issues related to housing, voting, and local law enforcement (Olivas, 2007).

Of the ten ISRT policies passed as of 2006, two were passed in 2001 (Texas and California), two in 2002 (Utah and New York), three in 2003 (Washington, Oklahoma, and Illinois), one in 2004 (Kansas), one in 2005 (New Mexico), and one in 2006 (Nebraska) (Flores & Chapa, 2009). Enactment dates—the dates on which a student is actually eligible to take advantage of the policy—and the primary identification strategy in this study range from the date of legislative approval to approximately one year after the signing of the bill. Under the enactment stipulations, then, the Texas policy became active in 2001; the California and Utah policies in 2002; New York, Washington, Oklahoma, and Illinois in 2003; Kansas in 2004; New Mexico in 2005; and Nebraska in 2006.

The policies also have different residency requirements. While a majority require a three-year residency and graduation from a high school in the state of residence (Texas, California, Utah,

Washington, Illinois, and Kansas), New York and Oklahoma require only a two-year residency. New Mexico is the only state to date with a one-year residency requirement, in addition to the usual requirement of graduation from a high school in that state. The policies also vary according to the time and location in which a GED can be earned. While California does not accept GED credentials from "adult" schools, New York allows any GED credential, but on the condition that a student applies to college within five years of completing the GED (National Immigration Law Center, 2006). Access to state financial aid is another benefit available only in some states. Texas, Oklahoma, and New Mexico (at the time the legislation passed) allow policy-eligible students to qualify for state financial aid. Since undocumented students do not qualify for any form of federal financial aid, this benefit might be an additional incentive for these students to enroll in postsecondary institutions in states that offer financial aid. However, it is not clear whether the amount of aid is similar across the three states or whether the application process in each state is clearly established and easily accessible to students and their families. Some school districts in Texas, for example, hold community workshops to coach families in how to fill out financial-aid paperwork, using strategies that work for those lacking particular identification documents (E. Morales, personal communication, November 2006).

Finally, three of the states that formally restricted race-conscious policies in college admissions through either a court mandate or a state referendum during a majority of the period examined also have an in-state resident tuition policy—Texas, with the Fifth Circuit Court of Appeals ruling in *Hopwood v. Texas* from 1996 to 2003;[3] California, with Proposition 209 beginning in 1997; and Washington, with Initiative 200 beginning in 1998. I have made an effort to account for a potential influence of these admissions policies where applicable.

Theoretical Framework and Review of the Literature

Costs, Benefits, and Uncertainties

For this study, I apply a cost-benefit framework developed by Becker (1964) as part of the human capital model to theorize the effect of a price reduction on college-enrollment behavior. Altonji (1993) extends this model by incorporating the concept of uncertainty, which I use to inform how undocumented Latino students, due to their vulnerable status in the United States, might choose to enroll in higher education as a result of a tuition subsidy that reduces the price of college. The price reduction is particularly important because it is mandated by a state law implemented by all public higher education institutions in each particular state.

According to Becker, investment in education incurs a cost, but it also increases human capital that translates into skills that can be "rented out" to employers in exchange for income. In deciding whether to prepare for, enroll in, or complete college, an individual weighs the costs and benefits of the educational investment—both monetary and nonmonetary. The monetary considerations typically include form of tuition, foregone earnings (costs), and higher future earnings (benefits). Nonmonetary costs may include the psychological stress associated with the investment, while nonmonetary benefits might include increased public and social prestige and better health outcomes. Within a basic human capital framework, the primary effect of an in-state resident tuition policy, which provides a tuition discount for students who would otherwise be required to pay international rates, is a reduction in price.

The typical cost-benefit analysis, however, may operate differently for a student who is undocumented and therefore susceptible to a number of uncertain factors and outcomes, including a lack of financial capital, insufficient command of English to do college-level work, risk of deportation, separation from family in the United States, and uncertainty of receiving any real returns from or opportunity to legally enter the United States labor market after investing in college. Altonji (1993) suggests that the decision to invest in college is further complicated when individuals have incomplete information and uncertain conditions when trying to make the most accurate cost-benefit analysis of their enrollment decision. Applying this framework, a student who is low income and undocumented may initially see the monetary costs of investing in a college education as enormous but may also expect that the benefits of receiving U.S. wages for doing college-level work will far outweigh the immediate direct and opportunity costs of attending college.

However, the uncertainties associated with nonmonetary costs and benefits may be too much to manage. The psychological costs of revealing one's undocumented identity (and perhaps that of one's family) by deciding to enroll in a public institution may be too great. Thus, for an undocumented student, the expected returns on a college education may have an unusually high level of uncertainty in institutions where their presence is not welcome or secure.

Applying the concept of uncertainty to the potential policy effects of an instate resident tuition policy, one might expect state support for this eligibility to reduce uncertainty by providing a safe space for undocumented students to pursue a college education while retaining a protected identity. In other words, a secondary effect of this policy may be the reduction of uncertainty in the college-enrollment process for these undocumented students.[4]

Price, Financial Aid, and Latino College Enrollment

The role that financial aid plays in the college-enrollment decisions of low-income and underrepresented minority students has received increased attention, with particular emphasis on how specific groups of students have responded over the last three decades. Research on the role of income and background status suggests that the response to financial aid differs by background and may be greater for low-income students and underrepresented minority students (Ellwood & Kane, 2000; Heller, 1997; Kane, 1994; St. John & Noell, 1989). Kane (1994), for example, finds that both Blacks and low-income Whites were sensitive to tuition increases in the 1980s. By the 1990s, Long (2004a) reports, cost continued to play an important role in the college-decision process for low-income students, although this was less of a factor for the cohort of students entering college in the 1990s than for those in the 1970s. Other research suggests that student response to different forms of aid also varies by background status. Perna (2000) finds that students respond differentially to particular forms of financial aid. In a study examining a national cohort of students graduating in 1992 (the National Education Longitudinal Sample of 1988) (NELS 88), she presents descriptive results suggesting that African Americans and Hispanics are more likely to receive grants than Whites, although African Americans are also more likely to receive loans than their White and Hispanic counterparts. Multivariate analyses of the same cohort also suggest that, when controlling for other factors, loans reduce the probability of enrollment for African Americans but not for the other race and ethnic groups examined. This study, however, focuses on four-year institutions, thereby not accounting for the institutions Hispanics are more likely to attend—community colleges (Adelman, 2005; Kurlaender, 2006). Nonetheless, these results add to the growing evidence regarding the differences in student decisions to invest in college by race and ethnicity, institutional type, and form of financial aid available (Heller, 1997; Perna, 2000; St. John, 1991).

The growing research on race and ethnicity—in particular the recent inclusion of a sizeable sample of Latino students in national datasets—has provided additional evidence on this group's enrollment-decision process and behavioral response to financial aid. However, few if any studies to date document the role of the complex relationship between citizenship and race/ethnicity in college-enrollment decisions as they relate to price and availability of aid. (See Erisman & Looney, 2007, as an exception.)

In a regional study examining the role of college access for Chicano students in California based on language status, Post (1990) found that costs were a large determinant of postsecondary plans for children of Spanish speakers but not for children of English speakers. In a recent examination of college price and aid response by race and ethnicity for students entering college in the 1990s, Alfonso (2004) suggests that Hispanics are more price sensitive to college costs than non-Hispanics. Additionally, a national study found that Hispanic parents were twice as likely as Black parents and White parents to have "no idea" how to pay for college, were less likely to receive any information on financial aid when their child was young, received information about financial aid later than Black parents and White parents, and indicated that the language in which information is available is critical (Sallie Mae Foundation, 2004).

These findings also showed that familiarity with financial aid options increased with time in the United States, although this pattern was not always consistent. More recently, Erisman and Looney (2007) provided detailed descriptions of the characteristics of immigrant student undergraduates according to citizenship status, using datasets from the Office of Immigration Statistics and the U.S. Census Bureau. They found that immigrant students from Latin America and the Caribbean were more likely to be living in poverty and to delay entry into higher education.

Finally, in examining where Hispanic students are most likely to enroll in college, the trends have remained remarkably consistent over the last three decades (Adelman, 2005; Hagy & Staniec, 2002; Kurlaender, 2005). A recent national study examining the role of generational status (not citizenship) also using the NELS 88 reports that both U.S.-born Hispanic students and Hispanic immigrant students are more likely than other racial and ethnic groups not to enroll in any postsecondary institution, followed by the second option of enrolling in a community college as their first-choice institution (Hagy & Staniec, 2002). In contrast, both first-and second-generation students of Asian origin were likely to enroll in a four-year institution as a first option.

Research Design

The Data

Did the introduction of an in-state resident tuition law in select states impact the college participation rates of students likely to be undocumented compared to similar students living states without an in-state resident tuition law? To answer this question, I use the Current Population Survey, a nationally representative sample sponsored by the U.S. Census Bureau and the U.S. Bureau of Labor Statistics, for 1998 through 2005. The dataset is particularly useful in answering this question, since it is also representative at the state level and provides sufficient observations for analysis as constructed. I do not include Nebraska in my analysis because it passed its tuition policy in 2006, and I am limited to data that do not extend far enough to measure this state's enrollment trends.

The CPS is a multistage, stratified monthly sample that contains information on approximately 60,000 housing units across the United States for the civilian population age 16 and older. In the CPS, households are interviewed each month for four months, ignored for eight months, and then interviewed again for four months. For this particular analysis, I use a subset of the CPS known as the Merged Outgoing Rotation Group files, which includes approximately 30,000 individuals nationally per monthly extract to answer how the in-state resident tuition policies affected college enrollment. Because the MORG dataset has multiple observations for most individuals over time, I calculate robust standard errors to account for the clustering of observations at the individual level (within person) and so that standard error estimates reflect the structure of the data. Data are representative at both the state and national level. I use logistic regression to estimate my equation.

Utilizing these data for my analysis has some limitations. Since no government agency in the United States, including the Census Bureau, directly counts the undocumented immigrant population due to obvious legal and ethical reasons, their numerical presence cannot be measured with certainty (Passel, 2005a; Passel, Van Hook, & Bean, 2004). However, the CPS does include undocumented immigrants in its survey, thus making it a principal source of information for current estimates of unauthorized immigration in the United States (U.S. Department of Labor, 2002). Undocumented individuals in this population are counted in the data category of foreign-born noncitizens, although noncitizenship does not equate with undocumented status. Instead, current estimates indicate that of all foreign-born individuals in the United States, the undocumented account for approximately 29% (10.3 million). Legal permanent residents comprise 29% of all foreign-born residents (10.4 million); naturalized citizens comprise 32% (11.3 million); refugee arrivals comprise 7% (2.5 million); and temporary legal residents comprise 3% (1.2 million) (Passel, 2005b).

Another limitation involves who the CPS undercounts in its monthly survey: the number of immigrants in the sample compared to the U.S. Census (Passel et al., 2004), and the number of high school dropouts, most notably minority males, since the survey excludes military and institutionalized populations (Orfield, 2004).

For this analysis, I focus on the Latino population in the sample and define Latino as any individual who has self-identified as Hispanic in the survey, has listed a Latin American country of national origin, and has at least one parent who is foreign-born and has listed a Latin American country of origin. Specifically, I use the sample of Latinos, using FBNC status as the identifier, in the states with the tuition policy in question (Texas, California, Utah, New York, Washington, Oklahoma, Illinois, Kansas, and New Mexico) as the treatment group. I use the same population in states without a tuition policy (the rest of the United States, including Washington, D.C.) as a control group.

I also limit the sample according to restrictions dictated by each state policy, such as years of residency and high school graduation. First, I use year of entry into the United States as a proxy for residency for the foreign born. For example, I limit the sample to individuals who entered the United States by the last year in which they would qualify for the benefit (based on CPS year categories). In Texas this might be 1998, while in Oklahoma, which requires two years of residency, a student would have had to enter the United States by 2001.

Second, I test two educational completion samples, "All Grades" and "HS Diploma/GED Completer," excluding all individuals who have completed a B.A. or higher. I also test my results for individuals within various age ranges (e.g., 18–24, 18–20, 21–24) within separate gender samples, and within separate samples of geographic concentration characteristics, such as metropolitan versus nonmetropolitan areas. The age categorization allows me to explore whether the "take-up" of the policy—i.e., whether an eligible student chooses to make use of the tuition policy benefit—is likely to occur with recent high school graduates or older students or both. The gender comparisons allow me to test as independent samples the factors that may influence the responses of females or males in particular states to the policy intervention. The tests for geographic concentration, which vary considerably across the nine states, allow me to examine how the role of urban concentration may interact with this type of financial assistance to affect the college-enrollment rates of this population.

I focus my results on the High School Diploma/GED Completer sample, but also include the more expanded All Grades sample (no high school/GED completion restriction; selected results for this sample are shown in Appendix B) for the following reasons. First, the various tuition policies differ in their requirements regarding previous postsecondary attainment and or years of consecutive U.S. high school attendance. Since various community colleges offer courses that lead to a GED or high school diploma, including courses such as English as a Second Language or GED preparation courses, it is possible that an individual without a high school diploma may have accessed a postsecondary institution without an intended degree declaration through this initial pathway. Illinois, California, and Kansas allow students who have previously accessed a postsecondary institution to qualify for the tuition benefit. Other states (New York, Texas, and Utah) are more restrictive in terms of the method and timing with which a student accessed any postsecondary education.

Second, the CPS asks about educational attainment levels based on U.S. education-completion categories. I allow for an expanded sample in the event that an educational trajectory in a country other than the United States, such as Mexico, is not accurately captured in the survey. Other potential measurement errors include not being able to reach all individuals in their primary language during the survey administration (U.S. Census Bureau, 2006). Finally, this expanded sample allows for the possibility that the policy is also acting as a welcoming signal, in that students who abide by these requirements are likely to feel less threatened and thus access public postsecondary institutions in states with an in-state tuition policy whether or not they qualify for the tuition discount.

In addition to using states without the tuition policy as a control group, I test the potential effects of the policy on a separate sample of Latinos who are U.S. citizens (individuals who are U.S.-born as well as individuals who are naturalized in the United States) as a robustness check and to assess potential measurement error on the citizenship question. Due to the vulnerable status of undocumented individuals in the United States, individuals may not have answered the question about their citizenship status truthfully when surveyed. For example, if the parameter of interest is positive and significant for both the foreign-born and U.S.-citizen Latinos (naturalized or U.S. born), then I will be less able to conclude that this policy had an effect on the population of interest, foreign-born noncitizen Latinos. However, with no other available and sufficiently large individual-level representative dataset in the United States to capture the exact percentages of the undocumented along with educational attainment rates, the CPS is still one of the best national datasets with which to estimate their behavior, using the FBNC category as a proxy for undocumented status. Table 1 displays summary statistics for the dataset that includes the percentage of foreign-born Latinos, as well as year-of-entry restrictions for students ages 18–24 in states with and without the in-state resident tuition policies.

Analytic Strategy

In my analysis, I capitalize on the passage of each state's policy as a plausible source of exogenous variation in measuring the effects of financial aid incentives on college enrollment, using a quasi-experimental method to measure the "causal" impact of aid policies (Dynarski, 2003, 2004; Kane, 1994, 2003; Long, 2004b). Specifically, I employ a differences-in-differences strategy to estimate the effect of eligibility for the nine in-state resident tuition policies on the overall college enrollment of FBNC Latino students, relative to this same population group in states without the tuition policy. This study examines the intent-to-treat effect—that is, students may not actually use the benefit even if they are eligible.

To answer whether the state resident tuition policies increased the college participation among FBNC Latino students in states with a tuition policy, I use the MORG subsample to estimate the following multivariate regression model (subscripts are suppressed):

$$(1) \text{LOGISTIC (INCOLL = 1)} = \beta_0 + \beta_1 \text{ DIMMIGTUITION} + \beta_2 \text{ FBNC} +$$
$$\beta_3 \text{ (DIMMIGTUITION} * \text{FBNC)} + \beta_4 \text{ STATEDUMMIES} +$$
$$\beta_5 \text{YEARDUMMIES} + \beta_6 \text{ (STATEDUMMIES*FBNC)} +$$
$$\beta_7 \text{(YEARDUMMIES*FBNC)} + \beta_8 X + \beta$$

where INCOLL is a binary variable and a measure of 18-to-24-year-old Latino FBNCs who were enrolled in college during the week prior to being surveyed. DIMMIGTUITION is a binary variable equal to 1 in states, months, and years with an in-state tuition policy for undocumented immigrants. This variable captures the policy interventions in each of the nine states by month and year of the policy enactment date, and also includes year of entry restriction for each state's residency requirement. FBNC is a binary variable set to 1 if a Latino student is classified as a foreign-born noncitizen.

β_3 represents the coefficient of primary interest and is the interaction term of DIMMIGTUITION and FBNC. Because undocumented Latino students do not qualify for any federal financial aid, and because Latino immigrant families are more likely than the general population to have incomes below 150 percent of the federal poverty level (Erisman & Looney, 2007), I hypothesize that there will be a different effect on the college-enrollment rates of FBNC Latino students in states with an in-state resident tuition policy than on the rates of similar students in states that did not enact an ISRT policy change. Therefore, if β_3 is nonzero, positive, and statistically significant, then I will reject the null hypothesis that the tuition policy has no effect, which will be suggestive evidence that states with a tuition policy have a positive effect on the college-enrollment rates of FBNC Latino students in the U.S. The coefficients $\beta_4 - \beta_7$ are dummy variables that account for all states and years in the sample and act as state- and year-fixed effects. The state-fixed effects account for intrastate variation and control for the average differences in any observable or unobservable predictors not explained by other covariates in my outcome, such as state unemployment rate and year-specific trends. I include year-fixed effects to control for general trends over time in the outcome variable of "currently enrolled in college" for all states in the sample. I also interact the state- and year-fixed effects with foreign-born noncitizens in the sample to allow for variance in immigration trends by state and year (as seen in β_6 and β_7), and to account for observable and unobservable characteristics among this population.

X, captures the effect of individual covariates in order to measure relevant demographic characteristics that are correlated with educational attainment, as well as local economic conditions that may affect an individual's schooling decisions (age, gender, marital status, and living in a metropolitan area). I include the unemployment rate to account for state-specific economic shocks in the various state labor markets. In addition, to account for lower college enrollment over the summer terms, I include a term for month-fixed effects in order to capture enrollment variation over the course of the academic year. Finally, I include a control variable for states not allowed to implement affirmative action practices during the period of analysis (Texas, California, and Washington) since Latinos are a primary beneficiary of affirmative action. Since Latinos are more likely to attend community colleges, which

TABLE 1

Summary Statistics
Sample: All Latinos and Latino Foreign-Born Noncitizens, Ages 18–24

| | All Latinos | | | | Foreign-Born Noncitizen Latinos | | | |
| | Policy States | | Non-Policy States | | Policy States | | Non-Policy States | |
	Pre-Policy (1)	Post-Policy (2)	Pre-Policy (3)	Post-Policy (4)	Pre-Policy (5)	Post-Policy (6)	Pre-Policy (7)	Post-Policy (8)
Pct. FBNC	0.3757	0.3453	0.3923	0.4183				
Age	20.9901	20.9840	21.0740	21.0805	21.1678	21.1733	21.1772	21.2769
	(0.0204)	(0.0195)	(0.0239)	(0.0201)	(0.0281)	(0.0283)	(0.0303)	(0.0260)
Female	0.4879	0.4880	0.4723	0.4704	0.4579	0.4535	0.4406	0.4283
Married	0.2434	0.2243	0.2568	0.2392	0.2783	0.2824	0.2861	0.2867
Employed	0.6522	0.6238	0.6703	0.6534	0.6535	0.6498	0.6688	0.6760
	(0.0048)	(0.0046)	(0.0055)	(0.0047)	(0.0065)	(0.0067)	(0.0071)	(0.0062)
Live in metro area	0.9223	0.9235	0.8705	0.8521	0.9381	0.9347	0.8883	0.8616
Pct. HS diploma & no BA	0.5748	0.6048	0.5476	0.5661	0.4765	0.4873	0.4821	0.4726
Pct with BA or higher	0.0236	0.0280	0.0346	0.0357	0.0179	0.0238	0.0230	0.0280
Average year of entry to U.S.	5.4574	5.6732	6.4772	7.5119	9.8041	11.6480	9.5407	12.3001
	(0.0961)	(0.0955)	(0.1076)	(0.1008)	(0.1025)	(0.1039)	(0.1227)	(0.1024)
Observations	12,929	14,719	9,217	13,025	6,586	6,522	5,345	6,888

Source: U.S. Current Population Survey, Merged Outgoing Rotation Groups. *Note:* Data in this sample include individuals ages 18–24 who entered the U.S. before 1998 of all educational completion rates. For "average year of entry," a value of 11 = entry in 1988–1989; 12 = entry in 1990–1991; 13 = entry in 1992–1995; 14 = entry in 1994–1997. Policy states in analysis include Texas, California, Utah, New York, Washington, Oklahoma, Illinois, Kansas, and New Mexico. Robust standard errors in parentheses. FE = Fixed Effects.

723

are nonselective institutions, issues of eligibility for affirmative action policies in selective institutions may not affect the majority of this sample (Adelman, 2005). However, the data do not allow me to examine the academic preparation of this sample, so I am not able to discern whether foreign-born Latino noncitizens who are high school graduates are likely to enter selective institutions. As such, I test my results with and without this variable. The variable ε represents an error term.

Threats to Validity and Strategies for Addressing Potential Limitations

Sources of potential bias that could affect results of the research and how they are addressed in this analysis are worth mentioning. First, external events other than the tuition policy change could affect FBNC Latino student enrollment in higher education during this time period. In states including Texas, California, Washington, and Florida, these might be the effects of a policy change, such as the retraction of affirmative action and other race-conscious programs since 1998. Three of these states (Texas, California, and Florida) implemented various versions of a percentage plan, each of which had different requirements for gaining access to its state's selective public higher education systems (Horn & Flores, 2003; Marin & Lee, 2003).

Another event may be general changes in immigration trends over the years. Moreover, the economic recession from 2001 may bias my results if the states experienced the recession differently from one another. To address the issue of state policies banning affirmative action practices in admissions and recruitment, I include an additional variable, NOAFFAM, to account for states that experienced this policy retraction. I do not include a measure for the presence of a percentage plan because I am able to assess only whether a student decided to enroll in college but not where he or she ultimately enrolled.

To address the issue of changes in immigration over time and in location, I include state- and year-fixed effects interacted with the variable FBNC to capture any such changes in each state across the country by year on the outcome of "currently enrolled in college." Another potential source of bias involves measurement error in reporting the citizenship status of undocumented individuals in this vulnerable category. To test the reliability of the citizenship question, I examine the effect of tuition policies on Latino U.S. citizens (naturalized and U.S. born) as an additional test for accuracy in measuring my outcome.

Finally, as an additional validity check to verify that an effect is occurring for Latinos in states with a tuition policy, I test my results on different racial and ethnic groups, such as African American and Asian students who are U.S. citizens. If there is an increase in college enrollment for the population most likely to benefit from the ISRT policy—students likely to be undocumented residents—the trend should not occur among racial and ethnic groups that are U.S. citizens not likely to be affected by the policy.

Results

Program Take-Up: The Odds of College Enrollment

I use logistic regression analysis to fit the model of whether students living in states with in-state resident tuition policies were more likely to enroll in college (via the outcome "enrolled in college") than not, compared to students in the rest of the United States. In the tables that follow, I present estimates of odds ratios and robust standard errors from the fitting of the regression model within the sample of all Latinos, using the primary variable of interest (DIMMIGTUITION*FBNC), the interaction of FBNC Latinos within the policy states during the years (and months) in which a policy was enacted. I also provide estimates clustered at the state level for select models in the event that standard errors at the individual level are too optimistic, using a group-level regressor and not allowing for group-level random effects (Moulton, 1986).

Table 2 presents detailed estimated odds ratios and robust standard errors for Latino FBNCs who are in the more restricted sample of HS Diploma/GED Completers. The data show that there is

TABLE 2

Impact of In-State Resident Tuition Policies on College Enrollment of Latino Foreign-Born Noncitizens, 1998–2005

Sample: Latinos, HS-GED Completers, Ages 18–24 Outcome: Enrolled in College; Control Group: U.S. States without a Tuition Policy

HS-GED Completers	Basic Model (1)	Add BG Characteristics (2)	Add Local/State Conditions (3)	Add St. Policy Control (4)	Add State & Year FE (5)	Full Model: FBNC Interaction with FEs (6)	Cluster by State (7)
Effect of all tuition policies	1.4196*** (0.1459)	1.3480*** (0.1473)	1.3969*** (0.1401)	1.4073*** (0.1459)	1.3502*** (0.1422)	1.5440*** (0.2260)	1.5440*** (0.2049)
Tuition policy states (w/enactment date)	1.2856*** (0.0533)	1.2512*** (0.0528)	1.2036*** (0.0579)	1.1689*** (0.0588)	1.2607*** (0.0813)	1.2193*** (0.0865)	1.2193*** (0.0708)
FBNC	0.4333*** (0.0222)	0.4926*** (0.0257)	0.4781*** (0.0249)	0.4766*** (0.0249)	0.4844*** (0.0258)	1.9645e+09*** (2.0606e+09)	1.9645e+09*** (2.7159e+08)
Age		0.8617*** (0.0078)	0.8570*** (0.0078)	0.8573*** (0.0078)	0.8556*** (0.0079)	0.8561*** (0.0079)	0.8561*** (0.0088)
Female		1.5224*** (0.0527)	1.5367*** (0.0534)	1.5352*** (0.0533)	1.5343*** (0.0536)	1.5357*** (0.0538)	1.5357*** (0.0559)
Ever married		0.2547*** (0.0147)	0.2570*** (0.0149)	0.2566*** (0.0149)	0.2630*** (0.0154)	0.2614*** (0.0154)	0.2614*** (0.0232)
Metro			1.6819*** (0.1124)	1.6546*** (0.1114)	1.6790*** (0.1235)	1.6917*** (0.1256)	1.6917*** (0.1786)
State unemp. rate			1.0081 (0.0214)	1.0066 (0.0215)	0.9935 (0.0448)	0.9896 (0.0452)	0.9896 (0.0407)
States w/o affirmative action				1.0731* (0.0435)	0.5114* (0.2038)	0.5898 (0.2320)	0.5898*** (0.0393)
Month fixed effects			Yes	Yes	Yes	Yes	Yes
State and year FE	No	No			Yes	Yes	Yes
State and year FE incl. FBNC interaction	No	No			No	Yes	Yes
Observations	24,445	24,445	24,445	24,445	24,445	24,402	24,402

Robust standard errors in parentheses; * significant at 10%; ** significant at 5%; *** significant at 1%.

Source: U.S. Current Population Survey, Merged Outgoing Rotation Groups.

Note: States with policy intervention include Texas (2001); California, and Utah (2002); New York, Washington, Oklahoma, and Illinois (2003); Kansas (2004); New Mexico (2005). Nebraska, passed in 2006, is not included in this analysis. Robust standard errors were calculated to account for clustering within person over time and so that standard error estimates would reflect the structure of the data. Results for clustering at state level included in select tables. FE = Fixed Effects.

a significant positive effect in the odds of college enrollment *after* the enactment of the tuition policies in states with the resident tuition legislation (Texas, California, Utah, New York, Washington, Oklahoma, Illinois, Kansas, and New Mexico) (column 6).

Specifically, column 6 in Table 2, which represents the full model with all fixed effects, indicates that FBNC Latinos are 1.54 times more likely than not to have enrolled in college after the enactment of the tuition policies, compared to the same population in the rest of the United States. The model in column 6 also indicates that being female increases the odds of college enrollment 1.53 times, as did residence in a metropolitan area (1.69 times). Conversely, having been married significantly decreases the odds of college attainment after the policy enactment by 0.26 times. The odds ratios are all significant at the $p < 0.01$ level. I found no effect for the control variable "living in a state without an affirmative action policy" on college enrollment.

Results clustered at the state level shown in column 7 indicate no change in significance level on the effect of the policy, although this variable has slightly lower standard errors. The major difference in this specification is that the covariate for states without affirmative action is now significant at the $p < .01$ level.

Table 3 presents the odds of college enrollment by ages 18–20, or students who may be classified as recent high school graduates, and ages 21–24, representing older students. The age range at which a Latino FBNC student living in a state with a tuition policy attends college after the enactment of the policy varies by the educational attainment samples of All Grades and HS Diploma/GED Completers. For example, while the odds of college enrollment are significant across the age ranges of the All Grades sample (columns 1–4), I find mixed results in the HS Diploma/GED Completer sample. In this sample, the policy appears to have increased the college-enrollment odds of older students ages 21–24. The data indicate that these students are 1.7 times more likely to have enrolled in college after the implementation of the policies than similarly aged students living in states without a policy (column 8).

Table 4 provides a separate examination of the samples by gender and by age group. Although I find an effect on the odds of college enrollment as a result of the policy for both the female and male sample separately for the wider age range of 18–24 (Table 4, columns 1 and 4), I find a stronger effect in the male sample comprised of respondents age 21–24. In this sample of males who have completed a high school diploma or GED, I find that Latino FBNC students are approximately 1.9 times more likely than their similarly aged counterparts in states without a tuition policy to enroll in college after the implementation of the tuition policies. The college-enrollment odds are slightly lower for the female sample of HS Diploma/GED Completers at 1.5 times, although the effect is significant at the $p < 0.05$ level. Interestingly, state unemployment rate has no significant effect on any of the specifications in the HS Diploma/GED Completer sample. Living in a state without affirmative action appears to significantly decrease the odds of college enrollment for females but not males (Table 4, column 1).

Table 5 presents as separate samples the estimated odds ratios for students living in metropolitan versus nonmetropolitan areas by age group. I find a significant effect for the tuition policies on the college-enrollment odds for students in the sample residing in a metropolitan area in the HS Diploma/GED Completer sample. Results for this specification indicate that students in the metropolitan residence sample are 1.52 times more likely to have enrolled in college after the policy's enactment than students in similar areas in states without a tuition policy ($p < 0.01$). I find no effect of the tuition policy on college enrollment for students who reside in a nonmetropolitan area in any of the specifications examined.

Additional Robustness Checks

To test whether results regarding the effects of the tuition policies are indeed measuring the behavior of Latino FBNCs, or whether the results may instead be a result of measurement error or a trend that may be affecting all Latinos, I test the robustness of my results using the current estimated fitted regression model on my outcome of "enrolled in college" on U.S.-citizen Latinos comprised of both U.S.-born and U.S.-naturalized Latinos.

TABLE 3

Impact of In-State Resident Tuition Policies on College Enrollment of Latino Foreign-Born Noncitizens, 1998–2005

Sample: Latinos All Grades and HS-GED Completers, Ages 18–20 and 21–24 Outcome: Enrolled in College; Control Group: U.S. States without a Tuition Policy

All Grades & HS-GED Completers	All Grades Ages 18–20		All Grades Ages 21–24		HS-GED Completion Ages 18–20		HS-GED Completion Ages 21–24	
	Main Model (1)	Full Model: FBNC Inter. with FEs (2)	Main Model (3)	Full Model: FBNC Inter. with FEs (4)	Main Model (5)	Full Model: FBNC Inter. with FEs (6)	Main Model (7)	Full Model: FBNC Inter. with FEs (8)
Effect of all tuition policies	1.4923***	1.8078***	1.5569***	1.8514***	1.3143*	1.4777*	1.5006***	1.7040***
	(0.1819)	(0.3046)	(0.19983)	(0.3404)	(0.1947)	(0.3120)	(0.2081)	(0.3403)
Tuition policy states (w/enactment date)	1.2141***	1.2589***	1.1121	1.1664	1.2453***	1.2784**	1.0985	1.1369
	(0.0714)	(0.1045)	(0.0738)	(0.1097)	(0.0833)	(0.1237)	(0.0755)	(0.1112)
FBNC	0.3774***	0.0000***	0.2825***	1.7274	0.5025***	3.9046	0.4477***	1.6166e+09***
	(0.0220)	(0.0000)	(0.0185)	(3.4827)	(0.0353)	(4.5968)	(0.0313)	(1.9031e+09)
Age	1.2218***	1.2213***	0.8069***	0.8050***	1.0946***	1.0929***	0.7940***	0.7924***
	(0.0274)	(0.0277)	(0.0154)	(0.0156)	(0.0311)	(0.0314)	(0.0160)	(0.0162)
Female	1.6056***	1.6030***	1.7612***	1.7755***	1.4345***	1.4294***	1.6445***	1.6659***
	(0.0652)	(0.0657)	(0.0803)	(0.0814)	(0.0696)	(0.0703)	(0.0786)	(0.0804)
Ever married	0.2022***	0.2092***	0.2389***	0.2424***	0.2442***	0.2503***	0.2627***	0.2629***
	(0.0211)	(0.0220)	(0.0150)	(0.0155)	(0.0283)	(0.0292)	(0.0172)	(0.0176)
Metro	1.5866***	1.5397***	1.7066***	1.7347***	1.7326***	1.7114***	1.5854***	1.6379***
	(0.1148)	(0.1262)	(0.1537)	(0.1706)	(0.1506)	(0.1698)	(0.1488)	(0.1681)
State unemp. rate	0.9639	0.9603	1.0303	0.9985	0.9779	1.0035	1.0304	0.9726
	(0.0234)	(0.0511)	(0.0294)	(0.0589)	(0.0278)	(0.0634)	(0.0303)	(0.0604)
States w/o affirmative action	1.0413	0.7245	1.1492***	1.0211	1.0462	0.7122	1.1188**	0.9230
	(0.0479)	(0.3507)	(0.0609)	(0.5219)	(0.0559)	(0.4491)	(0.0615)	(0.4556)
Month fixed effects	Yes	Yes	Yes	Yes	Yes	Yes	Yes	Yes
State and year FE incl. FBNC interaction	No	Yes	No	Yes	No	Yes	No	Yes
Observations	17,778	17,677	23,231	23,149	9,631	9,584	14,814	14,785

Robust standard errors in parentheses; * significant at 10%; ** significant at 5%; *** significant at 1%.

Source: U.S. Current Population Survey, Merged Outgoing Rotation Groups.

Note: States with policy intervention include Texas (2001); California, and Utah (2002); New York, Washington, Oklahoma, and Illinois (2003); Kansas (2004); New Mexico (2005). Nebraska, passed in 2006, is not included in this analysis. Robust standard errors were calculated to account for clustering within person over time and so that standard error estimates would reflect the structure of the data. FE = Fixed Effects.

TABLE 4

Impact of In-State Resident Tuition Policies on College Enrollment of Latino Foreign-Born Noncitizens, 1998–2005

Sample: Latinos, HS-GED Completers by Gender and by Age Group: 18–24, 18–20, 21–24

Outcome: Enrolled in College; Control Group: U.S. States without a Tuition Policy

HS-GED Completers	Females Full Model with All FE			Males Full Model with All FE		
	Ages 18–24 (1)	Ages 18–20 (2)	Ages 21–24 (3)	Ages 18–24 (4)	Ages 18–20 (5)	Ages 21–24 (6)
Effect of all tuition policies	1.5046** (0.3055)	1.5533 (0.4626)	1.6482* (0.4575)	1.6691** (0.3427)	1.4408 (0.4300)	1.9429** (0.5576)
Tuition policy states (w/enactment date)	1.3828*** (0.1313)	1.2918* (0.1702)	1.4129*** (0.1871)	1.0160 (0.1046)	1.2597 (0.1828)	0.8309 (0.1166)
FBNC	2.0571 (2.3898)	3.1686 (3.5266)	9.9536* (13.4153)	1.5568e+09*** (2.3429e+09)	1.3466 (1.3467)	6.2988e+09*** (8.9107e+09)
Age	0.8791*** (0.0110)	1.1526*** (0.0462)	0.8194*** (0.0226)	0.8268*** (0.0112)	1.0383 (0.0450)	0.7569*** (0.0238)
Ever married	0.2589*** (0.0175)	0.2518*** (0.0322)	0.2611*** (0.0206)	0.2451*** (0.0270)	0.2151*** (0.0521)	0.2538*** (0.0314)
Metro	1.5255*** (0.1473)		1.3677** (0.1852)		1.6009*** (0.2134)	
	1.8584*** (0.2094)		2.1935*** (0.3386)		1.5980*** (0.2497)	
State unemp. rate	0.9571 (0.0574)	0.9455 (0.0813)	0.9641 (0.0807)	1.0506 (0.0688)	1.0919 (0.1029)	0.9993 (0.0896)
States without affirmative action	0.3829** (0.1824)	0.4095 (0.3028)	0.6080 (0.3862)	1.1016 (0.6641)	0.4846 (0.4669)	1.6927 (1.2966)
Month fixed effects (FE)	Yes	Yes	Yes	Yes	Yes	Yes
State and year FE incl. FBNC interaction	Yes	Yes	Yes	Yes	Yes	Yes
Observations	12,600	5,004	7,530	11,751	4,484	7,052

Robust standard errors in parentheses; * significant at 10%; ** significant at 5%; *** significant at 1%

Source: U.S. Current Population Survey, Merged Outgoing Rotation Groups.

Note: States with policy intervention include Texas (2001); California, and Utah (2002); New York, Washington, Oklahoma, and Illinois (2003); Kansas (2004); New Mexico (2005). Nebraska, passed in 2006, is not included in this analysis. Robust standard errors were calculated to account for clustering within person over time and so that standard error estimates would reflect the structure of the data. FE = Fixed Effects.

TABLE 5

Impact of In-State Resident Tuition Policies on College Enrollment of Latino Foreign-Born Noncitizens, 1998–2005

Sample: Latinos, HS-GED Completers by Metropolitan Area Status and by Age Group: 18–24, 18–20, 21–24,

Outcome: Enrolled in College; Control Group: U.S. States without a Tuition Policy

HS-GED Completers	Metropolitan Area Full Model with All FE			Nonmetropolitan Area Full Model with All FE		
	Ages 18–24 (1)	Ages 18–20 (2)	Ages 21–24 (3)	Ages 18–24 (4)	Ages 18–20 (5)	Ages 21–24 (6)
Effect of all tuition policies	1.5226***	1.5183*	1.6832**	1.6098	1.1948	2.2385
	(0.2286)	(0.3279)	(0.3455)	(1.4715)	(1.4927)	(2.5336)
Tuition policy states (w/enactment date)	1.2422***	1.2815**	1.1611	0.9958	1.1574	0.9237
	(0.0924)	(0.1301)	(0.1189)	(0.2975)	(0.5015)	(0.3751)
FBNC	2.4707e+09***	0.2439	1.0355e+09***	25.0414**	0.3209	3.3739e+08***
	(3.4671e+09)	(0.3531)	(1.5810e+09)	(40.2609)	(0.4739)	(5.5861e+08)
Age	0.8554***	1.0892***	0.7977***	0.8462***	1.1191	0.6865***
	(0.0083)	(0.0328)	(0.0170)	(0.0284)	(0.1256)	(0.0563)
Ever married	0.2558***	0.2525***	0.2543***	0.3112***	0.2038***	0.3428***
	(0.0160)	(0.0315)	(0.0181)	(0.0583)	(0.0771)	(0.0745)
Female	1.5249***	1.3968***	1.6702***	1.8441***	2.0867***	1.8419***
	(0.0557)	(0.0719)	(0.0839)	(0.2448)	(0.3945)	(0.3549)
State unemp. rate	0.9912	1.0415	0.9450	1.0647	0.8452	1.3204
	(0.0500)	(0.0725)	(0.0640)	(0.1272)	(0.1468)	(0.2327)
States without affirmative action	0.8682	2.6660	0.8506	2.0988	1.0364	4.2738
	(0.5499)	(2.9116)	(0.5924)	(1.4755)	(1.2059)	(3.8997)
Month fixed effects (FE)	Yes	Yes	Yes	Yes	Yes	Yes
State and year FE incl. FBNC interaction	Yes	Yes	Yes	Yes	Yes	Yes
Observations	22,001	8,617	13,359	2,194	864	1,183

Robust standard errors in parentheses; * significant at 10%; ** significant at 5%; *** significant at 1%

Source: U.S. Current Population Survey, Merged Outgoing Rotation Groups.

Note: States with policy intervention include Texas (2001); California, and Utah (2002); New York, Washington, Oklahoma, and Illinois (2003); Kansas (2004); New Mexico (2005). Nebraska, passed in 2006, is not included in this analysis. Robust standard errors were calculated to account for clustering within person over time and so that standard error estimates would reflect the structure of the data. FE = Fixed Effects.

In addition, to explore whether the effect of an increase in college enrollment is a result of the tuition policies and not a trend affecting other underrepresented minority groups, such as African American or Asian students, I test my results on students who are African American and Asian U.S. citizens. If the tuition policy does indeed have an effect on the college-enrollment odds of foreign-born noncitizen Latinos, then we should not see any effects for other U.S.-citizen Latinos (to the extent that undocumented residents are truthful about their citizenship status according to the categories provided in the CPS). The policy should also not have an effect for students who are African American or Asian U.S. citizens. As hypothesized, the data indicate that there is no effect for any of the United States citizen groups in the full fixed-effects models (Table 6, columns 2, 4, and 6), further confirming the likelihood that the tuition policies have had a significant impact on the college-enrollment odds of students most likely to benefit from this legislation: Latino FBNCs.

Implications for Policy and Research

Did the introduction of tuition policies targeted at undocumented students in the states examined increase their college participation, compared to a similar population of students who live in U.S. states without the tuition benefit? Despite variation in immigration rates, history, and incorporation of Latino immigrant students into each respective state's school system, the data in this analysis indicate that the policies significantly increased the college-enrollment rates of Latino foreign-born noncitizens, a large percentage of whom are undocumented. Foreign-born noncitizen Latinos are indeed more likely to enroll in college after the implementation of the tuition policies than their counterparts in states without the tuition benefit. However, whereas the odds of college enrollment are higher for females in the larger sample of all Latino FBNC students, more complex results emerge when examining males and females separately. Living in a metropolitan area is also a consistent indicator of increased college enrollment odds, while having been married decreases the odds of enrollment by a significantly large margin.

The results of the study are particularly relevant to the current state and national policy context in terms of higher educational opportunities for this population across the nation. Of similar importance is the potential direction in which to advance research on the topic of undocumented immigrants, as the country increasingly moves toward data-driven policy decisions. Research on this topic has most notably emerged from legal scholarship, with a number of scholars now investigating this topic from expanded philosophical, educational, demographic, and political perspectives. This chapter contributes to that line of inquiry by providing an econometric perspective regarding the measured impact of the ISRT policies on the college enrollment of students likely to be undocumented. Additional questions, however, remain unanswered regarding (a) the academic performance and persistence of students who benefit from these policies including their employment prospects and a continued path to U.S. citizenship; (b) issues of data collection as it relates to research and policy decisions regarding this population of students and their families; and (c) the sustainability of the in-state resident tuition policies within the current state and federal policy immigration context including the effects of retraction of these policies or passage of laws that ban educational benefits for the undocumented (Olivas, 2009).

This study has shown that the availability of an ISRT policy positively and significantly affects the college decisions of students who are likely to be undocumented as measured by an increase in their college enrollment rates. However, we know less about how they perform in postsecondary institutions by sector and selectivity. Using student-level administrative data, research by Flores and Horn (forthcoming) finds that students identified as ISRT beneficiaries by a selective public institution in Texas are likely to persist through college at the same rate as their U.S.-born Latino counterparts, whom they are most likely to resemble. Additional research into the role and quality of institution type as they relate to the persistence behavior in states where ISRT beneficiaries are able to enroll would provide further insight into the cost-effectiveness of the policy and the potential economic contribution to states by students who are completing college.

TABLE 6

Impact of In-State Resident Tuition Policies on College Enrollment on U.S. Citizens By Race and Ethnicity, 1998–2005

Sample: Latino, Black, and Asian Students, HS-GED Completers Ages 18–24 Outcome: Enrolled in College; Control Group: U.S. States without a Tuition Policy

HS-GED Completers	Latino U.S. Citizens		Black U.S. Citizens		Asian U.S. Citizens	
	Main Model (1)	Full Model: FBNC Inter. with FEs (2)	Main Model (3)	Full Model FBNC Inter. FEs (4)	Main Model (5)	Full Model: FBNC Inter. with FEs (6)
Effect of all tuition policies	0.9362 (0.0441)	1.0924 (0.0833)	1.0961 (0.0691)	1.0393 (0.0920)	1.3178*** (0.1170)	0.8515 (0.1111)
Tuition policy states (w/enactment date)	1.2850*** (0.0303)	1.1190*** (0.0329)	1.2133*** (0.0276)	1.1192*** (0.0317)	1.2315*** (0.0275)	1.1331*** (0.0312)
FBNC	0.7460*** (0.0190)	1.0471 (0.3880)	0.6259*** (0.0140)	1.7923 (0.9156)	1.6999*** (0.0651)	0.6743 (0.3011)
Age	0.8526*** (0.0027)	0.8527*** (0.0027)	0.8549*** (0.0027)	0.8555*** (0.0027)	0.8527*** (0.0027)	0.8528*** (0.0027)
Female	1.3818*** (0.0162)	1.3845*** (0.0163)	1.4026*** (0.0165)	1.4051*** (0.0166)	1.3818*** (0.0162)	1.3830*** (0.0163)
Ever married	0.2925*** (0.0070)	0.2984*** (0.0070)	0.2824*** (0.0068)	0.2883*** (0.0069)	0.2924*** (0.0070)	0.2984*** (0.0070)
Metro	1.3625*** (0.0226)	1.3357*** (0.0239)	1.3906*** (0.0232)	1.3539*** (0.0243)	1.3331*** (0.0222)	1.3149*** (0.0236)
State unemp. rate	0.9869** (0.0061)	1.0034 (0.0121)	0.9934 (0.0061)	1.0023 (0.0120)	0.9827*** (0.0061)	1.0005 (0.0122)
States without affirmative action	1.0826*** (0.0247)	0.9654 (0.0629)	1.0143 (0.0225)	1.0465 (0.0686)	0.9986 (0.0222)	0.9717 (0.0621)
Month fixed effects (FE)	Yes	Yes	Yes	Yes	Yes	Yes
State and year FEincl. FBNC interaction	No	Yes	No	Yes	No	Yes
Observations	183,592	183,592	183,592	183,592	183,592	183,592

Robust standard errors in parentheses; * significant at 10%; ** significant at 5%; *** significant at 1%

Source: U.S. Current Population Survey, Merged Outgoing Rotation Groups.

Note: States with policy intervention include Texas (2001); California, and Utah (2002); New York, Washington, Oklahoma, and Illinois (2003); Kansas (2004); New Mexico (2005). Nebraska, passed in 2006, is not included in this analysis. Robust standard errors were calculated to account for clustering within person over time and so that standard error estimates would reflect the structure of the data. FE = Fixed Effects.

The question of data availability on this topic, however sensitive, is of the utmost importance. U.S. government databases like the one used for this study are the largest and most representative sources of state-level data on foreign-born noncitizens currently available to researchers. However, such databases are not designed to capture critical educational achievement variables, such as high school grades, course-taking patterns, parents' detailed income characteristics, and other influential factors that predict college enrollment and persistence (Ellwood & Kane, 2000). In contrast, existing national education databases that have such variables are too outdated to capture recent policy interventions and/or do not contain detailed citizenship information that would help answer questions on the diverse and growing immigrant population in the United States.

While studies on generational status have provided important contributions, current policy debates about citizenship status require particular information that goes beyond time spent in the United States. To this end, state participation in higher education data-collection entities can contribute extensively. These entities provide the most current and detailed data available to researchers. State administrative databases that can sensitively identify students as beneficiaries of these policies would provide ideal data for future analyses to confirm current results and to evaluate the future performance of these students in the state higher education systems in which they enroll.

Further analyses could be conducted on the impact of a college degree for these individuals. Recent research, for example, has begun to document the returns from a college education at the larger societal level. Moretti (2004) argues that the social returns to a college education exceed the private returns, finding that a percentage point increase in the supply of college graduates raises the wages of high school dropouts by 1.9%, the wages of high school graduates by 1.6%, and the wages of college graduates by 0.4%. With these results in mind, the larger benefits of educating a significant portion of the nation's largest minority extend beyond a personal income advantage. Furthermore, given the consistently low high school graduation rates of Latino students across the nation (Swanson, 2004), increasing the college-enrollment and completion odds for those who do graduate from high school despite the barriers faced by citizenship status is worth exploring in more detail.

In the interim, the number of legal challenges to the ISRT policies is on the rise and threatens their sustainability (Olivas, 2008, 2009). Future research might examine the effects of a policy retraction or the effect of a ban as initiated by a state legislature or voter referendum (Dynarski, 2003). If current trends regarding the passage of restrictions for undocumented immigrants continue, analyses regarding the likelihood of such events occurring would also add to the research on this topic (Desjardins, 2003; Doyle, 2006; McLendon, Hearn, & Deaton, 2006). What is certain is that activity on matters relating to the educational opportunities of immigrant students is all but static. Current data systems at the local, state, and national level should be compared and revised to answer the critical policy questions and legal challenges that continue to emerge on the topics of immigration and educational policy.

APPENDIX A

States That Allow Undocumented Students to Gain Resident Tuition Status as of 2006

State	Bill Number	Date Passed	Date Enacted	State Financial Aid for Undoc.	Affirmative Action Ban	% Plan/Year
Texas	H.B. 1403 (77th Leg)	June 16, 2001	June 16, 2001	Yes	1996 (Hopwood)	Yes: 1998 (Top 10%)
California	A.B. 540 (2001–02 Cal. Sess)	October 12, 2001	January 1, 2002	No	1997 (Prop 209)	Yes: 2001 (Top 4%+ELC)
Utah	H.B. 144 (54th Leg., Gen Session)	March 6, 2002	July 1, 2002	Partial: to 1 state program only	No	No
New York	S.B. 7784 (225th Leg., 2001 NY Sess)	June 25, 2002	August 1, 2003	No	No	No
Washington	H.B. 1079 (H.B. 1079, 58th Leg., Reg. Sess)	May 7, 2003	July 1, 2003	No	1998 (I 200)	No
Oklahoma	S.B. 596 (49th Leg., 1st Sess)	May 12, 2003	May 12, 2003	Yes	No	No
Illinois	H.B. 60 (93rd Leg., Reg. Sess.)	May 18, 2003	May 20, 2003	No	No	No
Kansas	K.S.A. 76–731A	May 20, 2004	July 1, 2004	No	No	No
New Mexico	N.M.S.A. 1978 Ch. 348, Sec. 21-1-1.2 (47th Leg. Sess.)	April 5, 2005	April 5, 2005	No	No	No
Nebraska	L.B. 239	April 2006	April 2006	No	No	No

Source: Some information from Olivas (2004), Rincon (2008), and National Immigration Law Center (2006).
Note: Texas amended the statute in its 2005 legislative session.

733

APPENDIX B

Impact of In-State Resident Tuition Policies on College Enrollment of Latino Foreign-Born Noncitizens, 1998–2005

Sample: Latinos, All Grades by Gender and by Age Group: 18–24, 18–20, 21–24
Outcome: Enrolled in College; Control Group: U.S. States without a Tuition Policy

HS-GED Completers	Females Full Model with All Fixed Effects			Males Full Model with All Fixed Effects		
	Ages 18–24 (1)	Ages 18–20 (2)	Ages 21–24 (3)	Ages 18–24 (4)	Ages 18–20 (5)	Ages 21–24 (6)
Effect of all tuition policies	1.5919*** (0.2759)	1.5643* (0.3749)	1.7829** (0.4454)	1.9754*** (0.3485)	2.0887*** (0.4809)	1.9781** (0.5352)
Tuition policy states (w/enactment date)	1.3851*** (0.1183)	1.2834** (0.1438)	1.4615*** (0.1853)	1.0553 (0.0977)	1.2292* (0.1493)	0.8703 (0.1172)
FBNC	0.0000*** (0.0000)	0.0000*** (0.0000)	0.0000*** (0.0000)	5.4170 (10.2603)	0.0000*** (0.0000)	28.0225 (56.9231)
Age	0.9345*** (0.0097)	1.2906*** (0.0414)	0.8220*** (0.0215)	0.8981*** (0.0099)	1.1642*** (0.0386)	0.7817*** (0.0232)
Ever married	0.2282*** (0.0144)		0.2058***		0.2405*** (0.0181)	
	0.2217*** (0.0228)		0.1992***	(0.0233) (0.0442)	0.2343*** (0.0273)	(0.0181) (0.0273)
Metro	1.4200*** (0.1215)	1.2144* (0.1346)	1.6228*** (0.2058)	1.9018*** (0.1877)	1.9712*** (0.2428)	1.8128*** (0.2698)
State unemp. rate	0.9585 (0.0509)	0.9164 (0.0663)	0.9992 (0.0788)	1.0232 (0.0594)	0.9985 (0.0767)	1.0183 (0.0862)
States without affirmative action	0.7903 (0.3411)	0.3778* (0.1877)	0.8676 (0.5797)	1.0401 (0.6178)	0.5353 (0.4619)	1.3091 (1.0220)
Month fixed effects (FE)	Yes	Yes	Yes	Yes	Yes	Yes
State and year FE incl. FBNC interaction	Yes	Yes	Yes	Yes	Yes	Yes
Observations	19,549	8,419	11,027	21,256	9,136	11,777

Robust standard errors in parentheses; * significant at 10%; ** significant at 5%; *** significant at 1%

Source: U.S. Current Population Survey, Merged Outgoing Rotation Groups.

Note: States with policy intervention include Texas (2001); California and Utah (2002); New York, Washington, Oklahoma, and Illinois (2003); Kansas (2004); New Mexico (2005). Nebraska, passed in 2006, is not included in this analysis. Robust standard errors were calculated to account for clustering within person over time and so that standard error estimates would reflect the structure of the data.

Impact of In-State Resident Tuition Policies on College Enrollment of Latino Foreign-Born Noncitizens, 1998–2005

Sample: Latinos, All Grades by Metropolitan Area Status and by Age Group: 18–24, 18–20, 21–24
Outcome: Enrolled in College; Control Group: U.S. States without a Tuition Policy

All Grades	Metropolitan Area Full Model with All Fixed Effects			Nonmetropolitan Area Full Model with All Fixed Effects		
	Ages 18–24 (1)	Ages 18–20 (2)	Ages 21–24 (3)	Ages 18–24 (4)	Ages 18–20 (5)	Ages 21–24 (6)
Effect of all tuition policies	1.7239*** (0.2239)	1.7865*** (0.3098)	1.8562*** (0.3522)	2.2576 (1.6785)	1.4938 (1.5707)	2.8866 (3.0149)
Tuition policy states (w/enactment date)	1.2593*** (0.0860)	1.2923*** (0.1136)	1.1833* (0.1168)	0.9866 (0.2382)	0.9504 (0.3087)	1.1460 (0.4162)
FBNC	2.7351 (6.3357)	0.0000*** (0.0000)	3.1465e+09*** (4.2068e+09)	0.0000*** (0.0000)	0.0000*** (0.0000)	0.0000*** (0.0000)
Age	0.9193*** (0.0074)	1.2302*** (0.0292)	0.8120*** (0.0164)	0.8780*** (0.0241)	1.1382 (0.0950)	0.6913*** (0.0529)
Ever married	0.2277*** (0.0134)	0.2166*** (0.0243)	0.2331*** (0.0159)	0.2523*** (0.0430)	0.1403*** (0.0449)	0.3195*** (0.0659)
Female	1.6554*** (0.0538)	1.5583*** (0.0670)	1.7798*** (0.0848)	2.1569*** (0.2478)	2.3836*** (0.3492)	2.0136*** (0.3696)
State unemp. rate	0.9895 (0.0448)	0.9918 (0.0587)	0.9785 (0.0629)	1.0534 (0.1077)	0.9085 (0.1297)	1.2218 (0.2025)
States without affirmative action	0.7573 (0.4012)	0.6728 (0.4168)	1.1155 (0.8019)	0.5896 (0.4913)	1.0908 (1.0445)	3.0063 (2.5723)
Month fixed effects (FE)	Yes	Yes	Yes	Yes	Yes	Yes
State and year FE incl. FBNC interaction	Yes	Yes	Yes	Yes	Yes	Yes
Observations	36,466	15,736	20,655	3,992	1,804	1,938

Robust standard errors in parentheses; * significant at 10%; ** significant at 5%; *** significant at 1%

Source: U.S. Current Population Survey, Merged Outgoing Rotation Groups.

Note: States with policy intervention include Texas (2001); California and Utah (2002); New York, Washington, Oklahoma, and Illinois (2003); Kansas (2004); New Mexico (2005). Nebraska, passed in 2006, is not included in this analysis. Robust standard errors were calculated to account for clustering within person over time and so that standard error estimates would reflect the structure of the data.

Notes

1. Passel, Van Hook, and Bean (2004) use the term "unauthorized" rather than "undocumented" for greater technically accuracy.
2. Estimating the undocumented population in the United States has involved a series of methodological developments since the 1980s. I rely on the latest estimates by Passel (2005a) and Passel, Van Hook, and Bean (2004), which account for various changes in demographic trends, including the number of refugees and asylees, and changes in immigration policy categories.
3. The 2003 U.S. Supreme Court *Grutter* decision allowed the use of race in college admissions in Texas and other states without a state ban on race-conscious policies (Coleman, Palmer, Sanghavi, & Winnick, 2007). However, institutions of higher education are not required to reinstitute this practice. Texas A&M University, for example, does not use race in college admissions. In contrast, The University of Texas at Austin reinstituted this practice in 2005 (Chapa & Horn, 2007).
4. Public colleges and universities are not required to act as immigration agents and report undocumented students to federal authorities. One exception is Arizona, through a 2006 referendum known as Proposition 300 (Redden, 2007; Stone, 2006).

References

Adelman, C. (2005). *Moving into town—and moving on: The community college in the lives of traditional-age students.* Washington, DC: U.S. Department of Education.

Alfonso, M. (2004, April). *What students of different racial/ethnic groups do after high school: An empirical analysis with focus on why students attend two-year colleges.* Paper presented at the annual meeting of the American Educational Research Association, Montreal, Canada.

Altonji, J. G. (1993, January). The demand for and return to education when education outcomes are uncertain. *Journal of Labor Economics, 11,* 48–83.

Batalova, J., & Fix, M. (2006). *New estimates of unauthorized youth eligible for legal status under the DREAM Act.* Washington, DC: Migration Policy Institute.

Bean, F., & Lowell, B. L. (2007). Unauthorized migration. In M. Waters, R. Ueda, & H. Marrow (Eds.), *The new Americans: A guide to immigration since 1965* (pp. 70–82). Cambridge, MA: Harvard University Press.

Becker, G. (1964). *Human capital: A theoretical and empirical analysis.* New York: Columbia University Press.

Castillo, J. (2007, May 10). After delay, bill challenging in-state tuition law all but dead. *Austin American-Statesman,* p. B1.

Chapa, J., & Horn, C. L. (2007). Is anything race neutral? Comparing "race-neutral" admissions policies at the University of Texas and the University of California. In G. Orfield, P. Marin, S. M. Flores, & L. M. Garcés (Eds.), *Charting the future of college affirmative action: Legal victories, continuing attacks, and new research* (pp. 157–172). Los Angeles, CA: The Civil Rights Project at UCLA.

Coleman, A. L., Palmer, S. R., Sanghavi, E., & Winnick, S. Y. (2007, March). *From federal law to state voter initiatives: Preserving higher education's authority to achieve the educational, economic, civic, and security benefits associated with a diverse student body* [Electronic version]. New York: The College Board.

DesJardins, S. L. (2003). Event history methods. In J. Smart (Ed.), *Higher education: Handbook of theory and research* (Vol. 18, pp. 421–472). London: Kluwer.

Dixon, D. (2006, March). *Characteristics of the Asian-born in the United States* [Electronic version]. Washington, DC: Migration Policy Institute.

Doyle, W. R. (2006). Adoption of merit-based student grant programs: An event history analysis. *Educational Evaluation and Policy Analysis, 28*(3), 259–285.

Dynarski, S. (2003). Does aid matter? Measuring the effect of student aid on college attendance and completion. *American Economic Review, 93,* 279–288.

Dynarski, S. (2004). The new merit aid. In C. Hoxby (Ed.), *College choices: The economics of where to go, when to go, and how to pay for it* (pp. 63–97). Chicago: University of Chicago Press.

Ellwood, D. T., & Kane, T. J. (2000). Who is getting a college education? Family background and the growing gaps in enrollment. In S. Danziger & J. Waldfogel (Eds.), *Securing the future: Investing in children from birth to college* (pp. 283–324). New York: Russell Sage.

Erisman, W., & Looney, S. (2007, April). *Opening the door to the American dream: Increasing higher education and success for immigrants.* Washington, DC: Institute for Higher Education Policy.

Feder, J. (2006, December 8). *Unauthorized alien students, higher education, and instate tuition rates: A legal analysis.* Washington, DC: Congressional Research Service.

Flores, S. M., & Chapa, J. (2009). Latino immigrant access to higher education in a bipolar context of reception. *Journal of Hispanic Higher Education, 8*(1), 90–101.

Gonzales, R. (2007, October). Wasted talent and broken dreams: The lost potential of undocumented students. In *Focus,* 5, p. 13. Newletter of the Immigration Policy Center, Washington, DC.

Hagy, A., & Staniec, J. F. O. (2002). Immigrant status, race, and institutional choice in higher education. *Economics of Education Review, 21,* 381–392.

Hebel, S. (2007, November 2). Arizona's colleges are in the crosshairs of efforts to curb illegal immigration. *Chronicle of Higher Education,* p. A15.

Heller, D. E. (1997). Student price response in higher education: An update of Leslie and Brinkman. *Journal of Higher Education, 68,* 624–659.

Hopwood v. Texas, 78 F. 3d 932 (5th Cir. 1996); cert. denied, 518 U.S. 1033 (1996).

Horn, C. L., & Flores, S. M. (2003). *Percent plans in college admissions: A comparative analysis of three states' experiences.* Cambridge, MA: The Civil Rights Project at Harvard University.

Immigrant Legal Resource Center. (n.d.). AB 540 Dream Act. Retrieved April 25, 2007, from http://www.ilrc.org/ab540_2.html.

Kane, T. J. (1994). College attendance by Blacks since 1970: The role of college cost, family background, and the returns to education. *Journal of Political Economy, 102,* 878–911.

Kane, T. J. (2003). *A quasi-experimental estimate of the impact of financial aid on college-going.* Working Paper No. 9703. Cambridge, MA: National Bureau of Economic Research.

Kobach, K.W. (2007). Immigration nullification: In-state tuition and lawmakers who disregard the law. *N.Y.U. Journal of Legislation & Public Policy, 10,* 473–523.

Kurlaender, M. (2006). Choosing community college: Factors affecting Latino college choice. *New Directions in Community Colleges* (Vol. 133, pp. 7–16). San Francisco: Jossey-Bass.

Leticia A. vs. Board of Regents of the University of California, I, No. 588982-4, slip op. at 2.

Long, B. T. (2004a). How have college decisions changed overtime? An application of the conditional logistic choice model. *Journal of Econometrics, 121,* 271–296.

Long, B. T. (2004b). How do financial aid policies affect colleges? The institutional impact of the Georgia HOPE Scholarship. *Journal of Human Resources, 39,* 1045–1066.

Margon, S. (2004, May). *Naturalization in the United States* [Electronic version]. Washington, DC: Migration Policy Institute.

Marin, P., & Lee, E. (2003). *Appearance and reality in the sunshine state: The Talented 20 Program in Florida.* Cambridge, MA: The Civil Rights Project at Harvard University.

McLendon, M. K., Hearn, J. C., & Deaton, R. (2006). Called to account: Analyzing the origins and spread of state performance-accountability policies for higher education. *Educational Evaluation and Policy Analysis, 28,* 1–24.

Moretti, E. (2004). Estimating the social return to higher education: Evidence from longitudinal and repeated cross-sectional data. *Journal of Econometrics, 121,* 175–212.

Moulton, B. R. (1986). Random group effects and the precision of regression estimates. *Journal of Econometrics, 32,* 385–397.

National Immigration Law Center. (2006,April). Basic facts about in-state tuition for undocumented immigrant students. Retrieved on December 3, 2006, from http://www.nilc.org/immlawpolicy/DREAM/in-state_tuition_basicfacts_041706. pdf.

Olivas, M. (1995). Storytelling out of school: Undocumented college residency, race, and reaction. *Hastings Constitutional Law Quarterly, 22,* 1019–1086.

Olivas M. (2004). IIRIRA, the Dream Act, and undocumented college student residency. *Journal of College and University Law, 30,* 435–464.

Olivas, M. (2007). Immigration-related state and local ordinances: Preemption, prejudice, and the proper role for enforcement. *University of Chicago Law Review 2007*, 27–56.

Olivas, M. (2008, July/August). Colleges and undocumented students. *Change*, pp. 20–21.

Olivas, M. (2009). Undocumented college students, taxation, and financial aid: A technical note. *Review of Higher Education, 32*(3), 407–416.

Olivérez, P., Chavez, M. L., Soriano, M., & Tierney, W. (2006, October). *College and financial aid guide for AB 540: Undocumented immigrant students.* Los Angeles: University of Southern California, Center for Higher Education Policy.

Orfield, G. (Ed.). (2004). *Dropouts in America: Confronting the graduation rate crisis.* Cambridge, MA: Harvard Education Press.

Passel, J. S. (2005a, March 21). *Estimates of the size and characteristics of the undocumented population.* Washington, DC: Pew Hispanic Center. Retrieved September 1, 2005, from http://pewhispanic.org/reports/report/php?ReportID=44.

Passel, J. S. (2005b, June 14). *Unauthorized migrants: Numbers and characteristics.* Background briefing prepared for Task Force on Immigration and America's Future. Washington, DC: Pew Hispanic Center. Retrieved on September 1, 2005, from http://pewhispanic.org/reports/.

Passel, J. S., Van Hook, J., & Bean, F. D. (2004). *Estimates of legal and unauthorized foreign-born population for the United States and selected states, based on Census 2000.* Report to the Census Bureau. Washington, DC: The Urban Institute.

Perna, L. W. (2000). Differences in the decision to attend college among African Americans, Hispanics, and Whites. *The Journal of Higher Education, 71*, 117–141.

Perry, A. (2006). Toward a theoretical framework for membership: The case of undocumented immigrants and financial aid for postsecondary education. *Review of Higher Education, 30*(1), 21–40.

Plyler v. Doe, 457 U.S. 202 (1982).

Post, D. (1990). College-going decisions of Chicanos: The politics of misinformation. *Educational Evaluation and Policy Analysis, 2*, 174–187.

Redden, E. (2007). An in-state tuition debate. *Inside Higher Education.* Retrieved on March 1, 2007, from http://www.insidehighered.com/news/2007/02/28/ immigration.

Rincon, A. (2008). *Undocumented immigrants and higher education.* New York: LFB Scholarly.

Sallie Mae Fund. (2004). *Caught in the financial aid information divide: A national survey of Latino perspectives on financial aid.* PowerPoint presentation. Retrieved on March 20, 2006, from www.thesalliemaefund.org/news/TRPI%20 Presentation.ppt.

St. John, E. P. (1991). What really influences minority attendance? Sequential analyses of the High School and Beyond sophomore cohort. *Research in Higher Education, 32*, 141–158.

St. John, E. P., & Noell, J. (1989). The effects of student financial aid on access to higher education: An analysis of progress with special consideration of minority enrollment. *Research in Higher Education, 30*, 563–581.

Stone, M. (2006, November 21). *Prop. 300 passed, but now what?* ASU Web Devil. Retrieved on December 2, 2006, from http://www.asuwebdevil.com/issues/2006/11/21/news/698975.

Swanson, C. B. (2004). Sketching a portrait of public high school graduation: Who graduates? Who doesn't? In G. Orfield (Ed.), *Dropouts in America: Confronting the graduation rate crisis* (pp. 13–40). Cambridge MA: Harvard Education Press.

Taylor, S. (2006, September 12). Strayhorn confirms she opposes Texas' DREAM Act. *Rio Grande Guardian.* Retrieved on April 25, 2007, from http://www. criminaljusticecoalition.org/files/userfiles/Strayhorn_confirms_she_opposes_Texas__DREAM_Act.pdf.

Texas Comptroller. (2006). *Undocumented immigrants in Texas: A financial analysis of the impact to the state budget and economy.* Retrieved on February 19, 2009, from http://www.window.state.tx.us/specialrpt/undocumented/.

U.S. Census Bureau. (2006, October). *Current population technical paper 66.* Retrieved on January 4, 2009, from http://www.census.gov/prod/2006pubs/tp-66.pdf.

U.S. Department of Labor. (2002, March). *Current population survey: Design and methodology.* Technical Paper 63RV. Washington, DC: Bureau of Labor Statistics.

CHAPTER 42
THE NEW MERIT AID

SUSAN DYNARSKI

Introduction

Merit aid, a discount to college costs contingent upon academic performance, is nothing new. Colleges and private organizations have long rewarded high-achieving, college-bound high school students with scholarships. For example, the privately funded National Merit Scholarship program, established in 1955, annually awards grants to 8,000 entering college freshmen who perform exceptionally on a standardized test. Private colleges have long used merit scholarships to lure students with strong academic credentials.

While merit aid has a long history in the private sector, it has not played a major role in the public sector. Historically, government subsidies to college students have not been merit based. At the federal level, aid has been need based and strongly focused on low-income students. Eligibility for the two largest federal aid programs, the Pell Grant and Stafford Loan, is determined by a complex formula that defines financial need on the basis of income, assets, and family size. The formula is quite progressive: 90 percent of dependent students who receive federal grants grew up in families with incomes less than $40,000.[1]

At the state level, subsidies for college students have historically taken the form of low tuition at public college and universities. Most states have long had *some* form of merit aid, but these programs have traditionally been small and limited to the most elite students. For example, New York rewards each high school's top scorer on the Regents exam with a scholarship. While such small merit programs abound, the vast bulk of state spending on higher education takes the form of low tuition, made possible by the $50 billion in subsidies that states annually provide their postsecondary institutions. These institutional subsidies are highest at the flagship universities, which draw the highest-achieving students. In this sense, these institutional subsidies are, by far, the largest "merit aid" program in the United States. Access to this state subsidy has traditionally been controlled not by state governments but by the schools, who decide which students are sufficiently meritorious to gain admission.

Recently, however, state legislatures have gotten into the business of defining academic merit and awarding merit aid to hundreds of thousands of students. Since the early 1990s, more than a dozen states have established broad-based merit aid programs. The typical program awards tuition and fees to young residents who have maintained a modest grade point average in high school. Many require a high school grade point average (GPA) of 3.0 or above, not a particularly high threshold: In 1999, 40 percent of high school seniors met this standard.[2] Georgia, for example, gives a free ride at its public colleges and universities to residents who have a GPA of 3.0 in high school.[3] In Arkansas, the GPA cutoff is 2.5, exceeded by 60 percent of high school students.

This new breed of merit aid differs from the old style in both its breadth and, plausibly, its effect on students' decisions. The old style of merit aid was aimed at top students, whose decision to attend college is not likely to be contingent upon the receipt of a scholarship. By design, if not by intent, this elite form of merit aid goes to students whose operative decision is not whether to attend college, but which high-quality, four-year college to choose. By contrast, the new, broad-based merit aid programs are open to students with solid although not necessarily exemplary academic records. Such students may be uncertain about whether to go to college at all. When offered a well-publicized, generous scholarship, some of these students may decide to give college a try. Even among students who would have gone to college without the scholarship, the incentives of merit aid may have an effect on schooling decisions. For example, some may choose a four-year school over a two-year school, or a private school over a public school.[4] Those students planning to go to college out of state may instead decide to stay closer to home in order to take advantage of a merit scholarship.

This chapter will examine how merit aid affects this array of schooling decisions, using household survey data to measure the impact of the new state programs. I start with a case study of the Georgia Helping Outstanding Pupils Educationally (HOPE) Scholarship, the namesake and inspiration of many of the new state programs. I then extend the analysis to other states that now have broad-based, HOPE-like programs. In the empirical analysis, I pay particular attention to how the effect of merit aid has varied by race and ethnicity.

Merit aid might affect the decisions not only of students but also of institutions. Do colleges increase their tuition prices, in order to capture some of the subsidy? Do they reduce other forms of aid? Does the linkage of scholarships to grades lead to grade inflation at high schools and colleges? A number of studies have addressed these questions, and I will review the evidence on these topics. Finally, I will briefly discuss the political economy of merit aid. Why has it arisen where it has and when it has? What are the prospects for its continuation and growth, given the current, poor fiscal prospects of the states?

State Merit Aid: A Primer

Broad-based state merit aid became common in a very short span of time. In 1993, just two states, Arkansas and Georgia, had programs in place. By 2002, thirteen states had introduced large merit aid programs. Most of this growth has occurred quite recently, with seven programs starting up since 1999. As is clear from the map in figure 1, merit aid is heavily concentrated in the southern region of the United States. Of the thirteen states with broad-based merit aid programs, nine are in the South. Table 1 summarizes the characteristics of the thirteen broad-based merit programs. As was discussed earlier, dozens of states have some form of merit aid in place. The state programs detailed in table 1 were chosen because they have particularly lenient eligibility criteria, with at least 30 percent of high school students having grades and test scores high enough to qualify for a scholarship.[5]

For example, the Arkansas award requires a GPA of 2.5, a standard met by 60 percent of high school students nationwide. The state also requires a minimum on the American College Test (ACT) of 19, a score exceeded by 60 percent of test takers nationwide and well below the Arkansas state average of 20.4. Five other states, like Arkansas, condition eligibility on a minimum GPA and test score. Six states use only GPA to determine eligibility. Of the states that require a minimum GPA, four require a GPA of 3.0, while two make awards to those with a GPA of 2.5.

Only one state—Michigan—bases eligibility solely on standardized test performance. For the class of 2000, 31 percent of Michigan students had test scores sufficiently high to merit an award. However, this overall eligibility rate masks substantial heterogeneity: Just 7.9 percent of African American students met the Michigan requirement. Civil rights groups have protested that this wide gap in eligibility indicates that Michigan's achievement test is an inappropriate instrument with which to determine eligibility for a state-funded scholarship. Similar objections were raised in Arkansas, which initially based eligibility for its program only on performance on standardized tests but later broadened the criteria to include academic performance in high school.

These controversies point to a shared characteristic of merit programs: their scholarships flow disproportionately to white, non-Hispanic, upper-income students. One reason is that blacks, Hispanics, and low-income youths are relatively unlikely to attend college, so *any* subsidy to college students will flow disproportionately to white, upper-income youth. But even among those non-white, Hispanic, and low-income youths who do attend college, academic performance is a barrier to merit aid eligibility.

For merit programs that are based on standardized tests, it is unsurprising to see (as in Michigan) a large gap in the eligibility rates of whites and African Americans, as the correlation between

1993

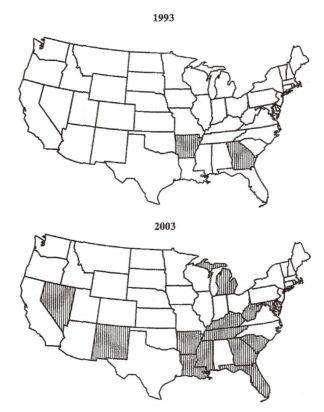

2003

Figure 1   States with broad-based merit aid programs.

standardized test performance and race is well documented. However, even those programs with only a GPA cutoff will experience large racial differences in eligibility, since academic performance in the classroom varies considerably by race and ethnicity. Forty percent of high school seniors have a 3.0 GPA or higher, while only 15 percent of African Americans and Hispanics meet this standard. Further, blacks and Hispanics receive relatively low grades in college, which threatens their ability to keep any merit scholarship they are able to win with their high school grades.

Since nonwhite youths are less likely to qualify, it is plausible that merit aid programs will have little positive impact upon their college attendance. Further, if the new merit aid crowds out state spending on need-based aid or leads to higher tuition prices, the programs may actually *decrease* low-income, nonwhite college attendance, since these populations will face the resulting cost increases but will be disproportionately ineligible for the new merit scholarships. Merit aid would therefore tend to widen existing gaps in college attendance, as it flows to those who already attend college at the highest rates. A countervailing force is that blacks and Hispanics may be relatively sensitive to college costs. Among those blacks and Hispanics who are eligible, a merit program could have a relatively large impact on schooling decisions. It is therefore an empirical question, to be investigated by this chapter, whether merit programs narrow or widen existing racial and ethnic gaps in postsecondary schooling.

Case Study: The Georgia HOPE Scholarship

In 1991, Georgia Governor Zell Miller requested that the state's General Assembly consider the establishment of a state-run lottery, with the proceeds to be devoted to education. The Georgia General Assembly passed lottery-enabling legislation during its 1992 session and forwarded the issue to voters, who approved the required amendment to the state's constitution in November of 1992. The

TABLE 1

Merit Aid Program Characteristics, 2003

State	Start	Eligibility	Award (in-state attendance only, exceptions noted)
Arkansas	1991	initial: 2.5 GPA in HS core and 19 ACT renew: 2.75 college GPA	public: $2,500 private: same
Florida	1997	initial: 3.0–3.5 HS GPA and 970–1270 SAT/20–28 ACT renew: 2.75–3.0 college GPA	public: 75–100% tuition/fees[a] private: 75–100% average public tuition/fees[a]
Georgia	1993	initial: 3.0 HS GPA renew: 3.0 college GPA	public: tuition/fees private: $3,000
Kentucky	1999	initial: 2.5 HS GPA renew: 2.5–3.0 college GPA	public: $500–3,000[a] private: same
Louisiana	1998	initial: 2.5–3.5 HS GPA and ACT > state mean renew: 2.3 college GPA	public: tuition/fees + $400–800[a] private: average public tuition/fees[a]
Maryland	2002	initial: 3.0 HS GPA in core renew: 3.0 college GPA	2-year school: $1,000 4-year school: $3,000
Michigan	2000	initial: level 2 of MEAP or 75th percentile of SAT/ACT renew: NA	in-state: $2,500 once out-of-state: $1,000 once
Mississippi	1996	initial: 2.5 GPA and 15 ACT renew: 2.5 college GPA	public freshman/sophomore: $500 public junior/senior: $1,000 private: same
Nevada	2000	initial: 3.0 GPA and pass Nevada HS exam renew: 2.0 college GPA	public 4-year: tuition/fees (max $2,500) public 2-year: tuition/fees (max $1,900) private: none
New Mexico	1997	initial: 2.5 GPA 1st semester of college renew: 2.5 college GPA	public: tuition/fees private: none
South Carolina	1998	initial: 3.0 GPA and 1100 SAT/24 ACT renew: 3.0 college GPA	2-year school: $1,000 4-year school: $2,000
Tennessee	2003	initial: 3.0–3.75 GPA and 890–1280 SAT/19–29 ACT renew: 3.0 college GPA	2-year school: tuition/fees ($1,500–2,500)[a] 4-year school: tuition/fees ($3,000–4,000)[a]
West Virginia	2002	initial: 3.0 HS GPA in core and 1000 SAT/21 ACT renew: 2.75–3.0 college GPA	public: tuition/fees private: average public tuition/fees

Note: HS = high school.

[a]Amount of award rises with GPA and/or test score.

first lottery tickets were sold in June of 1993. $2.5 billion in lottery revenue has flowed into Georgia's educational institutions since 1993. The legislation and amendment enabling the lottery specified that the new funds were not to crowd out spending from traditional sources. While it is not possible to establish conclusively that such crowdout has not occurred, spending on education has risen substantially since the lottery was initiated, both in absolute dollars and as a share of total state spending. Roughly equal shares of lottery funds have gone to four programs: the HOPE Scholarship, educational technology for primary and secondary schools, a new pre-kindergarten program, and school construction.

Residents who have graduated since 1993 from Georgia high schools with at least a 3.0 GPA are eligible for HOPE.[6] Public college students must maintain a GPA of 3.0 to keep the scholarship; a similar requirement was introduced for private school students in 1996. The HOPE Scholarship pays for tuition and required fees at Georgia's public colleges and universities. Those attending private colleges are eligible for an annual grant, which was $500 in 1993 and had increased to $3,000 by 1996. A $500 education voucher is available to those who complete a General Education Diploma (GED). The first scholarships were disbursed in the fall of 1993. Participation in HOPE during its first year was limited to those with family incomes below $66,000; the income cap was raised to $100,000 in 1994 and eliminated in 1995.

Two administrative aspects of HOPE differentially affected low- and upper-income youths. Since income is highly correlated with race and ethnicity, these administrative quirks may explain any racial and ethnic heterogeneity we observe in HOPE's effect. First, until 2001, HOPE awards were offset by other sources of aid. A student who received the maximum Pell Grant got no HOPE Scholarship except for a yearly book allowance of $400.[7] Insofar as blacks and Hispanics are disproportionately represented in the ranks of those who receive need-based aid, their HOPE awards would have been reduced more frequently than those of their white, non-Hispanic peers. Second, also until 2001, students from families with low incomes faced a more arduous application process for HOPE than did other students. Georgia education officials, concerned that students would forgo applying for federal aid once the HOPE Scholarship was available, mandated that applicants from families with incomes lower than $50,000 complete the Free Application for Federal Student Aid (FAFSA). The rationale for the $50,000 income threshold was that few students above that cutoff were eligible for need-based, federal grant aid.[8] The four-page FAFSA requests detailed income, expense, asset, and tax data from the family. By contrast, those with family incomes above $50,000 filled out a simple, one-page form that required no information about finances other than a confirmation that family income was indeed above the cutoff. As a consequence of the two provisions just discussed, low-income students faced higher transaction costs and lower average scholarships than did upper-income students.

In 2000–2001, 75,000 students received $277 million in HOPE Scholarships. Georgia politicians have deemed HOPE a great success, pointing to the steady rise in the number of college students receiving HOPE. The key question is whether the program actually changes schooling decisions or simply subsidizes inframarginal students. In the next section, I discuss the data and empirical strategy I will use to answer this question.

Data

Any empirical analysis of state financial aid policy quickly comes face to face with frustrating data limitations. The data requirements appear minor, since eligibility for merit aid is determined by a very short list of characteristics: state of residence at the time of high school graduation, high school GPA, standardized test score, and, in some states, parental income. In order to use this information in an evaluation of the effect of merit aid, we would want these characteristics for repeated cohorts of high school students, both before and after merit aid is introduced in their state, so that schooling decisions of eligible and ineligible cohorts could be compared.[9] Finally, we need a data set with state-level samples large enough to allow for informative analysis.

No publicly available data set meets all of these requirements. Surveys that are limited to college students do not, by their nature, allow us to examine the college attendance margin. For example, the National Postsecondary Student Aid Survey (NPSAS) surveys college students about their aid packages and contains detailed information from students' aid applications. By design, this data set cannot inform us about those students who decided *not* to go to college. Without making strong assumptions about how those who do not go to college differ from those who do, we cannot use the NPSAS to examine how aid affects the college attendance rate.

The NPSAS can be used to answer other questions of interest, however. For example, we might be interested in whether merit aid leads to higher tuition prices, or more or less government spending on other forms of aid. Or we might be interested in how the racial composition of a state's schools changes, if at all, after the introduction of a merit aid program. The NPSAS, as well as data that institutions gather about their students and report to the government through the Integrated Postsecondary Education Data System (IPEDS), can answer questions of this type.[10]

The National Longitudinal Surveys (NLSs) of Youth of 1979 and 1997 are particularly rich sources of data, containing information about academic performance on standardized tests, grades, parental income, and schooling decisions.[11] In a few years, the NLSY97 will be a useful resource for evaluating the newer merit aid programs, in particular those introduced in the late 1990s. The only weakness of the NLSY97 is that it is unlikely to interview enough youths in any one state to allow for detailed examination of a single merit aid program. Observations from multiple merit states could be pooled, however, as is done with the Current Population Survey in this paper.

Another potentially fruitful option for research in this area is data from administrative sources. Kane (2003) and Henry and Rubinstein (2002) take this approach in evaluations of programs in California and Georgia, respectively.[12] Kane matches enrollment data from California's public universities and colleges to federal aid applications and high school transcripts. He then uses regression-discontinuity methodology to estimate the effect of California's merit program on schooling decisions. Henry and Rubinstein use data from the College Board on high school grades and SAT scores in order to examine whether the Georgia HOPE Scholarship has led to grade inflation in high schools.

The Current Population Survey and the Analysis of State Aid Policy

The bulk of the analysis in this paper is based on a publicly available survey data set, the Current Population Survey (CPS). The CPS is a national household survey that each October gathers detailed information about schooling enrollment. Data on type of school attended, as well as basic demographics such as age, race, and ethnicity, are included in the CPS. While the CPS is the world's premier labor force survey, from the perspective of this chapter it has some key limitations.

First, the CPS lacks information about academic performance. We therefore cannot narrow the analysis to those whose academic performance makes them eligible for merit aid, and thereby measure the effect on schooling decisions of offering a merit scholarship among those who qualify (an effect I will denote π). From a policy perspective, the question we *can* answer is quite relevant: How does the existence of a merit aid program affect the schooling decisions of a state's youths? To answer this question, I will estimate a program effect (denoted β) that is the product of two interesting parameters: (1) π, the behavioral response to the offer of aid of youths eligible for the scholarship and (2) δ, the share of youths eligible for the scholarship:[13]

$$\beta = \pi\delta$$

When considering the effect of a financial aid program such as the Pell Grant, we generally are interested only in π. We assume that the parameters that determine Pell eligibility, such as family size and income, cannot easily be manipulated by those eager to obtain the grant. By contrast, merit aid is a program that *intends* to induce behavior that will increase the share that is aid-eligible. Policymakers consistently cite their desire to give students a financial incentive to work hard in high school and college as their motivation for establishing merit aid programs. Estimating π while ignoring δ would therefore miss half the story. Fortunately, data constraints prevent us from making this mistake!

A more serious weakness of the CPS is that it provides family background data for only a subset of youths. Highly relevant variables such as parental income, parental education, and other measures of socioeconomic status are available only for those youths who live with their families or who are temporarily away at college.[14] The probability that a youth has family background information available is therefore a function of his or her propensity to attend college. Under these circumstances, we cannot limit the analysis to those who have family background data without inducing bias in analyses in which college attendance is an outcome of interest.[15] In the analysis, therefore, I will make use only of background variables that are available for all youths.

Is State of Residence of Youth Systematically Mismeasured in the CPS?

A final weakness of the CPS is that it explicitly identifies neither the state in which a person attended high school nor the state in which he or she attends college. In this paper, I proxy for the state in which a person attended high school with current state of residence. This is a reasonable proxy, for two reasons. First, among eighteen-to-nineteen-year-olds, the group studied in this chapter, migration across state lines for reasons other than college is minimal. Second, when youths *do* go out of state to college, according to CPS coding standards they are recorded as residents of the state of origin, rather than the state in which they attend college.

The key question is whether these standards are followed in practice. We are confident that this protocol has been followed for those youths (78 percent of the sample) who appear on their parents' record.[16] Whether the CPS correctly captures the state of residence for the other 22 percent is an important question, as error in the collection of these data will bias the chapter's estimates.

If state of residence is simply a noisy measure of state of origin for this 22 percent, then the paper's estimates will be biased toward zero. But consider the following scenario, in which we will be biased toward finding a *positive* effect of merit aid on the probability of college attendance. Say that HOPE has no effect on the college entry margin but does affect whether students go to college in state. If the CPS incorrectly codes the state of residence as the state in which one is attending college, then any drop in the outward migration of Georgia college students induced by HOPE will mechanically induce an increase in the observed share of Georgia youths attending college.

A few simple tabulations can give us a sense of whether this is a problem. If the scenario laid out in the previous paragraph holds, then we should observe relative growth in the *size* of the college-age population in Georgia after HOPE is introduced. To test this hypothesis, I predicted the size of Georgia's college-age population by aging forward the high school–age population. Specifically, I compared the population of eighteen-to-nineteen-year-olds in a given state to the population of sixteen-to-seventeen-year-olds in the same state two years earlier. This is an admittedly crude prediction of cohort size. It will be wrong for any number of reasons, among them immigration and incarceration of teenagers (prisons are not in the CPS sampling frame). However, the relevant issue is not how error-ridden this prediction is, but whether the sign and magnitude of its error *change systematically* when a merit program is introduced in a state. In particular, does the population of college-age youths expand unexpectedly when a state introduces a merit program?

Figure 2 plots the difference between the predicted and actual cohort sizes, with the difference normed by the predicted size. I plot the normed error for Georgia and the average normed error for the other states in the Southeast and the United States.[17] For measurement error to be inducing positive bias in the paper's estimates, the errors should grow relatively more negative in Georgia after HOPE is introduced. There is no such clear trend. The large negative errors in Georgia in 1993 through 1995 are somewhat disturbing, even though a muted version of this pattern also appears in the U.S. and Southeastern series. In figure 3, I show the same series for West Virginia, a southern state that had no merit program during this period. This state's pattern is almost identical to that of Georgia, suggesting that Georgia's shifts in cohort size are random noise and that the paper's estimates will not be contaminated by this source of bias.

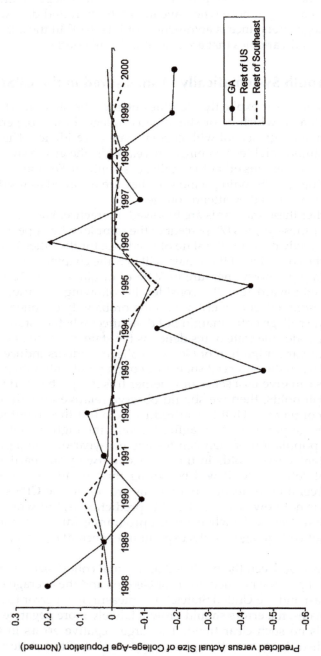

Figure 2 Does measurement error in state of residence bias the estimates?

Note: The figure plots the difference between the predicted and actual population of college-age youth, with the difference normed by the predicted population. The predicted population of eighteen-to-nineteen-year-olds in a state is the number of sixteen-to-seventeen-year-olds in that state two years earlier. The data used are the October Current Population Surveys.

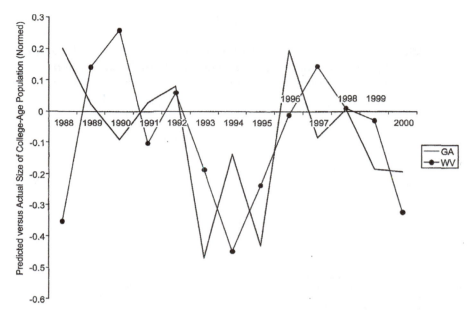

Figure 3 Does measurement error in state of residence bias the estimates?

Note: The figure plots the difference between the predicted and actual population of college-age youth, with the difference normed by the predicted population. The predicted population of eighteen-to-nineteen-year-olds in a state is the number of sixteen-to-seventeen-year-olds in that state two years earlier. The data used are the October Current Population Surveys.

Georgia HOPE Analysis

I begin by examining how the college attendance rate has changed in Georgia since HOPE was introduced, compared to how it has evolved in the other Southern states that have not introduced merit programs. The outcome of interest is whether an eighteen-to-nineteen-year-old is currently enrolled in college. I start with a parsimonious specification, in which an indicator variable for being enrolled in college is regressed against a set of state, year, and age effects, along with a variable, HOPE, that is set to 1 in survey years 1993 through 2000 for those who are from Georgia. In this equation, the HOPE variable therefore indicates that a young person of college age resides in Georgia after HOPE is in operation.

The estimating equation is as follows:

$$(1) \qquad y_{iast} = \beta_0 + \beta_1 HOPE_{st} + \delta_s + \delta_t + \delta_a + \varepsilon_{iast},$$

where y_{iast} is an indicator of whether person i of age a living in state s in year t is enrolled in college; δ_s, δ_t, and δ_a denote state, year, and age fixed effects, respectively; and ε_{iast} is an idiosyncratic error term. I use ordinary least squares (OLS) to estimate this equation, correcting standard errors for heteroskedasticity and correlation of the error terms within state cells.

Recall that HOPE (1) decreases the price of college, (2) decreases the price of in-state colleges relative to out-of-state colleges, and (3) decreases the price of four-year colleges relative to two-year colleges. The corresponding predicted behaviors for Georgia residents are (1) increased probability of college attendance, (2) increased probability of in-state attendance relative to out-of-state attendance, and (3) increased probability of four-year attendance relative to two-year attendance.

Column (1) of table 2 shows the college attendance results. The estimates indicate that the college attendance rate in Georgia rose 8.6 percentage points relative to that in the other Southern, non-merit states after HOPE was introduced. The estimate is highly significant, with a standard error of 0.8 percentage points. This estimate is quite close to the estimate in Dynarski (2000), which was

TABLE 2

Estimated Effect of Georgia HOPE Scholarship on College Attendance of Eighteen-to-Nineteen-Year-Olds (Southern Census Region)

	(1)	(2)	(3)	(4)
HOPE Scholarship	.086	.085	.085	.069
	(.008)	(.013)	(.013)	(.019)
Merit program in border state			−.005	−.006
			(.013)	(.013)
State and year effects	Y	Y	Y	Y
Median family income		Y	Y	Y
Unemployment rate		Y	Y	Y
Interactions of year effects with black, metro, Hispanic		Y	Y	Y
Time trends				Y
R^2	.020	.059	.059	.056
No. of observations	8,999	8,999	8,999	8,999

Notes: Regressions are weighted by CPS sample weights. Standard errors (in parentheses) are adjusted for heteroskedasticity and correlation within state cells. Sample consists of eighteen-to-nineteen-year-olds in Southern Census region, excluding states (other than Georgia) that introduce merit programs by 2000. See table 1 for a list of these states.

based on CPS data for 1989 through 1997.[18] The result suggests that HOPE did, as predicted, increase the share of youths attending college.

I next probe the robustness of this result by adding a set of covariates to this regression. For reasons discussed earlier, I limit myself to covariates that are available for the entire sample and exclude any that require that a youth and his or her parents appear on the same survey record, such as parental education and income. Control variables indicate whether a youth lives in a metropolitan area, is African American, or is Hispanic. These three variables are each interacted with a full set of year effects, so that the effect of these attributes on schooling decisions is allowed to vary flexibly over time. I also include the state's unemployment rate and the median income of families with children who are near college age. These two variables are intended to capture any Georgia-specific economic shocks that may have affected college attendance decisions. Results are in column (2). The coefficient does not change, although the standard error increases to 1.3 percentage points.

I next examine whether the effect of merit aid extends across state borders. Since students travel across state lines for college, changes in postsecondary education policy in one state will reverberate in neighboring states. If more Georgians want to go to college, and the supply of colleges is inelastic, students from Florida, for example, will be pushed out of school when HOPE is introduced. The estimating equation is as follows:

$$(2) \qquad y_{iast} = \beta_0 + \beta_1 \text{HOPE}_{st} + \beta_2 \text{border\_merit}_{st} + \beta_3 X_{st} + \beta_3 X_i + \delta_s + \delta_t + \delta_a + \varepsilon_{iast}$$

β_2 captures the effect of having a merit program in a neighboring state. X_{st} and X_i are the state-year and individual covariates discussed in the previous paragraph and used in column (2). Results are in column (3). The results weakly suggest that having a merit program on one's border has a small, negative effect on college attendance, indicating the presence of supply constraints. The point estimate is fairly imprecise, however: -0.5 percentage points, with a standard error of 1.3 percentage points.[19]

An identifying assumption of the preceding analysis is that Georgia and the control states were on similar trends in their college attendance rates before HOPE was introduced. If they were instead on divergent trends the estimates will be biased. In particular, if attendance was rising in Georgia relative to the other states before 1993, then we will falsely attribute to HOPE the continuation of this trend. The inclusion of these preexisting trends in the equation will eliminate this source of bias. In column (4), I add to the regression separate time trends for Georgia and the nonmerit states.[20] The point estimate drops moderately, to 6.9 percentage points, indicating that Georgia was trending

TABLE 3

Effect of Georgia HOPE Scholarship on Schooling Decisions
(October CPS, 1988–2000; Southern Census Region)

	College Attendance (1)	2-Year Public (2)	2-Year Private (3)	4-Year Public (4)	4-Year Private (5)
No time trends					
Hope Scholarship	.085	−.018	.015	.045	.022
	(.013)	(.010)	(.002)	(.015)	(.007)
R^2	.059	.026	.010	.039	.026
Add time trends					
Hope Scholarship	.069	−.055	.014	.084	.028
	(.019)	(.013)	(.004)	(.023)	(.016)
R^2	.056	.026	.010	.029	.026
Mean of dependent variable	.407	.122	.008	.212	.061

Notes: Specification in "No time trends" is that of column (3) in table 2. Specification in "Add time trends" adds trends estimated on pretreatment data. In each column, two separate trends are included, one for Georgia and one for the rest of the states. Sample consists of eighteen-to-nineteen-year-olds in Southern Census region, excluding states (other than Georgia) that introduce a merit program by 2000. No. of observations = 8,999. Standard errors in parentheses.

away from the rest of the South before HOPE. However, there is still a substantial relative increase in attendance in Georgia that cannot be explained by this trend.

The Effect of HOPE on School Choice

I next examine whether HOPE has affected decisions other than college entry. In particular, I examine the type of college that a student chooses to attend. The October CPS contains information about whether a student attends a public or private college and whether it is a two- or four-year institution. I use this information to construct four variables that indicate whether a person attends a two-year private school, a two-year public school, a four-year private school, or a four-year public school. I then run a series of four regressions in which these are the outcomes, including the same covariates as in the richest specification of table 2. I show results that both do and do not include time trends. The results are shown in table 3. The attendance results of the previous table are included for ease of comparison.

The HOPE Scholarship appears to increase the probability of attendance at four-year public institutions substantially, by 4.5 percentage points (no time trends) to 8.4 percentage points (time trends included). Attendance at four-year private schools also rises, although the estimates are smaller than those (2.2 to 2.8 percentage points). There is a somewhat smaller rise in the probability of attendance at two-year private schools (about 1.5 percentage points) and a drop at two-year public schools (of 1.7 to 5.5 percentage points). All but two of the eight estimates are significant at conventional levels.

These shifts in schooling decisions are in the expected direction. Any subsidy to college will both pull students *into* two-year public schools (from not going to college at all) and push them *out* of two-year public schools (into four-year colleges). The HOPE Scholarship appears to push more students out of two-year, public institutions than it pulls in, producing a net drop at these schools. Most of these students appear to shift toward four-year public institutions, although some also shift into the private sector.[21]

The Effect of HOPE on Migration to College

We might expect that HOPE would also affect whether students choose to attend college in their home state. Data from both the University System of Georgia (USG) and the Department of Education's

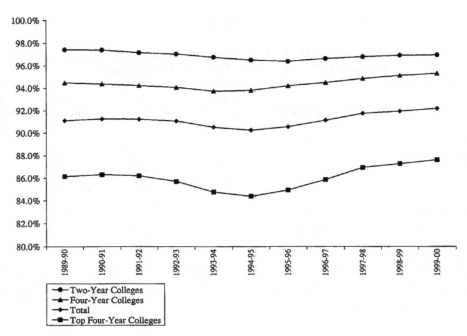

Figure 4   University System of Georgia students, Georgia residents as share of total enrollment.

Residence and Migration Survey suggest that HOPE has had the effect of encouraging Georgia residents who would have attended a four-year college out of state to stay in Georgia instead. Data from the Residence and Migration Survey indicate that in 1992 about 5,000 Georgians were freshmen at two- and four-year colleges in the states that border Georgia. This represented an average of 3.4 percent of the border states' freshman enrollment. By 1998, just 4,500 Georgians crossed state lines to enter college in the border states, accounting for an average of 2.9 percent of freshman enrollment in those states. This drop in migration was concentrated in a group of border schools that have traditionally drawn large numbers of Georgians. At the ten border schools drawing the most Georgia freshmen in 1992, students from Georgia numbered 1,900 and averaged 17 percent of the freshman class. By 1998, the ten top destinations enrolled 1,700 Georgians, who represented 9 percent of freshman enrollment. Jacksonville State College in Florida, for example, drew 189 Georgian freshmen in 1992 and only 89 in 1998; the share of the freshman class from Georgia dropped from 17 to 11 percent.

Further supporting the conclusion that Georgia's four-year college students are now more likely to attend college in state is a shift in the composition of Georgia's four-year colleges. Figure 4 shows data from the USG on the share of freshman enrollees that are Georgia residents at Georgia's two- and four-year public colleges. The data are separately plotted for the two-year, four-year, and elite four-year colleges in the state. Here we see a definite shift toward Georgia residents since HOPE was introduced, with the effect most pronounced at four-year colleges (especially the top schools) and least evident at the two-year schools. This pattern fits with our understanding that four-year students are most mobile when making college attendance decisions.

The Differential Impact of HOPE by Race and Ethnicity

The effect of merit programs may vary across racial and ethnic groups for a number of reasons. First, as was discussed earlier, academic performance in high school is strongly correlated with race and ethnicity. Second, the rules of the programs are sometimes such that they are likely to have a lesser impact on low-income youths. Until recently, Georgia did not offer the grant to those youths who had substantial Pell Grants and low college costs. Mechanically, then, the program would have had a

TABLE 4

Effect of Georgia HOPE Scholarship on College Attendance Analysis by Race and Ethnicity (October CPS, 1988–2000; Southern Census Region)

	No Time Trends	Time Trends
Merit program	.096	.140
	(.014)	(.013)
Merit · black/Hispanic	−.030	−.147
	(.023)	(.039)
R^2	.059	.056

Notes: Specification in first column is that of column (3) in table 2. Specification in second column adds trends estimated on pretreatment data. Separate trends are included for four groups: white-control, white-treat, nonwhite-control and nonwhite-treat. Sample consists of eighteen-to-nineteen-year-olds in Southern Census region, excluding states other than Georgia that introduce a merit program by 2000. Standard errors in parentheses.

lower impact on African Americans and Hispanics, who tend to have lower incomes: in Georgia, 94 percent of African American but just 62 percent of white sixteen-to-seventeen-year-olds live in families with incomes less than $50,000.[22] The numbers for the rest of the United States are similar.[23] Third, states that have merit programs may reduce need-based aid or appropriations to colleges. Both of these effects would tend to make college more expensive for those who don't qualify for the merit programs to which the money is being channeled. Finally, the elasticity of schooling with respect to a given grant may differ across demographic groups. A priori, it is not clear whether blacks and Hispanics would be more or less elastic than other students in their schooling decisions.[24]

To explore how the effect of merit aid programs varies by race and ethnicity, I repeat the analysis of the preceding section but allow the effect of HOPE to differ across racial and ethnic groups. I divide the population into two mutually exclusive categories: (1) white non-Hispanics and (2) Hispanics of any race plus blacks.[25] I then estimate the effect of merit aid separately for each group. The estimating equation is

$$(3) \qquad y_{iast} = \beta_0 + \beta_1 \text{Merit}_{st} + \beta_2 \text{Merit}_{st} \times \text{black\_hisp}_i + \beta_3 \text{border\_Merit}_{st} + \beta_4 X_{st} + \beta_5 X_i$$
$$+ \delta_s + \delta_t + \delta_a + \varepsilon_{iast}.$$

Results for Georgia are in table 4, for specifications that do and do not include preexisting time trends.[26] The point estimates are somewhat unstable, changing substantially when time trends are included. But the two sets of estimates agree that HOPE had a substantially greater effect on white attendance than black and Hispanic attendance. The estimated effect of HOPE on the white attendance rate is 9.6 to 14.0 percentage points, while that on blacks and Hispanics is –0.7 to 6.6 percentage points. The results indicate that HOPE has increased racial and ethnic gaps in college attendance in Georgia.

The Effect of Broad-Based Merit Aid in Other States

The Georgia program was one of the first, largest, and best-publicized merit aid programs. It has also been, by far, the best-studied program; at this point, dozens of papers have analyzed its impact. In the absence of sound empirical research on the effect of the other merit programs, the Georgia experience has been extrapolated in predicting their effects.[27] However, as is shown in table 1, there is heterogeneity in program rules, which may well lead to heterogeneity in the programs' effects. Further, initial college attendance rates and the supply of postsecondary schools vary across the merit aid states, which may affect the impact of the merit programs on schooling decisions. For all these reasons, results from one state may not provide a good prediction of the effect of another state's merit program.

Fortunately, many of the merit aid programs in table 1 have now been in existence sufficiently long to allow us to separately estimate program effects for each state. I will limit my analysis to the South, where all but three of the programs in table 1 are located. A benefit of focusing on the Southern merit states is that they have a natural control group: the nonmerit Southern states. The programs of three Southern states (Maryland, Tennessee, and West Virginia) are excluded, as they were introduced after 2000, the last year of the sample. That leaves seven merit programs, located in Arkansas, Florida, Georgia, Kentucky, Louisiana, Mississippi, and South Carolina.

I follow the approach used in the analysis of HOPE, creating a variable that indicates a year and state in which a merit program is in place. I estimate the following equation:

(4) $y_{iast} = \beta_0 + \beta_1 merit_{st} + \beta_2 border\_merit_{st} + \beta_3 X_{st} + \beta_4 X_i + \delta_s + \delta_t + \delta_a + \varepsilon_{iast}$

Results are in table 5. The estimated overall effect of the seven merit programs is 4.7 percentage points. The estimate is highly significant, with a standard error of 1.1 percentage points. In column (2), I allow this affect to vary across the seven states, by replacing the single merit dummy with a set of seven dummies, one for each state's program. The specification of column (2) is otherwise identical to that of column (1), and so the appropriately weighted average of the seven coefficients is the

TABLE 5

**Effect of All Southern Merit Programs on College Attendance
of Eighteen-to-Nineteen-Year-Olds**

	All Southern States (N = 13,965)			Southern Merit States Only (N = 5,640)		
	(1)	(2)	(3)	(4)	(5)	(6)
Merit program	.047 (.011)			.052 (.018)		
Merit program, Arkansas		.048 (.015)			.016 (.014)	
Merit program, Florida		.030 (.014)			.063 (.031)	
Merit program, Georgia		.074 (.010)			.068 (.014)	
Merit program, Kentucky		.073 (.025)			.063 (.047)	
Merit program, Louisiana		.060 (.012)			.058 (.022)	
Merit program, Mississippi		.049 (.014)			.022 (.018)	
Merit program, South Carolina		.044 (.013)			.014 (.023)	
Merit program, year 1			.024 (.019)			.051 (.027)
Merit program, year 2			.010 (.032)			.043 (.024)
Merit program, year 3 and after			.060 (.030)			.098 (.039)
State time trends			Y			Y
R^2	.046	.046	.047	.035	.036	.036

Notes: Specification is that of column (3) in table 2, with the addition of state time trends where noted. Sample consists of eighteen-to-nineteen-year-olds in Southern Census region, with the last three columns excluding states that have not introduced a merit program by 2000. Standard errors in parentheses.

4.7 percentage points of column (1). Six of the estimates are highly significant. Five are clustered between 4.9 (Mississippi) and 7.4 (Georgia). Well below Mississippi are Florida and South Carolina, with estimated effects of 3.0 and 0.2 percentage points, respectively.

We might suspect that the merit states are somehow different from the nonmerit states and that the nonmerit states therefore form a poor control group for these purposes. We can test the sensitivity of our results to the choice of control group by dropping the nonmerit states from the sample and estimating the effect of merit aid purely from the staggered timing of its rollout across the states. In this approach, the merit states form their own control group. Figure 5 graphically illustrates the identification strategy. During the first years of the sample (1988–1990), before the first merit program is introduced, all of the states are in the control group. In 1991, Arkansas moves into the treatment group, followed in 1993 by Georgia. By 2000, all of the states are in the treatment group. This approach assumes that the states that eventually have a merit program are on similar trends in the schooling outcomes of young people. The assumption is that the year in which a state's merit program begins is quasi-random, uncorrelated with any state-specific trends in or shocks to schooling decisions.

Results are in columns (4) and (5) of table 5. The estimated overall effect is insensitive to the choice of control group, with the estimate rising only slightly from 4.7 to 5.2 percentage points. The state-specific coefficients are somewhat more sensitive to the choice of control group. For five of the states, the two approaches yield similar results. The two exceptions are Arkansas and Florida, for whom the estimates vary substantially between column (2) and column (4). Arkansas's estimate drops from 4.8 to 1.6, while Florida's rises from 3.0 to 6.3.

Only South Carolina has a consistently small and insignificant effect, which may be explained by its requirement that students score at least 24 on the ACT. Nationally, just 30 percent of test takers scored above South Carolina's ACT cutoff in 2000, while 88 percent met Missouri's requirement and about 60 percent met the requirements of Arkansas (19), Florida (20), and Louisiana (19.6).[28] The South Carolina legislature has come under pressure to loosen the scholarship requirements and has responded by adding another route to eligibility. As of 2002, students can qualify for a scholarship by meeting two of three criteria: 24 on the ACT, a GPA of 3.0, and graduating in the top 30 percent of one's high school class (Bichevia Green of the South Carolina Commission on Higher Education, personal communication, June 14, 2002). Further, the ACT requirement has been dropped completely for those attending two-year institutions. It will be of interest to see if the effect of South Carolina's program on college attendance rises with this shift in policy.

Next, I examine whether the inclusion of preexisting time trends affects the results. Preexisting trends could contaminate the results for both control groups. The merit states may be on different time trends from the nonmerit states, and they may be on different trends from each other. I estimate a trend for the entire 1988–2000 period for each state. Deviations from these trends after a state introduces merit aid are then attributed to the new program.[29]

Results are in columns (3) and (6). As was true in the specification without time trends, the merit-only control group produces somewhat larger estimates. Both approaches indicate that the effect of merit aid evolves over time, with the effect rising from 2.4 percentage points in the first year

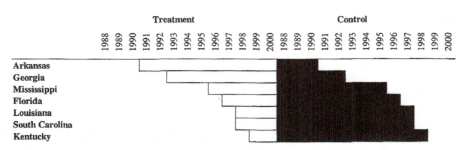

Figure 5 Timing of introduction of state merit programs.

a program is in effect to 6.0 percentage points in year three and beyond. When the merit states are used as their own control group, the effect rises from 5.1 percentage points in year one to 9.8 percentage points in the third year. Note that these are not cumulative effects but period-specific program effects.

The effect of merit aid may rise during the first years of a program for several reasons. It may take time for information about the new programs to diffuse. It also takes time for high school students who are inspired to work harder to increase their overall GPAs. Those who are high school seniors when a program is first introduced can do little to increase their cumulative GPAs, while those who are freshmen have four years to increase their effort. The pool of eligible youths may thereby expand over time.

The effect could also *diminish* over time, if many college students fail to qualify for scholarship renewals and their younger peers are discouraged from taking up the scholarship. Further, in the presence of supply constraints, the effect of latecomer programs would be smaller than that of earlier programs, as attendance grows and the supply grows tighter. The results in table 5 indicate that, across the merit states, the incentive and information effects dominate the discouragement effect.

The Effect of Merit Aid on College Choice

The analysis of the previous section indicates that the state merit aid programs have increased college attendance. I next examine whether these programs have also affected the choice of college, as was true in Georgia. I use the analytical framework of the previous section, although I will only show results that pool the merit states in order to gain precision. All of the Southern states are included in the sample; results are similar, but less precise, when the sample is limited to the Southern merit states. I show results that do and do not include time trends.

Table 6 indicates that, overall, the Southern merit programs have had a strong effect on the choice of college, with a considerable shift toward four-year public schools of 4.4 percentage points, which is about the same as the overall attendance effect. There are no effects on other choices of college. As was discussed earlier, this is probably the result of equal-sized shifts toward and away from

TABLE 6

**Effect of All Southern Merit Programs on Schooling Decisions
of Eighteen-to-Nineteen-Year-Olds (All Southern States; N = 13,965)**

	College Attendance (1)	2-Year Public (2)	2-Year Private (3)	4-Year Public (4)	4-Year Private (5)
No time trends					
Merit program	.047	−.010	.004	.044	.005
	(.011)	(.008)	(.004)	(.014)	(.009)
R^2	.046	.030	.007	.030	.020
State time trends					
Merit program, year 1	.024	−.025	.009	.034	.010
	(.019)	(.012)	(.005)	(.012)	(.007)
Merit program, year 2	.010	−.015	.002	.028	−.001
	(.032)	(.018)	(.003)	(.035)	(.011)
Merit program, year 3 and after	.060	−.037	.005	.065	.022
	(.030)	(.013)	(.003)	(.024)	(.010)
R^2	.047	.031	.009	.032	.022

Notes: Specification is that of column (3) in table 2, with the addition of state time trends where noted. Sample consists of eighteen-to-nineteen-year-olds in Southern Census region. Estimates are similar but less precise when sample is limited to Southern merit states. Standard errors in parentheses.

two-year public schools, by students on the margin of college entry and four-year-college attendance, respectively. The time trend specification gives similar results, although here there is more indication of a net drop in the probability of attendance at two-year public colleges.

Do All Merit Aid Programs Have the Distributional Impact of HOPE?

Many of the merit programs are quite new. Of the seven programs examined in table 5, three had been operative for fewer than four years by 2000. In this section, I examine the four more mature programs—those of Georgia, Florida, Arkansas, and Mississippi—in greater depth. An advantage of focusing on the older programs is that these states have sufficient postprogram observations to allow for the finer cuts of the data needed to examine heterogeneity in the effect of aid across demographic groups. Given the strong impact of HOPE on the racial/ethnic gap in schooling, it is of interest to examine whether the other programs have had a similar impact.

In table 7, I examine how the effect of the four programs varies by race and ethnicity. The control group is the nonmerit states. I show the results of specifications that do and do not include preprogram time trends.[30] While the estimates do change when time trends are included, and some are quite imprecisely estimated, a consistent story emerges from the table. The estimates are in concord with those of table 5, which showed that each of these four programs had a strong impact on the college attendance rate. However, table 7 shows that the *relative* effects on blacks and Hispanics differ substantially across programs. In particular, Georgia is an outlier in its relatively low effect on blacks and Hispanics, as compared to its effect on whites.

Georgia's HOPE has had the largest impact of all the state programs on the college attendance of whites, with the estimated effect ranging from 9.6 to 14.0 percentage points (without and with time trends, respectively). Analogous effects in the other states are substantially smaller, with no state's estimates for white non-Hispanics larger than 6 percentage points. Further, the effect of Georgia HOPE on blacks and Hispanics is 3.0 to 14.7 points *lower* than the effect on whites. In the other three states, the estimated effect of merit aid on blacks and Hispanics is consistently *more positive* than its effect on white non-Hispanics.

TABLE 7

Effect of Merit Aid on College Attendance Analysis by Race and Ethnicity
(October CPS, 1988–2000; Southern Census Region)

	Georgia (N = 8,999) (1)	Florida (N = 10,213) (2)	Arkansas (N = 8,949) (3)	Mississippi (N = 8,969) (4)
No time trends				
Merit program	.096	.001	.054	.002
	(.014)	(.022)	(.023)	(.011)
Merit · black/Hispanic	−.030	.077	.045	.120
	(.020)	(.021)	(.026)	(.032)
R^2	.059	.055	.061	.058
Time trends				
Merit program	.140	.030	.060	.016
	(.013)	(.021)	(.024)	(.015)
Merit · black/Hispanic	−.147	.000	.043	.083
	(.039)	(.030)	(.043)	(.033)
R^2	.056	.052	.059	.055

Notes: Specification in "No time trends" is that of column (3) in table 2. Specification in "Time trends" adds trends estimated on pretreatment data. In each column, separate trends are included for four groups: white-control, white-treat, nonwhite-control and nonwhite-treat. In each column, sample consists of eighteen-to-nineteen-year-olds in Southern Census region, excluding states (other than the treatment state) that introduce a merit program by 2000. Standard errors in parentheses.

This is an important finding, as Georgia's is the only program whose distributional effect has been examined in depth, and the assumption has been that, in other states, merit aid would similarly widen the racial gap in college attendance (see, e.g., Cornwell, Mustard, and Sridhar 2003 and Dynarski 2000). The results in table 7 indicate that the other mature merit aid programs have not had this effect, with nearly all of the estimates suggesting that merit aid has actually *narrowed* the gap.

Why is Georgia different? Its HOPE Scholarship diverges from the other three programs in two key dimensions. First, of the four programs analyzed in table 7, Georgia's has the most stringent GPA requirements. Georgia requires a high school GPA of 3.0, while Arkansas and Mississippi require a GPA of only 2.5. Florida's high school GPA requirement is similar to Georgia's, but its renewal requirements are less stringent. While Georgia requires that a HOPE scholar maintain a GPA of 3.0 in college, in Florida a college GPA of 2.75 allows a student to keep the scholarship. A college GPA of 2.75 also qualifies a student for renewal in Arkansas, and only a 2.5 is required in Mississippi.

Scholarship renewal rates for blacks are substantially lower than those of whites in Georgia, indicating that the college GPA requirement hits them particularly hard. Blacks at the University of Georgia are twice as likely as whites to lose their scholarship after the freshman year (Healy 1997). A study at the Georgia Institute of Technology also found that blacks were substantially more likely than whites to lose their scholarships. This differential disappeared after accounting for differences in ability (as measured by SAT scores; Dee and Jackson 1999). More generally, since blacks and Hispanics have relatively low high school and college grades, less stringent GPA requirements will disproportionately benefit this group.

A second key difference between HOPE and the other state programs is its treatment of other sources of aid and associated paperwork requirements for students potentially eligible for aid. During the period under analysis, HOPE was reduced dollar for dollar by a student's other aid, and low-income students were required to fill out extensive paperwork in order to establish their eligibility for other aid. The net impact of these requirements was that lower-income students had to work harder for less aid than their well-off counterparts.[31] In stark contrast, Arkansas gives *larger* awards to low-income students, by allowing students who receive the Pell to keep their Academic Challenge Scholarships and by excluding from eligibility students from families with incomes above $55,000.[32]

Additional Effects of Merit Aid on Individuals and Institutions

The analysis in this paper has focused on the effect of merit aid on two critical margins: the decision to attend college and the type of college chosen. I have touched on another outcome that is quite important, at least to legislators: the decision to attend college within one's home state. I have found that merit aid moderately increases college attendance and shifts students from two-year schools toward four-year schools. The data also suggest that Georgia's merit aid program has increased the probability that a student will attend college in his or her home state. It remains to be determined whether merit aid keeps those students in state after they have completed their education, which is the ultimate goal of legislators who hope to use merit aid to staunch a perceived "brain drain." It also remains to be settled whether the merit programs have increased completed schooling, as opposed to attempted schooling.[33]

There are many other margins of behavior that merit aid may affect. Thoroughly addressing all of these potential effects would expand this lengthy chapter into a book. Here I will provide a necessarily brief discussion of these issues.

Additional Effects of Merit Aid on Individuals

A goal of merit aid is to increase academic effort in high school and college. The carrot of merit aid may cause students to work harder in high school and college in order to qualify for and then maintain their scholarships. This increased effort would be reflected in higher grades, test scores, and college attendance rates. However, observed academic performance may also improve for unintended reasons, in that pressure from students and parents on teachers may lead to grade inflation at both the high school and college level.

A small literature has examined the effect of merit aid on academic effort. Henry and Rubenstein (2002) show that the average high school GPA of freshmen entering the Georgia public universities rose from 2.73 in 1992 to 2.98 in 1999. In order to test whether this increase reflects greater effort or grade inflation, they examine SAT scores of entering freshmen, which are not subject to the same parental and student pressures as high school grades. The authors find that the average SAT score of entering freshmen in Georgia rose along with grades after HOPE was introduced, from 968 to 1010. While these results are suggestive, they are not conclusive, since this study examines only students in Georgia. It is quite possible that the increases in grades and SAT scores in Georgia are part of a broader secular trend rather than a consequence of HOPE.

Grades at the college level may also be affected by merit aid. First, students may work harder in their courses in order to keep their scholarships. This is an intended effect of the merit programs. Two unintended effects may also increase college grades. Professors may feel pressured to give higher grades so as not to threaten their students' continued eligibility for HOPE, and students may choose less demanding course loads for the same reason. Note that determining whether merit aid increases effort in college is inherently difficult. While the SAT is a well-accepted metric of the preparation of high school students, there is no equivalent instrument used to measure the achievement of college students.

Whether due to increased effort, less demanding course loads, or grade inflation, college grades at the University of Georgia are on the rise, with the proportion of freshman grades below a B dropping from 40 percent in 1993 to 27 percent in 1996 (Healy 1997). In New Mexico, Binder and Ganderton (2002) found support for the hypothesis that this is due, in part, to students taking fewer courses per semester, and therefore concentrating more effort on each course. They found support for the hypothesis that students respond to a merit program by taking on less-demanding course loads. They found that credit hours per semester dropped after the Success program was introduced. This work on New Mexico is the only conclusive empirical research regarding the question of effect of merit programs on academic effort in college.

Even the largest estimates of the effect of merit aid on schooling decisions suggest that the great majority of aid goes to inframarginal families—that is, to families whose schooling decisions are unaffected by their receipt of aid.[34] For these families, of interest is which margins of behavior *are* affected by the windfall receipt of scholarship funds. Do students use these funds to reduce the number of hours they work while in school? Do they increase their spending on leisure activities? Do families save the money, for retirement or later bequests to their children? One study suggests that at least part of the money is used for increased current consumption. Cornwell and Mustard (2002) examine new car registrations in Georgia and comparison states and find that car purchases rose faster in Georgia after the introduction of HOPE than before. They reach similar conclusions by examining the correlation between car registrations and the number of HOPE recipients at the county level within Georgia, finding an elasticity of new car registrations with respect to HOPE recipients of about 2 percent.

Impact of Merit Aid on Institutions

Dynarski (2000) compares the cost of attendance (room, board, tuition, and fees) at four-year schools in Georgia to that in the rest of the Southeast. She concludes that prices rose faster at public schools in Georgia than in comparable states after HOPE was introduced. Long (2002) subjects this question to a more thorough analysis, controlling for college selectivity and state characteristics. She separately examines the various components of the cost of attendance: tuition, room and board, and institutional financial aid. She finds that the increase in posted schooling prices in Georgia is fully explained by increases in room and board, which are not covered by HOPE. Further, she finds that institutional financial aid dropped as a result of the introduction of HOPE. Long hypothesizes that schools may have been under pressure from the state not to raise tuition, since any increases here would have to be met by increased HOPE outlays. Increases in room and board and drops in aid, however, could slip by with less attention. Private schools faced no such incentives to manipulate the form taken by their price increases, and accordingly their price increases are more evenly divided between tuition and room and board after HOPE.

Cornwell, Mustard, and Sridhar (2003) provide insight into how a merit aid program affects the composition of institutions of higher education. They examine enrollment data for two- and four-year colleges in Georgia and the rest of the Southeast. Their empirical results show how the changing schooling choices of Georgia's young people translated into major shifts in the demographic composition of Georgia's schools. They find that enrollment expanded after the introduction of HOPE, relative to enrollment in comparable states. They also find a sharp rise in the enrollment of black students at Georgia's four-year colleges. Given the relatively small increase in the college attendance rate of blacks found in the present analysis, their increased presence at Georgia's four-year colleges probably reflects a shifting of black students from out-of-state colleges to Georgia schools.

The Politics and Finance of Merit Aid

State merit aid programs grew during the 1990s, a period characterized by strong economic growth and overflowing state coffers. Recently, merit programs have begun to feel the pinch of the recent economic downturn. As state legislators struggle to balance their budgets, merit aid programs dependent upon legislative appropriations (Arkansas, California, Louisiana, Maryland, and Mississippi) find themselves in direct competition with other state priorities such as elementary and secondary education and health care. Arkansas, the first state to introduce a broad-based merit aid program, has temporarily closed the program to new enrollees. Although current scholarship recipients can renew their awards, no new students are being admitted to the program. Funding for Louisiana's program barely avoided the chopping block during the state's last legislative session.

Those merit programs with committed revenue streams have been relatively buffered from the economic and political effects of the recession. Six states (Florida, Georgia, New Mexico, West Virginia, South Carolina, and Kentucky) fund their programs with revenues from a state lottery, while two (Nevada and Michigan) use funds from the tobacco litigation settlement. With their dedicated funding sources, merit aid in these states is not vulnerable to legislators seeking to cut spending in the face of sinking tax revenues. This puts merit aid in a unique position, since other sources of funding for higher education at the state level are not protected in the same way. For example, public universities are experiencing leaner times this fiscal year as their state appropriations are reduced. Aid for low-income students is also vulnerable. West Virginia's need-based aid program could not deliver scholarships to all those low-income students who were eligible during the 2002–2003 academic year. The same year, the state's new merit program, which has no income cap, was launched with full funding.

A similar dynamic has emerged at the federal level. The fastest-growing subsidies for college students—tax credits, savings tax incentives, and loans—are programs whose funding is not contingent upon legislative appropriation. By contrast, spending on the Pell Grant program, which funds the most needy students, is determined by annual legislative appropriation.

While lottery funding protects merit aid funding from downturns in tax revenue and associated drops in appropriations, using lotteries to fund merit scholarship is a particularly regressive form of redistribution. The high-achieving college students who receive merit funds are relatively likely to be white and from upper-income families. Lottery spenders, by contrast, tend to be disproportionately concentrated in the bottom of the income distribution. Through both the revenue and spending channels, then, lottery-funded merit programs are regressive in their impact.

Why have merit aid programs spread so rapidly and maintained such strong political support? One possibility is that merit aid is a politically astute way to build support for spending on postsecondary education. Consider three alternatives for subsidizing college: merit aid, subsidized public tuition, and need-based aid. Merit aid has a political advantage over low tuition in that it has a high profile. Parents (voters) generally do not understand that the public university tuition they pay is kept artificially low by state appropriations to the schools. As a result, they may be unsympathetic to legislative efforts to increase funding through this route. If, instead, their child receives a "scholarship" that pays for tuition, the perceived benefit is personal and immediate, inducing political support for the spending. This gives merit- and need-based aid a political edge over tuition subsidies as politically viable methods of subsidizing college costs.

A second dynamic gives merit aid an edge over the other subsidy options. Since students "earn" merit aid, families may feel a more personal connection to the program and fight for its continuation. In this way, a merit program is akin to Social Security: In both cases, voters are fiercely supportive of transfers that they perceive as earned rewards rather than unconditional entitlements.

A third political advantage of merit aid, again held in common with Social Security, is that it is broad based in its constituency. In most states, students of any income level qualify for a merit scholarship as long as they earn the required grades. All families are therefore potential recipients of, and political supporters of, merit aid scholarships. By contrast, the bulk of need-based aid flows to a relatively narrow slice of the population. The price of this highly progressive spending on need-based aid is that many voters do not perceive themselves as its potential beneficiaries. William Julius Wilson (1987) and Theda Skocpol (1991) have argued that robust welfare states are characterized by benefits that are widely available and, therefore, widely supported. They argue that means-tested antipoverty programs are politically weak because their scope is narrow. A similar dynamic could explain strong political support for merit-based aid paired with weak political support for need-based aid.

Do these political realities indicate that a progressive aid system is politically unviable? Skocpol and Wilson point out that politically popular "universal" programs can provide political cover for redistributive transfers. As Social Security shows, a universal program can be layered with transfers that channel extra dollars toward those with greater need. This does not necessarily require new spending, as existing need-based programs could simply be relabeled in a way that enhances their political viability. For example, federal need-based grants could be delivered to needy students through the tax system by making the Hope and Lifetime Learning tax credits refundable.[35] This would eliminate one layer of paperwork (the FAFSA) yet allow aid eligibility to still be determined with the detailed financial information that is provided in tax filings. More important, funding for low-income students would be shifted into a program with broad-based political appeal and a guaranteed funding stream.

Conclusion

This paper has examined how merit aid programs in seven states have affected an array of schooling decisions, with particular attention to how the effects have varied by race and ethnicity. I find that merit aid programs typically increase the attendance probability of college-age youths by 5 to 7 percentage points. The programs are therefore effective at getting more students into college. In fact, as I discuss presently, the merit programs appear to be *more* effective than need-based aid at achieving this goal.

The merit programs also shift students toward four-year schools and away from two-year schools. Why? Four-year colleges are far more expensive than two-year colleges, but merit aid programs generally reduce the direct cost (tuition and required fees) of each option to zero. It is therefore expected that a greater proportion of students would choose the four-year option than they would in the absence of merit aid. An open question is whether this shift toward four-year colleges is socially beneficial. Four-year colleges are more expensive to run than two-year colleges, so a shift toward these schools will increase the total cost of educating college students. Further, marginal students who cannot handle the rigors of a four-year college may drop out of school altogether, whereas at a two-year institution they may have received the support they needed to persist. A countervailing factor is that some students who would not have considered going on for a BA will do so once they are enrolled in a four-year school.[36] The current analysis does not allow us to address which of these effects dominates.

The merit programs also appear to close racial and ethnic gaps in schooling, at least in three of the four states whose programs are old enough to allow analysis by race. Merit aid programs in Arkansas, Florida, and Mississippi have closed gaps, with Georgia's the only program to widen them. I attribute the Georgia program's unique distributional effect to its relatively stringent academic requirements and a recently eliminated provision that channeled the most generous scholarships to higher-income students. This leaves open the question, however, of why merit aid does not simply have a race-*neutral* effect on schooling in states that do not have Georgia's unusual provisions.

One possible explanation for the role of merit aid in closing gaps in schooling is the simplicity and transparency of these programs. First, these programs are well publicized, and knowledge among potential recipients is unusually high; one survey found that 70 percent of Georgia high school freshmen could name the HOPE program without prompting, while 59 percent could identify its eligibility requirements (Henry, Harkreader, Hutcheson, and Gordon 1998). Second, unlike need-based aid, merit aid programs have minimal application procedures, and the applicant knows at the time of application both whether he is eligible and the amount of the award. By contrast, need-based aid requires that the applicant complete a complicated set of forms and wait for months to find out the actual award amount, which is a complicated function of family finances.

Collecting information about college costs and completing application forms may be particularly challenging to parents for whom English is a second language or who have not gone to college themselves. A program with low transaction and information costs may therefore find a particularly large response among nonwhite, low-income populations. This strong response among the eligible may more than compensate for the fact that a smaller proportion of nonwhites meet the academic requirements of merit aid.

This interpretation of the present results is consistent with a set of studies that have shown little effect of the need-based Pell Grant on schooling decisions (e.g., Kane 1995; Hansen 1983) but a large effect of simpler, more transparent subsidy programs (e.g., Dynarski [2003] on the Social Security student benefit program and Kane [1994] on tuition prices). Kane and Hansen both find no impact of the need-based Pell Grant on college attendance. By contrast, Kane, in his 1994 study, finds that tuition prices have a substantial impact on college attendance. Dynarski finds that the Social Security student benefit program, which had minimal application requirements, had a large impact on college attendance and completed schooling.

Whereas a benefit of a program with few paperwork requirements is that it may move more youths into school, a cost is the loss of targeting. Unlike the Pell Grant, a merit aid program subsidizes many middle- and upper-income students. A merit aid program is therefore relatively more costly to run than need-based aid. However, a merit aid program is no more costly than subsidized public tuition prices, which also benefit students regardless of income. Further, as was discussed earlier in this chapter, merit aid has a substantial advantage over both need-based aid and subsidized tuition in that it has a broad and loyal base of political support in states that have introduced the programs.

Notes

1. Calculated from data in National Center for Education Statistics (1998a, table 314).
2. As I will discuss later in the paper, this figure varies quite dramatically by race and ethnicity. Source: Author's calculations from the 1997 National Longitudinal Survey of Youth (NLSY). This is the share of students with a *senior year* GPA of at least 3.0 and so is probably an upper bound on the share of students who achieve this GPA for their entire high school career. Unfortunately, NLSY does not contain GPA data for the entire high school career.
3. As the paper will discuss, the merit programs require that a high level of academic performance be maintained in college. In Georgia, a GPA of 3.0 must be maintained in college, a considerably higher hurdle than a 3.0 in high school.
4. Two-year colleges are generally cheaper than four-year colleges. Most merit aid programs make them both free.
5. The eligibility estimates are based on national data from the NLSY97. Many of the states listed in table 1 do not have enough observations in the NLSY97 to allow state-specific estimates of the share of students whose GPA qualifies them for their state's merit program. For all states, therefore, I use the national grade distribution to impute the share in a state that meets the eligibility criteria. When available, state-level data on the ACT and SAT are used to measure the share of students who meet these criteria. Note that these estimates are used only to choose the merit programs to be analyzed; they are not used in the paper's regression analyses.
6. The high school GPA requirement is waived for those enrolled in certificate programs at technical institutes. For high school seniors graduating after 2000, only courses in English, math, social studies, science, and foreign languages count toward the GPA requirement.

7. As a result of this provision and the scaling back of the state's need-based State Student Incentive Grants (SSIGs), some low-income students have actually seen their state aid reduced since HOPE was introduced (Jaffe 1997). This contemporaneous shift in SSIG spending has the potential to contaminate the paper's estimates. However, SSIG spending was so miniscule—$5.2 million in 1995, before the program was scaled back—that the impact of its elimination on the estimates is likely to be inconsequential.

8. In 1995, only 3.7 percent of dependent students from families with incomes over $40,000 received federal grant aid, while 57 percent of those from families with income under $20,000 did so (National Center for Education Statistics 1998a).

9. Alternatively, we could make use of the sharp discontinuities in the eligibility requirements to estimate the effect of merit aid from a single cohort. Kane (2003) uses this approach in an evaluation of California's CalGrant program, comparing the college attendance of those very slightly above and very slightly below the grade point cutoff. This approach requires very large samples; Kane uses an administrative data set that is a near-census of potential college entrants.

10. Papers that use college-based surveys in this way include Long (2002) and Cornwell, Mustard, and Sridhar (2003), both of which evaluate the Georgia HOPE Scholarship.

11. The U.S. Department of Education's longitudinal surveys of the high school cohorts of 1972, 1982, and 1992 contain similarly rich data. But because each survey contains a single cohort, we cannot use these data to observe schooling decisions in a given state both before and after merit aid is introduced.

12. California's program is not among the programs discussed in this chapter, as it is relatively narrow in its scope due to income provisions that exclude many middle- and upper-income youth.

13. This formulation ignores any heterogeneity in π, the effect of the offer of aid on those who are eligible. It is almost certain that this effect is not homogeneous. For example, the offer of aid will probably have a different effect on those whose grades place them just on the margin of eligibility and those whose grades are so strong that they are well within this margin.

14. These youths appear on their parents' CPS record and so can be linked to parental data. Other youths will show up in the CPS as members of their own households.

15. Cameron and Heckman (1999) discuss this point.

16. We cannot restrict the analytical sample to this subset because, as discussed earlier, whether a youth is on his or her parents' record is correlated with whether he or she is in college.

17. That is, I calculate the prediction error for each state-year and divide it by the predicted value for that state-year. I take the average of these normed, state-year errors separately for the Southeastern United States and the entire United States, in both cases excluding Georgia. Each state-year is treated as a single observation; I have not weighted by population. The Georgia series is substantially more volatile than those of the Southeast and United States; however, any state's error will look volatile compared to averages for the region and country. See figure 3 for an example of an equally volatile state.

18. The standard error is substantially smaller, however, than that in Dynarski (2000), which conservatively corrected standard errors for correlation at the state-year level. Bertrand, Duflo, and Mullainathan (2002) conclude that, in this type of application, the appropriate correction is for correlation at the state level.

19. I have also tested the inclusion of the interaction of having a merit program in one's own state and having a merit program in a neighboring state. The interaction is never large or significant, and its inclusion does not affect the paper's estimates.

20. The time trends are estimated using pre-1993 data.

21. Note that the coefficients for the four schooling options do not sum to the overall attendance effect. This is because the type of school is unknown for some students, who appear as college attenders but not as attending a specific type of school.

22. Author's estimates from the CPS. Note that this refers to the nominal income distribution. This is appropriate, since the Georgia rules were written in nominal rather than real terms.

23. These figures for the share with income below $50,000 may appear high. This is because the unit of observation is not the family but the child. Since lower-income families have more children, the distribution of family income within a sample of children has a lower mean and median than the distribution of family income within a sample of families.

24. Dynarski (2000) develops a model of schooling choice that demonstrates this ambiguity. Dynarski (2002) reviews the evidence on the relative price elasticities of the schooling of low- and upper-income youths.

25. I would prefer to separately examine effects on blacks and Hispanics. I have attempted to do so, but the Hispanic results are too imprecisely estimated to be informative.

26. When time trends are included, they are estimated separately by state and race/ethnicity. Trends are estimated for four separate groups: (1) non-Hispanic whites in Georgia; (2) non-Hispanic whites in the

rest of the Southern nonmerit states; (3) blacks and Hispanics in Georgia; and (4) blacks and Hispanics in the rest of the nonmerit Southern states.

27. An exception is the study by Binder and Ganderton (2002), which examined the effect of New Mexico's merit program. They conclude that New Mexico Success has not affected the college attendance rate but, like HOPE, has shifted students toward four-year schools.

28. These figures refer to the national ACT distribution, which has a mean of 21. The black and Hispanic distributions have lower means, of 16.9 and 19, respectively. Fewer members of these groups will meet the state ACT cutoffs.

29. In this specification, a simple merit dummy will not properly identify the effect of the merit aid program, as such an approach would inappropriately attribute part of the aid-induced change to the trend. We can solve this problem by replacing the merit dummy with either a separate time trend or year effects after merit aid is introduced in a state. Wolfers and Stevenson (forthcoming) use this approach to estimate the effect of divorce law reform, which occurred in different states in different years.

30. In the analysis of each program, four preprogram trends are estimated: two for white non-Hispanics (one for the treatment state and one for the control states) and two for blacks/Hispanics (one for the treatment state and one for the control states).

31. Georgia recently eliminated this aspect of its program. As more data become available, it will be of interest to examine whether this change has altered the distributional impact of HOPE.

32. This is the income cutoff for a family of four. Median income for a family of four in Arkansas is $45,000, so a large share of students falls under these income guidelines.

33. Data limitations, rather than conceptual difficulties, hamper the analysis of this particular margin of behavior. At a minimum, we require data on the completed schooling of adults, along with information about the state in which they graduated high school. As of 2002, these data are not available in any survey large enough for informative analysis of the existing merit programs. The 2000 Census microdata may prove useful in this context, and I am currently examining this question using these data.

34. It is important to note that merit aid is not unique in this way. Estimates of the effects of other forms of student aid also indicate that aid largely goes to those whose observable schooling decisions are unaffected by the receipt of aid. Targeting of subsidies is a classic topic of public economics; there is no transfer program that is 100 percent effective in limiting its subsidy to those whose decisions are contingent on the receipt of the subsidy.

35. Those who assail the need-based aid system for its complex application process will probably be horrified by this suggestion, as the federal tax system is also notoriously complex. But the Earned Income Tax Credit has proved to be an effective mechanism for transferring money to low-income families, and a refundable education tax credit has the potential to do the same for low-income students.

36. Rouse (1995) addresses the effect of community colleges on college entry and completion.

References

Bertrand, Marianne, Esther Duflo, and Sendil Mullainathan. 2002. How much should we trust differences-in-differences estimates? NBER Working Paper no. 8841. Cambridge, Mass.: National Bureau of Economic Research.

Binder, Melissa, and Philip Ganderton. 2002. Incentive effects of New Mexico's merit-based state scholarship program: Who responds and how? In *Who should we help? The negative social consequences of merit scholarships* (report by the Civil Rights Project), ed. Donald Heller and Patricia Marin, 41–56. Cambridge, Mass.: Harvard University Civil Rights Project.

Cameron, Stephen, and James Heckman. 1999. Can tuition policy combat rising wage inequality? In *Financing college tuition: Government politics and educational priorities*, ed. Marvin Kosters, 76–124. Washington, D.C.: American Enterprise Institute.

Cornwell, Christopher, and David Mustard. 2002. Merit-based college scholarships and car sales. University of Georgia, Department of Economics. Manuscript.

Cornwell, Christopher, David Mustard, and Deepa Sridhar. 2003. The enrollment effects of merit-based financial aid: Evidence from Georgia's HOPE Scholarship program. University of Georgia, Department of Economics. Manuscript.

Dee, Thomas, and Linda Jackson. 1999. Who loses HOPE? Attrition from Georgia's college scholarship program. *Southern Economic Journal* 66 (2): 379–390.

Dynarski, Susan. 2000. HOPE for whom? Financial aid for the middle class and its impact on college attendance. *National Tax Journal* 53 (3): 629–661.

———. 2002. The behavioral and distributional consequences of aid for college. *American Economic Review* 82 (2): 279–285.

———. 2003. Does aid matter? Measuring the effect of student aid on college attendance and completion. *American Economic Review* 93 (1): 279–288.

Hansen, W. Lee. 1983. The impact of student financial aid on access. In *The crisis in higher education*, ed. Joseph Froomkin, 84–96. New York: Academy of Political Science.

Healy, Patrick. 1997. HOPE scholarships transform the University of Georgia. *The chronicle of higher education*, November 7, 1997, A32.

Henry, Gary, Steve Harkreader, Philo A. Hutcheson, and Craig S. Gordon. 1998. Hope longitudinal study, first-year results. Georgia State University, Council for School Performance. Unpublished manuscript.

Henry, Gary, and Ross Rubenstein. 2002. Paying for grades: Impact of merit-based financial aid on educational quality. *Journal of Policy Analysis and Management* 21 (1): 93–109.

Jaffe, Greg. 1997. Free for all: Georgia's scholarships are open to everyone, and that's a problem. *Wall Street Journal*, June 2, 1.

Kane, Thomas. 1994. College entry by blacks since 1970: The role of college costs, family background, and the returns to education. *Journal of Political Economy* 102 (5): 878–911.

———. 1995. Rising public college tuition and college entry: How well do public subsidies promote access to college? NBER Working Paper no. 5164. Cambridge, Mass.: National Bureau of Economic Research.

———. 2003. A quasi-experimental estimate of the impact of financial aid on college-going. NBER Working Paper no. 9703. Cambridge, Mass.: National Bureau of Economic Research.

Long, Bridget Terry. 2002. Merit-based financial aid and college tuition: The case of Georgia's HOPE scholarship. Harvard University, Graduate School of Education. Unpublished manuscript.

National Center for Education Statistics, U.S. Department of Education. 1998a. *Digest of education statistics*. Washington, D.C.: Government Printing Office.

———. 1998b. *State comparisons of education statistics: 1969–70 to 1996–97*. Washington, D.C.: Government Printing Office.

Rouse, Cecilia. 1995. Democratization or diversion? The effect of community colleges on educational attainment. *Journal of Business and Economic Statistics* 13 (2): 217–224.

Skocpol, Theda. 1991. Targeting within universalism: Politically viable policies to combat poverty in the United States. In *The urban underclass*, ed. Christopher Jencks and Paul Peterson, 411–436. Washington, D.C.: Brookings Institution.

Wilson, William Julius. 1987. *The truly disadvantaged*. Chicago: University of Chicago Press.

Wolfers, Justin, and Betty Stevenson. Forthcoming. 'Til death do us part: The effect of divorce laws on suicide, domestic violence and intimate homicide. *Journal of Political Economy*.

CHAPTER 43
RACE-CONSCIOUS STUDENT FINANCIAL AID: CONSTRUCTING AN AGENDA FOR RESEARCH, LITIGATION, AND POLICY DEVELOPMENT[1]

EDWARD P. ST. JOHN, BRITANY AFFOLTER-CAINE, AND ANNA S. CHUNG

The *Gratz* and *Grutter* decisions did not settle issues related to the legality of race-conscious strategies for outreach and student aid (Ancheta, 2006; Banks, 2006). Programs that are race exclusive may be especially vulnerable, although there still may be a sound basis for defense. Changes in college prices resulting from the decline in federal need-based grant aid (Advisory Committee on Student Financial Assistance, 2002), the rise of state merit programs (Heller & Marin, 2002), and the emergence of targeted, market-oriented grant aid as tools in institutional enrollment management (McPherson & Schapiro, 1997) have increased inequality in the opportunity to enroll in college across racial groups since 1980 (St. John, 2003). This condition has only been partially mitigated by race-conscious aid programs;[2] however, the extent to which the legal challenges to race-conscious aid awards as targeted[3] forms of grant aid, actually dismantle these programs, it will be increasingly important to adapt other forms of aid (including other merit and targeted aid programs) to ensure diversity in enrollment in institutions whose missions align with this goal.

This chapter examines how research can inform advocates of equal educational opportunity about: 1) responses to legal challenges to race-conscious aid; and 2) the redesign of merit and targeted grant programs to improve diversity and equalize opportunity. We examine federal, state, and institutional student aid in relation to the gap in enrollment opportunity and the role of race-conscious student aid. The review of federal student aid provides context for the legal issues facing states and institutions that choose to respond to legal challenges to race-conscious aid programs. The sections on state and institutional aid provide case studies of legal analyses related to financial aid and educational opportunities across race/ethnic groups. The conclusion discusses how research can inform legal and policy agendas for improving diversity in higher education. The policy agenda for advocates of equal opportunity must recognize the complexities of public finance introduced by the new emphasis on privatization[4] of public higher education (Priest & St. John, 2006).

Federal Student Aid

It is sad as well as ironic that the federal efforts to desegregate colleges, dating back to a series of U.S. Supreme Court decisions in the 1940s and 1950s, started in earnest in 1977 after the *Adams* decisions ordered states to develop plans for desegregation in 19 states with historically black colleges (St. John, 1998; Williams, 1988), but were quickly followed by the Middle Income Students Assistance Act of 1978 (MISAA)—legislation that is symbolic of the shift away from equal opportunity as the goal of federal student financial aid programs. Perhaps the most important indicator, with respect to the goal of ensuring equal educational opportunity in the United States, is whether the financial aid strategies used by states and the federal government have improved or accentuated the gap in college enrollment rates across groups. The review of the government role starts with a review of trends in enrollment, then examines changes in federal and state student aid policies.

The Opportunity Gap

A substantial enrollment gap opened after the maximum Pell award for individuals failed to keep pace with rising college costs.[5] This gap persisted through the 1980s and 1990s. Compared to whites, the differential was 7.7 percentage points for African Americans and 11.7 for Hispanics in 1990. These differentials had lessened only slightly by 2000 (to 4.8 and 7.9 percentage points, respectively). In short, there has been a slight reduction in the gap since 1985, the period of the most severe inequality, but the equality of the mid-1970s has not been restored.

Federal Pell grants played a crucial role in equalizing educational opportunity from 1973 until 1978, when financial aid for middle-income students became a priority. And Pell grants rapidly declined in their purchasing power after they were fully implemented, as is evident in Figure 2. In 1975 the maximum Pell award actually exceeded the average tuition in public colleges, but the half-cost provisions limited the maximum award to half of the total cost of attendance, so many public college students did not get these awards. As the purchasing power of Pell decreased, these cost provisions were dropped from the Pell program.

A comparison of Figures 1 and 2 illustrates that the rise in the unfunded Pell gap corresponds directly with the growth in inequality of enrollment opportunity. The decline in the purchasing power of Pell grants explains most of the increase in the gap during this period: the reforms in K-12 education and growth of encouragement programs, the policies thought to be linked to access, simply are not viable explanations (St. John, 2003; St. John, 2006). However, as is evident from the review of other policies below, state and institutional financing strategies also contributed modestly to the increased inequality.

The shift in funding students, especially through the development of loan programs that use private capital, continues to be a major stimulus for privatization. To deconstruct the underlying issues in this shift, we examine trends in funds for students through loan programs, funds through federal grants, and the purchasing power of Pell grants (award maximums in relation to costs of attending four-year colleges).

Federal Funding of Grant Programs

Historically, before the Education Amendments of 1972, the federal government used targeted, specially directed grants (Finn, 1978; St. John, 2003) as the primary means of financing students. The GI Bill of Rights and subsequent veteran benefit programs targeted ex-servicemen, and the Social Security Survivor Benefits targeted dependents of deceased working people. Both programs were funded at substantially higher levels than any other federal programs before 1975, when the Basic Educational Opportunity Grants (now the Pell program) was fully implemented. The 1964 War on Poverty legislation funded Work Study programs and college access efforts, and the 1965 Higher Education Act marked the federal government's move into grants for the poor. The shift away from targeted grants to need-based grants only took hold as the major federal role in student financial aid after 1973, and Pell grants were not fully implemented for another three years.

The Pell Grant program has been the major federal need-based grant program since it was implemented, as Basic Educational Opportunity Grants, in 1973. Pell Grants provide a need-based, voucher-like grant awarded directly to students by the federal government. The college disburses funds, but the amount of funds colleges receive and disburse through Pell is dependent on the number of low-income students who enroll.

Other than Pell, the federal government funds Leveraging Educational Assistance Partnerships (LEAP), Supplemental Educational Opportunity Grants (SEOG), and other grants. SEOG is an artifact of an earlier period when the federal government gave block grants to colleges as a means of funding students. LEAP is funded at one-third by the federal government and two-thirds by states. It is woefully under funded, given its potential for improving unequal opportunity. If LEAP had

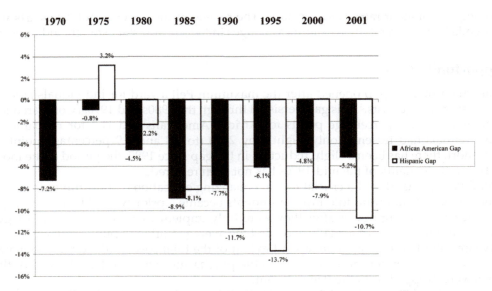

Figure 1   Differentials in college enrollment rates for Hispanic and African American compared to white 18- to 24-year-old high school graduates.

Note: Adapted from St. John, 2003; Data from *Digest of Education Statistics 2002*, p. 10, Table 4.

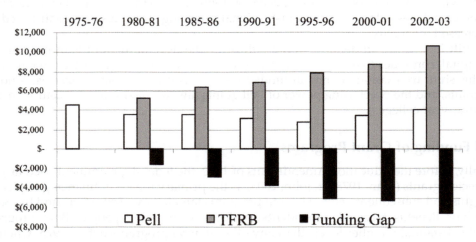

Figure 2   The gap between the actual maximum Pell award and university attendance costs (tuition, fees, room and board).

Data Source: TFRB data from Table 5b; Pell data from Table 7, *Trends in Student Aid,* College Board Current dollars adjusted to 2003 constant dollars (CPI 2003 annual). TFRB not available for 1975.

(Figure published previously in St. John, Tuttle, & Musoba, 2006.)

been appropriately reconstructed, almost two million students could have gone to college in the 1990s (St. John, Chung et al., 2002).

The story of federal funding for Pell (Figure 3) is far from compelling. Funding rose slightly during the 1980s, from about $5 billion in 1980 to nearly $7 billion in 1990–91, as the Reagan administration retargeted the program on low-income students. One of the ironies of this period was that it was possible to redirect funds from middle-income to low-income students by lowering the maximum award (St. John & Byce, 1982). Reductions in the award maximum did not hurt low-income students who enrolled in four-year colleges in the early 1980s because there was a half-cost provi-

Millions of constant dollars (2002 base year)

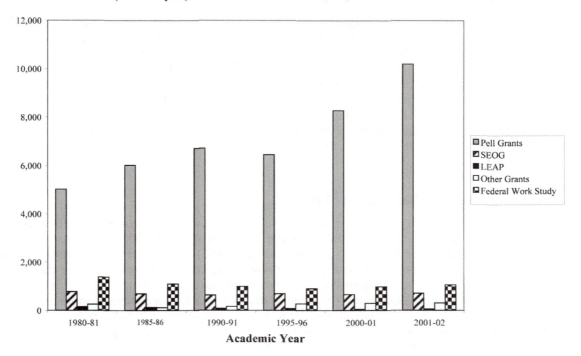

Figure 3   Federal grant aid for postsecondary education.

Source: *Trends in Student Aid 2002*, Table 2, p. 7, Appendix B, p. 19. The College Board, 2002.

Note: Dollar amounts for 2001–02 are estimates. Figure from St. John & Wooden (2006).

sion: it was not possible to secure a grant of more that half the cost of attendance, and during this time public colleges still had low tuition. However, as tuition rose, the half-cost provision was dropped (St. John, 2003).

Funding for Pell actually dropped during the early Clinton years as the federal government, sadly, allowed inequalities in enrollment opportunities to grow (Ellwood & Kane, 2000; St. John, 2003). There has been some increase in funding for Pell in recent years, growing to more than $10 billion in 2001–02, indicating that the G. W. Bush administration has been more responsive to the equity issue than the Clinton administration was. However, the increase in funding for Pell does not mean that low-income students have been better able to pay the costs of attending, as was noted in the discussion of the purchasing power of Pell above.

Federal Privatization and Unequal Opportunity

Privatization of public higher education may have been stimulated by federal policy, including the extensive use of private capital for college students who borrow to pay the higher costs of attending college (St. John & Wooden, 2006). The growth in federal loans, coupled with the decline in the purchasing power of Pell grants, has been a major catalyst for the growth in educational inequality since 1980. However, states are more directly responsible because they did not adapt to these new conditions in ways that maintain or improve equity in opportunity to enroll in higher education. Quite the opposite: state financing strategies have worsened the inequalities in opportunity since 1980, rather than reconstructing their financing policies in ways that enhance equity. Race-conscious aid in states and institutions is appropriately viewed in this changing context of state finance, as well as of being an artifact of changes in federal policy.

State Financing and Equal Opportunity

State financial strategies play an important role in equalizing access to higher education for diverse groups, especially for low-income students and people of color. In addition, the structural capacity of state systems (i.e., the number of seats available at public four-year, public two-year and private colleges as a percentage of the population) also influences access to postsecondary education, along with college enrollment levels, rates and persistence. That is, students cannot earn a postsecondary degree if sufficient openings do not exist at postsecondary institutions regardless of financial aid levels.

It is important to consider the role of state capacity in relation to state finance strategies when considering financial inequality in access. After reviewing changes in the state role, a case of the Michigan Merit Program is reviewed, to illustrate how research might inform litigation and policy development.

Understanding the Challenge in States

A recent study of financial access examined the statistical associations between state finance strategies and college enrollment rates in the 1990s (St. John, Chung, et al., 2004). The study found the percentages of students enrolled in 1) private colleges and 2) public two-year colleges were positively associated with overall college enrollment rates, indicating that the capacity of the state system as a whole was crucial to expanding access to higher education. Enrolling in private colleges had a particularly strong association. It also found that funding for need-based and non-need grants were positively associated with enrollment rates, but need-based grants had a more substantial effect (the standardized coefficient was twice the size). Controlling for demographic variables, state tax rates, and student financial aid, tuition was not significantly associated with enrollment rates.

Historically, states developed publicly funded colleges as a means of expanding opportunity to higher education and, with awareness of this aim, most states maintained low tuition. In constant dollars, tuition was relative stable throughout the 1970s. But tuition began to soar in the 1980s due to cuts in federal need-based grants and in state funding for institution. In a tax cutting era, triggered by the 1978 passage of Proposition 13 in California and the Reagan tax cuts, costs were shifted to students, sometimes rapidly during recessions when state revenue declined. While state officials in higher education agencies used to argue that funding colleges was necessary to ensure that residents had access to higher education, they now rationalize tuition increases (Mumper, 2001). With the advent of state need-based grant aid in the early 1970s, a more diverse pattern of public financing emerged. High tuition coupled with large grants was often considered more economical, and some states followed this strategy for expanding access. Minnesota has provided an excellent model for coordinating state subsidies to colleges, tuition, and student aid (Hearn & Anderson, 1989, 1995), but few states achieved this level of coordination. In spite of the great diversity in the financial strategies used by states, it is possible to consider a standard for state financing that promotes equal opportunity for high- and low-income students who are similarly qualified.

Coordination of Need-Based Grants with Other Finance Policies: Given the role of tuition and grants in determining financial access to postsecondary education for low-income students, it is important to ask: What standard of equity should be maintained in states? It has been proposed that setting funding for state need-based grants at a level equivalent to about one-quarter of revenue from public college tuition charges would significantly address the needs of low-income and lower-middle-income students (St. John, 2006; St. John, Chung, et al., 2004). This equity standard would apply to the state investment in need-based grants on top of Pell Grants, funded at current levels and adjusted for inflation. In addition, it would refer to the overall funding level for need-based grants and not the average award for a student. That is, states would fund need-based grants at a level of at least one-quarter of the average public college tuition charges, but any given student might receive need-based grants of more than that, depending on his or her financial need. The average award would equal about half the average tuition charge. The total grants—Pell, state, and institutional grants—plus loans at the legal limit for the neediest students should equal total cost of attendance. The equity standard provides a basis for defining the state share of grants, given rising tuition charges in public colleges.

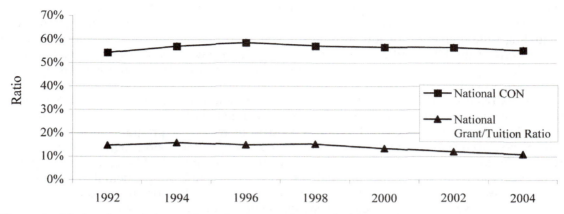

Figure 4   National trends in continuation rate and grant/tuition ratio.
Source: Calculated from NASSGAP reports and IPEDS data by authors.

When the equity standard is met, states can fund grants equaling need for low- and lower-middle-income students. Since states essentially save a dollar of general funds for each tuition dollar charged at public colleges, it is more economical for states to invest one quarter of the "tax savings" from privatization into need-based aid rather than simply lowering tuition for all, as a means of ensuring equalized opportunity. This standard appears reasonable and logical, given the foundation provided by Pell Grants.

Nationally there has been a slight decline in state funding for need-based grants in relation to tuition charges since 2000, along with a slight decline in college continuation rates (Figure 4). During the same period there was a corresponding decline in the continuation rate (the ratio of high school graduates in the spring to college freshmen in the next fall). Underrepresented students of color are more seriously affected by this pattern because a larger percentage of these student groups are from families with low incomes.

Merit Grants: If states provided sufficient need-based grants to meet financial need and equalize opportunity for college enrollment and persistence for equally prepared students, then there would not be a need to adjust state grant programs to remove prejudice in awards and to reduce gaps in opportunity. However, these inequalities are increased when total government grants (state and federal need-based grants) fall short of a reasonable equity standard in states.

The recent expansion of merit grants in states has been associated with increased inequality (Heller & Marin, 2004). Inequality in K-12 schools also adds to the inequality that underlies merit aid programs. One approach to adapting merit grant programs is to index merit measures by the high school (Goggin, 1999; St. John, Simmons, & Musoba, 2002). Indexing SAT scores for the high school (i.e., using the positive or negative differential between the individual and the school average in lieu of the SAT) predicts college success as well as the actual SAT, indicating that competition with peers is a good indicator of future success (St. John, Hu, et al., 2001). The case study below considers how new conceptions of merit might inform the reconstruction of state grant programs to ensure more equity in education opportunity.

The literature on merit grants has often included non-need grants in the same category as need-based aid. Some studies refer to the category as merit-based (e.g., Heller & Rasmussen, 2002), while others used the term non-need (mostly merit) to recognize the complexity of state reporting (e.g., St. John, Chung et al., 2004), but neither approach fully recognized the complexity of targeting grants to attract special groups, including minority and low-income students.

Targeted State Grants: Targeted state grant programs have also gained some attention in states in recent years. For example, Indiana's Twenty-first Century Scholars Program (St. John, Musoba, et al., 2002) has received attention from Congress (Advisory Committee on Student Financial Assistance, 2002), becoming the model for revision of the Higher Education Act. This Indiana program provides a small grant supplement to students who would have received aid anyway, increasing the total grant modestly and guaranteeing it will be linked to tuition. Fear of college costs can be minimized for low-income families. The central targeting feature of the Indiana program—guaranteeing aid equaling tuition charges for low-income students who prepare for college—was included in some versions of the HEA and has been implemented in a few other states, like Oklahoma and Texas. A similar program has recently been proposed in Wisconsin. These programs are appropriately treated as need-based grant aid.

Indiana's Twenty-first Century Scholars are reported as need-based in the National Association of State Grant Aid Programs (NASSGAP) surveys and would have been counted as part of the need-based aid in the trend analyses, which is one of the reasons why these programs have not grown as rapidly as non-need (mostly merit) grants. However, revising student aid programs to include this feature can be costly and it requires a long-term financial commitment, obligating states to pay for students years in the future. Other alternatives, such as targeting supplemental aid to minority groups with lower rates of enrollment and persistence, such as the Wisconsin Lawton program, also merit consideration as alternative means of equalizing opportunities.

Race-Conscious State Programs: Before leaping to the conclusion that race-conscious student financial aid can solve the problem of the growing gap in inequality, it is important to consider trends in the use of race-based student financial aid. Table 1 provides trend information in the number of states that have at least one race-conscious grant or scholarship program, as compiled from the NASSGAP surveys (1984–2003).

The NASSGAP surveys of state grants are important sources of information that have been used in most studies of state grant programs. These reports distinguish two forms of grants: need-based programs that make awards based on financial need, possibly in combination with other factors; and non-need grants, which are awards made on criteria other than financial need. While merit grants, such as Georgia's Hope Scholarships, comprise a substantial portion of the non-need grants, they are not the only form of aid lumped into this category. Race-conscious state grant programs

TABLE 1

Number of States with at Least One Publicly Funded Financial Aid Program that Was Race-, Sex-, or Disability-Conscious, 1984–2003

Population	84	85	86	87	88	89	90	91	92	93	94	95	96	97	98	99	00	01	02	03
African Americans	7	10	10	10	10	13	16	17	21	22	23	23	23	23	24	24	24	24	24	23
Hispanic	8	11	11	11	11	14	16	17	21	22	23	23	23	23	24	24	24	24	24	23
Women	0	1	1	1	1	1	2	2	2	2	2	2	2	2	2	2	1	1	1	1
Native American	13	15	15	15	15	17	19	20	24	25	26	26	26	26	27	27	27	27	26	25
Minority (multiple categories)	7	9	9	9	9	12	14	15	19	20	21	21	21	21	22	22	22	22	22	21
Minority (any and all race/sex conscious)	13	15	17	17	17	20	22	23	27	27	28	29	29	29	29	29	29	29	29	28
Disabled or dependents	4	4	5	5	5	5	5	5	5	5	5	3	3	3	3	3	3	3	3	3
Number of states	16	18	21	21	21	23	25	26	30	29	24	31	31	31	31	31	31	31	31	30

Source: These tables are based on data present in NASSGAP annual reports and state data (state statutes, financial aid coordinating boards, university system administrators and resources). Some dates are approximated based on available data, particularly if relatively old and terminated financial aid program.

Includes programs targeting either graduates or undergraduates. In some cases programs are counted as a single program even though they are funding both graduates and undergraduates when reporting of funds could not be disaggregated. In the cases where the same program was reported as two separate pools of funding, they are counted as individual programs.

Data for the academic year 1989–1990 were not available and were therefore approximated. The change in figures is due to detailed descriptions of programs available at financial aid coordinating boards that specified several programs were initiated in 1989.

Total is the number of states with at least one program that was race, sex or disability conscious. Since some state programs encompassed more than one underrepresented population, the total is not necessarily the sum of the columns.

that do not have a financial need component would be reported as non-need grants, even if they did not have any merit criteria. And other targeted programs, such as tuition equalization grants for state residents attending private colleges, would be reported as non-need. In contrast, targeted programs restricted to middle-school students who qualify for the federal lunch program (e.g., Indiana's Twenty-first Century Scholars) are reported as need-based because of the central role of financial need. These distinctions are important precisely because the dichotomies used in the past to distinguish among state grant programs may not be adequate to the task of building an understanding of targeted grant aid, especially race-conscious grants.

The number of states reporting they have programs that are either race-conscious or race-exclusive have grown steadily. In 1984, 16 states reported at least one program. Most of these states reported specialized programs for both African Americans and Native Americans. The total number of states reporting programs grew to 31 in 1996–2001. In 2003, 30 states reported having these programs even though legal challenges were being raised by this time.

It is also important to note that the number of race-exclusive grant programs also increased substantially during the period (see Table 2), as did the total number of programs. Most states with a program had more than one such program. Between 1984 and 2001 the number of race-exclusive programs grew from 22 to 55 and this number only dropped to 53 by 2003. In contrast the number of states that had race-sensitive programs grew from 5 in 1984 to 15 in 2000 and dropped to 12 by 2003.

These trends in the number of state programs that consider race as part of the award criteria reveals that the emphasis on race-conscious programs has increased during the period of privatization. The parallel between the growing inequality since 1980 and the rise in race-conscious grant programs is prima facie evidence that states at least implicitly recognize that the privatization process (i.e., shifting costs of higher education from taxpayers to students) added to the inequalities in educational opportunity. While implementation of these programs alone has not resolved the problems, since inequalities in educational opportunity persist, these programs may mitigate some effects of privatization on the disparity in opportunity.

TABLE 2

Number of Publicly Funded Financial Aid Programs That Are Race-, Sex-, or Disability-Exclusive or Sensitive, 1984–2003

	1984		1985		1990		1995		2000		2001		2002		2003	
Population	S	E	S	E	S	E	S	E	S	E	S	E	S	E	S	E
African Americans	3	9	3	14	7	29	8	39	8	40	8	39	9	37	8	37
Hispanic	3	9	3	15	6	31	8	38	8	40	8	39	10	37	8	37
Women	0	0	0	1	1	2	1	1	1	0	1	0	1	0	1	0
Native American	4	19	3	25	6	39	7	47	9	48	9	47	10	45	9	45
Minority (multiple categories)	4	9	3	15	7	29	9	36	8	38	8	37	9	35	8	35
Minority (any and all categories)	4	19	4	25	8	44	11	52	15	53	12	52	13	50	12	50
Disabled or dependents	1	3	1	3	1	5	0	4	0	3	0	3	0	3	0	3
Total programs	5	22	5	28	9	49	11	56	15	56	12	55	13	53	12	53

E refers to race-exclusive program. S refers to race-sensitive program.

Source: These tables are based on data present in NASSGAP annual reports and state data (state statutes, financial aid coordinating boards, university system administrators and resources). Some dates are approximated based on available data, particularly if relatively old and terminated financial aid program.

Research on the effects of race-conscious student grant programs is needed to build an understanding of the role they play in reducing inequalities caused by privatization. Such research can inform the legal and policy agendas of advocates of equal educational opportunity. If these programs eventually do not stand up to the equal rights claims currently being used by those in government and the non-profit sectors who litigate against race-conscious programs, then new policies must be crafted to remedy the inequalities created by the privatization process as implemented by the federal government and states.

State Contexts

A major challenge facing states that do not have adequate need-based grants is how to restructure student financial aid to reduce inequality. The best solution is to raise need-based grants to a level sufficient to at least equalize enrollment opportunity across income groups. Many states have used targeted grants for students of color as a partial remedy, but the future of this strategy is not certain. The alternative of redesigning merit grant programs also deserves consideration, a problem examined below.

Case Study 1: Research Informing Redesign of State Aid Programs

The most perplexing challenge facing states in their efforts to recraft public finance policies and grant programs is to address the competing arguments for raising standards and rewarding merit on the one hand, with arguments about equal educational opportunity on the other. In her commentary on the U.S. Supreme Court decisions in the Michigan cases, Lani Guinier (2003) argued that in the period ahead there is a need for more experimentation with alternative measures of merit. She argues that new approaches, like the Texas Top Ten Percent Plan, warrant further testing. One of the problems states face in the design of merit programs is that the conventional measures of merit do not fully recognize the unequal opportunities to prepare. Top ten percent programs have worked well in admissions, equalizing enrollment opportunities for prepared minority students (Chapa, 2006). The case study summarized below illustrates the potential of using alternative merit criteria in the redesign of state merit grant award programs.

The Michigan Merit Program:[6] The State of Michigan implemented the Michigan Merit Scholarship Program, making awards to students in the First Cohort (students in the high school class of 2000) based on scores on high school tests administered by the Michigan Educational Assessment Program (MEAP). The American Civil Liberties Union (ACLU), the National Association for the Advancement of Colored People (NAACP), and other groups brought suit against the State of Michigan based on the inequity in award distribution. Analyses for the plaintiffs demonstrated that the original method of awarding merit aid results in a distribution of student aid that is inequitable across racial/ethnic groups (Heller, 2001).

The method the State of Michigan used to award the Merit Scholarships appears to restrict opportunity for diverse groups in ways that penalize students for attending poor-quality schools. Indeed, when the fact that many college-qualified, low-income students cannot afford to attend is taken into account, the Michigan Merit Scholarship Program appears to discriminate against low-income students. The merit criteria in use at the time of litigation resulted in over awards to whites compared to their proportion of the population (see Table 3).

Therefore, it is desirable to modify the uses of MEAP tests in ways that provide an incentive for schools to make improvements in the academic preparation of students, but that do not discriminate against any particular group of students. Whites received 72% of the awards, but were only 53% of the high school population. In contrast, African Americans received 3% of the awards and were 12% of the population. There were similar disparities for other groups.

An alternative method for awarding merit aid involves creating a merit index that adjusts the award criteria to the quality of the high schools students attend. The idea of the merit index that adjusts standardized tests for high school quality was proposed as a more equitable approach for college admission (Goggin, 1999). The development of a merit index involves adjusting test scores and other merit criteria for the averages for the high schools students attend, then using these rankings in admissions decisions. This approach helps achieve greater racial balance because schools remain segregated in spite of court decisions in desegregation cases (Fossey, 1998, 2003).

Prior empirical tests of this method to date have focused on adjusting standardized test scores to refine admission policies. Initial analyses indicate that a merit index yields a more ethnically diverse population of admitted students than does the strict application of a standardized test, such as the SAT (St. John, Simmons, & Musoba, 2002). Further, a merit index that adjusts SAT scores for high school contexts predicts college success about as well as the SAT (St. John, Hu, & Weber, 2001).

While the extant research confirmed that the merit-index approach achieved the goals of rewarding merit in admissions while increasing diversity and equity, the method had not yet been extended to awarding merit aid. Conceptually, it had been previously argued that the same logic applied to merit aid (St. John, Simmons, & Musoba, 2002), but the Michigan case presented special problems relative to the implementation of a merit index. Specifically the legislation creating the program required that an assessment test be used that included consideration of the state tests. There was a range of interests among the plaintiffs that encouraged a broader assessment framework, but ultimately the proposal was constrained by the legislation. A two-stage analysis process is summarized below.

Stage 1: The alternative method of using a MEAP-Merit Index: There are a variety of ways to construct a MEAP-Merit Index that would adjust the rankings of students within their schools. Using school-based rankings—for either GPA or a combination of GPA and test scores—provides an adjustment for school context that does not penalize students for attending troubled schools. As a preliminary test of the merit-index approach, our initial paper used data files with the raw test scores and the award information to develop the following preliminary simulation. Table 4 presents the simulations of award ratios by group, had the state used a school-based ranking of MEAP scores, making awards to the top 25% of each high school's senior class.

As is evident from this simulation, the awards using these alternative merit criteria would have more closely reflected the race/ethnic composition of the population. For example, 58% of the awards would have gone to whites while 54% of the cohort was white. The percentage of African Americans who were eligible for merit awards would have increased to 11%, a percentage close to their share of the population. The distribution of awards for other groups would also have been similar to their representation in the population.

Stage 2: Analysis of a GPA-Merit Index: Based on this initial report, the litigants agreed to collect data from a sample of twenty percent of the state's high schools.[7] A random sample of twenty percent of the high schools was drawn within each type of locale in the state, as a means of ensuring representation of diverse types of schools.[8] For each senior, high schools were asked to provide information on ethnicity, cumulative GPA, and the MEAP scores. This data was adequate to test the alternative of using a GPA-Merit Index. The approach is similar conceptually to the Texas Top Ten Percent Plan.

While the sample mirrored the geographical distribution of high schools across the state, the responding high schools were not evenly distributed. The highest response rates were from high schools in cities and small towns, the types of schools that would benefit the most from alternative methods. A total of eight urban high schools were sampled and all responded, while 11 of the 14 high schools in small towns responded. In contrast, lowest response rates were from mid-sized cities (4 of 10 responses); and rural areas inside of large metropolitan areas (13 of 25 responses) were the areas that benefited the most from the original award criteria. A total of 14,356 students were included in the sample. The overall response rate (61.6%) was adequate, but it was necessary to adjust for the inconsistencies in reporting. The ethnic distribution of the sample differed slightly from the population, given these school responses.

The method used to adjust to these uneven response rates across local types was to compare awards using the original criteria for the MEAP[9] to awards using the GPA-Merit Index[10] with the sample population. This provided a means of judging whether the use of the GPA ranking would improve diversity of awards compared to the original award criteria.

TABLE 3

Actual Composition of Scholarship Qualification by Racial/Ethnic Group

		Native American	Asian/Pacific Islander	African American	Hispanic	White	Multiracial	Other	Missing	Total
Qualified	N	219	964	1,217	601	30,729	599	745	7,635	42,709
	%	0.5%	2.3%	2.8%	1.4%	71.9%	1.4%	1.7%	17.9%	100.0%
Otherwise	N	751	923	13,833	1,760	35,110	1,286	1,634	26,013	81,310
	%	0.9%	1.1%	17.0%	2.2%	43.2%	1.6%	2.0%	32.0%	100.0%
Total	N	970	1,887	15,050	2,361	65,839	1,885	2,379	33,648	124,019
	%	0.8%	1.5%	12.1%	1.9%	53.1%	1.5%	1.9%	27.1%	100.0%

Source: Data were collected by the State of Michigan in *White v. Enger.* Analyses by the lead author and C. G. Chung.

TABLE 4

Simulation of Racial/Ethnic Composition of Awardees, with Top 25% within Individual Schools (using at least one MEAP test)

		Native American	Asian/Pacific Islander	African American	Hispanic	White	Multiracial	Other	Missing	Total
Qualified	N	128	404	2,698	356	13,641	416	419	5,607	23,669
	%	0.5%	1.7%	11.4%	1.5%	57.6%	1.8%	1.8%	23.7%	100.0%
Not Qualified	N	728	1,076	10,276	1,499	36,773	1,128	1,592	16,660	69,732
	%	1.0%	1.5%	14.7%	2.1%	52.7%	1.6%	2.3%	23.9%	100.0%
Total	N	856	1,480	12,974	1,855	50,414	1,544	2,011	22,267	93,401
	%	0.9%	1.6%	13.9%	2.0%	54.0%	1.7%	2.2%	23.8%	100.0%

Source: Data were collected by the State of Michigan in *White v. Enger.* Analysis by the lead author and C. G. Chung.

When the original award criteria were used on the sample population (Table 5), the inequality in the distribution of awards was similar to the actual awards:

- American Indians represented 0.5% of the sample and 0.5% of the population that qualified under the original criteria.
- Asians represented 2.0% of the sample and 1.8% of the scholarship-qualified population.
- Blacks were 17.3% of the sample, but only 6.5% of the scholarship-qualified group.
- Whites were 77.9% of the sample and 89.9% of the scholarship-qualified group.
- Hispanics were 1.7% of the sample and 1.2% of the scholarship-qualified group.[11]

These results echo the findings from earlier analyses (e.g., Heller, 2001), indicating disproportional qualification across groups, especially for African Americans and whites. The simulations with the GPA-Merit Index estimated awards for 20%, 25%, 30%, and 35% of high school classes. These analyses provided a more balanced award distribution. The summary of the analysis of the 25% award level (Table 6) follows:

- American Indians and Alaska Natives were 0.5% of the sample and 0.3% of the scholarship-qualified group.
- Asians were 2.0% of the sample and 2.1% of the scholarship-qualified group.
- Blacks were 17.3% of the population and 16.4% of the scholarship-qualified group.
- Whites were 77.9% of the sample and 79.5% of the scholarship-qualified group.
- Hispanics were 1.7% of the sample and 1.4% of the scholarship-qualified group.

The Potential for Redesign

These simulations illustrate that it is possible to redesign the award criteria for merit programs in ways that recognize the differences in educational opportunities available to students.

The success of the Texas Top Ten Percent Plan in diversifying campuses without reducing student success, as measured by persistence, illustrates that changing award criteria did not change educational quality or impair academic success. In the Michigan merit case, the plaintiffs eventually lost the case because *intentional* discrimination could not be proven even though inequality in awards was evident. Changing merit grant programs to provide incentives for all students is fairer, relative to the equity standard, than the current system. Clearly the current approach to merit awards in Michigan favors students who attend better quality schools, but it does not necessarily reward students with the highest merit relative to their peers. The reconstruction of state merit grant programs represents an alternative that should be tried out in practice.

Reconstructing State Policy

The research on state grant programs consistently shows a relationship between funding for state grants and opportunity for enrollment for diverse students. Targeted programs like Indiana's Twenty-first Century Scholars Program enable more low-income students to enroll in college, while the reconstruction of merit programs using alternative merit criteria can increase the fairness in the ways these awards are made. These sorts of adjustments are necessary within the current system of public finance to overcome the inequalities that have emerged as a consequence of privatization of higher education.

There are no published evaluation studies of race-conscious state grant programs, although some studies are in development. It is highly likely that such studies will find a positive association between state funding for grants and both enrollment and persistence opportunities for students of color. Such findings are likely because they would be consistent with a large body of research (Heller, 1997; St. John, 2003). Questions remain about whether race-conscious aid could stand up to legal challenges, especially if research demonstrates that these grant programs improve diversity.

TABLE 5

MEAP Qualification by Ethnicity, Using Traditional Award Criteria

	American Indian or Alaska Native		Asian		Black		Native Hawaiian or Other Pacific Islander		White		Hispanic		Unknown		Total	
	N	%	N	%	N	%	N	%	N	%	N	%	N	%	N	%
Qualified *	20	0.5	77	1.8	277	6.5	1	0.0	3,852	89.9	50	1.2	6	0.1	4,283	100.0
Otherwise **	58	0.6	206	2.0	2,201	21.9	7	0.1	7,338	72.8	195	1.9	68	0.7	10,073	100.0
Total	78	0.5	283	2.0	2,478	17.3	8	0.1	11,190	77.9	245	1.7	74	0.5	14,356	100.0

* Qualified if the performances are 1 or 2 in all four 2001 MEAP tests (Math, Science, Reading and Writing).

** "Otherwise" includes those who are not qualified, who do not take all four tests and who are missing in test results.

Source: Data were collected by the State of Michigan in *White v. Enger.* Analysis by the lead author and C. G. Chung.

TABLE 6

Top 25% of GPA by Ethnicity Using GPA-Merit Index

	American Indian or Alaska Native		Asian		Black		Native Hawaiian or Other Pacific Islander		White		Hispanic		Unknown		Total	
	N	%	N	%	N	%	N	%	N	%	N	%	N	%	N	%
Top 25%	10	0.3	71	2.1	568	16.4	2	0.1	2,750	79.5	50	1.4	6	0.2	3,457	100.0
Otherwise *	68	0.6	212	1.9	1,910	17.5	6	0.1	8,440	77.4	195	1.8	68	0.6	10,899	100.0
Total	78	0.5	283	2.0	2,478	17.3	8	0.1	11,190	77.9	245	1.7	74	0.5	14,356	100.0

* "Otherwise" includes those who are missing in GPA report.

Source: Data were collected by the State of Michigan in *White v. Enger.* Analysis by the lead author and C. G. Chung.

Changes in Institutional Student Aid

Given the failure of federal and state financial aid policies to ensure equal education opportunity, it is interesting to note that the gap in opportunity has narrowed slightly since 1995 (refer back to Figure 1). While federal and state grants have declined in relation to student tuition, colleges and universities have increased their investments. This section first reconsiders campus-based strategies for awarding student financial aid, then presents a case study of strategies for targeting grants to increase diversity in institutions that are also trying to improve selectivity.

Trends in Institutional Aid

Institutional grants and scholarships have the potential of reducing financial inequities. However, most institutional grant aid is awarded on a mixture of merit and need criteria, as institutions use aid to leverage prestige (Hossler, 2004; McPherson & Schapiro, 1997). Aid leveraging involves giving higher awards to students with higher scores as a means of increasing average SAT scores. However, institutional grant aid can reduce or increase financial equality, depending on how it is implemented.

Institutional aid is a vital part of the nation's decentralized student aid system. It has eased the effect of the rise in college costs on regular enrollment. However, college campuses cannot be expected to solve the inequalities created by the decline in the purchasing power of federal and state grants. As the analysis of net price after grants (below) reveals, institutional grant aid has not been sufficient to overcome the inequalities in educational opportunities that are now evident. While institutional aid helps promote enrollment—and played a role in increasing the enrollment rates for high school graduates in the 1990s—it does not equalize opportunity for all academically qualified low-income students because many institutions also consider merit as part of the award process.

New Targeted (and Hybrid) Strategies: Targeted grant aid has a long history. Colleges routinely recruit athletes with scholarships, alter admissions and/or reduce tuition for legacy students (children of alumni), and so forth. In the past two decades colleges have targeted aid to middle-income students with relatively high achievement as a means of improving enrollment and prestige (Hossler, 2004, 2006; Martin, 2005).

Targeted grant aid, commonly referred to as leveraging, now predominates institutional aid packaging, especially in private colleges (Martin, 2005; McPherson & Schapiro, 1997). Most campuses cannot afford to provide the additional need-based aid required to enable all admitted students to enroll. Thus, they target aid at students who are likely to enroll with financial support, maximizing the return on institutional investment. Leveraging has been used by institutions to save money compared to need-based aid and yield more students with the desirable characteristics (average test scores, diversity, etc.). The use of this approach is a possible explanation for the narrowing of the gap for African Americans in the late 1990s (Figure 1). African Americans are more responsive to student aid than are whites (Martin, 2005). In Indiana for example, low-income students who have taken the Twenty-first Century Scholars pledge are more likely to enroll in private colleges than the otherwise average high school student in the state (St. John, Musoba et al., 2002), an artifact of strategic investment by private colleges. The additional support required to attract these students who bring large state and federal grants with them is less costly than the discounting necessary to attract other students.

Improving Diversity: It can be extremely difficult for colleges and universities to improve diversity in states that have inadequate need-based grants. While minority students are more responsive to grants, they also have greater unmet financial need than majority students. Only elite institutions—privates like Princeton University and publics like University of North Carolina—have been able to make and maintain the commitment to meet financial need for low-income students. These institutions can afford to make this commitment because of their admission criteria and their ability to attract large numbers of qualified applicants who can afford to pay the full cost of attendance.

Institutions in states with substantial need-based grant programs also have opportunities to attract large numbers of minority and low-income students because the additional costs of aid are modest. However, this situation does not exist in most states, which has made it difficult for many institutions to enable enrollment by relatively large numbers of minority students. In these instances the common use of aid leveraging can undermine opportunity for low-income students because the total grant amount required to attract minority students is substantially larger than the amounts being offered to middle-income students with some merit indicators.

Targeted aid can be adapted to improve diversity. For example, the Gates Millennium Scholars (GMS) program (St. John, 2004) has proven effective at improving opportunity for high-achieving, low-income students of color. This program sets a GPA threshold (minimum high school grade point average of B+), requires students to be eligible for the federal Pell Grant program, and uses noncognitive criteria to select among eligible applicants. This billion dollar investment by the Bill and Melinda Gates Foundation appears to be expanding the pool of minorities completing college. Recent evidence also suggests that the promise of financial support for graduate education improves the odds that GMS graduates will apply for and enroll in graduate schools (St. John & Hu, 2005).

Case Study 2: Using Targeted Merit Awards to Improve Diversity

This case involved assessing the impact of financial aid on enrollment of admitted applicants at an eastern university law school, along with simulations of an alternative award approach at the school. The law school, like others in the country, is adjusting to new competitive market conditions. During recent years the law school has raised admissions standards as a means of improving prestige. However, with the rising admissions standards, the institution has sought ways to maintain diversity. Merit aid has become an important instrument for both attracting better qualified students among admitted applicants and for maintaining diverse enrollment. There is substantial literature indicating differences in responsiveness to student financial aid for students of color compared to majority students, a topic covered elsewhere (e.g., Carter, 2006; Hu & St. John, 2001; Martin, 2005; St. John, Paulsen, & Carter, 2005). However research on the influence of merit aid on enrollment by minority graduate students is limited and the topic of price response among admitted law school applicants has seldom been studied for whites and students of color.

As part of the defense in a case, our research team worked with the university to compile a database of applicants and enrollees for three successive cohorts of applicants. Logistic regression analyses were conducted using a proven model (St. John, 1992, 1999) to establish the relationship between amounts of grant awards and enrollment decisions. Analyses were conducted for the combined sample of three student cohorts, as well as for both whites and minority students. The results of the regression analysis are summarized below, before the presentation of the simulations, which are the focus of this case statement.

Analysis of Enrollment: The enrollment model for all students predicted 67% of cases correctly and was reasonable according to other model indicators.[12] A summary of findings from the analyses includes the following:

- *Enrollment by Minorities:* In the analyses of enrollment by all admitted students, African Americans and Hispanics were less likely to enroll than were whites. This was consistent with the descriptive data that indicated that admitted Hispanics and African Americans were more difficult to attract to the law school than were other race/ethnic groups.

- *Ability Indicators:* LSAT scores were negatively associated with enrollment in the law school by admitted applicants, indicating the school was not attracting its highest achieving applicants into the law school after admission. However, as predicted by the breakdown of enrollment rates, having "A" grades was positively associated with enrollment, compared to having "B" grades, even controlling for the effects of prior graduate enrollment. In addition, students with "C" grades were less likely to enroll than students with "A" grades.

- *Undergraduate College Characteristics:* College selectivity was significant in enrollment decisions for whites but not for minorities. In both the model for whites and for all students, being from a low-selective college was positively associated with enrollment.

- *Differences Across Cohorts:* The cohort year was significant for whites, but not for minorities. In the model for all students, those in both the 2003 cohort and the 2005 cohort were more likely to enroll than were students in the 2004 cohort.

- *Student Financial Aid:* The amount of aid awarded was significant and positively associated with enrollment in the analyses of whites and minorities, but not in the combined model. It appears that differences in aid programs, as well as differences in price response, influenced these findings.

Simulations: The simulations used the regression model for the population, considering the otherwise-average[13] students broken down by gender and race (Table 7). The aid amounts were varied in the simulations, to demonstrate the impact of aid on enrollment probability for different types of admitted applicants. The other variables in the model were set as the largest or modal group (usually the comparison group coded as zero in the model). The enrollment year was set at 2005 in the simulation. Raising the amount of award improves the enrollment odds for each group. However, it would require a lower award level to raise the odds that otherwise-average white students would enroll. For example, awards of $10,000 would raise the odds of enrollment to at least 50% for whites, while an award of $30,000 is required to raise the odds of enrollment to 50% or greater for minority students. There appears to be more competition from other law schools for minorities with high LSAT scores.[14]

The reasons for these differentials in probabilities of enrollment are related to factors outside of the model, as well as factors in the model. As explained under limitations and analyses above, African Americans and Hispanics have higher financial need than whites, on average, meaning it takes more money from external sources to pay for graduate school. Even among enrolled students, a larger percentage of minorities than whites had need-based grants of some type. However, the availability of need-based grants was very limited at the law school, a factor that could contribute to the lower enrollment rate for admitted and qualified minorities compared to admitted and qualified whites.

It is evident from these simulations that it costs more to attract high-achieving minority students than similarly qualified whites when merit-based aid is used. Given the high costs of attending law school and the relatively low supply of high-scoring minority applicants, highly targeted programs are the most cost effective means for this law school (and probably for other law schools) to maintain diverse enrollments.

The simulations provided further insight into the consequences of the differentials in student price response. The baseline probability that an admitted minority student would enroll was only 27%. It takes a substantial investment to raise these odds above even 50%, especially for minority students with high scores. To attract students of color with LSAT scores of 160—that is to raise the probability of enrollment to 50%—would require a scholarship of $40,000 for Hispanics under the market conditions of 2005, and an award of $50,000 for African Americans. The minority award program in use achieved this objective with a substantially lower award, probably because of the mentoring and other support provided through the program.

Implications of the Case: These simulations illustrate how both measures of merit and race can be used to develop financial aid strategies in campuses that are trying to improve prestige. On the one hand, students with high test scores were less likely to enroll, which is why targeting aid to this group was desirable. In addition, minority students were less likely to enroll controlling for the effects of student financial aid, which is part of the reason why it would take a more substantial investment to attract high-achieving minority students to enroll. The specific measures of price response to aid offers will vary by campus, but each institution can build its own approach to equalizing enrollment opportunity for equally prepared students, a basic tenet of equity in higher education access.

Improving Diversity on Campuses

With respect to the role of student financial aid in promoting diversity within higher education, we need to consider three types of markets: local markets of colleges that compete for students at a low

TABLE 7

Simulations of the Effects of Grant Award Amounts on the Probability of Enrollment by Admitted Students by LSAT, Race, and Gender at the Law School

Award amount	LSAT score	African American		Hispanic		White	
		Female	Male	Female	Male	Female	Male
	155	15.13%	15.34%	23.78%	24.07%	46.40%	46.79%
	160	7.43%	7.54%	12.31%	12.48%	28.03%	28.35%
$0	165	3.48%	3.54%	5.94%	6.03%	14.91%	15.11%
	155	24.03%	24.32%	35.63%	35.99%	**60.57%**	**60.94%**
	160	12.46%	12.63%	19.94%	20.19%	40.86%	41.25%
$10,000	165	6.02%	6.11%	10.07%	10.22%	23.72%	24.00%
	155	35.94%	36.31%	49.26%	**49.66%**	**73.15%**	**73.46%**
	160	20.16%	20.41%	30.40%	30.74%	**55.07%**	**55.46%**
$20,000	165	10.20%	10.35%	16.43%	16.64%	35.55%	35.91%
	155	**49.88%**	**50.28%**	63.27%	63.64%	**82.86%**	**83.08%**
	160	30.93%	31.27%	43.66%	44.05%	**68.50%**	**68.84%**
$30,000	165	16.77%	16.99%	25.85%	26.16%	**49.45%**	**49.85%**
	155	**63.84%**	**64.21%**	75.34%	75.64%	**89.56%**	**89.70%**
	160	44.27%	44.66%	**57.89%**	**58.28%**	**79.41%**	**79.67%**
$40,000	165	26.33%	26.64%	38.22%	38.59%	63.45%	63.81%
	155	**75.80%**	**76.09%**	**84.43%**	**84.63%**	**93.83%**	**93.92%**
	160	**58.50%**	**58.88%**	**70.92%**	**71.25%**	**87.25%**	**87.43%**
$50,000	165	38.81%	39.18%	**52.32%**	**52.71%**	**75.49%**	**75.78%**
	155	**84.75%**	**84.95%**	**90.58%**	**90.71%**	**96.43%**	**96.48%**
	160	**71.43%**	**71.75%**	**81.23%**	**81.47%**	**92.39%**	**92.50%**
$60,000	165	**52.94%**	**53.33%**	**66.06%**	**66.42%**	**84.53%**	**84.73%**

Source: Analyses of institutional data on admissions and enrollment provided to the authors for this project.

cost (i.e., community colleges and some low-cost four-year colleges); high-prestige colleges that attract high-achieving students; and colleges seeking to use aid to raise prestige. Strategies for using financial aid to promote diversity will differ in these cases.

At campuses that compete locally for students, the opportunities to use institutional funds for student financial aid are usually limited. Instead colleges are largely dependent on state and federal student financial aid for students with financial need. Controlling educational costs provides a means of constraining tuition increases. In public colleges facing this condition, state support also has a substantial impact on prices and their ability to attract low-income students. Research also indicates that minorities and low-income students enroll in local institutions in high numbers because of financial constraints. So diversity in most of these institutions reflects the local demographic diversity, at least if high schools are equal and there is adequate state and grant aid. Student financial aid has limited utility as an instrument for promoting diversity at most of these campuses.

At the other extreme, the elite colleges have taken steps to make sure that low-income students know the colleges will provide necessary need-based aid. These colleges tend to have the resources to meet financial need, but the numbers of institutions able and willing to use this strategy has declined in recent decades (McPherson & Schapiro, 1997). Elite privates like Princeton and Harvard have a long history of meeting financial need, although some Ivy League institutions, like Cornell (Ehrenberg, 2002), have shifted away from this approach to make more extensive use of targeted merit aid. In recent years a few elite public institutions—including the University of Michigan, the

University of North Carolina, and the University of Virginia—have made the pledge to meet financial need for low-income students who gain admission. Taking this step enables these institutions to attract more diverse applicants, both economically and ethnically.

Finally, a growing number of institutions have developed targeted financial aid programs to attract students with desirable characteristics. A number of forces have motivated this shift, including the desire to rise in national rankings. It is possible that if institutions treat race as a sole criteria in the awarding of aid that their aid policies will be challenged by the Office of Civil Rights. As the case study above illustrates, it is possible for colleges and universities facing these conditions to use market analyses as a basis for developing financial aid awards that equalize the odds of enrollment by high-achieving students from different racial/ethnic groups.

The practice of targeting financial aid to yield students with desired characteristics is widespread but not well understood, especially with respect to the role of diversity. At campuses that are trying to simultaneously improve quality and diversity, it may be necessary to tailor targeted aid programs to achieve this goal. The same methods have been used by campuses to attract students in different majors and to attract other high priority groups.

Many researchers have focused on student aid as though there were two types, need-based and merit-based. The newer forms of targeted grant and scholarship aid can be either merit- or need-based and very often consider both criteria in the award process, as the simulations above illustrate. The tendency to use targeted financial aid can undermine diversity, unless race is considered along with other factors in the award process. As was the case in the analysis of merit-based state grants above, this case study of institutional student financial aid illustrates the need to recraft award criteria to ensure equal opportunity for enrollment of equally prepared students. In the case of merit aid (considered in case 1), the need is to create a more just measure of merit. In the case of targeted aid (considered in case 2), the challenge is to package student aid to equalize opportunity to equally able students from diverse backgrounds.

Conclusions

The current period of litigation over race-conscious student aid programs is especially troubling, given the decline in government need-based grants. Efforts to desegregate the nation's system of higher education have been undermined by the privatization of public colleges and the increased emphasis on high tuition and loans. This new system discriminates because minority populations in the United States are more likely to have low incomes, which means minorities face an unequal burden in paying the costs remaining after grants compared to whites.

Targeting grants to enable enrollment by students of color with a documented record of achievement provides a reasonable means for colleges and universities to contend with the discriminatory effects of government aid policies. While the current discrimination in access to four-year colleges may be an unintended consequence of federal and state policies on student grants, there is nonetheless substantial evidence that the reduction of federal grants has been accompanied by growing inequality. Targeting student aid—linking grants to different forms of merit—has become the predominant means of attracting students and may be the only workable alternative to full funding of need-based aid, as means of equalizing enrollment opportunity across racial groups within colleges and universities. As a conclusion, before deriving lessons learned, we briefly consider our findings relative to the issues of justice and fairness that underlie the issues considered.

Evaluation research can be especially helpful in efforts to defend race-conscious programs and in the design of targeted programs that do not explicitly consider race. Workable models for institutional research have a long history (St. John, 1992); and case study 2 above, illustrates how such research can be used. There are also well-tested methods for studying the effects of state grants, including fixed-effect regression studies (e.g., St. John, 2006); studies of state student resources (St. John, 1999; St. John, Hu, & Weber, 2000, 2001); and difference-in-difference studies (Dynarski, 2002, 2004). State-level studies of race-conscious grant programs should be a high priority for the defense of these programs.[15]

Rethinking the Strategies

Before 1960 higher education was accessible to fewer students and can be thought of as having been more elite. There was also a long history of racial discrimination in educational opportunity. While school desegregation began after *Brown v. Board of Education* in 1954, higher education desegregation did not begin in earnest until after the second *Adams* decision in 1977. By that time, there had already been a long history of federal student financial aid programs: the GI Bill started in 1945; the first generally available need-based grant programs began as a result of the National Defense Education Act; and the Higher Education Act and the Education Amendments of 1972 firmly established need-based student financial aid. In the middle 1970s, it has been argued, there was a system that had relatively equal access for prepared students who applied to college, meeting both the basic and equity standards reasonably well.

However, the system of low tuition and high grants was relatively expensive for taxpayers. In the late 1970s middle-income families advocated for student aid, leading to the Middle Income Students Assistance Act of 1978, which expanded eligibility for Pell to middle-income students. Soon thereafter tax rates emerged as a major issue, rolling back tax rates and public investment in higher education. College enrollment rates expanded as this new movement toward a privatized system that used private loan capital and charged students for a larger share of college costs. The new system was more reasonable for tax payers but the savings in tax dollars were accompanied by increased inequality in enrollment opportunity, a larger disparity in enrollment rates for African Americans and Hispanics compared to whites. Just savings were not realized given the disparity in enrollment rates.

Now the advocates of equal educational opportunity are faced with a challenging question: how can the current system be adapted to improve equity? One option is to argue for increased investment in need-based grants (Heller & Marin, 2004, 2002; McPherson & Schapiro, 1997; St. John, 2003; St. John, Chung et al., 2002). Another option is to take steps to encourage the redesign of the newer aid strategies—merit and targeted aid—to improve equity. What we advocate is a value-centered logic that adapts to the issues being debated: encouraging adaptation to improve equal opportunity, while promoting major system changes that improve justice in that system.

Lessons Learned

1. *State race-conscious aid programs have more than doubled in number over the past two decades as an appropriate response to the inequalities created by privatization.* The number of states with race-specific programs has more than doubled since 1984, the first year for which there is a national record. It is a crucial time to begin the process of evaluating the impact of both race-specific and race-sensitive grant programs, to test whether they meet the intent of reducing inequality. Whether or not such research will serve as a defense for these programs remains uncertain. However, if such research exposes the nature of unequal educational opportunity, along with the efficacy of student financial aid as a remedy, then this research can also be used in litigation. Researchers can support efforts to redesign other need-based, merit, and targeted-aid programs to ensure equal opportunity is not further eroded when and if these programs are lost.

2. *Need-based student financial aid helps equalize opportunities for equally prepared students with unequal financial means, but these programs are woefully inadequate.* Erosion of the purchasing power of the federal Pell Grant program since 1980 has been accompanied by increasing privatization of public colleges symbolized by rising tuition, decline in the purchasing power of state grants, and higher costs after grants for low-income students at public and private four-year colleges. No matter what standard of preparation is used, prepared low-income students have less opportunity to enroll in four-year colleges than high- or middle-income students (Fitzgerald, 2004; Lee, 2004). These conditions add to inequalities in enrollment opportunities for Hispanics and African Americans compared to whites. Not only should increased state and federal spending on need-based aid be advocated for, but better coordination of finance strate-

gies is also needed. States can probably achieve greater equity for the same investment through coordination without impairing institutional quality.

3. *It is possible to redesign state merit grant programs to improve equal opportunity.* While merit grant programs have been widely criticized by advocates of equal opportunity because they have added to inequality, the option of redesigning these programs has not been sufficiently considered. The success of the top ten percent programs indicates that alternative measures of merit that are indexed to students' schools can yield diverse enrollment. Similar methods can be used to redesign state merit programs to reward competition and high quality within schools. This may be a necessary adaptation to merit aid programs given the very substantial inequalities in high schools.

4. *Targeted financial aid programs are now widely used by colleges to attract students with desired characteristics and can be adapted to improve diversity.* While race-exclusive programs, a form of targeted grant aid, may be difficult to maintain in the future, other forms of targeted aid can be adapted to improve equity in enrollment opportunity. A greater emphasis should be placed on adapting targeted aid programs to consider race along with other factors to ensure that equally prepared students from different backgrounds have equal odds of enrolling. Evaluation targeted grants improve opportunity to enroll and persist for students from underrepresented minority groups.

5. *The agenda for advocates of equal educational opportunity should be expanded to include the redesign of merit and targeted aid programs, in addition to the defense of race-conscious aid programs and advocacy for need-based student aid.* Advocates of equal opportunity have been in a defensive position. New coalitions can and should be built. Part of this effort involves engaging in research that will help illuminate the linkages between current policies and inequalities in opportunities to prepare for and enroll in college. The new agenda should also involve advocacy, including using research that exposes how policy links to inequality as part of the arsenal for reform. Better information may help us to build more workable coalitions.

Notes

1. This chapter incorporates research previously conducted with support from two studies: one conducted for the NAACP Legal Defense Fund, the other for plaintiffs in *White v. Engler*. C. G. Chung assisted with analyses for the *White v. Engler* case. This support is gratefully acknowledged. The opinions expressed in the paper are the authors' and do not reflect policies or positions of funding organizations.

2. *Race-conscious* grants target underrepresented students of color. *Race-sensitive* grants consider race along with other factors. *Race-exclusive* grants are limited to students of color and may also consider merit, need, or both.

3. *Targeted* grants are defined as awards that emphasize a group of people, based on their characteristics. This form of aid could be reported as need-based, or non-need based. Since states report on all non-need grants in the same category, targeted race-conscious grants are often categorized with merit grants in analyses of student aid (e.g., Heller & Rasmussen, 2002). Given the importance of understanding the role of student financial aid in ensuring diversity in college enrollment, it is necessary to distinguish targeted grants from purely merit and need-based awards.

4. *Privatization* is the trend toward reduced government (federal, state and local) financial support of postsecondary education, increasingly shifting the financial burden to individuals to fund their postsecondary educations within public institutions. For related research, see Heller, 2006.

5. The Pell Grant maximum award actually declined in the late 1980s (as discussed in reference to Figure 2).

6 This case study substantially revises an early discussion of these analyses by St. John & Chung (2004). This case study includes simulation results not previously published.

7. Most of the members of the plaintiffs' coalition favored GPA or need over the MEAP test. After conference calls to discuss alternatives, we developed a format for a data collection.

8. Rural and urban schools had the highest levels of poverty and were the most likely to benefit from award criteria that included appropriate equity consideration. However, the suburban districts had the greatest representation in the program under the original award criteria. It was important that efforts be made to have all types of districts represented in the sample.

9. The original criteria included some alternative methods of qualification (using a specialized vocational test), but very few students met these criteria. Therefore we did not request information on the alternative test to reduce confusion about the data collection. The MEAP-only analysis is essentially similar to the original award criteria.

10. The GPA-Merit Index was essentially class rank.

11 The simulations also considered students of "unknown" ethnic origin and Native Hawaiian or other Pacific Islander. Both of these groups were extremely small.

12. Interestingly the model for minority students only predicted substantially better than the model for all students. However, since it was appropriate to use the overall model for simulations, we summarize only the general model here.

13. All variables set at the mode for the admitted student population, except of the variables included in the simulation (i.e., race, gender, and grant amount). An otherwise-average student is one who has variables other than race and gender set at the mode for the group

14. External competition is not a variable in the model. However, it is the most reasonable explanation for the variation in the odds of enrollment for minority students with high LSAT scores.

15. In fact, the legal defense of one state program is now underway and state records are being analyzed, with backing of the NAACP Legal Defense Fund and the state agency. However, it is not possible to report on this effort at the present time.

References

Advisory Committee on Student Financial Assistance. (2002). *Empty promises: The myth of college access in America.* Washington, DC: U.S. Department of Education.

Ancheta, A. N. (2006). *Law, higher education, and race-conscious recruitment, retention, and financial aid policies.* Paper presented at the Harvard Civil Rights Project and UCLA School of Education Conference, "Is Access to Higher Education Shrinking? The Impact of Race-Conscious Policies & Their Alternatives," on January 14, in Los Angeles.

Banks, R. R. (2006). *The challenges to student body diversity policies in higher education.* Paper presented at the Harvard Civil Rights Project and UCLA School of Education Conference, "Is Access to Higher Education Shrinking? The Impact of Race-Conscious Policies & Their Alternatives," on January 14, in Los Angeles.

Carter, D. F. (2006). Key issues in the persistence of underrepresented minority students. In E. P. St. John & M. Wilkerson (Eds.), *Improving academic success: Using persistence research to address critical challenges* (pp. 33–46) New Directions for Institutional Research, 130. San Francisco: Jossey-Bass.

Chapa, J. (2006). *Race-neutral policy: Progress or regression for growing minority population? Understanding the experiences of the U. of Texas and the U. of California under different race-neutral policies.* Paper presented at the Harvard Civil Rights Project and UCLA School of Education Conference, "Is Access to Higher Education Shrinking? The Impact of Race-Conscious Policies & Their Alternatives," on January 14, in Los Angeles.

The College Board. (2002). *Trends in student aid 2002.* Washington, DC: Author.

Dynarski, S. (2002). Race, income, and the impact of merit aid. In D. E. Heller & P. Marin (Eds.), *Who should we help? The negative social consequences of merit aid scholarships* (pp. 73–91). Cambridge, MA: The Civil Rights Project, Harvard University.

Dynarski, S. (2004). The new merit aid. In C. Hoxby (Ed.), *College choices: The economics of where to go, when to go and how to pay for it* (pp. 63–100). Chicago: University of Chicago Press.

Ehrenberg, R. G. (2002). *Tuition rising: Why college costs so much.* Cambridge, MA: Harvard University Press.

Ellwood, D. T., & Kane, T. J. (2000). "Who is Getting a College Education?: Family Background and the Growing Gaps in Enrollment." In S. Danziger and J. Waldfogel (Eds.), *Securing the Future* (pp. 283–324). New York: Russell Sage.

Finn, C. E., Jr. (1978). *Scholars, dollars, and bureaucrats: Federal policy toward higher education.* Washington, DC: The Brookings Institute.

Fitzgerald, B.K. (2004). Missed Opportunities: Has College Opportunity Fallen Victim to Policy Drift? *Change, 36(4),* 10.

Fossey, R. E. (1998). Desegregation is not enough: Facing the truth about urban schools. In R. E. Fossey (Ed.), *Race, the courts, and equal education: The limits of the law, vol. 15 of Readings on Equal Education* (pp. 5–20). New York: AMS Press.

Fossey, R. E. (2003). Desegregation is over in the inner cities: What do we do now? In L. F. Miron & E. P. St. John (Eds.), *Reinterpreting urban school reform: Reinterpreting urban school reform: Have urban schools failed, or has the reform movement failed urban schools?* (pp. 15–32). Albany, NY: State University of New York Press.

Goggin, W. J. (1999). *A "merit-aware" model for college admissions and affirmative action*: The Mortenson Research Seminar on Public Policy Analysis of Opportunity for Postsecondary Education.

Guinier, L. (2003). Admission policies as political acts: Guardian at the gates of our democratic ideal. *Harvard Law Review, 117,* 113–224.

Hearn, J. C., & Anderson, M. S. (1989). Integrating postsecondary education financing policies: The Minnesota model. In R. H. Fenske (Ed.), *Studying the impact of student aid on institutions* (pp. 55–74). New Directions for Higher Education, No. 62. San Francisco: Jossey-Bass.

Hearn, J. C., & Anderson, M. S. (1995). The Minnesota finance experiment. In E. P. St. John (Ed.), *Rethinking tuition and student aid strategies* (pp. 5–26). New Directions for Higher Education, No. 89. San Francisco: Jossey-Bass.

Heller, D. E. (1997). Student price response in higher education: An update to Leslie and Brinkman. *The Journal of Higher Education, 68*(6), 624–659.

Heller, D. E. (2001). *White, et al. v. Elger, et al.: Supplementary analysis of Merit Scholarship Program First Cohort (High School Class of 2000)*, from mimeo.

Heller, D. E. (2006). State support of higher education: Past, present, and future. In D. M. Priest & E. P. St. John (Eds.), *Privatization in public universities: Implications for the public trust* (pp.11–37). Bloomington, IN: Indiana University Press.

Heller, D. E., & Marin, P. (Eds.). (2004). *State merit scholarship programs and racial inequality.* Cambridge, MA: The Civil Rights Project, Harvard University.

Heller, D. E., & Marin, P. (Eds.). (2002). *Who should we help? The negative social consequences of merit aid scholarships.* Cambridge, MA: The Civil Rights Project, Harvard University.

Heller, D. E., & Rasmussen, C. J. (2002). Merit scholarships and college access: Evidence from Florida and Michigan. In D. E. Heller & P. Marin (Eds.), *Who should we help? The negative social consequences of merit aid scholarships* (pp. 25–40). Cambridge, MA: The Civil Rights Project, Harvard University.

Hossler, D. (2004). Refinancing public universities: Student enrollments, incentive-based budgeting and incremental revenue. In E. P. St. John & M. P. Parsons (Eds.), *Public financing of higher education: Changing contexts and new rationales* (pp. 145–163). Baltimore: Johns Hopkins University Press.

Hossler, D. (2006). Student and families as revenue: The impact on institutional behaviors. In D. M. Priest & E. P. St. John (Eds.), *Privatization in public universities: Implications for the public trust* (pp. 109–128). Bloomington, IN: Indiana University Press.

Hu, S., & St. John, E. P. (2001). Student persistence in a public higher education system: Understanding racial/ethnic differences. *The Journal of Higher Education, 72*(3), 265–286.

Lee, J. B. (2004). Access revisited: A preliminary reanalysis of NELS. In E. P. St. John (Ed.), *Readings on equal education: Vol. 19. Public policy and college access: Investigating the federal and state roles in equalizing postsecondary opportunity* (pp. 87–96). New York: AMS Press.

Martin, R. E. (2005). *Cost control, college access, and competition in higher education.* Cheltenham, UK: Edward Elger.

McPherson, M. S., & Schapiro, M. O. (1997). *The student aid game: Meeting need and rewarding talent in American higher education.* Princeton, NJ: Princeton University Press.

Mumper, M. (2001). The paradox of college prices: Five stories with no clear lesson. In D. E. Heller (Ed.), *The states and public higher education policy: Affordability, access, and accountability* (pp. 39–63). Baltimore: The Johns Hopkins University Press.

National Association of State Grant Aid Programs. (1983–2006). *Annual Survey Reports, 15th–35th, except for the 29th* (No. ED253172). Harrisburg, PA; Albany, NY; and Springfield, IL: Pennsylvania Higher Education Assistance Agency & The New York State Higher Education Services Corporation, & The Illinois Student Assistance Commission.

National Association of State Student Grant Aid Programs. (1983–2006). Annual Survey Reports, 15th–35th, except for the 29th (No. ED253172). Harrisburg, PA; Albany, NY; and Springfield, IL: Pennsylvania Higher Education Assistance Agency & The New York State Higher Education Services Corporation, & The Illinois Student Assistance Commission.

Priest, D. M., & St. John, E. P. (Eds.). (2006). *Privatization of public universities.* Bloomington, IN: Indiana University Press.

St. John, E. P. (1992). Workable models for institutional research on the impact of student financial aid. *Journal of Student Financial Aid, 22*(3), 13–26.

St. John, E. P. (1998). Higher education desegregation in the post-Fordice legal environment: An historical perspective. In R. E. Fossey (Ed.), *Readings on equal education: Vol. 15. Race, the courts, and equal education: The limits of the law* (pp. 101–122). New York: AMS Press.

St. John, E. P. (1999). Evaluating state grant programs: A study of the Washington state grant programs. *Research in Higher Education, 40*(2):149–170.

St. John, E. P. (2003). *Refinancing the college dream: Access, equal opportunity, and justice for taxpayers.* Baltimore, MD: Johns Hopkins University Press.

St. John, E. P. (Ed.) (2004). *Improving access and college success for diverse students: Research on the Gates Millennium Scholarship Program.* New York: AMS Press.

St. John, E. P., (2006). *Education and the public interest: School reform, public finance, and access to higher education.* Netherlands: Springer.

St. John, E. P., & Byce, C. (1982). The changing federal role in student financial aid. In M. Kramer (Ed.), *Meeting student aid needs in a period of retrenchment* (pp. 21–40). New Directions for Higher Education, No. 40. San Francisco: Jossey-Bass.

St. John, E. P., & Chung, C. G. (2004). The impact of GMS on financial access: Analyses of the 2000 cohort. In E. P. St. John (Ed.), *Readings on equal education: Vol. 20. Improving access and college success for diverse students: Studies of the Gates Millennium Scholars Program* (pp. 115–153). New York: AMS Press, Inc.

St. John, E. P., Chung, C. G., Musoba, G. D., & Simmons, A. B. (2004). Financial access: The impact of state financial strategies. In E. P. St. John (Ed.), *Readings on equal education: Vol. 19. Public policy and college access: Investigating the federal and state roles in equalizing postsecondary opportunity* (Vol. 19, pp. 109–129). New York: AMS Press, Inc.

St. John, E. P., Chung, C. G., Musoba, G. D., Simmons, A. B., Wooden, O. S., & Mendez, J. (2002). *Expanding college access: The impact of state finance strategies.* Indianapolis, IN: Lumina Foundation for Education.

St. John, E. P., & Hu, S. (2005, in review). *Studies of the effects of the GMS program, Prepared for the Bill & Melinda Gates Foundation.* Seattle, WA.

St. John, E. P., Hu, S., Simmons, A. B., & Musoba, G. D. (2001). Aptitude v. merit: What matters in persistence? *Review of Higher Education, 24*(2), 131–152.

St. John, E. P., Hu, S., & Weber, J. (2000). Keeping public colleges affordable: A study of persistence in Indiana's public colleges and universities. *Journal of Student Financial Aid, 30*(1), 21–32.

St. John, E. P., Hu, S., & Weber, J. (2001). State policy and the affordability of public higher education: The influence of state grants on persistence in Indiana. *Research in Higher Education, 42*, 401–428.

St. John, E. P., Musoba, G. D., Simmons, A. B., & Chung, C. G. (2002). *Meeting the access challenge: Indian's Twenty-first Century Scholars Program.* Indianapolis, IN: Lumina Foundation for Education.

St. John, E. P., Paulsen, M. B., & Carter, D. F. (2005). Diversity, college costs, and postsecondary opportunity: An examination of the college choice-persistence nexus for African Americans and Whites. *The Journal of Higher Education, 76*(5), 545–569.

St. John, E. P., Simmons, A. B., & Musoba, G. D. (2002). Merit-aware admissions in public universities: Increasing diversity. *Thought & Action, 17*(2), 35–46.

St. John, E. P., Tuttle, T. J., & Musoba, G. D. (2006). Access and equal opportunity in higher education in the United States: The effects of education and public finance policies. In A. Oduaran & H. S. Bhola (Eds.), *Widening access to education as social justice* (pp. 329–353). Dordrecht, The Netherlands: Springer.

St. John, E. P., & Wooden, O. S. (2006). Privatization and federal funding for higher education. In D. M. Priest & E. P. St. John (Eds.), *Privatization in public universities: Implications for the public trust* (pp.38–64). Bloomington, IN: Indiana University Press.

Williams, J. B. (1988). Title VI regulation of higher education. In J. B. Williams (Ed.), *Desegregating America's colleges and universities: Title VI regulation of higher education* (pp. 33–53). New York: Teachers College Press.

Chapter 44
Do Community Colleges Provide a Viable Pathway to a Baccalaureate Degree?

Bridget Terry Long

Michal Kurlaender

Community colleges have become an important entryway for students intending to complete baccalaureate degrees. However, many question the viability of the transfer function and wonder whether students suffer a penalty for starting at 2-year institutions. The authors examined how the outcomes of community college entrants compared with those of similar students who initially entered 4-year institutions within the Ohio public higher education system. Using a detailed data set, the authors tracked outcomes for 9 years and used multiple strategies to deal with selection issues: propensity score matching and instrumental variables. The results suggest that straightforward estimates are significantly biased, but even after accounting for selection, students who initially began at community colleges were 14.5% less likely to complete bachelor's degrees within 9 years.

Community colleges play an important role in American higher education. For many, they offer open, affordable access to postsecondary schooling. According to data from the Integrated Postsecondary Education Data System of the National Center for Education Statistics and to Wirt et al. (2000), nearly half of all undergraduates at public institutions attend community colleges, and low-income, minority, and first-generation students are more likely to attend community colleges than 4-year institutions. Although community colleges serve a diverse set of needs, their success is often measured by their ability to facilitate students' transfer to 4-year institutions, and in recent years, community colleges have become an increasingly important pathway to baccalaureate degrees. Capacity constraints at many 4-year institutions have prompted states to rely on the community college sector to accommodate much of the continued expansion of higher education (Evelyn, 2002).[1] In addition, rising admissions requirements and escalating tuition costs at 4-year institutions have limited access to these schools for some students (Mills, 2006).

The viability of the community college transfer function has long been a source of debate. On one hand, the "democratization" view suggests that community colleges have increased overall access to postsecondary education by making higher education possible for many students through open admissions and low costs (Leigh & Gill, 2003; Rouse, 1995, 1998). On the other hand, some posit that community colleges serve as a "diversion" by channeling students into vocational courses and weakening their educational progress through increased flexibility and nontraditional patterns of attendance (e.g., delayed entry, part-time enrollment, combining employment with schooling; Brint & Karabel, 1989; Dougherty, 1994; Grubb, 1991). In reality, many community college students face a number of personal and structural barriers to transfer, including financial concerns, limited information, and the lack of coordination between 2-year and 4-year institutions. As such, estimates from the most recent national longitudinal postsecondary study reveal that only 37% of students who graduated from high school in 1992 and began at community colleges eventually transferred to 4-year colleges (Adelman, 2005).

Although previous research has highlighted the reduced likelihood of baccalaureate attainment for students who begin at community colleges, the bulk of research in this area focuses on students who graduated from high school over 15 years ago and even 30 years ago.[2] Given the recent trends highlighted above, a more timely analysis is needed to reexamine and extend our understanding of the current function of community colleges.[3] In this chapter, we provide a new perspective on the role of community colleges for a cohort of students who entered Ohio public colleges and universities in fall 1998.

This study makes several important contributions to the existing literature on community colleges. First, we used a detailed, robust data source that is an improvement over the data used in many previous studies. We tracked students over a longer period of time than any other study to our knowledge (9 years) and across multiple institutions to capture transfer behavior and periods of stopping out and returning to college. Also, because our data set was a complete census of everyone in the public higher education system in Ohio, attrition in our sample was small.[4] Given that not all community college students aim to complete baccalaureate degrees, one must also account for degree intent in this sort of analysis (Alfonso, 2006; Alfonso, Bailey, & Scott, 2005). Our data set included important information on students' degree intent, so we were able to disentangle the many populations that community colleges serve to focus on students with 4-year degree objectives. Finally, unlike many other state unit record data sets, ours contained information on family background to control for other differences between students.[5]

Research on the transfer function of community colleges must address a number of empirical difficulties, which have been undertaken with varying degrees of success in past studies. Students do not randomly choose their colleges, and the types of students who first attend community colleges differ from those who initially enroll in 4-year institutions. To address this selection, past studies have used a variety of strategies: a Heckman two-stage sample selection model (Alfonso, 2006), propensity score matching (Melguizo, Kienzl, & Alfonso, 2007; Stephan & Rosenbaum, 2006), or instrumental variables (IV; Rouse, 1995). Each method has its own strengths and weaknesses, so, unlike in any other study, we used two different methodologies (propensity scores and IV) to triangulate the impact of starting at a community college on baccalaureate attainment. This also allowed us to explore the relative effectiveness of each method in dealing with selection. The propensity scoring method gets its strength from the wealth of observable information available on students' characteristics and preparation. In contrast, the use of IV accounts for unobservable differences by considering, among other things, the importance of college proximity in college choice. Distance is a particularly relevant issue in the choices of Ohio students, so our use of distance as an instrument to deal with selection is more convincing than in other contexts. We examined the postsecondary outcomes of students who initially entered higher education through the community college system in comparison with those of students who began at 4-year institutions. The chapter is organized as follows: In the next section, we discuss the relevant literature; we then describe our empirical strategies, detail our results, and offer our conclusions.

Literature Review

The standard human capital model, developed by Becker (1993), provides some insight for why students might choose to attend community colleges over 4-year institutions. First, in an effort to minimize costs, students may select to attend community colleges because they are less expensive than 4-year institutions and can reduce the total costs of a bachelor's degree. Community colleges also give students time to improve their educational records and therefore increase their likelihood of being admitted to higher quality, degree-granting, 4-year institutions. Hilmer (1997) found that students chose higher quality universities if they first attended community colleges, with the largest quality increases being observed for students who came from poor families or who performed poorly in high school.

Partly because community college participants vary widely in their educational backgrounds and purposes of participation, it is difficult to characterize the performance of community colleges in the educational attainment process. Although community colleges were originally designed to serve as "junior colleges" to 4-year programs, today, they constitute an incredibly diverse set of institutions with varied missions and courses of study (Alfonso et al., 2005). In addition to serving traditional-age students who recently graduated from high school, community colleges enroll many older, nontraditional students, who may take classes for personal enrichment rather than attempting to complete degrees. Moreover, community colleges attract students who are often "experimenting" with postsecondary education, without necessarily the drive to complete degrees (Grubb, 1991). Nevertheless, community colleges' success is often measured by their ability to facilitate students' transfer to 4-year institutions and complete bachelor's degrees.

Many question whether community colleges offer a genuine path to attaining a baccalaureate degree. As noted above, the increased flexibility and nontraditional patterns of attendance afforded by community colleges may weaken students' progression through postsecondary education and make transferring to 4-year colleges less likely (Brint & Karabel, 1989; Dougherty, 1994; Grubb, 1991). Furthermore, the administrative costs of transferring to a 4-year college may be exceedingly prohibitive for many students (Anderson, Sun, & Alfonso, 2006). Some also argue that the educational system is fraught with market failures as a result of a lack of information about the process for postsecondary entry (e.g., financial aid procedures and admissions standards at 4-year institutions) and other barriers that may limit the opportunity sets of students from disadvantaged backgrounds (Hilmer, 1998).

On the other hand, the democratization view suggests that community colleges have increased overall access to postsecondary education through open admissions and low cost. In fact, Rouse (1995), using the HSB data set, found that starting at 2-year colleges did not affect the likelihood of attaining bachelor's degrees for those students intending to transfer to 4-year colleges. Although Rouse did estimate a negative "diversion" effect, the democratization effect of increased access to higher education was estimated to be larger. Using a slightly different methodology, Leigh and Gill (2003), using the NLSY79 and controlling for a student's desired level of education, found similar results to those of Rouse.

There has also been a substantial amount of research describing who uses the transfer route from community colleges. Using the NELS, Adelman (2005) reported that among 12th graders in 1992 whose first postsecondary institutions were community colleges, 37% transferred to 4-year colleges, and 60% of those who transferred had earned bachelor's degrees by 2000. Using administrative data on a cohort of students initially enrolled in California community colleges in 1999–2000, Moore and Shulock (2007) reported that among the 60% of degree seekers attending California community colleges, about 25% transferred to universities and/or earned associate's degrees within 6 years. Overall, several researchers have concluded that those who transfer from community colleges to 4-year colleges are of higher social classes, have more academic preparation, are less likely to be minorities, and are less likely to be women than those who do not transfer (Dougherty, 1987, 1994; Dougherty & Kienzl, 2006; Grubb, 1991; Lee & Frank, 1990; Whitaker & Pascarella, 1994; Surette, 2001).

Questions also exist about whether community college students experience the same returns to education as their counterparts who entered 4-year colleges initially. Kane and Rouse (1995) used transcript data from the National Longitudinal Study of the Class of 1972 (NLS72) and the NLSY79 to compare the returns to college credit at 2-year and 4-year colleges. Controlling for family income and measured ability, they found that wage differentials for both 2-year and 4-year college credits were positive and of similar magnitude. In separate work, Leigh and Gill (1997), also using the NLSY79, examined whether returns to a community college education differed for adults who returned to college compared with continuing high school graduates. They found positive returns of essentially the same magnitude. Finally, Hilmer (2000) examined whether the return to university quality differed for community college transfer students and direct attendees. Using the HSB data, he found that the return to university quality differed dramatically across both educational paths, and institutional quality ranged with the length of time spent at the initial institution having a significant negative effect on transfer students.

Researchers have also debated whether there is a return to getting an education at a community college without completing a degree. Kane and Rouse (1995) found a positive return to attending a 2-year college even when a degree was not obtained. Grubb (1995) also found similar results after corrections to his NLS72 data in a revision of a 1993 article in which he concluded that economic benefits may accrue to even modest levels of community college participation.

Although these studies have laid the foundation on the impact of community colleges on baccalaureate attainment and labor market outcomes, this study provides an important comprehensive update using data on students aged 17 to 20 years who entered Ohio public colleges and universities in fall 1998. The data included important details such as educational intent and family background and tracked students over 9 years across public institutions within the state. In addition, by taking a state-level perspective, we were able to provide insight that is difficult to obtain in studies using national data. States differ greatly in how they choose to use community colleges within their statewide higher education systems. In some states, community colleges are the primary access points (e.g., California), whereas other states focus all remediation there (e.g., Florida), and still others favor 4-year college entry, with the community colleges primarily serving less traditional needs, such as older students and workforce retraining efforts (e.g., Massachusetts). Because of this state-level variation, it can be difficult to fully understand community college dynamics when looking at national data. For instance, marginal community college students (i.e., those on the fence between 4- and 2-year colleges) differ by state, making it hard to interpret some of the patterns observed in national data. Interpretation might differ greatly if looking at a community college student in California compared with one in Massachusetts, because their backgrounds, preparation, and aspirations are likely to be different as a result of their contrasting state higher education structures. By using state-level data, we were able to be much more specific about who the marginal students were and to take into account the state context in our interpretation.

This study also sheds light on a previously unstudied, important context: the fifth largest public higher education system in the country. Although the external validity of our results is limited by our focus on a particular state, the higher education system, population demographics, and diverse labor markets within Ohio are similar to larger national trends and those of many neighboring states (Mortenson, 2002), so our results could be used to reflect on issues facing many other states. It is worth noting, however, that because our study and many others on this topic focused on traditional-age college students, we can say little about the many older students who attend community colleges.

Empirical Framework and Method

Data

We used a longitudinal, administrative data set of students in the Ohio public higher education system. Maintained by the Ohio Board of Regents (OBR), the data include information from several sources, including applications, college transcripts, and entrance exams and their accompanying questionnaires. Therefore, we had access to detailed information about each student's family background, high school preparation, postsecondary intentions, college performance and course-taking behavior, and degree completion.[6] In addition, because the data covered the entire public higher education system in Ohio, we were able to track students across schools and determine the outcomes of individuals who may have continued their educations or completed their degrees at different postsecondary institutions from the ones they originally entered. With these data, we examined several student outcomes, including baccalaureate degree completion (after 4, 6, and 9 years), total credit hours completed, and stop-out behavior (within 1, 2, and 6 years).[7] One drawback to the data was that it did not include students who transferred to private colleges or transferred out of the state; these students may have been incorrectly designated as dropouts. However, this potential measurement error was likely to be very small because, according to analysis of Integrated Postsecondary Education Data System data, the percentage of students thought to transfer to such schools was a small fraction of the total number of observed dropouts.[8]

We focused on first-time freshmen aged 17 to 20 years who began their postsecondary studies during fall 1998 and followed them for 9 years until spring 2007. Because of our focus on baccalaureate completion, we restricted the sample to individuals who had demonstrated the intent to complete 4-year degrees either on their college applications or by starting at a 4-year university. The OBR collects information on the educational intent of all community college students on their applications, with eight possible options, and we defined baccalaureate degree intent as having designated the intention (a) "to obtain a bachelor's degree," (b) "to obtain an associate degree for transfer," or (c) "to transfer before completing a degree or certificate."[9] Responses to this question about educational intent are completed privately and in no way affect outcomes such as admissions or access to certain classes, so we believe the variable to be a fairly accurate depiction of educational goals at the time of college entry. In fall 1998, 60% of first-time community college students indicated intent to obtain bachelor's degrees or transfer to 4-year colleges with or without associate's degrees.[10]

We also restricted the sample to students who took the ACT.[11] This requirement further emphasizes that the sample, particularly the community college students, had some baccalaureate degree intent, because most 4-year colleges require students to take either the ACT or the SAT, though most schools do not require a minimum score. The ACT restriction was also necessary because this source provided information on student achievement and other important controls for the models. Because of this restriction, our results may reflect a more conservative estimate of the penalty felt by community college students, because we may have inadvertently excluded some students who did want baccalaureate degrees but failed to prepare for admission to 4-year universities. Finally, because of the use of proximity as an instrument, we restricted the sample to Ohio residents (i.e., distance would not serve as a good instrument for Florida residents attending Ohio colleges). Beyond these sample requirements, we dropped observations without complete college transcripts or ZIP code information.[12]

Although we focused on students in Ohio, our results have external validity. The percentage of Ohio public school students who graduate from high school and enter college the following fall is near the national average (Mortenson, 2002), and the higher education system, demographics, and diverse labor markets within Ohio are similar to those of many neighboring states and to national conditions. Moreover, Ohio plays a prominent role in higher education, with the fifth largest public higher education system in the United States (after California, Florida, New York, and Texas; National Center for Education Statistics, 2000). Although our results could be used to reflect on community college issues in some other states, caution should be taken when making comparisons with states with very different postsecondary systems, such as California.

Basic Empirical Strategy

Our research question was how the outcomes of community college entrants compare with those of similar 4-year college students. We addressed this question using regression techniques, beginning with a basic ordinary least squares (OLS) model estimating the impact of beginning at a community college on the total number of college credits completed:

$$CREDITS_i = {}_{1i} + {}_1COMMCOLL_i + {}_2X_{1i} + {}_{1i,} \tag{1}$$

where $COMMCOLL_i$ is a dummy variable equal to one if a student initially began at a community college and zero otherwise, and $_1$ is the parameter associated with beginning at a 2-year college. X_i is a vector of background controls, including student demographics (race, gender, age, and age squared), family background (parents' income and parents' income squared), and student ability (percentile ACT score and ACT score squared).[13] The error term is represented by $_i$. For the outcomes variables that are dichotomous in nature (e.g., degree completion within 9 years), we used probit models instead of OLS.

Our regression models controlled for observable differences between students in the sample to isolate the impact of beginning at a community college. However, other factors may influence who chooses to initially attend a community college rather than a 4-year institution. Stated more formally, our probit and OLS estimates could have led to biased estimates if $_{1i}$ were correlated with college choice because of unmeasured factors. For this reason, we used two additional empirical strategies to deal with selection. The first was to use propensity scores to match similar students on observable characteristics, and the second used an IV approach.

Addressing Selection Using a Propensity Matching Approach

Students' choices about whether to enroll in 2-year or 4-year colleges are subject to their preferences, financial constraints, academic profiles, beliefs about the prospects of benefiting from the respective institutions, and other unobservable characteristics. To address the bias that results from this potential selection, we first used a propensity score blocking technique to model selection into 2-year colleges compared with nonselective 4-year institutions. Propensity scores are useful for establishing a comparison group that is similar, on average, to a treatment group (in this case 2-year colleges) along a set of observed characteristics. First, we assembled a set of variables to predict the choice of 2-year versus 4-year postsecondary entry and estimated the following binomial logistic regression model:

$$\Pr(COMMCOLL)_i = {}_{3i} + X_{3i} + {}_{3i,} \tag{2}$$

where $\Pr(COMMCOLL)_i$ is the probability for the ith student to enter postsecondary study as a function of variety demographic characteristics and academic performance indicators, X_i (summary information on the estimation of the propensity score is included in Appendix Table A1). Thus, the propensity score is a "single number that indicates the extent to which one person is similar to another along a collection of observed characteristics" (Agodini & Dynarski, 2004). A histogram of the estimated propensity score for the 2-year entrants compared with the 4-year starters is shown in Appendix Figure A1.

Next, we used the propensity score (fitted probabilities of 2-year selection from this model) to stratify the sample into an optimal number of subclasses or "blocks." In stratifying the sample, we sorted from the lowest to the highest estimated propensity scores, discarding the observations with estimated propensity scores less than the minimum or greater than the maximum estimated propensity score for treated units (Dehejia & Wahba, 1999). The goal was to stratify the sample into groups of respondents with similar observed chances of postsecondary entry via 2-year versus 4-year institutions. The strata were chosen so that the covariates were "balanced" within each stratum, meaning that there were no statistically significant differences in means of covariates between those who started at 2-year colleges and those who started at 4-year institutions (Dehejia & Wahba, 1999).[14] Mean propensity scores for 2-year entrants (treated) and 4-year entrants (control) by strata are presented in Appendix Table A2. We then conducted our subsequent substantive models testing the effect of starting at a community college as fixed-effects models on the propensity score blocks, thereby evaluating the within-stratum difference in the outcomes between 2-year and 4-year entrants (Dehejia & Wahba, 1999).[15] Although the approach does not solve the selection problem on unobservable variables, it is an effective way to control for observed heterogeneity in the type of postsecondary entry (Morgan, 2001; Rosenbaum & Rubin, 1983; Rubin, 1997).

Addressing Selection Using an IV Approach

Our second strategy to address the issue of selection was an IV approach. To create a valid instrument, one must identify a variable that influences the choice of a 2-year versus a 4-year institution while not affecting the outcomes of interest (i.e., persistence, degree completion, and stop-out behavior). In this study, we used distances as instruments. Previous research has shown that students are more likely to attend one school over another on the basis of how close the colleges are to their homes (Long, 2004; Rouse, 1995). More specifically, our instruments were the distance from a student's home to the closest 2-year college and the distance to the closest nonselective 4-year university.[16] The instrumental approach is described as follows:

$$\text{CREDITS}_i = {}_{4i} + {}_1\text{COMMCOLL}_i + {}_2X_{i4i} + {}_{4i,} \tag{3}$$

where $\text{COMMCOLL}_i = f(\text{DIST\_2YR}_i, \text{DIST\_NONSEL4YR}_i) + {}_i$. As in the earlier equations, CREDITS_i is the outcome variable, and COMMCOLL_i is a dummy variable equal to one if a student began at a 2-year college. The difference with this approach was that COMMCOLL_i is instrumented for in the second part of the equation, with the distances from a student's home to the closest 2-year college and nonselective 4-year university, represented by DIST_2YR_i and DIST_NONSEL4YR_i, respectively.

There have been several critiques of using distance as an instrument. First, Rouse (1995) and Card (1995) advised that the estimates should be interpreted with caution, because families that value education might choose to live in close proximity to colleges, and therefore, distance could be endogenous. If so, the instruments would be invalid, because residence would also be correlated with educational outcomes (because of family preferences). Additionally, the relevance of distance is problematic when using national data sets because of differences in the way distance is perceived across the country and extreme variation in the geographical dispersion of colleges across a state.[17] However, these concerns are limited in this context. First, in Ohio, the colleges and universities are purposely distributed throughout the state so that each resident is within 30 miles of a school. During the 1960s and 1970s, with the goal of improving college access in Ohio, Governor James Rhodes influenced the locations of colleges so that every state resident was located within 30 miles of a college campus (Ohio Board of Regents, 2001). Therefore, the 4-year and 2-year colleges are scattered throughout the state, and each resident is close to one or both of each type of college, regardless of underlying preferences. Proximity is a particularly relevant factor in Ohio's enrollment patterns. The median distance from a student's home to the college of attendance was only 26 miles in our sample, with nearly 60% of students attending colleges within 50 miles of their homes. In addition, we focused on traditional-age college students, whose residential decisions were likely due to parental decisions made when the students were in high school or even earlier, long before college choice decisions (Rouse, 1995).

The results of the first stage of the IV approach are displayed in Appendix Table A3.[18] In addition to the instruments, the regression also included the following exogenous variables: a dummy variable for female students (with male students as the baseline), dummy variables for Black, Hispanic, Asian, and Native American students (with White students as the baseline), age, age squared, parental income, parental income squared, a dummy indicating missing values for parental income, and a student's math and English ACT scores. The signs of the estimates of the first stage of IV were as expected: Our sample of students was more likely to choose to initially attend community colleges the closer the nearest 2-year college and the farther away the nearest 4-year nonselective university. The test of joint significance for the instruments suggested that they had substantial explanatory power in the first stage ($F = 3{,}263.11$).

Results

Descriptive Analysis: Comparing Students with 4-Year Degree Intent

Table 1 displays summary statistics for our sample. The sample focused on students who began their postsecondary studies at 17 to 20 years old, who not only indicated 4-year degree intent but also took the ACT, an additional sign of aspirations to get a baccalaureate degree. As discussed above, previous empirical work suggests that community college students enter postsecondary schooling with lower academic credentials on average than their counterparts at 4-year institutions (as measured by high school grade point averages and ACT scores). However, the differences are not large between students at nonselective 4-year universities in Ohio and those at community colleges. Thus, for most of our analysis, we focused more explicitly on students at nonselective 4-year institutions as the main comparison group with community college students.[19]

TABLE 1

Descriptive Statistics

Variable	Public 4-Year Selective Universities	Public 4-Year Nonselective Universities	Public 2-Year Community Colleges
Age in 1998	18.351 (0.4995)	18.432 (0.5898)	18.425 (0.6446)
Percentage female	0.5500	0.5387	0.5498
Percentage White	0.8655	0.7991	0.8973
Percentage African American	0.0730	0.1178	0.0544
Percentage Hispanic	0.0151	0.0171	0.0142
Percentage Asian	0.0245	0.0148	0.0073
High school GPA	3.297 (0.4467)	2.959 (0.5901)	2.816 (0.5871)
Grades in high school math	3.204 (0.7829)	2.758 (0.9905)	2.548 (1.0249)
Grades in high school English	3.326 (0.7195)	2.959 (0.8589)	2.805 (0.9084)
ACT composite score (maximum = 36)	23.553 (3.838)	20.730 (4.2603)	19.550 (3.7237)
ACT math score	23.515 (4.480)	20.488 (4.6840)	19.198 (3.8956)
ACT English score	22.938 (4.397)	19.965 (4.8705)	18.692 (4.5223)
In math remediation	0.0807 [11,255]	0.2749 [7,421]	0.4639 [6,889]
In English remediation	0.0237 [11,255]	0.2372 [7,421]	0.2700 [6,889]
Percentage full-time	0.8188	0.6708	0.5550
Stopped out within 1 year	0.0431	0.1103	0.1642
Stopped out within 2 years	0.0852	0.1886	0.2761
Stopped out within 6 years	0.1810	0.3406	0.4392
Total credit hours after 6 years	110.893 (43.058)	85.218 (52.016)	66.230 (48.247)
Received bachelor's degree within 4 years	0.3647	0.1525	0.0564
Received bachelor's degree within 6 years	0.6900	0.4372	0.2118
Received bachelor's degree within 9 years	0.7291	0.4972	0.2587
Observations	13,683	7,422	7,388

Source: Ohio Board of Regents Higher Education Information System student entrance, student enrollment, and course enrollment files, along with test score and student background information from ACT Inc.

Note: GPA = grade point average. The sample consisted of the fall 1998 entering cohort aged 17 to 20 years who had intent to complete baccalaureate degrees. Because of the estimation techniques used, we also limited the sample to students who took the ACT (because of the information it provides on background) and Ohio residents (because we used residential proximity to an Ohio college as an instrumental variable). Values in parentheses are standard deviations. If the entire sample was not used in the calculation of the statistic, the number of observations is shown in square brackets. In Ohio, the selective public institutions require a certain academic standard but are not considered highly selective by national norms; in contrast, the nonselective 4-year universities are open-admissions schools.

The bottom part of Table 1 displays the mean enrollment and educational outcomes of students at each type of college. Students at each type of institution experienced very different outcomes. Among all students who started at 2-year colleges, nearly 44% had dropped out or stopped out 6 years after starting, compared with 34% who started at nonselective 4-year institutions and 18% who started at selective 4-year institutions. The rates of departure were consistently higher for those who started at community colleges compared with 4-year institutions, regardless of the timing of exit. More important, it is hard to ignore the vast differences in bachelor's degree receipt between those who started at 2-year colleges and those who began at 4-year institutions. Among community college students with the demonstrated intention to get 4-year degrees, only 26% obtained bachelor's degrees within 9 years of starting. Meanwhile, nearly 2 and 3 times as many students who began at nonselective (50%) and selective (73%) 4-year institutions did so. However, these comparisons do not account for differences between the students at each type of institution and should not be interpreted as causal effects. Community college students were also less likely to be enrolled full-time, with 56% of 2-year students enrolling fulltime as first-time freshmen, compared with 82% of students enrolled at selective 4-year institutions and 67% of students enrolled at nonselective 4-year institutions. This may be a decision endogenous to college choice, because community colleges offer more flexibility to be able to attend part-time.

Is There a Community College Penalty? Results of the Regression Analysis

Table 2 displays the relative likelihood that students who began at different types of institutions completed degrees within 6 or 9 years of initial enrollment. The 6-year benchmark, or 150% of the time needed to complete a 4-year degree full-time, is commonly used in the literature to calculate graduation rates, but we also show 9-year graduation rates because many community college students enroll in higher education part-time. Table 2 reports marginal effects estimated by probit regression models of starting at a community college. However, linear probability models produced similar results.[20]

The estimates suggest that students who started at community colleges compared with 4-year institutions, in particular, in comparison with selective 4-year universities, were significantly less likely to have completed baccalaureate degrees during the time frame. Specifications 1 and 6 show the simple comparison without any controls in the model. As shown in the upper part of the table, community college students were 43% less likely to complete bachelor's degrees than students who began at selective 4-year colleges. However, given differences between students who began at community colleges versus 4-year schools, the following specifications controlled for student demographic characteristics (race, gender, and age), parents' income, and student ability (ACT scores). Even after accounting for these differences, although lower in magnitude (from –0.426 to –0.363), the estimated penalty nevertheless persisted. There was also an estimated penalty, albeit a smaller one, for students who attended nonselective 4-year institutions in comparison with their counterparts at selective 4-year institutions. The F test comparing the results of attending a community college versus a nonselective 4-year university suggested that the estimates were statistically different from each other.

The bottom part of Table 2 limits the sample only to students at nonselective institutions, both 4 year and 2 year. As discussed above, these students were much more similar across institutions. Again, we note the lower likelihood of degree completion among those who started at community colleges. We also note that the estimated penalty was smaller once we omitted the comparison with selective 4-year institutions. In comparison with the results in the upper part of the table, however, there was only a modest change in the size of the estimate when including controls for background and ability (from –0.225 to –0.202). This suggests that the sample of students at nonselective schools was already very similar, so the covariates did not explain much of the variation in outcomes (below, we focus on comparisons between 2-year and nonselective 4-year entrants). The lower likelihood of graduation for community college entrants remained larger even after extending the time frame to 9 years. Nevertheless, selection into 2-year versus 4-year colleges may still be influenced by a variety of factors not accounted for in our model, so we turned to alternate specifications that addressed potential selectivity bias.

Comparing the Probit to the Propensity Score and IV Results

Table 3 presents a series of fitted models investigating the effect of starting at a 2-year college versus a nonselective 4-year institution on a host of outcomes: bachelor's degree receipt within 9 years (column 1), 6 years (column 2), and 4 years (column 3) and total credit hours earned after 6 years (column 4). In addition, the last column looks at the negative outcome of stopping out within 6 years without completing a degree (column 5). Panel A presents the results without any correction for selection, panel B presents the propensity score specification results, and panel C presents the results with the IV specification. The results using discrete outcomes were run using probit models. However, the results were robust to using linear probability models instead.

Looking at each outcome across the three specifications, students who started at community colleges had a significantly smaller likelihood of degree receipt, fewer total credits earned, and an increased likelihood of stopping out without a degree. However, as expected, after controlling for selection, the size of the estimated penalty fell. In terms of 9-year graduation rates, the negative effect of starting at a community college fell from 0.217 (Specification 1) to 0.211 when using propensity score methods (Specification 2), a very minor difference. However, using the IV approach to control for unobserved differences between community college and nonselective 4-year entrants

TABLE 2

The Role of the Initial Institution on Degree Completion (probit models with marginal effects reported)

	Outcome: Completed a Bachelor's Degree within 6 Years				Outcome: Completed a Bachelor's Degree within 9 Years
Variable	Baseline	Adding Demographics	Adding Parents' Income	Adding ACT Percentile	
All 4- and 2-year institutions					
	Specification				
	1	2	3	4	5
Initially attend 2-year college	−0.4259** (0.0069)	−0.4274** (0.0071)	−0.4175** (0.0072)	−0.3626** (0.0081)	−0.3544** (0.0084)
Initially attend nonselective 4-year college	−0.2136** (0.0076)	−0.1920** (0.0078)	−0.1799** (0.0079)	−0.1415** (0.0082)	−0.1266** (0.0083)
Pseudo-R^2	.09	.11	.12	.14	.14
Observations	28,493	28,493	28,493	28,493	28,493
Nonselective 4- and 2-year institutions only					
	Specification				
	6	7	8	9	10
Initially attend 2-year college	−0.2254** (0.0075)	−0.2409** (0.0075)	−0.2396** (0.0076)	−0.2023** (0.0078)	−0.2174** (0.0081)
Pseudo-R^2	.05	.07	.07	.12	.11
Observations	14,810	14,810	14,810	14,810	14,810

Note. The sample was the fall 1998 entering cohort aged 17 to 20 years who had intent to complete baccalaureate degrees. Values in parentheses are standard errors. Because of the estimation techniques used, the sample was also limited to ACT takers and Ohio residents. The baseline included only the variables for which a student initially attended (the shown coefficients). The second column adds the following demographic controls: a dummy variable for female students (with male students as the baseline); dummy variables for Black, Hispanic, Asian, and Native American students (with White students as the baseline); age; and age squared. The third column adds parental income, parental income squared, and a dummy indicating missing values for parental income. The fourth column adds math and English ACT scores. The last column includes all the controls (the same as the fourth column).

*Significant at 10%. **Significant at 5%.

796

TABLE 3

The Role of the Initial Institution: Comparing Estimation Strategies (probit models with marginal effects)

Outcome	Completed Bachelor's Degree within			Total Credit Hours in 6 Years	Stop Out within 6 Years
	9 Years	6 Years	4 Years		
(A) Probit results					
	Specification 1	2	3	4	5
Initially attend 2-year college	−0.2174** (0.0081)	−0.2023** (0.0078)	−0.0693** (0.0046)	−15.3948** (0.8085)	0.0796** (0.0083)
Pseudo-R^2/R^2	.11	.12	.13	.1285	.04
(B) Propensity score probit results					
	Specification 6	7	8	9	10
Initially attend 2-year college	−0.2110** (0.0082)	−0.1953** (0.0079)	−0.0642** (0.0045)	−14.4028** (0.8035)	0.0734** (0.0083)
Pseudo-R^2/R^2	.12	.13	.14	.1465	.04
(C) Instrumental variables probit results					
	Specification 11	12	13	14	15
Initially attend 2-year college	−0.1451** (0.0170)	−0.0983** (0.0164)	−0.0194** (0.0090)	−5.5882** (1.6446)	0.0488** (0.0169)
Overidentification test (X^2, $df = 1$)	0.371	1.227	1.760	0.204	7.801
Overidentification test p value	.5427	.2681	.1846	.6517	.0052
Pseudo-R^2/R^2	.08	.08	.11	.1198	.03

Note. The sample was students aged 17 to 20 years who entered a 2-year or nonselective 4-year college during fall 1998 and had intent to complete baccalaureate degrees. Values in parentheses are standard errors. Because of the estimation techniques used, the sample was also limited to ACT takers and Ohio residents. All regressions had 14,810 observations. The results for "total credit hours" were estimated using ordinary least squares instead of probit models. R^2 values are displayed for the "total credit hours" results; all others are pseudo-R^2 values. The number of blocks with the propensity score estimates is 10. Each regression included the following controls: a dummy variable for female students (with male students as the baseline); dummy variables for Black, Hispanic, Asian, and Native American students (with White students as the baseline); age; age squared; parental income; parental income squared; a dummy indicating missing values for parental income; and the student's math and English ACT scores. The results using discrete outcomes were run using probit models. However, the results are robust to using linear probability models instead.

*Significant at 10%. **Significant at 5%.

consistently resulted in the smallest estimate of the penalty (0.145 in terms of degree completion within 9 years; Specification 11). For credit hours completed, over 6 years, there was a difference of 15.4 credits in the simple comparison (Specification 4), but this dropped to 14.4 credits in the propensity score results and 5.6 credits in the IV estimate (Specification 14). Therefore, although propensity scores likely address some small part of the selection bias in the straightforward results, the IV strategy, by dealing with unobservable differences, seems to have done a better job addressing concerns about the comparability of students across types of schools. For the IV estimates, we also report overidentification tests under the null hypothesis that the instruments were valid. The test was X^2 distributed in the number of overidentifying restrictions.[21] As is evident in Table 3, the test consistently failed to reject the null hypothesis in all cases except for Specification 15 (stop-out behavior within 6 years), so we have confidence in the results.

Although the penalty experienced by community college students was much smaller once accounting for bias, there was still an important difference in outcomes not explained by initial selection into 2-year versus 4-year institutions. Even after adjusting for selection bias, our analyses still found a consistent, albeit more modest, negative effect of beginning at a community college. Focusing on the IV estimates, the penalty became larger once taking into account a longer period of time: The difference in rates of degree completion were not all that different within 4 years (–0.019), because few students who began at nonselective 4-year universities were able to do this, but the gap grew once giving students 6 (–0.98) and 9 years (–0.145). Likewise, the difference in total credits earned within 6 years was equivalent to nearly two average college courses.

This conclusion is similar to those made in earlier work (Alfonso, 2006; Leigh & Gill, 2003; Rouse, 1995; Sandy, Gonzalez, & Hilmer, 2006). However, these studies were based on cohorts of students who graduated from high school 15 or even 25 years ago. Meanwhile, there has been increasing pressure on community colleges to fill the role of an alternative pathway to a baccalaureate degree because of capacity constraints, rising admissions requirements, and escalating tuition costs at many 4-year institutions. With our focus on a cohort that is the most recently available to investigate 9-year outcomes (having entered college in fall 1998), we provide a timely estimate of the impact of starting at a community college.

How Does the Community College Penalty Differ by Student Type?

Earlier work on college access and degree receipt has pointed to important differences by race and gender in the educational attainment process. As such, we asked whether the penalty of community college entry was greater for women versus men, Black versus White students, and lower achieving versus higher achieving students. To answer these questions, we tested three sets of interactions (Tables 4, 5, and 6). It is important to note that the comparison of estimates across strategies becomes more complicated using the interactions because of the need to take into account the overall effect, interaction coefficient, and baseline dummy variable. Panel B of each table adds these coefficients together to calculate the overall effect for each group.

Table 4 summarizes the results for gender for our two most important outcomes: baccalaureate degree completion within 9 years and total credit hours completed within 6 years. Each of the models included an interaction between the variable of interest (starting at a community college) and a dummy variable equal to one for female students. As shown in the table, there was a statistically significant interaction between 2-year entry and being female for the simple probit and propensity score estimates (although negative and similar in size, the IV estimates were not statistically significant). This suggests that women experience a larger penalty for initially entering a community college than men. However, because women tend to do better than men overall in terms of educational outcomes (regardless of where they attend college), the overall effects were still more negative for men, as shown in panel B. Looking at the overall effects, it is still clear that correcting for selection using propensity score or IV models reduced the estimate of the community college penalty for both men and women.

We next tested for whether the community college penalty was greater for Black versus White students. Table 5 summarizes the results by race; the sample was limited to Black and White students only, so the total sample size was 13,836. Each of the models included an interaction between

TABLE 4

The Role of Initial Institution on Educational Outcomes by Gender: IV Results (probit models with marginal effects reported)

Variable	Completed Bachelor's Degree within 9 Years			Total Credit Hours (6 Years)		
	Probit Results	PS Results	IV Results	Probit Results	PS Results	IV Results
	Specification					
	1	2	3	4	5	6
(A) Estimated coefficients						
Initially attend 2-year college	-0.1915**	-0.1841**	-0.1165**	12.8725**	-11.8093**	-2.9279
	(0.0121)	(0.0122)	(0.0256)	(1.1809)	(1.1724)	(2.4406)
Initially attend 2-year college × female dummy variable	-0.0483**	-0.0499**	-0.0503	-4.6203**	-4.7436**	-4.7042
	(0.0163)	(0.0164)	(0.0326)	(1.5770)	(1.5619)	(3.1661)
Female dummy variable	0.0889**	0.0908**	0.0904**	11.3608**	11.5337**	11.4751**
	(0.0117)	(0.0117)	(0.0187)	(1.1533)	(1.1425)	(1.8036)
Overidentification test (X^2, $df = 3$)	—	—	3.713	—	—	0.139
Overidentification test p value	—	—	.2942	—	—	.9867
Pseudo-R^2/R^2	.11	.12	.08	.1290	.1471	.1201
(B) Overall effect of starting at a community college						
Male students	-0.1915	-0.1841	-0.1165	-12.8725	-11.8093	-2.9279
Female students	-0.1509	-0.1432	-0.0764	-6.1320	-5.0192	3.8430

Note. IV = instrumental variables; PS = propensity score. The sample was students aged 17 to 20 years who entered nonselective 2- or 4-year colleges during fall 1998 and had intent to complete baccalaureate degrees. Values in parentheses are standard errors. Because of the estimation techniques used, the sample was also limited to ACT takers and Ohio residents. All regressions had 14,810 observations. The results for "total credit hours" were estimated using ordinary least squares instead of probit models. R^2 values are displayed for the "total credit hours" results; all others are pseudo-R^2 values. The number of blocks with the propensity score estimates is 10. Each regression included the following controls: a dummy variable for female students (with male students as the baseline); dummy variables for Black, Hispanic, Asian, and Native American students (with White students as the baseline); age; age squared; parental income; parental income squared; a dummy indicating missing values for parental income; and the student's math and English ACT scores.

*Significant at 10%. **Significant at 5%.

799

TABLE 5

The Role of Initial Institution on Educational Outcomes by Race (Black and White students only) (probit models with marginal effects reported)

	Completed Bachelor's Degree within 9 Years			Total Credit Hours (6 Years)		
	Probit Results	PS Results	IV Results	Probit Results	PS Results	IV Results
Variable						
Specification	1	2	3	4	5	6
(A) Estimated coefficients						
Initially attend 2-year college	−0.2112**	−0.2043**	−0.1281**	−14.7258**	−13.6650**	−3.6118**
	(0.0087)	(0.0088)	(0.0182)	(0.8720)	(0.8665)	(1.7655)
Initially attend 2-year college × black dummy variable	−0.1203**	−0.1162**	−0.1590**	−8.5411**	−8.5039**	−18.0057**
	(0.0343)	(0.0344)	(0.0657)	(2.9982)	(2.9950)	(6.7629)
Black dummy variable	−0.0547**	−0.2914**	−0.0133	−8.5703**	−45.4329**	−2.1279
	(0.0180)	(0.0178)	(0.0313)	(1.8182)	(3.0703)	(2.7534)
Overidentification test (X^2, $df = 3$)	—	—	10.359	—	—	8.272
Overidentification test p value	—	—	.0158	—	—	.0407
Pseudo-R^2/R^2	.11	.12	.08	.1306	.1490	.1203
(B) Overall effect of starting at a community college						
White students	−0.2112	−0.2043	−0.1281	−14.7258	−13.6650	−3.6118
Black students	−0.3862	−0.6119	−0.3004	−31.8372	−67.6018	−23.7454

Note. PS = propensity score; IV = instrumental variables. The sample was students aged 17 to 20 years who entered nonselective 2- and 4-year colleges during fall 1998 and had intent to complete baccalaureate degrees. Values in parentheses are standard errors. Because of the estimation techniques used, the sample was also limited to ACT takers and Ohio residents. All regressions had 13,836 observations because non-White and non-Black students were dropped from the sample for this analysis. The results for "total credit hours" were estimated using ordinary least squares instead of probit models. R^2 values are displayed for the "total credit hours" results; all others are pseudo-R^2 values. The number of blocks with the propensity score estimates is 10. Each regression included the following controls: a dummy variable for female students (with male students as the baseline); dummy variables for Black, Hispanic, Asian, and Native American students (with White students as the baseline); age; age squared; parental income; parental income squared; a dummy indicating missing values for parental income; and the student's math and English ACT scores.
*Significant at 10%. **Significant at 5%.

800

the variable of interest (starting at a community college) and a dummy variable equal to one for being a Black student. We note that the interaction variable was statistically significant across all the models. In other words, a differential effect was found for Black versus White students, with Black students experiencing worse outcomes from beginning at a community college than White students. Again, the size of the estimate decreased once accounting for selection using the propensity score and IV strategies. However, the overidentification tests for the IV models cause us to be wary of these results. Focusing on the propensity score estimates instead, the results suggest that Black students had worse educational outcomes (i.e., a lower overall likelihood of graduation) and that attending a community college only exacerbated the educational gap between Black and White students. Controlling for the propensity score differences (i.e., the likelihood of initially choosing to attend a community college), Black students were much less likely to complete degrees or more credits than White students. This is possibly because within a propensity score block, White students had better academic preparation for college than Black students.

Finally, we looked at whether there were differences by previous academic achievement level. One might hypothesize that community colleges are the best entry point for students with weaker academic achievement in that they may specialize in providing the necessary preparation for more challenging work at the 4-year level. Work by Light and Strayer (2000) suggests that lower achieving students who attend less selective schools are more likely to complete college than their counterparts at more selective institutions. On the other hand, others have argued that in fact students perform better, regardless of their demonstrated ability, in more academically challenging environments. For example, some have found that attending a more selective institution, regardless of relative academic preparation, is associated with higher graduation rates (Alon & Tienda, 2005; Kane, 1998). These hypotheses would lead to different conclusions about whether the penalty of starting at a community college differs (and in what direction) for students of different demonstrated abilities.

Table 6 summarizes the results for models in which we included interactions between the type of college entrance and a categorical measure of ACT score: low (0 to 17) and high (23 to 36), with the categories left out being average scores (18 to 22). Without controlling for bias, it appeared that higher ability students at community colleges were at a real disadvantage over students of average ability. In the propensity score analysis, students with higher ACT scores were less likely to complete degrees or more credits than students with more average ACT scores. This is because within a propensity score block, students with more average ACT scores were likely to otherwise have better performance on other indicators (years of high school math or English, high school rank, etc.) or may otherwise have been different on other demographics (race, parental income, etc.) and therefore had better outcomes overall. But it may be the case that there were unobservable differences we did not catch, for example, that students with higher scores who entered community colleges were less motivated, actually lacked the right preparation to succeed, or had other demands on their time. Once we accounted for this, higher ability students did not suffer any special penalty in terms of graduation, and the interaction results were not statistically significant in terms of credits completed. On the other hand, students with lower ACT scores also seemed to do worse at community colleges than the average student in terms of degree completion (the results for credits completed were not statistically significant). These results were robust across the estimation strategies and lend credence to the idea that students do better if at nonselective 4-year institutions.

Conclusion

Although community colleges serve an important function in postsecondary education, comparatively little education research has assessed their effectiveness or examined their students. Although several studies have examined the consequences of attending a community college, many questions remain about both the goals and intentions of community college students and their postcollegiate outcomes. The increased flexibility and nontraditional patterns of attendance afforded by community colleges may weaken a student's progression through postsecondary education and make transferring to a 4-year college less likely (Grubb, 1991). Furthermore, the administrative costs of transferring to a 4-year college may be exceedingly prohibitive for many students.

TABLE 6

The Role of Initial Institution on Outcomes by Preparation: IV Results (probit models with marginal effects reported)

Variable	Completed Bachelor's Degree within 9 Years			Total Credit Hours (6 Years)		
	Probit Results	PS Results	IV Results	Probit Results	PS Results	IV Results
	1	2	3	4	5	6
(A) Estimated coefficients	Specification					
Initially attend 2-year college	-0.1981**	-0.1871**	-0.1308**	-13.6647**	-12.0216**	-3.5609
	(0.0016)	(0.0117)	(0.0231)	(1.1816)	(1.1596)	(2.3114)
Initially attend 2-year college × high ACT score	-0.0794**	-0.0621**	-0.0121	-11.4030**	-9.0981**	-6.1703
	(0.0186)	(0.0192)	(0.0403)	(1.9837)	(1.9530)	(4.0394)
Initially attend 2-year college × low ACT score	-0.0414**	-0.0423**	-0.0745*	-1.6363	-1.3450	-4.7433
	(0.0198)	(0.0201)	(0.0387)	(1.9221)	(1.8896)	(3.8159)
High ACT score dummy variable	0.1663**	-0.0361**	0.1488**	17.0388**	-4.9744**	16.4880**
	(0.0135)	(0.0163)	(0.0210)	(1.3107)	(1.6080)	(2.0191)
Low ACT score dummy variable	-0.0962**	0.0445**	-0.0826**	-11.7951**	4.6348**	-10.8974**
	(0.0139)	(0.0173)	(0.0241)	(1.4546)	(1.6327)	(2.3609)
Overidentification test (X^2, $df = 5$)	—	—	5.800	—	—	3.742
Overidentification test p value	—	—	.3262	—	—	.5871
Pseudo-R^2/R^2	.09	.12	.05	.1068	.1460	.0957
(B) Overall effect of starting at a community college						
High ACT	-0.1112	-0.2853	0.0059	-8.0289	-26.0941	6.7568
Middle ACT	-0.1981	-0.1871	-0.1308	-13.6647	-12.0216	-3.5609
Low ACT	-0.3357	-0.1849	-0.2879	-27.0961	-8.7318	-19.2016

Note. IV = instrumental variables; PS = propensity score. The sample was students aged 17 to 20 years who entered nonselective 2- and 4-year colleges during fall 1998 and had intent to complete baccalaureate degrees. Values in parentheses are standard errors. Because of the estimation techniques used, the sample was also limited to ACT takers and Ohio residents. All regressions had 14,810 observations. The results for "total credit hours" were estimated using ordinary least squares instead of probit models. R^2 values are displayed for the "total credit hours" results; all others are pseudo-R^2 values. The number of blocks with the propensity score estimates is 10. "High ACT" is a dummy variable for having a composite ACT score of 23 to 36, "middle ACT" is for scores of 18 to 22, and "low ACT" is for scores of 17 and lower. Each regression included the following controls: a dummy variable for female students (with male students as the baseline); dummy variables for Black, Hispanic, Asian, and Native American students (with White students as the baseline); age; age squared; parental income; parental income squared; a dummy indicating missing values for parental income; and dummy variables for having a high ACT score (23 to 36) or a low ACT score (17 or lower).
*Significant at 10%. **Significant at 5%.

Using a detailed data set of individuals in a large, public higher education system, we provide a timely examination of the experiences of community college students who intend to get 4-year degrees. Our study, beyond using straightforward regression models, used two additional research strategies to account for the fact that students do not sort into community colleges and 4-year institutions randomly. Accounting for selection using both propensity score methods and IV gave us the opportunity to measure and compare differences in postsecondary outcomes in two ways. In addition, we used a longer time span of data (9 years) than any other study, had access to important information on transfer behavior and student degree intent, and shed light on a context that has not previously been studied.

Although we did not specifically test a democratization or diversion theory of community colleges, we did ask whether, for those who divert (or perhaps detour) to bachelor's degrees via community colleges, there is a cost. We found that in fact there is a cost in terms of degree completion, credit accumulation, and the risk for dropping out to initially entering postsecondary study through community colleges. In other words, we found a persistent community college penalty. Moreover, this penalty persisted even after controlling for key student demographic and academic achievement variables. It was also evident after accounting for students' self-selection into community colleges using two different empirical methodologies. Selection into type of postsecondary institution is clearly a factor that biases straightforward estimates of the penalty of starting at a community college. We also found that the penalty of starting at 2-year rather than nonselective 4-year institutions varied by type of student, with female students experiencing a different penalty than male students.

As noted above, these results may be a conservative estimate of the "community college penalty" because of our sample restriction that students must have taken the ACT; the results of this study do not reflect the penalty experienced by students who want baccalaureate degrees but fail to prepare for admission into 4-year universities, a group that is likely to have less academic preparation. As shown by the summary statistics in Table 1, the results are representative for more traditional-age, primarily White college students on the margin between attending 2- and 4-year institutions who have slightly below average ACT scores (somewhere in the 25th to 50th percentiles in scores).[22]

These findings are particularly relevant in today's debates about how to improve educational attainment given the growing importance of community colleges as a pathway to a baccalaureate degree. Amid rising demands for skilled workers coupled with the increasing numbers of individuals seeking higher education, community colleges have been forced to accommodate much of the expansion in postsecondary schooling. However, one must acknowledge that, on average, the outcomes of students who initially enter higher education through the 2-year system appear to lag behind those of students who enter via 4-year colleges. Our conservative estimates suggest that these students are 14.5% less likely to complete baccalaureate degrees within 9 years. This has significant consequences, especially for low-income and minority students, who disproportionally rely on community colleges as the primary portal for postsecondary entry. Because of the "penalty" experienced by community college students, caution should be exercised when designing policies that might shift enrollment patterns more toward 2-year colleges. On the other hand, because community colleges are less expensive, it is worth comparing the size of the penalty to the difference in costs between 2-year and 4-year institutions. In addition, greater focus is warranted on institutional policies and programs that support community college students and help them transfer to 4-year institutions to reach their intended goal of obtaining baccalaureate degrees.

Appendix

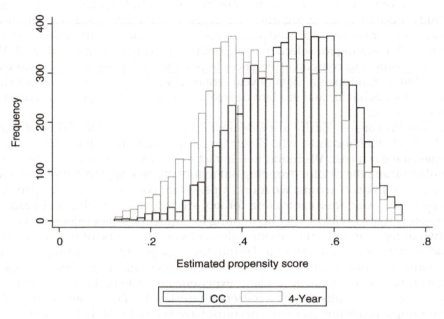

Figure A1   Histogram of the estimated propensity score for the 2-year community college (CC) versus nonselective 4-year college starters.

TABLE A1

Logit Coefficients from the Model Estimating the Probability of Entering a Public 2-Year College

Variable	Community College versus Nonselective 4-Year University
Female	0.0234 (0.0363)
Black	−1.2707*** (0.0682)
Hispanic	−0.3737** (0.1379)
Asian	−0.8822*** (0.1759)
Native American	−0.0360 (0.3414)
Age	−0.1256*** (0.0283)
Parent income	−2.27 ◊ 10^{-6}** (7.82 × 10^{-7})
Parent income missing dummy	0.0086 (0.0709)
High school GPA	0.3533 (0.2430)
High school GPA squared	−0.1244** (0.0438)
High school GPA rank	0.0833 (0.1090)
Years of high school math	−0.0961** (.0324)
Years of high school English	−0.0911* (0.0513)
High school math grades	1.5928*** (0.1281)
Missing high school math grades dummy	0.4193*** (0.1226)
High school English grades	0.0039 (0.0340)
Missing high school English grades dummy	0.3444** (0.1702)
ACT percentile	−0.0112*** (0.0008)
Private high school	−0.3452*** (0.0539)
Constant	3.3205 (0.6629)
R^2	.0672
Observations	14,819

Note. GPA = grade point average. The sample was limited to fall 1998 first-time students aged 17 to 20 years who had 4-year degree intent, took the ACT, and were Ohio residents. Values in parentheses are standard errors.
*Significant at 10%. **Significant at 5%. ***Significant at 0.01%.

TABLE A2

Mean Propensity Scores for 2-Year Entrants (treated) and Nonselective 4-Year Entrants (control) by Strata (blocks)

| Blocks | Mean Propensity Score | | Number of Observations | | t Value, Mean (Control)–Mean (Treatment) |
	Community College (Treatment)	4-Year College (Control)	Community College (Treatment)	4-Year College (Control)	
Block 1	.2099	.2076	79	315	−0.5738
Block 2	.2672	.2654	50	231	−1.2420
Block 3	.3286	.3280	501	1,190	−0.5486
Block 4	.3679	.3673	197	313	−1.4686
Block 5	.3905	.3898	422	674	−1.3004
Block 6	.4215	.4221	580	637	1.1514
Block 7	.4704	.4692	1,227	1,210	−1.6696
Block 8	.5501	.5488	2,274	1,845	−1.4120
Block 9	.6191	.6184	745	542	−1.0513
Block 10	.6748	.6746	812	454	−0.1740

TABLE A3

First-Stage Instrumental Variables Results (probit models with marginal effects)

Variable	Choose 2-Year College
Distance to closest 2-year college (per 100 miles)	−0.0942** (0.0458)
Distance to closest nonselective 4-year university (per 100 miles)	1.3510** (0.0236)
Female	−0.0134 (0.0098)
Black	−0.1698** (0.0168)
Hispanic	−0.0201 (0.0357)
Asian	−0.1747** (0.0420)
Native American	−0.0289 (0.0970)
Age	−3.8844** (0.3523)
Age squared	0.1038** (0.0095)
Parental income (per $1,000)	0.0006 (0.0008)
Parental income squared (per $1,000,000)	−0.0000 (0.0000)
Parent income missing dummy	0.0398 (0.0246)
ACT math score	−0.0188** (0.0015)
ACT English score	−0.0096** (0.0013)
Test of joint significance of instrumental variables	3,263.11
Pseudo-R^2	0.24
Observations	14,810

Note. The sample was students aged 17 to 20 years who entered 2-year or nonselective 4-year colleges during fall 1998 and had intent to complete baccalaureate degrees. Values in parentheses are standard errors. The variables listed are the instruments for the selection of a 2-year college (over a nonselective 4-year university). The regression also included the following exogenous variables: a dummy variable for female students (with male students as the baseline); dummy variables for Black, Hispanic, Asian, and Native American students (with White students as the baseline); age; age squared; parental income; parental income squared; a dummy indicating missing values for parental income; and the student's math and English ACT scores.
*Significant at 10%. **Significant at 5%.

Notes

1. As noted by Evelyn (2002), some states are even considering using community colleges to award bachelor's degrees in areas of specific need to those states.

2. Studies using the National Longitudinal Survey of Youth (NLSY79; e.g., Leigh & Gill, 1997, 2003) focused on students who were 14 to 22 years old when first interviewed in 1979, suggesting that they graduated from high school in the 1970s or 1980s. Studies using the High School and Beyond (HSB; e.g., Rouse, 1995) data set focused on students who graduated from high school in 1982. Studies using the National Education Longitudinal Study (NELS; e.g., Alfonso, 2006; Roksa, 2006) focused on students who graduated from high school in 1992.

3. Other recent developments that have likely affected the role of community colleges include increases in high school graduation requirements, which may have improved the academic preparation of some students while influencing others to drop out and seek their General Educational Development certificates at community colleges, and the increasing use of loans beginning with the 1992 Higher Education Act Reauthorization, which may have affected students' choice between 2- and 4-year college options. At the same time, many community colleges opted out of giving students federal student loans because of government rules that penalize colleges with high default rates.

4. Regardless of where students enroll or how many times they change institutions, they are tracked within the system using their unique Social Security numbers. This was not the case, however, in many other studies that used national data sets. Although these sources were designed to be nationally representative, they suffered from attrition over time, especially in the later follow-ups. For example, the fourth follow-up study of NELS had a target of 15,649 students, but only 12,144 were considered completed cases, resulting in a response rate of 77.6% (National Center for Education Statistics, [NCES] 2002, p. 206). Adjusting the sample weights in response to this attrition may not be an adequate solution, because there are likely to be important, unobservable differences between those in the sample and those missing. Therefore, information from these databases on behavior several years out of high school may not truly be nationally representative.

5. Most state administrative databases lack significant detail on community college students because information on academic preparation and test scores is not required for admission, and financial aid records are often not part of the data systems. (Even when included, not all students complete aid applications and so are missing from the data sets.) Therefore, many studies based on administrative data have only basic demographic information (e.g., Leigh & Gill, 2007; Moore & Shulock, 2007). Efforts to supplement the data with student surveys often have low response rates. For example, the City University of New York administrative data used by Bailey and Weininger (2002) was supplemented with a survey of students' social backgrounds and places of birth, but the response rate was only 31.4% (sample weights had to be developed for the analysis). An exception is the Florida administrative data used by studies such as that of Calcagno, Crosta, Bailey, and Jenkins (2007). As a K–20 data warehouse, it also includes information on high school preparation, test scores, and family income (if a free application for federal student aid was submitted). At the other end of the spectrum, the State University of New York data used by Ehrenberg and Smith (2004) was grouped so that analysis could not be done at the individual level. In contrast, the data used in this study had degree intent information from the college applications and details about family incomes, high school preparation and achievement, and high school types from the student surveys that accompany college entrance exams (i.e., the ACT and SAT).

6. We used three main files submitted by all public colleges and universities in Ohio to the OBR's Higher Education Information System: student entrance, student enrollment, and course enrollment. In addition, we used test score and student background information that is the result of an OBR data match with ACT, Inc. All of these files, which also denote the institutions, are linked by students' Social Security numbers (we received an anonymous version of the data), and students may have files from multiple institutions if they attended more than one school during the time period. These data were available for each term (fall, spring, summer, and, for those on the quarter system, winter) from fall 1997 to spring 2007.

7. In our study, students who ended college attendance sometime during the 9-year period, did not return to any statewide public institution, and had not completed bachelor's degrees were considered stopouts or dropouts. The multiple measures of stop-out behavior denoted the last time a student was enrolled in college.

8. Although we could not track students who transferred to private institutions or public out-of-state institutions, this was not likely to be a large group. The Integrated Postsecondary Education Data System,

an NCES annual database of postsecondary institutions in the United States, tracks the number of transfers at each institution but does not record the states of residence of transfer students. However, it does track the states of residence of incoming freshmen. Assuming that the distribution of transfer students matched the geographical distribution of the incoming freshman class, one would expect about 650 Ohio students to transfer to nonpublic or non-Ohio schools. If we further assume that all 650 transfer students just finished their first year of school, then about 4.3% of observed dropouts in our data were actually transfer students.

9. The other options were (d) "to obtain knowledge for personal interest," (e) "to upgrade skills for current job by taking only selected courses," (f) "to train for a new career by taking only selected courses," (g) "to obtain a certificate," and (h) "to obtain an associate degree for the job market." Students who began at 4-year institutions were not asked about intent and were assumed to want baccalaureate degrees.

10. The percentage at community colleges intending to obtain bachelor's degrees was slightly smaller in our data than that found in other surveys (e.g., NELS, the Beginning Postsecondary Study). Beyond slight differences in the way the question was posed to students in each survey, one reason for the different percentages may be related to how the questions were asked. There are concerns that students in other surveys reported higher educational aspirations, which may not match the realities surrounding college admission and/or enrollment (i.e., academic preparation, financial constraints, etc.) (Rosenbaum, 2001). The low-stakes method by which degree intent was collected in our data set could mean that our survey yielded more honest answers.

11. Approximately two thirds of high school students in Ohio take the ACT. Our data set included the highest score of a student and his or her most recent responses to the ACT survey, which includes self-reported information on high school preparation and performance as well as the intended plan of study in college.

12. After applying the basic sample restrictions (age 17 to 20 years, 4-year degree intent, took the ACT, and Ohio residency), we had to drop 1,092 observations (3.1% of the sample) because of missing complete college transcript information and 3,517 observations (10% of the sample) because of missing ZIP code information. Although the number missing ZIP code information was large, it was driven mainly by the fact that Kent State University did not submit any ZIP code information, resulting in our dropping its students from the sample (2,396 observations, or 68% of those missing ZIP code information).

13. To maintain the largest sample size possible, students missing parental income information were included by creating a "missing parental income" dummy variable. This was necessary for 1,316 observations, or 8.9% of the sample. However, for this reason, the coefficients on parental income should not be used in interpretation.

14. To ensure that the individual covariates were balanced within each stratum, we included additional higher order terms of the background variables (see Appendix Table A1).

15. For a more detailed discussion of propensity score "binning" procedures, see Dehejia and Wahba (1999, 2002); Conniffe, Gash, and O'Connell (2000); and Rosenbaum and Rubin (1983). Several studies have demonstrated that propensity score impacts are not sensitive to the ways in which matching is conducted (Dehejia & Wahba, 2002; Smith & Todd, 2005).

16. These distances were calculated from the student's high school to the nearest of each type of postsecondary institution. In Ohio, the nonselective 4-year universities are open-admissions schools.

17. These critiques have focused on the power of proximity as a predictor. Clearly, distance might be perceived differently in Nevada than in New Jersey. Also, the geography of college locations differs greatly by state, and this creates very different norms in college attendance patterns by distance. However, we focused on one state where students have a strong pattern of attending the colleges closest to their homes.

18. These first-stage results apply to the instrumental variables estimates discussed below.

19. It is worth noting that our sample characteristics were different from those of college students generally because we limited the sample by age and to those who indicated wanting 4-year degrees and who took the ACT. In the general population, one would find much starker differences between students at selective 4-year colleges and those at community colleges. Meanwhile, the data suggest that the student bodies at nonselective 4-year colleges and at community colleges had much more similar backgrounds and academic preparation, even without our sample restrictions. Students at nonselective 4-year and 2-year (i.e., community) institutions tended to be older and were more likely to be non-White and to have lower academic performance levels. Students at these schools were also more likely to attend part-time or less than part-time.

20. For instance, Specification 9, with all of the controls, yielded a probit estimate of –0.2023 (SE = 0.0078). Using OLS instead, the estimate was –0.1913 (SE = 0.0074). Likewise, Specification 10 yielded a probit estimate of –0.2174 (SE = 0.0081). Using OLS instead, the estimate was –0.2046 (SE = 0.0076).

21. Intuitively, it was a test of whether, after eliminating its correlation with choice (instrumented) and the other covariates, the educational outcomes were still correlated with the distance variables.

22. The average composite ACT score in 1997–1998 was 21 (ACT Inc., 2008).

References

ACT Inc. (2008). *The 1998 ACT high school profile report—National data.* Retrieved May 14, 2008, from http://www.act.org/news/data/98/tsum.html

Adelman, C. (2005). *The toolbox revisited.* Washington, DC: U.S. Department of Education.

Agodini, R., & Dynarski, M. (2004). Are experiments the only option? A look at dropout prevention programs. *Review of Economics and Statistics, 86*(1), 180–194.

Alfonso, M. (2006). The impact of community college attendance on baccalaureate attainment. *Research in Higher Education, 47*(8), 873–903.

Alfonso, M., Bailey, T., & Scott, M. (2005). The educational outcomes of occupational sub-baccalaureate students: Evidence from the 1990s. *Economics of Education Review, 24*(2), 197–212.

Alon, S., & Tienda, M. (2005). Assessing the "mismatch" hypothesis: Differences in college graduation rates by college selectivity. *Sociology of Education, 78*(4), 294–315.

Anderson, G., Sun, J. C., & Alfonso, M. (2006). Effectiveness of statewide articulation agreements on the probability of transfer: A preliminary policy analysis. *Review of Higher Education, 29*(3), 261–291.

Bailey, T. R., & Weininger, E. (2002). Performance, graduation, and transfer of immigrants and natives in the City University of New York community colleges. *Educational Evaluation and Policy Analysis, 24*(4), 359–377.

Becker, G. (1993). *Human capital: A theoretical and empirical analysis with special reference to education.* Chicago: University of Chicago Press.

Brint, S., & Karabel, J. (1989). *The diverted dream: Community colleges and the promise of educational opportunity in America, 1900–1985.* New York: Oxford University Press.

Calcagno, J. C., Crosta, P., Bailey, T. R., & Jenkins, D. (2007). Stepping stones to a degree: The impact of enrollment pathways and milestones on community college student outcomes. *Research in Higher Education, 48*(7), 755–801.

Card, D. (1995). Using geographic variation in college proximity to estimate the return to schooling. In L. N. Christofides, E. K. Grant, & R. Swidinsky (Eds.), *Aspects of labor market behaviour: Essays in honour of John Vanderkamp* (pp. 201–222). Toronto, Canada: University of Toronto Press.

Conniffe, D., Gash, V., & O'Connell, P. (2000). Evaluating state programmes: "Natural experiments" and propensity scores. *Economic and Social Review, 31*(4), 283–308.

Dehejia, R. H., & Wahba, S. (1999). Causal effects in nonexperimental studies: Reevaluating the evaluation of training programs. *Journal of the American Statistical Association, 94*(448), 1053–1062.

Dehejia, R. H., & Wahba, S. (2002). Propensity score-matching methods for nonexperimental causal studies. *Review of Economics and Statistics, 84*(1), 151–161.

Dougherty, K. (1987). The effects of community colleges: Aid or hindrance to socioeconomic attainment? *Sociology of Education, 60*(2), 86–103.

Dougherty, K. (1994). *The contradictory college: The conflicting origins, impacts, and futures of the community college.* Albany: State University of New York Press.

Dougherty, K., & Kienzl, G. S. (2006). It's not enough to get through the open door: Inequalities by social background in transfer from community college to four-year colleges. *Teachers College Record, 108*(3), 452–487.

Ehrenberg, R., & Smith, C. (2004). Analyzing the success of student transitions from 2- to 4-year institutions within a state. *Economics of Education Review, 23*(1), 11–28.

Evelyn, J. (2002). Budget cuts force community colleges to consider turning away students. *Chronicle of Higher Education, 48*(46), A25–A26.

Grubb, W. N. (1991). The decline of community college transfer rates: Evidence from National Longitudinal Surveys. *Journal of Higher Education, 62*(2), 194–222.

Grubb, W. N. (1995). Postsecondary education and the sub-baccalaureate labor market: Corrections and extensions. *Economics of Education Review, 14*(3), 285–299.

Hilmer, M. J. (1997). Does community college attendance provide a strategic path to a higher quality education? *Economics of Education Review, 16*(1), 59–68.

Hilmer, M. J. (1998). Post-secondary fees and the decision to attend a university or a community college. *Journal of Public Economics, 67*(3), 329–348.

Hilmer, M. J. (2000). Does the return to quality differ for transfer students and direct attendees? *Economics of Education Review, 19*(1), 47–61.

Kane, T. (1998). Misconceptions in the debate over affirmative action in college admissions. In G. Orfield & E. Miller (Eds.), *Chilling admissions: The affirmative action crisis and the search for alternatives* (pp. 17–31). Cambridge, MA: Harvard Education.

Kane, T., & Rouse, C. (1995). Labor market returns to two- and four-year college. *American Economic Review, 85*(3), 600–614.

Kyung, W. (1996). In-migration of college students to the state of New York. *Journal of Higher Education, 67*(3), 349–358.

Lee, V., & Frank, K. (1990). Students' characteristics that facilitate the transfer from two-year to four-year colleges. *Sociology of Education, 63*(3), 178–193.

Leigh, D. E., & Gill, A. M. (2003). Do community colleges really divert students from earning bachelor's degrees? *Economics of Education Review, 22*(1), 23–30.

Leigh, D. E., & Gill, A. M. (2007). *Do community colleges respond to local needs? Evidence from California.* Kalamazoo, MI: W. E. Upjohn Institute for Employment Research.

Light, A., & Strayer, W. (2000). Determinants of college completion: School quality or student ability. *Journal of Human Resources, 35*(2), 299–332.

Long, B. T. (2004). How have college decisions changed overtime? An application of the conditional logistic choice model. *Journal of Econometrics, 121*(1&2), 271–296.

Melguizo, T., Kienzl, G., & Alfonso, M. (2007, April). *Evaluating the effect of community college attendance on educational attainment: Application of propensity score matching methods.* Paper presented at the annual meeting of the American Educational Research Association, Chicago.

Mills, K. (2006). Enrollment squeeze: Virginia's community colleges cope with increasing demand and a changing world. *National CrossTalk, 14*(1). Available at http://www.highereducation.org/crosstalk/ct0106/news0106-enrollment.shtml

Moore, C., & Shulock, N. (2007). *Beyond the open door: Increasing student success in the California community colleges.* Sacramento: Institute for Higher Education Leadership & Policy, California State University, Sacramento.

Morgan, S. L. (2001). Counterfactuals, causal effect heterogeneity, and the Catholic school effect on learning. *Sociology of Education, 74,* 341–374.

Mortenson, T. (2002, September). *Chance for college by age 19 by state in 2000* (No. 123). Oskaloosa, IA: Postsecondary Education Opportunity.

National Center for Education Statistics. (2002). *National Education Longitudinal Study of 1988: Base-year to fourth follow-up data file user's manual* (NCES 2002-323). Retrieved April 21, 2008, from http://nces.ed.gov/pubs2002/2002323.pdf

Ohio Board of Regents. (2001). *Ohio colleges and universities 2001: Profile of student outcomes, experiences and campus measures.* Columbus: Author.

Ohio Board of Regents. (2002). *Making the transition from high school to college in Ohio 2002.* Columbus: Author.

Roksa, J. (2006). Does vocational focus of community colleges hinder students' educational attainment? *Review of Higher Education, 29,* 499–526.

Rosenbaum, J. (2001). *Beyond college for all: Career paths for the forgotten half.* New York: Russell Sage.

Rosenbaum, P. R., & Rubin, D. B. (1983). The central role of the propensity score in observational studies for causal effects. *Biometrika, 70,* 41–55.

Rouse, C. E. (1995). Democratization or diversion? The effect of community colleges on educational attainment. *Journal of Business Economics and Statistics, 13*(2), 217–224.

Rouse, C. (1998). Do two-year colleges increase overall educational attainment? Evidence from the states. *Journal of Policy Analysis and Management, 17*(4), 595–620.

Rubin, D. B. (1997). Estimating causal effects from large data sets using propensity scores. *Annals of Internal Medicine, 127*(8), 757–763.

Sandy, J., Gonzalez, A., &. Hilmer, M. (2006). Alternative paths to college completion: Effect of attending a two-year school on the probability of completing a four-year degree. *Economics of Education Review, 25*(5), 463–471.

Smith, J. A., & Todd, P. E. (2005). Does matching overcome LaLonde's critique of nonexperimental estimators? *Journal of Econometrics, 125,* 305–353.

Stephan, J. L., & Rosenbaum, J. (2006, August). *Do some colleges improve students' chances of completing degrees? How propensity scores change the question.* Paper presented at the annual meeting of the American Sociological Association, Montreal, Canada.

Surette, B. J. (2001). Transfer from two-year to four-year college: An analysis of gender differences. *Economics of Education Review, 20*(2), 151–163.

Whitaker, D., & Pascarella, E. (1994). Two-year college attendance and socioeconomic attainment: Some additional evidence. *Journal of Higher Education, 65*(2), 194–210.

Wirt, J., Choy, S., Gruner, A., Sable, J., Tobin, R., Bae, Y., et al. (2000). *The condition of education 2000* (NCES 2000-062). Available at http://nces.ed.gov/pubs2000/2000062.pdf

PART VII

CRITICAL PERSPECTIVES ON RACE AND RACISM IN HIGHER EDUCATION

LORI D. PATTON AND ROBERT T. TERANISHI, ASSOCIATE EDITORS

Interpretations of the federal government's slow responsiveness to Hurricane Katrina, a September 2009 *Newsweek* cover story that asked "Is your baby racist," the blatant omission of slavery in the Virginia Governor's 2010 proclamation of Confederate History Month, and ongoing debates regarding immigration along the Mexico border are all issues wherein race and racism emerged as salient to the national discourse. A cursory overview of trends in U.S. higher education would reveal similar patterns. The differential treatment and isolation experienced by students of color, the preponderance of anti-affirmative action efforts, and inadequate numbers of faculty and administrators of color are *some* examples of race salience in the postsecondary education context. Furthermore, Harper and Patton (2007) noted, "The reality is that many people, including college students, administrators, and faculty, make racist statements, engage in racially oppressive actions, and maintain exclusive memberships in racially segregated social networks" (p. 1).

Despite mission statements that espouse commitments to fostering diverse and inclusive campus environments, much remains to be addressed regarding issues of race and racism before such goals can be successfully met. Put plainly, race still matters. As Princeton University Professor Cornel West eloquently stated, "To engage in a serious discussion of race in America, we must begin with the flaws of American society—flaws rooted in historic inequalities and longstanding cultural stereotypes" (1994, p. 6). Indeed, the flaws of American society are many, one being the racism that has persistently plagued institutions of higher education. The purpose of this section is to highlight scholarship that focuses on critical and emerging perspectives on race. Featured herein is the work of scholars who use Critical Race Theory (CRT) and perspectives on Critical Whiteness Studies to frame important problems of education policy and practice. The chapters were extracted from a growing body of critical race scholarship that is concerned with how distinctions of race and other aspects of identity play out in the day-to-day operation of colleges and universities.

Collectively, the 10 chapters in this section are critical of Eurocentric values that largely determine what is important and rewarded in our field. They also uniquely bring to the fore voices of underrepresented and marginalized communities that are often silenced in debates about equity and diversity in higher education. Furthermore, these chapters place social justice at the center of the conversations about how race and racism continue to serve as mechanisms that stratify access, opportunities, and outcomes. Four additional factors compelled our selection of these readings. First, we wanted to include research that critically examines more nuanced features of the social boundaries of race and its differential impact on particular groups. Second, we chose scholarship that is critical of the role of policy and its implications for access, equity, and the institutional experiences of persons of color. Third, we were interested in presenting a set of studies that employ CRT in varied ways to demonstrate the strength of the framework's explanatory power. Finally, we wanted to identify scholarship that was interdisciplinary in nature. Thus, many chapters in this section draw from other fields of study to underscore the fact that our understanding of racism in higher education has to be situated in larger social and intellectual contexts.

The first two chapters focus on policies pertaining to access and equity in postsecondary education. In Chapter 45, Otoniel Jimenez Morfin, Victor H. Perez, Laurence Parker, Marvin Lynn, and John Arrona tackle diversity as race neutrality in higher education. They contend that colleges and universities engage in shallow measures of affirmative action rather than taking advantage of opportunities to address stagnant or declining enrollments of students of color. Using the *Grutter v. Bollinger* and *Gratz v. Bollinger* cases as a backdrop, the authors employ CRT as a framework to interpret the political nature of higher education, where diversity as a compelling interest is (mis)used to simply reproduce race neutrality as an institutional practice at selective predominantly white institutions. In Chapter 46, Shaun R. Harper, Lori D. Patton, and Ontario S. Wooden use CRT to analyze the effects of federal and state policies on African American students throughout the lifespan of U.S. higher education. By juxtaposing policy efforts that were progressive with those that ultimately deteriorated, the authors draw attention to issues such as affirmative action and HBCU desegregation policies that limit access and continually manufacture inequitable outcomes for African Americans. The authors call for more extensive policy analyses and the enactment of new legislative efforts to address the representation and success of this population.

Another set of readings addresses the effects of racism on faculty and students. In Chapter 47, William A. Smith, Tara J. Yosso, and Daniel G. Solórzano and discuss race-related stress among faculty of color at predominantly white institutions and use counterstorytelling (a CRT method) to disrupt dominant narratives about faculty work. They examine how racial microaggressions accumulate and cause many faculty of color to experience what Smith has termed "racial battle fatigue." Through counterstorytelling, they conclude that a clear connection exists between external factors such as racism and the psychological well-being of faculty of color. Similarly, Daniel G. Solórzano, Miguel Ceja, and Tara J. Yosso explore in Chapter 48 how racial microaggressions shape the campus climate for students of color. They draw attention to the subtle ways in which microaggressions are performed and how African American students subsequently respond. Moreover, the authors discuss how racial microaggressions themselves as well as corresponding behaviors ultimately converge to shape the college environment. Using students' voices, the authors challenge notions of race neutrality and the "level playing field" often referred to in affirmative action discourse.

In Chapter 49, Shaun R. Harper also uses the counternarrative tradition in CRT to challenge dominant, deficit views of Black male college students. He critiques research that focuses exclusively on these students' underachievement, disengagement, and attrition from colleges and universities—a set of acts he refers to as "Niggering." Harper uses data from the National Black

Male College Achievement Study—a multi-institution research study of undergraduate men who had cumulative grade point averages above 3.0, held multiple leadership positions on their campuses, and earned numerous merit-based awards and honors for their college achievements—to show how these students successfully navigated their ways to and through college, despite the odds that were stacked against them. This chapter makes explicit what is racist about the cyclical reinforcement of low expectations for a particular student population.

CRT is also used as a framework to examine the experiences of Asian Americans and Pacific Islanders (AAPIs) in higher education. In Chapter 50, Robert T. Teranishi, Laurie B. Behringer, Emily A. Grey, and Tara L. Parker discuss the persistence of the model minority myth ascribed to AAPI populations and how this myth determines, and in some ways undermines, the positionality of these groups within a higher education context. CRT is employed to challenge normative frameworks that typically address race through a black-white paradigm. The authors focus on college access and admissions, the varied experiences of AAPI students, and AAPI leadership in higher education as three central areas in which greater emphasis should be devoted in terms of research, policy, and practice.

Bryan McKinley Jones Brayboy offers in Chapter 51 an emerging perspective called "Tribal Critical Race Theory," a spin-off from CRT. Through the generation of TribalCrit, the experiences of and issues faced by Indigenous Peoples in the U.S. are illuminated. Key to TribalCrit is the acknowledgement that colonization is endemic and shapes much of how we understand the experiences of American Indian communities. Brayboy draws attention to the contentious and dynamic relationship between Indigenous Peoples and the federal government. This emergent framework engages in sensemaking about American Indians as both a racial and a legal/political group, and how liminal spaces shift when issues such as assimilation, low graduation rates, language preservation, and intertribal conflict emerge. Taken as a whole, the tenets of TribalCrit can serve as a powerful explanatory tool for understanding the educational experiences of American Indians as well as generating future research and policies that can benefit tribal communities.

CRT recognizes the experiential knowledge possessed by people of color. In Chapter 52, Dolores Delgado Bernal engages a paradigmatic shift by centering the knowledges generated by students of color. She uses CRT and Latina/Latino Critical Theory (LatCrit), another spin-off of CRT, to expose the ways in which Eurocentric epistemologies often silence the voices of students of color. Using Chicana/Chicano students' experiences as an example, she introduces critical raced-gendered epistemologies to validate and illuminate knowledge production among students of color. Delgado Bernal's chapter clearly indicates a necessity for higher education researchers to consistently question how knowledges are validated, by whom they are validated, and to what extent they are validated. She also offers implications for how critical raced-gendered epistemologies can shape education research and practice, while disrupting Eurocentric knowledges as the sole way of knowing.

In Chapter 53, Lindsay Perez Huber, Corina Benavides Lopez, Maria C. Malagon, Veronica Velez and Daniel G. Solórzano use LatCrit to theorize and respond to three questions regarding "racist nativism" in U.S. history as it pertains to immigrants of color. These authors contend that white supremacy is a disease that dictates how we understand White people, determines who is "native," and provides the basis upon which all others are measured as non-native. They rely on legal, political, and historical contexts, many situated in education, to challenge ideologies that fail to illuminate white supremacy as the driving force behind racist nativism.

Finally, David S. Owens reminds us in Chapter 54 that in order to address racial oppression, whiteness must be interrogated. The author theorizes whiteness in a way that acknowledges its structural and functional properties. He also describes how understanding whiteness can contribute to the promotion of anti-racist knowledge production. While this chapter is not specifically situated in the postsecondary domain, the author provides a critical lens through which higher education can be understood as a social system where whiteness produces and reproduces racial inequities. Owens suggests that by recognizing whiteness, both structurally and functionally, it can be disrupted and challenged.

Conclusion

These chapters bring much-needed attention to historical and current trends that sustain racial stratification in U.S. higher education. Together, they respond to a demand for new and more critical perspectives on educational practices and policies that determine access, equity, and outcomes for diverse populations. Considering that many colleges and universities are more diverse now than at any other moment in their histories, researchers such as those whose work is included in this section are exploring the causes and consequences of persistent racial gaps and hostile campus racial climates. Given the shifting landscape of U.S. higher education, critical race frameworks can be used to reveal the extent to which postsecondary institutions are responsive to the unique needs of and issues faced by students, faculty, and administrators of color.

References

Gratz v. Bollinger, 539 U.S. 244 (2003).

Grutter v. Bollinger, 539 U.S. 306 (2003).

Harper, S. R., & Patton, L. D. (Eds.). (2007). *Responding to the realities of race on campus. New Directions for Student Services* (No. 120). San Francisco: Jossey-Bass.

West, C. (1994). *Race matters*. New York: Vintage Books.

CHAPTER 45

HIDING THE POLITICALLY OBVIOUS

A CRITICAL RACE THEORY PREVIEW OF DIVERSITY AS RACIAL NEUTRALITY IN HIGHER EDUCATION

OTONIEL JIMENEZ MORFIN

VICTOR H. PEREZ

LAURENCE PARKER

MARVIN LYNN

JOHN ARRONA

What have colleges and universities done to increase student of color enrollment since the 2003 U.S. Supreme Court decisions in *Grutter v. Bollinger* and *Gratz v. Bollinger*? This chapter provides a critical race theory (CRT) snapshot of selective data and institutions since these landmark decisions. We find that even though *Grutter* gives the go-ahead to use affirmative action, higher education has failed politically to take on this challenge. When taken together, the *Gratz* and *Grutter* decisions allow higher education institutions to engage in symbolic affirmative action measures that appear as diversity measures but are operationalized as race neutral when one examines the data of continuing overall declines of students of color at many institutions. The authors conclude with a CRT call for a more expansive affirmative action with higher education administrators doing more to justify affirmative action through *Grutter*.

The conflict surrounding affirmative action in higher education reached an apparent resolution the spring of 2003 with two landmark U.S. Supreme Court rulings. *Grutter v. Bollinger* (2003) and *Gratz v. Bollinger* (2003) related to the use of race as a compelling government interest related to affirmative action in higher education admissions. In the *Gratz* decision, the U.S. Supreme Court ruled that the process of assigning points related to race for the weighting of undergraduate admissions decisions violated the Equal Protection Clause of the 14th Amendment. Students should have been treated as individuals under a comprehensive review process. However, in *Grutter*, the U.S. Supreme Court upheld racial diversity as a compelling state interest with respect to state institutions of higher education taking affirmative measures to diversify their colleges and universities. Writing for the majority, Justice Sandra O'Connor stated that admissions decisions based on comprehensive evaluations of candidates can use race as one of many factors to consider when evaluating applicants. Furthermore, the majority opinion held that in the higher education context, an important function of the democratic process is that the institutions and programs responsible for preparing our future leaders reflect the diversity and talent in our nation.

The initial reaction to the U.S. Supreme Court's upholding of diversity as a compelling interest in the *Grutter* decision was one of victory for affirmative action supporters and anger among politically conservative groups (see for example, Greenhouse, 2003; Lewis, 2003). But in the aftermath of this landmark ruling, the policy question must be raised as to what institutions of higher education are doing to affirm diversity as it was defined by the Court in the *Grutter* decision. We posit that critical race theory (CRT) provides a view of what some of the more selective colleges and universities are or are not doing with regards to undergraduate admissions. From a CRT perspective, whereas *Grutter* should have bolstered support for affirmative action in higher education through diversity as a compelling governmental interest, the politics of higher education has imposed a climate of racial neutrality in terms of actual institutional practice.

Our CRT analysis of the politics of higher education in a post-*Grutter* world will begin with a general discussion of what CRT is, how it has evolved, and why it is important to study racial inequality and discrimination. Part two of this chapter will briefly review the University of Michigan Law School's argument for diversity and the U.S. Supreme Court majority opinion in *Grutter* and how the Court viewed diversity related to undergraduate admissions differently in the *Gratz* holding. In Part three, we will present and discuss from a CRT perspective some preliminary evidence from institutions of higher education to provide a preview as to what is and is not being done to address student diversity after *Grutter*. In Part four, we will link this evidence to other previous research on CRT and higher education and discuss the limitations of the law to serve the purposes of diversity. The concluding section will return to the original question raised in this chapter and offer some CRT policy perspectives to address the pervasive political racial neutrality after *Grutter*.

Defining CRT, Its Evolution, and Inroads into Education

Matsuda, Lawrence, Delgado, and Crenshaw (1993) articulated six unifying themes that have defined CRT:

1. Critical race theory recognizes that racism is endemic to American life.
2. Critical race theory expresses skepticism toward dominant legal claims of neutrality, objectivity, colorblindness, and meritocracy.
3. Critical race theory challenges ahistoricism and insists on a contextual/historical analysis of the law. . . . Critical race theorists . . . adopt a stance that presumes that racism has contributed to all contemporary manifestations of group advantage and disadvantage.
4. Critical race theory insists on recognition of the experiential knowledge of people of color and our communities of origin in analyzing law and society.
5. Critical race theory is interdisciplinary.
6. Critical race theory works toward the end of eliminating racial oppression as part of the broader goal of ending all forms of oppression. (p. 6)[1]

In general, CRT views racism as a normal daily fact of life in society, and the ideology and assumptions of racism are so ingrained in the political and legal structures as to be almost unrecognizable (Crenshaw, Gotanda, Peller & Thomas, 1995; Delgado & Stefancic, 2000b). Legal racial designations have complex, historical, and socially constructed meanings that ensure the location of political subordination of racially marginalized groups. As a form of oppositional scholarship, CRT challenges the experience of White European Americans as the normative standard. CRT grounds its conceptual framework in the distinctive contextual experiences of people of color.[2] Literary knowledge and storytelling are used to challenge existing social constructions of race and racial oppression (Delgado, 1989). A key aspect of the narrative scholarship in CRT is its focus on how the stories of racism are quite personal and appear so for a reason: They attempt to make the reader question whether any person should be subjected to the treatment detailed in the story (Johnson, 1994, p. 817).[3] Moreover, CRT challenges liberalism and the inherent belief in the law to create an equitable, just society. CRT advocates have pointed out the legal racial irony and liberal contradiction of the frustrating legal pace of meaningful reform that has eliminated blatant hateful expressions of racism and yet has kept intact exclusionary relations of power as exemplified by the conservative backlash of the courts, legislative bodies, voters, and so forth against special rights for racially marginalized groups (Bell 1988; Delgado, 1987; Matsuda, 1987).

Bell (1980) posited that racial progress on civil rights only comes for African Americans when Whites make even more substantive gains to retain their legal, social, and material superiority in U.S. society. Bell articulated the interest-convergence principle, which can be defined as persons of color in U.S. society only receiving political, economic, or other major gains when these gains can be shown to somehow serve the interests of White European Americans. Bell's interest-convergence principle gives justification as to how and why *Brown* benefited White European Americans in large measure during the civil rights era. That is, *Brown* helped improve America's image in an international community that was becoming increasingly critical of the United States' civil rights legacy. As Bell argued, interest convergence, or the transient alignment of White European American elite self-interest and the interest of Blacks, has served as a powerful explainer for why, during certain periods of U.S. civil rights history, White European Americans saw it in their best interest to support a progressive civil rights agenda. As an example, Bell points to the international context of the 1950s, in which the United States had championed the cause of freedom and democracy after World War II and the fight against communist tyranny, which in turn prompted sharp rebuke and criticism from international leaders as to the hypocrisy of this stance when one looked at the virulent racism directed toward Blacks in the Jim Crow south. Bell argued that White European Americans in the elite positions of legal, political, and economic power saw it to their advantage in the international context to converge their interest with Blacks by moving forward for a short time period on a progressive civil rights agenda, exemplified by the U.S. Supreme Court decision in *Brown*.[4] Therefore, despite the genuine intent of some aspects of the civil rights movement to champion the rights of Blacks discriminated by the "separate but equal" legal standard set forth in *Plessy v. Ferguson* (1896), interest convergence in CRT demonstrates how White European Americans will only support policies that will result in a clear political or social advantage for them along with a lesser benefit for persons of color. Furthermore, White European Americans are quite willing to tolerate disadvantageous conditions (i.e., poverty, poor schools, health care) for persons of color as long as the former group is not compromised or threatened. Harris's (1993) landmark *Harvard Law Review* article entitled *Whiteness as Property* examined the role of law in shaping the way in which Whiteness is associated with status and power, thereby connected to property rights of ownership. Whiteness was ideologically and legally linked to the law and property in the way that private acquisition of property such as land and other material possessions and wants are linked. This ideological concept led to Whiteness being associated with ownership and power over Tribal Nations and African Americans. For instance, the connection of Whiteness to property rights was used against American Indian tribes through the taking of land and relegation of these groups to reservations and subordinate dependent nation tribal status within the United States. The connection of Whiteness to property has also been used legally against African Americans regarding slavery and White ownership of African chattel and subsequent separate-but-equal Jim Crow laws. In higher education, Harris posits that the U.S. Supreme Court legitimizes White property rights through the *Bakke* decision (1978). According to Harris's interpretation of Justice Powell's opinion, *Bakke* was an innocent victim with regard to how his property rights as a qualified medical school applicant were taken by a lesser qualified minority student under the University of California (UC)–Davis medical school admissions plan. Harris argued that the Court was willing to validate *Bakke's* expectation of a right to admission because the UC–Davis plan was not in fact color-blind with decisions being based on merit. The Court assumed that a fair admissions process based on the seemingly objective criteria used (i.e., standardized test scores) should hold legal sway over a seemingly rigid quota system. Therefore, despite Powell's description of an admissions process that was inclusive of race and other areas of difference, which later became the legal standard in *Grutter* (2003), Harris argued that the *Bakke* majority opinion should have been viewed as a decision protecting the property rights of White Americans in higher education.

Since the inception of CRT, a number of scholars have worked to frame CRT and explain its relevance to education. Ladson-Billings and Tate (1995) were among the first education scholars to do this. Building on Cheryl Harris's (1993) *Whiteness as Property* article, they established a set of propositions connecting "race and property as a central construct" toward understanding the "property functions of Whiteness" in relation to schooling (pp. 58–59). Their critical race analysis "move[d] beyond the boundaries of the educational research literature to include arguments and new perspectives from law and the social sciences" (p. 48) and demonstrated the centrality of racial inequalities in U.S. schools. Ladson-Billings and Tate (1995) portrayed U.S. racism as a persistent historical and ideological construct that could account for inequalities such as dropout rates and school suspension rates for African Americans and Latinos. They also made important links between property values in the United States and the quality of schools. In addition, they illustrate how poverty and low social status is racialized with African Americans and other people of color routinely having access to low-value property. This, in turn, affects the inherent value of the schools attended by those students. Ladson-Billings and Tate expand their analysis of property to include notions of educational property, such as curriculum and pedagogy in urban schools.

Tate (1997) provided an in-depth review of the legal literature that encompasses CRT and describes the relationship between education theory and the law, focusing first on pseudoscientific research on race and its role in shaping the field of education. He connects the nature of educational discourse to the legal history of the United States:

> Both educational research and the law have often characterized "raced" people as intellectually inferior and raised doubts about the benefit of equitable social investment in education and other social services. This paradigmatic kinship built on conceptions of inferiority suggests the need for a theory that explicates the role of race in education and the law. (Tate, 1997, p. 202)

After explaining the rationale and the historical precedents for CRT, Tate discusses the intellectual terrain that mapped out CRT. Tate suggests that CRT as a theory of race and racism in the law was influenced by fields such as sociology, theology, political science, and education. Although CRT is interdisciplinary, it also owes much to its predecessor in the law—Critical Legal Studies (CLS), which is based on Marxian and Gramscian critiques of the social order. CLS scholars viewed the law as ideological and often biased against society's dispossessed. In that sense, they critiqued the notion that the law was objective. In addition, they rejected the individualist nature of the law with its firmly entrenched individual rights discourse. As Tate explains, this aspect of the CLS critique was in conflict with the way some CRT scholars viewed the rights discourse in the American law in terms of the lack of attention paid to race and placing racism in the center of the legal analysis. Instead, class was the major tool of analysis; therefore, CRT scholars began to formulate a discourse that focused on issues of race and racism in the law (Crenshaw et al., 1995).

To summarize, CRT makes racism the center of legal review and critique in terms of how the law is developed and administered regarding its impact on people of color. The central themes of storytelling and counternarratives, interest convergence, and Whiteness as property have been used as benchmark lenses of analysis under CRT. More recently, Tate (2005) challenged those who apply CRT to education to make its links to the law and legal criticism more explicit in terms of an analysis of court decisions and its CRT ramifications in educational policy and research. Dixson and Rousseau (2005) argued for using CRT's grounding in the law and its untapped potential in educational research to build more complex understandings of the origins and impact of racism in educational settings. In the next section, we will attempt to make this education link to case law through a discussion of the U.S. Supreme Court decisions in *Grutter v. Bollinger*, and *Gratz v. Bollinger*, and then in subsequent sections, use CRT to analyze the general higher education response to this landmark case.

A Summary of *Grutter v. Bollinger* and *Gratz v. Bollinger*

The University of Michigan implemented a series of admissions policies in the early 1990s that sought to diversify its student body (Green, 2004). Consequently, the law school admissions criteria focused on the academic ability of its applicants, combined with a flexible assessment of applicant capabilities to determine admission to the law school. Part of this flexible assessment was defined under the rubric of diversity, which would potentially enrich the experience of the entire law school's incoming class. The law school argued that racial diversity should be one of many factors to be considered in the admissions review in terms of achieving a critical mass of underrepresented students of color, which would potentially make a unique and noticeable contribution to the law school at Michigan.

Barbara Grutter, a White Michigan resident who had an undergraduate GPA of 3.8 and a 161 LSAT score and was denied admission to the law school filed suit alleging that they had discriminated against her on the basis of her race in violation of the Fourteenth Amendment, Title IV of the Civil Rights Act of 1964, and 42 U.S.C 1981. She claimed that the University of Michigan Law School used race as a predominant factor in the admissions process, that she was a victim of reverse discrimination because of her race, and that lesser qualified students of color were admitted.

The district court decision in *Grutter* was in favor of the plaintiff, but on the appeal, the Federal 6th Circuit Court of Appeals reversed. The U.S. Supreme Court granted certiorari to decide the legal question of national importance: Is diversity a compelling state interest that can justify the narrowly tailored use of race in the selection of applicants for admission to public institutions of higher education?

Using strict scrutiny under equal protection analysis to determine the constitutionality of racial classifications if they are narrowly tailored to further compelling governmental interests, the U.S. Supreme Court, by a 5-to-4 majority, held that diversity was a compelling interest and that the University of Michigan Law School's admissions policy was indeed narrowly tailored to further this interest. Writing for the majority, Justice O'Connor articulated three key reasons for supporting the University of Michigan in this case. First, there was no indication that the use of race in the admissions process operated as a quota. Race was used in a flexible way and was considered along with many other diversity factors. This was in line of reasoning with former Justice Powell's opinion in the *Bakke v. Regents of University of California* (1978), in which he established that race could be one of many variables to ensure diversity in admissions. Second, diversity was a compelling state interest because the function and role of law schools, such as the University of Michigan, is to prepare the future political, social, and business leaders of our nation. The diversity standard attempts to reflect the diversity of population at large and prepares students for a diverse workforce. Third, a critical mass was important under the diversity standard because students could be potentially educated through a wide exposure to different ideas from students of different backgrounds, and race could be considered as part of that diversity to achieve this important government goal. To be sure, O'Connor did not define a critical mass in actual numbers, but she and the majority did agree that a critical mass served the purpose of contributing to cross-racial understanding, breaking down racial stereotypes, and helping achieve overall better understanding of different races.

The diversity standard was also at issue in the *Gratz* holding in terms of how far an undergraduate admissions process can go in attempting to ensure a racially diverse freshman class. Jennifer Gratz, a White European American female applied to admission to the University of Michigan's liberal arts and sciences college in the fall of 1995. When she was rejected, she too claimed reverse discrimination based on her race and said that race was a determining factor in why she was rejected whereas other students of color with lower standardized test scores and grade point averages were admitted. The Court found that the University of Michigan's use of a point system—in which students are awarded points based on their geographic region, high school grade point average, standardized test score, quality of high school attended, and underrepresented minority status—established a system of admissions that violated the compelling government interest of diversity. The Supreme Court majority held that this system was not narrowly tailored to achieve the educational diversity that the University of Michigan sought to justify in their undergraduate admissions system. Relying on Powell's reasoning in *Bakke*, the Court majority reasoned that undergraduate applicants were not reviewed and assessed on an individual basis to evaluate their potentially unique contribution to the freshman class. This reasoning led to the Court invalidating the numerical system of undergraduate admissions used by the University of Michigan.

A CRT Preview of Higher Education Post-*Grutter*

Given that the general concept of affirmative action was defended, a diversity standard was articulated in *Grutter*, and the use of a rigid system of admissions was held in violation of the Constitution in *Gratz*, we would expect that many selective colleges and universities would have embraced *Grutter* and moved toward a comprehensive admissions process resulting in more racial diversity. To review what has been done so far in this area, we used CRT through an analysis of data to see what initial progress, if any, has been made in higher education since the U.S. Supreme Court upheld the diversity standard in *Grutter* in 2003. To be sure, students of color have made some progress in overall college access in the post–civil rights era. In the eyes of many, students of color are achieving academic success at unprecedented levels in U.S. colleges and universities. The American Council on Education's (2001) *Annual Status Report of Minorities in Higher Education* notes that in 1997, students of color achieved their greatest percentage gain in enrollment at both the undergraduate and graduate levels. These students experienced an almost 3% enrollment increase at the undergraduate level and more than 5% increase at the graduate and professional school levels. The U.S. Department of Education, National Center for Education Statistics (2000) reported similar increases for students of color, noting that there were nearly 1.3 million minority students enrolled at these institutions in 1988 and slightly more than 2 million in 1998. By comparison, there were roughly 6.5 million White students enrolled in 4-yr institutions in 1988 and 1998. The number of baccalaureate degrees conferred to students of color also demonstrated increases. The U.S. Department of Education, National Center for Education Statistics (2002) reported that in the 1976 to 1977 academic year, White students received 88% of total baccalaureate degrees at degree-granting institutions, African American students received 6.4%, Hispanic students received 2%, Asian Pacific Islander students received 1.5%, American Indian and Alaskan Native students received 0.4%, and nonresident undocumented students received 1.7%. The percentage of students of color receiving baccalaureate degrees has increased ever since, with very small drops in isolated years. For example, during the 1980 to 1981 academic years, White students received 86.4% of total baccalaureate degrees, and students of color received 13.6%. In the 1990 to 1991 academic years, White students received 83.5% of total baccalaureate degrees, whereas students of color received 16.5%. In the 2000 to 2001 academic year, White students received 74.7% of baccalaureate degrees and students of color received 25.3%, with African American, Hispanic, and Asian Pacific Islander students leading at 8.9%, 6.2%, and 6.3%, respectively (U.S. Department of Education, National Center for Education Statistics, 2002). Similarly, the number of doctoral degrees conferred on students of color, who are U.S. citizens, increased by 4.4% from 1997 to 1998.

Nevertheless, despite these tremendous increases, students of color remain significantly behind their White peers in enrollment and completion across the postsecondary landscape. To be blunt, Whites remain overrepresented in elite institutions of higher education. Asian Americans have been given tentative honorary White status in the admissions process as long as it does not result in majority Asian American students on these campuses (Takagi, 1993). This was also evident in the 1st year in California when race was no longer used as a criterion for admission to the UC campuses after the passage of Proposition 209. In the fall of 1998, the number of African Americans, Chicano, and Latino and Latina students plummeted at UCLA, UC–Berkeley, and UC San Diego (Morfin, 2005), and this trend has continued at UCLA in terms of the lower numbers of Chicano and African American applications, admissions, and enrollment at the undergraduate level (see Charts 1 to 4, University of California, Office of the President fact-sheets, 2005).[5] One major point drawn from these data is that although African American students are applying to UCLA in high numbers, their admission rates are very low compared to other groups, and their actual enrollment at UCLA is even lower. These talented students may be going to other institutions. Yet given the *Grutter* decision, the rationale for diversity at an institution such as UCLA is made even more compelling with this large discrepancy among applications, admissions, and enrollment of African Americans. Even more crucial is the projected Chicano and Chicana and Latino and Latina student enrollment in the California K–12 schools versus their lower projected percentages in the UC and California State University systems. This future trend data (which resembles projections elsewhere in the United States) indicates that states must address diversity as a compelling government interest, and this interest is directly tied to the state's changing demographics and future state needs from higher education.

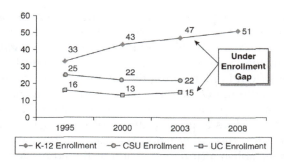

Figure 1 California K–12/CSU/UC Latina and Latino freshman enrollment.

Note: CSU = California State University; UC = University of California.
Sources: California State Department of Finance, November 2000; UCOP, 2004; provided by Daniel G. Solórzano (UCLA).

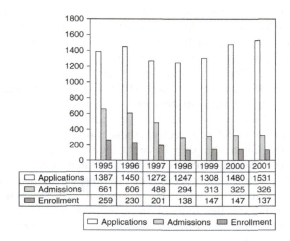

Figure 2 African American applications, admissions, and enrollment at UCLA.
Source: University of California, Office of the President (2005).

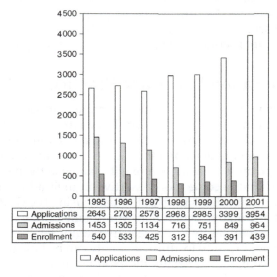

Figure 3 Chicano application, admission, and enrollment at UCLA.
Source: University of California, Office of the President (2005).

Based on this evidence, our position is that colleges and universities have not been aggressive in terms of taking advantage of the diversity principle established in the 2003 U.S. Supreme Court ruling. Selingo (2005, p. A21) reported that although the *Grutter* decision gave the "green light" in support of affirmative action, the conservative local and state political context may be a factor in stopping many institutions from implementing the diversity standard as a compelling government interest in admissions. Even though *Grutter* salvaged a form of affirmative action, it can be argued that the victory in reality was a loophole for the retreat from race and that *Gratz* was a political public relations policy way for universities to go on public record against the use of quotas or rigid point systems. The UC system has no affirmative action as a result of Proposition 209. Even though the university may attempt to re-establish affirmative action in the admissions process, what needs to be pondered is if the will and desire exists. For example, when *Gratz* and *Grutter* were decided, President Atkinson of the UC system applauded the U.S. Supreme Court's ruling in *Grutter*, but argued that the UC was constrained to re-implement affirmative action because of proposition 209. Was the UC system really constrained by the proposition or by a lack of administrative leadership?[6] In a survey of 29 institutions with competitive admissions policies, *The Chronicle of Higher Education* (Selingo, 2005) found that 7 institutions experienced a drop in the percentage of African American and Latino and Latina freshmen from 2002 to 2004. At 11 colleges, the percentage of Latino and Latina freshmen rose, but African American enrollment fell, whereas 11 institutions experienced gains in African American and Latino and Latina enrollment during this period. One of the institutions that suffered a drop in both categories was the freshman class of 2004 at the University of Illinois at Urbana–Champaign, where of the 7,248 students enrolled; 410 were Black, whereas the figure for the previous year for Black students was 602. Latino student enrollment for 2004 also saw a decrease—dropping to 483 from 503 in 2003—and the number of American Indian students also fell, from 25 in 2003, to 19 in 2004 (Lamothe, 2004). From a CRT perspective, these figures should be cause for alarm and action for higher education leaders. Given that they have the legal justification to pursue diversity as a compelling government interest, the argument for affirmative action can be made on both political and philosophical grounds through the perspective of opening up institutional doors to minority students. Otherwise, the soft affirmative action responses will not deal with the locked-in qualities of current racial discrimination that is tied to the material conditions of many students of color and their families in lower socioeconomic areas of the United States. Roithmayr (2004) argues that for affirmative action to really work post-*Grutter*, much more is needed in terms of politically addressing disparities in housing, wealth, employment, public services, and finances. A more comprehensive view of affirmative action argues for fundamental social justice changes resulting in opening societal doors and subsequent preparation for college access, which is still foreclosed to many groups of color that live in lower socioeconomic areas. Narrowly tailored programs will not markedly lower racial disparities in admissions and achieve a critical mass unless they are done in consort with broader remedies to address societal lock-in discrimination and hostile racial campus climate issues.

CRT and Higher Education Policy and Practice

The data reported in the previous section illustrate a picture of missed opportunity by some institutions of higher education from a CRT perspective. To be sure, some of these institutions have attempted to increase their enrollment of African American and Latino and Latina students for the fall 2005 freshman class or have openly defended their use of affirmative action (Schmidt, 2005; Sewell, 2005). Furthermore, we hope this snapshot picture will change in the near future if more institutions become aware of this issue and become more assertive in their admissions and enrollment initiatives. But the missed opportunity stems from not initially using the *Grutter* decision as a way to affirm a broader concept of affirmative action that would take on the problem of underrepresented racial groups of color on predominantly White selective campuses.

This picture of missed opportunity to affirm diversity can be linked to other CRT research in the higher education context that has documented the experiences of students and faculty of color and the historical evolution of racism in educational policy in higher education. To illustrate this point, we can draw from Anderson's (2002) historical findings of institutional racism at the University of Michigan from student interviews that were reported in university reports such as this passage:

> On Tuesday, January 27, 1987, a group of Black women were holding a meeting in a dormitory lounge in Couzens Hall. A racist flier was slipped under the door. It announced the beginning of a "hunt" against Black people and used a variety of pejorative terms: Be it known that due to severe drought and fire this past season, and due to decreased animal populations; the hunting of DEER, BEAR, RABBIT, QUAIL and POSSUM, has been prohibited. . . . The government has provided by special decree for a substitute animal to be hunted, so that no hunter will lose his skill during the season. . . . There will be an OPEN SEASON on PORCH MONKEYS (Regionally known as Jigaboos, Saucerlips, Jungle Bunnies, and Spooks). (Anderson, 2002, p. 86)

> The incidents of the past year remind us, however, that persons who are not white who accept the University of Michigan's offer to join this community experience a world that the university does not advertise. They are thrown into the company of white students who are amused by the kinds of 'humor' displayed on a certain radio [The Tenacious Slack Show] show. They are likely to be subjected to ridicule, abuse, and threat within University-controlled residence halls, even within their own dormitory rooms. In the classroom students of color encounter instructors who make openly racist comments, inside and outside of class. . . . If the testimony of the students, faculty, and staff who testified at the [Hood] hearings is accurate the show [Tenacious Slack Show] is only a symptom of a pervasive atmosphere on this campus. (Kennedy & Payton, 1987, as cited in Anderson, 2002, pp. 91–92)

The aforementioned passages are excerpted from a report conducted by Anderson (2002) on the historical documentation of racism at the University of Michigan. The evidence gathered from news articles and other archival sources from university hearings on racial harassment paints a portrait of a campus policy culture that supports the overall goal of affirmative action but a campus climate that has historically racially profiled African American and Latino and Latina students. Most of the evidence in this report illustrates how these students felt that the campus did not belong to them or that they were not fully accepted as students. Toward the end of the report, Anderson (2002) concludes that there are general perceptions of a more positive racial climate in terms of current campus diversity. However, these examples represent some of the past racial barriers that minorities had to face and overcome at the University of Michigan. Furthermore, these incidents and the historical patterns of past discrimination connect to the current debate about the meaning of diversity and affirmative action. Researchers who explore the experiences of students and faculty of color in higher education also use critical race counterstorytelling often as a way in which to tell important stories about social justice in higher education.

For example, Solórzano (1998) used counterstorytelling as a method to examine how Latino and Latina postdoctoral students who were awarded prestigious fellowships still suffered from the discrimination of invisibility as they were continually ignored by the faculty and administrators at their Research I home institutions. These students experienced racial microaggressions, or small and subtle acts of racist aggression, at three elite predominantly White universities, which had a decidedly negative impact on the overall racial climate of these campuses. Solórzano and Yosso (2001) conducted a CRT and LatCrit qualitative research study, which used counterstorytelling as a method to explore the experiences of Latina faculty and graduate students at a predominantly White institution. Their findings creatively chronicled their experiences with discrimination, self-doubt, and confusion as they grapple with surviving in hostile contexts. Villalpando and Delgado Bernal (2002) used both empirical data and counterstorytelling to tell a story about a Latina faculty member engaged in the battle for tenure at a predominantly White university. The story is told from two perspectives: a "majoritarian" story that focuses on the professor's deficits and her supposed pro–student of color (i.e., perceived anti-White) teaching practices. The counterstory, on the other hand, focuses on the researchers' strength as community-oriented scholars who engage in research and teaching that makes a difference in the lives of marginalized peoples. The article underscores the contradictions between the experiences and perspectives of faculty of color in higher education and the predominantly White faculty who evaluate their professional academic work by an unexamined set of cultural norms, standards, and beliefs. These conflicting worldviews—left unresolved in the two mirroring narratives—ground the authors' critical race analysis of the barriers that impede the success of faculty of color in these mirrored perspectives on a Chicana faculty member's qualifications for tenure. Taylor (2000) used CRT as a tool to explore the "backlash against affirmative action" in Washington State. He offered a critical race counterargument that deconstructed the core of arguments for race neutrality and colorblindness. In addition, he argued that CRT could not only be used to help situate arguments for affirmative action, but it could also be used as a way to enliven strong activist agenda for multicultural education in higher education. Finally, Solórzano and Yosso (2001) used critical race counterstories as a method for exploring affirmative action debates in higher education. The counterstory is set in the midst of student intervener arguments in the Michigan case and evokes the spirit of Thurgood Marshall to illustrate the complexity of the arguments in the complex legal battles over affirmative action. They use majority opinions, dissents, and compromises from the *Bakke* (1978) decision while also reaching back to the broader historical struggles of *Brown* I and *Brown* II (1954, 1955). This nuanced counterstory relies on history, legal analysis, and fictionalized historical accounts as a way to illuminate the lived history of the students of color who participated in the efforts to challenge the normative social experiences and assumed legal standard of equal opportunity for all at predominantly White Research I institutions.

To summarize, the research highlighted in this section points to missed opportunities to engage in positive affirmative action. CRT research in higher education has illustrated how faculty of color have to deal with microaggressions and racial harassment. The CRT studies have also shed light on how students of color have to tolerate a hostile racial climate and racial profiling on predominantly White campuses. From a CRT perspective, the counterstories show how different their narratives of racial discrimination are from the mainstream White European American students, such as those given by plaintiffs in the *Grutter* and *Gratz* cases, and faculty and what we have to learn from the mistakes of the past so we are not doomed to repeat them (Delgado & Stefancic, 2000a).

Conclusion: Diversity as a Compelling State Interest Equal to the Politics of Racial Neutrality?

A CRT analysis of education and affirmative action law, particularly in terms of the evidence generated through counternarratives and counterstories, can serve as a potential link with other movements (e.g., gender, social class) in terms of galvanizing progressive coalitions for political opportunity and activism. The diversity as compelling state interest standard should be fostered and moved on by higher education leaders. As the chancellor of Syracuse University, Nancy E. Cantor, said, "What needs to happen is that every major institution in this country has to be fired up to make this front and center. . . . We have to see to it as our responsibility to maintain and foster the commitment to diversity" (Selingo, 2005, p. A23).

However, from a CRT perspective, the unresolved issue is that the diversity standard set in *Grutter* does not completely address the remedial usage of race and provide a social justice remedy that takes on historical racial discrimination and influences current institutional racism (Yosso et al., 2005). From an interest-convergence perspective, the *Grutter* and *Gratz* decisions represent socially palatable reasons regarding diversity in higher education because rigid numerical systems for admissions were struck down, but an individualized student review to create a critical mass was accepted by the Court.

Furthermore, students from low-income families and students of color who access selective Research I post-secondary institutions face new legal and political challenges from right-wing conservative forces (e.g., Cato Institute, Center for Individual Rights, Heritage Foundation, Mountain States Legal Defense), which seek to undermine other higher education diversity goals. From a CRT perspective, what we are witnessing is the conservative legal groups' political emphasis on a color-blind interpretation of civil rights law as a strong movement driven to dismantle an array of outreach and recruitment efforts (Yosso, Parker, Solórzano, & Lynn, 2005). This, in turn, will create a host of new legal and political challenges for groups. CRT should be one of many intellectual tools used to aggressively counter this trend on behalf of fighting racial discrimination, both overt and institutional (Yosso et al., 2005).

Ladson-Billings (2004) argued that *Brown*, despite its symbolic importance, had limited effectiveness for substantively changing educational opportunity for the vast majority of Black students, Latino and Chicano students, and other students of color. What is needed is for us to see *Brown* as a first potential step to a different way to envision a future for real education to happen, particularly in terms of potential coalitions of poor and middle-class Whites and other racial minority groups to demand higher quality schooling that provides them with future opportunities (Ladson-Billings, 2004). In doing so, we believe that through CRT, affirmative action through *Grutter* now has to be seen broadly in terms of the following: (a) changing the material conditions of the lives of low-income persons and persons of color through a wide range of measures (e.g., affordable housing, better health care, job training and higher wages, etc.), (b) challenging conservative forces to "ante up" more resources and energy to eliminate racial inequities at the elementary and secondary school levels, and (c) proactively recruit and retain students and faculty of color and deal with the microaggressions that they face and the sometimes hostile racial climate documented by CRT researchers in higher education. From a CRT and praxis perspective (Yamamoto, 1997), it might be that students and/or parents and communities of color and their allies may put their own political pressure on higher education administrators in the future to enforce the compelling government interest of diversity that was central to the *Grutter* decision.

Notes

1. As critical race theory (CRT) continues in different directions, it has taken up new discourses and has offered new challenges to legal doctrine in American jurisprudence. Carbado and Gulati (2003) identify two strands within CRT, which he refers to as first-generation and second-generation scholarship. They argue that the first generation of CRT scholars, such as Bell (1980) Crenshaw (1988), Crenshaw et al. (1995), Harris (1993, 2002), Angela Harris (1994), and Williams (1987, 1991), focused mainly on the material manifestations of racism as a way to argue for social justice and focused much-needed attention on the inclusion of the subjugated voices of racially marginalized peoples into the debates on race, racism, law, and society. The second generation of scholars have taken Bell, Delgado, Williams and Crenshaw's ideas and extended them to address issues of gender, ethnicity, language, culture, sexuality, and other key markers of difference. Borrowing heavily from postmodernism, poststructuralism and critical theory, these works focus more attention on teasing out the multivaried meanings of race and their interaction with other forms of domination. This new hybridity is clearly laid out in *Crossroads, Directions and a New Critical Race Theory,* edited by Valdes, Culp, and Harris (2002). This work seeks to shift CRT in a new direction by discussing how CRT as a legal framework of analysis interfaces with concepts of identity (e.g., gender, sexual orientation), the impact of globalization on understandings about race, critical postcolonial thought on race and racism, critical race activism, and the development of coalitions across difference. For example, Valdes (2000) has discussed how upper class queer males from Latin American countries may come to the United States as queer nonracialized persons, but when they come to a racially polarized city such as Miami, they might be placed in a racialized group and face racial discrimination and homophobia. However, he observes that their social class position allows them entry into other sectors of the city's political economy that are off-limits to Miami's low-income population. Iglesias (1999) and Valdes et al. (2002) argue for using this new form of CRT as a way to think about race and other areas of difference as a set of shifting bottoms and rotating centers, in which not one category (e.g., race, social class, sexual orientation) dominates but multiple ways. These ways of thinking about race can become potential avenues of solidarity for common legal causes.

2. Carbado and Gulati (2002) argue that initially, CRT was conceived as an effective tool in terms of articulating the nuances of racism in a legal theoretical sense, particularly in terms of formal and informal barriers to job entry, law school admission, and so forth. In addition, they contend that CRT has helped to articulate a conception of race that is operationalized as a social construction at the larger level of institutional entry. Yet CRT has not been as effective in terms of paying attention to the interpersonal way in which race is produced, and the new approaches in CRT begins to deal directly with this issue. For example, Carbado and Gulati (2002) emphasized that CRT often ignores the racial productivity of the choices people of color make about how to present themselves as racialized persons. As a general matter, CRT's race-as-a-social-construction thesis does not include an analysis of the race-producing practices that are reflected in the daily negotiations people of color perform in an attempt to shape how (especially White) people interpret their non-White identities. Therefore, Cabado and Gulati make the

case for using CRT with a combination of law and economics. It is important to use CRT with a more nuanced analysis that combines CRT analysis and applies the use of econometric principles to show how and why race is operationalized within the economic sphere of the workplace. Carbado and Gulati argue that CRT can be used to explore the ways employers will use, for example, ideal racial profiles of model minorities in a consumerist culture in which race is commercialized. From their perspective, second-generation CRT analyses need to focus on the development of workplace identity and the interactions of class, gender, sexuality, and race in forming a unique set of experiences for men and women in the workplace.

3. There have been numerous critiques of CRT generally and specifically in the use of storytelling in the law. One of the more substantive critiques has come from Daniel Farber and Suzanna Sherry (1997). In *Beyond All Reason: The Radical Assault on Truth in American Law,* they argue that (a) outsiders' stories are not typical of outsider experiences and therefore unrepresentative; (b) outsiders' stories overemphasize the unique perspective of the author and/or "the voice of color" and thus are not generalizable to the overall outsider population; (c) because storytelling lacks clarity and analysis, they are not academically rigorous; and (d) storytelling distorts the truth.

4. Dudziak (2000) provides strong added historical documentation to the thesis that it was in the self-interest of powerful political forces to move on civil rights if only to disrupt the Communist ideological campaign of the Soviet Union in Africa, Asia, and Central and South America.

5. The sources for this compiled chart information was retrieved December 14, 2005, from http://www.ucop.edu/news/factsheets/flowfrc0503.pdf

6. UC President Richard C. Atkinson issued the following statement (June 23) regarding the U.S. Supreme Court's decisions on affirmative action:

> As a supporter of affirmative action, I am gratified by the Supreme Court's decision today in the University of Michigan law school admissions case. The court's action to uphold the principles of affirmative action sends an important message that diversity can be one of many compelling considerations in admitting students to our nation's most-selective universities. As president of the University of California, I also respect the decision of the California voters, who in 1996 eliminated consideration of race and ethnicity in state university admissions. The University of California will continue to comply with Proposition 209, and we will continue to work through other legal means to achieve excellence and diversity on our campuses.

Retrieved December 13, 2005, from http://www.universityofcalifornia.edu/news/michigancase.html

References

American Council on Education. (2001). *Eighteenth annual report on minorities in higher education.* Washington, DC: Author.

Anderson, J. D. (2002). *Expert witness report on history of race relations and minority student opportunities at the University of Michigan.* Unpublished manuscript.

Bakke v. Regents of the University of California, 438 U.S. 265 (1978).

Bell, D. A. (1980). Brown v. Board of Education and the interest-convergence dilemma. *Harvard Law Review, 33,* 1–34.

Bell, D. A. (1988). White superiority in America: Its legal legacy, its economic costs. *Villanova Law Review, 33,* 767–779.

Brown v. Board of Education, 347 U.S. 483 (1954).

Brown v. Board of Education, 349 U.S. 294 (1955).

Carbado, D. W., & Gulati, M. (2003). The law and economics of critical race theory. *Yale Law Review, 112,* 1757–1828.

Crenshaw, K. W. (1988). Race, reform, and retrenchment: Transformation and legitimation in antidiscrimination law. *Harvard Law Review, 101,* 1331–1387.

Crenshaw, K. W., Gotanda, N., Peller, G., Thomas, K. (Eds.). (1995). *Critical Race Theory: The key writings that formed the movement.* New York: The New Press.

Delgado, R. (1987). The ethereal scholar: Does critical legal studies have what minorities want? *Harvard Civil Rights-Civil Liberties Law Review, 22,* 301–322.

Delgado, R. (1989). Storytelling for oppositionists and others: A plea for narrative. *Michigan Law Review, 87,* 2411–2441.

Delgado, R., & Stefancic, J. (2000a). California's racial history and constitutional rationales for race-conscious decision making in higher education. *UCLA Law Review, 47,* 1521–1614.

Delgado, R., & Stefancic, J. (Eds.). (2000b). *Critical race theory: The cutting edge* (2nd ed.). Philadelphia: Temple University Press.

Dixson, A. D., & Rousseau, C. K. (2005). And we are still not saved: Critical race theory ten years later. *Race Ethnicity and Education, 8,* 7–28.

Dudziak, M. A. (2000). *Cold war civil rights: Race and the image of American democracy.* Princeton, NJ: Princeton University Press.

Farber, D., & Sherry, S. (1997). *Beyond all reason: The radical assault on truth in American law.* New York: Oxford University Press.

Gratz v. Bollinger, 539 U.S. 244 (2003).

Green, D. O. (2004). Fighting the battle for racial diversity: A case study of Michigan's institutional responses to *Gratz* and *Grutter, Educational Policy, 18,* 733–751.

Greenhouse, L. (2003, June 24). Justices back affirmative action by 5 to 4, but wider vote bans a racial point system. *New York Times,* pp. A1, A25.

Grutter v. Bollinger, 539 U.S. 306 (2003).

Harris, A. P. (1994). The jurisprudence of reconstruction. *California Law Review, 82,* 741–785.

Harris, C. I. (1993). Whiteness as property. *Harvard Law Review, 106,* 1707–1791.

Harris, C. I. (2002). Critical race studies: An Introduction. *UCLA Law Review, 49,* 1215–1239.

Iglesias, E. (1999). Identity, democracy, communication, power, Inter/national labor rights and the evolution of LatCrit theory, *Miami Law Review, 53,* 575–682.

Johnson, A. M., Jr. (1994). Defending the use of narrative and giving content to the voice of color: Rejecting the imposition of process theory in legal scholarship. *Iowa Law Review, 79,* 803–852.

Ladson-Billings, G. (1998). Just what is critical race theory and what's it doing in a *nice* field like education. *International Journal of Qualitative Studies in Education, 11,* 7–24.

Ladson-Billings, G. (2004). Landing on the wrong note: The price we paid for Brown. *Educational Researcher, 33,* 3–13.

Ladson-Billings, G., & Tate, W. F. (1995). Toward a critical race theory of education. *Teachers College Record, 97,* 47–68.

Lamothe, E. Jr. (2004, September 27). UI sees significant drop in minorities. *Champaign-Urbana News Gazette,* pp. A1, A8.

Lewis, N. A. (2003, June 24). Some on the right see a challenge: Angry groups seeking a Justice against affirmative action. *New York Times,* pp. A1, A25.

Matsuda, M. (1987). Looking to the bottom: critical legal studies and reparations. *Harvard Civil Rights-Civil Liberties Law Review, 22,* 323–399.

Matsuda, M., Lawrence, C., Delgado, R., & Crenshaw, K. (1993). *Words that wound: Critical Race Theory, assaultive speech, and the First Amendment.* Boulder, CO: Westview.

Morfin, J. O. (2005, November 30). Access and equity issues at UCLA in a post affirmative action era. Unpublished doctoral dissertation, University of Illinois at Urbana-Champaign.

Plessy v. Ferguson, 163 U.S. 537 (1896).

Roithmayr, D. (2004). From *Brown* to *Bakke* to *Grutter*: Constitutionalizing and defining racial equality: Tacking left: A radical critique of *Grutter*, vol. 21. *Constitutional Commentary 191.* Retrieved December 12, 2005, from Lexis-Nexis database.

Schmidt, P. (2005, April 22). U of Wisconsin vows to defend an aid program based on race. *The Chronicle of Higher Education,* p. A29.

Selingo, J. (2005, January 14). Michigan: Who really won? *The Chronicle of Higher Education,* pp. A21, A23.

Sewell, T. A. (2005, October 13). Minority enrollment rebounds from 2004 at U of I. *Daily Illini,* pp. A1, A5.

Solórzano, D. (1998). Critical race theory, racial and gender microaggressions, and the experiences of Chicana and Chicano scholars. *International Journal of Qualitative Studies in Education, 11,* 121–136.

Solórzano, D., & Yosso, T. J. (2001). Critical race and LatCrit theory and method: Counterstorytelling Chicana and Chicano graduate school experiences. *International Journal of Qualitative Studies in Education, 14,* 471–495.

Solórzano, D., & Yosso, T. J. (2002). A critical race counter-story of race, racism, and affirmative action. *Equity and Excellence in Education, 35,* 155–168.

Takagi, D. Y. (1993). Asian Americans and racial politics: A postmodern paradox. *Social Justice, 20,* 115–128.

Tate, W. F. (1997). Critical race theory and education: History, theory and implications. In M. Apple (Ed.), *Review of research in education* (vol. 22, pp. 195–250). Washington, DC: American Educational Research Association.

Tate, W. F. (2005). Ethics, engineering and the challenge of racial reform in education. *Race, Ethnicity and Education, 8,* 121–127.

Taylor, E. (2000). Critical race theory and interest convergence in the backlash against affirmative action: Washington state and initiative 200. *Teachers College Record, 102,* 539–561.

University of California, Office of the President. (2005). *Factsheets.* Retreived from http://www.ucop.edu/news/factsheets/flowfrc0503

U.S. Department of Education, National Center for Education Statistics. (2000). *Enrollment in higher education.* Washington, DC: Government Printing Office.

U.S. Department of Education, National Center for Education Statistics. (2002). Higher education general information survey, degrees and other formal awards conferred surveys, and integrated postsecondary education data system completion surveys. Washington, DC: Government Printing Office.

Valdes, F. (2000, February 25). *Law, culture, identity: LatCrit reflections on comparative racialization, antisubordination politics, and legal reform.* Presented at UCLA Law Review Symposium.

Valdes, F., Culp, J. C., & Harris, A. (Eds). (2002). *Crossroads, directions, and a new critical race theory.* Philadelphia: Temple University Press.

Villalpando, O., & Delgado Bernal, D. (2002). A critical race theory analysis of barriers that impede the success of faculty of color. In W. A. Smith, P. G. Altbach, & K. Lomotey (Eds.), *The racial crisis in American higher education: Continuing challenges for the twenty-first century* (pp. 243–269). Albany: State University of New York Press.

Williams, P. J. (1987). Alchemical notes: Reconstructing ideals from deconstructed rights. *Harvard Civil Rights-Civil Liberties Law Review, 22,* 401–433.

Williams, P. J. (1991). *The alchemy of race and rights: Diary of a law professor.* Cambridge, MA: Harvard University Press.

Yamamoto, E. (1997). Critical race praxis: Race theory and political lawyering in the post-civil rights America, *Michigan Law Review, 95,* 821–947.

Yosso, T. J., Parker, L., Solórzano, D. G., & Lynn, M. (2005). From Jim Crow to affirmative action and back again: A critical race theory discussion of racialized rationales and access to higher education. In R. Flodden (Ed.), *Review of Research in Education, 28,* (pp. 1–27). Washington, DC: American Educational Research Association.

CHAPTER 46
ACCESS AND EQUITY FOR AFRICAN AMERICAN STUDENTS IN HIGHER EDUCATION: A CRITICAL RACE HISTORICAL ANALYSIS OF POLICY EFFORTS

SHAUN R. HARPER, LORI D. PATTON, AND ONTARIO S. WOODEN

Higher education has been characterized as "one of the greatest hopes for intellectual and civic progress in this country. Yet for many Americans, however, it has been seen as part of the problem rather than the solution" (Boyer, 1997, p. 85). Some have acknowledged that higher education is a public good through which individual participation accrues benefits for the larger society (Institute for Higher Education Policy, 1998; Kezar, Chambers, & Burkhardt, 2005; Lewis & Hearn, 2003). Despite this, recent analyses have confirmed that too few African Americans are offered access to the socioeconomic advantages associated with college degree attainment (Harper, 2006; Perna et al., 2006). In some ways, the recurrent struggle for racial equity is surprising, given the number of policies that have been enacted to close college opportunity gaps between African Americans and their White counterparts at various junctures throughout the history of higher education.

Though presumably for the best, Tyack and Cuban (1995) acknowledge that education policy-making does not always lead to sustainable progress. Much evidence exists to confirm this has been the case with policies created to increase access and ensure equity for African American students in higher education. Such efforts are described in this chapter. While various scholars have offered insights into the educational histories of African Americans (e.g., Allen & Jewell, 1995; Anderson, 1988; Gasman, 2007; Katz, 1969), comprehensive analyses of the underlying catalysts, low sustainability, and ultimate effects of policy efforts throughout the lifespan of higher education are scarce. This chapter seeks to fill that void. Policies that have affected participation and degree attainment rates for this population across various time periods are reviewed and discussed below. We juxtapose historically noteworthy progressive steps toward access and equity with recent indicators of backward movement. Implications of these policy shifts are considered and critiqued at the end of the chapter. But first, the lens through which we analyzed these policies is described in the next section.

Analytical Framework

Critical Race Theory (CRT) is used as an analytical framework in this chapter. This race-based epistemology is particularly useful here because it provides a lens through which to question, critique, and challenge the manner and methods in which race, white supremacy, supposed meritocracy, and racist ideologies have shaped and undermined policy efforts for African American student participation in higher education. CRT is interdisciplinary in nature, incorporating intellectual traditions and scholarly perspectives from law, sociology, history, ethnic studies, and women's studies to advance and give voice to the ongoing quest for racial justice (Bell, 1987; Delgado & Stefancic, 2001). Solórzano (1998) notes, "A critical race theory in education challenges ahistoricism and the unidisciplinary focus of most analyses, and insists on analyzing race and racism in education by placing them in both a historical and contemporary context using interdisciplinary methods" (p. 123). While no single definition exists for CRT, many scholars agree on the centrality of seven tenets:

1. Racism is a normal part of American life, often lacking the ability to be distinctively recognized, and thus is difficult to eliminate or address (Delgado, 1995; Delgado & Stefancic, 2001; Ladson-Billings, 2000; Solórzano, 1998). Racial microaggressions—" subtle insults (verbal, nonverbal, and/or visual) directed toward people of color, often automatically or unconsciously" (Solórzano, Ceja, & Yosso, 2000, p. 60)—replace more overt demonstrations of racism in most settings. A CRT lens unveils the various forms in which racism continually manifests itself, despite espoused institutional values regarding equity and social justice.

2. CRT rejects the notion of a "colorblind" society. Colorblindness leads to misconceptions concerning racial fairness in institutions; tends to address only the most blatant forms of inequality and disadvantage; and hides the commonplace and more covert forms of racism. "Instead of tackling the realities of race, it is much easier to ignore them by embracing colorblind ideologies . . . it creates a lens through which the existence of race can be denied and the privileges of Whiteness can be maintained without any personal accountability" (Harper & Patton, 2007, p. 3). Critical race theorists continuously critique institutional claims of liberalism, neutrality, objectivity, color blindness, and meritocracy (Crenshaw, 1997). These ideas camouflage the socially constructed meanings of race and present it as an individualistic and abstract idea instead of addressing how racial advantage propels the self-interests, power, and privileges of the dominant group (Solórzano, 1998).

3. CRT gives voice to the unique perspectives and lived experiences of people of color. According to Solórzano (1998), "CRT recognizes that the experiential knowledge of women and men of color is legitimate, appropriate, and critical to understanding, analyzing, and teaching about racial subordination in the field of education" (p. 122). In acknowledging the validity of these lived experiences among persons of color, CRT scholars can place racism in a realistic context and actively work to eliminate it. CRT uses counternarratives as a way to highlight discrimination, offer racially different interpretations of policy, and challenge the universality of assumptions made about people of color.

4. CRT recognizes interest-convergence, the process whereby the white power structure "will tolerate or encourage racial advances for Blacks only when they also promote white self-interests" (Delgado, 1995, p. xiv). In this proposition, the argument of CRT scholars is that white people have been the main beneficiaries of civil rights legislation (Ladson-Billings, 2000). Delgado and Stefancic (2001) contend that efforts to eradicate racism have produced minimal results due to the insufficient convergence of interests by both white elites and African Americans. Consequently, racism continues to persist. Bell (2000) contends, "We cannot ignore and should learn from and try to recognize situations when there is a convergence of interests" (p. 9).

5. Revisionist History is another tenet of CRT. According to Delgado and Stefancic (2001), "Revisionist history reexamines America's historical record, replacing comforting majoritarian interpretations of events with ones that square more accurately with minorities' experiences" (p. 20). In essence, this suggests that American history be closely scrutinized and reinterpreted as opposed to being accepted at face value and truth. It requires a more nuanced understanding as well as taking a critical perspective toward examining historical events.

6. CRT also relies on *Racial Realists,* or individuals who not only recognize race as a social construct, but also realize that "racism is a means by which society allocates privilege and status" (Delgado & Stefancic, 2001, p. 17). Racial Realists recognize the hierarchy that determines who receives benefits and the context in which those benefits are accrued. In addition, they point to slavery as the inception of prejudice and discrimination. In essence, there is a coming to terms with the reality that racism is a permanent fixture in society, including on college and university campuses (Harper & Patton, 2007). Bell (2005) contends that racial realism is a mindset that requires individuals to understand the permanency of racism while still working to create a set of strategic approaches for improving the plight of historically excluded groups.

7. CRT continuously critiques claims of meritocracy that sustain white supremacy (Bergerson, 2003). Valdes, McCristal Culp, and Harris (2002), explain three central beliefs of mainstream culture that must consistently be challenged: (a) blindness to race will eliminate racism; (b) racism is a matter of individuals, not systems; and (c) one can fight racism without paying attention to sexism, homophobia, economic exploitation, and other forms of oppression or injustice. When such beliefs are maintained in society through legal, educational, and sociopolitical channels, students of color, low-income persons, and other disenfranchised populations are silenced.

CRT is particularly useful for examining policies affecting African American students in higher education, as racial subordination is among the critical factors responsible for the continued production of racialized disparities and opportunity gaps. Moreover, CRT is especially useful in this chapter because it addresses what Taylor (1999) describes as " widespread historical illiteracy" and reinforces the notion that African American participation in higher education cannot be taken for granted or assumed to be a privilege that has always existed. On the contrary, this presence was precipitated by an "up-and-down" struggle for equity, access, and progressive policies mandated via judicial and legislative action. Through the use of CRT, we offer a critique of the progressive and regressive policy efforts associated with African American student participation in higher education.

Progressive Steps in the History of Higher Education

The earliest access for African Americans was initiated in the 1820s. In 1823, Alexander Lucius Twilight completed his studies and was awarded a degree from Middlebury College in Vermont (Bennett, 1988; Ranbom & Lynch, 1988). Two other African Americans graduated three years later from Amherst and Bowdoin, respectively. The occasional awarding of degrees signified the onset of a movement to gradually extend college opportunity to freed slaves. Oberlin College became the first institution to openly admit African Americans (Brazzell, 1996; Roebuck & Murty, 1993; Rudolph, 1990). Although some institutions had graduated one or two African Americans prior to the founding of Oberlin in 1833, no others had adopted policies specifically permitting them to attend in large numbers.

Established in 1837 as an elementary and high school for the education of freed slaves, Cheyney State Training School (now Cheyney University) frequently claims to be the first historically Black institution in America (Bennett, 1988; Roebuck & Murty, 1993). However, Ashmum Institute (now Lincoln University) was the first all-African American institution to remain in its original location, award baccalaureate degrees, and develop completely into a degree-granting college (Roebuck & Murty). Wilberforce University was established two years later. These three institutions, each created expressly for freed slaves and their children, ignited what would eventually become a major access movement for African Americans—the establishment of Historically Black Colleges and Universities (HBCUs).

One additional stride toward educational opportunity occurred in 1862 when Oberlin College student Mary Jane Patterson became the first African American female college graduate. That an African American woman was granted access to postsecondary education denotes progress, especially considering the inadequate representation of educated African Americans and the status of women during that era (Katz, 1969). However, serious, systematic policy efforts for African Americans up to this point in American history had been minimal at best.

After the Civil War, only 28 of the nation's nearly four million newly freed slaves had received bachelor's degrees from American colleges (Bowles & DeCosta, 1971; Roebuck & Murty, 1993). Although the lives of those educated few had changed tremendously, much work was needed to increase African American access to higher education. Upon passage of the Thirteenth Constitutional Amendment in 1865, two additional Black colleges, Virginia Union and Shaw, were established. Additionally, northern churches and white missionary groups provided funds and teachers to start more than 200 private institutions for African Americans in the South (Anderson, 1988; Drewry & Doermann, 2001; Gasman, 2007). The American Baptist Home Mission Society, the Freedman's Aid Society of the Methodist Episcopal Church, and the American Missionary Association were among these groups.

Many religious groups were active in the abolition movement and endeavored to continue their benevolence by addressing the poor state of literacy among freed African Americans. According to Allen and Jewell (2002), "these missionaries perceived Blacks as hapless victims of a corrupt and immoral system that inculcated values antithetical to ' civilization' and viewed as their God-given task to both 'civilize and educate' the freedmen" (p. 243). White Baptists, Methodists, Presbyterians, and other religious groups invested significant time and money into the establishment of schools for the training of African American teachers and preachers throughout the South. "Many included in their titles 'normal,' 'college,' and 'university,' though they were largely elementary and secondary schools . . . founded with haste and limited financial backing, many ceased to operate following 1900" (Roebuck & Murty, 1993, p. 25). The emergence of these institutions, as well as increased access to others, suddenly altered the racial makeup of higher education. This demographic shift did not occur without opposition though, as many southern conservatives saw higher education for African Americans as a threat to white supremacy (Allen & Jewell).

Fisk, Morehouse, Hampton, Howard, and the Atlanta Baptist Female Academy (now Spelman College) are among the 40 surviving private HBCUs founded between 1865 and 1890 (Drewry & Doermann, 2001). Most of these institutions (excluding Hampton) emphasized the liberal arts. The white founders and financial supporters were reluctant to entrust control of the institutions to African Americans; therefore, the schools continued to be governed almost exclusively by white administrators and teachers until the 1930s and 1940s. (Allen & Jewell, 2002; Anderson, 1988; Gasman, 2007; Roebuck & Murty, 1993). In addition to maintaining the leadership and governance of these private colleges, missionary groups also held strict control over curricula. Nearly everything that was taught to the former slaves did not reflect their own cultural history and heritage, but instead focused on white, European, and Westernized values and culture.

One of the biggest access-related policies for public higher education, and subsequently for African Americans, was introduced in 1862 with the implementation of the first Morrill Land Grant Act. The Act ushered in the agricultural and mechanical arts educational movement, which provided funds and 30,000 acres of land for the establishment of public institutions in every state (Rudolph, 1990). Ten years after the passage of the Act, Alcorn College in Mississippi became the first land-grant institution to be established for African Americans. Regarding the Morrill Land Grant Act of 1862, Nevins (1962) asserts, "The law annexed wide neglected areas to the domain of instruction. Widening the gates of opportunity, it made democracy freer, more adaptable, and more kinetic" (p. vi).

Access was specifically extended to African Americans with the passage of the second Morrill Act of 1890, which mandated that funds for education be distributed annually on a "just and equitable" basis to African Americans in seventeen states (Brazzell, 1996; Bowles & DeCosta, 1971). This Act led to the establishment of 17 Black state-supported institutions, which joined the list of existing private Black colleges and 54 other Black institutions founded under the first Morrill Act (Rudolph, 1990). The Act also legalized the segregation of Black and white Public institutions and emphasized a curricular focus on mechanics, agriculture, and the industrial arts. This federally-supported model of vocational education, though attractive to some African Americans, promoted the idea that they were intellectually less capable than whites and should be offered a separate and lower-caliber education (Anderson, 1988; Davis, 1998).

Roebuck and Murty (1993) also posit that public HBCUs were created for the following reasons: "To get millions of dollars in federal funds for the development of white land-grant universities, to limit African American education to vocational training, and to prevent African Americans from attending white land-grant colleges" (p. 27). Regardless of the factors inspiring their founding, these institutions and their missionary-supported private counterparts collectively produced more than 3,400 African American college graduates by the turn of the century (Anderson, 1988).

The public HBCUs founded during this period were generally of poorer quality than their white public counterparts established under the 1862 Morrill Act. These institutions were forced to operate with inadequately trained faculty and substandard instructional facilities. Unlike the private HBCUs, Kujovich (1993/1994) reports that African American administrators were often selected to lead public HBCUs, as white southerners were unwilling to manage the poorly funded

Black institutions. The *Plessy v. Ferguson* court case of 1896 ruled that states could continue the racial segregation of public schools only if accommodations and facilities were equal (Anderson, 1988). Ideally, advances toward parity for the public Black land-grant institutions were to occur under the "separate, but equal" rule of *Plessy*. Unfortunately, public HBCUs remained disproportionately underfunded. Sekora (1968) reports that even after *Plessy*, white land-grant institutions were still receiving state appropriations at a rate of 26 times more than Black colleges. Similarly, Bowles and DeCosta (1971) found that the per-pupil state expenditure rate for African Americans equaled about one-fourth the rate for whites.

Despite these inequities, the Morrill Land Grant Acts and related legislation provided venues for the education of African Americans without much challenge. That is, the emergence and continuation of these institutions with public financial support went on uncontested because they provided an alternative to enrolling Negro students en masse at white colleges and universities. Although a few African Americans were allowed to matriculate at predominantly white institutions (PWIs) throughout this era, 90% of all African American degree-holders in the late 1940s had been educated at HBCUs (Davis, 1998). On the eve of desegregation, African Americans accounted for less than one percent of entering first-year students at PWIs.

In 1954, the U.S. Supreme Court ruled in *Brown v. Board of Education* that racial segregation, including the operation of "separate, but equal" facilities in public education would no longer be legal (Brown, 2001). This ruling did not immediately signal a victory for African Americans, as many whites were not receptive to the court's ruling. Kelly and Lewis (2000) suggest were it not for the Supreme Court's 1955 "with all deliberate speed" ruling, many probably would have given up their quest for desegregation. That the Supreme Court had to reinforce the decision a year later showed the seriousness of the anti-integration stance taken by some whites. Although primary and secondary schools were at the heart of this case, the precedent clearly applied to public postsecondary institutions. Conceivably, this policy would immediately extend access to previously segregated educational institutions. Brown (2001) contends, however, "the mandate to desegregate did not reach higher education until one decade after Brown, when President Lyndon B. Johnson signed the Civil Rights Act of 1964" (p. 49). Title VI of the Act provided that "no person in the United States, on the grounds of race, color, or national origin, be excluded from participation in, or the benefits of, or be subjected to discrimination under any program or activity receiving federal financial assistance" (Malaney, 1987, p. 17). Title VI also restricted the distribution of federal funds to segregated schools.

Desegregation, as well as equal opportunity for African Americans and HBCUs, was significantly enhanced upon the implementation of another piece of important legislation—the Higher Education Act of 1965. Title III of the Act, *Strengthening Developing Institutions,* favored HBCUs by providing certain subsidies for their survival. "The term 'developing institutions' was incorporated into the legislation as an apparent effort to avoid designating Black higher education institutions as the primary recipients of the federal assistance made available in the funding" (Roebuck & Murty, 1993, p. 40). Title III funds were provided for faculty and curriculum improvement, student services, exchange programs for faculty and students, and various administrative improvement policies. The Act sought to support HBCUs during the period in which increased numbers of African American students were beginning to seek educational opportunities elsewhere.

U.S. President John F. Kennedy first introduced the term "affirmative action" in a civil rights speech given on the campus of Howard University, an HBCU (Bowen & Bok, 1998). The term was soon followed by elaborate plans to remedy the problem of persistent exclusionary practices and decades of unfair treatment of women and racial/ethnic minorities in all facets of American life: housing, business, government, employment, and education. In 1965, U.S. President Lyndon B. Johnson officially brought Kennedy's vision to fruition with the signing of Executive Order 11246, which required federal contractors to increase the number of minority employees as an "affirmative step" toward remedying years of exclusion for minority workers in those firms; affirmative action was systematically enacted that year. This policy, like others mentioned in this section, positively affected African American participation in higher education.

Under this new legislation, African Americans were afforded opportunities to matriculate at institutions that were once completely inaccessible to non-whites. Notwithstanding, their enrollments at major colleges and universities would not reach noticeable increases until the late 1960s and early 1970s. Kelly and Lewis (2000) report that Black enrollments increased from 27% in 1972 to 34% in 1976, before dropping steadily during the subsequent decade.

40 Years of Regression in Access and Equity

Policy efforts enacted through the late-1960s opened many doors for African American students in higher education. However, to characterize the current status of African Americans as inequitable would be a gross understatement. Over a century of gainful policy efforts have been undermined by the following: the steady underrepresentation of African American students at PWIs; continued over-reliance on racially-biased college entrance exams; consistent attempts to dismantle affirmative action; increased statewide admissions standards for public postsecondary education, without corresponding advances in public K–12 schools; reports of racism and negative African American student experiences at PWIs; low African American male student persistence and degree attainment rates; forced desegregation of HBCUs; inequitable funding for HBCUs; and the decline of need-based federal financial aid. Where does one begin? A list this extensive could make it hard to believe there were ever serious policy efforts enacted on behalf of African Americans.

While each issue noted above somehow contributes to the demise of previous policy efforts, it is simply impossible to provide detailed discussion about each in this one chapter. Therefore, we attempt to untangle pieces of the aforementioned web of policy issues by discussing them in two categories: (a) Enrollment declines, inequitable funding, and forced desegregation at HBCUs; and (b) access, affirmative action, and race-based admissions at PWIs.

Enrollment Declines, Funding Inequities, and Forced HBCU Desegregation

Brown v. the Board of Education and Title VI of the Civil Rights Act were meant to increase educational access for African Americans and other minorities; to some degree, they did just that. However, new opportunities for matriculation at PWIs quickly yielded negative consequences for HBCUs. As noted above, "over 90 percent of African American students (approximately 100,000 in 1950) were educated in traditionally Black schools" (Fleming, 1984, p. 7). According to Hoffman, Snyder, and Sonnenberg (1992), these numbers dipped significantly to 18.4% in 1976, then again to 17.2% in 1990. More recent data indicate that in 2004, PWIs enrolled 88.1% of all African Americans in higher education (U.S. Department of Education, 2007). HBCUs have clearly forfeited control over the education of African American students. Their collective inability to match the enrollment figures of earlier years, among other factors, presents negative financial repercussions.

The funding picture of HBCUs, which has remained consistently grim throughout their existence, has gotten extremely complex within the past 40 years. It is difficult to ascertain the effectiveness of various back-and-forth fiscal policies for Black colleges. Signed by U.S. President Ronald Regan, Executive Order 12320 established financial support for HBCUs (Roebuck & Murty, 1993). In the 1986 reauthorization of the Higher Education Act, Congress passed the Historically Black College Act as Part B of Title III, which authorized $100 million exclusively for HBCUs. In addition to Title III funds, public HBCUs also rely on state appropriations. As was the case with the distribution of funds associated with the Morrill Acts, public HBCUs still receive disproportionately lower state appropriations than their predominantly white counterparts (Minor, 2008).

According to Lum (2001), the average per-student allocation of state appropriated funds during the 2000–2001 school year at public HBCUs was $6,064, compared to $10,266 at public PWIs. Hoffman (1996) also found that per-student allocations at HBCUs were on average 12% less than those given to PWIs. These figures clearly signify failed attempts to create financial parity between HBCUs and PWIs. Among a long list of other reasons, attempts to desegregate public HBCUs have been inspired by a desire to increase the institutions' funding to the levels enjoyed by the public white institutions in those states.

Policies to transform the racial demography of HBCUs have received considerable attention in the higher education literature (see Conrad, Brier, & Braxton, 1997; Darden, Bagakas, & Marajh, 1992;

Brown, 2001; Hebel, 2001; Hossler & St. John, 1997; Southern Education Foundation, 1998). The *Adams v. Richardson* and *United States v. Kirk Fordice* cases "stand as the judicial guidepost for desegregation in those states that historically operated racially segregated dual systems of higher education" (Brown, 2001, p. 50). Hossler and St. John say the *Adams* case focused on desegregating state systems of higher education, which would subsequently increase the representation of African Americans at PWIs, as well as whites at HBCUs. *Fordice* mandated states to strategically employ efforts to eliminate all policies and practices that mirror a dual system of operation and keep public institutions racially identifiable.

These cases have placed extreme pressure on HBCUs to alter recruitment practices by redirecting their efforts to enrolling more non-African American students. This has been difficult for some institutions, as their poorer facilities, lack of resources, and largely regional reputations are unattractive to most white prospective college goers (Hebel, 2001). Although *Fordice* compliance has been repeatedly emphasized at HBCUs, states have failed to respond to the inequitable distribution of public funds between HBCUs and PWIs (Brown, 2001; Hossler & St. John, 1997). While *Fordice* and *Adams* have created obstacles for HBCUs, settlements from the *Ayers* and *Knight v. Alabama* (1995) cases have yielded rewards for HBCUs in the states of Mississippi and Alabama, respectively. These two cases revealed years of unequal funding for public HBCUs post-*de jure* segregation. Collectively, these cases and the desegregation mandates accompanying them continue to present negative consequences for HBCUs, as they have been forced to rethink their missions and purposes (Minor, 2008). These institutions and their long-standing commitments to offering college opportunity for African American students are critically important, as Perna et al.'s (2006) study of 19 southern states revealed: "Public 4-year HBCUs are the only sector [of higher education] in which Blacks consistently approach or achieve equity in enrollment and degree completion" (p. 223).

Access, Affirmative Action, and Race-Based Admissions Policies at PWIs

Much like the HBCU desegregation literature, numerous books and articles have provided detailed discussion and multiple perspectives on access with regard to affirmative action and race-based admissions (see Allen, 2005; Bowen & Bok, 1998; Reisberg, 2000; Skrentny, 2001; Southern Education Foundation, 1998; St. John, Simmons, & Musoba, 1999; Trent, 1991; Tierney, 1996; Yosso, Parker, Solórzano, & Lynn, 2004). The affirmative action policies of the mid-1960s dramatically increased educational opportunities for African Americans, particularly at PWIs. In fact, Bowen and Bok (1998) say race-based college admissions policies "have led to striking gains in the representation of minorities in the most lucrative and influential occupations" (p. 10).

Despite its momentum, attempts to dismantle affirmative action at postsecondary institutions began in 1973 with the original filing of the landmark case, *Regents of the University of California v. Bakke* (Trent, 1991). Allan Bakke, a white male applicant who was denied admission to the University of California-Davis, believed he would have been admitted were it not for affirmative action programs. At the time of his application, there were two tracks by which applicants could gain admission to the medical school. The regular track denied candidates whose undergraduate grade point averages fell below 2.5 on a 4.0 scale. The "special" admissions track did not require candidates to have a 2.5 grade point average, and "disadvantaged" candidates were approved for entry on a case-by-case basis until 16 special admissions selections had been made.

During a four-year period, 63 minority students were admitted under these special arrangements and 44 under the general program. In 1973 and 1974, special applicants were admitted with lower scores than Bakke's. After being rejected the second time, he filed a lawsuit seeking mandatory admission to UC-Davis. A 1978 Supreme Court decision prohibited racial quotas, but allowed universities to consider race a factor among many in the pursuit of diversity (*Regents of the University of California v. Bakke*, 1978).

Policies to reform affirmative action across the nation have also been influenced by *Hopwood v. The University of Texas Law School*, in which a federal judge ruled that race could not be used to give preferential treatment to minority law school applicants in Texas (Southern Education Foundation, 1998; St. John et al., 1999). Cheryl Hopwood, a white woman from a working-class family, and three other students disputed their rejection by the University of Texas Law School. The court required schools to review applicants individually instead of using race as a proxy. The *Hopwood* case called into question the Supreme Court's ruling in *Bakke*. The Supreme Court's refusal to review this case raised questions about how to lawfully create admissions policies that take race into consideration.

Anti-affirmative action legislation has since restricted African American student access to post-secondary institutions in Texas and California. In fact, African American students at the University of Texas-Austin comprised 4.1–5.6% of the total student body between 1988 and 1996. "In fall 1997, the first year in which *Hopwood* banned race as a consideration in admissions and financial aid policies, African Americans made up just 2.7% of the first-time freshmen" (Southern Education Foundation, 1998, p. 50). Even more dramatic, California Institute of Technology, one of the nation's top universities, enrolled no African American first-year students during the 1999–2000 school term (Reisberg, 2000). According to data from the National Center for Education Statistics (2008), African Americans comprised less than 3% of undergraduates at both the University of California, Berkeley and UCLA in Fall 2006.

Policies that previously ensured access and the increased participation of African Americans in higher education have taken a downward turn in some states. Other states (e.g., Michigan, Oregon, and Arizona) have recently considered changes in their race-sensitive admissions policies that would further exclude racial/ethnic minorities (Allen, 2005; St. John et al., 1999). Continuing to challenge the admission of African Americans and other racial/ethnic minority students in higher education with regard to affirmative action policy were two recent cases at the University of Michigan. *Gratz v. Bollinger*, involving the University's undergraduate admissions policies, and *Grutter v. Bollinger*, which challenged Michigan's law school admissions policies, were filed in 1997. Regarding the Michigan cases, Allen (2005) noted:

> The battle lines were drawn for a struggle that engaged the nation's attention. At root were core sociocultural beliefs, values, and ideals about race, equity, and fairness in America. In this sense, the court cases symbolized a long national debate, joining *Dred Scott*; *Plessy v. Ferguson*; *Brown v. Board of Education of Topeka*; *Bakke v. Regents of the University of California* [sic]; and a plethora of other court cases that wrestled with race, equity, and opportunity in America. (p. 18)

In the first case, Jennifer Gratz, who applied for admission for fall 1995 and Patrick Hammacher who applied for admission for fall 1997, both white in-state applicants, were denied early admission and were later denied admission to the College of Literature, Science, and the Arts (*Gratz v. Bollinger*, 2003). The second case involved Barbara Grutter, a white applicant with a 3.8 undergraduate GPA and a 161 LSAT score, who applied for admission to the law school for fall 1996. She was first wait-listed for admission, but later rejected (*Grutter v. Bollinger*, 2003).

The issue in the *Gratz* case was whether the use of racial preferences in admissions to the undergraduate programs violated the Equal Protection Clause of the Fourteenth Amendment, Title VI of the Civil Rights Act, or 42 U.S.C. 1981. At issue in the *Grutter* case was whether diversity was a compelling interest that could justify the narrowly tailored use of race in selecting applicants for admission to public universities. More than 60 *amicus curiae* or "friend of the court" briefs were filed and separate decisions were made with different results in the two cases. In the undergraduate admissions case, the court found the admissions policy unlawful in a 6–3 decision, while the law school admission policy was upheld with a 5–4 decision. For the undergraduate admissions policies, the decision meant that schools could not award points to applicants based solely on race, but race could be used as a "plus" factor and in an individualized evaluation of applicants. Supreme Court Justice Sandra Day O'Connor wrote:

> Today we hold that the Law School has a compelling interest in attaining a diverse student body . . . The Law School's educational judgment that such diversity is essential to its educational mission is one to which we defer. The Law School's assessment that diversity will, in fact, yield educational benefits is substantiated by respondents and their *amici*. (as cited in NACUA, 2003, p. 2)

These decisions put to rest, at least in the short-term, the debates regarding the use of race in college admissions decisions; thus signifying a temporary victory for African American student access to higher education. However, there are already additional challenges to the use of race in admissions policies and campus leaders and policymakers will again be called upon to show the benefits of increased minority student participation in higher education. This most likely will further complicate or reduce African American student access to PWIs.

Discussion and Critical Race Analysis

In examining policy efforts for African Americans throughout the lifespan of higher education, there were numerous events, tumultuous and triumphant, that led to the current state of access and equity. In this section, we offer an analysis of these policies using CRT. Taylor (1999) purports, "the central tenets of CRT have yet to be extended into analyses of higher education, and their potential to inform strategies for reform has yet to be fully explored" (p. 182). Therefore, we critique some progressive and regressive policies enacted on behalf of African American students.

Parker (1998) discusses the importance that CRT attributes to linking history with contemporary social constructions of race. We have provided some historical policy insights associated with college access and equity, and now endeavor to demonstrate the historical centrality of race in policy efforts and the relevance of race when considering the current status of African American student enrollments at colleges and universities. To do so, we use CRT as a lens through which to examine history, and acquire a more sophisticated understanding of the realities of present dilemmas.

Racism: Indoctrinated, Normal, and Real

We begin our analysis by calling attention to the reality that racial issues have resurfaced at almost every juncture in the history of American education. Many policies described throughout this chapter were race-driven. Specifically, they were embedded within a mainstream, racist, and hegemonic framework that has consistently questioned the worthiness of African Americans as educated citizens and the legitimacy of their presence in higher education. The source of this racism goes beyond education, but for the purpose of this discussion, we contend that the question of worthiness was rooted in the idea that African Americans, based on the color of their skin, were intellectually inferior. In essence, it was ingrained into the fabric of education that African Americans did not possess the mental capacity to learn, nor had they any real need for formal postsecondary education. Our point is that from its inception, the United States was founded on racist principles that have permeated the systems upon which this country functions; education is no exception.

Due to enslavement and the construction of Africans as property, white privilege has been inextricably linked to African American subordination and serves as a foundation for white superiority in an oppressive educational system (Ladson-Billings & Tate, 1995). The systemic subordination of African Americans was grounded in erroneous assumptions and judgments that were generated and subsequently cemented into the educational system; thus creating later challenges for this population in their pursuit of higher education. African Americans proved their intellectual worthiness in education thanks to early trailblazers like Alexander Lucius Twilight and Mary Jane Patterson. However, their accomplishments did not impede the consistent use of racism to maintain systemic exclusion and subordination (consider the elusive neutrality of the SAT discussed later).

Despite the odds, the number of degree holders increased and more African Americans participated in higher education. The Civil Rights Movement and later court cases such as *Brown v. Board of Education* emerged and legislation was passed (e.g., Title VI), requiring states to expand access to previously excluded groups. Although these mandates allowed African American students to attend PWIs in larger numbers, the doors to these institutions were neither instantly nor easily opened, confirming that African Americans were not welcomed or perceived as worthy of being educated. Race was used to indicate intellectual inferiority, promote their exclusion from white institutions, and ultimately keep African Americans from disturbing the white status quo in higher education. Even when legislative mandates were passed and policies were enacted, the decisions were largely race-based and geared toward promoting white interests as opposed to eliminating inequities. Although race has and continues to be central to the problems concerning African American college access and equity, its presence and consequences are hardly recognizable without performing a critical examination to uncover it. This type of examination easily leads to one conclusion: racism is real and unlikely to be eradicated despite incremental changes.

While our prediction may appear pessimistic, we are suggesting that if African Americans and other historically excluded populations continue to work within a paradigm based on an unrealistic goal, true progress and change will never be attained with substantial measure. Our position is consistent with Derrick Bell's (2005) perspective: "Racial equality is, in fact, not a realistic goal" (p. 73). He recommends that African Americans adopt a "racial realism" approach, which requires acknowledgement of subordination in a racist society. Upon accepting that race and racism are persistent and dynamic fixtures in American culture, we can avoid the continued frustrations associated with reaching for an unattainable goal and focus more realistically on strategies and approaches that will more comprehensively address racial inequities in higher education.

In concert with this idea, Bell (2005) also suggests African Americans have placed too much trust into policies guaranteeing equal rights. This fallacy is based on the belief that legislators and politicians will enact espoused promises for access and equity. As history has shown, the end results more often than not are disappointing discard for African Americans, particularly when the supposed outcomes of various policy efforts are piecemeal, slow moving, or ultimately overturned, as has been the case with affirmative action. As we discussed earlier, many academic programs and admissions policies that were supposed to be designed to increase college access for African Americans have received great opposition and been criticized for giving these individuals an unfair advantage over white students. Unsurprisingly, once these programs were halted, there were dramatic decreases in the number of students for which the programs were originally intended to serve (Southern Education Foundation, 1998).

Understanding the Convergence of Interests

Interest-convergence is another tenet of CRT that resonates throughout the history of African Americans in higher education. For the purposes of this discussion, we focus on four areas: (1) White missionary involvement in the establishment of HBCUs; (2) legislation such as the Morrill Acts, *Brown v. Board of Education,* and Title VI; (3) state support for Black colleges; and (4) affirmative action and race-based approaches to college admission.

White missionary involvement. Earlier, we noted that religious missionaries were central to the founding of Black colleges (Anderson, 1988; Drewry & Doermann, 2001; Gasman, 2007). However, the question of why such support was offered merits attention. What gains and outcomes did Christian and philanthropic whites receive? It would seem naïve to think the altruistic "out of the kindness of my heart" motive was primary. Therefore we offer four possible explanations, each grounded in the interest-convergence principle. First, given the institution of slavery and the disgraceful rate of illiteracy among freed slaves, providing educational assistance to African Americans was a sure way to clear the conscious of white Christians. It is conceivable that White "benevolence" was more about alleviating their own guilt than it was about educating African Americans. Second, higher education for African Americans may have perceivably threatened the permanency of white supremacy (Allen & Jewell, 2002). Thus, white power could be maintained by providing the financial support for establishment of Black schools, which would ensure that the institutions were governed by white financers who would offer a curriculum grounded in whiteness, thus indoctrinating the superiority of whiteness into African American education.

In keeping with the indoctrination of "white as superior," our third proposition is that African Americans, deemed intellectually inferior, could at best be educated enough to remain relegated to a trade or vocation that would be useful toward advancing a labor force to serve the needs of White industrialists and farmers. Lastly, we offer that through the very establishment of separate schools, it was clear that African Americans were deemed unworthy and unwelcome at white institutions. The establishment of HBCUs ensured there would be no need for African Americans to attend the same institutions as the sons and daughters of the supposedly well-meaning White missionaries. While this analysis is certainly retroactive in nature, we argue that the interest of education converged for African Americans and White people, but came at a hefty price for the former, and at the self-interest of the latter.

(De)segregation legislation. "One cannot fairly discuss the legal struggle for educational opportunity for Blacks in the United States without first reviewing the history of the Supreme Court's role in protecting a racial social order that sought to place Whites in a superior and controlling position and relegate Blacks to an inferior, subservient one" (Byrd-Chichester, 2001, p. 12). The Morrill Land Grant Act of 1890 and the *Plessy v. Ferguson* decision firmly supported segregation and ultimately legalized the "separate but equal" doctrine. We argue that if in fact equality existed there would have been no reason to establish separate or segregated institutions. The mere acceptance of separation among the races and the inequitable distribution of resources to fund educational facilities imply the superiority of one race over the other. Public Black colleges were also disadvantaged by the limited curricular focus on vocational education. Ultimately, the establishment of separate facilities, namely public HBCUs, met a specific interest for African Americans and Whites. However, equality for African Americans during this time was not likely to occur because it fundamentally advanced White supremacy (Byrd-Chichester, 2001).

Interests in relegating African Americans to an industrial education and the need for continued monetary support at HBCUs converged, with the greatest rewards garnered by the White majority. Regarding the Booker T. Washington and W. E. B. Du Bois debates over the curricular foci of Black colleges (vocational vs. liberal arts), Bell (2005) asserted, "Whites welcomed Washington's conciliatory, non-confrontational policy, and deemed it sufficient self-acceptance for the society's involuntary subordination of Blacks in every area of life" (p. 86). The outcome of the debate rested with white people in powerful positions, who decided that African Americans were best suited for vocational education (Allen & Jewell, 2002). As we unravel and reinterpret historical policy efforts for African Americans in higher education, it becomes clear that the foundation of early legislation impacting this population is better characterized as "pseudo-equality" under the guise of legally legitimized segregation and separatism.

At some point in history "separate but equal" became unfashionable. Perhaps it was the recognition that "separate" was obviously "unequal," but our analysis now turns to the *Brown v. Board of Education* ruling which is purported to be the legislation that dismantled the *Plessy* doctrine. Bell (2004) examines the sociopolitical circumstances that shifted the enactment of this ruling. He argues that despite previous legal battles over school desegregation, the *Brown* decision was made amid the backdrop of several sociopolitical factors including the return of African American soldiers from Vietnam and the mass publicity surrounding the murder of Emmett Till. It was highly unlikely that soldiers would return to the U.S. to be subjected to second-class citizenry after having recently defended the country abroad. Delgado and Stefancic (2001) contend that such treatment would have surely led to domestic unrest. In addition, the gruesome murder of Emmett Till and other racially-motivated violence against African Americans had created a tarnished international image of the U.S., a country known to impose its supposed democratic values upon other nations. Thus, the *Brown* decision was one vehicle by which the U.S. could respond to these issues, if not in depth, at least on the surface (Delgado & Stefancic, 2001). The ruling would help soften its international image and calm ensuing domestic tensions, while secondarily serving as a major breakthrough in educational access and finally offering a long overdue policy response to the *Plessy v. Ferguson* ruling (Taylor, 1999).

Several scholars (Bell, 2000, 2004; Crenshaw, 1997; Delgado & Stefancic, 2001; Taylor, 1999; Yosso et al., 2004) caution us to refrain from succumbing to overwhelmingly positive assertions about the *Brown* decision without first subjecting this policy as well as other historical events to close scrutiny. For example, one consequence of the *Brown* decision was the belief that African Americans would receive a better education at white institutions. "*Brown* has taken on a somewhat twisted meaning—namely, it implies that Blacks have to be in the company of Whites in order to earn or progress, an argument which implies that Blacks are inferior" (Byrd-Chichester, 2001, p. 15). A more realistic examination would likely yield a revisionist historical perspective (Delgado & Stefancic, 2001). It is perhaps fitting to consider a revisionist lens in examining the current status of African American students in higher education and our assertion that despite *Brown*, "separate but equal" remains largely undisrupted.

> We tend to characterize *Brown* as having successfully interred *Plessy*. Quite clearly, separate but equal is no longer the law of the land. But I think it would be a mistake to focus solely on the rejection of the formal doctrine while failing to uncover the continuity of *Plessy's* social vision. (Crenshaw, 1997, p. 283)

State support for Black colleges. The state's role in higher education for African Americans is a trend that has repeatedly manifested itself throughout history. While some of the most notable policies were associated with the Morrill Acts and public funding for higher education, the relationship between the state and postsecondary institutions has gone back and forth around issues of equity. The allocation of state funds for public PWIs and HBCUs has always been unjustifiably disparate. HBCUs established under the Morrill Acts were generally of poorer quality than public PWIs, and per-pupil state allocations were always significantly lower for the Black colleges (Roebuck & Murty, 1993). Apparently, limited progress has been made as inequities persist (Minor, 2008). Current funding gaps and declining African American student enrollments are evidence that HBCUs still need equitable resourcing and higher state appropriations in order to reach parity with PWIs.

The mission of HBCUs to educate African American students is being threatened by state-imposed desegregation mandates that would provide the additional funding needed to improve facilities and expand capacity in all its forms. This places HBCU leaders in a precarious position as they work to advance and promote these institutions. If there is a true commitment to improving the condition of HBCUs and a genuine interest in increasing African American participation in higher education, it would seem only logical and fair for historically Black institutions to receive greater funding from the states in which they are located. Byrd-Chichester (2001) maintains that a major issue in the desegregation of HBCUs is whether the court-mandated remedies will enhance the education of African Americans or serve as another barrier to access. Moreover, we wonder what measures are being taken to ensure that public PWIs in those same states are being held equally accountable for student diversity.

In short, pressure for desegregation should be equally applied. However, HBCUs and PWIs remain separate and receive unequal treatment under the law. Interest-convergence is central in this example, particularly with regard to desegregation, because PWIs are being encouraged to diversify their student populations (while maintaining their white cultural norms), but HBCUs on the other hand are being forced to do so under a mandate that threatens their historical mission and purpose. The problem is that HBCUs were never exclusive, while PWIs on the other hand remain covertly exclusive. The interests of PWIs are ultimately protected because White people serve in powerful positions that affect state appropriations and allow them to make major decisions affecting both institutional types. As Taylor (1999) shared in his analysis of desegregation trends at Tennessee State University (an HBCU), most Black colleges continue to argue against state mandates that threaten their viability and existence, while PWIs will balk at suggested changes in the status quo that would threaten their racial identifiability.

The gradual abortion of affirmative action. The issue of interest-convergence becomes evident once again with the dismantling of affirmative action programs that have helped facilitate African American student entrée to PWIs. While viewed as remedies to racial inequality, affirmative action programs have received a wealth of criticism that has had longlasting effects (Byrd-Chichester, 2001; Yosso et al., 2004). One such criticism has been that these programs promote reverse discrimination against white people. In considering interest-convergence, the ultimate issue is that in order to effectively achieve any form of equity, sacrifices must be made and opportunity must be distributed. Thus, the onus lies with the white majority who must share a portion of what has long been perceived as their rightful ownership of certain colleges and universities.

However, there is a problem with how much of the ownership should be shared, with whom, and for how long. When benefits to African Americans and other marginalized populations are considered too excessive, the situation becomes problematic for those who argue the existence of reverse discrimination or believe African Americans and Whites have reached parity. In essence, the interest-convergence principle is once again manifested in that white people will only support efforts for African Americans when their own interests are not threatened, or when they too stand to gain particular benefits. When the interests do not converge, it is clear that many white persons will champion policies that limit African American student access and further exacerbate racial inequities in higher education.

Conclusion

To achieve the racial justice promised in many early policy initiatives, more research regarding the status of African Americans in higher education are needed. That is, policymakers in public and institutional sectors must be made aware of the structural barriers that produce racial disparities in college access and attainment. Harper (2008) described numerous ways in which promises of the *Brown v. Board of Education* case had been realized by an elite group of African American undergraduates. Necessary are policy initiatives that make more accessible the social, political, and economic gains he described.

While on the one hand it may appear to some that tremendous strides have been made for African Americans throughout the lifespan of higher education, we have made clear in this chapter that much remains to be done to ensure equity and increase participation. Several areas that warrant urgent policy attention with regard to access and equity in higher education were identified in this chapter. The contemporary issues described herein must remain on the agendas of public policymakers, college and university administrators, and others who are concerned about the education of African Americans. Equally important are critical and ongoing analyses of policies that were supposedly enacted to improve educational outcomes for this population, as many have regressed in recent years.

CRT was useful for illustrating how various policy decisions have caused African Americans to essentially take three steps forward and two steps back over the lifespan of higher education. Unfortunately, progressive change has not occurred vigorously since the 1970s. This should concern public policymakers as it poses troublesome implications for the economic and sociopolitical status of African Americans. Increasing access to the public good of higher education is beneficial to everyone—public interests converge when more Americans across racial/ethnic groups earn college degrees and assume societal roles that enhance global competitiveness, decrease crime and poverty, and help the U.S. enact its espoused democratic ideals (Harper, 2006; Kezar et al., 2005; Lewis & Hearn, 2003). Consistent attacks on affirmative action; funding inequities for public institutions that annually offer college opportunity to more than a quarter million African American students; the implementation of policy initiatives that distract HBCUs from their original missions; and infrequent policy analyses will continually manufacture insufficient access and equity barriers for those who could ultimately benefit from college participation. While it is important to acknowledge and honor historical advances, contemporary times call for new policy efforts to solve persistent problems.

References

Adams v. Richardson, 351 F.2d 636 D.C. Cir. (1972).

Allen, W. R. (2005). A forward glance in a mirror: Diversity challenged—access, equity, and success in higher education. *Educational Researcher, 34*(7), 18–23.

Allen, W. R., & Jewell, J. O. (1995). African American education since *An American Dilemma: An American Dilemma* revisited. *Daedalus, 124*(1), 77–100.

Allen, W. R., & Jewell, J. O. (2002). A backward glance forward: Past, present, and future perspectives on historically Black colleges and universities. *The Review of Higher Education, 25*(3), 241–261.

Anderson, J. D. (1988). *The education of Blacks in the south, 1860–1935.* Chapel Hill: University of North Carolina Press.

Bell, D. A. (1987). *And we are not saved: The elusive quest for racial justice.* New York: Basic Books.

Bell, D. A. (2000). *Brown v. Board of Education:* Forty-five years after the fact. *Ohio Northern Law Review, 26,* 1–171.

Bell, D. A. (2004). *Silent covenants:* Brown v. Board of Education *and the unfulfilled hopes for racial reform.* New York: Oxford University Press.

Bell, D. A. (2005). Racial realism. In R. Delgado & J. Stefancic (Eds.), *The Derrick Bell reader* (pp. 55–96). New York: New York University Press.

Bennett, L. (1988). *Before the Mayflower: A history of Black America* (6th ed.). New York: Penguin.

Bergerson, A. A. (2003). Critical race theory and white racism: Is there room for white scholars in fighting racism in education? *Qualitative Studies in Education, 16*(1), 51–63.

Bowen, W. G., & Bok, D. (1998). *The shape of the river: Long-term consequences of considering race in college and university admissions.* Princeton, NJ: Princeton University Press.

Bowles, F., & DeCosta, F. A. (1971). *Between two worlds: A profile of Negro education.* New York: McGraw-Hill.

Boyer, E. L. (1997). *Selected speeches, 1979–1995.* Princeton, NJ: Carnegie Foundation for the Advancement of Teaching.

Brazzell, J. C. (1996). Diversification of postsecondary institutions. In S. R. Komives & D. B. Woodard (Eds.), *Student services: A handbook for the profession* (3rd ed., pp. 43–63). San Francisco: Jossey-Bass.

Brown v. Board of Education of Topeka, 347 U.S. 483 (1954).

Brown II, M. C. (2001). Collegiate desegregation and the public Black college: A new policy mandate. *The Journal of Higher Education, 72,* 46–62.

Byrd-Chichester, J. (2001). The federal courts and claims of racial discrimination in higher education. *Journal of Negro Education, 69*(1), 12–25.

Conrad, C., Brier, E., & Braxton, J. (1997). Factors contributing to the matriculation of White students in public HBCUs. *Journal for a Just and Caring Education, 3*(1), 37–62.

Crenshaw, K. W. (1997). Color blindness, history, and the law. In W. Lubiano (Ed.), *The house that race built* (pp. 280–288). New York: Pantheon.

Darden, J. T., Bagakas, J. G., & Marajh, O. (1992). Historically Black colleges and the dilemma of desegregation. *Equity & Excellence, 25,* 106–112.

Davis, J. E. (1998). Cultural capital and the role of Historically Black Colleges and Universities in educational reproduction. In K. Freeman (Ed.), *African American culture and heritage in higher education research and practice* (pp. 143–153). Westport, CT: Praeger.

Delgado, R. (1995). *Critical race theory: The cutting edge.* Philadelphia, PA: Temple University Press.

Delgado, R., & Stefancic, J. (2001). *Critical race theory: An introduction.* New York: New York University Press.

Drewry, H. N., & Doermann, H. (2001). *Stand and prosper: Private Black colleges and their students.* Princeton, NJ: Princeton University Press.

Fleming, J. (1984). *Blacks in college: A comparative study of students' success in Black and in White institutions.* San Francisco: Jossey-Bass.

Gasman, M. (2007). *Envisioning Black colleges: A history of the United Negro College Fund.* Baltimore: Johns Hopkins University Press.

Gratz v. Bollinger, 123 S. Ct. 2411 (2003).

Grutter v. Bollinger, 123 S. Ct. 2325 (2003).

Harper, S. R. (2006). *Black male students at public flagship universities in the U.S.: Status, trends and implications for policy and practice.* Washington, DC: Joint Center for Political and Economic Studies.

Harper, S. R. (2008). Realizing the intended outcomes of *Brown:* High-achieving African American male undergraduates and social capital. *American Behavioral Scientist, 51*(7), 1029–1052.

Harper, S. R., & Patton, L. D. (2007). Editors' notes. In S. R. Harper & L. D. Patton (Eds.), *Responding to the realities of race on campus.* New Directions for Student Services (No. 120, pp. 1–5). San Francisco: Jossey-Bass.

Hebel, S. (2001, June 8). A new push to integrate public Black colleges. *The Chronicle of Higher Education, 47*(39), A21.

Hoffman, C. M. (1996). *Historically Black colleges and universities, 1976–1994.* Washington, DC: U.S. Department of Education, National Center for Education Statistics.

Hoffman, C. M., Snyder, T. D., & Sonnenberg, B. (1992). *Historically Black colleges and universities, 1976–1990.* Washington, DC: U.S. Department of Education, National Center for Education Statistics.

Hopwood v. Texas, 78 F.3d 932, 5th Cir., (1996).

Hossler, D., & St. John, E. P. (1997). Rethinking college desegregation. *Journal for a Just & Caring Education, 3*(1), 9–36.

Institute for Higher Education Policy. (1998). *Reaping the benefits: Defining the public and private value of going to college.* Washington, DC: Author.

Katz, W. L. (Ed.). (1969). *History of schools for the colored population.* New York: Arno Press.

Kelly, R. D. G., & Lewis, E. (2000). *To make our world anew: A history of African Americans.* New York: Oxford University Press.

Kezar, A. J., Chambers, T. C., & Burkhardt, J. C. (Eds.). (2005). *Higher education for the public good: Emerging voices from a national movement*. San Francisco: Jossey-Bass.

Knight v. Alabama, 900 F.Supp. 272. 282–86, N.D. Ala. (1995).

Kujovich, G. (1993/1994, Winter). Public Black colleges: The long history of unequal funding. *Journal of Blacks in Higher Education, 2,* 73.

Ladson-Billings, G. (2000). Racialized discourses and ethnic epistemologies. In N. K. Denzin & Y. S. Lincoln (Eds.) *Handbook of qualitative research* (2nd ed., pp. 257–277). Thousand Oaks, CA: Sage.

Ladson-Billings, G., & Tate, W. F. (1995). Toward a critical race theory of education. *Teachers College Record, 97*(1), 47–69.

Lewis, D. R., & Hearn, J. (Eds.). (2003). *The public research university: Serving the public good in new times*. Lanham, MD: University Press of America.

Lum, L. (2001). Will historic inequities ever be remedied? *Black Issues in Higher Education, 18*(3), 32–39.

Malaney, G. D. (1987). A review of early decisions in Adams v. Richardson. In A.S. Pruitt, (Ed.), *In pursuit of equality in higher education* (pp. 17–22). Dix Hills, NY: General Hall.

Minor, J. T. (2008). Segregation residual in higher education: A tale of two states. *American Educational Research Journal, 45*(4), 861–885.

National Association of College and University Attorneys. (2003). *NACUANOTE: U.S. Supreme Court decisions in University of Michigan Admissions Cases*. Washington, DC: Author.

National Center for Education Statistics. (2008). *Integrated Postsecondary Education Data System*. Washington, DC: U.S. Department of Education, Institute of Education Sciences.

Nevins, A. (1962). *The state universities and democracy*. Urbana: University of Illinois Press.

Parker, L. (1998). "Race is . . . race ain't": An exploration of the utility of critical race theory in qualitative research in education. *Qualitative Studies in Education, 11*(1), 43–55.

Perna, L. W., Milem, J., Gerald, D., Baum, E., Rowan, H., & Hutchens, N. (2006). The status of equity for Black undergraduates in public higher education in the south: Still separate and unequal. *Research in Higher Education, 47*(2), 197–228.

Ranbom, S., & Lynch, J. (1988). Timeline: The long road to educational equality. *Educational Record, 69*(1), 16–22.

Regents of the University of California v. Bakke, 438 U.S. 265, 287, 98 S. Ct. 2733, 2746, 57 L. Ed.2d 750 (1978).

Reisberg, L. (2000, April 28). A top university wonders why it has no Black freshmen. *The Chronicle of Higher Education, 46*(34), A52.

Roebuck, J. B., & Murty, K. S. (1993). *Historically Black colleges and universities: Their place in American higher education*. Westport, CT: Praeger.

Rudolph, F. (1990). *The American college and university: A history*. Athens: University of Georgia Press.

Sekora, J. (1968). Murder relentless and impassive: The American academic community and the Negro college. *Soundings, 51,* 259.

Skrentny, J. D. (2001, February 16). Affirmative action and new demographic realities. *The Chronicle of Higher Education, 47*(23), B7.

Solórzano, D. (1998). Critical race theory, racial and gender microaggressions, and the experiences of Chicana and Chicano scholars. *International Journal of Qualitative Studies in Education, 11,* 121–136.

Solórzano, D., Ceja, M., & Yosso, T. J. (2000). Critical race theory, racial microaggressions, and campus racial climate: The experiences of African American college students. *Journal of Negro Education, 69*(1), 60–73.

Southern Education Foundation. (1998). *Miles to go: A report on Black students and postsecondary education in the South*. Atlanta, GA: Author.

St. John, E. P., Simmons, A. B., & Musoba, G. D. (1999). *Merit-aware admissions in public universities*. Bloomington, IN: Indiana Education Policy Center.

Taylor, E. (1999). Critical race theory and interest convergence in the desegregation of higher education. In L. Parker, D. Deyhle, & S. Villenas (Eds.), *Race is . . . race isn't: Critical race theory and qualitative studies in education* (pp. 181–204). Boulder, CO: Westview Press.

Tierney, W. G. (2006). Affirmative action in California: Looking back, looking forward in public academe. *Journal of Negro Education, 65*(2), 122–132.

Trent, W. T. (1991). Student affirmative action in higher education: Addressing underrepresentation. In P. G. Altbach & K. Lomotey (Eds.), *The racial crisis in American higher education* (pp. 107–132). Albany: State University of New York Press.

Tyack, D., & Cuban, L. (1995). *Tinkering toward utopia: A century of public school reform.* Cambridge, MA: Harvard University Press.

U.S. Department of Education. (2007). *Digest of education statistics, 2006.* Washington, DC: National Center for Education Statistics.

United States v. Fordice, 505 U.S. 717, 112 S.Ct. 2727 (1992).

Valdes, F., McCristal Culp, J., & Harris, A. P. (2002). Battles waged, won and lost: Critical race theory at the turn of the millennium. In F. Valdes, J. McCristal Culp, & A. P. Harris (Eds.), *Crossroads, directions and new critical race theory* (pp. 1–6). Philadelphia, PA: Temple University Press.

Yosso, T. J., Parker, L., Solórzano, D. G., & Lynn, M. (2004). From Jim Crow to affirmative action and back again: A critical race discussion of racialized rationales and access to higher education. *Review of Research in Education, 28,* 1–25.

CHAPTER 47

CHALLENGING RACIAL BATTLE FATIGUE ON HISTORICALLY WHITE CAMPUSES: A CRITICAL RACE EXAMINATION OF RACE-RELATED STRESS

WILLIAM A. SMITH, TARA J. YOSSO, AND DANIEL G. SOLÓRZANO

The young black reporter looked at me patiently as I paused to gather my thoughts. Noticing that I was clenching my cup, she smiled reassuringly and calmly said, "I know this must be difficult to talk about, but please let me reassure you, my point is to get this out to our readers, to let people know more about what happened, and—" I interrupted, "Well, as I mentioned to you when you contacted me, I don't know exactly what happened, but I do want to make sure that folks know what this man was about. What he was doing. I think the link to what happened is his work—our work." I paused to sip my kava kava herb tea and take my stack of paperwork and notes out of my crocheted bag. Angela, Corky, Huey, and others had warned me about sharing too much information with reporters, but this newspaper had a reputation for serving the black community in Boston for many years. I hoped I was making the right decision to trust this woman. "Well, Monday, March 6, 1972, was for all intents and purposes just another day . . ."

We open this chapter with a counterstory preview to entice readers to engage in a framework called critical race theory (CRT). CRT draws on many areas of academic scholarship and centers the experiences of people of color to document voices and knowledges rarely taken into account in traditional academic spaces or mainstream mass media venues. CRT scholarship combines empirical and experiential knowledges, frequently in the form of storytelling, chronicles, or other creative narratives. These counternarratives can often expose traditional educational discourse as racialized, gendered, classed storytelling.

Indeed, traditional stories about race do not seem like stories at all. Such "everyday" narratives perpetuate myths that darker skin and poverty correlate with bad neighborhoods and bad schools. This chapter and counterstory utilize CRT in education to challenge the silences of "race-neutral" storytelling in order to discuss the race-related stress faculty of color confront when navigating through historically white universities.

Racial Microaggressions and Racial Battle Fatigue

Racism is structured into the rhythms of everyday life in the United States (Feagin, 2000). Pierce (1970) defines racism as a "public health and mental health illness" (p. 266) based on the delusion or false belief, in spite of contrary evidence, that innate inferiority correlates with dark skin color. He argues that in examining racism ". . . one must not look for the gross and obvious. The subtle, cumulative miniassault is the substance of today's racism . . ." (Pierce, 1974, p. 516). He further describes these assaults as racial microaggressions. In adapting Pierce's (1970, 1974, 1980, 1989, 1995) work, we define racial microaggressions as 1) subtle verbal and nonverbal insults directed at people of color, often automatically or unconsciously; 2) layered insults, based on one's race, gender, class, sexuality, language, immigration status, phenotype, accent, or surname; and 3) cumulative insults, which cause unnecessary stress to people of color while privileging whites. Critical race scholars have expanded on Pierce's research to address how people of color are experiencing and responding to racial microaggressions within and beyond the academy. For example, Carroll (1998) extends Pierce's work to describe that being black in the U.S. means living in a society permeated by mundane and extreme racism and punctuated by incessant microaggressions. She finds that African Americans are faced with mundane extreme environmental stress—MEES. Smith (2004a, 2004b) focuses on the stress aspects of racism, explaining that constant exposure to MEES reveals the cumulative effects of racial microaggressions. He argues that the stress associated with racial microaggressions causes African Americans to experience various forms of mental, emotional, and physical strain—racial battle fatigue.

The stress ensuing from racism and racial microaggressions leads people of color to exhibit various psychophysiological symptoms, including suppressed immunity and increased sickness, tension headaches, trembling and jumpiness, chronic pain in healed injuries, elevated blood pressure, and a pounding heartbeat. Likewise, in anticipation of a racial conflict, people of color may experience rapid breathing, an upset stomach, or frequent diarrhea or urination. Other symptoms of racial battle fatigue include constant anxiety, ulcer, increased swearing or complaining, insomnia or sleep broken by haunting conflict-specific dreams, rapid mood swings, difficulty thinking or speaking coherently, and emotional and social withdrawal in response to racial microaggressions or while in environments of mundane racial stressors. Ultimately, these symptoms may lead to people of color losing confidence in themselves, questioning their life's work or even their life's worth.

Indeed, constantly battling racial stress takes a toll on the lives of people of color. Izard (1972, 1977) documented that African Americans tend to perceive incidents of racism as personal threats, and this leads to an increase in their emotional stress level. Krieger and Sidney (1996) reported that 80% of 1,974 black women and men experienced racial discrimination and self-reported attempts to respond to unfair treatment, showing that both experiences of discrimination and efforts to respond to unfair treatment were associated with increased blood pressure. Similarly, Williams, Neighbors, and Jackson (2003) concluded that perceptions of discrimination appear to induce physiological and psychological arousal. Systematic exposures to such psychosocial stressors may have long-term health consequences.

Experiencing racial discrimination as a stressful life event can reduce one's personal sense of control and elicit feelings of loss, ambiguity, strain, frustration, and injustice. Smith (2004b) concluded that this activates a stress-response system, originally evolved for responding to acute physical and emotional emergencies. However, given the pervasiveness of racism in U.S. society and its institutions, this emergency stress-response system is constantly "switched on" to cope with chronic racial microaggressions (and macroaggressions).

The accumulative stress from racial microaggressions produces racial battle fatigue. The stress of unavoidable front-line racial battles in historically white spaces leads to people of color feeling mentally, emotionally, and physically drained. The stress from racial microaggressions can become lethal when the accumulation of physiological symptoms of racial battle fatigue are untreated, unnoticed, misdiagnosed, or personally dismissed. Our critical race counternarrative, which follows, acknowledges experiences with and responses to racial microaggressions and racial battle fatigue reported by faculty of color in predominantly white institutions.

Critical Race Theory (CRT)

CRT provides a useful tool to identify, analyze, and challenge racism in education and society. Through a CRT lens, the ongoing racism on college and university campuses comes into focus, revealing that race conditions have not improved significantly as we move further into the 21st century as compared with reports from the racially tumultuous 1960s (Carroll, 1998; Smith, Altbach, & Lomotey, 2002). Faculty and students of color must cope with daily incidents of racial microaggressions from white students, faculty, and administrators as they daily navigate institutions developed to benefit whites (Bonilla-Silva & Forman, 2000; Bowman & Smith, 2002; Ladson-Billings, 1996; Smith, 2004a, 2004b, 2004c; Solórzano, Ceja, & Yosso, 2000).

Originating in schools of law, the critical race movement seeks to account for the role of race and racism in the U.S. and to challenge the many forms of racism and its intersections with other forms of subordination such as gender and class (Delgado, 1995a). Latina/Latino critical race theorists have expanded the CRT framework in law to discuss issues of subordination on the basis of immigration status, culture, language, and sexuality (Arriola, 1997; Espinoza, 1998). Similarly, a multiracial coalition of scholars have worked since at least the mid-1990s to extend CRT to the field of education and implement its tenets into educational research, pedagogy, curriculum, and policy (Ladson-Billings & Tate, 1995; Lynn, Yosso, Solórzano, & Parker, 2002; Solórzano, 1997, 1998; Solórzano & Delgado Bernal, 2001; Tate, 1994, 1997).

Acknowledging CRT's roots in scholarly traditions such as ethnic studies, U.S./third-world feminisms, Marxism/neoMarxism, cultural nationalism, internal colonialism, and critical legal studies, Solórzano (1997) identified at least five tenets shared by CRT scholarship. These tenets acknowledge the critical strengths of other scholarly traditions while they reveal, critique, and address some of these frameworks' blind spots (e.g., Marxism's blind spots regarding race and gender, cultural nationalism's blind spots on gender, class, and sexuality). The basic perspectives, research methods, and pedagogy of CRT in education learn from these academic and community traditions.

- *The* inter*centricity of race and racism.* CRT starts from the premise that race and racism are endemic and permanent in U.S. society (Bell, 1987) and asserts that racism intersects with forms of subordination based on gender, class, sexuality, language, culture, immigrant status, phenotype, accent, and surname (see Espinoza, 1998).

- *The challenge to dominant ideology.* CRT in education challenges claims of objectivity, meritocracy, color blindness, race neutrality, and equal opportunity and asserts that these claims act as a camouflage for the self-interest, power, and privilege of dominant groups in U.S. society (see Solórzano, 1997).

- *The commitment to social justice.* CRT seeks to advance a social justice agenda. Such a goal emphasizes that the larger purpose of educational research, teaching, and policy is the transformation of society through the empowerment of oppressed groups (see Solórzano & Delgado Bernal, 2001).

- *The centrality of experiential knowledge.* CRT recognizes that the experiential knowledge of people of color is legitimate, appropriate, and critical to understanding, analyzing, and teaching about racial subordination. CRT explicitly listens to the lived experiences of people of color through counterstorytelling methods such as family histories, biographies, scenarios, parables, *cuentos* (stories), *testimonios*, *dichos* (proverbs), chronicles, and narratives (see Olivas, 1990).

- *The interdisciplinary perspective.* CRT challenges traditional mainstream frameworks by analyzing racism, classism, sexism, and homophobia in historical and interdisciplinary terms (see Delgado, 1984, 1992).

Composite Counterstorytelling

Although CRT scholarship arguably serves counternarrative functions in general, some scholars seek to be more explicit in presenting their research through the genre of storytelling. There are at least three types of such counterstories evidenced in the CRT literature: autobiographical (e.g., Aguirre, 2000; Williams, 1991), biographical (e.g., Olivas, 1990), and multimethod/composite (e.g., Bell, 1987, 1992, 1996; Delgado, 1995b, 1996, 1999, 2003a, 2003b; Yosso, 2006). For our purposes, we focus on multimethod/composite stories. Composite counternarratives draw on multiple forms of "data" to recount the racialized, sexualized, classed experiences of faculty and students of color (see Delgado Bernal, 1998).

The counterstory that follows draws on findings from various research projects to address the experiences and responses of faculty of color to the pervasiveness of racism and racial battle fatigue in and around college and university campuses. Methodologically, we started by finding and unearthing sources of data. Our first form of "data" came from primary sources, namely interviews with African Americans, primarily professors, at universities across the country.[1]

Next, we analyzed secondary data from social science and humanities scholarship, addressing experiences with and responses to racism in higher education (e.g., Allen & Solórzano, 2001; Bonilla-Silva & Forman, 2000; Ladson-Billings, 1996; Willie & Sanford, 1995). In sifting through this literature, we drew connections with the interview data and uncovered the concepts of racial microaggressions (Pierce, 1970, 1974, 1980, 1989, 1995; Solórzano, 1998; Solórzano, Ceja, & Yosso, 2000) and resilience (e.g., Yosso, 2006). To recover and recount the story evidenced in the patterns and themes of the data, we added a final source of data—our own professional and personal experiences.[2] This included our individual reflections as well as the multiple voices of family, friends, colleagues, and acquaintances. Such experiential knowledge echoed the related research literature and the interview findings, which helped us to better understand the relationship between microaggressions, stress responses, and resistance (Clark, Anderson, Clark, & Williams, 1999; Prillerman, Myers, & Smedley, 1989; Smith, 2004a, 2004b, 2004c; Solórzano & Delgado Bernal, 2001).

Once we compiled, examined, and analyzed these various sources of data, we created composite characters to help tell the story. We attempted to engage these characters in a real and critical dialogue about our data from the interviews, related literature, and personal/professional experiences. As such, the characters personify our research and our analysis process. In the tradition of Du Bois (1920) and Freire (1973), the dialogue emerged between the characters much like our own discussions in this process emerged—through sharing, listening, challenging, and reflecting. We differentiate our work from that of fictional storytelling. Certainly there are elements of fiction in the story, but the "composite" characters are grounded in real-life experiences, actual empirical data, and contextualized in social situations that are also grounded in real life, not fiction.

Introducing the Characters and Setting the Scene

We tell this counterstory from the perspective of a composite character named Alice Canon, a professor of psychiatry at the University of California–Los Angeles. As part of an interview with a reporter from a black community newspaper, Alice is reflecting on her work with her colleague, Chet Toboa, a professor of psychiatry and education at Harvard University. Professor Toboa disappeared about two years ago, in 1972, and this is one of several trips Alice has made back to Boston. She is continuing to conduct what was a collaborative research project about the experiences of faculty of color in historically white colleges and universities.[3]

Guided by CRT's five tenets and the concepts of racial microaggressions and racial battle fatigue, this counterstory invites the reader to approach the counterstory as a pedagogical and empirical case study: to listen for the story's points and reflect on how these points compare with her or his own version of reality (however conceived). We listen in to Professor Canon's interview with a newspaper reporter as she recounts the events preceding the disappearance of Dr. Chet Toboa.

The Supposed Scandal: Questions About Chet's Disappearance

"You probably have read the official versions of this scandal, but the story begins well before Chet went 'missing'." The reporter wasn't quite convinced, so I showed her a few old newspaper clippings. "It was a scandal that white folks couldn't get enough of for a while."

I showed her the Sunday, April 9, 1972, *Boston Globe* article with the headline of "Harvard Professor Missing." The *Chicago Defender* newspaper and *Jet* and *Ebony* magazines each ran front-page cover stories, under the headlines of, respectively, "Harvard Yard Suspected of Murder"; "1922 or 1972? The Professional Lynching of a Black Professor"; and "The Academic Klan: Powerful Organizations Suspected of Murdering Distinguished Black Professor."[4] I looked up from the clippings and sarcastically stated, "Most of those in the academic, medical, social science, and black communities knew this was a scandal as soon as the word got out. We were asking questions that no one could answer in their superficial scandal headlines: Was it just the typical race-related hatred for blacks in this hostile era? Was it Professor Toboa's standing up against some of the most powerful institutions in the country? Was it his refusal to accept tenure if his academic department did not hire another minority professor? Was it his role in starting black professional organizations? None of us had answers, but opinions were endless for how this terrible and unexpected situation occurred."

"Of course there were the usual racialized assumptions. Many whites claimed that this had nothing to do with race. Since Chet was a well-respected Harvard professor whose research was international in scope, some felt the only possible explanation was an international conspiracy led by the Soviet Union. Other whites went as far as to suggest that it was spontaneous human combustion that resulted in his disappearance. When they were pushed further on this point to explain what happened to the ashes, they suggested 'the janitor must have swept them up not knowing what they were.' I always thought that was the funniest theory. Most blacks, Chicanos, and Puerto Ricans pointed to some combination of racial conspiracies. Some suggested that orders were handed down from President Nixon to the FBI and J. Edgar Hoover, as one of the director's last assignments before dying in May of that year." I could see the reporter wanted to hear my theory, so I smiled reassuringly and explained, "As you probably know, Chet and I are first cousins and we basically grew up together like brother and sister. My theory isn't so over-dramatic. But let me tell you about our research because I think that's what your readers will really dig."

Alice's Theory About the Disappearance: Introducing a Racialized Research Agenda

"As I mentioned, March 6, 1972, was a relatively ordinary day, at least in Los Angeles. I was back in California, teaching a clinical seminar course and it was about 64 degrees with blue skies. The meeting took place in New York where it was slightly colder than usual. It dipped down to 33 degrees that night when Chet was seen watching Wilt 'The Stilt' Chamberlain assist the Los Angeles Lakers in a win against Willis Reed and his New York Knicks. He attended with Bumpy Johnson, a longtime friend who most folks thought of as a notorious Harlem gangster. Chet and Bumpy met years before when Bumpy gave a generous donation to our aunt who lived in South Carolina. She had been out of work and struggling to make ends meet after some jealously angry white men burned down her modest but successful business. The three white men fingered for the arson mysteriously came up missing, never to be seen or heard from again. Many black folks suspected Bumpy had something to do with it since he was in Charleston visiting shortly after the situation occurred, but—with a certain sense of pride—no one ever said an accusatory word. I think Bumpy actually inspired some of Chet's work. What a case study in racism, that Bumpy. Like too many young black brothers subjected to daily interpersonal and institutionalized racism, Bumpy's initial responses of anger and resentment led to his incarceration for a large part of his youth. Bumpy in turn admired Chet, who had also grown up in Harlem, but had channeled his anger to challenge racism through education and participation in the civil rights movement. Anyway, Bumpy and Chet ended up seeing one of Wilt's last professional basketball games and LA beat New York." I smiled as I held up a picture of me around that time period and another of Chet. The reporter commented that it must have been quite a shock for folks to see a research team made up of a woman with an Afro and multicolored shawl and a man in a three-piece gray suit, let alone an academic with a gangster like Bumpy Johnson. I responded that the clothes don't make the man, and if anything, Chet's dapper style was not too different from Bumpy's. If she only knew, I mused to myself, remembering that some of my friends had crushes on Chet when we were finishing ninth grade and he was the 6'4" zoot-suit-wearing high school valedictorian.

I explained that Chet and I were developing a U.S. minority mental health research agenda. As professors and clinicians of psychiatry, we had documented the health effects of minorities living and working in extreme conditions or dealing with the daily effects of racism. We had become increasingly concerned with the mental and physiological health outcomes of blacks, Chicanos, and Puerto Ricans, especially as they were becoming "integrated" into historically white spaces and institutions. Chet also kept a journal of his private therapy sessions as well as his personal conversations with other black, Chicano, and Puerto Rican professionals, professors, students, and other community members about what he labeled as their experiences with "racial microaggressions." I pulled out one of Chet's earlier articles and read aloud: "Chet defined racial microaggressions 'as subtle, innocuous, preconscious, or (un)conscious degradations and put-downs, often kinetic but capable of being verbal and/or kinetic, and/or purposefully malicious or violent.'"[5]

I continued speaking, "So we were able to trace a rise in a new form of stress-related psychological and physiological disease that resulted from constant experiences with racial microaggressions. Chet's preliminary diagnosis of the cumulative effects of racial microaggressions was 'racial battle fatigue.' Unlike typical stress, racial battle fatigue referred to the cumulative result of a natural race-related stress response to distressing mental and emotional conditions. These conditions emerged from constantly facing racially dismissive, demeaning, insensitive and/or hostile racial environments and individuals. Chet found a pattern that showed that this race-related stress kills gradually and stealthily. It takes an unending toll through various psychosomatic physical ailments, such as hypertension and poor health attitudes and behaviors that combine to give minorities a morbidity and mortality profile similar to those living in the developing world rather than in the industrialized world." The reporter's raised eyebrows indicated she was interested in racial battle fatigue and whether it was connected to Chet's disappearance. I didn't want to let her know that I wondered the same thing myself. My research with Chet initially began after a long conversation during a family reunion about the source of some of my physical ailments and Chet's high stress levels.

Revealing Experiences of Racial Microaggressions and Symptoms of Racial Battle Fatigue at the Black Faculty Association Meeting: Friday, February 4, 1972

"So the month before the March 6th meeting, Chet was preparing to address the East Coast Black Faculty Association in Mather Hall at Harvard University. As you may know, Mather Hall was named after Increase Mather, who was part of the upper-crust Boston slave owning society and a Harvard-educated preacher. He also presided over Harvard for 16 years as its sixth president (1685–1701). The association held its meetings in Mather Hall to remind them that within the institutional fabric of Harvard and outside of its campus, this multiheaded monster of racism and elitism was ever present, despite their laudable achievements. This special meeting was called to provide an update on the developments toward addressing the growing concerns about the racial violence aimed at black faculty and students at Harvard, as well as other schools across the East Coast and the country. In addition, Chet and I wanted to seek further input on the impending March 6th meeting. Chet was the current chair of the association."

I paused and showed the reporter that I had the actual transcriptions of association meetings because they had been trying out a new system where they audiotaped their meetings and had a volunteer write up the minutes at a later date. I didn't tell her that in retrospect I suspected that one of the newer association members was an FBI informant and he had suggested the audiotaping. Initially, I had told Chet it was odd, but he didn't seem too worried.

As I continued, I referred to the transcripts. "The Sergeant at Arms called the special meeting to order and Dr. Coleman, a black male history professor interrupted and said, 'Get on with it, Jesse. We know why we're here.'" I smiled thinking about how informal this formal group of black scholars could be.

"And then Chet, who was always known to be courteous despite the circumstances, welcomed everyone and explained who would be at the meeting on the 6th. He listed the senior-level administrators from each of the universities across the country that had been invited and who had ongoing campus racial unrest, including Harvard, Cornell University, University of Michigan, University of California–Berkeley, and University of California–Los Angeles. He also noted that key members from the Department of Health, Education, and Welfare (HEW) would be there. HEW is a federal office that has broad popular support for unprecedented amounts of federal funds that are allocated for social programs, so many people were pleased they accepted the invitation. The list also included the American Council on Education, which is the major coordinating body for all the nation's higher education institutions; the National Institute of Mental Health, which has a major budget to fund research projects, new service initiatives, and train mental health professionals; the American Psychological Association, our professional organization that has significant influence on the national practice of psychiatry; and the American Board of Psychiatry and Neurology, which awards the credentials of specialist psychiatrists after the successful completion of its examination."

"Now Chet turned it over to me because even though he was scheduled to be the main presenter Monday the 6th, I had done most of the groundwork in organizing the meeting. We were trying to be strategic and we knew that folks would probably respond more positively to a black man, like you said, in a three piece suit rather than a black woman with an Afro and a reputation for being a rebel-rouser and hanging out with Angela Davis, 'Corky' Gonzalez, Dolores Huerta, Huey P. Newton, Cesar Chavez, Kathleen Cleaver, Stokely Carmichael—who was calling himself Kwame Ture at this point—Carmen Valentin, and Jim Brown, the former NFL fullback. Anyway, I outlined the six major points we prepared for the meeting and Chet passed out mimeograph copies while I spoke. I'll read here my words:

'As some of you may know, Professor Toboa and I have been working together for a few years, following up on our epidemiological findings, which suggest that a positive correlation exists between increased white-black, white-Chicano, and white-Puerto Rican social integration and racial microaggressions. With each civil rights effort, or with each attempt at breaking down barriers of racial segregation in historically white spaces, minority health seems to suffer. We have identified that this experience of dealing with constant racial microaggressions leads to a phenomenon we are calling racial battle fatigue. These negative racial events and life crises clearly contribute to minorities' higher rates of affective disorders. Unfortunately, traditional research and healthcare practices inappropriately focus exclusively on poor diets, culture, poverty, and inadequate education as the source of blame in black and brown poorer physical health statistics."

"And here," I noted, "a colleague raised her hand and asked, 'Am I understanding correctly that this work is based on the premise that staying at the microsocial, proximal level of analysis offers a better prospect of obtaining ecologically valid and practical knowledge about racial microaggressions, emotions, coping strategies, and the racial battle fatigue phenomena?' Chet responded, 'Yes. However, I believe researchers must be free to choose which approach they want to use, proximal or distal, just as it is appropriate to ask which approach provides more useful information and in-depth analysis.'"

I explained to the reporter that many of our colleagues knew the growing bias toward quantitative, large-scale research projects when it came to swaying the interests of major government funders. Then I continued, "These transcripts don't really pick up on the emotion of the room, but I remember pretty clearly. It was quite tense and so, at first, I emphasized a few words sarcastically to bring a little humor to the situation. I said,

> 'We believe that each of these *leading* and *prestigious* institutions'—and Chet looked at me sideways to remind me that some of our colleagues might not appreciate that humor, so I continued on in a more serious tone. 'These institutions and organizations need to 1) be more cognizant of the needs and interests of minorities; 2) elevate minorities in the hierarchy of each institution; 3) be held responsible for the abundance of unsophisticated, anti-intellectual, racist, and sexist scholarship funded, produced, and rewarded in these institutions; 4) acknowledge that racism and white resistance to integration should be seen as a public health crisis for the stress, violence, and terror it inflicts on the aggrieved; 5) consider classifying racist behaviors as a psychological disorder in the *Diagnostic and Statistical Manual of Mental Disorders*; and 6) eliminate the homosexual classification that considers homosexuality as a physical disease, a "third sex," or a psychological aberration.'"

I looked up from the transcript and explained, "That last statement caused a mild disturbance in the room. People began to whisper to each other their concern about grouping racism with homosexuality. A young conservative black economics professor, Gleason Golightly,[6] stood up to make his objections clearly known for the record." I turned back to reading the transcriptions: "Professor Golightly said,

> 'So what you are telling us is that for the purposes of discrimination, sexual orientation—or, more accurately, sexual behavior—must be treated like race. Do you really think that is a legitimate claim? When I got up this morning I was a black man. When I drove my car through South Boston and was stopped, it was because I was a black man. When I go to bed tonight, I will still be a black man. If we are going to treat sexual orientation and race the same, then what you are saying is sexual orientation—read: behavior—is like race, a condition beyond the individual's control. If you want us, or this group that you will be addressing next month, to accept this kind of reasoning, then why should we stop at this form of sexual passion? If we're going to ask for special considerations for homosexuals, shouldn't everybody else's irrepressible sexual orientations be protected? Shouldn't adulterers, pedophiles, rapists, and other sorts of sexual aberrants be entitled to the same protections?'"

I sat back in my chair and said, "The room erupted after Golightly finished his diatribe. Whatever discomforts association members may have felt about this issue were replaced with even more contempt for Golightly's message and him as the messenger. Golightly's positions usually had an adverse effect for swaying people his way. This was also true for the more conservative blacks who appeared moderate in comparison. The Sergeant at Arms had to call the room to order."

"Now I could never really hide my disdain for Golightly, but I was always cordial. So I spoke up, and the transcripts actually caught me here. I'd been doing this for years, and usually only if you were sitting very close to me would you hear it. I said, 'Look here, 'Notlikely,' I am not fully comfortable with including this as part of our proposal but for very different reasons than yours. What I do understand is that if we allow these organizations to continue to mistreat and misrepresent one group, then blacks will never be free.'" I told the reporter that at this point the majority of the room rose to their feet to applaud my comments, much to Golightly's chagrin.

I referred back to the transcripts and explained, "Chet began to talk over the ovation to bring order to the room and said, 'I will briefly try to answer part of Professor Golightly's question and show the connection we are trying to draw.' Chet's strategy was not to change Golightly's name, but to stare him down as he challenged his reactionary comments. Chet looked right at Golightly and said, 'Many psychiatrists, psychologists, ministers, priests, rabbis, and even professors believe that homosexuality is a curable condition. However, the various 'cures' they propose are highly offensive and perilous, including castration, hypnosis, nausea producing drugs, electric shock, brain surgery, breast amputations, and aversion therapy. This is no different than the ideology held by the physician Sam Cartwright, who believed that blacks had 'drapetomania' and 'dysaesthia aethiopis' which justified our enslavement.'"[7]

"Then Chet addressed the rest of the room, using his fingers to infer quotation marks over the questionable words in these racist theories: 'Cartwright also theorized that the black skin of Afro-Americans in conjunction with a deficiency of red blood cells led to smaller brain sizes in blacks, which resulted in both less intelligence and lower morals. The 'cure' for the first disease was 'whipping the devil out of them' to prevent them from 'their crazy desire to run away from slavery.' Cartwright believed that the second disease caused a slave to refuse to work and the 'cure' was to give the slaves harder work to stimulate the blood to the brain and free them from their infliction. Even the so-called father of American psychiatry and one of the 'founding fathers' of this country, Benjamin Rush, believed that the only 'cure' for blacks would be when our skin color turns white. This is why he and others believed that blacks and whites should always be segregated from one another. What we are witnessing today are the modern forms of these ideologies.'"[8]

The reporter shook her head in disgust. I described the silence in the room after Chet's statement. "He pretty much put any lingering doubts about whether we were on the right track to rest, but an awkward silence and depression began to cover the room, so I spoke up and told them, 'Look, if we can convince these powerful organizations about the errors of their ways and the troubles ahead, then we can be more effective in influencing national policies and practice about the health consequences of minorities fighting against racism.'"

I paused and explained to the reporter that through our interviews over the years, Chet and I had collected more than 300 personal statements from minority professors across the country in varying fields. So we put up on the overhead projector the major themes we had found so far and asked the association members to think about whether their experiences fit into those themes or if we were any missing patterns that should be added. As I read a few examples of faculty experiences with racial microaggressions, I also noted the psychophysiological symptoms as each person had described them.

"A black male philosophy professor began the discussion about the pattern of racialized classroom experiences. This older man explained that his wife was concerned because he had been complaining much more than he had in the past and he began swearing and just seemed to be withdrawing both emotionally and socially. He explained,

'This is a very sensitive area for me. You might guess correctly that there are not many black philosophy professors. So I spend a lot of time sharing my struggles with black professors in other fields and their struggles are all the same. In spite of our efforts to demonstrate competency, black professors are challenged more on our intellectual authority than our white counterparts. In most of these challenges, students question our knowledge directly or indirectly in a way that is inappropriate or disrespectful. These challenges might include arguments on basic points of the discipline. For example, students might argue that the sociological imagination is not defined as I defined it. They might question the validity of lecture material or use more indirect forms of resistance. For instance, this particular white student simply thought he knew everything and that he certainly couldn't learn anything from me. He went so far as to say, when I was trying to explain something, 'That's wrong, that's just wrong, that's not true.' This is very, very difficult because you can't go off on him because you've got to be respectful and you've got to be this professional person, but it's very, very hurtful, particularly from someone who was not an excellent student.'"

The young reporter nodded as if she heard something familiar in the statement. I continued reading the examples. "Here's a black female developmental psychologist who had been experiencing tension backaches and elevated blood pressure and spoke about constant microaggressions in the classroom. She said,

'Our white colleagues do not understand how our classroom experiences qualitatively differ from theirs. White students expect the traditional hierarchy of society to prevail in the class. That is, white male on the top, and black woman on the bottom. And they can't get ready for the fact that a black woman is teaching this class! And that the white males are not in charge. . . . I think that if I were white, that I wouldn't have to go through those sorts of things in my classroom . . . but at every turn I have to remind students that I am the professor. I'm not just the instructor . . . I have a Ph.D. . . . I have to tell students, 'Look. I graduated summa cum laude; I got two master's degrees and my Ph.D. . . . I published these books and these articles, blah, blah, blah,' to let them know that I may be black, but what you think about in terms of what it means to be black is not necessarily what I am, if it's a negative perception . . . being uneducated and being illiterate and not able to think and basically being an affirmative action kind of a person. So those are the kinds of things that I think make my job more difficult. Much more difficult than white professors. And it's unfortunate that the so-called standardized evaluation process that we have been using in colleges and universities does not take these things into consideration. In fact, if you raise the subject, the college will look at you like you're crazy because they don't deal with that. And they're actually being honest because they don't understand the sheer level of complexity on the part of the professor and the student in dealing with these kinds of issues. So I'm not blaming my colleagues. I'm just saying they're really very ignorant. Ignorant about what goes on in my classes and the extent to which I have to use measures above and beyond what they have to use to even survive in the classroom.'"

The reporter continued to nod in agreement and I read one more example of classroom experiences with microaggressions. "This next one is a black female chemistry professor. This very accomplished woman had little confidence in her university and maintained even less confidence in herself. She shared a pretty blatant example with us." I found my place in the transcript and began to read, remembering vividly the pained expression on this woman's face as she shared this incident with us. "She said,

'The first time I walked as an instructor into a classroom in a large research university, I immediately experienced such a racially stressful event. I wrote my name on the board, turned around, and, to my utter dismay, a white male student was staring at me with contempt and holding up his middle finger to me. 'Can this be happening to me?' I asked myself. I began my lecture, but I was having an out-of-body experience as the young man continued to stare at me in contempt, still 'shooting a bird' until, finally, I could no longer pretend that this was not happening. So I walked slowly toward him and deliberately stared him straight in the eye as I lectured. It was the longest walk . . . but it would be one that I would repeat many times in the years to come, in different circumstances.'"

I flipped through the next few pages of the transcription to make sure I was staying on track. I continued, "A few of the professors also shared their experiences that follow in with the theme of a subtle yet stunning and cumulative nature of racial microaggressions. And these here certainly suggest that the cumulative effect of microaggressions is racial battle fatigue. For example, a black male psychiatry professor who admitted to having sleep broken by haunting conflict-specific dreams said,

'What is it like to be a black person in white America today? One step from suicide! The psychological warfare games that we have to play every day just to survive. We have to be one way in our communities and one way in the workplace or in the business sector. We can never be ourselves all around. I think that may be a given for all people, but us particularly; it's really a mental health problem. It's a wonder we haven't all gone out and killed somebody or killed ourselves.'"

I shared one last example of the overall cumulative effect of racial microaggressions with the reporter. "A black male psychiatry professor reporting insomnia and rapid breathing in anticipation of conflict, explained,

'If you can think of the mind as having 100 ergs of energy, and the average man uses 50% of this energy dealing with the everyday problems of the world—just general kinds of things— then he has 50% more to do creative kinds of things that he wants to do. That's a white person. Now, a black person also has 100 ergs. He uses 50% the same way a white man does, dealing with what the white man has to deal with, so he has 50% left. But he uses 25% fighting being black, with all the problems of being black in America and what it means.'"

"And then I told the faculty, 'So that's what brings us to you today, to ask humbly if you would share with us some of your stories so we can add your voices to the testimony we give next month. We would like for these folks to hear your story about the racial attacks—or what we call racial microaggressions—you may have had to endure just trying to be a black professor on a white campus." I paused from reading the transcript and shared with the reporter the inspiring scene that followed. "One after another, each professor in the room stood up to share stories of the racial microaggressions they faced on and around historically white campuses. We could see as we had read the examples out loud that these professors were realizing they were no longer struggling with incidents and symptoms of racial battle fatigue in isolation, now they had a name for their pain. Although some were hesitant to share their psychophysiological symptoms in that large group setting, they noted that our dataset reflected their own experiences and remarked that our thematic analysis had reached saturation. Even Golightly conceded to experiencing racial microaggressions. Although he tried to dismiss their effect on his personhood, I noticed he tended to yawn and demonstrate extreme fatigue after drinking multiple cups of black coffee."

I smiled at the ever-patient reporter and said, "So there it is. The meeting adjourned and each person stayed until they shared their experiences. Chet was frustrated at the multiple experiences of racism his colleagues had been subjected to, but he didn't let too much of this anger show. Instead, he assured them that their voices would be heard at the meeting Monday the 6th. Many expressed doubt as we headed off campus whether folks from the organizations and universities would really listen, but they thanked me for organizing the meeting and they thanked Chet in advance for bringing their stories and this research to such a forum."

Will Institutions Listen to and Learn From Effects of Racism? Waiting for an Update: April 7, 1972

So I left a message for Chet the morning of Friday, April 7th, to let him know I had arrived safely from my red-eye flight from California and that I'd see him at the association meeting shortly. I was anxious to hear about any recent reports stemming from the meeting. I didn't tell the reporter that it was strange that he hadn't called to give me an update earlier, but I didn't think much of it because I knew he believed his university phone and perhaps his home phone had been wiretapped. I also knew Chet usually volunteered at the hospital a few days a month and also visited the prison hospital on occasion, so I figured he may have been busy. He would often remind me of how he would much rather be involved in clinical work, challenging racism as a kind of street therapist who helped young black youth learn to recognize and respond to racial microaggressions before racism took its toll on their mental and physical health.[9]

I described to the reporter that the association meeting was scheduled for every first Friday of the month while school was in session. "So since we hadn't had our usual meeting in March, everyone was in attendance for that April 7th meeting. Most of us assumed Chet would be on time in one of his customary three-piece Brooks Brothers suits and his camel brown Allen-Edmonds shoes, with his calming and reassuring smile despite how grave the circumstances. By the time I got to Mather Hall at 11:50 a.m., the room was packed. Since no one had heard from Chet since last Wednesday, members thought that he had been planning something special in response to what was rumored to be disappointing news. At noon, the Sergeant at Arms called the meeting to order but Chet did not show."

The reporter asked me to pause briefly so she could start a new tape. I took the opportunity to drink some tea as I noted to myself that recounting the story today was the first time that a lump in my throat had not developed. My emotions had grown numb over the years thinking about the racial microaggressions that I have continuously experienced. But I have always gotten exceptionally angry when I think about how Chet was treated.

Once the new tape was recording, I continued, "After waiting for 20 minutes we decided to check his office. Several colleagues volunteered to join me and walk across campus to check on him. As we approached his building, the Cambridge police met us in the hallway. They were looking for Chet's office. One of the Harvard faculty members said that we were on our way to get him for a meeting and inquired what was wrong. An officer indicated that a missing person's report had been filed and they were sent to investigate Dr. Toboa's whereabouts. By this time there's almost a mob of folks heading up to Chet's office. And of course there was no elevator in that building, so we were all crammed together going up the stairs to the third floor! When we got there, the door was wide open. On his desk was an opened envelope, with a return address labeled 'Committee on Campus and Community Culture and Climate.' We learned this letter was delivered via certified mail Tuesday, April 4th, but there was no letter to be found. Instead, there was a note written on the back of the envelope, in what looked to be Chet's writing. It referred to Supreme Court Justice Brown's opinion in the *Plessy v. Ferguson* case of 1896 and simply read: 'It is only in black people's minds that racial conditions in America are oppressive.'"[10]

I excused myself momentarily to refill my mug with hot water and searched through my bag for another kava kava herb tea as the young reporter looked at the writing on the empty envelope, still sealed in the police protective covering. I brushed away a few tears as I stirred some honey into my tea, lost in my thoughts for a moment before I sat back at the table and continued. "Not much is really known about what happened to Chet. The department secretary reportedly saw him when he picked up his mail earlier that day. No one saw him leave his office or the building, even though folks were there until late in the evening."

"Noticing that there were various awards and certificates strewn all over the floor, the police asked us not to touch anything, and I think that's what caused us to finally start getting scared that something may have happened to Chet. So we were pretty much silent, almost frozen with fear and concern, but you know, right then in the silence of the moment, we heard Chet's little transistor radio playing on the shelf." I closed my eyes and began to sing softly the song that was playing:

> "People get ready there's a train a comin'
> Don't need no baggage, you just get on board"

I opened my eyes and saw a blank stare from the young reporter, so I explained that Curtis Mayfield and the Impressions recorded "People Get Ready" in 1965. The song symbolically described how people felt in the midst of the civil rights movement, that there was a train coming, that history was moving with a sense of inevitability. I continued singing:

> "People get ready for the train to Jordan
> Picking up passengers coast to coast
> Faith is the key, open the doors and board 'em
> There's hope for all those that love Him most"

I paused again to explain that the song goes on from there to issue a warning, and I sang this part to the young reporter as well:

> "There ain't no room for the hopeless sinner
> Who would hurt all mankind just to save his own
> Have pity on those whose chances grow thinner
> For there's no hiding place from the Kingdom's throne."

I smiled thinking that since this interview was being recorded, someday my singing might become part of an FBI file, as seemed to be the trend in the last few years with many of my politically active friends. Realizing the reporter was waiting for me to continue, I explained, "Well, as you might imagine, the police quickly regained their composure and finished digging around his office, asking each of us to 'stay in touch.' I walked with the other faculty back to Mather Hall and broke the news to the larger group that Chet had gone missing, and many of us were brought in for questioning over the next few weeks."

The reporter thanked me for my time and confirmed my summer contact information for possible follow-up questions. She noted that this would probably be a series of articles. She hadn't connected the date Chet received the certified letter, April 4th, with the anniversary of the assassination of Martin Luther King, Jr., and I was sure that would be a future follow-up question. Both Dr. King and Dr. Toboa were about nonviolent, peaceful resolutions. Both had visions of a better condition for *all* people. Each tried to break down the same system, which took an ultimate toll on each of their lives. I had learned not to worry too much about such ironies, but deep down, I knew it was no coincidence.

Alice's Epilogue

I walked to a small campus cafeteria to grab a quick bite before heading to the airport. The interview had gone longer than I anticipated. Out of the corner of my eye I saw a familiar face across the yard. It was the janitor I had met in Chet's building. I thought back to when the university decided to move another professor into Chet's office and asked me to prepare his work for the archives. It had been such a short time since Chet's disappearance, yet the office was almost all cleaned out by the time I got there.

The janitor was sweeping up Chet's office as I arrived. He smiled and tipped his cap. Maybe he recognized my picture from one of Chet's family photos he used to have in his office, I don't know, but he knew who I was immediately. Before leaving me to go through the stack of Chet's papers, the janitor handed me a small book that he said I might find useful. Given the huge task before me, I didn't even open the book until a few hours later. I realized it was Chet's personal journal and I wondered how the janitor came across it and why the police never mentioned it. I flipped through it briefly, stopping at one of the pages titled "I almost killed a white man today." Chet sketched out a scene, which apparently took place at an airport, where a white man verbally accosted him. He had just returned from a trip to McCurdo Base in the Antarctic, where he was studying how military personnel and scientists adapted and survived the stressors of extreme climates after a year of residency. Chet had mentioned some of this early work to me, and how he was comparing the extreme climates of Antarctica with the extreme climates of racism that blacks had been trying to survive for centuries in the Americas.[11] I sighed, thinking of how Chet must have looked in his full-grown beard, snow shoes in his bag, facing an extreme climate of hostility in the Boston airport terminal. Certainly there have been multiple incidents he described to me where he was belittled in front of colleagues with comments like "When I was talking about those blacks, I didn't mean you, you're different," or nonverbal exchanges such as being followed at the supermarket or not served at a restaurant. One night he was detained while walking to his apartment near Harvard. Police insisted that he "assume the position" because he "fit the description" of a burglar. I turned the pages to read a more recent journal entry. It was apparently inspired by the poem "Whitey on the moon," by Gil Scott-Heron.[12] Most of the lines had been edited from the original poem.

Whitey needs more room

Those rats done sent us all to hell, 'cause Whitey needs more room
Bit my sister then wished her well, 'cause Whitey needs more room
Can't live in those precious hills, 'cause Whitey needs more room
Ten years from now still taking pills, 'cause Whitey needs more room

No relief from the front-line, Black
One step forward 10 steps back
Feel my blood pressure going up
And as if all that crap wasn't enough

Those rats done sent us all to hell, 'cause Whitey needs more room
Bit my sister then wished her well, 'cause Whitey needs more room
Never got our 40 acres and a mule, 'cause Whitey needs more room!
Need national guards just to go to school? Hmm . . . only Whitey's in the room!

You know I've just about had my fill of Whitey needing room

I think I'd like to take my shot and send Whitey—Pow! Bang! Zoom!—to the moon.

Thinking back now about that creative entry, I marveled at Chet's multiple hidden talents. For me, the journal was a gentle reminder that things are never quite what they seem. I waved at the janitor, hoping he might have a moment and walk over. The janitor smiled and tipped his cap, but headed in the opposite direction. My questions would have to wait because I knew the plane would not. As I hailed a taxi to the airport, I realized that something in the janitor's smile back when he gave me Chet's journal and again today gave me an unexplainable sense of calm. The gloomy feelings I had from recounting so many memories of Chet began to ease, like the Boston sky, where the sun had finally broken through the cloud cover only to begin its descent into the horizon.

Discussion

Through this counterstory, we introduce the concepts of microaggressions and racial battle fatigue as a way to examine some of the implications of racism on the health and lifespan of faculty of color in historically white colleges and universities.

Our counterstory characters confirm that a few or even one microaggression may cause serious emotional and physical stress. Yet as Carroll (1998) reminds us, in a society plagued by racism, people of color endure a lifetime of mundane, extreme, environmental stress. In this context, people of color expend a tremendous amount of psychological energy managing and negotiating microaggressions.

The counterstory examines some of the effects of racial microaggressions on faculty of color by allowing brief entry into a moment in the lives of two composite characters—Professors Canon and Toboa. The composite characters analyze and personify data on racial battle fatigue. Indeed, as the black faculty recount their individual experiences with racial microaggressions, their collective experiences begin to demonstrate how a lifetime of microaggressions and their corresponding cumulative stress leads to racial battle fatigue. The psychophysiological symptoms of racial battle fatigue may cause lowered self-esteem, social withdrawal from perceived racial stressors, and many negative health complications, which can diminish one's quality of life and even shorten one's lifespan. The research presented through the counterstory shows that faculty of color report various psychophysiological symptoms as a result of battling an accumulation of racial microaggressions on historically white college and university campuses. Lomas (2003) explains that this tradition of listening to and recounting testimonios (life experiences) of subordinated groups can transform both the storytellers and listeners/readers. She asserts that "in making sense of the text as a whole the reader is forced to go outside the text itself and examine the real world in relation to the text" (pp. 2–3). In format and content, the counterstory told in this chapter attempts to build on the transformative capacity of narratives.

This chapter and counterstory show that people of color experience racial microaggressions, but the cumulative effect of this seemingly innocuous form of racism—racial battle fatigue—remains underresearched. Without further research in this area, the racial battle fatigue symptoms experienced by people of color will remain misdiagnosed or even dismissed. As historically white colleges and universities maintain structural barriers that deny access to students of color while perpetuating a discourse of tolerance and diversity, racial microaggressions and ensuing racial battle fatigue will continue to be an area in need of study. For example, research should address some of the coping mechanisms people of color engage in response to racial microaggressions and racial battle fatigue.

CRT, with its epistemological insistence on recognizing the knowledges of people of color and methodological flexibility in utilizing counternarratives, represents a useful framework for challenging both macro and micro forms of racism in education. Counterstorytelling holds pedagogical potential in its accessible story format embedded with critical conceptual and theoretical content. CRT counterstories can foster community building among subordinated groups by recognizing shared experiences with racism, sexism, classism, and other forms of subordination. The evidence is clear: External stressors can permanently alter physiological functioning. For people of color, racism increases the degree of stress that one endures and this directly correlates to the physiological arousal that is an indicator of stress-related diseases (Smith, 2004b). It is our humble hope that this counterstory and the painful realities of racial battle fatigue shared herein can help strengthen traditions of social, political, and cultural survival and resistance.

Endnotes

1. Each interview is from one of four data sources and has been slightly edited only to reflect the language use of the era: Feagin and Sikes (1994), Harlow (2003), Smith (1993–2005), and Smith (2004b).
2. We acknowledge that our own racialized, gendered, and classed experiences inform this counterstory. We do not purport to be neutral or objective in the process of sifting through the data and finding themes and patterns.
3. We use historically white institutions instead of predominantly white institutions to distinguish that the gross numbers or percentages of white students have less to do with the majority populations than with the historical and contemporary racial infrastructure that is in place, the current campus racial culture and ecology, and how these modern-day institutions still benefit whites at the expense of blacks and other groups of color.
4. While the early 1970s were rife with very real racial violence and scandalous headlines, the headlines listed here are fictitious.
5. See Pierce (1975, 1995).
6. We humbly and gratefully borrow the character of Professor Gleason Golightly from Chapter 9 of Bell (1992). Such a conservative "minority" viewpoint upholds white privilege by blindly clinging to the majoritarian story while dismissing the lived reality of people of color. Although whites most often tell majoritarian stories, people of color often buy into and even tell majoritarian stories. Being a "minority" majoritarian storyteller such as Golightly often means receiving benefits provided by those with racial, gender, and/or class privilege.

7. See Citizens Commission on Human Rights (1995).
8. See Citizens Commission on Human Rights (1995).
9. See Pierce (1970).
10. We paraphrase Justice Brown's majority opinion of the court in *Plessy v. Ferguson*, 163 U.S. 537, 538 (1896).
11. See Carroll (1998).
12. For the original poem, see Scott-Heron (2001).

References

Aguirre, A., Jr. (2000, Summer). Academic storytelling: A critical race theory story of affirmative action. *Sociological Perspectives, 43*(2), 319–339.

Allen, W. R., & Solórzano, D. (2001). Affirmative action, educational equity, and campus racial climate: A case study of the University of Michigan Law School. *La Raza Law Journal, 12*(2), 237–363.

Arriola, E. (1997). LatCrit theory, international human rights, popular culture, and the faces of despair in INS raids. *Inter-American Law Review, 28*(2), 245–262.

Bell, D. (1987). *And we are not saved: The elusive quest for racial justice.* New York, NY: Basic Books.

Bell, D. (1992). *Faces at the bottom of the well: The permanence of racism.* New York, NY: Basic Books.

Bell, D. (1996). *Gospel choirs: Psalms of survival in an alien land called home.* New York, NY: Basic Books.

Bonilla-Silva, E., & Forman, T. A. (2000, January). "I'm not a racist but . . .": Mapping white college students' racial ideology in the USA. *Discourse and Society, 11*(1), 50–85.

Bowman, P. J., & Smith, W. A. (2002). Racial ideology in the campus community: Emerging cross-ethnic differences and challenges. In W. A. Smith, P. G. Altbach, & K. Lomotey (Eds.), *The racial crisis in American higher education: Continuing challenges for the twenty-first century* (Rev. ed., pp. 103–120). Albany, NY: State University of New York Press.

Carroll, G. (1998). *Environmental stress and African Americans: The other side of the moon.* Westport, CT: Praeger.

Citizens Commission on Human Rights. (1995). *Creating racism: Psychiatry's betrayal* [Brochure]. Los Angeles, CA: Author.

Clark, R., Anderson, N. B., Clark, V. R., & Williams, D. R. (1999, October). Racism as a stressor for African Americans: A biopsychosocial model. *American Psychologist, 54*(10), 805–816.

Delgado, R. (1984). The imperial scholar: Reflections on a review of civil rights literature. *University of Pennsylvania Law Review, 132*, 561–578.

Delgado, R. (1992). The imperial scholar revisited: How to marginalize outsider writing, ten years later. *University of Pennsylvania Law Review, 140*, 1349–1372.

Delgado, R. (Ed.). (1995a). *Critical race theory: The cutting edge.* Philadelphia, PA: Temple University Press.

Delgado, R. (1995b). *The Rodrigo chronicles: Conversations about America and race.* New York, NY: New York University Press.

Delgado, R. (1996). *The coming race war? And other apocalyptic tales of America after affirmative action and welfare.* New York, NY: New York University Press.

Delgado, R. (1999). *When equality ends: Stories about race and resistance.* Boulder, CO: Westview Press.

Delgado, R. (2003a). Crossroads and blind alleys: A critical examination of recent writing about race. *Texas Law Review, 82*, 121–152.

Delgado, R. (2003b). *Justice at war: Civil liberties and civil rights during times of crisis.* New York, NY: New York University Press.

Delgado Bernal, D. (1998, Winter). Using a Chicana feminist epistemology in educational research. *Harvard Educational Review, 68*(4), 555–582.

Du Bois, W. E. B. (1920). *Darkwater: Voices from within the veil.* New York, NY: Harcourt Brace.

Espinoza, L. G. (1998). Latino/a identity and multi-identity: Community and culture. In R. Delgado & J. Stefancic (Eds.), *The Latino/a condition: A critical reader* (pp. 17–23). New York, NY: New York University Press.

Feagin, J. R. (2000). *Racist America: Roots, current realities, and future reparations.* New York, NY: Routlege.

Feagin, J. R., & Sikes, M. P. (1994). *Living with racism: The black middle-class experience.* Boston, MA: Beacon Press.

Freire, P. (1973). *Education for critical consciousness.* New York, NY: Seabury Press.

Harlow, R. (2003, December). "Race doesn't matter, but . . .": The effect of race on professors' experiences and emotion management in the undergraduate college classroom. *Social Psychology Quarterly, 66*(4), 348–363.

Izard, C. E. (1972). *Patterns of emotions: A new analysis of anxiety and depression.* New York, NY: Academic Press.

Izard, C. E. (1977). *Human emotions.* New York, NY: Plenum Press.

Krieger, N., & Sidney, S. (1996, October). Racial discrimination and blood pressure: The CARDIA study of young black and white adults. *American Journal of Public Health, 86*(10), 1370–1378.

Ladson-Billings, G. (1996, Spring). Silences as weapons: Challenges of a black professor teaching white students. *Theory into Practice, 35*(2), 79–85.

Ladson-Billings, G., & Tate, W. F. (1995, Fall). Toward a critical race theory of education. *Teachers College Record, 97*(1), 47–68.

Lomas, C. (2003, August). *Latina feminisms: Reflections on theory, practice, and pedagogy emerging in telling to live.* Paper presented at the 16th annual MALCS Summer Institute, San Antonio, TX.

Lynn, M., Yosso, T. J., Solórzano, D., & Parker, L. (2002, February). Critical race theory and education: Qualitative research in the new millennium [Special issue: Critical race and qualitative research]. *Qualitative Inquiry, 8*(1), 3–6.

Olivas, M. A. (1990). The chronicles, my grandfather's stories, and immigration law: The slave traders chronicle as racial history. *Saint Louis University Law Journal, 34,* 425–441.

Pierce, C. (1970). Offensive mechanisms. In F. B. Barbour (Ed.), *The black seventies* (pp. 265–282). Boston, MA: Porter Sargent.

Pierce, C. (1974). Psychiatric problems of the black minority. In S. Arieti (Ed.), *American handbook of psychiatry* (pp. 512–523). New York, NY: Basic Books.

Pierce, C. (1975). The mundane extreme environment and its effect on learning. In S. G. Brainard (Ed.), *Learning disabilities: Issues and recommendations for research* (p. xx). Washington, DC: National Institute of Education, Department of Health, Education, and Welfare.

Pierce, C. (1980). Social trace contaminants: Subtle indicator of racism in TV. In S. B. Withey & R. P. Abeles (Eds.), *Television and social behavior: Beyond violence and children* (pp. 249–257). Hillsdale, NJ: Lawrence Erlbaum.

Pierce, C. (1989). Unity in diversity: Thirty-three years of stress. In G. L. Berry & J. K. Asamen (Eds.), *Black students: Psychosocial issues and academic achievement* (pp. 296–312). Newbury Park, CA: Sage.

Pierce, C. (1995). Stress analogs of racism and sexism: Terrorism, torture, and disaster. In C. V. Willie, P. P. Rieker, B. M. Kramer, & B. S. Brown (Eds.), *Mental health, racism, and sexism* (pp. 277–293). Pittsburgh, PA: University of Pittsburgh Press.

Prillerman, S. L., Myers, H. F., & Smedley, B. D. (1989). Stress, well-being, and academic achievement in college. In G. L. Berry & J. K Asamen (Ed.), *Black students: Psychosocial issues and academic achievement* (pp. 198–217). Newbury Park, CA: Sage.

Scott-Heron, G. (2001). *Now and then: The poems of Gil Scott-Heron.* Edinburgh, Scotland: Payback Press.

Smith, W. A. (1993–2005). *National study on African Americans.* Unpublished interview database, University of Illinois at Chicago and the University of Utah.

Smith, W. A. (2004a). *Battle fatigue on the front lines of race: Teaching about race and racism at historically white institutions.* Manuscript submitted for publication.

Smith, W. A. (2004b). Black faculty coping with racial battle fatigue: The campus racial climate in a post–civil rights era. In D. Cleveland (Ed.), *A long way to go: Conversations about race by African American faculty and graduate students* (pp. 171–190). New York: Peter Lang.

Smith, W. A. (2004c). *The impact of racially primed white students on black faculty: Manifestations of racial battle fatigue on historically white campuses.* Manuscript submitted for publication.

Smith, W. A., Altbach, P. G., Lomotey, K. (Eds.). (2002). *The racial crisis in American higher education: Continuing challenges to the twenty-first century* (Rev. ed.). Albany, NY: State University of New York Press.

Solórzano, D. (1997, Summer). Images and words that wound: Critical race theory, racial stereotyping, and teacher education. *Teacher Education Quarterly, 24*(3), 5–19.

Solórzano, D. (1998, January). Critical race theory, racial and gender microaggressions, and the experiences of Chicana and Chicano scholars. *International Journal of Qualitative Studies in Education, 11*(1), 121–136.

Solórzano, D., Ceja, M., & Yosso, T. (2000, Winter/Spring). Critical race theory, racial microaggressions, and campus racial climate: The experiences of African American college students. *Journal of Negro Education, 69*(1/2), 60–73.

Solórzano, D., & Delgado Bernal, D. (2001, May). Examining transformational resistance through a critical race and LatCrit theory framework: Chicana and Chicano students in an urban context. *Urban Education, 36*(3), 308–342.

Tate, W. F. (1994, October). From inner city to ivory tower: Does my voice matter in the academy? *Urban Education, 29*(3), 245–269.

Tate, W. F. (1997). Critical race theory and education: History, theory, and implications. *Review of Research in Education, 22*, 195–247.

Williams, D. R., Neighbors, H. W., & Jackson, J. S. (2003, February). Racial/ethnic discrimination and health: Findings from community studies. *American Journal of Public Health, 93*(2), 200–208.

Williams, P. J. (1991). *The alchemy of race and rights: Diary of a law professor.* Cambridge, MA: Harvard University Press.

Willie, C. V., & Sanford, J. S. (1995). Turbulence on the college campus and the frustration-aggression hypothesis. In C. V. Willie, P. P. Rieker, B. M. Kramer, & B. S. Brown (Eds.), *Mental health, racism, and sexism* (pp. 253–275). Pittsburgh, PA: University of Pittsburgh Press.

Yosso, T. J. (2006). Critical race counterstories along the Chicana/Chicano educational pipeline. New York, NY: Routledge.

CHAPTER 48

CRITICAL RACE THEORY, RACIAL MICROAGGRESSIONS, AND CAMPUS RACIAL CLIMATE: THE EXPERIENCES OF AFRICAN AMERICAN COLLEGE STUDENTS

DANIEL SOLÓRZANO

MIGUEL CEJA

TARA YOSSO

Microaggressions are subtle insults (verbal, nonverbal, and/or visual) directed toward people of color, often automatically or unconsciously. Using critical race theory as a framework, the study described in this chapter provides an examination of racial microaggressions and how they influence the collegiate racial climate. Using focus group interview data from African American students at three universities, it reveals that racial microaggressions exist in both academic and social spaces in the collegiate environment. The study shows how African American students experience and respond to racial microaggressions. It also demonstrates how racial microaggressions have a negative impact on the campus racial climate.

. . . one must not look for the gross and obvious. The subtle, cumulative miniassault is the substance of today's racism. . . (Pierce, 1974, p. 516)

In and of itself a microaggression may seem harmless, but the cumulative burden of a lifetime of microaggressions can theoretically contribute to diminished mortality, augmented morbidity, and flattened confidence. (Pierce, 1995, p. 281)

These two epigraphs by psychiatrist Chester Pierce over a 21-year period speak volumes about an important, persistent, and underresearched social problem in the United States: racial microaggressions. Little is known about microaggressions, and yet this subtle form of racism has a dramatic impact on the lives of African Americans. Pierce and his colleagues have defined racial microaggressions as "subtle, stunning, often automatic, and nonverbal exchanges which are 'put downs' of blacks by offenders" (Pierce, Carew, Pierce–Gonzalez, & Wills, 1978, p. 66). They further maintain that these "offensive mechanisms used against blacks often are innocuous" and that the "cumulative weight of their never-ending burden is the major ingredient in black–white interactions" (p. 66). Additionally, Davis (1989) defined racial microaggressions as "stunning, automatic acts of disregard that stem from unconscious attitudes of white superiority and constitute a verification of black inferiority" (p. 1576).

Racial microaggressions, or unconscious and subtle forms of racism, though pervasive, are seldom investigated (Delgado & Stefancic, 1992; Johnson, 1988; Lawrence, 1987; Solórzano, 1998). Occasionally, African American students get a glimpse into the world of unconscious racism as demonstrated in comments such as those related to us by students who participated in the study described in this chapter: "When I [a White person] talk about those Blacks, I really wasn't talking about *you*," "You [a Black person] are not like the rest of them. *You're* different," "If only there were more of *them* [Black people] like *you* [a Black person]," and "I don't think of *you* [a Black person] as Black." Referring to White authority figures in particular (i.e., judges and other criminal justice authorities), Davis (1989) has suggested that Whites are capable of such utterances because "cognitive habit, history, and culture [have made them] unable to hear the range of relevant voices and grapple with what reasonably might be said in the voice of discrimination's victims" (p. 1576). Subsequently, as Pierce (1974) maintained, each Black person "must be taught to recognize these microaggressions and construct his future by taking appropriate action at each instance of recognition" (p. 520).

Race, Racism, and Racial Microaggressions

Our study of the collegiate racial climate and the effect of racial microaggressions begins by defining race and racism. One can argue that dominant groups often attempt to legitimate their position via ideological means or a set of beliefs that explains or justifies some actual or potential social arrangement. According to Banks (1995), an examination of U.S. history reveals that the "color line" of race is a socially constructed category, created to differentiate racial groups and to show the superiority or dominance of one race—in particular, Whites—over others. Yet, does racial domination require a rationalizing ideology? If racism is the ideology that justifies the dominance of one race over another, then how do we define racism?

For the purposes of this study, Lorde's (1992) definition of racism is perhaps the most concise: "the belief in the inherent superiority of one race over all others and thereby the right to dominance" (p. 496). Marable (1992) defined racism as "a system of ignorance, exploitation, and power used to oppress African-Americans, Latinos, Asians, Pacific Americans, American Indians and other people on the basis of ethnicity, culture, mannerisms, and color" (p. 5). His definition is especially important because it shifts the discussion of race and racism from a Black–White discourse to one that includes multiple faces, voices, and experiences. Embedded in both definitions, however, are at least three important points:

1. one group believes itself to be superior,
2. the group that believes itself to be superior has the power to carry out the racist behavior, and
3. racism affects multiple racial and ethnic groups.

Lorde's and Marable's definitions posit that racism is about institutional power, a form of power that people of color—that is, non-Whites—in the United States have never possessed.[1] It is also important to note that overt racist acts are usually not socially condoned and that examples of overt racism in the public discourse are rare. For example, Kennedy (1989) found that "although overt forms of racial domination described thus far were enormously destructive, *covert* color bars have been, in a certain sense, even more insidious [emphasis in original]" (p. 1752). Indeed, it is typically in subtle and covert ways (i.e., private conversations) that racism manifests itself. These innocuous forms of racist behavior constitute racial microaggressions.

Stereotype Threat and Racial Microaggressions

Any exploration of the racial microaggressions concept must include examination of the cumulative nature of racial stereotypes and their effects. Steele and Aronson's (1995) work reveals that racial stereotypes are deeply woven into the fabric of U.S. society, yet their daily effects are often misunderstood. Specifically, Steele and Aronson examined how such stereotypes may interfere with Black students' abilities to achieve high scores on standardized tests widely believed to measure aptitude or intelligence. Their research found that when African American college students were prompted to indicate their race before taking a Graduate Record Examination (GRE), their tests scores were significantly lower than when they were not prompted to note their race. Steele and Aronson described this phenomenon as "stereotype threat" or:

> . . . a social–psychological predicament that can arise from widely known negative stereotypes about one's group . . . the existence of such a stereotype means that anything one does or any of one's features that conform to it make the stereotypes more plausible as a self-characterization in the eyes of others, and perhaps even in one's own eyes. We call this predicament stereotype threat and argue that it is experienced, essentially, as a self-evaluative threat. (p. 797)

Steele and Aronson's stereotype threat research does "not focus on the internalization of inferiority images or their consequences," but rather examines the "immediate situational threat that derives from the broad dissemination of negative stereotypes about one's group—the threat of possibly being judged and treated stereotypically, or of possibly self-fulfilling such a stereotype" (p. 798). In other words, in a high-stakes testing situation, if African American students are reminded of stereotypes that they are intellectually inferior to Whites, their test performance is depressed.

In the present study, we used a critical race framework to examine how racial climate impacts the undergraduate experiences of African American students through racial microaggressions. We argue specifically that stereotype threat can affect the high-stakes game of college academic achievement in particular. The prospect of conforming to a negative stereotype about African Americans might be enough to undermine an African American college student's performance and achievement and thereby negatively contribute to the collegiate racial climate at his or her institution of higher learning. Our study thus explored the linkages between racial stereotypes, cumulative racial microaggressions, campus racial climate, and academic performance.

Racial Climate and the Undergraduate Experience

In this study, campus racial climate is broadly defined as the overall racial environment of the college campus. Understanding and analyzing the collegiate racial climate is an important part of examining college access, persistence, graduation, and transfer to and through graduate and professional school for African American students. As reported by Carroll (1998); Guinier, Fine, and Balin (1997); Hurtado (1992); and Hurtado, Milem, Clayton–Pedersen, and Allen (1999), when a collegiate racial climate is positive, it includes at least four elements: (a) the inclusion of students, faculty, and administrators of color; (b) a curriculum that reflects the historical and contemporary experiences of people of color; (c) programs to support the recruitment, retention and graduation of students of color; and (d) a college/university mission that reinforces the institution's commitment to pluralism.[2] In its negative form, these researchers conclude, these elements are less likely to exist on college campuses.

Our research approach provides a critical framework that can be used to study how race and racism, in their micro-level forms, affect the structures, processes, and discourses of the collegiate environment. Utilizing the experiences of African American students as guides, our analysis of collegiate racial climate also takes into account the intersection of racism with other forms of discrimination such as sexism and classism. We assert that a positive collegiate racial climate can facilitate and lead to important, positive academic outcomes for African American students. In contrast, a negative or nonsupportive campus climate is associated with poor academic performance and high dropout rates among African American students (Allen, Epps, & Haniff, 1991; Carroll, 1998; Hurtado et al., 1998).

From this conceptual foundation, our study extends Pierce's construct of racial microaggressions to examine collegiate racial climate and answer the following research questions:

1. How do African American college students experience racial microaggressions?
2. What impact do these racial microaggressions have on African American students?
3. How do African American students respond to racial microaggressions?
4. How do racial microaggressions affect the collegiate racial climate?

Critical Race Theory, Racial Microaggressions, and Campus Racial Climate

To address racial microaggressions and campus racial climate, we utilized critical race theory (CRT), which draws from and extends a broad literature base in law, sociology, history, ethnic studies, and women's studies. Though initially utilized in legal studies, CRT has been extended to areas such as education (Ladson–Billings & Tate, 1995; Solórzano, 1997, 1998; Tate, 1997), women's studies (Wing, 1996), and sociology (Aguirre, 2000). For our purposes, we introduce some of the tenets of CRT to our discussion of campus racial climate, as it represents a paradigm shift in the extant discourse about race and racism in education. CRT offers insights, perspectives, methods, and pedagogies that guide our efforts to identify, analyze, and transform the structural and cultural aspects of education that maintain subordinate and dominant racial positions in and out of the classroom (see Matsuda, Lawrence, Delgado, & Crenshaw, 1993; Tierney, 1993).

The basic CRT model consists of five elements focusing on: (a) the centrality of race and racism and their intersectionality with other forms of subordination, (b) the challenge to dominant ideology, (c) the commitment to social justice, (d) the centrality of experiential knowledge, and (e) the transdisciplinary perspective (Solórzano, 1997, 1998; Solórzano & Delgado Bernal, in press; Solórzano & Yosso, 2000).[3] Each of these five themes is not new in and of themselves, but collectively they represent a challenge to the existing modes of scholarship. The critical race theory framework for education is different from other CRT frameworks because it simultaneously attempts to foreground race and racism in the research as well as challenge the traditional paradigms, methods, texts, and separate discourse on race, gender, and class by showing how these social constructs intersect to impact on communities of color. Further, it focuses on the racialized, gendered, and classed experiences of communities of color and offers a liberatory and transformative method for examining racial/ethnic, gender, and class discrimination. It also utilizes transdisciplinary knowledge and the methodological base of ethnic studies, women's studies, sociology, history, and the law to forge better understandings of the various forms of discrimination. Indeed, critical race theory names racist injuries and identifies their origins.

When the ideology of racism is examined and racist injuries are named, victims of racism can find their voice. Further, those injured by racism discover that they are not alone in their marginality. They become empowered participants, hearing their own stories and the stories of others, listening to how the arguments are framed, and learning to make the arguments themselves. In this chapter, we take each of these five themes and, where applicable, apply them to the study of racial microaggressions, collegiate racial climate, and the experiences of African American college students.

Methodology

We used a qualitative, focus-group research design to illustrate in greater detail how African American students experience the racial climate of their college campuses. Focus groups are guided group discussions that allow the generation of a wealth of understanding about participants' experiences and beliefs about a particular topic of inquiry. Focus groups have four strengths that enrich the research process in that they provide a methodology to: (a) explore and discover concepts and themes about a phenomena about which more knowledge is needed, (b) add context and depth to the understanding of the phenomena, (c) provide an interpretation of the phenomena from the point of view of the participants in the group, and (d) observe the collective interaction of the participants. Qualitative focus-group analysis examines these students' lived experiences and shows how they can provide a depth of understanding, afford outsiders with greater insight, and be a guide to further research on collegiate racial climate and the impact of racial microaggressions on African American college students. Indeed, the purpose of a qualitative focus group methodology is to illustrate and elucidate the analytical categories of the relationship between racial microaggressions and campus racial climate.

Participants

The study participants consisted of a group of African American students who were attending three elite, predominantly White, Research I universities (two public and one private) in the United States. Thirty-four African American students (18 females, 16 males) participated in 10 focus groups that were convened on the campuses of each institution.

Instrumentation

The focus group interviews covered seven areas of inquiry:

1. the types of racial discrimination experienced by students;
2. how students responded to racial discrimination;
3. how racial discrimination affected the students, including their ability to perform academically;
4. the advantages of having a critical mass of African American students on campus;
5. whether or not the racial climate for African American students had improved or worsened on the students' campuses in the past few years;
6. whether or not the participants would recommend their college to other African American students; and
7. advice on how better to conduct the study.

Procedures

The focus groups did not represent a random student sample. Focus group participants were recruited using a purposive sampling technique, defined as "a procedure by which researchers select a subject or subjects based on predetermined criteria about the extent to which the selected subjects could contribute to the research study" (Vaughn, Schumm, & Singagub, 1996, p. 58). All focus group conversations were tape-recorded with the permission of the participants, and transcripts were made of each taped focus group. Additionally, extensive field notes, research memos, and information from debriefing meetings were compiled for each focus group. The transcripts were later coded and subjected to a thematic analysis.

Data Analysis

We used a grounded theory approach to investigate the concepts of racial microaggressions and collegiate racial climate. Specifically, we analyzed the transcripts, research memos, and field notes by immersing ourselves in the data and systematically analyzing the data for thematic patterns (Glaser & Strauss, 1967; Strauss & Corbin, 1990). This was accomplished by:

1. identifying the types of, reactions to, and effects of racial microaggressions;
2. determining whether patterns could be found in the types of, responses to, and effects of racial microaggressions;
3. deciding if certain types of, responses to, and effects of racial microaggressions could be collapsed into similar categories; and
4. finding examples of transcribed text that illustrate the different types of, reactions to, and effects of racial microaggressions.

Results

The following sections describe our findings from the focus group data and offer some general comments on how the racialized context of the college campus leads to a negative and marginalized perception of African American students. Figure 1 shows the relationship between racial microaggressions and campus racial climate. Using Figure 1 as a guide, we examine the different types of racial microaggressions that take place in academic and social spaces at the postsecondary level. Second, we explore the effects racial microaggressions have on African American students. Third, we describe the counter-spaces African American students create to challenge the racial microaggressions they face. Finally, we discuss the implications of these findings for the study of racial climate on the college campus.

Racial Microaggressions within Academic Spaces

As mentioned above, racial microaggressions take various forms, including both verbal and non-verbal assumptions about, and lowered expectations for, African American students. Overall, the students in our study described a very tense racial climate both inside and outside their classrooms.

Racial Microaggressions Within the Classroom Setting. Many students spoke of feeling "invisible" within the classroom setting. An African American female student noted that being viewed as a numerical racial minority seemed to translate into being ignored in class: "I think that when the professors see that there's fewer of you, they're less likely to address your concerns." The students in this study also shared that their experiences as African Americans were omitted, distorted, and stereotyped in their course curriculum. For instance, a female student stated: "When she [the professor] gets to talking about the subject of racism, she doesn't say 'racism,' and I'm like, 'No, it's racism.' She doesn't quite understand."

The African American students in this study also provided examples of racial microaggressions in faculty–student interactions such as instances when faculty maintained low expectations of them, even in the face of contradictory evidence:

> . . . I was doing really well in the class, like math is one of my strong suits. . . . We took a first quiz . . . and I got like a 95 . . . he [the professor] was like, "Come into my office. We need to talk," and I was like, "Okay." I just really knew I was gonna be [told], "great job," but he [said], "We think you've cheated. . . We just don't know, so we think we're gonna make you [take the exam] again." . . . And [then] I took it with just the GSI [graduate student instructor] in the room, and just myself, and I got a 98 on the exam.

Ongoing negative interactions with faculty seemed to instill a sense of self-doubt in some of the African American students we interviewed. Many students mentioned the importance of having other African American students in their classes to provide support against stereotype threat. According to one African American female student:

> They look at you [and think], "Oh that's another dumb Black girl in the class." That's how they make you feel. . . . So you don't feel like [saying], "Well, maybe it isn't me" 'cause you second-guess yourself. You're by yourself. If you have more African American students there, then there would be more of a voice, beside your one single voice. . . . [I]f there's more backup [other African American students] there, then you'll feel more comfortable. . . . Then you [won't] say, "Maybe I'm stupid! Maybe I don't understand what's going on."

The students also commented on the racial segregation evident among in-class study groups of their peers. For instance, an African American male student commented on his frustration, noting that he felt isolated because others did not believe he could be Black and still be intelligent:

> . . . [in] a technical field, [as] an engineer, oftentimes you'll feel like other students don't want to approach Black students for their groups, especially when [they think the Blacks are] just not technically smart . . . as maybe an Asian student. And, I'll notice they'll make some [study] groups [and] maybe you'll be the last one asked. So you feel more of a need to establish yourself . . . you need to prove yourself.

An African American female stated that racial discrimination in study group formation was obvious:

> I've had times when a guy in the class . . . [said], "Well, I don't want to work with you because you're Black." And he told me to my face. . . . And it was upsetting 'cause . . . I came here thinking that it wouldn't be like this, and that was naïve.

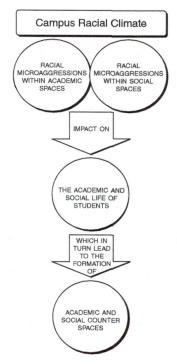

Figure 1   Racial microaggressions and collegiate racial climate.

Another African American female recalled a friend's experience:

> [A Black male student] thought he was going to be pre-med. And he was in this chemistry lab, and nobody wanted him to be in the [work] groups, so his partner . . . turned out to be this deaf girl. I'm sure everybody's looking at them like, "They're never going to pass."

Several of the students we interviewed indicated that beyond feeling like a numerical minority, they also felt personally diminished by nonverbal microaggressions perpetrated by their White counterparts. Other students agreed that merely "looking like" a person of color can be cause for White professors, students, and college staff persons to draw negative assumptions about minorities and lower their expectations of them. They further recognized that being stereotyped carries very real consequences beyond feeling bad about oneself. Some indicated feeling "drained" by the intense scrutiny their everyday actions received in the context of negative preconceived notions about African Americans. Others acknowledged as racial microaggressions the subtle and overt daily put-downs they encountered—or attempted to avoid—in their interactions with some Whites in the academic setting. Such incidents put these African American college students on the defensive to keep from succumbing to stereotype threat.

Importantly, several students indicated that key among the most negative racial assumptions Whites on their campuses held about them had to do with how African American students entered the university—in other words, those assumptions related to how Whites felt about affirmative action. An African American female described some of the assumptions that many students had about how Black students entered the university. Her comments reveal the subtle, yet pervasive nature of racism within a negative campus racial climate:

> Most of my experiences in regards to racism have come from students. . . . Like, a couple of our class discussions were about the whole Proposition 209 issue and affirmative action, and [the White] students really thought that the only reason Black students were getting into these universities was because of affirmative action. A lot of them could not fathom that we *earned* our way in here.

Another African American female echoed the above perception:

> Every time I leave my room I'm conscious of the fact that I'm Black. I'm really conscious of the fact that people are looking at me and [saying], "She's here on affirmative action."

Still another African American male described the frustration that his race leads others to make assumptions about his academic abilities and inabilities:

> . . . a lot of people don't accept the fact that I'm here on academics, and actually I got a scholarship for academics. All my scholarships were in academics, and they were not in sports.

Racial Microaggressions Outside the Classroom Setting. Students' responses also provided evidence of a negative racial climate outside their classrooms. Some expressed a generalized feeling of discomfort and racial tension as a result of microaggressions experienced in other academic spaces on their campuses. For example, one student asserted that he experienced a distinct level of discomfort when he entered the business school on his campus, noting that "it is like a little environment in itself" and that "a lot of African Americans don't feel comfortable there." Another targeted racism and racial microaggressions within her campus's science department particularly: "I've noticed that in the sciences here at this school, many of the people are racist, including the students and professors." Another recalled an encounter with a White faculty member:

> I was [in the department building] and I was walking down the hallway . . . [and] one of the teacher's doors was open. . . . She's like, "Oh, I should have locked the door. My purse is in there." I was just [thinking to myself], wow . . . maybe [she] should have kept that to [herself] or something, like, oh, I reminded you that you should lock your door!

Other students noted feeling that their very presence in non-classroom campus settings was unwanted and assumed to be inappropriate. For example, one noted the following:

> Last time we went to the library . . . to study . . . obviously, it's finals time . . . people are *going* to study. But when we walked in there looking for somewhere to sit down, it's like . . . they've never seen Black people before in their lives, or they've never seen Black people study before!

Such incidents and feelings of discomfort contribute to the development of a negative racial climate and serve to discourage several of the African American students we interviewed from taking advantage of student services on their campuses. As one African American female student explained:

> I decided to go see a counselor because I wanted to do pre-med and I wanted to make sure I was on the right track. . . . [The counselor] was very discouraging . . . not supportive at all. She finally said, "Well, I don't think that you should take all of those classes. You're not gonna be able to do that.". . . . I personally thought [she discouraged me] was because I was African American.

Whether inside or outside the classroom, racial microaggressions within academic spaces are filtered through layers of racial stereotypes. That is, any negative actions by or deficiencies noted among one or more African American students are used to justify pejorative perceptions about *all* African American students, while the positive actions or attributes of one or a few African American students are viewed as rare cases of success amidst their racial group's overall failure.

Racial Microaggressions Within Social Spaces on Campus. The students in our study related several instances of racial microaggressions experienced outside their academic environments, in social spaces both on and off campus. Indeed, our findings suggest that the collegiate racial climate fosters more covert or subtle racism within academic spaces and more overt racism within social spaces on campus. As an African American male student revealed: "With school events, it's definitely racial. They [the campus police] regulate and try to shut down [Black social functions], and make [us] leave through certain doors." A female student corroborated:

> It's so annoying that everywhere we go, we've got to [be] watched. At the Black parties at the Union, everybody else [Whites and other groups of students] can go [out the front door] . . . when there is a Black party, we had to go out the back door.

Another student described a racial microaggression that took the form of an unspoken yet understood double standard applied to African American students. In her words: "When it comes time for Black students to do things on campus . . . there's a whole set of rules that you have to abide by, whereas the other students, it's like, "Well, you all have a good time." These microaggressions, many of which are directed at African American students by the campus police, appear to be based on notions that African Americans pose a threat to and in these public spaces on their college campuses. For example, an African American male student related an incident that occurred when a group of Black students was playing football on a campus parking lot:

> . . . it's 11 o'clock [at night] and all of a sudden, [campus police] sweeps up. . . . There's a total of four or five cars, and then we have two cops on the bikes, all here for us who are not displaying any type of violence or anything like that . . . but we're upset. And we're saying at the same time, we're feeling restricted because if we act in a way that we want to react—number one, we're going to go to jail; number two—it's just going to feed into the stereotype that we're supposed to be violent. . . . We actually just stood there out there and just really pleaded our case for at least a good 45 minutes. And they were not trying to hear us at all. We had to leave the parking lot. . . . Once again, it reminded me I'm a Black man [on a predominantly White campus].

Effects of Racial Microaggressions

Racial microaggressions in both academic and social spaces have real consequences, the most obvious of which are the resulting negative racial climate and African American students' struggles with feelings of self-doubt and frustration as well as isolation. This means that the African American students on the campuses studied must strive to maintain good academic standing while negotiating the conflicts arising from disparaging perceptions of them and their group of origin. Additionally, they must navigate through a myriad of pejorative racial stereotypes that fuel the creation and perpetuation of racial microaggressions. As a female focus group participant explained:

> It's not fair on the African American students. [I have] to be on my guard every time I go in to talk to a professor, every time I go in and talk to the advisor, every time I go and talk to *anybody*. I'm like, are they here really to help me or are they going to lead me down the path that I don't want to go down?

The students also noted that being a member of a racial minority on their predominantly White campuses placed them in a position where they were perceived by others to represent the voice of their entire race. Steele and Aronson (1995) identify this "spokesperson pressure" as a part of stereotype threat. An African American male student explained it in the following manner:

> . . . a lot of times if they're having a discussion on whatever topic, you feel like you're going to get called on, just because they want a Black perspective and you're the only [person] that can speak on it. . . . It's definitely had an impact on how [Black students] perform in school. . . . A lot of times you're gonna be the only one in certain classrooms.

An African American female simply iterated that the role was "tiring."

The sense of discouragement, frustration, and exhaustion resulting from racial microaggressions left some African American students in our study despondent and made them feel that they could not perform well academically. These stresses contrast those cited by White college students, whose greatest stress typically originates from personal issues (Muñoz, 1986). As one female African American student admitted, the cumulative effects of stereotype threat made her feel "helpless." Another concluded: "All the beliefs and thoughts I had coming here [to the predominantly White campus] were extinguished." Another female student stated that her overall academic performance had been negatively affected by the racial climate on her campus, asserting that the experience was "kind of intimidating" because in several of her classes, she was the only Black person in the class; thus, it was harder for her "to participate and get involved and get interested."

Several students commented that racial microaggressions had affected their academic performance in overt ways such as pushing them to drop a class, changing their major and even leaving the university to attend school elsewhere. As one African American female student maintained:

> In many respects, I was naive, but now I'm cynical. . . . When I took my science courses, I had to fight every day through all the racism I felt. . . . Each time I took a new class, the same thing happened over and over and over and over again. Many times I was the only African American in the class. [The White students and professors] were like, "You know what, I don't think she knows what she's talking about," or . . . "Well, you got here because of affirmative action, not your grades or your merit." And when you try and voice something to somebody, they don't want to hear it. They're not *about* to hear it! And they're like, "Well, you need to be along with your other peers." I'm upset. I'm tired of it. That's why I changed my major to English.

Another African American female student maintained that the racial microaggressions she had endured at her university had pushed her to the point of exit:

> I can't stand this school and I'm ready to leave. And that for me is how I feel. I know this is the real world and I've learned that. . . . I know how I'm going to take what I want to do to get what I need to get. . .

Yet another female student related the experiences of an African American friend who was transferring to an historically Black university:

> . . . she got a B in physics before she came. She took physics again . . . she did her problems, got everything [in], and got a D on her exam. She looked at her friend's exam; he was a White person, and he had gotten an A, and they had the same, almost the same exact answers on the exam. . . . So she went up to the [graduate student instructor] and asked him . . . "What's going on?" He [says] to her, "Well, I have not really been around Black people, or people like you before . . . I don't think you did well on the test." So she went up to the professor, and the professor didn't do anything. She went to the chancellor. The chancellor had her drop the class. . . . Her parents are the ones who are paying for her education, but see, the first thing [the chancellor] asked her was whether or not she was on financial aid. So now she's mad, upset, and going to be transferring to Howard University.

Creating Counter-Spaces as a Response to Racial Microaggressions

In response to the daily barrage of racial microaggressions that they endure both in and outside of their classes, the African American students who participated in our focus groups indicated that they are creating academic and social "counter-spaces" on and off their campuses. These counter-spaces serve as sites where deficit notions of people of color can be challenged and where a positive collegiate racial climate can be established and maintained. Counter-spaces on the three campuses participating in our study were created within African American student organizations, organizations or offices that provide services to African American and other students, Black fraternities and sororities, peer groups, and Black student-organized academic study halls. Some of these counter-spaces were co-created with African American faculty and exist within classrooms. Others existed within more social settings.

As Solórzano and Villalpando (1998) have determined, academic counter-spaces allow African American students to foster their own learning and to nurture a supportive environment wherein their experiences are validated and viewed as important knowledge. According to our focus group participants, social counter-spaces were important because they afforded African American students with space, outside of the classroom confines, to vent their frustrations and to get to know others who shared their experiences of microaggressions and/or overt discrimination. For example, one male student explained that he sought out such a counter-space for support at his university:

> . . . that was one of the reasons why I chose to live on the African American theme floor [among the campus dormitories] . . . because if I go home [at the end of the day] and I don't have the support, then that can really be discouraging. . . . [Y]ou need some type of support to get through this thing . . . and if you're a freshman coming in, you don't know African American faces . . . you need somewhere to start.

Two African American female students shared similar conclusions:

> . . . I just feel more comfortable dealing with African American people in every aspect . . . counseling, financial aid. I just look for the first African American face I find because I feel like they're going to be more sympathetic.

> You know how you have African American crews, African American fraternities, and so forth. And then my sophomore year here, I was thinking about joining an African American sorority, and [a White fellow student] said, "Why do you want to join a African American sorority? Are those other sororities not good enough? You think that we're only White?" I said, "I don't think they're only White. It's just that . . . I don't want to say [they're] anti-African American, but I don't feel welcome in your sorority." And she said, "What do you think we are, the Klan?" [and] I was like, "Okay, we're not going to go there."

Many social counter-spaces also serve as academic counter spaces and vice-versa. For example, some students indicated that their study groups evolved into friendship groups and community outreach groups that provide them with educational, emotional, and cultural support. As a female African American student related:

> . . . the benefit that I have gained from [a study group of African American students] is that my involvement in the African American community has grown, and that's where I found a lot of my support. Even in terms of academics, I go study with the "homies" all the time. Go to [a certain student lounge] and you're going to see a million African American faces, and it's going to be cool. . . . You might not get that much studying done, but it's a cool little network that's created because classes are so uncomfortable.

It was noted, however, that the social counter-spaces had a "down side" among their positive attributes. As one African American male explained: "Trying to be involved in all these things [Black-focus organizations] and deal with activities to make sure your voice is heard can adversely effect your study habits."

Marginalized students are often familiar with their groups' voices being silenced in the classroom discourse or with having their personal and/or group experiences and beliefs discounted. These negative experiences occur in addition to the pervasiveness of the cultural-deficit discourse in the academy (Valencia & Solórzano, 1997). Perhaps as a response to their position of marginality on their campuses, the students in our study seemed to create academic and social counter-spaces along racial or gender lines. Nonetheless, in separating themselves from racially or gender-uncomfortable situations, this group of African American college students appeared to be utilizing their counter-spaces on their own terms. This confirms that the creation of such counter-spaces is an important strategy for minority students' academic survival (Solórzano & Villalpando, 1998).

Conclusion

In a 1998 study, educator and researcher Grace Carroll asked African American college students in her classes and workshops to answer the following three questions:

1. Have you ever been the only African American person in a class or meeting and a so-called black issue comes up and suddenly you feel all eyes are on you—that you are supposed to have the "appropriate response"—that you speak for all African Americans?

2. Have you ever watched the news and a particularly violent crime is described and your first reaction is: "God, I hope the perpetrator is not black"?

3. Have you ever been in a store, bar, or restaurant and felt you were next in line for service only to see that a white patron got served instead? (p. 3)

Carroll noted that her participants usually answered "yes" to each of the questions, concluding that their responses indicated the presence of "mundane extreme environmental stress" (p. 1), which is similar to what we define here as racial microaggressions. The students in the present study would probably also have answered "yes" to the above questions.

This study of racial microaggressions has helped us to extend and apply a racial microaggressions analysis to the study of campus racial climate. It has further allowed us to recognize, document, and analyze racial microaggressions from the perspective of African American students and listen to the voices of those who experience and are affected by racial microaggressions. Indeed, race, racism, racial stereotypes, and the campus racial climate must continue to be viewed through the lenses of African American and other students of color. The experiences of these students demonstrates that even at high levels of accomplishment (i.e., at elite undergraduate universities), where educational conditions might on the surface appear to be equal, inequality and discrimination still exist—albeit in more subtle and hidden forms. Perhaps, the study of the cumulative impact of racial microaggressions at each point in the educational system offers further evidence of the very different road that African American students must travel. It also reveals the strength they possess in overcoming both macro-level and micro-level barriers along that road.

The experiences related by this group of African American student participants raise two additional questions specifically related to the contemporary affirmative action discourse:

1. Is the educational playing field level for African American students as they make their way through the collegiate system?

2. Should a student's success and persistence in the face of racial discrimination be considered as a factor in the undergraduate, professional school, and graduate admissions process?

The answer from the students in our study to the first question would be a resounding "NO!" The answer to the second would be a resounding "YES!" Indeed, their descriptions of racial microaggressions challenge the anti-affirmative action ideology of college as an equal, colorblind, and race-neutral institution. They resonate with the essence of Pierce's (1970) comment: "It is my fondest hope that the day is not far remote when every black child will recognize and defend promptly and adequately against every offensive microaggression" (p. 280). Thirty years later, Pierce's vision has not yet come to pass. Indeed, very little is known about who, when, where, and how racial microaggressions are initiated and defended against. Without careful documentation and analysis, racial stereotypes, the threats that they pose and the assaults they justify in the form of racial microaggressions, can easily be ignored or downplayed. Nonetheless, these findings demonstrate that the cumulative effects of racial microaggressions can be devastating. It is our hope that further research into these subtle forms of and responses to racism and sexism will advance examinations of the conditions and concerns of African American and other students of color and move educators toward making Professor Pierce's hope a reality.

Notes

1. In this study, people, faculty, scholars, and students of color are defined as those persons of African American, Latino, Asian American, and Native American ancestry. It should be noted that each of these descriptors has a political dimension that this chapter does not discuss.

2. Our definitions of pluralism and collegiate racial diversity are synonymous. We define both as manifestations of a situation in which underrepresented racial and ethnic groups are present on the college campus and viewed as equals on the college campus; and where *all* students are willing to affirm one another's dignity, ready to benefit from each other's experience, and willing to acknowledge one another's contributions to the common welfare of students and faculty on the college campus.

3. For three comprehensive annotated bibliographies on critical race and theory, see Delgado and Stefancic (1993, 1994).

References

Aguirre, A. (2000). Academic storytelling: A critical race theory story of affirmative action. *Sociological Perspectives, 43,* 319–339.

Allen, W. R., Epps, E. G., & Haniff, N. Z. (Eds.). (1991). *College in Black and White: African American students in predominantly White and historically Black public universities.* Albany: State University of New York Press.

Banks, J. (1995). The historical reconstruction of knowledge about race: implications for transformative teaching. *Educational Researcher, 24,* 15–25.

Carroll, G. (1998). *Environmental stress and African Americans: The other side of the moon.* Westport, CT: Green-wood Press.

Davis, P. (1989). Law as microaggression. *Yale Law Journal, 98,* 1559–1577.

Delgado, R., & Stefancic, J. (1992). Images of the outsider in American law and culture: Can free expression remedy systemic social ills? *Cornell Law Review, 77,* 1258–1297.

Delgado, R., & Stefancic, J. (1993). Critical race theory: An annotated bibliography. *Virginia Law Review, 79,* 461–516.

Delgado, R., & Stefancic, J. (1994). Critical race theory: An annotated bibliography—1993, A year of transition. *University of Colorado Law Review, 66,* 159–193.

Glaser, B., & Strauss, A. (1967). *The discovery of grounded theory.* Chicago: Aldine.

Guinier, L., Fine, M., & Balin, J. (1997). *Becoming gentlemen: Women, law school, and institutional change.* Boston: Beacon Press.

Hurtado, S. (1992). The campus racial climate: Contexts of conflict. *Journal of Higher Education, 63,* 539–569.

Hurtado, S., Milem, J., Clayton–Pedersen, A., & Allen, W. (1998). Enhancing campus climates for racial/ethnic diversity: Educational policy and practice. *Review of Higher Education, 21,* 279–302.

Johnson, S. (1988). Unconscious racism and the criminal law. *Cornell Law Review, 73,* 1016–1037.

Kennedy, R. (1989). Racial critiques of legal academia. *Harvard Law Review, 102,* 1745–1819.

Ladson–Billings, G., & Tate, W. (1995). Toward a critical race theory of education. *Teachers College Record, 97,* 47–68.

Lawrence, C. (1987). The id, the ego, and equal protection: Reckoning with unconscious racism. *Stanford Law Review, 39,* 317–388.

Lorde, A. (1992). Age, race, class, and sex: Women redefining difference. In M. Anderson & P. H. Collins (Eds.), *Race, class, and gender: An anthology* (pp. 495–502). Belmont, CA: Wadsworth.

Marable, M. (1992). *Black America.* Westfield, NJ: Open Media.

Matsuda, M., Lawrence, C., Delgado, R., & Crenshaw, K. (1993). *Words that wound: Critical race theory, assaultive speech, and the First Amendment.* Boulder, CO: Westview Press.

Muñoz, D. (1986). Identifying areas of stress for Chicano undergraduates. In M. Olivas (Ed.), *Latino college students* (pp. 131–156). New York: Teachers College Press.

Pierce, C. (1970). Offensive mechanisms. In F. Barbour (Ed.), *The Black seventies* (pp. 265–282). Boston: Porter Sargent.

Pierce, C. (1974). Psychiatric problems of the Black minority. In S. Arieti (Ed.), *American handbook of psychiatry* (pp. 512–523). New York: Basic Books.

Pierce, C. (1995). Stress analogs of racism and sexism: Terrorism, torture, and disaster. In C. Willie, P. Rieker, B. Kramer, & B. Brown (Eds.), *Mental health, racism, and sexism* (pp. 277–293). Pittsburgh: University of Pittsburgh Press.

Pierce, C., Carew, J., Pierce–Gonzalez, D., & Wills, D. (1978). An experiment in racism: TV commercials. In C. Pierce (Ed.), *Television and education* (pp. 62–88). Beverly Hills, CA: Sage.

Solórzano, D. (1997). Images and words that wound: Critical race theory, racial stereotyping, and teacher education. *Teacher Education Quarterly, 24,* 5–19.

Solórzano, D. (1998). Critical race theory, racial and gender microaggressions, and the experiences of Chicana and Chicano scholars. *International Journal of Qualitative Studies in Education 11,* 121–136.

Solórzano, D., & Delgado Bernal, D. (in press). Critical race theory, transformational resistance, and social justice: Chicana and Chicano students in an urban context. *Urban Education.*

Solórzano, D., & Villalpando, O. (1998). Critical race theory, marginality, and the experience of minority students in higher education. In C. Torres & T. Mitchell (Eds.), *Emerging issues in the sociology of education: Comparative perspectives* (pp. 211–224). Albany: State University of New York Press.

Solórzano, D., & Yosso, T. (2000). Toward a critical race theory of Chicana and Chicano education. In C. Tejeda, C. Martinez, & Z. Leonardo (Eds.), *Demarcating the border of Chicana(o)/Latina(o) education* (pp. 35–65), Cresskill, NJ: Hampton Press.

Solórzano, D., & Yosso, T. (in press). Critical race theory: Counterstorytelling the Chicana and Chicano graduate school experience. *International Journal of Qualitative Studies in Education.*

Steele, C., & Aronson, J. (1995). Stereotype threat and the intellectual test performance of African Americans. *Journal of Personality and Social Psychology, 69*, 797–811.

Strauss, A., & Corbin, J. (1990). *Basics of qualitative research: Grounded theory procedures and techniques*. Newbury Park, CA: Sage.

Tate, W. (1997). Critical race theory and education: History, theory, and implications. *Review of Research in Education, 22*, 195–247.

Tierney, W. (1993). *Building communities of difference: Higher education in the twenty-first century*. Westport, CT: Bergin & Garvey.

Valencia, R., & Solórzano, D. (1997). Contemporary deficit thinking (The Stanford Series on Education and Public Policy). In R. Valencia (Ed.), *The evolution of deficit thinking in educational thought and practice* (pp. 160–210). New York: Falmer Press.

Vaughn, S., Schumm, J, & Singagub, J. (1996). *Focus group interviews in education and psychology*. Thousand Oaks, CA: Sage Publications.

Wing, A. (Ed.). (1997). *Critical race feminism: A reader*. New York: New York University Press.

CHAPTER 49

NIGGERS NO MORE: A CRITICAL RACE COUNTERNARRATIVE ON BLACK MALE STUDENT ACHIEVEMENT AT PREDOMINANTLY WHITE COLLEGES AND UNIVERSITIES

SHAUN R. HARPER

A methodological approach popularized by critical race theorists is used in this chapter to oppose dominant discourse concerning the social and educational status of Black men in America. Specifically, this counternarrative on student achievement was derived from face-to-face individual interviews with 143 Black male undergraduates at 30 predominantly White colleges and universities across the USA. Exemplified via five composites constructed from the overall sample are resistant responses to subordination and racist stereotyping; confrontations with the cyclical reproduction of low expectations for Black male leadership and achievement; and an industrious rejection of what I refer to throughout the chapter as 'niggering'. Also offered herein are implications for postsecondary faculty, administrators, and researchers.

The thought of the inferiority of the Negro is drilled into him in almost every class he enters and in almost every book he studies . . . If you teach the Negro that he has accomplished as much good as any other race, he will achieve and aspire to equality and justice without regard to race. (Woodson 1933, 2, 192)

The manufacturing of social, educational, economic, and political inferiority has managed to persist since the publication of Carter G. Woodson's epic book, *The mis-education of the negro*. It remains the case that Black men are continually reminded of our distress and subordination. In America, we have long been regarded as criminals, irresponsible fathers, descendants of dysfunctional families, self-destructive drug addicts, materialistic lovers of flashy possessions, and violent rapists of White women (Anderson 2008; Gadsden and Smith 1994; Gordon, Gordon, and Nembhard 1994; Jenkins 2006; Mandara 2006; White and Cones 1999). These attributes are typically used to render us collectively undeserving of trust, respect, equitable pay and workplace promotion, and fairness. Perceptions of us, unfortunately, are hardly better in schools and colleges. The typical Black boy in a K-12 educational setting is taught almost exclusively by White women who combine an insufficient anticipation for his academic achievement with high expectations for disruptive behavior, intellectual stupidity, and a dispassion for learning that will ultimately culminate with high school dropout (Davis 2003; Davis and Jordan 1994; Jackson and Moore 2008; Noguera 2003; Toldson 2008). His same-race male counterpart who makes it to postsecondary education encounters a different set of negative perceptions, which are later described in this chapter. Those who view and treat Black males in such troubled ways associate us, perhaps unconsciously, with one of the most racially offensive terms in American history: Niggers.

In the USA, the label Nigger (also referred to as 'the N-word') has been long assigned to a person of African ancestry who is thought to be of a lower social class and possesses a strong predisposition toward civil disobedience and failure, especially in comparison to White Americans (deCoy 1967). In his 2002 book, *Nigger: The Strange Career of a Troublesome Word*, Harvard law professor Randall Kennedy offers etymology, examples of historical and present use, and attitudinal and behavioral characteristics commonly associated with the term. Derived from the Latin word for the color black, Nigger had become a familiar insult to enslaved Africans prior to the mid-1800s. Although the word has multiple meanings, it is used most often derogatorily by White supremacists to stigmatize what they view as a filthy, good-for-nothing cadre of hopeless Americans—Kennedy calls this *Nigger-as-insult*. He quotes the master of ceremonies at a White citizens' banquet in the 1960s who publicly proclaimed: 'Throughout the pages of history there is only one third-rate race which has been treated like a second-class race and complained about it—and that race is the American Nigger' (9). More than 40 years later, Blacks, especially Black men, continue to be caricatured as second- and third-rate citizens through the media, the preponderance of deficit-oriented discourse regarding our lives, and the inequitable distribution of resources, justice, and opportunity. Kennedy also notes that some Blacks use the term as 'a shorthand way of reminding themselves and everyone else precisely where they perceive themselves as standing in American society—the message being, "Always remember you's a Nigger"' (39).

While Kennedy (2002) cites several dozen examples of how Nigger has been used over time (including in over 4200 court opinions), he makes clear that the N-word is also a way of viewing a race of people—not just a racial epithet used to verbally insult them. Likewise, deCoy (1967) contends that beyond its insult function, Nigger is an actionable term employed to categorically subordinate Black persons. Put differently, a Black male student could be 'niggered' in various ways (e.g., being told that he is unlikely to accomplish much in life; that he is no good, just like the rest of them; and that being successful in school is an anomaly for people like him). Another example is how a White teacher responded to Malcolm X's articulation of his aspiration to pursue a career in law—she encouraged him to consider carpentry instead, a profession that was more realistically accessible by Niggers (Kennedy). Malcolm was niggered by his teacher's avowal of low expectations for his goals. A third example could be derived from Jenkins's (2006) article, 'Mr. Nigger: The Challenges of Educating Black Males within American Society', wherein she notes the following contradictions in education policy and practice:

> On one hand, the society espouses rhetoric of concern and desire to elevate Black males, but on the other hand, practices a policy of oppression, prejudice, and disregard. Put differently, the experience of the Black man in America seems to be one in which he is called 'mister', but is treated with a 'niggardly' regard. And the result is the positioning of Black males at the lower rungs of society and their experiencing underachievement in almost all aspects of life. (127)

Continuing to claim an ethic of care for Black males without tending to racism and structural barriers to achievement and justice constitutes niggering.

deCoy (1967) predicted a certain group of educated Blacks would eventually proclaim they are 'Niggers no more' (95). Offered in this chapter is a critical race counternarrative on Black men who do just that—those who reject the ways they are niggered in scholarship produced about them and by educators who continually stigmatize them. My counternarrative is situated in the postsecondary educational context for three reasons. First, as evidenced in the next section, almost everything published about Black male collegians negatively portrays them as underachieving and unlikely to succeed. Second, young Black men who are not enrolled in college are probably thought to be more susceptible to niggering, while college matriculation is likely presumed to offer some sort of immunity to those who enroll. But, numerous examples confirm that niggering occurs in similar ways at predominantly white institutions (PWIs) higher education. And third, insufficient insights into how Black men productively refuse to be niggered have been offered in previous higher education research. Thus, little is known about psychological resistance and the sociopolitical strategies employed by those who consciously decide to defy racist stereotypes, exceed expectations, and offer more affirming views of their individual selves and the Black male collective.

Using Nigger instead of the euphemistic N-word was not compelled by some desperate attempt to add shock value to this chapter. Instead, being called a Nigger, especially by a White person, usually incites emotional hurt and a range of other injurious feelings within the insulted Black person (Kennedy 2002). It is possible that being continually treated like a Nigger engenders a stronger, more cumulatively aggravating series of responses than simply being called one. Protecting readers from the penetration of this word and all that is associated with it (historically and presently) seemed unfair to those of us who are persistently harmed by it in schools, colleges, and society. To understand, even partially, how Black men are niggered on college and university campuses requires some grappling with the very word that characterizes their experiential realities.

Niggered Males in College: A Literature Review

> The images created of Black men in our society often confine them to environments shaped by drugs, crime, athletics, and academic failure. In education, we have contributed to this negative portrait by the disproportionate amount of research that emphasizes remediation and disadvantage. (Fries-Britt 1997, 65)

Jackson and Moore (2008) similarly assert that most discourse on Black male school achievement focuses on deficits and advances a 'doom and gloom trajectory for these individuals in the educational enterprise . . . In the research literature, there has been little attention given to solving educational problems for [Black] males, but more emphasis placed on documenting it' (847–8). Although most of the scholarship Jackson and Moore cite is published in the K-12 domain, research on Black male college students has an analogous orientation. On its own, the almost exclusive fascination with problems encountered by this population reflects the act of niggering described earlier in this chapter. Specifically, anyone who takes time to read about them could confidently conclude that Black male undergraduates are troubled, their future is bleak, they all do poorly, and there is little that can be done to reverse longstanding outcomes disparities that render them among the least likely to succeed in college. Presented in this section is a synthesis of what is presently known about these students at PWIs.

Black male collegians, like many other students of color on predominantly White campuses, are expected to experience psychological stress and have tumultuous college adjustment experiences (Hinderlie and Kenny 2002; Smedley, Myers, and Harrell 1993). Low-expectations from their K-12 teachers follow them into college (Bonner and Bailey 2006), thus they often find themselves overwhelmed by the academic rigor of their courses and insufficiently prepared to meet their professors' expectations. In their study of the enablers of college student retention, Berger and Milem discovered that 'being Black [was] the third largest negative predictor of persistence' (1999, 657). Their inability to integrate into the campus because it is often so unlike their home environments is one of the main factors commonly used to explain Black student attrition. This college dropout dilemma is exacerbated by gender, as more than two-thirds (67.6%) of Black men who start college do not graduate within six years, which is the lowest college completion rate among both sexes and all racial/ethnic groups in higher education (Harper 2006a).

Although they are unlikely to find supportive relationships outside their same-race peer groups at PWIs, Black men need them to achieve high levels of satisfaction with their college experiences (Strayhorn 2008a); those who are satisfied stand the best chance of persisting toward baccalaureate degree attainment. Also essential to retention is active engagement in educationally purposeful activities, both inside and outside the classroom. But unfortunately, Black men have come to be known as one of the most disengaged populations on college and university campuses. For instance, in his analysis of data from the College Student Experiences Questionnaire, Cuyjet (1997) found that Black men devoted less time to studying, took notes in class less often, spent significantly less time writing and revising papers, and participated less often in class-related collaborative experiences than did Black female respondents to the national survey. Furthermore, Black women in comparison to their same-race male peers were more engaged in campus activities, served on more campus committees, and held more leadership positions at their institutions. For nearly a decade now, the Black male engagement problem has been a topic of discussion among administrators at national higher education conferences (Cuyjet 2006; Roach 2001; Schmidt 2008). Although there are many explanatory factors for these disengagement trends, one thing is known for sure: An insufficient sense of belonging at the institution stifles engagement and diminishes one's inclination to persist toward baccalaureate degree attainment (Bean 2005).

Black male students' sense of belonging at PWIs hinges in large part upon interacting with peers from different racial/ethnic groups (Strayhorn 2008b). Yet, their individual and collective belongingness at PWIs is threatened by the constant reinforcement of racist stereotypes that stigmatize them as dumb jocks, Black male criminals from the local community who do not belong on campus, affirmative action beneficiaries who were undeserving of admission, and underprepared 'at-risk' students who all emerged from low-income families and urban ghettos (Cuyjet 2006; Fries-Britt and Turner 2001; Smith, Allen, and Danley 2007; Smith, Yosso, and Solórzano 2007; Solórzano, Ceja, and Yosso 2000). Even high-achieving Black male collegians are met with suspicion from professors who doubt their intellectual competence as well as White peers who pass them over in selecting group members for collaborative work (Fries-Britt 1997). Moreover, there is an erroneous assumption that Black male college achievers are socially disconnected from their same-race male peers and thus accused of 'acting White' (Harper 2006b), a hypothesis that has been repeatedly disproven in the K-12 education literature (Ainsworth-Darnell and Downey 1998; Spencer et al. 2001).

At PWIs, niggering is also evidenced by the misperception that all Black men are the same and the inability of White persons on these campuses to recognize the different cultural backgrounds of Black male students. Harper and Nichols (2008) found tremendous within-group heterogeneity among the Black male undergraduates in their study. But a lack of institutional acknowledgment of these important differences led to a series of problems, including the transference of racist stereotypes about themselves onto each other; unproductive competition among them; and social distance in environments where same-race peer support was needed most. Harper and Nichols also found that two groups in particular, Black fraternity members and Black male student-athletes, were especially vulnerable to stereotypes and misperceptions. Despite their historical significance, the five national Black fraternities have become increasingly niggered over that past two decades by those who portray their members as violent murderers who beat Black male pledges to death (Jones 2004). Similarly, Black men who participate in intercollegiate sports (especially football and men's basketball, the two most financially lucrative sports on campus) are commonly thought to be intellectually inferior to their non-athletic peers and more interested in athletic accomplishment than academic achievement (Beamon 2008; Donnor 2005). One could easily summarize their status as Niggers with balls who enroll to advance their sports careers and generate considerable revenue for the institution without learning much or seriously endeavoring to earn their college degrees.

For the most part, the dominant narrative concerning Black men at PWIs is the same as in other sectors. As noted here, a niggered view of these students is continually perpetuated on campuses as well as in published research regarding their experiences. In light of what the literature reports, insights into the following questions are warranted: (1) Is there an overlooked population of Black male students who are not disengaged and academically underperforming; (2) if so, what are their experiential realities and navigational approaches at PWIs; and (3) how do these Black men resist niggering in its various forms on their campuses? The critical race counternarrative presented later in this chapter was derived from a qualitative exploration of these questions.

Methodology and Methods

Methodology

Honoring a scholarly tradition exceptionally executed by eminent critical race theorist Derrick Bell (see Bell 1987, 1992), Solórzano and Yosso (2002) introduce counter-storytelling as a useful approach to education research. They define this as a method of telling the stories of people who are often overlooked in the literature, and as a means by which to examine, critique, and counter majoritarian stories (or master narratives) composed about people of color. Master narratives are dominant accounts that are often generally accepted as universal truths about particular groups (e.g., Blacks are hopeless and helpless)—such scripts usually caricature these groups in negative ways. Solórzano and Yosso note that research and theoretical models that seek to explain outcomes inequities and achievement differences in education often support majoritarian viewpoints through the constant amplification of deficiency among students of color. As such, a counterstory 'exposes deficit-informed research that silences and distorts epistemologies of people of color. Although social scientists tell stories under the guise of "objective" research, these stories actually uphold deficit, racialized notions about people of color' (23).

Solórzano and Yosso (2002) identify three different types of counternarratives: Personal stories, other people's stories, and composite stories. The third was selected for use in this chapter, as it entails relying on data collected from multiple persons of color who have experienced a particular context or similar phenomena. Accordingly, composite stories are useful for representing the often disregarded experiences of a larger group through a smaller subset of 'characters' who represent the group. Solórzano and Yosso differentiate critical race storytelling from fiction in the following ways: 'We are not developing imaginary characters that engage in fictional scenarios. Instead, the "composite" characters we develop are grounded in real-life experiences and actual empirical data' (36). Hence, data collected from persons of color are juxtaposed with research published about them by others to identify contradistinctions and offer insights into overlooked experiential realities. Additionally, to qualify as a counternarrative, various elements of critical race theory must be incorporated.

The counternarrative presented in this chapter is derived from a large, multi-campus qualitative research study focused on Black male college achievement. It challenges the master narrative that has been constructed for this group—the story of Niggers that is often reinforced through literature such as that reviewed in the previous section. Composite characters in the story reject commonly held assumptions regarding their limited potential for leadership and college success by describing resistant responses to niggering and their politically effective navigation of predominantly White educational environments. Theirs is not a story of deficits. Furthermore, the counternarrative offered herein advances the following elements of critical race theory summarized by Solórzano and Yosso (2002): *The intercentricity of race and racism with other forms of subordination* (namely gender stigmatization); *the challenge to dominant ideology* (meaning, Black men as Niggers); *the centrality of experiential knowledge* (as reflected in descriptions of their postsecondary navigational journeys); and *the commitment to social justice* (demonstrated through the empowerment of achievers—a subordinated and often overlooked racial group).

Data Source and Research Design

This chapter is based on findings from the National Black Male College Achievement Study, the largest-ever empirical research study of Black male undergraduates. Data were collected from 219 students at 42 colleges and universities in 20 states across the USA. Six different institution types were represented in the study. Only data collected from the 143 participants attending the 30 predominantly White colleges and universities were included in analyses for this chapter.

This study was guided by the phenomenological approach to qualitative inquiry, which focuses on understanding and describing the 'lived experiences' of people who have experienced a similar phenomenon or been exposed to a common set of conditions (Creswell 2007; Holstein and Gubrium 1998). In this study, the phenomenon was being an actively engaged Black male college achiever (as opposed to a troubled, low-achieving Nigger) at a PWI. A phenomenological account gets inside the experience of a person or group of people and describes what participants have experienced, how they have experienced it, and their sensemaking regarding various effects relative to the phenomenon (Moustakas 1994). The researcher and readers of a phenomenological study should be able to say, 'I understand better what it is like for someone to experience that' (Polkinghorne 1989, 46). Given that the master narrative on Black male undergraduates focuses almost exclusively on disengagement and deficits, understanding better what it is like to succeed in higher education was the aim of the National Black Male College Achievement Study.

TABLE 1

Participating institutions in the National Black Male College Achievement Study.

Institution type	College/University
Public research universities	University of Illinois
	Indiana University
	University of Michigan
	Michigan State University
	The Ohio State University
	Purdue University
Highly-selective private research universities	Brown University
	Columbia University
	Harvard University
	University of Pennsylvania
	Princeton University
	Stanford University
Private Historically Black colleges and Universities[a]	Clark Atlanta University
	Fisk University
	Hampton University
	Howard University
	Morehouse College
	Tuskegee University
Public Historically Black Universities[a]	Albany State University
	Cheyney University
	Florida A&M University
	Norfolk State University
	North Carolina Central University
	Tennessee State University
Liberal arts colleges	Amherst College
	Claremont-McKenna College
	DePauw University
	Haverford College
	Lafayette College
	Occidental College
	Pomona College
	Saint John's University (MN)
	Swarthmore College
	Vassar College
	Wabash College
	Williams College
Comprehensive state universities	Brooklyn College, City University of New York
	California State Polytechnic University, Pomona
	California State University, Long Beach
	Lock Haven University
	Towson University
	Valdosta State University

[a]The 12 Historically Black Colleges and Universities were not included in analyses for this chapter.

Sampling and Data Collection

Criterion sampling methods were used in this study (Patton 2002). Administrators such as presidents, provosts, and deans of students nominated and senior student leaders (e.g., student government association presidents) helped identify Black male undergraduates who had earned cumulative

GPAs above 3.0; established lengthy records of leadership and engagement in multiple student organizations; developed meaningful relationships with campus administrators and faculty outside the classroom; participated in enriching educational experiences (e.g., study abroad programs, internships, service learning, and summer research programs); and earned numerous merit-based scholarships and honors in recognition of their college achievements. These criteria were used because decades of research on undergraduate students clearly indicate that those who are actively engaged in educationally purposeful activities on college and university campuses are more satisfied with their experiences, have a higher likelihood of navigating institutional obstacles with success, and come to enjoy a more robust set of educational outcomes than do their peers who approach the college experience more passively (Bean 2005; Pascarella and Terenzini 2005). Assuming these claims are true, it is then conceivable that much can be learned from accessing the narratives of actively engaged Black male student leaders on predominantly White campuses, a population about whom very little has been written in education research.

Each Black male achiever participated in a two–three-hour face-to-face individual interview on his campus; when necessary, some follow-up interviews were conducted via telephone. A semi-structured interview technique was used, which simultaneously permitted data collection and participant reflection (Patton 2002). Although standard questions and interview protocol were used, discussions often became conversational, thus allowing participants to reflect on their racialized experiences. Some interview questions pertained directly to resistant responses to racism and stereotypes, as well as participants' reactions to the niggering of Black men in society and on their campuses.

Data Analysis

Several techniques prescribed by Moustakas (1994) were systematically employed to analyze data collected from interviews with all 219 participants. I first bracketed my thoughts and assumptions as I read each line of the participants' transcripts. Margins of the transcripts were marked with reflective comments regarding my initial reactions and interpretations. After bracketing, 166 recurring topics were identified and reduced to simple code words. Using the NVivo® qualitative data analysis software program, these code words were applied to sentences, concepts, and passages of text in each participant's transcript. This process resulted in the production of 166 code reports that captured insights into various aspects of the participants' shared experiences. An additional step included a written trajectory analysis statement (Harper 2007) for each of the 219 participants—how he navigated his way to higher education, what the critical moments were during his first-year adjustment period, strategies that proved most effective in responding to racist situations, and so on. These statements were comprehensive versions of what Moustakas calls textural summaries (*what* the participant experienced) and structural summaries (*how* he experienced the phenomenon), which are essential components of the phenomenological data analysis process.

For the purposes of this chapter, I consulted each participant's trajectory statement and highlighted relevant examples of educational experiences that counter the master narrative on Black male college students—anything concerning his academic achievement, the impetus for his leadership and engagement, his negotiation of support from peers and professors, and his productive handling of racist stereotypes was highlighted. In addition, I printed and read code reports on the following topics: Perspectives regarding the social condition of Black men, views on the status of Black male collegians, reactions to the representation of Black males in the media, the positive aspects of Black fraternity membership, the positive outcomes associated with intercollegiate sports participation (which only included perspectives from student-athletes in the study), and 11 separate reports pertaining to lived experiences with and responses crafted to specific types of stereotypes encountered on campus. The 16 code reports each included statements from participants across the 30 predominantly White colleges and universities represented in the study. These reports, along with highlighted text from the 143 trajectory statements, were used to craft a dialog between five composite characters in my critical race counternarrative.

Researcher's Positionality and Trustworthiness

I am a Black man. Like others described thus far in this chapter, I have been niggered in schools, professional work settings, and various social milieus. For example, in tenth grade, a White male educator told me the following: 'You ain't ever gonna be shit'. While that statement was hurtful (and obviously inaccurate), his low expectations for my success were consistent with those possessed by most other White teachers who saw in me limited educational potential throughout my K-12 schooling experience. Moreover, I feel niggered whenever someone labels me exceptional (meaning, I am not like 'the rest of *those* Niggers'), when White people are visibly shocked to hear I am a faculty member at an Ivy League university, and each time I synthesize the deficit-laden scholarship that has been published on Black men in the USA. Given these and countless other lived experiences, I make no claims of objectivity in composing the critical race counternarrative that is offered in the next section.

Similar to the five composite characters, I too am continually insulted by the one-sided depiction of Black men as Niggers in the media, in research, and in the minds of Whites who have been afforded only one view of us. But unlike the 143 participants upon whom the counternarrative is based, my postsecondary education occurred at a Historically Black University. Thus, many of the navigational approaches and resistant responses they describe were unnecessary in the context I encountered 16 years ago. Notwithstanding this important difference and my rigorous execution of systematic analytical procedures, I recognize myself as one who also rejects the ongoing niggering of Black men. As an attempt to establish a reasonable level of trustworthiness, I emailed the counternarrative to 25 participants in the study who attended different PWIs. Nineteen responded (13.3% of the sample) to confirm my accurate characterization of their lived experiences, viewpoints, responses to racism, and navigational strategies; their suggestions for revision (all of which were minor) are reflected in the version presented in the next section.

The Counternarrative

Following the release of Professor Harper's book, *Black male student success in college,* an important convening was held in Philadelphia for the 219 men upon whom the book is based. The achievers, now all college graduates, were brought together to consider ways they could pool their social and political capital to collectively advance Black communities and strengthen Black male representation at the highest levels of leadership and policymaking in various sectors. Of the 219 who were invited, 158 were able to attend—Tyson, Corey, Khaseem, Michael, and DeSean were among them. Each of these men graduated with honors from five different PWIs just a few months prior to the event. They had not met each other prior to being assigned to sit at the same table during the opening luncheon.

Michael was the first to comment on how empowering it was to be in the same room with so many accomplished young Black men. 'Yeah, this is something that could've happened on our campus when I was in college, but never did', Corey remarked. Khaseem asked, 'Why do you think that is?' While Corey was taking a moment to reflect, Khaseem suggested that it was because the university Corey attended failed to even recognize there were smart, talented Black male achievers on the campus. 'Exactly', Corey confirmed. 'No one ever asked me or other Black male student leaders what enabled us to get good grades or what compelled us to take on leadership positions. Instead, they were spending all their time trying to figure out why brothas' were struggling'. Khaseem followed up by asking, 'You know that is racist, right?' Tyson jumped in and agreed with Khaseem's analysis. He too felt a unidirectional placement of institutional emphasis on failure only exacerbated the racist culture of low expectation that had long existed for Black male students. Tyson asked if anyone had been consulted by an administrator or professor on campus who attempted to pursue insights into what enabled him to be successful at the institution—no one could recall such inquiries.

DeSean made an important statement that steered the lunchtime discussion in a different direction. 'I refused to let them nigger me', he boldly proclaimed. Intrigued by this remark, Khaseem invited DeSean to elaborate. He told his tablemates that he felt Black men were all viewed as Niggers on his campus, but he refused to be treated as such. Thus, he immediately became involved in the Student Government Association and the Residence Hall Council during his freshman year. It was through these student organizations that he deliberately went about presenting a more positive view of Black men. DeSean offered additional examples of how he used his memberships and leadership in mainstream clubs and organizations to foster relationships with White administrators who had grown accustomed to viewing Black men as disengaged. Tyson confessed to using a similar approach and added that he purposely sought to engage younger cohorts of Black male students (usually freshmen), in hopes that the collective Black male image on campus would improve. Just before he graduated, Tyson even started a magazine similar to *Remix,* which is published by the Harvard University Black Men's Forum. Like *Remix,* Tyson's publication presented Black men as thoughtful, politically engaged, and socially conscious.

Khaseem didn't like the approach that Tyson and DeSean described. He asked, 'Do you really think that by you holding leadership positions on campus, publishing a men's magazine, and getting a few other Black dudes involved, that White administrators began to see you differently?' Before they could respond, Khaseem started talking about his approach. 'I like what you said, DeSean, about not letting them nigger you. I had the same refusal'. But Khaseem went on the tell how he used the Black Student Union, the NAACP chapter on campus, and other activist groups to disrupt stereotypical views Whites held about Black men and other students of color at his institution. 'I was one of those dudes who called attention to racism whenever I saw, heard about, or experienced it firsthand on campus', he said. 'I wasn't interested in trying to show *them* some differentiated representation of Blackness. Instead, I sought to awaken their consciousness regarding their own racist miscategorization of me'.

'Right on my brotha', Corey exclaimed. He too immediately confronted racist stereotyping whenever it occurred. For example, he recalled an instance when a White faculty member was offensively shocked by a thoughtful contribution he made to a class discussion. Instead of leaving class with the psychological burden of wondering if the professor was so surprised because he didn't expect a Black man to have anything smart to contribute, Corey said he asked the faculty member right then and there why he was so visibly astonished. 'I used to do the same thing', Michael added:

> Whenever White students would say something that was even remotely racist or stereotypical, I would call 'em on it immediately. I refused to let them get away with it. I was also unwilling to be stuck with the emotional internalization of their stupidity. As a self-protective strategy, I confronted *it* without making it seem like I was confronting *them,* per se. I did this by asking questions like, 'why did you assume I would know where to buy weed? Or what made you think I was an athlete?' This was an effective approach that forced them to examine their own misconceptions about Black men; but more importantly, it protected me.

Michael went on to describe an event that Kappa Alpha Psi Fraternity hosted annually that illuminated racist stereotypes experienced by Black men on campus. In addition to naming the stereotypes they had encountered, Michael and his fraternity brothers also shared strategies with the audience (which was primarily Black) about how to productively respond to White people who attempted to caricature them in racist ways. 'Oh, you were in a fraternity?', Khaseem asked. 'You sound surprised', Michael replied. 'Unlike the headlines you read about Black fraternities, mine added considerable value to my undergraduate experience.' He then elaborated on the educational benefits conferred to him vis-à-vis meaningful community service endeavors in which his fraternity was engaged; the social support he received from his chapter brothers, which was often very necessary given the extreme Whiteness of the campus environment; how his fellow fraternity brothers were role models for him because they were among the most actively engaged student leaders at the institution; and the sense of peer-imposed accountability he felt to make good grades. Regarding the last point, Michael noted:

> To be in my chapter, you had to earn good grades. If you got bad grades, it brought the whole chapter's academic profile down. The brothers in leadership weren't having that, which actually forced many of us to strive for the highest grades. Consistent with our fraternity's mission, we were a group of Black male achievers.

As a member of Omega Psi Phi, Tyson shared similar reflections on the numerous benefits associated with fraternity membership that have been overshadowed by negative press in recent years. He indicated that he and his chapter brothers were intentional about ensuring campus administrators, faculty, and other students understood that 'Omega men weren't a bunch of rowdy, violent Niggas'. DeSean jumped in to offer a similar perspective, but situated it in a different context. He was a college student-athlete, a football player to be exact. Reportedly, he refused to be mislabeled as a Nigga who came to the university only to play ball. Thus, he committed himself firmly to academic achievement and making the most of college beyond athletics. Although the majority of his teammates (including Whites) were not engaged in clubs and organizations on campus, DeSean saw this as an important way to protect himself from many of the negative outcomes that are often reported about student-athletes in general and Black male football players in particular.

'I'm impressed that you guys were so committed to positive representations of us as Black men', Khaseem remarked:

> I am just so sick of the way we are portrayed in the media and how we're niggered on college campuses. It is so tragic that we are continually oppressed by a discourse of deficit. Like you guys, I challenge this in various ways because I know there are smart, talented Black men all across America—in fact, look around . . . there are over 150 here in this room right now.

Khaseem's perspective was shared by Corey who also conveyed his disdain for the lack of visibility given to Black men like him and others seated at the table:

> Wherever I go, I make them see me. Not as the 'magical Negro' who stands out from the rest of them. But instead, as the Black male achiever who others attempt to hide in plain sight. I made sure they knew I had a 3.7 GPA—not because I sought to brag about it, but I wanted to contradict the widely held belief that Niggers don't get good grades. I agreed to speak publicly whenever I was asked to do so because they needed to know that Barack Obama isn't the only Black man who can talk intelligently. I didn't do this alone. I empowered other Black men on campus to rise up—we collectively decided we would be Niggers no more.

Discussion and Implications

There are Black men like Tyson, Corey, Khaseem, Michael, and DeSean on every college and university campus. But as indicated in the counternarrative, their experiences are often overshadowed by the master narrative that amplifies Black male underachievement, disengagement, and attrition. Continuing to focus exclusively on the problems encountered by Black men and our deficits is racist—it only niggers us further. Each of the 143 participants represented through the composite characters agreed that solutions to some of the most vexing problems concerning educational achievement, fatherhood, and leadership in Black communities are possessed by those who achieve in schools and colleges, are responsible and loving fathers, and are impactful leaders in their respective domains. But yet, solutions are rarely sought from these Black men. Likewise, those who are members confirmed that Black fraternities continue to do much good for individuals and communities, despite the now dominant discourse regarding their negative attributes. Study participants who played on intercollegiate sports teams made clear there is no universal disregard for learning and bachelor's degree attainment among Black male student-athletes.

Data collected from Black male undergraduates at 30 PWIs in the national study offer these insights into the previously stated research questions: (1) There is an overlooked population of Black males on college campuses—they are academic achievers and student leaders who thrive inside and outside the classroom; (2) they often simultaneously experience both racism and success, which calls for a multifaceted navigational strategy that includes engagement in student organizations, meaningful interactions with supportive same-race peers, and the strategic publicity of their educational achievements to White persons who possess deficit views of Black men; and (3) these achievers resist niggering in its various forms through positive self-representation in campus leadership positions and the immediate confrontation of racist stereotyping whenever it occurs on campus.

Many perspectives offered in this study are consistent with Harper and Nichols's (2008) most salient finding that not all Black men are the same. Nevertheless, our experiences are often presented as the same in the literature—as troubled, oppressed, and hopeless. Scholars who undertake future research projects concerning Black men must deliberately counterbalance popular negative dispositions with achievement-oriented pursuits. In almost all the interviews, each participant indicated that no one had endeavored to understand how he was productively navigating the institution, what compelled him to be actively engaged and take advantage of institutional resources, which personal and institutional factors led to his placement on the Dean's List, and how he developed resistance to racist stereotypes that are often internalized in dispiriting ways by his same-race peers. These are important questions that are urgently worthy of further exploration. Educational responses to the problems that Cuyjet (2006) and others describe are likely to be half-baked, at best, if experiential insights are only derived from Black men who do not achieve. As long as educational disparities that disadvantage Black men (such as those reported by Harper 2006a) exist, studies that reveal their undercurrents and perpetuation remain necessary. But equally important and largely missing in social science and education research are published insights that also reveal enablers of equitable outcomes and Black male student achievement.

In the final chapter of his book, Kennedy (2002) discusses contemporary condemnation of those who use Nigger to insult Black persons. Regarding public exclamation of the N-word, he notes 'political prudence counsels strict avoidance' (136). Despite the fashionable disapproval of Nigger-as-insult in many contexts, acts of niggering remain commonplace in education and society, as reported by participants in this study and documented elsewhere in the social science literature. Necessary is greater castigation of educators who persistently stereotype and hold low expectations for Black male students in schools and colleges. Contributing to the cyclical reproduction of marginalization, disengagement, and outcomes inequities that disadvantage Black male collegians should bring about the same shame and consequences as being caught calling them Niggers. Meaning, those who *do* racist things to Black males and other students of color should be subjected to the same social scrutiny as those who publicly say racist things. Similarly, there should be something embarrassing about publishing only deficit-laden scholarship that depicts Black men as 'at risk', disengaged Niggers.

Acts of resistance participants described in the interviews would be unnecessary if White educators and administrators stopped stereotyping and stigmatizing Black men. That is, Black male undergraduates could focus more on achieving academically if they did not constantly encounter racist assumptions in college classrooms regarding their intellectual inferiority (Bonner and Bailey 2006; Fries-Britt 1997; Smith, Yosso, and Solórzano 2007). Likewise, the time and energy these students devote to recovering from what Smith, Allen, and Danley (2007) call 'racial battle fatigue' can be more profitably invested into outcomes productive educational activities offered outside the classroom. While I agree with Bell's (1992) perspectives on the permanence of racism in the USA, I still wish to see oppressive stereotypes that distract Black male collegians from their academics replaced with higher expectations for their achievement, less shock when they do well or say something thoughtful, and lower tolerance for racist caricaturing of them by their White classmates. This is unlikely to occur if White faculty and administrators possess only one view of Black men—the view that is repeatedly presented in the literature, media, and public discourse. It would be unnecessary to proclaim we are Niggers no more if we were not niggered in almost every social domain, academic publication, and in the minds of many Whites with whom we interact.

References

Ainsworth-Darnell, J.W., and D.B. Downey. 1998. Assessing the oppositional culture explanation for racial/ethnic differences in school performance. *American Sociological Review* 63, no. 4: 536–53.

Anderson, A. 2008. *Against the wall: Poor, young, Black, and male*. Philadelphia, PA: Penn Press.

Beamon, K.K. 2008. Used goods: Former African American college student-athlete's perception of exploitation by Division I universities. *Journal of Negro Education* 77, no. 4: 352–64.

Bean, J.P. 2005. Nine themes of college student retention. In *College student retention: Formula for student success*, ed. A. Seidman, 215–44. Westport, CT: Praeger.

Bell, D. 1987. *And we are not saved: The elusive quest for racial justice.* New York: Basic Books.

Bell, D. 1992. *Faces at the bottom of the well: The permanence of racism.* New York: Basic Books.

Berger, J.B., and J.F. Milem. 1999. The role of student involvement and perceptions of integration in a causal model of student persistence. *Research in Higher Education* 40, no. 6: 641–64.

Bonner II, F.A., and K.W. Bailey. 2006. Enhancing the academic climate for African American men. In *African American men in college,* ed. M.J. Cuyjet, 24–46. San Francisco, CA: Jossey-Bass.

Creswell, J.W. 2007. *Qualitative inquiry and research design: Choosing among five approaches.* 2nd ed. Thousand Oaks, CA: Sage.

Cuyjet, M.J. 1997. African American men on college campuses: Their needs and their perceptions. In *Helping African American men succeed in college,* ed. M.J. Cuyjet (New Directions for Student Services, no. 80, 5–16). San Francisco: Jossey-Bass.

Cuyjet, M.J. 2006. African American college men: Twenty-first century issues and concerns. In *African American men in college,* ed. M.J. Cuyjet, 3–23. San Francisco: Jossey-Bass.

Davis, J.E. 2003. Early schooling and academic achievement of African American males. *Urban Education* 38, no. 5: 515–37.

Davis, J.E., and W.J. Jordan. 1994. The effects of school context, structure, and experience on African American males in middle and high school. *Journal of Negro Education* 63: 570–87.

deCoy, R.H. 1967. *The Nigger bible.* Los Angeles, CA: Holloway House.

Donnor, J.K. 2005. Towards an interest-convergence in the education of African American football student-athletes in major college sports. *Race, Ethnicity and Education* 8, no. 1: 45–67.

Fries-Britt, S.L. 1997. Identifying and supporting gifted African American men. In *Helping African American men succeed in college,* ed. M.J. Cuyjet (New Directions for Student Services, no. 80, 65–78). San Francisco: Jossey-Bass.

Fries-Britt, S.L., and B. Turner. 2001. Facing stereotypes: A case study of Black students on a White campus. *Journal of College Student Development* 42, no. 5: 420–9.

Gadsden, V.L., and R.R. Smith. 1994. African American males and fatherhood: Issues in research and practice. *Journal of Negro Education* 63, no. 4: 634–48.

Gordon, E.T., E.W. Gordon, and J.G.G. Nembhard. 1994. Social science literature concerning African American men. *Journal of Negro Education* 63, no. 4: 508–31.

Harper, S.R. 2006a. *Black male students at public universities in the U.S.: Status, trends and implications for policy and practice.* Washington, DC: Joint Center for Political and Economic Studies.

Harper, S.R. 2006b. Peer support for African American male college achievement: Beyond internalized racism and the burden of 'acting White'. *Journal of Men's Studies* 14, no. 3: 337–58.

Harper, S.R. 2007. Using qualitative methods to access student trajectories and college impact. In *Using qualitative methods in institutional assessment,* ed. S.R. Harper and S.D. Museus (New Directions for Institutional Research, no. 136, 55–68). San Francisco: Jossey-Bass.

Harper, S.R., and A.H. Nichols. 2008. Are they not all the same? Racial heterogeneity among Black male undergraduates. *Journal of College Student Development* 49, no. 3: 199–214.

Hinderlie, H.H., and M. Kenny. 2002. Attachment, social support, and college adjustment among Black students at predominantly White universities. *Journal of College Student Development* 43, no. 3: 327–40.

Holstein, J.A., and J.F. Gubrium. 1998. Phenomenology, ethnomethodology, and interpretive practice. In *Strategies of qualitative inquiry,* ed. N.K. Denzin and Y.S. Lincoln, 137–57. Thousand Oaks, CA: Sage.

Jackson, J.F.L., and J.L. Moore III. 2008. The African American male crisis in education: A popular media infatuation or needed public policy response? *American Behavioral Scientist* 51, no. 7: 847–53.

Jenkins, T.S. 2006. Mr. Nigger: The challenges of educating Black males within American society. *Journal of Black Studies* 37, no. 1: 127–55.

Jones, R.L. 2004. *Black haze: Violence, sacrifice, and manhood in Black Greek-letter fraternities.* Albany, NY: State University of New York Press.

Kennedy, R. 2002. *Nigger: The strange career of a troublesome word.* New York: Vintage.

Mandara, J. 2006. The impact of family functioning on African American males' academic achievement: A review and clarification of the empirical literature. *Teachers College Record* 108, no. 2: 206–23.

Moustakas, C. 1994. *Phenomenological research methods.* Thousand Oaks, CA: Sage.

Noguera, P.A. 2003. The trouble with Black boys: The role and influence of environmental and cultural factors on the academic performance of African American males. *Urban Education* 38: 431–59.

Pascarella, E.T., and P.T. Terenzini. 2005. *How college affects students, Volume 2: A third decade of research.* San Francisco: Jossey-Bass.

Patton, M.Q. 2002. *Qualitative research methods.* 3rd ed. Thousand Oaks, CA: Sage.

Polkinghorne, D.E. 1989. Phenomenological research methods. In *Existential-phenomenological perspectives in psychology,* ed. R.S. Valle and S. Hailing, 41–60. New York: Plenum.

Roach, R. 2001. Where are the Black men on campus? *Black Issues in Higher Education* 18, no. 6: 18–24.

Schmidt, P. 2008, October 10. Colleges seek keys to success of Black men in classroom. *Chronicle of Higher Education* 55, no. 7: A1, A3.

Smedley, B.D., H.F. Myers, and S.P. Harrell. 1993. Minority-status stresses and the college adjustment of ethnic minority freshmen. *Journal of Higher Education* 64, no. 4: 434–52.

Smith, W.A., W.R. Allen, and L.L. Danley. 2007. Assume the position . . . you fit the description: Psychosocial experiences and racial battle fatigue among African American male college students. *American Behavioral Scientist* 51, no. 4: 551–78.

Smith, W.A., T.J. Yosso, and D.G. Solórzano. 2007. Racial primes and black misandry on historically white campuses: Toward critical race accountability in educational administration. *Educational Administration Quarterly* 43, no. 5: 559–85.

Solórzano, D.G., M. Ceja, and T.J. Yosso. 2000. Critical race theory, racial microaggressions, and campus racial climate: The experiences of African American college students. *Journal of Negro Education* 69, no. 1: 60–73.

Solórzano, D.G., and T.J. Yosso. 2002. Critical race methodology: Counter-storytelling as an analytical framework for education research. *Qualitative Inquiry* 8, no. 1: 23–44.

Spencer, M.B., E. Noll, J. Stolzfus, and V. Harpalani. 2001. Identity and school adjustment: Revisiting the 'acting White' assumption. *Educational Psychologist* 36, no. 1: 21–30.

Strayhorn, T.L. 2008a. The role of supportive relationships in facilitating African American males' success in college. *NASPA Journal* 45, no. 1: 26–48.

Strayhorn, T.L. 2008b. Fittin' in: Do diverse interactions with peers affect sense of belonging for Black men at predominantly white institutions? *NASPA Journal* 45, no. 4: 501–27.

Toldson, I.A. 2008. *Breaking barriers: Plotting the path to academic success for school-age African-American males.* Washington, DC: Congressional Black Caucus Foundation.

White, J.L., and J.H. Cones III. 1999. *Black man emerging: Facing the past and seizing a future in America.* New York: Routledge.

Woodson, C.G. 1933. *The mis-education of the Negro.* Washington, DC: Associated Publishers.

CHAPTER 50
CRITICAL RACE THEORY AND RESEARCH ON ASIAN AMERICANS AND PACIFIC ISLANDERS IN HIGHER EDUCATION

ROBERT T. TERANISHI, LAURIE B. BEHRINGER,
EMILY A. GREY, AND TARA L. PARKER

In 2008, the National Commission on Asian American and Pacific Islander Research in Education (CARE) published a report on Asian American and Pacific Islander (AAPI) participation in higher education, in collaboration with the College Board and a team of researchers at New York University. Immediately following the publication's release, the report received widespread news coverage, to which a number of people responded. Those responses were overwhelmingly positive and supportive of the efforts of our project. There were inquiries, however, that we often pondered. We received an e-mail, for instance, that pointed us to a Web blog titled, "Why Can't You Be Content to Be the Model Minority?" This question is an appropriate one to consider: Is there something bad about a positive stereotype? We believe this question exemplifies a fundamental problem caused by the way AAPIs have been positioned within America's equity agenda, particularly as it pertains to higher education.

The treatment of AAPIs has been driven by assumptions and stereotypes that characterize the population as the model minority: a group with "stellar educational achievement" who overcame all barriers as a minority group to take over some of America's most selective colleges and universities. This consistent message about the AAPI population exists in the academic and policy arenas and the mainstream media. Consider how the *New York Times* characterized the population in a 1997 article declaring that Asian Americans were exhibiting exceptional academic achievement and that others ought to learn from these excellent students (Kristof, 2006).

The purpose of the CARE Project is to interrogate the evidence of this claim theoretically and empirically. While the project has made progress toward a deeper understanding of AAPIs and their educational needs, there continues to be a great deal of work that still needs to be done, particularly as it relates to educational policy. One fundamental area that needs to be addressed toward including AAPIs in higher education policy is that of transcending dominant conceptual framings, which have historically served as the foundation for how we approach educational problems and solutions. Existing paradigms about race, equity, and higher education policy may very well underlie the lack of understanding and responding to the needs and experiences of AAPIs in higher education.

In this chapter, we offer critical race theory (CRT) as an alternative theoretical perspective that permits the examination and transcendence of conceptual blockages, while simultaneously offering alternative perspectives on higher education policy and practice and the AAPI student population. We do so through a reflection of some findings from our project, our experiences as current and past members of the CARE research team at New York University, and our broader interests as scholars who seek to challenge racial inequality in higher education. In this chapter, we focus on issues related to college access and admissions, the AAPI college student experience, and AAPI administrators and higher education leadership. We examine each of these issues through the lens of CRT, which we assert is an effective tool for critically examining the position of AAPIs in higher education policy and practice.

Critical Race Theory

Critical race theory has been applied to the study of racial stratification in higher education to challenge dominant paradigms and place the educational experiences of students of color in broader social, institutional, legal, and historical contexts (Delgado, 1995). Solórzano (1998) explains that "critical race theory in education challenges the traditional claims of the educational system and its institutions to objectivity, meritocracy, color and gender blindness, race and gender neutrality, and equal opportunity" (p. 122). CRT has been particularly useful for the critique of deficit thinking—the framing of racial inequities as a result of individual deficiencies—by providing alternative pedagogies and methodologies through which scholars and students can "unlearn" stereotypical thinking about race (Smith-Maddox and Solórzano, 2002). This is extremely important for the study of AAPIs, given the extent to which stereotypes and assumptions may have driven the treatment of this population. Thus, an understanding of the educational experiences of AAPIs can be informed by CRT by acknowledging the unique racialized status of AAPIs, as well as their social, political, and structural positions in society.

Conceptually, CRT in education challenges the ways in which the theoretical framing of race in education policy and practice has implications for the AAPI population. CRT challenges the notion that normative framing is an effective lens through which to examine educational equity issues. Essentially, normative framing is typically invoked to identify how different racial groups are unevenly distributed across a particular outcome (for example, participation or graduation). Alternatively, CRT perspectives focus on the needs of marginalized populations, which are often overlooked, as opposed to the agenda served by normative frameworks. Therefore, CRT can be an effective lens for examining and challenging normative paradigms, which define mainstream policy discourse and determine appropriate concerns for education research.

For AAPIs, normative frameworks position the experiences, outcomes, and representation of AAPIs relative to blacks and whites, which often results in the conclusion that problems related to race in American society are dichotomous, with blacks and Latinos at one end of the racial spectrum and AAPIs and whites on the other (Chang, Witt, Jones, and Hakuta, 2003). The pervasiveness of this black-white paradigm has contributed to a precarious positioning of the AAPI educational experience (Green and Kim, 2005).

Critical Race Theory in Higher Education Research

Critical race theory can inform the assessment of policies and programs aimed at addressing racial inequities. Using a CRT lens can yield outcomes that better address the true needs of the beneficiaries of such policies and programs within higher education (for example, faculty and students). Specifically, Gillborn (2005) emphasizes CRT's utility in understanding the drivers of the policy, the beneficiaries as a result of the policy, and the short-and long-term effects of the policy.

We use CRT in this chapter to make suggestions for future policies and programs that might better address the AAPI population. We focus mainly on three tenets of CRT as particularly effective conceptual tools for understanding how AAPIs are positioned within and affected by research, policies, and practices in higher education: (1) taking account of the voices of AAPI students, which often go unheard and remain in the margins in America's equity agenda; (2) the issue of interest convergence, which posits that equality is pursued when the interests of the majority are furthered; and (3) an emphasis on social justice as a central theme in the purpose of higher education.

Voices of the Students

Critical race theory encourages the storytelling of people of color to better understand their individual experiences, which contribute to understanding a more holistic reality. Qualitative scholars use CRT to highlight individual experiences and the voices through which these experiences are told by providing thick descriptions of students' stories related to campus environments and college experiences (Patton, 2006; Solórzano, Ceja, and Yosso, 2000). Solórzano, Ceja, and Yosso (2000), for example, used CRT to understand African American experiences with racial microaggressions and campus racial climates, while Patton (2006) used it to understand students' perceptions of black culture centers on campus.

Interest Convergence

Another element of CRT, interest convergence, suggests that equality and equity will be pursued when the interests of people of color converge with the interests of whites. For example, Bell (1980) considered the U.S. Supreme Court's decision in *Brown v. Board of Education* through an interest convergence framework. Specifically, Bell argued that the much celebrated *Brown* decision was a result of the government's desire to improve its international image around issues of race. Interest convergence has been used to analyze educational issues and is useful for examining the underlying presumptions and reasoning behind policies and decision making. As a result, the implicit beneficial or harmful effects of policies and decision-making processes on disparate populations, which often remain unquestioned and unchallenged, are revealed.

Social Justice

Higher education scholars who use CRT as a framework through which to analyze students' experiences and postsecondary education policies illuminate a social justice component of CRT (Smith, Yosso, and Solórzano, 2007). Inherent in their approaches is the call to identify elements of the educational system in the United States that are perceived to be oppressive to students and families of color (Stovall, 2006). To facilitate processes of policy, program, practice development, or elimination on college campuses, shareholders might be well served by engaging in conversations that challenge dominant institutional discourses and the charged assumptions that are foundational to these discourses (Iverson, 2007).

College Access and Admissions

Asian American and Pacific Islander students, within higher education access and admissions debates, are either misrepresented or used by the opposing factions within the debate to further their own interests of maintaining or dismantling affirmative action. In both cases, AAPIs' authentic stories and voices have largely been silenced; that is, the dialogues about Asian Americans and Pacific Islanders and the policies that either ignore the community or position it in a convenient fashion to align with whites in some instances, or all people of color in others, are held and created without precise and sufficient information about AAPIs or consideration of their perspectives. We see evidence of this in three important higher education admissions issues: access and choice, affirmative action, and admissions policies.

College Access and Choice

Scholars note that the persistent attention received by AAPI students enrolled in or applying to elite four-year institutions has obscured the reality that a significant proportion of Asian American and Pacific Islander college students attend two-year colleges (Lew, Chang, and Wang, 2005). Moreover, recent literature that examines the breadth of research tackling issues affecting community college students suggests that few peer-reviewed journal articles of recent years specifically focus on AAPIs at two-year schools (Liu, 2007).

Also obscured, because of assumptions related to the model minority myth, are the academic, economic, linguistic, and other challenges that many AAPI community college students face. The argument that AAPI students comprise too small a number for quantitative research to be statistically significant is an important one, particularly as many have called for the need to disaggregate data collected on the AAPI student population in order to examine ethnicity-level data (see, for example, Museus, 2009). More important is that researchers find alternative methods to investigate AAPI students' realities at moderately, less, and nonselective colleges and universities. Using CRT to guide qualitative studies at the campus level is an effective and valuable way to generate much-needed information about AAPI students. Employing CRT to examine classroom issues, such as re-mediation courses and English language learning, and pipeline issues, like persistence and transfer, will contribute to our understanding of AAPI realities beyond black-white paradigms.

Affirmative Action

Positioning AAPI students in the affirmative action debate has been useful for those on both sides of the issue. Some assert that AAPI students "lose seats" to blacks and Latinos when affirmative action policies are in effect and, thus, affirmative action is unfair, while others argue that AAPIs are likely to "take over" elite universities without the presence of affirmative action policies, thus reducing op-portunities for whites. In either case, Asian American and Pacific Islander students have been used to argue for pro- and anti-affirmative action campaigns in ways that researchers claim are incorrect (Wu and Kidder, 2006). In reality, when affirmative action policies have been eliminated in certain states, as they have been in California, AAPI students have comprised smaller numbers on elite college campuses. Inkelas (2003a, 2003b) has studied in depth the ways in which AAPI students express their views on affirmative action. Although CRT is not an explicitly stated framework in these studies, it is easy to see how privileging students' voices can be used to better understand policies that affect AAPIs. Similarly, the value of a CRT lens and the illumination of students' voices is evident in its power to allow a more expansive view of the issue than narrower frameworks, such as the black-white paradigm. Finally, understanding the interest convergence aspect of affirmative action debates can inform broader and more accurate policy analysis.

Admissions Policies

The term *negative action* is used to refer to a policy, rarely articulated by admissions offices, that un-fairly influences AAPI college applicants. Scholars use the term to classify practices, such as admitting legacy students and instituting quotas for racial groups that give less weight to academic merit and leave fewer seats for AAPIs. Kang (1996) asserts that an institution employs negative action practices when an AAPI student who is denied admission would have, with the same application, been offered admission if he or she were white; simply stated, AAPIs are held to higher admissions standards than their white peers. The case of Jian Li, an Asian American applicant to Princeton University who was denied admission and sued the school in 2006 claiming discriminatory admissions practices, made na-tional headlines. Some, however, suggest that Li's case is an example of negative action in that his im-pressive exam scores, grade point average, and extracurricular activities in high school could not overcome a ceiling that the school may have placed on AAPI acceptances (Liu, 2008).

Other policies that must be examined at the college or university level are those that involve in-stitutional reporting on students, faculty, and staff. Researchers have suggested that two practices be implemented to provide accurate and useful data collection: disaggregating AAPI data by ethnic-ity and ensuring that AAPI data are not aggregated with Asian foreign national data (National Commission on Asian American and Pacific Islander Research in Education, 2008). Aggregating all AAPIs into one racial category prevents scholars and practitioners from examining and serving the needs of many Asian Americans and Pacific Islanders who are neglected in the shadows of persist-ent stereotypes about the academic abilities and financial positions of AAPIs. Equally important is the need to count citizens and residents separately from international students and employees; ded-icated services should be directed to both groups, but it is vital that resources are appropriately ap-plied in a knowledgeable manner.

AAPI College Students' Experiences

Examining the experiences of AAPI college students through the lens of critical race theory sug-gests several major gaps in policy and practice within higher education. First, student develop-ment theories often ignore the role of race in the student experience. Second, the impact of the campus racial climates on AAPIs is often overlooked, and research on racial climates focuses pri-marily on the experiences of whites and blacks (Ancis, Sedlacek, and Mohr, 2000; Loo and Rolison,

1986). Finally, although AAPIs report lower levels of student satisfaction and well-being, complete research on how and why it occurs is lacking. The lack of adequate research on the experiences of AAPIs results in the development of policies and practices that do not fully reflect the needs of the AAPI population.

Student Development Theories

Many fundamental student development theories that today's practitioners use overlook potential differences in student development processes by race and ethnicity. Patton, McEwen, Rendón, and Howard-Hamilton (2007) argue that these theories are "raceless" (p. 41) because they do not incorporate race or the impact of race on student identity and experiences, and they may even contain some inherent levels of racism. Instead, such theories assume that the experiences and development of students are similar, regardless of their race or ethnicity. However, race can play a substantial role in the student experience, especially for AAPIs and other minority groups. Because the voices of minority students such as AAPIs are not reflected in them (Kodama, McEwen, Liang, and Lee, 2002), these theories may not be useful for developing policies and programs for AAPIs.

Kodama, McEwen, Liang, and Lee (2002) suggest that alternative student development theories, based on the specific experiences and development of AAPI students themselves, should be used to understand those students' experiences. They propose a revised model of psychosocial development that incorporates AAPI racial identity and external influences and suggest that AAPI students will reach higher levels of development if they understand themselves in relation to their families, their communities, and the larger society. Most contemporary models lack direct attention to these types of relationships. Kodama, McEwen, Liang, and Lee (2002) suggest that taking into account the experiences of AAPIs in relation to their families and cultures will help them "draw on their strengths and values, rather than viewing them as deficient in relation to dominant society ideals" (p. 56).

Campus Racial Climate

Campus racial climates can also shape students' experiences, perceptions, attitudes, and expectations (Hurtado, Milem, Clayton-Pedersen, and Allen, 1999), and an understanding of campus racial climates incorporates theories of race and racism in order to better understand these students' experiences. Unfortunately, the impact of racial climates on AAPIs is often ignored. Most of today's research focuses solely on the experiences of white and black students, although there has been a recent surge in the study of the experiences of Latinos (for example, Ancis, Sedlacek, and Mohr, 2000; Loo and Rolison, 1986). Osajima (1995) suggests that AAPIs are overlooked in the research on the impact of racial climate on students' experiences because of a binary black-white conceptualization of race. When AAPIs are discussed in the literature, it is often only in comparison to other groups rather than as a unique group themselves (Osajima, 1995). Critical race theory, however, emphasizes the importance of better understanding the AAPI student experience itself in the context of campus racial climates.

Psychological Well-Being and Help-Seeking

The minimal research that has been done on racial climate and its impact on AAPI students suggests that AAPIs perceive a negative campus climate and, as a result, report lower levels of satisfaction and greater degrees of personal and emotional problems. Cress and Ikeda (2003), for example, studied the impact of perceptions of negative campus climate on students' levels of depression. They found that AAPI students are both more likely to perceive a negative campus racial climate and to experience feelings of depression. They concluded that these findings may be a result of a lack of AAPI presence in the academic environment, a lack of faculty role models, or cultural conflicts in choice of major. Using the lens of critical race theory, it may be that AAPI students may be experiencing lower levels of psychological well-being as a result of the racism in the climate.

Related to the reported lower levels of satisfaction and well-being of AAPI students, those students are also much less likely than other racial groups to seek psychological help. Although they are more likely than Caucasians to seek help for academic and career guidance, they are less likely to seek help for emotional and interpersonal problems (Tracey, Leong, and Glidden, 1986). Shea and Yeh (2008) suggest that this may be a result of both institutional barriers, such as a lack of culturally competent personnel, and sociocultural barriers, such as a high level of stigma attached to seeking help within the AAPI community. They assert that an inverse relationship exists between help-seeking attitudes of AAPIs and adherence to Asian values and attitudes. Shea and Yeh found that AAPI students with higher levels of a perceived stigma attached to seeking psychological help reported more negative help-seeking attitudes. This research further emphasizes the need for student development theories that reflect the unique experiences of AAPIs. If AAPI students are reporting poorer levels of mental health and not seeking the help they need, then postsecondary educators may not be effectively meeting the developmental needs of this AAPI student population.

AAPI Leadership in Higher Education

AAPI representation in positions of leadership in higher education can also be effectively and critically examined through a CRT lens. Examinations of the representation of racial groups in higher education administration and leadership using normative perspectives completely disregard AAPIs. In fact, in most studies focused on issues related to the racial representation of college administrators and presidents, AAPIs are simply left out of the reporting of data. This practice is common despite the fact that the representation of AAPI administrators and institutional leaders is dismal by any measure. We present some data, based on our analysis of recent data on AAPI administrators and presidents, as a case in point.

AAPI Representation among College Administrators

According to a survey of higher education conducted in 2005, there were only 5,493 AAPI professional executive, administrative, and managerial staff in higher education (National Center for Education Statistics, 2008). That number was equal to 2.8 percent of all administrators. The representation of AAPIs in public two-year institutions was even lower, at 2.3 percent. The poor representation of AAPIs in higher education administration was particularly pronounced among college presidents. In 2003, AAPIs composed only 1 percent of college presidents; they were slightly more represented among presidents of four-year institutions (1.2 percent) than two-year colleges (0.8 percent). Although the representation of AAPIs as a proportion of all college presidents is quite glaring, it is also important to consider the actual numbers. Throughout all of higher education, there were only thirty-three AAPI college presidents in 2003. In the community college sector, that number was only nine.

The poor representation among AAPI presidents results in a threefold problem that warrants closer attention. First, consider the many colleges and universities with high concentrations of AAPI students in states like California, Hawaii, and New York. In these institutions, there is a lack of AAPIs among institutional leaders, which diminishes the likelihood that AAPI students see themselves as institutional leaders. Second, the AAPI student population has been growing over the past decade in the South and Midwest, and they are a growing presence in the community college sector. In these institutions, the implications of a lack of AAPI representation among leadership present problems for understanding and responding to these rapidly changing demographic trends. Finally, a lack of AAPI leadership often means lack of attention to the challenges facing the AAPI student population, especially among networks of high-level administrators who discuss institutional priorities and how to respond to emerging trends in the broader higher education community.

The Compelling Interest for More AAPI Leadership

AAPI leadership in higher education is essential for the leadership, insights, and skills to globalize collegiate studies and help in understanding diversity and nuance in the vast regions of Asia and the Pacific. We must begin with the talent that can be found among the few AAPI students, faculty, and administrators who are able and willing to take up such leadership positions. This is particularly important because representation problems are systemic, with reports suggesting that very few AAPI graduate students are working toward advanced degrees that might lead to positions in higher education administration. As such, improving the educational and career pipelines for AAPIs into leadership positions in higher education requires a greater awareness of the issues that affect AAPI students, which can be a catalyst for bringing more AAPI educators and policymakers into such positions of leadership (Committee of 100, 2005; Ong, 2008).

The inclusion of AAPI leaders in higher education is an essential ingredient for responding to broader problems that shape the participation, experiences, and outcomes of AAPI students. This is because the presence of AAPI leaders in higher education is a key factor for dispelling and replacing the myths about AAPI students so that our education system and broader society can fully develop and engage these students. These leaders play a central role in the development of a renewed public vision for implementing policies and practices that are based on facts about AAPI students. Greater representation of AAPIs among higher education leaders will lead to the changes needed to better serve AAPI students and the educational system as a whole.

Conclusion

Normative frameworks unfairly, and often incorrectly, position AAPI students as the least in need of academic, financial, social, or psychological support. Whether AAPIs are included in research and discourse on college admissions, affirmative action, campus climate, or college health and wellness services is often a matter of how AAPIs can be positioned to support the interests of other groups. We assert that, as an alternative to the existing dominant paradigms, using the lens of CRT to examine several key issues within higher education policy and practice for the AAPI student population yields important conclusions. The incorporation of the CRT perspective within higher education research is vital for the success of today's policies and practices, and particularly for better understanding how AAPIs are positioned within higher education, as well as developing a better understanding of AAPIs within higher education. Further research should make use of these conclusions and incorporate critical race theory in much-needed scholarship examining the voices and experiences of AAPIs and the policies and practices that serve, or fail to serve, them.

References

Ancis, J., Sedlacek, W., and Mohr, J. "Student Perceptions of the Campus Cultural Climate by Race." *Journal of Counseling and Development,* 2000, *78,* 180–185.

Bell, D. "Brown v. Board of Education and the Interest-Convergence Dilemma." *Harvard Law Review,* 1980, *93*(3), 518–533.

Chang, M., Witt, D., Jones, J., and Hakuta, K. *Compelling Interest: Examining the Evidence on Racial Dynamics in Colleges and Universities.* Stanford, Calif.: Stanford University Press, 2003.

Committee of 100. *The Committee of 100s Asian Pacific Americans in Higher Education Report Card.* New York: Committee of 100, 2005.

Cress, C., and Ikeda, E. "Distress Under Duress: The Relationship Between Campus Climate and Depression in Asian Pacific American College Students." *NASPA Journal,* 2003, *40,* 74–97.

Delgado, R. *Critical Race Theory: The Cutting Edge.* Philadelphia: Temple University Press, 1995.

Gillborn, D. "Education Policy as an Act of White Supremacy: Whiteness, Critical Race Theory and Education Reform." *Journal of Education Policy,* 2005, *20*(4), 485–505.

Green, D., and Kim, E. "Experiences of Korean Female Doctoral Students in Academe: Raising Voice Against Gender and Racial Stereotypes." *Journal of College Student Development,* 2005, *46*(5), 487–500.

Hurtado, S., Milem, J., Clayton-Pedersen, A., and Allen, W. *Enacting Diverse Learning Environments: Improving the Climate for Racial/Ethnic Diversity in Higher Education.* ASHE-ERIC Higher Education Report (Vol. 26). Washington, D.C.: George Washington University, Graduate School of Education and Human Development, 1999.

Inkelas, K. "Caught in the Middle: Understanding Asian Pacific American Perspectives on Affirmative Action Through Blumer's Group Position Theory." *Journal of College Student Development,* 2003a, *44*(5), 625–643.

Inkelas, K. "Diversity's Missing Minority: Asian Pacific American Undergraduates' Attitudes toward Affirmative Action." *Journal of Higher Education,* 2003b, *74*(6), 601–639.

Iverson, S. "Camouflaging Power and Privilege: A Critical Race Analysis of University Diversity Policies." *Educational Administration Quarterly,* 2007, *43*(5), 586–611.

Kang, J. "Negative Action Against Asian Americans: The Internal Instability of Dworkin's Defense of Affirmative Action." *Harvard Civil Rights Civil Liberties Law Review,* 1996, *31*(1), 1–47.

Kodama, C., McEwen, M., Liang, C., and Lee, S. "An Asian American Perspective on Psychosocial Development Theory." In M. K. McEwen and others (eds.), *Working with Asian American College Students.* New Directions for Student Services, no. 97. San Francisco: Jossey-Bass, 2002.

Kristof, N. "The Model Students." *New York Times,* May 14, 2006. Retrieved April 3, 2009, from http://select.nytimes.com/2006/05/14/opinion/14kristof.html.

Lew, J., Chang, J., and Wang, W. "UCLA Community College Review: The Overlooked Minority: Asian Pacific American Students at Community Colleges." *Community College Review,* 2005, *33*(2), 64–84.

Liu, A. "UCLA Community College Biography: Asian Americans in Community Colleges." *Community College Journal of Research and Practice,* 2007, *31*(7), 607–614.

Liu, A. "Affirmative Action and Negative Action: How Jian Li's Case Can Benefit Asian Americans." *Michigan Journal of Race and Law,* 2008, *13*(2), 391–431.

Loo, C., and Rolison, G. "Alienation of Ethnic Minority Students at a Predominantly White University." *Journal of Higher Education,* 1986, *57*(1), 58–77.

Museus, S. D. "A Critical Analysis of the Exclusion of Asian American from Higher Education Research and Discourse." In L. Zhan (ed.), *Asian American Voices: Engaging, Empowering, Enabling* (pp. 59–76). New York: NLN Press, 2009.

National Center for Education Statistics. "Digest of Education Statistics" (NCES 2008-022). Washington, DC: U.S. Department of Education, 2008.

National Commission on Asian American and Pacific Islander Research in Education. *Asian Americans and Pacific Islanders: Facts, Not Fiction: Setting the Record Straight.* New York: College Board, 2008.

Ong, P. *Trajectory of Civic and Political Engagement: A Public Policy Report.* Los Angeles: LEAP Asian Pacific American Public Policy Institute, 2008.

Osajima, K. "Racial Politics and the Invisibility of Asian Americans in Higher Education." *Educational Foundations,* 1995, *9*(1), 35–53.

Patton, L. "The Voice of Reason: A Qualitative Examination of Black Student Perceptions of Black Culture Centers." *Journal of College Student Development,* 2006, *47*(6), 628–646.

Patton, L., McEwen, M., Rendón, L., and Howard-Hamilton, M. "Critical Race Perspectives on Theory in Student Affairs." In S. Harper and L. Patton (eds.), *The Realities of Race on Campus.* New Directions for Student Services, no. 120. San Francisco: Jossey-Bass, 2007.

Shea, M., and Yeh, C. "Asian American Students' Cultural Values, Stigma, and Relational Self-Construal: Correlates of Attitudes Toward Professional Help Seeking." *Journal of Mental Health Counseling,* 2008, *30*(2), 157–172.

Smith, W., Yosso, T., and Solórzano, D. "Racial Primes and Black Misandry on Historically White Campuses: Toward Critical Race Accountability in Educational Administration." *Educational Administration Quarterly,* 2007, *43*(5), 559–585.

Smith-Maddox, R., and Solórzano, D. "Using Critical Race Theory, Paulo Freire's Problem-Posing Method, and Case Study Research to Confront Race and Racism in Education." *Qualitative Inquiry,* 2002, *8*(1), 66–84.

Solórzano, D. "Critical Race Theory, Race and Gender Microaggressions, and the Experience of Chicana and Chicano Scholars." *International Journal of Qualitative Studies in Education,* 1998, *11*(1), 121–136.

Solórzano, D., Ceja, M., and Yosso, T. "Critical Race Theory, Racial Microaggressions, and Campus Racial Climate: The Experiences of African American College Students." *Journal of Negro Education,* 2000, *69*(1/2), 60–73.

Stovall, D. "Forging Community in Race and Class: Critical Race Theory and the Quest for Social Justice in Education." *Race, Ethnicity and Education,* 2006, *9*(3), 243–259.

Tracey, T., Leong, F., and Glidden, C. "Help Seeking and Problem Solving Perception Among Asian-Americans." *Journal of Counseling Psychology,* 1986, *33,* 331–336.

Wu, F., and Kidder, W. "Asian Americans Aren't White Folks' 'Racial Mascots.'" *Diverse Issues in Higher Education,* 2006, *23*(17), 48.

CHAPTER 51
TOWARD A TRIBAL CRITICAL RACE THEORY IN EDUCATION

BRYAN MCKINLEY JONES BRAYBOY

In this chapter, I outline the central tenets of an emerging theory that I call Tribal Critical Race Theory (TribalCrit) to more completely address the issues of Indigenous Peoples in the United States. Tribal-Crit has it roots in Critical Race Theory, Anthropology, Political/Legal Theory, Political Science, American Indian Literatures, Education, and American Indian Studies. This theoretical framework provides a way to address the complicated relationship between American Indians and the United States federal government and begin to make sense of American Indians' liminality as both racial and legal/political groups and individuals.

Recently, I attended a celebration for the graduating cohort of the University of Utah's American Indian Teacher Training Program (AITTP).[1] The AITTP is a program that prepares American Indians to become teachers with the stipulation that they teach in Indian-serving schools upon their graduation. The program is rooted in the idea that American Indians can engage in the process of educating themselves, and can do so through both Indigenous wisdom and knowledges often found in dominant society. The eight graduates had worked for two years in an institution that often devalued their presence. They were joined by 180 family members and supporters for the celebration. During the course of the evening, each graduate had an opportunity to speak to the assembled group. Every graduate thanked the many family members who contributed to their academic successes, and each told a story about why they wanted to be a teacher and what it meant for their communities. One of the graduates said, "I struggled in school for a long time, not knowing whether or not I was able to do this work. Now I know I am." She continued by stating, "Now, I see a need in our community to have our students read, have their parents read with them, and to recognize that there is power in both the written word, and [our] stories. We can, and must, do both." Still other graduates of the teacher training program spoke that evening of the need for teachers in their communities and the contribution the program participants would make to those communities upon graduation from our teacher education program. One teacher said, "We need teachers who look like us, talk like us, and think like us. To know what it means to be [tribal name] is an important part of this. We can change the ways our children think about schools." The stories conveyed a foundation for what the graduates and other AITTP students were doing and why, and outlined a theory of what self-education in American Indian communities should be like. Many of the stories were dominated by the fact that individuals are parts of communities that they serve in order to make the community more complete. One man said, "I am only one person, but I'm one more [tribal name] teacher than we had. I have to give back; there is no other way." The newly licensed teachers also pointed to the fact that the knowledge and skill sets they acquired at the institution, combined with their Indigenous ways of knowing, would help them better meet the educational and cultural needs of their communities. One student, for example, stated, "We have to make sure that our people know how to read and write, and that they have someone in front of them who understands what it means to be Indian. This program has given me an opportunity to do the work I was born to do." In this statement, the new teacher highlighted the importance of making connections between different types and forms of knowledge in order to meet larger, community goals of self-education and sovereignty.

As students spoke, I was reminded of my own conflicts with academic colleagues regarding the knowledge sources necessary to do rigorous research and to be theoretically sound. I once had an encounter with a colleague who told me that people like me "told good stories" and later added that because I told good stories, I might not ever be a "good theorist." I was struck by the seeming disconnect between community stories and personal narratives and "theory." After this encounter with my colleague, I returned home to Prospect, North Carolina, one of the communities of the Lumbee tribe of which I am an enrolled member, and told several of my relatives and elders about my colleagues' comments. My mother told me, "Baby, doesn't she know that our stories are our theories? And she thinks she's smarter than you because she can't tell stories?"[2] My mother clearly hit on the reason why locating theory as something absent from stories and practices is problematic in many Indigenous communities and in the work of anthropologists who seek to represent Indigenous communities.

The eight American Indian graduates who spoke of their commitments to community and told stories of elders, family members, and their children were, in fact, outlining theories of sovereignty, self-determination, and self-education. They were not simply telling "stories;" rather, they had clearly shown me that for many Indigenous people, stories serve as the basis for how our communities work. For some Indigenous scholars (and others), theory is not simply an abstract thought or idea that explains overarching structures of societies and communities; theories, through stories and other media, are roadmaps for our communities and reminders of our individual responsibilities to the survival of our communities. These notions of theory, however, conflict with what many in the "academy" consider "good theory." At the heart of this conflict are different epistemologies and ontologies. In this chapter, I want to make connections between different forms of knowledge and their application through a community-oriented theoretical lens.

Much of my academic career has been spent in search of an acceptable theoretical frame that allows me to analyze the problems encountered by American Indians in educational institutions and the programs that are in place to uniquely serve American Indian communities. In the past, I have relied on theorists like Bourdieu, Fordham, Giddens, and Willis, but I feel that my analyses have yet to be complete because these scholars do not explicitly address issues that are salient for and to American Indians. In this chapter, I intend to outline the central tenets of an emerging theory that I call Tribal Critical Race Theory (TribalCrit) to more completely address the issues of Indigenous Peoples in the United States. I have constructed this theoretical framework because it allows me to address the complicated relationship between American Indians and the United States federal government and begin to make sense of American Indians' liminality as both racial and legal/political groups and individuals. It is this liminal space that accounts for both the political/legal nature of our relationship with the U.S. government as American Indians and with our embodiment as racialized beings. I wish to emphasize the liminality of our position (legally/politically and socially); I do not offer one expression of it at the exclusion of another.

Critical Race Theory: An Influential Framework

TribalCrit emerges from Critical Race Theory (CRT) and is rooted in the multiple, nuanced, and historically-and geographically-located epistemologies and ontologies found in Indigenous communities. Though they differ depending on time, space, place, tribal nation, and individual, there appear to be commonalities in those ontologies and epistemologies. TribalCrit is rooted in these commonalities while simultaneously recognizing the range and variation that exists within and between communities and individuals.

Critical Race Theory evolved in the mid-1970s as a response to Critical Legal Studies (CLS). CLS is left-leaning legal scholarship that argues that the law must focus on how it is applied to specific groups in particular circumstances. CLS exposes contradictions in the law and illustrates the ways that laws create and maintain the hierarchical society in which we live (Gordon, 1990). CRT is "a form of opposition scholarship" (Calmore, 1992: p. 2161) that grew from a discontent that CLS was not moving fast enough in its attempts to critique and change societal and legal structures that specifically focused on race and racism (Delgado & Stefancic, 2000). While CRT centers race and racism, it also focuses on other areas of subordination. Solórzano (1998) writes, "Although race and racism are at the center of a critical race analysis, they are also viewed at their intersection with other forms of subordination such as gender and class discrimination" (p. 122). CRT values experiential knowledge as a way to inform thinking and research. As a result, narrative accounts and testimonies are valued as key sources of data by CRT scholars. Listening seriously involves an ability to make connections between "traditional" community values and those of larger societal institutions like courts or schools. Like CRT, TribalCrit values narrative and stories as important sources of data.

In the mid 1990s, CRT was applied to research in education as an alternative way of viewing educational institutions and the difficulties facing people of color within these institutions[3] (Ladson-Billings & Tate, 1995). CRT in education posits that racism is endemic in society and in education, and that racism has become so deeply engrained in society's and schooling's consciousness that it is often invisible. CRT confronts and challenges traditional views of education in regard to issues of meritocracy, claims of color-blind objectivity, and equal opportunity (Crenshaw, 1989, 1993; Delgado Bernal, 2002; Delgado & Stefancic, 2000; Solórzano & Yosso, 2001a; Villalpando, 2003). Finally, CRT in education is activist in nature and inherently must contain a commitment to social justice. Embedded in this notion is a "liberatory or transformative response to racial, gender, and class oppression" (Solórzano & Yosso, 2001a, p. 8). Those who rely on CRT "integrate their experiential knowledge, drawn from a shared history as 'other,' with their ongoing struggles to transform a world deteriorating under the albatross of racial hegemony" (Barnes, 1990, p. 1865). Scholars utilizing CRT in education explicitly argue that their work must move toward eliminating the influence racism, sexism, and poverty have in the lives of students and faculty (Delgado Bernal & Villalpando, 2002; Parker, 1998; Solórzano & Yosso, 2001b).

While CRT serves as a framework in and of itself, it does not address the specific needs of tribal peoples because it does not address American Indians' liminality as both legal/political and racialized beings or the experience of colonization. CRT was originally developed to address the Civil Rights issues of African American people. As such, it is oriented toward an articulation of race issues along a "black-white" binary (much the way *Brown v. Board* is), and, until recently, other ethnic/racial groups have not been included in the conversation. As a result, Latino Critical Race Theory (LatCrit) and Asian Critical Race Theory (AsianCrit) have been developed to meet the specific needs of those populations. For example, LatCrit emphasizes issues that affect Latina/o people in everyday life, including immigration, language, identity, culture, and skin color (Delgado Bernal, 2002; Espinoza, 1990; Hernandez-Truyol, 1997; Montoya, 1994, Villalpando, 2003). AsianCrit emphasizes and critiques the nativistic racism embedded in the model minority stereotype, immigration and naturalization, language, and disenfranchisement issues that relate to Asian people in the United States (Chang 1993, 1998). While these theories have developed to meet the specific needs of Latinos/as and Asian Americans, they largely maintain the basic premise of CRT that racism is endemic in society. In contrast, the basic tenet of TribalCrit emphasizes that colonization is endemic to society (Brayboy, 2001).

An Overview of Tribal Critical Race Theory: The Beginning

In the following pages, I will outline nine tenets of TribalCrit, which can be briefly summarized as follows:

1. Colonization is endemic to society.
2. U.S. policies toward Indigenous peoples are rooted in imperialism, White supremacy, and a desire for material gain.
3. Indigenous peoples occupy a liminal space that accounts for both the political and racialized natures of our identities.

4. Indigenous peoples have a desire to obtain and forge tribal sovereignty, tribal autonomy, self-determination, and self-identification.

5. The concepts of culture, knowledge, and power take on new meaning when examined through an Indigenous lens.

6. Governmental policies and educational policies toward Indigenous peoples are intimately linked around the problematic goal of assimilation.

7. Tribal philosophies, beliefs, customs, traditions, and visions for the future are central to understanding the lived realities of Indigenous peoples, but they also illustrate the differences and adaptability among individuals and groups.

8. Stories are not separate from theory; they make up theory and are, therefore, real and legitimate sources of data and ways of being.

9. Theory and practice are connected in deep and explicit ways such that scholars must work towards social change.

While CRT argues that racism is endemic in society, TribalCrit emphasizes that colonization is endemic in society while also acknowledging the role played by racism. Much of what TribalCrit offers as an analytical lens is a new and more culturally nuanced way of examining the lives and experiences of tribal peoples since contact with Europeans over 500 years ago. This is central to the particularity of the space and place American Indians inhabit, both physically and intellectually, as well as to the unique, sovereign relationship between American Indians and the federal government. My hope is that TribalCrit can be used to address the range and variation of experiences of individuals who are American Indian.[4] Furthermore, TribalCrit provides a theoretical lens for addressing many of the issues facing American Indian communities today, including issues of language shift and language loss, natural resources management, the lack of students graduating from colleges and universities, the overrepresentation of American Indians in special education, and power struggles between federal, state, and tribal governments.

The primary tenet of TribalCrit is the notion that colonization is endemic to society. By colonization, I mean that European American thought, knowledge, and power structures dominate present-day society in the United States. Battiste (2002) argues, "Eurocentric thinkers dismissed Indigenous knowledge in the same way they dismissed any socio-political cultural life they did not understand: they found it to be unsystematic and incapable of meeting the productivity needs of the modern world" (p. 5). Additionally, Lomawaima & McCarty (2002) illustrate this point in the context of American Indian education:

> The goal has been "civilization" of American Indian peoples . . . [which] assumes that what is required is the complete and utter transformation of native nations and individuals: replace heritage languages with English, replace "paganism" with Christianity, replace economic, political, social, legal, and aesthetic institutions. (p. 282)

In this way, the goal, sometimes explicit, sometimes implicit, of interactions between the dominant U.S. society and American Indians has been to change ("colonize" or "civilize") us to be more like those who hold power in the dominant society. For example, boarding schools were intended to "kill the Indian and save the man"; more recently, American Indians' status as legal/political groups has been called into question with the goal of simply making them a "racial" group. The everyday experiences of American Indians, the Indigenous inhabitants of the Americas, have essentially been removed from the awareness of dominant members of U.S. society. These viable images have instead been replaced with fixed images from the past of what American Indians once were. The colonization has been so complete that even many American Indians fail to recognize that we are taking up colonialist ideas when we fail to express ourselves in ways that may challenge dominant society's ideas about who and what we are supposed to be, how we are supposed to behave, and what we are supposed to be within the larger population. Smith (1999) is particularly useful here when she discusses the ways that Indigenous identities have become regulated by governments to meet their interests rather than those of the people who take up these identities. She writes, "legislated identities which regulated who was an Indian and who was not . . . who had the correct fraction of blood quantum, who lived in the regulated spaces of reserves and communities, were all worked out arbitrarily (but systematically), to serve the interests of the colonizing society" (p. 22). This process of colonization and its debilitating influences are at the heart of TribalCrit; all other ideas are offshoots of this vital concept.

Second, TribalCrit builds on the notion that colonization is endemic in society and explicitly recognizes that the policies of the United States toward American Indians are rooted in imperialism, White supremacy, and a desire for material gain. Williams (1987, 1989) has methodically examined the early policies set forth by the U.S. and its treatment of American Indians. He argues that these policies were rooted in a self-interested reading of legal concepts that allowed White settlers to rationalize and legitimize their decisions to steal lands from the Indigenous peoples who already inhabited them. This process highlights a divergence in the ways that White settlers and Indigenous peoples viewed the relationship between people and land. Semantically, this plays out in a distinction between the concepts of habitation and ownership, which is evident in the actions of White settlers. It appears that because a group of people were rooted to lands on which they lived, they did not necessarily properly "own" those lands, leading to a series of events that left many Indigenous peoples dispossessed of lands that held not only life sustaining crops, but also spiritually sustaining properties.[5] Moreover, this "removal" of tribal peoples by the U.S. government was justified by arguing that Indigenous people needed to be moved "for our own good." For example, the U.S. government claimed that Indians were not only underutilizing the lands on which they lived, but that they would be unmolested in the new Indian Territory (which is present day Oklahoma). Tribal nations, of course, were molested and land rich in oil and natural resources was stolen for the monetary benefits of its "new owners." In essence, American Indians were being saved from themselves by being moved off their lands.

At the heart of the removals were the concepts of Manifest Destiny and the Norman Yoke, used as arguments in favor of the dispossessing of people from their tribal lands. Manifest Destiny posited that it was God's destiny for the new settlers to have the land. This concept gave European-Americans the moral authority to take the lands through whatever means necessary. Similarly, the Norman Yoke, originally established by Adam Smith as an economic term, was extended to justify taking lands and property from Indigenous people. Loosely defined, the concept argues that not only do individuals have a right to utilize and exploit natural resources on lands that are considered "vacant," but they also have a moral obligation to do so.

Manifest Destiny and the Norman Yoke are both concepts rooted in White supremacy. In this context White supremacy refers to the idea that the established, European or western way of doing things has both moral and intellectual superiority over those things non-western.[6] White supremacy has a long history and is still pervasive in the U.S. For example, the modern-day canon that revolves around an established set of readings or "classics" (Shakespeare and Dickinson are classics, but Louis Owens and Zitkala-Sa are not) is one way White supremacy gets played out in colleges and universities. White supremacy is viewed as natural and legitimate and it is precisely through this naturalization that White supremacy derives its hegemonic power.

An examination of the attack on affirmative action points to the ways that hegemonic power is played out in the academic and larger public discourse. Affirmative Action that "benefits" people of color is attacked, while that which benefits White women (the group which has benefited the most from affirmative action), the children of alumni (often called "legacies" which is, in and of itself, telling of how institutions think about these students' entitlement regarding potential admission to an institution), athletes who raise large sums of money for institutions even as they fail to graduate at record levels, and veterans of the United States Armed Services is either naturalized and made invisible or celebrated.

The third tenet of TribalCrit is that Indigenous peoples occupy a liminal space that accounts for both the legal/political and racialized natures of our identities. That is, we are often placed between our joint statuses as legal/political and racialized beings.[7] My intent here is to argue that American Indians are both legal/political and racialized beings; however, we are rarely treated as such, leaving Indigenous peoples in a state of inbetweenness wherein we define ourselves as both, with an emphasis on the legal/political, but we are framed as racialized groups by many members of society. The racialized status of American Indians appears to be the main emphasis of most members of U.S. society; this status ignores the legal/political one, and is directly tied to notions of colonialism, because larger society is unaware of the multiple statuses of Indigenous peoples. Currently, the different circulating discourses around what it means to be Indian as well as what constitutes American Indian education establish a context in which American Indians must struggle for the right to be defined as both a legal/political and a racial group. Even though our status as a legal/political group has been repeatedly articulated in government policy, legal code, and the everyday lives of American Indian individuals and communities, it remains a point of debate and contention in most popular settings. For example, conservative groups who have attacked federally funded programs for American Indians invoke arguments—by utilizing the fourteenth amendment and the Civil Rights Act of 1964—that position American Indians solely as a racialized group. In fact, these programs are rooted in what President George W. Bush stated in an April 30, 2004 Executive Order:

> The United States has a unique legal relationship with Indian tribes and a special relationship with Alaskan Native entities as provided in the Constitution of the United States, treaties, and federal statutes. This Administration is committed to continuing to work with these federally recognized tribal governments on a government-to-government basis, and supports tribal sovereignty and self-determination.

This Executive Order clearly outlines that American Indians have a unique relationship with the federal government. The idea that the U.S. government has a unique relationship with federally recognized tribes is an important one for this argument. I recognize that there are Indigenous Peoples who may not be federally recognized and are state recognized. These groups need not be excluded from the conversation; as Deloria & Lytle (1984) and Wilkins (2002) have argued, these American Indian groups were nations before the Constitution was signed, and therefore their status as nations should be without question. The idea that there are tribal groups who are federally recognized and those who are not is constructed by the federal government and ignores what Deloria & Lytle (1984) call the "extraconstitutionality" of "non-recognized" groups.[8]

Fourth, TribalCrit is rooted in a belief in and desire to obtain and forge tribal autonomy, self-determination, self-identification, and ultimately tribal sovereignty. Tribal autonomy is the ability of communities and tribal nations to have control over existing land bases, natural resources, and tribal national boundaries. Autonomy is also linked to the ability to interact with the U.S. and other nations on a nation-to-nation basis. Self-determination is the ability to define what happens with autonomy, how, why, and to what ends, rather than being forced to ask permission from the United States. Self-determination rejects the guardian/ward relationship currently in place between the U.S. government and tribal nations.[9] Knowledge of these current relationships allows researchers ways to better analyze interactions between Indigenous students and the institutional structures. Ultimately, these analyses may lead to a reconceptualization of the parameters for engaging Indigenous students within institutions. Finally, self-identification is the ability and legitimacy for groups to define themselves and to create what it means to be Indian. As such, self-identification may or may not reject the "sign" Indian—or that which signifies what a "real Indian" is or looks like (often an ecology-loving, bead-wearing, feather-having, long-haired, tall, dark man or woman)— and its meanings to others (e.g. see Vizenor, 1994, 1998; Vizenor & Lee, 1999). This call for self-identification influences the way that colleges and universities examine issues of identification in the admissions process and may push for stricter ways of determining whether or not potential students and faculty members are committing "ethnic fraud." Additionally, this requires institutions to keep better records of who has identified as American Indian, rather than placing the figures under the dreaded catchall "Other" category.

Fifth, TribalCrit problematizes the concepts of culture, knowledge, and power and offers alternative ways of understanding them through an Indigenous lens. In so doing, TribalCrit migrates away from western/European notions of culture, knowledge, and power and moves to notions that have been circulating among Indigenous peoples for thousands of years. In TribalCrit, culture is simultaneously fluid or dynamic, and fixed or stable. Like an anchor in the ocean, it is tied to a group of people and often a physical place. For many Indigenous people, culture is rooted to lands on which they live as well as to their ancestors who lived on those lands before them. However, just as the anchor shifts and sways with changing tides and the ebbs and flows of the ocean, culture shifts and flows with changes in contexts, situations, people, and purposes. Like all humans, Indigenous people are shaped by their cultural inheritance, and they engage in cultural production.[10]

Knowledge is defined by TribalCrit as the ability to recognize change, adapt, and move forward with the change. There are at least three forms of knowledge that TribalCrit addresses, and they exist in accord with one another. Cultural knowledge is an understanding of what it means to be a member of a particular tribal nation; this includes particular traditions, issues, and ways of being and knowing that make an individual a member of a community. Knowledge of survival includes an understanding of how and in what ways change can be accomplished and the ability and willingness to change, adapt, and adjust in order to move forward as an individual and community. Finally, academic knowledge is that acquired from educational institutions. In many of our communities this is often referred to as "book knowing" or "book smarts." While Indigenous ways of knowing and "book smarts" are often seen as diametrically opposed, these different forms of knowledge do not necessarily need to be in conflict (Barnhardt & Kawagley, 2005; Battiste, 2002; Harrison & Papa, 2005; Kawagley, 1995; Medicine, 2001). Rather, they complement each other in powerful ways. This blending of knowledges—academic and cultural ones—creates knowledge that is key to survival (Barnhardt & Kawagley, 2004, 2005; Deloria, 1970; Medicine, 2001). The exercise of these various forms of knowledge is always context-specific and the different forms must be integrated with one another in order to achieve successful resistance and, thus, survival. For example, knowledge learned in school can be used in conjunction with tribal knowledge toward social justice for these communities. This strategic use of multiple forms of knowledge generates power that is situated, dynamic, and historically influenced.

Among Indigenous intellectuals and others, the notion of power is elusive and complicated but certain themes do emerge. Power is not a property or trait that an individual has to exercise control over others; rather, it is rooted in a group's ability to define themselves, their place in the world, and their traditions (Deloria, 1970; Stoffle & Zedeño, 2001; Vizenor, 1998; Warrior, 1995). Deloria (1970) argues, "Few members of racial minority groups have realized that inherent in their peculiar experience on this continent is hidden the basic recognition of their power and sovereignty" (p. 115). There is a clear link here between knowledge—in the form of experience—and power. Power through an Indigenous lens is an expression of sovereignty—defined as self-determination, self-government, self-identification, and self-education. In this way, sovereignty is community based. By this I mean that the ideas of self-determination, -government, -identification, and -education are rooted in a community's conceptions of its needs and past, present, and future. Deloria (1970) extends and crystallizes this point when he writes, "Since power cannot be given and accepted . . . The responsibility which sovereignty creates is oriented primarily toward the existence and continuance of the group" (p. 123). Power, as I define it, is the ability to survive rooted in the capacity to adapt and adjust to changing landscapes, times, ideas, circumstances, and situations. However, for Indigenous peoples, survival is more than simply staying together as a group. Vizenor's (Vizenor, 1998; Vizenor & Lee, 1999) concept of survivance is useful for articulating the uniqueness of the American Indian experience with persevering in hostile contexts. Survivance, which combines survival and resistance, calls for adaptation and strategic accommodation in order to survive and develop the processes that contribute to community growth (Deloria, 1970).

Power for many American Indians leads to that which Deloria advocates regarding the process of sovereignty for individual tribal nations. Of Deloria, Warrior (1995) writes:

> [Deloria] also advocates a position that is not merely a call for the United States to break down into tribes closed off from the rest of the world. Rather he recognizes that the withdrawal of a group to draw on its own resources does not cut it off from other groups' influences on its future . . . they need to confront a set of challenges for which no culture has all answers. (pp. 91–92)

In other words, the ability to determine a place in the world (power) is enabled by knowledge American Indian communities have that is rooted in both Indigenous and European sources of knowing. Thus, a group's own sense of themselves governs decisions regarding how to best attend to issues of tribal sovereignty and its critical components of tribal autonomy, self-determination, -identification, -government, and -education.

There is a dialogical relationship between culture, knowledge, and power: culture is the base for knowledge that ultimately leads to power. While I believe that culture serves as a basis for the relationship, there are reciprocal ties to knowledge and power. Culture reminds individuals, in a group, who they are. Its dynamic nature allows for adaptability to change. Knowledge relates to culture in that it offers links to what people know. Ultimately, knowledge is important in the process of recognizing that no single culture has solutions to the myriad problems encountered by groups. Knowledge also allows groups to change, adapt, and move forward in a vision related to power in the form of sovereignty. The ways that groups define themselves, their places in the world (at least in part, recognizing that places are co-constructed by many things), and their cultures is a form of power. Importantly, an Indigenous conception of power defines power as an energetic force that circulates throughout the universe—it lies both within and outside of individuals; hence both the tribal nation and the individual are subjects in the dialogic.

The sixth key component of TribalCrit is a recognition that governmental policies and educational policies toward Indigenous peoples have, historically, been oriented toward a problematic goal of assimilation. While I have, up to this point, argued that the governmental relationship between tribal peoples and the U.S. allows for the possibilities of self-education and -determination for American Indians, the way in which these policies have been interpreted and carried out has instead been rooted in assimilation. According to Klug and Whitfield, "early treaties emphasized that education 'appropriate' for Indian students was to be provided" (2003, p. 31). While trust responsibility and sovereignty were supposed to be the guiding principles of Indian education, "appropriate" is a relative term whose meaning was left to officials at the Bureau of Indian Affairs (BIA) to define. Often "appropriate" education was assumed to be that which eradicated Indianness or promoted Anglo values and ways of communicating. All of these attempts at assimilation through "appropriate" education failed.

TribalCrit explicitly rejects the call for assimilation in educational institutions for American Indian students. Deyhle's (1995) work on cultural integrity highlights the fact that individuals, in order to be successful as both academics and as Indigenous people, must maintain a strong sense of their Indigenous identity as distinctive and as a source of pride. By cultural integrity, I mean a set of beliefs (and actions directly linked to these beliefs) that are typically shared among a group of people. The beliefs are "distinct and independent tradition[s]" (Deyhle, 1995, p. 28). Maintaining cultural integrity means that experiences in school certainly affect a person, but they need not do so at the expense of their home culture (Fordham, 1996; Ogbu, 1987, 1993). TribalCrit rejects the past and present rhetoric calling for integration and assimilation of American Indian students in educational institutions because, rather than cultivating and maintaining cultural integrity, assimilation requires students to replace this cultural knowledge with academic knowledge.

Today, TribalCrit would argue, education for American Indians is not always rooted in the goal of assimilation, although some assimilation seems to be an inevitable outcome of education that occurs through the formal structures of western schooling. Education, according to TribalCrit, might also teach American Indian students how to combine Indigenous notions of culture, knowledge, and power with western/European conceptions in order to actively engage in survivance, self-determination, and tribal autonomy. The University of Utah's American Indian Teacher Training Program attempts to do this by combining Indigenous ways of knowing and being with the courses necessary for teaching licenses. The students highlighted at the beginning of this chapter are products of this program; each of the newly licensed teachers from the program is required to teach in Indigenous communities as part of a payback agreement for the funding they receive. Their role is to assist young American Indian elementary and secondary students in participating in the formal schooling structures while maintaining and valuing their cultural heritage. In this way, schooling and students' sense of Indigenous self do not necessarily conflict.

The seventh tenet of TribalCrit emphasizes the importance of tribal philosophies, beliefs, customs, traditions, and visions for the future; it honors the adaptability of groups and recognizes the differences within individuals and between people and groups. Growing out of a foundation in culture, knowledge and power, the beliefs, thoughts, philosophies, customs, and traditions of Indigenous individuals and communities serve as a foundation from which to analyze the schooling practices, self-education, and experiences of Indigenous peoples. These concepts must be recognized as being viable and important for the lives of the individuals and members of the group. This recognition leads to different ways of examining experiences and theoretical frames through which to view the experiences. There must be recognition that the ways of knowing for American Indians are vital to our self-education and self-determination (Barnhardt & Kawagley, 2005; Battiste, 2002; Lomawaima & McCarty, 2002).

The debate around the place of Indigenous ways of knowing in Western educational institutions is often framed is through discussions of competition and cooperation. A host of studies illustrate that Indigenous students are enculturated into a way of cooperation rather than the competitive nature of schooling (Brayboy, 1999; Deyhle, 1992, 1995; Deyhle & Margonis, 1995; Erickson & Mohatt, 1982; Foley, 1995, 1996; Philips, 1983). Cooperation is then viewed—by the institution and its powerbrokers—as an inability to work alone or to be self-sufficient, rather than a potential source of strength and a way to more fully address issues of concern to both individuals and communities (Burkhart, 2004; Deloria, 1969/1988). The notion that American Indians should be more rooted in individualism is one of the key factors that led to the creation of boarding schools in the late 19th century (Lomawaima, 1994, 1995). In my own work, Indigenous students in Ivy League universities struggled against being perceived as "not being self-motivated" and "unable to be independently successful" (Brayboy, 2004a, 2005). These students were guided to Ivy League universities by the requests and needs of their communities, suggesting that success is never independent but instead tied to communal conceptions of power and survivance (Brayboy, 1999, 2004a, 2005). This cooperation is not only tied to working on projects together, but also to the utility and necessity of community cooperation in assisting students in their academic quests. The idea and purpose of the students' attendance was for them to gain skills and credentials at the institution that they could use in ways that would benefit the community. These sentiments were also echoed by the American Indian graduates of the University of Utah in the opening vignette. In this way, formal, western education becomes a tool of empowerment and liberation for the community. A concrete example rests with a woman named Heather who told me in the spring of 1995, when she was an undergraduate student at an Ivy League university, "I have always wanted to be a lawyer; my father and mother and my elders told me that's what I was going to be, so I wanted it . . . I do this because it will mean a better life for my people, my siblings, my cousins and nieces and nephews . . . I can handle anything for those reasons; and I have." Heather's experiences in both undergraduate and law school were harsh and oppressive. She managed, however, to utilize her skills and credentials in powerful ways. She worked for her tribe's law firm and was a key litigator and negotiator in a new deal around the use of natural resources on her tribal nation's reservation. In the process, she blended her knowledge as an attorney with her knowledge as a tribal member to benefit her entire society.

Thus, within many tribal communities, individuality is devalued while contributing to the success of a community is valued. There is a clear discrepancy here in terms of what is valued in the context and situation of colleges and universities and what is valued in an individual's community. Burkhart (2004) puts it more simply when he writes, "Native philosophy tells us, 'We are, therefore I am'" (p. 25). Individuals are parts of communities rather than individuals alone in the world. TribalCrit, then, recognizes the importance of tribal philosophies, values, and beliefs—such as community and cooperation—in the experiences of American Indian peoples.

Contrary to recent calls for "scientifically based" research as being the only justifiable form of research, the eighth tenet of TribalCrit honors stories and oral knowledge as real and legitimate forms of data and ways of being. Stories are not separate from theory; they make up theory. As in the opening vignette, stories serve as a way to orient oneself and others toward the world and life. Cora Weber Pillwax (cited in Battiste, 2002) says, "Stories . . . are to be listened to, remembered, thought about, meditated on. [They] are not frivolous or meaningless, no one tells a story without intent or purpose" (p. 25). Likewise Basso (2000) argues that stories serve a central purpose in orienting Western Apache to what it means to be an "Apache." Stories are, he argues, moral tools with psychological implications, in that they remind individuals of particular ways of being, and they "stalk" those who step out of line in perpetuity. These stories do not have to be told by accomplished academics or writers; rather, the stories valued by TribalCrit are the foundations on which Indigenous communities are built. Many Indigenous people have strong oral traditions, which are used as vehicles for the transmission of culture and knowledge. The form and content of these stories, however, differ from the types of knowledge privileged by educational institutions. As a result, American Indian students have often struggled with acquiring the academic language of educational institutions and have been viewed as deficient. In contrast, TribalCrit recognizes that the legitimacy given to ways of communicating (written and verbal) prioritized by schools, colleges and universities does not necessarily mean that oral story-telling should be devalued.

Oral stories remind us of our origins and serve as lessons for the younger members of our communities; they have a place in our communities and in our lives (e.g. see Basso, 2000; Battiste, 2002; Olivas, 1990). They also serve as guideposts for our elders and other policy-makers in our tribal communities. Additionally, for researchers in institutions of higher education, there is a saliency in stories. TribalCrit recognizes that the statistical power of the "n" is not necessarily the marker of a "good, rigorous" study. Stories may also be informative of structural barriers or weaknesses. In this respect, "proof" is thought of in different ways.

Stories as "data" are important, and one key to collecting these data is "hearing" the stories. There is a difference between listening to stories and hearing them, and this is central to TribalCrit. Listening is part of going through the motions of acting engaged and allowing individuals to talk. Hearing stories means that value is attributed to them and both the authority and the nuance of stories are understood. When stories are heard, they lead the hearer to explore the range and variation of possibilities of what can happen and has happened (Basso, 1996, 2000; Battiste, 2002, Burkhart, 2004; Medicine, 2001, Williams, 1997). Stories often are the guardians of cumulative knowledges that hold a place in the psyches of the group members, memories of tradition, and reflections on power. Hearers ultimately understand the nuances in stories and recognize that the onus for hearing is placed on the hearer rather than the speaker for delivering a clearly articulated message. Additionally, one must be able to feel the stories. You tell them, hear them, and feel them—establishing a strong place for empathy and for "getting it."

The final component of TribalCrit is that there must be a component of action or activism—a way of connecting theory and practice in deep and explicit ways. Building on what Williams (1997) has called Critical Race Practice, TribalCrit must be praxis at its best. Praxis involves researchers who utilize theory to make an active change in the situation and context being examined. For TribalCrit scholars who embrace this line of thinking in their work, we must expose structural inequalities and assimilatory processes and work toward debunking and deconstructing them; it also works to create structures that will address the real, immediate and future needs of tribal peoples and communities (Burkhart, 2004). Deloria (1969/1988) is particularly useful here when he writes, "Abstract theories create abstract action. Lumping together the variety of tribal problems and seeking demonic principle at work is intellectually satisfying. But it does not change the real situation" (p. 86). Later he, argues, "Academia, and its by-products, continues to become more irrelevant to the needs of the people" (Deloria, 1969/1988, p. 93). Utilizing a TribalCrit lens, I would argue that no research should be conducted with Indigenous Peoples that is not in some way directed by a community and aimed toward improving the life chances and situations of specific communities and American Indians writ large. The research must be relevant and address the problems of the community; there is little room for abstract ideas in real communities. Ultimately, then, we have come full circle because TribalCrit research and practice—or better still, praxis—moves us away from colonization and assimilation and towards a more real self-determination and tribal sovereignty.

Conclusions

TribalCrit endeavors to expose the inconsistencies in structural systems and institutions—like colleges and universities—and make the situation better for Indigenous students. TribalCrit practitioners take part in the process of self-determination and in making institutions of formal education more understandable to Indigenous students and Indigenous students more understandable to the institutions.

The tenets I discuss above should serve as a starting point for future dialogue on what I have named Tribal Critical Race Theory.

There are a number of tenets within TribalCrit that are important for the experiences of and issues faced by Indigenous Peoples. Aspects of TribalCrit could certainly be taken up by scholars in other disciplines and applied more generally; however, my focus is on education. Further, I want to acknowledge that many of the tenets are intimately linked to others. In the context of this chapter, I discussed them as distinct ideas for heuristic purposes.

Ultimately, TribalCrit holds an explanatory power; it is potentially a better theoretical lens through which to describe the lived experiences of tribal peoples. TribalCrit is based on a series of traditions, ideas, thoughts, and epistemologies that are grounded in tribal histories thousands of years old. While I draw on older stories, traditions, ontologies, and epistemologies, the combination itself is new. As such, I hope that this chapter will initiate a process of thinking about how Tribal Critical Race Theory might better serve researchers who are unsatisfied with the theories and methods currently offered from which to study American Indians in educational institutions specifically, and larger society more generally. TribalCrit has the potential to serve as a theoretical and analytical lens for addressing the educational experiences of American Indian students, teachers, and researchers in the areas of classroom participation, language revitalization, lack of Native students graduating from high schools and colleges, multiple literacies, overrepresentation of Native students in special education, pedagogy, teacher-training, and many other areas. My hope is that, in addressing these issues and experiences through a TribalCrit lens, research will lead both to a better understanding of the needs of Indigenous communities and to changes in the educational system and society at large that benefit Indigenous communities.

I also hope that TribalCrit helps to further a larger conversation about methods of conducting research and analyzing data in ways that center Indigenous ways of knowing and lead to American Indian sovereignty and self-determination. As one of the American Indian teachers at the graduation celebration said, "We can change the ways our children think about schools." It is my hope and belief that TribalCrit begins to allow us to change the ways that Indigenous students think about schools and, perhaps more importantly, the ways that both schools and educational researchers think about American Indian students.

Notes

1. I am the founder and principal investigator of a program that is now 4 years-old. I am also an Indigenous man (Lumbee) who is a former secondary social studies teacher.

2. In my community, regardless of how old we are or what degrees we hold, we are often still referred to in the diminutive by our parents and elders. It is illustrative of how our community works and how knowledge is created by the older generation. It is also a clear indication of who holds power in these issues.

3. For a comprehensive overview of the introduction of CRT to education see, Parker, Deyhle, and Villenas (1999), Solórzano and Delgado Bernal (2001), Solórzano and Yosso (2002), and Yosso, Parker, Solórzano, and Lynn (2004).

4. Elsewhere, I have addressed how complicated this is, because American Indians are so widely diverse (Brayboy, 2004a, b). Missing from this analysis, too, are the complicated demarcations among groups who are federally versus state recognized, landed groups versus non-landed groups, and those who have economic development activities (like casinos and natural resources management) and those who do not. Space does not allow me to fully delve into the nuances of these differences; however, I have begun to address them elsewhere (Brayboy, in progress).

5. I am grateful to Kristin Searle for pointing out this important distinction. Feld and Basso (1996) outline and highlight the importance of rootedness to place.

6. For example, see Hall (1997), hooks (1995), Ladson-Billings (1998, 2000), Richardson and Villenas (2000), Spivak (1988), Thompson (1999), Villalpando (2003), and Villenas and Deyhle (1999).

7. There are certainly times in which American Indians may place themselves in one of these roles at the potential exclusion of the other. These moments are often strategic in nature, or come from individuals who are not aware of the unique legal/political status that American Indians hold.

8. This argument deserves a significant amount of time and space. I have addressed it more fully elsewhere (Brayboy, in progress).

9. I find the guardian–ward relationship problematic and wrongly taken up. Rather, the fiduciary relationship of trustee and beneficiary may be more appropriate in dealings with the U.S. government. Wilkins and Lomawaima (2002) more fully address issues of an Indigenous view of trust.

10. For a fuller discussion of the culture concept, see Borofsky et al. (2001). The article in American Anthropologist highlights the contested nature of culture. I recognize the term is contested, however, I choose to utilize it in this chapter (Wagner, 1981).

References

Barnhardt, R., & Kawagley, A. O. (2004). Culture, chaos and complexity: Catalysts for change in Indigenous education. *Cultural Survival Quarterly, 27*(4), 59–64.

Barnhardt, R., & Kawagley, A. O. (2005). Indigenous knowledge systems and Alaska native ways of knowing. *Anthropology & Education Quarterly, 36*(1), 8–23.

Basso, K. T. (1996). *Wisdom sits in places: landscape and language among the Western Apache.* Albuquerque, NM: University of New Mexico Press.

Basso, K. H. (2000). Stalking with Stories. In B. A. Levinson (Ed.), *Schooling and the symbolic animal: Social and cultural dimensions of education* (pp. 41–52). Lanham, MD: Rowman & Littlefield.

Barnes, R. (1990). *Race consciousness: The thematic content of racial distinctiveness in Critical Race scholarship.* Harvard Law Review, 103, 1864–1871.

Battiste, M. (2002). Indigenous knowledge and pedagogy in first nations education: A literature review with recommendations. Ottawa: Indian and Northern Affairs Canada.

Borofsky, R., Barth, F., Scweder, R. A., Rodseth, L., & Stolzenberg, N. M. (2001). WHEN: A conversation about culture. *American Anthropologist, 103*(2), 432–446.

Brayboy, B. M. (1999). Climbing the Ivy: Examining the experiences of academically successful Native American Indian students in two Ivy League universities. Unpublished doctoral dissertation, University of Pennsylvania.

Brayboy, B. M. (November 2001). Toward a Tribal Critical Theory in higher education. Paper presented at the Association for the Study of Higher Education, Richmond, VA.

Brayboy, B. M. (2004a). Hiding in the Ivy: American Indian Students and visibility in elite educational settings. *Harvard Educational Review, 74*(2), 125–152.

Brayboy, B. M. (2004b). "Those Indians are taking over": A Tribal Critical Theory analysis of a legal challenge to Indian Education. Paper presented at the Council on Anthropology and Education Canterbury Convocation, San Francisco, November 19.

Brayboy, B. M. (2005). Transformational resistance and social justice: American Indians in Ivy League Universities. *Anthropology & Education Quarterly, 36*(3), 193–211.

Brayboy, B. M. (in progress). *A tribal critical race theory in education.* Unpublished book manuscript.

Burkhart, B. Y. (2004). What Coyote and Thales Can Teach Us: An Outline of American Indian Epistemology. In A. Waters (Ed.), *American Indian thought: Philosophical essays* (pp. 15–26). Malden, MA: Blackwell Publishing.

Bush, G. W., President of the United States (2004, April 30). Executive Order American Indian and Alaska Native Education. Washington, DC: the White House. Retrieved July 19, 2005, from http://www.whitehouse.gov/news/releases/2004/04/20040430-10.html.

Calmore, J. (1992). Critical Race Theory, Archie Shepp, and Fire music: Securing an Authentic Intellectual life in a multicultural world. *Southern California Law Review, 65,* 2129–2231.

Chang, R. S. (1993). Toward an Asian American legal scholarship: critical race theory, poststructuralism, and narrative space. *California Law Review, 19,* 1243.

Chang, R. S. (1998). Who's Afraid of Tiger Woods? *Chicano-Latino Law Review, 19,* 223.

Crenshaw, K. (1989). Demarginalizing the intersection of race and sex: A Black feminist critique of antidiscrimination doctrine, feminist theory, and antiracist politics. *University of Chicago Legal Forum, 1989,* 139–167.

Crenshaw, K. (1993). Mapping the margins: Intersectionality, identity politics and the violence against Women of Color. *Stanford Law Review, 43,* 1241–1299.

Delgado, R., & Stefancic, J. (2000). Introduction. In R. Delgado, & J. Stefancic (Eds.), *Critical Race Theory: The cutting edge* (2nd ed., pp. xv–xix). Philadelphia: Temple University Press.

Delgado Bernal, D. (2002). Critical race theory, Latcrit theory, and critical raced gendered epistemologies: Recognizing students of color as holders and creators of knowledge. *Qualitative Inquiry, 8*(1), 105–126.

Delgado Bernal, D., & Villalpando, O. (2002). An apartheid of knowledge in academia: The struggle over the 'Legitimate' knowledge of faculty of color. *Journal of Equity & Excellence in Education, 35*(2), 169–180.

Deloria, V. (1970). *We talk, you listen: New tribes, new turf.* New York: Macmillan.

Deloria, V. (1988). Chapter 4: Anthropologists and other friends. In *Custer died for your sins: An Indian manifesto* (pp. 78–100). Norman, OK: University of Oklahoma Press.

Deloria, V., & Lytte, C. M. (1984). *The nations within: The past and future of American Indian sovereignty.* Austin: University of Texas Press.

Deyhle, D. (1992). Constructing failure and maintaining cultural identity: Navajo and Ute school leavers. *Journal of American Indian Education, 31*, 24–47.

Deyhle, D. (1995). Navajo youth and Anglo racism: Cultural integrity and resistance. *Harvard Educational Review, 65*(3), 403–444.

Deyhle, D., & Margonis, F. (1995). Navajo mothers and daughters: Schools, jobs, and the family. *Anthropology & Education Quarterly, 26*(2), 135–167.

Erickson, F., & Mohatt, G. (1982). Cultural organization of participation structures in two classrooms of Indian students. In G. Spindler (Ed.), *Doing the ethnography of schooling* (pp. 132–174). New York: Holt, Rinehart & Winston.

Espinoza, L. G (1990). Masks and other disguises: Exposing legal academia. *Harvard Law Review, 103*, 1878–1886.

Feld, S., & Basso, K. H. (1996). Introduction. In S. Feld, & K. H. Basso (Eds.), *Senses of place* (pp. 3–11). Santa Fe, NM: School of American Research Press.

Foley, D. E. (1995). *The Heartland Chronicles.* Philadelphia: University of Pennsylvania Press.

Foley, D. (1996). The silent Indian as cultural production. In B. A. Levinson, D. E. Foley, & D. C. Holland (Eds.), *The cultural production of the educated person* (pp. 79–92). Albany: SUNY Press.

Fordham, S. (1996). *Blacked out: Dilemnas of race, identity, and success at Capital High.* Chicago: University of Chicago Press.

Gordan, R. (1990). New developments in legal theory. In D. Kairys (Ed.), *The politics of law: A progressive critique* (pp. 413–425). New York: Pantheon Books.

Hall, S. (1997). Introduction: Who needs identity? In S. Hall, & P. duGay (Eds.), *Questions of cultural identity* (pp. 1–17). London: Sage.

Harrison, B., & Papa, R. (2005). The development of an Indigenous Knowledge Program in a New Zealand Maori-language immersion school. *Anthropology & Education Quarterly, 36*(1), 57–72.

Hernandez-Truyol, B. (1997). Indivisible identities: Culture clashes, confused constructs and reality checks, symposium: LatCrit theory: Naming and launching a new discourse of critical legal scholarship. *Harvard Latino Law Review, 2*, 199–230.

hooks, b. (1995). *Killing rage: ending racism.* New York: Holt & Co.

Kawagley, A. O. (1995). *A Yupiaq worldview: A pathway to ecology and spirit.* Prospect Heights, IL: Prospect Waveland.

Klug, B. J., & Whitfield, P. T. (2003). A brief history of American Indian education. In B .J. Klug, & P. T. Whitfield (Eds.), *Widening the circle: Culturally relevant pedagogy for American Indian children* (pp. 29–53). New York: Routledge Falmer.

Ladson-Billings, G. (1998). Just what is critical race theory and what's it doing in a nice field like education? *International Journal of Qualitative Studies in Education, 11*(1), 7–24.

Ladson-Billings, G. (2000). Racialized discourses and ethnic epistemologies. In N. Denzin, & Y. Lincoln (Eds.), *Handbook of Qualitative Research* (2nd ed.). Thousand Oaks, CA: SAGE Publications.

Ladson-Billings, G., & Tate, W. (1995). Toward a Critical Race Theory of Education. *Teachers College Record, 97*, 47–68.

Lomawaima, K. T. (1994). *They called it prairie light: The story of Chillocco Indian Boarding School.* Lincoln: University of Nebraska Press.

Lomawaima, K. T. (1995). Educating Native Americans. In B. James, & B. Cherry McGee (Eds.), *Handbook of research on multicultural education* (pp. 331–342). New York: Macmillan.

Lomawaima, K. T., & McCarty, T. L. (2002). When tribal sovereignty challenges democracy: American Indian education and democratic ideal. *American Educational Research Journal, 39*(2), 279–305.

Medicine, B. (with Sue Ellen Jacobs). (2001). My elders tell me. In *Learning to be an Anthropologist and Remaining "Native"* (pp. 73–82). Chicago: University of Illinois Press.

Montoya, M. (1994). Mascaras, trenzas, y grenas: Un/masking the self while un/braiding Latina stories and legal discourse. *Chicano-Latino Law Review, 15*, 1–37.

Ogbu, J. (1987). Variability in minority responses to schooling: A problem in search of an explanation. *Anthropology & Education Quarterly, 18*, 312–334.

Ogbu, J. (1993). Variability in minority school performance: A problem in search of an explanation. In E. Jacob, & C. Jordan (Eds.), *Minority education: Anthropological perspectives* (pp. 83–111). New York: Ablex.

Olivas, M. A. (1990). The chronicles, my Grandfather's stories, and Immigration law: The slave traders chronicle as racial history. *Saint Louis University Law Journal, 34*, 425–441.

Parker, L. (1998). "Race is . . . race ain't": an exploration of the utility of critical race theory in qualitative research in education. *Qualitative Studies in Education, 11*(1), 43–55.

Parker, L., Deyhle, D., & Villenas, S., (Eds.), (1999). *"Race is . . . race isn't": Critical Race Theory and qualitative studies in education.* Boulder, CO: Westview.

Philips, S. U. (1983). *The invisible culture: Communication in classroom and community on the Warm Springs Indian Reservation.* Prospect Heights, IL: Waveland Press.

Richardson, T., & Villenas, S. (2000). "Other" encounters: Dances with whiteness in multicultural education. *Educational Theory, 50*(2), 255–273.

Solórzano, D. G. (1998). Critical Race Theory, race and gender microagressions, and the experience of Chicana and Chicano Scholars. *International Journal of Qualitative Studies in Education, 11*(1), 121–136.

Solórzano, D., & Delgado Bernal, D. (2001). Examining transformational resistance through a Critical Race and LatCrit Theory framework: Chicana and Chicano students in an urban context. *Urban Education, 36*(3), 308–342.

Solórzano, D. G., & Yosso, T. J. (2001a). From racial stereotyping and deficit discourse toward a critical race theory in teacher education. *Multicultural Education, 9*(1), 2–8.

Solórzano, D. G., & Yosso, T. J. (2001b). Critical Race and LatCrit Theory and method: Counterstorytelling Chicana and Chicano Graduate school experiences. *International Journal of Qualitative Studies In Education, 14*(4), 471–495.

Solórzano, D., & Yosso, T. (2002). Critical race methodology: Counterstorytelling as an analytical framework for education research. *Qualitative Inquiry, 8*(1), 23–44.

Smith, L. T. (1999). *Decolonizing methodologies: Research and indigenous peoples.* Dunedin/London: University of Otago Press/Zed Books.

Spivak, G. (1988). Can the subaltern speak? In C. Nelson, & L. Grossberg (Eds.), *Marxism and the interpretation of culture* (pp. 217–313). Urbana: University of Illinois Press.

Stoffle, R. W., & Zedeño, M. N. (2001). American Indian Worldviews I: The concept of "power" and its connection to people, places, and resources. In R. W. Stoffle, M. N. Zedeño, & D. B. Halmo (Eds.), *American Indians and the Nevada test site: A model of research and consultation* (pp. 58–76). Washington, DC: U.S. Government Printing Office.

Thompson, A. (1999). Colortalk: Whiteness and Off White [book review]. *Educational Studies, 30*(2), 141–160.

Villalpando, O. (2003). Self-segregation or self-preservation? A critical race theory and Latina/o critical theory analysis of findings from a longitudinal study of Chicana/o college students. *International Journal of Qualitative Studies in Education, 16*(5), 619–646.

Villenas, S., & Deyhle, D. (1999). Critical Race Theory and ethnographies challenging the stereotypes: Latino families, schooling, resilience and resistance. *Curriculum Inquiry, 29*(4), 413–445.

Vizenor, G. (1994). *Manifest Manners: Postindian warriors of survivance.* Hanover, NH: Weslyan University Press.

Vizenor, G. (1998). *Fugitive Poses: Native American Indian scenes of absence and presence.* Lincoln: University of Nebraska Press.

Vizenor, G., & Lee, A. R. (1999). *Postindian conversations.* Lincoln: University of Nebraska Press.

Wagner, R. (1981). *The invention of culture.* Chicago: University of Chicago Press.

Warrior, R. A. (1995). *Tribal Secrets: Recovering American Indian intellectual traditions.* Minneapolis: University of Minnesota Press.

Wilkins, D. E. (2002). *American Indian politics and the American political system.* Oxford: Rowman & Littlefield.

Wilkins, D. E., & Lomawaima, K. T. (2002). *Uneven ground: American Indian Sovereignty and federal law.* Norman, OK: University of Oklahoma Press.

Williams, R. (1987). Jefferson, the Norman Yoke, and American Indian lands. 29 *Arizona Law Review, 2,* 165–194.

Williams, R. (1989). Documents of barbarism: The contemporary legacy of European Racism and colonialism in the narrative traditions of federal Indian law. *Arizona Law Review, 95,* 237–278.

Williams, R. (1997). Vampires anonymous and critical race practice. *Michigan Law Review, 95,* 741–765.

Yosso, T. J., Parker, L., Solórzano, D. G., & Lynn, M. (2004). From Jim Crow to affirmative action and back again: A critical race discussion of racialized rationales and access to higher education. *Review of Research in Education, 28,* 1–27.

CHAPTER 52

CRITICAL RACE THEORY, LATINO CRITICAL THEORY, AND CRITICAL RACED-GENDERED EPISTEMOLOGIES: RECOGNIZING STUDENTS OF COLOR AS HOLDERS AND CREATORS OF KNOWLEDGE

DOLORES DELGADO BERNAL

For too long, the histories, experiences, cultures, and languages of students of color have been devalued, misinterpreted, or omitted within formal educational settings. In this chapter, the author uses critical race theory (CRT) and Latina/Latino critical theory (LatCrit) to demonstrate how critical raced-gendered epistemologies recognize students of color as holders and creators of knowledge. In doing so, she discusses how CRT and LatCrit provide an appropriate lens for qualitative research in the field of education. She then compares and contrasts the experiences of Chicana/Chicano students through a Eurocentric and a critical raced-gendered epistemological perspective and demonstrates that each perspective holds vastly different views of what counts as knowledge, specifically regarding language, culture, and commitment to communities. She then offers implications of critical raced-gendered epistemologies for both research and practice and concludes by discussing some of the critiques of the use of these epistemologies in educational research.

I have to say that I think my high school was pretty discriminatory because I feel that I wasn't tracked into a college program and I think I had the potential to be. Except because I was from the other side of the tracks, no one really took the time to inspire me. . . . I had a high school English teacher who had asked us to write an essay. And I had written it about the death of my sister. And when she gave it back to me, she gave me a D. And she said it was all wrong. And I just couldn't get how she was, first of all, insensitive, and then second of all, criticizing me on an experience she didn't have and that only I could write about. And so that's when I think I started to feel the discrimination, almost in the way, I guess in the expectations of what you talk about or what you don't talk about in school. And what's academic and what's not academic.

—Angela, a graduating Chicana college student

Actually, after my second semester of my sophomore year, I took my first Chicano studies course, "Chicano Life History" with Ledesma, and that just opened my eyes to everything, a passion. . . . That class helped me a lot . . . *y tambien* [and also] basically gave me identity 'cause I was lost. . . . So, if the students were exposed to that . . . it would make a huge difference, *learning our history y todo* [and all]. . . . I wish that somehow I could [teach at] the elementary school 'cause I think it's important that we start that early, just giving that gift of giving someone their . . . history *y todo* [and all]. . . . And I don't think it should even be a gift, it's a right. It's a right; unfortunately, it's not happening [in schools].

—Chuy, a graduating Chicano college student

Although students of color are holders and creators of knowledge, they often feel as if their histories, experiences, cultures, and languages are devalued, misinterpreted, or omitted within formal educational settings. The above quotes address how two undergraduate students of color reflect on what counts as valid knowledge in schools and how this has directly affected their lives.[1] Angela speaks to how she learned as a young high school student that her real life experiences "from the other side of the tracks" were not considered an acceptable source of knowledge from which to draw on in academic settings. Her personal experience embodied knowledge that her teacher seemed to disregard, perhaps because she did not consider it to be objective or authoritative knowledge. Chuy points to how his cultural and/or ethnic history was omitted from the curriculum until he was in college and how this has motivated him to want to teach younger students. He expresses his disappointment in the schools' focus on a Eurocentric history that denies the history of students of color. Both students are addressing epistemological questions that deal with power, politics, and survival as well as the need for educators to recognize the knowledge, histories, and experiences of students of color.

Epistemology, in general, refers to the nature, status, and production of knowledge (Harding, 1987) and the way one knows and understands the world. However, the concept of epistemology is more than just a "way of knowing" and can be more accurately defined as a "system of knowing" that is linked to worldviews based on the conditions under which people live and learn (Ladson-Billings, 2000). Ladson-Billings argues that "there are well-developed systems of knowledge, or epistemologies, that stand in contrast to the dominant Euro-American epistemology" (p. 258). Indeed, a number of education scholars have begun talking about critical raced and raced-gendered epistemologies that emerge from a social, cultural, and political history different from the dominant race (e.g., Delgado Bernal, 1998; Dillard, 1997, 2000; Gordon, 1990; Ladson-Billings, 1995, 2000; Scheurich & Young, 1997). These raced and raced-gendered epistemologies directly challenge the broad range of currently popular research paradigms, from positivism to constructivism and liberal feminism to postmodernism, which draw from a narrow foundation of knowledge that is based on the social, historical, and cultural experiences of Anglos (Stanfield, 1994). As part of the challenge to popular research paradigms, this chapter demonstrates how critical race theory (CRT) and Latina/Latino critical theory (LatCrit) give credence to critical raced-gendered epistemologies that recognize students of color as holders and creators of knowledge.

In this chapter, I refer to critical raced-gendered epistemologies that offer unique ways of knowing and understanding the world based on the various raced and gendered experiences of people of color. In my mind, there is not just one raced-gendered epistemology but many that each speak to culturally specific ways of positioning between a raced epistemology that omits the influence of gender on knowledge production and a White feminist epistemology that does not account for race. Collins (1998) speaks to this balance when she states, "Black feminism must come to terms with a White feminist agenda incapable of seeing its own racism, as well as a Black nationalist one resistant to grappling with its own sexism" (p. 70). Whereas White feminisms often define themselves against a male-centered perspective, critical raced-gendered perspectives avoid male-female polarisms, instead examining how oppression is caught up in multiply raced, gendered, classed, and sexed relations. In other words, these systems of knowledge, or critical raced-gendered epistemologies, emerge from the experiences a person of color might have at the intersection of racism, sexism, classism, and other oppressions.

To demonstrate how critical raced-gendered epistemologies recognize students of color as holders and creators of knowledge, I first discuss how CRT and LatCrit provide an appropriate lens for qualitative research in the field of education. I then look to how different epistemological perspectives view students of color. More specifically, I compare and contrast how a Eurocentric perspective and a specific raced-gendered perspective offer very different interpretations of the educational experiences of Chicana/Chicano students.[2] I then offer implications of critical raced-gendered epistemologies for both research and practice. I conclude by discussing some of the critiques against the use of these epistemologies in educational research. Throughout this chapter, I emphasize how a critical raced-gendered epistemology recognizes students of color as holders and creators of knowledge who have much to offer in transforming educational research and practice. Indeed, I argue that students of color represent what Castillo (1995) describes as holders of knowledge who can transform the world into a more just place.

> Today, we grapple with our need to thoroughly understand who we are . . . and to believe in our gifts, talents, our worthiness and beauty, while having to survive within the constructs of a world antithetical to our intuition and knowledge. . . . Who, in this world of the glorification of material wealth, Whiteness, and phallic worship would consider us holders of knowledge that could transform this world into a place where the quality of life for all living things on this planet is the utmost priority? (p. 149)

CRT and LatCrit as a Lens for Educational Research

Although numerous frameworks could be used to move toward a critical raced-gendered epistemology in educational research, in this chapter, I use a lens that builds on the work of CRT and LatCrit.[3] As theoretical frameworks in the field of law, CRT and LatCrit explore the ways that so-called race-neutral laws and policies perpetuate racial and/or ethnic and gender subordination. They emphasize the importance of viewing laws and lawmaking within the proper historical and cultural context to deconstruct their racialized content (Crenshaw, Gotanda, Peller, & Thomas, 1995). These frameworks challenge dominant liberal ideas such as colorblindness and meritocracy and show how these ideas operate to disadvantage people of color and further advantage Whites (Delgado & Stefancic, 1994). "The task for critical race scholars is to uncover and explore the various ways in which racial thinking operates" (Flores, 2000, p. 437) to move toward a more just society.

LatCrit is similar to CRT. However, LatCrit is concerned with a progressive sense of a coalitional Latina/Latino pan-ethnicity (Valdes, 1996), and it addresses issues often ignored by critical race theorists. I see LatCrit theory adding important dimensions to a critical race analysis. For example, LatCrits theorize issues such as language, immigration, ethnicity, culture, identity, phenotype, and sexuality (Espinoza, 1990; Garcia, 1995; Hernández-Truyol, 1997; Johnson, 1997; Martinez, 1994; Montoya, 1994). LatCrit is a theory that elucidates Latinas/Latinos' multidimensional identities and can address the intersectionality of racism, sexism, classism, and other forms of oppression. It is a theory that has a tradition of offering a strong gender analysis so that it "can address the concerns of Latinas in light of both our internal and external relationships in and with the worlds that have marginalized us" (Hernández-Truyol, 1997, p. 885). Indeed, this tradition and its necessary intersectionality offers an important lens from which to envision a raced-gendered epistemology, especially for Chicanas/Latinas. LatCrit is conceived as an anti-subordination and antiessentialist project that attempts to link theory with practice, scholarship with teaching, and the academy with the community (*LatCrit Primer*, 1999). LatCrit is not incompatible or competitive with CRT.

> Instead, LatCrit is supplementary, complementary to [CRT]. LatCrit . . . at its best, should operate as a close cousin—related to [CRT] in real and lasting ways, but not necessarily living under the same roof. (Valdes, 1996, pp. 26-27)

To use CRT and LatCrit together as a lens for educational research, I adapt and borrow from both groups of theorists. CRT and LatCrit in education can be defined as a framework that challenges the dominant discourse on race, gender, and class as it relates to education by examining how educational theory, policy, and practice subordinate certain racial and ethnic groups (Solórzano & Delgado Bernal, 2001; Solórzano & Yosso, 2000). Critical race and LatCrit theorists acknowledge that educational structures, processes, and discourses operate in contradictory ways with their potential to oppress and marginalize and their potential to emancipate and empower. CRT and LatCrit are transdisciplinary and draw on many bodies of progressive scholarship to understand and improve the educational experiences of students of color (Parker, Deyhle, & Villenas, 1999).

Solórzano (1998) outlines the following five defining elements of CRT in relationship to educational research. I believe these elements form the basis of both CRT and LatCrit, and I offer examples of how they support raced-gendered epistemologies.

1. *The importance of transdisciplinary approaches.* CRT and LatCrit's transdisciplinary approach allows educational researchers to draw on the strengths and research methods of various disciplines in understanding and improving the educational experiences of students of color. Ethnic studies and women's studies, in particular, "have opened the way for multiple theoretical and epistemological readings in the field of educational research," and scholars of color have provided "a needed critique as well as an 'endarkenment' on society as a whole" (Dillard, 2000, p. 676).

2. *An emphasis on experiential knowledge.* For too long, the experiential knowledge of students of color has been viewed as a deficit in formal learning environments. Critical raced-gendered epistemologies allow this experiential knowledge to be viewed as a strength and acknowledge that the life experiences of students of color are "uniquely individual while at the same time both collective and connected" (Dillard, 2000, p. 676). An emphasis on experiential knowledge also allows researchers to embrace the use of counterstories, narratives, *testimonios*, and oral histories to illuminate the unique experiences of students of color.

3. *A challenge to dominant ideologies.* CRT and LatCrit give meaning to the creation of culturally and linguistically relevant ways of knowing and understanding and to the importance of rethinking the traditional notion of what counts as knowledge. Raced-gendered epistemologies also push us to consider pedagogies of the home, which offer culturally specific ways of teaching and learning and embrace ways of knowing that extend beyond the public realm of formal schooling (Delgado Bernal, 2001). Because power and politics are at the center of all teaching and learning, the application of household knowledge to situations outside of the home becomes a creative process that challenges the transmission of "official knowledge" and dominant ideologies.

4. *The centrality of race and racism and their intersectionality with other forms of subordination.* Raced-gendered epistemologies emerge from ways of knowing that are in direct contrast with the dominant Eurocentric epistemology, partially as a result of histories that are based on the intersection of racism, sexism, classism, and other forms of subordination. This means that the research process must recognize that multiple layers of oppression are followed by multiple forms of resistance (Solórzano & Yosso, in press).

5. *A commitment to social justice.* Critical raced-gendered epistemologies are grounded in raced and gendered histories, and their legacy of resistance to racism and sexism can translate into a pursuit of social justice in both educational research and practice. Indeed, research and practice grounded in a critical raced-gendered epistemology seek political and social change on behalf of communities of color.

These five defining elements come together to offer a unique way to approach educational research and to move researchers and educators into spaces of moral and critical practice.[4] I concur with Gloria Ladson-Billings (2000), who states, "The 'gift' of CRT is that it unapologetically challenges the scholarship that would dehumanize and depersonalize us" (p. 272). I, therefore, also believe that CRT and LatCrit can help to uncover the possibilities of raced-gendered epistemologies in educational research and practice.

How Different Epistemological Perspectives View Chicana/Chicano Students

In this section, I present an example of how the educational experiences of one group of students of color, Chicanas/Chicanos, may be interpreted very differently based on the different epistemological perspectives educators and/or researchers employ. First, I outline a Eurocentric perspective and illustrate how this perspective has been used as the basis for a deficit understanding of Mexican culture throughout the 1900s and into the 21st century. Then, I outline a specific raced-gendered perspective and demonstrate how we can reconceptualize the so-called deficits of Mexican culture into assets and view Chicana/Chicano students as holders and creators of knowledge.

A Eurocentric Perspective

Western modernism is a network or grid of broad assumptions and beliefs that are deeply embedded in the way dominant Western culture constructs the nature of the world and one's experiences in it (Foucault, 1979, 1988). In the United States, the center of this grid is a Eurocentric epistemological perspective based on White privilege. The Council on Interracial Books for Children (1977) defines this perspective as (a) the belief that the perspective of the Euro-Americans is the norm and (b) the practice of ignoring and/or delegitimizing the experiences, motivations, aspirations, and views of people of color. Traditionally, the majority of Euro-Americans adhere to a Eurocentric perspective founded on covert and overt assumptions regarding White superiority, territorial expansion, and "American" democratic ideals such as meritocracy, objectivity, and individuality. What this means is that their way of knowing and understanding the world around them is very naturally and subconsciously interpreted through these beliefs. For example, the notion of meritocracy allows people to believe that all people—no matter what race, class, or gender—get what they deserve based primarily on an individual's own merit and how hard a person works. Those who believe that our society is truly a meritocratic one find it difficult to believe that men gain advantage from women's disadvantages or that Euro-Americans have any significant advantage over people of color. This way of knowing and understanding the world is at least partially based on White privilege, which is "an invisible package of unearned assets" (McIntosh, 1997, p. 120) or a system of opportunities and benefits that is bestowed on an individual simply for being White. Tatum (1999) writes about the invisibility of White privilege, yet points out its very real effects and states that "despite the current rhetoric about affirmative action and reverse discrimination, every social indicator, from salary to life expectancy, reveals the advantages of being White" (p. 8). But because, especially to Whites, this privilege is often invisible, it is legitimized and viewed as the norm or the point of departure. Standards (especially those in education) are based on this norm, and individuals or knowledges that depart from this norm are often devalued and subordinated.

The insidious nature of a Eurocentric epistemological perspective allows it to subtly (and not so subtly) shape the belief system and practices of researchers, educators, and the school curriculum while continuing to adversely influence the educational experiences of Chicanas/Chicanos and other students of color. For example, throughout the 20th century, the Euro-American social belief system about Mexicans helped support the many political, economic, and cultural reasons for their de jure and then de facto school segregation (Delgado Bernal, 2000). First, some individuals openly argued that Mexican students should be segregated from White students because they were genetically and physically inferior. One school official stated, "We segregate for the same reason that the Southerners segregate the Negro. They are an inferior race, that is all" (Taylor, 1934, p. 219). Another common assertion was that the standard of cleanliness among Mexican children was lower than that of Anglos. "I don't believe in mixing. They are filthy and lousy, not all, but most of them," declared one school board member (Taylor, 1934, p. 217).

Indeed, the beliefs about Mexicans held by many educators shared a common trait during this period. Tate (1997) observed that educators' beliefs were "premised upon political, scientific, and religious theories relying on racial characterizations and stereotypes about people of color that help support a legitimating ideology and specific political action" (p. 199). A case in point is how prohibiting Spanish-language use among Mexican school children was a social philosophy and a political tool used by local and state officials to justify school segregation and to maintain a colonized relationship between Mexicans and the dominant society (Delgado Bernal, 1999). Today, bilingualism often continues to be seen as "un-American" and considered a deficit and an obstacle to learning.

A Eurocentric epistemology that is based on White superiority, capitalism, and scientific theories of intelligence has provided the cornerstone of de jure and de facto segregated schooling for Mexicans and the historic and current devaluation of the Spanish language (Crawford, 1992; G. G. González, 1990; Menchaca & Valencia, 1990; San Miguel, 1987). The epistemological orientation that for generations has viewed Chicanas/Chicanos as "culturally deficient" and characterized them as ignorant, backward, unclean, unambitious, and abnormal, remains unchanged and has been unaffected by major judicial and policy decisions throughout the Southwest (Donato, 1997; González,

1990; Moreno, 1999). In fact, a belief in the cultural and linguistic deficiency of Chicana/Chicano students remains in place in the 21st century and is supported by political action and ideological domination that continues to exclude and silence Chicanas/Chicanos and other Latinas/Latinos. Villenas and Deyhle (1999) powerfully stated one way in which this exclusion and silencing takes place at the institutional level through the curriculum.

> In the schools, the colonization of the mind is continued through the instilling of a historical amnesia that renders Latino/indigenous peoples as "immigrants," foreigners who have no claim to the Americas, while European Americans are constructed as the natural owners and inheritors of these lands. The rich knowledge, beliefs and worldviews of Latino and Mexicano/Chicano communities are not validated, let alone taught. (p. 421)

The message that Chicana/Chicano students are inferior and not agents of knowledge continues to affect the institutional level and also translates into overcrowded and underfinanced schools, low graduation rates, and overrepresentation of these students in special education classes (Kozol, 1991; Valencia, 1991). A CRT and LatCrit lens "can unveil and explain how and why 'raced' children are overwhelmingly the recipients of low teacher expectations and are consequently tracked, placed in low-level classes and receive 'dull and boring' curriculums" (Villenas & Deyhle, 1999, p. 415). In the next section, I use a CRT and LatCrit lens to examine how a specific raced-gendered epistemology offers a very different understanding of the knowledge and experience that Chicanas/Chicanos bring to their formal schooling.

A Chicana Feminist Perspective

I view raced-gendered epistemologies as dynamic and encompassing various experiences, standpoints, and theories that are specific to different groups of people of color. In earlier work, I have proposed a particular raced-gendered epistemology by outlining the characteristics of a Chicana feminist epistemology in educational research (Delgado Bernal, 1998). This epistemological orientation challenges the historical and ideological representation of Chicanas and is grounded in the sociohistorical experiences of Chicanas and their communities. Chicana feminist ways of knowing and understanding are partially shaped by collective experiences and community memory. Community and family knowledge is taught to youth through legends, *corridos,* and storytelling. It is through culturally specific ways of teaching and learning that ancestors and elders share the knowledge of conquest, segregation, patriarchy, homophobia, assimilation, and resistance. If we believe "in the wisdom of our ancient knowledge," as Ana Castillo (1995, p. 148) suggests, then the knowledge that is passed from one generation to the next can help us survive in everyday life. Therefore, adopting a Chicana feminist epistemology will expose human relationships and experiences that are probably not visible from a Eurocentric epistemological orientation. Within this framework, Chicanas and Chicanos become agents of knowledge who participate in intellectual discourse that links experience, research, community, and social change.

As a case in point, I draw from my current research, which focuses on the knowledge Chicana/Chicano college students learn in the home and successfully employ when confronted with challenges and obstacles that impede their academic achievement and college participation (Delgado Bernal, 2001). The life history interview and focus group data with more than 50 Chicana/Chicano college students are educational "counterstories" that are told from a nonmajoritarian perspective—offering stories that White educators usually do not hear or tell (Delgado, 1989, 1993). My analysis of these "counterstories" indicates that the students develop tools and strategies for daily survival in an educational system that often excludes and silences them. In fact, the communication, practices, and learning that occur in the home and community can be viewed as a cultural knowledge base that helps students survive the daily experiences of racism, sexism, and classism. What are often perceived as deficits for Chicana/Chicano students within a Eurocentric epistemological framework—limited English proficiency, Chicano and/or Mexicano cultural practices, or too many nonuniversity-related responsibilities—can be understood within a Chicana feminist perspective as cultural assets or resources that Chicana/Chicano students bring to formal educational environments.

The application of household knowledge, specifically in the form of bilingualism, biculturalism, and commitment to communities, interrupts the transmission of "official knowledge" and even helps students navigate their way around educational obstacles. For instance, the students in my study experienced their bilingualism in various ways throughout their educational journey. Most of them felt that their bilingualism had a positive impact on them academically and socially. They seemed to draw strength from using both Spanish and English in academic and social settings. As one young woman put it, "It's a great resource to my community, the people that I work with, the university itself." Students stated over and over again that knowledge in Spanish helped them acquire English and that their bilingualism had been an asset to their education. A few students also spoke passionately about their bilingualism in terms of identity and the importance of maintaining their home language.

In addition, students discussed how they and others benefited from their bicultural insights. Many also spoke of how they consciously rejected assimilation and attempted to hold onto different aspects of their culture while they learned from other cultures. As one female sophomore said,

> I think I'm acculturated, and I don't think I've assimilated by the simple fact that I have decided to learn about all these other cultures. . . . I am not giving up my own, and I think when you assimilate you give something up to gain something.

In spite of a Eurocentrism that has fostered a history of cultural repression in the United States, these students embrace the cultural and linguistic strengths and assets of Chicana/Chicano family education. As Mesa-Bains (1999) explained, it is important to affirm how our biculturalism and family knowledge have contributed to this country.

> Our *quinceaneras*, our *bailes*, our *bodas*, our *pastorelas*, our *fiestas patrias*, our foods, our music, and our arts are all part of the cultural contributions we have made to the vibrant life of the United States. . . . In such a time of growing xenophobia it is important to affirm for ourselves and for others the myriad ways in which we have enriched this country, from our historic beginnings as ancient people to our contemporary lives. (p. 107)

The students also voiced a very strong commitment to their families or the Mexican communities from which they came, a commitment that translated into a desire to give back and help others. Many of the students spoke of their role as examples for their younger siblings and in promoting education or ideas of social justice. One woman commented that "I'm teaching [my younger brothers] to be responsive to women, to believe in them, to not be like the other *machistas* at home." In addition, the words of the students I interviewed paralleled Villalpando's (1996) national research, which found that in comparison to White students, Chicana/Chicano students enter college with higher levels of altruism, stronger interests in pursuing careers serving their communities, and stronger interests in "helping their communities." Students spoke of their commitment to their families and communities as a source of inspiration and motivation to overcome educational obstacles. This male freshman spoke about his commitment to helping out other people in his community after he graduates from college.

> I kind of want a good income, but the only way I'll accept that is if I do something good . . . and I'm active in the community, and I'm helping out other people, I'm not just helping myself. . . . I've always seen it as you're just a wasted person if you just help yourself.

The voices of these students illustrate the vastly different worldviews about what is considered "valid knowledge." They see their home knowledge—their bilingualism, biculturalism, and commitment to communities—as a critical tool that has helped them navigate through educational obstacles, go onto college, and make a positive difference to others. As documented in the previous section, this contrasts with educators who operate within a traditional Eurocentric epistemological framework and often see the home knowledge of Chicana/Chicano students as lacking, limited, and inferior to the "norm." Situated within a particular raced-gendered framework, my work rejects the dominant culture's text and vision of what Chicana/Chicano students know and of who they are. At the same time, this epistemological orientation allows educators to better understand the different knowledges Chicana/Chicano students bring from their homes and communities.

Implications of a Critical Raced-Gendered Epistemology

Methodological and Pedagogical Insights

The focus of this chapter is epistemology, particularly those systems of knowing that counter a dominant Eurocentric epistemology, yet, it is interconnected to the critical race methodologies and pedagogies discussed in this volume. As Pillow (2000) states, "One cannot separate the epistemologies of feminist or race theory from their methodological and epistemological practices" (p. 23). None of the three—epistemology, methodology, and pedagogy—can be isolated from one another, as they are closely interdependent and directly influence the research process. Thus, I believe a critical raced-gendered epistemology offers the following methodological and pedagogical insights.

A critical raced-gendered epistemology allows educational researchers to "bring together understandings of epistemologies and pedagogies to imagine how race, ethnicity, gender, class, and sexuality are braided with cultural knowledge, practices, spirituality, formal education, and the law" (F. González, 2001, p. 643). F. González (1998, 2001) works from a prism of CRT, LatCrit, and U.S. third-world feminisms to develop a methodological approach that affirms the community and cultural knowledge of students of color. She names this methodological approach *trenzas y mestizaje*—the braiding of theory, qualitative research strategies, and a sociopolitical consciousness. This approach incorporates various qualitative strategies to examine and appreciate the cultural knowledge of students of color. F. González (2001) describes *trenzas y mestizaje* and elaborates

> on how a braiding of different ways of knowing, teaching, and learning brings cultural knowledge to the fore of discourses on human rights, social justice, and educational equity as well as to inform the formulations of holistic educational policies and practices. (p. 643)

In addition, it is through a raced-gendered epistemology that Trinidad Galván (2001) proposes how "womanist" pedagogies speak directly to third-world women's knowledge and experiences. She explores three pedagogical formations (spirituality, well-being, and *convivencia*) as the teaching, learning, and creation of knowledge among a group of *Mexicana campesinas*. These pedagogical formations expand our traditional notion of pedagogy "by situating it among groups of people traditionally unheard and spaces continually unexplored" (p. 607), thus extending our understanding of Mexicana/Mexicano knowledge. Therefore, researching from within a critical raced-gendered epistemology allows the experiential knowledge of communities of color to be viewed as a strength and an asset. It also allows us to "create *nuevas teorías* (new theories) that understand, penetrate, define, and elucidate the content and meaning of our multidimensional identities" (Hernández-Truyol, 1997, p. 884).

A critical raced-gendered epistemology, grounded in CRT and LatCrit, also supports methodological and pedagogical approaches that affirm experiences and responses to different forms of oppression and validates them as appropriate forms of data. By incorporating a counterstorytelling method based on the narratives, *testimonios*, or life histories of people of color, a story can be told from a nonmajoritarian perspective—a story that White educators usually do not hear or tell (Delgado, 1989, 1993). At the same time, counterstorytelling can also serve as a pedagogical tool that allows one to better understand and appreciate the unique experiences and responses of students of color through a deliberate, conscious, and open type of listening. In other words, an important component of using counterstories includes not only telling nonmajoritarian stories but also learning how to listen and hear the messages in counterstories. Legal scholar Williams (1997) believes that counterstorytelling and critical race practice are "mostly about learning to listen to other people's stories and then finding ways to make those stories matter in the legal system" (p. 765). Likewise, learning to listen to counterstories within the educational system can be an important pedagogical practice for teachers and students as well as an important methodological practice for educational researchers.

Insights for Policy and Practice

As my research on Chicana/Chicano college students demonstrates, CRT and LatCrit give credence to culturally and linguistically relevant ways of knowing and understanding and to the importance of rethinking the traditional notion of what counts as knowledge. The implications of this go beyond the methodological and pedagogical to affect both policy and practice. Rather than focus on the failures of students of color, an endarkened feminist epistemology allows us to ask how cultural knowledge contributes to the educational success of some students and how educational institutions can respond appropriately.

For example, universities that have language or diversity requirements might develop innovative curricular and pedagogical ways to include the bilingualism and biculturalism of students into the curriculum. In other words, institutions can acknowledge and give credit for these resources while helping students develop these resources even further. Rather than view students with limited English skills as a liability to the university (because the university has to provide language development classes for these students), the university should see these students as an asset. These are students who might be able to work as tutors in the university language department.

In addition, elementary, secondary, and postsecondary schools can incorporate the family knowledge of bilingual students by sending out information to parents in languages other than English. This would allow parents, especially at the elementary and secondary level, to stay involved and better understand the process of their children's formal education. It would also nurture the family and school relationship that is so important at all levels of formal schooling. Too often, students of color believe they have to choose either family and culture or school success (Nieto, 1996). Yet, researchers have found that for Latina/Latino students attending college full-time, maintaining family relationships is among the most important aspects that facilitates their adjustment to college (Hurtado, Carter, & Spuler, 1996). Other studies demonstrated that when college students maintain a supportive relationship with their parents, they are better adjusted and more likely to graduate (Cabrera, Castaneda, Nora, & Hengstler, 1992).

Finally, the national movement to dismantle race-based admissions policies at universities ignores current societal inequalities and the fact that the admissions process is based on a very Eurocentric measure of knowledge. Legislation that outlaws considerations of race and/or ethnicity in the university admissions process is supported by a myth of meritocracy and continues to validate a very subjective and highly selective admissions process (Delgado Bernal, 1999; Villalpando, in press). If race and/or ethnicity is not to be part of the admissions equation, educators need to think about creative ways to move away from a solely Eurocentric measure of knowledge to one that weighs "other" knowledges that emerge from communities of color (e.g., bilingualism, biculturalism, commitment to communities). Legal scholar Delgado (1995) argues for "an overhaul of the admissions process and a rethinking of the criteria that make a person a deserving . . . student" (p. 51). He and many others have argued for admission standards that would result in an increased number of women and students of color gaining admission, yet, he points out that these recommendations are often ignored and never instituted. A critical raced-gendered epistemology enables educators to consider creative admissions, curricular, and pedagogical policies that acknowledge, respect, and nurture the ways of knowing and understanding in communities of color.

Critiques of a Critical Raced-Gendered Epistemology

Without a doubt, there are those who will argue against the use of a critical raced-gendered epistemology in general and more specifically within the area of educational research and practice. Some of the potential critiques will probably parallel the numerous critiques already given against CRT and LatCrit within legal studies, and others may be unique to the field of education. In this section, I will briefly address two potential arguments that critics may put forth in relationship to a critical raced-gendered epistemology: the essentialist argument and the argument against the use of personal stories and narratives.

The Essentialist Argument

As Brayboy (2001) noted, postmodernists and other progressive scholars may be uncomfortable with CRT because they believe that it essentializes race and treats all people of color the same. The essentialist argument is rooted in a critique of identity politics that is based on a unidimensional characteristic, such as race or ethnicity. Identity politics is "an approach that is founded on parochial notions of race and representation" (Darder & Torres, 2000) and ignores or glosses over differences based on class, gender, sexuality, and culture. Rightly, critics argue that an essentialist notion of identity is simplistic and does not allow for the myriad experiences that shape who we are and what we know.

What many critics do not understand is that critical race theorists and LatCrits "have pushed the envelope of the ways in which we talk about race and racism, so that we focus on the intersectionality of subordination" (Solórzano & Yosso, in press). What this means is that one's identity is not based on the social construction of race but rather is multidimensional and intersects with various experiences. Certainly, "critical legal scholarship of race (and gender or sexual orientation) in recent times has interrogated and helped debunk various essentialisms and power hierarchies based on race . . . and other constructs" (Valdes, 1996, p. 3). LatCrit in particular has pushed scholars forward in analyzing identity construction of racially subordinated people at both the individual and group levels (Johnson, 1998) and within postidentity politics (Valdes, 1996). They have added layers of complexity to the formation of identity and construction of knowledge by looking at the intersections of immigration (Garcia, 1995; Johnson, 1996-1997), migration (Johnson, 1998), human rights (Hernández-Truyol, 1996; Iglesias, 1996–1997; Romany, 1996–1997), language (Romany, 1996), gender (Rivera, 1997), and class (Ontiveros, 1997).

With increased globalization and transnational labor and communication, we have to move beyond essentialist notions of identity and of what counts as knowledge. So although race and gender are central components of a critical raced-gendered epistemology, they are but two of the many components that are woven together, and they are anything but static. Dillard (2000) pointed out that the "intent here is not to present race/ethnicity or gender as being essentialist, unchangeable, or immovable. Instead, these positionalities must be seen as shifting and dynamic sets of social relationships which embody a particular endarkened feminist epistemological basis" (p. 670). Although a critical raced-gendered epistemology is anti-essentialist, it also allows us to grasp core values within communities of color such as education, self-determination, resistance, family, and freedom. Researching from within this framework offers a way to understand and analyze the multiple identities and knowledges of people of color without essentializing their various experiences.

The Argument Against Personal Stories and Narratives

There have been numerous critiques in legal studies regarding the use of stories and narratives by CRT and LatCrit theorists (see Farber & Sherry, 1997, for one of the more substantial critiques). The argument against using personal stories and narratives is a critique against alternative ways of knowing and understanding and is basically an argument over subjectivity versus objectivity. The critique states that CRT and LatCrit theorists

> relentlessly replace traditional scholarship with personal stories, which hardly represent common experiences. The proliferation of stories makes it impossible for others to debate. . . . An infatuation with narrative infects and distorts [their] attempts at analysis. Instead of scientifically investigating whether rewarding individuals according to merit has any objective basis, [they] insist on telling stories about their personal struggles. (Simon, 1999, p. 3)

It is interesting that the critics do not acknowledge that Eurocentrism has become the dominant mind-set that directly affects the mainstream stories told about race. Because Eurocentrism and White privilege appear to be the norm, many people continue to believe that education in the United States is a meritocratic, unbiased, and fair process. These individuals might find it difficult to accept the notion that a critical raced-gendered epistemology is important to educational research and practice. Yet, the stories, beliefs, and perspectives regarding race and gender in the United States often ignore the stories, beliefs, perspectives, and experiences of people of color in general and women of color in particular. Delgado (1993) points out that "majoritarians tell stories too. But the ones they tell—about merit, causation, blame, responsibility, and social justice—do not seem to them like stories at all, but the truth" (p. 666). In other words, they believe their stories are based on facts, and because Eurocentrism and White privilege are invisible, they fail to see how subjective their stories are.

A critical raced-gendered epistemology does not position the debate between objectivity and subjectivity. Rather, it sees all stories as subjective and the production of knowledge as situated. And those working from this perspective understand that education in the United States has a way to go before it is a meritocratic, unbiased, and fair process. Working from within a critical raced-gendered epistemology does not mean that one is interested in replacing an old body of knowledge that purports to be the truth with an alternative body of knowledge that claims to be the truth. It does mean that one acknowledges and respects other ways of knowing and understanding, particularly the stories and narratives of those who have experienced and responded to different forms of oppression. This has not been the case in education, where for too long, family cultural narratives have not been considered a legitimate part of research or practice. Many researchers have begun to demonstrate how the cultural resources and funds of knowledge such as myths, folktales, *dichos*, *consejos*, kitchen talk, autobiographical stories, and pedagogies of the home are indeed educational strengths and strategies found in communities of color (e.g., Collins, 1998; Delgado Bernal, 2001; Delgado-Gaitan, 1994; Moll, Amanti, Neff, & González, 1992; Silko, 1996; Suárez-Orozco & Suárez-Orozco, 1995; Villalpando, in press; Villenas & Deyhle, 1999; Villenas & Moreno, 2001). Tapping into these strengths and strategies is an important first step in moving away from a Eurocentric epistemological orientation to a critical raced-gendered perspective.

Conclusion

By comparing and contrasting the experiences of Chicana/Chicano students through a Eurocentric and a critical raced-gendered epistemological perspective, I demonstrated that each perspective holds vastly different views of what counts as knowledge, specifically regarding language, culture, and community commitment. The Eurocentric perspective has for too long viewed the experiential knowledge of students of color as a deficit or ignored it all together. The focus on Eurocentric knowledge and history can be alienating and frustrating for students such as Angela and Chuy, who were quoted at the beginning of this chapter. To recognize all students as holders and creators of knowledge, it is imperative that the histories, experiences, cultures, and languages of students of color are recognized and valued in schools.

Together, CRT and LatCrit form a lens for educational research that acknowledges and supports systems of knowing and understanding that counter the dominant Eurocentric epistemology. CRT and LatCrit's emphasis on experiential knowledge allows researchers to embrace the use of counter-stories and other methodological and pedagogical approaches that view the community and family knowledge of communities of color as a strength. In addition, critical raced-gendered perspectives in educational research become a means to resist epistemological racism (Scheurich & Young, 1997) and claim one's cultural knowledge as a legitimate and valid body of knowledge. Through a CRT and LatCrit lens, students of color can be seen as holders and creators of knowledge who have the potential to transform schools into places where the experiences of all individuals are acknowledged, taught, and cherished.

Notes

1. To protect the privacy of students, they are identified with a pseudonym and/or their gender and class status at the time of the interview.
2. Chicana and Chicano are cultural and political identities that were popularized during the Chicano movement of the 1960s. They are composed of multiple layers and are identities of resistance that are often consciously adopted later in life. The term *Chicana/Chicano* is gender inclusive and is used to discuss both women and men of Mexican origin and/or other Latinas/Latinos who share a similar political consciousness. Because terms of identification vary according to context and not all Mexican-origin people embrace the cultural and political identity of Chicana/Chicano, it is sometimes used interchangeably with Mexican.
3. In discussing raced-gendered epistemologies, I clearly draw from a rich body of U.S. third-world feminist literature that I do not discuss in detail in this chapter. I put this literature together with critical race

theory (CRT) and Latina/Latino critical theory (LatCrit) to form a lens that allows me to address how some knowledges and ways of knowing are subordinated within educational institutions.

4. Although CRT and LatCrit emerge from legal studies, they have intellectual roots in ethnic studies and women's studies. Their methodologies (i.e., storytelling, narratives), pedagogies, and underlying assumptions echo many of those found in these disciplines. Therefore, it is important to note that each of the defining elements "is not new in and of itself, but collectively, they represent a challenge to the existing modes of scholarship" (Solórzano, 1998, p. 123).

References

Brayboy, B. M. (2001, April). *Racing toward an interviewing methodology for the "Other": Critical race theory and interviewing.* Paper presented at the American Educational Research Association, Seattle, Washington.

Cabrera, A. F., Castaneda, M. B., Nora, A., & Hengstler, D. (1992). The convergence between two theories of college persistence. *Journal of Higher Education, 63,* 143–164.

Castillo, A. (1995). *Massacre of the dreamers: Essays on Xicanisma.* New York: Plume.

Collins, P. H. (1998). *Fighting words: Black women and the search for justice.* Minneapolis: University of Minnesota Press.

Council on Interracial Books for Children. (1977). *Stereotypes, distortions, and omissions in U.S. history textbooks.* New York: Racism and Sexism Resource Center for Educators.

Crawford, J. (1992). *Hold your tongue: Bilingualism and the politics of English only.* Reading, MA: Addison-Wesley.

Crenshaw, K. W., Gotanda, N., Peller, G., & Thomas, K. (Eds.). (1995). *Critical race theory: The key writings that formed the movement.* New York: New Press.

Darder, A., & Torres, R. D. (2000). Mapping the problematics of "race": A critique of Chicano education discourse. In C. Tejeda, C. Martinez, & Z. Leonardo (Eds.), *Charting new terrains of Chicana(o)/Latina(o) education* (pp. 161–172). Cresskill, NJ: Hampton.

Delgado, R. (1989). Storytelling for oppositionists and others: A plea for narrative. *Michigan Law Review, 87,* 2411–2441.

Delgado, R. (1993). On telling stories in school: A reply to Farber and Sherry. *Vanderbilt Law Review, 46,* 665–676.

Delgado, R. (1995). The imperial scholar: Reflections on a review of civil rights literature. In K. W. Crenshaw, N. Gotanda, G. Peller, & K. Thomas (Eds.), *Critical race theory: The key writings that formed the movement* (pp. 46–57). New York: New Press.

Delgado, R., & Stefancic, J. (1994). Critical race theory: An annotated bibliography 1993, a year of transition. *University of Colorado Law Review, 66,* 159–193.

Delgado Bernal, D. (1998). Using a Chicana feminist epistemology in educational research. *Harvard Educational Review, 68,* 555–582.

Delgado Bernal, D. (1999). Chicana/o education from the civil rights era to the present. In J. F. Moreno (Ed.), *The elusive quest for equality: 150 years of Chicano/Chicana education* (pp. 77–108). Cambridge, MA: Harvard Educational Review.

Delgado Bernal, D. (2000). Historical struggles for educational equity: Setting the context for Chicana/o schooling today. In C. Tejeda, C. Martinez, & Z. Leonardo (Eds.), *Charting new terrains of Chicana(o)/Latina(o) education* (pp. 67–90). Cresskill, NJ: Hampton.

Delgado Bernal, D. (2001). Learning and living pedagogies of the home: The mestiza consciousness of Chicana students. *International Journal of Qualitative Studies in Education, 14*(5), 623–629.

Delgado-Gaitan, C. (1994). *Consejos:* The power of cultural narratives. *Anthropology & Education Quarterly, 25,* 298–316.

Dillard, C. B. (1997, March). *The substance of things hoped for, the evidence of things not seen: Toward an endarkened feminist ideology in research.* Paper presented at the American Educational Research Association annual meeting, Chicago.

Dillard, C. B. (2000). The substance of things hoped for, the evidence of things not seen: Examining an endarkened feminist epistemology in culturally engaged research. *International Journal of Qualitative Studies in Education, 13,* 661–681.

Donato, R. (1997). *The other struggle for equal schools: Mexican Americans during the civil rights era.* Albany: State University of New York Press.

Espinoza, L. (1990). Masks and other disguises: Exposing legal academia. *Harvard Law Review, 103,* 1878–1886.

Farber, D., & Sherry, S. (1997). *Beyond all reason: The radical assault on truth in American law.* New York: Oxford University Press.

Flores, L. A. (2000). Constructing national bodies: Public argument in the English-only movement. In T. A. Hollihan (Ed.), *Argument at century's end: Proceedings of the 11th SCA/AFA conference on argumentation* (pp. 436–453). Annandale, VA: National Communication Association.

Foucault, M. (1979). *Discipline and punish: The birth of the prison.* New York: Vintage.

Foucault, M. (1988). *Madness and civilization: A history of insanity in the age of reason.* New York: Vintage.

Garcia, R. J. (1995). Critical race theory and Proposition 187: The racial politics of immigration law. *Chicano-Latino Law Review, 17,* 118–154.

González, F. (1998). The formations of Mexicananess: Trenzas de identidades multiples. Growing Up Mexicana: Braids of multiple identities. *International Journal of Qualitative Studies in Education, 11,* 81–102.

González, F. (2001). Haciendo que hacer: Cultivating a Mestiza worldview and academic achievement, Braiding cultural knowledge into educational research, policy, practice. *International Journal of Qualitative Studies in Education, 14*(5), 641–656.

González, G. G. (1990). *Chicano education in the era of segregation.* Cranbury, NJ: Associated University Presses.

Gordon, B. M. (1990). The necessity of African-American epistemology for educational theory and practice. *Journal of Education, 172,* 88–106.

Harding, S. (Ed.). (1987). *Feminism and methodology.* Milton Keynes: Open University Press.

Hernández-Truyol, B. E. (1996). Building bridges: Bringing international human rights home. *La Raza Law Journal, 9,* 69–79.

Hernández-Truyol, B. E. (1997). Borders (en)gendered: Normativities, Latinas and a LatCrit paradigm. *New York University Law Review, 72,* 882–927.

Hurtado, S., Carter, D. F., & Spuler, A. J. (1996). Latino student transition to college: Assessing difficulties and factors in successful adjustment. *Research in Higher Education, 37,* 135–157.

Iglesias, E. M. (1996–1997). International law, human rights, and LatCrit theory. *Inter-American Law Review, 28,* 177–213.

Johnson, K. R. (1996–1997). The social and legal construction of nonpersons. *Inter-American Law Review, 28,* 263–292.

Johnson, K. R. (1997). Some thoughts on the future of Latino legal scholarship. *Harvard Latino Law Review, 2,* 101–144.

Johnson, K. R. (1998). Immigration and Latino identity. *Chicano-Latino Law Review, 19,* 197–212.

Kozol, J. (1991). *Savage inequalities: Children in America's schools.* New York: HarperCollins.

Ladson-Billings, G. (1995). Toward a theory of cultural relevant pedagogy. *American Educational Research Journal, 32,* 465–491.

Ladson-Billings, G. (2000). Racialized discourses and ethnic epistemologies. In N. K. Denzin & Y. S. Lincoln (Eds.), *Handbook of qualitative research* (2nd ed., pp. 257–277). Thousands Oaks, CA: Sage.

LatCrit Primer. (1999, April 29–May 5). Fact sheet: LatCrit. Presented at the 4th annual LatCrit conference, Rotating Centers, Expanding Frontiers: LatCrit Theory and Marginal Intersection, Lake Tahoe, Nevada.

Martinez, G. A. (1994). Legal indeterminacy, judicial discretion and the Mexican-American litigation experience: 1930–1980. *U.C. Davis Law Review, 27,* 555–618.

McIntosh, P. (1997). White privilege: Unpacking the invisible knapsack. In B. Schneider (Ed.), *An anthology: Race in the first person* (pp. 119–126). New York: Crown Trade Paperbacks.

Menchaca, M., & Valencia, R. R. (1990). Anglo-Saxon ideologies and their impact on the segregation of Mexican students in California, the 1920s–1930s. *Anthropology and Education Quarterly, 21,* 222–249.

Mesa-Bains, A. (1999). As Latinos in America. In E. J. Olmos, L. Ybarro, & M. Monterey (Eds.), *Americanos: Latino life in the United States. La Vida Latina en Los Estados Unidos* (p. 107). Boston: Little, Brown.

Moll, L. C., Amanti, C., Neff, D., & González, N. (1992). Funds of knowledge for teaching: Using a qualitative approach to connect homes and classrooms. *Theory into Practice, 31,* 132–141.

Montoya, M. (1994). *Mascaras, trenzas, y grenas:* Un/masking the self while un/braiding Latina stories and legal discourse. *Chicano-Latino Law Review, 15,* 1–37.

Moreno, J. F. (Ed.). (1999). *The elusive quest for equality: 150 years of Chicano/Chicana education.* Cambridge, MA: Harvard Educational Review.

Nieto, S. (1996). *Affirming diversity: The sociopolitical context of multicultural education* (2nd ed.). White Plains, NY: Longman.

Ontiveros, M. L. (1997). Rosa Lopez, Christopher Darden, and me: Issues of gender, ethnicity, and class evaluating witness credibility. In A. K. Wing (Ed.), *Critical race feminism: A reader* (pp. 269–277). New York: New York University Press.

Parker, L., Deyhle, D., & Villenas, S. (1999). *Race is . . . race isn't: Critical race theory and qualitative studies in education.* Boulder, CO: Westview.

Pillow, W. S. (2000). Deciphering attempts to decipher postmodern educational research. *Educational Researcher, 29*(5), 21–24.

Rivera, J. (1997). Domestic violence against Latinas by Latino males: An analysis of race, national origin, and gender differentials. In A. K. Wing (Ed.), *Critical race feminism: A reader* (pp. 259–266). New York: New York University Press.

Romany, C. (1996). Gender, race/ethnicity and language. *La Raza Law Journal, 9,* 49–53.

Romany, C. (1996-1997). Claiming a global identity: Latino/a critical scholarship and international human rights. *Inter-American Law Review, 28,* 215–221.

San Miguel, G. (1987). *Let all of them take heed: Mexican Americans and the campaign for educational equality in Texas, 1910–1981.* Austin: University of Texas Press.

Scheurich, J. J., & Young, M. D. (1997). Coloring epistemologies: Are our research epistemologies racially biased? *Educational Researcher, 26*(4), 4–16.

Silko, L. M. (1996). *Yellow woman and a beauty of the spirit: Essays on Native American life today.* New York: Touchstone.

Simon, T. W. (1999). Racists versus anti-semites?: Critical race theorists criticized. *Newsletter on Philosophy, Law, and the Black Experience, 98*(2), 1–11.

Solórzano, D. G. (1998). Critical race theory, race and gender microaggressions, and the experience of Chicana and Chicano scholars. *International Journal of Qualitative Studies in Education, 11,* 121–136.

Solórzano, D. G., & Delgado Bernal, D. (2001). Examining transformational resistance through a critical race and LatCrit theory framework: Chicana and Chicano students in an urban context. *Urban Education, 36,* 308–342.

Solórzano, D. G., & Yosso, T. (2000). Toward a critical race theory of Chicana and Chicano education. In C. Tejeda, C. Martinez, & Z. Leonardo (Eds.), *Charting new terrains of Chicana(o)/Latina(o) education* (pp. 35–65). Cresskill, NJ: Hampton.

Solórzano, D. G., & Yosso, T. (in press). Maintaining social justice hopes within academic realities: A Freirean approach to critical race/LatCrit pedagogy. *Denver Law Review.*

Stanfield, J. H., II. (1994). Ethnic modeling in qualitative research. In N. K. Denzin & Y. S. Lincoln (Eds.), *Handbook of qualitative inquiry* (pp. 175–188). Newbury Park, CA: Sage.

Suárez-Orozco, C., & Suárez-Orozco, M. (1995). *Transformations: Migration, family, life, and achievement motivation among Latino adolescents.* Stanford, CA: Stanford University Press.

Tate, W. F. (1997). Critical race theory and education: History, theory, and implications. *Review of Research in Education, 22,* 195–247.

Tatum, B. (1999). *Why are all the Black kids sitting together in the cafeteria? And other conversations about race.* New York: Basic Books.

Taylor, P. S. (1934). *An American-Mexican frontier, Nueces County, Texas.* Chapel Hill: University of North Carolina Press.

Trinidad Galván, R. (2001). Portraits of mujeres desjuiciadas: Womanist pedagogies of the everyday, the mundane and the ordinary. *International Journal of Qualitative Studies in Education, 14*(5), 603–621.

Valdes, F. (1996). Foreword: Latina/o ethnicities, critical race theory and post-identity politics in postmodern legal culture: From practices to possibilities. *La Raza Law Journal, 9,* 1–31.

Valencia, R. R. (Ed.). (1991). *Chicano school failure and success: Research and policy agendas for the 1990's.* London: Falmer.

Villalpando, O. (1996). *The long term effects of college on Chicano and Chicana students: "Other oriented" values, service careers, and community involvement.* Unpublished doctoral dissertation, University of California, Los Angeles.

Villalpando, O. (in press). Self-segregation or self-preservation? A critical race theory and Latina/o critical theory analysis of a study of Chicana/o college students. *International Journal of Qualitative Studies in Education.*

Villenas, S., & Deyhle, D. (1999). Critical race theory and ethnographies challenging the stereotypes: Latino families, schooling, resilience and resistance. *Curriculum Inquiry, 29,* 413–445.

Villenas, S., & Moreno, M. (2001). To *valerse por si misma:* Between race, capitalism and patriarchy—Latina mother/daughter pedagogies in North Carolina. *International Journal of Qualitative Studies in Education, 14*(5), 671–687.

Williams, R. A. (1997). Vampires anonymous and critical race practice. *Michigan Law Review, 95,* 741–765.

CHAPTER 53
GETTING BEYOND THE 'SYMPTOM,'
ACKNOWLEDGING THE 'DISEASE':
THEORIZING RACIST NATIVISM

LINDSAY PEREZ HUBER, CORINA BENAVIDES LOPEZ,
MARIA C. MALAGON, VERONICA VELEZ, AND DANIEL G. SOLÓRZANO

An important tenet of Latina/o critical race theory (LatCrit) is to challenge dominant ideologies that mask racist beliefs and practices perpetrated against People of Color in the United States, particularly Latinas/os. In this chapter we utilize a LatCrit framework to theorize further the concept of racist nativism in the current sociopolitical moment, which is marked by significant anti-immigrant sentiment. In doing so, we hope to understand better the contemporary experiences of People of Color and Latinas/os specifically. We show how many racial and ethnic groups throughout US history have experienced racist nativism, but argue that those targeted by it today tend to be Latinas/os in general, and Mexican immigrants in particular. In conceptually extending the notion of racist nativism we endeavor to go beyond the 'symptoms' of racism and toward naming the 'disease' that plagues US society—white supremacy. We argue that the legacy of white supremacy not only remains with us today, but profoundly informs our racialized perceptions of a white American identity, whereby white Americans are perceived as native to the US and all others as non-native.

The persistent inflow of Hispanic immigrants threatens to divide the United States into two peoples, two cultures, and two languages. Unlike past immigrant groups, Mexicans and other Latinos have not assimilated into mainstream U.S. culture, forming instead their own political and linguistic enclaves—from Los Angeles to Miami—and rejecting the Anglo-Protestant values that built the American dream. The United States ignores this challenge at its peril. (Huntington, 2004, p. 30)

Different frames of analysis—which have stemmed from economic concerns to homeland security apprehensions in a post 9/11 era—have informed discourses about immigration reform differently. The epigraph above, quoting Harvard political scientist Samuel P. Huntington, is indicative of how the issue of immigration is currently being framed in the US, and who this framing targets—namely, Latina/o immigrants. Huntington's commentary is emblematic of what we see as racist nativist sentiment, rooted in white supremacy and directed at Latina/o immigrants in general and at Mexican immigrants in particular. In this chapter we begin to theorize the concept of racist nativism, first as a way of challenging the dominant discourse about immigration, and second in order to understand better the experiences of Immigrants of Color[1] in the US who continue to be subjected to racist nativist attitudes.

The racist nativist framing of the immigration issue has become acutely evident in current legislation concerning immigration policy, such as US House Resolution (HR) 4437.[2] According to Lakoff and Ferguson (2006), the 'problems' that become central to the framing of immigration remedies like HR 4437 have primarily to do with undocumented[3] immigrants, but particularly those of Latina/o descent:

> sneaking across the border . . . forg[ing] documents to get work, skirting labor laws, and deceiving employers who attempt to follow the law . . . tak[ing] jobs away from legal immigrants and ordinary Americans, bear[ing] children who will be American citizens even if they are not, and us[ing] local services like schools and hospitals, which may cost a local government a great deal. (p. 2)

By strategically framing the problem in this way, the authors of HR 4437, and other pieces of similar anti-immigrant legislation, have diverted attention away from the social structures, cultural values, and racist beliefs and actions that have historically marginalized and exploited immigrants. Instead, they have effectively blamed immigrants themselves for many of the country's social ills, including rising crime rates, the health care crisis, and lower educational standards. This framing of the issue distorts the 'symptoms' caused by the so-called immigration problem and takes us further away from understanding the actual 'disease.' We argue that this disease is white supremacy.[4]

In our attempt to define and understand racist nativism today, we situate our analysis within notions of white supremacy that have shaped the historic relationships between US society and immigrants, particularly of Latina/o descent.[5] While racist nativism has affected numerous groups in different ways, from nineteenth-century Italian immigrants to twentieth-century Asian Americans, we argue that today racist nativism targets Latinas/os generally and Mexican immigrants in particular. Utilizing critical race theory (CRT), and specifically Latina/o critical race theory (LatCrit), as a framing tool, we propose a working definition of racist nativism that brings us to a better understanding of the 'disease' that informs the exploitative and contradictory relationship between US dominant society and immigrant communities. Rather than merely proffering a simplistic definition of racist nativism, at the outset we delineate the logical process used in arriving at our definition. Through this process we justify our description of racist nativism and take significant steps towards theorizing a conceptual framework that will inform further work in this area and its application to many fields of inquiry.

We begin by providing key definitions of race, racism, and nativism. Using CRT and LatCrit, we build on these definitions to arrive at a more nuanced concept of racist nativism. These definitions are crucial because they place notions of white supremacy and privilege at the core of our conceptualization of racist nativism. We then address several questions which could potentially de-legitimize our definition of racist nativism, as a preemptive measure. In addressing these questions, we provide several examples of how racist nativism has affected different immigrant groups at various points in US history. Finally, we conclude by proposing steps for future research.

Race and Racism

A proper understanding of race[6] is needed before we proceed to examine the ways in which racism, and particularly racist nativism, works to marginalize People of Color in the US. While several critical theorists have provided their own definitions for understanding 'race,' most agree that it is a socially constructed category (Haney López, 2000; Omi & Winant, 1994; Solórzano & Yosso, 2002b). Although a social construction, race powerfully manifests itself in the everyday lives of people, particularly People of Color. As these manifestations become socially contested in the competition for various forms of power, race not only differentiates between racial groups, it also promotes a hierarchy that justifies the superiority of one race over others (Bonilla-Silva, 2001).

Racial hierarchies are legitimized through an ideology that positions one race as superordinate to all others (Solórzano, 1998; Solórzano & Yosso, 2002b). Racial hierarchies operate on the basis of *white supremacy*—that is to say, on the basis of a system of racial domination and exploitation whereby power and resources are unequally distributed to privilege whites and oppress People of Color (Bonilla-Silva, 2001; Dubois, 1999; Roediger, 1999). This right to white dominance is masked by notions of individualism, meritocracy, and color-blindness (Bonilla-Silva, 2003). White supremacy not only positions whites as the *entitled* beneficiaries of unearned societal privilege and status, it also normalizes white values, beliefs, and experiences as those dominant and therefore legitimate in US society (Delgado & Stefancic, 2001; Gillborn, 2006; Sue, 2003). Gillborn (2006) points to the normalization of white supremacy when he states, '[T]he racialized nature of politics, policing, education and every other sphere of public life is so deeply ingrained that it has become normalized—unremarked, and taken for granted' (p. 319).

Acknowledging white supremacy as the core of racism, Audre Lorde (1992) defines racism as 'the belief in the inherent superiority of one race over all others and thereby the right to dominance' (p. 496). Manning Marable (1992) adds that racism is a system of 'ignorance, exploitation, and power' used to oppress People of Color (p. 5). Using both Lorde (1992) and Marable (1992) as a reference, Daniel Solórzano (1998, p. 124) identifies three important characteristics of racism: (1) the belief that one group is superior; (2) this 'superior' group has the power to carry out racist acts; and (3) various racial/ethnic groups are affected.

Albert Memmi (1968) provides a powerful definition of racism that further centralizes white supremacy. His work acknowledges that racism is based on both real and 'imagined' racial differences. For example, an individual may be the victim of racism targeting Mexican immigrants even though he/she identifies as Persian. According to Memmi (1968), '[R]acism is the generalized and final assigning of values to real or imagined differences, to the accuser's benefit and at his victim's expense, in order to justify the former's own privileges and aggression' (p. 185). In a system of power, domination, and oppression that both Lorde and Marable make explicit in their definitions, this justification of white privilege through racism is based on white supremacy. Combining both these definitions, we argue that racism is the *assigning of values to real or imagined differences, in order to justify white supremacy, to the benefit of whites and at the expense of People of Color, and thereby to defend the right of whites to dominance.*

As we will see, this definition of racism is necessary to our notion of racist nativism. Employing a LatCrit analytic framework, we demonstrate how it is that racism particularly affects Latinas/os in the US. This focus on Latina/os is significant because discussions of race and racism are typically contextualized within a white/Black racial binary (Hacker, 1992; West, 1993). The definition of racism we utilize here positions and justifies white supremacy as central to understanding the experiences of *all* People of Color in the US. However, before arriving at a definition of racist nativism, it is necessary first to define nativism and explain its relationship to racism.

Nativism

The concept of nativism has been approached in a multitude of ways by scholars. Higham (1955), for example, defines it as the 'intense opposition to an internal minority on the grounds of its foreign (i.e. "un-American") connections' (p. 4). Furthermore, Higham describes how nationalism functions as the 'ideological core' of nativism. He explains how this nationalistic ideology justifies the fear 'that some influence originating abroad threaten[s] the very life of the nation from within' (p. 4). The issue of nationalism is important to nativism because it not only illuminates the process of defending national identity from perceived threats, it also engenders a fear of the foreigner.

In his typology of nativism, Higham (1955) identifies three different kinds of antiforeign tradition that have predominated in American society: (1) anti-Catholicism; (2) anti-radicalism; and (3) racism. Although each of these sentiments is associated with a particular period in US history, Higham contends that nativism is a recurring phenomenon as well as a racialized one. Indeed, the tradition of racism Higham highlights describes how notions of Anglo-Saxon superiority justified the belief 'that the United States belongs in some special sense to the Anglo-Saxon "race"' (p. 9). Here we see how nativism was rooted in notions of white supremacy that deemed Anglo-Saxons to be native to the United States.

From a CRT perspective, the connection between nativism and racism becomes necessary in arriving at a definition of racist nativism as it applies today. We make this conceptual link by applying our description of racism to defining nativism. We say, following Lorde (1992), that nativism is 'belief in the inherent superiority of the [native] over the [non-native] and thereby the right to dominance.' Marable (1992) follows suit, regarding nativism as a system of 'ignorance, exploitation, and power' used to oppress non-natives. Similarly, following Memmi's definition of racism, nativism may be depicted as 'the generalized and final assigning of values to real or imagined differences, to the [native's] benefit and at the [non-native's] expense, in order to justify the former's own privileges and aggression.' Using our combined definition of racism, then, we thus construe nativism as *the practice of assigning values to real or imagined differences, in order to justify the superiority of the native, to the benefit of the native and at the expense of the nonnative, thereby defending the native's right to dominance.*

Crucial to all these definitions is the distinction of the native from the non-native. While some would argue that such distinctions can easily be based on legal (i.e., citizenship) status, we maintain that perceptions of native-ness are too sociologically complex to be left up to legal designations. Before examining these perceptions, though, it is first necessary to justify why we seek to theorize about *native-ness* and not about *foreignness* in our understanding of nativism. We argue along with De Genova (2005) that:

> while the opposition of 'native' and 'foreign' is surely crucial, what is ultimately decisive in defining anti-immigrant politics of nativism is precisely not a preoccupation with the foreignness of any particular migrant or other internal minority so much as with the 'native'-ness of U.S. citizens and the promotion of the priority of the latter—exclusively on the grounds of their being 'native.' (p. 60)

This distinction between native and foreign is important to our definition of nativism because it centers on the natives, their identity, and their potential action to oppress others based on perceptions of being native. This, De Genova (2005) contends, is the power of nativism. It allows us to connect nativeness to nativism in the same powerful way that we can relate white supremacy to racism—by tracing the 'symptom' back to the 'disease.' It also positions the oppressor as central to our definitions of nativism and racism. Centering nativism in this way allows us to conceptualize better who is the native and who is the non-native.

To start this process, we must examine what it means to be 'American' and how this identity relates to a perception of being native. According to Saito (1997), being '"American" connotes Anglo-European heritage, Christian or Western religious traditions, and belief in representative democracy' (p. 268). At the time of the framing of the US Constitution in 1787, notions of what it meant to be American were not just left to individuals' perceptions, but were clearly articulated in legal documents. Saito cites the *Federalist Papers* of 1787, the Dred Scott decision of 1857, the Naturalization Act of 1790, and other historical legal documents to demonstrate how the idea of what it means to be an American became explicitly tied to being white. The notion of whiteness was privileged because it became strategically equated to Anglo-European heritage, Western religious traditions, and other values and beliefs deemed dominant and supportive of the 'American spirit' in the Federal Constitution. Being an American, or being perceived as such, and thus enjoying the privileges that come with that identity, had much, if not everything, to do with being white. Whiteness, thus, became the most important requirement for profiting from the privilege of being native to US soil.

Understanding this relationship between native-ness and whiteness allows us to return to our definition of racism—a definition based on white supremacy. Although we have made historical connections between native-ness and whiteness, our understanding of racism argues that racial oppression has been and continues to be defined by white supremacy. From this perspective the values, beliefs, and perceptions associated with whiteness are closely allied with a dominant national identity that maintains and supports not only a racial hierarchy with whites on top, but a normalized belief that whites are inherently native. Thus, the native, as perceived in mainstream society, is intrinsically tied to perceptions of whiteness, while the non-native refers to all others. This distinction between the native and the non-native leads directly to our definition of racist nativism. It powerfully positions white supremacy as fundamental and central in linking the concepts of racism and nativism.

Racist Nativism

According to Sánchez (1997), the end of the twentieth century was marked by three types of racial nativism.[7] The first involved antipathy toward languages other than English, and by default the speakers of those languages. As evidenced by 'English Only' proposals like California's Proposition

227, this type of antagonism stems from the fear of linguistic difference being a threat to American national identity. The second type of racist nativism, closely related to multicultural and affirmative action initiatives, is premised on the belief that 'contrived, misguided, and sometimes secretive government policies have tilted against white people in the 1990s' (Sánchez, 1997, p. 1020). The last type of racist nativist sentiment in Sánchez's typology, as embodied in California's Proposition 187, is engendered by the idea that immigrants are exploiting welfare, education, and health care systems in the US, thus posing a possible threat to the depletion of such resources for use by 'true' Americans.

Sánchez's (1997) work is important because it provides a detailed account of how racist nativism has been manifested in contemporary society—that is, of the 'symptoms' of today's racist nativism. But how do we begin to isolate the actual 'disease'? Based on our conceptualizations thus far, we start by merging our notion of racism with that of nativism and thus define racist nativism as the assigning of values to real or imagined differences, in order to justify the superiority of the native, who is to be perceived white, over that of the non-native people and Immigrants of Color, and thereby defend the right of whites, or the natives, to be dominant.

As with nativism and racism, we acknowledge that racist nativism is a concept that needs to be situated within a particular sociohistorical and political context. We argue that different Communities of Color have historically been perceived as non-native within US society. We further recognize that different groups within a larger community have experienced racist nativism in different ways, at different times, and in different locations. We contend that today's anti-immigrant climate challenges us to re-conceptualize racist nativism as it currently affects the lived experiences of Communities of Color. What we offer is one step closer toward that re-conceptualization. In what follows we defend our definition of racist nativism and situate it within the current anti-immigrant climate. We conclude by arguing for its importance in understanding the daily experiences of Latinas/os in the US.

Three Frequently Asked Questions about Racist Nativism: Steps Toward Theorizing

In this section we address three questions commonly asked about racist nativism. These questions have advanced our thinking concerning its application to the experiences of white ethnics, People of Color, and specifically Latinas/os. In answering these questions we demonstrate how racist nativism has consistently been used as a tool by white elites[8] to dominate various immigrant groups and maintain white supremacy. In addressing these questions we endeavor to advance theorizing about racist nativism and deepen our understanding of its role in the historical and contemporary subordination of People and Immigrants of Color, particularly Latina/o immigrants, in the US.

Racist Nativism in the Late Nineteenth Century, or, What about White Ethnics?

During the early nineteenth century, whiteness was constructed to encompass only one group: northern European Anglo-Saxon Protestants. This group was considered racially superior to all other groups, and was the only group deemed native to the US.[9] Later, in the early twentieth century, their self-professed racial superiority was scientifically 'proven' by eugenics (Grant, 1916; Kamin, 1974). As eugenics research grew in popularity, it legitimized the racism, discrimination, and violence directed at other white ethnic immigrants entering the country and became pivotal in differentiating natives from non-natives along perceived racial lines. Only northern Europeans and their descendents were regarded as the 'true' founders of white America. Immigrants from southern and eastern Europe, such as Italians, Poles, and Czechs, were perceived as inferior 'races' and subjected to negative treatment.[10]

The widely accepted belief in the racial superiority of northern Europeans was manifested in racist nativist immigration policy at the time. For example, relying on racial categories developed in eugenics research, the Johnson-Reed Act (the Immigration Act of 1924) created a quota system to restrict the number of white ethnic immigrants entering the US. This quota system ensured that immigrants from northern and western Europe comprised the vast majority, 84%, of the total allowed immigration (Ngai, 2004). The Johnson-Reed Act also required official documentation (passports and visas) as proof of national identity before permission could be granted to enter the country. These requirements established geographic points of entry and created the US Border Patrol to regulate border entry, with the patrol being primarily deployed at the US–Mexico border. As a result, the Johnson-Reed Act established strict territorial borders that could not be crossed without proper documentation. The new restrictions placed on immigration and the requirements to uphold these restrictions led to the beginning of 'illegal' immigration to the US and the criminalization of those entering the country without the required authorization (Ngai, 2004).

How Was the Racist Nativism Experienced by White Ethnic Immigrants Different than That Experienced by People of Color?

It is now necessary to explain how racist nativism experienced by white ethnics in the late-nineteenth and early-twentieth centuries differed from racist nativism experienced by People of Color today. While white ethnics experienced a form of racist nativism during the turn of the twentieth century, they eventually became part of the white American identity. Higham (1955) suggests that by 1915, with the exception of Italians and Jews, most white ethnic immigrants were no longer distinguishable from northern European whites. Brodkin (2004) concludes that the complete assimilation of Jews was achieved shortly after World War II. We argue that the acceptance of white ethnic groups, like the Irish and Poles, and later the Italians and Jews, into the white American mainstream was a result of the privileges granted by white supremacy. With this acceptance, they became beneficiaries of white privilege. Although these groups were regarded as racially different from Anglo-Saxon Protestants, social, political, and economic interests converged to sustain white supremacy and maintain dominance.

The incorporation of white ethnics into the American mainstream can be seen as a strategic decision made by white elites to ensure they remained on top of the power and racial hierarchy. Derrick Bell (2004) posits that in order to maintain their position and power, white elites strategically allowed poor whites certain rights shortly before and during Reconstruction.[11] He argues, for example, that white elites strategically incorporated poor (less superior) whites into policy decisions concerning slavery only when elites realized they would enjoy some significant benefit. When white elites saw the potential class alliance of poor whites and Black slaves posing a threat to their power, they extended white privilege to form a race-based alliance. The elite's acceptance of poor whites maintained the Black/white racial divide in US society, even as the division was detrimental to the economic conditions of poor whites (Bell, 2004; Roediger, 1999). We argue that white privilege, as a product of white supremacy, distinguishes today's racist nativism from that previously experienced by white ethnic immigrants. White privilege has never been extended to racial/ethnic groups in the way we currently define and perceive race.

How Does Racist Nativism Play Out for People of Color in the US?

According to our definition of racist nativism, this form of racism is not only directed toward Latina/o immigrants in the US, but toward all People of Color.[12] Johnson (1997) explains that since 1965, Immigrants of Color have been perceived as not assimilating into the American mainstream, compared to earlier European immigrants. He contends that this racialized perception of one's 'American-ness' leads to the subordination of People of Color, regardless of citizenship status, in the US. Johnson states:

> As the Chinese, Japanese and Mexican experiences suggest, nativism generally is not limited to aliens of a particular immigration status but ordinarily is directed at all persons of a group, whatever their immigration status, perceived to be different and 'un-American.' Latinos and Asian Americans often are treated by society as foreigners, even if they are long-term lawful permanent residents or citizens. It would not be extraordinary for an Asian American citizen to be asked which country she is from or for a Latino citizen in the Southwest to be approached by Border Patrol officers. (p. 180)

Johnson identifies an important element of contemporary nativism—it is not determined by citizenship status, but by the perception of who is an 'American.' To be sure, the dominant perceptions of 'American-ness' have remained unchanged throughout history and continue to be based on whiteness. People of Color do not fit into this white American identity and are thus perceived as not belonging, foreign, and non-native.

We can see how perceptions of 'American-ness' manifest themselves through exclusionary immigration policies that specifically target non-whites. In the past, racist nativist policies have overtly targeted Asian immigrants. The 1882 Chinese Exclusion Act deemed Chinese immigrants ineligible for US citizenship, the 1907 'Gentleman's Agreement' severely restricted Japanese immigration by denying passports to laborers, and in 1942, during World War II, the US 'nullified' the citizenship of Japanese-Americans, removed them from their homes, and forced them into internment camps located throughout the country (Ngai, 2004). This exclusion was justified based on perceived racial differences which constructed Asians as non-natives, foreigners, and un-American.[13]

Overtly racist nativist immigration policies have also targeted Mexicans and Chicanas/os in the US. During the Great Depression of 1929, repatriation and deportation programs throughout the country forced Mexican immigrants and US-born Chicanas/os to Mexico. Acuña (2000) reports that an estimated 500,000 to 600,000 Mexicans and Chicanas/os were deported to Mexico, more than half of whom were US citizens. This massive deportation was a result of the perceived economic threat posed by Mexican workers to the white American labor force. Sánchez (1993) explains that it was mostly Mexican men and young Mexican families who faced deportation, based on racialized perceptions of these specific workers taking jobs from 'Americans.' However, when cheap Mexican labor was needed to support the US economy during World War II, the US created the Bracero Program, a guest worker program that allowed Mexican laborers to work in the US and then return home. When the country no longer needed this source of cheap labor, 'Operation Wetback' deported over one million Mexicans, regardless of immigration status (Acuña, 2000). Racist nativist immigration policy continues to target Mexicans and Chicanas/os, although not as overtly, which will be addressed in the following section.

How Does Racist Nativism Play Out for Latinas/os?

We have argued that various groups of immigrants and People of Color in the US have been and continue to be racialized as non-native regardless of their citizenship status. Additionally, we posit that in the current historical moment of anti-immigrant sentiment, racist nativism is directed towards Latinas/os in general and Mexican immigrants specifically. While various groups have experienced racist nativism at different points in time, it has consistently targeted Mexicans in the US, from the repatriation and deportation movements of the 1930s described earlier to the 2005 anti-Mexican legislative proposal of US House Resolution 4437.[14] Mexicans and Chicanas/os are perceived as foreigners, ironically, in a land that once belonged to them. The persistent opposition and resentment towards Mexican immigrants, especially in the southwest US, is due primarily to the consistent flow of Mexican immigrants into the country across the US–Mexico border. Passel (2006) reports that currently 66% of all undocumented immigrants living in the US are from Mexico. Thus, the policies directed at undocumented immigrants are de facto targeted at Mexican immigrants. The policies are informed by cultural deficit theory and, we argue, by the ideology of white supremacy (Johnson, 1997; Valencia, 2002). Negative portrayals of Mexican immigrants—as dangerous criminals, invaders, enemies, and, most extreme, as sub-human animal-like beings—are disseminated to the American public (and accepted) via the media (Chavez, 1998, 2001; Santa Ana, 2002).

The fear and exclusion of Mexican immigrants was seen most clearly in California during the 1990s. In 1994, voters in that state passed Proposition 187, an initiative that banned undocumented immigrants from receiving social benefits and services including healthcare and education.[15] In 1998, California's Proposition 227 banned bilingual education in public schools. While this law affected all English Learner (EL) students, it targeted Spanish-speaking students who, at the time, comprised 81% of all EL students in California's public schools (California Department of Education, 2006). Santa Ana (2002) observes that economic downturn, a factor frequently regarded as the cause of nativist sentiment, would be an incorrect explanation for the state-wide support these laws received. While California was experiencing a recession when Proposition 187 was passed, Proposition 227 was passed during a period of relative economic prosperity (Santa Ana, 2002).

Both propositions demonstrate the fear of the 'browning of California and the United States.' Santa Ana maintains these laws were about 'culture' (p. 240); we argue that they were about race.

De Genova (2005) states, 'The aggravated nativism of the mid-1990s, with its acute preoccupation with "illegal aliens," pervasively bore the particular imprint of a distinctly anti-Mexican racism' (p. 62). We argue that the 'aggravated nativism' directed towards Mexican immigrants has been and continues to be fueled by notions rooted in white supremacy. The following comments, made by (then) California senator W.A. Craven at a 1993 meeting of the Special Committee on US/Mexico Border Issues, illustrate this point: 'It seems rather strange that we go out of our way to take care of the rights of these individuals [undocumented Mexican immigrants] who are perhaps on the lower scale of our humanity' (Santa Ana, 2002, p. 86). Today, undocumented Mexican immigrants suffer the most violent forms of racist nativism, and legalized Mexican immigrants, as well as Chicanas/os, continue to be racialized as undocumented and perceived as non-Americans.

Conclusion

We have defined the concept of racist nativism in a way that helps us to understand better the current experiences of Latinas/os. In addition, we have outlined the process used to arrive at this working definition, by considering historical contexts and contemporary implications. Using LatCrit as a framing tool, we also demonstrated how racist nativism departs from the definition of nativism frequently used to describe, yet inaccurately capture, the experiences of Latinas/os. We have argued for the need to advance critical race theory beyond a race/class/gender paradigm to address the experiences of Latina/o undocumented communities in the US. In moving towards a more comprehensive understanding of immigration, we begin to reframe its discourse and its impact on policy and practice.

It is the role of CRT and LatCrit scholars to analyze, subvert, and intervene in the dominant conceptual frameworks that mask the oppressive experiences of Communities of Color. We argue that the current discourse on Latina/o immigrants inaccurately portrays the dynamics of power and privilege and, as such, further oppresses this community. We believe that our notion of racist nativism advances an epistemology that contributes a more nuanced—and indeed a more accurate analysis of Latinas/os' lived experiences. This reframing also calls for a methodological consideration grounded in qualitative research that can better describe and analyze the draconian effects of policy and practice on these communities.

Utilizing a LatCrit framework challenges the dominant paradigms of immigration discourse that have distorted and/or erased the experiences of undocumented Latinas/os. This analytical approach is not just an epistemological matter—it can also inform social action in contesting power, politics, and ethics. We advocate a wider analysis that moves beyond a paradigm that narrowly defines the intersections of race, class, and gender. As such, we seek to address and validate the lived experiences of People of Color as they pertain to the issues of skin color, immigration, generational status, bilingualism, and other factors of oppression. A LatCrit racist nativist framework allows scholars to draw properly not only from the lived experiences of the undocumented immigrants they study, but also from their own, and thus engage in a transformative praxis.

While this conceptual approach advances educational scholars' theoretical understanding of the current political and social climate, further studies examining the experiences of Latina/os must include qualitative data obtained from those students' experiences. Such data can go a long way toward identifying how Latina/os experience racist nativism. It is important to acknowledge that Latina/os actively resist these oppressive conditions, despite the challenges they confront. This can be seen, for example, in the recent mass demonstrations in cities like Chicago, Los Angeles, and Washington DC against HR 4437, and other various attempts by students—including engagement in class projects, such as essay compositions, theatrical plays/skits, sit-ins and critical dialog forums—that challenge and transform these conditions. The everyday experiences faced by Immigrants of Color, and particularly by undocumented immigrants, demonstrate their resilience, and resistance, to racist nativism, despite the risk of deportation and other consequences.

We have argued that while the political and social discourse surrounding immigration has been framed primarily as an anti-Mexican issue, other Latino/as—Puerto Ricans, Cubans, Dominicans, etc.—also experience racist nativism on a daily basis. We recognize that while the Latino community is subjected to the negative consequences of white supremacy, the manner in which racist nativism impacts individuals varies according to their legal status at a particular moment. A proper analysis of these issues requires the utilization of diverse methodologies, such as counterstorytelling, a powerful methodological tool uniquely suited to tapping into the personal experiences of those who confront racist nativism and the different ways that it manifests itself in their daily lives.

Counterstorytelling, according to Delgado (1989), can effectively subvert the white metanarratives that distort the lived experiences of Latina/o groups 'whose marginality defines the boundaries of the mainstream, whose voice perspective—whose consciousness—has been suppressed, devalued, and abnormalized' (p. 60). The white supremacy metanarratives remind the dominant white groups of their American identity, in relation to Latina/o immigrants, and also shape the reality of how they see their superior position as natural.

Solórzano and Yosso (2002a) argue that counterstorytelling can serve 'several pedagogical functions' (p. 156). Drawing from the work of Delgado (1989) and Lawson (1995), they contend that this method can:

1. build community among those at the margins of society;
2. challenge the perceived wisdom of those at society's center;
3. open new windows into the reality of those at the margins of society by showing the possibilities beyond the ones they live and showing that they are not alone in their position;
4. teach others that by combining elements from both the story and the current reality, one can construct another world that is richer than either story or the reality alone;
5. provide a context to understanding and transforming established belief systems. (p. 156)

Counterstorytelling reveals the effects of racist nativism that individual Latinas/os experience. For example, in one family, an older sibling and her parents might hold undocumented status in the US, affecting their access to schooling, health care, and employment. In the same family younger siblings, born in this country, experience and benefit from different opportunities granted through their US citizenship. Each has their own experiences and their own stories to tell about living in the US. We maintain that while every member of this family may experience racist nativism despite their generational and 'legal' status, the ways in which racist nativism manifests itself in the lives of each individual will differ. Counterstorytelling provides a more penetrating insight into the manner in which racist nativism oppresses different groups and individuals and exposes how it privileges others.

This framework of racist nativism, informed by LatCrit theory, challenges the dominant discourse that fails to acknowledge white supremacy as the disease that fuels the current passions surrounding immigration. It is critical to deconstruct and reframe this discourse in order to challenge the discussion effectively and move beyond the restrictive conceptual frameworks currently proffered throughout the political spectrum. Moving beyond these limited frameworks requires further theorizing, the documenting of policy, and a more adequate understanding of the lived experiences of Latina/o immigrants. Our attempt lays the groundwork required to dismantle the social structures and cultural values that continue to perpetuate racist nativism, and specifically white supremacy.

Notes

1. 'Immigrants of Color' is intentionally capitalized, rejecting the standard grammatical norm, to empower this group and to represent a grammatical move toward social and racial justice. This rule will also apply to 'People of Color' and 'Communities of Color' throughout this paper.
2. Called the Border Protection, Antiterrorism, and Illegal Immigration Control Act, HR 4437 was introduced by Republican representatives James Sensenbrenner (R-WI) and Peter King (R-NY) in December 2005. HR 4437 proposed that any undocumented immigrant in the US would be charged with a felony and prevented from ever gaining legal status in the US. The proposed law also seeks to charge anyone,

regardless of legal status, with a felony who assists an undocumented immigrant or conceals the 'legal' status of an undocumented immigrant from the US government. If implemented, this bill would not only affect undocumented immigrants, but their families, communities, and anyone that knows of their status and does not report them to authorities. HR 4437 would compromise the position of undocumented immigrants living in the US and is predicted to increase the separation of families and communities throughout the nation. Although it was voted down in the Senate in the spring of 2006, modified versions of HR 4437 are being proposed and debated that could prove detrimental to immigrants and their families. For more information on HR 4437 and the immigration debate, visit the National Council of La Raza's website at http://www.nclr.org/section//immigration_debate/

3. For the purpose of this paper we use the term 'undocumented immigrant' to identify individuals who reside in the US without proper documentation.

4. Our references to 'symptoms' and 'diseases' are borrowed from the words of US District Judge Robert L. Carter in his reflection on the Supreme Court case, *Brown v. Board of Education* (1954). He stated:

> [T]he NAACP lawyers erred. The lawyers did not understand then how effective white power could be in preventing full implementation of the law; nor did it realize at the time that the basic barrier to full equality for blacks was not racial segregation, a symptom, but white supremacy, the disease. (Tushnet, 1988, p. 1094)

5. We use the term 'Latina/o' to be inclusive of the racist nativism experiences of various ethnic subgroups. However, we acknowledge that racist nativism is not experienced in the same ways by all groups of Latinas/os. Racist nativism is context-specific. We must consider the political, historical, geographical, and phenotypical conditions of those who fall victim to racist nativism in order truly to understand their experiences.

6. It is important to mention that ethnicity is also a socially constructed category, used to demark differences of culture between groups of people. While not the focus here, it is important to note that the categorizations of race and ethnicity, and their overlapping dimensions, are important for understanding the complex mechanisms employed in categorizing groups, such as Latinas/os.

7. Sánchez uses the term 'racial nativism'; however, we chose to use the term 'racist nativism' to position power within a racial hierarchy. Furthermore, it should be noted that we define racist nativism differently to Sánchez, as we root our definition of racist nativism within white supremacy. However, Sánchez's work on racial nativism has been especially helpful in conceptualizing racist nativism as we describe it in this chapter.

8. We reference white elites, northern Europeans, and Anglo-Saxon Protestants as members of the same group and use these terms interchangeably throughout the chapter.

9. Madison Grant (1916), in his book *Passing of the Great Race*, explains how racial distinctions can be scientifically determined among Europeans with the 'cephalic index,' or measurements of the human skull (p. 16). According to Grant, eye, hair, and skin color can also be used to determine race. He states, 'In general, the Nordic race in its purity has an absolutely fair skin, and is consequently the *Homo albus,* the white man par excellence' (p. 23).

10. Higham (1955) describes the violence committed against white ethnics in the late 1800s and early 1900s. He provides stories and illustrations of two incidents in particular: one involving 11 Italian immigrants in New Orleans who were lynched in a public display among crowds of onlookers and another involving a Jewish factory worker in Atlanta who was executed while shackled to a crucifix.

11. Here, we borrow from the work of Derrick Bell (2004) on the processes of racial-sacrifice and interest-convergence covenants.

12. We define People of Color as non-white racial groups that include, but are not limited to, Latinas/os, African Americans, Asian Americans, and Native Americans. We argue that all People of Color can experience racist nativism, but focus on the historical experiences of Asians and Mexicans, both immigrant and US-born. The experiences of these groups in particular lend us accurate examples of how racist nativism, in the ways we have defined it, plays out in the lives of People of Color. We acknowledge that further theorizing is needed to understand how other People of Color experience racist nativism at different historical moments, such as African Americans, Native Americans, and, specific to a post–9/11 era, Arab and Muslim Americans.

13. See Saito (1997), Johnson (1997), and Ngai (2004).

14. Although this legislation targeted all undocumented immigrants, we argue that such policies are largely anti-Mexican, as the majority of the undocumented population in the US is from Mexico.

15. Shortly after Proposition 187 was passed, an injunction was issued that blocked the implementation of the law until the courts found Proposition 187 unconstitutional.

References

Acuña, R. (2000). *Occupied America: A history of Chicanos* (4th ed.). New York: Longman Press.

Bell, D. (2004). *Silent covenants: Brown v. Board of Education and the unfulfilled hopes for racial reform.* New York: Oxford University Press.

Bonilla-Silva, E. (2001). *White supremacy and racism in the post-civil rights era.* Boulder, CO: Lynne Rienner Publishers.

Bonilla-Silva, E. (2003). *Racism without racists: Color-blind racism and the persistence of racial inequality in the United States.* Lanham, MD: Rowman and Littlefield.

Brodkin, K. (2004). *How Jews became white folks and what that says about race in America.* New Brunswick, NJ: Rutgers University Press.

California Department of Education. (2006). *Language census data 1997–1998.* Retrieved January 5, 2007, from http://dq.cde.ca.gov/dataquest/lepbylang1.asp?cchoice=lepbylang1&cyear=1997-98&clevel=state&ctopic=lc&mytimeframe=s&submit1=submit

Chavez, L.R. (1998). *Shadowed lives: Undocumented immigrants in American society* (2nd ed.). Belmont, CA: Wadsworth.

Chavez, L.R. (2001). *Covering immigration: Popular images and the politics of the nation.* Los Angeles: University of California Press.

De Genova, N. (2005). *Working the boundaries: Race, space, and "illegality" in Mexican Chicago.* Durham, NC: Duke University Press.

Delgado, R. (1989). Storytelling for oppositionists and others: A plea for narrative. *Michigan Law Review,* 2411–2441.

Delgado, R., & Stefancic, J. (2001). *Critical race theory: An introduction.* New York: New York University Press.

Dubois, W.E.B. (1999). *Darkwater: Voices from within the veil.* New York: Dover Publications.

Gillborn, D. (2006). Rethinking white supremacy: Who counts in 'whiteworld.' *Ethnicities, 6*(3), 318–340.

Grant, M. (1916). *Passing of the great race.* New York: Charles Scribner's Sons.

Hacker, A. (1992). *Two nations: Black and white, separate, hostile, unequal.* New York: Charles Scribner's Sons.

Haney López, I.F. (2000). The social construction of race. In R. Delgado & J. Stefancic (Eds.), *Critical race theory: The cutting edge* (2nd ed., pp. 163–175). Philadelphia: Temple University Press

Higham, J. (1955). *Strangers in the land: Patterns of American nativism 1860–1925.* New Brunswick, NJ: Rutgers University Press.

Huntington, S.P. (2004, March/April). The Hispanic challenge. *Foreign Policy,* 30–45.

Johnson, K. (1997). The new nativism: Something old, something new, something borrowed, something blue. In J. F. Perea (Ed.), *Immigrants out! The new nativism and the anti-immigrant impulse in the United States* (pp. 165–189). New York: New York University Press.

Kamin, L.J. (1974). *The science and politics of I.Q.* Potomac, MD: Lawrence Erlbaum Associates.

Lakoff, G., & Ferguson, S. (2006). *The framing of immigration.* Berkeley, CA: The Rockridge Institute. Retrieved January 4, 2007, from http://www.rockridgeinstitute.org/research/rockridge/immigration/view?searchterm=none

Lawson, R.J. (1995). Critical race theory as praxis: A view from the outside. *Howard Law Review, 38,* 353–370.

Lorde, A. (1992). Age, race, class, and sex: Women redefining difference. In M. Anderson & P. Hill Collins (Eds.), *Race, class, and gender: An anthology* (pp. 495–502). Belmont, CA: Wadsworth.

Marable, M. (1992). *Black America.* Westfield, NJ: Open Media.

Memmi, A. (1968). *Dominated man: Notes toward a portrait.* New York: Orion Press.

Ngai, M. (2004). *Impossible subjects: Illegal aliens and the making of modern America.* Princeton, NJ: Princeton University Press.

Omi, M., & Winant, H. (1994). *Racial formation in the United States: From the 1960s to the 1990s.* New York: Routledge.

Passel, J.S. (2006). *The size and characteristics of the unauthorized migrant population in the U.S.: Estimates based on the March 2005 current population survey.* Washington, DC: Pew Hispanic Center.

Roediger, D.R. (1999). *The wages of whiteness: Race and the making of the American working class* (rev. ed.). New York: Verso.

Saito, N.T. (1997). Alien and non-alien alike: Citizenship, "foreignness," and racial hierarchy in American law. *Oregon Law Review, 76,* 261–346.

Sánchez, G. (1993). *Becoming Mexican American: Ethnicity, culture and identity in Chicano Los Angeles, 1900–1945.* New York: Oxford University Press.

Sánchez, G. (1997). Face the nation: Race, immigration and the rise of nativism in late twentieth century America. *International Migration Review, 31,* 1009–1030.

Santa Ana, O. (2002). *Brown tide rising: Metaphors of Latinos in the contemporary American public discourse.* Austin: University of Texas Press.

Solórzano, D.G. (1998). Critical race theory, race and gender microaggressions, and the experience of Chicana and Chicano scholars. *Qualitative Studies in Education, 11,* 121–136.

Solórzano, D.G., & Yosso, T. (2002a). Critical race methodology: Counter-storytelling as an analytical framework for education research. *Qualitative Inquiry, 8,* 23–44.

Solórzano, D.G., & Yosso, T. (2002b). A critical race counterstory of race, racism, and affirmative action. *Equity and Excellence in Education, 35,* 155–168.

Sue, D.W. (2003). *Overcoming our racism: The journey to liberation.* San Francisco: Jossey-Bass.

Tushnet, M. (1988). 1988 survey of books relating to the law: The NAACP's legal strategy against legal segregation, 1925–1950. *Michigan Law Review, 86,* 1083–1095.

Valencia, R. (2002). *Chicano school failure and success: Past, present and future* (2nd ed.). New York: Routledge-Falmer.

West, C. (1993). *Race matters.* Boston, MA: Beacon Press.

CHAPTER 54
TOWARDS A CRITICAL THEORY OF WHITENESS

DAVID S. OWEN

In this chapter I argue that a critical theory of whiteness is necessary, though not sufficient, to the formulation of an adequate explanatory account of the mechanisms of racial oppression in the modern world. In order to explain how whiteness underwrites systems of racial oppression and how it is reproduced, the central functional properties of whiteness are identified. I propose that understanding whiteness as a structuring property of racialized social systems best explains these functional properties. Given the variety of conceptions of whiteness in the literature, the several uses of the term are analysed and it is shown that there is a unifying concept underlying these various senses of whiteness. Lastly, some of the implications of this account of whiteness for anti-racist engagement are considered.

In this chapter I will argue that a critical theory of whiteness is necessary, though not sufficient, to the formulation of an adequate explanatory account of the mechanisms of racial oppression in the modern world, and that understanding these mechanisms is essential to the liberation of peoples of color around the globe. Although I would argue that whiteness has always been a central element in racial oppression, it is particularly salient in the post-civil rights era of formal (though not material) equality because it serves to underwrite perceptions, understandings, justifications and explanations of the social order that perpetuate distortions in the social system that are a legacy of our nation's history. As an element in a comprehensive theory of racial oppression, a critical theory of whiteness contributes an account of key sociocultural mechanisms of the functioning and reproduction of racial oppression. This is a programmatic chapter, and as such is a first attempt to sketch out some of the central concepts and parameters of a critical theory of whiteness. Although all aspects of such a theory cannot be fully explored in this chapter, I will indicate some dimensions for further development and will close by considering some of the implications of my arguments within the broader context of anti-racist practice.

The chapter is divided into four main sections. I begin by arguing for the need for a critical theory of whiteness as a necessary element in a more adequate account of racial oppression. In the second section, I consider the ontology of whiteness. Here, I identify the functional mechanisms by which whiteness reproduces a racialized social order followed by a preliminary account of whiteness as a structuring property of modern social systems. The third section engages in a semantic inquiry into the three basic senses of 'whiteness' that are used by critical whiteness scholars, and I propose a communications-theoretic framework for situating these disparate conceptions with respect to one another. Finally, I consider the objections that whiteness is indistinguishable from white supremacy, and that white supremacy and not whiteness should be the primary theoretical term. Since I maintain that a critical theory of whiteness is pragmatic in the sense that it is liberatory and aimed at disrupting and dismantling the system of white racial oppression, I also consider some of the implications this theory has for anti-racist engagement.

Why a Critical Theory of Whiteness?

The growth of scholarship in the emerging field of critical whiteness studies has provided at least prima facie evidence for the significance of examining whiteness and its relation to systems of racial oppression. However, once whiteness is identified and recognized as a central support of racial domination, then why not simply attack whiteness directly; say, by attempting to 'abolish' whiteness by fiat? One group of proponents of this strategy, the 'New Abolitionists', urges those racialized as white to refuse the advantages and privileges associated with whiteness and thereby abolish whiteness.[1]

There are, however, multiple problems with this strategy. The new abolitionists presume that whiteness is the sort of thing that *can* be refused, like a gift. They also presume that it functions in a one-dimensional mode such that it does not colonize and infect all aspects of the social sphere. Furthermore, they presume that whiteness is—at least with self-conscious effort—something that is readily recognizable and identifiable such that it can be singled out to be refused. The new abolitionists also presume that whiteness is fundamentally, if not exclusively, a social identity, and as such it is in the power of whites to refuse.

I will argue below that these assumptions are mistaken. The new abolitionists fail to account for the hegemonic systematicity of whiteness and its colonization of every dimension of the social world. The new abolitionists understand whiteness primarily as a social identity, but if we understand whiteness as a structuring property of the social system, as I will argue we should, then it cannot be simply abolished or refused by force of will. Whiteness, understood as a structuring property of the social world can, however, be exposed, challenged, resisted and disrupted. And this is precisely why a greater degree of clarity is necessary concerning what whiteness is and how it functions in the reproduction of the system of racial oppression. If whiteness in fact is systematically embedded in the social world, then local micro-critiques and refusals will be insufficient to disrupt its power to reproduce racial domination. Only a theoretical understanding of its central operational properties will provide us with the insight and understanding to devise effective strategies to disrupt and dismantle its hold on modern social systems.

Whiteness as Structure

While there are various historical accounts of the origins of the use of 'white' in a racialized sense, and Charles Mills' theory of the racial contract can be read as an account of the generation of the system of white supremacy, what these lack is an adequate socio-theoretic account of how whiteness functions to underwrite and maintain the system of white supremacy.[2] An account of the reproduction of whiteness and the modes by which it maintains white supremacy is especially important to explain the persistence of racial oppression in the post-civil rights era. A liberatory project that seeks the liberation of all who are imprisoned by racial oppression must be grounded on an explanation of the reproduction of whiteness, for knowing the means and mechanisms by which whiteness reproduces the system of white supremacy will be essential if those operations are to be disrupted, deconstructed and delegitimized.

Functional Properties of Whiteness

To gain a deeper understanding of whiteness and how it functions to reproduce the system of white supremacy, it will be useful then to begin with an analysis of its modes of operation. A survey of the literature identifies certain 'functional properties' that characterize aspects of how whiteness operates or functions as a socio-historical phenomenon that reproduces white supremacy. The *first* functional property is that whiteness defines a particular racialized perspective or standpoint that shapes the white subject's understanding of both self and the social world. As a structuring property, whiteness situates persons racialized as white in a social location that provides a particular and limited perspective on the world.[3] *Second*, whiteness defines a specifically racialized social location of structural advantage. Being located in a social position by whiteness is not merely a location of difference, but it is also a location of economic, political, social and cultural advantage relative to those locations defined by non-whiteness. A *third* property is that whiteness is normalized. What is associated with whiteness becomes defined as natural, normal or mainstream. This contributes to its transparency in the dominant cultural consciousness of the post-civil rights era. The *fourth* functional property is implied by the third: it is that whiteness is largely invisible to whites and yet highly visible to non-whites. Many critical whiteness scholars have argued that whiteness is invisible or transparent, but such a claim presupposes the perspective of whiteness. Whiteness is (largely) invisible only to whites, yet it tends to be less transparent to non-whites, as is suggested by the long history of African-American analyses of whiteness that includes W. E. B. Du Bois, Langston Hughes, James Baldwin, Richard Wright and Toni Morrison.[4] This differential visibility for different racialized groups is significant and reflects its social and cultural dominance and hegemony. *Fifth*, although whiteness must be distinguished from mere skin color, it nevertheless is embodied. As I will contend, whiteness is grounded in the interests, needs and values of those racialized as white, so it is founded on the ascribed racial identity of being white. But, as Marilyn Frye argues, whiteness—or as she calls it, whiteliness—is not the same as having light-colored skin. Rather, it is 'a deeply engrained way of being in the world'.[5] Whiteness shapes actions, social practices and dispositions, and thus constitutes a part of that 'know how' or practical knowledge that competent social actors possess. By means of ongoing processes of socialization and acculturation, it becomes part of our bodily dispositions and comportment within the world. A *sixth* functional property of whiteness is that its borders are continuously being redefined, entailing that analyses of whiteness's functioning must always be grounded in specific contexts of its manifestation. Whiteness is a socio-historical phenomenon, and theoretical analyses should not reify it as an essential form. Finally, a *seventh* functional property is that of violence; whiteness cannot be understood apart from the violence that it begets or apart from the violence that produced—and continues to produce—it. Not only does whiteness have its origins in the physical and psychic violence of the enslavement, genocide and exploitation of peoples of color around the world, but also it maintains the system of white supremacy in part by means of actual and potential violence.

A complete critical theory of whiteness will need to explain how each of these properties contributes to the reproduction of the system of white supremacy. Doing so will require accounting for three key modalities of the functioning of whiteness: its nature as a structuring property of social systems; its complex relation to embodiment; and its instantiation and reproduction of power in the formation of the social order. Due to constraints of space, I will address only the first, that of whiteness as a structuring property, and even then I can do so only in a preliminary way.

Whiteness as Structuring Property

The fundamental explanatory figure of whiteness is that of a structuring property of modern social systems. To say that whiteness structures the social order implies several things: first, it conditions social practices; second, it conditions cultural representations; and third, it conditions the formation of identity. The notion of structure has a complex and troubled history in social theory; a history I will bracket here. As I use it, 'structure' refers to the ordering or patterning of the elements of a social system such that: the ordering serves as a binding force across space and time; the ordering defines the perceived horizon of thought and action; and the ordering provides the resources for social reproduction.[6]

In order to better understand the reproductive function of whiteness, a deeper account is needed of social structures that explains both how they condition practices, representations and identities, as well as how they are reproduced over time. Anthony Giddens' theory of structuration provides just such an account, and so is a useful place to start.[7] Giddens proposes that the notion of structure be understood temporally, as a continuous process of structuration. Thus, structures should be understood, not as the fixed girders of society, but as continuously subject to reproduction and alteration. They are reproduced by means of social practices, and, at the same time, these structures frame the social practices and unacknowledged conditions of action. For Giddens, social systems are constituted by social practices, where 'the structural properties of social systems are both the medium and the outcome' of those practices.[8] The performance of social practices, then, reproduces both social structures (which in turn inform social practices) and the consciousness of social agents.

As a structure, however, whiteness does not simply situate elements of the social system relative to one another. Significantly, it also places those elements into a hierarchical relationship of superiority and subordination. The structuring property of whiteness locates whites in a structural position of superiority and advantage and non-whites in a structural position of inferiority, subordination and disadvantage. This hierarchical ordering is an essential aspect of the structuring function of whiteness.[9]

Thus understood, whiteness is a structuring property of modern social systems, and as such it shapes the formation of both the consciousness of agents in terms of their cognitive and evaluative frameworks and the patterning of social practices. Whiteness shapes the cognitive frameworks of agents because, first, it is a structuring property of the social system into which agents are socialized and acculturated, and, second, it constitutes part of the conditions (acknowledged and unacknowledged) of action. If the social world is systematically shaped by the needs, interests and values of whites, then individuals are always already being socialized and acculturated into whiteness, with the consequence that they will internalize cognitive and evaluative schemas that reflect this whiteness. Whiteness will condition the cognitive and evaluative presuppositions individuals possess, thus shaping their perceptions of and judgments concerning the social world. The dualistic nature as both medium and outcome of social practices also explains another commonly identified feature of whiteness: the fact that it is normalized and thus largely invisible to the dominant culture of the post-civil rights era. As a structuring property, whiteness is a fundamental feature of the way society is reproduced, and hence it typically does not give rise to the appearance of deviance from the norm. Therefore, whiteness *defines* the normal functioning of modern social systems. Moreover, we can now explain the persistence of structural racial inequalities in the post-civil rights era. When whiteness is normalized and overt forms of racial prejudice and discrimination are seen as extreme and rare, whiteness functions behind the scenes, so to speak, to shape the world to the advantage of those racialized as white. A normally functioning society becomes defined as one that is structured by whiteness, which therefore functions to reproduce a society that is understood to be free of fundamental racial contradictions. Thus, whiteness functions as a key support in reproducing the hegemonic racial order that is a legacy of our past. The critical theory of whiteness, then, is especially needed to account for the ways that a de facto system of white supremacy survives and thrives after the discrediting and dismantling of the formal *de jure* system of white supremacy.

Another significant consequence of understanding whiteness as a structuring property is that it can explain the *systematicity* of whiteness's structuring of the social system. As a structuring property, whiteness affects every aspect of the system. It shapes the consciousness of individuals and hence the cognitive and evaluative frameworks for action, the patterning of social practices, the terms and rules for the operation of social institutions of the economy, the educational system, the legal system, the representations of value that define the culture and so on. Thus, whiteness systematically informs—and deforms—every aspect of the social world.

Moreover, whiteness's dualistic nature—as medium and outcome of social practices—explains the *historical continuity* of the racialized social order. There is a fundamental ahistoricity in our culture that masks the ongoing very real and deeply structured effects of the past upon the present. Structuring properties are reproduced in every social practice, as well as modified or transformed. If whiteness is a structuring property of modern social systems, then it must be understood as deeply embedded in the everyday, normal functioning of those systems, and because of its hegemony within the system, it is reproduced largely behind the backs of social agents. Whiteness persists as a structuring property when nothing or little is done to disrupt it. Whiteness is the legacy of a racially fraught past and it functions in such a way that it maintains the legacy of racial inequality as a central aspect of modern social systems, while at the same time, masking the impact of that history upon the present.

Now, one of the defining features of any critical social theory is its reflexive historicity. A critical social theory abandons the historically transcendent point of view and explicitly takes into account its own embeddedness in history. The emphasis I placed above on the two virtues of systematicity and of accounting for the historical continuity of the system of racial oppression might suggest that this account reifies whiteness as a fixed social structure. But this is not the case. Whiteness should be understood as a structuring property of the social system that is co-original with the system of racial oppression. However, its degree of explicitness or invisibility varies with historical context. Prior to the civil rights era, whiteness functioned in part as an explicit ideology that was normalized, though certainly not invisible. In the post-civil rights era, whiteness functions in part as an implicit, invisible ideology that legitimates (and structures) the social order. Thus, a critical theory of whiteness is especially relevant in the present because whiteness now functions largely behind the backs of social actors to structure and legitimize the present (racialized) social formation.

Aspects of Whiteness

Having a basic understanding of whiteness as a structuring property in hand, I want to suggest that this understanding of whiteness is useful for unifying the various senses of whiteness that are found in the literature. I will propose that the various senses of whiteness can be fruitfully unified and related to one another under a framework suggested by Habermas' theory of communicative action.

Conceptions of Whiteness

As Paul Taylor suggests, there is a certain 'definitional murkiness' that pervades critical whiteness scholarship, and sometimes this seems intended to underscore the variable and contextualized meanings of whiteness.[10] So there may be a sense in which critical whiteness scholars self-consciously use this concept ambiguously. Nevertheless, I intend to show that the variety of uses of 'whiteness' can be understood as reflecting the various dimensions that constitute social life and that a communications-theoretic framework can provide a unity to this diversity. While I agree that the concrete modes of whiteness's instantiations in specific contexts are highly localized and variable, I also think that a general theory of whiteness is necessary because, as I maintain, whiteness is a structural phenomenon and thus a general critique is required in order to identify effective means of disrupting its systemic effects.

There are three primary senses of whiteness found in the literature.[11] The first understands whiteness as a social identity. For example, George Lipsitz construes whiteness as 'a social fact, an identity created and continued with all-too-real consequences for the distribution of wealth, prestige, and opportunity'.[12] For Lipsitz, then, whiteness is a particular social identity, but one with an especially profound effect on the individual's well-being. Not only does this identity—or lack of it—have significant consequences for one's life-chances, it also is an 'unmarked category against which difference is constructed'.[13] Another well-known example of whiteness as social identity is Ruth Frankenberg's analysis of the social construction of the racial identities of white women in *White Women, Race Matters*.[14] The second sense is whiteness understood as a cultural representation embodying a racialized meaning. A classic example of this is Richard Dyer's examination of cultural imagery in the western world, and 'how whiteness has been culturally constructed in those representations'.[15] He notes that whiteness is both ubiquitous and invisible to whites, consequently whiteness means that whites are represented everywhere, but not as white. Thus, Dyer examines the cultural significance or meaning of cultural representations of whiteness. Other examples of the use of whiteness as representation include Toni Morrison's analysis of whiteness in the tradition of American literature, and bell hooks' discussion of 'representations of whiteness in the black imagination'.[16] Finally, a third use of whiteness is as an asset or form of property. Peggy McIntosh famously defines white privilege as 'an invisible package of unearned assets which I [as a white woman] can count on cashing in each day, but about which I was "meant" to remain oblivious'.[17] Another influential example of this use of whiteness is Cheryl Harris' legal analysis of it as a form of property.[18] She argues that race has always been entangled with property, and that the law structures property rights simultaneously with the meaning and effects of whiteness. Essentially, Harris understands whiteness as a form of property that defines identities, is a resource to be used at will, and has systematic consequences for its possessor.

A Communications-Theoretic Understanding of Whiteness

These uses of whiteness—as a social identity, a form of representation and a valuable asset—overlap and are closely related to one another, and often they are used interchangeably, even by the same author. Despite the variety of meanings of whiteness and the contextual nature of these meanings, there is unity—a concept of whiteness—underlying these various conceptions. If whiteness is understood as a structuring property of the socio-cultural life-world, each of these conceptions of whiteness can be unified under one account and thus understood as expressions of the same socio-cultural structure in different dimensions of the social order. Thus understood, then, whiteness is a social structure that normalizes the interests, needs and values of those racialized as white. The consequence of a social system structured by whiteness is that whites occupy a location of structural advantage that generates material and psychological privileges and benefits.

Habermas' theory of communicative action is an explanation of the possibility of social order, and it provides the theoretical resources for a unified account of whiteness.[19] On this account, the social coordination of action occurs by means of two analytically distinguishable mechanisms: consent or influence. Consent is the foundational mechanism, while influence is derivative, and without an adequate conception of the consensual integration of individuals' actions, social order could not be explained. Actions are coordinated by means of consent when the actors achieve an intersubjectively valid understanding of the situation. Such an understanding would be nearly impossible if there were not a mass of shared background knowledge drawn upon by the actors in the process of achieving intersubjective understanding. Habermas refers to this as the background life-world, but he rejects Husserl's phenomenological conception of the life-world as subject-centered. Instead, Habermas proposes a communications-theoretic conception of the life-world that is constituted in and by communicative interaction and discourse. From the first-person perspective of the participant in communicative action, the life-world functions as a background of unacknowledged and largely unquestioned presuppositions drawn upon in communicative interactions. From the third-person perspective of observer, the life-world appears as the totality of socio-cultural facts. This totality is constituted by the structures of culture, society and personality. Culture is the stock of (what counts as) valid knowledge that interlocutors use in communicative interactions; society refers to the institutions that regulate social interactions and generate solidarity; and personality refers to the competencies of speaking and acting, the development of which are necessary conditions for engagement in communicative action and identity formation.

There is a dialectical relation between individual actors' attempts to coordinate action through communicative interactions and the background life-world. On the one hand, the action coordinating effects and mutual understanding of communicative actions are possible only when a significant degree of background knowledge and sets of socio-cultural facts are shared. On the other hand, the background life-world, with its stock of cultural knowledge and representations, its institutions that normatively structure behavior and its competent social actors, is constituted in and through communicative interactions. Thus, communicative interactions and the background life-world form an analytically distinguishable, but practically inseparable, dyad of structures and operations.

The theory of communicative action is useful for explaining the concept of whiteness in its variety of senses. The form of whiteness present in the post-civil rights era is a legacy of past white supremacist beliefs, attitudes, behaviors and institutions. As such, it can be understood as a deforming set of presuppositions embedded in the background life-world that shapes the shared cultural stock of knowledge, the establishment and maintenance of what are seen as legitimate inter-subjective relations and the formation of personality structures and social identity. Here, I use 'deformed' in the sense of a distortion of the social system to the unjust advantage of a particular group. Whiteness shapes the cultural stock of knowledge and representations that form the considerable reservoir of background presumptions we unavoidably draw upon in everyday communicative interactions. Dyer's analysis of whiteness uncovers how some of these representations are part of our cultural representations. Whiteness also structures the social institutions that normatively regulate behavior, and it serves as a set of deep presuppositions that underlie the functioning of the economic, political, legal and other systems. This was clearly shown in Harris' analysis of whiteness as a form of property, and can also be seen in Charles Mills' argument that race is the political system that has created the modern polity.[20] If I am correct, and whiteness is a structuring property of the sociocultural life-world, then it also shapes the formation of personality that allows competent speaking and acting by social subjects and the formation of identity. As I have mentioned above, much of the critical whiteness scholarship has focused on whiteness as a social identity, and we can now see how its embeddedness in the life-world directly affects the formation of the identities of social actors. Moreover, since these aspects of the life-world (culture, society and personality) are integrated with one another in communicative interactions, we can better understand the connections between whiteness as an identity, as a form of domination and as a set of cultural representations and meanings. Insofar as we also have an explanation for its ubiquity and hegemony as a fundamental entity in the social system, it structures the life-world as a whole. And if the life-world is so thoroughly structured by whiteness, then it is clearer just how whiteness impacts particular communicative interactions, distorts the communicative understandings that are achieved and also is reproduced in the mechanisms that reproduce the sociocultural life-world.

Of course, there are various objections that might be raised concerning the adequacy of Habermas' theory. Some have suggested that it has weaknesses and blind spots in explaining the functioning of power and domination; others have been concerned with its inadequate account of embodiment.[21] For my purposes here, however, these worries need not concern us. I am interested in simply drawing on its theoretical resources, not as a complete account of whiteness, but only to situate the uses of whiteness in a unified account. The comprehensive critical theory of whiteness certainly will need to give an account of the embodiment of whiteness and the means by which whiteness instantiates power. However, these aspects of the theory are beyond the scope of this chapter.

But why should we think that a unified account of whiteness is adequate or even that it will be more useful for liberation than an account that begins from the contextual differences in the meaning of whiteness? First, I contend that theorizing whiteness in a unified way is necessary if effective strategies are to be devised and actions to be taken to disrupt its functioning and dismantle its hold on modern social orders. One of the more significant features of whiteness is its hegemonic colonization of all aspects of the social world, and so microanalyses of how it manifests itself in highly specific locations and contexts, while useful, will not address its systemic nature. Moreover, this Habermasian analysis of the concept of whiteness emphasizes the reproduction of whiteness in the social order, and especially the way that it can be reproduced 'behind the backs' of social actors. This is a particularly important feature of whiteness. Only a comprehensive theoretical approach will uncover the root system of its functional properties so that it can be dug up and destroyed. Second, although a critical theory of whiteness must include an account of the ways whiteness intersects gender, class and sexual orientation, I do think that it is both possible and productive to say something general about how whiteness functions to reproduce a system of white supremacy. It is not clear how beginning with the multiple inflections of whiteness will yield critiques that can effectively disrupt its reproduction as a system-wide social structure.

In my judgment, then, Habermas' theory is useful for making sense of the diverse uses and meanings of the concept of whiteness by showing how each use of whiteness primarily represents one of the three dimensions of the life-world. Whiteness as a social identity highlights the structuring of competent social actors; whiteness as asset or property highlights the structuring of normative social relationships and practices; and whiteness as cultural representation highlights the structuring of meaning, knowledge and values. There are two significant implications of this account. First, whiteness infuses and infects all aspects of the life-world. Its effects are not restricted to one domain or another; instead, we are immersed in whiteness, as fish are immersed in water, and we breathe it in with every breath. Second, whiteness is fundamentally integrated into the structures and processes of social reproduction. As whiteness is integral to the life-world, it gets drawn upon as a resource and context-forming background in everyday communicative interactions; and in turn, these communicative interactions reproduce the structuring effects of whiteness upon the life-world. It is this feature of whiteness that I want to argue is especially important to examine and to understand if its largely invisible mode of operation is to be unmasked.

Contextualizing the Critical Theory of Whiteness

I now want to situate the critical theory of whiteness within the wider context of the struggle against racial oppression, for it is crucial that such a theory be developed not merely as an intellectual exercise but always in view of engaging with the struggle against racial oppression. I will begin by distinguishing the concept of whiteness from that of white supremacy; then I will argue that a critical theory of whiteness does not necessarily recenter the interests of whites; and finally, I consider further implications of such a theory.

White Supremacy and Whiteness

I have maintained throughout that a critical theory of whiteness is necessary to account for the ways that whiteness is reproduced as it functions to maintain white supremacy. There are two concerns that might be raised about this. First, one might have doubts about the distinction between whiteness and white supremacy, and second, one might question the priority given to whiteness. In this section I want to address these two concerns.

(a) *Mills* In a series of papers that build upon his groundbreaking *The Racial Contract,* Charles Mills has argued that political philosophers ought to reclaim the concept of white supremacy and make it central to their theorizing.[22] He suggests that 'one strategy for developing a critical race theory within political philosophy will entail self-conscious theorizing of a *racial polity*—in this case, a *white supremacist polity*—and a rethinking of the political around the axis of race'.[23] Such a shift in perspective would make visible the system of advantage and disadvantage in which whiteness 'is not merely full personhood, first-class citizenship, ownership of the aesthetically normative body, membership in the recognized culture; [but] it is also material benefit, entitlement to differential moral/legal/social treatment, and differential rational expectations of economic success'.[24] Thus, in a white supremacist polity, one characterized by a system of white advantage and non-white disadvantage, whiteness is equated with the benefits, entitlements and advantages attached to members of the class racialized as 'white'.

Mills understands white supremacy as 'a multidimensional system of domination, encompassing not merely the "formally" political that is limited to the juridico-political realm of official governing bodies and laws; but . . . [also as extended to] white domination in economic, cultural, cognitive-evaluative, somatic, and in a sense even "metaphysical" spheres'.[25] As a system of domination, white supremacy consists of interlocking elements that work in complementary ways to oppress, just as in Marilyn Frye's famous description of how the bars of a birdcage work together in a systematic way to contain and constrain a bird.[26] Mills, however, stresses that the dimensions of white supremacy include not only the 'formal' political institutions of the state such as the government, the law and the criminal justice system, but also the informal political dimensions of the economic, cultural, cognitive-evaluative, somatic and metaphysical. These are categorized as (informally) political by Mills in the sense that they are contributing factors in the collective distribution of goods, opportunities and burdens, and also in the sense that each of them contributes to the domination of one group over another.

Mills presents a powerful argument for a much needed racial revision of political theory. But there is an ambiguity in Mills' understanding of white supremacy that undercuts his intention to develop a 'critical race theory within political philosophy'.[27] The concept of white supremacy is comprised of two elements, each signaling an important aspect of modern racialized social formations: 'supremacy' refers to the role of domination and power in structuring the social formation; and 'white' refers to the particular social identity marked as superior and advantaged in that social formation. Mills, however, emphasizes and develops an analysis of one of these aspects—that of the political domination of 'supremacy'—while leaving the other—whiteness—relatively unexamined. Mills fails to develop an independent analysis of the *racial* dimension of white supremacy; such an analysis would be constituted by an examination of the social, cultural and historical dynamics that generate, transform and reproduce whiteness. Indeed, in *The Racial Contract* Mills recognizes the need to understand how white supremacy is reproduced. He says: 'What we need to do, then, is to identify and learn to understand the workings of a racialized ethic. How were people able consistently to do the wrong thing while thinking that they were doing the right thing?'[28] He goes on to suggest cognitive science as a possible resource for this inquiry, but I want to argue that a more adequate explanation would be grounded in an account of whiteness as a social construct that structures the social order such that it results in the de facto social, economic, political and cultural supremacy of those racialized as white. In deeply structuring the social formation, whiteness generates *as a consequence* the effects described by the concept of white supremacy.

Mills' descriptive conception of white supremacy, including its extension to the informal dimensions of racial domination, is useful as an organizing concept, but it does not explain the underlying sociocultural processes that reproduce the white supremacist social order. This is *not* to say that 'white supremacy' is neither useful, nor necessary, simply that it is not sufficient for a complete analysis of systems of racial oppression. Further analysis of the concept of whiteness and how it functions to reproduce a white supremacist social order is needed.

More recently, Mills has conceded this by acknowledging that the concept of white supremacy 'should be an overarching category for critical race theory', and as such it leaves room for a variety of 'theoretical options' to be developed, just as in feminism the organizing concept of patriarchy encompasses a variety of theoretical orientations.[29] Thus, one might think of the concept of white supremacy to be descriptive of modern social formations, but as a descriptive term it still requires a theoretical account that explains the generation and reproduction of white supremacist social orders. This explanatory need, I argue, is precisely what a critical theory of whiteness can satisfy.

(b) *McClendon*   The second concern that might be raised is whether beginning with an analysis of whiteness is not beginning from the derivative rather than the primary term. John McClendon makes such an argument in claiming that the recent philosophical interest in whiteness privileges the wrong concept. Placing whiteness at the center of the analysis, he argues, results in the 'dangerous . . . inclination to ascribe attributes that are more appropriate to white supremacy than to whiteness'.[30] For McClendon, whiteness is a social category that defines the properties and social location of persons racialized as white, and as such 'a description and definition of a white person does not of necessity entail a description and definition of a white supremacist'.[31] So while whiteness is a descriptive property possessed by whites, white supremacy 'entails an evaluation of particular practices and values connected to how certain white people relate to racialized social conditions within a complex of power relations and within determinate historical conditions'.[32]

McClendon is certainly correct that the focus of the analysis needs to be on the critique of the social formation of white supremacy as it is historically instantiated in modern social orders. But his claim that analyses of whiteness fail to account for the complex of power relations and the concrete historical conditions of white supremacy is predicated upon too narrow a conception of whiteness. Whiteness certainly is a social category of identity, but it also shapes social practices and cultural representations and meanings, thus an analysis of whiteness and its privileging in every dimension of the social order the interests, needs and values of persons racialized as white is more substantive than McClendon supposes. Indeed, the critique of white supremacy presupposes the analysis of whiteness and an explanation of its functioning in deforming the social order to privilege whites.

Not a Re-Centering of White Interests

McClendon's argument suggests another objection: namely, that white people have once again become the central focus of theorizing, replacing the proper object of concern—white racial domination. This is a familiar criticism of critical whiteness scholarship. When Du Bois at the beginning of *The Souls of Black Folk* examines the question 'How does it feel to be a problem?' he articulates a common assumption: that the so-called race problem is really a problem *of* people of color.[33] This assumption has been challenged by black social thinkers since at least Du Bois, and the rise of critical race theory has made influential the view that racial injustice is not a problem of people of color, but one, as Richard Wright once said, of whites.[34] But an adequate critical theory of whiteness does not place the interests and needs of white people at the center of its reflections. Rather, as I have stressed throughout this chapter, the *telos* of an adequate critical theory of whiteness (and this is one of the necessary conditions of its adequacy) must be the disruption of the structures and mechanisms that function to maintain racial oppression; its purpose must be in the service of liberation. A critical theory of whiteness that is grounded in the broader project of racial justice does not place whites on a pedestal for admiration and veneration; rather it turns a critical eye towards the consciousness and practices of those in the racially dominant position in a white supremacist society. Although a critical theory of whiteness is a necessary part of the struggle against racial justice, it does not itself constitute a comprehensive theory of racial oppression (or of racial liberation, for that matter). Although whiteness is a primary functional support for contemporary racial oppression, racism and how it operates to reproduce racial injustice cannot be fully explained by whiteness. A comprehensive theory of racial oppression would also need to account for, among other things, the historical rise of hierarchical racial classifications, the system of white supremacy, and the psychological functioning and impact of race and racism.

Implications for Struggles against Racial Oppression

If I am correct, and the usefulness of a critical theory of whiteness is to contribute socio-theoretic clarity to the struggle to disrupt and dismantle the structures of racial oppression, then what are the implications of this theory for anti-racist engagement?

To begin with, given the systematicity of the functioning of whiteness, disrupting its operations will require a pluralistic strategy. Structures of whiteness will need to be unmasked, challenged, disrupted and dismantled in the material dimensions of social life, in the ideologies that shape consciousness, and in the cultural representations that transmit its meaning. Whiteness' functioning in the legal system, economic institutions, the political process and other means of coordinating social interaction will need to be transformed. Whiteness' coloring of the representations, significations and meanings that circulate in the cultural sphere through various modes of discourse, literature, art and mass media will need to be called out and critiqued. And finally, perhaps most importantly, whiteness' colonization of the epistemes, cognitive and evaluative frameworks and epistemological presuppositions that constitute the modern collective consciousness of individuals will need to be resisted and challenged.

But is whiteness to be eliminated? Exposing, challenging, resisting and disrupting structures of whiteness have the purpose of dismantling the system of racial oppression, and insofar as whiteness contributes to this system, it too needs to be dismantled. However, focusing too much on the idealized *telos* of a world where racial distinctions no longer exist is misguided. A critical theory seeks to identify the concrete possibilities contained in the present in order to reshape the social order so that it possesses a greater degree of justice, if not perfect justice. Given that whiteness is implicated in all dimensions of the social world, it would be ineffective, and perhaps even reactionary, to insist on its outright abolition as an immediate practical goal. Instead, the critical theory of whiteness implies that the structures of whiteness that generate racial oppression need to be exposed, challenged and re-formed.

Who does the critical theory of whiteness suggest is responsible for creating change? This theory implies that the responsibility for change, the responsibility to engage, challenge, unmask, disrupt and attack the structures of whiteness that shape *all* aspects of modern social systems, lies with each and every member of those social systems. However, because of differential racializations, which means individuals occupy differential social locations, some members bear a greater responsibility for generating change because they also possess greater power to do so. Namely, whites, who are advantaged and benefited by unjust structures of whiteness, who have a 'possessive investment in whiteness', bear a greater responsibility to engage in projects of deconstructing those structures.[35] Moreover, whites can be especially effective in promoting the necessary structural transformations because they are in a structural position of power. This should not be understood to imply, however, that people of color are not capable of generating the necessary dismantling of whiteness, nor that people of color themselves bear no responsibility.

Despite having the greater moral responsibility, and dominating the means to create change, whites must not imagine that they possess adequate understanding and knowledge to work for change on their own. The structures of whiteness differentially situate individuals according to ascribed racial status, consequently not only do whites stand in a location of advantage, but their perspective is limited by that standpoint.[36] Whites must work to disrupt the structures of whiteness only on the basis of the insight and knowledge of those marginalized and oppressed by those structures. This is not to say that whites cannot be effective allies, only that they cannot imagine that their own resources are sufficient to ensure that their actions will produce effective and just outcomes.

My primary argument, then, has been that one essential element of the struggle for liberation from white supremacy is a critical theory of whiteness, where such a theory not only clarifies what we mean by the concept of whiteness, but also explains the mechanisms by which whiteness functions to reproduce a system of white supremacy. The value and fruitfulness of any such critical theory of whiteness, however, will necessarily be grounded in its capacity for concrete and effective guidance for liberatory praxis.

Notes

1. See Noel Ignatiev and John Garvey (eds) *Race Traitor* (New York: Routledge, 1996).
2. Charles W. Mills, *The Racial Contract* (Ithaca, NY: Cornell University Press, 1997).
3. This implies only that there is a structural difference in social location between those racialized as white and those racialized as black, Asian-American, Latino/Latina, American Indian and so on. Some historians have argued that there is a ranked ordering within whiteness; that it is not a homogenous category with the sole distinction being between whiteness and non-whiteness. (See, for example, Thomas A. Guglielmo, *White on Arrival: Italians, Race, Color, and Power in Chicago, 1890–1945* [New York: Oxford University Press, 2003].) I maintain simply that there is an underlying unity to the racialized structuring of the social system that is denoted by whiteness. Exploration of internal distinctions within the structure of whiteness is undoubtedly a necessary task for a critical theory of whiteness, but one that is beyond the scope of the present chapter.
4. See David R. Roediger (ed.) *Black on White: Black Writers on What It Means to Be White* (New York: Schocken, 1998).
5. Marilyn Frye, 'White Woman Feminist: 1983–1992', in *Willful Virgin* (Freedom, CA: Crossing Press, 1992), p. 151.
6. My conception of structure draws significantly from Giddens' conception (see Anthony Giddens, *Central Problems in Social Theory* [Berkeley: University of California Press, 1979], pp. 64ff.).
7. See Anthony Giddens, *The Constitution of Society: Outline of the Theory of Structuration* (Berkeley: University of California Press, 1984).
8. Giddens, *Central Problems*, p. 69.
9. One might ask at this point: why is an account of white supremacy then necessary if whiteness also accounts for relations of domination and subordination? White supremacy is still necessary to account for: the generation of the system of white racial domination (the critical theory of whiteness accounts for only its reproduction), as well as the normative critique of the hierarchical structure of domination/subordination that is instantiated in and reproduced by whiteness. I address this further in section IV.
10. Paul C. Taylor, 'Silence and Sympathy: Dewey's Whiteness', in George Yancy (ed.) *What White Looks Like* (New York: Routledge, 2004).
11. In an article critically examining the use of the concept of whiteness in labor history, Eric Arneson describes the concept as a 'moving target', that is, 'variously, a metaphor for power, a proxy for racially distributed material benefits, a synonym for "white supremacy", an epistemological stance defined by power, a position of invisibility or ignorance, and a set of beliefs about racial "Others" and oneself that can be rejected through "treason" to a racial category' ('Whiteness and the Historians' Imagination', *International Labor and Working-Class History* 60 [Fall 2001]: 3–32 (p. 9)).
12. George Lipsitz, *The Possessive Investment in Whiteness* (Philadelphia, PA: Temple University Press, 1998), p. vii.
13. Ibid., p. 1.
14. Ruth Frankenberg, *White Women, Race Matters: The Social Construction of Whiteness* (Minneapolis: University of Minnesota Press, 1993).
15. Richard Dyer, *White* (New York: Routledge, 1997), p. xiii.

16. Toni Morrison, *Playing in the Dark* (New York: Vintage, 1993); bell hooks, 'Representations of Whiteness', in *Black Looks: Race and Representation* (Boston, MA: South End Press, 1992).

17. Peggy McIntosh, 'White Privilege: Unpacking the Invisible Knapsack', in *White Privilege: Essential Readings on the Other Side of Racism*, 2nd edn, ed. Paula S. Rothenberg (New York: Worth Publishers, 2005). The notion of white privilege was arguably theoretically foreshadowed by Michael Omi and Howard Winant's concept of racial formation. See their *Racial Formation in the United States*, 2nd edn (New York: Routledge, 1994).

18. Cheryl Harris, 'Whiteness as Property', *Harvard Law Review* 106(8) (1993): 1707–91.

19. See Jürgen Habermas, *The Theory of Communicative Action*, 2 vols, trans. T. McCarthy (Boston, MA: Beacon Press, 1994, 1997).

20. Mills, *The Racial Contract*.

21. See, for example, the essays collected in Axel Honneth and Hans Joas (eds) *Communicative Action* (Cambridge, MA: MIT Press, 1991); Johanna Meehan (ed.) *Feminists Read Habermas* (New York: Routledge, 1995); Lewis Edwin Hahn (ed.) *Perspectives on Habermas* (Chicago, IL: Open Court, 2000).

22. See Charles W. Mills, 'The Racial Polity', in *Blackness Visible* (Ithaca, NY: Cornell University Press, 1998), pp. 119–37; Charles W. Mills, 'White Supremacy and Racial Justice', in *From Class to Race: Essays in White Marxism and Black Radicalism* (Lanham, MD: Rowman & Littlefield, 2003), pp. 195–218; Charles W. Mills, 'White Supremacy as Sociopolitical System: a Philosophical Perspective', in ibid., pp. 177–94; and Charles W. Mills, 'Racial Exploitation and the Wages of Whiteness', in Yancy, *What White Looks Like*, pp. 25–54.

23. Mills, 'The Racial Polity', p. 123.

24. Ibid., p. 135.

25. Mills, 'White Supremacy as Sociopolitical System', p. 186.

26. Marilyn Frye, 'Oppression', in *The Politics of Reality* (Freedom, CA: The Crossing Press, 1983), pp. 1–16.

27. See Mills, 'The Racial Polity', p. 123.

28. Mills, *The Racial Contract*, p. 94. I would extend this question to include the present: How *are* people able consistently to do the wrong thing while thinking that they *are* doing the right thing?

29. Mills, *From Class to Race*, p. 174.

30. John H. McClendon III, 'On the Nature of Whiteness and the Ontology of Race: Toward a Dialectical Material Analysis', in Yancy, *What White Looks Like*, p. 218.

31. 'I take it that whiteness derives from the more general category—race—just as blackness results from such a general category. What we mean by race entails offering concrete specifications about whiteness (and blackness) as a social category' (McClendon, 'On the Nature of Whiteness', p. 218).

32. Ibid., p. 219.

33. W. E. B. Du Bois, *The Souls of Black Folk* (New York: Vintage Books, 1990), p. 7. I argue elsewhere that Du Bois rejects this assumption in his reflections on this question. He goes on to uncover its unacknowledged assumptions, and in doing so, Du Bois presents one of the earliest analyses of whiteness. See David S. Owen, 'Whiteness and Du Bois' *The Souls of Black Folk*', unpublished MS, on file with the author.

34. Quoted in Lipsitz, *The Possessive Investment in Whiteness*, p. 1.

35. Ibid.

36. This is similar to the arguments of feminist standpoint theory. See Linda Alcoff (ed.) *Feminist Epistemologies* (New York: Routledge, 1992), and Sandra Harding (ed.) *The Feminist Standpoint Reader: Intellectual and Political Controversies* (New York: Routledge, 2004).

Credits and Permissions

Anderson, J. D. (1993). Race, meritocracy, and the academy during the immediate post-World War II era. *History of Education Quarterly, 33*(2), 151–175.

Baez, B. (2000). Race-related service and faculty of color: Conceptualizing critical agency in academe. *Higher Education, 39*(3), 363–391.

Bensimon, E. M. (2005). Closing the achievement gap in higher education: An organizational learning perspective. In A. J. Kezar (Ed.), *Organizational learning in higher education. New Directions for Higher Education* (No. 131, pp. 99–111). San Francisco: Jossey-Bass.

Bonilla-Silva, E., & Forman, T.A. (2000). "I am not a racist but . . .": Mapping White college students' racial ideology in the USA. *Discourse & Society, 11*(1), 50–85.

Brayboy, B. M. J. (2004). Hiding in the Ivy: American Indian students and visibility in elite educational settings. *Harvard Educational Review, 74*(2), 125–152.

Brayboy, B. M. J. (2005). Toward a tribal critical race theory in education. *The Urban Review, 37*(5), 425–446.

Connolly, M. (2000). What's in a name? A historical look at Native American-related nicknames and symbols at three U.S. universities. *Journal of Higher Education, 71*(5), 515–547.

Crum, S. (2007). The Choctaw Nation: Changing the appearance of American higher education, 1830–1907. *History of Education Quarterly, 47*(1), 49–68.

de los Santos, A. G., & Vega, I. I. (2008). Hispanic presidents and chancellors of institutions of higher education in the United States in 2001 and 2006. *Journal of Hispanic Higher Education, 7*(2), 156–182.

Delgado Bernal, D. (2002). Critical race theory, LatCrit theory, and critical raced-gendered epistemologies: Recognizing students of color as holders and creators of knowledge. *Qualitative Inquiry, 8*(1), 105–126.

Denson, N., & Chang, M. J. (2009). Racial diversity matters: The impact of diversity-related student engagement and institutional context. *American Educational Research Journal, 46*(2), 322–353.

Dynarski, S. (2004). The new merit aid. In C. M. Hoxby (Ed.), *College choices: The economics of which college, when college, and how to pay for it* (pp. 63–100). Chicago: University of Chicago Press.

Elenes, C. A. (2001). Transformando fronteras: Chicana feminist transformative pedagogies. *International Journal of Qualitative Studies in Education, 14*(5), 689–702.

Flores, S. M. (2010). State "Dream Acts": The effect of in-state resident tuition policies on the college enrollment of undocumented Latino students in the United States. *The Review of Higher Education, 33*(2), 239–283.

Fries-Britt, S., & Griffin, K. A. (2007). The black box: How high-achieving Blacks resist stereotypes about Black Americans. *Journal of College Student Development, 48*(5), 509–524.

Gasman, M. (1999). Scylla and Charybdis: Navigating the waters of academic freedom at Fisk University during Charles S. Johnson's administration (1946-1956). *American Educational Research Journal, 36*(4), 739–758.

Harper, S. R. (2009). Niggers no more: A critical race counternarrative on Black male student achievement at predominantly white colleges and universities. *International Journal of Qualitative Studies in Education, 22*(6), 697–712.

Harper, S. R., & Hurtado, S. (2007). Nine themes in campus racial climates and implications for institutional transformation. In S. R. Harper, & L. D. Patton (Eds.), *Responding to the realities of race on campus. New Directions for Student Services* (No. 120, pp. 7–24). San Francisco: Jossey-Bass.

Harper, S. R., Patton, L. D., & Wooden, O. S. (2009). Access and equity for African American students in higher education: A critical race historical analysis of policy efforts. *Journal of Higher Education, 80*(4), 389–414.

Hurtado, S., Milem, J., Clayton-Pederson, A., & Allen, W. (1998). Enhancing campus climates for racial/ethnic diversity: Educational policy and practice. *The Review of Higher Education, 21*(3), 279–302.

Iverson, S. V. (2007). Camouflaging power and privilege: A critical race analysis of university diversity policies. *Educational Administration Quarterly, 43*(5), 586–611.

James, T. (1985). Life begins with freedom: The College Nisei, 1942-1945. *History of Education Quarterly, 25*(1/2), 155–174.

Kezar, A. (2008). Understanding leadership strategies for addressing the politics of diversity. *The Journal of Higher Education, 79*(4), 406–441.

Krueger, A. B., Rothstein, R., & Turner, S. (2008). Was Justice O'Connor right? Race and highly selective college admissions in 25 years. In M. S. McPherson, & M. O. Schapiro (Eds.), *College access: Opportunity or privilege* (pp. 35–48). New York: The College Board.

Long, B. T., & Kurlaender, M. (2009). Do community colleges provide a viable pathway to a baccalaureate degree? *Educational Evaluation and Policy Analysis, 31*(1), 30–53.

Long, M. C., & Tienda, M. (2008). Winners and losers: Changes in Texas university admissions post-Hopwood. *Educational Evaluation and Policy Analysis, 30*(3), 255–280.

MacDonald, V. M., Botti, J. M., & Clark, L. H. (2007). From visibility to autonomy: Latinos and higher education in the U.S., 1965–2005. *Harvard Educational Review, 77*(4), 474–504.

Marin, P., & Flores, S. M. (2008). Bakke and state policy: Exercising institutional autonomy to maintain a diverse student body. In P. Marin & C. L. Horn (Eds.), *Realizing Bakke's legacy: Affirmative action, equal opportunity, and access to higher education* (pp. 219–239). Sterling, VA: Stylus.

Marullo, S. (1998). Bringing home diversity: A service-learning approach to teaching race and ethnic relations. *Teaching Sociology, 26,* 259–275.

Massey, D. S., & Mooney, M. (2007). The effects of America's three affirmative action programs on academic performance. *Social Problems, 54*(1), 99–117.

Mayhew, M. J., Grunwald, H. E., & Dey, E. L. (2005). Curriculum matters: Creating a positive climate for diversity from the student perspective. *Research in Higher Education, 46*(4), 389–412.

McCurtis, B. R., Jackson, J. F. L., & O'Callahan, E. M. (2009). Developing leaders of color in higher education: Can contemporary programs address historical employment trends? In A. J. Kezar (Ed.), *Rethinking leadership in a complex, multicultural, and global environment: New concepts and models for higher education* (pp. 65–92). Sterling, VA: Stylus.

Minor, J. T. (2004). Dilemmas of decision-making in historically Black colleges and universities: Defining the context. *Journal of Negro Education, 73*(1), 40–52.

Morfin, O. J., Perez, V. H., Parker, L., Lynn, M., & Arrona, J. (2006). Hiding the politically obvious: A critical race theory preview of diversity as racial neutrality in higher education. *Educational Policy, 20*(1), 249–270.

Ortiz, A.M., & Rhoads, R.A. (2000). Deconstructing Whiteness as part of a multicultural educational framework: From theory to practice. *Journal of College Student Development, 31*(5), 429–436.

Owen, D. S. (2007). Towards a critical theory of whiteness. *Philosophy & Social Criticism, 33*(2), 203–222.

Patton, L. D., & Catching, C. C. (2009). 'Teaching while Black': Narratives of African American student affairs faculty. *International Journal of Qualitative Studies in Education, 22*(6), 713–728.

Perez Huber, L., Benavides, C., Malagon, M., Velez, V. & Solórzano, D. (2008). Getting beyond the 'symptom,' acknowledging the 'disease': Theorizing racist nativism. *Contemporary Justice Review, 11,* 39–51.

Perkins, L. M. (1997). The African American female elite: The early history of African American women in the Seven Sister Colleges, 1880-1960. *Harvard Educational Review, 67*(4), 718–756.

Slaughter, S. (1997). Class, race and gender and the construction of postsecondary curricula in the United States: Social movement, professionalization and political economic theories of curricular change. *Journal of Curriculum Studies, 29*(1), 1–30.

Smedley, B. D., Myers, H. F., & Harrell, S. P. (1993). Minority-status stresses and the college adjustment of ethnic minority freshmen. *Journal of Higher Education, 64*(4), 434–452.

Smith, D. G., Turner, C. S. V., Osei-Kofi, N., Richards, S. (2004). Interrupting the usual: Successful strategies for diversifying the faculty. *Journal of Higher Education, 75*(2). 131–160.

Smith, W. A., Yosso, T. J. & Solórzano, D. G. (2006). Challenging racial battle fatigue on historically white campuses: A critical race examination of race-related stress. In C. A. Stanley (Ed.), *Faculty of color: Teaching in predominantly white colleges and universities* (pp. 299–327). Bolton, MA: Anker.

Solórzano, D., Ceja, M., & Yosso, T. (2000). Critical race theory, racial microaggressions, and campus racial climate: The experiences of African American college students. *Journal of Negro Education, 69* (1/2), 60–73.

St. John, E. P., Affolter-Caine, B., & Chung, A. S. (2007). Race-conscious student financial aid: Constructing an agenda for research, litigation, and policy development. In G. Orfield, P. Marin, S. M. Flores, & L. Garces (Eds.), *Charting the future of college affirmative action: Legal victories, continuing attacks, and new research* (pp. 173–204). Los Angeles: Civil Rights Project, UCLA School of Education.

Stanley, C. A. (2006). Coloring the academic landscape: Faculty of color breaking the silence in predominantly White colleges and universities. *American Educational Research Journal, 43*(4), 701–737.

Tapia, R., & Johnson, C. (2009). Minority students in science and math: What universities still do not understand about race in America. In R. Ehrenberg & C. Kuh (Eds.), *Doctoral education and the faculty of the future* (pp. 123–134). Ithaca: Cornell University Press

Tatum, B. D. (1992). Talking about race, learning about racism: The application of racial identity development theory in the classroom. *Harvard Educational Review, 62*(1), 1–24.

Teranishi, R. T., Behringer, L. B., Grey, E. A., & Parker, T. L. (2009). Critical race theory and research on Asian Americans and Pacific Islanders in higher education. In S. D. Museus (Ed.), *Conducting research on Asian Americans in higher education. New Directions for Institutional Research* (No. 142, pp. 57–68). San Francisco: Jossey-Bass.

Terenzini, P. T., Cabrera, A. F., Colbeck, C. L., Bjorklund, S. A., & Parente, J. M. (2001). Racial and ethnic diversity in the classroom: Does it promote student learning? *The Journal of Higher Education, 72*(5), 509–531.

Turner, C. S. V. (2002). Women of color in academe: Living with multiple marginality. *Journal of Higher Education, 73*(1), 74–93

Turner, C. S. V., González, J. C., & Wood, J. L. (2008). Faculty of color in academe: What 20 years of literature tells us. *Journal of Diversity in Higher Education, 1*(3), 139–168.

Umbach, P. D. (2006). The contributions of faculty of color to undergraduate education. *Research in Higher Education, 47*(3), 317–345.

Williamson, J. A. (2004). "This has been quite a year for heads falling": Institutional autonomy in the civil rights era. *History of Education Quarterly, 44*(4), 554–576.